COPING WITH CHANGE:

BRITISH SOCIETY, 1780-1914

Richard Brown

Published by Authoring History

http://richardjohnbr1066.wordpress.com/

© Richard Brown, 2012, 2013

All rights reserved. No part of this publication may be reproduced in any form, stored in or re-introduced into a retrieval system, or transmitted, in any form or by any means, electronic, mechanical, photocopying, recording or otherwise without the prior consent of the author.

The moral right of Richard Brown to be identified as the author of this work has been asserted in accordance with the Copyright, Designs and Patents Act 1988.

ISBN-13: 978-1492969129

ISBN-10: 1492969125

For Margaret

Contents

Contents	i
Acknowledgements	iii
Preface	iv
1 A contextual overview	1
2 An industrial economy	10
3 Agriculture and industry	33
4 Communications	45
5 Birth, Marriage and Death	81
6 Regulating work	142
7 Urban growth and housing	181
8 The public's health	225
9 Poverty and the Poor Laws	257
10 Voluntary action	294
11 Literacy and schooling, 1780-1870	312
12 A state system of education, 1870-1914	359
13 Crime	382
14 Punishment	415
15 Policing	450
16 Leisure	477
17 Government	505

18 Churches under pressure	532
19 Religion in decline?	588
20 Class	611
21 The working-classes	625
22 The middle-classes	674
23 The upper-classes	718
24 The end of the nineteenth century	742
Further Reading	747
Index	748
About the Author	762

Acknowledgements

One of the constant things about research and writing History is that it is ever-changing, a paradox given the finality of the past. I remember being told by an aged and eminent historian some decades ago that 'historians are like good wines, they mature with age'. The genesis of this book lies long in my past. In fact, its origins go back to when I first began teaching in the early 1970s. Much of my work at university focused on medieval history; I had only taken one course in modern history. It was a shock to the system, though hardly a surprise, when I found that most of my teaching would be modern and I quickly had to familiarise myself with the Industrial Revolution and its consequences. I spent most of the succeeding three decades teaching the subject at GCSE and Advanced Level with growing confidence and enjoyment. Though I retained my interest in medieval history, it was evident that this was not what I would spend any time teaching.

I am grateful to Monica Place, Christopher Daniels, Don Hunt and Bev Labbett, colleagues in my first school in Bury St. Edmunds, for helping me down the 'modern road'. Successive waves of students have had to put up with my teaching of the subject. Both in Suffolk and Bedfordshire I found them to be interested in and committed to studying History. I have always enjoyed teaching and much of that enjoyment came from teaching the rudiments of being a historian and from students' overwhelmingly positive reactions. Their often irreverent comments have made teaching what it should always be, a joint search for understanding and knowledge in an environment that is encouraging and entertaining. They will never know how grateful I am for their willingness to engage with my ideas and the ideas of other historians and writers and how far they have influenced the development of this work. For those of us who remember that teaching was once rather more than simply getting students through examinations or reaching targets, the mutual enjoyment of discovering the past and understanding its histories is something I still savour.

Finally and most importantly, Margaret has lived with this work in its developing manifestations for the past thirty years. Her support throughout has been pivotal in translating ideas into words and words into paragraphs. Her pithy comments have always been pertinent and have found their way into the book. Dedicating this work to her is scant recompense for the enormous contribution she has made to my work.

Preface

There are many parallels between Britain today and Britain during the 'long' nineteenth century. Both societies were coping with substantial and sustained population growth and the tensions this creates between different ethnic groups. Both had to cope with profound changes. Today the concern is with unfettered immigration from the European Union and especially 'economic migrants' from beyond Europe. In the nineteenth century, there was unease over Irish immigration and, after 1880, from the influx of poor Jewish refugees especially from Eastern Europe and Russia. Poverty, housing shortages and exploitation in the workplace are as much issues today as they were over a century ago. Our current fixation with the environment was paralleled by the Victorians who sought, and largely failed, to take remedial action necessary to counter the impact of industrial change and urban growth on society. Education, crime and the nature of leisure are equally issues on which the attitudes of Victorians have much in common with our anxieties today over educational standards, knife-crime and binge-drinking, for them it would have been the garrotting panic of the early 1860s and Fenian and anarchist terrorism. The surveillance society of the nineteenth century was the pervasive presence of the bobby on his beat whereas today we are saturated with CCTV and speed cameras. Debates over the role of government and the extent to which it should impinge on people's lives remain as important and unresolved to us as they were to our ancestors. The origins of the 'nanny state' lie in the debate over whether Britain should or should not be compelled to be vaccinated or bathed into health in the early 1850s. We are still almost as psychotically fixated with our position in society as Victorian working men and women and those from the middle- and upper-classes. Belief and unbelief remain controversial whether the 'Catholic aggression' in the nineteenth century or today's debates over female and gay priests, Islamic jihad or whether creationism should be part of the school curriculum.

Victorian preoccupations with how to manage the problems created by economic and demographic change were largely unresolved by 1914. There may have been some improvements in people's quality of life but these were small and unevenly distributed. For most people, life remained a constant battle for survival to keep above the poverty line especially for the very young and the old. The 'arithmetic of woe' was all-pervasive. Only through hard work, self-help and a modicum of luck could most people maintain any semblance of quality in their lives. The fear of poverty and yet the recognition that poverty was inevitable at some stage in the individual's life was ever-present. Today, in an increasingly digitalised society, it is not difficult to find similar circumstances. Poverty has not been eliminated; in fact, if anything, in the last two decades it has worsened with growing concerns about a 'benefit culture', 'fuel poverty', the problems associated with an increasingly aging population and the economic crisis of 'credit-crunch Britain' and fear of austerity and recession'. We now have free access to schooling and medical care but this has not necessarily resulted in a more meritocratic or necessarily a healthier society. Twenty-five years of the National Curriculum have not made students better educated or better prepared for their 'place' in the labour market. We still have a large number of students leaving schools with minimum standards of literacy and numeracy despite a progressive rise in the school-leaving age. The National Health Service and advances in medical technology mean people can be cured of diseases that would have killed them in Victorian Britain but we are now plagued with rising levels of obesity and alcohol-related diseases. People from poorer backgrounds, regardless of the plaudits of government, remain disadvantaged. The poor it appears are getting poorer and the rich richer, a return to something like the 'two nations' of Disraeli's England. In many respects, the social and political agenda thrust on to the Victorians remains unresolved. Statements about a 'broken society' that periodically punctuate contemporary political debate would have been familiar to many Victorian social commentators.

Coping with Change is a new and extended edition of *Society under Pressure*, a book originally published in my *Nineteenth Century British Society*, a series of five Kindle-books that examined the major social developments that occurred during the nineteenth and early-twentieth century. It develops the ideas and chronological scope that I initially put forward in my studies of Britain's social and economic development originally published in 1987, 1991 and 1992.[1] I have extended the scope of the book to cover the 'long nineteenth century' from 1780 to 1914. The opening chapters provide the economic context for the book especially the character of economic change and continuity. This is followed by three chapters that consider agricultural and industrial, communication and demographic developments. The next tranche of chapters examine the social

---

[1] Brown, Richard, *Change and Continuity in British Society 1800-1850*, (Cambridge University Press), 1987, 2008, Brown, Richard, *Society and Economy in Modern Britain 1700-1850*, (Routledge), 1991; Brown, Richard, *Economic Revolutions 1750-1850: Prometheus Unbound?*, (Cambridge University Press), 1992, 2008.

problems created by changes in towns, the public's health, housing, poverty, the nature of work, education and crime and leisure and the ways in which government sought to regulate these activities. Chapter 17 draws on these chapters and provides an overview of the nature of government in the nineteenth and early-twentieth century as it grappled with the practicalities of social reform. Religion is the subject of Chapters 18 and 19 while Chapters 20-23 consider the vexed nature of class in the nineteenth century. The book ends with a chapter on the end of the nineteenth century.

1 A contextual overview

Victorian Britain has not had a good press. Giles Lytton Strachey's reputation was established with his book *Eminent Victorians*, a collection of four short biographies of Victorian heroes, published in 1918 in which he concluded that his Victorian worthies had not just been hypocrites but had bequeathed to his generation the 'profoundly evil system' by which it is sought to settle international disputes by force. It was an energetic character assassination that 'destroyed for ever the pretensions of the Victorian age to moral supremacy'.[1] By the 1960s, its sexual morality is seen as prudish and hypocritical with different standards of behaviour applicable to men and women. Its culture was regarded as crass and crude, its flamboyance a caricature of proper art and architecture; its poetry sentimental and over-blown; its novels over-long and patronising. The Thatcher government of the 1980s and John Major's government in the 1990s spoke repeatedly of a return to 'Victorian values': self-help; a market-oriented, laissez-faire economy; the role of the family in social control; and national self-confidence, patriotism and pride forged through war, either directly as in the case of the Falklands or indirectly in government belligerence over the European Union. Successive Labour governments between 1997 and 2010 extolled the virtues of enterprise, hard work and wealth-creation exacerbating the gulf between the haves and have-nots. This contemporary perception of 'Victorian values' was, in many respects, simplistic and created stereotypes that represent neither the complexities of Victorian Britain nor the diverse impact they had on localities and individuals.[2]

---

[1] Roy Hatterley, *New Statesman*, 12 August 2002.
[2] Brown, Callum G., and Fraser, W. Hamish, *Britain since 1707*, (Longman), 2010, covers the subject in depth from a 'British' perspective. Bentley, M., *Politics Without Democracy 1815-1914: Perception and Preoccupation in British Government*, (Fontana), 1996, O'Gorman, Frank, *The long eighteenth century: British political and social history 1688-1832*, (Edward Arnold), 1997, Rubinstein, W. D., *Britain's Century: A Political and Social History, 1815-1905*, (Edward Arnold), 1998, and Pugh, M. D., *The Making of Modern British Politics 1867-1939*, (Blackwell), 2002, and *State and Society: British political and social history, 1870-1992*, (Edward Arnold), 1994, provide a more political focus. Clark, G. Kitson, *The Making of Victorian England*, (Methuen), 1966, and Burn, W. L., *The Age of Equipoise: A Study of the mid-Victorian Generation*, (Allen Unwin), 1964, are readable and elegant classics. Langton, J., and Morris, R. J., *Atlas of Industrialising Britain 1780-1914*, (Methuen), 1986, and Pope, R., (ed.), *Atlas of British Social and Economic History since c.1700*, (Routledge), 1989, provide a valuable spatial dimension.

The dominant image of the Industrial Revolution is one of 'a landscape of fire'. Blackened tubs of coal clanking to the pit-head and tipping into wagons and barges; brooding factories shrouded in steam and smoke and echoing with the persistent clatter of machines; bales of cotton piled high in warehouses and swung down into the holds of high-masted sailing ships. [3] Although this is not an altogether misleading picture, it fails to capture the multiple histories of industrialisation. This image of dramatic, revolutionary change fired the imagination and fears of many contemporary writers but it needs to be treated with some caution.[4] Many of the changes that occurred were remarkably traditional. Most historians accept that industrialisation was a long-drawn-out process and that it is inappropriate to think of it as simply a cataclysmic transformation. 'Change in slow motion' is now the dominant view of the economic revolution. The idea of an 'industrial revolution' only became commonplace during the 1830s and with good reason. Even with an exaggerated definition of 'revolutionised industry' only one worker in five was employed in those branches as late as 1841. Most were concentrated in a narrow band of counties and in those areas many industries were reliant on the strength and skill of the individual worker rather than the repetitive movements of machines. Factory workers were in a minority. Most work took place in small workshops or in the home by workers who used traditional manual machinery rather than new technology. In these industries women retained an important economic role while in the so-called 'revolutionised industries' their role was increasingly marginalised and the better-paid jobs monopolised by men.

This means that we have to revise our 'heroic' assumptions about the industrial revolution. Take, for instance, the place of the steam engine in the transformation of the cotton industry and its role in manufacturing industry more generally. For Musson, the 'steam revolution was predominantly in cotton' but even here the frontier

---

[3] On the iconography of industrialisation see Briggs, Asa, *Iron Bridge to Crystal Palace: Impact and Images of the Industrial Revolution*, (Thames and Hudson), 1979, and Klingender, Francis, *Art and the Industrial Revolution*, (N. Carrington), 1947, revised edition, (Paladin), 1975.

[4] On the nature of the 'industrial revolution', see, More, Charles, *Understanding the Industrial Revolution*, (Routledge), 2000, King, Steven, and Timmins, Geoffrey, *Making sense of the Industrial Revolution: English economy and society 1700-1850*, (Manchester University Press), 2001. See also, Berg, Maxine, and Hudson, Pat, 'Rehabilitating the Industrial Revolution', *Economic History Review*, Vol. 45, (1), (1992), pp. 24-50, and Temin, Peter, 'Two Views of the British Industrial Revolution', *Journal of Economic History*, Vol. 57, (1), (1997), pp. 63-82.

moved slowly. [5] By 1879, steam engines supplied 97 per cent of power in the cotton industry and 85 per cent in the woollen industry. Yet the textile industries accounted for nearly half of all manufacturing steam power. Most manufacturing operations were still largely unmechanised and whole areas of the industrial economy remained far from the advancing technological frontier. As mechanisation proceeded, it did not so much push back the boundaries of manual labour as create new relationships and dependencies between hand- and steam-powered technologies. What we have are parallel and interlocking systems of manufacture. Some industries were revolutionised, while others remained largely unchanged. Some regions saw revolutionary changes in the nature of work, others did not. The British economy in the eighteenth century was already highly integrated, a process brought to a peak by the emergence of railways on a rapidly integrating transport system. However, behind this was an intricate and changing mosaic of economic interdependence, a patchwork of distinctive local and regional communities.

Queen Victoria's long reign (1837-1901) provided underlying continuity to profound economic and social changes. The country had largely recovered from the effects of the French Revolutionary and Napoleonic wars (1793-1815) and, with the exception of the Crimean War (1854-1856) that claimed 25,000 British lives and cost about £70m, Britain remained free from conflicts in Europe until 1914. Elsewhere, with the exception of perennial and costly 'colonial' wars and the Boer Wars (1880-1881, 1899-1902), Britain remained at peace. This almost unparalleled period of peace and Britain's dominance as a world power created stability that assisted economic growth and social change. This sixty-year period was one of almost continuous national economic growth. Wealth was, however, unevenly distributed between regions and social groups and, by the last quarter of the nineteenth century Britain's economic and imperial power was increasingly called into question. Carefully prepared political propaganda and improving standards of living persuaded most social classes in Britain to share these beliefs and values. The materialism that underpinned mid-Victorian prosperity was tempered by a set of religious and moral values that both legitimated the accumulation of wealth and, in some at least generated a moral consciousness that contributed towards nineteenth-century social reform. Yet this deceptively reassuring framework was shot through

---

[5] Musson, A. E., *The Growth of British Industry*, (Batsford), 1978, p. 113.

with changes, challenges and contradictions that substantially altered the social and economic geography of Britain.[6]

There was an increasing democratisation of society.[7] Parliamentary reform led to the progressive extension of the franchise. The Reform Act 1832 retained the principle that property was the main qualification for the vote while increasing the total electorate by slightly under half to 217,000 males. There was, however, a significant redistribution of parliamentary seats: 43 new boroughs, most northern industrial and commercial towns, gained MPs in Parliament. The Second Reform Act further extended male franchise in England in 1867 and in Scotland the following year. Although the electorate was still entirely male and under one in ten of the population, together with a further redistribution of seats towards large urban centres, the political voice of the middle-classes and some of the skilled working-class was strengthened. The secret ballot was introduced in 1872 reducing opportunities for intimidation and the Third Reform Acts in 1884 and 1885 further extended the vote and redistributed more seats to industrial towns. By the 1890s, a significant proportion of men had the opportunity to express their views through the ballot box. The economic and demographic structure of Britain had been reflected in a redistribution of parliamentary seats and national politicians were beginning to realise that the views of an increasingly working-class electorate needed be taken seriously.

Changes and challenges were stimulated by urbanisation and economic expansion. Urban growth and industrialisation had a major impact on all regions and all sections of society. Though women and many ordinary working men were still excluded from the effects of parliamentary reform, all were affected by the massive economic and social changes. But its effects were contradictory. Economic growth offered new opportunities and opened new horizons but also provided new constraints and condemned many to poverty and hardship in rapidly growing industrial towns. Victorian economic expansion is epitomised by the growth of the railways. They offered

---

[6] Rubinstein, W. D., *Wealth and Inequality in Britain*, (Faber), 1986, and Kaelbe, H., *Industrialisation and Social Inequality in Nineteenth Century Europe*, (Berg), 1986 provide useful analyses of the issues. Humphries, Jane, 'Standard of Living, Quality of Life', in Williams, Chris, (ed.), *A companion to nineteenth-century Britain*, (Blackwell Publishers), 2004, pp. 287-304, summarises the debate. Burnett, J., *Plenty and Want*, (Scolar Press), 1969, new edition, 1989, is central to the period 1830-1914.

[7] Garrard, J. A., *Democratisation in Britain: elites, civil society and reform since 1800*, (Palgrave), 2002, and Roberts, Matthew, *Political movements in urban England, 1832-1914*, (Palgrave Macmillan), 2009.

new and growing opportunities to move between regions, to travel long distances for business or pleasure and cheapened the movement of news and goods. However, not everyone benefited. Railway construction extracted a substantial toll of misery and death; the growth of new routes quickened rural out-migration and assisted the long-term decline of many communities; in towns it led to extensive demolition of houses, increased overcrowding and contributed to a progressively more noisy and polluted environment. Many people were simply too poor to benefit from the railways. The social effects of the Victorian economic 'miracle' were complex, unstable and uneven.[8]

Changes in attitudes and values created greater national uniformity while perpetuating regional and local diversity. Attitudes to Protestant Nonconformists and Roman Catholics had gradually become more tolerant during the late-eighteenth century but they remained barred from public office. Anglicanism or the Church of England, the official state religion, dominated England and Wales despite substantial Nonconformist and Catholic minorities. In 1828, the Test and Corporations Acts that discriminated against Nonconformists were repealed and in 1829 the Roman Catholic Relief Act achieved Catholic Emancipation. In theory Catholics, Nonconformists and Anglicans should have had equal opportunities from the 1830s onwards from this 'free trade in religion'.[9] The effects of these acts varied considerably from region to region. While Nonconformists were readily accepted into society in England if less so in Wales, perhaps because many were in the successful middle-classes, Catholics were often subjected to discrimination. This especially occurred where the Catholic threat was perceived to be significant, or where Catholicism was equated with other negative things, such as immigrant Irish communities. Sectarian violence and

---

[8] McCloskey, Donald N., 'Did Victorian Britain Fail?', *Economic History Review*, Vol. 23, (1970), pp. 446-459. See also Crafts, N. F. R.., 'Victorian Britain Did Fail', and McCloskey, Donald N., 'No It Did Not: A Reply to Crafts', *Economic History Review*, Vol. 32, (1979), pp. 533-537, and pp. 538-541, respectively.

[9] 'Free trade' had various economic meanings in the late-eighteenth and nineteenth centuries. It could signify 'the opening of any market, ending colonial restrictions, establishing reciprocal agreements, eliminating tariffs, or protecting neutral commerce. The concept encapsulated Enlightenment thinking that increasing free commerce between nations would lead to world peace and people's hopes that free trade would result in more jobs and higher wages. Free trade also had a broader cultural meaning related to the ending of discriminatory regulation that advantaged some in society at the expense of others.

discrimination was common in Glasgow, Liverpool and other industrial cities in the nineteenth century.[10]

Discrimination was not confined to religion. The small Afro-Caribbean population in Victorian Britain, concentrated in London, Bristol and Liverpool, was discriminated against far more severely than even the Irish. Jews, migrating in substantial numbers from Eastern Europe from the 1880s, encountered similar segregation and racism. Victorian Britain was also male-dominated and sexual division was commonplace in all aspects of economy and society. In other areas of national life, however, there appears to have been some convergence of values. The dominant vision of self-help is said to characterise Victorian attitudes to work, thrift and community life. In reality, a vast range of popular institutions such as co-operatives, working men's clubs and friendly societies implemented often conflicting values in different ways in difference communities. Despite the gradual movement towards a national system of education, there were great variations in the quality of schooling and in the level of attendance in different localities.

Between the 1830s and the 1890s, significant changes were projected on to a backcloth of apparent national stability and security. There was not one Victorian Britain but many.[11] Trends towards greater uniformity at the national level were paralleled by an increasing diversity in the ways in which these trends worked in particular communities. However, from the 1880s, traditional political values were challenged by the rise of the labour movement. Social and cultural values were questioned by the rise of secularism, progressive involvement of women in work and in politics and the development of state welfare transformed society; and the effects of depression and global competition rocked the economy. Political initiatives for social reform during the nineteenth century and influences from the rest of Europe led to the formation of the Independent Labour Party in 1893. By 1906, the newly formed Labour Party had 29 seats in Parliament. This combined with the increasing membership of trade unions resulted in the growing politicisation of the working population and posed a challenge to the existing political structures.[12]

---

[10] See, Neal, F., *Sectarian Violence: the Liverpool Experience*, (Manchester University Press), 1988.

[11] Heffer, Simon, *High Minds: The Victorians and the Birth of Modern Britain*, (Random House Books), 2013, considers the period from the1840s to the 1880s.

[12] Rubinstein, David, *The Labour Party and British society, 1880-2005*, (Sussex Academic Press), 2006, Laybourn, Keith, *A century of Labour: a history of the Labour Party, 1900-2000*, (Sutton), 2000, and Tanner,

The tide of the international economy was turning against Britain. From the 1880s, imports of both foodstuffs and manufactured goods increased rapidly and the balance of trade worsened despite the upturn in economic growth between the 1890s and 1914. Competition for markets in textiles was inevitable once major importers in North America, India and the Far East began to supply their own domestic markets and to compete internationally. By 1914, Britain had been supplanted by the USA and Germany in steel-making, some of the new industries such as electrical and precision engineering and many branches of the metals and chemical industries and trailed the USA in the assembly industries, especially automobiles. However, it was still the leading manufacturing nation in the world.[13] Victorian social values were challenged on a number of fronts after 1890 and in some cases led to significant legislation. Most importantly the role of women in society changed. Although economic opportunities for women were beginning to broaden in the late-nineteenth century, in 1914, there were still only 212,000 women employed in engineering and munitions industries, 18,000 in transport and 33,000 in clerical work but Victorian domestic slavery still dominated. Attitudes to women gradually changed and, following energetic campaigning by suffragists and suffragettes, the franchise was extended in 1918 and 1928 to include women.[14] It was to take the First World War (1914-1918) for these challenges to have their full impact but between 1890 and 1914, they were clearly evident and beginning to confront existing perceptions.

Change was perceived and experienced by people living in different parts of Britain whose activities and cultures helped create regional diversity and distinctiveness. The outlook of businessmen and workers in Liverpool, Birmingham or Glasgow was different from that in London. The view of change and continuity from Scotland,

---

Duncan, *Political change and the Labour Party, 1900-1918,* (Cambridge University Press), 1990.

[13] The simplest analysis of movements in the economy can be found in Checkland, S. G., *The Rise of Industrial Society in England 1815-1885*, (Longman), 1964. Church, R., *The Great Victorian Boom 1850-1873*, (Macmillan), 1975, and Saul, S. B., *The Myth of the Great Depression 1873-1896*, (Macmillan), 1988, provide short analyses of these critical themes. Alford, B. W. E., *Britain in the World Economy since 1880*, (Longman), 1996, is an important contribution on Britain's relative decline to 1914.

[14] Pugh, Martin, *Votes for women in Britain 1867-1928*, (The Historical Association), 1994, is a very brief introduction to the subject while his *The March of the Women: a revisionist analysis of the campaign for women's suffrage, 1866-1914*, (Oxford University Press), 2000, provides an accessible introduction to the major problems of interpretation.

Wales or North East England was quite distinct from that in rural South East England. Within the national framework strong regional distinctiveness was based on persistent cultural and economic differences: Scotland and Wales had strong cultural and linguistic identities while the English regions had cultural characteristics that transcended successive economic and social changes. To be born and bred in, for instance, Cornwall or Yorkshire or the Fens was important for people of these areas and ever-increasing internal migration did not destroy such loyalties.

For many people between 1830 and 1914, the most important region remained their own locality. They identified with the neighbourhood, community or village where they had been born, worked, raised their own families, had their friends and lived out their lives. These home areas were, however, perceived differently by people of different age, gender, class and race. Irrespective of where they lived an active adult travelled more widely round a town or through the countryside than a child or an elderly person whose sense of place was more constrained and who identified mainly with the home and street rather than a larger region. Most women lived more circumscribed lives than men. Even when they worked outside the home, extra burdens of childcare and household duties meant that their time was more home-centred: the region or locality with which they identified was often smaller than that of their male counterparts. But lack of income constrained mobility for most people, regardless of age or sex.

The forces that produce structural and regional imbalances in contemporary Britain were apparent by the mid-nineteenth century. Divisions were not only geographical but also social, reflecting the varying degree to which people of different gender, class and race benefited from the opportunities in their localities. Some groups within society were consistently disadvantaged in all regions. Migration shifted the younger and more skilled workforce to areas of economic growth, so regions of economic decline, particularly the old industrial districts of northern and western Britain, were increasingly marginalised. Structural imbalances not only produced variations in regional prosperity, but also equally marginalised certain sectors of the population. Contemporary commentators were well aware of the disparities between the rich and poor as characterised by Disraeli's 'two nations' in 1845, one rich and one poor, one privileged and one underprivileged and Mrs Gaskell's *North and South* of 1855, the one industrial, the other rural. Disadvantage in Victorian Britain was at least as complex as that existing today. Where cultural identity was associated with the protection and promotion of a minority language, distinctive linguistic and cultural regions may be identified. The most distinctive minority languages of nineteenth century Britain were Welsh and Scottish Gaelic. Dialects also had distinct cultural associations. In regions such as South Wales, the Black Country, Lancashire, Yorkshire, North East England and London, they were reflected in contemporary social and political comment as shown in the work of the many dialect poets of the industrial regions.

The administrative geography of the early-nineteenth century England familiar to most people was still the parish and the shire. The parish provided the social and cultural focus of the church and chapel; the framework within which locally raised poor relief was dispensed; the body through which the roads were maintained; and via the parish vestry the means through which most aspects of rural life were regulated. [15] The shire was the link to national frameworks of civil and, in times of emergency, military organisation of the region. The county sessions reflected their place in the administration of justice; the offices of Sheriff and Lord Lieutenant provided links with central government and the Crown. [16] By the 1850s, these older administrative geographies were beginning to change in response to the new demands of an industrialising society. The Poor Law Amendment Act 1834 amalgamated parishes to create Poor Law Unions for the administration of the Poor Law and the provision of workhouses. Reform of urban administration, begun in 1835, progressively replaced ancient town and borough councils with elected municipal corporations. That process was not completed and then ineffectively and at the expense of separation of increasingly inter-related urban and rural areas until the Local Government Acts of 1888 and 1894. The result of these developments was the creation of a multiplicity of administrative boundaries created for different purposes such as health, education and housing that actually had meaning for the people who lived within them. The extent to which this was the case is, however, a matter of some debate. The economic and social developments of the nineteenth and early-twentieth centuries have to be seen within a framework of diverse lives and experiences. Neither change nor continuity was uniform.

---

[15] Snell, Keith D. M., *Parish and belonging: community, identity, and welfare in England and Wales, 1700-1950*, (Cambridge University Press), 2006.

[16] Eastwood, David, *Government and community in the English provinces, 1700-1870*, (Macmillan), 1997, and *Governing rural England: tradition and transformation in local government, 1780-1840*, (Oxford University Press), 1994.

2 An industrial economy

In the latter part of the eighteenth and the first half of the nineteenth century, Britain underwent what historians have called an 'industrial revolution' with factories pouring out goods, chimneys polluting the air, escalating exports and productivity spiralling upwards. This was an epic drama, of Telford, the Stephensons and the Darbys, Macadam, Brunel and Wedgwood, a revolution not simply of inventions and economic growth but of the spirit of enterprise within an unbridled market economy. This is, however, misleading. Industrial change was not something that occurred simply after 1780 but took place throughout the eighteenth century. There was substantial growth in a whole range of traditional industries as well as in the obviously 'revolutionary' cases of textiles, iron and coal. Technical change was not necessarily mechanisation but the wider use of hand working and the division of labour. Changes were the result of the conjunction of old and new processes. Steam power did not replace waterpower at a stroke. Work organisation varied: the 'dark satanic mills' were not all conquering. In 1850, factories coexisted with domestic production, artisan workshops, large-scale mining, and metal production. Change also varied across industries and regions.[1]

---

[1] Hudson, Pat, *The Industrial Revolution*, (Edward Arnold), 1992, is a valuable summary of research on both economic and social history. See, Daunton, M. J., *Progress and Poverty: An Economic and Social History of Britain 1700-1850*, (Oxford University Press), 1995, and *Wealth and welfare: an economic and social history of Britain, 1851-1951*, (Oxford University Press), 2007, Mokyr, Joel, *The Enlightened Economy: An Economic History of Britain 1700-1850*, (Yale University Press), 2009, Griffin, Emma, *A Short History of the British Industrial Revolution*, (Palgrave Macmillan), 2010, and Floud, Roderick, and Johnson, Paul A., (eds.), *The Cambridge economic history of modern Britain. Volume 1: industrialisation, 1700-1860*, (Cambridge University Press), 2004, and *The Cambridge economic history of modern Britain. Volume 2: economic maturity, 1860-1939*, (Cambridge University Press), 2004, for the most up-to-date studies. See also, Floud, R., *The People and the British Economy 1830-1914*, (Oxford University Press), 1997, and Griffin, Emma, *Liberty's Dawn: A People's History of the Industrial Revolution*, Yale University Press), 2013. The best approach to the notion of a 'slow growth' industrial revolution remains Crafts, N. F. R., *British Economic Growth during the Industrial Revolution*, (Oxford University Press), 1985. Ibid, Brown, Richard, *Economic Revolutions 1750-1850: Prometheus Unbound?*, combines text with sources.

What was the nature and extent of change?

The view that the industrial revolution represented a dramatic watershed between an old and a new world has increasingly been questioned by historians. Growth is considerably slower and longer than previously believed though few historians would go as far as Jonathan Clark:

> England was not *revolutionized*, and it was not revolutionized *by industry*. [2]

Change in the economy was multi-dimensional. There were dynamic industries like cotton and iron where change occurred relatively quickly and that may be called 'revolutionary'. In other industries, change took place far more slowly. Between 1750 and 1850, the British economy experienced rapid, and by international standards, pronounced structural change. The proportion of the labour force employed in industry (extractive, manufacturing and service sectors) increased while the proportion working in farming fell.[3] Much employment in industry continued to be small-scale, handicraft activities producing for local and regional markets. These trades were largely unaffected by mechanisation and experienced little or no increase in output per worker. Increased productivity was achieved by employing more labour.

The experience of cotton textiles, though dynamic and of high profile was not typical and there was no general triumph of steam power or the factory system in the early-nineteenth century. Nor was economic growth raised spectacularly by a few inventions. The overall pace of economic growth was modest. There was no great leap forward for the economy as a whole, despite the experiences of specific industries. Productivity in a few industries did enable Britain to sell around half of all world trade in manufacture and by 1850 Britain was 'the workshop of the world'. This, however, needs to be seen in the context of the characteristics of industrialisation. The 'industrial revolution' involved getting more workers into the

---

[2] Clark, J. C. D., *Revolution and Rebellion: State and society in England in the seventeenth and eighteenth centuries*, (Cambridge University Press), 1986, p. 39.

[3] The nature of industrial organisation and the persistence of a 'domestic' system is examined in Thomis, M., *The Town Labourer and the Industrial Revolution*, (Batsford), 1974, and *Responses to Industrialisation*, (David & Charles), 1976. Clarkson, L. A., *Proto-Industrialisation: The First Phase of Industrialisation*, (Macmillan), 1985, examines the literature critically.

industrial and manufacturing sectors rather than achieving higher output once they were there. The cotton and iron industries existed with other industries characterised by low productivity, low pay and lower levels of exports.

Between 1760 and 1800, there was a significant increase in the number of patents giving exclusive rights to inventors, what T. S. Ashton called 'a wave of gadgets swept over Britain'. [4] Between 1700 and 1760, 379 patents were awarded. In the 1760s, there were 205, the 1770s, 294, the 1780s, 477 and the 1790s, 647. Certain key technical developments pre-dated 1760. Coke smelting was developed by Abraham Darby in Shropshire in 1709 but it was not until the 1750s that it was widely used. James Kay developed the 'flying shuttle' in 1733 increasing the productivity of weavers but it was thirty years before advances were made in spinning. Registering patents was expensive and as a result some inventions were not patented. Samuel Crompton, for instance, did not register his spinning mule. [5] From the 1760s, there was a growing awareness of the importance of obtaining patents and the danger of failing to do so. This may account for some of the increase. Many of the patents covered processes and products that were of little economic importance, including medical and consumer goods as well as industrial technologies. Some patents represented technological breakthroughs while others improved existing technologies. Despite these reservations, there were important groupings of technological advances after 1760.

In the textile industries, there were advances in spinning thread with James Hargreaves' 'jenny' in 1764, [6] Richard Arkwright's water frame in 1769 and Samuel Crompton's 'mule' in 1779, weaving with Edmund Cartwright's power loom in 1785 and finishing with

---

[4] Ashton, T. S., *The Industrial Revolution 1760-1830*, (Oxford University Press), 1948, p. 48. See also, MacLeod, Christine, *Heroes of Invention: Technology, Liberalism and British Identity, 1750-1914*, (Cambridge University Press), 2007, and *Inventing the Industrial Revolution: The English Patent System, 1660-1800*, (Cambridge University Press), 1988. Allen, Robert C., *The British Industrial Revolution in Global Perspective*, (Cambridge University Press), 2009, and ibid, Mokyr, Joel, *The Enlightened Economy: An Economic History of Britain 1700-1850*, place technological ideas and change at the heart of the Industrial Revolution.

[5] See Calling, H., 'The development of the Spinning Mule', *Textile History*, Vol. 9, (1978), pp. 35-57.

[6] Aspin, Christopher, *James Hargreaves and the spinning jenny*, (Helmshore Local History Society), 1964.

mechanised printing by Thomas Bell in 1783. [7] James Kay's 'flying shuttle' had speeded up the process of weaving producing a bottleneck caused by the shortage of hand-spun thread. The mechanisation of spinning after 1764 reversed this situation. The new jennies allowed one worker to spin at least eight and eventually eighty times the amount of thread previously produced by a single spinner. Improvements by Arkwright and especially Crompton further increased productivity. The problem was now weaving. The power loom did not initially resolve the problem and the decades between 1780 and 1810 were ones of considerable prosperity for handloom weavers. [8]

Although the introduction of new machines for textile production, especially cotton occurred over a short timescale, their widespread use was delayed until the 1820s. [9] There were three main reasons for this. The new technologies were costly and often unreliable. Modifications were necessary before their full economic benefits were realised and it was not until the early 1820s that the power loom was improved and the self-acting mule was introduced. [10] There was worker resistance to the introduction of the new technologies and some employers continued to use hand workers because they were cheaper than new machines. [11] This was

---

[7] Hills, R. L., 'Hargreaves, Arkwright and Crompton: why three inventors?' *Textile History*, Vol. 10, (1979), pp. 114-126. See also, Aspin, Christopher, *The water spinners*, (Helmshore Local History Society), 2003, Fisk, Karen., 'Arkwright: cotton king or spin doctor?', *History Today*, Vol. 48, (3), (1998), pp. 25-30, and Merrill, J. N., *Arkwright of Cromford*, Matlock, 1986.
[8] Chapman, Stanley D., and Butt, John, 'The Cotton Industry 1775-1856' and Jenkins, D. T., 'The Wool Textile Industry 1780-1850', in Feinstein, C. H., and Pollard, Sidney, (eds.), *Studies in capital formation in the United Kingdom, 1750-1920*, (Oxford University Press), 1988, pp. 105-125, 126-140.
[9] Chapman, Stanley D., *The cotton industry in the Industrial Revolution*, (Macmillan), 1972, remains a good bibliographical essay. Thompson, James, 'Invention in the Industrial Revolution: the case of cotton textiles', in Prados de la Escosura, Leandro, (ed.), *Exceptionalism and industrialisation: Britain and its European rivals, 1688-1815*, (Cambridge University Press), 2004, pp. 127-144; Farnie, Douglas A., *The English Cotton Industry and the World Market, 1815-1896*, (Oxford University Press), 1976.
[10] Lazonick, W., 'Industrial relations and technical change: the case of the self-acting mule', *Cambridge Journal of Economics*, Vol. 3, (1979), pp. 231-262.
[11] Randall, A., *Before the Luddites: Custom, community and machinery in the English woollen industry 1776-1809*, (Cambridge University Press), 1991, places Luddism in a longer context and is particularly valuable for its

particularly evident in the Yorkshire woollen industry that lagged behind cotton in applying new technology. [12] Finally, the original spinning jennies were small enough to be used in the home but Arkwright's water frame was too large for domestic use and needed purpose-built spinning mills. These early factories used waterpower though increasingly steam engines were used. By 1800, a quarter of all cotton yarn was spun by steam but factories did not combine powered spinning and weaving until after 1815. By 1850, some factories employed large numbers of workers, but most remained small. In Lancashire in the 1840s, the average firm employed 260 people and a quarter employed less than 100. [13] The mechanisation of the textile industry was a process in technological innovation and modification rather than an immediate revolutionary process. [14]

This was even more the case in the iron industry. [15] In 1700, charcoal was used to smelt iron and was increasingly expensive leading to Britain relying on European imports. Although Abraham Darby perfected coke smelting in 1709 to produce 'pig' or cast iron it was not until demand for iron rose rapidly after 1750 that coke replaced

---

discussion of community and cultural opposition to new technology. Thomis, Malcolm, *The Luddites: Machine-breaking in Regency England*, (David & Charles), 1970, Binfield, Kevin, (ed.), *Writings of the Luddites*, (John Hopkins University Press), 2004, pp. 1-68, and Vincent, Julien, Bourdeau, Vincent, and Jarrige, François, *Les Luddites: Bris de machines, économie politique et histoire*, (Maisons-Alfort), 2006, pp. 17-54, consider the Luddite outbreaks.

[12] Crump, W. B., *The Leeds woollen industry, 1780-182,* (Thoresby Society), 1931, Rees, Henry, 'Leeds and the Yorkshire woollen industry', *Economic Geography*, Vol. 24, (1), (1948), pp. 28-34; Caunce, Stephen, 'Complexity, community structure and competitive advantage within the Yorkshire woollen industry, c.1700-1850', *Business History*, Vol. 39, (4), (1997), pp. 26-43; Smail, John, 'The sources of innovation in the woollen and worsted industry of eighteenth-century Yorkshire', *Business History*, Vol. 41, (1), (1999), pp. 1-15.

[13] Gatrell, V. A. C., 'Labour, power, and the size of firms in Lancashire cotton in the second quarter of the 19th century', *Economic History Review*, Vol. 30, (1977), pp. 95-139, considers the size of enterprises.

[14] Harley, C. K., and Crafts, N. F. R., 'Cotton textiles and industrial output growth during the industrial revolution', *Economic History Review*, Vol. 48, (1995), pp. 134-144, examines the sixty years between 1770 and 1830.

[15] Harris, J. R., *The British iron industry, 1700-1850*, (Macmillan), 1988, looks at the research while Davies, R. S. W., and Pollard, Sidney, 'The Iron Industry, 1750-1850', in ibid, Feinstein, C. H., and Pollard, Sidney, (eds.), *Studies in capital formation in the United Kingdom, 1750-1920*, pp. 73-104, considers investment.

charcoal as the fuel for smelting. [16] The stimulus for expansion in iron making came from the wars with France and the American colonies in the 1750s and 1770s and especially between 1793 and 1815. This led technological change. Henry Cort's puddling and rolling process of 1783-1784 that accelerated wrought iron production was of comparable importance to Darby's earlier discovery. [17] The new technologies led to a four-fold growth of pig iron between 1788 and 1806, a significant reduction in costs and virtually put an end to expensive foreign imports. The 'hot-blast' of 1828 further reduced costs. Rising demand for iron stimulated developments in the coal industry. Here the major technological developments were led by the need to mine coal from deeper pits. [18] Pumping engines, first Newcomen's and then Watt's helped in this process. Sir Humphrey Davy's safety lamp improved safety underground from inflammable methane gas or 'firedamp'. Increases in productivity were, however, largely achieved by employing more miners.

Contemporaries and later historians emphasised the importance of the steam engine to the industrial revolution but wind and water remained important as sources of mechanical energy. Windmills were used for grinding corn, land-drainage and some industrial processes. Waterpower was far more important and remained so until the mid-nineteenth century. Before 1800, most textile mills were water-powered and in 1830, 2,230 mills still used waterpower as against 3,000 using steam. [19] Metalwork, mining, papermaking and pottery continued to use waterpower. The development of steam power in the eighteenth century was gradual. Thomas Newcomen developed his steam-atmospheric engine in 1712 that was largely used for pumping water out of mines and though costly and inefficient was

---

[16] Raistrick, Arthur, *Dynasty of iron founders: the Darbys and Coalbrookdale*, (Longman, Green), 1953; Flinn, M. W., 'Abraham Darby and the coke-smelting process', *Economica*, ns, Vol. 26, (1959), pp. 54-59; Trinder, Barrie, *The industrial revolution in Shropshire*, 3rd edition, (Phillimore), 2000.

[17] Mott, R. A., *Henry Cort, the great finer: creator of puddled iron*, ed. P. Singer, (Metals Society), 1983.

[18] Pollard, Sidney, 'Coal Mining 1750-1850', in ibid, Feinstein, C. H., and Pollard, Sidney, (eds.), *Studies in capital formation in the United Kingdom, 1750-1920*, pp. 35-72. Just how important coal was to industrial development is viewed more sceptically in Clark, G., and Jacks, D., 'Coal and the industrial revolution, 1700-1869', *European Review of Economic History*, Vol. 11, (1), (2007), pp. 39-72.

[19] Harris, J. R., 'The employment of steam power in the 18th century', *History*, Vol. 52, (1967), pp. 133-148.

in widespread use by 1760. [20] Watt trebled the efficiency of the Newcomen engine by adding a separate condenser in the mid-1760s.[21] This made steam engines more cost-effective but they could still only be used for tasks involving vertical motion. The breakthrough came in 1782 with the development of 'sun and planet' gearing that enabled steam engines to generate rotary motion and power the new technologies in textiles. By 1800, about a fifth of all mechanical energy in Britain was produced by steam engines. Steam power was a highly versatile form of energy and its impact on British industry was profound.[22] It allowed industry to move into towns often on or near to coalfields where it could be supplied by canals. Though older means of generating energy remained important, the application of steam power to mining, iron-making, the railways and especially the booming cotton industry meant that by 1850 it was increasingly the dominant form of energy. The technologies of the Industrial Revolution were adopted in Britain rather than elsewhere because they were profitable in Britain. [23] This explains Britain's precociousness in invention: the famous inventions of the Industrial Revolution were invented in Britain because they generated enough profit to make the cost of developing and perfecting them worthwhile.

How important was technical advance to the industrial revolution? In 1776, Adam Smith in his *Wealth of Nations* seemed

---

[20] Mott, R. A., 'The Newcomen Engine in the Eighteenth Century', *Transactions of the Newcomen Society*, Vol. 35, (1964 for 1962-63), pp. 69-86, and Harris, J. R., 'Recent research on the Newcomen engine and historical studies', *Transactions of the Newcomen Society*, Vol. 50, (1980 for 1978-1979), pp. 175-192.

[21] Hills, R. L., *James Watt*, 3 Vols. (Landmark), 2002-2006, is a major study. See also, Hills, R. L., 'James Watt and his rotary engines', *Transactions of the Newcomen Society*, Vol. 70, (1), (1999), pp. 89-108,.

[22] Wrigley, E. A., *Energy and the English Industrial Revolution*, (Cambridge University Press), 2011, provides a valuable critique of developments in energy use and their significance. Tunzelmann, G. N. von, *Steam power and British industrialisation to 1860,* (Oxford University Press), 1978, Crafts, N. F. R., and Mills, Terence C., 'Was 19th century British growth steam-powered?: the climacteric revisited', *Explorations in Economic History*, Vol. 41, (2004), pp. 156-171, Tann, Jennifer, 'Fixed Capital Formation in Steam Power 1775-1825', in ibid, Feinstein, C. H., and Pollard, Sidney, (eds.), *Studies in capital formation in the United Kingdom, 1750-1920*, pp. 164-181, and Samuel, R., 'The workshop of the world: steam power and hand technology in mid-Victorian Britain,' *History Workshop*, Vol. 3, (1977), pp. 6-72.

[23] See, Allen, Robert C., *The Industrial Revolution in Miniature: The Spinning Jenny in Britain, France and India*, (Oxford University, Department of Economics), Working Paper, 375, 2007.

unaware that he was living in a period of technical change and mechanisation. For him, economic growth was achieved through the organisational principle of division of labour rather than the application of new technologies. Others followed Smith in assigning less importance to technical change than historians subsequently did. The effect of technological change was neither immediate nor widespread until after 1800. Cotton and iron set the pace of change but other industries, like glass and paper-making, shipbuilding and food-processing were also undergoing organisational and technological change. Change varied across industries and regions. Steam power did not replace waterpower at a stroke. Work organisation and the uses of newer technologies varied and in 1850 factories coexisted with domestic production, artisan workshops and large-scale mining and metal-producing organisations. Both revolutionary technologies and traditional techniques remained important to Britain's economic development

The pace of economic change and its geographical distribution after 1780 was also uneven. Dynamic growth took place in specialised economic regions. [24] Cotton was largely based in south Lancashire and parts of Derbyshire and Cheshire. Wool was dominant in the West Riding of Yorkshire. Iron dominated the economies of Shropshire and South Wales. Staffordshire was internationally renowned for its potteries. Birmingham and Warwickshire specialised in metal-working. Tyneside was more diverse with interests in coal, glass, iron and salt. London with its huge population, sophisticated manufacturing and service sectors and its docks, warehouses, engineering, shipbuilding, silk weaving, luxury trades, the machinery of government and the law, publishing and printing, financial centre and entertainment was an economic region in its own right. De-industrialisation was also regional in character. After 1780, the West Country and East Anglia textile industries declined. The iron industry disappeared from the Weald in Kent and the Cumberland coalfield waned.

Regional growth or decline depended largely on whether industries had access to waterpower as an energy source or as a means of processing, easy access to coal and other raw materials, and an ample labour force. In 1780, regions and their industries retained their rural character in varying degrees. Increasingly, however, industrial growth took on an urban character and the late-eighteenth and early-nineteenth centuries saw the rapid expansion of towns that specialised in various industries. Around each of these urban centres

---

[24] Hudson, Pat, (ed.), *Regions and industries: a perspective on the industrial revolution in Britain*, (Cambridge University Press), 1989.

clustered smaller towns and industrial villages whose artisan outworkers specialised in particular tasks. Walsall in the Black Country, for example, specialised in buckle-making; Coventry in ribbon production and tobacco boxes at Willenhall. The concentration of specialised commercial and manufacturing industries, especially skilled labour, in and around towns was a major advantage for entrepreneurs and businessmen. They were helped by the expanding communication network of roads and canal and after 1830 railways providing cheap supplies of raw materials and fuel as well as helping distribute finished products. For those who worked in these industries downturns in the economy or changes in fashion could have a devastating effect leading to high levels of unemployment and falling wages.

Economic change and population growth led to the rapid expansion of urban centres. [25] Towns, especially those in the forefront of manufacturing innovation, attracted rural workers hoping for better wages. They saw towns as places free from the paternalism of the rural environment and flocked there in their thousands. For some migration brought wealth and security. For the majority, life in towns was little different, and in environmental terms probably worse than life in the country. They had exchanged rural slums for urban ones and exploitation by the landowner for exploitation by the factory master and the landlord. Between 1780 and 1811, England's urban population rose from a quarter to a third, a process that continued throughout the century and by 1850, the rural-urban split was about even. The number of towns in England and Wales with 2,500 inhabitants increased from 104 in 1750 to 188 by 1800 and to over 220 by 1851. England was the most urbanised area in the world and the rate of urban growth had not peaked. London, with its one million inhabitants in 1801, was the largest city in Europe. The dramatic growth of the northern and Midland industrial towns after 1770 was caused largely by migration because of industry's voracious demand for labour. Regions where population growth was not accompanied by industrialisation or where deindustrialisation took place found their local economies under considerable pressure. Surplus labour led to falling wages and growing problems of poverty.

Population growth, economic and social change, technological advances, changes in the organisation of work, the dynamism of cotton and iron as well as urbanisation were bunched in the last twenty

---

[25] Clark, Peter, (ed.), *The Cambridge urban history of Britain, Vol. 2: 1540-1840*, (Cambridge University Press), 2000, and Daunton, Martin J., (ed.), *The Cambridge urban history of Britain, Vol. 3: 1840-1950*, (Cambridge University Press), 2000, are essential.

years of the eighteenth century and the first thirty years of the nineteenth. This was revolutionary change. However, change was itself a process that extended across the eighteenth century. The revolution in the economy did not begin in 1780 nor was it completed by 1830.

Why did economic change occur in Britain between 1780 and 1850?

Historians face significant problems in examining the industrial revolution. [26] There is the problem of what precisely the 'industrial revolution' was and its national nature has been questioned. How far was there a British industrial revolution or was economic change essentially local or regional? There is also the question of timing. When did the revolution begin? When did it end? Finally, historians increasingly recognise the diversity of economic experiences and the existence of both change and continuity of experience in the eighteenth and early-nineteenth century. The 'industrial revolution' is increasingly seen as a metaphor for the changes that took place in the British economy between 1780 and 1850. While it would be perverse to refrain from using a term 'hallowed by usage', it is important to recognise that change occurred slowly in most industries and rapidly in a handful. Contemporaries were aware that they were living through a period of change. The poet Robert Southey wrote in 1807:

> ...no kingdom ever experienced so great a change in so short a course of years. [27]

Cotton, iron and coal expanded and the spread of steam power were important but undue emphasis on them neglects the broader economic experiences of Britain. Similarly, the question 'Why did the industrial revolution take place in Britain rather than France or Germany?' misses the crucial point that economic change did not

---

[26] On the debate on the nature of the 'industrial revolution', Fores, Michael, 'The Myth of a British Industrial Revolution', *History*, Vol. 66, (1981), pp. 181-198, and a vigorous response Musson, A. E., 'The British Industrial Revolution, *History*, Vol. 69, (1982), pp. 252-258, can be supplemented with ibid, More, Charles, *Understanding the Industrial Revolution*, pp. 9-28, 158-173, ibid, King, Steven and Timmins, Geoffrey, *Making sense of the Industrial Revolution: English economy and society 1700-1850*, pp. 10-66.

[27] Southey, Robert, *Letters from England*, (Longman, Hurst, Rees and Orme), 1808, p. 73.

occur in Britain as a whole. [28] Growth was regional and industrialisation took place in particular locations like Lancashire, the Central Lowlands of Scotland and South Wales and around Belfast. Explaining the industrial revolution is a very difficult undertaking since economic change had an effect, however small, on all aspects of society. Some circumstances that were present in Britain made change possible and, in that sense, can be said to be causal. Others held back progress but change occurred despite them. [29]

What was 'economic growth' in the late-eighteenth and first half of the nineteenth centuries and what were its major characteristics? The main indicator of long-term growth is the income the country receives from goods and services or gross domestic product. During the eighteenth century, GDP grew slightly fluctuated around 1 per cent per year. Between 1800 and 1850, growth remained at over 2 per cent per year. Growth in GDP depends on three things: increases in labour, capital investment and productivity. Growing population accounted for the increase in labour after 1780 and grew at around 1 per cent per year between 1780 and 1800 and 1.4 per cent for the next fifty years. Increased capital investment was also evident after 1780. Between 1780 and 1800, capital investment rose by 1.2 per cent per year. This rose slightly to 1.4 per cent between 1800 and 1830 and, largely because of investment in railways to 2 per cent between 1830 and 1850. Increasing productivity is more difficult to estimate. Statistical data is far from reliable leading to major discrepancies in modern estimates. For instance, the production of coal in the late-eighteenth century is estimated to have grown annually at 0.64 per cent or alternatively at 1.13 per cent, twice as fast. The statistics also show only part of the picture and it is very difficult to extrapolate from specific data on specific industries to the economy as a whole. Total figures also blur the important differences between the experience of different industries and regions. It was not until the development of

---

[28] Crafts, N. F. R., 'Industrial Revolution in England and France: Some Thoughts on the Question 'Why was England First?'' and comment by Rostow, W. W., *Economic History Review*, Vol. 30, (1977), pp. 429-441, and 'Economic Growth in France and Britain, 1830-1910: A Review of the Evidence', *Journal of Economic History*, Vol. 54, (1984), pp. 49-67.

[29] Wrigley, E. A., *Continuity, chance and change: the character of the industrial revolution in England*, (Cambridge University Press), 1988, and ibid, Crafts, N. F. R., *British economic growth during the industrial revolution,* provide an excellent summary of the problems of studying the 'industrial revolution'.

the railways after 1830 that the notion of a British economy, as opposed to localised or regional economies had real meaning. [30]

If it is possible to identify a single cause for the industrial revolution, then a strong case can be made for population increase. Between 1780 and 1850, the population of England and Wales increased from over 7 million to nearly 18 million. This led to mounting demand for goods like food and housing. Nevertheless, the increase in demand for other goods such as more manufactured goods or more efficient means of communication did not necessarily follow from population expansion. The problem is one of timing. When did population growth and economic growth occur and did they correspond? Although historians broadly accept that population grew from the mid-eighteenth century, they do not agree about the economic growth. If population growth stimulated demand, you would expect economic and population growth broadly to coincide. However, they did not. Accelerated economic growth began in the last quarter of the eighteenth century while the maximum rate of population growth on mainland Britain was not achieved until after 1810.

Population began to expand after 1750 and some historians argue that this provided the final ingredient necessary to trigger off

---

[30] On the problems of measuring growth see, Berg, M., and Hudson, P., 'Rehabilitating the industrial revolution', *Economic History Review*, Vol. 45, (1992), pp. 24-50, Crafts, N. F. R., 'British economic growth 1700-1831: a review of the evidence', *Economic History Review*, Vol. 36, (1983), pp. 177-199, Crafts, N. F. R., and Harley, C. K., 'Output growth and the British industrial revolution: a restatement of the Crafts-Harley view', *Economic History Review*, Vol. 45, (1992), pp. 703-730, Harley, C. K., 'British industrialization before 1841: evidence of slower growth during the industrial revolution', *Journal of Economic History*, Vol. 42, (1982), Heim, C., and Mirowski, P., 'Interest rates and crowding out during Britain's industrial revolution', *Journal of Economic History*, Vol. 57, (1987), pp. 117-139, Hoppit, J., 'Counting the industrial revolution', *Economic History Review*, Vol. 43, (1990), pp. 173-193, Jackson, R. V., 'Rates of industrial growth during the industrial revolution', *Economic History Review*, Vol. 45, (1992), pp. 1-23, Mokyr, J., 'Has the industrial revolution been crowded out? Some reflections on Crafts and Williamson', *Explorations in Economic History*, Vol. 24, (1987), pp. 293-318, and Williamson, J. G., 'Why was British growth so slow during the industrial revolution?', *Journal of Economic History*, Vol. 44, (1984), pp. 687-712, and Crafts, N. F. R., 'Productivity Growth in the Industrial Revolution: A New Growth Accounting Perspective', *Journal of Economic History*, Vol. 64, (2004), pp. 521-535. For the period after 1830, see Matthews, R. C. O., Feinstein, C. H., and Odling-Smee, J. C., *British Economic Growth, 1856-1973*, (Stamford University Press), 1982.

industrialisation. Berg and Craft have shown that the origins of higher growth rates went back to the early decades of the century. In this scenario, population growth came after the beginnings of economic growth. [31] The impact of population growth causes problems for historians who argue for economic growth from the 1780s and those who see growth as something that began earlier in the century. It had favourable effects on economic growth in three important respects. Population growth provided Britain with an abundant and cheap supply of labour. [32] It stimulated investment in industry and agriculture by its impact on increased demand for goods and services. Finally, urbanisation made it profitable to create or improve services. For example, the building of the canal from the Bridgewater coalmines at Worsley to Manchester in the early 1760s took advantage of growing demand for domestic coal that made canal investment cost-effective. The role of population growth in the origins of Britain's industrial revolution was far from straightforward.

Britain was a relatively wealthy country in the mid-eighteenth century with a well-established system of banking. [33] After 1688, Britain underwent a revolution in public finance and the cost of borrowing declined sharply. Leading scholars have argued that easier credit for the government, made possible by better property-rights protection, lead to a rapid expansion of private credit. [34] This enabled

---

[31] Berg, Maxine, *The age of manufactures: industry, innovation and work in Britain 1700-1820*, (Basil Blackwell), 1985, 2nd edition, (Routledge), 1994, Berg, Maxine, and Hudson, Pat, 'Growth and change: a comment on the Crafts-Harley view of the industrial revolution', *Economic History Review*, 2nd series, Vol. 47, (1994), pp. 147-149.

[32] Tranter, Neil L., 'Population, migration and labour supply', in Aldcroft, Derek H., and Ville, Simon P., (ed.), *The European economy, 1750-1914: a thematic approach* (Manchester University Press), 1994, pp. 37-71, provides a long-term perspective.

[33] Collins, M., *Banks and Industrial Finance in Britain 1800-1939*, (Cambridge University Press), 1995, pp. 14-24, provides a succinct discussion of developments to 1870. Crouzet, F., (ed.), *Capital Formation and the Industrial Revolution*, (Methuen), 1967, contains valuable papers. See also, Capie, Forrest Hunter, 'Money and economic development in eighteenth-century England', in ibid, Prados de la Escosura, Leandro, (ed.), *Exceptionalism and industrialisation: Britain and its European rivals, 1688-1815*, pp. 216-32.

[34] Temin, Peter, and Voth, Hans-Joachim, *Prometheus Shackled: Goldsmith Banks and England's financial revolution after 1700*, (Oxford University Press), 2013, especially pp. 23-38, 148-175, challenges this traditional view suggesting that the 1688 political settlement, which led investors to feel more confident that the government would repay money, resulted in the diversion of capital from industrial enterprises and into the state, which then

people to build up savings and provided them with capital to invest.[35] After 1750, there was growing investment in roads, canals, and buildings and in enclosing land.[36] This process was sustained after 1780 through to the 1850s with continued investment in transport and enclosure and in the expansion of the textile and iron industries, and after 1830 by the development of railways. The annual rate of domestic investment rose from about £13 million in the 1780s to over £40 million by the 1830s. The ratio of gross investment to the gross national product rose from 6 per cent in the 1770s to 12 per cent by the 1790s and it remained at this level until 1850. Widespread capital investment was largely confined to a small, though important part of the economy rising in farming, communications and textiles, especially cotton and in iron and steel. Other areas of the economy were often undercapitalised relative to these industries.

Capital investment in farming was largely on enclosures, drainage and buildings.[37] Landowners ploughed back about 6 per cent of their total income into the land. This rose to about 16 per cent during the French wars when high wheat prices encouraged investment in enclosure but fell back after 1815 with the onset of depression and did not revive until the 1840s. In the 1780s, a third of all investment was in farming but by 1850, this had fallen to an eighth. By contrast, there was a rapid growth of investment in industry and communications. Annual investment in industry and trade rose from £2 million in the 1780s to £17 million by 1850. Between 1780 and 1830, there was an annual investment of £1.5 million on canals and roads and for the improvement of docks and harbours. These figures were dwarfed by investment in railways that peaked at £15 million per year in the 1840s, some 28 per cent of all investment. The increase in the availability of investment capital allowed economic growth to occur.

---

spent the money on activities with a low social rate of return. Low borrowing costs allowed the British government to go on a military and naval spending spree that starved the private sector of funds. Stiffling prvate credit resulted in markedly slower growth in the English economy. The Industrial Revolution began in Britain despite rather than because of the post-1688 Financial Revolution.

[35] Finn, M., *The character of credit: personal debt in English culture 1740-1914,* (Cambridge University Press), 2003.

[36] Ginarlis, J., and Pollard, Sidney, 'Roads and Waterways 1750-1850', in ibid, Feinstein, C. H., and Pollard, Sidney, (eds.), *Studies in capital formation in the United Kingdom, 1750-1920*, pp. 182-224.

[37] Holderness, B. A., 'Agriculture 1770-1860', in ibid, Feinstein, C. H., and Pollard, Sidney, (eds.), *Studies in capital formation in the United Kingdom, 1750-1920*, pp. 9-34

Britain was already a well-established trading nation. [38] Colonies were important sources of raw materials as well as markets for manufactured goods. London was a major centre for the re-export trade. The slave trade played a major role in the development of Liverpool and Bristol and its profits provided an important source of capital for early industrialisation. [39] By the 1780s, the export trade was expanding annually by 2.6 per cent. Cotton production depended on international trade and was responsible for half the increase in the value of exports between 1780 and 1830. [40] Cotton accounted for just over half Britain's exports by 1830 and three-quarters of all exports were associated with textiles. This represented a narrow trading base and helps to explain why the British economy underwent depression in the 1830s and early 1840s. British factories were over-producing for European and global markets already saturated with textile goods. The result was some changes in the nature of exports with iron growing from 6 per cent in the 1810s to 20 per cent by 1850 and the growing importance of coal.

In the 1780s, Europe was a major market for British goods and this remained the case in 1850. However, there were important changes in the destination of British goods. The United States increasingly became a focus for exports of manufactured goods and for importing raw cotton. [41] This process was helped by the opening up of the Latin American markets in the early-nineteenth century. [42] India was a huge market for cotton goods. Similar possibilities existed

---

[38] Mathias, Peter, and Davis, John Anthony, (eds.), *International trade and British economic growth: from the eighteenth century to the present day* (Blackwell Publishers), 1996, contains valuable papers. Crouzet, François, 'Britain's Exports and Their Markets, 1701-1913', in Emmer, Pieter C., Pétré-Grenouilleau, Olivier, and Roitman, Jessica V., (eds.), *A deus ex machina revisited: Atlantic colonial trade and European economic development*, (Brill), 2006, provides a longer-term perspective.

[39] Morgan, Kenneth, *Slavery and the British Empire: From Africa to America*, (Oxford University Press), 2007, and *Slavery, Atlantic Trade and the British Economy 1699-1800*, (Cambridge University Press), 2000, provide a good synopsis of current thinking.

[40] Edwards, M. M., *The growth of the British cotton trade, 1780-1815*, (Manchester University Press), 1967.

[41] Nash, R. C., 'The organization of trade and finance in the British-Atlantic economy, 1600-1830', in Coclanis, Peter A., (ed.), *The Atlantic economy during the seventeenth and eighteenth centuries: organization, operation, practice, and personnel*, (University of South Carolina Press), 2005, pp. 95-151.

[42] Platt, D. C., *Latin America and British Trade, 1806-1914*, (Oxford University Press), 1972.

in the Middle East and South America. Britain increasingly shifted trade towards less developed economies that provided growing imports of tropical products to Britain and other industrialised countries like Germany and France. Overseas trade has been highlighted by some historians as a primary cause of economic growth. The growth of export industries at a faster rate than other industries was closely linked to foreign trade. [43]

To what extent was the growth in trade between 1780 and 1850 central to Britain's economic development? It stimulated a domestic demand for the products of British industry. For example, in 1767, 16,000 sheep and 14,000 cattle passed through the Birdlip Hill Turnpike in Gloucester en route from south Wales to London. The coastal traffic of coal into London from the north-east rose from one million to three million tons per year between 1720 and 1790. [44] International trade gave access to raw materials that both widened the range and cheapened the products of British industries. It provided purchasing power for countries to buy British goods since trade is a two-way process. Profits from trade were used to finance industrial expansion and agricultural improvement. It was a major cause of the growth of large towns and industrial centres. The role of British trade must, however, be put into perspective. Changes in the pattern of British trade between 1780 and 1850 such as the export or re-export of manufactured goods in return for imports of foodstuffs and raw materials were relatively small and industrial developments from the 1780s consolidated already existing trends. Exports may have helped textiles and iron to expand but they made little impact on the unmodernised, traditional manufacturing sectors.

By 1750, Britain was already a highly mobile society. Travel may have been slow and, on occasions dangerous but it was not uncommon. Within a hundred years, the British landscape was scarred by canals and railways and traversed by improved roads and the movement of goods and people quickened dramatically. Turnpike roads and the emergence of a sophisticated coaching industry, canals with their barges carrying raw materials and the

---

[43] For the development of shipping see, Davies, R., *The Rise of the English Shipping Industry*, (Macmillan), 1962, and Hope, R. A., *A New History of British Shipping*, (John Murray), 1990.

[44] Ibid, Clark, Gregory, and Jacks, David, 'Coal and the Industrial Revolution, 1700-1869', and Hausman, William J., 'The English coastal coal trade, 1691-1910: how rapid was productivity growth?', *Economic History Review*, 2nd series, Vol. 40, (1987), pp. 588-602, and 'A model of the London coal trade in the 18th century', *Quarterly Journal of Economics*, Vol. 94, (1980), pp. 1-14.

manufactured goods of the industrial revolution, new harbours and the railways were symbolic of 'progress' as much as factories and enclosed fields. From the 1550s, the parish had responsibility for maintaining roads. This may have been adequate for dealing with local roads but the major or trunk roads were not maintained as well. Local people thought that the people who used these roads should pay for their upkeep. The result was the development of turnpike roads, financed by private turnpike trusts, which people were charged a toll to use. Britain's road system in the mid-eighteenth century was extensive but under-funded. Just over £1 million was spent annually. This was, however, insufficient to maintain the road system necessary to growing trade and manufactures. Turnpike roads, the first established in 1663, grew slowly in the first half of the eighteenth century. About eight new trusts were established each year. From the 1750s, this went up to about forty a year and from the 1790s, to nearly sixty. By the mid-1830s, there were 1,116 turnpike trusts in England and Wales managing slightly more than a sixth of all roads, some 22,000 miles. Parallel to this organisational development, there were improvements in the quality of road building associated particularly with Thomas Telford and John Loudon Macadam. [45]

What contribution did turnpike and parish roads make to improved communication in Britain between 1780 and 1850? Spending on parish roads did not increase markedly though there was a significant growth in spending by turnpike trusts. This reached a peak of £1.5 million per year in the 1820s. The problem was that improvements to the road system were patchy and dependent on private initiatives. Despite this, there were significant reductions in journey times between the main centres of population. In the 1780s, it took ten days to travel from London to Edinburgh; by the 1830s, 45 hours. This led to a dramatic increase in the number of passengers carried by a rapidly expanding coaching industry. The road system transported all kinds of industrial material and manufactured goods. There was a significant growth of carrier firms after 1780. In London, for example, there were 353 firms in 1790 but 735 in the mid-1820s and a five-fold increase in the number of carriers in Birmingham between 1790 and 1830. These firms were, however, unable to compete with the canals or the railways and concentrated on providing

---

[45] Albert, W., *The turnpike road system in England, 1663-1840*, (Cambridge University Press), 1972, and Pawson, E., *Transport and economy: the turnpike roads of 18th-century Britain*, (Academic Press), 1977. See also, Buchanan, B. J., 'The Evolution of the English Turnpike Trusts: Lessons from a Case Study', *The Economic History Review*, Vol. 39, (2), (1986), pp. 223-243.

short distance carriage of goods from canals and railway stations to local communities. The major problem facing early industrialists was the cost of carrying heavy, bulky goods like coal or iron ore. The solution was to use water, rivers, coastal transport and from the 1760s, canals. [46]

The first phase of canal development took place in the 1760s and early 1770s beginning with the construction of the Bridgewater canal. The second phase, in the 1790s, has rightly been called 'canal mania' with the completion of several important canals and the setting-up of fifty-one new schemes. By 1820, the canal network was largely completed linking all the major centres of industrial production and population. Canals dramatically enhanced the efficiency of the whole economy by making a cheap system of transport available for goods and passengers. The price of raw materials like coal, timber, iron, wood and cotton tumbled. The needs of farming, whether for manure or for access to markets for grain, cheese and butter, were easily satisfied where farmers had access to canals. Canals were a means of overcoming the fuel crisis that threatened to limit industrial growth by making cheap, abundant coal supplies available. [47] The building of canals also created massive employment and spending power at a time when growing industries were looking for mass markets. It is difficult to exaggerate the importance of canals to Britain's industrial development between 1780 and 1830. [48]

From 1830, railways were the epoch-making transport innovation. Between 1830 and 1850, 7,000 miles of track was laid with railway 'manias' in the 1830s and between 1844 and 1847 when investment was at its peak. Their economic importance lay in their ability to move both people and goods quickly that no other single mode of transport had previously been able. They offered lower costs and greater speed attracting passengers, mail and high-value goods. Mail went to new railways in six months and coaches running in direct competition lost out. Canals were able, by cutting their rates and improving their services, to continue to carry goods for several years.

---

[46] Ward, J. R., *The finance of canal building in 18th-century England*, (Oxford University Press), 1974.
[47] See also the role of coastal traffic, Ville, S., 'Total factor productivity in the English shipping industry: the north-east coal trade, 1700-1850', *Economic History Review*, Vol. 39, (1986), pp. 355-370, and 'Shipping in the port of Sunderland, 1815-1845', *Business History*, Vol. 32, (1990), pp. 32-51.
[48] Turnbull, G., 'Canals, coal and regional growth during the industrial revolution', *Economic History Review*, Vol. 40, (1987), pp. 537-560.

In 1840, the volume of traffic carried by canal from Liverpool to Manchester was more than twice that carried by railway.

The decline of the coaching industry was, however, rapid. In 1824, about fifty coaches went through Dunstable on the A5 in Bedfordshire. *Pigot's Directory*, 1839 clearly shows the effects of the opening of the London-Birmingham railway the previous year. The number of coaches was greatly reduced. The records of the Puddlehill Trust show that only twelve coaches a day passed through in early 1838. Local carriers fared better and *Pigot's* noted that Deacon's conveyances from *The King's Arms* went to and from Leighton Buzzard to meet the trains from London and Birmingham. Dunstable suffered greatly during 1838-1839 from the decline of the coaching industry and the more general slump in the economy. Twenty years later, Charles Lambourn noted:

> ...the people were panic-struck and dismay was visible on every countenance, the hope of their gains was pain...it was a fearful time...[49]

This was later supported by William Derbyshire:

> A period of great depression ensued, upon the extinction of the traffic of the road, which continued for some years; but after awhile, the business men of the town, directed their whole attention to the extension and development of the Straw trade, which had existed in Dunstable for more than 200 years, although it had hitherto been carried on to a very limited extent...[50]

His view of the effects of dramatic end of road traffic may well be based on the experiences of his own family but evidence from both *Pigot's Directory* and the 1841 Census suggest the slump was short-lived.

The Victorians had no hesitation in assuming a direct link between railways and economic growth though historians are today far less convinced. There was increased demand for coal and iron. In the 1840s, 30 per cent of brick production went into railways and between 1830 and 1845, some 740 million bricks were used in railway construction. Towns grew up round established engineering centres at Swindon, Crewe, Rugby and Doncaster. Food could be transported more cheaply and arrive fresher. There is, however, no doubting the social and cultural impact of railways. 64,000 passengers were carried in 1843 rising to 174,000 by 1848 with an increase in the third-class

---

[49] Lambourn, Charles, *The Dunstapalogia*, (James Tibbet,) 1859, p. 208
[50] Derbyshire, W. H., *The History of Dunstable*, 2nd edition, (James Tibbet), 1882, p. 97.

element from 19,000 to 86,000 in the same period. The Great Exhibition of 1851 reinforced this increased mobility of population.[51]

Between 1780 and 1850, great output was achieved by the transport industry, as in manufacturing industry, by applying a rapidly increasing labour force to existing modes of production as well as using new techniques and applying steam-driven machinery. Historians have emphasised the importance of canals and railways that respectively in the eighteenth and nineteenth centuries in reducing transport costs. However, coastal and river traffic and carriage of goods and people by road remained important and the horse was the main means of transport well beyond 1850.

British society in the eighteenth and nineteenth century was profoundly conservative. How was a society with highly traditional structures able to generate changes in so many areas of economic life? By 1780, British society was capitalist in character and organisation. Its aristocracy was remarkably 'open', allowing the newly rich and talented to 'climb'. The most successful merchants, professional and businessmen in each generation were funnelled off into landed society. Success brought wealth and the ultimate proof of success in business was the ability to leave it. In France, where social mobility was discouraged there was political and social discontent and ultimately political revolution. In Britain, where social climbing was not obstructed, there was an industrial revolution. [52]

Britain was already a highly market-oriented society. [53] Imports, whether smuggled or not, were quickly moved to market. There were 800 market towns in England and Wales in the 1780s reflecting the intensity of production and the ability of particular areas to specialise in particular products. Domestic goods, both agricultural and

---

[51] Auerbach, Jeffrey A., *The Great Exhibition of 1851: a nation on display*, (Yale University Press), 1999, and 'The Great Exhibition and historical memory', *Journal of Victorian Culture*, Vol. 6, (1), (2001), pp. 89-112.

[52] Laqueur, Thomas W., 'Literacy and Social Mobility in the Industrial Revolution in England', *Past & Present*, Vol. 64, (1974), pp. 96-107, and Sanderson, Michael, 'Literacy and Social Mobility in the Industrial Revolution in England: A Rejoinder', *Past & Present*, Vol. 64, (1974), pp. 108-112.

[53] Hatton, T. J., et al., '18th-century British trade: homespun or empire made?', *Explorations in Economic History*, Vol. 20, (1983), pp. McKendrick, N., 'Home demand and economic growth: a new view of the role of women and children in the Industrial Revolution', in McKendrick, N., (ed.), *Historical perspectives: studies in English thought and society in honour of J. H. Plumb*, (Cambridge University Press), 1974, pp. 152-210, and Mokyr, J., 'Demand versus supply in the industrial revolution', *Journal of Economic History*, Vol. 37, (1977), pp. 981-1008.

manufactured, were bought and sold directly at the network of markets or through middlemen, who acted as a channel between producer and consumer. Until 1830, the key to economic growth was the mounting home demand for consumer goods. Growing consumption influenced trade and economic growth. Possessing and using domestic goods enhanced social status or displayed social rank. Lower food prices after 1780 may well have stimulated a consumer boom: people had more disposable income. There was a dramatic increase in the number of permanent shops in major urban centres and many of the characteristics of modern advertising emerged with circulars, showrooms and elaborate window displays. [54] Changing patterns of consumption created an environment in which manufacturers could exploit known and growing demand. [55]

Finally, entrepreneurial skill and 'enterprise' played a major role in the development of the late-eighteenth and early-nineteenth century economy. [56] In his book *The Protestant Ethic and the Spirit of Capitalism* published in 1905, the German sociologist Max Weber argued that religious factors were crucial for spurring European economic growth. Weber's view centred on Calvinism maintaining that it encouraged Europeans to be thrifty, rational, and concerned with material gain. [57] An ideology approving bourgeois innovation was crucial and new and its development was a consequence of the social and intellectual foundations established by the Scientific Revolution and the Enlightenment, what Mokyr calls the Industrial

---

[54] Berg, Maxine, and Clifford, Helen, 'Selling Consumption in the Eighteenth Century: Advertising and the Trade Card in Britain and France', *Cultural and Social History*, Vol. 4, (2007), pp. 145-170.

[55] Weatherill, Lorna, *Consumer behaviour and material culture in Britain, 1660-1760*, 3rd edition, (Routledge), 1997, Wagner, Tamara S., and Hassan, Narin, (eds.), *Consuming culture in the long nineteenth century: narratives of consumption, 1700-1900*, (Lexington Books), 2007.

[56] Burns, T., and Saul, S. B., (eds.), *Social Theory and Economic Change*, (Tavistock Press), 1967, is a useful collection of papers, providing useful summaries of Hagen E. H., *On the Theory of Social Change*, (Dorsey Press), 1962, and McClelland, D., *The Achieving Society*, (Van Nostrand), 1961. Payne, P. L., *British Entrepreneurship in the Nineteenth Century*, (Macmillan), 1974, 2nd ed., 1988, is a good bibliographical essay. Campbell, R. H., and Wilson, R. G., (eds.), *Entrepreneurship in Britain 1750-1939*, (A. & C. Black), 1975, is a short collection of contemporary writings with an extremely useful introductory essay.

[57] Holton R. J., *The Transition from Feudalism to Capitalism*, (Macmillan), 1985, and Marshall, G., *In Search of the Spirit of Capitalism: an essay on Max Weber's Protestant ethic thesis*, (Hutchinson), 1982, are useful studies of the nature and development of capitalism.

Enlightenment, Jack Goldstone the Engineering Culture [58] and Deirdre McCloskey, the Bourgeois Revaluation. [59] Entrepreneurs were responsible for three things. They organised production and brought together capital (their own or others') and labour. They selected the geographical site for operations, the technologies to be used, bargained for raw materials and found markets for their products. They often combined the roles of financiers, capitalists, work managers, merchants and salesmen. Three main explanations for the place of entrepreneurs in leading economic change have been identified by historians. There was a gradual though incomplete change in the ways people viewed social status from one based on birth to one where it related to what individuals achieved. Status was based more on what you did, less on who you were born. This was a reflection of the openness and mobility of British society. [60] Nonconformity seems to have been a crucial experience for many of the first-generation entrepreneurs encouraging a set of values outwardly favourable to economic enterprise. Finally, entrepreneurs were able effectively to exploit advances in technology and industrial organisation. Most entrepreneurs were not pioneers of major innovations or inventions but realised how best to utilise them. James Watt would not have been as successful but for the entrepreneurial skills of Matthew Boulton. This allowed them to manufacture and market goods effectively within a highly competitive consumer society. Entrepreneurial success was based on such successful transactions, not necessarily on a multi-talented genius who could do it all. British society did not prevent entrepreneurs from using their talents and motivation. [61]

There was no blueprint for the 'industrial revolution'. Population growth stimulated demand that entrepreneurs were able to satisfy. Developments in transport led to reductions in the cost of

---

[58] Goldstone, Jack A., *Why Europe? The Rise of the West in World History 1500-1850*, (McGraw-Hill), 2008, and 'Engineering Culture, Innovation and Modern Wealth Creation', in C. Karlsson, C., Johansson, B., and Stough R. R., (eds.), *Entrepreneurship and Innovations in Functional Regions*, (Edward Elgar), 2008, pp. 23-49.
[59] McCloskey, Deirdre N., *The Bourgeois Virtues: Ethics form an Age of Commerce*, (University of Chicago Press), 2006.
[60] Miles, Andrew, 'How open was nineteenth-century British society?: social mobility and equality of opportunity, 1839-1914', in Miles, Andrew, and Vincent, David, (eds.), *Building European society: occupational change and social mobility in Europe, 1840-1940*, (Manchester University Press), 1993, pp. 18-39.
[61] Daunton, Martin J., 'The entrepreneurial state, 1700-1914', *History Today*, Vol. 44, (6), (1994), pp. 11-16.

production making manufactured goods cheaper. Investment in industry often brought good returns. The state made little attempt to control growth. Foreign trade brought raw materials and profits that could be invested in enterprise. The social structure was adaptable and relatively flexible. Each of these factors helped create an environment in which change could occur.

3 Agriculture and industry

This chapter considers the question of agricultural and industrial change between 1780 and 1914.[1] A clear understanding of the economic profile of England and its social consequences is essential for grasping the major social transformation that occurred in this period.

Agriculture: an overview

External as much as internal forces increasingly influenced the Victorian countryside.[2] The poor harvests and deep depression especially in the arable sector in the 1820s and 1830s[3] was followed by recovery as rising home markets took agriculture into a so-called 'Golden Age' from the late 1840s to the early 1870s.[4] The dominance of wheat production ended as grain prices collapsed under the flood of cheap imports from the New World after 1875. Free trade meant that British farmers could not respond. Markets for stock and dairy products and perishable cash and fruit crops benefited from rising real wages and growing demand, but they too experienced foreign competition with the development of refrigeration and canning after 1870. The agricultural depression of the late 1880s and 1890s was widespread and crippling. It reflected the decline of

---

[1] Chambers, J. D., and Mingay, G. E., *The Agricultural Revolution 1750-1880*, (Batsford), 1966, remains the most straightforward introduction to the subject. Beckett, J. V., *The Agricultural Revolution*, (Blackwell), 1989, is a brief but essential study. Overton, Mark, *Agricultural Revolution in England: The Transformation of the Agrarian Economy 1500-1850*, (Cambridge University Press), 1996, restates the case for revolution after 1750.

[2] Jones, E. L., *The Development of English Agriculture 1815-1873*, (Macmillan), 1968, is a useful, if dated, bibliographical study. Mingay, G. E., (ed.), *The Victorian Countryside*, 2 Vols. (Routledge), 1980, is a collection of invaluable and readable essays. See also Allen, Robert C., 'Agriculture during the industrial revolution, 1700-1850', in ibid, Floud, Roderick, and Johnson, Paul A., (eds.), *The Cambridge economic history of modern Britain, Volume 1: industrialisation, 1700-1860*, pp. 96-116. Mingay, G. E., (ed.), *The Agrarian History of England and Wales, Vol. 6, 1750-1850*, (Cambridge University Press), 1989, and Collins, E. J. T., (ed.), *The Agrarian History of England and Wales, Vol. 7, 1850-1914*, (Cambridge University Press), 2000, are similarly invaluable.

[3] Wilkes, A. R., 'Adjustments in arable farming after the Napoleonic wars', *Agricultural History Review*, Vol. 28, (1980), pp. 90-103.

[4] Thompson, F. M. L., 'The second agricultural revolution, 1815-80', *Economic History Review*, Vol. 21, (1968), pp. 62-77.

agriculture's share of national income from one-fifth in 1850 to one-twelfth by the 1980s. [5]

The achievements of British farming from the 1830s to the mid-1870s were impressive. There was widespread adoption of existing improvements and new techniques for dealing with difficult clay soils, poor light soil and the marshlands spread to all types of farming. There was more intensive farming using chemical as well as natural fertilisers producing substantially higher yields. By the 1870s, many agricultural labourers and craftsmen, especially the young, had left the countryside because of the push of low wages, the pull of job opportunities, a livelier urban life style and better and cheaper transport drew local trade towards the larger county towns and regional centres and with it many professional and service activities. [6]

A diverse and changing economy

In 1850-1851, James Caird argued that, in an increasingly market economy farming could only succeed as a business by maximising profits by increased yields and/or reducing the real cost of working the land. [7] Faced with increasing foreign competition, British agriculture needed flexibility in cropping and land use and the key to success was to adapt varying soil and climatic conditions to profitable products.

Despite this increasing adaptability, Britain's three major land use and farming systems exerted a powerful influence. Upland farmers raised sheep and cattle, with some dairying near industrial centres, in an overwhelmingly pastoral setting and on small family farms. The drier lowland areas of eastern Britain were dominated by arable farming. The wetter lowland and heavy, water-retentive land saw farming increasingly focus on grassland for fattening and dairying as the price of grain plummeted in the 1870s. After 1870, a fourth

---

[5] Jones, E. L., 'The Changing Basis of English Agricultural Prosperity, 1853-73', *Agricultural History Review*, Vol. 10, (1962), pp. 102-119; Collins, E. J. T., and Jones, E. L., 'Sectoral advance in English agriculture, 1850-1880', *Agricultural History Review*, Vol. 15, (1967), pp. 65-81, with summary by Whetham, E. H., *Agricultural History Review*, Vol. 16, (1968), pp. 46-48; Caunce, Stephen, 'A golden age of agriculture?', in Inkster, Ian, (ed.), *The golden age: essays in British social and economic history, 1850-70*, (Ashgate), 2000, pp. 46-60, re-examines the issue.
[6] Rew, Sir Robert Henry, *Report on the Decline in the Agricultural Population of Great Britain, 1881-1906*, (Darling & Son Ltd.), 1906.
[7] Caird, James, *English agriculture in 1850-51*, (Brown, Green and Longman), 1852; see also his 'Fifty years of progress of British agriculture', *Journal of the Royal Agricultural Society of England*, 3rd series, Vol. 1, (1890), pp. 20-36, and Harvey, N., 'Sir James Caird and the landed interest', *Agriculture*, Vol. 60, (12), (1954), pp. 586-589.

system of intensive cash-crop arable farming characterised high-quality, high-yielding soils close to major urban centres: the Fens for London; the moss-lands for south Lancashire. [8]

The recovery from the agricultural depression, considerable urban growth, improved railway access to markets and innovation from the 1840s were reflected in the mosaic of regional patterns of farming. Up to the early 1870s wheat dominated all types of soil in arable lowland Britain, occupying between 25 and 50 per cent of tillage and combined, especially on lighter soil, with barley. In wetter, cooler areas oats with barley were usual. In both systems root crops, rotation grasses and clovers were standard fodder crops.

Crops as percentage of arable in England and Wales 1836-1911

Crops	1836	1871	1911
Wheat	26.8	23.0	16.3
Barley	15.7	14.3	12.6
Oats	12.6	11.4	18.1
All cereals	55.1	49.1	47.4
All roots	N.K.	16.7	16.0
Fallow	9.4	3.5	2.9
All tillage	79.5	79.5	76.4

Sources: Data for 1836 estimated from the Tithe Commutation Survey; for 1871 and 1911 from *Annual Agricultural Returns*.

From the early 1870s, the price of grain fell dramatically as railways opened up the American prairies and cheap bulk ocean transport reduced costs. Wheat prices fell from an average of 55s to 28s a quarter between 1870 and 1890. Barley similarly fell in price. Oats, an important fodder crop especially for the increasing number of horses for draught and transport, did relatively better. Pastoral farmers did not feel the results of depression so severely but even they were hit by refrigeration. How did farmers respond to this challenge?[9]

The number and density of stock increased substantially in most areas. Consumption of milk and dairy products increased and

---

[8] Holderness, B. A., 'The origins of high farming', in Holderness, B. A. and Turner, M. E., (eds.), *Land, labour and agriculture, 1700-1920: essays for Gordon Mingay*, (Hambledon), 1991, pp. 149-164; Perry, P. J., 'High farming in Victorian Britain: prospect and retrospect', *Agricultural History*, Vol. 55, (1981), pp. 136-166.

[9] Coppock, J. T., 'Agricultural Changes in the Chilterns, 1875-1900', *Agricultural History Review*, Vol. 9, (1961), pp. 1-16.

dairying dominated the pastures round cities. [10] Liquid milk production was the most profitable form of stock farming. Numbers of dairy cattle rose steadily after 1870, beef cattle fell slightly and sheep flocks were considerably reduced. By 1914, 70 per cent of milk production went direct to the consumer. There was an increasing demand for vegetables and fruit. From the 1880s, canning, jam making and preserving were using both home and imported products for processing at large ports but many manufacturers were in specialist fruit or vegetable areas. In many areas cash crops of potatoes, green vegetables and legumes were added to previously grain-dominated rotations.

Improvements and innovations

Specialisation reflected farmers' abilities to adapt to the market by investment in improved techniques and equipment. From the 1840s, the flow of capital into farming was heralded by the reform of the 'old' Poor Law in 1834, which significantly reduced the costs to farmers of the rural poor, the Commutation of Tithes Act 1836 and the recovery of prices. The Corn Laws has provided protection for arable farmers since 1815 and their repeal in 1846 did not result immediately in the demise of the grain farmer; that has to wait until the 1870s and foreign competition. The result of improved conditions was higher levels of investment in land management, buildings and machinery between the 1830s and the early 1870s and these were little improved upon over the next half-century.

More effective under-drainage was developed, especially on heavy clay soils. [11] Although it is difficult to quantify around half of cultivated land in England was in need of drainage in 1850. There had been earlier attempts but they had limited success. There were two developments that stimulated change: the perfecting of cheap, machine-made pipes in the 1840s and the availability of £2m in loans under the Public Draining Acts of 1846 and 1850. Some 4-5 million acres were tackled between 1846 and 1876. [12] Fertilisers, especially

---

[10] See, for example, Dalton, Roger T., 'The railway milk trade and farming in the north Midlands, c.1860-1914', *Midland History*, Vol. 28, (2003), pp. 100-119.

[11] On this issue see, Phillips, A. D. M., *Underdraining of farmland in England during the nineteenth century*, (Cambridge University Press), 1989, and Sturgess, R. W., 'The agricultural revolution on the English clays', *Agricultural History Review*, Vol. 14, (1966), pp. 104-121, Vol. 15, (1967), pp. 82-87..

[12] Phillips, A. D. M., 'Arable land drainage in the nineteenth century', in Cook, Hadrian F., and Williamson, Tom, (eds.), *Water management in the*

imported nitrates and potash, had an important contribution to make. Their impact was helped by a significant trend towards more scientific farming associated with Justus von Liebig and Sir John Lawes. [13] Although agricultural improvers advocated the use of machinery, effective mechanisation was slow to develop and spread. [14] Cheap labour, not least in the harvest gangs of women, children and itinerant Irish, gave little incentive to invest in machinery and the machine breaking in the Swing riots of 1830 reflected widespread opposition to its use. There had been substantial improvements in the quality and design of implements in the years before 1830 but as long as implement manufacture was small-scale and local, the pace of change was slow.

The Great Exhibition of 1851 was a splendid showcase for agricultural machinery, but their general adoption as judged from catalogues, farm sales and inventories was limited before the High Farming of the 1850s and 1860s. Attempts to mechanise harvesting date from the late eighteenth century but modern reapers came after 1848 with the large-scale production of the American McCormick reaper. Many developments awaited improvements in motive power. Plough horses had ousted oxen from all but the heaviest land but steam did not achieve general success in harvesting or ploughing. Many farmers, especially on small family farms, could not afford mechanisation. Harvesting was not generally mechanised until movement from the land and restriction on child labour together with rising wages made hand methods increasingly uneconomic. Although the 1880s depression saw fewer innovations, there was more widespread use of machinery: in 1871, only a quarter of British grain was harvested by machine, by 1900 this had risen to four-fifths.

Finally, there was large-scale investment in farm buildings, particularly on large estates. By 1850, larger farms sometimes had a boiler-house and engine to drive equipment, process stock food or

---

English landscape: field, marsh and meadow, (Edinburgh University Press), 1999, pp. 53-72.

[13] Dyke, G. V., *John Lawes of Rothamsted: pioneer of science, farming and industry*, (Hoos), 1993. Catt, John A., 'Long-term consequences of using artificial and organic fertilisers: the Rothamsted experiments', in Foster, Sally M., and Smout, Thomas Christopher, (eds.), *The history of soils and field systems*, (Scottish Cultural), 1994, pp. 119-134.

[14] Walton, John R., *A study in the diffusion of agricultural machinery in the 19th century*, (Oxford University, School of Geography, Research Papers, 5), 1973, and 'Mechanization in agriculture: a study of the adoption process', in Fox, H. S. A., and Butlin, Robin Alan, (eds.), *Change in the countryside: essays on rural England, 1500-1900*, (Institute of British Geographers), 1979, pp. 23-42.

run a saw mill. Stock farms increasingly provided winter shelter for milking and fat-stock, as well as piggeries, hen houses and the like. While most farms were still made of local materials, cheap rail transport introduced slate, machine-produced bricks and cast-iron into the buildings and their equipping, especially on large estates. The decline of farming from the 1870s saw much neglect of both farm buildings and of labourers' cottages. [15]

There was a progressive switch to a market-oriented farming economy after the 1840s and this was reflected in tenure and size of farms and estates. Eighteenth century enclosures had increased the number of small holders and had produced a three-fold structure of landlord, tenant farmer and landless labourers. Large estates dominated England and especially Scotland but the balance between tenant and family farms was more equal in Wales. Changes in farming methods contributed to substantial falls in agricultural labour from 1850 but there was an increase in the number of smallholdings. Although mixed, stock and cash-crop farmers adapted well to the post 1870s depression, bankruptcies of grain producers in the late 1870s and 1880s and of small stock farmers in the early 1890s reflected poor harvests, increasing grain imports and the fall in wheat, wool and then meat prices. [16] Great estates reached their peak of dominance in the 1870s when in England and Wales 1,700 of the 270,000 landowners held over 43 per cent of the land and in Scotland the 25 largest owners held one-third of the land. While very small units were largely removed from many areas by enclosure and in later nineteenth-century depopulation, small acreage typified intensive cash-crop production in the Fens and south-west Lancashire and in vegetable, fruit and market gardening production. [17] From the depressed 1880s, there was a drive to increase smallholdings: Acts to extend allotments

---

[15] Phillips, A. D. M., 'Rebuilding rural England: farm building provision, 1850-1900', in Baker, Alan R. H., (ed.), *Home and colonial: essays on landscape, Ireland, environment and empire in celebration of Robin Butlin's contribution to historical geography*, (Historical Geography Research Group), 2004, pp. 39-51, and 'Landlord investment in farm buildings in the English Midlands in the mid-nineteenth century', in ibid, Holderness, B. A., and Turner, M. E., (eds.), *Land, labour and agriculture, 1700-1920: essays for Gordon Mingay*, pp. 191-210.

[16] Oddy, Derek J., 'The growth of Britain's refrigerated meat trade, 1880-1939', *Mariner's Mirror*, Vol. 93, (2007), pp. 269-280.

[17] See, for example, Beavington, F., 'The development of market gardening in Bedfordshire 1799-1939', *Agricultural History Review*, Vol. 23, (1975), pp. 23-47, and Martin, J. M., 'The social and economic origins of the Vale of Evesham market gardening industry', *Agricultural History Review*, Vol. 33, (1985), pp. 41-50.

in 1882 and in 1887 empowered local councils to compulsorily purchase land for that purpose. [18]

The worst of the depression for arable farmers was over by the mid-1890s by which time wheat prices had fallen by 50 per cent over twenty years. Their position was, at best, stabilised up to 1914. Contraction of grain production was most marked in low-output areas and where land could be successfully converted to grass as in northern and western Britain and in many parts of midland England. Wheat and barley remained important in eastern England where good farmers on the better soils made it pay. On heavy land that was costly and difficult to work, many arable farmers continued to go out of business. By 1913, permanent grassland occupied over one third of the country's cultivated area and over one sixth was agriculturally unproductive. The switch to grassland was most marked on midland clay and in western districts: nearly 70 per cent of Wiltshire's farmland was under permanent pasture by 1914 and one-fifth of its arable under grass ley. Increases in fruit, market garden and field vegetables were reflected in intensive cultivation of specialist crops.

Responses to agricultural change

The landscape and economy of rural Britain were substantially reshaped after 1830. Despite substantial advances in 'new farming', many parts of Britain were still backward in the 1830s and 1840s. The stimulus of High Farming transformed grain growing and enhanced commercial meat and then milk production and this was reflected in investment in soil improvement, stock, machinery and farm buildings. These had greatest impact on the bigger estates and large tenant farms of lowland arable and grazing districts and on milk and vegetable producers near the urban markets. [19]

---

[18] On the problems facing farming after 1870, see, Perry, P. J., *British farming in the Great Depression, 1870-1914: an historical geography*, (David & Charles), 1974, Perren, Richard, *Agriculture in Depression 1870-1940*, (Cambridge University Press), 1995, Thompson, F. M. L., 'An anatomy of English agriculture, 1870-1914', in ibid, Holderness, B. A., and Turner, M. E., (eds.), *Land, labour and agriculture, 1700-1920: essays for Gordon Mingay*, pp. 211-240. Perren, Richard, 'The Landlord and Agricultural Transformation, 1870-1900', *Agricultural History Review*, Vol. 18, (1970), pp. 36-51, and the debate in Vol. 27, (1979), pp. 42-46.; Perry, P. J., 'Where was the 'Great Agricultural Depression'? A geography of agricultural bankruptcy in late Victorian England and Wales', *Agricultural History Review*, Vol. 20, (1972), pp. 30-45.

[19] Taylor, David, 'The English dairy industry, 1860-1930: the need for a reassessment', *Agricultural History Review*, Vol. 22, (1974), pp. 153-159,

By 1874, the High Farming boom was over. The depression to the 1890s was initially largely a grain crisis that most affected high-cost clay-land farmers. Large-scale cereal growers on lighter soils could adjust by growing more fodder, keeping more animals or producing cash crops. Land use changed substantially from the late 1870s. Marginal land went out of cultivation on a massive scale: some went over to forestry like the Brecklands; some to sporting estates; others tumbled down to weedy pasture and scrub. There was a good deal of conversion of arable, especially cereal, to grassland with permanent pasture on heavier soils and longer temporary grass leys within arable rotations. The grassland/arable boundary was displaced eastward. Despite the endorsement of free trade after 1846, the problems of the late-nineteenth century brought many basic issues concerning agricultural policy into the political arena. The agricultural lobby was still powerful and many of them were prominent witnesses to the Royal Commissions on the Depressed State of the Agricultural Interest of 1879-1882 and the 1883 Royal Commission. Most legislation of the period favoured tenants, for example the outlawing of restrictive leases in Agricultural Holdings Acts of 1875, 1883 and 1906 or offered palliatives such as allotments and smallholdings to landless labourers. But the plight of farming failed to shift belief in free trade and state aid came only after 1914. [20]

Few rural areas were wholly remote from urban influences in this period. Many were affected by urban sprawl and suburbanisation made possible by improved transport and greater affluence. The urbanisation of the countryside was increasingly recognised in planning legislation as planners sought to recreate the perceived advantages of rural living within new and extended urban communities. This can be seen in the Garden City Movement. In 1898, Ebenezer Howard published *Tomorrow: a peaceful path to real reform* and in 1900, the Garden City Association was founded. Its aims were both to provide a new urban environment in small communities of around 6,000 people within a garden city with a maximum population of 30,000 and, at the same time, revitalise the countryside. Howard's vision sought to combine urban amenities with rural beauty. In 1903, the First Garden City Company was formed

---

and 'Growth and structural change in the English dairy industry, c1860-1930', *Agricultural History Review*, Vol. 35, (1987), pp. 47-64.

[20] Fisher, J. R., 'The Farmers' Alliance: an agricultural protest movement of the 1880s', *Agricultural History Review*, Vol. 26, (1978), pp. 15-25; Mutch, Alistair, 'Farmers' Organizations and Agricultural Depression in Lancashire, 1890-1900', *Agricultural History Review*, Vol. 31, (1983), pp. 26-36.

and, mainly through the initiative of Thomas Adams and Raymond Unwin, Letchworth was built in the first decade of the twentieth century.

The importance of agriculture, as a contributor to the national economy and as an employer of labour, declined during the second half of the nineteenth century. In 1831, agriculture, forestry and fisheries contributed 23.4 per cent of the total national income but this fell progressively during the remainder of the century: 20.3 per cent in 1851, 14.6 per cent in 1871, 8.6 per cent in 1891 and 6.1 per cent in 1901. The benefits that High Farming brought to the landed interest were short-lived and illusory. Those who opposed the repeal of the Corn Laws in 1846 were proved correct but not until the 1870s and 1880s when British farmers found that they could not compete with foreign imports. Faced by falling profits farmers either adapted or went under.

Industry and industrialisation

If the early industrial revolution was an age of cotton and wool, the Victorian era was an age of coal and iron.[21] Mechanisation and steam power transformed transport through the development of the railway system and, from around 1850, of marine transport. While many goods were still largely hand-made, steam powered machines with standardised and eventually in some cases semi-automatic systems of production achieved substantial improvement in productivity and lowering of labour costs in textiles, heavy industry and engineering. By the 1880s, they began to permeate some sectors of consumer industry, for example, clothing and footwear, furniture-making and food processing.

Britain's industrial leadership was reflected in its domination of

---

[21] The most straightforward studies of British industry are ibid, Musson, A. E., *The Growth of British Industry*, and Church, R., (ed.), *The Dynamics of Victorian Business*, (Allen and Unwin), 1983. For the textile industry Chapman, S. D., *The Cotton Industry in the Industrial Revolution*, (Macmillan), 2nd edition, 1987, and Jenkins, D. T., and Ponting, K. G., *The British Wool Textile Industry 1770-1914*, (Scolar Press), 1987, are the more accessible introductions. For the iron industry see Ashton, T. S., *Iron and Steel during the Industrial Revolution*, 3rd edition, (Oxford University Press), 1963, Birch, A., *The Economic History of the British Iron and Steel Industry 1784-1879*, (Kelley), 1967, and Harris, J. R., *The British Iron Industry 1700-1850*, (Macmillan), 1988, that summarises research. Flinn, M. W., *A History of the British Coal Industry, Vol. 2: The Industrial Revolution*, (Oxford University Press), 1984, and Church, R. A., *A History of the British Coal Industry, Vol. 3: Victorian Pre-Eminence 1830-1913*, (Oxford University Press), 1986, are detailed studies.

an extending global economy: international trade expanded at over 3 per cent per annum throughout the greater part of this period, averaging 4.6 per cent between the 1840s and 1870s and falling back only during the Great Depression of the 1880s. Britain imported more than it exported leading to an adverse trade balance but earnings from overseas and other 'invisible' trade in services, shipping and insurance generally kept the annual balance of payments in surplus, notably so from the mid-1850s. As the competitiveness of British industry was challenged from the late 1880s, especially by the USA and Germany, the value and proportion of imported manufactures grew substantially, especially of luxury goods and products of some newer industries. Britain continued to depend largely on exports of textiles, iron and steel products, machinery and increasingly coal but by the 1890s foreign competitors were making greater progress in trade in chemicals, newer types of machinery and electrical goods.

These trends are reflected in changes in the basis of the nation's wealth and the structure of its labour force. The value of land and farm buildings fell to less than a quarter of the national capital by the late 1880s and the agricultural labour force fell from one quarter in 1831 to only one tenth by 1891. By then manufacturing, industry, trade and transport employed over two-thirds of the workforce and accounted for rather more of the national product. By 1901, nearly 1.5 million worked in textiles, mainly in fully mechanised mills, well over a million in metal manufacture, machine-tool making and vehicle manufacture and almost a million in mining and quarrying.

Continuous growth of 2.2 to 3.3 per cent in the national product of Victorian Britain was accounted for largely by sustained growth of between 2.7 and 3.5 per cent per annum in manufacturing, mining and building. By the late-nineteenth century Britain's growth was outstripped by the USA (4.5 per cent) and Germany (2.8 per cent). In addition the steadily increasing output per head of the British industrial workforce (1.0 to 1.3 per cent per annum) was far behind that achieved in the USA (1.9 to 3.2 per cent) and in the 1880s and 1890s in Germany (1.7 to 2.1 per cent). Much of Britain's increased industrial output was achieved through greater mechanisation of a traditionally trained workforce in established industries, rather than by application of science and technology to new industries. The increased coal output was achieved by greater use of labour rather than, as was evident in the USA and Germany the use of machinery.[22]

---

[22] Broadberry, Stephen N., 'Anglo-German productivity differences 1870-1990: a sectoral analysis', *European Review of Economic History*, Vol. 1, (1997), pp. 247-267, Ritschl, Albrecht O., 'The Anglo-German Industrial Productivity Puzzle, 1895-1935: A Restatement and a Possible Resolution',

Technological advance and progressive mechanisation had considerable implications for the organisation of many industries. New skills of machine-minding rather than individual craftsmanship; of engineers rather than wrights; of process workers often on specific parts of a product rather than the sole creators of finished articles; bigger units of manufacture, whether factory or workshop, and larger firms.

The result was a newly structured workforce with a hierarchy from a skilled 'aristocracy of labour' of perhaps a sixth of the whole, with a mass of semi-skilled machine operatives and casual unskilled labourers. In 1851, factory industries employed 1.75 million as against an estimated 2.5 million in traditional craft industries. Within twenty years two million, about half the industrial workforce, were employed in 23,346 factories as against a little over half a million in 106,988 workshops. Handicraft workers were found not only in traditional rural industries (stocking and knitwear, gloving and straw hat-making) and individual artisan crafts (tailors and dressmakers, smiths, bakers, building workers etc.) but also, increasingly, in the workshops and 'putting-out' systems of the urban 'sweated trades' (clothing, furnishing, box-making, toy-making). These trades continued to employ many, especially juvenile and women workers, but used little power, underlining the importance of small-scale, unmechanised industry before the widespread adoption of electric power after 1900.

Nevertheless the scale of organisation of both the productive unit and the firm increased in late-Victorian Britain. In 1830, most firms were individual, often family, concerns and with some exceptions, for example in smelting and processing (brewing for instance), production units were small. Even large factories seldom employed more than a few hundred workers. While some big companies employed thousands of workers their workforces were often dispersed among hundreds of small workshops. In 1850, the Dowlais Company employed some 7,000 workers at eighteen sites but the metal trades of Birmingham and the cutlery industry of Sheffield operated in small, simply equipped workshops and even the machine-tool trade was largely small-scale. The spread of mechanisation and standardised production into the hosiery, knitwear, shoemaking and clothing trades and into engineering, iron manufacture and shipbuilding and the improvements in transport resulted in an

---

Journal of Economic History, Vol. 68, (2), (2008), pp. 535-565, and Broadberry, Stephen N., and Burhop, Carsten, 'Resolving the Anglo-German Industrial Productivity Puzzle, 1895-1935: A Response to Professor Ritschl', *Journal of Economic History*, Vol. 68, (3), (2008), pp. 930-934.

increase in the size of companies and their productive units.

Late-Victorian competition for markets eliminated many of the small, less competitive firms, producing notable concentrations in textiles, coal, chemicals and some processing industries. Integration of processes within industries and between large firms with complementary interests (for example, coal and steel; related branches of chemicals; food refining and processing) saw the emergence of the first modern industrial giants, though this should not be exaggerated. In the 1880s, the top one hundred firms provided one tenth of British output; by 1909, after a number of big industrial mergers they produced 15 per cent. The average workplace in the 1890s was still small, lightly mechanised and used little motive power, though the situation was beginning to change rapidly. Footwear manufacture was one of the most widespread early Victorian handicraft industries but large-scale factory production was firmly established by the 1880s. By 1895, 70 per cent of England's 123,000 footwear workers were employed in factories, some of them very large, and by 1905 82.5 per cent were factory workers.

Concentration of production in factories was accompanied by considerable geographical concentration of manufacturing with some notable specialisation within particular industries. Comparative advantages in raw materials, as in the case of coal and heavy industry and of inherited skills encouraged specialisation. By 1851, the North West was dominated by textiles (one third of its workers) and engineering (one-quarter); the West Midlands had nearly two-fifths of Britain's metal workers and one third of those in metal working and engineering. These emphases remained in 1891 and were strengthened in South Wales, northern England and western Scotland by growing dependence on mining, heavy industry and shipbuilding. Concentration of individual industries and processes was even more striking producing a vulnerable dependency on a limited industrial base in many places as in the specialist Lancashire cotton towns, shipbuilding at Barrow, Sunderland or Greenock and above all in coal-mining communities. That dependency could be socially claustrophobic and eventually, as was proved after 1918, economically disastrous. There was a decline in British manufacturing and trade competitiveness from the Great Depression of 1873-1896 and a transition to a broader-based economy. The impact of this varied from industry to industry and region to region and was a process that was more clearly evident in the years after 1918.

4 Communications

The popular image of Victorian England is of a society whose members travelled by train. While there is little doubt of the massive impact that railways had on British society, its landscapes and its attitudes, for most people most of the time the railways were not the main means of transport. [1]

Why did Britain remain a horse-drawn society?

Victorian England has justifiably been called 'a horse drawn society':

> Railways paraded the power of the machine across the whole country, they eroded localism and removed barriers to mobility and they created new jobs and new towns. Their very modernity and success in generating new traffic, however, also generated expansion in older forms of transport, for all the feeder services bringing freight and passengers to the railway stations were horse-drawn. This, coupled with the needs of road transport within the larger towns, produced a three or fourfold increase in horse-drawn traffic on Victorian roads. The result, in employment terms, was that there were consistently more than twice as many road transport workers as there were railwaymen until after 1891 and that in the early twentieth century the road transport men, by now including some handling electric trams and soon to include others on motor vehicles, remained easily the largest group of transport workers. [2]

In early 1830, twenty-nine coaches operated daily between Liverpool and Manchester; by early 1831, there were four and only one remained two years later. One of the leading coach owners considered 'annihilation' as the most appropriate word to describe the effects of railways. But this experience was untypical of other parts of the country. Where the new railways ran roughly parallel to long-established trunk roads there was certainly little future for stage coaching. Where roads traversed or fed into the route of the railway

---

[1] Bagwell, P. S., *The Transport Revolution since 1770*, (Batsford), 1974, Dyos, H. J., and Aldcroft, D. H., *British Transport: an economic survey from the seventeenth to the twentieth century*, (Leicester University Press), 1969, (Penguin), 1976, Freeman, Michael J., and Aldcroft, Derek H., (eds.), *Transport in Victorian Britain*, (Manchester University Press), 1991, and Perkin, H., *The Age of the Railway*, (Routledge), 1970, are valuable general surveys.

[2] Thompson, F. M. L., *The Rise of Respectable Society: British Society 1830-1900*, (Fontana), 1988, p. 47. See also his *Victorian England: the horse-drawn society: an inaugural lecture*, (Bedford College), 1970, and 'Nineteenth-century horse sense', *Economic History Review*, Vol. 29, (1976), pp. 60-81.

a very different situation existed and horse-drawn vehicles still played a very important part in the overall provision of transport services.[3]

Initially the effect of railways on towns that had previously been important staging posts was disastrous. In 1839, Doncaster found employment for seven four-horse coaches, 20 two-horse coaches, nine stage wagons and 100 post horses; the total horse population was 258.[4] In 1845, after the town had had railway links for five years, only one four-horse coach, three stage wagons and 12 post horses were still in service and the number of horses had fallen to 60. Trade had suffered badly and the value of property had fallen between 25 and 30 per cent. Where coaches acted as 'feeders' there were still opportunities for them to stay on the road and, in some cases, increase their business. The completion of the early skeleton network by about 1840 provided many opportunities for opening up new combined coach and railway routes for passenger traffic. In April 1839, the well-known coach magnate George Sherman expressed the opinion that after the railway had driven most of the coaches off the long distance routes:

> ...there would be as much to employ more horses as there ever was through the extra ordinary quantity of omnibuses and cabs that were appearing on the streets.[5]

In 1839, there were 600 omnibuses in London and this increased to 1,300 by 1850. There was a parallel increase in hansom cabs: 12 in 1823 to over 4,400 by the 1840s. Such was the importance of horse transport in London that, during the cab strike of July 1853, the city ground to a halt:

> There was not only a dearth, but an absolute famine of locomotion, and never since the days of Charles II, when Hackney-coaches were first invented, have the sight-seeing and outgoing public been reduced to such an extremity of helplessness as by the cabmen's strike of yesterday.[6]

The result was a significant increase in the cost of horses: in 1872 the London and South Western were paying £54 17s for the same

---

[3] Hart, Harold W., 'Stage-coach and train in conflict', *Journal of the Railway & Canal Historical Society*, Vol. 24, (2), (1978), pp. 42-45.

[4] Scowcroft, P. L., 'From pack horse to motor lorry: freight transport by road in Doncaster and district', *Journal of the Railway & Canal Historical Society*, Vol. 32, (1997), pp. 260-264.

[5] Cit, Bagwell, P. S., *The Transport Revolution, 1700-1985*, (Routledge), 1998, p. 131.

[6] 'London without Cabs', *The Times*, 28 July 1853.

type of animal that had only cost them £44 10s five years earlier. The increased demand for horses was certainly not confined to London; there is also significant evidence from the provinces. Thompson commented:

> Without carriages and carts the railways would have been like stranded whales, giants unable to use their strength, for these were the only means of getting people and goods right to the doors of houses, where they wanted to be. [7]

There was also an increase in privately owned heavy carriages: from 30,000 in 1840 the number grew to 120,000 by 1870. Over the same period the number of light two-wheeled carriages increased six times. By 1902, 12 out of every 1,000 people in Great Britain owned some kind of private horse-drawn vehicles. This compared with 14 per 1000 in 1870 and 4 per 1000 in 1840, and it was not until 1926 that the number of car owners exceeded the number of persons who had owned horse-drawn carriages in 1870.

Road traffic

The road system in Britain in 1780 was administered by two separate bodies. Turnpike trusts, local bodies run by boards of trustees, were given powers to levy tolls on the users of a specified stretch of road and used the revenue obtained to improve and maintain it. From the 1660s and especially after 1720, most of Britain's major roads were turnpike. This only constituted about a sixth of all roads and the remainder were the responsibility of the parish and were toll free. Until 1835, they were repaired by statute labour a highway rate. [8]

Turnpike trusts were under increasing financial pressure after 1830 largely caused by over-investment, falling income and competition from railway. In 1838, there were 1,116 turnpike trusts, private, profit-making bodies, managing some 22,000 miles of road compared to the 104,770 managed by parish authorities. Neither was well equipped to meet the challenge of the railways. In the first place

---

[7] Ibid, Thompson, F. M. L., *The Rise of Respectable Society: British Society 1830-1900*, p. 49.

[8] The Highways Acts of 1555 and 1562 placed the burden of the upkeep of roads on parishes. Annually, one or two unpaid Surveyors of Highways were appointed by local Justices of the Peace who were responsible for organising the four days of statute labour (six days after 1563) when the whole parish was to work on the highways. The 1691 Highways Act authorised the levying of a Highwats Rate levied, like Poor and Church Rates, on the owners of land but this could onloy be done with the approval of the Quarter Sessions.

both operated on too small a scale to be run economically: the average turnpike road was under 20 miles long and parish roads even less. They were also in financial difficulties: turnpikes were in debt for over £7 million (four times their annual income) and parishes had considerable difficulty collecting the highway rates. Reform was necessary, extended through the century and was a tediously slow process.[9] Some amalgamation of turnpikes had already occurred by 1830. In 1826, for example, north London set up the Metropolitan Turnpike Trust uniting under one management the administration of 122 miles of roads formerly controlled by separate trusts.[10] In 1844, following the Rebecca riots, trusts in South Wales were brought under the control of county road boards.[11] This process was not followed in other areas of the country where trusts suffered from increasing indebtedness and their roads lay unrepaired. Parliament was aware of the need for reform and Royal Commissions and Select Committees recommended consolidation and abolition.

It was not until the Local Government Board took over responsibility for roads from the Home Office in 1872 that the dissolution of the trusts quickened. Many turnpike trusts were wound up under General Acts of Parliament between 1873 and 1878. The transfer of resources and sale of assets to repay loans were supervised by the Local Government Board that acted as arbiter in the case of disputes. Toll-houses were sold, gates torn down and responsibility for the main roads passed to Highway Boards. Bond-holders were paid off with any residual funds, though some did not get a satisfactory return on their investment. For instance, investors in the Harwell to Streatley Turnpike Trust were repaid less than a half of their capital and bondholders received less than a fifth of the face value of their investment in the Stokenchurch Trust. In contrast the Besselsleigh Trust handed over its roads free of debt though some of the Highways Authorities that inherited responsibility for the road complained that they were in 'a uniform (bad) state of repair throughout'. In 1871, there were 851 trusts, by 1881 this had been reduced to 184 and by 1890 only two remained. The last trust on the Anglesey section of the

---

[9] Barker, Theo, and Gerhold, Dorian, *The rise and rise of road transport, 1700-1990*, (Cambridge University Press), 1998, provides an excellent summary of developments in a neglected area.

[10] See, Spiro, Robert H., 'John Loudon McAdam and the Metropolis Turnpike Trust', *Journal of Transport History*, Vol. 2, (1955-6), pp. 207-213.

[11] The Rebecca Riots are examined in Williams, David, *The Rebecca Riots*, (University of Wales Press), 1955, and Jones, David J. V., *Rebecca's Children: A Study of Rural Society, Crime and Protest*, (Oxford University Press), 1989.

Holyhead road ceased to function on 1 November 1895.

Reform of the parish roads occurred equally slowly. Parish responsibility for roads other than turnpikes was confirmed by the General Highways Act of 1835. This legislation also abolished statute labour and permitted parishes to levy a highway rate. Parishes, even when it was obvious that they could not maintain their roads, were unwilling to surrender their authority and consequently the clause in the 1835 Highway Act allowing them to unite for highway purposes remained a dead letter. This did not help bring about uniformity of practice. In 1848, the Public Health Act placed roads under local boards of health in the newly constituted urban administration areas and the Highways Act of 1862 united most of the parishes for road administration purposes under Highway Boards. Initially, the vestry levied a rate on the parish to meet the precepts of the Highway Boards, but in 1878 a common fund was established to help pay for half the cost of maintaining the 'disturnpiked' main roads. Quarter Sessions paid the balance out of the county fund and took responsibility for main roads. The pattern became more orderly from 1872 but it was not until 1894 that the chaos that previously existed was finally sorted out. The Local Government Act 1888 transferred responsibility for main roads to the new County Councils. The Local Government Act 1894 dissolved the unpopular Highway Boards and the care of minor roads was devolved to the new Rural and Urban District Councils.

The reform of road administration occurred at the same time as a reawakening of interest in long-distance road transport from the 1880s. There were several reasons for this. A revival of horse-drawn coach transport for carriage of the new parcel post, started by Royal Mail in 1883, because of the terms offered by railway companies. Success on the London-Brighton route in 1887-1888 led to the scheme being extended to other routes. There was also a revival of four-in-hand coaching primarily as a leisure activity. Finally, the bicycle became available for the less well off. [12] The British bicycle industry had its origins in the late 1860s in Coventry. It was the Rover safety bicycle with rear wheel chain drive, first produced in Coventry in 1885 that extended the craze.[13] This was aided by the introduction of the pneumatic tyre by J. B. Dunlop in 1888 considerably increasing the comfort of cycling and helping to make the new means of

---

[12] Herlihy, David V., *Bicycle: The History*, (Yale University Press), 2006, provides a global view of the development and impact of cycling.
[13] Thompson, Steve, 'The cycling craze of the 1890s in Wales', *Transactions of the Honourable Society of Cymmrodorian*. Vol. 14, (2008), pp. 114-126.

recreation socially acceptable to women. [14] Specious medical arguments that excessive riding of bicycles could lead to overstrain of the heart, spinal deformities and was a danger to women's reproductive systems had been deployed to restrict the physical mobility and personal freedom of women. [15]

Let it at once be said, an organically sound woman can cycle with as much impunity as a man. Thank Heaven, we know now that this is not one more of the sexual problems of the day. Sex has nothing to do with it, beyond the adaptation of machine to dress and dress to machines. With cycles as now perfected, there is nothing in the anatomy or the physiology of a woman to prevent their fully and freely enjoyed within the limits of common sense...[16]

When the motorcar became a more common mode of transport in the 1920s and women took to the wheel, similar warnings were made that this new machine was not suitable for women: it would lead to nervous strain and exhaustion and driving for any period of time might encourage hysteria and neurasthenia. By 1885, there were already 400,000 cyclists in Britain and the 1890s saw the bicycle reach the peak of its popularity: in 1896 for example they were issued to all police stations in the country. By 1900, the Raleigh Cycle Factory was producing 12,000 cycles a year. [17] Finally, the 12 mph speed limit established in the 'Red Flag' legislation of 1865 was repealed in 1896. Though originally designed to limit the speed of 'steam-carriages', the decision liberated the newly developed motor vehicles for which good roads were essential.

As the proportion of people living in large towns and cities rose, the problems of urban transport assumed an ever-growing importance. Suburban railways met some of the demand but during the second and third quarters of the century an attempt was made to meet this by expanding the provision of horse-drawn short stage and

---

[14] See, Cooke, Jim, 'John Boyd Dunlop 1840-1921, inventor', *Dublin Historical Record*, Vol. 49, (1996), pp. 16-31.

[15] See Strange, L. S., and Brown, R. S., 'The bicycle, women's rights, and Elizabeth Cady Stanton', *Women's Studies*, Vol. 31, (2002), pp. 609-626, and Vertinsky, Patricia, *The Eternally Wounded Woman: Women, Doctors and Exercise in the late Nineteenth Century*, (Manchester University Press), 1989, pp. 76-81.

[16] Fenton, W. H., 'A Medical View of Cycling for Ladies', *The Nineteenth Century*, no. 39, (May 1896), p. 797.

[17] Lloyd-Jones, Roger, and Lewis, Mervyn J., *Raleigh and the British bicycle industry: an economic and business history, 1870-1960*, (Ashgate), 2000, and Rosen, Paul, *Framing production: technology, culture, and change in the British bicycle industry*, (MIT Press), 2002, pp. 1-40.

omnibus services. The number of horses engaged in commercial passenger transport rose from 103,000 in 1851 to 464,000 by 1901. The carriage and the horse-drawn omnibus (each of which required 11 horses a day to keep running) were essentially middle-class conveyances. The working-classes largely still went by foot. A survey of London in 1854 found that to reach their place of work 52,000 people used their own or hired carriages, 88,000 used horse-drawn omnibuses, 54,000 used suburban trains and 30,000 river steams but 400,000 people still walked to work. [18] After 1875, there was a rapid expansion of the tramway network, especially the growth of the electric tram from the turn of the century, with fares sufficiently low to give general access to the working-class. By 1900, 1 million passengers were carried each year on electric trams rising to 3.3 million by 1913. This produced, for the first time, genuine mass transport. Traffic jams are not the product of the car: urban traffic congestion was a consequence of the nineteenth century horse.

The growth in passenger traffic on the roads was paralleled by a growth in good traffic, nearly all horse drawn. An estimated 161,000 horses were pulling freight vehicles in Britain in 1851. By 1891, the figure was 500,000, by 1901 702,000 and by 1911 832,000. Throughout the nineteenth century three things need to be noted about transport than have been generally overlooked. Walking remained of central importance both as a mode of transport and as a way of carrying and delivering goods, from the porters, packmen, coster girls and street vendors of urban areas to the carriers, peddlers and postmen of the countryside. There was the sheer diversity of experience of transport. Just as today, people did not restrict themselves to one mode of transport. Finally, the gradual adoption of the bicycle which in its flexibility and ease of use and its speed since it was four times faster than walking, foreshadowed automobile travel

British motor transport had a greater impact on social life than it did on the economy in the period up to 1914. [19] The country's

---

[18] Taylor, Sheila, and Green, Oliver, (eds.), *The moving metropolis: a history of London's transport since 1800*, (Laurence King in association with London's Transport Museum), 2001. See also, Voice, David, *The Age of the Horse Tram: A history of horse-drawn passenger tramways in the British Isles*, (Adam Gordon), 2009.

[19] O'Connell, Sean, *The car and British society: class, gender and motoring 1896-1939*, (Manchester University Press), 1998. See also, Saul, S. B., 'The motor industry in Britain to 1914', *Business History*, Vol. 5, (1962), pp. 22-44, and Church, Roy A., *The rise and decline of the British motor industry*, (Macmillan), 1984, (Cambridge University Press), 1995, pp. 3-13. Thoms, David, and Donnelly, Tom, *The motor car industry in Coventry since the 1890s,* (Taylor & Francis), 1985, pp. 14-70, provides a valuable case-study

roads were in no fit state to accommodate the noisy new vehicles with their solid rubber or even metal tyres. They generated huge clouds of dust and this was a major cause of their unpopularity. Cottages and market gardens whose properties fronted by roads popular with motorists were angry that the quality of their crops and hence the saleability of their land had fallen sharply: on the London to Portsmouth road, for example, the fall was in the order of 25 to 35 per cent. Animosity also had a class dimension: cars were only for the wealthy who seemed to drive oblivious of their effects on others.

Canals

Britain's complex river system and its coastal waters had been used to move raw materials, goods and people before the changes in the industrial economy from the 1750s. Coal had, for instance, been carried by sea from the North-East to London since the seventeenth century. Transporting raw materials or goods by water was cheaper than using road transport simply because barges pulled by a horse could carry more than pack mules. The Bridgewater canal, completed in 1761, was a response to the growing market in Manchester for coal reducing the price of coal in the rapidly expanding city by half. The potential of canals as a means of opening up Britain's growing manufacturing sector was quickly recognised. As a result, canal projects proliferated from the 1770s linking the major industrial centres to each other and to ports such as Liverpool and Hull facilitating the movement of heavy raw materials such as coal and iron ore and the export of finished products. Despite the high cost of construction, there was a dramatic increase in the number of schemes promoted in the 1790s resulting in a 'canal mania' in the early 1790s with Parliament authorising twenty schemes in 1793. By 1830 there were over 4,000 miles of inland waterways in Britain. [20]

It is no longer possible to accept at face value the view that with the coming of railways, canals ceased to be economically viable.[21] It is true that from carrying more goods than railways in the mid-1840s, the canals sank to a situation where they carried only just over one-

---

while Lewchuk, Wayne, *American technology and the British vehicle industry*, (CUP Archive), 1987, pp. 112-151, considers the technology and management of the industry to 1914.

[20] Hadfield, Charles, *The Canal Age*, 2nd ed., (David & Charles), 1981, remains a valuable study.

[21] Armstrong, John, 'Inland navigation and the local economy', in Kunz, Andreas, and Armstrong, John, (eds.), *Inland navigation and economic development in nineteenth-century Europe*, (Philipp von Zabern), 1995, pp. 307-311.

tenth the tonnage carried by railways in 1898.[22] As with roads, most canals were fulfilling the more humble role of local feeders of traffic to the main line railways rather than acting as the principal arteries of trade as they had been before 1850. Between 1845 and 1872, government failed to prevent the absorption of key sections of the canal network by the railway companies. A firmer stand was taken in 1873, when the Railway and Canal Traffic Act banned further mergers without parliamentary consent, but it was too late. By 1883, more than one third of the canal mileage had passed under railway control. The monopoly position of the railways for long-distance good traffic had been established and railways owning canals had a vested interest in not maintaining or using them effectively.

There was a major campaign to promote the fuller use of Britain's canals in the late Victorian and Edwardian period but the initiative came from commerce and towns rather than from the canals' own management. There were three main reasons for this upsurge in interest. The high costs of carriage by railways hit communities furthest removed from the sea. They had the greatest interest in the improvement of communications to the ports. The loss of overseas markets to foreign competition after 1870 was, manufacturers believed, in part the result of higher transport costs than in Europe and America. Certainly where there was effective competition, as for example with the success of the Manchester Ship Canal, it was rightly believed that canals could keep down railway costs.[23] Finally, businessmen were critical of railway control of canals before Select Committees in 1872 and 1883 and this was reinforced by the Royal Commission on Canals, which published its report and evidence between 1906 and 1910. Despite this, government did not implement its recommendations especially the nationalisation of English and Welsh canals. The Liberal government was preoccupied with the problems of industrial strife, the demands of the Suffragettes and the Irish question. The management of canals was a lesser issue. War in 1914 marked the nemesis for canals and they had a much less significant role in the movement of goods when the war ended.

---

[22] Foxon, L. T., 'Part load traffic on a Cheshire canal 1846-1870', *Journal of the Railway & Canal Historical Society*, Vol. 33, (2000), pp. 344-347; Thorn, Patrick, 'Crowley & Co, canal carriers 1811-73', *Journal of the Railway & Canal Historical Society*, Vol. 33, (1999), pp. 82-91, considers a Wolverhampton family.

[23] Farnie, Douglas A., 'Cotton waterway: 100 years of Manchester and its ship canal', *History Today*, Vol. 44, (6), (1994), pp. 25-29.

Railways

The railway in the modern sense was very much an innovation of the late 1820s.[24] The industry was established in the next half-century in a series of promotional and speculative 'manias' in the late 1830s, mid-1840s and mid-1860s. By 1870, over 70 per cent of the final route mileage had been constructed. There were three striking characteristics of the railway industry. There was its novelty. The Liverpool and Manchester railway, opened in September 1830, combined the essential features: specialised track, mechanical traction, and facilities for public traffic and provision for passengers.[25] The scale of this new technology was also soon apparent. The capital raised by the companies in the United Kingdom amounted to £630 million by 1875, dwarfing the fixed-capital formation of basic industries such as coal, iron, textiles and steel. Gross revenue, running at £19 million a year in the 1850s, rose to £52 million a year in 1870-75, equal to the output value of the woollen industry and double that of coal. Permanent employment reached 56,000 in 1850 and by 1873 the figure had risen to 275,000 or 3.3 per cent of the male labour force. Finally concentration was also visible at an early stage. The great mania of 1845-1847 left 61 per cent of the UK railway capital and 75 per cent of gross traffic revenue in the hands of 15 major companies. By 1870, the same number of companies controlled 80 per cent of the capital and 83 per cent of the revenue. The remaining 415 railway companies shared the rest.

---

[24] Simmons, Jack, *The Railway in England and Wales, 1830-1914: The system and its working*, (Leicester University Press), 1978 remains essential on the development and operation of the system. On the construction of railways, Coleman, Terry, *The Railway Navvies*, (Penguin), 1968, is an eminently readable book. On the impact of railways see Gourvish, T. R., *Railways and the British Economy 1830-1914*, (Macmillan), 1980, Reed, M. C., (ed.), *Railways in the Victorian Economy: Studies in Finance and Economic Growth*, (David & Charles), 1969, Hawke, G. R., *Railways and Economic Growth in England and Wales 1840-1870*, (Oxford University Press), 1970, Freeman, Michael, *Railways and the Victorian Imagination*, (Yale University Press), 1999, Woolmar, Christian, *Fire and Steam: A New History of the Railways in Britain*, (Atlantic Books), 2008, and Kellett, J. R., *Railways and Victorian Cities*, (Routledge), 1969. See, Parris, H., *Government and the Railways in the Nineteenth Century*, (Routledge), 1965, on state regulation.

[25] The role of the Stephensons can be examined in Rolt, L. T. C., *The Railway Revolution: George and Robert Stephenson*, (St Martin's Press), 1962, and Thomas, R. H. G., *The Liverpool and Manchester Railway*, (Batsford), 1980.

Investment

For the twenty years after 1830, when the first passenger steam railway opened, an extraordinary amount of capital and labour was invested in Britain's railway network. By 1850, nearly 6,000 miles of line had been built, with another 1,000 under construction; between 1844 and 1846 Parliament authorised about 8,500 miles of line, three times more than had already been built. Between 1843 and 1850, £109 million was spent on railways, and investment in the network grew by about 20 per cent per year.

In the period up to 1870, investment was very largely the story of three great 'manias', peaking in 1839-1840, 1847 and 1865-1866. [26] In the late 1830s, railway investment consumed nearly 2 per cent of national income but this rose to about 4.5 per cent of gross national product in 1845-1849. In 1847, nearly 7 per cent of total national income and more than 60 per cent of gross domestic investment went toward British railways. We should not neglect the continuing importance of railway investment after 1850: over 60 per cent of the capital raised between 1825 and 1875 occurred after 1850. So what role did this play in the growth process? While railway promotion was an undoubted influence on general economic activity from the 1830s, its role was to support rather than lead. Decisions to invest in railways tended to concentrate in the upswing of the trade cycle but, because of the timescale involved in promotion and construction, actual investment lagged behind. So there is a clear distinction between peaks of economic activity in 1836 and 1845 and high levels of railway investment in 1839-1840 and 1847. Kellett commented:

...in the investment booms of 1837 and 1846...the whole character of the investing class changed. An entirely new range of small shareholders pressed forward to offer their savings, or even the working capital from their businesses....Because of the relatively high unit cost of these shares, it can be assumed that the majority, if not all of this numerous group were from the middle class, were politically enfranchised, and therefore proportionately influential in making their disappointment felt when they saw their investments more than halved in value in 1846 and 1847. Their resentment was increased by the knowledge that a great part of their loss could be assigned not to legitimate business miscalculations but to the sharp practices... [such as] misleading prospectuses, payments of dividends out of capital, rigged Board Meetings, accounts 'audited by daring amateurs. [27]

---

[26] Lewin, Henry Grote, *The Railway Mania and Its Aftermath, 1845-1852*, (Railway Gazette), 1936. See also, Kenwood, A. G., 'Railway investment in Britain, 1825-1875', *Economica*, ns, Vol. 32, (1965), pp. 313-322.

[27] Ibid, Kellett, J. R., *Railways and Victorian Cities*, p. 29.

This level of investment was spurred by the promise of high returns. Although the opening of the first major lines in the early 1840s coincided with an economic depression, once the economy began to recover railway stock began to yield dividends as high as 10 per cent.[28] This level of speculation could not be sustained. By 1850, most of the country's main railway network had been completed and new lines were only marginally profitable. In 1848 the second 'railway mania' came to a sudden end. Dividends fell sharply after 1846, and by 1849 the average dividend of British railway stock had dropped to 1.88 per cent.[29] The growth of investment in British railways slowed from about 20 per cent per year to 5 per cent in the 1850s and 1860s, and to just 2 per cent in the 1870s and 1880s.

Technological change, commercial viability and parliamentary attitudes were all important in stimulating investment. Gladstone's Act of 1844, which referred to the possibility of a state purchase after 21 years of new companies earning 10 per cent or more, helped encourage over-optimism about the industry's future profitability during the second 'mania'. After 1860, investment fluctuations tended to coincide with those of the economy as a whole, with a peak in 1865-1866, a trough in 1869 and a further peak in 1874-1875. Railway investment encouraged radical changes in the structure of the British capital market. The volume of railway business from the mid-1830s was such that the London Stock Exchange not only expanded but shifted its emphasis towards company securities. Railway investors were protected by limited liability from the start and it is logical to assume that the industry acted as a model for the companies that sprang up in the wake of the 1855-1862 legislation.[30]

One problem is that the duplication of lines led to the railway industry being over-capitalised. The actual network was even more inefficient than is commonly alleged as a result of the excessive competition between towns that national government was too weak to control. Although Parliament was in a position to regulate excessive competition between the private railway companies that built the

---

[28] Campell, Gareth, and Turner, John D., 'Dispelling the Myth of the Naive Investor during the British Railway Mania, 1845-1846', *Business History Review*, Vol. 86, (1), (2012), pp. 3-41.

[29] Campbell, Gareth, 'Deriving the railway mania', *Financial History Review*, Vol. 20, (1), (2013), pp. 1-27, Campbell, Gareth, Turner, John D., Walker, Clive B., 'The role of the media in a bubble', *Explorations in Economic History*, Vol. 49, (4), (2012), pp. 461-481.

[30] On railway investment see, Alborn, Timothy L., *Conceiving Companies: Joint-stock Politics in Victorian England*, (Routledge), 1998, pp. 173-256, and Reed, M. C., *Investment in Railways in Britain, 1820-1844: A Study in the Development of the Capital Market*, (Oxford University Press), 1975.

system, competition between towns to build railways as expressions of civic status discouraged Parliament from sufficiently regulating inter-company competition.[31] New estimates of the profitability or return on capital employed for major British railway companies shows that return on capital employed was generally below the cost of capital after the mid-1870s and fell until the turn of the century.[32] Addressing issues of cost inefficiency could have restored return on capital employed to an adequate level in the late 1890s but not in 1910. Declines in return on capital employed adversely affected share prices and returns to shareholders were negative after 1897. Optimal portfolio analysis shows that, whilst railway securities would have had a substantial weight prior to this date, investors would have been justified selling their shares afterwards.

Construction

Historians have distinguished between the railway as a producer of transportation services and as a construction enterprise. While it is not always easy to isolate the economic effects of railway enterprise, there is no doubt that the construction phase was a major activity in its own right.[33] Before 1850, the employment generated by railway building dwarfed that created by railway operation. Between 1830 and 1870, about 30,000 miles of track were laid to form routes totalling 15,500 miles with associated demands for men and materials, especially unskilled labour and iron products.

Between 1831 and 1870, 60,000 men were engaged annually in building railways, or about 1 per cent of the occupied male labour force.[34] This may not appear particularly dramatic but during the short 'mania' the numbers employed were considerable: 172,000 annually between 1845 and 1849 and 106,000 between 1862 and 1866. The construction booms produced sudden surges in demand for especially unskilled labour. The outcome, in the late-1840s, was a substantial boost to effective demand in the economy at a time of depression. Wages paid during this period amounted to £11 million

---

[31] Casson, Mark, 'The Efficiency of the Victorian British Railway Network: A Counterfactual Analysis', *Networks and Spatial Economics*, Vol. 9, (3), (2009), pp. 339-378.

[32] Mitchell, B. R., Chambers, D., and Crafts, N. F. R., *How good was the profitability of British Railways, 1870-1912?*, Working Paper, University of Warwick, Department of Economics, Coventry, 2009.

[33] Joby, R. S., *The railway builders: lives and works of the Victorian railway contractors*, (David & Charles), 1983.

[34] On navvies, see, ibid, Coleman, Terry, *The railway navvies*, and Brooke, David, *The Railway Navvy: 'That Despicable Race of Men'*, (David & Charles), 1983.

or 2 per cent of GNP. In the mid-1860s, constructional wage costs were high once again, averaging £7 million or so between 1862 and 1866. Railway construction also brought demands for professional expertise based on specialist work. Engineering, law, accountancy and surveying all received an important stimulus. Civil engineers increased fourfold between 1841 and 1851. Both navvies and specialists were not immune from cutbacks once railway booms subsided. The number of parliamentary agents increased from 27 to 141 between 1841 and 1851 but fell back to 70 by 1861. The navvy workforce dwindled to fewer than 36,000 by 1852 and after the 1860s boom it was probably no more than 33,000 in 1870. The long-term benefits of the attraction of labour to railway building were limited, especially after 1850. Of more lasting importance was the permanent employment offered by companies open for traffic, which exceeded 100,000 by 1856 and 200,000 by the late 1860s. [35]

There is general agreement that the construction of Britain's railways had its greatest impact on the iron industry. Wrought iron rails were the major product purchased, but there was also a substantial demand for iron in other areas of railway enterprise. It is, however, important not to overestimate the long-term significance of this additional demand. Pig iron requirements were of major importance in the 1840s, particularly in terms of home demand, but the same cannot be said of the construction phase as a whole. Between 1844 and 1851, about 18 per cent of United Kingdom pig iron output went into railway enterprise. However, after 1852 as iron exports grew steadily, the railway's share of iron output fell back to under 10 per cent. Railways were not essential to the expansion of the iron industry; of more importance were the diffusion of Neilson's hot-blast technique in the 1830s and the surge of export demand, much of it was in for railway iron after 1840. Steel rails began to replace iron in the 1860s but the substantial shift did not occur until the 1870s.

Railway construction stimulated demand for other products, notably coal, engineering products, timber and building materials. The evidence for linkages is rather thin. In terms of total production,

---

[35] Kingsford, P. W., *Victorian Railwaymen: the emergence and growth of railway labour, 1840-1870*, (Frank Cass), 1970, and McKenna, Frank, *The Railway Workers, 1840-1970*, (Faber), 1980. See also, Grinling, Charles H., 'Railway Employment', *Journal of the Railway & Canal Historical Society*, Vol. 202, (2008), pp. 91-98, first published in the *Windsor Magazine* in 1905, and McKenna, F., 'Victorian railway workers', *History Workshop*, Vol. 1, (1976), pp. 26-73, and *The railway workers, 1840-1970*, (Faber), 1980.

the direct impact of railway on the coal industry was small but as much as 10 per cent of output was used for making iron for railway uses. About 20 per cent of engineering's output went in the form of railway rolling stock in the late-1830s and 1840s. Brick production also received a direct stimulus: 25-30 per cent of the total production went into railways in the 1840s. [36]

Operation

Railway traffic, both passenger and freight grew steadily during this period. Passenger numbers rose from 24.5 million in 1842, to 72.9 million in 1850 and spiralled to 507 million by 1875; freight tonnage grew from 5.4 million in 1842 to 38 million in 1850 to 119.6 million in 1875; and, total revenue from £4.8 million in 1842 to £61.3 million in 1875. Although some companies created new traffic, the principal aim was to supply improved facilities for existing customers.

The trunk-line railways that eventually dominated the industry established themselves as specialist high-tariff businesses. As the industry expanded there were two significant changes in the composition of the business handled. There was an increased emphasis on freight from the mid-1840s. [37] During the decade 1835-1845, the major companies concentrated on passenger traffic, deriving three quarters of their gross revenue from this source. By 1850 the proportion had fallen below half. Also, there was a shift in passenger traffic to third class: in 1845-1846 third class passengers made up half of total numbers and produced a fifth of the total revenue; by 1870 the proportions had risen to 65 and 44 per cent respectively. [38]

---

[36] For the problems of construction, see, James, Leslie, *A chronology of the construction of Britain's railways 1778-1855*, (Ian Allan), 1983, Clifford, David, *Isambard Kingdom Brunel: the construction of the Great Western Railway*, (Finial), 2006, and Richards, P. S., 'Labour supply and construction of the London & Birmingham Railway', *Journal of the Railway & Canal Historical Society*, Vol. 14, (1968), pp. 2-6.

[37] Le Guillou, M., 'Freight rates and their influence on the Black Country iron trade in a period of growing domestic and foreign competition, 1850-1914', *Journal of Transport History*, new series, Vol. 3, (1975), pp. 108-118, Joby, R. S., 'Goods traffic on the Eastern Counties Railway from 1839', *Journal of the Railway & Canal Historical Society*, Vol. 32, (1997), pp. 251-260, and Hughes, M. J., 'Transport of livestock by rail', *Journal of the Railway & Canal Historical Society*, Vol. 32, (1997), pp. 299-305.

[38] Leunig, Timothy, 'Time is Money: A Re-Assessment of the Passenger Social Savings from Victorian British Railways', *Journal of Economic History*, Vol. 66, (2006), pp. 635-673, Andrews, Frank W. G., 'Passenger services on the South-Eastern Railway in 1845', *Journal of the Railway & Canal Historical Society*, Vol. 32, (1998), pp. 603-614, an excellent case-

Railways were slow to exploit their freight-carrying advantages. As late as 1835, locomotive technology was confined to a few lines and not until the early 1840s that locomotives were capable of hauling heavy goods trains. It was only with the company amalgamations of the late 1840s and the improvement of long-distance traffic interchange via the Railway Clearing House that railways were able to challenge canals and so extend their markets. [39] Railways could carry freight in quantity and this was the key to their success. There is general agreement that railways stimulated an overall reduction in transport costs, both by introducing lower rates and by forcing competitors to cut their own charges. However, the extent of the reductions and the effects on markets and commodities are more difficult. Between 1830 and 1850, railways undercut road coaches by between 15 and 20 per cent and canals by a more substantial figure of 30-50 per cent. Retailing was transformed and new traffic was encouraged in perishable goods especially meat, fish, fresh milk and vegetables. [40] The extension of services was accompanied by an improvement in communications and the telegraph, postal services and newspapers were all highly dependent on rail facilities. Faster and cheaper travel also stimulated the growth of leisure facilities, particularly in the coastal resorts. The railway reduced the cost and greatly improved the quality and volume of Britain's transport.

Economic growth and railways 1830-1900

Nineteenth century writers had little hesitation in assuming a direct link between the growth of the railway network and the pace of economic change. Historians today are more cautious. How much did railways really contribute to British economic growth between 1830 and 1870? Hawke posed the question: 'To what extent did the economy depend on railways in 1865?', or more exactly, what would have been the cost of dispensing with railways and transporting

---

study, Parton, Alan, 'Passenger transport in Surrey, c.1800-1870', *Surrey Archaeological Collections*, Vol. 78, (1987), pp. 109-118, and Hawke, G., 'Railway passenger traffic in 1865', in McCloskey, D. N., (ed.), *Essays on a mature economy: Britain after 1840*, (Princeton University Press), 1971, pp. 367-392.

[39] Bagwell, P. S., *The Railway Clearing House in the British economy, 1842-1922*, (Allen & Unwin), 1968.

[40] See, Robinson, R., 'The evolution of railway fish traffic policies, 1840-66', *Journal of Transport History*, 3rd series, Vol. 7, (1986), pp. 32-44, Dalton, Roger T., 'The railway milk trade and farming in the north Midlands c.1860-1914', *Midland History*, Vol. 28, (2003), pp. 100-119, and Atkins, P. J., 'The growth of London's railway milk trade, c. 1845-1914', *Journal of Transport History*, ns, Vol. 4, (1977-8), pp. 208-226.

passengers and goods by road and canal?[41] Hawke is concerned with 'social saving theory' and concludes that railway services in 1865 represented a social saving of between 7 and 11 per cent of the net national income of England and Wales. He recognises that social savings were much lower in the earlier years: about 2.5 per cent in 1850 and 6.5 per cent in 1855.

By 1870, the essential features of the railway industry, its basic network and organisational structure and traffic patterns had been established. But maturity did not mean stagnation. From 1870 to 1914, there was a four-fold increase in passengers and a three-fold increase in freight. Route-mileage increased by 50 per cent, capital by 150 per cent and gross revenue by nearly 200 per cent. Inland transport was essentially rail transport in the late-nineteenth century, though this is not to ignore the important role of road transport, and especially road haulage, as a short-distance feeder. There is no doubt that the contribution of railways to the economy was much greater than it had been in the 1860s. But historians have directed attention to the declining profitability of the industry and its relevance to the wider debate on British retardation and weakening competitiveness after 1870. So how were railways performing?

The net rate of return on capital fell steadily from 4.55 per cent in 1870-1874 to 3.38 per cent in 1900-1904. However, it was not until the 1890s that returns fell below the 4.0 per cent level of the 1860s and there was a recovery from 1901 to 3.6 per cent by 1910-1912. After two decades of recovery between 1850 and 1870, the industry's earning power fell back to the level of the early 1860s and that operating margins narrowed significantly. These developments can be explained by seeing railways as the victims of the increased demand for traffic. Traffic growth occurred largely in those sectors were profits were lowest: third class passengers and small consignments of short-haul bulk freight. The emphasis of the railway companies was on expanding links by constructing branch lines at the expense of operating costs.[42]

There were four distinct periods affecting the working environment and these corresponded broadly with changing price trends. There was a sharp rise in costs in the early 1870s. Revenue and costs per train-mile fell between 1873 and 1890 when the additional costs of an improve quality of service were offset by the

---

[41] Ibid, Hawke, G. R., *Railways and Economic Growth in England and Wales 1840-1870,* pp. 2-31.
[42] Crafts, N. F. R., Mills, Terence C., Mulatu, Abay, 'Total factor productivity growth on Britain's railways, 1852-1912: A reappraisal of the evidence', *Explorations in Economic History*, Vol. 44, (2007), pp. 608-634.

falling price of materials, especially coal. In the 1890s, and notably between 1896 and 1901, there was a serious escalation of costs. After 1900 the situation changed again and there was a substantial improvement in operating efficiency; almost all of this occurred in the freight area.

The railways' difficulties were exacerbated by the challenging nature of the economy between 1896 and 1901. Operating costs increased sharply, traffic growth slowed down and the extra burdens of newly raised capital put pressure on profit levels. All this was accompanied by legislation seeking to control two areas of railway economy: charges and labour costs. The Railway Regulation Act 1893, which aimed to restrict excessive working hours, and the Railway and Canal Traffic Act 1894, which established the 1892 rates as new maximum charges, were examples of the many efforts to make the railways conform to public expectations. [43] The degree to which the railway companies were responsible for this situation is a matter of some disagreement. Derek Aldcroft suggests that much of the problem was due to managerial shortcomings and there is evidence that while managers were aware of the need to prune uneconomic services, they frequently yielded to pressure from customers. [44] The results, in the case of uneconomic lines, were economies by squeezing labour and reducing the quality of services. Other historians emphasise the more hostile political environment in which railways were placed after 1870: governments were prepared to legislate on passenger fares and safety in the 'public interest'. The Railway and Canal Traffic Act 1873, the Cheap Trains Act 1883 and the legislation of 1888-1894 were all part of a significant shift in political attitudes. Railways were seen more as public corporations than as profit-making businesses. It is in this environment railways experienced diminishing returns, while producing substantial benefits for society as a whole.

British railway companies developed into powerful regional monopolies, which then contested each other's territories. When denied access to existing lines in rival territories, they built duplicate lines instead. Plans for an integrated national system, sponsored by William Gladstone, were blocked by Members of Parliament because of a perceived conflict with the local interests they represented. Each town wanted more railways than its neighbours, and so too many lines

---

[43] Cain, Peter J., 'Traders versus railways: the genesis of the Railway and Canal Traffic Act of 1894', *Journal of Transport History*, new series, Vol. 2, (1973), pp. 65-84.

[44] Aldcroft, D. H., 'The efficiency and enterprise of British railways, 1870-1914', *Explorations in Entrepreneurial History*, new series, Vol. 5, (1968), pp. 158-174.

were built. The costs of these surplus lines led ultimately to higher fares and freight charges that ultimately impaired the performance of the economy. [45]

Railways and society

The impact of railways on Victorian society was immense. [46] In 1851, William Johnston, a barrister summed up contemporary attitudes to the railway:

> ...the most important event of the last quarter of a century in English history...this dependence magnitude of the capital they have absorbed – the changes they have produced in the habits of society – the new aspect they have given, in some respects, to the affairs of government – the new feeling of power they have engendered – the triumphs and disappointments of which they have been the cause – above all, the new and excessive activities to which they have given rise – must lead all who reflect upon the subject to admit that the importance of the general result of these great undertakings can scarcely be exaggerated. [47]

This was echoed later when H. G. Wells suggested:

> The nineteenth century, when it takes its place with the other centuries in the chronological charts of the future, will, if it needs a symbol, almost certainly have as that symbol a steam engine running upon a railway. [48]

Railways provided the speediest means of transport during the nineteenth century. At first some railways charged first-class passengers more than they would have had to pay making the same

---

[45] Casson, Mark, *The World's First Railway System: Enterprise, Competition and Regulation on the Railway Network in Victorian Britain*, (Oxford University Press), 2009, uses counterfactual analysis to construct an alternative network to represent the most efficient alternative rail network that could have been constructed given what was known at the time. It reveals how weaknesses in regulation and defects in government policy resulted in enormous inefficiency in the Victorian system.

[46] On the impact of railways, see, Simmons, Jack, *The Victorian Railway*, (Thames & Hudson), 1991, ibid, Freeman, Michael J., *Railways and the Victorian imagination*, and Evans, A. K. B. and Gough, J. V., (eds.), *The Impact of the Railways on Society in Britain: essays in honour of Jack Simmons*, (Ashgate), 2003.

[47] Johnston, William, *England As It Is: political, social and industrial, in the middle of the nineteenth century*, 2 Vols. (J. Murray), 1851, Vol. 1, p. 260.

[48] Well, H. G., *Anticipations of the Reactions of Mechanical and Scientific Progress upon Human Life and Thought*, (Chapman & Hall), 1902, p. 4.

journey inside a coach and second-class passengers more than they would have been charged for an outside seat. It was not long, however, before railways began to give fares a competitive edge over the charges of coach travel. It was a policy that resulted in a rapid increase in the volume of passenger traffic. By the early 1840s, half fares for those under twelve were generally widely available making family rail travel more widespread and still further augmented the volume of passenger travel. Initially the poor were not encouraged to travel unless it was in search of work or to fulfil urgent family responsibilities. Railway companies made no provision for that type of traveller who had gone by carrier's wagon rather than by the outside of a coach because it was cheaper. Robert Stephenson told the Select Committee on Railways in July 1839 that there was:

>...a class of people who had not yet had the advantage from the railways which they ought, that is the labouring classes.

The practice of providing third-class carriages on trains spread gradually. It was not, however, until the Railway Act 1844 with its clauses making the provision of third-class accommodation on at least one train a day in each direction obligatory, that the working-class could count on penny-a-mile travel under minimum conditions of comfort. [49] Between 1849 and 1870, the number of third-class passengers increased nearly six fold whereas the increase in other areas was only fourfold. The boost to third-class travel was further increased after 1874 when the Midland Railway abolished second class and greatly improved the comfort for third-class passengers. Other companies followed suit and by 1890 the difference in the standards of accommodation had been substantially narrowed.

Freight traffic did not increase as rapidly as passenger travel partly because of the relative cheapness of inland navigation. One problem the early railway companies faced was through-traffic: getting goods from one part of the country to another through different

---

[49] Bailey, Mark F., 'The 1844 Railway Act: A Violation of *laissez-faire* Political Economy?', *History of Economic Ideas*, Vol. 12, (2004), pp. 7-24, McLean, Iain, and Foster, C., 'The political economy of regulation: interests, ideology, voters and the UK Regulation of Railways Act 1844', *Public Administration*, Vol. 70, (1992), pp. 313-331. See also, Prest, John, 'Gladstone and the railways', in Jagger, Peter J., (ed.), *Gladstone*, (Hambledon), 1998, pp. 197-212 and Hodgkins, David, 'Gladstone and Railways, Part 1', *Journal of the Railway & Canal Historical Society*, Vol. 197, (2007), pp. 501-508, and 'Gladstone and Railways, Part 2: Gladstone, the Minister', *Journal of the Railway & Canal Historical Society*, Vol. 198, (2007), pp. 574-582.

companies' lines. Although a Railway Clearing House was established in January 1842 it was five years before it began to operate effectively and there was a substantial reduction in the cost of freight. In the early 1850s, the volume of freight carried by railway first exceeded that carried by canals. The movement of coal was the mainstay of British railways; the tonnage carried always well over half the total of freight traffic. In 1865, for example, 50 million tons of coal was carried compared to 13 million tons of other minerals (especially iron) and nearly 32 million tons of other merchandise. Up to 1914, the volume of mineral traffic increased at a faster rate than traffic in other goods. Despite this, the mineral trade was less profitable than the other type of freight, earning only 45 per cent of freight revenue in 1913. The railways made available, at a lower cost, the fuel that was the lifeblood of the basic industries. On the other hand the presence of about 1,400,000 mostly small wagons, many of which were used to carry coal, cluttered up the tracks and led to congestion on the railway network. Railways' contribution to the prosperity of coal mining came through their cheapening of delivery costs and the consequent vast extension of the use of coal in manufactures and in domestic heating.

The growth of the iron industry was sustained by orders of rails, locomotives and rolling stock. The demand for locomotives and rolling stock was so great that it accounted for at least 20 per cent of the engineering industry's output in the later 1840s. Railways spread the engineering industry into areas that were previously regarded as agricultural: for example, the South Eastern Railway established its locomotive and carriage works at Ashford in Kent in 1845 and the Great Western Railway decided to set up a similar establishment at Swindon five years earlier. [50] Though railway engineering made significant early achievements, its later progress was unimpressive.

The dominance of the chief mechanical engineer over development policy in many of the larger railway companies acted as an important constraint in innovative developments. These engineers were highly individualist and liked to be known for the distinctive features on the locomotives they designed. This led to little standardisation of design, with consequently little attempt to maximise economy of operation. Considerations of engineering excellence took precedence over better cost accounting and the need for more adequate statistics on the operating efficiency of freight trains. This did not mean that there were no improvements in the efficiency of the locomotive after 1850. The replacement of wrought iron with steel rails meant that weightier and more powerful locomotives could be

---

[50] Peck, A. S., *The Great Western at Swindon works*, (Oxford Publishing Co.), 1983.

used. The substitution of coke for coal as fuel after 1870 made feasible higher steam pressure, greater speeds and heavier trains. Some lines were electrified before 1914 but the mileage was very small: 314 out of 23,911 route miles of track. Railway costs meant that manufacturing centres were able to undercut the largely hand-based local centres of production. The economic and social life of towns and villages became less diversified.[51] A comparison of local directories demonstrates this very clearly. By 1900, although the names of trades had sometimes survived, the character of the business that went on behind the shop front had changed radically. Tradesmen had, in many cases, ceased to be craftsmen. They became dealers or shopkeepers, selling goods made in some remote manufacturing centre elsewhere in Britain or even in America or Germany.

One effect of the railways was the elimination of local differences in farm prices. Not only could farmers bring in fertilisers, they could send their produce to market more easily and cheaply. This had important consequences for people's diet. Take, for example, the transformation of the system of marketing livestock. Traditionally meat was supplied to London and other large centres of population 'on the hoof'. Animals were driven from the farms to the final fattening grounds near the main markets. In early 1830, 34 drovers guided 182,000 sheep a year from south Lincolnshire to London while a further 52 men drove 26,520 oxen on the same route. It was an expensive and time-consuming operation. When the rail link from Cambridge to London was opened, the greater part of the journey could be completed in less than a day cutting costs considerably. The gradual disappearance of the long-distance droving industry occurred in Scotland in the 1850s and 1860s and led to the emergence of new markets at railheads like Lairg, Lockerbie and Lanark. The fat-stock farmer could now expect a better financial return because less of his product was being wasted in the process of marketing and the customer could get a cheaper and fresher product. A similar process can be seen in the transformation of Britain's fisheries and the expansion of the east coast fishing ports.

Railway investment broadened the social spread of those involved in risk capital. Before 1830, the investment habit was largely confined to the members of the mercantile and landed interests whose opportunities for obtaining a secure return on their savings had been strictly limited. Railways demanded a quite unprecedented volume of capital and in order to obtain it companies were obliged to lower the

---

[51] Everrit, Alan, 'The Railways and Rural Tradition 1840-1940', in ibid, Evans, A. K. B., and Gough, John, (eds.), *The impact of the railway on society in Britain: essays in honour of Jack Simmons*, pp. 181-198.

denomination of shares allowing people from the lower middle and even upper working-class to invest. The result was a permanent change in investment trends: before 1830 little over one twentieth of national income was invested annually, by 1850 the proportion was one tenth; more people were investing more money. Investors, engineers and architects supported railway expansion for different reasons but most recognised the opportunities it had to offer. Shareholders such as George Hudson recognised opportunity, new enterprises and large profits to be made. Engineers such as George Stephenson saw new machines to be built and old records to conquer. Others such as Thomas Grey believed that the railways would benefit Victorian society as a whole and raise the basic standard of living in the nation. In his *Appeal to the Public* in 1837, George Godwin, an associate of the Institute of British Architects, identified the advantages of railways and attempted to gain the support of the middle- and upper-classes by informing them of the 'intrinsic goodness' of railways. [52] He claimed that rails would reduce the cost of transporting goods and considering that, 'In some instances the cost of conveyance forms a greater part of the price of an article', many luxuries would become more affordable and would be enjoyed by more people. [53]

However, those who supported railways were often faced by concerted, if localised opposition. The first phase of opposition extended roughly from the mid-1820s to the mid-1840s, during which a large number of lines were sanctioned by Parliament, and the amalgamations of 1845 and was marked by an almost universal aversion to the railways. People who owned property on land that had been designated as railway right-of-way or land rumored to be so worried that their houses would be destroyed or at the very least made uninhabitable. A Quaker who called himself 'Ebenezer' wrote in 1831:

> On the very line of this railway, I have built a comfortable house; it enjoys a pleasing view of the country. Now judge, my friend, of my mortification, whilst I am sitting comfortably at breakfast with my family, enjoying the purity of the summer air, in moment my dwelling, once consecrated to peace and retirement, is filled with dense smoke of foetid gas; my homely, though cleanly, table covered with dirt; and the features of my wife and family almost obscured by a polluted atmosphere. Nothing is heard

---

[52] Godwin, George, *An Appeal to the Public, on the Subject of Railways*, (J. Weale, 59 High Holborn), 1837.
[53] Ibid, Godwin, George, *An Appeal to the Public, on the Subject of Railways*, p. 19.

but the clanking iron, the blasphemous song, or the appalling curses of the directors of these infernal machines. [54]

Farmers were concerned about their crops and produce: no one knew the effects of railway development on the average hen's laying capacity, or cows' grazing habits. Many of those who had worked along the canals or on the highways or in one of the hundreds of roadside inns that flourished at the zenith of coach travel felt their livelihoods threatened by the new locomotives. Many of these arguments were ridiculed by transportation historians of the early twentieth century and by railway proponents of the day, but they expressed genuine contemporary concerns reflecting the pervasiveness of the railway's influence on daily life and demonstrated fears, among all classes, about what the nature of that influence would be. [55]

The second phase of opposition, from the 1840s to the 1880s was a response to the railway manias and fears of railway monopolies and a reaction against perceived 'railway vandalism'. Railways, once so strongly opposed, were now using their economic power to push new lines through previously off-limits areas. The debates on railway vandalism centred largely on city centres, particularly central London and national historic sites, spawning societies for the preservation of antiquities. For example, in 1845-1846, the proposed line to Dorchester threatened the Maumbury Rings that had successively been a henge, amphitheatre and Civil War fort. In 1846, the Wilts Somershire & Weymouth railway company was forbidden to approach the Rings beyond a certain distance. Local opposition was not always successful and in 1844, the Brighton Lewes & Hastings Railway was allowed to construct its line through the ruins of St. Pancras Priory at Lewes, the earliest Cluniac monastery in Britain.

John Ruskin was among those firmly against railways, particularly the railway's 'vandalism' of personal homes and national treasures alike. In 1844, the proposed Kendal and Windermere rail line threatened to violate William Wordsworth's Lake District. Ruskin responded with a literary campaign against the line and Wordsworth wrote poems and letters that were published in the *Morning Post* to gain the support of the public and specifically address

---

[54] *Leeds Intelligencer*, 13 January 1831.
[55] Drinka, George F., *The Birth of Neurosis: Myth, Malady and the Victorians*, (Simon & Schuster), 1984, provides a general discussion of the cultural impact of the railway on the Victorian psyche. See also Schivelbusch, Wolfgang, *The Railway Journey: The Industrialization of Time and Space in the Nineteenth Century*, (Basil Blackwell), 1980.

the members of the Board of Trade and the House of Commons. [56] The line was eventually built in 1847, Wordsworth had successfully raised the question of need to preserve Britain's landscape heritage and although, until 1876, further lines were built the core of the Lake District remained untouched. Both side of the railway debates claimed the moral high ground but almost everyone had ulterior motives.

Few Victorian or Edwardian novelists followed Dickens, who while pointing out some of the railway's bad effects upon the city, recognised its positive ones as well. [57] More commonly, writers described the impact of railways in an urban setting as largely destructive and the artificial and intrusive sound of the train's whistle, often described as a 'scream', was often cited as the perfect symbol of that destructiveness. Bulwer-Lytton described how 'just as our travellers neared the town, the screech of a railway whistle resounded towards the right, a long train rushed from the jaws of a tunnel and shot into the neighbouring station.' [58] Wilkie Collins described the effect of railways on the city:

> It was a very lonely place — a colony of half-finished streets, and half-inhabited houses, which had grown up in the neighbourhood of a great railway station. I heard the fierce scream of the whistle, and the heaving, heavy throb of the engine starting on its journey, as I advanced along the gloomy Square in which I now found myself. [59]

He also compared past and present when a character arrived at the exact spot the tracks enter the ancient city of York:

> He reached the spot where the iron course of the railroad strikes its way through arches in the old wall. He paused at this place — where the central activity of a great railway enterprise beats, with all the pulses of its loud-clanging life, side by side with the dead majesty of the past, deep under the old historic stones which tell of fortified York and the sieges of two centuries since. [60]

Kellett argued that railway companies 'renewed and determined

---

[56] The two letters were dated 16 October and 9 December 1844.
[57] Dickens, Charles, *Dombey and Son*, Vol. 1, 1852, pp. 318-319
[58] Bulwer-Lytton, Edward, *What Will He Do with it?*, (B. Tauchnitz), 1857, p. 6.
[59] Wilkie Collins, William, *Basil, A Story of Modern Life*, 3 Vols. (Richard Bentley), 1852, (James Blackwood), 1856, p. 128.
[60] Wilkie Collins, William, *No Name: A Novel*, (Harper & Brothers), 1863, p. 80.

invasion of the central core of the Victorian city in the 1860s' ultimately made them owners of between 8 and 10 per cent of the most valuable central land often with negative effects for both the companies themselves and urban life.[61] By 1890, the principal railway companies had expended £100 million, more than one eighth of all railway capital, on the provision of terminals, had bought thousands of acres of central land, and undertaken the direct work of urban demolition and reconstruction on a large scale. Promoters had also underestimated the expenses involved making decisions without any sensible cost-benefit calculations with the result that many railways lost enormous sums of money. The Great Western Railway, for example, put up the money for the Metropolitan line and negotiated access to Victorian Station ten years before they considered how useful this arrangement would be and how many trains would be needed and surprised by heavy traffic from Windsor and Ealing, it opened unprofitable stations where there was little demand. Railway companies built enormously expensive stations while neglecting their rolling stock and in the 1860s spent between ¼ and ½ percent of the nation's total income on less than half a dozen stations.

...in the North the railway company that played the most active part in carving out new termini for itself in Manchester and Liverpool – the Manchester, Sheffield, and Lincolnshire – paid such poor dividends that the shareholders ironically suggested that the company's initials stood for 'Money Sunk and Lost'.[62]

Railway companies were largely unaware of the wider effects, particularly the social costs, of building in urban centres. As early as the 1840s, people realised the scale of these costs since appropriating land in urban centres forced up real estate prices, devastated working-class housing, added to congestion and even when residential housing was left standing it was not renewed. It is conspicuous that where the railways passed no residential improvement took place. They were frozen, as far as renovation or improvements were concerned, as completed as if time has stopped in 1830. Capital sunk in replacing residential housing in such an environment with a more up-to-date equivalent was obviously considered capital wasted. The best plan for a proprietor was to patch the properties up, accept a lower class of tenant, and wait until a major alteration made it possible to abandon residential use altogether: until commercial or business offer was

---

[61] Ibid, Kellett, J. R., *Railways and Victorian Cities*, p. 69.
[62] Ibid, p. 80.

made, a corporation clearance or street widening scheme swept the district away, or the railways themselves enlarged their approaches. [63]

Novelists Diana Mullock Craik and George Gissing characterised a place positively because the railway has not touched it. Gissing tells us:

> No corner of England more safely rural; beyond sound of railway whistle, bosomed in great old elms, amid wide meadows and generous tillage; sloping westward to the river Dee, and from its soft green hills descrying the mountains of Wales. [64]

In *The Ogilvies*, Mrs Craik regarded as place as a city precisely because a railway has not yet entered it:

> Yet there is much that is good about the place and its inhabitants. The latter may well be proud of their ancient and beautiful city – beautiful not so much in itself as for its situation. It lies in the midst of a fertile and gracefully undulated region, and consists of a cluster of artistically irregular and deliciously old-fashioned streets, of which the nucleus is the cathedral. This rises aloft with its three airy spires, so light, so delicately traced, that they have been christened the Ladies of the Vale has an air of repose, an old-world look, which becomes it well. No railway has yet disturbed the sacred peace of its antiquity, and here and there you may see grass growing in its quiet streets, – over which you would no more think of thundering in a modern equipage than of driving a coach-and-four across the graves of your ancestors. [65]

Elizabeth Gaskell pointed out in *North and South* and *Cranford* that much of the beauty and charm of ancient cities derived from their prosperous citizen's wilful ignorance of the economic, intellectual, and spiritual impoverishment of the lower classes, a point wryly made by Mrs Craik when she describes the 'melancholy emphasis' of 'the line where the threatened railway was to traverse this beautiful champaign, and bring at last the evil spirit of reform and progress into the time-honoured sanctity of the cathedral town.' [66]

Despite this, railways were regarded as symbolic of the progressive spirit. Sponsors of railway companies were often also supporters of parliamentary reform, municipal reform and free trade. In 1907, the author of a survey of the Essex economy wrote:

> It was not easy to lay down rails in the soft Essex soils and a good deal of the country is still untouched by railroads and therefore quietly

---

[63] Ibid, p. 340.
[64] Gissing, George, *The Crown of Life*, (F. A. Stokes), 1899, p. 87.
[65] Craik, Diana Mullock, *The Ogilvies*, (B. Tauchnitz, 1863), p. 71.
[66] Ibid, pp. 83-84.

unprogressive in spirit. [67]

It is certainly true that the arrival of the railway was often accompanied by the introduction of other changes. The railway first came to the Isle of Wight in 1864, after sustained opposition from local landowners for nearly twenty years.[68] The editor of the local newspaper grumbled that many of the visitors bought by the railway had great difficulty in finding the beauty spots and that not only improved signposting but also better roads and gas lighting were urgently needed. Two months later he announced the formation of a gas company, 'the prospects of success being so very encouraging'. The 'progressive spirit' can be seen in other respects.

The development of the railway system resulted in the general acceptance of Greenwich Time as a standard. [69] Before 1840, different parts of the country operated at different times. The Great Western timetable of 30 July 1841 said:

> London time is about four minutes earlier than Reading time, seven and a half minutes before Cirencester and 14 minutes before Bridgwater.

The disadvantages of not having a standard time applicable to all parts of the United Kingdom were increasingly obvious. The result was the gradual standardisation of time during the 1850s. There is no denying the influence of railways in starting that standardisation of language and speech that was carried forward more speedily by the influence of radio and television. The railways of Wales, for example, were powerful agencies in the decline of Welsh speaking in the principality.

The creation of a national railway system was one of the preconditions, together with technological changes in printing, the growth in literacy levels and the abolition of stamp duty in newspapers in 1836 and the 1850s, for the establishment of mass circulation daily newspapers. In 1830, only 41,412 daily papers left London through the postal system. Railways extended the radius of circulation and newspapers could be delivered to all but the remotest parts of the country within a day of publication. In 1866, the railway companies agreed that the standard charge for newspapers should be half the

---

[67] Page, William, and Round, J. Horace, (eds.), *Victoria County History of the County of Essex*, Vol. 2, 1907, p. 488.
[68] See the comments in Somerville, Alexander, *The Whistler at the Plough*, (James Ainsworth, Piccadilly), 1858, pp. 392-393.
[69] Guilcher, Goulven, 'Railway Time', *Journal of the Railway & Canal Historical Society*, Vol. 199, (2007), pp. 639-643.

ordinary parcel rate. As early as 1848, potential demand was so great that the firm of W.H. Smith & Son chartered six special trains to get newspapers through to Glasgow within ten hours of publication in London.

Railways contributed to the increasing secularisation of British society through the development of leisure and the development of tourism. The holiday began as a holy day. At the Bank of England there were 44 such holidays in 1808 though this had been reduced to four by 1834. Elsewhere, however, there was a new movement in the opposite direction: in many factories holidays were declared at the will of the owners as a device for saving wages when business was slack. Every important form of leisure activity that existed in the Victorian period and which some supposed to have been introduced by the railways had their origins in the eighteenth or early-nineteenth century. Holidays were not something created by railways for the few, but arguably were for the masses.

Railways were quick to recognise the opportunities presented by train excursions. [70] One way of filling empty seats in passenger coaches and so offset high overhead costs was to provide excursion tickets at lower prices than the standard tickets: in 1846, for example, the Bodmin & Wadebridge Company ran a cheap train for those wishing to see a public execution. The first trunk line to show a positive attitude to the promotion of leisure traffic was the London & Brighton and in 1844 it became the chief pioneer of excursion trains in southern England. But it was the Great Exhibition in 1851 that provided the greatest opportunity for railways to promote excursion travel. Without the railways the Exhibition could not have reached the imaginative ambitions of those who planned it and, in the end, those ambitions were surpassed. The train had come to Dorchester four years earlier, excursions were arranged to London and more than forty years later Thomas Hardy conjured up the impact of the Exhibition on 'South Wessex':

...[it] formed in many ways an extraordinary chronological frontier or transit-line, at which time there occurred what one might called a precipice in Time...we had presented to us a sudden bringing of ancient and modern into

---

[70] Jordan, Arthur, and Jordan, Elisabeth, *Away for the day: the railway excursion in Britain, 1830 to the present day*, (Silver Link), 1991, and Reid, Douglas A., 'The 'iron roads' and 'the happiness of the working classes': the early development and social significance of the railway excursion', *Journal of Transport History*, 3rd series, Vol. 17, (1996), pp. 57-73.

absolute contact... [71]

When the Exhibition closed, railways stood higher in general estimation than they had done before. Their system was now revealed as a working unit, able to concentrate attention and energy from the most populous parts of the island on a single object in London. The running of these trains quickly came to be accepted by all the railway companies having substantial passenger business. There were other special events when their services were again in demand: the Manchester Art Treasures Exhibition in 1857, the International Exhibition in London in 1862 and big exhibitions in Glasgow in 1888 and 1901. The seaside traffic grew; excursions carried race-goers into the suburbs of the great towns balanced later by those bringing passengers into towns to see football and cricket matches. It is difficult to estimate the quantity of the excursion traffic as only the Royal Commission on Railways 1865-1867 dealt with the issue, and then only cursorily.

When excursion trains first appeared, it was common practice to run them on Sundays. Sunday observance affected the provision of railway services from the start and there was a conflict between the prompting of conscience and the pressing claims for business efficiency. The Sunday timetable, as the system developed in the 1840s and 1850s, differed from one railway to another but two generalisations can be made. First, the Post Office was empowered to compel railways to carry mail at any time it appointed; and since it had both to deliver and collect letters on Sundays it insisted on the provision of Sunday mail trains. This was uneconomic for the railway companies and so nearly all mail trains also carried passengers. Secondly, on all British railways the Sunday service was very much less liberal than that offered on weekdays unlike continental Europe where there was very little difference.

In Scotland, there were many lines on which no Sunday trains of any kind ran in the Victorian age: the suburban system in Glasgow, for example, was almost wholly shut down. In England and Wales the policy of providing Sunday trains was often criticised and sometimes strongly opposed. The clergy of the diocese of Winchester complained that their congregations were much reduced in the summer time. In 1846, Francis Close, the Evangelical parson of Cheltenham wrote, when Sunday trains began to serve the town:

---

[71] Hardy, Thomas, 'The Fiddler of the Reels', *Scribner's Magazine*, May 1893, reprinted in Hardy Thomas, *The Fiddler of the Reels and Other Stories*, (Dover Publications Inc.), 1998, p. 70.

Another page of Godless legislation, another national sin invokes the displeasure of the Almighty. [72]

His ranting was ignored and the trains continued to run. This heavy-handed approach was not, however, the only approach used. The case against running trains was sometimes stated with considerable restraint. The Sabbatarians treated Sunday as both a day of observance and as a day of rest. However, some secularly minded people argued that what was at issue here was really a battle of classes. The Sabbatarians seemed to them to be denying to the poor what would remain accessible to the rich, who kept their own carriages and could travel as they chose. Ought not the railways, as an instrument of social mobility, be available to all? The Duke of Wellington, hardly a radical thinker, thought they should. Two accidents, in 1858 and 1861, of excursion trains were seen as a judgement of God on the sin of providing Sunday excursion trains. [73]

There were signs by the 1850s of support for increased railway facilities on Sundays but the control by the anti-travel lobby seemed to be growing stronger. In 1856, Parliament turned down attempts to open the chief London museums and galleries on a Sunday afternoon by an eight-to-one majority. In 1861, 5.7 per cent of the system was closed on Sundays; by 1871, it was 18.9 per cent. By 1914, about 3,700 miles of the system in England and Wales were closed on a Sunday, a little over 22 per cent of the whole. The railways' Sunday business had never been large and was carried out at a substantially higher cost than the weekday business. There were therefore strong arguments for keeping it down. Railway companies needed to relay track and daylight hours were only available on Sundays: most of the

---

[72] Letter to the *Cheltenham Examiner*, cit, Goding, John, *Norman's History of Cheltenham*, (Longman, Green, Longman, Roberts & Green), 1863, pp. 570-571, something Close repeated in 1853, p. 600. See also, Richardson, R. C., 'The 'Broad Gauge' and the 'Narrow Gauge': Railways and Religion in Victorian England', in ibid, Evans, A. K. B., and Gough, John, (eds.), *The impact of the railway on society in Britain: essays in honour of Jack Simmons*, pp. 101-116.

[73] It was 111 years before another bad accident occurred to an excursion train running on a Sunday. On railway accidents and their impact on Victorian neurosis see, ibid, Schivelbusch, Wolfgang, *The Railway Journey: The Industrialization of Time and Space in the Nineteenth Century*, pp. 129-149, and Harrington, Ralph, 'The Railway Accident: Trains, Trauma and Technological Crises in Nineteenth-Century Britain', in Micale, Mark S., and Lerner, Paul, (eds.), *Traumatic Pasts: History, Psychiatry and Trauma in the Modern Age 1870-1930*, (Cambridge University Press), (2001), pp. 31-56.

conversion of the gauge on the Great Western Railway was carried out at weekends. The Sabbatarians began to revive at the end of the century. The Anti-Sunday-Travelling Union launched a new periodical, *Our Heritage*, in 1895 that was critical of all the railways' Sunday services. Protesters soon began to lobby management and disturb shareholders meetings. Their doctrine no longer represented prevalent thinking. The successful body in these years was on the other side: the National Sunday League founded in 1855 to support the Sunday opening of museums and parks. The Sunday service was often very slow. The policy of the various companies was to impose a strict rigidity of their own as far as timetabling was concerned. In part this was because of their anxiety not to offend Sabbatarian susceptibilities, the requirement of carrying mail and the demands of railwaymen for additional Sunday pay. Railways had begun by offering emancipation: opportunities to travel over substantial distances on Sunday. In doing so it violated the old Protestant Sunday in Britain. Despite opposition the railways' intervention enlarged the choice open to those individual consciences. In this sense they can be seen as progressive.

With the development of the Victorian excursion system can tourism and the family holiday. There are several reasons for the close relationship between tourism and the railways, unlike on the Continent. The smallness of Britain was itself an invitation to provide this kind of service. A quick trip to the coast was an attractive proposition. This combined with a large increase in average wages between 1860 and 1913 of 72 per cent and the increase in paid holidays. Victorian working men had more money to spend and more leisure time in which to spend it than workers in France and Germany. British governments ignored the excursion business because it was the affair of the railway companies, and theirs alone, to determine when and where these trains should run. As a result there was a continually increasing provision of excursions to match public demand.

The railway companies fostered the habit of taking short holidays over the weekend. In doing so it developed a practice that emerged in the late eighteenth century. The London & South Western seems to have been the first railway to encourage such behaviour: in 1842, it offered tickets at reduced fares from London to Southampton and Gosport on Saturday for return either on the same day, or Sunday or Monday. In 1844, the South Eastern ran six excursions to Dover with the option of extending the journey to France for the weekend. The motive here was profit. Other railways had different motives. Mark Huish, manager of the North Western, did not like Sunday trains for religious reasons (he was a strong Nonconformist). He believed that the weekend ticket provided a substitute for Sunday travel. The Saturday-Monday holiday does not seem to have acquired the name 'week-end' until 1870. By the late 1880s, the habit had evidently grown. *Bradshaw*, the railway guide, shows early morning trains running up to London to Mondays only from Eastbourne, Hastings, Ramsgate and Yarmouth as well as from Llandudno to Liverpool, Manchester and Birmingham. By 1914, there were ten such trains altogether but there never seems to have been any in Scotland. For the middle-classes the development of this type of service had two advantages. It gave them the opportunity to take weekend holidays and allowed the family to live away from the major conurbations and the husband could go home for the weekend.

There are major problems for historians in examining Victorian tourism and the impact railways made. There are no parliamentary enquiries or official statistics. Census returns give little information since they were taken in April when few tourists were on the move. As the tourist traffic grew, in extent and complexity, many of the British railway companies put part of it into the hands of agents or outside firms. The 'tour' was nothing new; guidebooks had been produced since the seventeenth century, the Grand Tour was part of the education for the wealthy in the eighteenth century.[74] By 1824, steamboats were plying the east coast from London to Leith, the port of Edinburgh; one was named *The Tourist*. In 1845, two men appreciating what could be done with railways and steamers came forward with offers to arrange this kind of travel, guaranteeing accommodation on trains and ships in return for a single payment: Joseph Crisp in Liverpool and Thomas Cook in Leicester. Cook offered two tours by train from Leicester to Liverpool and on by a steamboat to North Wales in 1845. The following year he organised a tour to Scotland. Cook never had any monopoly in the travel business, nor with his liberal principles would he have sought one. But his firm remained much the most famous. His outstanding quality was his imagination, served by intense energy and in the early 1860s his lack of real business sense resulted in the firm moving from Leicester to London and his son John Mason Cook playing a more active role on the strict business side. The result was the genesis of the package holiday.[75]

---

[74] On this see Black, Jeremy, *The Grand Tour*, (Allan Sutton), revised edition, 1992.

[75] See, Cook, Thomas, *Letters from the sea and from foreign lands descriptive of a tour round the world*, (Thomas Cook & Son), 1873, reprinted, (Routledge), 1998, Pudney, John Sleigh, *The Thomas Cook story*, (M. Joseph), 1953, and Simmons, Jack, 'Thomas Cook of Leicester', *Leicestershire Archaeological and Historical Society*, Vol. 49, (1975, for

The railways' excursion and tourist business had come to be very substantial indeed before 1914. In the early years, down to 1851, the pleasure of travel was combined with the discomfort and fear of travelling by the new trains. Improvisation was the characteristic feature of tourism. By the 1860s, the business had become, as a general rule, to be well managed. Trains were more tolerable to travel in and excursions had become an accepted part of the British railway system. Seaside resorts strove hard to achieve rail links with London or the great industrial centres. When Torquay achieved this ambition in 1848 a public holiday was declared in the town. [76] The railway did not reach Bournemouth until 1870 but in the following decade its population grew from 5,896 to 16,859 and by 1911 reached 78,674. Excursions became most obvious in the mass movements on or around the principal public holidays. There would have been little point in Parliament passing the Bank Holidays Act 1871 had there not existed a railway system capable of carrying thousands of wage earners and their families to the seaside and back in a day at remarkably cheap rates. [77]

Urban growth and creation was influenced by the emergent railway system.[78] Some towns owed their very existence to the enterprise of a railway company. [79] Others would not have grown if the railway had not helped to provide access to markets for the goods they produced and yet others had their character radically altered as a result of the extension of railway communications. In 1841, Crewe did not appear in the national census. There were only two small parishes of Monks Copenhall and Church Copenhall with a population of 747. Communications in the area were poor; roads were covered with 'excessively deep' ruts. By the end of 1842, four routes converged at this point of the railway system establishing links with Manchester, Birmingham, Chester and Liverpool. In late 1841, the Grand

---

1973-4), pp. 18-32. Brandon, Piers, *Thomas Cook: 150 Years of Popular Tourism*, (Secker and Warburg), 1991, takes a longer perspective.

[76] Travis, John, *The Rise of Devon Seaside Resorts 1750-1900*, (University of Exeter Press), 1993, pp. 94-123.

[77] Barton, Susan, *Working-class organisations and popular tourism, 1840-1970*, (Manchester University Press), 2005, recounts how short, unpaid and often unauthorised periods of leave from work became organised and legitimised through legislation, culminating with the Holidays with Pay Act of 1938.

[78] Gregory, Ian N., and Henneberg, Jordi Marti,'The Railways, Urbanization, and Local Demography in England and Wales, 1825-1911', *Social Science History*, Vol. 34, (2), (2010), pp. 199-228.

[79] Simmons, Jack, *The railway in town and country 1830-1914*, (David & Charles), 1986, pp. 171-196, examines railway towns.

Junction Railway started to build its locomotive and carriage works there and the town grew very rapidly. [80] By 1901, the year in which it produced its 4,000th locomotive, Crewe had a population of 42,074. Less spectacular was the development of Wolverton in Buckinghamshire. In 1838, the London & Birmingham Railway decided to establish its engine works on a site conveniently placed between the two cities. Population grew: from 417 in 1831 to 2,070 by 1851. By 1907, there was employment for 4,500 men and boys in the railway carriage works. Swindon became the engineering centre for the Great Western Railway employing 14,000 men by the turn of the century. Railway workshops were not always built in rural settings and it is easy for historians to overlook those in the urban environment. Stratford, in east London, fulfilled the same role for the Great Eastern Railway as Swindon was for the Great Western. Dozens of towns, though not the creation of railway companies, owed their rapid development to the presence of good communications. The spectacular emergence of Barrow in Furness as a major industrial centre after 1840 was associated with the expansion of iron mining and smelting; the Furness Railway played a decisive role in opening up the district that had earlier been remote and difficult of access. Middlesbrough, though not so geographically remote, was a parallel case in that the railway was an essential agency in the growth of the iron and steel industry.

The railways' influence in opening up new urban centres continued up to 1914. After 1860, the construction of branch lines helped to create or enlarge residential suburbs of large towns and cities rather than establish completely new industrial towns. However, the early development of railways was not entirely constructive and when the railway companies extended their ownership of property within already existing cities their role was also partly destructive. By 1900, the railways had over five per cent of the central areas of London and Birmingham, more than seven per cent of the corresponding districts of Glasgow and Manchester and nine per cent of central Liverpool. This led to considerable dispossession of the powerless and the poor. In building new stations, goods yards and stables in the centre of big cities, railway companies avoided large factories. It was far cheaper and less complicated to buy up large numbers of individual houses, especially where one landlord owned them. As a result railways contributed to the creation of urban ghettos and inner city deprivation.

As well as those dispossessed by the building of a new depot,

---

[80] Drummond, Diane K., *Crewe: railway town, company, and people, 1840-1914*, (Scolar Press), 1995.

there was usually an influx of labour into an area as more casual labour would be needed. At the same time as the number of houses and rooms were reduced, demand increased. Those displaced, it was suggested, should find new homes outside the city centre. But, one witness to the Royal Commission on Metropolis Railway Termini commented:

> ...the poor man was chained to the spot; he had neither the leisure to walk nor the money to ride....[81]

'Money to ride' implied travelling at the normal third-class, penny-a-mile rate established from 1844 and this proved to be too expensive. Parliament did attempt to require railway companies to provide workmen's trains at very cheap concessionary rates. In the Cheap Train Act 1883, Parliament intervened in a more comprehensive manner and extended what some railway companies had already begun to do. The result was a dramatic increase in workmen's tickets. An average of 26,000 was issued daily in the London area in 1882. By 1912, a quarter of all suburban rail passengers travelled with these tickets. With parliamentary encouragement the railways had made some contribution to the dispersal into healthier districts of the people living in the grossly overcrowded city centres. However, the continued existence of slums a generation after the passage of the 1883 Act makes it wholly misleading to suggest that the housing problem could be solved simply by a policy of concessionary fares.

The importance of the railways to social developments between 1830 and 1914 cannot be underestimated. Railways impinged on the lives of all sections of society, increased mobility, improved diet as well as introducing a degree of uniformity on the diversities of regional and local experience. They engendered wonder and fear, changed the landscape of the country whether rural or urban, and liberated society from the constraints and slowness of existing modes of travel. Yet railways could not have been as successful as they were without those modes of travel. Roads provided short-distance feeders to railway stations; canals still carried heavy goods; and Britain was still a horse-driven society in 1914.

---

[81] Cit, ibid, Bagwell, P. S., *The Transport Revolution since 1770*, p. 121.

5 Birth, Marriage and Death

Population growth between 1780 and 1914 played a major role in determining the directions of Victorian Britain.[1] In 1803, Thomas Robert Malthus (1766-1834) published a second edition of his *An Essay on the Principles of Population*, a work that had been first published anonymously five years earlier.[2] The main tenets of his argument were radically opposed to contemporary thinking. He drew attention to the consequences of untrammelled population growth, arguing that it would double every twenty-five years and that existing resources would not rise sufficiently to support such growth. Although the ultimate check on population for Malthus appeared to be want of food arising from the different ratios according to which population and food supplies increased, the immediate checks 'are all resolvable into moral restraint, vice and misery'. Of these, the 'positive checks', as Malthus called them, included:

> ...all unwholesome occupations, severe labour and exposure to the seasons, extreme poverty, bad nursing of children, great towns, excesses of all kinds, the whole train of common diseases and epidemics, wars, plague and famine.[3]

The 'preventive checks' could largely be equated with 'restraint

---

[1] Tranter, N., *Population and Society 1750-1940: Contrasts in Population Growth*, (Longman), 1985, provides the most straightforward discussion of the problems. Wrigley, E. A., and Schofield, R. S., *The Population History of England 1541-1871*, (Edward Arnold), 1980, revised edition, (Cambridge University Press), 1988, is a standard work, difficult but essential. Baker, T., and Drake, M., (eds.), *Population & Society in Britain 1850-1980*, (Batsford), 1982, is a seminal collection of articles. Woods, R., *The Population History of Britain in the Nineteenth Century*, (Macmillan), 1992, and Mitchison, R., *British Population since 1860*, (Macmillan), 1977, are short bibliographical guides. Woods, R., *The Demography of Victorian England and Wales*, (Cambridge University Press), 2000, provide detailed analysis.

[2] Malthus, T. R., *An Essay on the Principle of Population, Or, A View of Its Past and Present Effects on Human Happiness: With an Inquiry Into Our Prospects Respecting the Future Removal Or Mitigation of the Evils which it Occasions*, various editions. Winch, Donald, (ed.), *An Essay on the Principle of Population*, (Cambridge University Press), 1992, is an annotated version of the 1803 edition while Gilbert, Geoffrey (ed.), *An Essay on the Principle of Population*, (Oxford University Press), provides an accessible copy of the 1798 edition. Winch, D., *Malthus*, (Oxford University Press), 1987, is a good short discussion.

[3] Ibid, Winch, Donald, (ed.), *An Essay on the Principle of Population*, p. 23.

from marriage which is not followed by irregular gratifications', while:

> ...promiscuous intercourse, unnatural passions, violations of the marriage bed and improper arts to conceal the consequences of irregular connections, are preventive checks that clearly come under the head of vice.[4]

In England, Malthus argued, the checks on population were much affected by social class, the opportunities for employment and the physical, especially urban, environment. Self-imposed restraint on marriage operated with 'considerable force throughout all the classes of the community'. He doubted whether 'moral restraint' would work, especially among the poor though he supported a public tax-funded elementary school system to lift the working-classes out of poverty and irresponsible breeding and into middle-class self-control and responsibility. But he strongly opposed state relief arguing that, by making the poor comfortable, it would encourage them to have larger families that continued their misery. This pessimistic view of humanity's future drew criticism that his vision of unavoidable mass starvation was a 'doctrine of despair' while the social critic Thomas Carlyle dubbed Malthus' economic analysis 'the dismal science'. The population model Malthus developed was one in which the rate of demographic growth was influenced by mortality, fertility and net migration. When the rate of population growth begins to rise there will be an increase in the price of food that will reduce the level of real wages. Lower real wages might lead to increased mortality or affect the prospects of marriage that will automatically increase the level of temporary or permanent celibacy. As a result, fertility will fall and the growth of population slow down as it would if mortality were to be increased.

There is much in what Malthus wrote that is relevant to the post-1800 period but during the nineteenth century ways were found to escape from the weight of Malthus' law.[5] The association between population growth rates and food prices appears to have been broken even during Malthus' lifetime, a process made possible by Britain's reliance on food imports and by increasing both the yields produced on existing farms and by expanding the amount of land under cultivation. While the relationship between mortality and real wages

---

[4] Ibid, p. 24.
[5] See, Komlos, John, 'The industrial revolution as the escape from the Malthusian trap', *Journal of European Economic History*, Vol. 29, (2000), pp. 307-331, and Thomas, Brinley, 'Escaping from constraints: the industrial revolution in a Malthusian context', in Rotberg, R. I., and Rabb, Theodore Kwasnik, (eds.), *Population and history: from the traditional to the modern world*, (Cambridge University Press), 1986, pp. 169-193.

persisted, the latter began a long-term improvement. Mortality was probably reduced as a result, though difference between classes persisted. Improving standards of living were only one of many potential reasons for falling mortality. Marital fertility took the place of nuptuality as the principal influence on changes and variations in general levels of fertility. Family limitation came to be widely practised. Finally, the closed system described by Malthus was thrown open to new forms of destabilising influences. Cities grew at the expense of villages and the Empire at the expense of Britain.

Although analysis of population before the 1830s is problematic for historians, after 1850, information drawn from censuses can be matched with data from civil registration to construct a more accurate and comprehensive picture. To call the nineteenth century 'the age of statistics' is highly appropriate. The first decennial census was conducted in 1801 and the civil registration of births, deaths and marriages was begun in England and Wales in 1837 and in Scotland in 1855. While civil registration did not replace the recording of ecclesiastical events, like baptism and burial, it did mean that parish registers lost their position as the principal source for demographic study.[6] The availability of a series of population censuses makes it a far simpler task to chart the changing size, composition and distribution of population and to trace the characteristics of individuals and households from census to census. The creation of the General Register Offices in London in 1837 and Edinburgh in 1855 and especially the contribution of William Farr (1807-1883) brought a sense of rigour to what could merely have become a matter of data collection. Farr was responsible for the first official English life tables, preparing special reports on cholera and devising classifications of cause of death.[7] Despite the various methodological

---

[6] On the nature of the nineteenth century census and problems in using them see Lawton, R., (ed.), *The Census and Social Structure*, (Cass), 1978, and Wrigley, E. A., (ed.), *Nineteenth Century Society: Essays in the Use of Quantitative Methods for the Study of Social Data*, (Cambridge University Press), 1972, 2008. Armstrong, W. A., *Stability and Change in an English County Town: a social study of York 1801-1851*, (Cambridge University Press), 1974, shows how census material can be used.

[7] Eyler, J. M., *Victorian Social Medicine: the ideas and methods of William Farr*, (John Hopkins University Press), 1979, 'William Farr on the cholera: the sanitarian's disease theory and the statistician's method', *Journal of the History of Medicine and Allied Sciences*, Vol. 27, (1973), pp. 79-100, and 'The changing assessments of John Snow's and William Farr's cholera studies', *Sozial- und Präventivmedizin*, Vol. 46, (4), (2001), pp. 225-232. See also, Donnelly, Michael, 'William Farr and Quantification in Nineteenth-Century English Public Health', in Jorland, Gérard, Opinel,

problems in using the data, the development of civil registration from 1837 and the considerable improvement in the population censuses from 1841 mean that it is the demography of the first half of the nineteenth century that remains obscure in comparison with later decades.

How did population grow?

Between 1831 and 1911, Britain's population continued to grow steadily. Although rates of increase slackened from about 1850, especially in Scotland, annual increments rose from around 250,000 in the 1830s to nearly 400,000 in the 1890s, mostly in towns and industrial areas. Ireland, with its falling population after 1841, was the exception. [8]

Population 1801-1911 (in millions)

Census	England and Wales	Scotland	Ireland
1801	8.89	1.61	7.54
1831	13.90	2.36	7.77
1841	15.91	2.62	8.18
1851	17.93	2.89	6.55
1861	20.07	3.06	5.80
1871	22.71	3.36	5.42
1881	25.97	3.74	5.18
1891	29.00	4.03	4.71
1901	32.53	4.47	4.46
1911	36.07	4.76	4.39

From the 1830s, rural population growth slackened and progressive losses through migration led to continuous decline of population in virtually all agricultural areas between mid-century and 1914. All regions were affected, though the greatest relative loss was on the marginal uplands of Britain and on largely farming economies, both lowland and upland. Despite substantial overseas emigration much of the rural surplus was absorbed in urban labour markets.

Annick, and Weisz, George, (eds.), *Body counts: medical quantification in historical and sociological perspective*, (McGill-Queen's University Press), 2005, pp. 251-265.

[8] Cullen, L. M., *An Economic History of Ireland since 1660*, ((Batsford)), 1970, O'Grada, C., *Ireland: A New Economic History 1780-1939*, (Oxford University Press), 1995, and Kennedy, L., and Ollerenshaw, P., (eds.), *An Economic History of Ulster 1820-1939*, (Manchester University Press), 1985..

Demographic indices

Period	CBR	CDR	LE	IMR
1801-1825	40.20	25.38	39	167
1826-1850	36.04	22.54	40	151
1851-1875	38.82	22.22	41	154
1876-1900	32.38	19.26	46	149
1901-1925	24.02	14.26	53	105
1926-1950	16.16	12.24	64	55

CBR: crude birth rate; CDR: crude death rate; LE: life expectancy at birth; IMR: infant mortality rate

By the end of the nineteenth century, the economic influences on population growth had changed. The dominant influence of food prices, previously the major element in real wages, on marriage rates and levels of fertility was no longer the key determinant of population growth. Earnings were driven mainly by the secondary and tertiary sectors that employed most people and shaped labour demand and population mobility. The mortality decline had contributed significantly to accelerating population growth from the 1740s but this was halted between the 1820s and early 1870s by the toll exacted by high urban mortality. Not until improvements in urban health, in child and, from the turn of the century, infant mortality, did mortality rates resume their downward trend.

From the 1870s, the fertility decline, initiated among the middle-classes spread rapidly as widespread adoption of birth control led to a fall in crude birth rates from 36.3 per thousand in 1876 to 28.7 in 1900 that then fell rapidly to around 15 in the 1930s. However, its youthful structure still predisposed Britain's population to grow. Annual births remained at over one million throughout the period 1890-1914, peaking at 1.08 million in 1903 and with deaths falling from 670,000 per annum in 1891 to 578,000 in 1913; it was only increased emigration that kept population growth in check.

Overseas migration played an important part in reduced rates of population growth throughout the Victorian period. In England and Wales net losses were 0.04 to 0.2 per cent. In all some 10 million emigrants left Britain between 1815 and 1914 as compared with a total population increase of 29 million. That the balance was not more adverse was due to substantial immigration, especially from Ireland. Over 1.8 million people left England and Wales in the depressed 1880s and 1.9 million in the 1900s. All parts of the country contributed, though losses were relatively greatest from the most depressed rural counties and declining mining areas such as Cornwall.

Up to 1850, half the emigrants were unskilled, many of them agricultural labourers; by 1900, that proportion had fallen to one third and four out of five emigrants were from large towns and industrial areas.

What happened to mortality?

Levels of mortality changed little between the 1820s and the 1870s after which they moved hesitantly downwards to the turn of the century. There were three major factors influencing health and mortality. Socio-economic forces such as rising real wages and improved living standards and diet offered some improvement though not to the urban poor. Bio-medical factors also offered few major breakthroughs in curative medicine before the late-nineteenth century despite better hospital provision and improved treatment and containment of epidemic diseases especially those of childhood such as scarlet fever, diphtheria and measles. Finally, environmental conditions put considerable pressure on the larger towns in which an increasing proportion of the population lived but housing improvement was restricted. Only with effective legislation to improve sanitation, water supply and housing and to apply effective measures of preventive medicine, especially the control of epidemic diseases were these gradually eliminated. [9] Medical science may have changed slowly but improving public and private medicine and, from 1850 onwards, more and better-run hospitals improved health and life expectancy, especially among the middle-classes. [10] The introduction of school medical services in the 1900s helped through regular eye, dental and hair inspections since head lice were a universal scourge in poorer areas. [11]

---

[9] Woods, Robert, and Shelton, Nicola, *An atlas of Victorian mortality*, (Liverpool University Press), 1997, provides a graphic representation. Winter, J. M., 'The Decline of Mortality in Britain, 1870-1950', in ibid, Barker, T., and Drake, M., (eds.), *Population and Society in Britain*, pp. 101-120, and Millward, R., and Bell, F. N., 'Economic Factors in the Decline of Mortality in late-nineteenth Century Britain', *European Review of Economic History*, Vol. 2, (1998), pp. 263-288, consider the evidence.

[10] Hardy, A., *Health and Medicine in Britain since 1860*, (Longman), 2001, and Hardy, A., *The Epidemic Streets: Infectious Disease and the Rise of Preventive Medicine 1856-1900*, (Oxford University Press), 1993.

[11] Houlbrooke, R., (ed.), *Death, Ritual and Bereavement*, (Routledge), 1989, contains some useful papers and Barnard, S. M., *To Prove I'm not Forgot: Living and Dying in a Victorian City*, (Manchester University Press), 1990, provides a specific case study on Victorian attitudes to death. Woods, Robert, 'Physician, heal thyself: the health and mortality of Victorian

The unprecedented and unplanned growth of overcrowded cities lacking proper water supply and waste disposal facilities was directly reflected in the increasing incidence of the sanitation diseases in the first two thirds of the nineteenth century. While most epidemic diseases resisted cure, prevention and treatment could limit their impact. During the epidemic years of 1831-1832, 1847-1849 and in the 1860s, average mortality of about 22 per thousand rose to 24-25 per thousand. Excess mortality in large cities and industrial areas was reflected in the contrast, identified by William Farr, between the 'Healthy Districts' (rural and suburban areas) that had an average life expectancy at birth of 51.5 years in the late 1830, and the 'Poor Districts' (unhealthy inner cities and many industrial areas) where it was less than 29. The return to generally declining mortality in the last third of the nineteenth century reflects the chronology of the most significant improvements in public health and urban sanitation. [12] In the 1870s, the establishment of the Local Government Board and the passing of a series of Public Health Acts introduced a period in which local authorities adopted an increasing role in initiating civic improvements to safeguard public health. The majority of urban authorities took over the function of supplying water. A wide range of preventive measures were implemented throughout the country, governing municipal sanitation, the content of food, and the urban environment, particularly overcrowding. The elimination of typhoid and cholera, demonstrated the effectiveness of large-scale preventive health measures. From the 1880s, life expectancy increased and by 1911, it was 47.5 and 66.3 years respectively for County Boroughs and Rural Districts.

The close link between high population density, overcrowding and death rates, especially among infants and children underlined the continuing important of environmental and socio-economic factors in health and mortality. The principal reason for the wide discrepancies in life expectancy until after 1890 was high levels of infant mortality. In late-nineteenth century England between 15 per cent and 20 per cent of all deaths occurred to those under the age of one year with about 25 per cent for those under five years. Infant mortality in the unhealthiest cities was more than double than in healthy rural areas and twice that of suburban areas. In Glasgow, intra-urban mortality in the 1870s ranged from 21 to 46 per thousand with even wider

---

doctors', *Social History of Medicine*, Vol. 9, (1996), pp. 1-30, looks at the medical profession.

[12] Millward, Robert, and Bell, Frances N., 'Economic factors in the decline of mortality in late-nineteenth century Britain', *European Review of Economic History*, Vol. 2, (1998), pp. 263-288.

discrepancies between wards of 69 to 166 per thousand. The mortality of infants born to unmarried mothers was substantially higher than that of legitimate children and roughly one third of all infant deaths occurred during the first month of life. [13]

Over three-quarters of the fall in mortality between 1848 and 1901 was brought about by a decline in diseases such as scarlet fever, diphtheria and measles and those caused by infected water and food such as typhoid, cholera and, most significantly, dysentery and diarrhoea, a major cause of child deaths in summer months. There was also considerable improvement in the prevention of respiratory tuberculosis thanks to better housing, nutrition and nursing. There was no improvement of other bronchial deaths, including pneumonia and influenza, to which growing air pollution undoubtedly contributed. Even in the countryside substantial differences in mortality reflected environmental and nutritional contrasts. In the Fens, for example, damp and humid summer heat tainted food and increased mortality in areas where babies were weaned young. Where children were breast fed and/or had access to fresh milk, as in many areas of upland England infant mortality was often below average.

Why did infanticide become an issue?

In West London, on the evening of 1 September 1856, a grisly discovery was made. The bodies of new-born twins were found wrapped in a blood-stained petticoat and chemise in the front garden of a house at Pentridge Villas, Notting Hill. Mr Guazzaroni, the surgeon who conducted the post-mortem at the Kensington workhouse, found that the twins had died because of intentional suffocation and exposure. A verdict of wilful murder by persons unknown was returned at the coroner's inquest but the twin's mother

---

[13] Woods, Robert, 'On the historical relationship between infant and adult mortality', *Population Studies*, Vol. 47, (1993), pp. 195-219, and *Children remembered: responses to untimely death in the past*, (Liverpool University Press), 2006, and Woods, R., et al., 'The causes of rapid infant mortality decline in England and Wales, 1861-1921', *Population Studies*, Vol. 42, (1988), pp. 343-366, and Vol. 43, (1989), pp. 113-132. See also, Williams N., & Mooney, G., 'Infant Mortality in an "Age of Great Cities": London and the English Provincial Cities Compared, *c.*1840-1910', *Continuity and Change*, Vol. 9, (1994), pp. 175-212, Reid, A., 'Locality or Class? Spatial and Social Differentials in Infant and Child Mortality in England and Wales, 1895-1911', in Corsini, C. A., & Viazzo, P., (eds.), *The Decline of Infant and Child Mortality: The European Experience 1750-1990*, (Martinus Nijhoff), 1997, pp. 129-154, and Graham, D., 'Female Employment and Infant Mortality: Some Evidence from British Towns, 1911, 1931 and 1951', *Continuity and Change*, Vol. 9, (1994), pp. 212-246.

was never traced. Infanticide was disturbingly common in Victorian Britain.[14] Lionel Rose estimates that of 113,000 deaths of children under the age of one in 1864, 1,730 were due to 'violence' with only 192 of those being classified as homicides. Contemporaries maintained that Britain was suffering from an epidemic of child-killing blamed on 'puerperal insanity', a form of post-natal mania that accounted for as much as 15 per cent of female asylum admissions in some years.[15]

From the early 1840s, questions were being openly asked on the floor of the House of Commons where Thomas Wakley, coroner, surgeon and MP shocked his audience by claiming that infanticide,[16] 'was going on to a frightful, to an enormous, a perfectly incredible extent.'[17] By the 1860s, the problem was believed to have reached crisis proportions and figured as one of the great plagues of society, alongside prostitution, drunkenness and gambling. According to some experts, it was impossible to escape from the sight of dead infants' corpses, especially in the capital, for they were to be found everywhere from interiors to exteriors, from bedrooms to train compartments. One observer commented:

---

[14] Rose, Lionel, *Massacre of the Innocents: Infanticide in Britain 1800-1939*, (Routledge), 1986, and more generally Jackson, Mark, (ed.), *Infanticide: Historical Perspectives on Child Murder and Concealment*, (Ashgate), 2002, Thorn, Jennifer, (ed.), *Writing British infanticide: child-murder, gender, and print, 1722-1859*, (University of Delaware Press), 2003, and McDonagh, Josephine, *Child Murder & British Culture, 1720-1900*, (Cambridge University Press), 2003, pp. 97-183.

[15] Puerperal psychosis is now a well-recognised event, affecting perhaps one in every 500 births in the UK. It normally happens in the first month of the new child's life and takes the form of a severe episode of mania similar to that suffered by manic depressives. Patients may become confused and delusional, and in the most extreme cases try to harm themselves or their new child. See, Marland, Hilary, 'Getting away with murder? Puerperal insanity, infanticide and the defence plea', in ibid, Jackson, Mark, (ed.), *Infanticide: historical perspectives on child murder and concealment, 1550-2000*, pp. 168-192, and 'Disappointment and desolation: women, doctors and interpretations of puerperal insanity in the nineteenth century', *History of Psychiatry*, Vol. 14, (2003), pp. 303-320.

[16] William Ryan described infanticide as 'the murder of a new-born child' although no specific time was applied to the term 'new-born'; it is not restricted to days after the birth. Ryan, William Burke, *Infanticide: Its Law, Prevalence, Prevention and History*, (J. Churchill, New Burlington Street), p. 3

[17] *Hansard's Parliamentary Debates*, 3rd Series, Vol. 76, 1844, col. 430-431.

...bundles are left lying about in the streets...the metropolitan canal boats are impeded, as they are tracked along by the number of drowned infants with which they come in contact, and the land is becoming defiled by the blood of her innocents. We are told by Dr Lankester that there are 12,000 women in London to whom the crime of child murder may be attributed. In other words, that one in every thirty women (I presume between fifteen and forty-five) is a murderess. [18]

Even *The Times* was forced to concede at the end of a long list of Herod-like statistics on the subject that 'infancy in London has to creep into life in the midst of foes'. [19] At every new 'epidemic' of dead babies found abandoned on the streets of the capital, there was a public outcry focussed on society's responses. In 1870, in London, 276 infants were found dead in the streets and even in 1895, this figure reached 231. For the Ladies' Sanitary Association, civilisation itself was under threat:

...an annual slaughter of innocents takes place in this gifted land of ours... we must grapple with this evil, and that speedily, if we would not merit the reproach of admitting infanticide as an institution into our social system.[20]

Many of the women involved were from the lower classes and many of the babies were illegitimate. However, pleading this form of temporary insanity when taken to court was frequently met with a sympathetic response from judges, despite the obvious suspicion that some cases were murders. The problem of infanticide was brought into strong focus by the case of Mary Newell. [21] Born in south Oxfordshire, Mary had been a servant since she was 16. Without work in the summer of 1857, aged 21, she travelled to Reading where she met as old acquaintance, poulterer William Francis who invited her for a drink at his house. Mary ended up pregnant and Francis showed no further interest in her. Although she soon found employment within two months she left and single, pregnant and unemployed and having failed to persuade Francis to marry her, she was admitted to Henley workhouse on 11 January 1858. In May, she

---

[18] Ibid, Ryan, William Burke, *Infanticide: Its Law, Prevalence, Prevention and History*, pp. 45-46.
[19] *The Times*, 29 April 1862.
[20] Baines, Mrs M. A., *Excessive Infant Mortality: How can it be stayed?*, (J. Churchill and. Sons), 1865.
[21] National Archives: PCOM 4/36/37, and the review of Ryan, William Burke, 'Infanticide: its Law, Prevalence, Prevention and History', *The British and Foreign Medico-Chirurgical Review or Quarterly Journal of Practical Medicine and Surgery*, Vol. 31, (1863), pp. 1-27.

gave birth to a son, Richard and remained at the workhouse until August when she walked the eight miles to Reading to seek help from Francis who refused. Unclear what to do and confused, Mary wandered round all night and eventually she undressed her baby son, laid him by the bank of the Thames and let him roll in.

At Mary's trial, there was outrage at Francis' attitude as it was believed that had he shown any willingness to help, the baby would not have died. Although he admitted his neglect at the trial, this did little to moderate local feeling and after the verdict he was attacked by a mob, beaten and left semi-naked, an event repeated when news of the trial's outcome reached his new home at Wallingford. Mary was condemned to death but was in such a state that she was committed to the local asylum. A petition was launched asking Queen Victoria to commute her sentence and it was signed by the local mayor, magistrates and nearly 800 others. A deputation of people from Reading visited the Home Office to lobby and this intervention appears to have saved Mary's life.

Infanticide was an act of murder and as such, the guilty parties could be exposed to the full force of the law. Yet, on this politically delicate question, sentencing by the courts depended as much on the facts as on the medical interpretation placed on them. Victorian leniency towards infanticide was shaken in 1865 when a woman from London, Esther Lack, killed her three children by slitting their throats. After the court backed an insanity plea, one newspaper openly questioned the willingness of courts finding in favour of such defendants. Evidence from London shows that most women charged with infanticide between 1837 and 1913 were in their early to mid-20s though some were as young as 16 and that the younger the woman, the more likely she was to be acquitted or guilty only of the lesser offence of concealing a birth. However, it was not until the 1922 Infanticide Act that the death penalty was abolished for women who murdered their new-born babies if it could be shown that the woman in question had had her balance of mind disturbed as a direct result of giving birth.

The advent of the life insurance business brought a further motive for murder but in particular infanticide. Arsenic poisoning was difficult to identify since its symptoms were similar to those of dysentery, gastritis and other causes of natural death and magistrates were generally unwilling to squander public funds while the chances of detection were so small. [22] Families could enrol their children in a

---

[22] See, Whorton, James C., *The Arsenic Century: How Victorian Britain was Poisoned at Home, Work and Play*, (Oxford University Press), 2010, pp. 27-33.

'burial club' for a halfpenny a week and when the child died the club would pay out as much as £5 towards funeral expenses. Since a cheap funeral cost around £1, this left a valuable surplus for feeding the remaining children and some families enrolled each child in several clubs to increase the pay-out. There was a saying in Manchester, though it existed across the country that a burial-club baby was unlikely to survive for long. The burial-club scandal became so widespread that legislation was passed in 1850 prohibiting insuring children under 10 for more than £3. However, the lure of life insurance remained a potent cause of infanticide. Mary Ann Cotton, a former school-teacher from County Durham murdered most of her 15 children and step-children, as well as her mother, three husbands and her lodger, before she was hanged in 1873.

The harshest decisions were certainly those meted out to professional 'baby farmers' found guilty of infanticide. One of the first and most sensational trials was that of Margaret Waters, the so-called 'Brixton Baby Farmer' in 1870, who was found guilty of conspiracy to obtain money by fraud and the murder of a baby. [23] She was executed amid extensive popular agitation and press coverage. In a sense the pattern had been set and when, in 1879, Annie Took was similarly found guilty of smothering and dismembering an illegitimate physically handicapped child she had been paid £12 to look after, she too was executed. Other high-profile baby farmers such as the Edinburgh murderess Jessie King in 1887 [24] and Amelia Dyer[25] suffered a similar fate. Yet not all of these criminals were sentenced to death and other cases that received front-page coverage such as those of Catherine Barnes and Charlotte Winsor resulted in verdicts of life imprisonment.

There was a growing body of evidence by the 1870s that infanticide was a crime committed primarily by women and, more often than not, by the mothers or the surrogate mothers of the infants.

---

[23] On Margaret Waters' case, see HO 12 193/92230 for her statement and the judge's reply.

[24] One of the children in her care apparently died from an overdose of whisky. King was executed on 11 March 1889 in Calton Prison, and had the unenviable distinction of being the last but one woman to be hanged for murder in Scotland.

[25] Dyer's reputation as a mass-murderess stems from her modus operandi for after strangling her victim with tape, she placed it in a carpet bag (nicknamed the 'travelling coffin') and threw it into the Thames. She stated in her confession 'You'll know all mine by the tape around their necks'. Fifty-seven-year-old Dyer was responsible for at least 17 deaths before her arrest in 1896. See, Vale, Alison, *Amelia Dyer, angel maker: the woman who murdered babies for money*, (Andre Deutsch), 2007.

Undoubtedly, the more 'acceptable' of these two explanations was the latter, that these crimes were the work of depraved, unscrupulous women who had lost all sense of their maternal instincts and indulged in a commercial trade with life itself inside a profession known popularly as 'baby farming'. [26] The term first appeared in *The Times* in the late 1860s, and, according to one medical practitioner of the period, was coined 'to indicate the occupation of those who receive infants to nurse or rear by hand for a payment in money, either made periodically (as weekly or monthly) or in one sum'. [27] It was regarded with a great deal of suspicion in many quarters, as an 'occupation which shuns the light' [28] and not simply a primitive form of child-care. However, its popular appeal and social function were immense at a time when illegitimacy was stigmatised and single mothers excluded from the most elementary means of supporting their child.

By the latter part of the nineteenth century, the system had become well-established. The 'baby farmer' was usually a woman of a mature age and poor working-class background who would offer either to look after the 'unwanted' child or ensure that it was 'passed on' to suitable adoptive parents. The fee for this transaction varied according to the specifics of the contract but was usually situated between £7 and £30. [29] In the majority of cases there was also a tacit understanding between the two parties that, in the harsh conditions of life in working-class areas of the nation's cities, the child's chances of survival would be extremely slim. What particularly outraged public feeling was that this trade had a visible, almost respectable, side to it for it was practised openly through advertising in national, regional and local newspapers. Not surprisingly under such circumstances, the financial considerations involved in this extensive traffic in infant life gradually became the focus of deep suspicion. For the *British Medical Journal* of 1868, these 'baby farmers' would not have:

> ...the slightest difficulty in disposing of any number of children, so that

---

[26] See, Behlmer, George K., *Child abuse and moral reform in England 1870-1908*, (Oxford University Press), 1982, pp. 25-42, 150-156, and 211-221.

[27] Curgenven, J. B., *On Baby-farming and the Registration of Nurses, Read at a meeting of the Health Department of the National Association for the Promotion of Social Science, March 15, 1869*, (National Association for the Promotion of Social Science), 1869, p. 3. See also, Greenwood, James, *The Seven Curses of London*, (S. Rivers), 1869, pp. 29-57.

[28] *North British Daily Mail*, 2 March 1871.

[29] Ibid, Rose, Lionel, *Massacre of the Innocents. Infanticide in Great Britain 1800-1939*, p. 94.

they may give no further trouble, and never be heard of, at £10 a head. [30]

Baby farms were denounced as nothing more than 'centres of infanticide', a convenient way for women to solve the problem of unwanted and illegitimate births. It was, for instance, widely believed that these babies were often left to wilt away and die, sometimes helped along with a little soother known as 'Kindness'. These rumours found credence in the fact that at this time it was common practice, not only among those whose looked after children, but also among mothers themselves, to use a certain 'Godfrey's Cordial' to quieten the babies, and that this, if dosed incorrectly, could lead to 'the sleep of death'. [31]

Little however was known about the role of the mothers in this trade. *The Times* had no doubts that the women who sent their children to baby farmers were 'complicitous and selfish 'and not naive and impoverished victims in their own right. [32] Yet a survey of those implicated in the more spectacular trials of the period suggests that most were guilty only of having a child outside of wedlock. Crime reports invariably refer to the biological mothers' occupation as that of bar-maid, prostitute, factory or mill worker, domestic servant. Much more rarely are there references to 'outraged' middle-class girls and unfaithful upper-class women having recourse to the infamous baby farmers. In the Margaret Waters case, for instance, the court heard of 17-year-old Jeanette Cowen, who had been raped by the husband of a friend and, on the birth of her son, her father arranged 'adoption' procedures with Waters without the mother's consent. Evelina Marmon, a barmaid from Bristol, confided her 10-month-old child to the safe keeping of Amelia Dyer because she was temporarily unable to look after it. She was unaware that the baby had been strangled and disposed of until the trial, as Dyer sent her regular reports about its progress. The illegitimate child of Elizabeth Campbell, who died in childbirth, was 'adopted' for a generous fee by Jessie King to avoid a family scandal but nobody apparently suspected that any harm would befall the child.

The problem of 'baby farming' proved intractable, despite the sustained pressure of such groups as the Infant Life Protection Society that called for the registration and control of all people in charge of

---

[30] Cit, Altick, Richard D., *Victorian Studies in Scarlet*, (W. W. Norton & Co.), 1970, p. 285

[31] See, Findlay, Rosie, "More Deadly Than The Male'...? Mothers and Infanticide In Nineteenth Century Britain', *Cycnos*, Vol. 23, (2), (2006), URL: http://revel.unice.fr/cycnos/document.html?id=763

[32] *The Times,* 4 July, 24 September 1870.

babies on a professional basis. [33] Not only was this activity an integral part of the social regulation of the nation's sexuality, it also fulfilled a valuable economic role by allowing working-class women to occupy paid employment. Government interference in such a private sphere was therefore problematic in the extreme. The breakthrough only came through a private member's initiative which became the Infant Life Protection Act in 1872. This reform made registration obligatory with the local authority for any person taking in two or more infants under one year of age for a period greater than 24 hours. Furthermore, deaths of infants in such care had to be communicated to the Coroner within 24 hours. It was a timid start since the scope of people exempted from the Act was significant; relatives, day-nurses, hospitals and even foster women were all excluded and no 'authentication' of contracts between parent and baby farmer was required. Moreover since the registration of all births, live and dead did not become compulsory until 1874, unless the authorities actually knew that a baby had been born, it was possible for it to die, be killed or be disposed of without anyone even noticing its existence. Only after other sensational 'epidemics' of infanticide in the ensuing years did a further Infant Life Protection Act force its way through Parliament in 1897. This Act finally empowered local authorities to control the registration of "nurses" responsible for more than one infant under the age of five for a period longer than 48 hours. [34]

---

[33] The Infant Life Protection Society, created in 1870 and the National Society for the Prevention of Cruelty to Children established in 1889 campaigned relentlessly for the introduction of better 'policing' of working-class families: Allen, Anne, and Morton, Arthur, *This is your child: the story of the National Society for the Prevention of Cruelty to Children*, (Routledge & K. Paul), 1961, pp. 15-33. They recommended more foundling hospitals to be set up as well as public nurseries for the children of the poor, as they believed that working-class mothers' lack of education and standard of living both conspired against infant life. See, Arnot, Margaret L., 'Infant death, child care and the state: the baby farming scandal and the first infant life protection legislation of 1872', *Continuity and Change*, Vol. 9, (2), 1994, p. 290, and 'An English Crèche', *The Times*, 8 April 1868.

[34] The Prevention of Cruelty to Children Act was passed in 1889 to protect children under the age of fourteen from ill-treatment. Although in 1881 the Midwives Institute was founded, it took almost another twenty years before the first Midwives Act was passed in 1902; the Central Midwives Board were to govern training and practice of midwives in England and Wales, and it was illegal to practise without qualification (Scotland 1915 and Northern Ireland 1922).

What happened to fertility?

Martial fertility levels had already stabilised by the 1830s. [35] The lower marriage age that had contributed to the increased natural growth of the early industrial revolution after 1780 gave way after the depressed 1820s and 1830s to later marriage, a slight increase in the proportion of women who never married and lower birth rates of 35-36 per thousand women in the 1840s compared with over 40 per thousand around 1800. [36] From the 1870s, there was further decline in marital fertility and a fall in birth rates from 36.3 per thousand in 1876 to 28.7 in 1900 then fell rapidly to around 15 in the 1930s. However, its youthful structure still predisposed Britain's population to grow. Births remained at over one million annually throughout the period 1890-1914, peaking at 1.08 million in 1903 and with deaths falling from 670,000 per annum in 1891 to 578,000 in 1913, it was only increased emigration that kept population growth in check.

Why fertility declined is difficult to explain. The birth-rate in England and Wales declined at roughly the same speed and at the same time in most other European countries. This was not, however, a unitary phenomenon and the reasons why this occurred in Britain were different from those in Finland or Spain. In Britain, it appears that low fertility was achieved by spacing of births and that this correlated to later marriage but this was not a uniform process. Szreter has demonstrated that there was an intricate interplay between family-building strategies, gender and labour relations as well as broader cultural and economic change and that 'no single factor or

---

[35] Wrigley, E. A., 'Explaining the rise in marital fertility in England in the "long" eighteenth century', *Economic History Review*, Vol. 51, (1998), pp. 435-464.

[36] Soloway, R. A., *Demography and Degeneration*, (University of North Carolina Press), 1990, and Szreter, Simon, *Fertility, class and gender in Britain 1860-1940*, (Cambridge University Press), 1996, deal with the controversial question of declining fertility in contrasting ways. Woods, R., and Smith, C. W., 'The decline of marital fertility in the late-nineteenth century: the case of England and Wales', *Population Studies*, Vol. 37, (1983), pp. 207-225, and Woods, R., 'Social class variations in the decline of marital fertility in late 19th century London', *Geografiska Annaler*, Vol. 66, (1984), pp. 29-38, are important papers. Gillis, J. R. et al., (eds.), *The European Experience of Declining Fertility: A Quiet Revolution, 1850-1970*, (Blackwell), 1992, and Lestheaghe, R. and Wilson, C., 'Modes of Production, Secularization and the Pace of the Fertility Decline in Western Europe 1870-1930', in Coale, A. J., and Watkins, S. C., (eds.), *The Decline of Fertility in Europe*, (Princeton University Press), 1986, pp. 262-291, provide a European perspective.

national set of factors can explain 'the' fertility decline.'[37]

Working-class family size remained high throughout the period. Late-nineteenth and early-twentieth century working-class wives have often been characterised as fatalistic in their attitudes towards childbirth. The few working-class women who have left a record of their conscious decision to limit their families usually mention the plight of their mothers as the decisive factor. It is not, however, sufficient to interpret the failure to limit fertility entirely to fatalism. The letters published by the Women's Co-operative Guild in 1915 make it very clear that women with large families bitterly regretted it, chiefly because of the hard work necessary to sustain a large family.[38] What comes across in the letters is an overwhelming ignorance about female physiology and sexuality;[39] the difficulties of gaining access to information about contraception and family planning;[40] and, a lack of privacy in their homes that would have made the use of female methods of birth control extremely difficult.[41] The social taboo place on discussion of birth control and sexuality meant that little information was likely to be obtained by women. There is also little evidence to suggest that the use of contraceptives and substances to prevent conception percolated down from the privileged to the less privileged.

Sex education was as contentious then as it is today and for young girls was usually assigned to their mothers. William Stead wrote of his friend Annie Besant's ignorance of sexuality:

> She had kept her daughter ignorantly innocent of the nature of men and women, through the customary conventional delusion that ignorance is the same as innocence. It was then, as always, a blunder, and in her case a fatal blunder... No doubt it seems almost incredible to those who do not know women, and the immense capacity which blank ignorance has of ignoring facts, that a woman as intelligent as Mrs Besant could have left her home a bride absolutely unaware of what she ought to have known; but it is unfortunately by no means an isolated phenomenon. To the criminal

---

[37] Ibid, Szreter, Simon, *Fertility, class and gender in Britain 1860-1940*, p. 595.
[38] Women's Co-operative Guild, Davies, Margaret Llewelyn, (ed.), *Maternity: Letters from Working Women*, (G. Bell), 1915, pp. 1-10, 18-20, demonstrated the strain of repeated pregnancies on women's health and lives.
[39] Ibid, pp. 39-40, 59, 115-117.
[40] Ibid, pp. 52-53, 59-60, 93-95.
[41] Ibid, pp. 27-28, 787-78, 112-113.

wickedness of parents in this respect there seems sometimes to be literally no limit. [42]

However, this was increasingly felt to be an unsatisfactory approach and by the 1890s, there was considerable support for girls being taught 'some of the necessary physical facts'. The content of that education remained a difficult question. The Reverend Edward Lyttleton was quite clear in 1900 that more sex education was needed but that girls required less information than boys. He argued:

> ...for most girls it would be enough for the parent to advise that the seed of life is entrusted by God to the father in a very wonderful way, and that after marriage he is allowed to give it to his wife. [43]

The problem was that sex education was inextricably linked to different views about female sexual character and the religious emphasis on moral restraint. There were certain limitations on marriage. New appliance methods of birth control (the rubber condom, Dutch cap and douche) were developed, marketed and adopted during the last decades of the nineteenth century but were beyond the financial reach of the majority of working-class couples until after 1914. [44] Since marital fertility was reduced, it must be assumed that some combination of sexual abstinence since at least the beginning of the nineteenth century, coitus interruptus or withdrawal, regarded by Szreter as the principal way of limiting family size in the last decades of the nineteenth century, [45] accurate use of the safe period and induced abortion were the most likely means by which family limitation was brought about. [46]

---

[42] Stead, W. T., 'Mrs Annie Besant', *The Review of Reviews*, Vol. 4, (October 1891), pp. 349-367, reprinted as *Annie Besant: A Character Sketch 1891*, (sn), pp. 25-26.

[43] Lyttleton, Edward, *The Training of the Young in the Laws of Sex*, (Longman, Green), 1900, p. 85.

[44] Cook, Hera, *The Long Sexual Revolution: English Women, Sex and Contraception, 1800-1975*, (Oxford University Press), 2004, shows how the growing effectiveness of contraception gradually eroded the connection between sexuality and reproduction. The increasing control over fertility was crucial to the remaking of heterosexual physical sexual behaviour and had a massive impact on women's lives.

[45] Ibid, Szreter, Simon, *Fertility, class and gender in Britain 1860-1940*, p. 432.

[46] Banks, J. A., *Feminism and Family Planning in Victorian England*, (Liverpool University Press), 1964, McLaren, A., *Birth Control in Nineteenth-Century England*, (Croom Helm), 1977, and Soloway, R. A.,

Nineteenth and early-twentieth century writings on birth control provide a revealing source for attitudes towards female sexuality and social roles. Advocates of birth control were seen as supporters of atheism, depravity and social unrest especially by organised religion and the medical profession. Effective birth control shattered the link between sexuality and reproduction and created the real possibility of greater sexual freedom and control for women as well as helping to reduce family size. Michael Ryan, an evangelical physician argued in 1837:

> None can deny that, if young women in general were absolved from the fear of consequences, the great majority of them...would rarely preserve their chastity. [47]

Chastity according to Ryan was a consequence of fear of pregnancy. Birth control brought the possibility of unrestrained female sexuality and with it the breakdown of sexual control and social order. Medical opposition to birth control was expressed in a mixture of warnings about the injurious results for health and the associated moral decline. *The Lancet*, virulent in its condemnation of contraception commented in 1869:

> A woman on whom her husband practises what is euphemistically called 'preventative copulation', is, in the first place necessarily brought into the condition of mind of a prostitute... [48]

There was, however, an unresolved problem in medical thinking grounded in class. Self-denial was recommended as fertility control. However, the working-classes could not be expected to show restraint such was 'the natural predominance of the animal life in the illiterate.' [49] Doctors were generally unwilling to recommend contraception but also assumed that there was little restraint in working-class sexuality. This reinforced the widespread anxiety in the assumed sexual depravity and unrestrained breeding of the poor.

Birth Control and the Population Question in England 1877-1930, (University of North Carolina Press), 1982, provide a useful introduction to a vexed subject.

[47] Ryan, Michael, *The Philosophy of Marriage, in its social, moral and physical relations: With an Account of the Diseases of the Genito-urinary Organs, which Impair Or Destroy the Reproductive Function, and Induce a Variety of Complaints: with the Physiology of Generation in the Vegetable and Animal Kingdoms...*, (John Churchill), 1837, p. 12.

[48] 'Checks on Population', *The Lancet*, 10 April 1869, p. 500.

[49] Ibid, 'Checks on Population', p. 500.

Medical conservatism was illustrated when in 1888 H. A. Allbutt, a doctor on the staff of the Leeds Medical School, was struck off the Medical Register for publicising birth-control methods in one chapter of his popular *The Wife's Handbook* published two years earlier. Since the book was clear designed for married women, it was surprising that the General Medical Council took such extreme action. Its action reflected the official and strict Victorian mores and the illiberal attitude of most doctors rather than the general sexual practices of the day. The Council condemned the book as being 'to the detriment of public morals' stating that it was published at so low a price that brought it within the reach of the youth of both sexes.[50]

There were, however, strong public advocates of birth control and of the right of women to choose whether and when to have children. Francis Place and Richard Carlisle popularised methods of contraception in the 1820s. An early Malthusian League was established by Charles Bradlaugh during the 1860s to promote the doctrines of restraint within marriage but even the most tentative attempt to discuss family limitation met with furious opposition from the press and public opinion. In 1876, Bradlaugh and Annie Besant decided to republish the American Charles Knowlton's pamphlet advocating birth control, *The Fruits of Philosophy, or the Private Companion of Young Married People*, whose previous British publisher had already been successfully prosecuted for obscenity. In 1877 Annie Besant also published her own pamphlet on birth control, *The Law Of Population: Its Consequences, and Its Bearing upon Human Conduct and Morals* that sold about 40,000 copies in three years.[51] The two activists were both tried in 1877 and were sentenced to heavy fines and six months' imprisonment, but their conviction was overturned by the Court of Appeal on a legal technicality.[52] Although this did not initiate the spread of birth-

---

[50] For the attitude of the medical profession to birth control between 1850 and 1914, see, ibid, McLaren, Angus, *Birth Control in Nineteenth-Century England*, pp. 116-140.

[51] Besant, Annie, *The Law Of Population: Its Consequences, and Its Bearing upon Human Conduct and Morals*, originally published in *National Reformer*, 7, 14, 21, 28 October, 4 November 1877, (Freethough Publishing Company), 1877, reprinted in Saville, John, (ed.), *A Selection of the Social and Political Pamphlets of Annie Besant*, (Augustus Kelley), 1970, Section II, no. 10.

[52] Chandrasekhar, Sripati, (ed.), *Reproductive Physiology and Birth Control: The writings of Charles Knowlton and Annie Besant*, (Transaction Publishers), 2002, pp. 21-45, and Manwell, Roger, *The Trial of Annie Besant and Charles Bradlaugh*, (Elek, Pemberton), 1976, discuss the trial. See also, Royle, Edward, *Radicals, Secularists and Republicans: Popular*

control practices, the publicity surrounding the trial and the formation of a new Malthusian League to campaign for the abolition of all penalties against public discussion of contraception and the education of the public about the importance of family planning were a major boost to the birth-control cause. [53] Before 1876, the circulation of *Fruits of Philosophy* had been about a thousand per year but by August 1881, it had increased to 18,500. Opponents in the middle- and upper-classes felt increasingly pressure from what they called 'the evil in our midst'. [54]

Abortion was probably the most important female initiative in family limitation in this period, particularly among the very poor. In the 1890s and early 1900s, the *British Medical Journal* traced the diffusion of abortion involving the use of lead plaster from Leicester to Birmingham, Nottingham, Sheffield and though some of the larger Yorkshire towns. By 1914, abortion was common in 26 out of the 104 registration districts north of the Humber. Among northern textile workers, poverty and the need to work probably played the most important part in the decision to seek an abortion, but it is also important to recognise that working-class women saw abortion as a natural and permissible strategy. Withdrawal was undoubtedly the main method by which the decline in working-class fertility was achieved. One of the main reasons for this was the cost of sheaths: 2 to 3 shillings for a dozen when the average weekly wage for labourers did not rise above 20 shillings a week. Withdrawal was a cheaper, if less reliable, method. It also raises the issue of women's sexual dependency and that some degree of male co-operation was necessary.

Despite religious and cultural beliefs that delayed the adoption of family limitation in some sectors of society, increasing secularisation caused barriers to be broken down. The argument that family limitation represented the diffusion of birth control from the professional and upper middle-classes (the maid learning from her mistress) to the lower classes does not stand up to close examination. Among the first to limit family size were 'skilled' non-manual and commercial workers such as shopkeepers, and clerks who were also prominent among cautious late-marriers. There were considerable

---

Freethought in Britain, 1866-1915, (Manchester University Press), 1980, pp. 12-19.
[53] For the early development of the League, see Ledbetter, Rosanna, *A History of the Malthusian League, 1877-1927*, (Ohio State University Press), 1976, pp. 3-24.
[54] Banks, J. A., and Banks, Olive, 'The Bradlaugh-Besant Trial and the English Newspapers', *Population Studies*, Vol. 8, (1), (1955), pp. 22-34.

differences in marital fertility between different types of area in 1891. Relatively low birth rates in textile districts and residential towns, with large numbers of single women in domestic service and middle-class households, contrasts with earlier and more universal marriages with larger families among iron and steel-making and coal-mining communities where the abundant use of high-paid boys and young men in the mines reduced incentives to limit families, while fewer opportunities for female employment and the stereotyping of women meant that girls married earlier. [55]

Social factors such as the availability of marriage partners in areas of high emigration or persistent out-migration throughout rural England limited marriage levels and affected births. [56] Limitations on marriage in certain occupational groups, for example, living-in domestic servants and farm labourers, also affected local fertility patterns. [57] The general increase in the mean age of marriage to about 25.8 years for women and some two years higher for men by 1850, and further increased from the 1870s, also reflected changing economic circumstances and the desire for more spending power and independence. [58] There were considerable differences between

---

[55] Williams, N., and Galley, C., 'Urban-rural Differentials in Infant Mortality in Victorian Britain', *Population Studies*, Vol. 49, (1995), pp. 401-420, and Williams, N., and Mooney, G., 'Infant mortality in an "age of great cities": London and the English provincial cities compared, c.1840-1910', *Change and Continuity*, Vol. 9, (1994), pp. 185-212.

[56] Anderson M., & Morse, D. J., 'High Fertility, High Emigration, Low Nuptiality: Scotland's Demographic Experience, 1861-1914', *Population Studies*, Vol. 47, (1993), pp. 5-25, 319-343.

[57] Seccombe, W., 'Starting to Stop: Working Class Fertility Decline in Britain', *Past and Present*, Vol. 126, (1990), pp. 151-180, and debate with R. Woods, *Past and Present*, Vol. 134, (1992), pp. 200-211. See also Seccombe, W., *Weathering the storm: working-class families from the industrial revolution to the fertility decline*, (Verso), 1993.

[58] Lewis, Jane, (ed.), *Labour and Love: Women's experience of home and family 1850-1940*, (Basil Blackwell), 1986, is a good starting-point on the experience of home and family. Lane, Penny, *Victorian Families in Fact and Fiction*, (Macmillan), 1997, provides a novel analysis of the issues. O'Day, Rosemary, *The Family and Family Relationships 1500-1900*, (Macmillan), 1995, takes a longer perspective. Banks, J. A., *Victorian Value: Secularism and the Size of Families*, (Routledge), 1981, is concerned with the implications of changing gender-ratios in the late-nineteenth century and continues the argument about birth control. Gillis, J. R., *For Better, For Worse; British marriages, 1600 to the present*, (Oxford University Press), 1985, takes a long perspective on marriage while Dyhouse, Carol, *Feminism and the Family in England 1880-1939*, (Cambridge University Press), 1991, looks at the politics of the family.

industrial areas, where there were more and earlier marriages and rural areas where marriages tended to be later and between different social classes. Urban labourers and miners married young; prudent white-collar workers, shopkeepers and the middle-class postponed marriage until they felt able to afford it. Many single children who moved to the city, whether as a domestic servant or an industrial or office worker often lived for a time in lodgings before taking on family responsibilities. Hence the large number of households with lodgers reflected in census enumerators' books.

Across society, the 'perceived relative cost' of having a child played a critical role in determining when and if couples decided to have children. Among the middle-class, the expense of raising children with rising costs for domestic servants and school fees, as well as a growing desire for greater freedom and more money to spend on luxuries and entertainment, were obvious incentives to having fewer children. Economic and cultural incentives limiting the number and spacing of births were strong where women were prominent in the workforce. In the mills of Lancashire or West Yorkshire or in the Potteries women might delay having children or have a smaller family and return to work as soon as possible. Evidence from Bradford, Leeds and Middlesbrough suggests that after 1860 working-class parents pursued higher living standards, not to emulate the better-off but to give their children better lives than they had experienced. [59] To achieve this, they chose to have fewer children, allowing more resources and attention for each family member. This explanation places a new stress on the nature of rising working-class consumption. Expectations of rising living standards placed the greatest pressures on working mothers, who had to pursue them by both wage labour and domestic labour and made them the most susceptible to the appeal of family limitation. However, it is also clear that fathers also had incentives to family limitation, something underestimated in previous studies. Increasing numbers of women involved in shop and, from the 1890s, office work might also have deferred marriage and limited their families. Among the middle-class, the increasing expense of raising children with rising costs for domestic servants and school fees, as well as a growing desire for greater freedom and more money to spend on luxuries and entertainment, were obvious incentives to having fewer children. Even within geographical areas there were often significant differences in rates of marriage. In London, there was a very close relationship between the proportion of women

---

[59] Atkinson, Paul David, *Cultural Causes of the Nineteenth-Century Fertility Decline: A Study of Three Yorkshire Towns*, Doctoral thesis, University of Leeds, 2010.

married and the percentage of women employed in domestic service. In Hampstead the proportion married was 0.274 while in Poplar, in the East End, it was 0.638 in 1861 and little had changed by 1891.

As child mortality gradually declined from the 1860s, there was less need for large families and more incentive to put space between births so as to avoid excessive pressure on mothers and households. The average family size fell from 6.2 children in the 1860s, to 4.1 for those marrying in the 1890s and to 2.8 for the 1911-marriage cohort. The rapid decline in the average age at which the mother's last child was born, from age 41 to 34 over this period is a clear reflection of deliberate spacing and limitation of births within marriage. In the nineteenth century marriage set the bounds for sexual activity. This does not mean that illegitimacy, bridal pregnancy, prostitution and adultery were uncommon, especially in certain localities, but it does give marriage a direct demographic importance that is all but lost today. Illegitimacy or bastardy existed in the nineteenth century and in East Anglia and eastern England in general was sufficiently large for one to begin to doubt the importance of marriage as a social and legal event. [60] But elsewhere in England, and especially off the coalfields, non-marital fertility was low enough in 1851 at only 5 per cent or 6 per cent of births were illegitimate for the institution of marriage still to be accepted as having particular importance as a regulator of fertility rates. By 1911, only 4 per cent of all births were illegitimate in England and Wales. It can be asked whether the forces that resulted in decline in marital fertility also led to the reduction of non-marital fertility. [61]

If there was a reduction in fertility caused by the introduction of successful methods of family limitation, was it the result of initiatives by men or women or through co-operation between them? Banks rejected the argument that fertility controls resulted from economically rational behaviour. [62] The introduction of compulsory elementary education following the 1870 and 1880 Education Acts may have led to a re-evaluation of the cost of children. This legislation seriously reduced the contribution children could make to the family budget. Generally, however, there is little evidence of a link between

---

[60] Levene, Alysa, Williams, Samantha, and Nutt, Thomas, (eds.), *Illegitimacy in Britain, 1700-1920*, (Palgrave), 2005, contains several relevant papers; see also Crafts, N. F.R., 'Illegitimacy in England and Wales in 1911', *Population Studies*, Vol. 36, (1982), pp. 327-331.

[61] Anderson M. 'Fertility Decline in Scotland, England and Wales and Ireland: Comparisons from the 1911 Census of Fertility, *Population Studies*, Vol. 52, (1998), pp. 1-20.

[62] Banks, J. A., *Victorian Values: Secularism and the Size of Families*, (Routledge), 1981, pp. 123-126.

male wage levels and fertility. For instance, the size of agricultural labourers' families, one of the poorest paid occupational groups, remained high. Banks stresses the importance of the development of a meritocratic career pattern for men and a resulting future-time perspective on the part of all the mainly middle-class occupational groups whose fertility rates fell fastest during the late-nineteenth century. The fertility rate of railway workers declined rapidly following the expansion of promotion hierarchies after 1880.[63]

It was the occupational status and attitudes of the husband that was the dominant factor. Sidney Webb observed that the thrifty of all classes were limiting the size of their families: 'prudence, foresight and self-control'.[64] However, in attributing prime importance to male decision-making on birth control, Banks is dismissive of the part women may have played. It is perfectly possible to accept that male co-operation was needed for fertility to fall, while also arguing that the opinions of wives may also have had an important effect on husbands. Precisely who made decisions within the family is difficult to determine yet the process by which family size was negotiated by husband and wife is crucial. Evidence suggests that the couples who were most successful in controlling their fertility were those who discussed the issue and reached agreement. Gittins concludes that couples, whose worlds increasingly centred on the home rather than on the culture of the workplace or on the spouses' respective circles of friends, most frequently achieved their ideal family size.[65] She argues that effective family planning, as opposed to desperate efforts to avert births through abortion was not a feature of urban working-class life until the 1920s and 1930s. The critical factor in limiting fertility appears to have been role-relationships within marriage and the quality of joint decision-making and communication within marriage. Where role-relationships were segregated, fertility rates tended to be high. However, where role-relationships were more integrated and the husband spent a significant part of his non-working hours with his wife and children, fertility was negotiated and consequently lower.

Middle-class women found themselves in a less favourable position. At least working-class women engaged in paid employment and there was ambivalence on the part of politicians and policy makers to their behaviour in this respect. The separation of spheres

---

[63] Ibid, p. 105.
[64] Webb, Sidney, *The Decline in the Birth-Rate*, (Fabian Society), 1907, pp. 6-8.
[65] Gittins, Diana, *Fair sex, family size and structure in Britain,1900-1939*, (St Martin's Press), 1982.

was far more clearly defined for middle-class women. Lydia Becker, a leading Victorian feminist, compared the position of middle-class women unfavourably with that of working-class women:

> What I most desire, is to see married women of the middle-classes stand on the same terms of equality as prevail in the working-classes and the highest aristocracy. A great ladies or factory women were independent persons, the women of the middle-classes are nobodies, and if they act for themselves they lose caste.[66]

The comparison failed to take account of the burden borne by working-class women but Becker was rebelling against the notion that middle-class women should be 'kept' by their husbands or fathers, brothers or other male relatives.

The home was the centre of the middle-class woman's world and she bore sole responsibility for its management. The interests and concerns of middle-class men and women were often profoundly different. Both lived in their own insulated worlds, segregated from the other: the breakfast- or morning-room served as the ladies' sitting room and the drawing room was where ladies received calls and took tea; the library, the study and the billiard room were male territory. Not only were their worlds generally separate, they were also profoundly unequal since the majority of middle-class women were financially dependent in their husbands. The domination of the Victorian husband was reflected in law until the 1880s and in emotional and sexual relations.

The vast majority of middle-class Victorian women led an insulated and limited existence within a tightly knit family circle. By the 1890s, the isolation of suburban life was beginning to become a characteristic feature of middle-class women. It is difficult to build an accurate picture of what middle-class women did in their homes. The notion of the perfect Victorian lady certainly did not apply to most middle-class women who had to pay great attention to household budgeting and routine to survive on between £100 and £300 per year. Much was sacrificed, even in the less well-off households, to provide the domestic help necessary to achieve a certain degree of gentility. Middle-class couples began to limit their families in the 1860s but whether this was a decision by the husband or wife is a matter of some debate. Branca maintains that middle-class women were asserting control over their lives both by seeking the assistance of doctors and

---

[66] Letter from Lydia Becker; neither the date nor the recipient are known, cit, Blackburn, Helen, *Women's Suffrage: A Record of the Women's Suffrage in the British Isles*, (Williams & Norgate), 1902, p. 42.

by deciding to use birth control. [67] Banks, by contrast, suggests that the lead in fertility control was taken by men in professional occupations who were concerned not about the burden but the cost of childrearing. It is unlikely that middle-class women would have been able to procure birth control literature on their own initiative. Nor was middle-class women's ready access to doctors likely to be of use in the search for birth control information, as many doctors believed that it led to serious illness. [68]

Clergymen, expressing public outrage during the trials of birth control propagandists in the 1880s, were nevertheless clearly limiting their own numbers of children. The motivation of middle-class family planning was complicated. The age of marriage remained high as couples waited to amass resources to sustain the 'paraphernalia of gentility'. Concern with the health of wives was one reason why births in the later years of marriage seem to have been curtailed. The growing cost of running middle-class households, making it difficult to afford large families, was another. With the rise of corporate business, there was less need for large numbers of sons and nephews who now required expensive schooling rather than informal apprenticeship in the family firm. Whether decisions to limit the size of middle-class families were rational or not, economic considerations clearly played a significant part.

Did the family decline?

The impact of the industrial revolution and the employment of women caused considerable pessimism among many contemporaries such as Richard Oastler and Lord Shaftesbury. According to Oastler, the transition from domestic to factory system was nothing less than catastrophic: 'a violation of the sacred nature of the home'. Leaving aside the polemic, two points are clear. The pessimistic critique stems from a contrast of the impact of factories with the presumed conditions of family life under the domestic system. Critics rarely went outside the textile industry in making comparisons. The problem was that the textile industry was not typical of work in nineteenth century Britain. It was highly mechanised and firmly based on division of labour. This significantly weakens the pessimist's case.

It has been argued that the domestic system was based on an integrated family unit of reproduction, production and consumption.

---

[67] Branca, Patricia, *Silent Sisterhood: Middle class women in the Victorian Home*, (Croom Helm), 1975, pp. 115-118.
[68] Ibid, Banks, J. A., *Victorian Values: Secularism and the Size of Families*, pp. 143-145.

Patriarchal control and moral guidance were exerted over both wives and children. In this context, the advent of the factory affected the 'independent' economic status of the family. Engels argued that it destroyed the pride and status of the breadwinner, now dependent on the factory earnings of his wife and children.[69] Women were no longer able to carry out their domestic functions effectively and the family's dietary needs suffered. Daughters were not instructed in the family virtues and were exposed early to sexual temptation and activity. The contrast was drawn, by Marx and others, between the artisan as an independent seller of his own labour and the slave-trader selling his own and his wife's and children's labour in the factory. Smelser challenged this view of the breakdown of the family arguing, on the basis of the Lancashire cotton industry, first that the separation of working-class children from their families did not really begin until after the 1820s with the introduction of powered weaving.[70] Technological changes between 1820 and 1840, especially the introduction of the self-acting mule led to a redefinition of the economic functions of the textile family and sharply differentiated the roles of its members. Finally, mule spinning was very much a family affair with operative spinners hiring their own relatives as scavengers and piercers. This was codified in many early spinners' trade union rules that attempted to limit recruitment to the kinship unit. As a result, traditional family values were perpetuated. Smelser has not been without his critics but he raised an alternative view of the question of the family to the contemporary pessimism.

Assembling the basic features of family structure for this period appears to be a straightforward task. There is much information in published census reports, social surveys and in descriptive and literary sources. The problem is that these sources do not always allow historians to answer the questions they want to ask. For instance, we know that marriage was far more central to the matrix of family life than it had been in the early-nineteenth century but we are unclear why. We know that the average number of children born to each marriage between 1870 and the 1900s fell from just under six to just over three but we do not know precisely how far contemporary views of 'the family' were limited to parents and children. Censuses often equated 'family' with 'household' and the number of household rose from just over 5 million in 1871 to almost 8 million in 1911. Average household size was about 4.75 persons, rising slightly

---

[69] Engels, F., *The Condition of the Working-class in England*, Leipzig, 1845, pp. 147-148.
[70] Smelser, Neil, *Social Change in the Industrial Revolution*, (Routledge), 1959, pp. 225-264.

between 1871 and 1891 and falling to 4.4 persons by 1911. In each census, nearly 70 per cent of the population lived in medium-sized households of between three and six people. One-person households were rare throughout the period, though their number arose in the 1900s reflecting partly the new phenomenon of metropolitan 'bedsitterland' and partly the flight of younger people from the countryside. By 1914, nearly half the population lived in households where there was one occupant per room or less giving rise to the notion of 'a room of one's own' as one of the touchstones of ideal family life.

How was sexuality represented

The view that women and men naturally have distinctive and separate characteristics is today treated with justifiable disdain. [71] This was not the case in the eighteenth and nineteenth centuries. The Christian position was clear. God created Adam first and then, in what James Simpson [72] the pioneer of chloroform saw as the first case of anaesthesia 'caused a deep sleep to fall upon the man and while he slept took one of his ribs and...made [it] into a woman...'[73] Women were subject to the rule of man. This view was reinforced in the *New Testament* where St Paul stated, 'as the church is subject to Christ, so let wives also be subject in everything to their husbands'. [74] This view dominated medieval and early-modern thinking. In the seventeenth and eighteenth centuries, these theological arguments were gradually undermined by the development of medical science though both remained important and widely accepted well into the nineteenth century. [75]

Early-modern medicine, still grounded in the notion of the four 'humours' maintained that men were more perfectly and physically

---

[71] I have explored this issue in greater detail in my *Sex, Work and Politics: Women in Britain, 1830-1918*, (Authoring History), 2012, pp. 9-75.

[72] Simpson used this argument against those in the Church who believed that the pain of childbirth was punishment for Eve's responsibility for the Fall.

[73] *Genesis*, 2: 18-22.

[74] *Letters to the Ephesians*, 4: 24.

[75] Laqueur, Thomas, *Making Sex: The Body and Gender from the Greeks to Freud*, (Harvard University Press), 1990, provides an invaluable overview on this issue. More specific studies are: Gallagher, Christine, and Laqueur, Thomas, (eds.), *The Making of the Modern Body: Sexuality and Society in the Nineteenth Century*, (University of California Press), 1987, and Hitchcock, Tim, *English Sexualities 1700-1800*, (Macmillan), 1997. Reay, Barry, *Popular Cultures in England 1550-1750*, (Longman), 1998, pp. 4-35, provides an excellent overview of current thinking.

formed because they were hotter and drier than women. They were active, intelligent and superior. Women by contrast had weaker brains than men because their lack of body heat reduced the amount of blood sent to the brain. They were governed by their lower organs especially the uterus where they had an excess of blood. [76] This led to lust, hysteria and irrational behaviour. Sexual differences were not based on anatomy. Men and women were regarded as identical apart from the fact that female genitalia had failed to emerge externally because of their lower body temperature. Thomas Laqueur termed this a 'one-sex' model of sexual difference and argues that during the eighteenth century a 'two-sex' model to explain sexual differences replaced it. The focus moved from differences in body temperature to differences in the structure of nerves. Women had finer nerves and this made them more sensitive than men to external emotions and, contemporaries argued made them prone to mental disorders and hysteria. Maudsley argued, 'their nerve-centres being in a state of greater instability, by reason of the development of their reproductive functions, they will be more easily and more seriously deranged.' [77] The reasoning may have changed but the subordinate realities for women remain unaltered. [78] Popular medical texts, conduct books, popular literature, novels and periodicals promoted the culture of female domesticity with vigour and considerable popularity. [79] Influential though these concepts are in gender studies, it is questionable how significant Laqueur's 'one-sex' theory was in practice. Medical books may have seen women's bodies as variants on maleness in which women were regarded as inverted men rather than as uniquely female, but doctors were a minority in early modern society and we should not assume that their theories were accepted by the wider world.

---

[76] It was believed that menstruation was necessary because women had insufficient body heat to purify their blood.
[77] Maudslay, Henry, 'Sex in Mind and in Education', *Popular Science Monthly*, Vol. 5, June 1874, p. 206.
[78] See Kent, Kingsley, *Gender and Power in Britain 1640-1990*, (CRC Press), 1999, pp. 186-188, for discussion of Maudslay's view.
[79] Conduct books were designed for moral instruction and included examination of the purposes of marriage and domestic relationships. Two, Richard Allestree *The Whole Duty of Man*, (Printed for T. Garthwait), 1659, laid down in a plain and familiar way for the use of all, but especially the meanest reader and an anonymous author's *New Whole Duty of Man: Containing the Faith as well as Practice of a Christian*, (Edward Wicksteed), 1744, were widely read. The former went through sixty-four editions between 1659 and 1842; the latter thirty-seven editions between 1744 and 1850.

Sexuality and desire were not universal, a-historical conditions but part of the discourse of gender that allows the development of political control of the body. The creation of a modern culture of sex was a central part of the Enlightenment especially the view that sex was a private matter and that morality cannot be imposed by force.[80] Changing attitudes to sexuality in the eighteenth and early-nineteenth centuries are, however, difficult to chart with any precision.[81] There are studies of middle-class attitudes, notably by Peter Gay, Jeffrey Weeks and Michael Mason, but we still do not know a great deal about working-class sexuality. This has led to historians taking different positions on the issue. Lawrence Stone, for example, argues that sexual permissiveness grew in the eighteenth century, a process reversed in the nineteenth century.[82] Others, by contrast, see the eighteenth century as one of increasing sexual repression. The critical issue is how far attitudes to sexuality changed in the late-eighteenth and nineteenth centuries and, if so, when that change occurred. Foucault saw an explosion of sexual discourses during the late-eighteenth and nineteenth centuries as corresponding to revolutionary changes in economic, demographic and social structures. Laqueur[83] argues that changes in attitudes to sex were part of the Industrial Revolution:

> Desire, whether for sexual gratification or for consumer goods, lies at the heart of theories of capitalism.[84]

The market economy is based on openness of exchange in stark contrast to a society based on ranks and order in which convention and sumptuary laws were designed to keep desire under control.

---

[80] On this process see, Dabhoiwala, Faramerz, *The Origins of Sex: A History of the First Sexual Revolution*, (Allen Lane), 2012.
[81] Weeks, Jeffrey, *Sex, Politics and Society: the regulation of sexuality since 1800*, (Longman), 2nd edition, 1989, is the best introduction to changing notions of sexuality. Gay, Peter, *The Bourgeois Experience: Education of the Senses*, (Oxford University Press), 1984, and Mason, Michael, *The Making of Victorian Sexuality*, and *The Making of Victorian Sexual Identity*, (Oxford University Press), 1994, debunks the myth of Victorian 'repression'.
[82] Stone, Lawrence, *The Family, Sex and Marriage in England 1500-1800*, (Weidenfeld & Nicolson), 1977.
[83] Laqueur, Thomas, 'Sex and Desire in the Industrial Revolution', in O'Brien, Patrick and Quinault, Roland, (eds.), *The Industrial Revolution and British Society*, (Cambridge University Press), 1993, pp. 100-123.
[84] Ibid, Laqueur, Thomas, 'Sex and Desire in the Industrial Revolution', p. 114.

Freedom of exchange and of labour was economically desirable, but sexual freedom was not. Consuming goods was acceptable, with observers in the 1790s noting that the rural poor was 'panting to imitate London fashions', consuming sex was not. However, recent research on the early modern period suggests that the Foucauldian notion of multiple expressions of sexuality should be pushed back into the sixteenth and seventeenth centuries. [85] Reay's study of Kent in the nineteenth and early-twentieth century supports the view that there was considerable continuity of attitudes to sexuality especially in rural Britain across the early-modern-modern divide. [86]

Nineteenth century writings emphasise the preoccupation of Victorian doctors and moralists in defining 'healthy' and 'unhealthy' or deviant female sexuality. However, they were overwhelmingly middle-class in character. Some authors, such as William Acton, argued that women were only capable of a limited or negligible sexual response: 'the best mothers, wives and managers of households know little or nothing of sexual indulgence. Love of children, home and domestic duties are the only passions they feel'. [87] Mary Scharlieb, in 1913, favoured self-control by men and women as a solution to a common problem. [88] The suffragettes went one step further and advocated 'votes for women and chastity for men'. [89] How did the idea that women were passionless develop? Until the 1720s, many believed that women's lust was unquenchable but that they could become spiritual and less carnal through God's grace. This view was reversed and in the nineteenth century, women were increasingly seen as less lustful than men. Middle-class society effectively denied women's sexuality yet ironically sharpened the awareness of women as reproductive and sexual individuals. Women were viewed as 'the Sex', not simply defined by their reproductive systems but controlled by them as well. However, many contemporaries maintained a more positive view of female sexuality. Dr George Drysdale believed that sexual pleasure was natural and beneficial to both sexes. [90] Priscilla

---

[85] Ibid, Reay, Barry, *Popular Cultures in England 1550-1750*, pp. 33-35.
[86] Reay, Barry, *Microhistories: Demography, society and culture in rural England, 1800-1930*, (Cambridge University Press), 1996, pp. 179-212.
[87] Acton, William, *The Functions and disorders of the reproductive organs in childhood, youth, adult age, and advanced life*, (Lindsay and Blakiston), 1865, p. 134.
[88] Scharlieb, Mary, *The seven ages of woman: a consideration of the successive phases of woman's life*, (Cassel), 1913, pp. 73-77, 99-100.
[89] See Pankhurst, Christabel, *The great scourge and how to end it*, (E. Pankhurst), 1913, pp. vii-viii.
[90] Drysdale, George R., *The elements of social science; or, Physical, sexual, and natural religion*, (Truelove), 1861, pp. 53-75.

Barker argued in 1888 that the passion of lust was stronger in the female sex, an interpretation redolent of Adam and Eve. [91] James Walvin rightly maintains:

> It is hard to think of any aspect of Victorian life that has been more comprehensively misunderstood and misrepresented than sexuality. [92]

Why were the middle-classes anxious about working-class sexuality?

The Registrar General reported that in 1842, 6.7 per cent of births were illegitimate and that during the century as a whole the figure was around 6.0 per cent.[93] Albert Leffingwell wrote of the 'annual harvest of sorrow and shame' shown by the tables of illegitimate births produced by the Registrar General in the 1880s.[94] The fallen woman, clasping an infant, the badge of her shame, was a commanding icon in Victorian art and literature.[95] In Elizabeth Gaskell's *Ruth* (1853) and E. M. Forster's *Howard's End* (1910), Ruth Hilton's son Leonard and Forster's Leonard Bast (literally as Bastard) sought to hide the stain of their illegitimacy. The critical question is whether the rhetoric corresponded to lived experience.

Reay concludes that the 'experience of rural Kent suggests that bearing children outside marriage should be seen not as a form of deviancy but rather as part of normal sexual culture.' [96] Half the brides in Reay's three-parish sample were pregnant when they married or had actually given birth before their marriage. This paralleled the experience in villages and small towns in Bedfordshire, Cambridgeshire, Hampshire, Leicestershire and Devon. There is

---

[91] Barker, Priscilla, *The secret book containing private information and instruction for women and young girls: By a woman*, (This pamphlet to be had, wholesale and retail, for gratuitous distribution or otherwise, of Mrs. Priscilla Barker, Authoress, 'Phrenological House,' Trafalgar St., Brighton), 1888.

[92] Walvin, James, *Victorian Values*, (Longman), 1987, p. 120.

[93] Wrigley, E. A., Davies, R. S., Oeppen, J. E., and Schofield, R. S., *English Population History from Family Reconstitution 1580-1837*, (Cambridge University Press), 1997, pp. 219-224, deals with the problems of determining levels of illegitimacy. For their persistence see, Klein, Joanne, 'Irregular Marriages: Unorthodox Working-Class Domestic Life in Liverpool, Birmingham and Manchester, 1900-1939', *Journal of Family History*, Vol. 30, (2005), pp. 210-229.

[94] Leffingwell, A., *Illegitimacy and the Influence of the Seasons upon Conduct*, (Sonnenschein), 1892, p. 7.

[95] Nead, Lynda, *Myths of Sexuality: representations of women in Victorian Britain*, (B. Blackwell), 1990, especially plates 48-50.

[96] Ibid, Reay, Barry, *Microhistories*, p. 180.

little evidence that pre-nuptial pregnancy was regarded as shameful or that social pressure was used to force a pregnant bride to marry quickly. Though there is some evidence of teenage promiscuity, Reay finds that about a third of pregnant brides were between 16 and 19 and it appears that most women were sexually active around the time they married rather than when they reached sexual maturity. Reay's conclusions call into question the contemporary middle-class views of Leffingwell and others that women who had illegitimate children were either deviant or powerless. [97]

Evidence from urban Britain suggests levels of illegitimacy lower than in the countryside with London having the lowest national levels around mid-century. There was, however, considerable diversity in the urban experience. Bristol, Birmingham, Liverpool, Portsmouth and Sheffield had low rates while in Nottingham, Preston and Bolton rates were almost twice as high, though none as high as Norwich. The reasons for this are difficult to identify with certainty though there may be a link between high urban illegitimacy and levels in its rural hinterland. Both Norwich and Nottingham were in counties with high levels of illegitimacy. Of the eight counties with the highest rates in 1842, five predominantly rural counties remained in this group sixty years later: Cumberland, Norfolk, North Riding, Nottinghamshire and Shropshire. This indicates a regional dimension to sexuality that lasted through the century. However, elsewhere in urban Britain, non-marital fertility was low enough in 1851 for marriage still to be regarded as having particular importance as a regulator of sexuality. By 1911, only 4 per cent of all births were illegitimate in England and Wales. The social stigma of illegitimacy was not as pronounced as contemporary middle-class commentators would have historians believe. Social attitudes to sexuality were much more complex and varied. [98]

Pre-nuptial pregnancies were class specific. Women from higher social groups were less likely to be pregnant. Middle-class observers regarded their own class as sufficiently rooted in home, work and family to prevent or at least limit pre-nuptial sex. Below this, however, pre-nuptial pregnancy and intercourse were

---

[97] Sheetz-Nguyen, Jessica A., *Victorian Women, Unwed Mothers and the London Foundling Hospital*, (Continuum), 2012, provides a case-study of women who successfully petitioned the Foundling Hospital for admission of their infants were not East End prostitutes, but rather unmarried women, often domestic servants, determined to maintain social respectability.

[98] On illegitimacy in nineteenth century Britain, see Finn, Margot, Lobban, Michael, and Taylor, Jenny Bourne, (eds.), *Legitimacy and Illegitimacy in Nineteenth-Century Law, Literature and History*, (Palgrave Macmillan), 2010.

widespread phenomena. This was seen as a challenge to established order and consequently something that needed, especially with regard to women, to be controlled. Contemporaries often looked at the working-classes through the medium of illicit sexual behaviour. Engels spoke of their 'unbridled search for pleasure', their shared sleeping arrangements and the ways work was organised:

> The moral consequences of the employment of women in factories are even worse....A witness in Leicester said that he would rather let his daughter beg than go into a factory; that they are perfect gates of hell; that most of the prostitutes of the town had their employment in the mills to than for their present situation. [99]

Another, in Manchester:

> ...did not hesitate to assert that three-fourths of the young factory employees, from fourteen to twenty years of age, were unchaste... If the [factory] master is mean enough...his mill is also his harem; and the fact that not all manufacturers use their power, does not in the least change the position of the girls. [100]

The problem for writers such as Engels and for reformers such as James Kay and Peter Gaskell, writing in the 1830s and 1840s was that there was little evidence to support their assertions about illicit, urban sexual behaviour. In addition, most of the evidence used in the debate about working-class sexual behaviour comes from areas of textile production. Kay noted that though crime can be 'statistically classed':

> ...the moral leprosy of vice cannot be exhibited with mathematical precision. Sensuality has no record... [101]

Gaskell maintained that statistics on illegitimacy were 'worse than useless' and showed higher levels of illegitimacy in rural than urban areas. [102] There is little here to support the assertions of

---

[99] Ibid, Engels, F., *The Condition of the Working-class in England*, p. 158.
[100] Ibid, Engels, F., *The Condition of the Working-class*, pp. 176-177.
[101] Kay, James, *The Moral and Physical Condition of the Working-classes Employed in the Cotton Manufacture in Manchester*, (Ridgway), 1832, p. 62.
[102] Gaskell, Peter, *Artisans and Machinery: The Moral and Physical Conditions of the Manufacturing Population*, (Blackwood and Sons), 1836, p. 100.

Edward Shorter that urbanisation led to a 'sexual revolution'.[103] Middle-class anxieties were grounded in concerns about working-class female sexuality and their economic autonomy. Because of their view of the proper role of women in the family, many middle-class commentators focussed their criticism less on the conditions under which women laboured than on the moral and spiritual degradation said to follow from female employment. For them the dangers posed by class and changed sexual attitudes were closely linked. For evangelicals like Lord Ashley, sexual freedom inevitably led to social dangers especially the loss of middle-class control. Consequently, they exaggerated the situation and misread the evidence to support bourgeois, male ideological assumptions. There was a lack of concrete evidence to support the case for working-class immorality or early marriages. Despite this, the sexual perspectives of Gaskell and Kay tumbled into their fears about the sexual consequences social mobility. It became 'licentiousness capable of corrupting the whole body of society, like an insidious disease...'[104] Sexual freedom posed a threat to the stability of society to such an extent that 'Morality is worthy of the attention of the economist.'[105]

The problem that historians face is one of continuity and change. Traditional, essentially pre-industrial sexual attitudes among the working-class remained important throughout the nineteenth century. These can be seen particularly in rural Britain where sexual relationships could begin at betrothal and where evidence of a woman's fertility might be economically necessary. This was gradually weakened by the transformation of working-class sexual experience caused less by urbanisation than by the effects of developing industrial capitalism on society as a whole. Jeffrey Weeks argues, 'The key factor seems to have been proletarianisation rather than urbanisation that is the generalisation of the wage-labour relationship'.[106] There was a fall in the age of marriage from around 28 years in the 1750s to 24 by the 1820s. This increased the years of potential childbearing and he suggests these changes were motivated in part by economic factors: 'children could be a positive asset, as sources of domestic labour and increased income'.[107] He also shows the weakening of customary control over sexual relations in the

---

[103] Ibid, Shorter, Edward, *The Making of the Modern Family*, pp. 86-124.
[104] Ibid, Kay, James, *The Moral and Physical Condition of the Working-classes*, pp. 81-82.
[105] Ibid, Kay, James, *The Moral and Physical Condition of the Working-classes*, p. 82.
[106] Ibid, Weeks, Jeffrey, *Sex, Politics and Society*, p. 62.
[107] Ibid, Weeks, Jeffrey, *Sex, Politics and Society*, p. 63.

context of growing social mobility where illegitimacy was often the result not of rampant promiscuity but 'Marriage Frustrated'. [108] The effect of this was to diminish female control and sexual autonomy. In the second half of the nineteenth century, illegitimacy and irregular marriages declined, as working-class women became more conservative in their sexual behaviour. This was less the result of the diffusion of middle-class values than a pragmatic response to the loss of control over the consequences of pre-nuptial relations.

In what respects did the working-class adopt middle-class values in the last third of the nineteenth century? Social factors such as the availability of marriage partners in areas of high emigration or persistent out-migration throughout rural England limited marriage levels and affected births. Limitations on marriage in certain occupational groups, for example, living-in domestic servants and farm labourers, also affected local fertility patterns. The general increase in the mean age of marriage to about 25.8 years for women and some two years higher for men by 1850 and from the 1870s further increases reflected changing economic circumstances and the desire for more spending power and independence. How far these changes were the result of middle-class attitudes or of the emergence of a distinctive working-class culture impervious to middle-class guidance is a matter of considerable debate.

The problem for historians lies in the gulf within the working-class between skilled workers and, what middle-class moralists called 'the residuum'. There is evidence of the transmission of middle-class moral values and the pursuit of 'respectability' among skilled workers. However, there is little doubt that this ideology of respectability was grounded in their general experience and growing sense of class identity. The demands of skilled workers to take an active role in local institutions were a source of social tension with the middle-class. The assimilation of middle-class sexual mores was not as straightforward as contemporaries believed. By 1900, it had become clear that middle-class 'civilising' evangelism had not created a working-class in its own image. Most workers were not chaste or temperate by middle-class standards but had adopted their own values. The changed sexualities of the working-class cannot be seen as evidence of the success of middle-class social control but was produced from deeply felt experiences of the class itself.

---

[108] See, Levine, David, *Family Formation in an Age of Nascent Capitalism*, (Academic Press), 1977.

Middle-class respectability and sexual control

In men, in general, the sexual desire is inherent and spontaneous, and belongs to the condition of puberty. In the other sex, the desire is dormant, if not non-existent, till excited; always till excited by intercourse...If the passions of women were ready, strong and spontaneous, in a degree even approaching the form they assume in the coarser sex, there can be little doubt that sexual irregularities would reach a height, of which, at present, we have happily no conception. [109]

Greg had exposed the fear felt by middle-class society by the thought of unregulated female sexuality. He distinguished between active male sexuality and passive female sexuality. It had its social expression in the notion of the 'double standard'. Sexual activity was regarded as a sign of 'masculinity' while in women it was represented as deviant or pathological behaviour. The concept of double standards was based on the division between madonna and whore, between the 'respectable' or the 'fallen'.

Women were seen as either controlling or heightening male sexual behaviour and their sexual identity determined whether they were seen as respectable members of society. This definition of female sexuality was class specific. The notion of the middle-class woman's sexual respectability was contrasted not only with the prostitute but also with all working-class women especially the unrespectable poor. Working-class women, like prostitutes were regarded as potential health hazards and as a general public danger because of their uncontrolled and uncontrollable breeding.

William Acton argued that sexual desire was unknown to the virtuous woman. He said:

...a perfect ideal of an English wife and mother...so pure-hearted as to be utterly ignorant of and averse to any sensual indulgence, but so unselfishly attached to the man she loves, as to be willing to give up her own wishes and feelings for his sake. [110]

This image of the passionless respectable woman was, however, one aspect of a more complex view of female sexualities in the nineteenth century. Other doctors argued that respectable women did experience sexual desire and that, far from being deviant was extremely healthy. George Drysdale, an active campaigner for family

---

[109] Greg, W. R., 'Prostitution', *Westminster Review*, Vol. 53, (1850), pp. 456-457.
[110] Ibid, Acton, William, *The Functions and Disorders of the Reproductive Organs*, p. 114.

limitation and a supporter of the mid-century women's movement attacked the values of respectable morality:

> To have strong sexual emotions is held to be rather a disgrace for a woman, and they are looked down upon as animal, sensual, coarse and deserving reprobation. The moral emotions of love are indeed beautiful in her; but the physical ones are rather held unwomanly and debasing; this is a great error... If chastity must continue to be regarded as the highest female virtue; it is impossible to give women real liberty. [111]

Drysdale's view did not fit with the dominant discourse of woman's mission. This was based on the relationship between woman's nature and woman's duty. Because of the ambiguity of woman's nature, control and regulation were justified to enable women to fulfil their domestic duty. Sexual control was part of the far wider dependency of women. The issue of dependency was not one of repressive male power over women. Dependency was regarded as a natural part of respectable femininity. Male protection of women was not represented as control but as a shield to protect them against the harshness of public life. Contemporary doctors supported this view. The major features of respectable femininity were believed to develop naturally during puberty and were part of women's biological development. Edward Tilt wrote in 1852:

> That what makes men more bold, will generally awaken greater timidity in women. Puberty, which gives man the knowledge of greater power, gives to woman the conviction of her dependence. [112]

The notion of female respectability was accepted by many, though not all middle-class women. Adultery was regarded as the extreme form of sexual deviancy. Female unchastity was a betrayal: betrayal of father, husband, home and family. It violated women's femininity and its effects were both permanent and irrevocable. For women, a fall from virtue was final. Men's natural urges and sexual lapses were seen as regrettable but unavoidable. Acton believed that male sexual impulses could be controlled but not repressed. Male adultery was accommodated within the dominant codes of morality. Male sexuality rested on the twin contradictions of motherhood and prostitution. Maternity and sexuality were separated by the representation of prostitution as existing exclusively to gratify male

---

[111] See ibid, Drysdale, George R., *The elements of social science; or, Physical, sexual, and natural religion,* pp. 172-173.
[112] Tilt, Edward, *The Elements of Health and Principles of Female Hygiene,* (Lindsay and Blakiston), 1852, p. 173.

sexual lusts. Many Victorians believed that it was the prostitute who kept middle-class women pure by satisfying the sexual needs of middle-class men:

> Herself the supreme type of vice, she is ultimately the most efficient guardian of virtue. But for her, the unchallenged purity of countless happy homes would be polluted... On that degraded and ignoble form are concentrated the passions that might have filled the world with shame. [113]

Prostitution acted as a sexual safety valve and did not corrupt the home in the ways in which female adultery did. This meant that adultery must be committed with a woman who was either without a family or who did not belong to the respectable classes and whose family was therefore considered to be of little account.

The view that historians until recently had of nineteenth century middle-class sexuality was a caricature. Prudery, as repugnance of sexual contact and the cold, highly functional asexuality within the privacy of marriage was complemented by male permissiveness within the public arena. This is not to suggest that these attitudes were untrue but asks to what extent they were typical and representative of the experience of the middle-class as a whole. The dominant attitudes to male and female sexuality were both a means of female sexual control and of male sexual license. There was, Jeffrey Weeks argued:

> ...no Golden Age of sexual propriety, and the search for it in the mythologised past tells us more about present confusions than past glories. [114]

The idea of the prudish, sexually repressed Victorians, who covered the legs of pianos lest they inflame passions and cautiously guarding themselves against any temptation no matter how slight, has been successfully challenged and shown to be both inaccurate and misleading. Sex and sexuality were unavoidable issues for the Victorians.

Comings and goings

Mobility and migration, both internal and international were important in Britain's growing population. Four aspects of migration are of particular significance. There was massive emigration from the outer rural periphery, especially the west of Ireland and the Scottish

---

[113] Lecky, William, *The History of European Morals*, (D. Appleton and Co.), 1869, Vol. 2, p. 299.
[114] Ibid, Weeks, Jeffrey, *Sex, Politics and Society*, pp. 22-23.

Highlands that caused general depopulation. The countryside in general also suffered net losses to the towns. The great industrial and commercial centres of central Scotland, the English North and Midlands and South Wales, not only increased in numbers, but also expanded physically until they coalesced into the amorphous conurbations so well known in the twentieth century. Finally, London should be treated as a special case since it not only maintained its British primacy, but also its share of the total population. The new problems associated with managing and servicing such a massive concentration of people that reached nearly 5 million by 1901 imposed many strains, not least in terms of transport, social inequalities and sanitation. There were different kinds of movement within Britain during the nineteenth century. [115]

Rural-Rural
Temporary harvest migration: Local inter-village movement including marriage migration.
Rural-Urban
This was usually a series of 'stepwise' moves up the urban hierarchy. Most common during early phase of urban growth: short distance movement to nearest town.
Urban-Urban
This was increasingly common between large cities after about 1860 and led to movement up the urban hierarchy from small town to the nearby city.
Urban-Rural
There was reverse mobility of high-status households from urban centres to rural suburbs.
Intra-Urban
Frequent short distance moves mostly in same area of city.

Many people saw rural to urban migration as the dominant feature of migration between 1830 and 1890. This view is misleading since net in-migration was less important in most places than natural increase in urban growth. Only newer settlements, resort towns, residential suburbs especially round London and newly established industrial centres depended largely on migration for growth. While many left the countryside for towns, inducing nation-wide rural depopulation, and there was substantial and changing movement

---

[115] Lawton, R., and Pooley, C. G., *Britain 1740-1950: An Historical Geography*, (Edward Arnold), 1991, p. 128

between towns, natural increase was of growing importance in urban population development.[116]

The motives for and effects of migration were highly varied after 1830. It is possible to produce a classification of migratory moves that demonstrate the complexity of migratory experiences and the way in which inter-urban and urban-suburban movement became increasingly important as the century progressed. This classification suggests that the rural to urban move was not a single, discrete event but part of an overall life history of individual migration from the countryside, to an adjacent village and then to a local town. In Suffolk, for instance, evidence from successive censuses shows that individuals and families moved to villages or towns up or down the railway line from Cambridge to Ipswich. An individual might move several times up the urban hierarchy perhaps reaching a large city in the 1850s and subsequently moving between and within cities to end up in an outer suburb in the 1890s. Such a migration history may be closer to reality than the simple stereotype of rural-urban migration. Three principal points on migration in mid-century can be highlighted. Most migration was directed at those counties and regions experiencing rapid industrialisation and urbanisation. The majority of individual moves were relatively short distance through a series of stepwise movements. Longer distance moves tended to be selective by occupation and age: such migrants were often significantly more skilled and literate than non-movers.[117]

Census birthplace data, though imperfect, offers a series of pictures of lifetime inter-county population movement after 1841. For instance, successive censuses show individuals and families moving up and down the railway line between Cambridge and Bury St. Edmunds. Most studies emphasise the dominance of London as the target of long distance migration. Industrial areas outside London tended to rely heavily on regional networks of migration, though exchanges of migrants between industrial regions increased through the century. In some instances, this migration was seasonal as in the hat industry in Bedfordshire and Hertfordshire where predominantly girls and women moved to the hat-making centres for the season and then returned home. A quarter of the population of Dunstable, a leading hat-making community, were lodgers in the 1841 Census.

---

[116] See, Saville, John, *Rural depopulation in England and Wales, 1851-1951*, (Routledge), 1957, and Long, Jason, 'Rural-Urban Migration and Socioeconomic Mobility in Victorian Britain', *Journal of Economic History*, Vol. 65, (2005), pp. 1-35.

[117] Redford, Arthur, *Labour migration in England, 1800-1850*, (Oxford University Press), 1926, remains important.

Between 1851 and 1891, the limited occupational opportunities of a small town like Lancaster attracted migrants over only a short distance and it relied largely on its rural hinterland.

Larger towns such as Bolton and Preston had wider spheres of attraction that increased in the late-nineteenth century. Although competing with Liverpool and Manchester, they offered significant and specific employment opportunities and exchanged migrants with the larger towns. Specialist employment opportunities attracted particular migrant streams over long distances. The substantial Welsh-born population of Middlesbrough in the 1870s was drawn almost exclusively from South Wales and reflected a well-established migration stream between areas with similar industrial structures. Several Welsh iron masters moved to Middlesbrough to exploit expanding economic opportunities on Teesside and continued to recruit Welsh labour over a considerable period of time. Similarly St Helen's glass industry recruited many skilled workers from other glass-making areas, supporting the view that longer-distance migrants were often more skilled, better educated and of higher social status.

Most rural areas lost population but in those districts closest to expanding towns, population rapidly stabilised. By 1900, population may have increased as urban growth spilled over the surrounding countryside. Around London improvements in communication and pressure on space led to early and rapid suburbanisation. Around Liverpool, villages on Deeside were attracting residential migrants by the 1890s after decades of population loss. In remoter rural areas, population losses were more general and continuous and were made worse in some cases by the coming of the railway. Initially railways provided labour but they subsequently offered an easy outlet for migrants, especially with the decline of rural industry in the face of competition from urban-based factories.

Though most ordinary working people walked to most places with an occasional use of the railway, by 1900 not only were most towns and many villages connected into the national rail network but the cost of transport could be met by a larger proportion of the population. Increasing provision of third class coaches with better facilities, after 1883 at a standard rate of only 1d per mile on most trains, led, by the early-twentieth century, to nearly 95 per cent of all railway passengers travelling third class. Public transport was also essential to suburban growth, especially in London. From the 1860s with the opening of the Metropolitan Line in 1863 and the South London line in 1867, railways linked the City with residential suburbs and by 1910 a basic underground network stretched from Clapham to Finsbury Park and Hampstead. Cheap workmen's fares allowed working-class commuters to move to inner suburbs and helped to push the middle-classes further into the countryside.

Manchester, Liverpool, Birmingham, Glasgow and Newcastle all had quite well developed suburban rail services by 1914. But in smaller towns, suburban dwellers relied on the omnibus and especially the tram to connect home and work. The Tramways Act 1870 marked the beginning of tramway networks in most towns and from 1891 municipal authorities could take over the running of the tramway system. Even in London the tram and the omnibus competed effectively with suburban railways. The movement to the suburbs was an expression of rising social and economic aspirations. Families moving from terraced housing to the new semi-detached suburbs were a distinct section of the population: they had skilled jobs, with regular hours and often worked in the expanding sectors of the economy. The centres of cities lost population and increasingly became simply places where people worked and where the unskilled and semi-skilled working-classes lived. Round the centres of cities were the inner suburbs where the skilled working-classes lived. Round them the semi-detached leafy suburbs of the white-collar and blue-collar workers, who acquired a new way of life and set of values as well as a pleasant environment.

What impact did such movements have on the communities left by migrants and the places to which they moved? How did it affect the lives of individuals and families? In areas where there was a marked imbalance between inflow and outflow in numbers, demographic or social characteristics, the impact of migration could be devastating. In many parts of rural England, for example, there was a substantial deficit of young men. Elsewhere results were more subtle. Most large cities lost and gained vast numbers through migration, but socio-economic structures were little changed. Those who left were replaced largely by people of similar socio-economic backgrounds. In smaller settlements atypical change is most striking: the short-term impact of navvy gangs involved in railway construction on villages and small market towns; the recruits to defence establishments in such towns as Portsmouth, Plymouth and Aldershot, the short-term impact of rapid industrial growth in new towns like Middlesbrough and Crewe or in expanding mining areas. But in most places the long-term impact of migration was gradual and more easily assimilated.

During the nineteenth century, retaining Britain's population was increasingly viewed not as the basis for economic and commercial growth but as a cancer that threatened the basis of British society. [118]

---

[118] Richards, Eric, *Britannia's Children: Emigration from England, Scotland, Wales and Ireland since 1600*, (Hambledon Continuum), 2004,

Emigration provided a solution that allowed the poor to escape from the impoverished rural and urban slums to the expanding colonies, themselves a source of wealth for Britain's continuing prosperity and greatness. Where these emigrants came from within the British Isles, their religion, when and why they left the country, what they took with them in the form of skills and capital and where they settled really did matter. Emigration figures show that between 1821 and 1915 some 10 million people left Great Britain and a further 6 million left Ireland for non-European destinations. More than half went to the USA and a further fifth to Australasia. The impact of emigration needs to be assessed with some caution. Emigration was far more important for Irish and Scottish populations than it was for England: between 1853 and 1900 net emigration represented 9 per cent of natural increase in England and Wales but 25 per cent in Scotland. It is also important to note that of the 4,675,000 who left England and Wales, only about 2,250,000 were permanent migrants.

Poverty, persecution, famine, all provided justification for emigration and was encouraged by government, charities and by individuals and parishes. Whether this was the British state 'shovelling out the poor' as some colonial commentators believed, its aim was to populate the empire with British citizens as well as alleviating social distress in Britain and Ireland. Books, children's literature, souvenirs, paintings, public monuments and lectures all transmitted narratives of martial heroism from the mid-nineteenth century reinforcing the notion that emigration was not only practical but also, in some ways, heroic. [119] Foreign missionary representatives canvassed working-class Sunday schools and chapels and middle-class philanthropists for subscriptions but the missionary presence at local level extended far beyond this. [120] The effectiveness of missionary organisations was such that contemporaries could

---

and Murdoch, Alexander, *British Emigration, 1603-1914*, (Palgrave), 2004, provide a detailed overview. Belich, James, *Replenishing the Earth. The Settler Revolution and the Rise of the Anglo-World, 1783-1939*, (Oxford University Press), 2009, and Harper, Marjorie, and Constantine, Stephen, *Migration and Empire*, (Oxford University Press), 2010.

[119] MacKenzie, J. M., 'Heroic myths of empire,' in MacKenzie, J. M., (ed.), *Popular Imperialism and the Military*, (Manchester University Press), 1992, pp. 10-38, considers the heroic reputation of Henry Haverlock, David Livingstone, Charles Gordon and T. E. Lawrence.

[120] Thorne, Susan, "The Conversion of Englishmen and the Conversion of the World Inseparable': Missionary Imperialism and the Language of Class in Early Industrial Britain', in Cooper, Frederick, and Stoler, Laura Ann, (eds.), *Tensions of Empire: Colonial Cultures in a Bourgeois World*, (University of California Press), 1997, pp. 238-262.

justifiably claim that 'many a small tradesman or rustic knows more of African or Polynesian life than London journalists'. [121] Popular culture was saturated by imperial images from sauce bottles and biscuit tins to plays and in due course films, all of which amounted to populist propaganda on an industrial scale.

Young men tended to make up the vast majority of migrants, although couples and family units were also prominent. For instance, of the 103 individuals who arrived in Melbourne, Victoria in February 1867 on the *Alhambra*, there were seven married women en route to join their husbands and most were male with an average age of twenty-seven. Migrants came from many different types of occupations. For instance, most Welsh emigrants were miners or worked in the iron, steel, copper and tin industries. However, general labourers and worker of the building trades and textile workers, engineers, farmers, clerical and commercial workers were also represented. There was also an explosion of voluntary organisations, strongly motivated by evangelical zeal, and some state involvement in sponsoring migration as a means of improving the life chances of children. Although this was not a new solution to child poverty, pauper children had been sent to the Cape Colony, Western Australia and Canada from at least the late-eighteenth century, the enthusiastic adoption of the practice by all the main child rescue agencies from the late 1860s meant that many thousands of children were uprooted and sent abroad. [122] The main pressure for child rescue and the religious impulses which powered it can be laid at the door of four men, Thomas Barnardo, Thomas Bowman Stephenson, Edward de Mountjoie Rudolf and Benjamin Waugh, the founders of Dr Barnardo's Homes, National Children's Homes, the Church of England Central Homes for Waifs and Strays and the National Society for the Prevention of Cruelty to Children. Their success in attracting financial and other support for their work owed much to their ability to tailor their publicity to contemporary ideas about childhood, the threats posed to it by urban life and the irresponsibility of many poor parents. Magazines and pamphlets were interspersed with skilfully manipulated illustrations and photographs in case mere words failed to convey the message. Removing children from poor and inadequate homes was a Christian duty and in the best interests of the child.

Immigration also contributed to Britain's growing population. Between 1844 and 1870, more than 7,000 people applied to become

---

[121] *London Quarterly Review*, Vol. 7, (1856), p. 238.
[122] Ibid, Harper, Marjorie, and Constantine, Stephen, *Migration and Empire*, pp. 247-276, provides an up-to-date analysis of child migration.

British citizens under the 1844 Nauturalisation Act. They included a large number of immigrants notably France and the German states, some of whom were political exiles especially in the aftermath of the European revolutions in 1848 but there were also people from Belgium, Holland, Switzerland, Spain, Russia, Poland, Sweden and the Italian states. The majority settled in London, establishing immigrant communities, such as 'Little Italy' in Clerkenwell that still exist today. Many Italian immigrants were ice cream makers, plasterers, confectioners, restaurateurs, and shop keepers, while many German immigrants settled in the East End of London working in the sugar refineries and in the meat and baking trades. [123]

There were many Asian and Black people living in Britain.[124] They formed an integral part of British society, whether labouring as servants in country houses, enlisting in the armed forces, marrying in parish churches, engaging with literary and artistic life or challenging the repressive laws of the day. It was Britain's subsequent involvement in the slave trade that had the greatest influence over the size and pattern of its Black population. By the 1780s, there were 20,000 black people in Britain of whom over half lived in London. London's Blacks vociferously contested slavery and in 1772 Lord Mansfield ruled that slave who has deserted his master could not be taken by force to be sold abroad. London's Blacks and Asians (Lascars) lived among many whites in such areas as Mile End, Stepney, Paddington, and the St Giles areas. The majority were living, not as slaves and servants in wealthy homes, but as free people, householders or tenants. The abolition of the British slave trade in 1807 and of slavery in the British Empire in 1833 led to a steady decline in numbers and visibility of London's Blacks From the 1870s, small black dockside communities developed in London's Canning Town and in Liverpool and Cardiff, Bristol and Plymouth as new shipping links are established with the Caribbean and West Africa. By the end of the nineteenth century very few Black people remained in England. The descendants of Black slaves in England had largely 'disappeared' through intermarriage with white people. Without doubt, the children from mixed African, African-Caribbean, Asian and white relationships represent the largest and longest surviving Black ethnic groups within Britain. Indians first arrived in Britain mainly because Britain traded with, and later colonised, India but it was only in the

---

[123] Panayi, Panikos, *Immigration, Ethnicity and Racism in Britain, 1815-1945*, (Manchester University Press), 1994, pp. 23-75,

[124] Fryer, P., *Staying Power: The History of Black People in Britain*, 2nd ed., (Pluto), 2010, Visram, R., *Asians in Britain: 400 years of History*, (Pluto), 2002.

1840s that large numbers of Indians began to migrate, mainly to the Caribbean, as indentured labourers. Some of these migrants or their descendants eventually settled in Britain. Africans appear to have been more numerous than Asians in Britain largely because African people had been travelling to Europe in larger numbers since the medieval period.

Concerns about the level of immigration became a populist issue from the 1880s. Control of aliens was based on the principle that race-mixing caused degeneration of a biological stock and appeared in 1853 and was particularly influential in Germany where the term 'anti-Semitism' first appeared as a biological rather than religious concept in 1879. Jews in Britain had long been received more liberally than in many other European countries but there was a change of mood, reflected in literature as well as reality, by the end of the century. [125] This began with the immigration of Jewish refugees from the Russian Empire and Romania in the 1870s. Many settled in the East End of London where local Conservative politicians fanned anti-Jewish sentiments into an anti-immigrant agitation. The numbers involved were relatively modest: the number of aliens in the United Kingdom was 135,640 in 1881, 219,523 in 1891 and 280,925 by 1901. Despite this, the insecurity and frustration caused by poverty, unemployment, casual labour, overcrowding a crime that were pervasive in the 1880s and 1890s, were projected on to Jewish immigration by East Enders who blame it for social problems that had existed in London before the 1880s. Calls for immigration controls came from the British Brothers League, a grassroots organisation in the East End that, from 1901 to 1905, organised constant demonstrations and rallies through the East End against immigration. There was also widespread support for this within the labour movement and from within the socialist movement with the TUC demanding controls in 1896. Much of the alarm was stoked by exaggerated media reports. Despite the average annual number settling being 4,000 to 5,000, even the respected Whitaker's Almanac claimed in 1902 that 140,000 Jewish immigrants arrived in Britain each year without mentioning that a significant number continued on to the United States. A Select Committee in 1889 and the Royal Commission on Alien Immigration in 1903 both rejected the contention that immigrants were unclean or unhealthy and concluded that fears about alien immigration were largely unfounded. But, the Royal Commission recommended controls over certain categories of 'undesirable aliens' that became law in the

---

[125] Feldman, David, *Englishmen and Jews: Social Relations and Political Culture 1840-1914*, (Yale University Press), 1994.

Aliens Act 1905. [126] The 1905 Act was followed up with further legislation in 1914 and 1919 that gave the state the power to deport people who had settled in the UK and made it a criminal offence for 'an alien' to 'promote industrial unrest'.

In Victorian Britain population migration affected most people at some time in their lives and was taken for granted as part of lifetime experience, without severe long-term effects on either individuals or communities. The search for work was the dominant motive, especially in longer distance movement targeted on specific labour markets. Short distance moves remained dominant throughout the century and involved a host of individual reasons, leading migrants towards familiar areas and leaving open the possibility of return, something generally precluded from those who emigrated to Britain's burgeoning colonies or to the United States.

Why did Irish migrants settle in Britain?

Unlike Canada, Australia and the United States that have substantial information on numbers of Irish immigrants, Britain does not. [127] There was no consistent measurement of Irish migration into Britain largely because there were no legal boundaries between the two islands. Migrants were not counted in and out as they were when

---

[126] On this issue see Wray, Helena, 'The Aliens Act 1905 and the Immigration Dilemma', *Journal of Law and Society*, Vol. 33, (2006), pp. 302-323, Pellew, Jill, 'The Home Office and the Aliens Act, 1905', *Historical Journal*, Vol. 32, (1989), pp. 369-385, and Gainer, Bernard, *The alien invasion: the origins of the Aliens Act of 1905*, (Heinemann), 1972.

[127] The best short studies of the Irish in Britain are Fitzpatrick, David, "A peculiar tramping people': the Irish in Britain, 1801-70' in Vaughan, W. D., (ed.), *A New History of Ireland, Vol. V, Ireland under the Union, I: 1801-70,* (Oxford University Press), 1989, pp. 623-660 and 'The Irish in Britain, 1871-1921' in Vaughan, W. D., (ed.), *A New History of Ireland, Vol. VI, Ireland under the Union, II: 1870-1921,* (Oxford University Press), 1996, pp. 653-702, Swift, Roger, *The Irish in Britain, 1815-1914: Perspectives and Sources*, (The Historical Association), 1991 and MacRaild, D. M., *The Irish in Britain 1800-1914*, (Dundalgan Press), 2006. For more detailed treatments, see Davis, Graham, *The Irish in Britain, 1815-1914*, (Gill & Macmillan), 1991 and MacRaild, D. M., *Irish Migrants in Modern Britain, 1750-1922*, (Macmillan), 1999, *The Irish Diaspora in Britain, 1750-1939*, 2nd edition, (Palgrave Macmillan), 2010. Important collections of essays include Swift, R., and Gilley, S., (eds.), *The Irish in Victorian Britain 1815-1939*, (Pinter Publishing), 1989, *The Irish in the Victorian City*, (Croom Helm), 1985, and *The Irish in Victorian Britain: the Local Dimension*, (Four Courts Press), 1999, and MacRaild, Donald M., (ed.), *The Great Famine and Beyond: Irish Migrants in Britain in the Nineteenth and Twentieth Centuries*, (Irish Academic Press), 2000.

emigrating overseas and the most important source of emigration data for Ireland measured only aggregate overseas migration. [128] Consequently, the census returns for the United Kingdom remains the only reliable source of data, and then only a snapshot every ten years and this was not systematically used for examining Irish immigration until the 1980s.

Just when the Irish began crossing the Irish Sea is unclear though there were already Irish names among Liverpool's citizens by 1378 [129] and London already had a significant Irish population by the early fifteenth century when legislation was passed in 1413 restricting their entry and movement. Liverpool and Whitehaven, ports of significance to the Irish trade saw some Irish settlement in the early modern period but these communities were small. As migration became more common, drovers, peddlers and travelling salesmen were often Irish. However, it was the seasonal movement of harvesters that represented the most important incursion of Irish migrants to Britain by the mid-eighteenth century. This continued parallel to permanent settlement and did not peak until the late-nineteenth-century. Itinerancy was by no means the domain simply of the Irish and 'tramping' was a central feature of British society in the eighteenth and nineteenth centuries. Skilled workers were forced into itinerancy throughout their careers; in fact, being a 'journeyman' was an integral part of becoming a 'master'. [130]

> The tramp, the navvy, and the pedlar might be one and the same person at different stages of life, or even at different seasons of the year... the nomadic phase and the settled were often intertwined. [131]

---

[128] These sources were the annual series of returns by the United State immigration authorities, the Emigration Commissioners' returns and, from 1876, the Returns of the Registrar General for Ireland.

[129] Muir, Ramsay, *History of Liverpool*, (Williams & Norgate), 1907, p. 304.

[130] Journeymen tramped the country in search of work (by the day: *journée*) in part to extend their experience and knowledge of their trade but also to escape increasingly uncertain employment prospects in their immediate locality. See, Hobsbawm, E. J., 'The Tramping Artisan', in his *Labouring Men: Studies in the History of Labour*, (Weidenfeld & Nicholson), 1964, pp. 34-63, and Humphries, Jane, 'English Apprenticeship: A Neglected Factor in the First Industrial Revolution', in David, Paul A., and Thomas, Mark, (eds.), *The economic future in historical perspective*, (Oxford University Press), 2001, pp. 73-102.

[131] Samuel, Raphael, 'Comers and Goers', in Dyos, H. J., and Wolff, Michael, (eds.), *The Victorian City: Images and Realities*, 2 Vols. (Routledge), 1973, Vol. 1, pp. 123-160, at pp. 152-153.

Large numbers of Irish had been coming from Ireland since the early-eighteenth century to meet seasonal demands for labour and were vital to Britain's booming economy. [132] Many worked as temporary summer harvesters outside the capital and by 1794, for example, open field farmers in Bedfordshire relied on itinerant Irish labour for harvesting crops. [133] In the 1820s, 6,000-8,000 Irish were making the harvest migration to Scotland each year and this had risen this had grown to 25,000 over the agricultural season by the 1840s.[134] Non-agricultural labourers in Scotland earned nearly four times their counterparts in Ireland and agricultural wages were twice as high in Scotland as in Ireland in 1800. The disparity between wages and incomes in the two countries increased between 1830 and 1850.[135] There was especially high demand for labour in the London area where supplying fresh milk led to an increase of small cow keepers in the suburbs who cultivated hay extensively to provide cattle feed.[136] The Irish provided the labour necessary for hay harvesting, arriving in the summer and returning home in the autumn.

---

[132] Collins, E. J. T., 'Migrant labour in British agriculture in the nineteenth century', *Economic History Review*, 2nd series, Vol. 29, (1976), pp. 38-59, examines the importance of migrant labour to the agrarian economy. On the continued importance of migrant labour to agriculture, see, Rogaly, Ben, *Intensification of Work-Place Regimes in British Agriculture: The Role of Migrant Workers*, (University of Sussex), 2006.

[133] The Irish dimension is explored in Johnson, J. H., 'Harvest migration from nineteenth century Ireland', *Institute of British Geographers*, Vol. 41, (1967), pp. 97-112, Kerr, B.M. 'Irish seasonal migration to Great Britain, 1800-38', *Irish Historical Studies*, Vol. 3, (1943), pp. 365-380, Ó Gráda, C., 'Seasonal migration and post-Famine adjustment in the west of Ireland', *Studia Hibernica*, Vol. 13, (1973), pp. 48-76, Moran, G., "A passage to Britain': seasonal migration and social change in the west of Scotland, 1870-1890', *Saothar*, Vol. 13, (1988), pp. 22-31, Barber, Sarah, 'Irish migrant agricultural labourers in nineteenth century Lincolnshire', *Saothar*, Vol. 8, (1982), pp. 10-22, and O'Dowd, Ann, *Spalpeens and Tattie Hokers: History and Folklore of Irish Migratory Agricultural Workers in Ireland and Britain*, (Irish Academic Press), 1991.

[134] Handley, J. E., *The Irish in Scotland*, (John S. Burns), 1964, p. 16.

[135] Cullen, Louis M., 'Incomes, Social Classes and Economic Growth in Ireland and Scotland, 1600-1900', in Devine, T. M., and Dickson, David, (eds.), *Ireland and Scotland 1600-1850: Parallels and Contrasts in Economic and Social Development*, (John Donald), 1981, p. 250. Ibid, Handley, J. E., *The Irish in Scotland*, p. 8, stated that wages in Scotland were five to six times higher than those in Ireland

[136] Hill, Bridget, *Women, Work and Sexual Politics in Eighteenth-century England*, (Routledge), 1993, pp. 164-172, provides a succinct discussion of the importance of itinerant labour to England's economy.

The scale of the traffic is illustrated in a survey in 1841 showing that 57,651 deck passengers travelled from Ireland to Britain between mid-May and August 1841. It estimated that 40,000 later returned and noted 'the comparatively small cost to Great Britain at which this useful labour is annually purchased at the moment it is required'. [137] As many as 100,000 harvest labourers a year in the 1860s, moved around Britain over the summer and autumn months, gathering hay, corn, potatoes, turnips and whatever might earn them the cash needed to pay rents or debts back home in Ireland. Itinerant labour was also a major force in the building trades as labourers and as navvies for road building, canal digging and railway construction. MacRaild [138] suggests that 10 per cent of the navvying workforce was Irish and between 1790 and 1820 up to 90 per cent of labourers employed in canal construction in Scotland were Irish. [139] Most itinerant workers were men, although in the 1870s women from Kerry were said to migrate regularly to the iron furnaces of South Wales. Despite the obvious economic benefits of itinerant labour to Britain, its benefits for Ireland were less clear.

In his long and rhetorically subtle pamphlet *Chartism*, first published in December 1839, Thomas Carlyle commented on the Irish presence in the early Victorian city that 'Crowds of miserable Irish darken all our towns' but also 'England is guilty towards Ireland and reaps at last, in full measure, the fruit of fifteen generations of wrongdoing.' [140] *Chartism* marked Carlyle's first direct intervention in contemporary social and political concerns reflecting his personal insights into the true causes of the social distress that he had witnessed at first hand, journeying from London to Scotland earlier that summer. During the 1840s, Carlyle increasingly saw the crisis in Ireland as related to difficulties facing contemporary 'English' society and he treated it as a distinctive symptom of a malaise that afflicted all European societies. Morrow suggests that Carlyle's views on Ireland reflected the illiberal and authoritarian attitudes that underwrote his social and political thought, but they were not, as has sometimes been suggested, premised on anti-Irish prejudices derived from racial stereotypes. [141]

---

[137] *Census: Ireland*, 1841, pp. xxvi-xxvii.
[138] Ibid, MacRaild, D. M., *Irish Migrants in Modern Britain, 1750-1922*, p. 47.
[139] Ibid, Handley, J. E., *The Irish in Scotland*, p. 28.
[140] Swift, Roger, 'Thomas Carlyle, *Chartism*, and the Irish in early Victorian England, *Victorian Literature and Culture*, Vol. 29, (1), (2001), pp. 67-83.
[141] Morrow, John, 'Thomas Carlyle, 'Young Ireland' and the 'Condition of Ireland Question', *Historical Journal*, Vol. 51, (2008), pp. 643-667. See also his broader discussion 'Formality and Revolution: Carlyle on

Carlyle was not alone in his response to Irish immigration in the 1830s and 1840s. James Kay [142] and Friedrich Engels [143] both took a critical stance in their discussion of the Irish of 'Little Ireland' in Manchester. It was the smallest of the Irish settlements in Manchester covering four acres immediately south of Oxford Road railway station but with a population of 1,510 in the 1841 Census. Most of its residential housing was only occupied from the early 1820s until it was finally boarded up and demolished in the late 1840s. Other Irish areas in Manchester had larger populations, worse housing and suffered more severely from the recurrence of cholera, typhus and typhoid but 'little Ireland' became the generic term for a concentration of poor, unskilled Irish living in slum housing in an industrial area throughout Britain in the nineteenth century.

By the mid-nineteenth century, itinerant labour was viewed with increasing suspicion. Many definitions of rogues, vagabonds and vagrants emphasised their deviant opposition in contrast to sedentary, decent and civilised society. In *London Labour*, Henry Mayhew proclaimed a racial distinction between the sedentary and the mobile to demonise the latter:

> Of the thousand millions of human beings that are said to constitute the population of the entire globe, there are -- socially, morally, and perhaps even physically considered -- but two distinct and broadly marked races, viz., the wanderers and the settlers -- the vagabond and the citizen -- the nomadic and the civilized tribes...The nomadic or vagrant class have all an universal type, whether they be the Bushmen of Africa or the 'tramps' of our own country.[144]

Modernity', in ibid, Morrow, John, and Scott, Jonathan, (eds.), *Liberty, Authority, Formality: Political Ideas and Culture, 1600-1900*, pp. 153-172.
[142] Kay, James, *The Moral and Physical Condition of the Working Classes Employed in the Cotton Manufacture in Manchester*, (Ridgway), 1832, pp. 34-36; Selleck, R. J. W., *James Kay-Shuttleworth. Journey of an Outsider*, (Woburn Press), 1994, pp. 46-103 provides context.
[143] Engels, F., *The Condition of the Working-class in England*, 1844, translated, with foreword by V. Kiernan, (Penguin), 1987 pp. 97-99, 123-126 on 'Little Ireland'; see also, Busteed, M. A., ''The most horrible spot'? The legend of Manchester's Little Ireland', *Irish Studies Review*, Vol. 13, (1996), pp. 12-20, and George, A. D. and Clark, S. C., 'A note on "little Ireland", Manchester', *Industrial Archaeology*, Vol. 14, (1979), pp. 36-40.
[144] Mayhew, Henry, *London Labour and the London Poor: The Condition and Earnings of Those that will work, cannot work, and will not work*, 4 Vols. (Charles Griffin and Company), 1851-1852, Vol. I, p. 3.

In the winter of 1848-1849, the Houseless Poor Society sheltered 8,068 individuals from Ireland. [145] In Victorian society it was difficult to isolate the illicitly nomadic from the decent and sedentary. The Irish poor, much as their British counterparts, shared lives of intermittent mobility and stability, economic misfortunes and hostility.

After 1815, Irish migrants settled in increasing numbers in the big towns and cities and by the 1830s contemporaries wrongly viewed the dirt, disease and overcrowding in cities as the result of waves of Irish migrants. By the end of the eighteenth century, Irish people lived in most parts of London especially around the docks where they were the most numerous non-native labour. [146] There was a rapid increase in the size of the Irish community in Liverpool that by 1800 made up 6 per cent of the total population, by 1831 numbered 24,156 and increased threefold by 1841.[147] Irish migrants, many of them Ulster Protestant weavers, spread across the central Lowlands of Scotland by 1800. In 1831, around 35,000 Irish-born lived in Glasgow. By the 1830s, the Irish presence had reached as far north as Aberdeen where there was a largely Catholic community of around 3,000 in 1836. Shortage of native handloom weavers helps account for the increase in Irish migration to Manchester after 1800 reaching around 35,000 by the mid-1830s. Iron smelting encouraged Irish migrants to Scotland, the Lake Counties and South Wales. [148] In 1841, almost half of Irish-born migrants in Britain lived in London, Liverpool, Manchester or Glasgow

Those who turned seasonal migration into permanent settlement were often involved in work that British people found dirty, disreputable or otherwise disagreeable; jobs such as petty trading, keeping lodging houses and beer houses. [149] By 1840, three-quarters

---

[145] Ibid, Mayhew, Henry, *London Labour and the London Poor*, Vol. I, pp. 416-417.

[146] Lees, L. Hollen, *Exiles of Erin: Irish Migrants in Victorian London*, (Manchester University Press), 1979, pp. 45-48, and Jackson, J.A., 'The Irish in East London', *East London Papers*, Vol. 6, (1963), pp. 105-119.

[147] Belchem, John, (ed.), *Liverpool 800: Culture, Character & History*, (Liverpool University Press), 2008, and Belchem, John, *Irish, Catholic and Scouse: The History of the Liverpool Irish 1800-1939*, (Liverpool University Press), 2007, provide the context.

[148] MacRaild, D. M., *Culture, Conflict and Migration: Irish in Victorian Cumbria*, (Liverpool University Press), 1998, pp. 29-32

[149] For discussion of the debate on the impact of Irish labour on British labour markets, see, Williamson, Jeffrey, 'The impact of the Irish on British

of the stall-holders in Manchester were Irish. The stereotype of the Irish community as unskilled needs to be viewed with caution. Heavy dock work may have dominated labour experience in the city but one in ten Irish workers were mechanics and a few were middle-class. [150] In Manchester, Irish labour was concentrated in the less-skilled aspects of the building trade but was also well represented among the more skilled bricklayers and masons. The Ulster Irish were especially well suited to hand loom weaving as many had experience in the linen industry in Ireland while in Scotland and England, the Irish obtained higher-paid jobs because of their willingness to use new machinery unlike the more conservative native spinners and weavers.

...we find them useful labourers, and their services are of considerable importance to us; at present we could not do without them. In this part of the country, the Scotch do not show too much disposition for labouring work; they would rather go to trades. Even the hand-loom weavers, whose wages are so low, do not either themselves attempt to be labourers, or bring up their children to it. [151]

By the 1830s, there was an accelerated expansion of the demand for the kinds of jobs that the Irish performed and Irish men and women made a positive contribution to the growth of the British economy by undertaking employment which others resisted enabling some in the British workforce to move into higher occupational brackets. [152] Employers often took a favourable view of Irish labour. In 1830 for example, Sir R. Heron commented:

...the Irish labourers who found their way into Lincolnshire were very useful, and he had generally found them to be very orderly, well behaved men. [153]

However, others took a less charitable view and by the mid-1830s, the Irish were increasingly regarded as carriers of disease, a cause of crime and the major reason for the spiralling costs of poor

---

labour markets during the Industrial Revolution', in ibid, Swift, R., and Gilley, S., (eds.), *The Irish in Victorian Britain 1815-1939*, pp. 134-162.

[150] Ibid, MacRaild, D. M., *Irish Migrants in Modern Britain, 1750-1922*, pp. 51-52, especially Table 2.2.

[151] 'Report of the Select Committee of the State of the Irish Poor in Great Britain', *Parliamentary Papers*, Vol. xxxiv, 1836, p. 456.

[152] On this issue, see Harris, Ruth-Ann, *The Nearest Place was Wasn't Ireland: Early-nineteenth Century Irish Labour Migration*, (Iowa State University Press), 1994.

[153] *Hansard*, House of Commons, Debate, 9 March 1830, Vol. 23, cc5-6.

relief. [154] Charles Hindley, MP for Ashton-under-Lyne suggested that Irish migrants reduced the wages of English workers:

> There were vast numbers of the Irish poor in Manchester who contended for bread with the English weaver. He by no means objected to their right to do so. On the contrary, he thought we ought to make them welcome, and by every means to better their condition. Yet, certainly, the effect of their coming and entering into competition with the resident weavers was to increase the distress of the latter, and to render their condition almost as low as that of the Irish. [155]

It is, however, clear from Scottish evidence that this was not the case although this did not mean there was no competition for employment. In the iron industry and in coal mining, the Irish were in direct competition with the native population even though they were not displacing native labour supply but augmenting it through acceptance of positions that were unwanted by the native population.

For Ireland in the nineteenth century, the Famine in the 1840s was *the* climatic event. Not only did it exacerbate existing trends within Irish society but it led to a massive loss in its population either through famine-induced deaths or emigration. Ireland had experienced blights that attacked and destroyed potato plants in 1822, 1831, 1835, and 1837 but these were minor in comparison to the cataclysmic events between 1845 and 1851. [156] In 1845, a previously unknown fungus, *Phytophthora infestans*, arrived without warning and

---

[154] Lewis, Sir George Cornewall, 'A Report into the Condition of the Irish Poor in Great Britain, 1834', *Parliamentary Papers*, Vol. xxxiv, 1836, provides a detailed snap-shot of Irish settlement though it neglects the significant community in North-East England.

[155] *Hansard*, House of Commons, Debates, 21 December 1837, Vol. 39, cc 1410-1411.

[156] For detailed discussion of the Famine see, Edwards, R. Dudley, and Williams, T. Desmond, (eds.), *The Great Famine: Studies in Irish History 1845-52*, (Browne and Nolan), 1956, Woodham-Smith, C., *The Great Hunger: Ireland 1845-1849*, (H. Hamilton), 1962, Daly, Mary E., *The Famine in Ireland*, (Dundalgan Press), 1986, Kinealy, Christine, *This great calamity: the Irish Famine 1845-52*, (Gill & Macmillan), 1994, *A Death-Dealing Famine: The Great Hunger in Ireland*, (Pluto Press), 1997, and *The great Irish famine: impact, ideology and rebellion*, (Palgrave), 2002, O'Grada, Cormac, *Black '47 and Beyond: The Great Irish Famine in History, Economy, and Memory*, (Princeton University Press), 1999, and *The Great Irish Famine*, (Macmillan), 1989, and Donnelly, James S., *The Great Irish Potato Famine*, (Sutton), 2001. McAuliffe, Mary, O'Donnell, Katherine, and Lane, Leeann, (eds.), *Palgrave Advances in Irish History*, (Palgrave), 2009, pp. 84-89, provides a current view of the historiography.

destroyed Ireland's potato crop at a devastating pace cutting the means of sustenance of the most marginal sections of society. Initially, there were few excess deaths even in counties such as Cork and Kerry, where excess mortality was later severe, until the summer and autumn of 1846. Near total failure of the potato crop in 1846 was made worse by harsh weather conditions. Excess mortality increased from the summer of 1846 and peaked in 1847-1848 though it persisted in some areas into 1850 and 1851. For those who survived the devastating effects of the Famine, emigration to Britain, the United States or British colonies such as Canada and Australia proved an attractive prospect. [157]

Britain's Irish population doubled between 1841 and 1861. In 1841, in England and Wales there were 291,000 Irish-born and 126,000 in Scotland respectively 1.8 per cent and 4.8 per cent of the total population. After 1845, the Famine turned a flood of migrants into a torrent. By 1851, there were 520,000 Irish-born in England and Wales and 207,000 in Scotland and this reached 602,000 in England and Wales by 1861 though in Scotland, there was a slight reduction to 204,000. This magnified already existing perceptions among middle-class commentators that Irish immigration was the root cause of many contemporary social problems especially poverty, low standards of living, crime and urban squalor and among the working-classes, that Irish immigrants posed a threat to their labour. It was the enormity of the migration with its accompanying and highly visible horrors of destitution, disease and death that shocked British urban society and exposed the inadequacies of private and public provision for relieving poverty. Most ports with Irish connections and smaller towns across Wales, the west and into the Midlands, Yorkshire and the north experienced a dramatic increase in the number of migrants. Wandering Irish paupers soon reached inland parishes and even small rural villages suddenly faced a mounting problem. Ormskirk, a small market town in Lancashire not usually associated with Irish emigration contained over 1,100 Irish inhabitants out of a population of 6,000 in 1849.[158] The scale of migration destabilised existing Irish communities by increasing the proportion of poor and destitute compared to those who were employed and established.

Initially Famine migrants overwhelmed existing patterns of Irish settlement especially in the big cities, ports and towns near original

---

[157] Brown, Richard, *Famine, Fenians and Freedom, 1840-1882*, (Clio Publishing), 2011, pp. 1-88, examines the Irish diaspora to Britain, United States, Canada and Australia.

[158] Ibid, MacRaild, D. M., *Irish Migrants in Modern Britain, 1750-1922*, p. 58.

large Irish centres such as Liverpool. Between 1847 and 1848, one-third of outdoor relief payments in Manchester were made to Irish people. This was also a period of trade depression with many mills closed and more local people claiming relief as well. At least 50,000 Irish people received emergency relief aid in Liverpool in 1847 and at the height of the Famine between 1847 and 1848, over 40 per cent of those receiving outdoor relief in Liverpool were Irish, about twice the proportion of Irish people in Liverpool's population. The famine years of the 1840s also saw a huge influx of Irish into London. Many found work in the construction industry. By 1851, there were 108,500 Irish-born people in the city, plus a large number born in London of Irish descent. Men generally worked as labourers or in the port as dockers or stevedores, helping to build the canals, docks, roads, bridges and railways of the expanding industrial city. Women worked in domestic service or the clothing industry.

The impact of migration varied across Britain. [159] Glasgow, for example, experienced more immigration before the mid-1840s than after and in general Famine migrants did not head for the west of Scotland. [160] Handley estimated that approximately 115,000 Irish migrants arrived permanently in Scotland during the decade 1841-1851 of whom around 50,000 went to Glasgow. [161] The pace of migration to Glasgow from Ireland remained largely constant throughout the first half of the nineteenth century. While there was some increase, the percentage of Irish-born in Glasgow only increased from 16 per cent to 18 per cent between 1841 and 1851. Even though there was a temporary increase in arrivals during this period, it did not have the impact that it had elsewhere. [162] There were two main reasons for this. Ulster was the chief source of Irish migration to Ireland and it was less affected by the Famine and the industrial economy of west-central Scotland was largely unaffected by the depressed nature of the economy elsewhere in Britain and was able to absorb large amounts

---

[159] Collins, Brenda, 'Irish emigration to Britain during the famine decade, 1841-51,' *Familia*, Vol. 11, (1995), pp. 1-16, provides a succinct discussion.
[160] What follows draws on Day, Shawn, *Where's Poor Paddy? The Contrasting Results of Irish Migration to Glasgow and Liverpool 1790-1850*, unpublished, 2002.
[161] Ibid, Handley, J. E., *The Irish in Scotland*, p. 198.
[162] See, Gordon, Michèle, and Gründler, Jens, 'Migration, survival strategies and networks of Irish paupers in Glasgow, 1850-1900', in Gestrich, Andreas, King, Steven and Lutz, Raphael, (eds.), *Being poor in modern Europe: historical perspectives 1800-1940*, (Peter Lang), 2006, pp. 113-134.

of cheap unskilled labour.[163] Famine migration to Liverpool is in stark contrast to Glasgow. Liverpool was Britain's gateway to the United States and Britain's main imperial trade centre. It close links with Ireland made it a magnet for Famine migrants either as a route into England or a stage in their voyage to the United States or colonial destinations. 296,000 Irish arrived in Liverpool during 1847 alone and although 130,000 went to the United States, over 100,000 were classed as paupers. In all, between 1846 and 1852, some 600,000 Irish paupers landed in Liverpool but only just over half continued to the United States or Canada. This exodus came to a city with a total population of around 300,000 permanent inhabitants. By 1851, the Irish made up a third of the working class. At this same time Liverpool was experiencing a trough in its business cycle and there was already rampant unemployment among its native population. The situation was tense and despite the bulk of these migrants quickly took ship for Canada and America, friction with the existing population was widespread.

The different economic experiences of Glasgow and Liverpool account for differences in the intensity of sectarian conflict. There were limited occurrences of such violence in Glasgow, but they did not become a frequent occurrence until the 1870s.[164] Liverpool however is a different story and sectarian riots were reported as early as 1819. Class distinctions played a larger role in Glasgow in determining where people lived and this, combined with the more consistent rate of migration, allowed the natural growth of community without ethnic or religious segregation. The Irish were scattered throughout the central wards of Glasgow, amongst the Highlanders and other working class Scots.[165] Segregation was endemic to Liverpool, with specific areas dedicated to the Welsh, the Irish Protestant and even the ship owners.[166] There were huge concentrations of Irish in particular wards in Liverpool. In the districts of St. Bartholomew's, Vauxhall and the North-End in 1841, the

---

[163] This was not without its problems, see Walls, Patricia, and Williams, Rory, 'Sectarianism at work: Accounts of employment discrimination against Irish Catholics in Scotland', *Ethnic and Racial Studies*, Vol. 26, (4), (2003), pp. 632-661.
[164] Fraser, W. Hamish, and Maver, Irene, (eds.), *Glasgow, Vol. 2: 1830-1912*, (Manchester University Press), 1996, pp. 96-162.
[165] Sloan, William, 'Religious affiliation and the immigrant experience: Catholic Irish and Protestant highlanders in Glasgow, 1830-1850', in Devine, T. M., (ed.), *Irish immigrants and Scottish society in the nineteenth and twentieth centuries*, (John Donald), 1991, pp. 67-90.
[166] Smith, Joan, 'Labour Tradition in Glasgow and Liverpool', *Workshop Journal*, Vol. 17, (1984), p. 49.

proportion of Irish-born residents was respectively 51 per cent, 46 per cent and 42 per cent. [167] By 1851, there were more Irish in Liverpool than in Cork, Ireland's third largest city. The Famine migrants helped to define many of Britain's cities and endorsed their striking sense of Irishness.

The initial impact of the Famine migration consolidated existing regional patterns of Irish settlement in the big cities, ports or in towns near original large Irish centres such as Liverpool, Dundee, Glasgow and Cardiff that contained over three quarters of the Irish-born. After 1851, the Irish spread out from these major centres and the proportion of all Britain's Irish-born in the four main cities fell between 1841 and 1861 although they still contained a third of the total Irish-born in Britain in 1871. The Irish remained more mobile than the non-Irish but after 1861, they became increasingly dispersed. Migrants fanned out across the country leaving the large cities and major conurbations and moved into the network of small and medium-sized towns. This dispersal was far from evenly spread across England, Scotland and Wales. Although there were Irish in every county in Britain, it was a presence that was predominantly urban in character. Outside London and the military towns in south-east England, there were relatively few Irish and in East Anglia, Irish migrants were found in Norwich, King's Lynn and Ipswich rather than in the smaller communities. This was also the case in Scotland and Wales. Glamorganshire and Monmouthshire attracted the highest number of Irish-born in South Wales that in 1871 contained 18,532 migrants compared to only 3,475 in North Wales.

Attitudes towards the Irish were slow to change but by the 1870s the image of the poor outcast Irish migrant had begun to disappear. This was, in part, a consequence of the declining memory of the Famine Irish but was also due to the increasingly settled nature of Irish communities. Although the Irish remained a predominantly labouring population, in the larger towns a vibrant Irish middle-class emerged that included bankers and financiers, lawyers, teachers, politicians and members of the cultural community as writers and painters. The classic view of the Irish was as labourers in the poorest grades of work but this too was changing as some found more skilled and better-paid employment. For example, in 1871 a fifth of Irish workers in the Consett area in north-west Durham were skilled puddlers in the iron and steel industry.

The series of articles written by Hugh Heinrick, a Wexford-born schoolteacher in Birmingham published between July and November

---

[167] Ibid, Neal, Frank, *Sectarian Violence: The Liverpool Experience, 1819-1914*, p. 12.

1872 in *The Nation*, an Irish nationalist newspaper printed in Dublin provide a valuable snapshot of the Irish in England. [168] The survey indicated, much to Heinrick's dismay, the extent to which the Irish had been assimilated into English society, a process facilitated by intermarriage and upward mobility that sapped the strength of Irish communities. For Heinrick, the only salvation of the Irish as a distinct people lay in isolation and the function of nationalist politics was to separate them from the baneful influences of English society.

...while the Irishmen in England are true to Faith and Fatherland, there is no power in England, whether political or social, that can divert their destiny or check their progress. [169]

---

[168] Heinrick, Hugh, *A Survey of the Irish in England (1872)*, edited by Alan O'Day, (Hambledon), 1990, provides a contemporary Irish perspective on the Irish in nineteenth-century Britain, offering a slight counterweight to the profusion of often critical non-Irish sources. In this context the *Survey* stands alongside John Denvir's more impressive *The Irish in Britain: from the earliest times to the fall and death of Parnell*, (Kegan Paul, Trench, Trübner), 1892, as a major source for the study of the subject.

[169] Ibid, Heinrick, Hugh, *A Survey of the Irish in England (1872)*, p. 129.

6 Regulating work

In Kirkheaton churchyard near Huddersfield there is a fifteen foot stone obelisk topped by a flame that commemorates:

> The dreadful fate of 17 children who fell unhappy victims to a raging fire at Mr Atkinson's factory at Colne Bridge, February 14th 1818.

All the dead were girls; the youngest nine, the oldest eighteen. The fire started when about 5 am a boy aged ten was sent downstairs to the ground floor card room to collect some cotton rovings. Instead of taking a lamp, he took a candle that ignited the cotton waste and the fire spread quickly through the factory that became a raging inferno. The children were trapped on the top floor when the staircase collapsed. The entire factory was destroyed in less than thirty minutes and the boy who had inadvertently started the fire was the last person to leave the building alive. It is not surprising that child labour and calls to regulate it became a national issue in the early 1830s.

Technological change and the development of new work conditions had gained sufficient strength by the 1830s to necessitate a serious and sustained effort by the state to regulate their application. Both employers and workers believed themselves locked into an established system of attitudes, actions and responses. Employers regarded their position as defined by the laws of the free market over which they had little control. Insensitive, repressive and largely indifferent to the conditions of their workers, many were motivated by a belief in profit, a belief buttressed by their religious piety. Widespread drunkenness among the workforce, as escape from these pressures, seemed to confirm employers' belief that the workforce could and would not respond to better treatment. These attitudes percolated down into the workforce itself and there is ample evidence of the exploitation of and cruelty towards workers, especially children, by fellow workers.[1] Masters and workers had been related to each other by simple contract and face-to-face contact but industrialisation had created a new set of relationship patterns. Workers had become 'operatives', human extensions of new technology, 'dehumanised' and 'dehumanising'.

By no means were all factories similar and there was often a wide range of work experience within any one factory unit. Work in factories required regular attendance and consistent effort, respect for tools and machinery used but not owned, tolerance of close

---

[1] Newey, Katherine, 'Climbing boys and factory girls: popular melodramas of working life', *Journal of Victorian Culture*, Vol. 5, (2000), pp. 28-44.

supervision, a willingness to work under non-personal contract and the ability to work in close quarters with a large number of persons. In early-nineteenth century Britain, these were largely new kinds of skills. Many late-eighteenth and early-nineteenth century textile mills were rural and recruited labour from the local domestic industries. Families often moved together to a new factory so that all members of a household could gain employment. A weaver used to the workings of a small weaving shed would be familiar with many aspects of the work environment, if not the scale, of a factory. Boys would probably be apprenticed to weaving, power spinning or in the machine shop; girls might work in the carding room before moving to other low-technology jobs within the mill. Generally, as new technology was adopted, men took control of the new processes in spinning and weaving while women were left with the older machines and more poorly paid jobs. [2]

Increasingly, as factories moved to steam-powered sites, the labour force moved from rural mills to towns. The new large urban mills offered greater opportunities and a wider range of employment in towns was some insurance against recession and unemployment. But factory work altered labourers' lives in a variety of ways. Labour input per worker may have increased from around 2,500 hours a year to over 3,300 (10.54 hours a day on a six day week) largely because holidays declined in number, with both religious and political festivals as well as 'St. Monday' becoming less important. Most obvious was the loss of freedom and independence, especially for men who had previously been their own masters. Factory workers could no longer intersperse industrial work with agricultural labour or other activities. Many factory masters introduced rigid and draconian regulations to keep the workforce at their machines for long hours and to break their irregular work patterns. [3]

Child labour

Child labour was an essential part of Britain's labour supply from the late-eighteenth century through to the 1870s when elementary school attendance was given statutory force. [4] The most common

---

[2] Morgan, Carol E., 'The domestic image and factory culture: the cotton district in mid-nineteenth-century England', *International Labor and Working-Class History*, Vol. 49, (1996), pp. 26-46.

[3] Clark, Gregory, 'Factory discipline', *Journal of Economic History*, Vol. 54, (1994), pp. 128-163.

[4] For a debate on child employment see, Cunningham, H., 'The employment and unemployment of children, 1680-1851', *Past and Present*, Vol. 126, (1990), pp. 115-150, and Kirby, Peter, 'How many children were

explanation for the increase in supply of child labour was poverty--families sent their children to work because they desperately needed the income. Working-class children were seen as 'little adults; and were expected to contribute to the family income or enterprise. E. P. Thompson, though generally critical of the factory system, nonetheless conceded that 'it is perfectly true that the parents not only needed their children's earnings, but expected them to work.'[5] Cultural attitudes also played an important role in this process. Parents had worked when they were young and required their children to do the same. For factory owners, child labour was a cheap source of labour that allowed them to remain competitive. Managers and overseers pointed out that children were ideal factory workers because they were obedient, submissive, likely to respond to punishment and unlikely to form unions. In addition, since the machines had reduced many procedures to simple one-step tasks, unskilled workers could replace skilled workers.

The initial division of labour in factories was slanted towards child labour but once this generation of workers had grown up into adult factory workers, there was a shift towards adult male dominance of factory work and its new technologies. A survey in 1788 showed that 'children' made up two-thirds of the workforce on powered machines in 143 water mills in England and Wales.[6] By 1835 before the 1833 Factory Act had taken full effect, however, a survey of 982 mills in England and Scotland found that cotton mill workers under eighteen only made up 43 per cent of the workforce. [7] This downward trend in the use of child labour is supported by other local evidence: surveys in Manchester, Stockport and Preston in 1816-1819 showed that the share of cotton mill workers under eighteen were 47, 58 and

---

'unemployed' in 18th and 19th century England', and Cunningham's response in *Past and Present*, Vol. 187, (2005), pp. 187-215. Hopkins, E., *Childhood Transformed. Working Class Children in Nineteenth-Century England*, (Routledge), 1994, Horn, Pamela, *Children's Work and Welfare 1780-1880s*, (Macmillan), 1994, Kirby, Peter, *Child labour in Britain, 1750-1870*, (Palgrave), 2003, and Humphries, Jane, *Childhood and Child Labour in the British Industrial Revolution*, (Cambridge University Press), 2010, provide valuable insights into children's work and how and why it changed.
[5] Thompson, E. P., *The Making of the English Working Class*, (Gollancz), 1963, p. 339.
[6] Colquhoun, P., *Memorandum on Cotton Manufacture in Great Britain*, (n.d.), Manuscript E-46, Kress Library, Harvard but see also Colquhoun, P., *A representation of facts relative to the rise and progress of cotton manufacture in the cotton industry in Great Britain*, (n.p.), 1789.
[7] British Parliamentary Papers, 'First Annual Report of the Poor Law Commissioners', *Sessional Papers, House of Commons*, Vol. 35, (1835).

65 per cent respectively while the corresponding figures in 1835 were 39, 36 and 47 per cent. Although child labour remained important in 1830 and was regarded by factory managers as important poor for future factory workers as well as training them for this work, there was already a shift away from often inefficient employment of children to an experienced adult workforce. For factory managers, child labour functioned as a form of apprenticeship and, in the Factory Queries of 1833, 84 per cent of the responses from 194 cotton mill managers from Cheshire, Lancashire and Derbyshire asserted that workers employed from 'infancy' were preferable though they differed over when they should start work. [8] Some argued that children should begin work under 12 while others suggested that, as long as they began work before 15, they could be 'effective workers'. Many mill managers claimed that poor parents pressed them into accepting children under 12, while others acknowledged the advantage of the low wages of very young children.

Comparison between inexperienced migrant workers and experienced young factory workers suggests that the latter earned higher wages than inexperienced workers of the same age. The House of Lords Reports of 1818 and 1819 indicated that local males ages 19-21 averaged 10.6 years of factory experience and local females 8.4 years. [9] Wages for local male workers and women aged 19-21 were respectively 58 and 19 per cent higher than those for migrants with two years' experience. Workers recognised that child labour represented future competition for adult jobs. This was particularly a concern among mule-spinners, who held the best-paid jobs in the mills. In 1829, John Doherty, the secretary of the Manchester mule-spinners, proposed that only piercers who were sons or brothers of mule-spinners should be taught to spin while spinners sought to preserve their privileged position by controlling children's work experience.

The extent to which child labour was used is difficult to estimate with any accuracy. In the early-nineteenth century, the labour market for children was not a national market but rather a regional phenomenon with high levels of child labour in manufacturing

---

[8] British Parliamentary Papers, 'Factories Inquiry Commission Supplementary Report Part I,' *Sessional Papers, House of Commons*, Vol. 19, (1834).

[9] British Parliamentary Papers, 'Minutes of Evidence on the Health and Morals of Apprentices and others employed in Cotton Mills and Factories', *Sessional Papers, House of Lords*, Vol. 96, (1818), appendix, and 'Minutes of Evidence on the State and Condition of the Children employed in Cotton Factories', *Sessional Papers, House of Lords*, vol. 110, (1819), appendix.

districts with lower incidence in rural and farming districts. The House of Lords Reports of 1818 and 1819 suggested that nearly half of workers in factories started when they were under 10 and a further 27.9 per cent started between the age of 10 and 13. Children under 13 made up roughly 10 to 20 per cent of the workforce in cotton, wool, flax, and silk mills in 1833. The employment of youths between the age of 13 and 18 was higher than for younger children, comprising roughly 23 to 57 per cent of the workforce in cotton, wool, flax, and silk mills. The employment of children in textile factories remained high until the mid-nineteenth century. The 1841 Census showed than the textile industry employed 107,000 children and, although there was a decline by 1851, they still accounted for a significant proportion of workers in the industry.

Children and youth also involved in coal and metal mines in Britain. In 1842, the proportion of the workforce in coal and metal mines that were children and youth ranged from 19 to 40 per cent. A larger proportion of the workforce of coal mines used child labor underground while more children were found on the surface of metal mines 'dressing the ores', separating the ore from the dirt and rock. By 1842, one-third of underground labour in coal mines was under the age of 18 while a quarter of the workforce of metal mines were children and youth. After the Mines Act of 1842 was passed, which prohibited girls and women from working in mines, fewer children worked in mines. Even so in 1851, children and youth (under 20) were 30 per cent of all coal miners in Great Britain. In 1838, roughly 5,000 children were employed in the metal mines of Cornwall and by 1842, as many as 5,378 children and youth worked in the mines. In 1838 Lemon found that in 124 tin, copper and lead mines in Cornwall, 105 employed children who comprised from as little as 2 per cent to as much as 50 per cent of the workforce with an average of 20 per cent. [10] According to Jenkin the employment of children in copper and tin mines in Cornwall began to decline by 1870. [11]

Factory children fell into two types: parish apprentice children and free labour children. [12] Factory owners could not forcibly subjugate free labour children and compel them to work in conditions

---

[10] Lemon, Sir Charles, 'The Statistics of the Copper Mines of Cornwall', *Journal of the Royal Statistical Society*, Vol. 1, (1838), pp. 65-84.

[11] Jenkin, A. K. Hamilton, *The Cornish Miner: An Account of His Life Above and Underground From Early Times*, (George Allen and Unwin, Ltd.), 1927, p. 309.

[12] Honeyman, Katrina, *Child Workers in England, 1780-1820: Parish Apprentices and the Making of the Early Industrial Labour Force*, (Ashgate), 2007, pp. 175-199, 239-260, considers the exploitation of parish labour.

their parents found unacceptable. The situation, however, was very different for parish apprentice children and the first piece of factory legislation—the Health and Morals of Apprentices Act 1802—dealt specifically with parish not free child labour. These children, most of who were orphans, were legally in the custody of parish poor law officials and who were bound to these officials for long periods of unpaid apprenticeship. The conditions in which parish apprentices worked were often brutal, degrading and oppressive and, for both contemporaries and later historians, epitomised the 'evils' of factory system. For instance, the Sadler Report of 1832, regarded by the Hammonds as 'one of the main sources for our knowledge of the conditions of factory life at the time', painted a picture of unmitigated horror. [13] But Sadler was not an impartial observer and had falsified the evidence to support his case for a Ten Hours' Bill. R. H. Greg commented in 1837 that the work was:

...such a mass of ex-parte statements, and of gross falsehoods and calumnies, as probably never before found their way into any public document... [14]

While Friedrich Engels, hardly a supporter of capitalist factories, thought it a 'very partisan document, which was drawn up entirely by the enemies of the factory system for purely political purposes.'[15] There is, however, little doubt that factory conditions, especially in the smaller, older mills were frequently abysmal. They were poorly ventilated, noisy, and damp and poorly lit and were frequently unhealthy and dangerous places to work with large numbers of unguarded machines. Many of those who worked as children in the choking dust of coal mines died before they were twenty-five. In addition to poor working conditions, children laboured for up to fourteen hours a day, brutalised by overseers and adult workers. The cruelty and deprivation depicted by authors such as Charles Dickens and Thomas Hardy was commonplace during the Industrial Revolution and not just fictional exaggeration.

---

[13] Hammond, J. L., and Barbara, *Lord Shaftesbury*, (Constable), 1933, p. 16.
[14] Greg, R. H., *The Factory Question, Considered in Relation to Its Effects on the Health and Morals of Those Employed in Factories, and the "Ten Hours Bill" in Relation to Its Effects Upon the Manufactures of England, and Those of Foreign Countries...*, (J. Ridgway and Sons), 1837, p. 7.
[15] Engels, Friedrich, *The Condition of the Working Class in England*, (The Macmillan Co.), 1958, p. 192.

How and why was the 1833 Factory Act passed?

The emergence of the short-time or Ten Hour movement after 1830 has its origins in the late-eighteenth century when concerns about the deteriorating conditions in child employment emerged.[16] Early legislative efforts, however, depended largely on benevolent individuals. Sir Robert Peel senior was behind both the 1802 and 1819 Acts but he received considerable popular support from Lancashire cotton spinners, in liaison with at least three distinguishable groups. [17] The old labour aristocracies such as the east Midland framework-knitters, Yorkshire woollen croppers and the ubiquitous handloom weavers saw the factories with their technological innovations as threats to their social status and their

---

[16] Kydd, Samuel, *The History of the Factory Movement: From the Year 1802, to the Enactment of the Ten Hours' Bill in 1847*, 2 Vols. (Simpkin, Marshall, and Co.), 1857, Edler Von Plener, Ernst, *The English Factory Legislation, from 1802 Till the Present Time*, (Chapman and Hall), 1873, Cooke-Taylor, R. W., *The Factory System and the Factory Acts*, (Methuen), 1894, and Hutchins, B. L., Hutchins, Elizabeth L., and Harrison, Amy, *A history of factory legislation*, (P. S. King & Son), 1911, provide contemporary comment on the development of legislation. The shortest introduction to factory reform is Henriques, U., *The Early Factory Acts and their Enforcement*, (The Historical Association), 1971. Ward, J. T., *The Factory Movement 1830-1850*, (Macmillan), 1962, is the most detailed study though it has, in part, been superseded by Gray, R., *The Factory Question and Industrial England 1830-1860*, (Cambridge University Press), 1996. Driver, C., *Tory Radical: A Life of Richard Oastler*, (Oxford University Press), 1946, and Weaver, A., *John Fielden and the Politics of Popular Radicalism 1832-1847*, (Oxford University Press), 1987, are useful biographies. Hargreaves, John A., 'Reading on the edge of revolution? Richard Oastler (1789-1861)', in Hargreaves, John A., and Haigh, E. A. Hilary, (eds.), *Slavery in Yorkshire: Richard Oastler and the campaign against child labour in the Industrial Revolution*, (University of Huddersfield), 2012, pp. 201-228, is an importancorrective to Driver's biography. Finlayson, Geoffrey, *The Seventh Earl of Shaftesbury 1801-1885*, (Eyre Methuen), 1981, is a detailed biography that contains much on factory conditions. Nardinelli, Clark, *Child Labour and the Industrial Revolution*, (Indiana University Press), 1990, examines the most contentious of the questions surrounding factory conditions. Ward, J. T., (ed.), *The Factory System*, 2 Vols. (David & Charles), 1970, contains primary material.

[17] Innes, Joanna, 'Origins of the factory acts: the Health and Morals of Apprentices Act 1802', in Landau, Norma, (ed.), *Law, crime and English society, 1660-1830*, (Cambridge University Press), 2002, pp. 230-255, and Thomas, M. W., *The early factory legislation: a study in legislative and administrative evolution*, (Thames Bank Publishing Co.), 1948.

incomes. Some early pioneers of social medicine drew attention to the insidious effects of factory labour on health.[18] Finally, Northern clergymen of the old High Church tradition and those tinged with new Evangelical enthusiasm played important roles in successive factory campaigns. In 1836, Richard Oastler, who believed in the notion of a 'Christian commonweal' wrote in a letter of the Archbishop of York:

> ...his only object was to establish the principles of Christianity, the principles of the Church of England in these densely people districts....the Factory question was indeed....a Soul-question -- it was Souls against pounds, shillings and pence.... [19]

In 1815, Peel, supported by Robert Owen, the progressive owner of the New Lanark Mill on the River Clyde, attempted unsuccessfully to bring in legislation to ban children under the age of ten from any employment. He continued to campaign inside and outside Parliament and a parliamentary inquiry into child labour in factories resulted in the Cotton Mills Act of 1819. The Act required that no child under the age of nine was to be employed in cotton mills, with a maximum day of 16 hours for all those under 16. But once again the means of enforcing such legislation remained a serious problem and there were only two convictions while it operated. A further burst of agitation in the 1820s by the cotton spinners led only to John Cam Hobhouse obtaining minor changes to existing legislation in 1825 and 1831 but these too were limited in scope and implementation. [20] Lancashire cotton operatives who were strong supporters of factory legislation became disillusioned with the lack of enforcement of existing law and were demoralised by the collapse of strikes against wage reductions. It is, however, clear that the Factory Movement began in Lancashire rather than with the better known Yorkshire agitation begin by Richard Oastler in 1830 and that it was the militant Cotton Spinner's Union that first created the rudiments of a popular organisation and gained support from the radical press.

The early industrial reformers lacked the organisation needed to mobilise extra-parliamentary pressure. The campaign between 1825 and 1829 had achieved little but it was at this stage that Richard Oastler, a Tory land steward from Huddersfield, burst upon the scene

---

[18] See, for instance, the comments in Ure, Andrew, *The Philosophy of Manufactures: or, An exposition of the scientific, moral and commercial economy of the factory system of Great Britain*, (Charles Knight), 1835, pp. 374-403.
[19] Cit, ibid, Driver, C., *Tory Radical: A Life of Richard Oastler*, p. 306.
[20] On Hobhouse, see, Zegger, Robert E., *John Cam Hobhouse: a political life, 1819-1852*, (University of Missouri Press), 1973.

when he sent his celebrated letter on 'Yorkshire Slavery' to the *Leeds Mercury*.[21] For Oastler, emotionally bound by the established interconnected web of customs, loyalties, ties, memories and services, liberalism spoke of men as 'free agents' while in practice they were 'wage-slaves' created when 'Money' and 'Machinery' drove a wedge between the nation's old landed and labouring interests. For Oastler, the cause of anti-slavery and child labour were 'one and the same'. Most of the founders of the Ten Hour Movement were Tories and Anglicans from northern industrial towns, committed to reviving the aristocratic idea that, if necessary, might be promoted through state intervention against both the dismantling of the paternal system and the new entrepreneurial ethos. They were as deeply hostile to parliamentary reform and workers' organisations as they were to Nonconformists, orthodox political economy and the newly rich manufacturers. Many of those who financed the movement, like Michael Sadler, were themselves well-established factory owners and members of the Tory urban elite facing a challenge locally from Dissenting entrepreneurs.[22]

It is possible to identify four principal pressure groups that favoured factory reform. There were the mill operatives themselves and their supporters, of whom Richard Oastler was the most prominent. Their demands for a 10-hour working day was used in the debate over child labour both as a way of exposing the hardship faced by children and as a way of seeking a limitation on the working day of adults. In the laissez-faire atmosphere of the period, any direct attempt to achieve state regulation of the hours of adult males was doomed to failure. But because juveniles aged 10-13 were an essential part of the workforce it was hoped that restrictions on their hours would percolate through to the rest. The reformers did not oppose

---

[21] Creighton, Colin, 'Richard Oastler, factory legislation and the working-class family', *Journal of Historical Sociology*, Vol. 5, (1992), pp. 292-320; Ward, J. T., 'Richard Oastler on politics and factory reform, 1832-1833', *Northern History*, Vol. 24, (1988), pp. 124-145.

[22] Lawes, Kim, *Paternalism and Politics: The Revival of Paternalism in Early Nineteenth-Century Britain*, (Palgrave), 2000, pp. 150-183, examines Sadler's contribution to factory reform. See also, Sadler, Michael T., *Protest Against the Secret Proceedings of the Factory Commission, in Leeds*, (F. E. Bingley), 1833, *Reply to the Two Letters of John Elliot Drinkwater, Esquire, and Alfred Power, Esquire, Factory Commissioners*, (F. E. Bingley), 1833, and *Factory statistics: the official table appended to the report of the committee on the ten-hour factory bill vindicated in a series of letters addressed to J. E. Drinkwater*, (Hatchards), 1836; Drinkwater, J. E., Bethune, John Elliot, and Power, Alfred, *Replies to Mr. M. T. Sadler's Protest Against the Factory Commission*, (Baines and Newsome), 1833.

child labour as such but were merely against unregulated labour. They judged legislation not by its direct effect on child labour but by its indirect effect on the position of adult workers. There were also Tory humanitarians among whom Lord Ashley was most active. They were concerned about the moral and religious deprivation of young workers and the ineffectiveness of existing protective legislation. Others such as William Wordsworth, Robert Southey and William Cobbett looked back to a pre-industrial 'golden age' and blamed the industrial revolution for alienating workers from the land and forcing children to play a major role in the workforce. [23] Finally, a body of reformers came to the fore in the debates over amendments to the factory legislation that occurred in the 1840s. They included active supporters of laissez-faire principles, such as Thomas Babington Macaulay, but who argued for regulation on economic and moral grounds. Child labour, they suggested, damaged the health of youngsters who were then later in life not able to achieve their potential productivity. Restricting child labour was a rational means of promoting investment in the country's future workforce.

The early Ten Hour movement had a number of strands, loosely held together by a rhetoric that combined evangelical religion, the threat posed by unregulated economic change, populist radical ideas of fair employment and labour as property and patriarchal values. [24] Such rhetoric embodied notions of a 'moral economy' in opposition to the aggressive economic liberalism and free-market principles of the manufacturers' lobby. [25] Oastler spoke of the 'monstrous' nature of the factory system and the 'terrors' of child labour. He denounced political economy as 'earthly, selfish and devilish' and pointed to the abnormality of 'the tears of innocent victims (wetting) the very streets which receive the droppings of an Anti-Slavery Society'. These attributes cut across the political spectrum from traditionalist Tories to Whigs, to radical artisans and factory workers who shared many of these views. It was saturated in romantic imagery, of the 'golden age' of domestic production and of seeing their labour in terms of 'freedom', 'tyranny' and 'slavery'. Paternalism was not confined to Oastler and the Ten Hour movement

---

[23] On this issue, see, Stevenson, Warren, *The myth of the golden age in English Romantic poetry*, (Institut für Anglistik und Amerikanistik, Universität Salzburg), 1981.

[24] For what follows see Gray, Robert, 'The languages of factory reform in Britain c.1830-1860' in ibid, Joyce, Patrick, (ed.), *The historical meanings of work*, pp. 143-179.

[25] Lyon, Eileen Groth, *Christian Radicalism in Britain from the Fall of the Bastille to the Disintegration of Chartism*, (Ashgate), 1999, pp. 125-150, examines the Christian radicalism of the Factory movement.

and many manufacturers accepted their civic duty to engage actively in schooling, management of housing, charity and moral surveillance. Paternalistic controls over the labour force were justified in a language of mutual obligations and the mission of enlightened manufacturers as improvers of the poor. It was their competitive effectiveness and accumulation of capital that enabled employers to fulfil this moral mission and, in this sense, there was no contradiction between the economic ethics of political economy and the moral imperatives of industrial paternalism. Textile manufacturers found themselves in a vulnerable and isolated position when the factory issue exploded in the early 1830s and were divided over their response to it. 'Evils' were recognised, but in terms far removed from the language of wage-slavery. In the cotton districts, opponents pointed to the diminished rate of profit and increase in the cost of production if the hours of workers were reduced. Others emphasised the threat from foreign competition and the absolute rights of property.

During the winter of 1830-1831, there was a furious controversy in the Yorkshire press and rival views became polarised. [26] Oastler acted as the fulcrum of the agitation and as its central organiser. He possessed considerable oratorical skills and journalistic gifts; he controlled the central funds and he imparted a crusading verve to the movement. The question of child exploitation was a 'moral' one and Oastler became head of a network of 'short-time committees' that demanded the ten-hour day. A substantial number of pamphlets, petitions and tracts were issued and 'missionaries' were despatched throughout the textile areas of England and Scotland to highlight the horrors of child labour in the mills. Thousands of workers were willing to ignore the hostility of the Factory Movement's leaders to their political aspirations during the agitation for parliamentary reform 1830-1832, put aside their opposition to the excesses of the Church of England and turned a blind eye to the darker side of paternalism with its insistence on a harsh penal code, savage game laws and low wages and living conditions for the rural labourer and supported the Movement. [27]

In the event, the movement had little success with the Whig government and Peel and the opposition kept the agitation at arm's

---

[26] Royle, Edward,'Press and People: Oastler's campaign in 1830-32', in ibid, Hargreaves, John A., and Haigh, E. A. Hilary, (eds.), *Slavery in Yorkshire: Richard Oastler and the campaign against child labour in the Industrial Revolution*, pp. 145-172.

[27] For a short summary of the issues, see Ward, J. T., 'The Factory Movement', in Ward, J. T., (ed.), *Popular Movements 1830-1850*, (Macmillan), 1970, pp. 78-94.

length.[28] When Michael Sadler moved a Factories Regulation Bill in March 1832, he was obliged to accept the appointment of a Select Committee to take evidence from the operatives.[29] Meanwhile the factory masters organised a vigorous lobby to resist further legislation, arguing that shorter working hours could result only in a victory for foreign competition, leading to lower wages and unemployment. Sadler's seat was a casualty of the Reform Act and after the dissolution of Parliament in 1832 he sought but failed to be elected for Leeds in December. His replacement as parliamentary spokesman for the Ten Hour campaign, at the suggestion of the Reverend George Bull, was the young Evangelical Anthony Ashley Cooper.[30] The publication of Select Committee report in January 1833 brought the stark realities of conditions to Parliament and the wider public and led Anthony Ashley Cooper to introduce a Factory Bill.[31] There were largely justified criticisms, particularly from manufacturers that the Select Committee report was one-sided as it had only heard the workers' views. This led to an orchestrated petitioning campaign in the spring of 1833, for instance:

> *Mr. John Stanley* presented a Petition from the Master Manufacturers of Stockport, praying that further evidence might be taken before the Factories' Bill was passed, in order that they might have an opportunity of clearing their character of the imputations cast upon them in the ex-parte evidence brought forward by Mr. Sadler, and admitted by him to be intended only to establish his views. He concurred in the prayer of the petition, but could not concur in some of its statements. The Bill brought in some years ago by Sir John Hobhouse had not had a fair trial [and] had not been tried at all in the woollen, the silk, or the hemp factories, so that how far it would protect the children employed was not known. He considered that the petitioners had made out such a case as entitled them to have an inquiry either by a Committee or a Commission.[32]

---

[28] *Hansard*, House of Commons, Debates, 28 February 1832, Vol. 10, cc894-5, 7 March 1832, Vol. 610, cc1222-5, 14 March 1832, Vol. 11, cc204-205, .

[29] For Sadler's speech on the second reading of the Factories Regulation Bill see, *Hansard*, House of Commons, Debates, 16 March 1832, Vol. 11, cc340-98., and his speech referring to ten hours, 7 June 1832, Vol. 13, cc500-5.

[30] Gill, J. C., *The ten hours parson: Christian social action in the eighteen-thirties*, (SPCK), 1959, pp. 81-83, Finlayson, Geoffrey *The Seventh Earl of Shaftesbury 1801-1885*, (Methuen), 1981, pp. 72-86.

[31] *Hansard*, House of Commons, Debates, 8 February 1833, Vol. 15, cc390-3.

[32] *Hansard*, House of Commons, Debates, 22 March 1833, Vol. 16, cc970-1.

This resulted in the government setting up a Royal Commission to investigate the employment of children in factories.[33] Its work coincided with the parliamentary debate on the abolition of slavery in the British Empire. The Whigs had effectively taken reform out of the hands of the Ten Hour Movement and it became a government sponsored issue.

Why did the Whigs take control of factory reform? Extra-parliamentary agitation occurred not only in the context of conflict between capital and labour but of other economic and social rivalries. Social, ideological, religious and political rivalry between industrialists and neighbouring agriculturalists was exploited by operatives who turned for protection from millowners to county JPs. The result was an Anglican Tory-Radical alliance on the factory question, grounded in notions of paternalism rather than the tenets of political economy and less inhibited in its support of the industrial poor than Whig Radicals. This alliance was weakened by the reform agitation of 1831-1832 but remained important till the late 1830s and the onset of Chartism. Parallel to this Tory paternalist approach was one supported by some Whig radicals and a group of philanthropic millowners in which Nonconformity was a unifying force. The agitation in Yorkshire had already convinced the Whigs that factory legislation was inevitable. Determining the composition of the Royal Commission ensured that the range of options available to them would be wider and less unpalatable to manufacturers than a Ten Hours bill. The Royal Commission Report was placed in the hands of Edwin Chadwick. [34] The report, produced in forty-five days, looked at factory conditions more dispassionately than the Select Committee. Its conclusions were not based on humanitarian grounds, the position adopted by the Ten Hour Movement, but on the question of economic efficiency. Chadwick argued that human suffering and degradation led to less efficient production and that a good working environment would lead to health, happiness and an effective workforce. Its recommendations focused on the question of children's employment and it was consequently criticised for failing to deal with the issue of adult labour.

The resultant Factory Act 1833 restricted children aged 9-14 (by stages) to 8 hours actual labour in all textile mills (except lace-

---

[33] *Hansard*, House of Commons, Debates,3 April 1832, Vol. 17, cc79-115, 3 June 1833, Vol. 67, cc79-115.
[34] Finer, S. E., *The Life and Times of Sir Edwin Chadwick*, (Methuen), 1952, pp. 50-68, and Brundage, A., *England's 'Prussian Minister': Edwin Chadwick and the Politics of Government Growth 1832-1854*, (Pennsylvania University Press), 1988, pp. 22-24

manufacture), with 2 hours at school; young persons under 18 to 12 hours; and, four Factory Inspectors were appointed to enforce the legislation. [35] Previous Acts had been restricted to the cotton industry, but the 1833 Act also applied to the older woollen producing communities in and around Yorkshire which had been ignored in previous legislation. However, the silk industry was given special consideration after vigorous lobbying from manufacturers who argued that the industry would perish without the employment of young children. Silk manufacture used a large number of workers who were below age 16 and they accounted for almost 80 per cent of the workforce in some workshops and mills. The 1833 Act was confined to children's work and applied only to textile mills but it did establish a small inspectorate responsible to the Home Office to enforce the legislation. Inspection was essential for making effective enforcement possible and providing a continuous stream of information about the conditions of workers in a range of industries. Despite the rhetoric of Oastler that magistrates, who heard the overwhelming majority of cases, obstructed conviction under the legislation, there is significant evidence that they were not unsympathetic to prosecutions and were prepared to convict. [36] Despite intense criticism of the 1833 Act and the problems encountered in enforcement, it would be unfair to underestimate the Whig achievement. The debates in 1832 and 1833 led to the issue being publicly aired as never before. [37] The extra-parliamentary movement may have been frustrated by what had been achieved and the 1833 Act may have not been based on any real principles, but it did mark an important stage in the emergence of effective factory legislation and underpinned the developments of the 1840s.

How did factory legislation develop in the 1840s?

The Ten-Hour movement had been out-manoeuvred by the Whigs and its campaign against the 1833 Act proved ineffective. In October 1833, Oastler formed the Factory Reformation Society to continue

---

[35] Lord Ashley moved the second reading, *Hansard*, House of Commons, Debates, 17 June 1833, Vol. 18, cc914-5; further debate took place on 5 July 1833, Vol.19, cc219-54, 18 July 1833, Vol. 19, cc883-97; 9 August 1833, Vol. 20, cc449-53, 12 August 1833, Vol. 20, cc527-31, 13 August, 1833, Vol. 20, cc576-8.
[36] Peacock, A. E., 'The successful prosecution of the Factory Acts, 1833-55', *Economic History Review*, 2nd series, Vol. 37, (1984), pp. 197-210.
[37] See, Wing, Charles, *Evils of the Factory System Demonstrated by Parliamentary Evidence*, (Saunders and Otley), 1837, Part II, for important contemporary comment.

the campaign but a month later, Robert Owen and John Fielden announced a Society for Promoting National Regeneration with the impractical but popular demand for an 8-hour day with 12 hours pay. Oastler rejected 'Regenerationist' invitations and it failed during the general Owenite collapse of 1834 carrying with it much of the Short Time agitation. From 1834, the Factory Movement had a chequered history.

Oastler and his supporters became increasingly involved in anti-Poor Law campaigns and there were growing local differences. Lancashire reformers, experienced in evasions of previous legislation, demanded that mill engines should be stopped at set times to make enforcement certain, a policy Oastler supported but 'dare not ask for'. Some of the parliamentary spokesmen, such as Hindley and Brotherton, were prepared to compromise on the Ten Hours demand and adopted a gradualist approach by arguing for 11 hours.[38] In Scotland, committees in Aberdeen, Arbroath, Edinburgh and Paisley tended to rely on the support of professional men and Presbyterian ministers while the Glasgow committee was under working-class control until 1837. Yorkshire was less prone to division and controversy within the organisation but even here there were differences.[39]

The redefining of the factory question is part of the shaping of the Victorian state and the accommodation of interests within it. If the 1830s saw the elaboration of Benthamite responses to reform and vigorous resistance to them at both populist and elitist levels, the 1840s saw modifications to this project through its incorporation into a broader consensus that shaped the agenda of the 'condition of England' question. Across the political elite there was a growing recognition, in part a response to the mass Chartist movement that there was a 'softening' of the attitudes of the state after 1843 and that it began to make legislative and administrative concessions to Chartist grievances. The writing of the new public agenda owed something to expert knowledge and the role of the factory inspectorate. Initially the inspectors had been inclined to defer to the expertise of leading employers but the pressure of public agitation pushed them into taking a more independent line. In 1840, Leonard Horner, a leading inspector, presented the benefits of factory regulation in terms of moral order and economic efficiency appealing to the longer-term rational interests of employers and workers. The issue was not the

---

[38] For instance, *Hansard*, House of Commons, Debates, 9 May 1836, Vol. 33, cc737-88.

[39] See, Ward, J. T., 'The Factory Reform Movement in Scotland', *Scottish Historical Review*, Vol. 41, (2), (1962), pp. 100-123.

introduction of new legislation, but fulfilling the intention of existing law by taking action to remedy defects in the 1833 Act. The key issue was enforcement.

During the 1830s, Oastler and the Ten Hour had projected a vision in which the regulation of the factory and the protection of labour was the key to remedying social distress. In the 1840s, the factory question can be seen through the language of negotiation within a growing consensus in favour of further regulation. Two particular emphases worked to incorporate social criticism about the distress, moral degeneration and Chartist threat and the awareness of working-class conditions, into a liberal vision of a rationalised factory system. The development of state regulation increasingly resulted in distinctions being made between 'good' and 'bad' factories and of the need to improve the 'bad'. The agenda of the 'condition of England' extended into mines, child and female labour generally, the weavers, out-work and 'sweating' and urban conditions. As a result, the factory lost its centrality as a focus of social concern. Public opinion saw social problems as separate and the evils of the factory was by no means the worst form of social distress.

The pace of the campaign of the 1840s varied considerably. Ashley Cooper failed to inject 'ten hours' into unsuccessful bills in 1838, 1839 and 1841. [40] By 1840, the Inspectors were also in favour of further reform and hopes rose with the return of the Conservatives under Sir Robert Peel in 1841. [41] The issue of social reform was, in Peel's mind, linked to successful economic conditions. These would enable economic growth, create new jobs and so stimulate consumption. Peel was sceptical of the value of direct government intervention in solving social problems. Free market solutions were more effective. He recognised that government could not abdicate all responsibility in the 'social question' but, like many contemporaries, believed that its role should be severely limited and definitely cost-effective. Peel remained fixed in his opposition to the Ten Hour movement right up to the passage of the 1847 Factory Act. He accepted the argument of political economists that wages would fall under a ten-hour day and the cost of production would increase with consequences for rising prices. This was not a doctrinaire approach but one grounded in a genuine concern for the welfare of workers. In

---

[40] For Ashley's role in the 1840s, see ibid, Finlayson, Geoffrey, *The Seventh Earl of Shaftesbury 1801-1885*, pp. 173-270. See also, *Hansard*, House of Commons, Debates, 25 February 1839, Vol. 45, cc879-93, 4 August 1840, Vol. 55, cc1260-79.

[41] *Hansard*, House of Commons, Debates, 4 March 1839, Vol. 45, cc1164-87, for Ashley's comments on the Factory Commissioners' Report for 1838.

1841, this concern was mistaken by a West Riding short-time deputation as an acceptance of the ten hour principle. This led to widespread and misleading publicity, raising then shattering workers' hopes and intensifying their hostility to the government during 1842.

Peel was, however, prepared to accept intervention to control working conditions when convinced that the moral case was overwhelming. He opposed Ashley over ten-hour legislation because he believed that the moral case was weaker than the economic one. However, he was prepared to accept the moral arguments implicit in the Mines and Collieries Act 1842. Working conditions in collieries were dangerous and children and women played an important part in mining coal. In 1840, a Royal Commission was established to investigate the working conditions of children in coalmines and manufactories. Its findings were horrific with children as young as five or six working as 'trappers' (operating doors to enable air-coursing). There were also many comments about the poor health of the mining community. Artists were employed to go underground and make sketches of workers. [42]

These appeared in the Commissioners' *Report* published in 1842. They were graphic and immediate and public opinion was shocked. [43] Shaftesbury drafted a bill that became law at the end of 1842. [44] It banned the employment of women and boys under 10 underground but allowed parish apprentices between 10 and 18 could continue to work in mines. There were no clauses relating to hours of work and inspection could only take place on the basis of checking the 'condition of the workers'. Many women were annoyed that they could no longer earn much needed money. [45] Further legislation in 1850 addressed the frequency of accidents in mines. The Coal Mines Inspection Act introduced inspectors of coal mines, set out their powers and duties and placed them under the supervision of the Home Office. The Coal Mines Regulation Act of 1860 improved

---

[42] *Hansard*, House of Commons, Debates, 7 June 1842, Vol. 63, cc1320-64.
[43] Those who favoured reform also used literature as propaganda. In 1839-1840, Mrs Frances Trollope published her *The Life and Adventure of Michael Armstrong, the Factory Boy* in twelve shilling parts; see, Chaloner, W. H., 'Mrs Trollope and the Early Factory System', *Victorian Studies*, Vol. 4, (2), (1960), pp. 159-166.
[44] *Hansard*, House of Commons, Debates, 22 June 1842, Vol. 64, cc423-8, 1 July 1842, Vol. 64, cc936-8, and 5 July 1842, Vol. 64, cc999-1009, for third reading in the Commons, House of Lords, Debates, 1 August 1842, Vol. 65, cc891-3, on passing third reading in the Lords.
[45] John, Angela V., 'Colliery legislation and its consequences: 1842 and the women miners of Lancashire', *Bulletin of the John Rylands University Library of Manchester*, Vol. 61, (1978), pp. 78-114.

safety rules and raised the age limit for boys from 10 to 12. [46]

There was an obvious difference between Ashley's proposals and the government's own initiatives in social legislation. For Ashley, it was a crusade; the government was more concerned with the promotion of social and political order. Peel's good intentions were insufficient to dampen class and sectarian antagonisms that intensified during the industrial distress and disturbances of 1841 and 1842. The 'Plug Plots' of mid-1842 [47] speeded government action and in March 1843, the Home Secretary, Sir James Graham introduced a Factory Bill that would restrict children aged 8-13 to 6½ hours' work with three hours' daily education in improved schools largely controlled by the Church of England. Peel and Graham agreed on the importance of improving educational provision for the working population and making the educational clauses of the 1833 Factory Act effective. Graham also believed in the importance of education as a means of social control emphasising the moral content of schooling. [48] He was convinced that the riots in 1842 were the result of declining religious attendance. It was necessary, he told Parliament to:

> ...rescue the rising generation in the manufacturing districts from the state of practical infidelity... [only if] the education of the rising youth should be the peculiar care of the Government could the moral tone of the nation be elevated. [49]

For the state to sponsor religious training in factory schools meant, to some degree favouring the Church of England. Graham anticipated opposition and took exceptional care in drafting the educational clauses of the proposed bill. He consulted two of his

---

[46] On the Mines Act 1843, see, ibid, Finlayson, Geoffrey, *The Seventh Earl of Shaftesbury 1801-1885*, pp. 182-189, and Heesom, Alan, 'The Coal Mines Act of 1842, social reform, and social control', *Historical Journal*, Vol. 24, (1981), pp. 69-88. See also, MacDonagh, Oliver, 'Coal Mines Regulation: the first decade, 1842-52', in Robson, R., (ed.), *Ideas and Institutions of Victorian Britain: Essays in honour of George Kitson Clark*, (Barnes and Noble), 1967, pp. 58-86.

[47] Jenkins, Mick, *The General Strike of 1842*, (Lawrence & Wishart), 1980, surveys the wave of strikes with a particular emphasis on Lancashire.

[48] Ward, J. T., *Sir James Graham*, (Macmillan), 1967, and Erickson, A. B., *The public career of Sir James Graham*, (Blackwell), 1952, are complementary biographical studies. Donajgrodzki, A. P., 'Sir James Graham at the home office', *Historical Journal*, vol. 20 (1977), pp. 97-120, is a useful article.

[49] *Hansard*, House of Commons, Debates, 24 March 1843, Vol. 67, cc1411-77.

factory inspectors: Leonard Horner, who he believed had some influence with the Nonconformists, and Robert Saunders, who had the confidence of the Bishop of London. [50] He also drew on the educational expertise of James Kay-Shuttleworth. [51]

Graham's proposal for state assistance in the education of factory children was motivated by the need to raise the 'moral feeling' of the people as a counter to radical agitation but Nonconformists and Roman Catholics believed it favoured the Church of England unfairly.[52] Fear and prejudice came together in the massive campaign by Nonconformist pressure groups coordinated by the United Conference, stressing the virtues of 'voluntarism' and professing concerns about the 'Romanising' effects of the Oxford Movement. Within two months, it had organised a petition to Parliament containing over two million signatures. In June 1843, the education clauses were withdrawn but the government remained committed to proceeding with the remainder of the bill. [53] However, it was not until the following February that Graham submitted a truncated bill. The Factory Act 1844 actually effected considerable improvements: children (8-13) became 'half-timers', working 6½ hours; dangerous machinery was to be fenced in; women shared the young persons' 12 hour restriction; and, it was permissible for a factory to operate for fifteen hours in a day. [54]

Oastler mounted a major campaign but he was unable to graft a '10 hour clause' on to the revised factory bill. Ashley moved a ten hour amendment that carried with 95 Conservatives supporting it.[55] Peel refused to accept this or compromise with eleven hours and the bill was only passed by his threat of resignation unless his wayward

---

[50] For the broader context of the government's relationship with the Bishop of London, see Welch, P. J., 'Blomfield and Peel: A Study in Cooperation between Church and State, 1841-46', *Journal of Ecclesiastical History*, Vol. 12, (1961), pp. 71-84.

[51] *Hansard*, House of Commons, Debates, 1 May 1843, Vol. 68, cc1103-30, 22 May 1843, Vol. 69, cc668-9, consider the nature of the religious question in the proposed bill.

[52] Ward, J. T., and Treble, James H., 'Religion and education in 1843: reaction to the 'Factory Education Bill'', *Journal of Ecclesiastical History*, Vol. 20, (1969), pp. 79-110.

[53] Graham gave his reasons for withdrawing the educational clauses, *Hansard*, House of Commons, Debates, 15 June 1843, Vol. 69, cc1567-70.

[54] *Hansard*, House of Commons, Debates, 25 March 1844, Vol. 73, cc1482-525, 29 March 1844, Vol. 77, cc1666-71.

[55] *Hansard*, House of Commons, Debates, 15 March 1844, Vol. 73, cc1073-155.

supporters rescinded their earlier vote. [56] The debate on the ten hour amendment developed over the next two months and forced the government into a series of difficult manoeuvres. Initially, Peel and Graham argued against Ashley on economic grounds. Peel was prepared to pass laws preventing exploitation of children and women but he argued adult males were free agents and the law should not interfere with market forces. Even so, he doubted whether employers would pay a twelve hour rate for ten hours work. Graham warned the Commons that the reduction of two hours' work might damage British industry by reducing productivity, thus lowering profits and ultimately wages. Not all members of the House were convinced by this argument. There was also an important political motivation in supporting Ashley. The agricultural interest, upset of Peel's liberalised tariff policy and angered by the activities of the Anti-Corn Law League saw an easy opportunity for revenge against manufacturers. This mixture of motives accounts for the surprising victory on 18 March 1844 in committee of Ashley's amendment by 179 to 170. [57] However, four days later, when the specific clause of the Ten Hours' Bill was presented, the vote went against Ashley. [58]

Ashley returned to factory reform the following year. The Royal Commission on the employment of children had investigated abuses not only in mines and collieries but in numerous other unregulated industries. Ashley was determined to extend government regulation to these exempted industries and concentrated on calico printing. Since it was a textile industry, he thought that the restrictions on work contained in the 1844 Factory Act could be extended with relative ease. His proposal to limit the hours of children and women in calico printing was introduced to the Commons in February 1845 and initially attracted some support from the government. [59] The result on this occasion was a compromise. The government agreed with those parts of Ashley's bill that provided education for children under thirteen and prohibited the employment of children under eight and night work for children and women. However, it did not agree with restrictions on the hours of children between eight and thirteen years old arguing that the employment of children in calico printing was

---

[56] Stewart, R., 'The Ten Hours and Sugar Crises of 1844: Government and the House of Commons in the Age of Reform', *Historical Journal*, Vol. 12, (1969), pp. 35-57.

[57] *Hansard*, House of Commons, Debates, 18 March 1844, Vol. 73, cc1177-267.

[58] *Hansard*, House of Commons, Debates, 22 March 1844, Vol. 73, cc1371-464, Ashley lost by three votes: 183 to 186.

[59] *Hansard*, House of Commons, Debates, 18 February 1845, Vol. 77, cc638-68.

more necessary than in other industries. With Ashley's acceptance of the government's position, an effective compromise was reached and the measure passed into law. [60]

There was, however, considerable disappointment in the textile towns and this provoked compromises and local negotiations. A series of conferences sought to maintain unity by reviving the Ten Hours Bill in Parliament, and after a wide winter campaign Ashley Cooper moved for leave to introduce it in January 1846. [61] However, the debate over industrial conditions was now overshadowed by the nation-wide controversy over the Corn Laws. Ashley felt morally obliged to resign his seat and Fielden took his place as parliamentary leader but lost his seat in May. [62] As another campaign was mounted in the autumn, a gathering industrial recession weakened the case for opposition. Final Whig attempts to compromise on 11 hours were defeated and Fielden triumphed in May 1847 [63] with the Ten Hours Act receiving the royal assent in June. [64]

Northern rejoicing was still premature. From 1848, there were reports of evasions in Lancashire and of masters' campaigns to repeal the Act. Several employers resorted to the relay system that meant that hours of work could not be enforced: the 15 hours per day clause in the 1844 Act had not been repealed and the 1847 legislation did not limit the number of hours machines could operate. As a result, employers quickly recognised that they could abide by the letter of the new law and still keep their mills working for 15 hours by the use of a relay system. Working children, women and young persons were subjected to interrupted shifts (two hours on, one hour off, for example) so the adult workers could be kept at their machines for fourteen or more hours a day. Attempts by the factory inspectors to prosecute employers invariably failed in the magistrates courts. Gradually, a new campaign emerged to protect the Act but it was increasingly obvious that the Factory Movement was divided: Ashley Cooper and a 'liberal' group were prepared to accept some

---

[60] *Hansard*, House of Commons, Debates, 2 April 1845, Vol. 78, cc1368-89, House of Lords, Debates, 30 May 1845, Vol. 80, cc1027-33.

[61] *Hansard*, House of Commons, Debates, 29 January 1846, Vol. 83, cc378-411.

[62] See *Hansard*, House of Commons, Debates, 29 April 1846, Vol. 85, cc1222-50, for Fielden's proposal for ten hour legislation. See also, House of Commons, Debates, 13 May 1846, Vol. 86, cc466-536, and 22 May 1846, Vol. 86, cc997-1080.

[63] *Hansard*, House of Commons, Debates, 3 May 1847, Vol. 92, cc306-12, deals with the third reading that passed the Commons by 151 to 88.

[64] Ibid, Weaver, A., *John Fielden and the Politics of Popular Radicalism 1832-1847*, pp. 249-281.

compromise while Oastler was not.[65] A test case on the legal status of the relay system in the Court of Exchequer (*Ryder v Mills*) was heard in early 1850 and the employers' liberal interpretation of the law upheld.[66]

The Factory Act 1850 finally legislated for what was called a 'normal day'.[67] The term derived from the custom that developed in the eighteenth century limiting the hours of work of craftsmen in most trades to those that could be worked, with breaks between 6 am and 6 pm. The Act required that young persons and women should only work between these two customary times, starting and ending one hour later in winter, with one and a half hours for meals and ending at 2pm on Saturdays with half an hour for breakfast. This meant they would work 10½ hours a day Monday to Friday and 7½ hours on Saturdays increasing their working week from 58 to 60 hours. Although textile workers now worked a shorter working week than most manual labourers, their anger over what they saw as the betrayal of the ten-hour principle was intense. Attempts to include children in the 'normal day' failed and, as a result, men might work up to 15 hours, aided by relays of children beyond the hours allowed for women and young persons. Children only received their fixed day in the 1853 Factory Act.[68] This legislation effectively limited the running of textile factories to twelve hours each day with 1½ hours set aside for meals. Disraeli only restored the '10 hours' in 1874. In the meantime, however, similar legislation had been extended to a wide range of workers.

After campaigns lasting twenty years and the passage of factory legislation in 1833, 1844, 1847, 1850 and 1853, the regulation of factory labour amounted to this.[69] Adult males over 18 were unregulated but three 'protected' classes of workers had been established: children between the ages of 8 and 13; young persons between the ages of 14 and 18; and women. Children could not enter factories until they were 8 years old and their work was restricted to 6½ hours a day. However, those hours could be worked any time between 5.30 am and 8.30 pm and nothing prevented them being

---

[65] *Hansard*, House of Commons, Debates, 14 March 1850, Vol. 109, cc883-933.
[66] Ibid, Finlayson, Geoffrey, *The Seventh Earl of Shaftesbury 1801-1885*, pp. 295-296.
[67] *Hansard*, House of Commons, Debates, 6 June 1850, Vol. 111, cc823-56, 14 June 1850, Vol. 111, cc1234-83, House of Lords, Debates, 19 July 1850, cc5-10.
[68] *Hansard*, House of Commons, Debates, 5 July 1853, Vol. 128, cc1251-90; the legislation received the Royal Assent on 20 August 1853.
[69] Ibid, Ward, J. T., *The Factory Movement 1830-1850*, pp. 505-506.

used in relays throughout that time. Women and young persons were classed together and their hours were restricted to 10½ hours daily (exclusive of meals) between 6 am and 6 pm five days a week with an 8 hour day on Saturdays. Finally, the legislation was supervised by regional Inspectors and their assistants who made quarterly reports to the Home Office.

Factory reform had some bearing on the making of mid-Victorian industrial paternalism. The consensual rhetoric of factory reform could, however, have different meanings in particular contexts. For workers, the reforms were important as a symbol of 'industrial legality', especially where trade unions were relatively weak. The construction of women and children as protected categories reinforced notions of the adult male 'breadwinner' as an independent free labourer. Much of the debate concerned the drawing of boundaries; between morality and the market, dependent and free agents, the state and the rights of property, the household, the factory and the school. Factory reform reflected a recognition that the free market existed within a moral and legal framework.

How were working conditions improved after 1850?

The Ten Hours Act, together with the repeal of the Corn Laws, came to be regarded as part of the symbolic 'social settlement' underpinning the apparent social harmony of the mid-Victorian period. The absence of factory acts became part of a collective memory of the 'bad old days', an unacceptable face of capitalism that no doubt helped to make its current face seem more benign. From the 1860s, the factory agitation could be recalled as part of the general progress of society. For employers, the improvements associated with legislation became part of an image of the well-regulated factory as the site of the economic, social and moral progress that the Victorian middle-classes liked to represent as its mission. The factory inspectors saw themselves as agents of moral improvement among workers as much as their protectors from unscrupulous employers. The factory movement as such disappeared in the 1850s with considerable success to its credit. As yet the legislation applied only to textiles and mines and Ashley, who in 1851 became the seventh Earl of Shaftesbury, continued the battle in Parliament to extend legislation to unprotected trades. In many respects, however, 1850 remained the legislative high water mark.

Why were the early Victorian acts expanded after 1860?

The first phase occurred naturally, if somewhat illogically, on the hitherto excluded textile industries and their satellites such as bleaching and dyeing. This process had begun in 1845 when the 1844 Act was extended to calico printing. Next the great range of other child-employing industries where working conditions and arrangements were similar to those in cotton manufacture came under review. These included pottery, the metal trades, paper-making, chemicals, glassworks and printing. Finally the principle of comparability was applied to units of production, whatever their size.

In the 1850s, the colour green became extremely popular as it was seen as new and modern. New colouring agents made green greener than ever before. [70] Unfortunately, arsenic was an important part of the process and as a result was liberally released into the atmosphere. Green wallpaper was a killer and when one Limehouse family lost four children the green wallpaper in their bedroom was analysed and every square foot was found to contain a lethal dose. Manufacturers, however, persistently denied that there was a problem among them William Morris who used green pigments widely and never accepted that they were harmful. For those who worked with these green pigments, especially in the fashion trade, this could prove fatal. They developed sores, ulcers and skin loss and the death of Matilda Scheurer, aged 19, made headlines. There was no disagreement about what killed her, the issue was whether it justified restricting the use of arsenic in manufacture. A leading medical journal decided that it was not the business of the state to 'hinder...young women from destroying themselves for a beggarly livelihood'. [71] More importantly perhaps, arsenic was valuable for trade. Parliament agreed. In 1883, the National Health Society drew up a list of safeguards for the use of arsenic, but none of them became law.

The critical development in the 1860s was the extension of existing provisions to new industries. In 1860, the bleach and dye were brought under existing legislation and four years later the Factory Acts Extension Act applied existing law to six new industries. In 1862, Shaftesbury suggested the establishment of the Children's Employment Commission to inquire into the conditions in the unregulated trades. Among the first trades to be examined was paper-staining, application of pigments and patterns to wallpaper demonstrating just how vulnerable arsenic workers of all ages were to injury from their employment. Despite this, the Commission's report played down the dangers of paper-staining and consequently there was

---

[70] Ibid, Whorton, James C., *The Arsenic Century: How Victorian Britain was Poisoned at Home, Work and Play*, pp. 294-323.
[71] *Medical Times & Gazette*, Vol. 2, (J. & A. Churchill), 1861, 30 November 1861, p. 558.

no action to regulate arsenic. [72] What led to a reduction of arsenic in wallpapers and dresses was consumer concerns about the use of poisons but this varied considerably from one industry to another. It was not until the 1890s that occupation health and 'dangerous trades' received statutory recognition. In 1892, the provisions for ventilations, sanitation and protective clothing in white lead production were extended to arsenic employments. Three years later, a further Factory and Worshop Act mandated regular inspection of industries involving arsenic, lead and phosphorous requiring cases of poisoning to be reported to the government. In the following twenty years, an average of six cases a year were recorded and there were only nine fatalities.

By 1866, the Commission had published five reports that the Russell government was preparing to act on. The last report was published in 1867 and drew attention to the practice of employing women and children in gangs in some agricultural counties.[73] The minority Conservative government took up these plans and in 1867 produced two measures. The Factory Acts Extension Act applied existing law to all factories employing over 50 people in industries such as metalwork, printing, paper and glassworks, while the main effects of the latter were felt in clothing. The Workshops Regulation Act covered premises including private houses with less than fifty workers and was enforced by local authorities instead of the factory inspectorate with limited success. The jurisdiction of the inspectorate over the handicrafts had to wait until 1878. Children under eight years were forbidden to work and older children were required to have ten hours' schooling a week. Young people and women were also protected, and in all the measures affected 1.4 million people. By 1870, over a thousand lives were still being lost in mining accidents each year. In 1872, the Coal Mines Regulation Act introduced the requirement for pit managers to have state certification of their training. Miners were also given the right to appoint inspectors from among themselves. The Mines Regulation Act, passed in 1881, empowered the Home Secretary to hold inquiries into the causes of mine accidents. It remained clear, however, that there were many

---

[72] *Royal Commission on Employment of Children in Trades and Manufactures Not Regulated by Law, First Report*, (HMSO), 1863, pp. 119-142.

[73] These gangs worked long hours under so-called gang-masters who frequently exploited and abused their workers. By the Agricultural Gangs Act 1888 all gang-masters had to be licensed by JPs, no boy or girl under eight was to be employed, and a licensed gang-mistress was necessary when women and girls were included in the gang.

aspects of mining that required further intervention and regulation.

By the late 1860s, over a wide range of industries the abolition of infant labour, the reduction of the hours of children to six and a half, the principles of 'protected classes' of children, young persons and women in the mills and workshops, the 60 hour week all round, compulsory education over the age of eight and rudimentary forms of the modern working week and of factory safety and health codes had been achieved. The circle of exceptions was ever-widening but it remained and this meant continued gross abuse of infant, child, adolescent and female labour elsewhere. The next decade saw the consolidation of early Victorian factory reform. The electoral consequences of the 1867 Reform Act were felt much more powerfully in the general election of 1874 than in 1868. [74] Factory hours were an issue, especially in Lancashire during the election resulting in a spate of legislation on factories and trade unions introduced by Disraeli's Conservative administration (1874-1880). In 1874 and 1878, there were Factory Acts and in 1875 the Trade Union Act, Conspiracy and Protection of Property Act and the repeal of the remaining master and servant legislation. The 1874 Factory Act was the work of Richard Cross, Disraeli's Home Secretary. It finally established the ten-hour day, the historic working-class goal, as far as the factories and workshops embraced in the 1867 legislation were concerned. It carried forward for the first time in a quarter of a century the frontier of regulation: the minimum age of half-time employment was raised from eight, which it had been since 1844, to ten; the minimum age for full-time employment was raised from thirteen, established since 1833, to fourteen; and, women and young persons were specifically included in the body of 'protected persons', who were to receive the benefits of the ten-hour day. Men were deliberately excluded: they gained the ten-hour day not in their own right but through the accident of working side by side with the protected persons. The Factory Act 1878, followed from a Royal Commission established in 1876, and, though the more comprehensive act, it was essentially a consolidating Act pulling together all the provisions into one scheme. The Factory Code now applied to all trades, no child under the age of ten could be employed, 10-14 year olds could only work for half days and women no more than 56 hours a week.

In coal mining, only one inspector (Hugh Seymour Tremenheere, a barrister and previously an Inspector of Schools) was appointed in 1842 and it was not until the Coal Mines Inspection Act

---

[74] Maehl, W. H., 'Gladstone, the Liberals, and the election of 1874', *Bulletin of the Institute of Historical Research*, Vol. 36, (1963), pp. 53-69.

1850 that officials were empowered' to make underground inspections.[75] The number of inspectors was raised to four in 1850, six in 1852 and twelve in 1855. Even this gave each inspector an impossibly large area to administer and this was equally true of the factory inspectorate where a reorganisation in 1839 left each inspector some 1,500 mills to supervise with the assistance of four superintendents. The total establishment for the factory inspectorate was raised to about twenty in 1839 and by 1868, despite the extension of legislation in the 1860s there were still only 35 inspectors and sub-inspectors, each responsible for a distinct geographical area. In 1844, a central office, known later as the Factory Department or Factory Office, was established under Home Office supervision exercised through the Domestic Department and, after 1896, the Industrial Department. These departments also carried out the specific duties of the Home Secretary under the Factory Acts. In 1878, a chief inspector was appointed directly responsible to the Home Secretary for the operation of the central office and district inspectorates. The Home Office appeared to have a deliberate policy of paying inspectors especially those concerned with mining at a low level and openly admitted that this would not command the services of first rate men. Initially mining inspectors were paid £400 a year plus travelling expenses. This was more than a mine manager but substantially less than a mine agent. The inspectors were also hampered by inadequate budgets: in the mid-1860s, the mines inspectorate had a budget of only £10,000 while that of the factory inspectorate was about a third more.[76]

The inspectorates were never intended as an industrial police force supervising industry's every move. They were intended to create a moral climate of observance by the principle of inspection. Indeed, it was strongly believed that inspectors should not take the ultimate responsibility for running decent industrial establishments from employers. Almost inevitably the inspectors did not act in concert as a unified service; in fact the 1876 Royal Commission questioned whether any unified policy existed. It was therefore common for inspectors to have different prosecution rates and to concentrate on different sorts of offences. In matters of fencing and safety at work the inspectorate was often quite ineffectual in raising standards but in other areas there were much greater levels of success. Well over

---

[75] Edmonds, E. L., and O. P., 'Hugh Seymour Tremenheere, pioneer inspector of schools', *British Journal of Educational Studies*, Vol. 12, (1963), pp. 65-76.

[76] Crooks, Eddie, *The factory inspectors: a legacy of the industrial revolution*, (Tempus), 2005.

three-quarters of prosecutions were successful and at times the rate was over 90 per cent. This was, in part, the result of prosecuting only in those cases that had a good chance of success.

The legislation of the 1870s represented the consummation of the early Victorian endeavour. 'Protection' was an unchallenged principle. Despite the changes in emphasis and disagreements within the factory debate, the combatants of 1833 soon found common ground in the notion of 'freedom of contract' as expressed by John Stuart Mill in his *Principles of Political Economy*. Mill started from the proposition that individuals were the best judge of their own interests and should be free to pursue them without interference from the state. This can be seen in Cross's speech to the Commons in 1874 when he paid lip-service to the old Chadwick doctrine of the free agent:

> So far as adult males are concerned there could be no question that freedom of contract must be maintained and men must be left to take care of themselves.[77]

However, Mill recognised that there were situations when this was unacceptable and where state intervention was justifiable. He accepted that children and 'young persons' could not be the best judges of their own interest: for them 'freedom of contract' was often 'but another name for freedom of coercion'.[78] This is the essence of liberal paternalism. He also argued that in areas such as education, good judgement might depend upon being subjected to it and therefore compulsion was justifiable.[79] Finally, there were 'matters in which the interference of law was required, not to overrule the judgement of individuals respecting their own interests, but to give effect to that judgement'. So, if some employers wished to establish a ten-hour day, they might be restrained from pursuing what they conceive to be in their own best interests because their rivals resisted the innovation. In these circumstances, state intervention was justifiable if 'the judgement of individuals respecting their own interests' were to be given effect.[80]

The depression of the 1870s inclined some to argue that factory

---

[77] *Hansard*, House of Commons, Debates, 6 May 1874, Vol. 218, cc1740-1803, at cc1793-1794.
[78] Mill, J. S., *Principles of Political Economy with Some of Their Applications to Social Philosophy: With Some of Their Applications to Social Philosophy*, 2 Vols. (C. C. Little & J. Brown), 1848, Vol. 2, pp. 532-536.
[79] Ibid, pp. 528-532.
[80] Ibid, pp. 552-554.

reform had gone too far and indeed was a major cause of the country's failure to keep up with her new industrial competitors. By that time, however, the principle of state intervention was well established and could not be reversed. Children, young people and women at work were the responsibility of the state, secured by legal provisions enforceable through a bureaucratic machine. Their effectiveness depended on the efficiency of the inspectorate itself but its size meant that it was always unlikely that there would be comprehensive coverage. The legislation of 1874 and 1878 may have marked the culmination of the legislative process begun in 1833 but there were harbingers of a new era. In the early 1870s, several bills were introduced in the Commons proposing a nine-hour day for men as for protected persons; and the Royal Commission of 1876 entered at length into a consideration of occupational health in factories. These were early indicators that the battle was to move on to new ground.

Why was legislation after 1880 largely concerned with women's work?

Legislation restricting or prohibiting women's work in mines or limiting their duties or hours of work featured prominently in the factory reforms of the 1830s and 1840s. When the issue was revisited in the 1880s with women's employment as its primary target the political context was of a very different complexion. Despite the ability of women's organisations to lobby parliament, state intervention in areas of social and economic concern was a growing reality despite voices raised in support of the values of individualism. The extension of the Factory Inspectorate after 1878 and the appointment of women inspectors signalled a more serious intention of enforcement by the authorities than had the earlier, more permissive, legislation. There was, however, considerable opposition to the idea of women inspectors with Alexander Redgrave, the Chief Inspector of Factories stating in his 1879 annual report:

> I doubt very much whether the office of factory inspector is one suitable for women...The general and multifarious duties of an inspector of factories would really be incompatible with the gentle and home-loving character of a woman... [81]

After several years of campaigning by the Women's Protective and Provident League, the London Women's Trades Council and others and amid growing support in Parliament, the first 'Lady Inspectors', May Abraham and Mary Paterson were appointed in

---

[81] *Annual Report of the Chief Inspector of Factories and Workshops for 1879*, p. 98.

1893. They were based in London and Glasgow respectively and earned an annual salary of £200. Much of their early work involved enforcing the Truck Acts, investigating women's hours of employment and enforcing health and safety in laundries. [82]

The issue was difficult for Victorian feminists dividing them less along class lines than along lines of political belief. [83] Three positions emerged in the debate. There was outright laissez-faire opposition to any proposals that restricted women's freedom. Some women saw restriction as a progressive and humane response of the state. Finally there were those who applauded the principle of protective legislation but only where its application was not on the basis of gender. The reaction of working women varied but there is little doubt that the impact of government reform was unwelcomed by many late-Victorian and Edwardian working people. The significant point is that women were legislated for without consultation. It was a case of men legislating for women. Women, from markedly different ideological camps, agreed that there was clearly a need to curb the excesses of employers whose interpretation of the free market was detrimental to the health and safety of their workers. They also broadly agreed where government legislated for mixed employment as in the 1878 Factory Act. But the 1878 Act specifically exempted workplaces exclusively employing women and the sweated trades were left untouched. Domestic service, the largest employer of female labour, and agricultural work, despite the governmental investigation of this area from the 1840s, remained largely unregulated. [84] The problem that the anti-legislation lobby had was

---

[82] Anderson, Adelaide, *Women in the Factory: An administrative adventure, 1893 to 1921*, (E. P. Dutton and Co.), 1922, is a valuable contemporary account. McFeely, Mary Drake, *Lady Inspectors: The Campaign for a Better Workplace 1893-1921*, (Basil Blackwell), 1988, is a useful study of how women fared as factory inspectors. Liversey, Ruth, 'The politics of work: feminism, professionalisation and women inspectors of factories and workshops', *Women's History Review*, Vol. 13, (2), (2004), pp. 233-262, is a case study of the first women appointed as official government factory inspectors in Britain.

[83] On the divisive nature of feminist approaches to women's work after 1870 and restrictions on it, see Holloway, Gerry, *Women and Work in Britain since 1840*, (Routledge), 2005, pp. 75-95.

[84] Blackburn, Sheila C., '"To be poor and to be honest…is the hardest struggle of all": sweated needlewomen and campaigns for protective legislation, 1840–1914', in Harris, Beth, (ed.), *Famine and fashion: needlewomen in the nineteenth century*, (Ashgate), 2005, pp. 243-258, Malone, Carolyn, 'Campaigning journalism: the *Clarion*, the *Daily Citizen*,

that in championing women's rights to all available employment, they came close to sanctioning work that clearly endangered health and safety.

By the end of the nineteenth century it is possible to see the sexual division of labour clearly in operation. Women were concentrated into a few low paid industries, where the great majority of employees were female and in domestic service. Attention shifted to the sweated trades, those trades often carried on in domestic workshops or actually in a house, where hours were notoriously long and wages low. In 1888, a Select Committee of the House of Lords was appointed to report on the sweated trades and in 1892 another Royal Commission was established on labour conditions generally but which provided valuable information on both sweated and non-sweated trades. The Factory Act 1891 made the requirements for fencing machinery more stringent, prohibited employers from employing women within four weeks after childbirth and raised the minimum age at which a child could work from ten to eleven. In 1901, the Factories and Workshops Act raised the minimum working age was raised to 12, introduced regulations regarding education of children, meal times and fire escapes.

In the major industries a new practice had grown up that had a further influence on the limiting of hours. This was the setting up of Wages Boards or Trades Boards on which both employers and employees were represented. In determining wages, working hours were also taken into consideration and this was particularly important as there was still no legislation specifically restricting the working hours of men. The Nottingham Hosiery Board dated from the 1860s while the Midland Iron and Steel Board came into informal existence in 1872 and was re-constituted more formally in 1876. [85] The Midlands Mining Wages Board also began informally in 1874, with an official position from 1883 onwards. In addition, in the Birmingham area, the 'alliance system' was used from time to time. Under this arrangement employers would fix wages and employ only one union, while the workmen would all join the union and work only for employers in the alliance. In this way it was hoped to avoid competitive wage cutting by employers. [86]

---

and the protection of women workers, 1898-1912', *Labour History Review*, Vol. 67, (2002), pp. 281-297.

[85] Taylor, E., *The better temper: a commemorative history of the Midland Iron and Steel Wages Board, 1876-1976*, (Iron and Steel Trades Confederation), 1976.

[86] See, Treble, John G., 'Interpreting the record of wage negotiations under an arbitral regime: a game theoretic approach to the coal industry

In 1909, the Sweated Industries Act (sometimes called the Trades Board Act) was passed, made necessary by the continued sweating of workers in certain trades. [87] The Act required wage boards to establish and enforce minimum rates of pay for workers in four of the most exploited industries: chain-making, box-making, lace-making and the production of ready-made clothing. This piece of legislation was gender neutral and covered homeworkers as well as factory hands. But it included only the most notoriously low-paying industries and less than a quarter of a million workers. In May 1910, the Chain Trade Board announced a minimum wage for hand-hammered chain-workers of two and a half pence an hour, nearly double the existing rate for many women. At the end of the Trade Board's consultation period on 16 August 1910, many employers refused to pay the increase. In response, the National Federation of Women Workers called a strike of chain-makers at Cradley Heath. It lasted 10 weeks and attracted immense popular support from all sections of society. Nearly £4,000 of donations were received by the end of the dispute from individual workers, trade unions, politicians, members of the aristocracy, business community and the clergy. Mary Macarthur, the founder of the NFWW in 1906, used mass meetings and the media, including the new medium of cinema, to bring the situation of the striking women to a wider audience. [88] Within a month, 60 per cent of employers had signed the 'White List' and agreed to pay the minimum rate, the dispute finally ended on 22 October when the last employer signed the list. [89]

The growth in shop work, a consequence of the development of retailing with the emergence of department stores, led to further legislation. The Shop Hours Regulation Act 1886 limited the hours

---

conciliation boards, 1893-1914', *Business History*, Vol. 31, (1989), pp. 61-80.

[87] Blackburn, Sheila C., 'Ideology and social policy: the origins of the Trade Boards Act', *Historical Journal*, Vol. 34, (1991), pp. 43-64, '"Princesses and Sweated-Wage Slaves Go Well Together": Images of British Sweated Workers, 1843–1914', *International Labor and Working-Class History*, Vol. 61, (2002), pp. 24-44 and *A fair day's wage for a fair day's work?: sweated labour and the origins of minimum wage legislation in Britain*, (Ashgate), 2007, and Melling, Joseph, 'Welfare capitalism and the origins of welfare states: British industry, workplace welfare and social reform, c.1870-1914', *Social History*, Vol. 17, (1992), pp. 453-478.

[88] Hamilton, Mary A., *Mary Macarthur: A Biographical Sketch*, (Parsons), 1925, pp. 76-96, examines her contribution to the strike.

[89] Ibid, Blackburn, Sheila C., *A fair day's wage for a fair day's work?: sweated labour and the origins of minimum wage legislation in Britain*, pp. 121-142, examines the Cradley Heath dispute.

of work of persons under eighteen to seventy four hours a week. The Shop Hours Act 1904 empowered local authorities to fix shop closing hours where two thirds of the shops agreed. The 1911 Shops Act introduced a weekly half-day holiday for all staff and said that shops should have at least one early closing day. The Shops Act 1912 consolidated existing legislation regulating employment in shops.

Women, unionism and protection

By the end of the nineteenth century, it is possible to see the sexual division of labour clearly in operation. Women were concentrated into a few low paid industries -- where the great majority of employees were female -- and in domestic service. Outworkers and domestic servants were isolated and divided workers and were to remain outside any co-operative protection or trade unionism. For the most part, feminist activity concentrated on the reality of the working woman's situation and on the necessity that brought it about rather than on theoretical arguments in favour or against women's work of this kind. It was largely a pragmatic and practical concern with the organisation of benefit societies and unions, with working conditions or wages, with the evils and miseries of outwork that motivated organisation within the working-classes. Interested middle-class women ran many of these organisations, though there was significant working-class input as well.

Trade unions in this period were male-dominated and most had the interests of male trade unionists at heart. [90] Unions were threatened by the way in which female labour was being used to undercut male wages and to 'dilute' male craft skills. Their reaction did not help women workers but does not explain the lowly place of women in the labour market. Women's trade unions tended to have their most marked successes in recruiting in periods when male union activity was riding high. In 1832 1,500 women card-setters at Peep Green Yorkshire came out on strike for equal pay. The Lancashire cotton mill women were active in trade unions. In 1859, the North

---

[90] Drake, B., *Women in Trade Unions*, (Labour Research Department), 1920, reprinted (Virago), 1984is the classic starting-point on this subject. See also, Soldon, Norbert C., *Women in British Trade Unions 1874-1976*, (Gill & Macmillan), 1978, Gordon, Eleanor, *Women and the Labour Movement in Scotland 1850-1914,* (Oxford University Press), 1991, that focuses on the jute industry in Dundee and Lown, Judy, *With Free and Graceful Step? Women and industrialisation in nineteenth century England*, (Polity), 1987. See also, Taylor, Anne, *Annie Besant: A biography,* (Oxford University Press), 1992, and Harrison, Barbara, *Not only the 'dangerous trades': women's work and health in Britain, 1880-1914*, (Taylor & Francis), 1996.

East Lancashire Amalgamated Society was formed for both men and women and in 1884 the Northern Counties Amalgamated Association of Weavers was established for male and female workers. But the most significant development was the emergence of separate women's unions.

Thus the Women's Protective and Provident League (WPPL) was established in 1874 at a time when men's unions were enjoying some success, both in membership terms and in establishing their legality. Similarly it was in the brief period of 'new unionism' in the late 1880s and early 1890s when unskilled labour became politicised that the Women's Industrial Council (WIC) and a score of women's unions were established. [91] The late-nineteenth century saw considerable industrial action by women as they campaigned for better wages and working conditions: the famous Bryant and May's match girl strike of 1888 but also the Dewsbury textile workers in 1875, [92] the Aberdeen jute workers in 1884, Dundee jute workers in 1885 and Bristol confectionery workers. It is a reflection of this era of separate female unions that in 1906 there were 167,000 members of all unions and that by 1914 this had risen to nearly 358,000.

In June 1888, Clementina Black gave a speech at a Fabian Society in London on Female Labour. In the audience, Annie Besant was horrified when she heard about the pay and conditions of the women working at the Bryant & May match factory. Henri Hyde Champion, editor of the *Labour Elector*, suggested that Mrs Besant should take up the cause of the match-girls and the following day, she went to Bryant & May's factory and interviewed some of the workers. The women earned 1s 4d for a sixteen hour day whereas the 1847 Factory Bill limited the day of work to 10 hours. However, they did not always receive their full wage because of a system of fines imposed by the Bryant & May management for talking, dropping matches or going to the lavatory without authorisation. The women worked from 6.30 am in the summer (8.00 am in winter) to 6.00 pm. If workers were late, the fine was half-day's pay. On 23 June, Besant published 'White Slavery in London' in *The Link* drawing attention to the dangers of phosphorus fumes and complaining about the low wages paid to the women who worked at Bryant and May. [93]

---

[91] Mappen, E., *Helping women at Work: The Women's Industrial Council 1889-1914*, (Hutchinson), 1985.
[92] Reynolds, Melanie, '"A man who won't back a woman is no man at all": the 1875 heavy woollen dispute and the narrative of women's trade unionism', *Labour History Review*, Vol. 71, (2), (2006), pp. 187-198
[93] Beer, Reg, *Matchgirls' Strike 1888: the struggle against sweated labour in London's East End,* (National Museum of Labour History), 1988, Raw,

Three women who supplied information for Besant's article were sacked. With the support of Champion, Besant and a socialist journal, *The Link*, the women at the firm decided to form a Union. Besant became its leader helping Bryant & May workers to organise a Match girls Union with George Bernard Shaw as treasurer of a £400 fighting fund. Nearly 700 match girls picketed their employers but the owners of the factory declared that they would 'not take back the strikers especially the ring leaders'. In spite of the public opinion on the girls' side, phosphorus was already illegal in Sweden and the USA, and the fact that many people stopped buying Bryant & May matches; the British government had refused to follow their example, arguing that it would alter free trade. After a three week strike, on 21 July Bryant & May agreed to the requirements of the match girls: re-employment of the sacked women and end of the fines' system. The strike stopped and for the first time an unskilled workers' union had triumphed in picketing for increased pay and better working conditions.

Catherine Booth as an active member of the Salvation Army was also concerned about women making matches; who were risking their health when they dipped their match heads in the yellow phosphorus. These women suffered from 'necrosis' or gangrene of the bones known as 'Phossy Jaw' caused by the toxic fumes of the yellow phosphorus. The whole side of their faces turned green, then black, discharging foul-smelling infection and finally death. Annie Besant, Henry Hyde Champion, Catherine and William Booth, and William Stead persevered to fight against the usage of yellow phosphorus. In 1891, the Salvation Army, still campaigning, opened its own match-factory in Old Ford, East London. The workers, using harmless red phosphorus, produced six million boxes a year. Whereas Bryant & May paid their workers just over two pence a gross, the Salvation Army paid their employees twice this amount. William Booth organised guided tours of MPs and journalists round this 'model' factory. He also took them to the homes of those 'sweated workers' who were working eleven and twelve hours a day producing matches for manufactures like Bryant & May. This bad publicity forced the enterprise to reconsider its actions and in 1901, Gilbert Bartholomew, the managing director of Bryant & May, finally declared it had stopped using yellow phosphorus.

Louise, *Striking a Light: The Truth About the Match Girls Strike and the Women Behind it*, (Hambledon Continuum), 2009, Beaver, Patrick, *The match makers,* (Melland), 1985, and Satre, Lowell J., 'After the match girls' strike: Bryant and May in the 1890s', *Victorian Studies*, Vol. 26, (1982), pp. 7-31.

Despite the success of the match girl strike, a host of disincentives stood in the way of the successful unionisation of women. Male unions at this stage were barely acceptable and themselves faced the problems of recruitment and of sustaining membership. The economic competition that women posed as a cheaper labour supply further determined men not in unionising women but in deterring their existence in the workplace. The sporadic nature of women's work, interrupted by pregnancies and domestic duties, might mean that in many cases work for women was simply a strategy for survival. Constant interruption added to poor pay and monotonous work would certainly not encourage women to invest energy in their identity as workers; their concentration in the less skilled sectors of employment not only further discouraged any such identity but made them vulnerable too. Unskilled unions were late in taking off because such workers were, by virtue of their lack of skill, expendable. In addition, the high number of women whose source of income derived from occupations such as outwork or domestic service, where congregation with their peers was precluded, was without any means of organisation. Many working women were isolated through their work and essentially untouched in this organisational context.

The Women's Protective and Provident League (WPPL) was established in 1874. Throughout its principal function was to offer help to working women in their own setting up of unions. It was never a trade union itself but a mechanism for pooling funds, expertise and experience. It offered sickness benefits and a host of related activities. It has been criticised for offering welfare instead of militancy and it was certainly far more of a propaganda and educational body. This should not, however, obscure our understanding of its political significance. Its initial gains were no more than modest. Its overall membership fluctuated wildly, though in 1884 there were less than a thousand women in its unions. Nonetheless in that time the League had succeeded, albeit temporarily, in organising a number of London trades from boot and umbrella makers, tailoresses and laundresses to feather and flower workers and box makers. Its activities extended beyond London to other industrial centres like Dewsbury and Leicester. Emma Paterson the wife of a cabinet maker[94], who had founded the League, died in 1886 and control passed to Lady Emilie Dilke. Under her leadership many of the former policies of the WPPL were abandoned and a more militant approach adopted. The name was

---

[94] Goldman, Harold, *Emma Paterson: she led woman into a man's world*, (Lawrence and Wishart), 1974

changed to the Women's Trade Union and Provident League in 1889 and to the Women's Trade Union League two years later. It sought more secure funding with the introduction of a scheme of affiliation for unions with a female membership and also sought to broaden its appeal outside London and by 1891, had seventeen London unions and six provincial affiliates.

The 1890s saw both a growth of women's trade union membership and the creation of several new women's organisations. The Women's Trade Union Association (WTUA) was founded in 1889 by women dissatisfied with the stance of the Women's Trade Union League, amongst them Clementina Black, Amie Hicks, Clara James and Florence Balgarnie. Its aims differed little from the parent body and it was to be a short-lived venture merging in 1897 with the Women's Industrial Council then three years old.[95] In 1870, 58,000 women were members of trade unions but by 1896, that has risen to 118,000, a figure representing some 7.8 per cent of all union members. Unionism was strong in the textile and especially cotton industry where women often outnumbered male operatives. Women had since the 1850s been incorporated in mixed unions. The common characteristic of all these organisations was their concern with the singularity of women's position and women's requirements in the worlds of work and leisure and even within the working-class home. These spheres could not be divorced given the disrupted employment patterns of most women workers. Even when the Women's Trade Union League opted for a policy of encouraging women into unions of mixed rather than single-sex membership in the 1890s, other specifically female issues remained central planks of their overall philosophy. Given the extensive nature of women's exploitation, feminist activity was necessarily split into a series of autonomous but linked campaigns.

The interest shown by so many better-off middle-class women in tackling the problems of industrial conditions and practices rather than the home lives of women is significant. Their choice of organisations offered help in establishing autonomous unions rather than merely philanthropic aid and often pious moralising. There were certainly class tensions between the middle-class activists and working-class women. However, despite the mistakes the failures and lapses into philanthropy, feminist organisations in this central area of working-class women's work represented a serious attempt at broadening the notion of sisterhood beyond the parameters of class.

---

[95] Ibid, Mappen, E., *Helping Women at Work: The Women's Industrial Council 1889-1914.*

When and why did hours of work and safety become political issues?

If one explanation for the early opposition to factory reform was ignorance of conditions, this was no longer the case after the 1860s. In addition to Royal Commission and Select Committee reports, there were annual Reports of the Mines Inspectors and the Inspectors for Factories and Workshops that became more detailed as the century advanced. The working week after 1850 was gradually reduced in length. Although it was still a six day week, Saturday labour was less than before and only a half-day was worked in many trades from the 1870s onwards. Working men acquired four statutory holidays with the passing of the Bank Holiday Acts in 1871 and 1875. By 1900, a week's holiday a year was not unknown though it was more likely to be enjoyed by skilled than unskilled workers. In 1908, the Eight Hours Act was passed fixing the working day for miners. [96] Regulations grew increasingly complex in the area of safety at work. The Coal Mines Acts provide a good illustration of this. By 1900, safety regulations were very extensive and the 1911 Act added further regulations covering many different matters: the fixing of hours for engine men, the provision of baths and facilities for drying clothes at the bigger pits and the searching of men for matches and other forbidden items. Accidents still happened and the rules were not always obeyed but the contrast with the 1850s is striking. At other places of work employers found themselves under increasing pressure to make their premises safe.

The Employers Liability Act 1880 made employers responsible for injuries at work and gave the injured worker the right to sue. However, the burden of proof as well as other legal expenses was on the worker. The 1880 Act was repealed and replaced with a Workmen's Compensation Act in 1897. [97] After 1897, injured employees had only to show that they had been injured doing their job. The Act applied was to railways, mining and quarrying, factory work and laundry work. However, the courts took a restrictive interpretation of a 'workman' in 1905 in *Simpson v. Ebbw Vale Steel, Iron & Coal Company* in which a widow claimed for the death of a colliery manager who had been killed in an underground accident. Lord Collins, Master of the Rolls held that her dead husband was

---

[96] McCormick, Brian, and Williams, J. E., 'The miners and the eight-hour day, 1863-1910', *Economic History Review*, 2nd series, Vol. 12, (1959), pp. 222-238. See also, Duffy, A. E. P., 'The Eight Hours Day Movement in Britain 1886-1893', *The Manchester School*, Vol. 36, (3), pp. 203-222.

[97] Markham, Lester, V., 'The employers' liability workmen's compensation debate of the 1890s revisited', *Historical Journal*, Vol. 44, (2001), pp. 471-495.

outside the Act's scope, because though the act extended to non-manual workers the victim 'must still be a workman' and said the Act:

> ...presupposes a position of dependence; it treats the class of workmen as being in a *sens inopes consilii*, and the Legislature does for them what they cannot do for themselves: it gives them a sort of State insurance, it being assumed that they are either not sufficiently intelligent or not sufficiently in funds to insure themselves. In no sense can such a principle extend to those who are earning good salaries.

The Workmen's Compensation Act 1906 fixed the compensation that a workman could recover from an employer in case of accident. It gave to a workman, except in certain cases of 'serious and wilful misconduct', a right against his employer to compensation on the mere occurrence of an accident where the common law gives the right only for negligence of the employer. Exceptions were made at the top and bottom ends of the labour market, including non-manual workers employed on annual pay over £250, casual workers employed 'otherwise than for the purposes of their employer's trade or business', outworkers and family workers. National Insurance after 1911 and voluntary insurance before were no longer the only ways of coping with industrial injuries.

7 Urban growth and housing

Successive governments in the late-twentieth and early-twenty-first century have had to grapple with the problem of urban sprawl, the need for affordable housing and sustainable development.[1] This, combined with changing energy technology, has resulted in a sustained debate over the status of the countryside and to what extent and under what circumstances it is justifiable or expedient to impinge on it. While few disagree with the building of new housing or wind turbines, there are always those who object that the location is wrong: the view is sacrosanct, local facilities will not be able to cope, the character of the community will be irrevocably changed and so on. Notions of the 'country' and the 'town' have always roused strong feelings and evoked powerful images. They have also created fundamental opposites. The 'country' was seen either as a natural way of life, of peace, innocence and simple virtue or as a place of ignorance, backwardness and obstruction. Round the 'town' clustered either the idea of it as a centre of achievement, of learning and communication or as a place of worldliness, noise, ambition and corruption.

Like all stereotypes, these polarities contain elements of truth. Towns and cities were a growing feature of British society in this period. By 1851, Britain was overwhelmingly an urban society and that trend continued and accelerated through to 1914. The nineteenth century saw the transformation of British society from one where one in four people lived in towns or cities to one in which over two out of three people lived in built-up areas. This urbanisation was not without its cost in human misery and deprivation, in appalling housing and polluted conditions and in 'sweated' workshops. But towns were also places of elegance, of conspicuous spending and wealth, resplendent with their civil buildings and parks and their sense

---

[1] The issue of town and country is discussed in Williams, Raymond, *The Country and the City*, (Chatto), 1973, and some of its implications for an industrialising society in Weiner, M., *English Culture and the Decline of the Industrial Spirit 1850-1950*, (Cambridge University Press), 1982. The agenda for urban historians was set in Dyos, H. J., (ed.), *The Study of Urban History*, (Edward Arnold), 1973, and the extent to which developments occurred in the following decade in Fraser, D., and Sutcliffe, A. J., (eds.), *The Pursuit of Urban History*, (Edward Arnold), 1983. Waller, P. J., *Town, city and nation: England 1850-1914,* (Oxford University Press), 1983, is a succinct study. Clark, Peter, (ed.), *The Cambridge urban history of Britain, Vol. 2: 1540-1840*, (Cambridge University Press), 2000, and Daunton, Martin J., (ed.), *The Cambridge urban history of Britain, Vol. 3: 1840-1950*, (Cambridge University Press), 2000, are essential.

of 'civic pride' and were seen by many as symbols of 'progress'. Towns and cities were places of intense contrasts. This was not new since they had always been places of contrast. Many of the problems such as housing and sanitation existed in the medieval and early modern town. [2] What was new, however, was the scale and expansion of towns and cities and this exacerbated their problems.

How and why did urbanisation occur?

The economic changes that originated in the eighteenth century led to the rapid expansion of urban centres. Towns, especially those in the forefront of manufacturing innovation, attracted rural labour, which hoped for better wages and a sense of freedom. The notion that 'town air is free air' was nothing new; it had its origins in medieval Germany. But labourers saw towns as places free from the paternalism and dependency of the rural environment and flocked there in their thousands. [3] For some, migration brought wealth and security but for most, life in towns was little different, and in environmental terms probably worse, from life in the country. They had exchanged rural slums for urban ones and exploitation by the landowner for exploitation by the factory master. Poverty was universal and few, whether rural or urban, could escape from it.[4]

---

[2] On small towns, see, Clark, Peter, 'Small towns 1700-1840', in ibid, Clark, Peter (ed.), *The Cambridge urban history of Britain, Vol. 2: 1540-1840*, pp. 733-774, and Royle, Stephen A., 'The development of small towns in Britain', in ibid, Daunton, Martin J., (ed.), *The Cambridge urban history of Britain, Vol. 3: 1840-1950*, pp. 151-184

[3] On this issue, see, Feldman, David, 'Migration', in ibid, Daunton, Martin J., (ed.), *The Cambridge urban history of Britain, Vol. 3: 1840-1950*, pp. 185-206.

[4] The development of town and city can be approached through Briggs, Asa, *Victorian Cities*, (Penguin), 1968, Dennis, R., *Industrial Cities of the Nineteenth Century*, (Cambridge University Press), 1984, Dyos, H. J., and Wolff, M., (eds.), *The Victorian City: Images and Realities*, 2 Vols. (Routledge), 1973, and ibid, Waller, P. J., *Town, City and Nation, England 1850-1914*. There are several useful studies of specific cities: Olson, D. J., *The Growth of Victorian London*, (Batsford), 1976, Fraser, D., (ed.), *A History of Modern Leeds*, (Manchester University Press), 1980, Hopkins, E., *The Rise of the Manufacturing Town: Birmingham and the industrial revolution*, (Sutton), 1998, Daunton, M., *Coal Metropolis, Cardiff 1870-1914*, (Leicester University Press), 1977. See also, Williamson, J. G., *Coping with City Growth during the British Industrial Revolution*, (Cambridge University Press), 1990, that adopt a statistical approach to the issues of urban growth; and, Koditschek, T., *Class Formation and Urban Industrial Society: Bradford 1750-1850*, (Cambridge University Press), 1990, that considers in depth the social and economic development of a

Why was London so big?

Between a sixth and a fifth of the total population of England lived in London. Its functions were plural. It was the largest city in the world containing the country's biggest concentration of industry chiefly clothing, footwear and furniture. In the 1851 Census, 86 per cent of London's employers employed fewer than ten men but some large establishments could be found such as the Woolwich Arsenal with 12,000 people in 1900 and the main railway works of the Great Eastern Railway at Stratford employing around 7,000 a decade later. The port of London was the country's largest and, as the epicentre of railways, roads and shipping, London was undoubtedly the chief emporium of Britain and its empire. It was the functional and ceremonial seat of politics and diplomacy, the first place of finance and the professions and the most important stage for the world of art, literature and entertainment and the centre and magnet for all things for luxurious living and High Society.

Defining London is not easy for the historian. To the Metropolitan Board of Works and the London County Council (LCC), established in 1855 and 1888-1889 respectively, it was an administrative province. To the City Corporation, it was the jealously guarded enclave of about one square mile of almost immeasurable wealth. To the Registrar-General in charge of censuses, London was an over-spilling, almost indeterminate, urban area. Some statistical definition was given to the concept of Greater London in 1875 when it was made to correspond to the Metropolitan Police District with a radius of fifteen miles from Charing Cross. Overall, from 1861 to 1911, the population of the administrative county grew by 61 per cent and the Greater London conurbation by 125 per cent compared to 80 per cent in England as a whole. [5] The newspaper editor R. D. Blumenfeld wrote in his diary on 15 October 1900:

> Everybody wants to come to London; and little wonder, since the rural

---

'boom' town. Morris, R. J., and Rodger, R., (eds.), *The Victorian City: A Reader in British Urban History 1820-1914*, (Longman), 1994, collects together important papers and has an excellent introduction that puts urban growth in its context.

[5] Schwarz, Leonard D, 'London 1700-1840', in ibid, Clark, Peter, (ed.), *The Cambridge urban history of Britain, Vol. 2: 1540-1840*, pp. 641-672, and Dennis, Richard, 'Modern London', in ibid, Daunton, Martin J., (ed.), *The Cambridge urban history of Britain, Vol. 3: 1840-1950*, pp. 95-131, provide an excellent overview.

districts are all more or less dead, with no prospect of revival. [6]

One of the major causes of the expansion of London between 1830 and 1880 was migration. More women than men were migrants. Domestic service and the prospect of marriage were prevailing forces. In addition, women's opportunities of fieldwork were reduced in the late-nineteenth century and a more scientific and intensive milk trade was eliminating the ordinary milkmaid. The number of women returned in censuses as agricultural workers fell from 229,000 in 1851 to 67,000 by 1901. The majority of in-migrants were aged between 15 and 30, a situation that worsened the over-supply of unskilled, casual labour in the capital. The Royal Commission on the Poor Laws (1905-1909) showed than in London people aged over 60 made up 67 per 1,000 population compared to 102 per 1,000 in mainly rural areas. The greater the city the wider its magnetic attraction and in the case of London, this extended overseas.

East European pogroms brought an additional 100,000 to 150,000 Jewish immigrants to England between 1881 and 1914.[7] Leeds, Manchester and, to a lesser extent, Liverpool were also destinations but the heaviest concentration was in East London. Whitechapel's population in 1901 was 31.8 per cent alien. The proportion of foreign-born in the total population of London increased from 1.57 per cent in 1881 to 2.98 per cent in 1901. [8] The number of Irish-born immigrants, especially in the old East End, was highest before 1860 falling in the late-nineteenth century. Most migrants from the English countryside reached London from a short

---

[6] Blumenfeld, R. D., *In the Days of Bicycles and Bustles*, (Brewer and Warren), 1930, pp. 94-95.

[7] On Jewish migration in the second half of the nineteenth century and the role of Jewish labour in London, see Feldman, David, *Englishmen and Jews: Social Relations and Political Culture 1840-1914*, (Yale University Press), 1994, and Endelman, Todd M., *The Jews in Britain 1656 to 2000*, (University of California Press), 2000, pp. 79-182. See also, Stallard, Joshua Harrison, *London pauperism amongst Jews and Christians: An inquiry into the principles and practice of out-door relief in the metropolis, and the result upon the moral and physical condition of the pauper class*, (Saunders, Otley, and Co), 1867, Wechsler, R. S., *The Jewish garment trade in East London 1875-1914: a study of conditions and responses*, (Columbia University Press), 1979, and Berrol, Selma Cantor, *East Side/East End: Eastern European Jews in London and New York, 1870-1920*, (Praegar), 1994.

[8] Lees, L. Hollen, *Exiles of Erin: Irish Migrants in Victorian London*, (Manchester University Press), 1979, and Jackson, J. A., 'The Irish in East London', *East London Papers*, Vol. 6, (1963), pp. 105-119

distance and the proportion of migrants was proportional to the distance of their homes from the capital. Railways certainly increased the volume of migration but did not substantially alter its character. Most people moved in a series of short stages.

The proportion of migrants in London's population was falling in the nineteenth century. In the period 1851-1891, 84 per cent of London's increase in population came from the surplus of births, only 16 per cent from net immigration. This feature radically distinguished London from major European cities. Two causes were outstanding. The superior sanitary provision of England resulted in a falling death rate and there was an outflow of population to suburbs. This was particularly obvious in London. The square mile of the City had a resident population that peaked around 1850 at 130,000 but had dropped to 27,000 by 1901: this should be contrasted with the increase in its daytime or working population that rose from 170,000 in 1865 to 437,000 by 1921. Like other major cities and towns, population became increasingly segregated by income and class. The decline of the working-class population of the City resulted in them being jammed into the adjacent East End. Suburban railways and the underground, as well as enhanced omnibus services meant that the middle-class could move to the outer ring of Greater London; East and West Ham, Leyton, Tottenham, Hornsey, Willesden, Walthamstow and Croydon. [9]

What in an average English town was the work of one or two sanitary and housing departments was in London split across many bodies. [10] The options available to the LCC and before 1889 the Metropolitan Board of Works were unattractive and freedom of manoeuvre small. Each of the 28 Metropolitan Borough Councils (and before them, the vestries) had concurrent powers with the LCC.[11]

---

[9] On the development and impact of the underground, see Wolmar, Christian, *The Subterranean Railway: How the London Underground Was Built and How it Changed the City Forever*, (Atlantic Books), 2004. Jackson, Alan A., 'The London Railway Suburb 1850-1914', in Evans, A. K. B., and Gough, John, (eds.), *The impact of the railway on society in Britain: essays in honour of Jack Simmons*, (Ashgate), 2003, pp. 169-180.

[10] See, for example, Hardy, A., 'Parish pump to private pipes: London's water supply in the 19th century', in Bynum, W. F., and Porter, R., (eds.), *Living and dying in London*, (Wellcome Institute), 1991, pp. 76-93.

[11] The vestry had its origins in medieval England and was established as early as the fourteenth century to manage church affairs. However, in the early modern period it became a general administrative body. In large industrialising parishes or in places where the leading inhabitants formed executive committees, known as *'select vestries'*, most of the population were excluded. Inevitably the vestry began to involve itself in every aspect

Each was also a sanitary authority and it was their duty to overcome overcrowding and its associated problems. As a result, there was considerable difficulty in co-ordinating local government policy. The LCC could build but it was the responsibility of other local authorities to provide tenants with other services. Even when the LCC did build council properties the tenants were not generally displaced slum dwellers. The high price of land in London restrained the LCC's activities as it had to pay on average 35 per cent higher prices per acre than provincial local authorities.

Slum clearance failed to provide cheap alternative accommodation and made the housing situation worse. Low cost travel from homes built on cheaper suburban land was a potential solution. There was, however, a substantial time lag before transport and work, wages and rents made this possible. For this period most of the London's inner-city poor were cramped in overcrowded, high-rent housing in order to remain in walking distance of work. As C. F. G. Masterman, a British Liberal politician and journalist wrote in 1903:

> Place a disused sentry-box upon any piece of ground in South or East London and in a few hours it will be occupied by a man and his wife and family, inundated by applications from would-be lodgers. [12]

There was some improvement in overcrowding but in 1911, 27.6 per cent of people in the inner London area were living more than two per room. This situation was not helped by the higher rents of ordinary working-class homes: in 1908, they were 70 per cent higher than in Birmingham. The pressure was greatest in the East End. The housing problems of London serve to illustrate several points of general importance with regard to urban development in this period. London was a living laboratory for experiment in the housing question, for individual and company philanthropy, for private enterprise and for collective public action. From 1883, the exposures of Andrew Mearns' *The Bitter Cry of Outcast London* stimulated a debate that led to the Royal Commission on the Housing of the Working-classes (1884-1885). [13] There was little new in *The Bitter*

---

of local administration because it had the right to set parish rates to finance the work of its officials. Its influence only declined after 1834 when it lost its responsibilities for the poor law to the Poor Law Unions with their Boards of Guardians. In 1894, it was finally replaced by parish councils.

[12] Masterman, C. F. G., *From the Abyss: Of Its Inhabitants*, (R. B. Johnson), 1903, p. 12.

[13] Mearns, Andrew, *The Bitter Cry of Outcast London: An Inquiry into the Condition of the Abject Poor*, (James Clarke & Co), 1883, reprinted edited

Cry but its popularity can be explained by the sensationalist publicity it received in the *Pall Mall Magazine* and the climate of working-class discontent and middle- and upper-class insecurity existing in London in the 1880s. Mearns' choice of a memorable title helped boost sales of the work and his decision to focus on the homes of the poor not merely street life was a radical departure from earlier studies. The pamphlet hinted at horrors too dark to be included and this further stimulated people's shocked emotions. [14] It also gave stimulus to investigative social work in the Settlement Movement, [15] later investigative studies [16] and especially Charles Booth's *Life and Labour of the People in London*.

Unregulated and unrestrained individualism was put on trial as rents rose and accommodation shortages spiralled out of control. The conclusion that emerged from this experience was that national government could not permanently stand aside since the heart of the problem was the uneven distribution of wealth and resources. [17] Graduated direct taxation and state subsidies to local council housing were the courses that were eventually adopted. There was, and arguably still is, in the words of Joseph Chamberlain in 1883 on the Torrens and Cross housing legislation:

---

by A. S. Wohl, (Leicester University Press) 1970, and extracts in Keating, P., (ed.), *Into Unknown England 1866-1913*, (Fontana), 1976, pp. 91-111. There is some debate as to whether Andrew Mearns or William Preston was the author. The pamphlet was certainly either written or heavily revised by Rev. William C. Preston with Rev. James Munro helping with the research and composition of the work as well.

[14] Under William T. Stead, the *Pall Mall Magazine* devoted a great deal of space to promoting the pamphlet and between mid-October and early November 1883, published at least one article a day on 'Outcast London'. Supported by the *Daily News*, and with a combination of sensationalism and moral righteousness, Stead was able to keep the public's attention focused on the London poor for the next two months.

[15] Hamilton, Richard, 'A hidden heritage: The social settlement house movement 1884-1910', *Journal of Community Work and Development*, Vol. 2, (2), (2001), pp. 9-22, and Meacham, Standish, *Toynbee Hall and social reform, 1880-1914: the search for community*, (Yale University Press), 1987.

[16] See, Sims, G. R., *How the Poor Live: And, Horrible London*, (Chatto & Windus), 1898, and Wilson, Keith, 'Surveying Victorian and Edwardian Londoners: George R. Sims' *Living London*', in Phillips, Lawrence, (ed.), *A mighty mass of brick and smoke: Victorian and Edwardian representations of London*, (Rodopi), 2007, pp. 131-149.

[17] On the revival of the 'condition of England question', see, Haggard, Robert, F., *The Persistence of Victorian Liberalism: the politics of social reform in Britain, 1870-1900*, (Greenwood Publishing), 2001, pp. 27-52

...an incurable timidity with which Parliament...is accustomed to deal with the sacred rights of property.[18]

There were many Londons. Contemporaries noted the difference of East and West End, the character of north and south of the river and the enclaves of Westminster and the City. It was, however, the East End that dominated contemporary comment. Writers like Walter Besant [19] and George Gissing [20] focused attention on the enormity of its problems.[21]

The East End consisted of the parishes east of Bishopsgate Street, stretching north of the Thames to the River Lea. By 1900, however, new industrial developments, the opening of the Royal Albert Dock and the Great Eastern Railway's provision of workmen's train services meant that East London also now included the working-class dormitories east of the Lea and south of Epping Forest. By 1900, this swollen East London contained nearly two millions people. It was largely a one-class community with few amenities.[22] However, the work of East London displayed extraordinary variety largely carried out in small workshops rather than large factories. The East End spanned the working-class spectrum from the sweated trades, the casual and under-employed workers who predominated in the western areas and along the waterfront, to the regularly employed and

---

[18] Chamberlain, Joseph, *Fortnightly Review*, Vol. 40, (1883), p. 767.

[19] Besant wrote several books on London including *East London*, (Century Co.), 1901 and *South London*, (Chatto & Windus), 1899. In both he was highly critical of and was capable of dismissing as of no account the greater part of London that was not the City or West End. The *Lumpenproletariat* East London and artisan and petty-bourgeois South London were each for him a travesty of urban civilisation.

[20] George Gissing was the most gifted novelist to employ late-nineteenth century London as a backcloth to his fiction. Whether writing of working-class Clerkenwell and Hoxton, as in *The Nether World*, (Smith, Elder and Co.), 1889, and *Demos: A Story of English Socialism*, (Harper & Brothers), 1886 or artisan and petty-bourgeois Camberwell, in *In the Year of the Jubilee*, (Lawrence and Bullen), 1894, the picture of the streets was of drab squalor. Gissing's London was the London of defeat, a nightmare region; in *The Nether World*, p. 205, 'beyond the outmost limits of dread' and p. 167, 'a city of the damned'. His urban world was barren, barbaric and beyond redemption.

[21] Domville, E. W., '"Gloomy City, or, the deeps of Hell": the presentation of the East End in fiction between 1880 and 1914', *East London Papers*, Vol. 8, (1965), pp. 98-109.

[22] See Steffel, R. V., 'The evolution of a slum control policy in the East End, 1889-1907', *East London Papers*, Vol. 13 (1970), pp. 23-35.

quietly respectable artisans in the Poplar, Bow and Bromley districts. Each parish had its own character: some metal work but mainly cheap clothing, cigar and food preparation dominated Whitechapel; furniture, silk and toys predominated in Bethnal Green and Shoreditch; boots and shoes in Mile End; and weaving in Spitalfields.[23] East London contained many technical inventions but also a darker side with sub-contracting, sweating, irregular demand and low wages. Craftsmanship survived but rarely in its totality; for example, watch makers often made only one part of a watch and used mass-produced parts for the remainder

Charles Booth's study of East London is an important source for the social composition of East London and provides a valuable corrective to the gloom of contemporary novelists such as Gissing. [24] He divided society into eight classes from A to H: A to F spanned the lower classes and classes G and H were the lower middle and upper-middle-classes. Booth found that higher artisans (class F) made up about 13.5 per cent of the population. B to D made up 30 per cent, those with small regular earnings and intermittent earnings. Class E was varied but brought together most artisans and regular wage-earners and was the largest category at 42 per cent; the lowest class A was about 1.25 per cent of the population comprising 'some occasional labourers, street-sellers, loafers, criminals and semi-criminals'. This study is important in several respects. It rendered insupportable generalisations about a tidal wave of wretchedness and viciousness gaining on society and about to engulf it. Booth rejected the view that misery was all pervasive and irremediable.

Booth did, however, suggest that the state of East London had been worse in the past than in the 1890s. Certainly by 1860, there was a crisis in London's inner industrial areas as civic improvements elsewhere in the metropolis shunted thousands into adjacent working-class parishes and resulted in a cruel spiral of rising rents and increased overcrowding. [25] Workers found themselves under increasing pressure because there was insufficient cheap, plentiful or

---

[23] Leech, Kenneth, 'The decay of Spitalfields', *East London Papers*, Vol. 7, (1964), pp. 57-62. See also, Kerchen, Anne J., *Strangers, aliens and Asians: Huguenots, Jews and Bangladeshis in Spitalfields, 1660-2000*, (Routledge), 2005.

[24] Booth, Charles, *Life and Labour of the People in London: Vol. 4, The trades of East London*, (Macmillan), 1893.

[25] On conditions in London in the 1860s the standard work is Jones, Gareth Steadman, *Outcast London: a study in the relationship between classes in Victorian society*, (Oxford University Press), 1971, where the 'arithmetic of woe' can be seen graphically illustrated. See also the contemporary prints by the French artist Gustave Doré.

well-timed transport to, from and within the suburbs resulting in many working people being trapped in East London. The casual labour of the old East End was trapped within an economy of declining trades and conditions of employment deteriorated. By the early 1870s, London's shipbuilding had slumped beyond the point of recovery and by the 1880s most heavy engineering, iron founding and metal work had gone the same way. Competition from provincial furniture, clothing and footwear factories could only be met by reducing labour costs and led to the mounting importance of sweated trades. [26] London's industries found themselves increasingly under pressure and this had two consequences. The disadvantages of the least skilled were cruelly exposed and the 'respectable' working-class found themselves pushed down into competing for the same work and accommodation as the casuals: this marked a dilution of labour status.[27]

The conventional middle-class perception of East London was of a foggy, malarial urban landscape, a place where revolutionary tempers might grow to overthrow society. London was an image of their fear of the streets, aversion from crowds and anxiety about impersonality. London was a place of anonymity. Samuel Wilberforce, the Bishop of Oxford, said in a talk on 'the London we live in' in 1864:

> He looked out of the bedroom windows of the little inn in which he was staying at the surging crowd which passed and re-passed beneath him; and he could have screamed for someone who knew him or knew somebody who knew.... This feeling of isolation in the midst of a vast crowd was absolutely painful. [28]

The rapidity of growth startled the middle- and upper-classes. London was too extensive to be grasped, too impersonal to be understood. Many reacted to London as the poet Rudyard Kipling did to Chicago: 'Having seen it, I urgently desire never to see it again.'[29] The influence of London, throughout the southeast and further, was increasingly immeasurable. The capital city had grown

---

[26] See, Hall, P. G., 'The East London footwear industry: an industrial quarter in decline', *East London Papers*, Vol. 5, (1962), pp. 3-21, and Oliver, J. L., 'The East London furniture industry', *East London Papers*, Vol. 4, (1961), pp. 88-101.
[27] Brodie, Marc, *The politics of the poor: the East End of London 1885-1914*, (Oxford University Press), 2004.
[28] Cit, ibid, Waller, P. J., *Town, City and Nation, England 1850-1914*, p. 49.
[29] Kipling, Rudyard, *From sea to sea: letters of travel*, (Doubleday, Page and Co.), 1900, p. 276.

and spread to the point of virtual amorphousness, unorganised and unorganisable. The persistent feature of London in this period was the warning it gave about cities generally: their overwhelming power to defeat those who tried to control their overall movement and development.

Why did regional manufacturing centres emerge?

Friedrich Engels [30] wrote at the beginning of the chapter on 'The Great Towns' in his *The Condition of the Working-class in England*:

> What is true of London, is true of Manchester, Birmingham, Leeds, is true of all great towns. Everywhere barbarous indifference, hard egotism on one hand and nameless misery on the other, everywhere social warfare, every man's house in a state of siege, everywhere reciprocal plundering under the protection of the law... [31]

J. G. Kohl, a German visitor to Britain in the early 1840s, reported on the appearance of Birmingham:

> Birmingham, compared with Manchester is evidently deficient in large buildings and public institutions.... London has her Thames, Liverpool her Mersey....Birmingham has nothing of the kind, nothing but a dull and endless succession of house after house, and street after street. [32]

By the time he reached Leeds, Birmingham's ugliness was forgotten:

> The manufacturing cities of England are none of them very attractive or pleasing in appearance, but Leeds is, perhaps, the ugliest and least attractive town in all England. In Birmingham, Manchester and other such cities, among the mass of chimneys and factories, are scattered, here and there, splendid newsrooms or clubs, and interesting exchanges, banks, railway-stations or Wellington and Nelson monuments. Leeds has none of these. [33]

---

[30] Engels F., *The Condition of the Working-class in England in 1844*, Leipzig, 1845; various editions including W. O. Henderson and W. H. Chaloner, (Blackwell), 1958, Victor Kiernan (Penguin), 1987 and Tristram Hunt, (Penguin), 2009. Carver, T., *Engels*, (Oxford University Press), 1981, McLellan, D., *Engels*, (Fontana), 1977, and Hunt, Tristram, *The Frock-coated Communist: The Revolutionary Life of Friedrich Engels*, (Allen Lane), 2009, provide biographical detail.

[31] Ibid, Engels F., *The Condition of the Working-class in England in 1844*, p. 68.

[32] Kohl, Johann Georg, *England and Wales*, (Chapman & Hall), 1844, reprinted, (Augustus M. Kelley), 1968, p. 6.

[33] Ibid, Kohl, Johann Georg, *England and Wales*, p. 49.

The French social critic, Alexis de Tocqueville noted in 1835:

> At Manchester a few great capitalists, thousands of poor workmen and little middle-class. At Birmingham, few large industries, many small industrialists. At Manchester workmen are counted by the thousand.... At Birmingham the workers work in their own houses or in little workshops in company with the master himself.... the working people of Birmingham seem more healthy, better off, more orderly and more moral than those of Manchester (where) civilised man is turned back almost into a savage. [34]

Certainly, the built environments of Birmingham and Manchester were very different: there was less overcrowding in Birmingham and the quality of street cleansing and drainage was better than in Manchester and other Lancashire towns.

It is tempting to arrange England's industrial cities along a continuum from Manchester at one extreme, as Engels called it 'the classic type of a modern manufacturing town' by way of Leeds where factories in the woollen industry were smaller than in Lancashire cotton, to Sheffield and Birmingham, the principal examples of workshop industry. This is misleading to several respects. It ignores the major seaports, many of which like Liverpool were also industrial cities. It suggests falsely that the satellites of each of the major cities could also be ranged along a continuum paralleling that of the regional capital. Engels' view of Manchester as the archetypal manufacturing city is misleading and other writers stressed that it was not typical. [35]

It was, however, the great cities that Victorians contemplated when they considered the urbanisation of their society. These cities and towns were multi-purpose and multi-functional and most were, to a marked degree, specialists in one or two substantial activities. Their competitive positions as great cities were geared to the fortunes of particular trades. Certainly the early expansion of towns and cities in the late-eighteenth and early-nineteenth century led to differentiation between communities and the recognition that all towns experienced, or thought they experienced, the same problems. The major reasons for the growth of regional centres were similar to the causes of growth in London. However, by 1900 as the result of more government intervention, especially with regard to health and housing, increased

---

[34] Mayer, J. P., (ed.), Alexis de Tocqueville, *Journeys to England and Ireland*, (Transaction Publishers), 1988, p. 104.
[35] Trinder, Barrie, 'Industrialising towns 1700-1840', in ibid, Clark, Peter, (ed.), *The Cambridge urban history of Britain, Vol. 2: 1540-1840*, pp. 805-830, and Reeder, David and Rodger, Richard, 'Industrialisation and the city economy', in ibid, Daunton, Martin J., (ed.), *The Cambridge urban history of Britain, Vol. 3: 1840-1950*, pp. 553-592.

dominance of national and metropolitan influences, the spread of chain stores and the diffusion of ideas and fashions from London, towns came to be more alike.

The massive increase in urban population resulted in a substantial physical increase of the built-up areas of towns. That, in turn, triggered a fundamental restructuring of urban land usage. [36] As with London, there was increasing segregation within urban communities largely as a response to a series of technological transformations. [37] In 1800, small-scale craft industries based on workshops scattered throughout the town produced for the local market. By 1900, two changes had occurred. Large-scale, factory-based industries were established demanding extensive areas of land and accessibility to water and rail transport. The urban industrial region emerged. As a consequence, workshop-based craft industries were eventually displaced. For instance, the boot and shoemaker were eventually ousted by mass produced factory goods from the East Midlands; the tailor became a retailer of centrally produced off-the-peg garments. Manufacturing was concentrated into larger and distinctive regions within the town.

A whole series of changes also took place in retail technology though these were not completed until 1900. [38] Though they were not immediate or revolutionary, the end result was a radical change in the whole system. The weekly market was gradually replaced by, or transformed into, the permanent shopping centre. Up to 1850, the first stage was characterised by the building of a market hall. Michael Marks, for example, started in Leeds as a peddler or packman. By 1884, he had a stall in the open market that operated two days a week; from there he moved into the covered market that had been opened

---

[36] Englander, David, *Landlord and Tenant in Urban Britain, 1838-1918*, (Oxford University Press), 1983, and Offer, Avner, *Property and Politics, 1870-1914: Landownership, Law, Ideology and Urban Development in England*, (Cambridge University Press), 1981, 2010. See also, Gilbert, David and Southall, Humphrey, 'The urban labour market', in ibid, Daunton, Martin J., (ed.), *The Cambridge urban history of Britain, Vol. 3: 1840-1950*, pp. 593-628.

[37] Pooley, Colin G., 'Patterns on the ground: urban form, residential structure and the social construction of space', in ibid, Daunton, Martin J., (ed.), *The Cambridge urban history of Britain, Vol. 3: 1840-1950*, pp. 429-466.

[38] Benson, John, and Ugolini, Laura, (eds.), *A nation of shopkeepers: retailing in Britain, 1550-2000*, (I. B. Tauris), 2002, provides a good overview. Cohen, Deborah, *Household gods: the British and their possessions*, (Yale University Press), 2006, and Baren, Maurice E., *Victorian shopping*, (Michael O'Mara), 1998, look at what people bought.

in 1857 on a daily basis; the next stage was to open stalls in other markets and by 1890 he had five. The old core of the town, or part of it, that had been a mixture of land uses became more specialised into retail or professional uses.

Mass produced goods undermined old local craft production and specialist retailers of manufactured goods replaced the old combined workshop-retailing establishments. The railways enhanced this process by providing speedy transport of even perishable commodities. Part of this process was the wider occurrence of the lock-up shop to which the retailer commuted each day. By the 1880s, both multiple and department stores appeared, the former especially in the grocery trade. Thomas Lipton started a one-man grocery store in Glasgow in 1872; by 1899, he had 245 branches throughout Britain. The greater demand for professional services, itself related to urban growth, resulted in lawyers and doctors seeking central locations. But a variety of other uses also located themselves here offering services to business, auctioneers and accountants or to the public, such as lending libraries.[39] Transport technology greatly affected two aspects of towns. The developing railway system was a significant consumer of urban land and in 1800, movement was primarily on foot, 'the walking city'. By 1900, this had been transformed. The railway supplemented by the carriage, electric tram and omnibus were the main means of transport. [40]

Civic pride and civic rivalry among the industrial towns of the north were almost entirely materialistic in character and aesthetic issues played a lesser role. [41] The motives that inspired both were in part those of business. Sanitary reform made business sense as much as moral sense. Healthier workers would improve output and individuals and public authorities would be spared unproductive spending on hospitals and funeral charges. Certainly a social conscience inspired civic improvements but it is an error to neglect business needs. For the Victorians humanitarian and business aims

---

[39] Walton, John K., 'Towns and consumerism', in ibid, Daunton, Martin J., (ed.), *The Cambridge urban history of Britain, Vol. 3: 1840-1950*, pp. 715-744.

[40] Armstrong, John, 'From Shillibeer to Buchanan: transport and the urban environment', in ibid, Daunton, Martin J., (ed.), *The Cambridge urban history of Britain, Vol. 3: 1840-1950*, pp. 229-257.

[41] Morley, Ian, with a foreword by Richard Fellows, *British provincial civic design and the building of late-Victorian and Edwardian cities, 1880-1914*, (Edwin Mellen Press), 2008.

were complementary not contradictory. [42]

In 1800, the prevailing style of Georgian urban design was theatrical, the prevailing aim one of spectacle. [43] Cities and towns had been rebuilt and refashioned with elegant assembly rooms, town halls, residential squares, parades and public gardens, settings for the rituals that helped shaped a variety of interests, landed, commercial, financial, professional into the cultural consensus of 'polite society'. Classical styling established a common, nation-wide code for polite townscape as did other improvements to the fabric such as paving, lighting, street cleaning and the provision of piped water and sewage disposal. Noxious or dangerous trades were expelled to the districts of the poor. Other areas for the poor, notably town commons were liable to be enclosed for building genteel properties. The building of a genteel townscape emphasised a growing but never complete segregation between polite and impolite culture. The urban crowd, riotous and unpredictable, was always a threat. Aristocratic motives for restructuring towns and styles were in part patrician, an expression of an aristocratic conception of society, but they were also financial. Leading landowners in London, such as the Dukes of Bedford, Portland and Southampton, vied with each other to develop their estates. [44] Long-term leases realised long-term financial returns: urban land was cropped as effectively as arable soil.

The lives and living conditions of the poor were largely ignored. But after 1830, spectacle was increasingly replaced by surveillance. This reflected the attitudes of social reformers who frowned on spectacular public display and city life generally became an object of concern. The conditions of the poor could no longer be ignored; they ceased to have walk-on roles and became central to the condition of towns. Contemporaries developed the idea of the 'dangerous classes' especially as the working-classes tended to be concentrated in particular areas of urban communities. The spectre of contagious diseases like cholera rampaging through towns and cities and with it a variety of social pathologies prompted Victorian reformers into more

---

[42] Morris, R. J., 'Structure, culture and society in British towns', in ibid, Daunton, Martin J., (ed.), *The Cambridge urban history of Britain, Vol. 3: 1840-1950*, pp. 395-426.

[43] See, for example, Ayres, James, *Building the Georgian city*, (Yale University Press), 1998, Chalklin, C. W., *The provincial towns of Georgian England: a study of the building process, 1740-1820*, (Leicester University Press), 1974, Ison, W. W., *The Georgian buildings of Bath: from 1700 to 1830*, (Spire), 2004, and Summerson, J. H., *Georgian London*, (Pimlico), 1988, 2nd edition, (Yale University Press), 2003.

[44] See, for instance, Byrne, Andrew, *Bedford Square: An Architectural Study*, (Athlone Press), 1990.

vigorous strategies for social and environmental control. Metropolitan improvements ceased to be schemes to beautify London but came to be limited to ones that deal with specific evils such as traffic congestion, insanitary buildings and inefficient sewage disposal in which aesthetic considerations were secondary. There were a number of schemes, privately and publicly funded, to improve the physical fabric of poorer urban districts and, by extension, their moral and social condition. The wide streets, model housing estates and public parks were informed by the belief that slums nourished, if not caused, a variety of pathologies, not just physical disease but crime, laziness, irreligion and insurrection. At their core therefore schemes like this were concerned with principles of social discipline and public order.[45]

As towns and cities expanded, early Victorian reformers voiced their concern about the loss of open space for public recreation. The crisis was not actually as great as reformers believed; open country was only a short walk away in most cities. The issue was the use to which open space was put.[46] Middle-class reformers promoted 'rational recreation', constructive kinds of leisure as opposed to the dog racing, prize fighting and political rallies that occurred round the northern industrial towns. The first purpose-built public park was the Arboretum in Derby opened in 1840 and the first municipal park was the more extensive Birkenhead Park opened four years later (soon known as 'the people's park').[47] From the 1850s, new public parks and walks were built in most industrial towns and cities, often on the edges, sometimes by enclosing common land. Some were initially financed by large employers and then handed over to municipal corporations; others were municipal ventures from the outset. New cemeteries on the edge of cities were designed for rational recreation: Undercliffe Cemetery, high above Bradford, was run as a profit-making concern by local businessmen for families who walked beside extravagant tombs of the city's leading industrial families.[48]

From the reform of municipal corporations in 1835 environmental improvement was entwined with middle-class radicalism and attacks on what one Whig newspaper called 'a shabby

---

[45] Cunningham, Colin, *Victorian and Edwardian Town Halls*, (Routledge), 1981, provides insights into municipal building.

[46] Eyres, Patrick and Russell, Fiona, 'Introduction: The Georgian Landscape Garden and Victorian Urban Park', in Eyres, Patrick and Russell, Fiona, (eds.), *Sculpture and the garden*, (Ashgate), 2006, pp. 39-50.

[47] Elliott, Paul, 'The Derby Arboretum (1840): the first specially designed municipal public park in Britain', *Midland History*, Vol. 26. (2001), pp. 144-176.

[48] Clark, Colin, and Davison, Reuben, *In loving memory: the story of Undercliffe Cemetery*, (Sutton), 2004.

mongrel aristocracy'. [49] Between the mid-1830s and 1850s, there were bitter disputes between those who associated improvement with sewerage, drainage and water supplies and improvers who took a broader view of civil improvement and who sought to build a new civic townscape of broad open spaces and magnificent public buildings. With the revival of urban fortunes, it was improvement on the grand scale that captured the corporate imagination. In 1873, Joseph Chamberlain was elected Birmingham's mayor and re-elected in 1874 and 1875. [50] He focused on improving the physical condition of the town and its people. He organised the purchase of the two gas companies and the water works; he appointed a Medical Officer of Health, established a Drainage Board, extended the paving and lighting of streets, opened six public parks and saw the start of the public transport service. His Improvement Scheme saw the demolition of ninety acres of slums in the town centre. The council bought the freehold of about half the land to build Corporation Street. The experience of Birmingham was not, however, unique.

What kinds of new urban growth occurred?

New urban developments in the nineteenth century were, in part, the result of expansive capitalism. It is natural that they should excite polemicists. Did they favour some social groups more than others? This needs to be considered against the background of the new urban growths of the late Victorian period: the resort and pleasure towns, the suburban and satellite towns and planned communities of both businessmen and utopians.

Towns and leisure

By 1911, 55 per cent of English people were visiting the seaside on day excursions and 20 per cent were talking holidays requiring accommodation. The holiday industry involved about 1.25 per cent of the occupied population and 1.5 per cent of consumer expenditure. No previous society gave so many people the chance for

---

[49] Cit, Webb, Sidney and Beatrice, *The manor and the borough, Part 1*, (Cass), 1908, p. 770.

[50] On Chamberlain in Birmingham the most recent study is Marsh, Peter, *Joseph Chamberlain: Entrepreneur in Politics*, (Yale University Press), 1994. See also, Rodrick, Anne Baltz, *Self help and civic culture: citizenship in Victorian Birmingham*, (Ashgate), 2004, and Thompson, D. M., 'R. W. Dale and the "civic gospel"', in Sell, Alan P. F., (ed.), *Protestant nonconformists and the west Midlands of England: papers presented at the first conference of the Association of Denominational Historical Societies and Cognate Libraries*, (Keele University Press), 1996, pp. 99-118.

a holiday beside the sea. [51] John Glover-Kinde issued the song *I do like to be beside the seaside* in 1909 and the most copied artist of mid-nineteenth century England was W. R. Frith whose most popular painting, *Ramsgate Sands or Life at the Seaside*, was painted in 1853-1854. Seaside resorts were not places of production but of conspicuous expenditure where people wasted time and money: many contemporaries regarded them as parasites. Transport permitted the expansion of coastal resorts and presented each with a problem of how to define and preserve its character. The Kent resorts of Broadstairs, Ramsgate and Margate were popular before the railways arrived owing to cheap fares on the hoys and, after 1815, the Thames steam-packets. [52] Steamboat services had an impact in other areas. From Liverpool after the Napoleonic wars, boats went along the Lancashire, Cheshire and North Wales coastline as well as to the Isle of Man and there were comparable stirrings in the Bristol Channel. [53] Some resorts owed their early expansion to Court connections. George III visited Weymouth in 1784, then almost every August and September from 1789 to 1805. [54] Worthing and Southend were briefly favoured by royal princesses and Brighton owed its expansion to the patronage of the Prince Regent, later George IV.[55]

In the eighteenth century the seaside resort largely took second place to the spa and the appeal of the spas persisted into the nineteenth century. [56] The depression of the 1830s had taken its toll of their prosperity but railway links and individual initiative brought

---

[51] Walvin, James, *Beside the Sea*, (Penguin), 1978, and *The English Seaside Resort: A Social History 1750-1914*, (Leicester University Press), 1983.

[52] Whyman, John (ed.), *The early Kentish seaside (1736-1840): selected documents*, (A. Sutton for Kent Archives Office), 1985, and Stafford, Felicity, and Yates, Nigel (eds.), *The later Kentish seaside (1840-1974): selected documents*, (A. Sutton for Kent Archives Office), 1985.

[53] Belchem, John, "The playground of northern England': the Isle of Man, Manxness and the northern working class', in Kirk, Neville, (ed.), *Northern identities: historical interpretations of 'the north' and 'northerness'*, (Ashgate), 2000, pp. 71-86; see also, Belchem, John, (ed.), *A New History of the Isle of Man, Vol. 5: The Modern Period 1830-1999*, (Liverpool University Press), 2000.

[54] Fripp, John, 'Weymouth over the long eighteenth century: urban renaissance, or new leisure town?', *Proceedings of the Dorset Natural History and Archaeological Society*, Vol. 129, (2008 for 2007), pp. 49-58.

[55] Farrant, Sue, and Farrant, John Howard, 'Brighton, 1580-1820: from Tudor Town to Regency Resort', *Sussex Archaeological Collections*, Vol. 118, (1980), pp. 331-350.

[56] On this issue, see, Hassan, John, *The seaside, health and the environment in England and Wales since 1800*, (Ashgate), 2003, pp. 15-74.

renewed spa development after 1840. In 1841, A. B. Granville identified seventy spas. [57] Tenbury Wells and Droitwich grew as offshoots of John Corbett's salt-extracting business; Matlock and Buxton revived after the coming of the railway in 1863 and the support of the seventh Duke of Devonshire. There was also municipal investment: Bath Corporation made extensive renovations in the late 1880s and the expansion of Harrogate owed much to the vigorous corporation investment and rivalled some continental spas as an aristocratic and middle-class centre. [58] Spas also developed as locations for fashionable sport or as general tourist centres: Harrogate utilised its proximity to the Yorkshire Dales; Cheltenham promoted general tourism in the Cotswold; Leamington exploited Shakespeare country; Llandrindod Wells brought visitors to Wales. [59]

For recreation, the spas lagged in popularity behind the inland tourist centres and inland tourist centres ran second to seaside resorts. Between 1861 and 1871, the 48 places classified as seaside resorts had grown by 21.5 per cent. Seaside towns were not the same. They catered for different classes of visitors and often combined holiday facilities with other pursuits, usually shipping and fishing. But tourism in some areas thrived and in others barely stirred. The railway reached Cornwall in 1859 but it remained comparatively unexploited until after 1914: it lost population in every decade from 1861 to 1901 and grew merely 1.86 per cent between 1901 and 1911. Only one resort in the south-west enticed visitors in any quantity. Torquay's population quadrupled between 1841 and 1901. [60] It retained some port traffic and well as minor industry but its position as a social centre determined its expansion. Sir Lawrence Palk was active in the 1820s and 1830s in developing Torquay and the arrival of the railway in

---

[57] Granville, A. B., *The spas of England, and principal sea-bathing places*, 3 Vols. (H. Colburn), 1841. See also, Hembry, Phyllis May, edited and completed by Cowie, Leonard W., and Cowie, Evelyn Elizabeth, *British spas from 1815 to the present: a social history*, (Fairleigh Dickinson University Press), 1997.

[58] See, Walker, H. H., and Neesam, M. G., *History of Harrogate under the Improvement Commissioners, 1841-1884*, (Manor Place), 1986.

[59] Millward, Roy, 'Railways and the Evolution of Welsh Holiday Resorts', in ibid, Evans, A. K. B., and Gough, John, (eds.), *The impact of the railway on society in Britain: essays in honour of Jack Simmons*, pp. 211-224, Yates, Nigel, *The Welsh seaside resorts: growth, decline, and survival*, (Trivium Publications occasional papers, 1), 2006, Rees, Arfon D., 'Seaside, Llanelli: a changing landscape', *The Carmarthenshire Antiquary*, Vol. 39, (2003), pp. 95-104.

[60] Travis, John, *The Rise of the Devon Seaside Resorts, 1750-1900*, (University of Exeter Press), 1993, is a good case study.

1848 was greeted with a town holiday. It was promoted as an autumn and winter resort deliberately to offset the spasmodic conditions of the holiday trade. The late holiday season was largely a middle- or upper-class prerogative and to attract this clientele resorts needed to offer both creature comforts and the right tone. New middle-class resorts, such as Bournemouth and Eastbourne, were better able to lengthen their seasons, something working-class resorts like Southend and Blackpool could not do. [61] Exclusivity was encouraged. At Folkestone the resident Earls of Radnor were responsible for the new town that emerged on the cliffs to attract genteel society. At Skegness the prime mover was H. V. Tippet, agent of the Earl of Scarborough and Fleetwood commemorated its developer by name. [62]

The history of pleasure resorts is more complicated than that of the middle-class resorts. The outstanding new resort was Blackpool made by the customs of the textile trades: many northern textile towns had their 'wakes' (or holiday weeks) when factories closed and the towns emptied for the seaside. [63] In some places the whole town took a break, as in the July Glasgow Fair when excursion steamers on the Clyde and the railways to the Ayrshire coastal resorts were packed. The turning point was the late 1860s and 1870s. Bank Holidays (under an Act of 1871) gave working-class trippers time for holidays, though legislation to provide a week's holiday with pay did not come until 1938.

Real wages increased in the 1870s and friendly societies and holiday clubs encouraged the habit of saving, so the prospects of textile workers spending time at the coast increased. The organisation of holidays, some with pay but most without, resulted in the development of block bookings and bargain rates. Blackpool did not discourage middle-class visitors and Lytham St Anne's offered sanctuary for those affronted by Blackpool's common side. Blackpool was established as a mecca for entertainment: there were winter gardens, pleasure pavilions, aquarium, music halls, its three piers, ballrooms and theatres (Frank Matcham created the Grand Theatre in 1894) but its 500 foot imitation Eiffel Tower (1891-1894) was astonishing. Nowhere was everything gathered together, and in such proportions, as at Blackpool that gained a reputation as the premier, not just a plebeian, resort though Brighton vastly exceeded

---

[61] Yearsley, Ian, *A history of Southend*, (Phillimore), 2001.

[62] Fletcher, Allan, 'The role of landowners, entrepreneurs and railways in the urban development of the north Wales coast during the nineteenth century', *Welsh History Review*, Vol. 16, (1993), pp. 514-541, provides a good case study.

[63] Walton, John K., *Blackpool*, (Keele University Press), 1998.

it in size. As an older community, Brighton contained deeper pockets of resistance to the new tourist trends. Blackpool had three times as many lodging-houses and the seaside landlady was very much a creation of Blackpool. [64] But Brighton had three times as many hotels. Brighton resisted the influx of revelling lowborn Londoners and certain residents and hoteliers lobbied the railway companies to limit the number of cheap return tickets to London. It was, however, investment in amenities that turned the plebeian tide or at least stemmed it. Two substantial piers were built in 1866 and 1896 but the principal investment was in baroque hotels in the late-nineteenth century to seduce the rich and nouveaux riches from the French Riviera. Royal patronage was essential: first class ticket sales from London to Brighton doubled following the visit of Edward VII in 1909.

There was more to Brighton than grand hotels. In the 1870s, observers commented that both Brighton and Hastings were 'marine suburbs of London'. [65] Several other resorts qualified as satellites or suburbs. Southport, twenty miles north of Liverpool, is a good example. Connected by rail in 1848, its population rose from 5,000 in 1851 to 48,000 in 1901. Southport had all the trappings of a middle-class holiday centre but it also represented Liverpool wealth by the sea. The second home phenomenon was evident at resorts both inland and coastal. Leeds and Bradford businessmen colonised Scarborough as well as Ilkley and Harrogate. Wealthy Lancashire businessmen settled in the Lake District as well as in Cheshire. This was part of the general movement, temporary and permanent, from big cities.

Suburbia

Suburban growth is one of the great features of the nineteenth century.[66] It is possible to identify three phases of suburban growth in this period. In the first half of the century improved road communication, by private carriage or public coach, facilitated ribbon

---

[64] Walton, John K., *The Blackpool Landlady: A social history*, (Manchester University Press), 1978, and 'The Blackpool Landlady Revisited', *Manchester Region History Review*, Vol. 8, (1994), pp. 23-31.
[65] Smiles, Samuel, *The life of George Stephenson and of his son Robert Stephenson: comprising also a history of the invention and introduction of the railway locomotive*, (Harper), 1868, p. xviii.
[66] Reeder, D. A., *Suburbanity and the Victorian city*, (Leicester University Press), 1980, and Bond, Winstan, and Divall, Colin, (eds.), *Suburbanising the masses: public transport and urban development in historical perspective,* (Ashgate), 2003.

development. City merchants built grand villas in picturesque settings along the highways that radiated from the major cities, especially London. Then from the mid-nineteenth century a new wave emerged, aided by the railways, that threatened to engulf exclusive villadom with the lower- and middle-middle-classes. Finally, in the late-nineteenth century working-class dormitories threatened the status of suburbia again. Many contemporaries believed the development of suburbia to have spoiled the cities. The suburban dream equalled selfishness, a rejection of the obligation and commitment to the city where the suburbanite earned his living. Suburbs highlighted class distinctions residentially and the core of the cities became depopulated. Suburban development was prompted by a series of factors. There was the demographic upsurge; of particular importance was the expansion of the lower middle-class. Clerks increased from 2.5 per cent of all occupied males in 1851 to over 7 per cent in 1911: a rise from fewer than 150,000 to over 900,000 individuals. Though the composition of the class was varied and the single category concealed a range of character, responsibility and income, the clerk was the butt of snob jokes. [67]

Clapham, once among the most affluent Georgian suburb, remained in the 1860s a citadel of stockbrokers and merchants with easy access to open countryside. By 1900, Clapham was closed in and had deteriorated socially into a clerkly capital. Around provincial cities the same process is evident. Acock's Green, a village four miles from the centre of Birmingham, became unbearable for the upper middle-classes as it was engulfed by the expanding city. By 1903, it had become, as the *Birmingham Daily Mail* commented:

> ...abandoned to the smaller house -- the house adapted to the means of the family man of limited income who like to live just outside the artisan belt encircling the city. [68]

There was the ability of people to extend their journey to work. The combination of rising real wages and reduced hours of work by allowing more travelling time were necessary preconditions for the growth of mass suburbs. The presence of a responsive building industry, ready capital and compliant landowners was essential to

---

[67] Studies of suburbia have often focussed on London; see, for example, Dyos, H. J., *Victorian Suburb: A Study of the Growth of Camberwell*, (Leicester University Press), 1966 and Pullen, D.E., *Sydenham: from hamlet to suburban town*, (D. E. Pullen), 1974.
[68] Cit, ibid, Waller, P. J., *Town, City and Nation, England 1850-1914*, p. 148.

organise and effect the transfer. There was also the matter of taste and visions of family privacy and class exclusiveness. There were also certain negative conditions in, for instance, the prejudice against apartment building that ensured that English cities, if not Scottish ones, expanded outwards rather than upwards. Purpose-built flats for the poor only emerged after it was clear that they could not take advantage of decentralised housing. The need for cheap, central accommodation was undeniable for the poor who needed to be close to possible work. The exception was in the industrial north-east where two-storey flats were commonplace. Generally, relatively low-density housing spilling out of open towns was the norm. City centres were vacated for residential purposes, left to bankers by day and prostitutes by night gave a special tone to these constructions.

Suburbia tended to Conservatism in politics, a counterweight to urban Liberal radicalism and socialist collectivism. [69] Central city and suburban conflict fast replaced the town-country conflict that previously dominated politics. Lord George Hamilton's election for Middlesex in 1868 is commonly regarded as inaugurating the Conservative trend in suburban south-east England. By 1900, as a party organiser commented to a leading Liberal Lord Rosebery:

> ...as the middle and artisan classes had prospered or acquired their houses they have inclined to the Conservative party because they dread the doctrine which Sidney Webb thinks would be so popular.

The suburban movement represented the beginnings of the gradual move from a society in which most people rented accommodation to one in which many envisaged owning their homes. About 1,500 building societies existed in 1850 but by 1895 there were some 2,600 societies with 600,000 members placed on a statutory basis in 1874 and 1894. [70] In 1914, tenancies remained the norm for

---

[69] Coetzee, Frans, 'Villa Toryism reconsidered: conservatism and suburban sensibilities in late-Victorian Croydon', *Parliamentary History*, Vol. 16, (1997), pp. 29-47, and Roberts, Matthew,' "Villa toryism" and popular conservatism in Leeds, 1885-1902', *Historical Journal*, Vol. 49, (2006), pp. 217-246. Moore, J. R., 'Liberalism and the politics of suburbia: electoral dynamics in late-nineteenth-century South Manchester', *Urban History*, Vol. 30, (2003), pp. 225-250, gives a Liberal perspective.

[70] See, for example, Pooley, Colin G., and Harmer, Michael J., *Property ownership in Britain c. 1850-1950: the role of the Bradford Equitable Building Society and the Bingley Building Society in the development of homeownership*, (Granta Editions), 1999, and more generally Johnson, Paul A., *Saving and spending: The working-class economy in Britain, 1870-1939*, (Oxford University Press), 1985.

90 per cent of the population. The property-owning democracy was a product of the post-war periods. [71]

The suburbs were much criticised by contemporaries. Walter Besant in 1909 said they were:

> ...without any society; no social gatherings or institutions; as dull a life as mankind ever tolerated....[72]

Yet their benefits were plain. Thousands gained a precious privacy in a home of their own in quiet and healthy surroundings, within reach of the countryside. Shopping facilities, initially poor, improved dramatically with the displacement of the stall-holder and local craftsmen by the lock-up shop in the 1850s and the emergence of shopping centres in the 1880s containing branches of national retail chains like Boots, Liptons and Freeman, Hardy and Willis.[73] The infrastructure of suburbs was reinforced in other ways with the building of churches, schools, pubs and theatres.

There was also some decentralisation of industrial and business activity, some of which catered entirely for suburban needs: building and repair trades, bakeries and breweries, laundries, gas and electricity works. But lack of space and high rents and rates in city centres were driving other businesses to suburban sites. This development was generally part of the process of evolution of suburban sites. Camberwell, for example, began as a detached village outside London, became a satellite community and was fully absorbed as a suburb.[74] By 1900, a majority of its population of 259,000 both lived and worked in Camberwell itself. The extension in railway mileage between 1870 and 1912, from 13,562 to 20,038 miles, was the consequence of rural branch lines or suburban services. Many railways followed rather than anticipated suburban expansion. The growth in third-class suburban travel was of major importance in London. Outside London the railways were underused by commuters: the Nottingham Suburban Railway opened in 1889 could

---

[71] See, Daunton, Martin J., *A property-owning democracy?: Housing in Britain*, (Faber) 1987, for the period after 1900.

[72] Besant, Walter, *London in the Nineteenth Century*, (A. & C. Black), 1909, p. 262.

[73] See, Lancaster, Bill, *The department store: a social history*, (Leicester University Press), 1995, Benson, John, and Shaw, Gareth, (eds.), *The evolution of retail systems, c.1800-1914*, (Leicester University Press), 1991, and Chapman, S. D., *Jesse Boot of Boots the Chemists: a study in business history*, (Hodder & Stoughton), 1974.

[74] Boast, Mary, *The story of Camberwell*, rev. edition, (Southwark Local Studies Library), 2000.

not withstand the competition of trams and closed in 1916.

Planning towns

The distinctive tradition of English town planning was not extinguished by industrialisation but it was repressed. The term 'town planning' gained currency after 1900 as a result of debates in Germany and the USA. The problem with town planning in Britain, today as in the late-nineteenth century, was that too many planners thought in one-dimensional terms: architects concentrated on houses, engineers on roads and so on. [75] The need was to co-ordinate people and functions, to complement social and industrial organisation and to produce plans that would permit growth and change. Much of the planned developments of the late-eighteenth and nineteenth centuries were largely the work of individuals or individual employers.

Many of the model factories and towns were motivated by feelings of industrial paternalism such as providing adequate housing for the working-classes. Railway centres like Swindon and Crewe found captive workers caged in regulation housing. The enlightened employer had humanitarian, philanthropic and other motives to experiment. Robert Owen's New Lanark blended capitalism and paternalism. For the Oldknows, Ashworths and Gregs, the motives were more ones of social control. Some model factory villages did involve ideas beyond the utilitarian or disciplinarian. The factory estates outside Bradford and Halifax planned by Titus Salt, Edward Akroyd and Francis Crossley between 1850 and 1870 were essays in urban regeneration. In Somerset the Quaker family of shoemakers, C & J Clark Ltd, built model housing for their workers in the industrial village of Street after production was mechanised in the 1850s. It was in the industrial Midlands and north that the most significant extensions of the tradition were made: Lever's Port Sunlight in 1888, Cadbury's Bourneville in 1895 and Rowntree's New Earswick in 1902.[76] The Garden City was the ideal, the concept of Ebenezer

---

[75] On the development of urban planning see Sutcliffe, A., (ed.), *The Rise of Modern Urban Planning 1800-1914*, (Mansell), 1981, (Taylor and Francis), 1998, Meller, Helen, *Towns, Plans and Society in Modern Britain*, (Cambridge University Press), 1997, and Beach, Abigail, and Tiratsoo, Nick, 'The planners and the public', in ibid, Daunton, Martin J., (ed.), *The Cambridge urban history of Britain, Vol. 3: 1840-1950*, pp. 525-550, for an invaluable synthesis of recent research. See also, Hardy, Dennis, *From garden cities to new towns: campaigning for town and country planning, 1899-1946*, (E. & F. N. Spon), 1991.

[76] On Bournville see, Bailey, A. R., and Bryson, J. R., 'Quaker industrial patronage: George Cadbury and the construction of Bournville model

Howard author of *Tomorrow: A Peaceful Path to Real Reform* (1898), reissued in 1902 as *Garden Cities of To-morrow*.[77] Town and country, Howard argued, must be married in garden cities to enjoy the best of both, with low density housing, green belt and separate industrial and agricultural zones. The result was the first garden city at Letchworth.[78]

Decentralisation of housing, as in the development of suburbia and planning, reflected land values, social forces and cheaper transport. From the 1870s, a growing 'civic gospel' began to create progressive municipal involvement in provision and regulation of housing and such amenities as baths, markets, libraries, art galleries and museums, parks and recreation spaces, as well as gas, electricity and, by the late-nineteenth century, transport services.[79] This larger social role was a prelude to more interventionist planning principles and policies. By 1900, most large towns were involved in such 'municipal socialism'. The first direct state intervention in town planning per se was the Housing, Town Planning etc. Act 1909.[80] It was limited in scope to building and land-use plans for developing peripheral areas of towns and was permissive rather than mandatory. Where enlightened municipal officials, such as Liverpool's Chief Engineer James Brodie, and a philosophy of planning as in the University of Liverpool's Department and Lever Chair of Civil Design established in 1910 came together the result was a degree of quality of layout of suburbs and roads. But little was achieved before 1918.

---

village', *Quaker Studies*, Vol. 11, (2006), pp. 96-124, and Harrison, M., *Bournville: model village to garden suburb*, (Phillimore), 1999.

[77] Ward, Stephen V., 'Ebenezer Howard: his life and times', in Parsons, K.C., and Schulyer, David, (eds.), *From garden city to green city: the legacy of Ebenezer Howard*, (Johns Hopkins University Press), 2002, pp. 14-37, and Meacham, Standish, *Regaining paradise: Englishness and the early garden city movement*, (Yale University Press), 1998.

[78] Miller, Mervyn, *Letchworth: the first garden city*, rev. edition, (Phillimore), 2002.

[79] Hill, Kate, *Culture and Class in English Public Museums, 1850-1914*, (Ashgate), 2005, considers the development of museums as a means of educating the working-classes and the shift from private aristocratic leadership, toward a middle-class civic directorship and a growing professional body of curators as part of the emergence of a dominant urban middle-class culture. See also, Gunn, Simon, *The Public Culture of the Victorian Middle Class: Ritual and Authority in the English Industrial City 1840-1914*, (Manchester University Press), 2000.

[80] Herbert-Young, Nicholas, 'Central government and statutory planning under the Town Planning Act, 1909', *Planning Perspectives*, Vol. 13, (1998), pp. 341-355.

How can we interpret urbanisation?

Transport played an essential role in the development of bigger, functionally more specialised towns from 1830. The railways created new towns such as Swindon, Crewe, Ashford and Wolverton, workshops and company headquarters at strategic sites and junctions within their regional system. Railway companies also added new impetus to old-established towns such as Derby, Doncaster and Newton Abbot, while specialist suburbs or satellites focused on railway and engineering works developed at Springburn (Glasgow), Hunslet (Leeds), Gorton (Manchester) and Saltley (Birmingham). Railways also played a key role in the growth of specialist resorts and residential towns. It was only with the coming of railways and the establishment of a national rail network in the 1840s that a fully integrated urban system developed and the constraints of time and distance that kept all cities apart from London tightly bounded in the early Victorian period were progressively reduced. This profound social revolution led to a period of great change in the structure of the urban system and the extent, characteristics and internal and external relations of cities. The first phase of railway construction confirmed the new regional urban hierarchy of the nineteenth century in its focus on London, the provincial capitals and industrial centres.

Urbanism became more pervasive and individual towns became more populous. In 1831, some 44 per cent of the population of England and Wales and 32 per cent of Scotland's was urban dwelling. By 1891, the proportions had increased to 75 and 65 per cent respectively. Big towns grew at the expense of the small. In 1830, London was the only 'million' city but about one-sixth of Britain's population lived in large towns of over 100,000. By the 1890s, nearly two-fifths did so and, in addition to London, another five city-regions had over a million people: Glasgow, Manchester, Birmingham, Liverpool and possibly Leeds. Such regional capitals were major centres of commerce and industrial services. Major ports, such as Liverpool and Glasgow, rivalled and in some activities surpassed London.

There was also an increase in the size and number of manufacturing towns. Many were highly specialised. The total number of towns of over 2,500 in England and Wales doubled between 1831 and 1901 from 412 to 895. Up to 1850, the fastest growing towns were in the major manufacturing areas of the industrial revolution, the West Midlands, the Potteries, south Lancashire and west Yorkshire. By 1871, some of the new industrial towns like Cardiff and Middlesbrough had almost outstripped slow-growing historic centres such as Chester, York and Exeter. Towards 1900, renewed urban concentration of economic activity led to overspill of great cities into surrounding residential and satellite towns. In parallel, some older centres were revitalised as new industries sought out skilled labour from declining crafts or as shifting values drew industries back to older towns such as Norwich, Coventry, Northampton, Leicester and Derby.

One level in the urban hierarchy, the small country town lost ground and the percentage of Britain's population in towns under 10,000 had changed little by the 1890s. Rural depopulation reduced the demand for crafts and services in market and many county towns; cottage industries lost ground to factory production and increased accessibility by rail to the larger towns reduced the range of shopping and services, leading to a decline of many hitherto thriving little towns. Between 1830 and 1914, Britain became an overwhelmingly urban culture. It led to new ways of living and a range of environmental and governmental problems but it was largely ad hoc expansion rather than planned growth.

How far did the state intervene in housing?

It was the concentration of people in the burgeoning towns and cities of manufacturing Britain in the eighteenth and nineteenth centuries that led to a growing housing crisis. [81] The inflow of population to towns before 1830 was accommodated both by massive new buildings and the subdivision and change of use in existing buildings. Many separate builders and developers provided new building in a variety of different ways especially where there was no shortage of building land in and around towns. Where land for development was less readily available, housing development proved more problematic. For instance, in 1671, the estimated population of Dunstable in Bedfordshire was around one thousand living in 209 houses and the town followed national trends in growing in size during the eighteenth century.[82] In 1801, there were 296 families living in 245 houses with a population of 1,296 men, women and children. Two houses were empty giving an average of 5.3 people living in each house, rather

---

[81] For urban housing Chapman, S. D., (ed.), *The History of Working-class Housing: A Symposium*, (David & Charles), 1971, Gauldie, E., *Cruel Habitations: a history of working-class housing 1780-1918*, (Allen and Unwin), 1978, and Burnett, J., *A Social History of Housing 1815-1985*, (Methuen), 2nd edition, 1986, are major works. Rodger, R., *Housing in Urban Britain 1780-1914*, (Macmillan), 1989, (Cambridge University Press), 1996, is an excellent bibliographical study.

[82] Marshall, Lydia M., (ed.), *The Bedfordshire Hearth Tax Return for 1671*, (Bedfordshire Historical Record Society), Vol. 16, 1935.

higher than the 4.8 people for 1671. Between 1801 and 1841, the population of Dunstable doubled to nearly 2,600. The only new residential developments in this period were houses built on the medieval lanes; the rest of the increase came from building on waste land and infilling. There was, nevertheless, a doubling in the number of houses in the town in this forty-year period from 247 houses to 489 houses, an average of six new houses a year. Despite this, in 1841 there was considerable overcrowding with over half the houses having more than six inhabitants, a situation exacerbated by the large number of lodgers, generally women employed in the straw trade.

The landowner was not generally the builder, though small infill developments in gardens and yards could be carried out by the original owner. Usually land was sold to a middleman or developer who would finance and organise the building process. Landowners included municipal corporations, as for instance in Liverpool and Newcastle, charities, schools and churches, large private landowners and professional and businessmen with small parcels of land. Developers could include local merchants, tradesmen, professional men especially lawyers and builders who would raise capital locally to finance house construction. Land was conveyed freehold in perhaps half of all sales, or through a building lease. Urban house building before 1830 took many forms. Most cities had some grand housing for the rich and leisured classes, perhaps best typified by the sweeping terraces built by John Wood in Bath and the development of Edinburgh's New Town from the 1750s. Artisans' housing ranged from substantial terraced houses to small courts. In Birmingham a relatively affluent skilled craftsman might live in a two or three storey house with two rooms on each floor with an associated yard and workshop. It cost up to £200 to buy in 1800 and was rented for at least £8 per year. Only a minority of workers could afford such rents and many houses were multi-occupied by 1830. From the 1770s, rows of back-to-back houses were being constructed costing £60 to buy but could be rented for less than £5 a year.

However, as pressure on space increased many of these were also multi-occupied. Some of the worst housing conditions in 1830 were found in London where population pressures and constraints on space were far more acute than in provincial towns. Working-class families generally lived in a single room or cellar without proper sanitation or water supply and paid 2-3 shillings per week rent. Lodging houses were also common in London, and in the poorest districts as many as 15 people would sleep in one room, each paying

1 or 2 pence for a night's shelter. [83] It is hard to compare rural and urban housing conditions. Contemporary descriptions tend to focus on the horrors of urban living experienced by the very poor, but the situation was little different for the rural poor. The main difference was in the density of urban living. Living literally on top of or beneath neighbours in a multi-occupied tenement was a new experience for many requiring considerable adjustments in lifestyles and daily routine.

Why was there a free market in housing?

Victorian cities were in a state of constant social flux. Many residents in all large cities were migrants but they often did not stay long in one place: 45-55 per cent of urban populations either died or moved from a town within ten years. Most housing throughout the period 1830 to 1914 was rented and owner-occupancy rarely accounted for more than 10 per cent of the housing stock before 1918.[84]

Rented accommodation came in a vast array of types. In central areas most was provided through the construction of purpose-built working-class housing or was in large multi-occupied dwellings filtered down from the middle-classes who had moved to suburban villas or more spacious town houses. From 1850, terraced suburbs increasingly housed the skilled working-class. For those on low incomes, rent levels were crucial to housing availability. Although cheap housing had been built in many cities in the early-nineteenth century, by the 1850s, it was increasingly difficult to build new housing to rent at much below 5s per week, well beyond the means of those on low or irregular incomes. Such families had little option but to rent lodgings or take slum housing in the city centre. Income determined where you lived and construction costs controlled the type of housing that was built in different locations. In such areas as Whitechapel or St. Giles in London or dockside areas and commercial districts of Liverpool, slum housing could be obtained quite easily. Accommodation was confined and relatively expensive; for example a single room 12 feet square could be rented for 1s 6d or more per week in a provincial town and for rather more in London.

---

[83] Crook, Tom, 'Accommodating the outcast: common lodging houses and the limits of urban governance in Victorian and Edwardian London', *Urban History*, Vol. 35, (2008), pp. 414-436.

[84] Rodger, Richard, 'The Invisible Hand: Market Forces, Housing and the Urban Form in Victorian Cities', in ibid, Fraser, Derek, and Sutcliffe, Anthony, (eds.) *The Pursuit of Urban History*, pp. 190-211, and Baer, William C., 'Is speculative building underappreciated in urban history?', *Urban History*, Vol. 34, (2007), pp. 296-316.

It could be dirty and facilities were shared with the other tenants.

By 1850, construction of new housing in the central areas of towns had almost ceased, but lower-density terraced housing was expanding rapidly in new residential suburbs of all English and Welsh towns. In Scotland tenement construction continued to be the norm. A new terraced house with four rooms, its own privy and in-house water supply would probably cost 5-7 shillings per week to rent. Relatively few such properties were multi-occupied, though the family might take in a lodger. Working-class home ownership was feasible only for those with relatively stable incomes in prosperous areas because of repayments of around 10 shillings per month. High levels were found in parts of north east Lancashire, County Durham, the West Riding and South Wales. Housing provided by employers or by philanthropic organisations, like the Peabody Trust in London, was often locally significant but never accommodated more than a few per cent of the population.

The process of residential decentralisation with the construction of suburban housing estates by private enterprise gathered momentum after 1890. This was most clearly seen in London, but similar processes were operating in all large towns. In 1850, Ilford, for instance, was a quiet village on the main railway line from London to Ipswich, seven miles from Liverpool Street station. In 1891, there were some 11,000 people in the parish, but by 1901, the new urban district had expanded to 41,240 people and its population almost doubled again by 1911. Two London builders, W. P. Griggs and A. C. Corbett, encouraged by the good railway communication, acquired large areas of land and began to develop massive private housing estates. In 1906, on the Griggs estate a four-room house started at £260, a four-bedroom, double-fronted house at £375 and a five-bedroom house at £450. Both the builders and Ilford Council provided further incentives to move to the suburbs. Corbett gave loans to purchasers to cover some of the cash deposit while Ilford Council used the Small Dwellings Acquisition Act 1899 to give cheap mortgages. Ilford is a classic example of the ways in which improved transport, availability of land, the willingness of entrepreneurs and public bodies to invest and the demand for suburban living combined to restructure the city in the early-twentieth century.

In the Housing of the Working-class Act 1890, government intervened in the free market for the first time and, in so doing, fundamentally affected the expansion and planning of towns. Though the provision of council housing was slight before 1919, some councils had begun building houses before 1890 and the Act gave further impetus to such schemes. Some 24,000 council units were built in Britain before 1914 but most were concentrated in London (9,746 units), Liverpool (2,895 units) and Glasgow (2,199 units). These schemes were too few in number to make any real impact on housing needs and, in any case, rent levels and selection procedures tended to exclude the very poor.[85]

There was little fundamental change in housing between 1830 and 1914. Paying rent to private owners remained the norm, accounting for 90 per cent of all houses. Council housing accounted for only 1 per cent in 1914 and housing associations 9 per cent. Though all towns spawned a succession of new residential suburbs, these were mainly for the affluent working and lower-middle-class families who would leave the older parts of the city centre, and new skilled in-migrants. The poor remained trapped in low-cost, sub-standard housing. The spatial segregation of social groups was cleared structured by the economic realities, reflected in income and occupation that controlled access to different types of housing.

Why was housing such a problem in London

By the 1870s, it was clear that poor housing was one of the most serious elements in the public health problem and attention tended to concentrate on the larger cities, especially London. [86] The need for action had been recognised since the 1840s, though effective measures were few. In 1851, Shaftesbury introduced a pioneering Labouring Classes Lodging Act that attempted, albeit unsuccessfully, to raise money for building or leasing houses for the use of the poor. The 1868 and 1875 Acts promoted by the Liberal W. H. Torrens and the Conservative Richard Cross both accepted the principle that houses must be kept in good repair. The 1875 Act enabled demolition of grossly unsatisfactory property to be effected and solid dwellings built in their place. It was, however, permissive, and met with mixed success at best. Joseph Chamberlain used it in Birmingham, but more to clear the city centre for prestige buildings than to re-house the poor. Others were deterred by the cost and by 1881, only ten of the 87 municipal authorities had made use of it.

---

[85] See, for example, Durgan, Shirley, 'Providing for "the needs and purses of the poor": council housing in Chelmsford before 1914', *Local Historian*, Vol. 33, (2003), pp. 175-189, Damer, Seán. '"Engineers of the Human Machine": The Social Practice of Council Housing Management in Glasgow, 1895-1939', *Urban Studies*, Vol. 37, (2000), pp. 2007-2026, and Chinn, Carl, *Homes for people: council housing and urban renewal in Birmingham, 1849-1999*, (Brewin), 1999.
[86] Jones, G. Steadman, *Outcast London: A Study of the Relationship between Classes in Victorian Society*, (Oxford University Press), 1971, (Penguin), 1975, is a classic study of the impact of conditions on the working population in London.

Many observers pointed out that those dispossessed when their property was pulled down could not afford the rent for better property and simply moved into other overcrowded properties one or two miles away.

Building activity reached its peak in 1876, after which construction declined and rents rose at the time of bad trade when working people had little money to spare. The issue was whether state intervention could resolve the problem without, as Shaftesbury among others believed, enfeebling those it was designed to support. The idea of individual endeavour to relieve distress was closely related to the basic social and religious assumptions of mid-Victorian society. The organisers of charity were committed individualists but they believed that it needed organisation. The focus for the organisers' efforts was London because the social problems were most extreme and the giving most generous. The most important of the philanthropic organisations was the Charity Organisation Society founded in 1869. Octavia Hill, who had close links with COS, worked in the intractable area of the housing of the poor. [87] But even she insisted that housing should be made to pay. She would allow no arrears and no sub-letting and she turned out those who fell into debt.

Charity bodies and housing associations were alone unable to resolve the problem of London's housing. [88] The 1880s saw an increasing public concern with housing as the problems of the cities grew. The publication of *The Bitter Cry of Outcast London* in 1883 entered a passionate plea for state direction of a housing policy. There had been a parliamentary Select Committee on housing in 1881-1882 and a Royal Commission was established in 1884-1885 that was much more successful in setting out the problems than in suggesting practical remedies for them. Local authorities were exhorted to be more active, and cheap workmen's train fares were recommended to enable the poor to live away from the overcrowded centres of big cities. [89] The Commission's recommendations,

---

[87] Darley, Gillian, *Octavia Hill: A Life*, (Constable), 1990, is a major study of one of the foremost housing reformers of the nineteenth century. Hill, Octavia, *Homes of the London Poor*, (Macmillan), 1883, is her most important study of the issue. See also, Whelan, R., (ed.), *Octavia Hill and the social housing debate: essays and letters by Octavia Hill,* (IEA Health & Welfare Unit), 1998.

[88] See, for example, Tarn, J. N., 'The Peabody donation fund: the role of a housing society in the 19th century', *Victorian Studies*, Vol. 10, (1966), pp. 7-38, and Parker, Franklin, *George Peabody: a biography,* rev. edition, (Vanderbilt University Press), 1995.

[89] Morton, Jane, *"Cheaper than Peabody": local authority housing from 1890 to 1919*, (Rowntree Foundation), 1991, considers London.

however, skirted the essential issues. A codifying Housing Act was passed in 1885 and the Housing of the Working-class Act was passed in 1890. This legislation, however, was hardly the landmark that some historians have suggested. In effect before 1914, the State exhorted but refused to insist. The permissive principle remained dominant and what initiatives there were took place because of local government activities.

What was 'municipal socialism' and how effective was it?

The role of local authorities in improving amenities was a matter of importance and some controversy before 1914. A Medical Officer of Health was first appointed in Liverpool in 1847 but other cities did not do so until the 1860s, for example Manchester in 1868, or the 1870s. As the interventionist role of local authorities was defined, especially in the legislation of the 1870s and 1880s, the number of local authority employees increased. [90] This resulted in uncoordinated responses. Frederic Harrison commented in 1875 that local self-government might stand for 'local mis-government and local no-government'. [91] Ratepayers understood that increased staff meant increased rates and landowners saw their rents decline if they needed to improve their properties. Councillors wanted to maintain their autonomy and restrict the role of what they saw as meddlesome inspectors. Working-class people were invariably hostile seeing intervention as a threat to liberty and privacy. This was, in part, the same attitude that opponents of Chadwick had exhibited in the 1850s. But this is only part of the reason. Where borough health departments were small, the police were used to enforce sanitary legislation. Property and possessions were damaged by fumigation procedures whenever infectious diseases were suspected. Provision for compensation existed after 1875 but was rarely taken. To the working-classes, inspection was deeply suspected and slum clearance aroused even more bitter resistance than inspections. Communities were broken up and dispersed by health authorities.

In 1850, municipal priorities were public order, street maintenance and lighting and the provision of basic sanitary services. There was some investment in gas and water supply but the scale of public amenities and municipal trading that developed in the next half century was altogether grander. But was this 'socialist'? Although

---

[90] On the development of public utilities, see Foreman-Peck, James and Millward, Robert, *Public and Private Ownership of British Industry 1820-1990*, (Oxford University Press), 1994.

[91] Harrison, Frederic, *Order and Progress*, (Longman, Green and Co.), 1875, p. 226.

collectivism caused unease, there were some who did not see it as socialist. The Whig authority on local government, George Brodrick, said in April 1884 that Public Health and Education Acts were:

...founded on reasons of public utility, and not on the principle of equalising the lots of the higher and lower classes in the community. [92]

By contrast, Joseph Chamberlain speaking a year later in Warrington said:

The Poor-Law is Socialism, the Education Act is Socialism, the great part of our municipal work is Socialism; every kindly act of legislation by which the community recognises its responsibilities and obligations to its poorer members is socialistic....Our object is the elevation of the poor of the masses of the people -- a levelling up which shall do something to remove the excessive inequalities in the social condition of the people, and which is now one of the greatest dangers as well as the greatest injury to the State....[93]

In 1895, the later Conservative Prime Minister, A. J. Balfour, saw social legislation as:

The direct opposite and most effective antidote to socialist legislation...the adoption of what is good (in socialism) is the best preventative for what is bad. [94]

Social legislation was designed to raise the standard of living and provide efficient services that did not endanger existing institutions. A. K. Rollit, from 1890 to 1906 President of the Association of Municipal Corporations and a Tory Democrat, argued that the municipality should do what individuals 'cannot do, or do so well, for themselves'. The issue by the 1890s was not whether the state, locally or nationally, should intervene in matters of public concern but the level of that intervention and the balance between public and private utilities.

Chadwick's 1842 *Report* on the fifty largest towns had condemned private enterprise in providing clean and efficient water supplies. Legislation in 1847 and 1848 allowed municipalities to establish or to transfer privately owned, water companies. Additional

---

[92] See, Brodrick, George, C., *Literary Fragments*, (Spottiswoode & Co.), 1893, p. 188.
[93] Chamberlain, Joseph, *The Radical Platform, speeches by the Right Hon. J. Chamberlain*, 1885, p. 23.
[94] Balfour, A. J., speech in Manchester 16 January 1895, *Manchester Guardian*, 17 January 1895.

legislation in 1870 and 1875 cheapened and speeded up the process. Even so the assumption of water supply by local authorities was irregular: by 1871 only 250 of 783 urban districts provided some supply and by 1879 only 413 out of 944 urban districts were doing so while 290 were supplied by private companies. By 1914, two-thirds of the population were supplied by a public authority. There were various reasons for this situation. For the larger cities the massive cost of extending supplies brought local political turmoil. In Liverpool, the Rivington Pike scheme disrupted party political alignments for ten years after 1847, as did the Lake Vyrnwy scheme forty years later.[95] Supply was also a serious problem. Between 1850 and 1900, for instance, Manchester's population doubled and its daily water needs quadrupled from 8 to 32 million gallons. This meant piping water from areas where supplies could be found: Thirlmere in the Lake District, some eighty miles away, was tapped.[96] Finally, purity mattered and many rivers were seriously polluted by industrial effluent and untreated sewage. Waterborne diseases had not yet been eliminated and typhoid epidemics were common into the 1870s and isolated outbreaks, as in Cambridge in 1887 and Kings Lynn ten years later, still occurred.[97] To prevent contamination, as much as to ensure supply of water, there was a real need for co-ordination between local authorities.[98]

The municipalisation of gas contained some different features

---

[95] Roberts, Owen G., 'Developing the untapped wealth of Britain's 'Celtic Fringe': Water engineering and the Welsh landscape, 1870–1960', *Landscape Research*, Vol. 31, (2006), pp. 121-133, Pritchard, John Wyn, 'Water supply in Welsh towns, 1840-1900: control, conflict and development', *Welsh History Review*, Vol. 21, (2002), pp. 24-47.

[96] Ritvo, Harriet, 'Manchester v Thirlmere and the Construction of the Victorian Environment', *Victorian Studies*, Vol. 49, (2007), pp. 457-481.

[97] See the detailed case study by Richardson, Nigel, 'The Uppingham Typhoid Outbreaks of 1875-1877: A Rural Case-Study in Public Health Reform', *Social History of Medicine*, Vol. 20, (2007), pp. 281-296, 'Typhoid in Uppingham, Rutland, 1875-1877: reassessing the social context', *Local Historian*, Vol. 38, (2008), pp. 274-288, and *Typhoid in Uppingham: analysis of a Victorian town and school in crisis, 1875-1877*, (Pickering & Chatto), 2008.

[98] On the broader context see, Coopey, Richard, and Roberts, Owen G., 'Public Utility or Private Enterprise: Water and Health in the Nineteenth and Twentieth Centuries', in Borsay, Anne, (ed.), *Medicine in Wales c. 1800-2000: public service or private commodity?*, (University of Wales Press), 2003, pp. 21-39, Hassan, John, 'The water industry 1900-51: a failure of public policy?', in Millward, Robert, and Singleton, John, (eds.), *The political economy of nationalisation in Britain 1920-1950*, (Cambridge University Press), 1995, pp. 189-211.

from water but in both, as with tramways, the disturbance to public highways from the laying of services roused the municipal authorities' interest. [99] Nine municipalities took control of gas before 1850; another 18 in the 1850s, 22 in the 1860s, 76 in the 1870s, 24 in the 1880s, 50 in the 1890s and 25 between 1901 and 1910. Over two-thirds were northern and Midlands towns but several large cities including Liverpool, Sheffield, Newcastle and Bristol remained in the hands of private companies. [100] By 1910, local authority gas sales comprised 37 per cent of the total. The vast increase in domestic users was chiefly due to two inventions: the gas mantle and the slot meter. Towns and cities could take over gas companies in the same way as water companies. Gas companies, as local monopolies, could have exploited their position without municipal intervention.

By 1906, local authorities charged on average 2s 8d and private companies 2s 11d per thousand cubic feet of gas. The difference can be explained by the reluctance of local authorities to take over unprofitable concerns. It was the issue of profitability that roused arguments that were absent over water supply and a deceleration of the movement to municipal ownership can be seen from the 1880s partly because of the development of electricity. The threat from electricity in the 1880s to municipal gas profits led to the 1882 Act that limited an electricity company's licence to operate to 21 years after which a local authority has the right to purchase without compensation. This so discouraged the industry that in 1888 the licence was extended to 42 years. From the 1890s, however, municipal investment accounted for two-thirds of the organisation and distribution. [101]

As with electricity, technical economies and regional services were hindered by too rigid adherence to local government boundaries. This prevented local authority ownership and management of the majority of tramways. The Tramways Act 1870 chiefly licensed private enterprise and, though local authorities might

---

[99] Williams, Trevor, I., *A History of the British Gas Industry*, (Oxford University Press), 1981, pp. 1-60, Falkus, M. E., 'The British gas industry before 1850', *Economic History Review*, 2nd series, Vol. 20, (1967), pp. 494-508, Milward, Robert, and Ward, Robert, 'From private to public ownership of gas undertakings in England and Wales, 1851-1947; chronology, incidence and causes', *Business History*, Vol. 35, (3), (1993), pp. 1-21.

[100] See, for instance, Nabb, Harold, *The Bristol gas industry, 1815-1949*, (The Historical Association, Bristol Branch), 1987.

[101] Hennessey, R. A. S., *The electric revolution*, (Oriel Press), 1972, Byatt, I. C. R., *The British electrical industry, 1875-1914: the economic returns of a new technology*, (Oxford University Press), 1979.

build and lease tram systems, they could not operate them. By 1913, however, about 1,500 miles of local authority line existed and municipal ownership embraced 63 per cent of lines and 80 per cent of passengers carried.

There were other areas where local authorities could take a lead. The Housing Act 1890 determined public and private interests and some council housing was the consequence. Restrictions hedged other municipal ventures. Hull and several other towns established municipal telephone services; resort towns ventured into the entertainment business, Bournemouth even sponsored its own orchestra, Doncaster managed a racecourse, Worcester a dairy and Wolverhampton a cold store. Non-profit making activities were pursued with less vigour and voluntary provision was preferred. Consider public libraries. Their finances were limited by the maximum rate of halfpenny under the 1850 Act and from 1885 to 1919 by a penny rate. Take-up was patchy: by the late 1870s, only 86 rate-supported libraries existed. Since free-libraries were conceived as a service for the working-classes, the question whether those classes would really benefit and suspicion of the working-class public persisted. By 1910, a sizeable reading public had emerged with library loans doubling since 1896 from 26 to 46 million book issues. But fewer than 5 per cent of the population were registered borrowers. [102]

These enterprises did not, however, mark a transfer of control from private to municipal ownership, as many socialists wanted. 'Municipal socialism' was rarely, if ever, socialist. R. H. Tawney summed up the position in November 1914:

> The motive of nearly all these developments has been a purely utilitarian consideration for the consumer. They have not been inspired by any desire to introduce more just social arrangements....They have been inspired simply by the desire for cheap services....Clearly there are no germs of a revolution here. [103]

A review of municipal services inevitably results in a mixed account. It may be easy to scale down achievement but civic pride had genuine foundations. There is little doubt that improved sanitary

---

[102] Kelly, T., *A history of public libraries in Great Britain 1845-1975*, (Library Association), 1977, Pateman, John, 'Public Libraries and the Working Classes', *Library History*, Vol. 21, (2005), pp. 189-194, and McKitterick, David, 'Libraries, knowledge and public identity', in Daunton, Martin J., (ed.), *The organisation of knowledge in Victorian Britain*, (Oxford University Press), 2005, pp. 287-312.

[103] Winter, J. M., and Joslin, D. M., (eds.), *R. H. Tawney's Commonplace Book*, (Cambridge University Press), 2006, p. 80.

services in English towns enhanced the living standards of the nation.

By 1914, England could boast some remarkable civic creations but there was still a great deal wanting especially in respect of housing and town planning. In 1860, it was argued that municipalising essential services was a sound way of achieving efficiency and economy. By 1914, municipalisation had been widened to encompass 'desirable' as well as 'essential' services. But there was a widespread belief that the existing provision of services and the type of municipal management could not survive without major restructuring. Nationalisation, or the bringing of services under the State, provided one solution to this problem. Privatisation provided the alternative. The development of services after 1918 was, in many respects, a dialogue (albeit on occasions a dialogue of the deaf) between these two positions.

What was it like living in the countryside?

There is a tendency when considering nineteenth century Britain to concentrate on urban life and neglect its rural dimension. This reflects a period of unparalleled industrialisation, urbanisation and unprecedented urban problems. Yet in 1851, nearly half of the population of Britain lived in rural areas and many more had been born in the countryside or had experienced rural living. For much of the nineteenth century a rural view of the world continued to exert a significant influence in Britain. Successive Reform Acts may have redistributed power after 1832 to urban centres, but much political power and personal wealth remained in the countryside until the late-nineteenth century. [104]

Two further perceptions of rural life should be dispelled. The first was that rural life was in some way separate and distinct from that of towns. In fact, rural life in Britain had never been separate from the towns and, as nineteenth century urbanisation developed, the interconnectedness of rural and urban became stronger and more obvious. Few areas had no links with urban areas in the 1780s and by 1850, most rural dwellers had contact with the nearest market town; by the 1890s, upland Wales and the Highland and Islands of Scotland were being integrated socially and economically into a regional system

---

[104] The most useful general works on rural society are Horn, P., *The Rural World 1780-1850*, (Hutchinson), 1980, for the early period and Mingay, G. E., *The Social History of the English Countryside*, (Routledge), 1990, throughout though they need to be supplemented with Reay, Barry, *Rural Englands*, (Palgrave), 2004, and Short, Brian, (ed.), *The English Rural Community*, (Cambridge University Press), 1992. Howkins, A., *Reshaping Rural England*, (Harper Collins), 1991, deals with the post-1850 period.

focused increasingly on the larger towns. This connection took various forms. Improved communications, especially the railways, linked most villages into a comprehensive and complex transport system. Towns were economically dependent on rural labour and rural to urban migration created family links between town and countryside. There were also rural-based but urban-financed putting out industries. Through social interaction between rural and urban at fairs, markets and other meeting places. There was also a widespread belief that life in the countryside was in some ill-defined way 'better' than life in the towns. Commentators such as Engels misleadingly contrasted images of an idyllic rural life and the horrors of urban living:

> They did not need to overwork; they did no more than they chose to do and yet earned what they needed. They had leisure for healthful work in garden or field, work which, in itself, was recreation for them, and they could take part besides in the recreations and games of their neighbours....They were, for the most part, strong well-built people....Their children grew up in the fresh country air....while of eight or twelve hours work for them was no question. [105]

The reality was very different. In 1800, rural housing was a mixture of decaying older properties, poorly built new houses and a minority of decent stone or brick-built cottages for the more prosperous. The nature of work was, in some part, a determinant of the nature of rural housing. [106] Living space was more important for the domestic weaver or knitter who spent more time indoors than for the farm labourer who toiled for 12 hours a day in the field. By contrast, the single migrant who left home to seek work might have been hired at a hiring fair and either given accommodation as a lodger in the master's house (most common in the north and west of England) or housed and fed in sheds or outhouses along with other hired hands as in the arable counties of England in the early-nineteenth century.

Population growth since the mid-eighteenth century had led to a crisis in rural housing. [107] Many houses were permanently

---

[105] Engels, F., *The Condition of the Working Class in England*, (Penguin), 1987, p. 51.

[106] Broad, John, 'Housing the rural poor in southern England, 1650-1850', *Agricultural History Review*, Vol. 48, (2000), pp. 151-170, provides a long-term view.

[107] Armstrong, W. A., 'The Influence of Demographic Factors on the Position of the Agricultural Labourer in England and Wales, c1750-1914',

overcrowded with many rural parents bringing up six or more children in tiny two-room cottages. [108] Individual privacy was difficult and much of life, especially the development of friendships and courtship, was lived outside the home in lanes, woods and fields. Marriage was often delayed due to the lack of opportunity to set up home. Epidemic diseases such as smallpox or typhus spread rapidly in such overcrowded and insanitary conditions. Some landowners maintained 'closed' villages, where accommodation was limited to keep down the size of the population, and this exacerbated the problem of housing.[109]

By 1830, living conditions could be as unhealthy and harsh as in many towns. The quality of rural housing varied greatly and for the very poor it was often worse than its urban counterpart. [110] A combination of poor housing, lack of employment and poor social prospects frequently impelled town-ward migration rather than any specific urban attractions. The density of occupation of rural housing was often higher than that in towns. High natural increase in rural areas mostly offset migration losses and rural population densities continued to increase up to the 1840s. In many rural areas, the housing supply expanded more slowly than population; indeed some large landowners demolished cottages and took less responsibility for housing their labour force. Increasingly, urban housing had proper foundations, solid walls and slate roofs contrasting with the substandard character of much rural housing when first built. Most landowners accepted little responsibility for the provision of decent homes and, even in more prosperous areas such as North West

---

Agricultural History Review, Vol. 29, (1981), pp. 71-82, provides a long-term perspective.

[108] Hasbach, W., *A history of the English Agricultural Labourer*, (P. S. King & Son), 1908, translation of *Die englischen Landarbeiter in den letzten hundert Jahren und die Einhegungen*, (Duncker & Humblot), 1894, despite its age, contains much useful information but should now be read in conjunction with Armstrong, W. A., *Agricultural Workers 1770-1970*, (Batsford), 1988. Newby, Howard, *Country Life*, (Weidenfeld), 1987, is a major and readable study. Snell, K., *Annals of the Labouring Poor: Social Change and Agrarian England 1660-1900*, (Cambridge University Press), 1984, is a mine of information and interpretation.

[109] Holderness, B. A., "'Open' and 'close' parishes in England in the 18th and 19th centuries', *Agricultural History Review*, Vol. 20, (1972), pp. 126-139, Banks, Sarah, 'Nineteenth-century scandal or twentieth-century model? A new look at 'open' and 'close' parishes', *Economic History Review*, 2nd series, Vol. 41, (1988), pp. 51-73, and Spencer, D., 'Reformulating the 'closed' parish thesis: associations, interests, and interaction', *Journal of Historical Geography*, Vol. 26, (2000), pp. 83-98.

[110] Mingay, G. E., 'The rural slum', in Gaskell, S. M., (ed.), *Slums*, (Leicester University Press), 1990, pp. 92-143.

England, cottages were often small, cold and wet. In southern England, where there was more abject poverty, cottages often had mud walls, earth floors and neglected thatched roofs. [111] Such conditions persisted until the 1850s but during the remainder of the century, housing gradually improved as out-migration lessened pressure on housing stock and sanitary and housing reforms began to percolate into rural areas. On large estates and big arable farms, there was considerable rebuilding from the 1860s. Nevertheless, not all rural housing was bad: surviving nineteenth century houses include not only good quality homes of landowners, farmers and artisans, but well-built estate cottages and good-quality late-eighteenth century dwellings of rural factory workers.

For many rural families poor housing was combined with acute poverty. [112] Between 1815 and the mid-1830s, arable England underwent a deep depression. [113] Population growth led to a rural labour surplus that, except in areas where there was alternative employment, led to low wages. [114] James Caird found, in his agricultural survey of 1851, that there was considerable variety in wages between the 'high wage' north and west and 'low wage' south and east. [115] In the West Riding, wages were 13-14s per week but in

---

[111] For example, Sheppard, June A., 'East Yorkshire's Agricultural Labour Force in the mid-Nineteenth Century', *Agricultural History Review*, Vol. 9, (1961), pp. 43-54.

[112] On rural poverty, see Lee, Robert, *Unquiet country: voices of the rural poor, 1820-1880*, (Windgather), 2005, and *Rural society and the Anglican clergy, 1815-1911: encountering and managing the poor*, (Boydell), 2006 on Norfolk.

[113] Todd. A. C., 'An Answer to Poverty in Sussex, 1830-45', *Agricultural History Review*, Vol. 4, (1956), pp. 45-51, examines the problems in one area.

[114] Clark, Gregory, 'Farm wages and living standards in the industrial revolution: England, 1670-1869', *Economic History Review*, Vol. 54, (2001), pp. 477-505, provides a valuable longitudinal study. See also, Armstrong, A., *Farmworkers: a Social and Economic History 1770-1980*, (Batsford), 1988.

[115] Caird, James, *English Agriculture in 1850-51*, (Longman, Brown, Green and Longmans), 1852, pp. 480, 512, 514, 516. See also, Vaughan, W. E., 'Agriculture output, rents and wages in Ireland, 1850-1880', in Cullen, L. M., and Furet, François, (eds.), *Ireland and France, 17th-20th centuries: towards a comparative study of rural history*, (Éditions de l'Ecole des Hautes Études en Sciences Sociales), 1980, pp. 85-97, Houston, George, 'Farm wages in central Scotland from 1814 to 1870', *Journal of the Royal Statistical Society*, Series A, Vol. 118, (1955), pp. 224-228, and Molland, R. and Evans, G., 'Scottish farm wages from 1870 to 1900', *Journal of the Royal Statistical Society, ser. A: General*, Vol. 113, (1950), pp. 220-227.

southern counties like Berkshire and Suffolk floundered at only 7-8s per week. Northern wages were higher because of the greater prosperity of mixed and pastoral areas compared to wheat-growing counties and, particularly, to competition for labour from industrial towns where wages were generally higher. This led to widespread rural distress and rural protests such as riots in East Anglia in 1816 and 1822 and the more extensive Swing riots of 1830 across southern England. [116]

Rural industrial workers were usually better off. [117] In areas such as the south Pennines survival of a dual farming-weaving economy gave some protection against poverty though, as the textile industry became more mechanised and centralised in factories, the distress of rural textile workers mushroomed. The effects of rural poverty can be seen in malnutrition and associated ill-health. [118] A survey in 1863 showed that most English rural labourers relied heavily on a diet of bread and potatoes, with meat consumption varying from season to season and area to area, though men were generally better fed than

---

See contemporary analysis in Wilson, Arthur Fox, *Earnings of Agricultural Labourers By Great Britain Board of Trade*, (HMSO), 1905.

[116] Charlesworth, A., *An Atlas of Rural Protest in Britain 1548-1900*, (Croom Helm), 1983, is an excellent introductory work, containing useful maps and commentary. Griffin, Carl J., *Protest, Politics and Work in Rural England, 1700-1850*, (Palgrave Macmillan), 2013, provides a valuable synthesis. The 1816 East Anglia riots are explotred in Peacock, A. J., *Bread or Blood: a study of the agrarian riots in East Anglia in 1816*, (Gollancz), 1965. For 1830 see, Hobsbawm, E. J., and Rudé, George, *Captain Swing*, (Penguin), 1973, and Griffin, Carl J., *The Rural War: Captain Swing and the Politics of Protest*, (Manchester University Press), 2012. Dunbabin, J. P. D., *Rural Discontent in Nineteenth Century Britain*, (Faber), 1975, and Archer, John E., *"By a flash and a scare": incendiarism, animal maiming and poaching in East Anglia, 1815-1870*, (Oxford University Press), 1990, on arson as a form of protest. See also, Richardson, T. L. 'The agricultural labourers' standard of living in Lincolnshire, 1790-1840: social protest and public order', *Agricultural History Review*, Vol. 41, (1993), pp. 1-19, Jones, Peter, 'Swing, Speenhamland and rural social relations: the 'moral economy' of the English crowd in the nineteenth century', *Social History*, Vol. 32, (2007), pp. 271-290.

[117] Chartres, John, 'Rural industry and manufacturing', in ibid, Collins, E. J. T., (ed.), *The Agrarian History of England and Wales, Vol. 7: 1850-1914, part 2*, pp. 1101-1149.

[118] See contemporary analysis in Denton, John Bailey, *The Agricultural Labourer*, (Stanford), 1868, pp. 35-44, Wilson, Arthur Fox, *Earnings of Agricultural Labourers By Great Britain Board of Trade*, (HMSO), 1900.

the rest of the family. [119] Even so, the food supply in the countryside was rather better than that available to the urban poor: it was fresher and there were more opportunities to supplement it by poaching or from the cottage garden. [120] Despite increasing mechanisation agricultural work was still hard and poorly regulated. Rural labourers worked longer for less pay than most other workers and much of the welfare legislation passed between 1900 and 1914 did not apply to the agricultural sector.

The social composition of rural areas changed between 1830 and 1890 in several respects. Selective rural out-migration removed many younger and more active members of the community. Areas close to towns began to experience the urban to rural drift of wealthy families seeking a house in the countryside. Commuter villages grew around cities like Leeds, Manchester and especially London particularly where there were good rail connections. Rural resort areas also began to expand. In the late-nineteenth century, Windermere became the centre of an invasion of the Lake District for recreation. This was especially true of Manchester merchants who established second homes around its fringes and elsewhere. The image of the rural idyll had by the 1890s become firmly implanted as a middle-class vision of the countryside that they increasingly imprinted through residence, landownership and conservation movements. The National Trust was founded in 1895. [121] However, for many, the reality of rural life in the early years of the twentieth century remained harsh and often unpleasant. [122]

---

[119] Smith, Edward, 'Report to the Privy Council on the Food of the Poorer Labouring Classes', *Sixth Report of the Medical Officer of the Privy Council*, (George E. Eyre and William Spottiswoode), 1863, Appendix 6. Burnett, John, 'Country Diet', in Mingay, G. E., (ed.), *The Victorian Countryside*, (Routledge), 1981, Vol. 2, pp. 554-565, provides a summary.
[120] Freeman, Mark, 'Investigating rural poverty 1870-1914: problems of conceptualisation and methodology', in Bradshaw, Jonathan, and Sainsbury, Roy, (eds.), *Getting the measure of poverty: the early legacy of Seebohm Rowntree*, (Ashgate), 2000, pp. 255-274.
[121] Jenkins, Jennifer, 'The roots of the National Trust', *History Today*, Vol. 45, (1), (1995), pp. 3-9, and Moreau, Gilbert, 'Acquisition et gestion de patrimonie par les fondateurs du *National Trust*, 1895-1914', *Cahiers victoriens et édouardiens*, Vol. 48, (1999), pp. 159-172.
[122] Burchardt, Jeremy, *Paradise lost: rural idyll and social change in England since 1800*, (I. B. Tauris), 2002, pp. 67-76, 112-120.

8 The public's health

Britain became an increasingly urban society between 1832 and 1914. There is a flood of evidence for urban conditions in this period: reports, Blue Books, surveys, memoranda, diaries, books. [1] So what were urban conditions like in the 1800s? In what ways did those conditions change in the next century and why? [2] Although Dale Porter, [3] like Anthony Wohl and other social historians, paints a grim picture of London's environmental contamination, absence of adequate sanitation and lack of viable solutions to problems caused by human, animal, and industrial waste, he also asks the pointed question, how filthy was London actually? Cleanliness is in the eye of the beholder and there is a difference between the dismal levels of sanitation and public health that historians identify in hindsight and how most contemporaries perceived them.

Late Georgian London was generally considered clean and healthy by most people. Olsen cited evidence that visitors to London before 1830 were quite pleased by the healthy climate and sanitation of the capital. [4] He speculated that London's early Victorian reputation for filthiness stemmed most directly from the largely unexpected and shockingly swift cholera epidemic of 1832. This threw the medical profession into a panic since no one could explain what cholera was, let alone how to prevent it. Its horrifying symptoms and devastating if temporary mortality led the public and the media to

---

[1] On urban conditions and the problems of public health see Wohl, A. S., *Endangered Lives: Public Health in Victorian Britain*, (Methuen), 1985, and his *The eternal slum: housing and social policy in Victorian London*, (Edward Arnold), 1986. Walvin, J., *English Urban Life 1776-1851*, (Hutchinson), 1984, is an excellent, readable study on the early years of the period. Fraser, D., (ed.), *Municipal reform and the Industrial city*, (Leicester University Press), 1982, contains useful case studies. Porter, R., *Disease, Medicine and Society in England 1550-1860*, (Macmillan), 2nd edition, 1993, contains some useful ideas in its final chapters. Mort, Frank, *Dangerous Sexualities: Medico-Moral Politics in England since 1830*, (Routledge), 1987, 2nd edition, (Routledge), 1999, examines the impact of disease on perceptions of women. Smith, F. B., *The People's Health 1830-1910*, (Croom Helm), 1979, is a valuable study of social problems and the limited resources of nineteenth century medicine.

[2] Luckin, Bill, 'Pollution in the city', in ibid, Daunton, Martin J., (ed.), *The Cambridge urban history of Britain, Vol. 3: 1840-1950*, pp. 207-228.

[3] Porter, Dale H., *The Thames Embankment: Environment, Technology, and Society in Victorian London*, (University of Akron Press), 1998.

[4] Olsen, D. J., *The growth of Victorian London*, (Batsford), 1976, pp. 330-331.

over-dramatise its actual impact. Although cholera returned in 1848, 1853 and 1866, each time prompting cries for pollution control it actually killed fewer people than probably any other epidemic infection. John Snow's famous demonstration of the waterborne nature of the disease was not accepted until after the last of these epidemics. [5] In other words, like the development of ideas of Victorian ideas of the public interest and pollution, both so crucial in late-nineteenth-century conceptions of class, sexuality, gender, and the effects of literature and the arts and the filth of London and other cities were part verifiable fact and part a cultural response to the practical problem of cholera.

How were cities and towns run?

By the 1830s, the administrative and electoral map of Britain was at odds with its demographic and economic structures. [6] The antiquated legal structure of local government created three major sets of problems for urban government. Urban status was often unrelated to contemporary size and function. Major cities, such as Manchester and the east Lancashire cotton towns and the Black Country industrial centres, were without formal status. Manchester and Birmingham, for example, were unincorporated in the eighteenth century and, in theory, controlled by the county authorities. [7] Although they gained some control over their own affairs through local Improvement Acts, the system did not lend itself to effective local government.

Unincorporated industrial towns had no direct representation in Parliament and found it difficult to petition for change. In contrast,

---

[5] Snow, John, *On the Mode of Communication of Cholera*, (John Churchill), 1855. See also, Hempel, Sandra, *The Medical Detective: John Snow, Cholera and the Mystery of the Broad Street Pump*, (Granta), 2007, and Vinten-Johansen, Peter, Brody, Howard, Paneth, Nigel, and Rachman, Stephen, *Cholera, Chloroform and the Science of Medicine: A Life of John Snow*, (Oxford University Press), 2003.

[6] Despite their age, the development of local government is best examined in Webb, S., and B., *The Manor and the Borough*, 2 Vols. (Longmans, Green), 1908, and *The Parish and the County*, (Longmans, Green), 1906, Laski, H. J., Jennings, W. I., and Robson, W. A., (eds.), *A Century of Municipal Progress: The last hundred years, 1835-1935*, (Allen & Unwin), 1935.

[7] There was an important distinction between incorporated and unincorporated towns. Incorporated towns or boroughs had received charters, often in the Middle Ages, which gave them certain rights and the right to elect two MPs. In particular, they were run by elected corporations. Unincorporated towns were still run by the parish or by the old feudal leet courts.

many decayed towns had parliamentary representation, for example the rotten borough of Old Sarum had a handful of inhabitants in the 'pocket' of aristocratic landowners and retained borough status. [8] London's metropolitan area of some eight-mile radius from St Paul's had a population of 1.75 million in 1831 but lacked a coherent overall administrative structure. Even where administrations were in place in large towns, as in the incorporated boroughs in Liverpool, Bristol, Newcastle and Kingston upon Hull, their room for continued expansion was often tightly restricted. Incorporated towns also varied greatly in the way in which local government was organised. 'Closed' or corporate boroughs such as Leeds, Liverpool, Coventry, Bath and Leicester were often run by a corporation consisting of a small oligarchy appointed for life with vacancies filled by appointment by existing members. This led to the third problem. What effective control was there of a range of physical, environmental, health, economic and social issues that often affected areas outside existing corporation boundaries? Although London's parish vestries sought to provide better sanitation and health their efforts lacked integration. Despite the work of Improvement Commissions in larger English cities, there were severe limitations to the range of their activities. Under these circumstances it is not surprising that local government was slow to respond to the increasingly serious problems of urban life until after 1835. [9]

Between the 1830s and 1890s, urban and local government was restructured twice and there was significant parliamentary legislation on specific urban problems, together with a restructuring of the franchise and parliamentary and civic representation. [10] Parliamentary franchise was widened in 1832, 1867 and 1884-1885 creating a more equal relationship between parliamentary representation and property ownership and population size and increased the urban voice in national affairs. The introduction of single-member constituencies in the 1884-1885 legislation broke the link between the right to vote and

---

[8] Before it lost its two MPs in the 1832 Reform Act, Old Sarum had three houses and seven voters. Out of the 406 burgesses elected in the 1831 General Election, 152 were chosen by fewer than 100 voters and 88 by fewer than 50.

[9] Hennock, E. P., 'Urban Sanitary Reform a Generation before Chadwick?', *Economic History Review*, New Series, Vol. 10, (1), (1957), pp. 113-120, provides a useful discussion of local government sanitary initiatives in the early-nineteenth century.

[10] Davis, John, 'Central government and the towns' and Doyle, Barry M., 'The changing functions of urban government: councillors, officials and pressure groups', in ibid, Daunton, Martin J., (ed.), *The Cambridge urban history of Britain, Vol. 3: 1840-1950*, pp. 261-286, 287-314.

property ownership by introducing 'one man, one vote'. The Municipal Corporations Act 1835, and parallel legislation in Scotland in 1833 and 1834 and Ireland in 1839, laid the basis for municipal planning and control over a wide range of issues and recognised the reality of urban Britain by giving full urban status to many unincorporated towns. [11] Some, such as Manchester, Birmingham and Sheffield, were already very large; others such as Bradford, Bolton, Huddersfield, Wolverhampton and Brighton were growing rapidly. They also allowed the incorporation of adjacent townships over which urban development had spread, as reflected in the considerable boundary extensions of Liverpool and Leeds and of Glasgow in the 1830s.

The 1835 Act did not solve the problem of integrating urban government. Intervention through bye-laws in key issues such as health and sanitation, housing, public amenities, poverty was either piecemeal or, as in the case of the Poor Law and the provision of compulsory state education (made over to local government in 1919 and 1902 respectively) was reserved for central government. When new administrative divisions were established, they were often based on existing structures. The reformed Poor Law of 1834 created a framework of 624 Unions centred on old market towns and regional centres, a pre-industrial pattern of functional regionalism that had to be constantly adjusted to meet changing population distribution. By the 1860s, there was a growing recognition that urban administration needed to be more coherent if it was to implement legislation on health, housing and sanitation. In 1855, the Metropolitan Management Act, following the Royal Commission of 1854 attempted to create an integrated government for London by reorganising the previously haphazard structure into a Metropolitan Board to control sewage, highways, lighting and health in London's 36 Registration Districts with an 1861 population of 2.8 million. [12]

Elsewhere, despite the addition of 554 new urban areas between 1848 and 1868 in England and Wales, confusion remained. A Royal Commission to investigate local government was set up in 1869 and its Second Report began the transition to the Acts of 1888 and 1894 that established the late-nineteenth and early-twentieth century

---

[11] Finlayson, Geoffrey, 'The Municipal Corporation Commission and Report, 1833-5', *Bulletin of the Institute of Historical Research*, Vol. 36, (1963), pp. 36-52, and 'The politics of municipal reform, 1835', *English Historical Review*, Vol. 81, (1966), pp. 673-692.

[12] Owen, David, *The government of Victorian London 1855-1889: the Metropolitan Board of Works, the vestries, and the City Corporation*, (Harvard University Press), 1982.

framework of local government. The Public Health Act 1872 created an administrative framework of Urban and Rural Sanitary Districts under the Local Government Board set up the previous year. The Local Government Act 1875 and the Municipal Corporations Acts 1882 defined the principles and functions of a new system of urban administration. However, the Commissioners of the Board set up under the Local Government Boundaries Act 1887 and the decisions made under the Local Government Acts of 1888 and 1894 determined its geography. These Acts recognised that the needs of large towns could best be met by integrating all the functions of local government within all-purpose administrations of 63 Counties and 61 County Boroughs. London became an Administrative County incorporating its 41 Metropolitan Board Areas. In 1894, the remaining urban areas were consolidated into Municipal Boroughs and Urban Districts each with a range of powers but subordinate to their Administrative Counties for education, police and fire and some other services.

Why was urban life so unhealthy?

Bad housing, poor sanitation and overcrowding, that in turn bred epidemic disease, were closely associated with inner-city areas. Ursula Henriques suggests:

> In the first half of the nineteenth century no aspect of life suffered such cumulative deterioration as did public health. [13]

It was unhealthy to live in Victorian cities, though chances of illness and premature death varied considerably depending on who you were, where you lived, how much you earned and how well you were fed. Social class mattered. Not all towns had equally high mortality rates and death rates in the countryside could match those in middle-class suburban areas of cities. [14]

Contemporary opinion was most concerned about infectious diseases even though more people died from 'other causes' than from

---

[13] Henriques, U., *Before the Welfare State: Social administration in early industrial Britain*, (Longman), 1979, p. 117.

[14] On health, see Howe, G. M., *Man, environment and disease in Britain*, (Penguin), 1976, Woods, R., and Woodward, J., (eds.), *Urban disease and mortality in nineteenth-century England*, (Batsford), 1984, and ibid, Smith, F. B., *The People's Health 1830-1910*. Youngson, A. J., *The Scientific Revolution in Victorian Medicine*, (Croom Helm), 1979, is useful on medical developments.

all infectious diseases combined. [15] Such diseases as typhus and influenza were both endemic and epidemic: they killed large numbers of both rural and urban dwellers but particularly affected the young and malnourished of the urban slums. Smallpox became less important, in part because of the vaccination developed by Edward Jenner in the 1790s though it was not eradicated. [16] Typhus fever was endemic in London and epidemics occurred in all towns in 1817-1819, 1826-1827 and 1831-1832. [17] Influenza epidemics occurred in 1803 and 1831. As towns grew, polluted water became an increasingly pressing problem and was the cause of many diseases from infantile diarrhoea and typhoid fever and especially cholera. [18]

Nothing occupies a nation's mind with the subject of health like a widespread epidemic. In the 1830s and the 1840s, there were three massive waves of contagious disease: the first, from 1831 to 1833, included two influenza epidemics and the initial appearance of cholera; the second, from 1836 to 1842, saw major epidemics of influenza, typhus, typhoid and cholera. As Garrison observed, epidemics in the eighteenth century were 'more scattered and isolated' than previously and in the early-nineteenth century there had been a

---

[15] Brown, Michael, 'From Foetid Air to Filth: The Cultural Transformation of British Epidemiological Thought, ca. 1780-1848', *Bulletin of the History of Medicine*, Vol. 82, (2008), pp. 515-544, Condrau, Flurin, and Worboys, Michael, 'Epidemics and Infections in Nineteenth-Century Britain', *Social History of Medicine*, Vol. 20, (2007), pp. 147-158, and Mooney, Graham, 'Infectious Diseases and Epidemiologic Transition in Victorian Britain? Definitely', *Social History of Medicine*, Vol. 20, (2007), pp. 595-606.

[16] Hardy, A., 'Smallpox in London: factors in the decline of the disease in the nineteenth century', *Medical History*, Vol. 27, (1983), pp. 111-138. See also, Brunton, Deborah, *The politics of vaccination: practice and policy in England, Wales, Ireland, and Scotland, 1800-1874*, (University of Rochester Press), 2008.

[17] Hardy, A., 'Urban famine or urban crisis? Typhus in the Victorian city', *Medical History*, Vol. 32, (1988), pp. 401-425.

[18] On cholera, see, Hamlin, Christopher, *Cholera: The Biography*, (Oxford University Press), 2009, is a valuable global study. Longmate, N., *King Cholera*, (Hamish Hamilton), 1966, Morris, R. J., *Cholera, 1832*, (Croom Helm), 1976, Pelling, M., *Cholera, Fever and English Medicine 1825-1865*, (Oxford University Press), 1977, Durey, Michael, *The Return of the Plague: British Society and Cholera 1831-2*, (Gill and Macmillan), 1979, and Gilbert, Pamela K., *Cholera and nation: doctoring the social body in Victorian England*, (State University of New York Press), 2008. Hardy, A., 'Cholera, quarantine and the English preventive system, 1850-1895', *Medical History*, Vol. 37, (1993), pp. 250-269, looks at later developments.

marked decline in such illnesses as diphtheria and influenza. [19] Smallpox, the scourge of the eighteenth century, appeared to be controllable by the new practice of vaccination. Then, in the mid-1820s, England saw serious outbursts of smallpox and typhus, anticipating the pestilential turbulence of the next two decades.

The first outbreak of Asiatic cholera in Britain was at Sunderland during the autumn of 1831. From there the disease made its way north into Scotland and south toward London eventually claiming 52,000 lives. [20] It had taken five years to cross Europe from its point of origin in Bengal and by 1831 British doctors were well aware of its nature, if not its cause. The progress of the illness in a cholera victim was a frightening spectacle: diarrhoea increased in intensity and became accompanied by painful retching; thirst and dehydration; severe pain in the limbs, stomach and abdominal muscles; a change skin hue to a sort of bluish-grey. The disease was unlike anything then known. One doctor recalled:

> Our other plagues were home-bred, and part of ourselves, as it were; we had a habit of looking at them with a fatal indifference, indeed, inasmuch as it led us to believe that they could be effectually subdued. But the cholera was something outlandish, unknown, monstrous; its tremendous ravages, so long foreseen and feared, so little to be explained, its insidious march over whole continents, its apparent defiance of all the known and conventional precautions against the spread of epidemic disease, invested it with a mystery and a terror which thoroughly took hold of the public mind, and seemed to recall the memory of the great epidemics of the middle ages. [21]

Cholera subsided as rapidly as it had begun, but another sort of devastation had already taken hold. The previous June, following a particularly rainy spring, Britain experienced the first of eight serious influenza epidemics that occurred over the next sixteen years. The disease was often fatal, and even when it did not kill, it left its victims

---

[19] Garrison, F. H., *An introduction to the history of medicine: with medical chronology, bibliographic data, and test questions*, 2nd edition, (W. B. Saunders Company), 1913, p. 334.

[20] On the impact of 1831-1832 outbreak on localities see, Hardiman, Sue, *The 1832 cholera epidemic and its impact on the city of Bristol*, (Historical Association, Bristol Branch), 2005, Kidd, Alan J., and Wyke, Terry J., 'The cholera epidemic in Manchester 1831-32', *Bulletin of the John Rylands University Library of Manchester*, Vol. 87, (2005), pp. 43-56, O'Neill, Timothy P., 'Cholera in Offaly in the 1830s', *Offaly Heritage*, Vol. 1, (2003), pp. 96-107, and Walker, Martyn., 'The 1832 cholera epidemic in the east midlands', *East Midland Historian*, Vol. 1-2 (1991-2), pp. 7-14.

[21] Gairdner, William, T., *Public health in relation to air and water*, (Edmonston and Douglas), 1862, pp. 15-16.

weakened against other diseases. Burials in London doubled during the first week of the 1833 outbreak; in one two-week period they quadrupled. Whereas cholera, spread by contaminated water, affected mainly the poorer neighbourhoods, influenza was not limited by economic or social boundaries. Large numbers of public officials, especially in the Bank of England, died from it, as did many who worked in the theatre.

In the 1830s, the term 'fever' included a number of different diseases, among them cholera and influenza and a 'new fever', typhus was isolated. During its worst outbreak, in 1837-1838, most of the deaths from fever in London were attributed to typhus and new cases averaged about 16,000 in England in each of the following four years. This coincided with one of the worst smallpox contagions, which killed thousands, mainly infants and children. Scarlet fever or scarlatina was responsible for nearly 20,000 deaths in 1840 alone. [22] Although mortality rates for specific diseases were not compiled for England and Wales between 1842 and 1846, during this period there was a considerable decline in epidemics. It has been suggested that one reason was the expansion of railway building, with the consequent increase in wage levels and a better standard of living. A hot, dry summer in 1846, however, was followed by a serious outbreak of typhoid in the autumn of that year. Enteric fever, as it was then called, is a water-borne disease like cholera and tends to flourish where sources of drinking water are infected. That same year, as the potato famine struck Ireland, a virulent form of typhus appeared, cutting down large numbers of even well-to-do families. Irish migrants moved to cities especially Liverpool and Glasgow and the 'Irish fever' moved with them. By 1847, the contagion, not all of it connected with immigration, had spread throughout England and Wales, accounting for over 30,000 deaths. As had happened a decade earlier, typhus occurred simultaneously with a severe influenza epidemic that killed almost 13,000. Widespread dysentery and cholera returned in the autumn of 1848, affecting especially those parts of the island hardest hit by typhus and leaving about as many dead as it had in 1831. [23]

---

[22] See, Duncan, C. J., Duncan, S. R., and Scott, S.,' The dynamics of scarlet fever epidemics in England and Wales in the 19th century', *Epidemiology and Infection*, Vol. 117, (1996), pp. 493-499.

[23] On local effects of the 1848-1849 cholera epidemic see, Haines, Gary., 'Cholera and Bethnal Green in 1849', *East London History Society Newsletter*, Vol. 2, (3), (2002), pp. 20-24, Thomas, Amanda J., *The Lambeth Cholera Outbreak of 1848-1849: The Setting, Causes, Course and Aftermath of an Epidemic in London*, (McFarland & Co. Inc.), 2009, Cochrane, Margaret Ruth, and Cochrane, Robert Evan, *Death comes to Hedon: the cholera epidemic of 1849*, (Highgate), 1993, James, D. C., 'The

Diseases such as cholera, typhus, typhoid and influenza were more or less endemic, erupting into epidemics with the right climatic conditions and often coincided with periods of economic distress. The frequency of concurrent epidemics gave rise to the belief that one sort of disease brought on another; indeed, it was widely believed that influenza was an early stage of cholera. There were other contagions, however, that yearly killed thousands without becoming epidemic. Taken together, measles and 'whooping cough' accounted for 50,000 deaths in England and Wales between 1838 and 1840, and about a quarter of all deaths have been attributed to tuberculosis or consumption. Generally throughout the 1830s and the 1840s, trade was depressed and food prices were high. The poorer classes, often underfed, were less resistant to contagion. Also, during the more catastrophic years the weather was extremely variable, with heavy rains following prolonged droughts. Population, especially in the Midlands and in some seaport cities and towns, was growing rapidly without a parallel expansion in new housing and over-crowding contributed to the relatively fast spread of disease.

The Registrar General reported in 1841 that while mean life expectancy in Surrey was forty-five years, it was only thirty-seven in London and twenty-six in Liverpool. The average age of 'labourers, mechanics, and servants', at times of death was only fifteen. Mortality figures for crowded districts like Shoreditch, Whitechapel, and Bermondsey were typically half again or twice as high as those for middle-class areas of London. Such statistics made people aware of the magnitude of disease, but also served as effective weapons for sanitary reformers when they brought their case before Parliament. Two reports by the Poor Law Commission in 1838, one by Dr Southwood Smith,[24] the other by Doctors Neil Arnott and J. P. Kay, outlined causes and probable means of preventing communicable disease in poverty areas like London's Bethnal Green and Whitechapel. Chadwick's *Sanitary Report* in 1842 broadened the scope of inquiry geographically, as did a Royal Commission report in 1845 on the Health of Towns and Populous Places.

During the first decades of Victoria's reign, baths were virtually unknown in the poorer districts and uncommon anywhere. Most

---

cholera epidemic of 1849 in Cardiff', *Morgannwg*, Vol. 25, (1981), pp. 164-179, and Lloyd, T. H., 'The cholera epidemic of 1849 in Leamington Spa and Warwick', *Warwickshire History*, Vol. 2, (1973), pp. 16-32.

[24] See Lewes, Gertrude Hill, *Dr. Southwood Smith; a retrospect*, (Blackwood), 1898, and Webb, R. K., 'Southwood Smith: The Intellectual Sources of Public Service', in Porter, Dorothy, and Porter, Roy, (eds.), *Doctors, Politics and Society: Historical Essays*, (Ropodi), 1993, pp. 46-80.

households of all economic classes still used 'privy-pails'; water closets were rare. Sewers had flat bottoms, and because drains were made out of stone, seepage was considerable. If, as was often the case in towns, streets were unpaved, they might remain ankle-deep in mud for weeks. For new middle-class homes in the growing manufacturing towns, elevated sites were usually chosen, with the result that sewage filtered or flowed down into the lower areas where the labouring populations lived. Some towns had special drainage problems. In Leeds, for example, the Aire River, fouled by the town's refuse, flooded periodically, sending noxious waters into the ground floors and basements of the low-lying houses. As Chadwick later recalled, the new dwellings of the middle-class families were scarcely healthier, for the bricks tended to preserve moisture. Even picturesque old country houses often had a dungeon-like dampness, as a visitor could observe:

> If he enters the house he finds the basement steaming with water-vapour; walls constantly bedewed with moisture, cellars coated with fungus and mould; drawing rooms and dining rooms always, except in the very heat of summer, oppressive from moisture; bedrooms, the windows of which are, in winter, so frosted on their inner surface, from condensation of water in the air of the room, that all day they are coated with ice. [25]

In some districts of London and the great towns the supply of water was irregular. Typically, a neighbourhood of twenty or thirty families on a particular square or street would draw their water from a singly pump two or three times a week. Sometimes, finding the pump not working, they were forced to reuse the same water. When a local supply became contaminated the results could be disastrous. In Soho's St. Anne's parish, for instance, the faeces of an infant stricken with cholera washed down into the water reserve from which the local pump drew and almost all those using the pump were infected. Millbank Prison, taking its water from the sewage-polluted Thames, suffered greatly during every epidemic of water-borne disease.

Since it was widely believed that disease was generated spontaneously from filth (pythogenesis) and transmitted by noxious invisible gas or miasma, there was much alarm over the 'Great Stink' of 1858. The Thames had become so polluted with waste as to be almost unbearable during unusually hot summer months. People refused to use the river-steamers and would walk miles to avoid

---

[25] Chadwick, Edwin, *The General History of the Principles of Sanitation*, (Cassell and Company), 1889, p. 10.

crossing one of the city bridges. Parliament could carry on its business only by hanging disinfectant-soaked cloths over the windows. Ironically, the introduction of flush toilets was part of the problem since their use dramatically increased the volume of water and waste pouring into existing cesspits that overflowed into street drains before entering the River Thames. It should have been a blow to miasma theory when no outbreak of fever followed from this monstrous stench.

It was clear that the sewer system in London could not cope with the increased levels of waste and, although it had rejected the notion in 1855, the Metropolitan Board of Works now accepted the proposals of its chief engineer, Joseph Bazalgette. [26] Between 1859 and 1865, the key elements of the London sewerage system were created resulting in uncontaminated water supplies. Although the new sewerage system was in operation and water supplies gradually improved, they did not prevent a later epidemic during the 1860s, especially in east London. In 1867, Captain Henry Tyler of the Railway Inspectorate showed that the polluted River Lea was entering reservoirs of the East London Water Company, and so caused the epidemic. The water-borne explanation had now been proved beyond doubt and eliminating the source of pollution ended the last epidemic of cholera in the capital

As late as 1873, however, William Budd [27] could reluctantly report in his important book on typhoid:

> ...organic matter, and especially sewage in a state of decomposition, without any relation to antecedent fever, is still generally supposed to be the most fertile source. [28]

Resistance to the theory of polluted water as a source of infection contributed to the incidence of typhoid in the second half of the century as well as to the high mortality rates from cholera in epidemics

---

[26] On this, see, Halliday, Stephen, *The Great Stink of London: Sir Joseph Bazalgette and the cleansing of the Victorian capital*, (Sutton), 1999, and Cook, G. C., 'Construction of London's Victorian sewers: the vital role of Joseph Bazalgette', *Postgraduate Medical Journal*, Vol. 77, (2001), pp. 802-804.
[27] Dunnill, Michael S., *Dr William Budd: Bristol's most famous physician*, (Redcliffe), 2006.
[28] Budd, William, *Typhoid Fever, its Nature, Mode of Spreading and Prevention*, (Longmans, Green and Co.), 1873, p. 132. Cit, Gaw, Jerry L., *"A time to heal": the diffusion of Listerism in Victorian Britain*, (Diane Publishing), 1999, p. 24.

as late as 1854 and 1865-1866. [29] The general cleaning up of the cities and towns, however, produced a marked reduction in deaths from typhus, a disease transmitted by lice. The Registrar General remarked of the last quarter of 1871:

> Although the remarkably low death rate in town districts, last quarter, may be due to the somewhat unusual meteorological conditions which prevailed, [very heavy, cleansing, rain] it may be safe to assume that a portion of the improvement in their health is permanent, and is the result of the general awakening to the importance of sanitary measures which has been so conspicuous in the last few years. [30]

A systematic control of contagious disease had to await the introduction of preventive inoculation in the 1880s and 1890s but after 1850 the general health of the country measurably improved. [31]

For much of the century, doctors were confused about the causes, course and treatment of the disease. The unpredictable behaviour of the severe contagions also intensified anxiety. They would appear, perhaps then subside for a month or two, only to reappear in the same locality or somewhere else. The individual sufferer had no way of predicting the outcome of the disease in his own case. Influenza patients, observed the *London Medical Gazette* during the 1833 epidemic, 'might linger for the space of two or three weeks and then get up well, or they might die in the same number of

---

[29] For contemporary analysis, see Farr, William, *Report on the Cholera Epidemic of 1866 in England*, (George E. Eyre and William Spottiswoode), 1868, and Budd, William, 'On Asiatic Cholera in Bristol', *British Medical Journal*, Vol. 1 for 1867, pp. 413-420, and (Kerslake), 1871. There are fewer studies on the later outbreaks of cholera but see, for example, Roberts, Glynne, '"Closing the stable door after the horse has bolted": preventing the spread of smallpox and cholera in Caernarfonshire, 1870-1910', *Transactions of the Caernarvonshire Historical Society*, Vol. 55, (1994), pp. 109-128, Callcott, M., 'The challenge of cholera: the last epidemic at Newcastle upon Tyne', *Northern History*, Vol. 20, (1984), pp. 167-186, and Luckin, W., 'The final catastrophe: cholera in London, 1866', *Medical History*, Vol. 21, (1977), pp. 32-42.
[30] *Annual Reports of the Registrar-General of Births, Deaths and Marriages in England*, Vols. 34-35, (Great Britain General Registrar Office), 1873, pp. xlvi-xlvii
[31] Vaccination and inoculation remained contentious issues throughout the nineteenth century and there was an anti-vaccination movement as well as parental resistance to compulsion. On this see, Durbach, Nadja, *Bodily matters: the anti-vaccination movement in England, 1853-1907*, (Duke University Press), 2005.

days.'[32] Just as frightening was the uncertain progress of typhoid. Infectious diseases were spatially concentrated: deaths from tuberculosis, typhus and cholera focused mainly on inner-city slum districts. The main nineteenth century killer of adults was tuberculosis. Few families were untouched by its effects and even in 1900 it was responsible for around 10 per cent of all deaths nationally, despite a significant decline since 1850. Spread by a bacillus through droplet infection from coughs or saliva, tuberculosis is not highly contagious but its spread is encouraged by a combination of poverty, malnutrition and overcrowded living conditions. Though not immune, the middle-classes were better able to withstand tuberculosis than the poor, malnourished working-class.[33]

The number of victims of chronic food poisoning was also significant. Mineral poisons were often introduced into food and water from bottle stoppers, lead water pipes and wall paints or equipment used to process food and beverages. Moreover, the deliberate adulteration of food was a common and, until 1860, virtually unrestricted practice. For instance, because of people's dislike for brown bread, bakers regularly whitened their flour with alum. In 1858, a Bradford sweetshop owner ordered a delivery of plaster of Paris that was commonly used to adulterate sugar but a novice supplied arsenic instead. It went on sale in a batch of peppermint drops and within a few days 20 people were dead and hundreds seriously ill.[34]

Conditions for the processing and sale of foods were generally unsanitary. In 1848, the Spreading of Contagious or Infectious Disorders among Sheep, Cattle and other Animals Act introduced penalties for selling meat unfit for human consumption and gave powers for the destruction of such meat. An 1863 report to the Privy Council stated that one-fifth of the meat sold came from diseased cattle that had died of pleuro-pneumonia and anthracid or anthracoid diseases.[35] In 1860, the first pure-food act was passed, but, as was often the case in these early regulatory measures, it provided no mandatory

---

[32] Cit, Thompson, Theophilus, *Annals of influenza or epidemic catarrhal fever in Great Britain from 1510 to 1837*, (Sydenham Society), 1852, p. 289.
[33] Smith, Francis Barrymore, *The retreat of tuberculosis, 1850-1950*, (Croom Helm), 1988.
[34] Ibid, Whorton, James C., *The Arsenic Century: How Victorian Britain was Poisoned at Home, Work and Play*, pp. 139-141.
[35] See, Waddington, Keir, *The bovine scourge: meat, tuberculosis and public health, 1850-1914*, (Boydell & Brewer), 2006.

system of enforcement. [36] In 1872, further legislation was passed considerably strengthening penalties and inspection procedures. Cow's milk, was perhaps the most widely adulterated food. In 1877, a quarter of all the milk examined by the Local Government Board was seriously adulterated; in 1882, one-fifth of the 20,000 milk analyses made by the 52 county and 172 borough analysts was adulterated. Not until 1894 was the Local Government Board able to report that adulterated milk accounted for less than 10 per cent of all samples. However, throughout most of the nineteenth century, Britons had little protection against unwholesome food and drink.

What was the impact of such high rates of infectious disease? Death was only one, and not necessarily the most important, of the many effects of disease. For a poor family struggling to pay rent and buy food, illness, whether fatal or not, imposed additional strains: medical bills to pay, medicines to buy, extra heating costs and the problem of childcare if the mother was taken ill. If the primary wage-earner was off work the crisis would be more acute as not only did outgoings rise but income fell. Short-term crises were met by pawning clothes, borrowing from kin and raising short-term loans. Prolonged illness increased costs and reduced income to such an extent that it could cause or increased malnutrition for the whole family, leading to further illness or to eviction for non-payment of rent. Families might then have to move to inferior accommodation or to be separated from one another in the workhouse. There is little doubt that the high levels and concentration of infectious disease was a significant extra burden for working-class families in the Victorian city.

In certain respects, the health of the urban population began to improve as a result of a number of changes occurring after 1880. General increases in standards of living and especially improvements in diet and nutrition led to greater resistance to disease and lower mortality. Advances in medical knowledge and technology began to make real inroads into diseases that had been barely understood in 1780. The development of a state welfare policy towards health created a buffer that prevented some of the worst impacts of disease in family life though the impact of the embryonic welfare state was patchy before 1914. The Public Health Act 1890 was more effective than previous legislation in ensuring that towns took responsibility for the basic provision of pure water supply and proper sanitary conditions. The Housing Act 1890 placed emphasis on slum clearance but this only had a limited effect by 1914. The development

---

[36] Collins, E. J. T., 'Food adulteration and food safety in Britain in the 19th and 20th centuries', *Food Policy*, Vol. 18, (1993), pp. 95-109, provides a useful overview.

of town planning began to stress environmental considerations that influenced the layout of some suburban developments and created a healthier environment. This only had an effect if individuals were able to move from the inner-city areas to the new garden suburbs. While there had been some improvement in the quality of life for all living in urban communities between 1830 and 1914, the major determinant of health remained social class with the working-classes generally less healthy than the middle-classes.

Reforming Public Health

Poor housing, overcrowding and high levels of disease, often held to have been exacerbated by the massive influx of Irish migrants, were certainly perceived as problems by those with power and authority in the Victorian city and by politicians at Westminster. Despite prevailing laissez-faire attitudes, the development of municipal intervention in various areas of the urban environment reveals a genuine crisis in urban living conditions with an increasing gap between public expectations and the realities of urban life. Much as they might have wished to, neither local nor national politicians could ignore urban living conditions. Edwin Chadwick was the best-known propagandist, but increasing amounts of statistical and other information was discussed and publicised by local societies and used as propaganda by doctors and others with first-hand experience of life in the slums at the local level.[37] Such evidence was unlikely on its own to persuade ratepayers and their elected representatives to pass legislation and spend money improving housing and sanitation for the working-classes. Concerned by revolution in Europe especially in 1830 and 1848, politicians genuinely believed that poor living conditions could lead to mass disturbances and urban violence. Self-interest lay at the heart of political action.

The impact of cholera in 1832 and 1848 brought home, especially to the middle-classes that disease affected all classes. The poor were blamed for the disease, but it was in the interests of the middle-classes to improve conditions and prevent it recurring. Intervention was also rationalised through economic self-interest since a reduction in disease and improvement in housing would bring about

---

[37] Lewis, R. A., *Edwin Chadwick and the Public Health Movement 1832-1854*, (Longman), 1952, Finer, S. E., *The Life and Times of Sir Edwin Chadwick*, (Methuen), 1952, and Brundage, A., *England's 'Prussian Minister': Edwin Chadwick and the Politics of Government Growth 1832-1854*, (Pennsylvania University Press), 1988. Hamlin, C., *Public health and social justice in the age of Chadwick*, (Cambridge University Press), 1998, is essential.

a more efficient workforce and therefore benefit industrialists and entrepreneurs. But there were also important constraints. The contrast between political reaction to Chadwick's contribution to the *Poor Law Report* in 1834 and reaction to his 1842 public health report is instructive. In 1834, legislation rapidly followed the Report while it took six years to produce the public health legislation Chadwick wanted. In 1834, Chadwick was expressing commonly held assumptions held by a broad spectrum of society; in 1842, he was radical and original and his ideas had far less support.

Why did government not act?

Today services such sewage disposal, street lighting and paving are provided by one local authority. Before 1835, where councils existed they were often corrupt and inefficient; self-perpetuating rather than elected and unaccountable for the ways in which they used the local rates. In some towns, power was in the hands of the parish vestry elected by property owners. Most towns before 1835 tried to deal with 'nuisances' like water supply and drainage using Improvement Commissions. The problem was that each Commission dealt with a specific issue such as paving but there was little co-ordination between different Commissions leading to a disjointed approach to improvement. The Municipal Corporations Act 1835 allowed rates to be levied for street lighting, fresh water-supply and sewage disposal by local Acts of Parliament. Initially, this too did little to address the need for a co-ordinated response to health issues.

The chaotic nature of local government militated against effective reform and so too did self-interest. Various groups in towns opposed interference with the existing situation largely because they were in search of profit. Water companies, for example, only supplied water to those areas of a town where the householders could afford the fees. Builders exploited the demand for cheap jerry-built housing and paid little attention to drainage, ventilation or water supply. Private landlords were reluctant to pay the cost of sanitary improvements and were reluctant to accept any responsibility for the cleanliness of the working-classes. There is also the suggestion that middle-class families were either ignorant of the real conditions in which the working-classes lived or were prepared to ignore them. Middle-class houses were built on the edge of towns and were worlds apart from the inner-city slums. Finally there was the question of who was responsibility for public health. How far should central government dictate to local government with regard to the problem? Initially laissez-faire attitudes meant that central government was reluctant to intervene directly in public health issues while local authorities were resistant to solutions imposed on them.

Whatever the reasons, the second half of the nineteenth century saw unprecedented activity in the passing of both by-laws and national legislation affecting urban living conditions. Local legislation was in practice more important than that passed by Parliament: national legislation often included what had previously occurred at a local level. Although the Public Health Act 1848 did not induce any major changes in urban areas, it was the culmination of a concerted public health campaign in England and Wales in the 1840s, marking acceptance of the fact that public health was an issue of national importance. Not until the Sanitary Act 1866 were local Authorities obliged to provide a proper water supply, drainage and sewerage system but the legislation lacked teeth to enforce its powers. Many towns acted independently: Manchester, for instance, took control of the city's water supply in 1851. But powers to force Local Authorities to act to improve water supply and sanitation did not become effective until the 1875 and especially 1890 Public Health Acts.

Why was Edwin Chadwick's involvement in public health between 1832 and 1854 controversial?

During the 1840s, there were two contradictory trends in matters of social policy. On the one hand there was a tendency to extend public regulation and, on the other, a tendency to call a halt to further change. The public health movement had to operate within the pressures produced by these opposing forces, pressures that in the end brought Chadwick's resignation and ended a stage in the history of social policy. Public health was the fourth major area of policy, along with the poor law, factory reform and constabulary reform, with which Chadwick's name was connected. He promoted sanitary policies that tackled all aspects of the problem and thought out an administrative structure at both central and local levels but his comprehensiveness and broad planning antagonised powerful vested interests. Nor were the plans free from Chadwick's characteristic dogmatism and they showed his persistent inability to compromise or to modify his ideas.

The 1830s and early 1840s saw two complementary developments in sanitary reform: action by central government and investigation of urban conditions that identified the scale of the problem. In 1831, a Consultative Board of Health was established that issued a series of recommendations in the form of sanitary regulations. Later in the year, it was replaced by a Central Board of Health that called for the establishment of local boards of health composed of one or more magistrates, a clergyman, a number of substantial householders and one or more doctors. The local boards were to appoint district inspectors to report on the food, clothing and bedding of the poor, the ventilation and sanitation of their dwellings, space, means of cleanliness and their habits of temperance; houses were to be whitewashed. The Boards sought to remedy, by every means that individual and public charitable exertion could supply, such deficiencies as may be found. Over 1,200 local boards were established by Orders in Council, many continued after 1832 when the Central Board was disbanded. In 1832, faced with the crisis of cholera, the Cholera and Cholera (Scotland) Acts enabled the Privy Council to make orders for the prevention of cholera provided that any expense incurred should be defrayed out of money raised for the relief of the poor by the parishes and townships. Powers lapsed at the end of 1834. The 1840 Vaccination Act made free vaccination available as a charge on the poor rates.

The Sanitary Report 1842

Conditions of public health and sanitation were a concern of the Poor Law Commission set up in 1834. [38] Chadwick, one of the Poor Law Commissioners, organised an investigation into the sanitary condition of the poor. Doctors Neil Arnott and James Kay and another by Southwood Smith exposed the extent of preventable disease and appalling living conditions in in East London and Manchester in 1838. In 1840, the *Report* of the Select Committee on the Health of the Towns exposed squalid conditions in many industrial areas and recommended the institution of district boards of health. Chadwick's own *Report on the Sanitary Conditions of the Labouring Population of Great Britain* was published in 1842. [39] It was the result of two further years' exhaustive work and it put the whole discussion of public sanitary policy onto an entirely new footing. The 1842 *Sanitary Report* was complemented by a report the following year on interments in towns that exposed the terrible conditions of overcrowded graveyards of London. [40] These reports made a deep impression on public opinion and some 30,000 copies were initially printed. Chadwick's *Report* led to the Royal Commission for Inquiry into the State of Large Towns and Populous Districts being

---

[38] Ibid, Hamlin, C., *Public health and social justice in the age of Chadwick*, pp. 84-155, looks at the genesis of the *Sanitary Report*.
[39] Chadwick Edwin, *Report on the Sanitary Condition of the Labouring Population*, (W. Clowes and Sons), 1842, reprinted, Flinn, M. W., (ed.), (Edinburgh University Press), 1965. See also, ibid, Hamlin, C., *Public health and social justice in the age of Chadwick,* pp. 156-187.
[40] Select Committee on the Improvement of Health in Towns, *Supplementary Report on Internments in Towns*, 1843.

established in 1843. It published an interim report in 1844 and a final report the following year recommending the creation of a new government department and that the arrangements for drainage, paving, cleansing and water supply should come under one administration in each locality. [41] The *Report* deplored the extent of overcrowding, called for a central inspectorate of housing and recommended that local authorities should be able to demand that landlords clean and repair properties dangerous to public health. The Health of Towns Association was founded in December 1844 to diffuse the information obtained from recent inquiries on the physical and moral evils arising from existing sanitary conditions and to:

...substitute health for disease, cleanliness for filth, order for disorder, economy for waste, prevention for palliation, justice for charity, enlightened self-interest for ignorant selfishness and to bring to the poorest and meanest-- Air, Water, Light. [42]

Chadwick believed that disease was carried by impurities in the atmosphere (miasma theory) and that it was critical to get rid of impurities before they could decompose. [43] The medical basis of his ideas may have been flawed but the solution he proposed could have addressed the problem. The key to resolving the whole problem was the provision of a sufficient supply of pure water driven through pipes at high pressure. This would provide both drinking water and make it easier to cleanse houses and streets. Manure could be collected when it left the town and used as fertiliser in the surrounding fields. [44]

This solution presented many problems. Water companies normally provided water only on certain days a week and at certain times and did not provide it in either the quantity or at the pressure that Chadwick desired. Many houses in poorer districts had no water

---

[41] Ibid, Hamlin, C., *Public health and social justice in the age of Chadwick*, pp. 217-244.

[42] Paterson, R. G., 'The Health of Towns Association in Great Britain, 1844-49: an exposition of the primary voluntary health society in the Anglo-Saxon public health movement', *Bulletin of the History of Medicine*, Vol. 22, (1948), pp. 373-399.

[43] See, Hamlin, Christopher, 'Edwin Chadwick, 'mutton medicine,' and the fever question', *Bulletin of the History of Medicine*, Vol. 70, (1996), pp. 233-265.

[44] Goddard, Nicholas, '"A mine of wealth"? The Victorians and the agricultural value of sewage', *Journal of Historical Geography*, Vol. 22, (1996), pp. 274-290, and Sheail, John, 'Town wastes, agricultural sustainability and Victorian sewage', *Urban History*, Vol. 23, (1996), pp. 189-210.

supply at all and no proper means of sewage disposal. Where sewers did exist they were often very badly regulated. Chadwick wished to replace the large brick-arched constructions with smaller egg-shaped types developed by John Roe. In addition to his first two basic ideas, the atmospheric theory of infection and the cyclical theory of water supply and drainage, Chadwick maintained that proper central direction of sanitary planning should be combined with efficient local organisation, an idea parallel to his views on poor law and police. Several points stand out in the *Sanitary Report*. Members and officials of existing commissions of sewers were generally examined in an unsympathetic, even hostile way. There were two authoritative statements of the views of reformers, one by Southwood Smith from the scientific and medical viewpoint, the other by Thomas Hawksley giving an engineering perspective.[45] Complementing Hawksley's evidence, there was evidence from other professional men about the importance of properly made plans and surveys as the pre-requisite for sound planning.

The Public Health Act 1848

By the mid-1840s, the local state was beginning to intervene in towns and several of the larger towns obtained private Acts to dealing with nuisances. In 1847, the Improvement of the Sewerage and Drainage of Liverpool Act resulted in William Duncan becoming the Medical Officer for Liverpool, the first appointment in Britain.[46] Public reaction to public health legislation is often assumed to have mirrored the views expressed in Parliament or in influential provincial newspapers but the 871 petitions submitted to Parliament during the 1847 and 1847-1848 sessions clearly show that few issues stimulated more interest than public health.[47] The petitions indicated that the idea of national sanitary legislation had been embraced by a

---

[45] See also, evidence of Thomas Hawksley, *First Report of the Commissioners for Inquiring into the State of Large Towns and Populous Districts*, Minutes of Evidence, PP, (572), XVII.1, 1844, pp. 298-331.

[46] Fraser, W. M., *Duncan of Liverpool: being an account of the work of W. H. Duncan, Medical Officer of Health of Liverpool 1847-63*, (Hamish Hamilton), 1947.

[47] For instance, petitions were presented from 'Worcester, and a great number of other Places, in favour of the Health of Towns Bill', *Hansard*, House of Lords, Debates, 23 June 1848, Vol. 99, c1049. There were also petitions opposing the legislation, for instance, Penryn, House of Lords, Debates, 4 August 1848, Vol. 100, cc.1125-6.

geographically and socially diverse constituency. [48] Although the public health debate is characterised as one between those who favoured reform and those against it, the reasons for support or opposition were far from coherent and were concerned less with centralisation and more with local concerns and priorities. [49]

Central government did intervene passing the Nuisances Removal and Prevention of Epidemic Diseases Act in 1846 and the Public Health Act two years later. The 1846 legislation established procedures for the more speedy removal of nuisances when certified as such by two medical practitioners and empowered the Privy Council to make regulations for the prevention of contagious diseases. The prime motivation behind both pieces of legislation was not cholera but typhus that was most frequently mentioned in parliamentary debates and in the parliamentary reports in the previous decade. Some argued that cholera was too dangerous to be tackled using complex legislation and that the simpler 1832 Cholera Act was more appropriate. The recommendations of the Health of Towns Commission led to the passage of the Public Health Act in 1848. [50] The approach of cholera did not prevent the House of Commons delaying the Bill and stripping the General Board of all its major powers in the name of protecting the localities from central power. The fear of cholera had a marginal effect in reducing delays in late summer 1848 and the Bishop of London withdrew amendments in the Lords designed to strengthen the Bill because he felt that delay in the face of cholera was irresponsible. [51]

Nonetheless, the legislation represented a further dilution of laissez-faire attitudes and established a central General Board of Health with a five-year mandate based at Gwydir House in London with three Commissioners (Lord Morpeth, Lord Shaftesbury and Chadwick, with Southwood Smith as Medical Officer). Local Boards of Health would be set up in towns where the death rate was higher than 23 per thousand or more radically could be established where 10

---

[48] Hanley, James G., 'The Public's Reaction to Public Health: Petitions Submitted to Parliament, 1847-1848', *Social History of Medicine*, Vol. 15, (2002), pp. 393-411.

[49] See Sigsworth, Michael, and Warboys, Michael, 'The public's view of public health in mid-Victorian Britain', *Urban History*, Vol. 21, (1994), pp. 237-250.

[50] See, for instance, Lord Morpeth's speech introducing the Health of Towns Bill, *Hansard*, House of Commons, Debates, 30 March 1847, Vol. 91, cc617-636. The Public Health Act received the Royal Assent on 31 August 1848.

[51] *Hansard*, House of Lords, Debates, 7 July 1848, Vol. 100, cc231-5, 27 July 1848, Vol. 100, cc894-5.

per cent of ratepayers petitioned the Central Board asking that the Act be applied to their town. The Nuisances Removal and Diseases Prevention Act 1848 also gave the General Board power to issue orders and instructions but only on the authority and after an order by the Privy Council. [52] The Local Boards of Health would take over the powers of water companies and drainage commissioners, could levy a rate and had the power to appoint a salaried Medical Officer. They also had the power to pave streets etc. but this was not compulsory. [53]

The intended gains from the legislation were long-term. Setting up local boards of health with plans for drainage, sewerage and water supply would take time to implement. However, almost as soon as it was established in September 1848 and throughout 1849, the General Board of Health assumed the administrative burden for the expected cholera epidemic. In Sheffield, early medical intervention kept deaths down to 46 while in Dumfries nothing was done until Sutherland, one of the Board's two medical officers, visited the community and the London parishes resisted all attempts at intervention until September 1849. [54] The Nuisances Removal and Diseases Prevention Act 1848, regarded by some historians as the 'real cholera act of 1848', legislated for the removal of nuisances and the prevention of epidemic diseases in places where the Public Health Act was not in force and gave power for the Poor Law Commissioners to compel guardians to execute regulations and directions of the General Board of Health. [55]

There were several important weaknesses in the Act. The lifespan of the General Board of Health was limited to five years and, because it was not led by a minister, it lacked a voice in Parliament defending its actions. Its primary aim was to promote municipal sanitation but the legislation was permissive in character and many towns did not take advantage of the Act. Through its inspectors, it sought to persuade local authorities to inaugurate sanitary reform but

---

[52] Glen, William Cunningham, *The Nuisances Removal and Diseases Prevention Acts, 1848 & 1849: (11 & 12 Vict. Cap. 123 ; 12 & 13 Vict. Cap. 111): with Practical Notes and Appendix Containing the Directions and Regulations of the General Board of Health, with Index*, 3rd ed., (Shaw & Sons), 1849.

[53] Johnson, Cuthbert W., *The Acts for Promoting the Public Health, 1848n to 1851*, (Charles Knight), 1852, provides a contemporary commentary on the legislation.

[54] *Report of the General Board of Health on the epidemic Cholera of 1848 and 1849*, (W. Clowes & Sons), 1850, pp. 57-69, 107-110.

[55] Ibid, Hamlin, C., *Public health and social justice in the age of Chadwick*, pp. 275-301, examines the relationship between inspectors and local authorities between 1848 and 1854..

it had no powers to impose this. For Chadwick and his inspectors, sanitary reform was a matter of faith and they could not understand why the poor, surely they believed the beneficiaries of reform, often opposed their endeavours. It was based on preventative measures and was narrow in its focus. Such measures did bring about improvements but Chadwick disregarded contagionist theories and so alienated some in the medical profession. Finally, the Act did not legislate for Scotland or London that operated under the Metropolitan Commission of Sewers Act.

Some large cities avoided the legislation by obtaining private Acts of Parliament to carry out sanitary improvements. Leeds had already done this in 1842, Manchester in 1844 and Liverpool in 1847. However, evidence from the North-East suggests that some communities were prepared to implement the 1848 legislation. Sunderland Corporation worked with the General Board, not only co-operating with its proposals but developing their own initiatives. The idea that sanitary reform was resisted by local councils made up of tradesmen and shopkeepers did not apply to Gateshead Corporation, made up of this socio-economic group, that accepted the reforms while Newcastle Corporation with its wealthier socio-economic structure resisted state intervention at all costs. In these three communities, different groups including churches, medical practitioners, sanitary associations and the local press, played a central role in shaping public opinion and in the different responses to sanitary reform. In the absence of a medical consensus on the impact of environmental factors on typhus, typhoid and tuberculosis, it is hardly surprising that different communities came to different conclusions about what reform was needed. [56] These differences explain why the scale of the General Board's operations was modest. By July 1853, 164 places, including Birmingham, had been brought under the Act. In Lancashire only 26 townships took advantage of the Act and by 1858 only 400,000 of the county's 2.5 million people came under Boards of Health. [57]

The litmus test for the success or failure of the new policies took place in London.[58] A new Metropolitan Commission of Sewers had

---

[56] Mclean, David, *Public Halth and Politics in the Age of Reform: Cholera, the State and the Royal Navy in Victorian Britain*, (I. B. Tauris), 2006, provides a valuable case-study of South Devon.

[57] Midwinter, Eric C., *Social Administration in Lancashire, 1830-1860: Poor Law, Public Health and Police*, (Manchester University Press), 1969, 79-86.

[58] Bain, Alexander, *Autobiography*, (Longmans, Green, and Co.), 1904, pp. 196-210, provides a civil servant's view of Chadwick's attempted reforms in London and the 1848 Act.

been set up in December 1847 of which Chadwick was a leading member. [59] From the outset there were bitter rivalries in the Commission between him and the representatives of the old sewer commissions and the parish vestries. In 1850, Chadwick produced a new scheme for the water supply and for a system of publicly controlled cemeteries. Both schemes aroused a host of opponents and both were abandoned. The Treasury refused to advance money for the purchase of private cemeteries and the Metropolitan Water Supply Act 1852 left provision in the hands of water companies. [60] Hopes for any comprehensive sanitary reform in London had been dashed and there was growing opposition to the General Board across the country. In 1850, Lord Morpeth, who had worked effectively with Chadwick and acted as a constraint on his doctrinaire ideas, was replaced by Lord Seymour who was hostile to Chadwick. Feelings against the Board and in particular against Chadwick rose. The Central Board should have ended in 1853 but was given a year's extension because of a further outbreak of cholera.

Chadwick produced a report on what had been achieved but tactlessly again criticised the various vested interests. To the public Chadwick personified the autocratic, overbearing, centralising state and without parliamentary support or the backing of government he became a liability. In 1848, Chadwick's ideas may have been the solution for sanitary reform; by 1854, they had become the problem. He became the focus of a campaign in *The Times* and *Punch* that characterised him as trying to bullying the nation into cleanliness. It was Lord Seymour, who had left office in 1852, who demanded the removal of the Board members in 1854 and successfully carried an amendment against the government's bill to reorganise the Board. What ultimately proved fatal to the 1848 legislation was not cost or efficiency or the centralising role of the state but Chadwick's increasing inability to communicate with the different interests that he needed to persuade to support his sanitary ideal and then to alienate them by becoming even more doctrinaire in his attitudes. The tragedy is that many of those he antagonised shared Chadwick's goal for clean water and well drained towns but their approach was not dogmatic but practical, finding the right solution for the particular situation. With no aptitude for compromise and with few supporters left, on 12

---

[59] Hanley, James G., 'The metropolitan commissioners of sewers and the law, 1812-1847', *Urban History*, Vol. 33, (2006), pp. 350-368, Darlington, Ida, 'The London Commissioners of Sewers and their records', *Journal of the Society of Archivists*, Vol. 2, (1962), pp. 196-210.

[60] Allen, Michelle Elizabeth, *Cleansing the city: sanitary geographies in Victorian London*, (Ohio University Press), 2008, pp. 24-85.

August 1854, Chadwick resigned and though he lived until 1890, he never held public office again. Such was the odium in which he was held that his considerable public service was not recognised until he was knighted a year before his death. The General Board was reconstituted in August 1854 with a President responsible to Parliament but was finally abolished in 1858.

How was public health improved between 1854 and 1914?

Chadwick's retirement may have mollified those opposed to his view of sanitary reform, but the need to deal with the problem of disease and urban conditions remained. There was, however, a great difference between Parliament passing acts and enforcing an effective policy against the opposition of local authorities and property owners who saw sanitary reform as a source of unjustified expense. For all the efforts that had been made progress was slow and the death rate actually rose slightly between 1841-1845 and 1861-1865. In two respects, there were important developments in the mid-1850s. The Vaccination Act 1853 required parents and guardians to arrange for a smallpox vaccination of infants within four months of birth. Even though there were no provisions for enforcement, by the 1860s about two-thirds of children born were vaccinated and the death rate from smallpox fell as a result. There was also an important extension in the definition of 'nuisances'. The cholera epidemic of 1853-1854 and the influenza pandemic of 1855 led to the Nuisances Removal Act 1855. It consolidated the Acts of 1846 and 1848, enlarged the definition of nuisances and dealt with the sale of meat unfit for human consumption and with offensive trades. The act made obligatory the employment of one or more 'sanitary inspectors', previously inspectors of nuisances by each authority or jointly with other authorities and defined their powers of entry. It introduced the concept of overcrowding as being dangerous or prejudicial to health and also authorised the Privy Council to declare the Act in force in any part of England affected by or threatened with any epidemic of contagious disease and for the General Board of Health to issue regulations for house-to-house inspections, provision of medicines and interment of the dead.[61]

---

[61] Hamlin, Christopher, 'Public Sphere to Public Health: the Transformation of "Nuisance"', in Sturdy, Steve, (ed.), *Medicine, health and the public sphere in Britain, 1600-2000*, (Routledge), 2002, pp. 189-204, Brenner, J. F., 'Nuisance Law and the Industrial Revolution', *Journal of Legal Studies*, Vol. 3, (1973), pp. 403-433, and McLaren, J. P. S., 'Nuisance Law and the Industrial Revolution: Some Lessons from Social History', *Oxford Journal of Legal Studies*, Vol. 3, (1983), pp. 155-222.

Public health was far more complex than the pioneers of the 1840s had envisaged. For Chadwick, it was simply a matter of better sanitation and water supply. In reality, the problem had far wider environmental causes, pressure of population, bad housing and poor nutrition and Chadwick had persistently underestimated the importance of medical questions. In the twenty years after 1850, the progress that was made in public health was largely through scientific and medical developments. This can be seen in the statistical analysis of mortality by William Farr in the Registrar-General's department after 1839 and improvements in understanding how diseases were transmitted. Important independent investigations were made during the cholera epidemic of 1848-1849 by John Snow in London and a group of doctors including William Budd in Bristol with both diagnosing the cause of cholera as a living organism spread in drinking water and breeding in the human intestine.[62] Although the response to Budd's and Snow's 'water-borne theories' was ambivalent among the medical profession, their investigations provided good scientific reasons for suspecting sewage-tainted water apart from the smell. It was not until 1883 that Robert Koch's work in Alexandria showed conclusively that cholera germs were carried in water. The 1850s saw a sustained parliamentary campaign to improve the water supply of London which brought slow results. Indeed it can be argued that by 1870 analysis of the causes of health problems had run considerably ahead of effective administrative machinery for remedying them.

The eclipse of the career of Edwin Chadwick coincided with the rise of John Simon (1816-1904).[63] Trained as a doctor, he was appointed as the first medical officer of health for the City of London in October 1848. Simon worked with characteristic thoroughness and presented a series of annual and other reports to the Commissioners of Sewers. They were unofficially reprinted in 1854, with a preface in which Simon spoke strongly of 'the national prevalence of sanitary neglect,' and demonstrated the urgent need of control of the public health by a responsible minister of state.[64] The General Board of Health was reconstituted in 1854, and in 1855 was empowered to appoint a medical officer and Simon accepted the post in October 1855. The Board was subject to successive annual renewals of its

---

[62] Vandenbroucke, Jan P., 'Changing images of John Snow in the history of epidemiology', in Morabia, Alfredo, (ed.), *A history of epidemiologic methods and concepts*, (Birkhaeuser Verlag), 2004, pp. 141-148.
[63] Lambert, Royston, *Sir John Simon 1816-1904*, (MacGibbon & Kee), 1963, is the major biographical study.
[64] Simon, John, *Reports relating to the sanitary condition of London*, (J. W. Parker and Son), 1854.

powers and Simon's position was initially uncertain. He produced several valuable reports for the General Board of Health: on cholera and London's water supply in 1856, on vaccination in 1857 and reports on the sanitary state of the people of England and the constitution of the medical profession in 1858.[65] In the Public Health Act 1858, the Board was abolished and its functions and staff were transferred in part to the Local Government Act Office, a department of the Home Office and to the Medical Department of the Privy Council of which Simon remained medical officer. The 1858 Act was only made permanent in 1859 in face of strong opposition. [66] As medical officer of the Privy Council from 1858 he produced annual reports on the working of his department. Between 1858 and 1871, Simon trusted by his official superiors, was allowed a free hand and made the Medical Department into an effective instrument for change.

Much of Simon's work was deeply affected by the cholera outbreaks of 1848-1849 and 1853-1854, though initially he rejected Snow's theories and like other reformers he saw the problems of the city as moral as well as material. From his appointment to the Board of Health in 1855 till he resigned in 1876, the emphasis of his work shifted to statistical investigation and exact scientific enquiry. His reports were of significance in developing state intervention in public health issues.[67] In 1857, Simon had published his *Papers relating to the History and Practice of Vaccination*. Ten years later the law was strengthened by legislation that both tightened procedures and providing ways of improving the vaccine. [68] In the Vaccination Act 1871, following a very serious smallpox epidemic, Boards of Guardians were required by law to appoint a paid vaccination officer. Other infectious diseases that the reports gave attention were smallpox, which re-appeared in 1865-1866, typhoid, scarlatina and

---

[65] Stokes, T. N., 'A Coleridgean against the medical corporations: John Simon and the parliamentary campaign for the reform of the medical profession, 1854-1858', *Medical History*, Vol. 33, (1989), pp. 343-359.

[66] Hardy, Anne, 'Public health and the expert: the London Medical Officers of Health, 1856-1900', in Macleod, R. M., (ed.), *Government and expertise: specialists, administrators and professionals, 1860-1919*, (Cambridge University Press), 1988, pp. 128-142.

[67] Seaton, Edward, (ed.), *Public health reports by Sir John Simon*, 2 Vols. (J. & A. Churchill), 1887.

[68] Brunton, Deborah, *The politics of vaccination: practice and policy in England, Wales, Ireland, and Scotland, 1800-1874*, (University of Rochester Press), 2008, and Lambert, R. S., 'A Victorian national health service: state vaccination, 1855-71', *Historical Journal*, Vol. 5, (1962), pp. 1-18.

diphtheria. There were studies of 'industrial' diseases like the lung conditions produced among miners, potters and steel-grinders. An ineffective Adulteration of Foods Act was passed in 1860, the precursor of more far-reaching legislation in 1872 and 1875, by which local authorities had to employ public analysts to test food. The Alkali Act 1863 was the first of a series of enactments to deal with acid gas pollution. [69]

In 1866, Simon's *Eleventh Report* called for the consolidation of the legislation and administrative agencies relating to public health. Advances in scientific and medical knowledge, which had not existed under Chadwick, meant that effective legislation was now possible. The threat of cholera helped produce the Sanitary Act 1866 that gave local authorities increased powers to provide drainage and water supplies, stricter provision for the removal of nuisances and additional powers were given to regulate communicable diseases. It made the specific duty of authorities to inspect their districts and to suppress nuisances and in case of failure to do this and upon complains being made, the Home Secretary had the power to send an inspector and, if neglect was established, to order the authority to act. Although the legislation was badly drafted, it included the principle of uniform and universal provision of sanitary protection combined with compulsory powers of enforcement on local authorities that formed the basis for the administrative reforms of the 1870s.

In 1869, the Liberal Prime Minister William Gladstone had set up a Royal Commission to look into sanitary laws and administration. It reported in 1871 and its recommendations were embodied in the Public Health Act 1872. In August 1871, the ways in which public health policy was administered shifted. The Poor Law Board, Local Government Office of the Home Office and the Medical Department of the Privy Council were amalgamated to form a new department, the Local Government Board. Simon became its chief medical officer in the belief that his independent powers would be maintained. But neither Sir James Stansfeld, President of the Board, nor Sir John Lambert, the Permanent Secretary, were prepared to accept Simon's administrative independence. The Local Government Board was dominated by the old Poor Law officials and they took a different view from Simon keeping the medical scientific view out of policy-making in favour of the administrative principles inherited from the Poor Law.

---

[69] Macleod, R. M., 'The Alkali Acts administration, 1863-84: the emergence of the civil scientist', *Victorian Studies*, Vol. 9, (1965), pp. 85-112, and Garwood, Christine, 'Green Crusaders or Captives of Industry? The British Alkali Inspectorate and the Ethics of Environmental Decision Making, 1864-95', *Annals of Science*, Vol. 61, (2004), pp. 99-117.

Simon protested in vigorous minutes and appeals at the lessening of the influence of medical and scientific work on policy that were renewed when George Sclater-Booth became President in 1874. After a fierce battle with the Treasury, his office was 'abolished,' and he retired in May 1876.[70]

The shift towards administrative efficiency during the 1870s and 1880s resulted in legislation that either established organisational structures or consolidated existing legislation. The Public Health Act 1872 rationalised sanitary authorities throughout the country and made compulsory the appointment of medical officers of health. Finally, in 1875 a consolidating Public Health Act covered the whole field of public health, sanitation and nuisance prevention. Other legislation dealt with related fields: for instance, an act in 1875 regulating the sale of foods and drink, legislation in 1876 on the pollution of rivers and in 1879 the law on contagious diseases in animals was consolidated. The Diseases Prevention Act 1883 no longer pauperised the recipient of treatment in hospital with infectious diseases while the Infectious Diseases Notification Act 1889 persuaded a large number of local sanitary authorities to establish isolation hospitals, a situation extended into rural areas by the Isolation Hospitals Act 1893.

Why was public health reform only effective after 1870?

The early phase of public health reform was dominated by Edwin Chadwick, the later phase by Sir John Simon. Both left office disillusioned by their inability to implement reforms in the ways they wished. Paradoxically Chadwick resigned because of criticism of too much central control and Simon because of too little. Both believed that effective public health reform could only be achieved if the state took the leading role in both determining policy and controlling its administrative implementation. With some justification, they argued that local government was unable to fulfil these roles. However, the parameters of the public health debate had shifted by the early 1870s.[71] National administrative and especially inspectorial structures were in place to facilitate public health innovation providing the framework in which reformed local government could turn a legislative framework into a working system.

---

[70] See Brand, J. L., 'John Simon and the Local Government Board bureaucrats, 1871-6', *Bulletin of the History of Medicine*, Vol. 37, (1963), pp. 184-194.
[71] What follows draws on Szreter, Simon, *A central role for local government? The example of late Victorian Britain*, http://www.historyandpolicy.org/papers/policy-paper-01.html

Central to the implementation of national public health initiatives was the transformation of civic thinking associated initially with Joseph Chamberlain and Birmingham. For Chamberlain, elected mayor for three consecutive years between 1873 and 1875, 'true economy' lay in spending and investing in the homes, streets and schools of the working-classes and their families to enhance productivity, civilise the urban environment and contribute to the long-term prosperity of the city. The 'civic gospel' rippled out all over the country from its Nonconformist Birmingham epicentre and from the separate centre of municipal innovation of Glasgow. In other large cities including Manchester, Sheffield and Leeds, businessmen and professionals began to emulate Birmingham's and Glasgow's successful improvements. By 1900, smaller towns such as Wolverhampton, West Bromwich and Wakefield had followed suit. Lighting and paving streets, supplying homes with clean water, building sewers and connecting working-class houses to them were expensive capital investments paid for out of rates and taxes previously unacceptable to the electorate. The parish vestries of Victorian London eventually embraced the new spirit of civic government. Their key functions were integrated into a powerful London County Council created in 1889 to give the capital a governing body capable of providing strategic direction in providing services for its residents. Death rates had failed to improve for a generation and inner cities with their unregulated overcrowding and insanitary streets and housing had high levels of mortality. The expansion in municipal services and the creation of comprehensive public health measures made a significant contribution to levels of mortality and from the 1870s, the death rate fell steadily decade by decade.

Why were the constraints on and opposition to public provision of services that Chadwick and Simon encountered from the 1840s loosened from the 1870s? Existing private charity and philanthropy had proved insufficient to 'civilise' towns and ameliorate poverty. This was initially recognised in elementary education long regarded by many as the key to raising the standards and attitudes of the children of the poor. **Unitarian, Quaker, Baptist,** Congregationalist and even Anglican urban networks increasingly acknowledged that it was time to follow Britain's more successful continental rivals like Germany, Holland and France and fund educational provision on a larger scale. The only way to really break through the repeated generational cycles of families and whole districts trapped in poverty was to overhaul the scale of provision with a commitment to fund and administer education from the local rates. From 1870 onwards, central government also supplemented local rates from national taxation to provide a universal and national education system. Urban communities and their political elites realised that the problems of education, poverty, housing and public health were linked and that the only way to resolve them was for communities to take a proactive role through a more dynamic form of municipal self-government.

The changing and increasingly competitive nature of politics, locally and nationally, encouraged the sustained revolution into municipal activism in the last third of the nineteenth century. From 1835 until the late 1860s, local councillors were largely recruited from the 'shopocracy', small-scale property-holders who held most of the votes and who exercised them in favour of minimal local taxation. However, from 1867 through to 1884, a sequence of legislation brought an ever larger proportion of the upper, 'respectable' working-class and even some women onto the electoral rolls, swamping the votes of the 'shopocracy'. These individuals rented rather than owned property and had never personally received rate bills but whose families had an interest in voting for councillors committed to programmes for improving the urban environment and services. Being in favour of public health reform was no longer a matter of moral conscience but of political expediency.

Between 1870 and 1914, all of Britain's cities made substantial and ever-increasing investments in improving their environments, their housing, their social and health services, all of which disproportionately benefited the poor. This required significant public funding and the practical success of the new municipal activism rested on innovation in public finance in which Joseph Chamberlain, as a financial entrepreneur, was a crucial figure. Two devices were particularly important: long-term loans and a form of indirect taxation. It was important for the largest municipalities that they gained parliamentary authority to raise big loans at favourable long-term rates from the London money-markets, on the security of the city's rate-base. This postponed the initial costs of capital improvements and minimised the immediate fiscal cost for the current generation of ratepayers, whose political assent was necessary for these expensive schemes to go ahead. The second innovation, indirect taxation, took the form of using some of these loans to take over or build local monopoly services such as gas and lighting, electricity, transport and trams and water supply. They then ran them at a moderate profit that was used to fund local services or maintain the rates at a politically acceptable level. Local rates did eventually rise but by then the cities had their vital improvements. [72]

---

[72] Hennock, E. P., 'Finance and politics in urban local government in England, 1835-1900', *Historical Journal*, Vol. 6, (1963), pp. 212-225.

One other source of increased revenue for municipalities was in the form of subsidies from central government, derived principally from income and consumption taxes;

...the extent of local self-government during the nineteenth century appears stupefying. As a matter of principle Whitehall thrust every type of administration on to elected local bodies. [73]

Central government was prepared to use its legislative powers but preferred to coax local authorities to implement changes by partly defraying the costs of innovation through 'grants-in-aid' while leaving decisions on adoption to local councillors and their electorates. [74] The attack on inequality and urban misery was achieved by a doubling of government expenditure from 3 to 6 per cent of GNP after 1870 and especially the increase in local government's share of all forms of government expenditure that rose from 32 per cent in 1870 to 51 per cent in 1905.

Local pride often resulted in rivalry between towns to ensure that they benefited from these central subsidies. Moreover, when central government did legislate, it was almost always an attempt to apply across the country practices that had already been developed and thoroughly tested in particular localities. This was true for instance of public housing in Glasgow, free school meals in Birmingham or the notification system for monitoring infectious diseases used in Bolton. The direction of flow of new ideas and policy initiatives was a two-way process in which individual local authorities faced with concrete problems had the self-confidence, resources and the freedom to pioneer new approaches. Where these were seen to work, they were then adopted and applied nationally by the centre. With power and responsibility genuinely devolved by the centre to local authorities and with substantial revenue-raising powers, dynamic local businessmen and ambitious public service professionals were equally drawn to serve their local communities knowing they could really make a difference.

---

[73] Hanham, H. J., *The Nineteenth Century Constitution 1815-1914: Documents and Commentary*, (Cambridge University Press), 1969, p. 373.
[74] Baugh, G. C., 'Government grants in aid of the rates in England and Wales, 1889-1990', *Historical Research*, Vol. 65, (1992), pp. 215-237.

9 Poverty and the Poor Laws

Between 1800 and 1914, there were two period when state intervention in social policy significantly increased. The first was in the 1830s and 1840s and the second at the beginning of the twentieth century. Fundamental in the first burst of reforming activity was the New Poor Law of 1834 that gave conditional welfare for a minority, with public assistance at the price of social stigma. Some Edwardian reforms still retained conditions on take-up, as in the first old-age pensions in 1908, where tests of means and character eligibility were reminiscent of the Poor Law. Three years later, in 1911, there was a radical departure in the national scheme for insurance against ill-health and unemployment that conferred benefits as a result of contributions. It was still a selective scheme, limited to a section of the male population and entirely left out dependent women and children.

What was poverty?

The nineteenth century inherited the attitude that the existence of poverty was both right and proper. Many contemporary writers regarded poverty as a necessary feature of society, since only by feeling its pinch could the labouring poor be inspired to work. It was not poverty but pauperism or destitution that was regarded as a social problem.[1] Many early Victorians adopted the attitude that combined fatalism, 'For ye have the poor always with you' and moralism, destitution was the result of individual weakness of character.[2] In 1849, *Fraser's Magazine* commented:

> So far from rags and filth being the indications of poverty, they are in the large majority of cases, signs of gin drinking, carelessness and recklessness.[3]

Such people if congregated together in sufficient numbers

---

[1] A 'pauper' can simply be defined as an individual who was in receipt of benefits from the state. A labourer who was out of work was termed an able-bodied pauper, whereas the sick and elderly were called impotent paupers. Relief was given in a variety of ways. Outdoor relief was when the poor received help either in money or in kind. Indoor relief was when the poor entered a workhouse or house of correction to receive help. The Poor Law Amendment Act 1834 said that paupers should all receive indoor relief.
[2] *St Matthew*, 26: 8-11.
[3] 'Work and Wages', *Fraser's Magazine for Town and Country*, Vol. xl, (1849), p. 528.

seemed to constitute a social menace.[4] It was thinking of this sort that provided the impetus to poor law reform in 1834. Relief continued to be offered but only in the workhouse where the paupers would be regulated and made less comfortable than those who chose to stay outside and fend for themselves, the principle of 'less-eligibility'. Those who were genuinely in dire need would accept the workhouse rather than starve. Those who were not would prefer to remain independent and thus avoid the morally wasting disease of pauperism. The Poor Law of 1834 provided an important administrative model for future generations with central policy-making, supervision and inspection and local administration but the workings of this model were often profoundly disappointing to the advocates of 'less-eligibility' as a final solution to the problem of pauperism. But the issue was not pauperism on which contemporaries focused, but the debilitating effects of poverty itself.

Poverty is a term that is notoriously difficult to define. In simple terms, the failure to provide the basic necessities of life, food, clothes and shelter results in a state of poverty.[5] British society in the nineteenth century was poor by modern standards. The net national income per head at 1900 prices has been estimated as £18 in 1855 and £42 in 1900. The higher paid artisan might be unable to get work at a time of depression even if willing and anxious to do so. Most members of the working-class experienced poverty at some time in their lives and, compared to the middle-classes, their experience of poverty was likely to be a far more frequent, if not permanent one. It was not until near the end of the nineteenth century that poverty was first measured in any systematic fashion and most of the evidence of the extent and causes of poverty is from around 1900.[6] The number of paupers had long been known: they amounted to about 9 per cent of the population in the 1830s and this fell to less than 3 per cent by 1900. Far more people lived in poverty than ever applied for workhouse relief. In 1883, Andrew Mearns in his *Bitter Cry of Outcast London* claimed than as much as a quarter of the population of London received insufficient income to maintain physical health.[7]

---

[4] It is important to remember the 'revolutionary psychosis' that afflicted many within the ruling elite during the first half of the nineteenth century. Poverty was seen in this revolutionary light.
[5] On this subject the briefest introduction is Rose, M. E., *The Relief of Poverty 1834-1914*, (Macmillan), 2nd edition, 1986.
[6] Englander, David, and O'Day, Rosemary, (eds.), *Retrieved Riches: Social Investigation in Britain, 1840-1914*, (Scolar Press), 1995, examines the nature of social investigation.
[7] Mearns, Andrew, *The Bitter Cry of Outcast London: An Inquiry into the Condition of the Abject Poor*, (James Clarke & Co), 1883, pp. 15-18.

Impressionistic claims like this led Charles Booth to begin his scientific investigation of the London poor in 1886. He found that 30 per cent of the population of London and 38 per cent of the working-classes lived below the poverty line.[8]

Booth's conclusions were criticised by some who pointed to the unique position of London. However, B. Seebohm Rowntree[9] did a similar survey of his native York and in 1899 published conclusions that mirrored those of Booth.[10] He distinguished between 'primary poverty' and 'secondary poverty'.[11] Primary poverty was a condition where income was insufficient even if every penny was spent wisely. Secondary poverty occurred when those whose incomes were theoretically sufficient to maintain physical efficiency suffered poverty as a consequence of 'insufficient spending'. 10 per cent of York's population and 15 per cent of its working-classes were found to be in primary poverty. A further 18 per cent of the whole population and 28 per cent of the working-classes were living in secondary poverty. Rowntree also emphasised the changing incidence of poverty at different stages of working-class life, the 'poverty cycle' with its alternating periods of want and comparative plenty.[12]

Other surveys followed the work of Booth and Rowntree.[13] The

---

[8] Booth, Charles, *Life and Labour of the People in London*, 17 Vols. (Macmillan), 1889-1903. Norman-Butler, Belinda, *Victorian Aspirations: the Life and Labour of Charles and Mary Booth*, (Allen and Unwin), 1972, and Simey, T. S., and M. B., *Charles Booth: Social Scientist*, (Liverpool University Press), 1960, are sound biographies and Fried, A., and Elman, R., (eds.), *Charles Booth's London: a Portrait of the Poor at the Turn of the Century. Drawn from His 'Life and Labour of the People in London'*, (Harmondsworth), 1969, a useful collection of sources. O'Day, Rosemary, and Englander, David, *Mr Charles Booth's Inquiry: Life and Labour of the People in London Reconsidered*, (Hambledon), 1993, Gillie, Alan, 'Identifying the poor in the 1870s and 1880s', *Economic History Review*, Vol. 61, (2008), pp. 302-325, and Spicker, P., 'Charles Booth: the examination of poverty', *Social Policy and Administration*, Vol. 24, (1990), pp. 21-38, examine Booth's ideas. .

[9] On Rowntree see, Bradshaw, Jonathan, and Sainsbury, Roy, (eds.), *Getting the measure of poverty: the early legacy of Seebohm Rowntree*, (Ashgate), 2000, and Briggs, Asa, *Social Thought and Social Action: A study of the work of Seebohm Rowntree, 1871-1954*, (Longman), 1961.

[10] Rowntree, Seebohm, *Poverty: a study of town life*, (Macmillan), 1899, 2nd edition, (Macmillan), 1901.

[11] Ibid, Rowntree, Seebohm, *Poverty: a study of town life*, pp. 119-145.

[12] Ibid, Rowntree, Seebohm, *Poverty: a study of town life*, pp. 86-118.

[13] Hennock, E. P., 'Concepts of poverty in the British social surveys from Charles Booth to Arthur Bowley', in Bulmer, Martin, Bales, Kevin, and Sklar, Kathryn Kish, (eds.), *The Social Survey in Historical Perspective,*

most notable was the investigation in 1912-1913 of poverty in Stanley (County Durham), Northampton, Warrington and Reading by A. L. Bowley and A. R. Burnett-Hurst. [14] They found that the levels of poverty reflected different economic conditions and that among the working-class population primary poverty accounted for 6 per cent, 9 per cent, 15 per cent and 29 per cent in the respective towns. These conclusions questioned the assumption made by both Booth and Rowntree that similar levels of poverty might be found in most British towns. In fact, the diversity of labour market conditions was reflected in considerable variation in the levels and causes of poverty.

It is important to examine the reliance that can be placed on the results of early poverty surveys as few of their results can be accepted with complete confidence. Booth relied heavily on data from school attendance officers and families with children of school age, itself a cause of poverty in what he supposed to be a cross section of the population. Rowntree's estimates of food requirements were regarded as over-generous by nutritionists and he conceded after a second survey in 1936 that his 1899 poverty lines were 'too rough to give reliable results'. [15] Working-class respondents, confronted by middle-class investigators were notoriously liable to underestimate income. Most poor law and charity assistance was means tested and the poorer respondents, suspecting that investigators might have some influence in the disposal of relief, took steps not to jeopardise this. Income acquired illegally was likely to remain hidden. It is difficult to compare these levels with poverty at other times. Recent attempts by historians to assess approximate numbers that lived below Rowntree's poverty line in mid-nineteenth century Preston, York and Oldham all suggest poverty levels higher than those at the time of the 1899 survey. This is not surprising as between 1850 and 1900 money wages rose considerably and many more insured themselves against sickness and other contingencies.

1880-1940, (Cambridge University Press), 1991, and Hennock, E. P., 'The measurement of urban poverty: from the metropolis to the nation, 1880-1920', *Economic History Review*, Vol. 40, (1987), pp. 208-227.

[14] Bowley, A. L., and Burnett-Hurst, A. R., *Livelihood and Poverty: A Study in the Economic Conditions of Working-Class Households in Northampton, Warrington, Stanley and Reading*, (Routledge), 1915; see also, Carré, Jacques, 'A. L. Bowley et A. R. Burnett-Hurst étudient les familles ouvrières à Reading en 1915', in Carré, Jacques, (ed.), *Les visiteurs du pauvre: Anthologie d'enquêtes britanniques sur la pauvreté urbaine, 19e-20e siècle*, (Karthala), 2000, pp. 158-173.

[15] Rowntree, Seebohm, *Poverty and Progress: A Second Social Survey of York*, (Longman, Green and Co.), 1941, p. 461.

What caused poverty?

The causes of poverty revealed by the early poverty surveys were as surprising and disturbing to most contemporaries as the calculations of its extent. The common belief was that poverty was caused by idleness, drinking and other personal shortcomings, a belief that was used to justify the stigmatic nature of the Poor Law. Booth found that only a quarter of his 'submerged one-tenth' was impoverished chiefly by drink, idleness and 'excessive children'. More than half were in poverty as a result of insufficient earnings and a further 10 per cent due to sickness and infirmity. The crucial point was that a very considerable part of poverty was not 'self-inflicted' but derived from low wages and other circumstances over which the poor had little control. [16]

Low wage rates and unemployment must have both been serious causes of poverty earlier in the century when real wages were lower, when more men and women were engaged in declining domestic industries, in arable farming with its erratic labour requirements, and at casual work and occupations liable to be disrupted by poor weather, by uncertain transport or loss of power. In these circumstances slumps were accompanied by high food prices and few workers had the resources to make provisions against unemployment. However, the working of the trade cycle was still a major source of poverty in 1900. School medical reports show significant variety in the height and health of school children that reflect the amount of work available in their vulnerable early years.[17] The only unemployment figures historians have for the second half of the nineteenth century are those for trade unionists and they show a long-term average rate of between 4.5 and 5.5 per cent. These figures hide localised slumps such as the Lancashire 'cotton famine' during the American Civil War, the depression that impoverished Coventry when the silk trade was opened to foreign competition in 1860 and the effects of major strikes and lock-outs after 1890.

Old age was not as important a cause of poverty as low wages in

---

[16] In some respects, the recognition that poverty had different causes harked back to the distinction made in the 1601 Poor Law legislation (itself echoing the distinction made by JPs in 1563) between the able-bodied poor and the impotent poor both regarded as 'deserving poor' and the idle or 'undeserving' poor.

[17] Floud, Roderick, 'The dimensions of inequality: height and weight variation in Britain, 1700-2000', *Contemporary British History*, Vol. 16, (2002), pp. 13-26, and Jordon, T. E., 'Linearity, gender and social class in economic influences on heights of Victorian youths', *Historical Methods*, Vol. 24, (1991), pp. 116-123.

1900 but it was much more important than Booth and Rowntree at first suggested. [18] Booth did not pay sufficient attention to families in which the chief wage earner was elderly and as a result ascribed only 10 per cent of poverty to illness or infirmity. Rowntree said that only 5 per cent of primary poverty resulted from old age or illness but he omitted the numerous elderly inmates of workhouses and poor law infirmaries. [19] In 1890, well over a third of the working-class population aged 65 or over were paupers and in 1906, almost half of all paupers were aged 60 and above. This is not surprising since state pensions were not paid until 1909. [20] Sickness was still among the important causes of poverty in 1900 and was probably even more important earlier in the century. Chadwick and early public health campaigners pointed to the enormous economic cost of preventable disease and emphasised how poor rates were swollen by the deaths of working men and by the vicious circle of sickness, loss of strength and reduced earnings that delayed economic recovery. Rising wages after 1850 reduced the amount of poverty directly attributable to ill-health. This was aided by the increasing number of working men who joined friendly societies that provided sickness insurance.

Women were the chief sufferers from most of the causes of poverty.[21] They were prominent by a ratio of two to one among elderly paupers largely because of their outliving their husbands. Widows and spinsters also suffered from wage rates that reflected the assumption that all females were dependent. Working-class wives deserted by their husbands and the majority of unmarried mothers almost invariably became paupers. Women were also affected by hardships often hidden from investigators. The male breadwinner was almost always also the meat eater and there is ample evidence of the uneven distribution of income within the family that was to the detriment to the health of wives and children. Uncertain and fluctuating earnings made budgeting difficult and led too easily to dependence on pawnbrokers and retail credit to smooth economic fluctuations.

Drinking was the greatest single cause of secondary poverty in York in 1899 and an average working-class family spent a sum

---

[18] Thane, Pat, *Old age in English history: past experiences, present issues*, (Oxford University Press), 2000, pp. 147-193.
[19] Ibid, Seebohm Rowntree, B., *Poverty: a study of town life*, p. 121.
[20] Pugh, Martin, 'Working-class experience and state social welfare, 1908-1914: old age pensions reconsidered', *Historical Journal*, Vol. 45, (2002), pp. 775-796.
[21] See, Levine-Clark, Marjorie, *Beyond the reproductive body: the politics of women's health and work in early Victorian England*, (Ohio State University Press), 2004, especially pp. 116-130.

equivalent to a third of a labourer's earnings on it.[22] Heavy drinkers claimed that beer was necessary to their strength but drink was an extremely expensive way of obtaining nutrition. Some men could not easily avoid drinking especially as wages were often paid in public houses. Drinking was obviously a consequence of poverty as well as one of its causes. The public house was often warm and cheerful and full of friends and was certainly more attractive that squalid and overcrowded homes. One sign of the importance of drink among the causes of working-class poverty was extensive temperance activity. [23] The temperance movement has been characterised as overwhelmingly middle-class concerned to impose bourgeois value on a degenerate workforce. However, the middle-class did not have a monopoly of the Victorian virtues and temperance was as much a working-class trait as drunkenness.

Large families were also shown by Booth and Rowntree to be less important as a cause of poverty than many had believed. Nevertheless they were important and, like drink, were indirectly responsible for some of the poverty ascribed to low wages and other causes. Rowntree calculated that almost a quarter of those in primary poverty in York would have escaped had they not been burdened by five or more children. [24] Low earnings, irregular employment, large families, sickness and old age were the root causes of poverty in the nineteenth century rather than intemperance or idleness. By 1900 new levels of poverty were discovered showing clearly that official statistics for pauperism revealed only the tip of the iceberg and that comfortable assumptions based on the belief that poverty would melt away in the warm climate of economic prosperity must be considerably modified.

Why were the Poor Law reformed?

The reform of the Poor Laws extended the growing chasm between the middle-classes and the working population. The poor law, as it existed in the early 1830s was not a system but, in Sidney Checkland's

---

[22] Ibid, Seebohm Rowntree, B., *Poverty: a study of town life*, pp. 323-331. See, Dingle, A. E., 'Drink and working class living standards in Britain, 1870-1914', *Economic History Review*, 2nd series, Vol. 25, (1972), pp. 608-622.

[23] Harrison, Brian, *Drink and the Victorians*, (Faber), 1971, revised edition, (Keele University Press), 1995, is a work of major importance on the 'drink question' between the 1830s and the 1870s. It should be supplemented with the study by Lambert, W. R., *Drink and Sobriety in Victorian Wales*, (University of Wales Press), 1984.

[24] Ibid, Seebohm Rowntree, B., *Poverty: a study of town life*, pp. 121-122, 129-135.

words, 'an accretion', determined by statutes passed two centuries earlier in a different economic and social world without central organisation and left to the discretion and vagaries of local parishes. Any attempt to reconstruct the poor law would have to be both bold and grand. The old poor law, constructed in the late-sixteenth century, touched almost every aspect of domestic government. [25] It provided the only general social securities and the only general regulation of labour. But its main characteristic was perhaps the almost complete lack of either central control or uniform policy. [26] The old poor law also provided no clear answers to certain critical questions: was unemployment to be regarded as an offence or a misfortune? Was relief to be administered as a deterrent, as a dole or as a livelihood?

Between 1750 and 1820, there was an explosion in relief spending. Real per capita expenditures more than doubled between 1750 and 1800, and remained at a high level until the Poor Law was reformed in 1834. Relief expenditures increased from 1.0 per cent of GDP in 1750 to a peak of 2.7 per cent of GDP in 1820. The nature of pauperism changed considerably in the late-eighteenth and early-nineteenth centuries, especially in the rural south and east of England. There was a sharp increase in numbers receiving casual benefits, as opposed to regular weekly payments. The age distribution of those on relief became younger--those aged between 20 and 59 increased significantly while payments to those aged 60 and over declined. Finally, the share of relief recipients in the south and east who were male increased from about a third in 1760 to nearly two-thirds in 1820. Gilbert's Act in 1782 allowed parishes to join together to form

---

[25] Slack, P., *The English poor law, 1531-1782*, (Macmillan), 1990, and Marshall, J. D., *The Old Poor Laws 1795-1834*, (Macmillan), 2nd edition, 1985, are brief bibliographical essays on the debates until the late 1980s. Fideler, Paul A., *Social welfare in pre-industrial England: the old Poor Law tradition*, (Palgrave), 2006, is a more recent study. Hitchcock, Tim, King Peter, and Sharpe, Pamela, (eds.), *Chronicling Poverty: The Voices and Strategies of the English Poor 1640-1840*, (Macmillan), 1997, and Lees, Lynn Hollen, *The Solidarities of Strangers: The English Poor Laws and the People 1700-1948*, (Cambridge University Press), 1998, take a longer perspective.

[26] Innes, Joanna, 'The distinctiveness of the English poor laws, 1750-1850', in Winch, D. N., and O'Brien, P. K., (eds.), *The political economy of British historical experience, 1688-1914*, (Oxford University Press), 2002, pp. 381-407. Valuable local studies include Adams, Jenny, 'The old poor law in Suffolk, 1727-1834', *Suffolk Review*, Vol. 47, (2006), pp. 2-27, and Hampson, E. M., *Treatment of Poverty in Cambridgeshire 1587-1834*, (Cambridge University Press), 1934, reprinted 2009.

unions for the purpose of relieving the poor: the impotent poor should be relieved in workhouses while the able-bodied poor should either be found work or granted outdoor relief. In many respects, this legislation legitimised existing policies that found outdoor relief both less expensive and more humane than workhouse relief. [27]

Economic distress in the mid-1790s led to the introduction of 'allowances on aid of wages', generally though not accurately known as the 'Speenhamland system' after its first application in Berkshire in 1795. [28] The share of the population receiving poor relief in 1802-1803 varied significantly across counties, being 15 to 23 per cent in the grain- producing south and less than 10 percent in the north. What was initially perceived as a temporary expedient became a necessity for the labouring population in the depressed agrarian south after 1815. Escalating costs, changing ideological perceptions and the 'Swing' riots of 1830 led to an increasingly focused challenge to the existing system that was seen as corrupting, lenient and not cost-effective and for demands that more rigour should be imposed on the poor. [29]

Broadly speaking, opinion on the poor laws was divided into three: those who wished to retain them, those who wished to modify them and those who wished to abolish them. Humanitarians, sentimental radicals and paternalistic Tories belonged to the first group. They believed that there was a strong imperative of humane social responsibility in providing a basic measure of social security for

---

[27] Williams, Samantha, *Poverty, gender and life-cycle under the English poor law, 1760-1834*, (Boydell), 2011

[28] Neuman, Mark, 'A suggestion regarding the origins of the Speenhamland plan', *English Historical Review*, Vol. 84, (1969), pp. 317-322, Speizman, M. D., 'Speenhamland: an experiment in guaranteed income', *Social Service Review*, Vol. 40, (1966), pp. 44-55, Williams, Samantha, 'Malthus, marriage and poor law allowances revisited: a Bedfordshire case study, 1770-1834', *Agricultural History Review*, Vol. 52, (2004), pp. 56-82, and 'Poor relief, labourers' households and living standards in rural England c.1770-1834: a Bedfordshire case study', *Economic History Review*, Vol. 58, (2005), pp. 485-519.

[29] The debate over the poor laws is best approached through Poynter, J. R., *Society and Pauperism: English Ideas on Poor Relief 1795-1834*, (Routledge), 1969, and Cowherd, R. G., *Political Economists and the English Poor Laws*, (Ohio University Press), 1978. Boyer, G. R., *An Economic History of the English Poor Law 1750-1850*, (Cambridge University Press), 1990, is an important defence of Malthusian ideas. Himmelfarb, G., *The Idea of Poverty: England in the Early Industrial Age*, (Faber), 1984, is an extensive work on the subject. Brundage, Anthony, *The English poor laws, 1700-1930*, (Palgrave), 2002, provides a convenient overview.

the labouring poor and this seemed to them to outweigh its disadvantages. Those who wished to modify the existing system were to some degree motivated by the same sentiments but were alarmed by escalating costs and sought to reduce them. The third group was the most influential and powerful if the least numerous. Its guiding lights were political economy and Malthusianism. [30] They believed that labourers must operate within the framework of the free market economy and 'social discipline'. The latter had the better of the argument and by the early 1830s it was accepted among the middle-classes and many of the aristocratic elite, especially the Whigs that the poor laws encouraged indolence and vice. [31]

The Royal Commission set up in 1832 to investigate the workings of the poor law was weighted towards 'progressive' opinion and quickly confirmed what the Commissioners had set out to prove.[32] There may have been exaggeration of the abuses of the old poor law in the 1834 Poor Law Report. Mark Blaug[33] has shown that its economic consequences were not understood by contemporaries or later historians but there was no confusion about the purpose of those who framed the Poor Law Amendment Act, especially Edwin Chadwick its guiding force. Chadwick could not adopt any of the approaches argued by the three groups. He objected to the basic security conception of the humanitarians and to the notion of the 'parish in business'. [34] He also differed from the Malthusians and political economists in two important respects. The idea of abandoning any attempt at control was antithetical to his bureaucratic temperament. He did not agree with the Malthusian proposition that population must inevitably outrun resources and asserted that there was no economic problem that greater and freer productivity could

---

[30] Boyer, G. R., 'Malthus was right after all: poor relief and birth rates in south-eastern England', *Journal of Political Economy*, Vol. 97, (1989), pp. 93-114

[31] Blaug, Mark, 'The myth of the old Poor Law and the making of the new', *Journal of Economic History*, Vol. 23, (1963), pp. 151-184, remains an important paper. See also, Taylor, J. S., 'The mythology of the Old Poor Law', *Journal of Economic History*, Vol. 29, (1969), pp. 292-297.

[32] *Royal commission on administration and practical operation of the Poor Laws, Report and appendices*, Parliamentary papers, House of Commons, (1834), XXVII; Parliamentary papers, House of Commons, (1834,) XXVIII.

[33] Blaug, M., 'The Poor Law report re-examined', *Journal of Economic History*, Vol. 24, (1964), pp. 229-245.

[34] See, Dunkley, P., 'Whigs and paupers: the reform of the English poor laws, 1830-1834', *Journal of British Studies*, Vol. 20, (1981), pp. 124-149, and 'Paternalism, the magistracy and poor relief in England, 1795-1834', *International Review of Social History*, Vol. 24, (1979), pp. 371-397.

not solve. His primary objection to the old poor law was that it held down productivity by effectively pauperising the independent labourer and the laws of settlement immobilised a huge labour force that factories were crying out for. Chadwick wanted to 'de-pauperise' the able-bodied poor and drive them into the open labour market. This could be achieved, Chadwick believed, through the process of less eligibility because it would be in the labourer's interest to join the free labour market. This would induce the majority of able-bodied paupers to refuse poor relief and provide capital for development and productivity.

What were the aims of the 1834 Poor Law Amendment Act?

The 1834 Act did not aim to deal with the nature or lack of provision only with its excess. It had not been politically practical to abolish public relief completely but the relief for those unwilling to unable to make provision for themselves was to be on terms less favourable than those obtained by the lowest paid worker in employment (the principle of 'less eligibility'). This would eliminate abuse and fraud. Pauperism was a defect of character as there was always work available at the prevailing market price if it was sought strenuously enough. Hard work and thrift would always ensure a level of competence, at whatever level individuals were working. These values, reflecting emergent middle-class ideology, made a lasting impression on society for the rest of the century. The sense of shame at the acceptance of public relief, the stigma of the workhouse and the dread of the pauper 's funeral were central facets of the attitudes and anxieties of working people. They played a major role in the definition of 'respectability' that emerged among both the middle-classes and labourers. The 1834 Act embodied the ideology of the political economists but it could be presented by its opponents as an abuse of the poor: the poor law agitation before 1834 was aimed at amelioration but after 1834 the rigour of the system generated a counter-pressure in favour of easement. [35]

The 1834 Act was important in three respects. Unlike factory

---

[35] Brundage, A., *The Making of the New Poor Law: the politics of inquiry, enactment and implementation, 1833-39,* (Hutchinson), 1979, Checkland, S. G., and E., (eds.), *The Poor Law Report of 1834*, (Penguin), 1974, Digby, A., *The Poor Law in Nineteenth Century England and Wales*, (The Historical Association), 1982, Fraser, Derek, (ed.), *The New Poor Law in the Nineteenth Century*, (Macmillan), 1976, Rose, M.E., *The Relief of Poverty 1834-1914*, (Macmillan), 2nd edition, 1985, and Wood P., *Poverty and the Workhouse in Victorian England*, (Alan Sutton), 1991, are the most useful books on the introduction and operation of the 'new' poor law.

or mine reform, the thinking behind the act was rural rather than urban. This led to the adoption of a programme entirely unsuitable and largely unworkable in the industrial urban setting of northern England and accounted for the widespread opposition to its introduction after 1836. [36] A simple reversal from relaxation to rigour could succeed in the agrarian south to a considerable extent but matters were different in the industrial north. There the new poor law was politicised, first by the anti-poor law agitation and then by the effects of the introduction of the electoral principle into poor law affairs. Secondly, the legislation in 1834 was the result of a generalised view of a whole range of problems containing a moral rather than an economic and social view of the poor and within this framework aimed at internal consistency and comprehensiveness. Finally, it created the first effective element of centralised British bureaucracy intended to preside over a general social policy with central control and supervision with local administration.

The standardising intentions of national legislators almost immediately came into conflict with the attitudes and responses of those who dealt with the Poor Law locally. Localities could and did ignore or evade the instructions of the Commissioners. Outdoor relief could not be withheld in seasonal employment like agriculture or during trade depressions in industrial centres. Checkland has argued:

> ...this generated a kind of schizophrenia when placed alongside the concepts embodied in the governing Act of 1834... [producing] concessions to common sense and common humanity.[37]

Despite this there is no doubt that imposing 'rigour' resulted in much hardship under the Act. There are accounts of deficient diet, penal workhouses, families torn apart and the denial of dignity to the old. The poor were abused because of a combination of indifference to their plight and social zealotry because of the dogma enshrined in the enabling legislation.

The Act was intended as an attack on a structural problem: the conditions and behaviour of the labouring poor, especially in agrarian regions, the intention of reducing abuse and to stop confusion

---

[36] Poverty in the cities is analysed by Treble, J., *Urban Poverty in Britain 1830-1914*, (Batsford), 1979, Rose, L., *'Rogues and Vagabonds' Vagrant Underworld in Britain 1815-1985*, (Routledge), 1988, and Chinn, Carl, *Poverty amidst prosperity: the urban poor in England 1834-1914*, (Manchester University Press), 1995.

[37] Ibid, Checkland, S., and E., (eds.), *The Poor Law Report of 1834*, pp. 91-92.

between wages and relief. Can this be seen as an expression of middle-class values grounded in the ideology of political economy? In simplistic terms it probably can, but the relationship between political economy and poor law policy was in practice far more complex. The uniformity of support for political economy by the middle-classes can be easily over-exaggerated and the nature of the trade cycle resulted in their refusal to implement the full rigour of the legislation in their industrial centres.

The *Poor Law Report* may have been over-optimistic in believing that uniformity of practice was possible but its principles established attitudes to poverty, which still have current significance. Ursula Henriques maintains:

> In 1834 the new development was given a scope, a momentum and a character which made it irreversible. The change was more immediate and more complete in the south than in the north, but it was lasting....The Victorian workhouse and all it stood for....was perhaps the most permanent and binding institution of Victorian England. Not until the working-class had obtained the vote and entirely different attitudes to poverty in general and unemployment in particular began to creep in at the turn of the century did the principles of 1834 start to lose their grip. [38]

Chadwick's original proposals were modified in four important respects as the bill went through Parliament during 1834. Each of these changes had more widespread and serious consequences than was anticipated. Chadwick had given his proposed Central Board powers to forbid absolutely the granting of outdoor relief, but the act merely gave permission to 'regulate' it. This ambiguity clearly opened the way for a retreat towards the old allowance system. He had also given the Board the powers of a court of record with the capacity to commit offenders for contempt but this was dropped from the bill during its second reading. This stripped the Board of its coercive powers. Chadwick proposed that the Board should have powers to compel local guardians of the new unions to raise rates for, and to build new workhouses. The Act limited these coercive powers to a maximum of £50 per year or one-tenth of the annual rate. These sums were inadequate and meant that the Central Board could not force the local unions into action at all. This concession proved fatal to the system. If the Board could not compel the unions to build workhouses, the 'workhouse test' failed. [39] Finally, he proposed that

---

[38] Ibid, Henriques, Ursula, *Before the Welfare State*, p. 59.
[39] Besley, Timothy, Coate, Stephen, and Guinnane, Timothy W., 'Incentives, information, and welfare: England's New Poor Law and the workhouse test', in Guinnane, Timothy W., Sundstrom, William A., and

the law of settlement be abolished. This was rejected and the retention of parish responsibility for its own paupers struck another blow at his great objective of freeing the labour market. These alterations crippled the project in many ways. In particular the second and third points robbed the central authority of much of its initiating and discretionary power and left it weakened.

The government followed up its concessions to public opinion by concessions to the old idea of patronage. Patronage was at the heart of government in the 1830s and Chadwick was, in part because of his social origins, not appointed one of the three Poor Law Commissioners. The posts were raised in salary and by implication in rank from £1,000 to £2,000 per year and men from the ruling political elite were found to fill them. Chadwick, enraged by this situation, did however persuade the Whig government to accept him as a permanent secretary to the Commission with the vague understanding that he would be next in line for promotion. This proved the worst of all possible solutions. Of the Commissioners, Thomas Frankland Lewis, J. G. Shaw-Lefevre and George Nicholls, only the latter even understood let alone sympathised with Chadwick's views. The personal antipathy between Chadwick and the Lewises, father and son--Cornewall Lewis succeeded his father as commissioner in 1839--meant that from 1837 the Commission paid little attention to Chadwick's advice and from 1838 onwards it practically broke off all relations with him. The poor law administration was from the beginning divided into two camps. Most of the Assistant Commissioners, the executive in the field sided with Chadwick but they were under the direction and in the power of an increasingly anti-Chadwickian Commission. This conflict damaged the efficacy of administration and Chadwick suffered most from this situation. Public opinion held him responsible for the Commission's policy whereas in fact he had fought against the introduction of a system that was a parody of his own principles and projects and over which he had declining influence.

The Act as it was implemented may well have not been what Chadwick intended but he cannot escape some responsibility for this situation. His errors were not only tactical but political. He failed to protest sufficiently against the dropping of the coercive clauses, though it is unlikely whether this would have altered and eventual outcome, and had accepted the secretaryship, what proved to be a poisoned chalice. It is also important to recognise that there were important

---

Whatley, Warren, (eds.), *History matters: essays on economic growth, technology, and demographic change,* (Stanford University Press), 2004, pp. 245-270.

weaknesses in his conception of the problem of the poor. Chadwick prided himself in the introduction of the 'reign of fact' yet his analysis of the problem of the rural poor was seriously flawed. The *Poor Law Report* was cast in universal terms but it was really based on one feature of the problem, rural poverty, and even here the issues were misconstrued. On critical matters such as rural wage rates, numbers of unemployed and regional variations, very little reliable data was collected. It focused on spectacular cases of abuse and described the problem rather than quantifying it. Chadwick had little understanding of the nature of urban poverty or that the old poor laws operated differently in towns and cities that in the countryside.

The administrative aspect of his plan also suffered from important weaknesses. The first was the independent status of the Central Board. In the post-reform politics of the 1830s and 1840s, criticisms and protests about the new poor law were voiced in Parliament where the Commissioners had no responsible defender. Separation from parliament far from making the Commission strong and fearless, made it weak, confused and extraordinarily subject to political pressures. The second great weakness was the power still left to the local authorities. Chadwick refused to go to the full length of centralisation since he believed that a national instead of a local poor rate would be too expensive and demanded substantial administrative machinery. He expected that the self-interest of the local Guardians would operate in the interests of his general plan and believed that the plan would be more effective if it allowed some degree of representation for local taxation and for the election of members of the Boards of Guardians. [40] In fact, this proved a recipe for confrontation between central and local government: local taxation, because it is collected close to the individual, tends to be less popular than national taxation which often seems more impersonal and local electors also have greater control over the level of that taxation. The blame was not wholly Chadwick's. It was government that had removed its ultimate coercive powers over the local unions from the hands of the Commission and thus left the 1834 Act more permissive in nature than Chadwick wanted.

Despite the important changes from Chadwick's original proposals, much of his work survived and in a few instances his gravest errors were corrected in practice. At the same time, some of the foundations of modern central government had been laid. Some problems were left unresolved: the political status of the new type of central commission, its relationship to representative local institutions

---

[40] See, Brundage, A., 'Reform of the Poor Law electoral system, 1834-94', *Albion*, Vol. 7, (1975), pp. 201-215, on local elections.

and central responsibility for the actions of its subordinates. It is also true that without coercive powers the Central Board could not fully discharge its function and without being subordinate to the cabinet the board could not fully use the coercive powers it retained. These deficiencies were largely remedied by the Poor Law Amendment Act 1847. The substance of centralisation had been established.

To what extent was the 1834 Poor Law Amendment Act modelled on Benthamite principles? Jeremy Bentham had been Chadwick's mentor in the years before his death in 1832. [41] The close links between Bentham and Chadwick led historians to assume there was a connection between the former's ideas and the practical solutions put forward by the latter. The question that needs to be addressed is how significant was that connection. Benthamism or Utilitarianism flourished in England in the first half of the nineteenth century though it existed before that and its effect lasted long after. [42] Its main impact came through the writings of Jeremy Bentham and James Mill, and in modified ways through the work of the latter's son John Stuart Mill. Bentham was eager not only to establish a general formula for the happiness of the community but to apply his ideas to the detail of reform and his supporters were experts in economics, law, politics and administration. He believed that with the principle of utility as a clear first principle, politics and law need no longer be replete with inconsistency, obscurity, prejudice and confusion. [43] Bentham maintained that there was a natural harmony of interests between the individual and the community; an individual in pursuing his own interests also pursued the interests of the community. This may have necessitated bringing the interests of the individual into artificial harmony with the interests of the community through the various sanctions open to the community and this had crucial implications for the role of government in society. [44]

---

[41] Ibid, Finer, S. E., *The Life and Times of Sir Edwin Chadwick*, pp. 28-37.

[42] Pearson, Robert, and Williams, Geraint, *Political Thought and Public Policy in the Nineteenth Century*, (Longman), 1984, pp. 9-38, is perhaps the simplest introduction to a complex issue. See also, Quinn, Michael, 'A Failure to Reconcile the Irreconcilable? Security, Subsistence and Equality in Bentham's Writings on the Civil Code and on the Poor Laws', *History of Political Thought*, Vol. 29, (2008), pp. 320-343, and Schofield, Philip, *Utility and democracy: the political thought of Jeremy Bentham*, (Oxford University Press), 2006.

[43] Winch, D., *Riches and poverty: an intellectual history of political economy in Britain, 1750-1834*, (Cambridge University Press), 1996, provides the intellectual background.

[44] See, Roberts, David, 'Jeremy Bentham and the Victorian administrative state', *Victorian Studies*, Vol. 2, (1959), pp. 193-210.

The unreformed Poor Law system showed an absence of both uniform policy and central control and was clearly inadequate as a means of dealing with the problems of unemployment and poverty. In Benthamite terms, it was hopelessly outdated and failed to fulfil the principle of utility. Chadwick's *Report* and its principle of 'less eligibility' seemed to offer a simple, uniform and economic alternative to the complexities and cost of the old system. In addition to the principle that was to govern poor relief, Chadwick also detailed the administrative change that would be necessary to implement it. The subsequent legislation can be regarded as Benthamite in its operational principles and in the administration set up to regulate them. However, the underlying belief that the poor could always find work and that relief should only be given in the workhouse, proved to be the undoing of the system. In many areas, outdoor relief was still given in recognition of the harsh realities of unemployment, while in other areas wages declined as more people were forced on to the labour market. So the system was often seen as cruel if administered strictly; in order for it to be made more compassionate certain aspects of it had to be diluted or evaded.[45] The system of local uniformity under central control and inspection, as recommended by Chadwick, was never put into full operation but was established as the administrative model that was increasingly followed throughout the century.

Assessing Chadwick's role in the formulation of the 1834 legislation is a matter on which there has been some debate. In the 1840s and particularly the early 1850s, Chadwick was regarded with considerable suspicion by many of his contemporaries. This was, in part, the result of his prickly character and dogmatic and often overbearing and unbending nature. However, Chadwick did attack certain long-established traditions in British administration and social policy. His Benthamism and middle-class origins made him suspect in a bureaucracy still dominated by aristocratic patronage. The notion of a Civil Service grounded in merit and ability was still in the future. Added to this he was politically pushy and easily offended. His belief in a uniform system of poor law administration under central control offended those who believed in local autonomy and, within the limits of nineteenth century definitions, in 'democracy'. This helps to explain why no uniform system was introduced in the 1830s and was even more an issue when Chadwick moved into public health and the need to legislate positively in favour of cleaner towns. It is not surprising that Anthony Brundage called his study of Chadwick

---

[45] Henriques, U. R. Q., 'How cruel was the Victorian Poor Law?', *Historical Journal*, Vol. 11, (1968), pp. 365-371.

England's 'Prussian Minister', a term of contemporary abuse drawing comparisons between Chadwick's 'unEnglish' centralisation and the militaristic and highly centralist Prussian State.

Why did people oppose the 1834 Act?

Resistance to alterations in the provision of poor relief was not uncommon in the early-nineteenth century and grievances about the operation of the poor laws formed a significant feature of disturbances in southern England between 1830 and 1832. Whatever its demoralising character, the old poor law had at least provided flexible arrangements to deal with poverty and had come to be regarded by many labourers as their right in times of hardship. It was not surprising that the introduction and especially the implementation of the Poor Law Amendment Act of 1834 provoked widespread hostility and opposition. [46] The Act had a relatively easy passage through Parliament but even so there was some opposition. On 30 April 1834, *The Times* came out strongly against the Poor Law Bill and held an on-going debate about the legislation with the *Morning Chronicle*. The Tory publication, the *Leeds Intelliegencer* opposed the Act while the *Manchester Guardian* and the *Leeds Mercury* supported it. William Cobbett saw it, in his pamphlet *The Legacy to Labourers*, as an attack on the 'right' to relief and an assault on the traditional 'social compact' between the propertied and the poor. [47] Other saw it as an attack on the independence of local government. Working-class radicals regarded it as part of the attack on the livelihood of the poor by a penny-pinching government. The threat of the workhouse, with the expectation that it would break up families, impose starvation wages and treat paupers more severely than criminals lay at the heart of popular assumptions that those receiving poor relief would be humiliated and degraded even when their poverty was no fault of their own. This view was reinforced by the Anatomy Act of 1832 that made

---

[46] Opposition to the introduction of the 1834 Act can be found in Edsall, N., *The Anti-Poor Law Movement 1833-1844*, (Manchester University Press), 1971, and Knott, J., *Popular Opposition to the 1834 Poor Law*, (Croom Helm), 1985. See also, Green, David R., 'Pauper protests: power and resistance in early-nineteenth-century London workhouses', *Social History*, Vol. 31, (2006), pp. 137-159.

[47] See, Dyck, Ian, 'William Cobbett and the rural radical platform', *Social History*, Vol. 18, (1993), pp. 185-204, and *William Cobbett and rural popular culture, 1790-1835*, (Cambridge University Press), 1992, pp. 200-210.

unclaimed pauper corpses available for medical dissection. [48]

The first reaction to the implementation of the Act came in agricultural areas. From 1835, there were numerous disturbances in East Anglia and the southern counties, a situation aggravated by a hard winter that forced many unemployed labourers to apply for relief. Announcements of the implementation of the Act were greeted with hostility. In May 1835, a crowd assembled at Ampthill demanding 'Blood or bread', 'All money' and 'No bread' and dispersed only after the Riot Act was read. [49] In other places labourers occupied the workhouses demanding their customary rights. Attempts to separate male and female paupers under the new regulations were seen as part of a Malthusian plot to stop the poor from breeding; this was elaborated by rumours that workhouse food was laced with an anti-fertility substance or even poisoned. The most serious disturbances took place in Suffolk. Anglican clergymen openly opposed to the new law and strong local feeling was more evident than in many other parts of the country. The disturbances in southern England demonstrated the sensitivity of the population to changes in customary arrangements for poor relief. Reactions varied from locality to locality but there was little serious violence other than some property being damaged and a few people assaulted. There was often considerable local sympathy for the rioters and many gentry and parsons petitioned against the Act. However, the disturbances did little to disturb the implementation of the legislation and by mid-1836 the new system was operating across the agricultural south. The anti-poor law movement never gained the support and partial success it was to achieve when the system was applied to the North.

In Wales, Tories exploited working-class antipathy to the 1834 legislation and the Tory press, and especially *Yr Haul*, portrayed itself as the champion of the poor who, it said, were suffering because the Whigs wanted to relieve their own supporters and defended the poor who were now its victims:

> The poor tremble...they would rather die of famine on the fields and hills where they live than go into the workhouse to pine in slavery...[50]

---

[48] On this issue, see Richardson, Ruth, *Death, Dissection and the Destitute*, (Routledge), 1988, with its vivid description of the importance of the Anatomy Act to the climate of fear that helped nurture Chartism.

[49] Apfel, William, and Dunkley, Peter, 'English rural society and the New Poor Law: Bedfordshire, 1834-47', *Social History*, Vol. 10, (1985), pp. 37-68.

[50] *Yr Haul*, 1836, p. 214.

The anti-Poor Law agitation took an increasingly religious tone with the new workhouses seen as violating the laws of Christianity by separating families.[51] The agitation in Wales also demonstrated deep local aversion to outside interference, matched only in northern England.[52] The legislation was constantly referred to as a piece of 'English' legislation unsuited to Welsh conditions but Welsh opposition had few links with opposition in England. Also bitterly resented was the decision by Poor Law Commissioners, because of the low density of population, to create large Poor Law Unions separating some communities from their Union centres by many miles.

Nevertheless, opposition in Wales took time to gain momentum and initially the commissioners expected little opposition to the implementation of the legislation. The major problem they faced was what they called an 'unholy alliance' of magistrates, Anglican clergy and Nonconformists to capture control of the Boards of Guardians. This proved remarkably successful and in many Unions, the 1837 board elections were won by anti-Poor Law candidates. In south Wales, these victories had little practical effect since Unions had already been established and workhouse construction had gone too far to be easily reversed. In addition, wages in the iron-mining districts were comparatively high and Glamorgan was considered fairly free of the worst evils of pauperism.[53] This was not the case in central and northern Wales where reorganisation had not proceeded beyond the preliminary stage before opposition crystallised. By early 1838:

...the administration of the Poor Law in northern and central Wales had become a war of nerves in which the Poor Law Commissioners might not actually lose but which they had little prospect of winning.[54]

As in England, the 1834 Act politicised working people and reinforced increasingly negative views of the reforming Whigs.

Initially the Act was received favourably by the powerful provincial northern press largely because it seen as irrelevant to the industrial areas where poor rates were much lower than in the south. However, implementation from the end of 1836 aroused serious and

---

[51] *Y Diwygiwr*, 1837, p. 148.
[52] Ibid, Edsall, N., *The Anti-Poor Law Movement 1833-1844*, pp. 128-132, 136.
[53] Dewar, Ian, 'George Clive and the Establishment of the New Poor Law in South Glamorgan, 1836-8', *Morgannwg*, Vol. 11, (1967), pp. 46-70, and Thomas, J. E., 'The Poor Law in West Glamorgan, 1834-1930', *Morgannwg*, Vol. 18, (1974), pp. 45-69.
[54] Ibid, Edsall, N., *The Anti-Poor Law Movement 1833-1844*, p. 132.

sometimes violent opposition, much of it organised by Tory radicals such as Michael Sadler and Richard Oastler but they were soon joined by Feargus O'Connor, Joseph Rayner Stephens, and London-based radicals like Henry Hetherington and Bronterre O'Brien. These middle-class reformers, some already prominent in campaigning for factory reform, provided the organisation and leadership that resistance in the south had lacked. [55] Their campaign stressed the Christian duty of the rich to assist the poor and accepted Cobbett's argument that the Act denied basic rights. The problem was that the Commissioners misunderstood the nature of poverty in the industrial north assuming that it was the same as in the south and east. It was not. For most industrial workers poor relief was viewed not as an essential means of subsistence but as a support when they were suddenly thrown out of work because of a downturn in trade. For them, and local magistrates and poor law officials, the 'old' system worked effectively and they strongly objected to interference from London in their local affairs. The timing of implementation in the north was also unfortunate and occurred just as trade depression was beginning to affect many of the textile districts, greatly adding to the fears of the manufacturing population, especially the increasingly vulnerable handloom workers. This combined with the circulation of exaggerated stories of starvation and ill-treatment in the new workhouses and further inflamed passions.

The arrival of the Commissioners often led to violence though the leaders of the anti-poor law movement preferred to maintain control over their followers and direct the campaign in a peaceful direction without causing outright violence. This was not always possible. In June 1837, a crowd of people wrecked the workhouse in Huddersfield that led to implementation being postponed until the following year. [56] The sensitivity of the assistant commissioner to local circumstances was central to the degree of opposition. In the north-east Sir John Walsham was able to get the new system accepted. By contrast, in Lancashire and the West Riding Charles Mott was more confrontational and this encouraged widespread opposition. The *Halifax Guardian* opposed the poor law as 'unEnglish, pernicious and wicked' and published accounts of the ill-treatment of the poor. Riots by local ratepayers at Todmorden led to the military

---

[55] Rose, M. E., 'The anti-Poor Law movement in the North of England', *Northern History*, Vol. 1, (1966), pp. 70-91.
[56] Hargreaves, John A., '"A metropolis of discontent": popular protest in Huddersfield c.1780-1850', in Haigh, E. A. Hilary, (ed.), *Huddersfield: a most handsome town: aspects of the history and culture of a West Yorkshire town*, (Kirklees Cultural Service), 1992, pp. 189-220.

having to keep order. The new system was not introduced into Leeds until 1844 and Liverpool was given permission to return to the former system of administering relief under its own local Act.

By the end of 1838, the violent phase of resistance had died down as Unions were gradually established and the Poor Law Commissioners made concessions that allowed boards of guardians to give relief in Lancashire and Yorkshire on the traditional basis of the old poor law when the situation required it. By 1839, the campaign began to disintegrate as working-class resentment was appeased by the continued use of outdoor relief and rivalries between middle-class and working-class elements of the movement began to come to the fore. Increasingly, Chartism attracted the more radical supporters of the agitation. The anti-poor law movement in the North represented a temporary alliance between working- and middle-classes against what was widely regarded as an unjust and intrusive measure; in a sense it was also a local reaction against centralisation that cut across class lines. Eventually differences in emphasis and ideas between Tory radicals, who emphasised the value of paternalism, and the emerging Chartist leaders, with their belief in universal suffrage, ruptured the alliance.

Opposition to the 1834 Act did little to delay its implementation in southern England but in the north and Wales it was more successful. It delayed effective implementation until 1838 and even then local concessions meant that outdoor relief still continued to play an important role. The northern campaign demonstrated that exerting pressure through press, pamphlets and meetings was far more influential that the 'language of menace'. This stands in contrast to the more traditional, less organised and less successful reactions in the agricultural areas.

How did the Poor Law function between 1834 and 1847?

Despite opposition, the Poor Law Amendment Act was implemented with speed and determination. [57] Nine Assistant Commissioners were appointed and this rose to sixteen within a year. Poor Law Unions were created with some rapidity. By the end of 1835, 2,066 parishes had been incorporated into 112 Unions. In 1836, this reached 365 Unions of 7,915 parishes and by December 1839, 13,691 out of some 15,000 parishes had been incorporated into 583 Unions, leaving 799 largely Local Act or Gilbert Act Unions outside. The new Poor Law territorial system was nearly as complete as it would be until 1871,

---

[57] Fraser, D., (ed.), *The New Poor Law in the Nineteenth Century*, (Macmillan), 1976, is a collection of excellent essays on the operation of the system.

although some restructuring of Unions occurred later.

The resulting reduction in costs was considerable. By 1838, the Commissioners reported that the country had been relieved of some £2.3 million of 'direct annual taxation'. Although costs soon began to rise again, it was not until after 1900 that they reached pre-1834 levels. This was a success for those whose aim was reducing poor rate. For those who saw the 1834 Act as a measure of social rehabilitation, there was also some success. By 1835, the Commissioners were claiming that the new system was already delivering more prompt and adequate relief to the aged, infirm and sick and improving the education of pauper children. It was encouraging industry and moral habits in the able-bodied helping farmers to provide more employment and higher wages and improving the relationship between rural employers and their workers. There was a decline in chargeable bastardy and better sexual morals in the countryside. The Commission produced *annual reports* and the propaganda features of the 1834 *Report* reappeared regularly. It remains, with the help of regional studies, to see how far their claims were justified. The southern counties felt the impact of the new poor law even before the new Unions were created. Some places took the opportunity to reduce poor relief wholesale: the Uckfield Union in Sussex reduced its costs in one year from £16,643 to £8,733 of which only £5,675 was spent on the poor, the remainder being used to build a workhouse. Immediate reductions occurred in other areas, even if not on the Uckfield scale. In East Yorkshire, expenditure fell by 13 per cent in 1835 and by 27 per cent between 1834 and 1837. These examples hide the extent of opposition, the poor geographical construction of some Unions and the role of the landed classes. [58]

The Commissioners wanted the Unions to consist of a circle of parishes round a market town and some Unions did conform to this pattern. But many did not. Most of Anglesey formed a large Union of 53 parishes while five parishes in the east of the island were attached to Caernarfon to which they were linked by ferry and 16 more were

---

[58] Useful local studies include Rawding, Charles, 'The Poor Law Amendment Act 1834-65: a case study of Caistor Poor Law Union', *Lincolnshire History and Archaeology*, Vol. 22, (1987), pp. 15-23, Fletcher, Barry, 'Chichester and the Westhampnett Poor Law Union', *Sussex Archaeological Collections*, Vol. 34, (1996), pp. 185-196, Carter, Paul, (ed.), *Bradford Poor Law Union: papers and correspondence with the Poor Law Commission, October 1834-January 1839*, Yorkshire Archaeological Society, Record series, Vol. 157, (Boydell), 2004, and Song, Byung Khun, 'Continuity and change in English rural society: the formation of poor law unions in Oxfordshire', *English Historical Review*, Vol. 114, (1999), pp. 314-338.

attached to Bangor across the Menai straits. [59] In some rural areas, the Assistant Commissioners were compelled to obtain the support of the landed nobility by drawing the boundaries of Unions round their estates. In Northamptonshire, for example, the Union of Potterspuy encompassed the Duke of Grafton's interest, Aynho, the Cartwright's interest and Daventry, Charles Kingsley's interest. Brundage sees this as a process by which the great landowners created Unions to suit their own interests and so maintain their control over Poor Law administration. Dunkley challenges this view observing that in urban areas and in some rural districts lacking great landowners and yeomen farmers, shopkeepers and artisans secured control of the Boards of Guardians. [60] There was therefore considerable disparity in the size, shape, population and wealth of the Unions. Far from uniformity, the 1834 Act established considerable variety in local administrative areas.

The success of central policies was dependent on the character and efficiency of the Poor Law Union officials. The new government service included Clerks to the Boards, Relieving Officers, Workhouse Masters and Medical Officers. Some of these posts were part-time and the salaries varied according to the size and population of the Union. The officials in the front line were the Relieving Officer and Workhouse Master, sometimes one person holding two posts. The Relieving Officer decided the fate of applicants for relief; whether they should be relieved at home, enjoy free medical treatment, be assigned to public work or 'offered' the workhouse. He was also supposed to supervise outdoor relief. The Workhouse Master ran the House but served two masters, the Commission and the Board of Guardians, who not infrequently issued conflicting orders. He was required to fulfil the demands of Medical Officers for the supply and treatment of pauper patients. He needed to be of firm character and the Commissioners hoped that the Guardians would use their powers of patronage to appoint both Relieving Officers and Workhouse Masters

---

[59] Jones, David Llewelyn, 'The fate of the paupers: life in the Bangor and Beaumaris Union Workhouse 1845-71', *Transactions of the Caernarvonshire Historical Society*, Vol. 66, (2005), pp. 94-125.

[60] For the debate, see, Brundage, Anthony, 'The landed interest and the New Poor Law: a reappraisal of the revolution in government', *English Historical Review*, Vol. 87, (1972), pp. 27-48, Dunkley, Peter, 'The landed interest and the new Poor Law: a critical note', *English Historical Review*, Vol. 88, (1973), pp. 836-841, and Brundage, Anthony, 'The landed interest and the new poor law: a reply', *English Historical Review*, Vol. 90, (1975), pp. 347-351. See also, Brundage, Anthony, 'The English Poor Law of 1834 and the cohesion of agricultural society', *Agricultural History*, Vol. 48, (1974), pp. 405-417.

from the police or military NCOs. [61] Even so between 1835 and 1841, 90 Relieving Officers were dismissed for theft, neglect of duty, misconduct or drunkenness. The inevitable result of local patronage was the dismissal and then re-appointment of officials from the old poor law system.

Similar problems occurred in establishing professional Poor Law medical services. [62] Initially the Commissioners encouraged Unions to offer part-time medical posts at the lowest tender but this led to many complaints of neglect and ill-treatment before the Select Committee of 1837. After this Unions appointed qualified doctors at reasonable wages. From 1842, when the first General Medical Order was issued, attempts were made by the Commissioners to regulate improvements to the service. Unions were divided into medical districts each with its own Medical Officer. Workhouse infirmaries did provide indoor medical treatment and increased in number but they were often overcrowded and without adequate equipment or staff.

The Medical Act 1858 stated that Poor Law Doctors could not be employed by the Guardians unless qualified in both Medicine and Surgery and were registered. Despite this, conditions failed to improve in London until 1867, when the Metropolitan Poor Law Act began the process of taking the infirmaries out of Union control. [63] In 1885, the Medical Relief Disqualification Act removed some of the stigma of pauperism from those who received only medical assistance from the poor law and the poor law authorities administered three-

---

[61] See, Gutchen, R. M., 'Masters of workhouses under the New Poor Law', *Local Historian*, Vol. 16, (1984), pp. 93-99.

[62] See, for example, Green, David R., 'Medical relief and the new Poor Law in London', in Grell, Ole Peter, Cunningham, Andrew, and Jütte, Robert, (eds.), *Health care and poor relief in eighteenth and nineteenth century northern Europe*, (Ashgate), 2002, pp. 220-245, Hodgkinson, R. G., 'Poor law medical officers of England, 1834-71', *Journal of the History of Medicine and Allied Sciences*, Vol. 11, (1956), pp. 299-338, and Miller, Edgar, 'Variations in the official prevalence and disposal of the insane in England under the poor law, 1850-1900', *History of Psychiatry*, Vol. 18, (1), (2007), pp. 25-38.

[63] See, Anon, *The Lancet sanitary commission for investigating the state of the infirmaries of workhouses: reports of the commissioners on metropolitan infirmaries*, (The Lancet), 1866. On the operation of the poor laws in London after 1834 see, Green, David R., *Pauper Capital: London and the Poor Law 1790-1870*, (Ashgate), 2010, pp. 81-246.

quarters of all hospital beds.[64] In 1897, the Local Government Board passed an order forbidding the employment of Pauper Nurses, though they were still allowed to work in infirmaries under the supervision of a trained Nurse and the Local Government Board Order 1913 required that an institution with more than 100 beds for the sick must have an appropriately qualified Superintendent Nurse.

The well-regulated workhouse was the centrepiece of the new system.[65] Chadwick never intended that the deterrent workhouse test should apply to all. He intended to build new workhouses for orphans, the old and infirm while driving the able-bodied to provide for themselves and their families. Existing parish workhouses were to be included in the Unions for the separate treatment of classified paupers, the old, the young and the able-bodied. He hoped to extend this principle to the separate housing of lunatics, the blind and other special categories.[66] This proved impractical and a single large Union workhouse was more efficient with the result that the 'deserving poor' were treated little different from the 'undeserving' able-bodied. The Commissioners never intended that workhouses should be places of repression for the able-bodied. Paupers might be better fed and housed than in a labourer's cottage. But they would be put to heavy work and subjected to discipline including the denial of tobacco and alcohol and the separation of men from women. However, in practice, workhouses were increasingly seen as 'prisons without crime'. Dietaries published by the Commissioners were not wholly insufficient but took little notice of local eating habits and food was

---

[64] Brand, J. L., 'The parish doctor: England's poor law medical officers and medical reform, 1870-1900', *Bulletin of the History of Medicine*, Vol. 35, (1961), pp. 97-122.

[65] The workhouse is discussed in Longmate, N., *The Workhouse*, (Temple Smith), 1974, Digby, A., *Pauper Palaces*, (Routledge), 1978, Crowther, M., *The Workhouse System 1834-1929: The History of an English Social Institution*, (Methuen), 1984, and Driver, Felix, *Power and pauperism: the workhouse system 1834-1884*, (Cambridge University Press), 1993.

[66] Bartlett, Peter, *The poor law of lunacy: the administration of pauper lunatics in mid-nineteenth-century England*, (Leicester University Press), 1999, Ellis, Robert, 'The Asylum, the Poor Law and the Growth of County Asylums in Nineteenth-Century Yorkshire', *Northern History*, Vol. 45, (2008), pp. 279-293, Murphy, Elaine., 'The New Poor Law Guardians and the administration of insanity in east London, 1834-1844', *Bulletin of the History of Medicine*, Vol. 77, (2003), pp. 45-74, and Bartlett, Peter, 'The asylum and the Poor Law: the productive alliance', in Melling, Joseph and Forsythe, Bill, (eds.), *Insanity, institutions, and society, 1800-1914: a social history of madness in comparative perspective*, (Routledge), 1999, pp. 48-67. See also, Phillips, Gordon Ashton, *The blind in British society: charity, state, and community, c.1780-1930*, (Ashgate), 2004, pp. 160-199.

stodgy and monotonous. [67] Inmates had to wear workhouse uniform but the Commissioners resisted the attempts of some Guardians to clothe unmarried mothers in yellow as a badge of shame.

Was the Poor Law 'cruel' between 1834 and 1847?

The picture of a stern and uniform regime in the workhouse, a picture reinforced by radical writers calling them *'Bastilles'* belied the facts. Just how cruel the new poor law workhouses were is a question often obscured by propaganda and myth. They were often overcrowded but their character varied between areas. The character of the Master and Matron, the Union boards and the regional Assistant Poor Law Commissioner regulated the actual conduct of the workhouses. The new workhouses were often less crowded and insanitary than those built before 1834. The most resented deterrent effect of the new poor law, and the most obvious contrast with the old system, was the strict workhouse routine and the increasing stigma attached to pauper status.

The feature of the 1834 legislation that caught the attention of contemporary opinion was not the system of central administration but the threat of seeking relief, with special emphasis being paid to the workhouse test. Official records are stronger on administration that relief, but they do give more attention to the inmates of the workhouse than to those on outdoor relief. In many respects this is unfortunate since the majority of paupers were normally those in receipt of outdoor relief. The statistics of the period suggest that over 80 per cent of paupers remained on outdoor relief. In 1837, 11 per cent of all paupers had been workhouse inmates; by 1844, the figure was no more than 15 per cent. In 1844, the Outdoor Relief Prohibitory Order re-confirmed that the able-bodied should not be given outdoor relief but infrequent visits by Commissioners meant that this was never rigorously applied.

The workhouse test was designed to deter the able-bodied poor, but the majority of workhouse inmates were normally the physically and mentally disabled, the aged and a wide variety of sick. [68] In dealing with the able-bodied the workhouse test was invariably offered

---

[67] See, Johnston, V. J., *Diet in workhouses and prisons 1835-1895*, (Garland), 1985, pp. 13-36.

[68] Besley, Timothy, Coate, Stephen, and Guinnane, Timothy W., 'Incentives, information, and welfare: England's New Poor Law and the workhouse test', in Guinnane, Timothy W., Sundstrom, William A., and Whatley, Warren, (eds.), *History matters: essays on economic growth, technology, and demographic change*, (Stanford University Press), 2004, 245-270.

to those regarded as of bad character: aged or diseased prostitutes, ex-criminals, mothers with more than one illegitimate child, known alcoholics and vagrants. [69] Regarded as a refuge for undesirables, the workhouse gave its inmates a greater stigma than applied to those in receipt of outdoor relief. The Victorian workhouse was faced with the impossible task of providing a refuge for the impotent while deterring the scrounger. In that the mass of the poor regarded the workhouse with considerable dread the deterrent feature had been successfully conveyed, despite the fact that the majority of the inmates were usually unsuitable for such treatment. Indeed for the Webbs, the workhouse became 'shocking to every principle of reason and every feeling of humanity'. [70]

This dismal view corresponds to that of contemporary critics of the 1830s and 1840s such as *The Times* and the novelist Charles Dickens. The picture of the workhouse presented by its early opponents suggested a life of horror. [71] For even the mildly awkward there were savage beatings and solitary confinement in the most unsuitable of cells. For the majority, existence was endured on a starvation diet, families were ruthlessly separated in the interests of classification, accommodation was overcrowded and unhealthy and daily life was a monotonous routine supervised by unsympathetic officials. Finally, for those unfortunate enough to die in the workhouse, the end was a pauper burial without dignity or respect. There were, however, others in the 1830s and 1840s who took a more positive view of the new system and sought to answer the rabid criticisms of those opposed it. [72]

---

[69] Fillmore, Jacquelené, 'The female vagrant pauper', *Local Historian*, Vol. 35, (2005), pp. 148-158, and Henriques, U. R. Q., 'Bastardy and the new Poor Law', *Past & Present*, Vol. 37, (1967), pp. 103-129.
[70] Webb, Sidney, and Webb, Beatrice, *English Poor Law Policy*, (Longman, Green), 1910, p. 133.
[71] See, for example, Oastler, Richard, *Damnation! Eternal damnation to the fiend-begotten 'coarser-food', new Poor law, a speech*, (Henry Hetherington), 1837, Roberts, Samuel, *Mary Wilden, a Victim to the New Poor Law, Or, The Malthusian and Marcusian System Exposed: In a Letter to His Grace the Duke of Portland*, (Whittaker and Co.), 1839, *A few practical observations on the new poor law: showing the demoralizing & enslaving effects of this anti-Christian enactment: containing various facts illustrating the working of the new law*, (A. Redford), 1838, and especially, Baxter, G. R. W., *The book of the Bastiles: or, The history of the working of the new poor law*, (J. Stephens), 1841.
[72] For example, Nevile, Christopher, *The new poor law justified: with suggestions for the establishment of insurance offices for the poor*, (Ridgway), 1838, Spencer, Thomas, *The new poor law: its evils and their*

The picture was not simply a study in black. There was much variation between workhouses and those that paid most attention to the directives of the central authority probably provided better food and accommodation than was available to many of the poor who struggled to survive outside. In the case of children and the sick, foundations were being made for future progress, though developments were slow and partial until the mid-1860s. Most historians accept that the sensational stories of cruelties were either false or the result of survivals from the former regime. In a number of cases, such as the flogging of young girls at the Hoo Workhouse or the scandal at Andover, the local authority could be shown to have ignored the directives of the central authority. However, this did not excuse the inadequacy of the supervision that allowed such things to take place.

The effectiveness of the workhouse test in the north was never fully tested. From 1837 to 1842, much of industrial England was in the grip of severe depression. Whole communities went suddenly out of work and in these circumstances it was impossible for the new poor law to operate. The Outdoor Labour Test Order was introduced as a result by which the poor were supposed to do the 'labour test', hard and monotonous work in return for outdoor relief. Zealous opposition to the Poor Law became a central theme of Chartism and, because it posed a threat to public order, produced a ceaseless campaign against the Commissioners. The Central Board had only been given a five-year lease of life and it was so unpopular when it came up for renewal it was only extended for one year. The result was a tempering of the workhouse test and less eligibility principle in the north with a return to outdoor relief. By late 1842, the worst of the economic distress was over and the Commission was given five more years of life but its position was already compromised. A humanitarian attack began on the conditions in the new workhouses, criticism that gained strength from a series of mistakes, epidemics and scandals that provoked public inquiries and ultimately public demands for reform of the worst abuses. In 1842, the first scandal led to the withdrawal of the rule imposing silence at all meals; the bringing together of families separated into male, female and infant; and the first attempts to separate prostitutes, lunatics and infected persons from the general body of paupers. This process continued gradually until 1847 but events in the Andover Union were the last straw.

---

remedies, (John Green), 1841, and *Objections to the new Poor Law answered*, (John Green), 1841, and Gurney, John Hampden, *The new poor law explained and vindicated: A plain address to the labouring classes among his parishioners....*, (W. Walker), 1841.

What were the effects of conditions in the Andover workhouse?

The Andover scandal in the mid-1840s was not unique but it was highly publicised and used by those critical of or opposed to the new system. [73] Bone crushing was used in some workhouses as a 'useful' occupation for paupers. Sir Robert Peel's Home Secretary, Sir James Graham, disapproved of it as a means of employing the poor but Commissioner George Nicholls was a great enthusiast while a second Commissioner, Sir George Cornewall Lewis vacillating in his attitude. Andover was regarded, from the Commissioners' point of view, as a model union. All outdoor relief was stopped as soon as the workhouse was opened and it was one of the few unions not to relax this rule during the 'great freeze' of January 1838. The Board's ruthlessness shocked even the Rev. Thomas Mozeley, a convinced opponent of the old system. [74]

At Andover, the work was hard, the discipline strict and the diet scanty. No little indulgences were allowed to creep in. This was due to the choice of ex-sergeant Colin M'Dougal, a veteran of Waterloo, as workhouse master and his wife, Mary Ann, as matron. The local Guardians acknowledged that even this admirable couple had their faults but were only too ready to leave the management of the union's affairs to their domineering chairman. Attempts to end bone crushing at Andover in December 1844 were voted down by the chairman and his supporters. However, during the next few months ugly rumours began to circulate about inmates eating the marrow from the decomposing bones. The Guardians took no action, apart from suspending bone crushing during hot weather. Hugh Mundy, a local farmer frequently at odds with his colleagues whom he infuriated by paying his labourers ten shillings a week, two shillings more than his fellow landowners, went public. He turned to Thomas Wakley, who on Friday 1 August 1845, rose to ask the Home Secretary about paupers eating bone marrow at Andover. [75] Sir James Graham replied that he could not believe this situation but promised to institute an enquiry. The following day Henry Parker, the Assistant Commissioner responsible for Andover, was dispatched to ascertain the facts.

His enquiry began on Monday, 4 August 1845 and the following

---

[73] Wells, Roger, 'Andover antecedents? Hampshire New Poor-Law scandals, 1834-1842', *Southern History*, Vol. 24, (2002), pp. 191-227.

[74] Anstruther, Ian, *The scandal of the Andover workhouse*, (Geoffrey Bles), 1973.

[75] Sprigge, Samuel Squire, Sir, *The life and times of Thomas Wakley, founder and first editor of The Lancet, M.P. for Finsbury and coroner for West Middlesex*, (Longmans), 1897.

day he was able to report back to London that the charges were true. On 14 August, Parker was instructed to investigate any alleged 'neglect or misconduct on the part of the Master or officers of the workhouse'. M'Dougal offered his resignation on 29 September but when Parker, now summoned back to London, suggested consulting the Commission's solicitors about prosecution the lawyers advised against it. The Commission was left with a hostile press, a critical Parliament, a seriously alarmed public and no scapegoat. Parker now found himself cast in this role. When he drafted a letter from the Board to the Andover Guardians he was accused of trying to throw the blame on the Commissioners. On 16 October, Parker was called upon to resign and his only reward for years of devoted service was a suggestion that he should seek work with one of the expanding railway companies. If the Commissioners felt that they had saved themselves by dismissing Parker, they were mistaken. The former Assistant Commissioner published a long pamphlet in his own defence, which indicted his recent superiors, and his case was rapidly taken up by a group of anti-Poor Law MPs. [76]

The public were unhappy about Parker's dismissal and the Commissioners compounded their error by peremptorily ordering another Assistant Commissioner, William Day, to resign after years of loyal service, nominally because he had been ill for several weeks after falling down some steps. This provided too valuable an opportunity for Edwin Chadwick, still bitter about his treatment by the Commission, who encouraged MPs to keep the issue alive. On 8 November 1845, the Poor Law Commissioners tacitly acknowledged the justice of the attacks made on bone crushing by issuing a General Order forbidding it. This came too late. Public opinion was now seriously alarmed and the government bowed to it. On 5 March 1846, a Select Committee of the House of Commons was established to investigate the Andover scandal, the conduct of the Poor Law Commissioners and the circumstances surrounding Parker's resignation. The fifteen members of the 'Andover committee' included three well-known opponents of the workhouse, John Fielden, Thomas Wakley and Benjamin Disraeli and began work two weeks later. For the next three and a half months they heard evidence from witnesses and their words were reported at length in the press. The New Poor Law, the Whigs who had created it and the gentry who administered it were on trial. The *Report*, published in August 1846, filled two large volumes totalling several thousand pages with a

---

[76] Parker, H. W., *Letters to the Right Hon. Sir James Graham, Bart., One of Her Majesty's Principal Secretaries of State, &c. &c. &c: On the Subject of Recent Proceedings Connected with the Andover Union*, (Cross), 1845.

scathing indictment of everyone involved. The government announced that it proposed to take no action but it had privately decided that the Commission must go, partly to placate public opinion but also because it had done its work. The poor rates had been cut; outdoor relief for the able-bodied had been significantly reduced and almost the whole country had been unionised. The time had come when 'the three kings of Somerset House', as the Poor Law Commissioners had been nicknamed by their critics, could safely be replaced by a body with fewer dictatorial powers and directly responsible to Parliament.

When the Act that had extended the life of the Poor Law Commission ran out in 1847 it was not renewed and the Poor Law Board Act was passed in its place. It set up a new body, the Poor Law Board, consisting in theory of four senior ministers (the Home Secretary, the Chancellor of the Exchequer, Lord President of the Council and the Lord Privy Seal). In practice, like the Board of Trade, it was a mere fiction and never intended to meet. The real power lay with its President, who was eligible to sit in Parliament, and his two Secretaries, one of whom could become an MP. It was expected that the President would sit in the House of Lords and the Permanent Secretary in the Commons but in practice both ministers were usually MPs. The 1847 Act had two great merits. It remedied the weakness caused by the old board's independent status: the government was now genuinely responsible and there was a proper channel between the board and parliament. It stilled the long agitation against the new poor law and meant that the new board could undertake a common-sense policy of gradual improvement in peace. It was aided in this by the improved economic situation and by the fact that the laws of settlement were also swept away in 1847.

How did the Poor Law function after 1847?

The achievements of the Poor Law Board between 1847 and 1870 were limited but a beginning was made in several fields. In 1848, the first schools for pauper children were set up and these were extended by legislation in 1862. In the 1850s, outdoor relief was frankly admitted and regulated and by 1860, segregation of different classes of pauper into different quarters of the workhouse was virtually accomplished and the harshness of the old uniform regulations was softened. More and more money was being spent on the poor and unfortunate without protest. Pauperdom, especially for the able-bodied poor, was being increasingly regarded as misfortune rather than a crime or cause for segregation. Even so, the stigma of disfranchisement was not removed until 1885. By the 1860s, the Poor law service had moved away from controversy and into a phase of consolidation. The administration became less centralised, less doctrinaire and to some extent less harsh. Inspectors turned to advising on workhouse management rather than applying blind deterrent policies. The cost per capita for 1864-1868, for example, was the same as it had been twenty years earlier and was one third cheaper than forty years earlier. Boards of Guardians had more freedom to respond to local conditions and outdoor relief was given more frequently.

The Lancashire cotton famine of the early 1860s brought matters to a head. [77] The action that sparked depression overseas was the blockade of the southern American ports by Federal Navy. This cut off the supply of raw cotton to Europe, including Lancashire and Scotland. At the start of this depression, Lancashire mills had four month supply of cotton stockpiled. The impact did not hit immediately and they had enough time to stockpile another month.[78] Without raw further materials, production had stopped by October 1861 and mill closures, mass unemployment and poverty struck northern Britain leading to soup kitchens being opened in early 1862. Relief was provided by the British government in the form of tokens that were handed to traders so that goods could be exchanged to that amount. [79] Emigration to America was offered as an alternative; agents came to recruit for the American cotton industry

---

[77] Arnold, R. A., Sir, *The history of the cotton famine: from the fall of Sumter to the passing of the Public Works Act*, (Saunders, Otley and Co.), 1864, Henderson, W. O., *The Lancashire cotton famine, 1861-1865*, (Manchester University Press), 1934, and Farnie, Douglas A., 'The cotton famine in Great Britain', in Ratcliffe, B. M., (ed.), *Great Britain and her world 1750-1914: essays in honour of W. O. Henderson*, (Manchester University Press), 1975, pp. 153-178.

[78] For the impact of the famine see, Holcroft, Fred, *The Lancashire cotton famine around Leigh*, (Leigh Local History Society), 2003, Peters, Lorraine, 'Paisley and the cotton famine of 1862-1863', *Scottish Economic & Social History*, Vol. 21, (2001), pp. 121-139, Henderson, W.O., 'The cotton famine in Scotland and the relief of distress, 1862-64', *Scottish Historical Review*, Vol. 30, (1951), pp. 154-164, and Hall, Rosalind, 'A poor cotton weyver: poverty and the cotton famine in Clitheroe', *Social History*, Vol. 28, (2003), pp. 227-250.

[79] Shapely, Peter, 'Urban charity, class relations and social cohesion: charitable responses to the Cotton Famine', *Urban History*, Vol. 28, (2001), pp. 46-64, Boyer, George R., 'Poor relief, informal assistance, and short time during the Lancashire cotton famine', *Explorations in Economic History*, Vol. 34, (1997), pp. 56-76, and Penny, Keith, 'Australian relief for the Lancashire victims of the cotton famine, 1862-3', *Transactions of the Historic Society of Lancashire & Cheshire*, Vol. 108, (1957 for 1956), pp. 129-139.

and also for the Federal army. Workers also made the shorter move to Yorkshire for work in the woollen mills there. Blackburn alone lost approximately 4,000 workers and their families. On 31 December 1862, cotton workers met in Manchester and decided to support those against slavery, despite their own impoverishment. The workers felt bitter at the nominal relief provided by the government and also resented that other relief came from affluent donors from outside Lancashire, not from their own wealthy cotton masters. It was also felt that no distinction was made between those who were previously hard working and forced into unemployment and those who were 'stondin paupers' or drunkards. This built up bitterness and resentment that led to rioting especially in Stalybridge, Dukinfield and Ashton in 1863. Poor law and charity solutions proved inadequate and government, both central and local, thought that it was justifiable to intervene to create employment. As a result, government relief was changed and instead provided in the form of constructive employment in urban regeneration schemes, implemented by local government.

The Public Works (Manufacturing Districts) Act 1863 gave powers to local authorities to obtain cheap loans to finance local improvements. This Act, as much as anything, symbolised the failure of the nineteenth century poor law to cope with the problem of large-scale industrial unemployment. Poor law financing was changed in the Union Chargeability Act 1865 ending the system where each union was separately responsible for the cost of maintaining its own poor. Each parish now contributed to the union fund with charges based upon the rateable value of properties. This led to inequalities since the rateable value of houses was set locally across the country and, in many areas, Boards of Guardians, themselves often middle-class ratepayers kept rates as low as possible. The Metropolitan Poor Act 1867 spread the cost of poor relief across all London parishes and provided for administration of infirmaries separate from workhouses.[80] Lunatics, fever and smallpox cases were removed from management of the Guardians and a new authority, the Metropolitan Asylums Board provided hospitals for them.[81]

In 1871, the Local Government Act set up a new form of central

---

[80] Ashbridge, Pauline, 'Paying for the poor: a middle-class metropolitan movement for rate equalisation, 1857-67', *London Journal*, Vol. 22, (1997), 107-122.

[81] Powell, Allan, Sir, *The Metropolitan Asylums Board and its work, 1867-1930,* (The Board), 1930, and Ayers, G. M., *England's first state hospitals and the Metropolitan Asylums Board, 1867-1930*, (Wellcome Institute), 1971.

administration: the Local Government Board combined the work of the Poor Law Board, the Medical Department of the Privy Council and a small Local Government section of the Home Office. There were attempts by the Local Government Board and its inspectorate during the next decade to reduce the amount of outdoor relief by urging Boards of Guardians to enforce the regulations restricting outdoor relief more stringently and supported those boards that took a strict line. The Local Government Board and the Charity Organisation Society maintained that the ready availability of outdoor relief destroyed the self-reliance of the poor and that the shift from outdoor to workhouse relief would significantly reduce the demand for assistance, since most applicants would refuse to enter workhouses and thereby reduce Poor Law expenditures. A policy that promised to raise the morals of the poor and reduce taxes was popular with most Poor Law Unions.

The deterrent effect associated with the workhouse led to a sharp fall in numbers on relief. From 1871 to 1876, the number of paupers receiving outdoor relief fell by 33 per cent. The share of paupers relieved in workhouses increased from 12-15 per cent in 1841-71 to 22 per cent in 1880, and it continued to rise to 35 per cent in 1911. The extent of deterrence varied considerably across Poor Law Unions. Urban unions typically relieved a much larger share of their paupers in workhouses than did rural unions, but there were significant differences in practice across cities. In 1893, over 70 per cent of the paupers in Liverpool, Manchester, Birmingham, and in many London Poor Law unions received indoor relief; however, in Leeds, Bradford, Newcastle, Nottingham and several other industrial and mining cities the majority of paupers continued to receive outdoor relief.

This made using the poor law system as a device to cope with unemployment more difficult and led to the unemployed seeking relief from other sources. This trend was given official recognition in 1886 when Joseph Chamberlain, the President of the Local Government Board, issued a *Circular* that urged local authorities to undertake public works as a means of relieving unemployment. [82] The policy of the Chamberlain *Circular* of providing work for the unemployed was continued both by local authority and by some philanthropic bodies such as the Salvation Army. In 1904, with unemployment worsening, the Local Government Board encouraged the creation of joint distress committees in London to plan and co-ordinate schemes of work relief for the unemployed. The

---

[82] Hennock, E. P., 'Poverty and social theory: the experience of the 1880s', *Social History*, Vol. 1, (1976), pp. 67-91.

Unemployed Workmen Act 1905 made the establishment of similar distress committees in every large urban area in the country mandatory. The committees were also empowered to establish labour exchanges, keep unemployment registers and assist the migration or emigration of unemployed workmen. This Act marked the culmination of attempts to deal with unemployment through work relief schemes. [83]

The poor law system of the late-nineteenth century was gradually moving towards greater specialisation in the treatment of those committed to its care. This can be seen in the increase in expenditure on indoor relief by 113 per cent between 1871-1872 and 1905-1906, though the number of indoor paupers only increased by 76 per cent. In the conditions of the late-nineteenth century, the focus shifted from pauperism to an increasing awareness of poverty and to the growing demand for an attack on it. While the Boards of Guardians retained control over paupers, other agencies became more important in dealing with various kinds of poverty. School Boards from 1870 and local education authorities after 1902 played a vital role in exposing and dealing with child poverty. School meals and medical inspections developed out of the work of these bodies not out of the poor law system. At the other end of the age spectrum, opinion was moving in favour of old-age pensions in some form to take the poor out of the sphere of the poor law. A Royal Commission on the Aged Poor that reported in 1895 favoured the improvement of poor law provisions for old people but rejected the pension idea. Four years later, however, a parliamentary Select Committee on the Aged Deserving Poor reported in favour of pensions.

Poor relief costs rose to £8.6 million by 1906 and poor economic conditions in 1902 and 1903 had seen the numbers seeking relief rise to two million people. The result was the establishment in August 1905 of a Royal Commission on the Poor Laws and the Relief of Distress by the outgoing Conservative government chaired by Lord George Hamilton. The Commission included Poor Law guardians, members of the Charity Organisation Society and of local government boards as well as the social researchers Charles Booth and Beatrice Webb. [84] It spent four years investigating and in February 1909

---

[83] Harris, J., *Unemployment and Politics, 1886-1914*, (Oxford University Press), 1972, and Melling, J., 'Welfare capitalism and the origin of welfare states: British industry, workplace welfare, and social reform, 1870-1914', *Social History*, Vol. 17 (1992), pp. 453-478.

[84] Vincent, A. W., 'The poor law reports of 1909 and the social theory of the Charity Organisation Society', in Gladstone, David, (ed.), *Before*

produced two conflicting reports known as the *Majority Report* and the *Minority Report*. The *Majority Report* reiterated that poverty was largely caused by moral issues and that the existing provision should remain. However, it believed that the Boards of Guardians provided too much outdoor relief and that the able-bodied poor were not deterred from seeking relief because of mixed workhouses. The *Minority Report* took a different stance arguing that what was needed was a system radically different from current provision by breaking up the Poor Law into specialist bodies dealing with sickness, old-age etc. administered by committees of the elected local authorities. It also recommended that unemployment was such a major problem that it was beyond the scope of local authorities and should be the responsibility of central government. However, because of the differences between the two reports, the Liberal government was able to ignore both when implementing its own reform package and, despite the adoption of various social insurance programs in the early twentieth century, the Poor Law continued to assist the poor until it was replaced by the welfare state in 1948.

Beveridge: welfare before the welfare state, (Institute of Economic Affairs Health and Welfare Unit), 1999, pp. 64-85.

10 Voluntary action

If the development of the poor law system was an expression of the 'collectivist impulse', many groups and individuals were trying to tackle the worst evils on a voluntary basis.[1] In 1948, William Beveridge, the author of the modern welfare state, identified three distinct types of voluntary social service: first, philanthropy or the movement between the social classes, from the haves to the have-nots; secondly, mutual aid, the attempt by working men to support each other against the predictable crises in their lives: unemployment, sickness, disability, old age and to protect their dependants in the event of their early death; and finally, 'personal thrift' by making what provision was possible for oneself.[2]

Why was Victorian philanthropy controversial?

There were bodies to meet every conceivable need: charities for the poor, the sick, the disabled, the unemployed, the badly-housed, charities for the reclamation of prostitutes and drunkards, for reviving drowning persons, for apprentices, shop-girls, cabbies, costermongers, soldiers, sailors and variety artistes. Sir James Stephen wrote in 1850:

> For the cure of every sorrow...there are patrons, vice-presidents and secretaries...For the diffusion of every blessing...there is a committee.[3]

In 1833, Dr Thomas Griffith opened Wrexham's first dispensary with the support of local gentry. Such was the demand for medical care that money was raised to build a proper infirmary in 1838. The hospital cost over £1,800 to build and a bazaar in the Town Hall during the Wrexham Races raised £1,050. The management of

---

[1] Gosden, P. H. J. H., *Self-Help: Voluntary Associations in Nineteenth Century Britain*, (Batsford), 1973, provides a detailed study of ways in which working people provided for themselves against poverty. It should be considered in relation to Hopkins, E., *Self-Help*, (UCL), 1995. Prochaska, F., *The Voluntary Impulse*, (Faber), 1988 is brief and pithy. Checkland, O., *Philanthropy in Victorian Scotland: Social Welfare and the Voluntary Principle*, (John Donald), 1980, extends the argument. Finlayson, G., *Citizens, State and Social Welfare in Britain 1830-1990*, (Oxford University Press), 1994, is perhaps the best book on the subject of voluntary efforts.

[2] Beveridge, William H., *Voluntary Action, A Report on Methods of Social Advance*, (Allen & Unwin), 1948, pp. 10-15.

[3] Stephen, J., *Essays in Ecclesiastical Biography*, 2 Vols. (Longman, Brown, Green, and Longmans), 1850, Vol. 1, p. 382.

the infirmary reflected the contemporary values and would only treat those who could not afford to pay but patrons who regularly gave money could nominate poor people for medical treatment. As there was no government funding, all the money had to be raised by the community. Annual events such as the Wrexham Cyclists' Club Carnival, Hospital Saturday and the Wrexham Infirmary Annual Ball and church collections and workers' subscriptions all helped raise the money needed.

Charles Dickens captured the contradictions of Victorian philanthropy: the enormous need for charity in a society where want and plenty lived side-by-side and the inadequacy of much of the charity provided. Philanthropists appear throughout his novels, not just as a dramatic device to offer hope to impoverished characters but also as subjects in their own right. Some of his earlier characters have a positive role, such as Mr. Brownlow in *Oliver Twist*, the Cheeryble brothers in *Nicholas Nickleby* and Mr and Mrs Garland in *The Old Curiosity Shop*. But philanthropists were subjected to some acerbic ridicule in his later works. In *Bleak House* a novel mainly attacking the legal system, Mrs Jellyby and Mrs Pardiggle are respectively guilty of 'telescopic philanthropy' and 'rapacious benevolence', neither of them helping to save the life of the child Jo, who dies of pneumonia.
[4] In his final, unfinished, novel *The Mystery of Edwin Drood* Dickens ridiculed a selfish, paternalist attitude to philanthropy taking a direct swipe at the newly established Charity Organisation Society (COS). The character Mr. Honeythunder's 'Haven of Philanthropy' would have been unmistakable to the readers of the day as a parody of the COS, or 'Cringe or Starve' as it was known by critics. [5]

Victorian philanthropy is a highly controversial subject. In its own day it was much admired but by the 1960s, a reaction had set in. There was increasing awareness of the humiliation often involved in the ways recipients were offered 'charity' and of the social climbing that often went with charity dinners, charity balls and royal patronage. Derek Fraser expresses this view in a mild, but pointed way:

> The Victorian response to the powerlessness (or, as it was often conceived, the moral weakness) of the individual was an over-liberal dose of charity. The phenomenal variety and range of Victorian philanthropy was at once confirmation of the limitless benevolence of a generation and an implicit

---

[4] Dickens, Charles, *Bleak House*, (Sheldon), 1863, pp. 271-297. See also, Christianson, Frank, *Philanthropy in British and American fiction: Dickens, Hawthorne, Eliot, and Howells*, (Edinburgh University Press), 2007, pp. 75-103.
[5] Dickens, Charles, *The Mystery of Edwin Drood*, (Chapman and Hall), 1870, pp. 82, 85-86, 91-94, 300-310.

condemnation of the notion of self-help for all. It was small wonder that self-congratulation was so common a theme in contemporary surveys of Victorian philanthropy. So many good causes were catered for -- stray dogs, stray children, fallen women and drunken men... [6]

Neither the cynicism of today nor hero-worship of the past really explain the complexities of philanthropic activity in the Victorian period.

How did Victorian philanthropy work?

Victorian philanthropy is an umbrella term covering a wide range of different activities that took place at many different places and in almost every community by people for a variety of very mixed motives. [7] During this period philanthropy changed both in methods and scope. There were at least four different, though overlapping phases. Small-scale voluntary giving of the kind common in the eighteenth century: a landowner might look after his cottagers; a merchant might bequeath a sum of money for the relief of apprentices or indigent seamen or the aged poor of the parish. Pioneer work by individuals such as Florence Nightingale, [8] Lord Shaftesbury, [9] Dr Barnardo, [10] General Booth of the Salvation Army, [11] or Octavia Hill, the housing reformer, brought particular social evils to the public notice.

Who were the pioneers and what motivated them? Many of them were neither rich nor aristocratic, though they all had time to spare from the daily grind of earning a living. Lord Shaftesbury was an exception among the landed classes, most of whom confined their

---

[6] Fraser, D., *The Evolution of the British Welfare State*, 4th edition, (Macmillan), 2009, pp. 124-125.

[7] See, for example, Gorsky, Martin, *Patterns of philanthropy: charity and society in nineteenth-century Bristol*, (Boydell), 1999.

[8] Bostridge, Mark, *Florence Nightingale: the woman and her legend*, (Viking), 2008, is the most recent study but see also, Preston, M. H., *Charitable words: women, philanthropy, and the language of charity in nineteenth-century Dublin*, (Greenwood Publishing), 2004, pp. 127-174.

[9] See, ibid, Finlayson, G. B. M., *The Seventh Earl of Shaftesbury, 1801-1885*.

[10] Wagner, G. M. M., *Barnardo*, (Weidenfeld & Nicolson), 1979, and Williams, A.E., *Barnardo of Stepney: the father of nobody's children*, 3rd edition, (Allen and Unwin), 1966.

[11] Green, R. J., *The life and ministry of William Booth: founder of the Salvation Army*, (Abingdon Press), 2005. See also, Walker, Pamela J., *Pulling the devil's kingdom down: the Salvation Army in Victorian Britain*, (University of California Press), 2001.

charitable activities to their own tenants. Many philanthropists came from the comfortable upper middle-class. Elizabeth Fry, the prison reformer, was the daughter of a banker and the wife of another. William Tuke, who founded the York Retreat, a model for the humane management of asylums, was a prosperous grocer. Florence Nightingale was the daughter of a wealthy dilettante. Others had a more precarious social background. Octavia Hill was a banker's daughter but the family fell on hard times after her father's death and the girls had to support themselves by teaching. General Booth was the son of a speculative builder but was apprenticed to a pawnbroker at thirteen. Dr Barnardo went to work at the age of ten as a clerk in a wine merchant's office. Most philanthropists were people of religious conviction. Shaftesbury was a leading Evangelical Churchman and his work as a reformer reflected his faith. The Quaker contribution, by such families as the Frys, Tukes, Cadburys and Rowntrees, was particularly innovative. [12] Roman Catholics, Anglo-Catholics and Jewish groups were to develop their own organisations for social care in the second half of the century, but the Evangelicals led the way.

The major national societies and associations were often set up by the pioneers, but sometimes developed out of more widely supported local philanthropic effort. [13] In 1861, one survey estimated that there were 640 charitable institutions in London, of which nearly half had been founded in the first half of the century and 144 in the decade after 1850. By the late 1880s, the amount of money involved was substantial: voluntary societies in London alone were handling between £5.5 and £7 million a year. [14] *The Times* claimed that the income of London charities was greater than the governments of some European countries, '...exceeding the revenue of Sweden, Denmark and Portugal, and double that of the Swiss confederation.' [15]

The contribution of women to institutional charity, whether under male control or not, increased markedly after 1830. [16] In

---

[12] Isichei, Elizabeth Allo, *Victorian Quakers*, (Oxford University Press), 1970, pp. 212-251, considers philanthropy .Kennedy, Carol, *Business pioneers: family, fortune and philanthropy: Cadbury, Sainsbury and John Lewis*, (Random House), 2000.

[13] Prochaska, F. K., 'Victorian England: the age of societies', in Cannadine, David, and Pellew, Jill, (eds.), *History and philanthropy: Past, present and future*, (Institute of Historical Research), 2008, pp. 19-32.

[14] See, for example, Dennis, Richard J., 'The geography of Victorian values: philanthropic housing in London, 1840-1900', *Journal of Historical Geography*, Vol. 15, (1989), pp. 40-54.

[15] *The Times*, 9 January 1885.

[16] Prochaska, F. K., *Women and Philanthropy in Nineteenth Century England*, (Oxford University Press), 1980, Lundy, Maria, *Women and*

Birmingham, for example, many middle-class women became well known for their philanthropy and charitable work in the city: Mary Showell Rogers founded the Ladies Association for the Care of Friendless Girls; [17] Joanna Hill set up foster homes for pauper children; [18] Susan Martineau [19] helped establish a Homeopathic Hospital and worked to encourage poor people to save and Dr Mary Sturge was well known for her work at the Women's Hospital. [20] The reason lies partly in the piety and need for 'good work's' implicit in evangelicalism but also in the decline of middle-class female occupations. Throughout this period much of their work was paternalistic and conservative in character, concerned with the perennial problems of disease, lying-in and old age, drink and immorality. What was distinctive about women's philanthropic enterprise was the degree to which they applied their domestic experience and education, their concerns about family and relations to the world outside the home. [21] It was a short step from the love of family to the love of the family of man, a step reinforced by the stress on charitable conduct by all religious denominations. The Evangelical concern with the importance of a proper home and family life can be seen as a move towards the more formal subordination of women that took place even in the more radical sects like the Quakers. Service and duty were implicit in both

---

Philanthropy in nineteenth-century Ireland, (Cambridge University Press), 1995, and Preston, Margaret H., *Charitable Words: Women, philanthropy, and the language of charity in nineteenth-century Dublin*, (Greenwood Publishing), 2004. Mumm, Susan, 'Women and philanthropic cultures', in Morgan, Sue, and de Vries, Jacqueline, (eds.), *Women, Gender and Religious Cultures in Britain, 1800-1940*, (Routledge), 2010, pp. 55-57, succinctly discusses the historiography of women's philanthropy.

[17] Bartley, Paula, 'Moral Regeneration: Women and the Civic Gospel in Birmingham, 1870-1914', *Midland History*, Vol. 25, (2000), pp. 145-148.

[18] Hill, Florence Davenport, *Children of the State*, (Macmillan and Co.), 1889, pp. 17-19.

[19] Terry-Chandler, Fiona, 'Gender and 'The Condition of England' Debate in the Birmingham Writings of Charlotte Tonna and Harriet Martineau', *Midland History*, Vol. 30, (2005), p. 59.

[20] Oldfield, Sybil, (ed.), *Women Humanitarians: A biographical dictionary of British women active between 1900 and 1950: 'doers of the word'*, (Continuum), 2001, p. 238.

[21] Changing attitudes can be seen in the contrast between Loudon, Mrs, *Philanthropy: The Philosophy of Happiness, practically applied to the Social, Political and Commercial Relations of Great Britain*, (Edward Churton), 1835, and Burdett-Coutts, Angela Georgina, (ed.), *Woman's Mission: A Series of Congress Papers on the Philanthropic Work of Women, by Eminent Writers*, (S. Low, Marston & Company, Limited), 1893.

philanthropy and family life. Important though philanthropy was to women as an extension of the home and domestic experience, they also acted out of ideological impulse. [22] Women were not just practitioners but contributors to the intellectual debates about the role and purpose of philanthropy. Philanthropy should not be seen as a 'soft option' for women excluded from formal politics.

Practically every denomination had its own 'benevolent' society to cater for its own poor. [23] Anglicans, Nonconformists and Roman Catholics all maintained their own charitable funds and in 1859 the Jewish Board of Guardians was set up.[24] These religious societies were often the source of temporary charities in times of economic distress, either national or local. It is important to note that other types of society developed in this period. Visiting societies attempted to bridge the gap between the so-called 'Two Nations' through personal contact. The Metropolitan Association for Improving the Dwellings of the Industrious Classes was founded in 1841 to build new homes for the poor. This organisation practised what the Victorians called '5 per cent philanthropy', where donors could invest their money for a good cause while receiving a respectable but below-market rate of return. The Relief Association launched in 1843 was an Anglican charity led by Bishop Blomfield. These societies made a positive effort to go out and see people in their own homes, while other societies were seeking to provide a sort of refuge for the needy. Housing charities such as the Peabody Trust sought to provide cheap homes for the working-classes but it was only Octavia Hill's housing experiments that really reached the destitute. Finally, ragged schools associated with Mary Carpenter [25] and Lord Shaftesbury provided rudimentary education.[26]

Most of the major modern charitable societies had their origins in the Victorian period and it is important to ask what motivated such a torrent of charity for the poor. It would appear that charity was a response to four types of motivation. There is little doubt that many

---

[22] Richardson, Sarah, *The Political Worlds of Women: Gender and Politics in Nineteenth Century Britain*, (Routledge), 2013, pp. 63-81.

[23] Prochaska, F. K., *Christianity and social service in modern Britain: the disinherited spirit*, (Oxford University Press), 2006.

[24] Rozin, Mordechai, *The rich and the poor: Jewish philanthropy and social control in 19th century London,* (Sussex Academic Press), 1999

[25] See, Manton, J. *Mary Carpenter and the children of the streets*, (Heinemann), 1976.

[26] Swift, Roger, 'Philanthropy and the children of the streets: the Chester Ragged School Society, 1851-1870', Swift, Roger, (ed.), *Victorian Chester: essays in social history 1830-1900*, (Liverpool University Press), 1996, pp. 149-184.

in the upper- and middle-classes had a genuine and persistent fear of social revolution and believed that charity could lift the masses from the depths of despair and out of the hands of radical agitators. There was a society-wide increase in sensitivity to the suffering of others. Charity was a Christian virtue and many in the nineteenth century were moved to try and save souls in the belief that, as Andrew Reed with a lifelong concern with orphans and lunatics put it in 1840, 'the Divine image is stamped upon all'. [27] A study of 466 wills published in *Daily Telegraph* in 1890s showed that men left 11 per cent of their estates to charity and women left 25 per cent. Increasingly, religious activity became socially oriented and religion became imbued with an essentially social conscience. Charity was also seen as a social duty to be done and be seen to be done. Charitable activity was imbued with social snobbery and a royal or aristocratic patron could considerably enhance a society's prospects. Charity assumed the guise of a fashionable social imperative. Finally, charity was seen as a means of social control. Many philanthropists preached respectable middle-class values, cleanliness, sobriety, self-improvement and responsibility. The widespread practice of visiting was in effect a cultural assault on the working-class way of life. Poverty was seen by few as a function of the economic and social system. The majority assumed that it stemmed from some personal failing. Charity was a way of initiating a moral reformation, of developing the self-help mentality in individuals who would then be freed from the thraldom of poverty. Philanthropy was an essentially educative tool; in the words of C. S. Loch:

> Charity is a social regenerator...We have to use charity to create the power of self-help.[28]

Increasingly by the 1850s, doubts were expressed about the effectiveness of the multifarious charities. Two accusations were noted. There was a built-in inefficiency that was an almost inevitable result of the astonishing growth in the number of charities. There was a great deal of duplication of effort and much wasteful competition between rival groups in the same cause. There was sometimes conflict between London and the provinces in national organisations, and the same Church versus Dissent antagonism that characterised Victorian

---

[27] Reed, Andrew, and Reed, Charles, (eds.), *Memoirs of the Life and Philanthropic Labours of Andrew Reed, D. D.: With Selections from His Journals*, (Strahan & Co.), 1863, p. 384.
[28] Cit, Himmelfarb, Gertrude, *The de-moralization of society: from Victorian virtues to modern values*, (A. A. Knopf), 1995, p. 165.

politics plagued Victorian charity. Charity was, like the Poor Law, counter-productive, helping to promote that very poverty is sought to alleviate. Although it may be an over-generalisation to say that the whole concept of charity tended to degrade rather than uplift the recipient, the radical William Lovett once remarked:

> Charity by diminishing the energies of self-dependence creates a spirit of hypocrisy and servility. [29]

The problem was not lack of effort but the unscientific nature of much Victorian charity. The great divide in philanthropy was over whether to respond to immediate need, risking creating dependency or to help only the deserving, risking callousness. This was evident in the dispute between Thomas Barnardo and the COS. Inspired by his Christian faith, Barnardo began working with the poor in London's East End in the late 1860s. He had a natural flair for publicity coining a good slogan, 'No destitute child ever refused admittance' and had great success raising funds using faked 'before' and 'after' photos of rescued children. The COS regarded Barnardo as an indiscriminate almsgiver and sought to discredit him. After a protracted and ugly legal battle, during which Barnardo's right to the title 'doctor' was exposed as bogus since he never completed his studies and was forced to abandon the fake photographs, he was cleared of any wrongdoing.

The question of whether charity reached those who most needed it was one of the main reasons for the creation of the Society for the Organisation of Charitable Relief and the Repression of Mendicity or Charity Organisation Society in 1869. [30] District Committees were established first in Marylebone led by Octavia Hill, then in St George-in-the-East and, within a year, there were seventeen. There was a constant struggle to recruit enough volunteers to staff the committees and do the work. Tensions were later to surface between the local and the authoritarian central committee. In a paper read to the Social Science Association in 1869, significantly titled *The Importance of aiding the poor without almsgiving*, Octavia Hill set out

---

[29] Lovett, William, *Life and struggles of William Lovett in his pursuit of bread, knowledge, and freedom: with some short account of the different associations he belonged to and of the opinions he entertained*, (Trubner), 1877, p. 142.

[30] Roberts, M. J. D., 'Charity disestablished? The origins of the Charity Organisation Society revisited, 1868-1871', *Journal of Ecclesiastical History*, Vol. 54, (2003), pp. 40-61. Humphreys, Robert, *Poor relief and charity, 1869-1945: the London Charity Organisation Society*, (Palgrave), 2001, and Mowat, C. L., *The Charity Organisation Society, 1869-1913: its ideas and work*, (Methuen), 1961.

what was to be the approach of COS. Charity, was a work of friendly neighbourliness and essentially private, should help and not harm. Any gift that did not make individuals better, stronger and more independent damaged rather than helped them.

Social problems, the COS believed, were ethical in origin, the result of free moral choices made by 'calculating' individuals. Poverty should spur individuals on to better their lot, to the benefit of all and charity should step in to help the destitute only if they were morally upright and provide training in personal responsibility. Pauperism was regarded as a social evil, a degraded mentality, even, according to Thomas Mackay a disease requiring scientific treatment that should be deliberatively punitive and stigmatising. [31] In practice, the COS wanted outdoor-relief under the Poor Law system to wither away, with a return to the rationale of the 1834 Poor Law Amendment Act, restricting help to relief through workhouses. Over the years outdoor-relief had spread, and COS believed this was a corrupting sign of a dysfunctional society. It also meant that the Poor Law Guardians and the charities were competing for the same clients, each giving inadequate relief because of the other.

The COS was founded at the same time as an important policy statement from the Gladstone government known as the *Goschen Minute* instructing local Boards to co-operate with charities so that the Poor Law would relieve the undeserving in workhouses, charities the deserving poor and out-relief could be drastically reduced. George Goschen was President of the Poor Law Board and was concerned to tighten up the Poor Law, which he believed had become too generous, and its administration too lax. It is not clear who inspired who but the Goschen Minute formed the basis for the activities of the COS. Many of its members were also members of their local Boards of Guardians and they applied themselves with energy their tasks. Although most Boards were unsympathetic to the COS approach, in St George-in-the-East the COS had no less than six places and the chairman was Albert Peel who, from 1877 to 1898, also chaired the Central Poor Law Conference. In St. George's and later in Whitechapel and Stepney, outdoor-relief virtually disappeared and the Poor Law Board and COS worked hand-in-hand.

It is important to make a distinction between the social casework of COS and its social philosophy. [32] In its methods the COS was a

---

[31] Mackay, Thomas, *The State and Charity*, (Macmillan and Co.), 1898, pp. 1-17, 134-177, and *The English poor: a sketch of their social and economic history*, (J. Murray), 1889, pp. 206-240, provides a summary of his views.
[32] Bosanquet, Helen, *Social work in London, 1869 to 1912: a history of the Charity Organisation Society,* (John Murray), 1914, Whelan, Robert,

pioneering body that was of great significance in the development of professional social casework in the nineteenth century. From the 1890s, they produced training manuals for this purpose, for the use of their volunteers. They also believed that loans, pioneered by the Jewish societies, were less 'demoralising' than gifts. The social philosophy of the COS was rigorously traditional and it became one of the main defenders of the self-help individualist ethic long after it had been challenged on all sides. The COS had an essentially dualistic attitude to its work: it was professionally pioneering but ideologically reactionary. The early leaders Charles Bosanquet, Edward Denison, Octavia Hill and above all Charles Loch (secretary from 1875 to 1913) all believed that the casework methods should be geared to the moral improvement of the poor and that this was the real purpose of charity.[33] All charities had to be on their guard against fraudulent applicants and this, for the COS, was justification for indiscriminate charity being ended by the vetting of every applicant.

By 1900, there were more than forty COS district offices in London and some 75 corresponding societies in other parts of the country. Their enquiries into individual cases were detailed, severe and highly judgmental, based on the conviction that poverty was a personal failing and that the poor needed to be forced back into self-sufficiency. The COS came into conflict with Dr Barnardo and opposed the Salvation Army with particular bitterness claiming that its work actually created homelessness. Their approach was abrasive, to both potential clients and other more compassionate relief organisations, and earned much of the opprobrium that has been since directed against philanthropy in general. Some within the COS became 'reluctant collectivists', recognising the need for limited extension of state action to address the problems endemic in late-Victorian capitalism and the rise of socialist ideas. Loch's opposition to old-age pensions divided the COS in the 1890s but growing public support for pensions schemes resulted in its stance was attacked in the

---

Helping the Poor: Friendly visiting, dole charities and dole queues, (Civitas), 2001, Woodroofe, Kathleen, 'The Charity Organisation Society and the origins of social casework', *Historical Studies: Australia & New Zealand*, Vol. 9, (1959), pp. 19-29, and Fido, Judith, 'The Charity Organisation Society and social casework in London, 1869-1900', in Donajgrodzki, A.D., (ed.), *Social control in 19th century Britain*, (Croom Helm), 1977, pp. 207-230.

[33] Loch, C. S., *Charity and Social Life: a short study of religious and social thought in relation to charitable methods*, (Macmillan and Co.), 1910.

press in 1896. [34] This led to growing tensions since the District Committees resented being dictated to by the Council and being regarded as disloyal for advocating policies not approved by Loch. Loch answered this by speaking of two paths: one slow and difficult, leading to social independence, prosperity and stability for all; the other, that of liberal political expediency, dangerous, fatally expensive, and resulting in universal pauperisation. The dominance of the COS approach can be best seen in the Majority Report of the Royal Commission on the Poor 1905-1909. [35]

Despite the opposition of the COS to state intervention and its continued opposition to indiscriminate philanthropy, some of its approaches were genuinely innovative. In 1871, it established a medical sub-committee which deplored the fact that 180,000 out-patients were treated annually at St Bartholomew's Hospital without any enquiry and favoured the creation of charitable provident dispensaries and after-care centres especially for tuberculosis patients. A similar committee was set up to consider work with the 'physically and mentally defective' that pressed for better charitable provision for the blind and for the mentally ill and for children, the Invalid Children's Aid Association was created though, not surprisingly, the COS opposed the spread of free school meals. A Sanitary Aid Committee was created in 1882 and some local inspectors appointed who helped to raise standards of hygiene. To assist the able-bodied to find work, they created a series of employment enquiry offices, the precursor of Labour Exchanges. The COS attempted to place a mass of unregulated charitable activity on a more constructive basis, but earned a reputation for rigidity and harshness in its approach to poor people. Much of the criticism directed against philanthropy relates to the operation of this organisation in the late-Victorian period. If any group gave charity a bad name, it was the COS. The problem was that the COS propounded its views in a manner that was punitive, moralistic and highly offensive to other charities.

---

[34] Macnicol. John, *The politics of Retirement in Britain, 1878-1948*, (Cambridge University Press), 1998, pp. 85-111, examines the attitudes of the COS to pensions.

[35] Vincent, A. W., 'The poor law reports of 1909 and the social theory of the Charity Organisation Society', *Victorian Studies*, Vol. 27, (1984), pp. 343-363, see also, Lewis, Jane, 'The voluntary sector and the state in twentieth century Britain', in Fawcett, Helen, and Lowe, Rodney, (eds.), *Welfare policy in Britain: the road from 1945*, (Macmillan), 1999, pp. 52-68.

How effective were mutual aid and self-help?

Voluntary institutions in a variety of forms and established for a variety of reasons had been an important feature of associational culture since the religious fraternities and trade guilds of medieval society. Senses of locality were central to ideas about mutual responsibility, entitlement, a hostility to top-down charity, an acceptance of aid from neighbours, a site of friendship and belonging. Voluntary bodies gave a voice to those who were excluded, or felt excluded, from the political nation: minorities, dissenters, women and the working-classes. Institutionally self-governing, they provided scope for democratic participation and, it is argued, provided a check on the mechanisms of the central state and acted as a check on the fluctuations of the market by encouraging peaceful cooperation and solidarity based on common and shared interests.

Mutual aid started spontaneously on a local level. It became a custom for groups of men to meet in the local inn for a drink on payday, and to contribute a few pence a week to a common fund. From these simple beginnings, friendly societies, trade unions, housing associations, people's banks and co-operatives were all to develop. Rose's Act of 1793 required friendly societies to register and laid down rules for their operation. The provision made by friendly societies varied. Some were primarily burial societies, protecting the working-classes against the feared pauper's funeral. Some provided for widows and children, or for sick or aged members. Some were 'collecting' societies, pre-cursors of the People's Banks. Some were 'dividing' societies that had a share-out from time to time, often at Christmas. It was almost exclusively a male movement, though there were three 'female' clubs in the villages of Cheddar, Wrington and Shipham in the 1790s.

The late-eighteenth century saw the emergence of savings institutions aimed at the working-classes that were established to encourage the poor to exercise thrift in order to protect themselves against old age and illness. [36] All types of workers, and not exclusively artisans and skilled factory workers, sought to protect themselves by setting up specifically working-class voluntary associations.[37] Friendly

---

[36] Clark, Peter, *British Clubs and Societies 1580-1800: The Origins of an Associational World*, (Oxford University Press), 2000, provides a lucid examination of the development of associational institutions and culture.

[37] Hopkins, Eric, *Working Class Self-Help*, (UCL), 1994, Finlayson, Geoffrey, *Citizens, State and Social Welfare in Britain 1830-1990*, (Oxford University Press), 1994, Morris, R., 'Clubs, societies and associations', in Thompson, F. M. L., (ed.), *The Cambridge Social History of Britain 1750-1950, Vol. 3: Social agencies and institutions*, (Cambridge University

societies and savings banks encouraged workers to put by money in good times to offset the effects of unemployment, sickness and to a limited extent old age. Cooperative societies provided workers with good quality, cheap food. These working-class associations encouraged workers to maintain and protect and where possible improve their livelihoods by giving them control, even if limited, over their lives and lacked the deferential baggage associated with charity. Friendly societies have, until recently, received only limited attention from historians.[38] Far more has been written on trade unions despite them having only a quarter of the membership of friendly societies. By 1800, there were about 7,200 Friendly societies with 648,000 members, rising to over 800,000 by 1820.[39] Friendly societies developed in the newly industrialised and urbanised society. In 1821, 17 per cent of Lancashire's population were in societies, compared to 5 per cent in rural counties. This is explained by higher industrial wages but also because industrial workers felt greater need to make provision against sickness than those who worked on the land. Clubs were also prevalent in rural areas and, for instance in the East Riding of Yorkshire, unskilled agricultural labourers were prominent members. Membership fluctuated with economic conditions and the level of agricultural wages demonstrating the insecure status of its poorer members.[40] This was also evident in the large Hampshire Friendly Society where drop-out rates average about six per cent per year in the second half of the century. Urban studies suggest that divisions within the working-classes was reflected in membership of different societies. In Bristol, there was a division between the Odd Fellows with the highest subscription, the Foresters and then the Shepherds that had larger numbers of unskilled workers.[41] In Preston, membership of the Odd Fellows signalled aspiration to higher status while in Lancaster, residential proximity rather than

---

Press), 1990, pp. 395-443. Prochaska, Frank, *The Voluntary Impulse*, (Faber), 1988, is brief and pithy.

[38] Ibid, Clark, Peter, *British Clubs and Societies 1580-1800: The Origins of an Associational World*, pp. 350-387, Gosden, P. H. J. H., *Self-Help: Voluntary Associations in Nineteenth Century Britain*, (Manchester University Press), 1961, (Batsford), 1973, pp. 11-76, and Cordery, Simon, *British Friendly Societies, 1750-1914*, (Palgrave Macmillan), 2003.

[39] Gorsky, M., 'The growth and distribution of English friendly societies in the early Nineteenth Century', *Economic History Review*, Vol. 51, (3), (1998), pp. 489-511.

[40] Neave, D., *Mutual Aid in the Victorian Countryside: Friendly Societies in the Rural East Riding,* (Hull University Press), 1991.

[41] Gorsky, M., 'Mutual aid and civil society: friendly societies in nineteenth century Bristol', *Urban History*, Vol. 25, (1998), pp. 302-322.

occupation underpinned the societies' networks. [42]

Initially restricted to small local sick clubs, often patronised by local clergymen or schoolmasters, these eminently Victorian institutions soon evolved into a bewildering array of forms. Gradually, a three-tier federal structure of branch, district and unity emerged that combined significant local autonomy and participatory democracy with representation at district and national levels. Best known were the huge federated orders like the Foresters and Oddfellows, each of which boasted over half a million members by 1900. The provision made by friendly societies varied. Some were primarily burial societies, protecting the working-classes against the feared pauper's funeral. Some provided for widows and children, or for sick or aged members. [43] Some were 'collecting' societies, pre-cursors of the People's Banks. Some were 'dividing' societies that had a share-out from time to time, often at Christmas. The main financial benefits expected by a member of a local friendly society were a weekly allowance when he was sick and a funeral payment for his widow. Friendly societies were not charities but some did provide financial support but generally for specific purposes. [44] In Manchester in 1800, a Union of Friendly Societies collected donations and distributed food cheaply to the poor. Giving their members access to medical care explains why friendly societies were willing to donate funds for building and maintaining hospitals. For instance, between 1765 and 1814, sixteen friendly societies donated to Northampton General Hospital and secured places for their members. At the opening ceremony of Huddersfield Infirmary in 1831, Manchester Unity Odd Fellows, Royal Foresters, Ancient Order of Shepherds and various local societies were present.

Just how successful friendly societies were in practice is a matter of some disagreement. Societies were vulnerable during economic downturns, to loss of members because of their inability to pay and the risk of fraudulent claims. They may not have been the epitome of the values of the labour elite but equally it is unclear whether they creates a broad sense of working class solidarity. Women were largely

---

[42] D'Cruze, S., and Turnbull, J., 'Fellowship and Family: Odd Fellows' Lodges in Preston and Lancaster, c.1830-c.1890', *Urban History*, Vol. 22, (1), (1995), pp. 25-47.

[43] Winter, James, 'Widowed Mothers and Mutual Aid in Early Victorian Britain', *Journal of Social History*, Vol. 17, (1), (1983), pp. 115-125.

[44] Weinbren, Daniel, 'Supporting self-help: charity, mutuality and reciprocity in nineteenth-century Britain', in Bridgen, Paul, and Bernard, Harris, (eds.), *Charity and Mutual Aid in Europe and North America since 1800*, (Routledge), 2007, pp. 67-88, is an important discussion of the similarities and differences between charity and friendly societies.

excluded and many of the poor were unable to pay the subscriptions but there were also internal divisions within the organisations between labourers who rarely aspired to the managerial posts and skilled workers who monopolised them. There is no doubting their importance in providing social and medical welfare during the nineteenth century but they proved not to be a viable alternative to state social security as it evolved after 1908.

The first housing society was founded in Birmingham in 1781 and by 1874, there were some 2,000. They developed in two rather different ways. Housing associations had a philanthropic element, and built houses for the working-classes. Building societies were mainly a means of investment for the middle-classes. Many subscribers made quarterly payments; they were not weekly wage earners. Building societies were not friendly societies and their legal position was obscure until the passing of the Building Societies Act 1836. People's Banks grew naturally out of the collecting societies. As wages improved for some classes of skilled workers, they needed a safe place to keep their limited reserved. By the second half of the nineteenth century there were village banks and municipal banks among many other forms of savings institutions. The Post Office Savings Bank dated from 1861, an innovation of Sir Rowland Hill, who had introduced the penny post in 1840. The co-operative movement had its origins in the eighteenth century and in the pioneering work of Robert Owen. But the idea of linking labour directly to the sale of goods without the intervention of the capitalist class survived until in 1844 a group of flannel weavers in Rochdale set up a shop in a warehouse in Toad Lane to sell their own produce. [45] They sold at market prices but gave members of their society a dividend on their purchases that could be reinvested. This encouraged 'moral buying as well as moral selling'. Co-operative production did not last more than a few decades but co-operative retailing flourished.

---

[45] Brown, W. H., *The Rochdale pioneers: a century of Cooperation in Rochdale*, (Co-operative Wholesale Society Ltd.), 1944, and Hibberd, Paul, 'The Rochdale tradition in cooperative history: is it justified?' *Annals of Public & Co-operative Economy*, Vol. 39, (1968), pp. 531-557. Jackson, John, and Platt, John, *History of the Castleford Co-operative Industrial Society Ltd., 1865-1915,* (CWS), 1925, Childe, W. H., *Batley Co-operative Society Limited: A Brief History of the Society, 1867-1917*, (CWS), 1919, Rhodes, Jos, *Half a Century of Co-operation in Keighley, 1860-1910*, (CWS), 1911, and Hartley, W., *Fifty Years of Co-operation in Bingley: A Jubilee Record of the Bingley Industrial Co-operative Society Limited 1850-1900*, (T. Harrison), 1900, for the co-operative experience in West Yorkshire.

'Heaven helps those who help themselves'. Samuel Smiles announced at the beginning of *Self-Help* published in 1859.[46] An example of his own philosophy, he was apprenticed to a group of medical practitioners at the age of fourteen after his father died of cholera and studied in his spare time gaining a medical diploma from Edinburgh university. He abandoned medicine, first for journalism and then for the exciting world of the developing railway system. From 1854, he managed the South-Eastern Railway from London. His experience provided Smiles with his main theme:

> The spirit of self-help is the root of all genuine growth in the individual.... help from without is often enfeebling, but help from within invariably invigorates. [47]

Bad luck or lack of opportunity was no excuse. There were many examples of development by men who started from humble beginnings and achieved wealth and fame: Isaac Newton, James Watt, George Stephenson and Isambard Kingdom Brunel. Smiles preached a gospel of social optimism. *Self-Help* was followed by a series of other books with similarly promising titles: *Character* (1871), *Thrift* (1875) and *Duty* (1880). These never achieved the overwhelming success of *Self-Help* and over the years the message became somewhat repetitive; but it had made its mark.

By the 1880s, Britain's economic dominance was increasingly challenged by competition from Europe and the United States. A long economic depression from the mid-1870s to the mid-1890s stretched the Victorian welfare system beyond its limits. As a result, Jose Harris argued:

> Between 1880 and 1890 the uneasy synthesis of Poor Law, thrift, and charity which had relieved distress from want of employment since the 1830s broke down. [48]

---

[46] On Smiles see, Briggs, Asa, *Victorian People*, (Penguin), 1975, pp. 116-139, for a short introduction. Jarvis, Adrian, *Samuel Smiles and the Construction of Victorian Values*, (Alan Sutton), 1997, is a more detailed study.

[47] Smiles, Samuel, *Self Help with Illustrations of Character, Conduct and Perseverance*, (Ticknor and Fields), 1866, p. 15.

[48] Harris, J., *Unemployment and politics: a study in English social policy, 1886-1914*, (Oxford University Press), 1972, p. 51. This is evident in local studies such as Crocker, Ruth Hutchinson, 'The Victorian Poor Law in Crisis and Change: Southampton, 1870-1895', *Albion*, Vol. 19, (1), pp. 19-44.

It was increasingly clear that philanthropy, mutual aid and self-help could not resolve the national problems of poverty and unemployment. The London COS provided caseworkers to help only 800 people a year; model villages accommodated barely a few thousand; and the Ragged Schools movement at its height only numbered 192 schools. Social reformers such as Charles Booth and Seebohm Rowntree challenged the preconceptions that drove the COS and other charities. Pioneering work supported by charity and philanthropists was taken over by the state on a massive scale, including the provision of sanitation in cities. The debate on poverty had started to move on. George Sims' poem *Christmas Day in the Workhouse* was not written until 1903, but social reformers like Dickens had long been pointing to the inhumanity of the system. Dickens had pilloried the ideas of Malthus in his character Scrooge in *A Christmas Carol*, who justified his meanness on the grounds that he did not want to support 'surplus population'. Ricardian economic had blamed idleness on 'excess wages' but this was undermined by Alfred Marshall, whose revolutionary concept of 'unemployment' caused by trade cycles, made poverty a product of the economic environment rather than moral degeneracy.

By 1900, there was a growing political consensus in Britain that government needed to do more to address social problems and fear of political unrest pushed the ruling elite towards social programmes to ease the pressure. Winston Churchill argued:

> With a 'stake in the country' in the form of insurances against evil days these workers will pay no attention to the vague promises of revolutionary socialism. [49]

In Victorian Britain, philanthropy, mutual aid and self-help were contrasting and competing philosophies. The three voluntary movements were in many respects complementary to one another, providing different pieces of the jigsaw of future social service provision. Philanthropy highlighted the extent of social misery. At worst it was patronising and snobbish, but at best, it reached out to the poorest and most disadvantaged classes in a divided society and developed a public conscience about conditions. Mutual aid was an intensely practical movement for the better-off sections of the working-classes. It was not a way out of poverty, but it was a means for supporting and protecting members of society against sudden

---

[49] Cit, Addison, Paul, 'Church and Social Reform', in Blake, Robert and Louis, William Roger, (eds.), *Churchill*, (Oxford University Press), 1996, p. 62.

financial disaster. Self-help was tough-minded, of greatest value to the individualistic and hardworking who were prepared to strive in order to further their own ambitions. The problem for each of these approaches was that they could only address the symptoms of the problem of national poverty, not its causes.

11 Literacy and schooling, 1780-1870

In an agricultural society the old man is the wise one; in an industrial society he is a has-been.[1]

Education is a social activity. No society or state can afford to leave education to chance and consequently it became enmeshed in conflicting social and political agendas. Schools train children for their future role within society and, especially where this is hierarchical, their place in the hierarchy. When economic conflict gave rise to class-consciousness, the dominant class saw schooling as a means of controlling other classes by offering them education on their own terms. Education also became a matter of sectarian conflict where there was more than one faith and there was a struggle over whether the different churches should provide alternative systems of education or whether the state should fulfil their role. What people believed had close links with their economic position and social status of those and the conflicts between different beliefs influenced and possibly distorted the development of English education. Education was therefore a major focus for those who believed in social control, as an instrument for moulding public morals and social attitudes.

By the nineteenth century, education had become too important and too contentious for government and politicians to leave it alone. Baldwin Francis Duppa, Secretary of the Central Society of Education wrote in 1837:

> For schools to be efficient, it is necessary that they should be so ordered as to supply the wants peculiar to the class intended to be educated at them; that they would have a regard to existing evils, and that they should have reference, not to one class of faculties alone, but to all. [2]

The radical Robert Owen commented in 1816:

> For every day will make it more and more evident that the character of man is without a single exception, always formed for him; that it may be, and is, chiefly created by his predecessors; that they give him, or may give him, his ideas and habits, that are the powers that govern and direct his conduct. Man, therefore, never did, nor is it possible that he ever can, form his own character. [3]

---

[1] Cipolla, C. M., *Literacy and the Development in the West*, (Penguin), 1969, p. 17.
[2] Duppa, Baldwin Francis, 'Central Society of Education: Objects of the Society', *Central Society of Education*, 1837, p. 13.
[3] Owen, Robert, *A New View of Society*, (Cadell and Davies), 1813, 2nd

Education was a major support for the existing system but it could also act as a means for liberation, a force for subversion. Schooling emerged as the process of education became institutionalised. It entailed a move from experiential, non-formalised learning grounded in older educational agencies, for example, employment, the church and the family to formalised, rational, institutional learning in the school. The nineteenth century is pivotal in the development of English education since, for the first time, all children were officially required to attend school. The debate in the nineteenth century was, in part, about the degree to which schooling should be controlled, why and by whom.

How and why did literacy improve?

Literacy is difficult to define with any degree of accuracy and, in the first sixty years of the nineteenth century difficult to quantify.[4] The concept of literacy can be defined very broadly as a person's ability to read and sometimes write down the cultural symbols of a society or social group.[5] Literacy has always been a two-edged sword providing the means to expand experience but also leading to control over what people read. It is not surprising that the dominant culture wants to control literacy while subordinate groups call for freer access to the

---

edition, (R. Taylor), 1816, p. 45.

[4] On literacy see Cipolla, C. M., *Literacy and the Development in the West*, (Penguin), 1969 contains an excellent chapter on literacy and the industrial revolution. Altick, R. D., *The English Common Reader*, (Phoenix Books), 1963, Webb, R. K., *The British Working-class Reader 1790-1848: Literacy and Social Tension*, (Allen & Unwin), 1955, and Sanderson, M., *Education, Economic Change and Society in England 1780-1870*, second edition, (Macmillan), 1991, contain important material. Vincent, D., *Literacy and popular culture: England 1750-1914*, (Cambridge University Press), 1989, is an important study based on computerised research. Smith, O., *The Politics of Language 1791-1819*, (Oxford University Press), 1984, examines how ideas about language were used to maintain repression and class divisions.

[5] The concept of functional literacy has been developed to deal with the semantic problem of defining 'literacy'. It was originally coined by the United States Army during World War II and denoted an ability to understand military operations and to be able to read at a fifth-grade level. Subsequently, the United Nations Educational, Scientific and Cultural Organization (UNESCO) defined functional literacy in terms of an individual possessing the requisite reading and writing skills to be able to take part in the activities that are a normal part of that individual's social milieu.

'really useful knowledge' of the dominant culture. [6]

The economic innovations of the eighteenth and early-nineteenth centuries led to important changes in the working lives of many people who were increasingly drawn to work in factories. This disrupted earlier patterns of domestic and community life. Child employment meant that many children were denied the disciplines of schooling but new types of schools were established to compensate for these factory-related developments. Factory schools, Sunday schools, evening schools and infant schools were all developed to accommodate the consequences of industrialisation. These new schools adopted a new social agenda seeking not only to inculcate virtue but also remould their pupils to fit in with the needs of an industrial society. Schools began to place much greater emphasis on continuous and regular attendance with teachers developing elaborate pedagogies to ensure that all children remained busy at their allotted tasks.

Two developments flowed from this. Much greater attention was given to the education, training and competence of elementary school teachers. Rote methods were given much less attention and, instead, teachers were expected to be accomplished in more intellectual methods of instruction. They were expected not merely to inspect the contents of their pupils' minds by hearing memorised lessons but also to exercise the minds of their charges by questioning them on their lessons. There was also a major expansion of the school curriculum promoted alongside the spread of elementary education. Children began to be taught through secular as well as religious topics. It was assumed that if children knew how the world worked, they would be more ready to accept their allotted, if unnatural, place in the scheme of things. Another educational consequence of economic change was that writing began to enter the core curriculum of schooling. This did not meet with unqualified approval. Some argued that writing, a business skill, should not be taught in Sunday schools, while others claimed that it would promote crime, a view ridiculed in 1829:

'If you teach them to write,' it was said, 'they will learn to forge.' And upon the same principle, they ought, were it possible, to be precluded from the exercise of speech, because they may lie and blaspheme...This absurd objection, though urged at no remote period...can no longer find any one

---

[6] On 'useful knowledge', see Connell, Philip, *Romanticism, Economics and the Question of 'Culture'*, (Oxford University Press), 2001, pp. 76-83.

hardy enough to be its advocate. [7]

Many assumed that writing skills would elevate people above their proper station in life. Nevertheless, there was a powerful lobby that recognised the importance of writing skills to the prosperity and administration of the economy. The army of clerks expanded with industrialisation.

'Read or was read to': it is only in the course of the nineteenth century that reading gradually became a private rather than a public act for the mass of the population. Until the 1830s, if you could read, you were expected to read aloud and share your reading with family, friends and workmates. [8] A population with a significant proportion of 'illiterates' may not be ill-informed but may be at least as well informed as a population where the formal reading skill is widely diffused but seldom used. [9]

---

[7] Wood, John, *Account of the Edinburgh Sessional School: and the other parochial institutions for education established in that city in the year 1812; with strictures on education in general*, (John Wardlaw), 1829, p. 241, cit, 'The Art of Writing', *The Saturday Magazine*, Vol. 23, 7 October 1843, p. 143.

[8] Vincent, D., 'The decline of oral tradition in popular culture', in Storch R. D., (ed.), *Popular culture and custom in 19th-century England,* (Croom Helm), 1982, pp. 20-47.

[9] On popular literature Williams, R., *The Long Revolution*, (Penguin), 1961, contains important chapters on the growth of the reading public and the popular press. Ibid, Vincent, D., *Literacy and popular culture: England 1750-1914*, and Neuburg, V. E., *Popular Literature: A History and Guide*, (Penguin), 1977, are good introductions. James, L., *Print and the People 1819-1851*, (Peregrine), 1978 and *Fiction for the Working Man 1830-1850*, (Penguin), 1973, are more detailed. Cross, N., *The Common Writer: Life in nineteenth century Grub Street*, (Cambridge University Press), 1985, is the most useful study of nineteenth century writing. On the press Read, D., *Press and People 1790-1850: Opinion in Three English Cities*, (Edward Arnold), 1961, is excellent on the impact of the middle class press while Hollis, P., *The Pauper Press: A Study in Working-Class Radicalism of the 1830s*, (Oxford University Press), 1970, Wickwar, W. H., *The Struggle for the Freedom of the Press 1819-1832*, (Allen & Unwin), 1928, and Weiner, J., *The War of the Unstamped: the movement to repeal the British newspaper tax, 1830-1836*, (Cornell University Press), 1969, on the popular press. There has been a proliferation of regional and local studies on the role of the press: for example, Milne, M., *Newspapers of Northumberland and Durham*, (Graham), 1951, and Murphy, M. J., *Cambridge Newspapers and Opinion 1780-1850*, (Oleander Press), 1977. Shattock, J., and Wolff, M., (eds.), *The Victorian Periodical Press: Samplings and Soundings*, (Leicester University Press), 1982, contains several valuable articles. Koss, Stephen,

The spread of reading skills was aided by the technology of printing in the 1830s and 1840s with the steam-driven printing press. The speed of book production had changed little since the hand-operated Gutenberg-style presses were developed in mid-fifteenth century but steam-powered presses increases the impression per hour tenfold from 240 to 2,400 by the 1850s. As a result, the average price of books halved between 1828 and 1853. Stamp duty on newspapers and the tax on paper were both substantially reduced in 1836 and finally abolished in 1855 and 1861 respectively. The spread of writing in commercial institutions also received a technological stimulus with the invention of the mass-produced and low-cost steel-nib pen in the 1830s and the introduction of cheaper esparto grass paper in the 1860s. The quill was in common use until the early-nineteenth century but with the advent of the metal nib, the quill was fairly quickly overtaken for business purposes. However, it remains popular for personal use and for artistic work. Books and newspapers became more readily available with the Public Libraries Act of 1850[10] and communications were improved by the introduction of the Penny Post in 1840. [11]

There is some debate over whether levels of literacy were rising or falling in the first thirty years of the nineteenth century. The problem that historians face is that there is no agreed standard for measuring literacy in this period. Attempts have taken two main forms: a counting of institutions and of signatures on marriage registers and legal documents. Both are fraught with problems. Counting the number of schools tells historians little about the education that went on in them, the average attendance, length of the school year or average length of school life, all of which have a direct relevance to levels of literacy. Counting signatures may lead to an overestimation of literacy levels as individuals might be able to sign but have few other literacy skills. Conversely, the same evidence may lead to an underestimation of literacy skills. Writing requires a productive proficiency that reading does not and those who cannot sign may be able to read, but would be in danger of being classified as illiterate. Yet, it is agreed that signatures provide better figures and

---

The Rise and Fall of the Political Press in Britain, (Fontana), 1990, is a monumental study.

[10] Burch, Brian, 'Libraries and literacy in popular education', in Mandelbrote, Giles, and Manley, Keith A., *The Cambridge History of Libraries in Britain and Ireland, Vol. 2: 1640-1850*, (Cambridge University Press), 2006, pp. 371-387.

[11] Campbell-Smith, Duncan, *Masters of the Post: The Authorized History of the Royal Mail*, (Allen Lane), 2011, provides the context for the dramatic expansion of letter-writing.

these are more soundly based than attempts to count schools or scholars.

A survey of seventeen country parishes in the East Riding of Yorkshire found that male literacy was 64 per cent in both 1754-1760 and 1801-1810 and rose steadily afterwards. [12] Lawrence Stone argues that literacy was rising between the 1770s and 1830 based upon more widespread analysis seeing this as a result of the process of industrialisation and its demands for a more literate workforce. [13] This optimistic view has, however, been called into question as far as England as a whole was concerned. There are various reasons for questioning whether literacy did rise. The sharp rise in population from the 1760s began to swamp the existing provision of schools, especially charity schools funded by local patrons. [14] Private, charitable investment in education slackened after 1780 as people diverted their investment into more expensive and pressing outlets such as enclosure, canal and turnpike investment. The dynamic areas of growth in the education system were no longer the charity schools for the working population but private fee-paying schools for the upper-classes and grammar schools for the middle-classes. Children were also drawn into the new processes of industrialisation and there were increased opportunities to employ them from an early age. This too militated against working-class children receiving an education that would make and keep them literate, especially in industrial areas. [15] Under these circumstances it would not be surprising if literacy rates did sag. There is some statistical evidence for a fall in literacy in the last decades of the eighteenth century and the first decades of the nineteenth. Studies of Lancashire, Devon and Yorkshire suggest that there was a sharp fall in literacy in the 1810s and 1820s from around 67 per cent to fewer than 50 per cent. Stephen Nicholas has examined 80,000 convicts transported to Australia between 1788 and 1840 and he found that urban literacy continued to rise until 1808 and rural literacy to 1817 but then both fell consistently for the rest of the

---

[12] Baker, W. P., *Parish registers and illiteracy in East Yorkshire*, (East Yorkshire Local History Society), 1961

[13] Stone, L., 'Literacy and education in England 1640-1900', *Past and Present*, Vol. 42, (1969), pp. 69-139.

[14] Jones, Mary, *The Charity School Movement: A Study of Eighteenth Century Puritanism in action*, (Cambridge University Press), 1938, and Mason, J., 'Scottish Charity Schools of the Eighteenth Century', *Scottish Historical Review*, Vol. 33, (1), (1954), pp. 1-13.

[15] Sanderson, M., 'Literacy and social mobility in the industrial revolution in England', *Past and Present*, Vol. 56, (1972), pp. 75-104.

period.[16]

It was the Sunday school movement that from the 1780s countered these trends.[17] In 1801, there were some 2,290 schools rising to 23,135 in 1851 with over 2 million enrolled children. By then, three-quarters of working-class children aged 5-15 were attending such institutions. However, there are some limitations to making a strong case that Sunday schools sustained the literacy rate. Many schools ceased the teaching of writing after the 1790s. They have also been seen as either the creation of a working-class culture seeking respectability and self-reliance or as middle-class conservative institutions for the reform of their working-class pupils from above. A positive force in a worsening situation, they probably prevented literacy falling more than it did in areas vulnerable to decline. These divergent views illustrate the difficulty of extrapolating from specific examples to a general picture. England, especially urban England, was not a homogenous unit experiencing 'optimistic' or 'pessimistic' literacy trends before 1830.

From 1830, levels of literacy began to rise, a process that continued for the rest of the century, though inevitably with regional variations in pace. Literacy rates were published by the Registrar General for each census year in percentages.

	1841	1851	1861	1871
Male	67.3	69.3	75.4	80.6
Female	51.1	54.8	65.3	73.2

This was paralleled by growth in the average number of years of schooling for boys: 2.3 years in 1805 to 5 years in 1846-1851 to 6.6 years by 1867-1871. Various factors lay behind this, but first it is important to consider the motives both of educators and of educated that made this possible. The Churches were concerned with the salvation of souls and the winning back what they saw as the irreligious working-class urban population to Christianity. The Church of England felt itself under attack from a revival of Nonconformity and Roman Catholicism in the 1830s. By 1870, there were 8,798 voluntary assisted schools of which 6,724 were National Society

---

[16] Nicholas, Stephen, (ed.), *Convict Workers: Reinterpreting Australia's Past*, (Cambridge University Press), 1988; see also, Richards, E., 'An Australian map of British and Irish literacy in 1841', *Population Studies*, Vol. 53, (1999), pp. 345-359.

[17] Laqueur, T. W., *Religion and Respectability: Sunday Schools and Working-class Culture 1780-1850*, (Yale University Press), 1976, is the seminal work on a major educational movement.

Schools. At a secular level, the long period of radical unrest from the 1790s to the 1840s created deep anxiety about order and social control. Richard Johnson put it well when he says:

> The early Victorian obsession with the education of the poor is best understood as a concern about authority, about power, about the assertion (or the reasserting) of control.[18]

For instance, in Spitalfields much education was aimed at controlling the population in the interests of social and economic stability while in the north-eastern coalfields coal owners created schools attached to collieries in the 1850s as a means of social control following damaging strikes in 1844. [19]

The social control argument dated back to the Sunday Schools, the SPCK Charity schools and beyond. These suggested that schooling and literacy would make the poor unfit for the performance of menial tasks because it would raise their expectations. Even worse, the acquisition of literate skills would make the working-classes receptive to radical and subversive literature. This was the essential dilemma: to deny education to the poor and so avoid trouble or to provide ample education in the hope that it would serve as an agent of social control. By the late 1830s, the latter ideology dominated the minds of policy makers. Education was seen as a means of reducing crime and the rising cost of punishment. It was also recognised as a way of keeping the child or the child when adult out of the workhouse. In the 1860s, these views were joined by two other that presaged the 1870 Act. The military victories of Prussia and the northern States of America in the 1860s suggested that good levels of education contributed to military efficiency. At home, the Reform Act 1867 prompted concerns about the extent of education of those who would soon wield political power through an extended franchise: 'we must now education our masters' according to Robert Lowe, a leading Conservative politician. Education may have been of limited value for actual performance in some occupations, but it had important

---

[18] Johnson, Richard, 'Educational Policy and social control in early Victorian England', *Past & Present*, Vol. 49, (1970), p. 119.

[19] McCann, Phillip, and Young, Francis A., *Samuel Wilderspin and the Infant School Movement*, (Taylor & Francis), 1982, pp. 15-33, and McCann, Phillip, 'Popular Education, Socialisation and Social Control: Spitalfields 1812-1824', in McCann, Phillip, (ed.), *Popular Education and Socialisation in the Nineteenth Century*, (Methuen), 1977, pp. 1-49, consider Spitalfields. Colls, R., "Oh Happy English Children!': Coal, Class and Education in the North-East', *Past & Present*, Vol. 73, (1), pp. 75-99, looks at coalfield schools.

implications for the creation of an industrial society. This made it possible for people to be in touch with a basic network of information dispersal and could make labourers aware of the possibilities open to them or the products of consumers. A positive belief in the value of education on the part of the authorities replaced earlier assumptions that teaching the poor to read would merely lead to the diffusion of subversive literature and the wholesale flight of the newly educated from menial tasks.

The literacy rate was driven up by the injection of public money into the building and maintenance of elementary schools. This rose from £193,000 in 1850 to £723,000 in 1860 and £895,000 by 1870. The money was channelled largely into two religious societies: the Anglican National Society, founded in 1811, and the British and Foreign School Society, a Nonconformist body created three years later. These bodies raised money to build schools usually run on monitorial lines. However, by the early 1830s, it was obvious that they were unable to counter the defects in school provision, especially in the north. State funding began in 1833 with investment of about one per cent of national income. From the 1840s, under the guidance of the Privy Council for Education and its Secretary James Kay-Shuttleworth expenditure increased as grants were extended from limited capital grants for buildings to equipment in 1843, teacher training three years later and capitation grants for the actual running of schools in 1853. Closer control over these grants was instituted in 1862 with the system of payment by results and by a reduction of teacher training to try and control sharply rising expenditure.

Important though the role of the state and religious societies was in developing literacy levels, some historians have pointed to the large sector of cheap private education where the working-classes bought education for their children outside the church and state system. It has been suggested that at least a quarter of working-class children were educated in this way. Many in the working-classes spurned the new National and British schools and chose slightly more expensive, small dame and common day schools. Although their quality was maligned by publicists such as Kay-Shuttleworth who advocated a state-financed system, they were not regarded as part of the authority system and had no taint of charity or the heavy social control of the Churches. Parents often regarded the teachers as their employees and they fitted in with working-class lifestyles. [20]

---

[20] Gardner, Philip, 'Literacy, Learning and Education', in Williams, Chris (ed.), *A Companion to nineteenth-century Britain* (Blackwell Publishers), 2004, pp. 353-368.

There is no doubt, however, that the expansion of this type of education did result in the creation of a remarkably literate working-class. A major factor in rising literacy was the creation of a teaching profession in elementary schools. The religious societies had their own training colleges before the 1830s and from 1839 many Anglican dioceses established colleges to serve diocesan National Schools. The system received its most important stimulus from the Minutes of 1846 that established the training and career structure for teachers. The 1850s saw the rapid rise of a schoolteacher class: there were 681 certificated teachers in 1849 but 6,878 ten years later. A further important factor was the role of Her Majesty's Inspectors first appointed in 1839 to ensure that the state grant was spent properly. Their duties expanded into more educational roles, examining pupil teachers and the training colleges, calculating the capitation grants of the 1850s and then examining children in the subjects on which the grant was based in the 1860s. They encouraged the replacement of the monitorial system with class teaching. By 1870, their number has risen from 2 to 73.

Four things mopped up the illiteracy of deprived groups who, left to themselves, would have remained a hard core of illiterates: the ragged, workhouse, prison and factory schools. Ragged schools began during the early 1840s and the Ragged School Union dated from 1844. They charged no fees and took the poorest children for a basic education, depending for their support on a circle of philanthropists including Charles Dickens. By 1852, there were 132 Ragged Schools in London with 26,000 children and 70 outside the capital in 42 towns. By 1870, at their peak, there were 250 schools in London and 100 in the provinces until they were taken over by the School Boards. Workhouse and prison schools catered for children who had lost their freedom or who had fallen into the safety-net of the Poor Law. Their education was guaranteed in the 1834 Poor Law Amendment Act and the 1823 Prisons Act. Finally, factory schools were created by the 1833 Factory Act that obliged factory owners to ensure that their child workers received a regular education either in a factory schools or outside before being allowed to work. This was firmly enforced. All these measures helped the most disadvantaged groups of children.

What was learned was important and the development of a body of reading material accessible to the masses was a characteristic feature of the years after 1830. At the school level, the SPCK, acting as the publishing arm of the National Society, set up its Committee of General Literature and Education in 1832 to produce schoolbooks.[21]

---

[21] Society for Promoting Christian Knowledge, the oldest Anglican mission organisation was founded in 1698 in England to encourage Christian

The National Society gradually took over from the SPCK and in 1845 established its own book collection for National schools. The British Society similarly published secular books for schools after 1839. There was also concern among the governing elite to provide informative books for adults that would divert them away from the propaganda of radicalism. The Society for the Diffusion of Useful Knowledge, established in 1826, issued a library of cheap, short books on popular science, history and all types of secular subjects to combat the strong tradition of radical literature ushering in publishing for a mass audience. [22] The Society was particularly influential in spreading science to a broad and diverse population. It was deliberately inclusive in its audience, actively seeking to make its publications useful and appealing to a wide variety of readers of all classes, genders, educational levels and professions. By providing the same information, in the same format, for all readers, the Society democratised learning across the social boundaries of the period and broadened the horizon for future popularisers. The commercial market also played an increasingly important role for literate society with the sensationalist 'penny dreadfuls', serialisation of novels by authors such as Dickens, Gothic and romantic novels and the railway reading of W. H. Smith & Son.

Literacy rates had risen by the 1860s before the advent of state secular schools or free or compulsory education. However, one and a half million children, 39 per cent of those between 3 and 12 were not at school and there was a further million children without school places even had they chosen to attend. The 1870 Act filled in the gaps in areas where voluntary provision was inadequate. The building of non-sectarian schools, the work of 2,000 School Boards and

---

education and the production and 1709 in Scotland as a separate organisation for establishing new schools. See, Allen, William Osborne Bird, and McClure, Edmund, *Two Hundred Years: the History of the Society for Promoting Christian Knowledge, 1698-1898*, (SPCK), 1898, and Clarke, W. K. L., *A History of the SPCK*, (SPCK), 1959.

[22] Kinraid, R. B., *The Society for the Diffusion of Useful Knowledge and the democratization of learning in early-nineteenth-century Britain*, (University of Wisconsin-Madison), 2006. See also, Rauch, Alan, *Useful Knowledge: the Victorians, morality, and the march of intellect*, (Duke University Press), 2001, and Mandelbrote, Scott, 'The publishing and distribution of religious books by voluntary associations: from the Society for Promoting Christan Knowledge to the British and Foreign Bible Society', in Suarez, Michael F., and Turner, Michael L., (eds.), *The Cambridge History of the Book in Britain, Vol. 5: 1695-1830*, (Cambridge University Press), 2009, pp. 613-630.

compulsory education after 1880 finally led to the achievement of mass literacy by 1900.

What role did the state play in the development of education 1833-1870?

There were individuals at the beginning of the nineteenth century who favoured widespread popular mass education, but they did not have the backing either of government, influential taxpayers or those who benefited from employing children. The leaders of the Chartist Movement and the Radicals were in favour of some sort of national system of education but there was only a limited desire for the education of the population as a whole. Although, the Church of England, Nonconformist denominations and the Roman Catholic Church thought extending education was desirable, the government was unwilling to intervene or take the lead for fear of appearing to promote one group over the others.

How did elementary education develop?

English elementary education grew in the face of constant fear and opposition from sections of the upper- and middle-classes.[23]

---

[23] The most straight-forward study of education between 1830 and 1914 is the relevant chapters of Lawson, John and Silver, Harold, *A Social History of Education in England*, (Methuen), 1973. Smelser, Neil J., *Social paralysis and social change: British working-class education in the nineteenth century*, (University of California Press), 1991, is both a detailed history of educational development and a theoretical study of social change. The focus of much study has been on the education of the working population. Central to the period 1830-1870 are the contrasting views of West, E. G., *Education and the State*, (Institute of Economic Affairs), 1965, and *Education and the Industrial Revolution*, (Batsford), 1975, and Hurt, J. S., *Education in Evolution: Church, State, Society and Popular Education, 1800-1870*, (Rupert Hart-Davis), 1971. The work of Harold Silver is also important especially his *The concept of popular education*, (Methuen), 1965, and his collection of essays *Education as History*, (Methuen), 1983. Simon, B., *The Two Nations and the Educational Structure 1780-1870*, (Lawrence and Wishart), 1974, and Sutherland, G., *Elementary Education in the Nineteenth Century*, (The Historical Association), 1971, are essential reading. Johnson, Richard, 'Really useful knowledge: radical education and working-class culture 1790-1848', in Clarke, J., Critcher, C., and Johnson, R., (eds.), *Working-class Culture: Studies in history and theory*, (Hutchinson), 1979, pp. 75-112, is valuable. Burns J., 'From Polite Learning to Useful Knowledge 1750-1850', *History Today*, Vol. 36, (4), (1986), pp. 21-29, and Harrison, B., 'Kindness and Reason: William Lovett and Education', *History Today*, Vol. 37, (3), (1987), pp. 14-22, are interesting. Ibid, Sanderson, M.,

Education, it was believed, would teach the working-classes to despise their lot in life, enable them to read seditious literature and make them less deferential to their social superiors. This attitude persisted, especially among rural farmers and gentry, throughout the nineteenth century. In 1846, the Rev. John Allen, Inspector for Bedfordshire, Cambridgeshire and Huntingdonshire wrote the following that he maintained reflected rural opinion:

We cannot help having a school, but we think it advisable that as little as possible be taught therein. [24]

Overt hostility to any form of education may have retreated into the backwoods of rural England but there were many who wished to give the working-classes just enough education so that they could read the Bible, learn their duty to God and Man, and the place in life to which Providence had been pleased to assign them. William Lovett, the Chartist leader, denounced these educationalists as:

...favourable to the securing of their prey, another portion, with more cunning, were for admitting a sufficient amount of mental glimmer to cause the multitude to walk quietly and contentedly in the paths they in their wisdom had prescribed for them. [25]

In time this attitude also weakened, partly through the actions of Lord Ashley who, though an enemy of secular state schools, was an enthusiastic champion of working-class education. Its successor was the 'Morals before Intellect' view of those who demanded that working-class education should be primarily religious, because its primary purpose was to inculcate good morals and obedience. This was often found among High Churchmen who believed:

...no secular knowledge really desirable for the bulk of the population could be fitly taught apart from a constant reference to religion. [26]

Education, Economic Change and Society in England 1780-1870, provides a brief bibliographical statement.

[24] Kay, David, and Kay, Joseph, *The Education of the Poor in England and Europe*, (J. Hatchard and Son), 1846, p. 220.

[25] Lovett, William, *Life and Struggles of William Lovett in his pursuit of bread, knowledge, and freedom: with some short account of the different associations he belonged to and of the opinions he entertained*, (Trubner), 1877, p. 111. See also, ibid, Harrison, B., 'Kindness and Reason: William Lovett and Education'.

[26] Rev. Alexander Watson, curate of St John's, Cheltenham in 1846, cit, Henriques, Ursula, *Before the Welfare State*, (Longman), 1979, p. 201.

This also resonated among conservative landed gentry:

> I consider those schools to be the most promising where The Commandments and the Duty of God and Man are regularly taught, because without moral and practical religious training there can be no real education.[27]

Secular educationalists were, until the 1860s, a small, noisy group advocating moral without religious training. Modern historians often maintain that the purpose of early Victorian educationalists was the social control of one class by another or as Harold Silver puts it 'Rescuing the poor for religion and a concomitant stable society'. [28] But the concept of social control, though important in any examination of education, is oversimplified. As a label 'social control' is crude covering a multitude of stances from the crudely manipulative and instrumental attitude of Lord Londonderry building schools in his mining villages after the Chartist disturbances to the wholly sincere attempts to remake the working-class child in the middle-class image.[29] Among middle- and upper-class philanthropists it was an argument for enlightened self-preservation; to Ashley and Kay-Shuttleworth education would rescue the working-classes from crime and sedition. The means varied. Churchmen sought to inculcate religion and morals to buttress duty and obedience while liberals attacked sedition and socialism by developing popularised versions of classical political economy. Motives and means might have varied but there was a good deal of common ground among all educationalists. Lovett and Owen no less than Ashley and Kay-Shuttleworth looked to education to rescue the working-classes from vice and crime accepting the relationship between ignorance and criminality. Education as a means of 'improvement' embodied in the idea of the 'march of mind' and provided a counter-force to the Law and High Church preoccupation with faith, duty and obedience. The interesting question is not whether a given educational scheme was designed as social control but what sort of society it was intended to produce.

One reason why education in the 1830s appeared to be an instrument of class control was the decline of the parallel conception

---

[27] Sir Charles Anderson of Lea, near Gainsborough, Lincolnshire in evidence to the Newcastle Commission in June 1859, Parliamentary Paper, *Education Commission: Answers to the Circular of Questions*, Vol. 5, (HMSO), 1860, p. 9, cit, ibid, Henriques, Ursula, *Before the Welfare State*, p. 201.
[28] Ibid, Silver, Harold, *The concept of popular education*, p. 26.
[29] Johnson, Richard, 'Educational policy and social control in early Victorian England', *Past & Present*, Vol. 49, (1970), pp. 96-119.

of education as a means of social mobility. It had declined as the professional and industrial middle-classes turned to defensive measures against the working-classes forming below them. Education, as a result, became involved in the class struggle and became politicised. By the 1830s, there were voluntary Church schools teaching the Anglican catechism, voluntary Nonconformist schools teaching private morality from the Bible and public morality from readers of classical economics and voluntary Owenite schools propagating socialism. It was the dominance of the rescue motif, as interpreted by middle-class enthusiasts that prevented education from permanently dividing into forms of propaganda serving conflicting social and political aims.

What role did sectarian divisions play in the emergence of elementary day schools?

From the 1780s, working-class enthusiasts and middle-class reformers alike were much concerned with what might be done to extend working-class children's schooling through the voluntary principle. Among the most successful enterprises were Sunday schools. They originated in the eighteenth century and by the early 1830s it has been estimated that over a million children and adolescents were attending them. [30] Sunday schools fitted into the interstices of working-class struggles for economic survival very well. Sunday was the one day when schooling did not compete with physical labour. Chapel or church could be used as schoolroom; and teachers gave their services free, so that if fees were charged at all, they were very low. All Sunday schools taught reading and a minority writing and even arithmetic. From 1807, controversies ranged, especially among Methodists, as to the appropriateness of activities other than reading on a Sunday and the teaching of writing was usually a good guide to those schools under local and lay control rather than under religious domination. [31]

Sunday schools differed from most day schools because of their low running costs Regular weekday school required some sort of building and paid teachers, that in turn required an initial capital

---

[30] Robert Raikes of Gloucester has traditionally featured as pioneering Sunday schools in the 1780s but in fact teaching Bible reading and basic skills on a Sunday was already an established activity in some nonconformist and evangelical congregations.

[31] Orchard, Stephen, and Briggs, John H. Y., (eds.), *The Sunday school movement: studies in the growth and decline of Sunday schools*, (Paternoster), 2007, ibid, Laqueur, T. W., *Religion and Respectability, Sunday Schools and Working Class Culture 1780-1850*.

outlay, either from endowment or charitable subscription or both, as well as a reasonably regular and sizeable income from fees. The promotion of day schools led to the formation of two voluntary Religious Societies, designed to co-ordinate effort and spread best practice nationally. The National Society for Promoting the Education of the Poorin the Principles of the Established Church in England and Wales was formed in 1811 followed three years later, by the British and Foreign School Society (it replaced the Lancastrian Society formed in 1808). [32] The sectarian divide had been established: the Anglican National Society and the broadly NonconformistBritish and Foreign School Society.

The attractiveness of these voluntary schools was not enhanced by their teaching methods. Both favoured the monitorial or mutual system of teaching, by which a teacher taught the older children (or monitors) who then passed on what they had learnt to groups of younger children. [33] It was designed to enable a single teacher to cope with very large groups of children: almost the application of the factory principle to learning. It was mechanical in its approach relying on rote learning and memorisation but it was economical and this appealed to many contemporary adult observers. The reaction of the children to the monitorial system was ranged from the very critical to many of those who later wrote their autobiographies, whose remembered experience was more encouraging. To Charles Dickens, whose experience of schooling was less than positive, these schools provided a ready source for satire. [34] At the same time, many monitorial schools were more ambitious trying to teach reading, writing and arithmetic as an integrated package

These voluntary religious day schools offered an experience significantly different from the pattern of schooling familiar to the

---

[32] Binns, H. B., *A century of education: being the centenary history of the British and Foreign School Society, 1808-1908*, (T. C. & E. C. Jack), 1908.
[33] It was sometimes known as the 'Madras system' where the Anglican clergyman Andrew Bell first developed it or the 'Lancastrian system' after the Nonconformist Joseph Lancaster who independently developed the same system in England. See, Tschurenev, Jana, 'Diffusing useful knowledge: the monitorial system of education in Madras, London and Bengal, 1789-1840', *Paedagogica Historica*, Vol. 44, (2008), pp. 245-264.
[34] Dickens, Charles, *Hard Times: a novel*, (Harper & Brothers), 1854, pp. 18-19, 33, 35, 58, 65-66, 99, contains the best satirical account of the monitorial system in action under the teacher Mr McChoakumchild while in *The Life and Adventures of Nicholas Nickleby*, (Chapman and Hall), 1839, pp. 58-73, he caricatured the 'practical' nature of education at Mr Squeer's Dotheboys Academy.

working-classes and one that many of them chose to avoid. [35] The number and persistence of what middle-class contemporaries disparagingly called dame or private adventure schools is striking. Goldsmith, Cowper, Crabbe and other eighteenth century poets perpetuated the image of a white-capped widow reading to a crowd of unruly infants in a cottage but the same school adapted itself to industrialisation and urbanisation as a form of working-class educational self-help in both industrial districts and the countryside. Their flexibility and informality, willingness to accept attendance on an intermittent basis, parents paying when they could, fetching their child out to do an errand or job, were part of their attraction. It is difficult to generalise about them and in some contemporary reports they are viewed positively. However, their inadequacies were illustrated by a study conducted in 1838 by the Statistical Society of London that found nearly half of all pupils surveyed were only taught spelling, with a negligible number being taught mathematics and grammar. [36] They were small in size, seldom more than thirty children and often as few as ten. They met often in the teacher's home, in a back kitchen, basement or living room. The 1851 Census described dame schools as 'inferior' but they made up over 13,000 of the 29,425 private schools for which returns were made. Horace Mann commented:

In the case of 708 out of these 13,879 [inferior] schools, the returns were respectively signed by the master or mistress with a *mark*. [37]

They might simply be reading schools, taught indeed by an elderly woman or dame but writing and arithmetic could be tackled for an additional fee. They did not have the resources of the monitorial schools but they lacked the noise, numbers and barrack-room discipline. They functioned often as an extension of the child's familiar domestic environment rather than places separated from and often alien to it. [38] Despite the criticisms, dame school remained an important feature of education, especially for the young, until the

---

[35] Allen, J. E., 'Voluntaryism: a "laissez-faire" movement in mid-nineteenth century elementary education', *History of Education*, Vol. 10, (1981), pp. 111-124.
[36] *Journal of the Royal Statistical Society*, Vol. 1, (1839), pp. 451-452.
[37] *Census of Great Britain, 1851: Education in Great Britain, the official report of H. Mann*, (George Routledge and Co.), 1854, p. 29
[38] Higginson, J. H., 'Dame schools', *British Journal of Educational Studies*, Vol. 22, (1974), pp. 166-181, and Grigg, G. R., '"Nurseries of ignorance"? Private adventure and dame schools for the working classes in nineteenth-century Wales', *History of Education*, Vol. 34, (2005), pp. 243-262.

latter part of the century.

In competing for the custom of working-class parents and their children, the voluntary societies and the schools affiliated to them had one resource that the working-class private day schools lacked: access to central government and thus the possibility of mobilising its power and resources in their support. Day schools could not copy the mushroom growth of Sunday schools. They were more expensive to run, an expense reflected in fees ranging typically from two pence to five pence per week. They also competed directly with work and work almost always won. This competition made it difficult to get a child into a day school at all and even more so to keep him or her there. Despite these problems and pressures, in the decades between 1810 and 1860, the number of children attending day schools increased. In 1833, Lord Kerry's *Returns* on elementary educationconcluded that about 1.2 million or about a third of all children in England and Wales aged 4 to 14 were attending day schools; 1.549 million or under half were attending Sunday schools, of whom a third went to day school as well. He concluded that the proportion of children attending day schools was 1:11 of the population, an increase from the 1:17 in Lord Brougham's *Returns* in 1818. [39]

Why did the state intervene?

Everyone was agreed that any education worth the name had a moral and therefore a religious core. But if religious, which denomination? Anglicans, as members of the established church, argued that any school named in law and supported by government funds should be theirs. Nonconformists and Roman Catholics hotly disputed this. It was for this reason that the two voluntary day school societies were joined by the Catholic Poor School Committee, in 1849. This was the sectarian divide that dominated developments in elementary education up to 1902 and arguably beyond. [40]

Public provision for elementary education began with a grant of £20,000 in 1833 in aid of school buildings. This was channelled inevitably through the two religious societies because these alone could show any degree of efficiency. This was the beginning of a system of 'giving to them that hath'. Government initiatives and funding were most needed in areas of 'educational destitution' where

---

[39] This reduction continued: in 1851 the proportion was 1:8 and by 1858, 1:7: *Journal of the Royal Statistical Society*, Vol. 24, (1861), p. 209.
[40] Paz, D. G., *The Politics of Working-class Education 1830-1850*, (Manchester University Press), 1980, is the best analysis of early state intervention.

there were no middle-class enthusiasts to start schools. In 1839, therefore, the Whigs attempted to grasp the nettle of the 'religious problem' with a scheme that included grants to districts according to need and government training schools for teachers organised on a non-denominational basis. [41] The Tories mobilised against it in both Commons and Lords and the opposition of almost the entire bench of bishops brought most of the scheme down to defeat.

In 1843, Peel's Conservative government attempted to take the initiative in the education clauses of Graham's Factory Bill creating Anglican-run factory schools. Peel and his Home Secretary Sir James Graham agreed on the importance of improving educational provision for the working population and making the educational clauses of the 1833 Factory Act effective and in the importance of education as a means of social control and emphasised the moral content of schooling. Fear and prejudice came together in the massive campaign by nonconformist pressure groups coordinated by the United Conference, stressing the virtues of 'voluntarism' and professing concerns about the 'Romanising' effects of the Oxford Movement. Within two months, it had organised a petition to Parliament containing over two million signatures. In June 1843, the education clauses were withdrawn but the government remained committed to proceeding with the remainder of the bill. [42] When it was reintroduced the following year, it was shorn of its educational clauses. Thereafter there was a stalemate with neither side strong enough to break through to a new system. The amount of grant continued to rise but still the money went only to localities already making an effort. Middle-class enthusiasts broadly agreed that working-class children should be in school, not at work. The problem was which school they should attend and whether government aid could be deployed to ensure that there were schools within the reach of all working-class children. This was finally broken by the Education Act of 1870.

The debacle of 1839, where non-sectarian developments were effectively vetoed by the churches, did result in the creation of the Committee of the Privy Council on Education. Opposition continued from the Church of England resulting in the 'Concordat' of 1840

---

[41] On this issue see, Newbould, I. D. C., 'The Whigs, the Church, and Education, 1839', *Journal of British Studies*, Vol. 26, (1987), pp. 332-346, and Brent, Richard, *Liberal Anglican Politics: Whiggery, Religion and Reform, 1830-1841*, (Oxford University Press), 1987.

[42] Ward, J. T., and Treble, James H., 'Religion and education in 1843: reaction to the 'Factory Education Bill', *Journal of Ecclesiastical History*, Vol. 20, (1969), pp. 79-110.

under which the church authorities secured control of the appointment of the inspectors of state-aided schools and the right to frame the instructions for religious education, though not over non-Anglican schools. The most positive result of the Concordat was the appointment as secretary to the new Committee of Education of James Kay-Shuttleworth. [43] Resistance to state elementary education and the sectarian conflict made it impossible to start a national system using the established technique of a Royal Commission followed by a governing statute. A step-by-step approach was adopted: from the small grant of 1833 to the Privy Council Minutes of 1846 that governed the mid-century expansion. However, in the 1830s and 1840s, there were two other roots from which a national system of primary education might have grown: the new Poor Law and the Factory Acts. [44]

Chadwick saw education as a depauperising influence sharing the assumption that universal education would in some unexplained way cure unemployment and render poor relief largely unnecessary. His enthusiasm was shared by several of the Poor Law Assistant Commissioners, who believed that pauperism as well as crime could be eradicated by early training. The architect of poor law education was James Phillips Kay (Kay-Shuttleworth as he called himself after his marriage). Son of a Rochdale cotton manufacturer, trained as a physician in Edinburgh, founder-member of the Manchester Statistical Society and a writer on social questions, he was recruited as Assistant Commissioner for Norfolk and Suffolk in 1835. He found little or no education for pauper children: some were sent to local schools, but always the cheapest and worst and there was no industrial training. Kay began by persuading more enlightened guardians to employ young trainee teachers. [45] He claimed in his autobiography, that this improved the workhouse schools up to a point where the Guardians would be persuaded to take more interest in pauper education and perhaps consent to the creation of school districts. [46]

---

[43] Selleck, R. J. W., *James Kay-Shuttleworth: Journey of an Outsider*, (Woburn Press), 1994, is now the standard biography of this seminal figure.
[44] Ibid, Paz, D. G., *The Politics of Working-class Education 1830-1850*, pp. 44-69.
[45] On the early development of workhouse schools see, Kay-Shuttleworth, James, *Four Periods of Public Education as reviewed in 1832-1839-1846-1862 in papers*, (Longman, Green, Longman and Roberts), 1862, pp. 287-292. See also, Ross, A. M., 'Kay-Shuttleworth and the training of teachers for pauper schools', *British Journal of Educational Studies*, Vol. 15, (1967), pp. 275-283.
[46] Bloomfield, B. C., (ed.), *The autobiography of Sir James Kay Shuttleworth*, (Institute of Education, University of London), 1964.

When Kay was appointed Secretary to the new Committee of Council on Education in 1839, he selected an establishment in Norwood for his experiment in pauper education. In three years, he turned it into a model for the district school movement and a nursery of pupil teachers for elementary schools. After 1842, however, Peel's government slowed down the plans for district schools as it was not prepared to coerce the Unions and the movement never achieved more than three Metropolitan School Districts and six small rural ones. [47] The failure of the district-school movement was partly compensated by the growth of separate schools in the more enlightened Unions. By 1857, 57 of these were listed. Some smaller workhouses had detached schools on the workhouse site. School standards greatly improved after 1846 with the beginnings of poor law school inspection and the decline in the use of untrained pauper teachers. Poor Law education never aspired to becoming a basis or a model for state elementary education. [48] It was intended for workhouse children but there were, in 1855, some 277,000 children in families on outdoor relief not provided with any education except in refuges or mission or 'ragged' schools. It was on too small a scale even to fulfil its own task, a criticism evident once the Local Government Board took responsibility for their operation in 1872. [49] Workhouse schools provided national coverage but the stigma attached to the workhouse meant that they could never provide the nationwide system of elementary education that by the 1860s many regarded as essential.

The factory school was not new in 1833. [50] Voluntary provision

---

[47] Hill, Florence Davenport, *Children of the state: the training of juvenile paupers*, (Macmillan and Co.), 1868, pp. 63-78, considers critically the development of District Schools.

[48] Richson, Charles, *Pauper education: its provisions and defects; with certain objections to its extension, considered in a letter to the Right Hon. Sir Geo. Grey, Bart., M.P.*, (Rivington), 1850, and Browne, Walter, 'Facts and Fallacies of Pauper Education', *Fraser's magazine for town and country*, Vol, 18, (Longmans, Green), 1878, pp. 197-207, considers the problems posed by pauper education while Chance, William, *Children under the poor law: their education, training and after-care, together with a criticism of the report of the departmental committee on metropolitan poor law schools*, 2 Vols. (S. Sonnenschein & Co.), 1897, provides later, more positive analysis.

[49] See, for example, Local Government Board, *Annual Report*, Vol. 1, (HMSO), 1872, pp. 224-235.

[50] See, for example, Sanderson, Michael, 'Education and the Factory in Industrial Lancashire, 1780-1840', *Economic History Review*, new series,

can be traced back to the 1780s and was pioneered by enlightened manufacturers such as Henry Ashton at Turton Mill, the Peel family and Robert Owen. The factory master was traditionally responsible for the education of his apprentices but progressive millowners were often alienated by the education clauses in factory legislation: W. R. Greg, an enthusiastic organiser of factory schools, became a leading opponent of the 1833 Factory Act. [51] After 1833, much of the enthusiasm for the voluntary provision of factory schooling was lost.[52] The Factory Act 1833 made millowners responsible for the education of children workers who were not their apprentices but lived with their own parents. 80 per cent of all pupils attending factory schools were concentrated in Lancashire, Cheshire, the West Riding and Monmouthshire, where literacy levels were low and there is little to suggest any marked improvement in factory districts in the aftermath of the legislation. Inspectors were authorised to enforce attendance but the Act did not require employers to provide education themselves, only to obtain a certificate of school attendance for the previous week. Millowners unable or unwilling to provide their own schools tried to obey the law by sending their children to the local day schools. These arrangements were often unsuccessful. Factory education became embroiled in the sectarian debate over Graham's Factory Bill of 1843 and the Act eventually passed in 1844 without its education clauses. [53] The Newcastle Commission was damning in its indictment of the inadequacies of factory education. Factory education might have improved, at least in small mills, if the millowners had co-operated in setting up shared schools. The failures of factory education, especially its involvement in sectarian disputes, certainly delayed the spread of elementary education. Disgusted Nonconformists turned to the voluntarist movement and Anglicans seemed to prefer the perpetuation of ignorance to giving up their own control of education. Faced with such attitudes, the government contribution to the development of education in the mid-century had to be made largely be stealth.

Government intervention in education was made more difficult as a result of sectarian conflict. Grants provided the first form of

---

Vol. 20, (2), (1967), pp. 266-279. Robson, A. H., *The Education of Children Engaged in Industry, 1833-1876*, (K. Paul, Trench, Trubner), 1931.

[51] See Rose, Mary B., *The Gregs of Quarry Bank Mill: The Rise and Decline of a Family Firm, 1750-1914*, (Cambridge University Press), 1986, pp. 56-58.

[52] Robson, A. H., *The Education of Children Engaged in Industry, 1833-1876*, (K. Paul, Trench, Trubner), 1931.

[53] Ibid, Paz, D. G., *The Politics of Working-class Education 1830-1850*, pp. 114-125, considers the 1843 Bill.

intervention but during the 1840s and 1850s other forms of central control over education were instituted largely through the work of Kay-Shuttleworth whose period as secretary of the Committee of Council for Education lasted between 1839 and 1849. He believed that the key to better standards was better-paid and trained teachers. He set out to change the monitorial system into a sound preliminary to a professional training and to attract teachers of the right class and calibre by raising salaries. [54] By the Minutes of 1846 selected pupils would be apprenticed at the age of 13 to their teachers and would receive a grant of £10 increased annually to £20 when they were 18. [55] They were taught by the master for 90 minutes a day and had to pass the annual Inspector's examination. [56] They were to assist the master in teaching and he would train them in class management and routine duties and would be paid according to their level of success in the examinations. This system was not new. Kay-Shuttleworth had used it at Norwood. Although the first pupil-teachers came from pauper schools, he intended that the bulk of them should form a social link between the children of labourers in elementary schools and the school managers, who were clergy or gentry. They would therefore be mostly from the upper-working and lower-middle-classes. The apex of this ladder of recruitment and training was formed by the teacher training colleges. In 1839, there were four training colleges with model schools in the United Kingdom that took students through very inadequate courses of six weeks to three or four months. Beginning with the Battersea Training College in 1840, [57] by 1858 there were thirty-four colleges partly financed by the Education Department through Queen's Scholarships. [58]

The Minutes of 1846 may have led to the trained elementary

---

[54] Ross, A. M., 'Kay-Shuttleworth and the training of teachers for pauper schools', *British Journal of Educational Studies*, Vol. 15, (1967), pp. 275-283.

[55] These were the minutes of the Committee of Council on Education minutes of August and December 1846. See, Kay-Shuttleworth, James, *Public Education: as affected by the Minutes of the Committee of Privy Council from 1846 to 1852; with suggestions as to future policy*, (Longman, Brown, Green, and Longmans), 1853, pp. 54-112.

[56] Dunford, J. E., *Her Majesty's Inspectorate of Schools in England and Wales, 1860-1870*, (Museum of the History of Education, University of Leeds), 1980.

[57] For Kay-Shuttleworth's take on the Battersea Training College, see, ibid, Kay-Shuttleworth, James, *Four Periods of Public Education as reviewed in 1832-1839-1846-1862 in papers*, pp. 294-431.

[58] Dent, H. C., *The training of teachers in England and Wales, 1800-1975*, (Routledge), 1977.

teacher but did it really improve the standard of teaching?[59] To some degree any response to this question is subjective. Much school teaching was mechanical, overloaded with 'facts' for memorisation. The Teacher Training Colleges did provide a little teaching material, method and possible much-needed self-confidence. They were, however, severely criticised by the Newcastle Commission for their long hours, vast syllabuses, addiction to textbooks and the superficial nature of many of their courses. The main cause of poor teaching in elementary schools was generally considered to be the low wages of teachers. The Minutes attempted to solve the problem by state grants but the basic variations and inequities were left untouched. Salaries varied from area to area and school to school depending on endowments, contributions and school fees. By 1855, the average annual pay of a certificated schoolteacher was assessed at £90. Higher pay would have removed elementary teachers too far from the class of their pupils and weakened the sympathy and understanding supposed to be felt between them. The reality was often different. Elementary teachers were educated above their station and in the 1850s began to demand promotion of the Inspectorate, to leave the schools for better jobs or to go into the church

The growth of grants to elementary schools increased dramatically from the original £20,000 of 1833 to £724,000 by 1860. From 1856, the Committee of Council on Education had a Vice-President to represent it in parliament. Yet the 1850s were considered a period of comparative educational stagnation. This was partly because all reformers (except the voluntarists) were convinced that a national school system could not be completed without support from the rates. In addition, continuing sectarian bitterness defeated all attempts to secure rate support: bills in 1850, 1852, 1853 and 1862 all failed as did the recommendation of the Newcastle Commission in 1861. The continuation of central grants ensured the survival and increase of the Inspectorate; from 2 in 1840 they had become 23 with 2 Assistant Inspectors in 1852, 36 with 25 Assistants in 1861 and 62 with 14 Assistants in 1864. Grants and inspectors came together with the introduction of the payment by results principle in the reconstruction of the government grant in the Revised Code of 1862-1863.[60] The bulk of a school's grant, roughly half its income, was to

---

[59] Ibid, Kay-Shuttleworth, James, *Four Periods of Public Education as reviewed in 1832-1839-1846-1862 in papers*, pp. 437-551, provides an explanation of the Minutes of 1846.

[60] Mason, Donald, 'Peelite opinion and the genesis of payment by results: the true story of the Newcastle Commission', *History of Education*, Vol. 17, (1988), 269-281, and Marcham, A. J., 'The revised Code of Education,

be dependent upon satisfactory performance by each child over seven in examinations conducted by HMIs. It was unwelcome to those who thought that government should be doing more but was praised by those who thought expenditure was mushrooming out of control and who doubted that the grants were giving value for money. Grant aid to education fell almost by a quarter and expenditure in 1861 was not reached again until 1869. In effect, payment by results was a piece-rate system, putting teachers in the position of factory operatives.

Kay-Shuttleworth had, through the central government department, established an inspectorate and a system of training teachers. Under his successor Ralph Lingen (1849-1869) the work of the Education Department, as it became in 1856, steadily expanded but on more formal and bureaucratised lines. [61] The age of creative innovation was over and the department's primary goal was to manage the system as efficiently and economically as possible. Lingen saw his job as being to:

...stem the growth of a system of subsidies and to control the expansionist tendencies of inspectorate and educational public. [62]

A Royal Commission on Elementary Education, chaired by the Duke of Newcastle was appointed in 1858 and reported in 1861. [63] In general, it considered that the system of state aid had worked well, but argued that the objectives had been set too high for the majority of children who attended the schools. It was desirable that results should be tested to ensure that schools were providing value for money, a recommendation adopted by Robert Lowe, the minister who spoke for the Education Department in the House of Commons,

---

1862: reinterpretations and misinterpretations', *History of Education*, Vol. 10, (1981), pp. 81-99.

[61] Bishop, A. S., 'Ralph Lingen, Secretary to the Education Department, 1849-76', *British Journal of Educational Studies*, Vol. 16, (1968), pp. 138-163.

[62] Cit, Johnson, Richard, 'Administrators in education before 1870: patronage, social position and role', in Sutherland, Gillian, (ed.), *Studies in the growth of Nineteenth-century Government*, (Routledge), 1972, p. 135.

[63] *Report of the Commissioners appointed to inquire into the state of popular education in England; Reports of assistant commissioners etc.; Correspondence etc.* Parliamentary papers, [2794-I] H.C. (1861), Vol. XXI, pt. 1, 1; Parliamentary papers, [2794-II-VI] H.C. (1861), Vol. XXI, pt. I-VI; Parliamentary papers, H.C. 231 (1861), Vol. XLVIII, 295; Parliamentary papers, H.C. 354 (1861), Vol. XLVIII, 307; Parliamentary papers, H.C. 410 (1861), Vol. XLVIII, 341; Parliamentary papers, H.C. 325 (1861) and Vol. XLVIII, 305.

to establish the Revised Code in 1862 linking annual grants to pupil results. It also recommended involving local as well as central government in the provision of schools, allowing local government agencies to offer rate support to supplement government grants and suggested that this rate support should be dependent on the school's results, in effect a series of incentive payments.

The Revised Code established a system where the payment of government grant to a school depended on two things: a basic grant was paid for any child who attended a fixed number of times in the year; further grants were paid for any child, qualified by attendance, who passed examinations in any of the 3Rs. Pupils were tested in a higher 'standard' each year using a narrowly defined syllabus laid down by the Education Department for each standard. Regulations were later added allowing supplementary grants to be paid if senior pupils were taught various subjects but this was considered subordinate to the school's main work of teaching the basics. The emphasis on 'payment by results' was on finding the cheapest possible way of teaching literacy and numeracy to the children of the working-classes.[64]

Exactly what the Revised Code represented and what its impact was on elementary education disputed.[65] The main objective of the Kay-Shuttleworth system had been to buy efficiency by offering managers grants to stimulate school building and buy materials and equipment and paying teachers to become better qualified. The argument in 1861 was not whether public money should be used to promote efficiency but what was the most cost-effective way in which it could be used. The weakness of this system was that it lacked sanctions. The grant was simply an inducement for managers and

---

[64] *Minute...confirming the Alterations of the Revised Code of Regulations*, (George Edward Eyre and William Spottiswoode), 1862, prints the Regulations. Sylvester, David W., *Robert Lowe and Education*, (Cambridge University Press), 1974, pp. 40-116, considers the genesis, purpose and effects of the Revised Code.

[65] 'Payment by results' proved highly divisive issue; see for example, 'Popular Education—The New Code', *London Quarterly Review*, Vol. CCXXI, (1862), pp. 38-59, Menet, John, *The Revised Code: A Letter to a Friend, suggested by the pamphlets of the Rev. C. J. Vaughan, D.D., Vicar of Doncaster, and the Rev. J. Fraser, Rector of Upton*, (Rivingtons), 1862, and Kay-Shuttleworth, James, *Memorandum on Popular Education*, (Ridgway), 1868. See also, Rapple, Brendan A., 'A Victorian experiment in economic efficiency in education', *Economics of Education Review*, Vol. 11, (4), (1992), pp. 301-316, and Fletcher, Ladden, 'A Further Comment on Recent Interpretations of the Revised Code, 1862', *History of Education*, Vol. 10, (1), pp. 21-31.

teachers to improve efficiency but although school inspectors could check that schools were complying with the conditions of the grant, they had no powers of enforcement since the conditions of grant had no statutory basis. The Revised Code, by contrast, linked grants to performance in ways that inspectors were expected to enforce. The system may have improved regularity in attendance and there may also have been some improvement in the teaching of the 3Rs. However, few educational measures have been so comprehensively damned by contemporaries and most historians and it is difficult to find any grounds for dissenting from this view. The system lasted three decades and generated intense contemporary controversy including some of the bitterest discussion of education by outspoken critics such as Matthew Arnold and Sir James Kay-Shuttleworth. [66] By focusing on a satisfactory number of attendance and competence in the 3Rs in the annual inspection and introducing income sanctions for failing to reach satisfactory standards, the Revised Code meant that poor schools were derived of the means of improving. From being often friendly critics, school inspectors were now regarded as hostile judges of whether schools were giving 'value for money' effectively reducing teachers' salaries for every failure they identified. The examination came to be seen both as a test of individual achievement and as a guide to institutional standards.

The almost universal opposition to the new system by contemporary educationalists highlighted the problem of public elementary education. [67] This was reinforced by the failure of payment by results to achieve either efficiency or cheapness. The reduction in grants proved temporary and the cost to taxpayers was soon rising again. Attendance remained erratic, a situation made worse by the failure of the Code to introduce an enforcement agency to compel children to come to school, and made no impression on the large number of children who never attended school. As late as

---

[66] On Arnold and the Revised Code, see, Super, R. H., (ed.), *The Complete Prose Works of Matthew Arnold, Volume 2: Democratic Education*, (University of Michigan Press), 1962, pp. 212-251, Arnold, Matthew, *Reports on Elementary Schools, 1852-1882*, (Eyre and Spottiswoode), 1910, Smith, Peter, and Summerfield, Geoffrey, (eds.), *Matthew Arnold and the Education of the New Order: A selection of Arnold's writings in education*, (Cambridge University Press), 1979, and Connell, W. F., *The Educational Thought and Influence of Matthew Arnold*, (Routledge), 1950, pp. 203-242.
[67] Ellis, P. David, 'The Effects of the Revised Code of Education in the West Riding of Yorkshire', *Journal of Educational Administration and History*, Vol. 19, (1987), pp. 1-18, provides a valuable local study suggesting that, contrary to established belief, teachers and school managers generally accepted the Code's reforms, though with some reservations.

1873, only 15 per cent of children passed the annual examination in the standard corresponding to their age; 57 per cent were a year behind and 27 per cent two years. Kay-Shuttleworth summed up contemporary views in 1868:

> The Revised Code has constructed nothing; it has only pulled down. It had not simplified the administration...It has generally discouraged all instruction above the elements and failed in teaching them...It has not succeeded in being efficient, but it is not even cheap; for it wastes the public money without producing the results which were declared to be its main objective. [68]

It seems probable that public opinion was prepared for substantial state intervention in 1870 because the Revised Code had demonstrated the complete inability of voluntary provision to solve either the problem of attendance or standards. [69]

Until the late 1850s, much of the schooling of the working-classes was still informal or semi-formal. Efforts to bring government resources to bear had so far been hampered by the 'religious problem' and it took another twenty years to cut through this knot. Elementary education in the 1860s entered a period of some regression. The Newcastle Commission set low intellectual targets for the education of the poor and this can be compared with the hardening of Poor Law attitudes in the 1870s. [70] A national system of elementary education had to await the legislation of 1870 and 1880.

What was a 'middle-class' education?

Before 1850, no one seriously argued the need for the state to provide schools for middle- and upper-class children largely because it was thought the free market was functioning effectively. Certainly it seems there was considerable activity and formal schooling appears to have been becoming the norm for boys. This sense of activity had to remain an impressionistic one and is difficult to quantify. [71] In the

---

[68] Kay-Shuttleworth, James P., *Memorandum on Popular Education*, (Woburn Press), 1868, p. 30.
[69] Wardle, David, *English Popular Education, 1780-1970*, (Cambridge University Press), pp. 68-70.
[70] Several areas of social administration went through periods of administrative regression in the third quarter of the nineteenth century: education in the 1860s and the poor law and public health in the 1870s.
[71] For this area of education see Bamford, T. W., *The Rise of the Public Schools*, (Nelson), 1967, and Allsobrook, David, *Schools for the shire: The reform of middle-class education in mid-Victorian England*, (Manchester University Press), 1986.

early-nineteenth century, families who aimed to raise their sons as gentlemen and who could afford to do so employed tutors to educate their children at home. Home education was thought to be more conducive to virtue than in public schools with their low standards of morality and harsh corporal discipline. Rising urban populations and living standards brought an increase in middle-class families able to afford modest fees for private day schooling in their home towns. It was these demands that were to revitalise the grammar schools and subsequently the public boarding schools.

Grammar schools responded strongly to demands for middle-class education. Endowed often in the sixteenth century to provide free education for the poor, it was unclear what 'grammar school' were by 1800. [72] Many taught elementary subjects sometimes with classics, took all social classes, included girls and acted simply as the local village or parochial school. The first half of the nineteenth century saw a process of change in three areas. Grammar schools began to change their curriculum, often including commercial subjects alongside the classics. The new curriculum enabled the schools to charge fees. There was a decisive shift to a fee-paying middle-class clientele and away from the poorer former free pupils. [73] The move away from the original charitable intentions of the founders of grammar schools led to several disputes between trustees, who wanted to charge fees, and schoolmasters who did not. The most famous case was between the trustees and schoolmaster at Leeds Grammar School and led to a ten-year case in the Court of Chancery that resulted in Lord Eldon's judgement in 1805 that grammar schools could not use their endowments to teach non-classical subjects free of charge. The Grammar Schools Act 1840 made it lawful to apply the income of grammar schools to purposes other than the teaching of classical languages, but this change still required the consent of the schoolmaster. Some schools pressed further along the road and turned themselves into boarding schools, Victorian public schools in embryo. [74]

In the mid-nineteenth century, three factors revitalised those grammar schools that had already made the change and those that had

---

[72] Timpson, Richard S., *Classics or charity?: the dilemma of the 18th century grammar school*, (Manchester University Press), 1971.

[73] Edwards, Edward, *An inquiry into the revenues and abuses of the free grammar school at Brentwood*, (C. Roworth), 1823, demonstrates the problems of turning a free school into a fee-paying one.

[74] Carlisle, Nicholas, *A concise description of the endowed grammar schools in England and Wales*, 2 Vols. (Baldwin, Cradock and Joy), 1818, provides a detailed description of the development and state of grammar schools.

not. A new breed of headmaster seemed to appear at this time, of high Victorian moral purpose and strength of personality. Such men often took over ailing or mediocre grammar schools and made them centres of academic excellence: for instance, Reverend John William Caldicott at Bristol (1860), Augustus Jessop at Norwich (1859), Reverend John Mitchinson at King's School, Canterbury (1859) and Frederick Walker at Manchester (1859). [75] The schools were stimulated by the creation of a system of 'middle-class' examinations from the 1850s. T. D. Acland in Exeter started these as a private venture in 1856 but so great was demand that their administration was taken over by Oxford and Cambridge in 1858 and they became known as the Local examinations. For middle-class boys not intending to go to university, they were a valuable school-leaving qualification and gave grammar schools something to aim for, and a perception of how they measured up to a common standard. The Higher Locals began at Cambridge in 1868 and at Oxford in 1877. In 1873, the Oxford and Cambridge Schools Examining Board was established.

The third factor was the Taunton Commission that investigated some 800 endowed schools between 1864 and 1867. [76] Its investigations revealed the poor provision of secondary education, its uneven distribution and the misuse of endowments. It also showed that there were only thirteen secondary schools for girls in the country. It addressed the problem of middle-class parents who could not afford to send their children to public schools but who wanted a local grammar school offering a curriculum that would provide entry to universities or to the professions for their sons. The Commissioners recommended the establishment of a national system of secondary education based on existing endowed schools. This solution led to the abolition of free education in grammar schools excluding free boys from the lower middle-class, artisan and tradesman classes who had no university or professional ambitions and enable the curriculum to be determined by the market demand of fee-payers. The Endowed

---

[75] Hill, C. P., *The History of Bristol Grammar School*, (Pitman), 1951, pp. 78-107, Saunders, H. W., *A History of Norwich Grammar* School, (Jarrold and Sons Ltd.), 1932, Edward, David L., *A History of the King's School, Canterbury*, (Faber and Faber), 1957, Mumford, A. A., *The Manchester Grammar School, 1515-1915; A Regional Study of the Advancement of Learning in Manchester Since the Reformation*, (Longman, Green and Co.), 1919.

[76] *Schools Inquiry Commission: report of the commissioners plus Minutes of evidence etc.,* Parliamentary papers, [3966] H.C. (1867-8), Vol. XXVIII, pt. 1, 1; Parliamentary papers, [3966-I to XX] H.C. (1867-8) and Vol. XXVIII, pts. II to XVII.

Schools Act 1869 established three Commissioners who, by making schemes and regulations for some 3,000 endowments, created throughout the country the middle-class fee-paying academic grammar school. [77] Their defect was in failing to provide for the tradesman-artisan class who had to resort to the new Board Schools created after 1870.

Public schools differed from grammar schools because they catered for the upper and upper-middle-classes and were boarding establishments. [78] The body of Victorian public schools were made up of various groups. There were the ancient nine schools investigated by the Clarendon Commission in the 1860s (Eton, Winchester, Harrow, Charterhouse, Rugby, Westminster, Merchant Taylors', St. Paul's and Shrewsbury). To these were added certain grammar schools that had changed their status like Sedburgh and Giggleswick. [79] There were also waves of new foundations: nine in the 1840s including Rossall, Marlborough and Cheltenham and ten in the 1860s including Clifton and Malvern. Most were run as commercial ventures but many had wider purposes: schools at Lancing and Hurstpierpoint promoted high Anglicanism while those at Cranleigh and Framlingham stressed science and agriculture for farmers' sons. The schools achieved cohesion informally by playing inter-school games and formally by membership of the Headmasters' Conference that met first in 1869 initially comprising the non-

---

[77] Balls, F. E., 'The Endowed Schools Act, 1869, and the development of the English grammar schools in the 19th century', *Durham Research Review*, Vol. 19, (1967), pp. 207-218, Vol. 20, (1968), pp. 219-229, and Goldman, Lawrence, 'The defection of the middle class: The Endowed Schools Act, the Liberal Party, and the 1874 election', in Ghosh, Peter, and Goldman, Lawrence, (eds.), *Politics and culture in Victorian Britain: essays in memory of Colin Matthew*, (Oxford University Press), 2006, pp. 118-135.
[78] Chandos, John, *Boys together: English public schools, 1800-1864*, (Hutchinson), 1984, Huggins, M. J. W., and Rees, A. D. J., *The making of an English public school*, (Hiroona), 1982, and Simon, Brian, and Bradley, Ian C., (eds.), *The Victorian public school: studies in the development of an educational institution: a symposium*, (Gill and Macmillan), 1975.
[79] Card, Tim, *Eton established: a history from 1440 to 1860*, (John Murray), 2001, Tyerman, Christopher, *A history of Harrow School, 1324-1991*, (Oxford University Press), 2000, Quick, Anthony, *Charterhouse: a history of the school*, (James & James), 1991, Bettinson, G. H., *Rugby School*, (printed for the author and publisher by Harold Saunders), 1929, Carleton, J. D., *Westminster School: a history*, (Country life, Ltd.), 1934, 2nd edition, (R. Hart-Davis), 1965, Draper, Frederick W. M., *Four centuries of Merchant Taylors' school, 1561-1961*, (Oxford University Press), 1962, Oldham, J. B., *A history of Shrewsbury School, 1552-1952*, (Oxford University Press), 1952.

Clarendon public schools.

Public schools also underwent a process of changing vitality after 1830. Increasing numbers of middle-class children survived infancy and they could no longer conveniently be taught at home. They had to be sent away to school. Improvements in transport facilities, fast road-coaches and then railways, made possible a national market in education. Newly founded schools or old town grammar schools could set out to attract a regional or even national catchment of clients who would reside as boarders. The growing empire meant that many more families lived abroad but for cultural and climatic reasons they preferred their children to be educated in England in institutions that provided a home environment. Public schools were sought by newly prospering social groups who wished to confirm their status by assimilation with existing landed and professional elites. Thomas Arnold's reforms at Rugby and the spread of his masters into other schools raised the moral tone of public schools making them attractive to those who cared for their children's nurture and who had shunned the violence and neglect of welfare that characterised many public schools before 1830.

Important changes took place in the content of education in public schools. Science was accepted into the curriculum, especially in the 1860s. Various factors changed this situation: the introduction of science degrees in the 1850s; army reforms of the 1850s that placed an emphasis on competitive examining including two papers in science helped by the increase in the numbers of graduate science masters; and a new generation of headmasters with particular interests in science: for instance, H. M. Butler and F. W. Farrer at Harrow and Frederick Temple at Rugby. Almost as important as change in the formal curriculum was a change in the value systems of the public schools. Thomas Arnold raised the tone of the schools from the 1820s with 'godliness and good learning' with the aim of producing the Christian Gentleman. [80] From the 1850s, these ideals came to be replaced by a more secular and robust emphasis on manliness and character training. 'Muscular Christianity ', as advocated by Thomas Hughes and Charles Kingsley, equated virile good health with Christian values and in the 1860s was expressed in a concern for organised games, athleticism and militarism. [81] Arnold had effected a

---

[80] Copley, Terence, *Black Tom: Arnold of Rugby: the myth and the man*, (Continuum), 2002.
[81] Many schools began cadet corps in the 1860s, notably Eton, Winchester, Harrow and Rugby. See, Money, Tony, *Manly and muscular diversions: public schools and the nineteenth-century sporting revival*, (Duckworth), 1997, and Neddam, Fabrice, 'Constructing masculinities under Thomas

change in the ethos of public schools and the changes of the 1860s matched them with secular needs outside.

These developments made public schools highly attractive to social groups of parents somewhat below the traditional clientele and there was a marked change in the social intake of such schools after 1850. In the first half of the century, the social class of parents at eight leading public schools showed that the gentry provided 38.1 per cent of boys, titled persons 12.2 per cent, clergy 12.0 per cent and professional parents 5.2 per cent. There was an expected and large predominance of the rural elites of gentry, titled and clerical families. From the 1850s, there is clear evidence of the rise of business families beginning to send their sons to Winchester and as more businessmen's sons went to these schools so in turn more public school boys went into careers in business and industry. At Winchester this rose from 7.2 per cent of boys born in the 1820s to 17.6 per cent of those born in the 1850s. These upward trends in businessmen sending their sons to public school and in public schoolboys entering business were to be of great importance. There was a link between class, public school, education and business leadership in the larger companies from the 1860s. An extended public school network gradually replaced the older Nonconformistnetwork that had characterised the early industrial entrepreneurs.

The strong expansion of middle-class education both in grammar and public schools after 1830 was a response to the demands for education from parents. The Royal Commission under Lord Clarendon, established in 1859, looked at the nine 'ancient institutions' that still focussed on the classics and which found themselves facing stiff competition from newer and more progressive institutions. Clarendon was concerned that these newer schools were giving the middle-classes a better education that the upper-classes did not have and that this was socially dangerous. The problem of the decaying grammar schools led the government to concede another Royal Commission in 1864, under Lord Taunton, to look at all schools not looked at by either Clarendon or Newcastle. [82] The two Commissions took as a given the stratification of schooling for the

---

Arnold of Rugby (1828-1842): gender, educational policy and school life in an early-Victorian public school', *Gender & Education*, Vol. 16, (2004), pp. 303-326.

[82] Anon. *Report from the Select Committee of the House of Lords on the Public Schools Bill [H.L.]*, Parliamentary papers, H.C. 481 (1865), Vol. X, 263, and Shrosbree, Colin, *Public schools and private education: the Clarendon Commission, 1861-1864, and the Public Schools Acts*, (Manchester University Press), 1988, pp. 73-134.

middle-classes as it had developed in the first half of the century and formalised it into a hierarchy. At the top were the 'first grade schools' modelled on Eton and its eight correspondents, mostly boarding, with a classical education, sending boys to universities. Next came the 'second grade schools', mostly day, teaching a Latin but no Greek, whose boys would leave at sixteen. Finally there were 'third grade schools', all day, teaching a little Latin, sending boys into employment at fourteen. The three grades were conceived as parallel, separate tracks, only the common study of Latin allowing mobility via scholarships from one track to another for the very bright. The Public Schools Act of 1868 and the Endowed Schools Act the following year greatly helped the process.

The three-grade division proved over elaborate. However, an increasingly clear distinction emerged between schools for gentlemen and schools for those who aimed at respectability not gentility. The problem was not the grading but the opportunities open to the educated. Too many public schoolboys were being produced between 1851 and 1871 when there were fewer opportunities in the Church, law and medicine and young men with middle-class aspirations also outstripped the availability of careers. The fastest growing occupations lay in lower middle-class employment such as clerks and shop assistants to which ex-public schoolboys would be unlikely to be attracted. The Empire provided a safety valve as products of these new schools sought in colonial lifestyles a status they would have been denied at home.

How did the universities develop?

What was the function of the university? The debate on the role of universities in society had several dimensions. There was an important argument about research as a function of the university. Advocates of research in the 1860s such as Mark Pattison and Henry Halford Vaughan were influenced by German universities and accepted the discovery of new knowledge as part of their obligations.[83] They wished to move Oxford and Cambridge away from being merely advanced public schools towards a more liberal education with more

---

[83] See, Pattison, Mark, *Suggestions on academical organisation with especial reference to Oxford*, (Edmonston and Douglas), 1868, Sparrow, John, *Mark Pattison and the Idea of a University*, (Cambridge University Press), 1967, 2008, Jones, H. Stuart, *Intellect and character in Victorian England: Mark Pattison and the invention of the don*, (Cambridge University Press), 2007, Bill, E. G. W., *University reform in nineteenth-century Oxford: a study of Henry Halford Vaughan, 1811-1885*, (Oxford University Press), 1973

money on research on the sciences, history and archaeology. This viewpoint inevitably involved a clash with the established college position and the financial provision of scholarships and fellowships outside the classics and mathematics brought conflict with the curricular conservatism in college-based anti-research teaching. Until some changes were made to the autonomy of the colleges, there could be no change in teaching and the colleges would continue to exert a stranglehold not just over the universities but also the schools that aimed to send their boys to Oxford or Cambridge.

These were not glorious years for the 'ancient' universities. Cambridge [84] and Oxford [85] reposed in a social and curricular inertia that limited their value to society. [86] Their intake was socially remarkably stable and narrow: between 1752 and 1886, 51 per cent of Oxford students and 58 per cent of those at Cambridge came from two social groups, the gentry and the clergy. The future careers were even narrower: 64 per cent of Oxford and 54 per cent of Cambridge men went into the Church. The student body was limited by its connection with the Church of England and the requirement at both universities that graduates should subscribe to the Anglican Thirty-Nine Articles and excluded Nonconformists. They were thus isolated from the new potential clientele of Nonconformistbusiness families enriched by industrialisation. High costs, a course could cost over £300 per year also limited the social composition of courses. Oxford became socially exclusive in the second quarter of the nineteenth century. As a result, many people needed scholarships, the bulk of which were in classics and mathematics. This had an impact of the school curriculum and led to a focus on and perpetuation of classical educationin grammar and public schools. The provision of fellowships also had a similar effect. Most fellowships were tied to classics at Oxford and mathematics at Cambridge. In this way the whole financial scholarship-fellowship system locked the older subjects into the ancient universities.

---

[84] Searby, Peter, *A history of the University of Cambridge: Vol. 3: 1750-1870*, (Cambridge University Press), 1997, and Brooke, C. N. L., *A history of the university of Cambridge: Vol. 4: 1870-1990*, (Cambridge University Press), 1992.

[85] Brock, M. G., and Curthoys, Mark C., (eds.), *The history of the University of Oxford, Vol. 6: Nineteenth-century Oxford, part 1*, (Oxford University Press), 1997, and *The history of the University of Oxford, Vol. 7: Nineteenth-century Oxford, part 2*, (Oxford University Press), 2000.

[86] Anderson, R. D., *Universities and Elites in Britain since 1800*, (Macmillan), 1992, (Cambridge University Press), 1995, is a very useful, short summary of current research on the role of universities in nineteenth century society.

This was also tied into the power struggle within the institutions between the university and the colleges. At Oxford and Cambridge the colleges were powerful and wealthy and the universities relatively weak as financial and administrative entities. This suited colleges that ran like private companies. They were aware the classics and mathematics were very cheap subjects to teach and did not entail research or expensive equipment or even rapidly growing libraries. The colleges were not only conservative about new subjects for financial reasons, they also feared a tilting of the balance of power in favour of the universities. More university power as, for instance, in the building of common science laboratories, meant less college autonomy. Curriculum conservatism was rooted in a defence of a private financial system and resistance to the growth of centralised power in the university.

Curriculum conservatism was defended as a positive virtue in a lively debate about 'liberal education' in relation to universities. This was an important argument against those who attacked the classics as a patently useless form of study on crudely utilitarian grounds. This argument had two basic propositions. There is a distinction between ends and means. Some activities and qualities are ends in themselves and cannot be justified by reference to some ends beyond themselves. This is the essence of 'education for its own sake'. As well as being 'an end in itself', the study of the classics fitted a man for no particular occupation thereby fitting him for all. This was a belief that was to become very influential in the 1850s when the general intellectual training given by classics was regarded as the most suitable for civil service recruitment through public examinations. The culmination of the old liberal education ideal was expressed by John Henry Newman in his *Discourses on University Education* that he gave in Dublin in 1852. [87] Liberal education made the gentlemen and was 'the especial characteristic or property of a University and of a gentleman'. The end result of such education was 'a cultivated intellect, a delicate taste, a candid equitable dispassionate mind'. [88] The purpose was not vocational training but the general development of the intellect and of moral and social qualities for their own sake. This expressed what the ancient universities thought about themselves and what many others

---

[87] Newman, J. H., *Discourses on the scope and nature of university education: addressed to the Catholics of Dublin*, (James Duffy), 1852.

[88] Newman, J. H., *The idea of a university: defined and illustrated: I, in nine discourses delivered to the Catholics of Dublin: II, in occasional lectures and essays addressed to the members of the Catholic University*, (Longman), 1891, p. 110

conceived the purpose of a university education to be. [89]

From 1850, the ancient universities began a limited reform. Following Royal Commissions for both universities in 1852, an Act for Oxford in 1854 and for Cambridge two years later enabled Nonconformists both to matriculate and to graduate. This resolved one problem but created another for graduated Nonconformists were still barred from becoming fellows of colleges throughout the 1860s and this restriction was not finally removed until the Universities' Religious Tests Act 1871, that also ended the need for fellows to be ordained clergymen. There was also some curricular innovation. In 1848, Cambridge established new tripos in Natural Sciences and in Moral Sciences that included history and law. In Oxford two years later, the Schools of Law and Modern History and of Natural Sciences were established. Since both universities now claimed to teach science to degree level they both built laboratories: the Oxford Museum in 1855 and the New Museum at Cambridge in 1865. The watershed for Oxford and Cambridge came after 1870 with the Cleveland Commission of 1873 leading to the Act of 1877 and the revision of the statutes of colleges. The latter were obliged to release some of their funds for the creation of scientific professorships and university institutions. Only then, with this rebalancing of power between colleges and the universities was it possible to create an Oxford and Cambridge more oriented to research in science and scholarship, professional training, a widening curriculum and a strong professoriate.

Oxford and Cambridge had considerable defects that were only beginning to be resolved in the 1850s and 1860s but there was no effective civic university movement that could serve as an alternative. The Church of England had founded Durham University in 1832 but it became largely training college for clergy with 90 per cent of its students going into Holy Orders. [90] By trying to ape Oxford without having the latter's resources, it had very little success either with poor students or in the eyes of local industrialists who rejected it in favour of Newcastle as a centre of urgently needed mining education. Owens College, Manchester, founded in 1851 with £100,000 left by John Owen, a local textile manufacturer, fared little better. The intention was not to establish a technological university to serve industry but a college to give 'instruction in the branches of learning and science taught in the English universities'. It was to be the Oxford of the

---

[89] Harvie, Christopher, *The lights of liberalism: university liberals and the challenge of democracy, 1860-86*, (Allen Lane), 1976.
[90] Watson, Nigel, *The Durham Difference: The story of Durham University*, (James & James), 2007.

north. The Manchester business classes were unimpressed and it was not until the 1870s when it acquired a new sense of purpose in service to industry that it began to take its place in the forefront of the civic universities movement. [91]

A more dynamic root of the future civic universities lay in the emergence of provincial medical schools. The Apothecaries' Act 1815 made it illegal to practise as an apothecary unless licensed by the Society of Apothecaries. This stimulated the creation of medical schools to prepare students for the examinations and, from 1831, those of the Royal College of Surgeons. Schools were founded in Manchester (1825), Sheffield (1827), Birmingham (1828), Bristol (1828), Leeds (1830), Liverpool (1834) and Newcastle (1834). Both Durham and Owens before 1870 were abortive provincial initiatives stifled by the ancient universities and channelled into the dead end of being deferential and unsuccessful imitations rather than challenging alternatives. The medical schools, by contrast, provided one of the strands out of which civic universities were to emerge after 1870.

The origins of the University of London were rooted in an open antipathy to the ancient universities and not with any concern to replicate them. [92] Founded in 1828, it differed from existing institutions in three respects: it was free of religious tests and open to Nonconformists and unbelievers; it was to be cheaper than the ancient universities to cater for 'middling rich people'; and finally, there was a strong emphasis on professional training in the medical, legal, engineering and economic studies neglected at Oxford and Cambridge. It was to be useful and vocational. The Church of England did not regard the creation of the new University College in 'Godless Gower Street' with kindness and established their own rival King's College in 1828 as an exclusively Anglican institution but also with a focus on vocational training. From 1836, the University of London became the body managing examinations and degrees for its now constituent colleges, University and King's. From 1858, it became the examining body dealing not only with London institutions but providing external examinations for all comers.

The chief criticism levelled at universities in this period was that their neglect of science meant they contributed little to the needs of industrialisation. Oxford and Cambridge produced clergy, gentlemen and, after 1850, civil servants. They did not appeal to the commercial

---

[91] Fiddes, Edward, *Chapters in the History of Owens College and of Manchester University, 1851-1914*, (Manchester University Press), 1937.
[92] Harte, N. B., and North, John, *The world of University College, London, 1828-1990*, (London University Press), 1991, and Harte, N. B., *The University of London, 1836-1986: an illustrated history*, (Athlone), 1986.

classes or to the new professions; nor did Durham and Manchester before 1870. Only the London colleges thrived on a close linkage with the new business and professional classes. Nor did the university sector keep up with rising population and during the decade between 1855 and 1865 only one in 77,000 went to university. Higher education was still accessible to only a small minority.

Was technical education successful?

In the 1820s, there was an attempt to create a scientific culture and technical education for the working-classes.[93] George Birkbeck, a Glasgow doctor who had settled in London, was instrumental with Benthamite radicals in establishing the London Mechanics' Institute in 1823. His aim was to provide tuition in physics and chemistry for artisans and mechanics and became the model for a provincial movement. By 1826, there were 100 mechanics' institutes, by 1841 over 300 and had more than doubled to 700 by 1851.[94] In some cities, initially at least, they tried to serve a serious educative and scientific purpose. In Leeds, for example, local businessmen were strongly in favour of scientific education.[95] The movement, however, faced significant problems that led to its initial aims being diluted. Birkbeck questioned whether literacy levels in England were high enough to support further education of some rigour. His doubts were well founded and, as a result, many of the institutes took different paths in response to various other social pressures and local needs. Many concentrated on basic education in reading and writing while others became social clubs foreshadowing the working men's club

---

[93] Cronin, Bernard P., *Technology, industrial conflict, and the development of technical education in 19th century England*, (Ashgate), 2001, Summerfield, Penny, and Evans, E. J., (eds.), *Technical education and the state since 1850: historical and contemporary perspectives*, (Manchester University Press), 1990, and Roderick, G. W., and Stephens, M. D., (eds.), *Scientific and technical education in 19th century England: a symposium*, (David & Charles), 1972.

[94] Hudson, J. W., *The History of Adult Education*, (Longman, Brown, Green & Longmans), 1851, pp. 222-236, and Cliffe-Leslie, T. E., *An Inquiry into the Progress and Present Conditions of Mechanics' Institutes*, (Hodges and Smith), 1852, provide details of numbers and location of Institutes. For a useful case-study see, Tylecote, M. P., *The Mechanics' Institutes of Lancashire and Yorkshire before 1851*, (Manchester University Press), 1957.

[95] Garner, A. D., and Jenkins, E. W., 'The English Mechanics' Institutes: The case of Leeds 1824-42', *History of Education*, Vol. 12, (1), (1984), pp. 139-152.

movement of the 1860s while others became centres of radical political activity. [96]

Most institutes forgot their origins and were taken over by the middle-classes either as cultural centres for themselves or as institutions in which an attempt could be made to persuade the working-classes of the virtues of temperance or classical political economy; in Sheffield, 88 per cent of members were business or professional men. [97] Two things are clear about this movement. The institutes were not an entire failure, fulfilling a variety of useful roles relevant to their time and locality and whatever path away from the original intention was taken as a result of local circumstances. [98] Whatever Birkbeck had hoped, the mechanics' institutes did not prove to be a mass movement giving working men a scientific culture that the middle-classes had enjoyed since the mid-eighteenth century.[99]

In the mid-century, the state became involved in the promotion of technical education in national institutions focused in London. In 1845, the Royal College of Chemistry was established and the Government School of Mines followed in 1851. Both these institutions benefited from the Great Exhibition of 1851 whose profits of £186,000 together with a Government grant purchased the site in South Kensington where it was intended to gather various scientific institutions. In 1853, the School of Mines incorporated the nationalised College of Chemistry, the latter transferring to South

---

[96] Munford, W. A., 'George Birkbeck and Mechanics' Institutes', in English libraries, 1800-50 (University College London: School of Librarianship & Archives), 1958, pp. 33-58, and Kelly, Thomas, *George Birkbeck: pioneer of adult education*, (Liverpool University Press), 1957. See also, Royle, Edward, 'Mechanics' Institutes and the Working Classes 1840-1860', *Historical Journal*, Vol. 14, (2), (1971), pp. 305-321.

[97] See Inkster, I., 'Science and the Mechanics' Institutes, 1820-1850: The Case of Sheffield, *Annals of Science*, Vol. 32, (5), (1975), pp. 451-474.

[98] Mechanics' Institutes, largely inspired by British models emerged in the United States and throughout the British Empire. Although American Institutes were soon involved in large-scale technical research projects that were seen as 'useful' by American manufacturers and politicians, in Britain they appeared more concerned with remedying social disorder and no contemporary Institute sought to translate its utilitarian rhetoric of applied research into reality.

[99] Tylecote, M. P., *The mechanics' institutes of Lancashire and Yorkshire before 1851*, (Manchester University Press), 1957 provides a good regional study.

Kensington in 1872 and the former joining it piecemeal thereafter. [100] In 1853, government created the Department of Science and Arts that controlled the School and the College. It also tried to create science schools in the provinces but with limited success. More importantly, in 1859 the new Department began a series of science examinations for schools and paid grants to such schools for successful pupils under the Revised Code. In 1860, nine schools with 500 pupils participated but by 1870, there were 799 schools with over 34,000 pupils. This represented a considerable effort to introduce science teaching into schools, its standards secured by the financial control of inspectors.

So how successful was the development of technical education? Britain had won most of the prizes at the Great Exhibition of 1851 but its performance sixteen years later in the Paris Exhibition was poor. Despite government involvement in technical education, there was a strong feeling that Britain had fallen behind France and Prussia.[101] National unease generated the civic university movement of the 1870s and 1880s but found immediate expression in the 1868 parliamentary Select Committee on scientific education chaired by the ironmaster Bernhard Samuelson.[102] This began twenty years of various parliamentary inquiries into science, industry and education that led to improvements in technical education especially after 1890.[103]

Two major points emerge from this. The industrial revolution appears to have struck an economically efficient balance in its provision of education whatever its social deficiencies.[104] Little

---

[100] Roderick, G. W., and Stephens, M. D., 'Mining Education in England and Wales in the Second Half of the Nineteenth Century', *Irish Journal of Education*, Vol. 6, (2), (1972), pp. 105-120.

[101] Floud, Roderick, 'Technical education and economic performance: Britain, 1850-1914', *Albion*, Vol. 14, (1982), pp. 153-168.

[102] Samuelson chaired the Royal Commission on Technical Instruction in thre early 1880s, see Argles, M., 'The Royal Commission on Technical Instruction, 1881-4: Its inception and composition', *Journal of Education & Training*, Vol. 11, (1959), pp. 97-104.

[103] See, Stephens, M. D., and Roderick, G. W., 'The later Victorians and scientific and technical education', *Annals of Science*, Vol. 28, (1972), pp. 385-400, Bailey, Bill, 'The Technical Education Movement: A Late-nineteenth Century Educational 'Lobby'', *Journal of Further and higher Education*, Vol. 7, (3), (1983), pp. 55-68, and Betts, Robin, 'Persistent but misguided?: the technical educationists 1867-89', *History of Education*, Vol. 27, (3), (1998), pp. 267-277.

[104] Roderick, G. W., and Stephens, M. D., (eds.), *Where did we go wrong?: industrial performance, education, and the economy in Victorian Britain*, (Falmar Press), 1981.

serious effort was made before 1830 to maintain elementary education for the mass of the population but this did not have any real adverse effects on economic growth since most of the new occupations created did not require literate labour. After 1840, Britain was sufficiently rich to finance expensive projects like its railway building and the considerable expansion of investment in education. Expenditure on education was postponed but so too was a problem. While scientific and technical information circulated in middle-class institutions, for working men the attempt to create a technical education was less successful. Apart from the central institutions in South Kensington and the introduction of technical examinations into schools in the 1860s, there was a dangerous deficit in the provision of technical education. The roots of a great deal of anxiety about the level of educationvis-à-vis Germany in the 1870s and 1880s lay in the lack of development in the 1850s and 1860s. [105] Industrial success bred a lack of urgency to make rising literacy the basis for a higher level of working-class scientific training. Britain's economic challenge from the 1870s was, in part, a result of this. [106]

To what extent did educating women become important?

The education of women and girls had been an issue in England since the 1790s. [107] Certain social pressures had been given an extra urgency by 1850 by the claims of writers like Mary Wollstonecraft that equality of education with boys was a means of securing independence

---

[105] Haines, George, 'German Influence upon Scientific Instruction in England, 1867-1887', *Victorian Studies*, Vol. 1, (3), (1958), pp. 215-244.

[106] Sanderson, Michael, *Education and economic decline in Britain, 1870 to the 1990s*, (Cambridge University Press), 1999, pp. 3-54, summarises the contrary arguments.

[107] Purvis, June, *A History of Women's Education in England*, (Open University Press), 1991, covers the period between 1800 and 1914 and is the best introduction to the subject. It should be supplemented by: Hunt, Felicity, (ed.), *Lessons for Life: The Schooling of Girls and Women*, (Basil Blackwell), 1987, Bryant, Margaret, *The Unexpected Revolution: A study of the history of the education of women and girls in the nineteenth century*, (NFER), 1979, Dyhouse, Carol, *Girls Growing up in Late Victorian and Edwardian England*, (Routledge), 1981, Gorman, Deborah, *The Victorian Girl and the Feminist Ideal*, (Croom Helm), 1982, Burstyn, Joan, *Victorian Education and the Ideal of Womanhood*, (Croom Helm), 1980, and Fletcher, Sheila, *Feminists and Bureaucrats: A study in the development of girls' education in the nineteenth century*, (Cambridge University Press), 1984, 2008. Spender, Dale, (ed.), *The education papers: women's quest for equality in Britain 1850-1912*, (Routledge), 1987, is a valuable selection of documents on women's education.

for women,.[108] Women were still less educated than men. Female literacy rates in 1851 were still only 55 per cent compared to nearly 70 per cent for men. The lack of education was exacerbated by the steady rise in the proportion of women in the population from 1,036 females per 1,000 males in 1821 to 1,054 per 1,000 in 1871. This meant that there was a surplus of women over men and accordingly over a quarter of a million women had little expectation of marriage and the lifetime protection of husband and home. This situation was aggravated by the rising age of marriage that also left more single women waiting for, and often not achieving, marriage.

The education of women was a class-based as that of boys.[109] Well-to-do girls were educated at home or in small academies in 1830. The academic content was low and, with the transformation of the grammar schools, girls found themselves excluded from establishments they had previously attended. Lower class girls attended the National or British schools along with boys and were destined, if not for the drudgery of working-class marriage, then for factory work or the vast army of domestic service. The education girls received before 1870 was very similar to that followed by boys, with the addition of some sewing and knitting. The concern to develop a more distinctive curriculum with a focus on domestic science, cooking, laundry and needlework came after 1870 and especially in the 1880s and 1890s.

With more middle-class women relying on parents or putative husbands and children, they were forced to think in terms of earning their own living. This brought education to the forefront of feminist thinking. The problem between 1840 and 1870 was finding a career for unmarried middle-class ladies and of fashioning an education that would prepare them for it. Existing careers were limited and becoming a governess was often the only means of earning a living for women of gentle birth. In 1851, there were some 25,000 governesses in England but most had no proper training and often a limited education. Moreover, there were uneasy status incongruities: hired to impart ladylike qualities to her charges, the governess by taking paid employment was seen as having forfeited her own status as a lady. The gendered nature of elementary education can be seen after the 1870

---

[108] Godwin, Mary Wollstonecraft, *Thoughts on the Education of Daughters with Reflections of Female Conduct in the More Important Duties of Life*, (J. Johnson), 1787.

[109] See, Roach, John, 'Boys and girls at school, 1800-70', *History of Education*, Vol. 15, (1986), pp. 147-159.

Education Act with the curriculum for girls stressing 'domestic skills'.[110]

The Governesses' Benevolent Institution was formed in 1843 to help active governesses seek positions and aged ones to live in retirement.[111] Under its auspices, the central problem of education was tackled with the founding of Queen's College, an Anglican institution, in 1848 with an academic curriculum that developed sciences and languages as well as basic subjects and accomplishments (drawing, music, dancing, and needlework).[112] Queen's College was open to all girls over the age of twelve; soon preparatory and evening classes were offered as well. It received a Royal Charter in 1853 and this marked its independence from the Governesses' Benevolent Institution. Queen's College issued its own certificates of proficiency, and although it was possible to take a University of London degree, few did so. A similar institution, Bedford College, was opened in 1849.[113] Pupils from these colleges influenced many areas of feminist life in the 1860s and 1870s: *The English Woman's Journal*, the Social Science Association, the early suffrage and married women's property movements all stemmed from them. Ex-Queen's students dominated many areas of feminist development, for example, Sophia Jex Blake, the first English doctor and Octavia Hill, the social housing pioneer. But most important were Miss Beale and Miss Buss.

Dorothea Beale and her friend Frances Mary Buss created respectively the girls' public boarding school and the girls' grammar school.[114] In 1858, Miss Beale took over the recently founded Cheltenham Ladies College and turned it into the model of the high-

---

[110] Gomersall, Meg, 'Ideals and realities: the education of working-class girls, 1800-1870', *History of Education*, Vol. 17, (1988), pp. 37-53, Horn, Pamela, 'The education and employment of working-class girls, 1870-1914', *History of Education*, Vol. 17, (1988), pp. 71-82.

[111] For the organisation and rules of the Governesses' Benevolent Institution, see *The Church Guardian and Church of England Magazine*, (Seeley, Burnside and Seeley), 1846, pp. 237-240. See also, Hughes, Kathryn, *The Victorian Governess*, (Hambledon), 2001, pp. 181-188

[112] Kaye, Elaine, *A History of Queen's College, London 1848-1972*, (Chatto and Windus), 1972

[113] See, Tuke, D. M. J., and Tuke, M. J., *A History of Bedford College for women, 1849-1937*, (Oxford University Press), 1939.

[114] Dyhouse, Carol, 'Miss Buss and Miss Beale: gender and authority in the history of education', in Hunt, Felicity, (ed.), *Lessons for life, the schooling of girls and women 1850-1950*, (Basil Blackwell), 1987, pp. 22-38.

quality girls' boarding school. [115] St Leonards and Roedean were founded after 1870 based on its example. Miss Buss' North London Collegiate School began in 1850 in Camden Town to meet the problem of the lack of education for middle-class girls. [116] She believed in the important of home life in the upbringing of girls and it deliberately remained a day school. In both institutions the curriculum included subjects like science and Latin. Both institutions might have remained unique in their own areas had not feminist educators brought two powerful factors into play.

Public examinations were opened to girls. Oxford and Cambridge had started Local Examinations for boys' schools in 1858 providing an external common standard. The Victorians placed great stress on examinations as a means of raising academic performance and deciding the fitness of candidates for public office. Feminists saw that without the standard demanded of boys the new academic girls' education would not be taken seriously. Emily Davies, the future founder of Girton College and sister of a Principal of Queen's College, urged Cambridge to admit girls to its Locals that it did experimentally in 1863. Miss Buss sent 25 candidates and following this success Local school examinations were formally opened to girls by Cambridge, Edinburgh and Durham universities in 1865 and 1866 and Oxford followed suit in 1870. [117]

Girls' education was also strengthened and spread after it secured financial aid through endowments. In the 1860s, the Taunton Commission examined the issue of endowments for grammar schools. Feminists saw this as another crucial opportunity. Emily Davies insisted the Commission should examine girls' education and she, and Miss Beale and Miss Buss, gave evidence before it and Miss Beale edited the volume of the report devoted to girls. The result was the Endowed Schools Act 1869 and the creation of the Endowed Schools Commissioners to reform grammar school endowments. They created 47 new grammar schools between 1869 and 1875 and their successors, the charity Commission, created another 47 after

---

[115] Clarke, A. K., *A history of the Cheltenham Ladies' College, 1853-1953*, (Faber), 1953. See also, Raikes, E., *Dorothea Beale of Cheltenham*, (A. Constable), 1908.

[116] Scrimgeour, Ruby Margaret, (ed.), *The North London Collegiate School, 1850-1950: a hundred years of girls' education,* (Oxford University Press), 1950. See also, Ridley, A. E., *Frances Mary Buss and her work for education*, (Longmans), 1986.

[117] Roach, John, *Public Examinations in England, 1850-1900*, (Cambridge University Press), 1971, pp. 103-135, on girls' examinations.

1875. The North London Collegiate gained an endowment from the reorganisation. [118]

The early movement for higher education for girls and its outcome occupied the 1860s. The prime mover was Emily Davies.[119] She wanted higher education for women to widen the range of occupations open to them, fit them for public life, raise the standard of teaching in girls' schools, advance the cause of women's suffrage and match the experience of France, Germany and Italy where women were accepted into universities. She took a house in Hitchen in 1869 to prepare girls for Cambridge examinations and in 1873 moved to Cambridge itself founding Girton College. [120] At the same time Anne Clough moved to Cambridge in 1871 to set up what was to become Newnham College. [121] Owens College in Manchester admitted women in 1869. This was followed by London in 1878 and Oxford in 1879. [122] The timing of these events coincided with the development of civic universities in the 1870s that admitted women as a normal policy.

Some historians have argued that the improvement in middle-class girls' schooling was linked to the more general attempt at reforming secondary education and owed more to the attention of government through such bodies as the Taunton Commission than to feminist lobbying. [123] This view neglects the role of feminists in

---

[118] Sondheimer, Janet, and Bodington, P. R. (eds.), *The Girls' Public Day School Trust, 1872-1972: a centenary review*, (Girls' Public Day School Trust), 1972, and Kamm, Josephine, *Indicative Past: A Hundred Years of the Girls' Public Day School Trust*, (Allen & Unwin), 1971.

[119] Bennett, Daphne, *Emily Davies and the Liberation of Women, 1830-1921*, (Andre Deutsch), 1990, remains the best study but see also the relevant section of Caine, Barbara, *Victorian Feminists*, (Oxford University Press), 1992, Davies, Emily, *The Higher Education of Women*, (Portrayer), 2002, facsimile reprint of 1866 edition. See also, Robinson, Jane, *Bluestocking: The Remarkable Story of the First Women to Fight for an Education*, (Viking), 2009.

[120] See Stephens, B. N., *Emily Davies and Girton College*, (Constable & Co.), 1927.

[121] Clough, B. A., *A memoir of Anne Jemima Clough*, (E. Arnold), 1897, and Gardner, Alice, *A Short History of Newnham College, Cambridge*, (Bowes & Bowes), 1921.

[122] Stevenson, Julie, 'Women in higher education, with special reference to University College, London, 1873-1913', in Blanchard, I., (ed.), *New directions in economic and social history*, (Newlees), 1995, pp. 101-109.

[123] Moore, Lindy, 'Young ladies' institutions: the development of secondary schools for girls in Scotland, 1833-c.1870', *History of Education*, Vol. 32, (2003), pp. 249-272, Sperandio, Jill, 'Secondary schools for Norwich girls,

widening the concerns of that commission to include girls' education. Had Emily Davies and other feminists not pursued their case, the Commission would have looked only at the state of boys' education. Some historians stress that the demand for improved educational opportunities for women was part of a wider extension of democratic rights and liberty for individuals especially the call for women's suffrage after 1865. A second explanation suggests that industrialisation created a need for more education. This too is problematic. Industrialisation and the entrenching of capitalist values led to a focus upon separate spheres and upon domestic respectability and to a marginalising of the economic role of especially working-class women. [124] A final explanation sees the emergence of the women's educational reform movement much more centrally to the wider women's movement. Women saw education as the key to a broad range of activities and freedoms: as a means of training for paid employment, of alleviating the vacuity and boredom of everyday idleness and of improving their ability to fight for the extension of female opportunities in other areas. [125]

1850-1910: demanded or benevolently supplied?', *Gender & Education*, Vol. 14, (2002), pp. 391-410.

[124] See, Jordan, Ellen, *The women's movement and women's employment in nineteenth century Britain*, (Routledge), 1999, pp. 107-122, and Delamont, Sara, 'The Domestic Ideology and Women's Education', in Delamont, Sara, and Duffin, Lorna, (eds.), *The Nineteenth Century Woman*, (Croom Helm), 1978, pp. 164-187.

[125] See, Aldrich, Richard, 'Pioneers of female education in Victorian Britain', *History of Education Society Bulletin*, Vol. 54, (1994), pp. 56-61.

12 A state system of education, 1870-1914

The first two-thirds of the nineteenth century in England were years of extraordinary growth in popular education and literacy, reflecting the combined influence of increased private demand for basic instruction and the government-subsidised efforts of voluntary religious societies to construct schools for the working-classes. By 1858, the Newcastle Commission was able to report that there remained 'very few cases indeed in which children have been at no school whatsoever.' [1] Although most working-class children had at least some experience of formal schooling, the general pattern of irregular attendance and early withdrawal was clearly detrimental to educational progress. [2] The existing educational system of voluntary schools and state subsidies did not deliver an effective educational market for all and the development of a system of state-provided and controlled elementary education was an attempt by the state to address fundamental deficiencies in the rapidly expanding market for popular education.

Why was the Education Act 1870 so important?

Whatever the benefits of elementary education to the working-classes, the fees that were charged, however small, posed a problem. The Newcastle Commission reported:

> It is not to be denied that, in every division of my district, some parents are too poor to pay even the trifling sum charged by schools supported by the Committee of Council on Education. [3]

More significant than the monetary cost of school attendance was the loss of the child's contribution to the family economy. For many working-class families, sending their children to school would have entailed the loss of their financial independence. A government inspector of schools concluded in 1854:

> The earnings of the adult operative are insufficient to support himself and *children* up to fourteen years of age, hence the removal of them from

---

[1] *Report of the Commissioners Appointed to Inquire into the State of Popular Education in England*, Parliamentary Papers, 1861, Vol. 21, pt. I, p. 85.
[2] Ibid, pt. I, p. 178.
[3] Ibid, pt. III, pp. 236-237.

school in order to meet the wants of his household. Compel them to go to school, and you drive the family to the workhouse. [4]

For families living at or near the level of subsistence, times of financial hardship frequently meant withdrawing children from school. The alternative for Victorian workers was to borrow money at reasonable rates but there were major difficulties with this that made this alternative unrealistic. Three basic forms of credit were available to members of the working-classes in the late-nineteenth century: 'not-paying', pawning, and borrowing. [5] Each of these options was unsuited to the modest but protracted expenses associated with investments in schooling and the complete lack of discussion by contemporary observers of the possibility of taking out temporary loans confirms its impracticality. In short, for those Victorian parents incapable of paying school fees or of subsisting even temporarily without the financial contributions of their children, existing capital markets were of little help. [6]

The economic incentives to acquire a basic education offered by the Victorian job market increased significantly after 1840 as a result of structural changes in the British economy. As technology developed and the potential uses of literacy increased, the skills taught in elementary schools came to be valued by employers in a far wider range of industries. As James Fraser reported to the Newcastle Commission in 1858, 'prejudice against an educated labourer was rapidly passing away' even in agricultural districts due to the development of 'more scientific methods of cultivation' for which 'more intelligence is required in those who actually have to apply them.' [7] Literate workers were more likely to work in higher-status occupations than illiterates with the same background. Basic skills taught in elementary schools were increasingly necessary not only for the traditionally middle-class jobs of clerk or solicitor, but also for more modest occupations. Investments in elementary education, therefore, did generally offer an economic return for members of the Victorian working-classes. There was some resistance to this notion in some communities where the local economy was grounded in occupations that needed young labour and where elementary

---

[4] *Minutes of the Committee of Council on Education,* Parliamentary Papers, 1854-5, pp. 79-80.

[5] Johnson, Paul, *Saving and Spending: the working-class economy in Britain, 1870-1939,* (Oxford University Press), 1985, pp. 144-192.

[6] Ellis, A. C. O., 'Influences on School Attendance in Victorian England', *British Journal of Educational Studies*, Vol. 21, (3), (1973), pp. 313-326.

[7] Ibid, *Report of the Commissioners Appointed to Inquire into the State of Popular Education in England,* pt. II, p. 105.

education was less well regarded. In mining communities, for example, parents were notorious for not sending their children to school despite relatively high earnings. [8] Newcastle Commissioners acknowledged that the miners' choice to send their children to work in the pits rather than to school was not necessarily selfish or near-sighted. Rather, it represented a rational economic decision to equip their children with the experience and skills that would benefit them as miners, a career that offered high earnings relative even to the small number of jobs in the region requiring literacy and into which most of them would go.

It was not a lack of ideas that prevented the government from becoming involved in education early in the nineteenth century as Parliament was well aware of the state-mandated systems of education emerging on the continent in Prussia and France. Bills to establish rate aid for schools were presented in Parliament and defeated in 1807, 1820 and in 1833, when John Roebuck presented a bill that would also have made elementary education compulsory. The British government's earliest interventions in the market for popular education represented attempts to increase the supply of suitable education available to the working-classes at a price they could afford. As Henry Brougham informed his fellow members of the 'upper classes' in an 1825 pamphlet:

...the question no longer is whether or not the people shall be instructed—for that has been determined long ago, and the decision was irreversible—but whether they shall be well or ill taught. [9]

Forced to take a more active role after 1833, the government began an extended effort to improve the standard of education in the voluntary sector. The eventual substitution of statutory elementary schools financed by local taxation for voluntary and for-profit types of schooling represented an attempt to address the imperfections of the private educational market.

Why was state provision introduced in 1870?

The Elementary Education Act 1870 created school boards for those parts of England and Wales in that there were insufficient school

---

[8] Ibid, Colls, R., '"Oh Happy English Children!": Coal, Class and Education in the North-East'.

[9] Brougham, Henry, *Practical Observations upon the Education of the Poor: addressed to the working classes and their employers,* (Printed by Richard Taylor ... and sold by Longman, Hurst, Rees, Orme, Brown and Green ... for the benefit of the London Mechanics Institution), 1825, p. 32.

places for working-class children. These boards possessed power to enforce the attendance of their pupils. Ten years later this power became a duty that devolved also on the school attendance committee, a body created under legislation in 1876 in the non-school board areas. The idea of compulsory education was not new. Certain groups of children had been forced, under a variety of legislation that included the Factory Acts, the Reformatory and Industrial Schools Acts and the Poor Law Acts, to attend school before 1870 but the numbers involved were comparatively small. [10] What was new about the legislation of the 1870s was the extent of its operation. For the first time, the nation's children had to attend school on a full-time basis for a minimum of five years, a period that was extended to nine years for many by 1914. The new laws had an important effect on the working-class way of life. No longer could parents take for granted the services of their children in the home or their contributions to the family budget. Traditional working-class patterns of behaviour continued in defiance of the law. The state had interfered with the pattern of family life by coming between parent and child, reducing family income and imposing new patterns of behaviour on both parent and child.

The 1870 Act was the culmination of a thirty year struggle to establish an effective and nationwide elementary schooling system. There was broad agreement that this was necessary, but the sectarian interests of Anglicans, Nonconformists and Roman Catholics created obstacles to progress. As long as the provision of schools was a voluntary, charitable activity, the three religious societies could co-exist. But any attempt to establish education as the responsibility of the state and spend public money, created acute tensions. Anglicans, as members of the Established Church, claimed that any national system must be Anglican-based, a claim fiercely resisted by Nonconformists and Catholics. As the events of the 1830s and 1840s showed, each side was able to mobilise enough support to prevent successive governments from taking any large-scale action. Whatever its justification, the voluntary principle did not prove a success in promoting schools. Even many Nonconformists were coming round

---

[10] After 1832, a series of acts shored up, but did not radically modify, the voluntary school system. The Industrial Schools Acts of 1857, 1861 and 1866; the Reformatory Schools Acts of 1854, 1857 and 1866 and the Education of Pauper Children Act of 1862 all helped local authorities to tackle the problem of the education of the 'residuum', the class the voluntary schools had neglected. When the efforts of pre-1867 parliaments had failed and the voluntary system had lost credence as the means of educating the children of the nation, then and only then, did the 1870 Act belatedly and reluctantly 'fill the gaps'.

to the view that voluntarism had been given a fair trial and had failed. The Congregationalist Education Union that had originated in the 1840s to oppose state education was wound up in 1867 and the symbolic acceptance of defeat was registered when the great voluntarist Edward Baines accepted the practical case for state education. The Newcastle Commission and the controversies over the Revised Code were important because they reinforced the public interest in the subject that had been growing since the 1850s. Religion was one reason for the late growth of a national system of education but there were others.

Some of the conflict and bitterness was due to the social and political divisions that underlay and reinforced sectarian and theological disputes. By the 1840s, the Anglican Church was bitterly resented by its rivals: a national institution identified with a class and the Tory Party. Many Anglican clergymen regarded education as a means of crude social control. In this they were in agreement with the bulk of the Conservative Party that had frustrated Whig efforts in 1839-1840 to establish a national non-denominational system and that fought hard for the interests of the Church during the long debates in 1870. Paradoxically, the provisions of the 1870 Act had the effect of allying Catholics and Anglicans. Voluntary schools were to be in competition with the new board schools and Catholics were implacably opposed to this. Nonconformists naturally ranged themselves behind the Whigs and then the Liberals. However, at no point were they more than a vigorous pressure group within the party that, after 1867, was led by William Gladstonewho in 1838 had been 'desirous of placing the education of the people under the efficient control of the clergy'. [11] By 1870, he was prepared to accept the need for some government action on a non-denominational basis but refused, as did the majority of the Liberal Party, to act against the voluntary schools. It was impossible to devise a bill that would have satisfied both sides.

There was also a lack of parliamentary and administrative will to address the problems that did exist and an absence of local government structures that would provide the necessary local agencies. Municipal corporations had been reformed in 1835 but their powers were limited. In the counties, elected councils were not established until 1888. There were serious administrative problems in involving the state in popular education. Local rate support would certainly bring demands for local control that was bound to raise the denominational issue. There was the growing problem of expense of

---

[11] Cit, Morley, John, *The Life of William Ewart Gladstone*, 3 Vols. (Macmillan and Co.), 1903, Vol. 1, p. 109.

government grants that the Revised Code was supposed to have resolved and this was combined with the tension that, since education was a local service, it ought to be financed from local taxation, a proposal that was central to the National Public School Association founded in 1850. The final problem was one of timing. Education took up a good deal of parliamentary time in the mid-fifties. In 1855, for example, there were three bills before Parliament though all were withdrawn. It was not a period when the state was likely to move into a major new area of social policy because the government was tending to restrict its activities in central planning. The 1850s was the decade of administrative reform and retrenchment with reformers planning to achieve economies rather than extend the range of government activity. As a result, much of the pressure for a national system of elementary education came from outside parliament.

Elementary education was an area where national policies were greatly influenced by local initiatives, beginning first in Manchester[12] and later in Birmingham.[13] The National Public School Association had the support of Richard Cobden and, among others, a young Bradford manufacturer named W. E. Forster who later carried the 1870 Act through the Commons.[14] It campaigned for public, rate-supported, non-denominational education during the 1850s but ran out of steam after an 1857 bill failed to become law. During the 1860s, opinion in cities became increasingly concerned about the large numbers of children who were not in school.[15] Evidence of poor educational provision was beginning to accumulate. In 1861-1862, the first and second reports of the Royal Commission on Children's Employment in agriculture highlighted the poor state of education in the countryside. It was clear that the half-time system could not be introduced into agricultural work. Manchester was not the only major city to reveal its deficiencies. Very similar conclusions were reached by the Birmingham Education Society, founded in 1867, and the House of Commons return on the state of education in Birmingham, Manchester, Leeds and Liverpool in 1869 showed that many children

---

[12] See, Maltby, S. E., *Manchester and the movement for national elementary education, 1800-1870*, (Manchester University Press), 1918.

[13] Marcham, A. J., 'The Birmingham Education Society and the 1870 Education Act', *Journal of Educational Administration & History*, Vol. 8, (1976), pp. 11-16.

[14] Jackson, Patrick, *Education Act Forster: a political biography of W. E. Forster (1818-1886)*, (Fairleigh Dickinson University Press), 1997, and Reid, T. W., Sir, *Life of the Right Honourable William Edward Forster*, 2 Vols. (Chapman and Hall), 1888.

[15] On the impact of public opinion, see, Rich, E. E., *The Education Act 1870: a study of public opinion*, (Longman), 1970.

were attending no school at all and that existing private schools were very inefficient. [16] The Social Science Association argued, as a result of an extensive survey, that for every 100 children living with parents and not at work, 40 were at school and 60 were not. [17] Their conclusion was that only compulsory education could deal with the apathy of parents and the inadequacy of the voluntary system. Education bills were introduced in 1867 and 1868 but the latter was withdrawn when it was clear that a general election was imminent. When Gladstone formed his new Liberal government, Forster became Vice-President of the Committee of Council for Education, the man who spoke for education in the Commons. [18]

What were the main features of the legislation?

The Reform Act 1867 enfranchised the urban working-class. Both Disraeli and Gladstone accepted that self-improvement and rising levels of literacy were, in part, a justification for this development. There is, however, some debate on the degree to which reform in 1867 led to educational reform in 1870. Robert Lowe's statement that 'we must now educate our masters' has to be seen as partly rhetoric but it raised the issue of parental non-consumers and the degree to which they should be coerced into sending their children to school. It has been argued that the extension of education in 1870 was a matter of social policy not one of political necessity. The leadership that had long rested with Manchester now passed to Birmingham. Education was one of the major interests of the Birmingham municipal reformers and in 1869 they created the National Education League with George Dixon as President and Joseph Chamberlain as Chairman of the committee. [19] The League was a national movement that carried on the ideas of the National Public School Association and represented the non-sectarian and Nonconformist view of the way

---

[16] *Papers for The Schoolmaster*, New Series, Vol. 4, (1868), pp. 163-164, *Report of the first general meeting of members of the National Education League: held at Birmingham, on Tuesday and Wednesday, Oct. 12 & 13, 1869 ...,* (The Journal), 1869, pp. 22-23. See also, Rodrick, Anne B., *Self-Help and Civic Culture: Citizenship in Victorian Birmingham*, (Ashgate), 2004, pp. 88-109.
[17] *Transactions of the National Association for the Promotion of Social Science*, (John W. Parker), 1869, pp. 38-74, 391-399, 454-455.
[18] See Roper, Henry, 'Towards an Elementary Education Act for England and Wales, 1865-1870', *British Journal of Educational Studies*, Vol. 23, (2), (1975), pp. 181-208.
[19] Ibid, *Report of the first general meeting of members of the National Education League: held at Birmingham, on Tuesday and Wednesday, Oct. 12 & 13, 1869....*

ahead. In November 1869, the National Education Union was founded in Manchester with the protection of the interests of denominational schools as its primary objective. [20]

Forster introduced the bill in February 1870 and it became law on 9 August. [21] It did not design a new national system. It left the existing voluntary schools untouched with the same committees of managers. Where the existing school provision was inadequate or where a majority of ratepayers demanded it, school boards should be set up for boroughs and parishes with a single board for the whole of London, with the duty of building the schools that were necessary. These boards were to be elected triennially in the boroughs by the burgesses and in parishes by ratepayers, and were given the power to issue a precept on the rating authority to be paid out of the local rate. The religious question was resolved by allowing schools provided by the boards to be non-sectarian (the so-called Cowper-Temple clause) but giving parents the right to withdraw their children from any religious observance or instruction. Elementary education was not made free and school boards might make it compulsory for children to attend school. This was not extended to the voluntary schools. The Act essentially filled in the gaps creating a dual system of state schools and voluntary schools. [22]

The main feature of the debate was the major division of opinion not between Conservatives and Liberals but within the Liberal majority itself. The Conservatives on the whole supported the bill, though they disagreed over some issues. The original proposals were considerably modified by the Radical Nonconformist wing of the Liberal party, many of them recently elected MPs, who wanted to go further in a number of directions that the government had planned.

---

[20] Rich, E. E., *The Education Act, 1870: a study of public opinion*, (Longman), 1970, but see also the contemporary studies, Adams, Francis, *The Elementary Education Act, 1870: with analysis, index and appendix*, (Simpkin, Marshall, & Co.), 1870, and Munby, F. J., *A popular analysis of the Elementary Education Act, 1870: for the use of ratepayers, school managers, overseers, parents, and others outside the metropolis*, (John Heywood), 1870.

[21] Armytage, W. H. G., 'The 1870 Education Act', *British Journal of Educational Studies*, Vol. 18, (1970), pp. 121-133, Baker, Gordon, 'The romantic and radical nature of the 1870 Education Act', *History of Education*, Vol. 30, (2001), pp. 211-232. See also, *A Verbatim Report, with indexes, of the debate in Parliament during the progress of the Elementary Education Bill, 1870*, (National Education Union), 1870.

[22] Ibid, Jackson, Patrick, *Education Act Forster: a political biography of W.E. Forster (1818-1886)*, pp. 150-180, examines the passage of the legislation.

Some Radicals were strong Nonconformists who advocated the disestablishment of the Church of England. Prominent in this group was Edward Miall, a former Independent minister who had founded *The Nonconformist* in 1841 and who was a leading figure in the Society for the Liberation of the Church from State Patronage and Control (or Liberation Society for short). Henry Richard, Welsh MP with similar views pointed out the particular difficulties raised by the religious situation in Wales and the dislike of the Welsh people for Anglican teaching in schools. They argued that school instruction should be entirely secular so that religious agencies would be left to do their work outside schools. The pressures were not all from the religious side. Compulsory education was strongly advocated by the Cambridge economist Henry Fawcett and by Sir Charles Dilke, whose main contribution to was to propose that the ratepayers should elect the school boards. Free education, part of the programme of the National Education League, was little discussed and an amendment in favour of it soundly defeated.

Board schools financed from the rates as well as by government grants had the resources to grow. Voluntary schools had no source of local income comparable to rates and there was no way in which they could keep pace. In this sense the settlement of 1870 carried within it the seeds of its own destruction. By the 1890s, it was clear that provision for elementary education was uneven and annually growing more so. Nor was the structure one on to which provision for secondary education could be grafted. The Education Act 1902 put the Church on the rates. School Boards were abolished and, in return for rate aid, voluntary schools' committees of management came within the control of the new Local EducationAuthorities, county and county borough councils, some 140 of them. [23]

How did the relationship between the state and education develop, 1870-1914?

Forster's Education Act did not provide universal, free or compulsory education, but it did allow for the glaring deficiencies in English education to be removed. [24] A separate Act extended similar

---

[23] Murphy, James, *The Education act 1870: text and commentary*, (David & Charles), 1972, provides the legislation and how it worked.

[24] Simon, B., *Education and the Labour Movement 1870-1920*, (Lawrence and Wishart), 1979, is perhaps the broadest account of developments after 1870. Hurt, J. S., *Schooling and the Working-class 1860-1918*, (Routledge), 1979, is excellent on the 1870 Education Act and after and Sutherland, Gillian, *Policy-Making in Elementary Education 1870-1895*, (Oxford University Press), 1973, is fundamental on the changing nature of policy and

provisions to Scotland in 1872. Before 1870 the system was characterised as one of state subsidy of voluntary education, the period after by state supplementation of voluntary education. Board schools and voluntary schools existed side by side, in theory complementary, in practice in competition. The 1870 Act was a compromise that tried to make use of and not destroy existing educational resources but criticism of the legislation remained. [25] It did not solve the problem of elementary schooling overnight and it took a further thirty years to make a national system of elementary schools fully a reality.

How was Forster's Act extended to 1902?

Religious squabbling continued in the elections for School Boards and in the attempts, [26] particularly by Anglicans in county areas, to forestall the imposition of the School Boards. [27] Initially the advantage lay with the existing voluntary schools and even by 1880 only one sixth of children were in board schools but the potential for growth lay with School Boards and by 1900, 54 per cent of the elementary school population were in their schools. Many of the larger boroughs imposed by-laws making education compulsory, that in turn increased revenue, since grants were still related to attendance, and it was partly as a means of helping the rural voluntary schools that Disraeli's ministry turned its attention to compulsion. [28]

For these schools, Lord Sandon the Vice-President, told the

---

priorities. Sanderson, Michael, *Education and economic decline in Britain, 1870 to the 1990s*, (Cambridge University Press), 1999, examines the relationship between education and the economy.

[25] This is evident in Gregory, Robert, *The results and lessons of the first decade of the Education act of 1870: being a paper read at the Newcastle church congress on the 6th October 1881, and What do we mean by religious education being a paper read at the Edinburgh church conference on the 11th October, 1881*, (National Society's Depository), 1881, and Temple, Henry, *Injustice in the working of the Education Act of 1870: A speech delivered at the annual meeting of the English Church Union on Thursday, June 7, 1883*, (Rivingtons Waterloo Place, London and English Church Union Office, 35, Wellington Street, Strand), 1883.

[26] Richards, N. J., 'Religious Controversy and the School Boards 1870-1902', *British Journal of Educational Studies*, Vol. 18, (1970), pp. 180-196.

[27] Ibid, Jackson, Patrick, *Education Act Forster: a political biography of W.E. Forster (1818-1886)*, pp. 181-206, considers the implementation of the legislation through to 1874.

[28] Auerbach, Sascha, "'The Law Has No Feeling for Poor Folk Like Us!': Everyday Responses to Legal Compulsion in England's Working-Class Communities, 1871-1904', *Journal of Social History*, Vol. 43, (3), (2012), pp. 686-708.

Cabinet in 1875 it was a matter of 'life or death'. The result, in 1876, was Sandon's Education Act that set up School Attendance Committees and placed the responsibility for ensuring attendance firmly on parents. It also gave voluntary schools the right to make attendance compulsory. Various loopholes were removed by the incoming Liberal ministry when Mundella's Education Act 1880 made attendance compulsory for children between five and ten. [29] By the early 1890s, attendance within this age group was falling short at 82 per cent. Many children worked outside school hours: in 1901 the figure was put at 300,000 and truancy was a major problem due to the fact that parents could not afford to give up income earned by their children. Compulsory education was also extended to blind and deaf children under the Elementary Education (Blind and Deaf Children) Act of 1893, which established special schools. Similar provision was made for physically-impaired children in the Elementary Education (Defective and Epileptic Children) Act of 1899. Further legislation in 1893 extended the age of compulsory attendance to 11, and in 1899 to 12.

This inevitably sharpened the debate about fees, that averaged about 3d per week per child but many School Boards waived the fee for needy children. [30] The Elementary Fee Grant Act 1891 virtually established free elementary education and by 1895 only about one-sixth of the five million needy elementary children were paying fees. The availability of free education through School Boards made it easier to integrate pauper children into the general education system. An Act of 1873 had made school attendance a condition of outdoor relief for children, an option that had been open to guardians since Denison's Act of 1855 had empowered guardians to pay school fees. By 1900, the vast majority of Unions sent children to their local board school and so the distinctive badge of pauperism was gradually removed. The pernicious effects of payment by results were also removed. The system had been severely criticised by the Cross Commission that reported in 1888 and in the 1890 Code grants for examinable attainments in the 3Rs were abolished. [31]

It is important to recognise the achievements that resulted from

---

[29] See, Roper, H., *Administering the Elementary Education Acts, 1870-1885*, (Museum of the History of Education, University of Leeds), 1976.
[30] See for example, Lewis, Jane, 'Parents, children, schhol fees and the London School Board 1870-1890', *History of Education*, Vol. 11, (1982), pp. 291-312.
[31] Moore, Marianne, 'Social Control or Protection of the Child? The Debates on the Industrial Schools Acts, 1857-1894', *Journal of Family History*, Vol. 33, (2008), pp. 359-387.

the 1870 Act. The figures for the final decades of the century show the almost complete elimination of illiteracy as measured from parish registers. The gains were greater for women than men. Had it not been for the 1870 Act progress in literacy would have slowed down simply because illiteracy was concentrated in those classes and regions that were hardest to provide for under the voluntary system. The 1870 Act was responsible for the mopping-up operation by providing more school places and improvements in attendance and length of school life.

There were certainly improvements in attendance but by 1897 it was still only just over 80 per cent. Legislation helped but machinery of enforcement was necessary. The main pressure was that of the attendance officer (commonly called the 'board man') and ultimately a summons. This did not always prove effective and authorities were often unwilling to prosecute or convict parents especially in rural areas where cheap child labour was essential for farmers and parents. The Agricultural Children Act 1873 was intended to improve attendance, but fines were low if they were imposed at all. [32] The quality of literacy was governed by things other than directly educational ones. The factory legislation of the late 1860s and 1870s encompassed children in industries not covered before. From the 1870s, future patterns of leisure and holidays began to take rudimentary form. New skilled and semi-skilled occupations were being created and white-collar occupations were expanding. Literacy was essential in all of these areas.

The 1870 Act inevitably made access to higher than elementary education a more prominent issue. Apart from evening and adult education, such access became available mainly in two ways: the evolution of a higher stage within the elementary system or the use of scholarships from the elementary school to the grammar school.

Why was the Education Act 1902 significant?

The historian G. M. Young characterised the absence of any substantial educational provision in England and Wales for much of the nineteenth century as 'the great Victorian omission'. [33] The 1870 Education Act represented a significant move forward and by the 1890s, over 2,500 new school boards had been created in England and Wales and there were also some 14,000 committees of management for individual voluntary schools. However, this dual

---

[32] Horn, P. L. R., 'The Agricultural Children Act 1873', *History of Education*, Vol. 3, (2), (1974), pp. 27-39.

[33] Young, G. M., *Victorian England: Portrait of an Age*, (Oxford University Press), 1953, p. 165.

system of elementary education was uneven in administrative terms and voluntary schools were often at a financial disadvantage since they were funded not from the local rates but by direct government grants.

By 1900, the pattern of education that had evolved since 1870 was under considerable pressure. [34] The elementary system had developed what for many people seemed to be pseudo-secondary features in its higher-grade schools and evening classes. The still insecure financial basis of many grammar schools placed them withering pressure from school board initiatives. Board schools were also outpacing many voluntary schools that faced serious financial difficulties in a period of declining church attendance. The voluntary agencies were divided on the desirability of further state aid and intervention. State intervention in society was generally being more actively advocated and tolerated. The 1895 Bryce Commission [35] recommended the creation of a central authority for education and a Board of Education was created in 1899. [36] Local councils also entered the education field mainly under the Technical Instruction Acts as competitors of the school boards.

Such changes threatened the uneasy 1870 settlement. School boards came under fire before the end of the century, particularly for their higher-grade schools and what the church party considered excessive expenditure of ratepayers' money. Leading Conservatives, especially Sir John Gorst, attacked the boards and attempted to reduce their powers or transfer their powers to the county and county borough councils. The boards themselves, Nonconformist and labour bodies expressed hostility to such moves and defended their record. Sir Robert Morant, [37] who became Gorst's private secretary in 1899 and permanent secretary of the Board of Education from 1903, was able to engineer a test case. The Local Taxation Act of 1890 led the Government to put a tax on whisky and the so-called

---

[34] Dalglish, Neil, *Education Policy-making in England and Wales: The Crucible Years 1895-1911*, (Woburn Press), 1996.

[35] Anon. *Royal commission on secondary education: report of the commissioners plus Minutes of evidence etc.* Parliamentary papers, [C. 7862] H.C. (1895): Vol. XLIII, 1, [C. 7862-I-VIII] H.C. (1895), Vols. XLIV-XLIX.

[36] Gosden, P. H. J. H., 'The Board of Education Act, 1899', *British Journal of Educational Studies*, Vol. 11, (1962), pp. 44-60.

[37] Lowe, Roy, 'Personalities and policy: Sadler, Morant and the structure of education in England', in Aldrich, Richard, (ed.), *In history and in education: essays presented to Peter Gordon,* (Woburn), 1996, pp. 98-115. See also, Allen, B. M., *Sir Robert Morant; a great public servant*, (Macmillan), 1934, and Dugdale, B. E. C., 'Arthur James Balfour and Robert Morant', *Quarterly Review*, Vol. 260, (1933), pp. 152-168.

'whisky money' was used to fund technical education. However some school boards used the revenue to fund secondary education. In the Cockerton judgement in 1899, London School Board expenditure on high elementary classes was disallowed by the district auditor. [38] This allowed Morant and Gorst to achieve a dual objective: the prevention of further post-elementary developments in board schools and the possibility of using the borough and county councils as all-embracing educational authorities. The result was the 1902 Education Act. In drafting the bill, Morant was able to bring elementary and secondary education under one authority and at the same time bring relief to the voluntary schools:

> The 1902 Education Act was a deeply reactionary piece of legislation that consciously set out to dismantle the popular schooling system developed by the school boards that had been created by the 1870 education act. The purpose of this dismemberment was to buttress the control of education by religious groups and by the grammar schools... [39]

The debate on the education bill, steered by the Prime Minister A. J. Balfour through Parliament, saw a stalwart defence of board schools. [40] However, the separate administration of board schools, grammar schools, Science and Art Department grants, technical instruction committees and the independent management of voluntary elementary schools was confusing. The creation of 131 Local Education Authorities (LEAs) based on county and county borough councils and 202 minor authorities replaced 2,568 School Boards and 14,238 School Attendance Committees in elementary education alone. [41] It was, however, the notion of 'Church schools on the rates' that provoked fierce and sustained resistance especially from

---

[38] Taylor, Tony, 'The Cockerton case revisited: London politics and education, 1898-1901', *British Journal of Educational Studies*, Vol. 30, (1982), pp. 329-348.

[39] Manton, Kevin, 'The 1902 Education Act', *History Today*, Vol. 52, (12), (2002), p. 18.

[40] Simon, Brian, 'The 1902 Education Act: a wrong turning', *History of Education Society Bulletin*, Vol. 70, (2002), pp. 69-75, Reeder, David A., 'The Education Act of 1902 and local governance: some reflections on Brian Simon's critique', *History of Education Society Bulletin*, 70, (2002), pp. 101-108, Pugh, D. R., 'The 1902 Education Act: the search for a compromise'. *British Journal of Educational Studies*, Vol. 16, (1968), pp. 164-178, and Chambers, B., 'The 1902 Education Act: The Making of a Part III Authority', *History of Education Researcher*, Vol. 78, (2006), pp. 61-71.

[41] In Scotland, school boards survived until 1918 when they were replaced by elected county authorities, and in 1929 by the county councils

Nonconformists. [42] Opposition was especially intense about state-support for the Catholic Church. Inside and outside Parliament there was outcry against 'Rome on the rates'. Church of England schools generally heeded the rule that no pupil or teacher should be required to conform to religious belief or ritual. Roman Catholic schools were less enthusiastic and enforced religious observance more strictly. In 1917, the Church issued a canon expressly forbidding Catholic parents on pain of excommunication from sending their children to non-Catholic schools.

The Act also empowered LEAs to support teacher training colleges. Most of the existing colleges were church owned, though new non-denominational colleges, for example, Froebel, Edge Hill and Charlotte Mason had opened in the last years of the nineteenth century, as had teacher training departments in the universities, 16 of them by 1900. The expansion of LEA teacher training meant that by 1906 not all places at denominational colleges were being filled. The Board of Education therefore decided that if the church colleges wished to receive grant aid, they must forfeit the right to use denominational criteria in offering places. The Church of England and the Catholic Church protested, the government backed down and the churches were allowed to recruit up to half their students on the basis of their denominational allegiance. [43]

The most far-reaching effect of the 1902 Act was its influence on the structure of elementary and secondary education. It did not make it mandatory for local authorities to provide secondary education but it did require them to perform the functions previously performed by the school boards and the technical instruction committees. The result of this was a massive expansion in the physical provision of secondary schooling in the years up to 1914. [44] In 1904, the Board of Education published its Secondary Regulations, defining a four year

---

[42] See, Gullifer, N. R., 'Opposition to the 1902 Education Act', *Oxford Review of Education*, Vol. 8, (1), (1982), pp. 83-98, and Pugh, D. R., 'English Nonconformity, Education and Passive Resistance, 1903-6', *History of Education*, Vol.19 , (4), (1990), pp. 355-73, and 'The Church and Education: Anglican Attitudes, 1902', *Journal of Ecclesiastical History*, Vol. 23, (1972), pp. 219-232.

[43] Gore, Charles, *Objections to the Education bill, 1906, in principle and in detail*, (Murray), 1906, indicates the extent of opposition. See also, Dalglish, N., 'Lloyd George's Education Bill? Planning the 1906 Education Bill', *History of Education*, Vol. 23, (1994), pp. 375-384.

[44] Robinson, Wendy, 'Historiographical Reflections on the 1902 Education Act', *Oxford Review of Education*, Vol. 28, (2002), pp. 159-172, offers a valuable overview of a hundred years of historiography of the 1902 Education Act.

subject-based course leading to a certificate in English language and literature, geography, history, a foreign language, mathematics, science, drawing, manual work, physical training, and household crafts for girls. This was followed by the Elementary Code in 1907 that sought to clarify the aims and improve the quality of elementary education.

The government did not neglect the question of access for elementary school pupils to the new fee-charging secondary schools. The Free Place Regulations of 1907 made available enhanced government grants to all secondary schools prepared to offer at least a quarter of their places without fees to pupils who had spent at least two years at public elementary school and received £5 per head for each scholar. Would-be 'free placers' were expected to sit a simple qualifying examination that evolved into the 11+. Pressure of numbers soon made this as ferociously competitive as any of the existing scholarship tests. By 1912, 49,120 children, 32 per cent of the total population of maintained secondary schools, were 'free placers'.

There was much concern both within and outside Parliament that there should be more measures to ensure that children were healthier. The Boer War (1899-1902) revealed the extent of 'physical deterioration' when a government committee investigated the causes of the poor physical condition of potential recruits. The need for developments in child health, orchestrated by Morant and Margaret McMillan, was legislation in 1906 and 1907 and in setting up a medical department of the Board of Education.[45] In 1906, needy schoolchildren received further assistance under the Education (Provision of Meals) Act that allowed local authorities to provide meals free of charge when parents could not afford to pay. This was made compulsory under an Act of 1914. The Education (Administrative Provisions) Act of 1907 required education authorities to see that all schoolchildren under their care received a medical inspection. Free school meals and medical inspections were a further attack on the existing poor law system as well as a major advance in the role of the state in education.

How were grammar and public schools reformed?

Between the Endowed Schools Act 1869 and the appointment of the Bryce Commission in 1895, four main developments had taken place in secondary education. The endowments and management of the grammar schools had been widely reformed and their curriculum had

---

[45] Steedman, Carolyn, *Childhood, culture and class in Britain: Margaret McMillan, 1860-1931*, (Virago), 1990.

become subject to greater scrutiny and change. The middle-class character of the schools had been further reinforced though there were opportunities to recruit a small number of working-class children to the secondary system and, finally secondary education for middle-class girls had made considerable advances.

In spite of these reforms, many schools remained insecure. The Bryce Commission found in the 1890s many of them, mainly smaller schools, were prone to fluctuating numbers and decline. [46] Its report led to the establishment of the Board of Education and, after the Cockerton Judgement, to the 1902 Act. It recommended that for every 1,000 of the population, secondary education should be made available to just ten children, of whom eight would be in the third grade. This meant that, out of 4,000,000 children, 64,000 would be educated in the first and second grade schools and 256,000 in the third grade. 'It is obvious', the Commission commented, 'that these distinctions correspond roughly, but by no means exactly, to the gradations of society'. [47] It was the question of access to secondary schools that was becoming a major issue. The Education Act 1902 was central to the process of change for grammar schools.

The Endowed Schools Commissioners had power to make provision for girls and was widely used by them. By the time of their demise in 1874, they had created 27 schools for girls and schemes for another twenty were in the pipeline. The Charity Commissioners proceeded at a much slower pace but as further 45 girls' schools had been added by 1903. Parallel to these developments was the creation of proprietary schools for girls. In 1872, a Girls' Public Day School Company was formed to provide good and cheap academic day schools for girls of all classes above the level of elementary education. By 1880, it had opened eleven schools in London and eleven elsewhere and by 1901 the Company owned 38 schools educating girls from the age of 3-18. A handful of new girls' schools, such as Cheltenham, Wycombe Abbey and Roedean, were boarding, modelling themselves more or less on boys' public schools; but the vast majority were day schools. [48]

The elementary and endowed and private school systems remained broadly defined by the criteria of social class. It is not

---

[46] Rankin, James R., *The Bryce Commission: an historical study of its contributions to the development of English secondary education*, (Department of Education, University of Chicago), 1963.
[47] Roach, John, *Secondary education in England, 1870-1902: public activity and private enterprise*, (Routledge), 1991, pp. 3-86, 119-156.
[48] Avery, Gillian, *The best type of girl: a history of girls' independent schools*, (Deutsch), 1991.

surprising that the public schools managed to maintain their social identity though criticisms continued to be levelled against their traditions and preoccupation with games and athleticism. The public schools perpetuated an aristocratic element in English education and the proprietary and endowed schools continued to uphold it as an educational ideal. The sons of the expanding commercial and industrial middle-classes were trained in the older traditions and codes of gentlemen, an education that some argue left them ill-prepared for their role in an increasingly competitive world. [49] Modern subjects were often left optional and between 1860 and 1880 games became compulsory, organised and eulogised at all the leading public schools. There was no overall change in their structure, objectives or curriculum until after 1918.

Why did higher education expand after 1870?

The vast growth in and attempt to systematise secondary education was paralleled by significant, though relatively small, growth and innovation in the university sector. Higher education was still only accessible to a tiny minority. There were changes in the composition of the university population, in the structure of university government and in the curriculum. The 1870s saw the arrival at Oxford and Cambridge both of Nonconformists and of women. The 1871 legislation abolishing university tests untying both undergraduate places and fellowships and in the process allowed fellows to marry. The growing regiment of dons' wives was augmented by a small file of women students. Girton and Newnham at Cambridge in the early 1870s were joined by Somerville, Lady Margaret Hall and St Anne's at Oxford in 1879 followed by St Hugh's and St Hilda's in 1886 and 1892 respectively. [50] But numbers were small: in 1900-1901 296 women students at Cambridge and 239 at Oxford compared to 2,880 and 2,537 male students respectively. Women did not become full members of the university in Oxford until 1919 and in Cambridge until 1948 whereas they were admitted to all the University of London

---

[49] Berghoff, Hartmut, 'Public schools and the decline of the British economy, 1870-1914', *Past & Present*, Vol. 129, (1990), pp. 148-167.

[50] Howarth, Janet, "In Oxford but...not of Oxford': The Women's Colleges', in Brocks, Michael G., and Curthoys, Mark C., (eds.), *The History of the University of Oxford,* Vol. 7, part 2, *Nineteenth Century Oxford*, (Clarendon Press), 2000, pp. 237-307, and 'Women', in Harrison, Brian, (ed.), *History of the University of Oxford*, Vol. 8, (Clarendon Press), 1995, pp. 345-375.

degrees in 1878. [51]

The Royal and Statutory Commissions of the 1850s had begun the process of overhauling college statutes and strengthening the central institutions of university government. This was continued in the 1870s but the more ambitious plans were spoiled by the fall in colleges' income brought about by the agricultural depression. At the same time, a reassertion of control over teaching and pastoral responsibilities by many colleges very powerfully counter-balanced such trends towards centralisation. The assault on the dominance of Classics and Mathematics towards the end of the 1840s continued and in the early 1870s separate courses in History and Law emerged and the 1890s saw the arrival of courses in English and Modern Languages. Parallel to this was the emergence of research as a systematic postgraduate activity.

Change in Oxbridge, however, was a pale reflection of the changes outside it. By 1900, there were more students, women as well as men, in higher education in Great Britain outside than within Oxford and Cambridge. Universities were established at Newcastle in 1871 followed by University College of Wales, Aberystwyth in 1872; Leeds 1874; Mason College, Birmingham 1874; Bristol 1876; Firth College, Sheffield 1879; Liverpool 1881; Nottingham 1881; Cardiff 1883; Bangor 1883; Reading 1892; and, Southampton 1902. Many of these institutions began by taking external London degree examinations before seeking Royal Charters to enable them to grant their own degrees.[52] Other institutions, often also exploiting the external London examining umbrella, grew in London itself: medical schools attached to the teaching hospitals; in South Kensington the Royal School of Mines, the Royal College of Science and the Central Technical College formed the great Imperial College of Science and Technology in 1907; the London School of Economics and Political Science in 1895; and the women's colleges, Bedford (1849), Westfield (1882) and Royal Holloway (1886). [53] But the University of London only acquired a teaching as well as an examining role in 1899,

---

[51] Vernon, Keith, *Universities and the State in England, 1850-1939*, (Routledge), 2004, pp. 93-132, examines the development of provincial universities. Dyhouse, Carol, *No Distinction of Sex? Women in British Universities, 1870-1939*, (UCL Press), 1995.

[52] Walsh, J. J., 'The University Movement in the North of England at the End of the Nineteenth Century', *Northern History*, Vol. 46, (1), (2009), pp. 113-131.

[53] Bingham, Caroline, *A History of Royal Holloway College, 1886-1986*, (Constable), 1987, Sondheimer, Janet, *Castle Adamant in Hampstead: A History of Westfield College, 1882-1982*, (Westfield College), 1983.

following the University of London Act 1898 that brought all these and other institutions together in a complex and uneasy federation. By 1900-1901, full-time students outside Oxford and Cambridge totalled almost 8,000 in England and a further 1,250 in Wales.

Funding the civic university movement proved problematic and most universities operated with fewer resources than the endowments of Oxbridge. In individual cases, university colleges benefited from the generosity of local business: in Birmingham, for example, the Chamberlains played a central role. But this was not enough. From 1839, the University of London had small recurrent grants in recognition of the imperial and colonial as well as the domestic function of its examining role. In 1883-1884, the Welsh parliamentary lobby succeeded in securing short-term grant aid for the three Welsh colleges; and in 1880 the Treasury finally conceded the principle of grant aid to the English institutions outside Oxbridge. By 1906, direct Treasury grants to universities amounted to £100,000.

The full-time student population in all English and Welsh universities in 1914 only accounted for one per cent of the age group. Universities still catered for the elite. The advance of the new professional middle-classes gradually reduced the dominance of the landed gentry and clergy and outside Oxbridge, and by 1914, the children of the lower middle-classes and skilled artisans were beginning to appear.

How were women educated after 1870?

The 1870 Education Act widened the gap between the educations of different classes. It marked the increasing involvement of the state in the financing and control of elementary education.[54] The age of compulsory schooling was raised from ten, to eleven and then fourteen in 1880, 1893 and 1899 respectively. However, exceptions were made for part-time working under local by-laws. [55] From 1870 to 1914, the state also increased the number of grants for certain subjects taught in elementary schools and supported scholarship schemes for entry to secondary education. Both these measures

---

[54] Gomersall, Meg, 'Ideals and realities: the education of working-class girls, 1800-1870', *History of Education*, Vol. 17, (1988), pp. 37-53, Horn, Pamela, 'The education and employment of working-class girls, 1870-1914', *History of Education*, Vol. 17, (1988), pp. 71-82. Ibid, Roach, John, *Secondary education in England, 1870-1902: public activity and private enterprise*, pp. 201-242, examines middle-class girls' education in secondary schools.

[55] This half-time system was ended in the 1918 Education Act and fourteen became the national compulsory school leaving age.

further sharpened existing sexual divisions between working-class boys and girls. The Education Department influenced the elementary curriculum through the provision of grants and for working-class girls the influence was in the expansion of domestic subjects. [56] The Education Department Code of 1878 provided for compulsory domestic education for girls in the state sector. In 1882, grants were made for the teaching of cookery and in 1890 for laundry work. [57] The textbooks used in schools made it quite clear that the 'new' subjects should involve the learning of useful, practical skills and character building. Such habits were, of course, to prepare working-class schoolgirls to become good women, capable of being efficient wives and mothers. [58]

Writers such as Anna Davin and Carol Dyhouse link the expansion of domestic subjects with fears about the future of the British race and the decline of the British Empire. The *Report of the Inter-Departmental Committee on Physical Deterioration* (1904) contained many statements from the middle-classes about the low standards of living among the poor in congested urban areas and particularly the inadequacies of working-class wives. Since children were seen as a national asset, it was believed critical to educate working-class elementary schoolgirls for wifehood and motherhood. The results were, however, not always as anticipated by government officials. Working-class women interviewed by Elizabeth Roberts about their lives in the late-nineteenth and early-twentieth century stated that school domestic science was 'never any help'. It would appear that for many working-class girls, it was their mothers' training at home that was valued more than the unreal situations created in schools.

---

[56] Williams, Susan, 'Domestic science: the education of girls at home', in Aldrich, Richard, (ed.), *Public or private education?: lessons from history* (Woburn), 2004, pp. 116-126, Manthorpe, Catherine, 'Science or domestic science?: The struggle to define an appropriate science education for girls in early twentieth century England', *History of Education*, Vol. 15, (1986), pp. 195-213.

[57] Turnball, A., 'An isolated missionary: the domestic subjects teacher in England, 1870-1914', *Women's History Review,* Vol. 3, (1), (1994), pp. 81-100. Heggie, Vanessa, 'Domestic and domesticating education in the late Victorian city', *History of Education*, Vol. 40, (3), (2011), pp. 273-290, considers Manchester.

[58] For a detailed case studies, see, McDermid, Jane, *The schooling of working class girls in Victorian Scotland: gender, education and identity,* (Routledge), 2005, Allsopp, Anne, *The education and employment of girls in Luton, 1874-1924: widening opportunities and lost freedoms*, (Bedfordshire Historical Record Society), 2005.

The increased emphasis on the sexual division between boys and girls between 1870 and 1914 was evident also in the scholarship system whereby poor elementary pupils could be offered a free place in a fee-paying secondary school. The number of scholarships was severely limited. More were, however, offered to boys than girls and this was especially so after the Technical Instruction Act 1889 enabled counties and county boroughs to make grants to secondary schools for scholarship purposes. In addition to this handicap, working-class girls might also find themselves discriminated against both by their parents and teachers when they had scholastic ambitions for secondary schooling. In essence, working-class girls were being trained in domestic skills while a proportion of middle-class girls were offered at least a route out of that sphere.

Feminist philosophies were applied in the many new fee-paying schools rather than in the new state schools. There was some minor activity in feminist educational provision for working-class women and girls. A Working Women's College was established in London in 1864. The only means by which women were able to influence government and working-class schooling was through membership of School Boards. In the 1870s, many women took local government office, a new avenue of political participation opened to them in 1869. Women became eligible for election to Poor Law Guardianship positions and in 1870 to School Boards. [59] Between 1892 and 1895, 128 women were elected on to English and Welsh School Boards. However, they were not dealing primarily with girls' schooling but with the schooling of all working-class children and were often allotted to suitably 'feminine' committees such as the Needlework Sub-Committee.

How can we explain the development of mass education and how does it provide insights into girls' education? Britain needed an educated electorate after the extension of the vote to working men in 1867. Britain also needed an educated workforce that would be able to produce goods in the competitive international market as well as for home consumption A third explanation, grounded in a Marxist analysis, argues that education was seen by the middle-classes as a means of reforming, civilising and controlling a decadent working-class. None of these explanations take into account gender divisions. While the first two explanations may be relevant to the schooling of working-class boys, they had little relevance for working-class girls, since women did not have the right to vote and neither could they

---

[59] Martin, Jane, 'Entering the public arena: the female members of the London School Board, 1870-1914', *History of Education*, Vol. 22, (3), (1993), pp. 225-240.

enter the range of skilled jobs which, it was believed, would bring economic prosperity. However, some feminist historians argue that mass schooling was an attempt to impose a middle-class family form of a male breadwinner and an economically dependent wife and mother upon the working-class children. Such family forms would benefit all family members and the wider society and would provide a secure environment for the rearing of healthy children, the future workforce and for the care and comfort of the male wage earner.

Some conclusions

The development of education between 1830 and 1914 was largely a reflection of the class basis of English society. The working-classes, if they were schooled at all before 1870, went to elementary schools. The middle-classes filled the grammar schools while the public schools remained the preserve of the upper-classes. There were links between these three stages, a situation made more obvious after 1902 and the 'free-place' system, but movement from elementary school to grammar school was the exception rather than the rule. Children of all classes and of both sexes were better educated in 1914 than in 1830 but this did not have any real impact on the class bias of that education. Education mirrored the pyramidal nature of society rising to the one per cent who received a university education by 1914.

The growing intervention by the state, first with grants to voluntary schools and then with its school boards and local education authorities, marked a recognition that education for all was increasingly seen as a social service not something that ought to be provided by religious and voluntary organisations. The policy-making initiative moved from localities to central government. Acceptable standards were imposed from the centre and administered locally. Education was finally perceived as being too important to be left to chance.

13 Crime

There has been an unprecedented growth of academic research and publications in the history of crime.[1] Until the 1970s, most books dealing with crime tended to be 'popular' rather than narrowly 'academic' and concentrated on particular, notorious events or personalities and many depended on largely anecdotal and literary sources Since then, historians have increasingly turned their attention to crime and how former societies understood it and sought to deal with it.[2]

Why is defining crime a problem?

Some historians have made a distinction between 'real crime' such as murder, rape and theft and 'social crime' or offences that had a degree of community acceptance or that can be linked with social protest.[3] John Rule suggested that it is useful to think of two main types of social crime during the late-eighteenth and first half of the nineteenth century. Some crimes drew society's support because of their protest nature. In this category he included rioting over the high cost of food, over enclosures, recruiting for the army or navy or over turnpike tolls.[4] Other crimes were not regarded as criminal by those who committed

---

[1] Emsley, C., *Crime and Society in England 1750-1900*, fourth edition, (Longman), 2010, is the most recent general text and should be read in conjunction with his *Policing and its Context 1750-1870*, (Macmillan), 1983, and 'Crime in Nineteenth Century Britain', *History Today*, Vol. 38, (4), (1988), pp. 40-46, Gattrell, V., 'Crime, authority and the police ', in Thompson, F. M. L., (ed.), *The Cambridge Social History of Britain 1750-1950: Vol. 3 Social Agencies and Institutions*, (Cambridge University Press), 1900, pp. 243-310, and the older study by Tobias, J. J., *Crime and Industrial Society in the Nineteenth Century*, (Batsford), 1967. See also, Taylor, David, *Crime, policing and punishment in England, 1750-1914*, (Macmillan), 1998, and McLynn, Frank J., *Crime and punishment in eighteenth-century England*, (Routledge), 1989.

[2] Kilday, Anne-Marie, and Nash, David, (eds.), *Histories of Crime in Britain 1600-2000*, (Palgrave Macmillan), 2010, provides a valuable summary of current thinking.

[3] Taylor, H., 'Rationing Crime: The Political Economy of Criminal Statistics since the 1850s', *Economic History Review*, Vol. 51, (1998), pp. 569-590, and Sindall, R. S., 'The criminal statistics of nineteenth-century cities: a new approach', *Urban History*, Vol. 13, (1986), pp. 28-36, consider the problem of crime statistics.

[4] Shakesheff, T., *Rural conflict, crime and protest: Herefordshire, 1800 to 1860*, (Boydell), 2003, pp. 78-112, 141-175, provides a good local study on this issue.

them. 'Perks' or the appropriation of things from the workplace became increasingly the object of criminal prosecution by employers in the nineteenth century. Poachingfell into the same category. [5] The poor did not look upon it as a crime:

...they almost universally look upon game, when in a wild state, as not being the property of any individual. [6]

The degree to which the state criminalises certain types of behaviour and not others has always been a matter of debate. The traditional view is that humanitarian reformers such as Sir Samuel Romilly and Sir James Mackintosh gradually created awareness both inside and outside Parliament that England's Bloody Code needed drastic revision. [7] While such men stressed the barbarity of the legal code, other reformers like John Howard paved the way for improvement in the penal system. This view fitted well with the Whig notion of history as progress but implied a logic that neglected the economic, social and political context for change.

Eighteenth century Parliaments tended to pass laws to deal with local issues but gradually government concluded that crime was a 'national' issue. [8] Sir Robert Peel's reorganisation of the criminal law during the 1820s was symptomatic of this change. Yet national laws still had to be implemented at local level by local people, whose perceptions were not always the same as those in Parliament. The law had to be interpreted and enforced by local agents such as the magistracy who had their own assumptions, interests and prejudices and who could, on occasions, be at odds with each other. [9]

---

[5] Osborne, Harvey, and Winstanley, Michael J., 'Rural and Urban Poaching in Victorian England', *Rural History*, Vol. 17, (2006), pp. 187-212, and Hopkins, H., *The Long Affray: the poaching wars, 1760-1914*, (Secker and Warburg), 1985.

[6] A Bedfordshire JP to the Select Committee on Criminal Commitments and Convictions, *Parliamentary Papers 1826-7*, Vol. 6, p. 34.

[7] The 'Bloody Code' refers to the system of laws and punishments in England between 1688 and 1815. It was not referred to as such in its own time, but the name was given later owing to the sharply increased number of crimes that attracted the death penalty. In 1688, there were 50 offences on the statute book punishable by death, but that number had almost quadrupled by 1776 and it reached 220 by 1800.

[8] Innes, Joanna, *Inferior Politics: Social Problems and Social Policy in Eighteenth-Century Britain*, (Oxford University Press), 2009, pp. 78-108, considers local acts of the national Parliament.

[9] Zangerl, C. H. E., 'The Social Composition of the County Magistracy in England and Wales, 1831-1887', *Journal of British Studies*, Vol. 11, (1971),

Offenders in England and Wales were brought before three main kinds of court during the nineteenth century.[10] Trials were quick and, until the early-nineteenth century, lawyers were rarely present. The trial involved a confrontation between the prosecutor, normally the victim of the crime and the defendant, in which the defendant was expected to explain away the evidence presented against them with witnesses testifying on both sides. Since the law of evidence was not a fully developed, prosecutors, judges and where appropriate jurors had greater power and flexibility than they do today. Criminal prosecution was rather more like civil litigation. Private prosecution was expensive and only wealthy people could afford to pay for a lengthy court trial. The cost of the litigation meant that the poor often 'took the law into their own hands' but this did not preclude the use of the courts. For instance, in the Essex Quarter Sessions between 1760 and 1800, labourers were prosecutors in about a fifth of cases.

Before the appointment of professional prosecutors, criminal cases were initiated by complaints from private citizens, usually the victims, to local magistrates. Once the accused was arrested, they were examined by a magistrate whose role was to assess the allegations. If charged with a felony, the magistrate could commit the individual to prison to await trial at the Quarter Sessions or Assize or, if charged with a misdemeanour, bind them over to appear at the next meeting of the magistrates' court. During the eighteenth century, magistrates used the preliminary hearing to dismiss weak cases and only committed the accused to prison if they felt the evidence was sufficient to merit a trial. How far magistrates might go in examining the accused during these initial hearings was the source of some debate

---

pp. 113-125, Philips, D., 'The Black Country Magistracy 1835-1860', *Midland History*, Vol. 3, (1975), pp. 161-190, and Swift, R., 'The English Urban Magistracy and the Administration of Justice during the early-nineteenth Century: Wolverhampton 1815-1860', *Midland History*, Vol. 17, (1992), pp. 75-92.

[10] Cottu, Charles, *On the Administration of Criminal Justice in England: and the Spirit of the English Government*, (R. Stevens), 1822, provides a contemporary view. Bentley, D. J., *English Criminal Courts in the Nineteenth Century*, (Continuum), 1998, and Langbein, John H., *The Origins of the Adversary Criminal Trial*, (Oxford University Press), 2003. See also, King, Peter, *Crime, Justice and Discretion in England, 1740-1820*, (Cambridge University Press), 2000, and Cornish, William, Anderson J. Stuart, Cocks, Ray, Lobban, Michael, Polden, Patrick, and Smith, Keith, *The Oxford History of the Laws of England, Volumes XI, XII and XIII, 1820-1914*, (Oxford University Press), 2010, Vol. XI for detailed discussion of the development of the criminal justice system.

that was not resolved until 1848 when they were forbidden from interrogating the accused.

Victim-based prosecution in criminal justice was a unique feature of English system and was based on a distinction between heinous crimes, like murder, regarded as crimes against the Crown and ordinary crimes that were a matter for the community. After 1830, the 'new' police had some discretion in identifying behaviour as criminal or not and in deciding what action to take. It was largely victimless crimes that were open to such discretion: drunkenness, prostitution, street gaming and especially Sunday street-selling. Gradually after 1830, the police rather than the victim began to initiate prosecutions though the private prosecutor predominated until the 1880s. Peel was sympathetic to extending the Scottish system of a special public prosecutor in the mid-1820s and there were further attempts in the 1850s but legislation failed in the House of Commons largely because the opposition lobby of solicitors thought they would lose business. In was not until 1879 that the office of Director of Public Prosecution was established.

After 1820, magistrates' courts, known generally as police courts, saw an expansion of summary jurisdiction. They heard all but the most serious offences; 66 per cent of all cases in England and Wales in 1857 rising to 80 per cent by 1911. Misdemeanours, the least serious offences such as drunkenness, soliciting and vagrancy were dealt with summarily by magistrates sitting alone or in pairs on the bench, although those accused were allowed to employ a defence counsel. At the beginning of the nineteenth century, individual magistrates frequently tried summary offences in their own home but this was abolished in 1848 by the Summary Jurisdiction Act. After this, all summary trials took place at formally constituted Petty Sessions, before at least two magistrates. Petty Sessional courts had existed since the eighteenth century but in 1828, legislation had tightened up procedures and carefully defined Petty Sessional divisions within counties. In the larger towns and cities, stipendiary or paid magistrates, took on more and more of the burdens of summary justice. Magistrates' summary powers were extended to include some cases of petty larceny and assault with the passage of the Juvenile Offenders Acts in 1847 and 1850 and the Criminal Justice Acts of 1855 and 1879. [11] Summary jurisdiction benefitted the working-classes by making access to the courts quick and cheap but also entailed them

---

[11] The Juvenile Offenders Act of 1847 permitted summary trial for larceny by offenders aged under 14. This was raised to 16 in 1850. The Criminal Justice Act of 1855 extended summary jurisdiction with the consent of the accused to all cases of simple larceny.

'handing over' to the police and increasingly middle-class magistrates the right to sort out their conflicts. [12]

When the offence appeared more serious, the magistrate drafted a bill of indictment for a grand jury which, if satisfied that there was a case to answer, sent it for trial by jury in one of two venues. [13] More serious offences or felonies were prosecuted on indictment and were heard at Quarter Sessions that met four times a year in the county town and in those boroughs where the right for a borough session was included in its charter. These courts were held before a bench of county justices or magistrates appointed by a borough corporation, with a jury. Quarter Sessions were regarded as consistently poor throughout the nineteenth century due to failure by chairmen, who did not have to be legally qualified, to take proper note of evidence, often displaying open hostility to prisoners and the severity of its sentences compared to the Assizes.

The most serious offences were tried before professional circuit judges and juries at Assizes that generally sat twice a year. Before 1842, when legislation assigned all capital offences and those with life imprisonment for the first offence to the Assizes, the line between Assize and Quarter Sessions cases was rather blurred. It has been estimated that in the early-nineteenth century, trials lasted about 20 minutes with Assizes hearing 20-30 cases a day. Traditionally, English felony trials consisted of a relatively unstructured exchange between the victim of the felony or a hired prosecutor and the accused generally appearing without a lawyer. In cases of high treason, the right to make a defence had been established in 1696 [14] but it was not

---

[12] Davis, J., 'A poor man's system of justice: The London police courts in the second half of the nineteenth century', *Historical Journal*, Vol. 27, (2), (1984), pp. 309-335.

[13] Grand juries met to assess the indictments and decide whether there was sufficient evidence to try the case before a trial jury. At this point prosecutors and their witnesses, but not defendants, could testify. Those cases for which a grand jury believed the evidence was sufficient to warrant a trial were approved as 'true bills'; those rejected were labelled 'ignoramus' or 'not found' and the case was dropped. There were repeated calls throughout the nineteenth century for the abolition of the grand jury but it was not until 1933 that they were abandoned in favour of a committal procedure. See, Hostettler, John, *The Politics of Criminal Law Reform in the Nineteenth Century*, (Barry Rose Law Publishers), 1992, pp. 150-154, and *The Criminal Jury Old and New: Jury power from early times to the present day*, (Waterside Press), 2004, pp. 109-125.

[14] See, Shapiro, Alexander H., 'Political Theory and the Growth of Defensive Safeguards in Criminal Procedure: The Origins of the Treason

until 1836 that the Prisoners' Counsel Act recognised the defendant's right to legal counsel in felony trials and lifted many restrictions on the activities of defence lawyers. [15] This recognised the growing practice, which had developed during the previous century, of judges allowing counsel to examine witnesses on the defendant's behalf. [16] In the early-nineteenth century, there were two assizes per year held in the major county towns of most counties at Lent and during the summer. Emergencies, such as food riots or other types of public disorder could lead to a special assize being called. The metropolitan equivalent of the assizes was the court at the Old Bailey that, by the 1750s, held eight sessions a year. In 1834, it was enlarged and re-housed in the new Central Criminal Court. [17]

The King's or Queen's Bench was the monarch's personal court concerned with protecting the interests of the Crown. Cases could be referred to it where it was believed that a fair hearing in a particular locality was impossible. It was also a court of review for magistrates, who could ask it to rule on points of law. Judges at the Assizes normally consulted their colleagues on points of law but, in 1848, the Court for Crown Cases Reserved was set up for this. During the nineteenth century, there was no appeals procedure or court of appeals. A convicted criminal's only hope was the Royal Pardon, in practice delegated to the Home Secretary. A Court of Criminal Appeal was finally established in 1907. [18]

Were there criminal classes?

Today we are concerned about 'organised crime' as its tentacles sprawl across the globe. In the nineteenth century, contemporaries

---

Trials Act of 1696', *Law & History Review*, Vol. 11, (2), (1993), pp. 215-255.

[15] Beattie, J. M., 'Scales of Justice: Defence Counsel and the English Criminal Trial in the Eighteenth and Nineteenth Centuries', *Law & History Review*, Vol. 9, (2), (1991), pp. 221-267, examines the development of defence in felony cases.

[16] Langbein, John H., 'The Prosecutorial Origins of Defence Counsel in the Eighteenth Century: The Appearance of Solicitors', *Cambridge Law Journal*, Vol. 58, (1999), pp. 314-365.

[17] May, Allyson M., *The Bar and the Old Bailey, 1750-1850,* (University of North Carolina Press), 2003.

[18] In Scotland, the nineteenth century justice system consisted of two courts, the Sheriff Court and the High Court (based in Edinburgh). Both of these courts travelled on a circuit to different regional locations where cases would be tried. The most common crimes to be tried in the Sheriff Court were theft and assault while more difficult cases were referred to the High Court, the supreme criminal court of Scotland.

In Europe and North America were concerned by the existence of professional criminals and the more ambiguous 'criminal classes'. [19] The *Report of the Royal Commission on the Rural Constabulary* 1839, largely drafted by Edwin Chadwick, attempted to explain crime across England and Wales. [20] Criminality was rooted in the poorer classes, especially those who roamed the country: 'the prevalent cause of vagrancy was the impatience of steady labour'.[21] This idea of 'masterless men' had been a prevalent feature of social thinking since the sixteenth century but Chadwick and his fellow commissioners were either unaware of, or ignored the seasonal nature of much nineteenth century employment and the need of many, even urban dwellers, to spend time moving from place to place and from job to job. Poverty and indigence did not lead to crime, the *Report* insisted. Criminals suffered from two vices: 'Indolence or the pursuit of easy excitement'. [22] They were drawn to commit crimes by 'the temptation of the profit of a career of depredation, as compared with the profits of honest and even well paid industry'. [23] For Chadwick, criminals made a rational decision to live by crime because of its attractions. This analysis of why individuals became criminals was also not new.

However, what was new was that Chadwick and other reformers identified a group within the working-class that possessed the worst habits of the class as a whole. [24] The issue was one of 'bad' habits and

---

[19] What follows draws on ibid, Emsley, C., *Crime and Society in England 1750-1900*, pp. 177-178.
[20] Philips, David, 'Three "moral entrepreneurs" and the creation of a "criminal class" in England, c.1790s-1840s', *Crime, Histoire et Sociétés*, Vol. 7, (2003), pp. 79-107, considers Colquhoun, Chadwick and Miles. See also, Ekelund, Robert B., and Dorton, Cheryl, 'Criminal justice institutions as a common pool: the 19th century analysis of Edwin Chadwick', *Journal of Economic Behavior & Organization*, Vol. 50, (3), (2003), pp. 271-294.
[21] *First Report of the Commissioners appointed to enquire into the Best Means of Establishing an Efficient Constabulary Force in the Counties of England and Wales*, (W. Clowes and Son), 1839, p. 63
[22] Ibid, p. 64.
[23] Ibid, p. 128.
[24] The problems involved in defining a 'criminal class' are explored in Bailey, V., 'The fabrication of deviance: 'dangerous classes' and 'criminal classes' in Victorian England', in Rule J., and Malcolmson, R., (eds.), *Protest and survival: the historical experience; essays for E. P. Thompson*, (Merlin Press), 1993, pp. 221-256, McGowen, Randall, 'Getting to Know the Criminal Class in Nineteenth-Century England,' *Nineteenth-Century Contexts*, Vol. 14, (1990), pp. 33-54, Taylor, David, 'Beyond the bounds of respectable society: The "dangerous classes" in Victorian and Edwardian England', in Rowbotham, Judith, and Stevenson, Kim, (eds.), *Criminal conversations : Victorian crimes, social panic, and moral outrage* (Ohio

vices that were then identified as the causes of crime. The 1834 Select Committee enquiring into drunkenness concluded that the 'vice' was declining among the middle- and upper-classes but increasing among the working-classes with a notable impact on crime. [25] Employment and good wages led to greater consumption of alcohol that, on occasions, contributed to a greater incidence of violent behaviour. The problem, the Committee concluded, was the poor's lack of morality. 'Lack of moral training' was not a new issue in 1834, but it was taken up and emphasised by several educational reformers in the next two decades especially as concern grew about juvenile delinquency. Individuals such as Mary Carpenter, John Wade and James Kay-Shuttleworth argued that proper education would lead to a reduction of crime but that it was not secular education merely involving reading, writing and arithmetic that they wanted. Jelinger Symons explained:

When the heart is depraved, and the tendencies of the child or the man are unusually vicious, there can be little doubt that instruction per se, so far from preventing crime, is accessory to it. [26]

What was needed was Christian and moral education that would explain to the working classes their true station in life. This education had to instil in the young habits of industry. If bad parents or the efforts of ragged schoolsor Sunday Schools failed to do this, then reformatory schools would have to take over. Jelinger Symons again:

There must be a change of habit as well as of mind, and the change of habit mostly needed is from some kind of idleness to some kind of industry.

State University Press), 2005, pp. 3-22, Wiener, M., *Reconstructing the criminal: culture, law and policy, 1830-1914,* (Cambridge University Press), 1991, and *Men of blood: violence, manliness and criminal justice in Victorian England*, (Cambridge University Press), 2004 and Gray, Drew D., *London's Shadow: The Dark Side of the Victorian City*, (Continuum), 2010, pp. 167-208. See also, Carpenter, Mary, *Reformatory schools for the children of the perishing and dangerous classes and for juvenile offenders*, (C. Gilpin), 1851, and Adshead, Joseph, 'On juvenile criminals, reformatories, and the means of rendering the perishing and dangerous classes serviceable to the state', *Transactions of the Manchester Statistical Society*, (1855-6), pp. 67-122.

[25] Speech by James Silk Buckingham, *Evidence on Drunkenness presented to the House of Commons*, (Benjamin Bagster), 1834, pp. 2-24.

[26] Symons, Jelinger C., 'Special Report on Reformatories in Gloucestershire, Shropshire, Worcestershire, Herefordshire and Monmouthshire and in Wales', printed in the *Minutes of the Parliamentary Committee on Education*, Parliamentary Papers, 1857-58, p. 236.

We are dealing with a class whose vocation is labour; and whose vices and virtues are infallibly connected with indolence and industry. [27]

The economic and political instability of the 1830s and especially the 1840s saw people at opposite ends of the political spectrum share increasingly ominous visions of society. Friedrich Engels wrote:

...the incidence of crime has increased with the growth of the working-class population and there is more crime in Britain than in any other country in the world. [28]

Crime was an aspect of a new and worsening social war and a frightening portrait of a brutalised, savage poor, a truly dangerous class was provided by the Chartist G. W. M. Reynolds in his fictional *The Mysteries of London*. [29] While in Paris, Reynolds had been impressed by Eugène Sue's *Les Mystères de Paris* and his serial paralleled Sue's tale of vice, depravity, and squalor in the Parisian slums with a sociological story contrasting the vice and degradation of London working-class life with the luxury and debaucheries of the hedonistic upper crust. [30] The middle-classes in England readily

---

[27] Ibid, p. 238.
[28] Engels, F., *The Condition of the Working-class in England*, 1844, translated, with foreword by V. Kiernan, (Penguin), 1987, p. 146.
[29] *The Mysteries of London*, a penny dreadful was begun by Reynolds in 1844 and he the first two series of this long-running narrative of life in mid-nineteenth century London. Thomas Miller wrote the third series and Edward L. Blanchard the fourth series of this immensely popular title. Instalments were published weekly with a single illustration and eight pages of text printed in double columns and later bound together as single volumes. See, Carver, S. J., 'The wrongs and crimes of the poor: the urban underworld of *The Mysteries of London* in context', in Humpherys, Anne and James, Louis, (eds.), *G. W. M. Reynolds: nineteenth-century fiction, politics, and the press*, (Ashgate), 2008, pp. 149-162.
[30] *Les Mystères de Paris*, a *feulliton* or French newspaper serial, was one of the most influential novels of the nineteenth century. While it is little known today, when it first ran as a weekly serial it outsold Alexandre Dumas *pere*'s *The Count of Monte Cristo*, and was praised by Victor Hugo, who called its author, Eugène Sue, the 'Dickens of Paris.' An English translation was published in three volumes in 1844. See, Maxwell, Richard, 'G. M. Reynolds, Dickens and the Mysteries of London', *Nineteenth Century Fiction*, Vol. 32, (2), (1977), pp. 188-213, and Chevalier, Louis, *Classes laborieuses et classes dangereuses*, (Plon), 1958, translated *Labouring Classes and Dangerous Classes in Paris During the First Half of the Nineteenth Century*, (Routledge), 1973.

accepted this vision of their social inferiors if nothing else because the poor looked very different in physique as well as dress. [31]

Between the 1850s and the 1870s, a succession of middle-class commentators, as often as not guided by local policemen penetrated the dark recesses of working class districts. They then wrote up their exploits for the delight of the reading public as journeys into criminal districts where the inhabitants were best compared with Red Indians or varieties of black 'savages'. The writings of Henry Mayhew, a reporter for the *Morning Chronicle*, are justifiably the most eminent and he incorporated his findings in the massive, four volumes, *London Labour and the London Poor: A Cyclopaedia of the Conditions and Earnings of those that will work, those that cannot work and those that will not work* between 1851 and 1861-1862. Mayhew noted the different physical and mental characteristics of the nomadic street people:

> There is a greater development of the animal than of the intellectual and moral nature of man.... They are more or less distinguished for their high cheek-bones and protruding jaws -- for their use of a slang language -- for their lax ideas of property -- for their general improvidence -- their repugnance to continuous labour -- their disregard of female honour -- their love of cruelty -- their pugnacity -- and their utter want of religion. [32]

For Mayhew, these 'exotic people' lacked all of the virtues that respectable middle-class Victorian society held dear. Lurking among these people there was a separate 'class' of thieves who were mainly young, idle and vagrant and who enjoyed the literature that glorified pirates and robbers. In the final volume of *London Labour*, first published in 1861-1862, Mayhew concentrated on 'the Non-Workers, or in other words, the Dangerous Classes of the Metropolis'. Mayhew himself set out to define crime and the 'criminal classes'. Crime, he argued, was the breaking of social laws in the same

---

[31] Angelo, Michael, *Penny Dreadfuls and Other Victorian Horrors*, (Jupiter), 1977, pp. 80-81. See also, Maxwell, Richard, *The Mysteries of Paris and London*, (University of Virginia Press), 1992, pp. 1-58.

[32] Mayhew, Henry, *London Labour and the London Poor: The Condition and Earnings of Those that will work, cannot work, and will not work*, 4 Vols. (Griffin, Bohn, and Company), 1861-1862, Vol. I, p. 3. See also, Beier, A. L., 'Identity, Language, and Resistance in the Making of the Victorian "Criminal Class": Mayhew's Convict Revisited', *Journal of British Studies*, Vol. 44, (2005), pp. 499-515, and Englander, David, 'Henry Mayhew and the Criminal Classes of Victorian England: The Case Reopened', *Criminal Justice History*, Vol. 17, (2002), pp. 87-108.

way that sin and vice broke religious and moral laws. [33]

From the 1850s, many commentators confidently maintained that crime was being checked. There remained, however, an irredeemable, residuum that, with the end of transportation, could no longer be shipped out of the country. This group was increasingly called the criminal class: the backbone of this class was those defined by Mayhew as 'professional' and by legislators as 'habitual' criminals. *The Times* commented in a leading article in 1870 that these men:

>...Are more alien from the rest of the community than a hostile army, for they have no idea of joining the ranks of industrious labour either here or elsewhere. The civilised world is simply a carcass on which they prey, and London above all, is to them a place to sack. [34]

In the late 1860s, James Greenwood, a journalist, noted that many juveniles resorted to crime because of hunger, yet in general habitual criminals were rarely perceived as being brought to crime by poverty. [35] The problem that contemporaries had was to explain the persistence of crime in spite of the advantages and opportunities provided by the advance of civilisation and the expansion of education from the mid-century. Poor parenting, corrupting literature etc. were combined with the mixing of first-time offenders with habitual offenders in prisons, concepts of hereditary and ideas drawn from developments in medical science.[36]

Since the 1820s, phrenologists had visited prisons to make case studies of convicts in the belief that irrational mental faculties led to crime. [37] A visitor to Newgate prison in the 1830s said the prisoners

---

[33] See also, Mayhew, Henry, and Binny, John, *The criminal prisons of London, and scenes of prison life*, (Griffin, Bohn, and Co.), 1862.

[34] *The Times*, 29 March 1870, cit, ibid, Emsley, Clive, *Crime and Society in England 1750-1900*, p. 73.

[35] See, Greenwood, James, *The Seven Curses of London*, (Fields, Osgood, & Co.), 1869.

[36] Welshman, John, *Underclass: The History of the Excluded, 1880-2000*, (Continuum), 2007, examines later developments.

[37] Phrenology developed in the early-nineteenth century. It was based on 'feeling' the bumps on a person's skull. By doing this, phrenologists believed they could draw conclusions about the individual's personality. See, Stack, David, *Queen Victoria's Skull: George Combe and the Mid-Victorian Minds*, (Continuum), 2008, Parssinen, T. M., 'Popular science and society: the phrenology movement in early Victorian Britain', *Journal of Social History*, Vol. 8, (1974), pp. 1-20, Tomlinson, Stephen, 'Phrenology, education and the politics of human nature: the thought and influence of George Combe', *History of Education*, Vol. 26, (1997), pp. 1-22, and Van Wyhe, John, 'Was Phrenology a Reform Science? Towards a New

had 'animal faces'. From 1850, doctors like James Thompson, who worked in Perth prison, began collecting biological analyses of convicts providing an academic veneer to these perceptions of 'animal propensities' through empirical research.

The work of Charles Booth in the 1880s and 1890s, with its exposure of bad housing and inadequate diet, encouraged a perception of the residuum as the product of the inevitable workings of social Darwinism. Arnold White, who in the 1900s was the central figure in warning the public about the degeneration of the British race, first expressed his concerns in the 1880s. [38] The fundamental problem was not class but 'degeneracy' and hereditary and urban environment were the keys to understanding. Degeneracy was inherited or could be acquired when an individual adopted and deliberately persisted in a life of crime. The problem was made worse by the highly concentrated nature of cities that led to the 'creation of a large degenerate caste'. [39]

The key elements about the perceptions of the criminal class were, first, that the criminal class was perceived as overwhelmingly male; and secondly, these perceptions were primarily those of middle-class commentators who were speaking to a predominantly, though not exclusively, middle-class and 'respectable' audience. There were occasional references to women committing crimes, even to them being afflicted by criminal 'diseases', but in general, they were seen as accessories. [40] There was, however, a parallel between perceptions of the male criminal and the female prostitute. Prostitution was not in itself a criminal offence, but there was growing concern about 'the Great Social Evil' and from 1850 determined attempts at control. Dr William Acton 's *Prostitution, Considered in its Moral, Social and Sanitary Aspects, in London and Other Large Cities* did not see prostitution as the slippery slope of damnation and noted that young women often became prostitutes only for a short while. But there are important parallels between his list of the causes of prostitution and contemporary views of the causes of crime:

> Natural desire. Natural sinfulness. The preferment of indolent ease to

---

Generalization for Phrenology', *History of Science*, Vol. 42, (2004), pp. 313-331.
[38] See, White, Arnold, *The Destitute Alien in Great Britain: A Series of Papers Dealing with the Subject of Foreign Pauper Immigration*, (Charles Scribner's Sons), 1892, and *Efficiency and Empire*, (Methuen & Co.), 1901.
[39] Morrison, W. D., 'The Increase in Crime', *The Twentieth Century*, Vol. 31, (1892), p. 957.
[40] Zedner, L., *Women, Crime and Custody in Victorian England*, (Oxford University Press), 1991, pp. 51-92.

labour. Vicious inclinations strengthened and ingrained by early neglect, or evil training, bad associates, and an indecent mode of life. Necessity, imbued by the inability to obtain a living by honest means consequent on a fall from virtue. Extreme poverty. To this blacklist must be added love of drink, love of dress, love of amusement. [41]

Contemporaries across much of Europe and North America, as well as in Britain, were convinced that the crux of the question of what caused crime was the existence of a separate criminal class. There were individuals and groups who were 'professional criminals' and who made a significant part of their living from crime but whether there was a 'criminal class' is questionable. Contemporaries drew a dubious parallel, grounded in fear and a partial reading of criminal statistics between offenders who came largely from the working-classes and the causes of crime that were generally perceived as the vices of this class. In fact, there were perhaps no more than 4,000 'habitual criminals' in the 1870s and the scale of the problem was considerably less than the middle-classes believed. Most thefts and most crimes of violence were not the work of professional criminals. Court records suggest that the overwhelming majority of thefts that were reported and prosecuted were opportunist and petty. Most incidents of violence involved people who were either related or who were known to each other. Evidence from the Black Country and London suggests that no clear distinction can be made between a dishonest criminal class and a poor, but honest, worker. [42] The working-classes were more likely to be victims of crime in inner city areas than members of the middle-classes. Despite this, belief in a criminal class persisted and was convenient for insisting that most crime was something committed on law-abiding citizens by an alien and 'dangerous' group and, since no reformation was possible, justified the use of draconian punishment.

Crimes against individuals and property

Although there were several high profile crimes and criminals in the nineteenth and early-twentieth centuries, most criminal activity was small-scale, often involved a degree of violence and, despite the fears of the middle-classes largely involved members of the working-classes

---

[41] Acton, William, *Prostitution considered in Its Moral, Social & Sanitary Aspects*, (Churchill), 1857, p. 118.
[42] Philip, D., *Crime and Authority in Victorian England: The Black Country 1835-60*, (Croom Helm), 1977, pp. 13-21, 126-129, 287-288.

both as criminals and as victims. 43 There are major problems with the official crime statistics. How the police collated information or massaged the figures is often unclear and many crimes went unreported largely because the poorer sections of Victorian society, those most vulnerable to crime, had little faith in the police and many did not bother to report crimes as a result. 44 National figures of committals on indictment began in 1805, covering fifty crimes until 1834 when they become almost complete.

From the middle of the nineteenth century the annual publication of Judicial Statistics for England and Wales suggested that in general crime levels appeared to be declining in England and Wales. Indictable offences declined by 79 per cent between 1842 and 1891 and in London they declined by 63 per cent between the 1820s and 1870s. Much of the decline in London reflects a sharp drop in violent crime of about 68 per cent between the 1830s and the 1860s. Larceny indictments also decreased in London, from about 220 per 100,000 in the 1830s and 1840s to about 70 per 100,000 in the 1850s. This decline, however, stems at least partially from a revision of the criminal code in 1855 that removed minor larcenies from the indictable category and permitted courts to deal with them summarily. Although this revision treated simple assaults similarly, nearly all the decline in assaults had occurred by 1855. Other property crimes, particularly burglary, fraud, and embezzlement, increased during this period or remained steady. However, some areas experienced increases in crime. For example, as the industrialised Black Country, larceny committals to trial rose from 91 per 100,000 in 1835 to about 262 in 1860, an increase of 188 per cent, and committals to trial for offences against the person increased from about 6 per 100,000 to about 14 per 100,000, a 133 per cent increase. 45 This study suggests that rural areas and small towns exhibited sharply higher levels of criminality as they industrialised, while in heavily urbanised areas such as London studies found declines in serious criminality as they and their surrounding communities developed. 46

---

[43] See, Chassaigne, Philippe, 'Popular representations of crime: the crime broadside, a subculture of violence in Victorian Britain?', *Crime, Histoire et Sociétés*, Vol. 3, (1999), pp. 23-55.

[44] Williams, Chris A., 'Counting Crimes or Counting People: Some implications of mid-nineteenth century British policing returns', *Crime, Histoire & Sociétés*, Vol. 4, (2), (2000), pp. 77-93, focuses on Sheffield.

[45] Ibid, Philip, D., *Crime and Authority in Victorian England: The Black Country 1835-60*, p. 143.

[46] King, P., 'The Impact of urbanization on murder rates and on the geography of homicide in England and Wales', *Historical Journal*, Vol. 53, (2010), pp. 671-698.

The volume and composition of indictments were determined by various factors, particularly the legal definition of crime and the zeal of prosecutors and officials. It is clear that prosecution rates varied both between crimes and over time. As a result, criminal statistics offer a poor indication of the fluctuating level of crime. The pattern of indictments demonstrates starkly a determination to protect property and an assumption that it was endangered by the criminality of the lower orders. In contrast, the countless offences of nobles, gentry, shopkeepers, and tradesmen went largely unpunished and white-collar criminals were more familiar to readers of Charles Dickens than to officials of the criminal courts.

What were the main offences against the person?

It was offences against the person that provided the most spectacular and terrifying images of criminality in this period although they only accounted for about 10 per cent of all indictable crimes in the nineteenth century For example, the metropolitan garrotting panics of the mid-1850s and 1862-1863 that set a trend for describing a variety of robberies in London and the provinces, as 'garrotting ' and the butchery of Jack the Ripper in East London in the autumn of 1888 reverberated outside London. [47]

At the popular level, there were newspapers devoted to crime and this helped to feed people's interest. There were few restrictions on reporting and artists were used to draw scenes from the crime allowing them to print the kind of pictures that would not be allowed as photographs today. Madame Tussaud's opened in 1802 and had popular waxworks of criminals, especially murderers. Murder featured a great deal perhaps because it was, from the 1860s, the only

---

[47] In July 1863, Hugh Pilkington, an MP was garrotted and robbed in central London. This led to a 'garrotting scare'. There were 12 more recorded cases in October and 32 in November. Maybe the press reports of the original case led criminals to copy the tactic. Maybe the police or the public labelled certain kinds of robbery 'garrotting' that they would not previously have done; see, Davis, J. 'The London garrotting panic of 1862: a moral panic and the creation of a criminal class in mid-Victorian England', in ibid, Gatrell V. A. C., et al., (eds.), *Crime and the law: a social history of crime in Western Europe since 1500,* pp. 190-213, and Sindall, R. S., 'The London garrotting panics of 1856 and 1862', *Social History*, Vol. 12, (1987), pp. 351-359, and *Street Violence in the Nineteenth Century: Media Panic or Real Danger?*, (Leicester University Press), 1990. See also, Rudé, G., *Criminal and Victim: Crime and Society in Early-nineteenth-Century England,* (Oxford University Press), 1985, and Wood, J. Carter, *Violence and crime in nineteenth-century England: The shadow of our refinement,* (Routledge), 2004.

capital offence. There was huge public interest in celebrated nineteenth century horror crimes, like the Radcliffe Highway murders of 1811 when two families were battered to death, the activities of the poisoner William Palmer in the mid-1850s [48] and the Ripper murders. [49] But these were the dramatic and well-publicised exception rather than the norm. The statistics show that the number of murders stood at about 400 a year during the nineteenth century and that, then as now, most murders were normally committed by either relatives or by persons known to the victim. For instance, Mary Ann Cotton perhaps the most prolific serial killer of the century, a former school-teacher from County Durham murdered most of her 15 children and step-children, as well as her mother, three husbands and her lodger, before she was hanged in 1873. Murder by strangers or by burglars was exceptional though widely and luridly reported in newspapers. [50]

Homicide is regarded as a most serious offence and it is probably reported more than other forms of crime. [51] Between 1857 and 1890, there were rarely more than 400 homicides reported to the police each year, and during the 1890s the average was below 350. In Victorian England, the homicide rate reached 2 per 100,000 of the population only once, in 1865. Generally, it was about 1.5 per 100,000 falling to rarely more than 1 per 100,000 at the end of the 1880s and declining even further after 1900. These figures do not take into account the significant number of infanticides that went undetected. [52] The statistics for homicide are therefore probably

---

[48] Watson, Katherine, *Poisoned Lives: English Poisoners and their Victims*, (Hambledon), 2004, considers one type of homicide.
[49] Gray, Drew D., *London's Shadows: The Dark Side of the Victorian City*, (Continuum), 2010, examines the impact of the Ripper murders.
[50] D'Cruze, Shani, 'Murder and Fatality: The Changing Face of Homicide', in ibid, Kilday, Anne-Marie, and Nash, David, (eds.), *Histories of Crime in Britain 1600-2000*, pp. 100-119.
[51] Wiener, Martin J., 'Homicide and "Englishness": Criminal Justice and National Identity in Victorian England', *National Identities*, Vol. 6, (2003), pp. 203-214, and Conley, Carolyn A., 'Wars among Savages: Homicide and Ethnicity in the Victorian United Kingdom', *Journal of British Studies*, Vol. 44, (2005), pp. 775-795. Local studies include, Cockburn, J. S., 'Patterns of violence in English society: homicide in Kent, 1500-1985', *Past & Present*, Vol. 130, (1991), pp. 70-106, England, R. W., 'Investigating Homicides in Northern England, 1800-24', *Criminal Justice History*, Vol. 6, (1985), pp. 105-123, Emsley, C., *The English and Violence since 1750*, (Hambledon), 2007, and Conley, Carolyn A., *Certain other countries: homicide, gender, and national identity in late-nineteenth-century England, Ireland, Scotland, and Wales*, (Ohio State University Press), 2007.
[52] On infanticide, see Kilday, Anne-Marie, 'Desperate Measures or Cruel Intentions? Infanticide in Britain since 1600', in Kilday, Anne-Marie, and

closer to the real level of the offence. Two points are important. There was a high level of violence within the family. Physical punishment seems to have been accepted or at least tolerated across social groups until well into the nineteenth century. [53] Yet there were limits. Ill-treatment leading to death was exceptional but even here courts could find mitigating circumstances: Frederick Gilbert was acquitted of the manslaughter of his wife after the court noted that he was a good, sober man and his wife a drunkard. There appears to have been a decline in violence between working-class men and women in the third quarter of the century, possibly because of growing respectability and rising living standards that reduced stress on the male as the principal economic provider. [54]

Violence, or the threat of violence, was widespread; in the home, in the workplace, in the pub as well as on the streets. Most acts of violence are committed by known individuals, such as husbands and wives, parents and children, work-mates, and lovers, and were the consequence of everyday tensions over money, space, jealousy and countless other banal situations. A breakdown of assaults taken before Bedfordshire magistrates every five years between 1750 and 1840 shows that there were very high numbers of assaults on women of which a third were attacks by husbands on their wives. Only a third of these types of assault were prosecuted on indictment and one in ten cases failed because wives failed to given evidence in court and wife-beating rarely led to more than six-month imprisonment. There were a significant number of attacks on authority in the shape of constables or overseers of the poor. By contrast, some 85 per cent of these

---

Nash, David, (eds.), *Histories of Crime in Britain 1600-2000*, pp. 60-80. For more detailed nineteenth century discussion, see above pp. 40-47.

[53] On this issue see, ibid, Wood, J. Carter, *Violence and Crime in Nineteenth-Century England: The Shadow of Our Refinement*, pp. 1-69, who argues that violence was 'discovered' as a social problem in the late-eighteenth and early-nineteenth centuries as a traditional customary understanding that legitimated physical confrontation was challenged by an emergent middle- and upper-class culture. Ibid, Wiener, Martin, *Men of Blood* argues that, while there was an increasingly sharp distinction made between the separate spheres of men and women during the Victorian period, this had the effect of criminalising male violence. See also, Flanders, Judith, *The Invention of Murder: How the Victorians revelled in Death and Detection and created Modern Crime*, (Harper Press), 2011.

[54] Tomes, Nancy, 'A "Torrent of Abuse": Crimes of Violence between Working-class Men and Women in London, 1840-1875,' *Journal of Social History*, Vol. 11, (1977-8), pp. 328-345.

attacks led to prosecution. [55] Offences against the person made up over 10 per cent of committals made on indictment during the period 1834 and 1914 and about 15 per cent of summary committals in the second half of the century. Assaults on authority, in the shape of policemen formed a significant percentage of nineteenth century assaults and declined at a slower rate than common assault: 15 per cent of summary prosecutions in the 1860s rising to about 21 per cent in the 1880s. Most assaults were for resisting or obstructing the police in their duty.

Perhaps also the cult of respectability made wives even less likely to complain since such assaults were shameful and in the growing suburbs they were less public, less likely to disturb the neighbours, while the bruising was less visible than on the crowded stair of a tenement. In addition, there was the extent to which courts and the police were prepared to accept the uncorroborated word of the beaten wife. [56] In court, some juries reasoned: if a man's wife was a drunk, or did not have his dinner on the table when he came home from work, then why shouldn't he chastise her? Although magistrates took contrasting positions with regard to wife-abuse, increasingly brutality by husbands was seen as unmanly and cowardly and some magistrates took the view that no amount of provocation could justify any act of violence against women.

However, wife-abuse remained a significant problem and was denounced especially by Frances Power Cobbe. Campaigns around marital violence pre-dated the Ripper murders by a decade and one of the most powerful arguments that campaigners against 'wife-torture' had was the inadequacy of the law in protecting women from reprisals. The incidence of wife-beating declined from the 1870s in part because of the increase in penalties such as the power of police magistrates to have offenders flogged and exposed in the public pillory contained in the Wife Beaters Act 1882 but also because of improved living standards and the diffusion of middle-class family values.

Cobbe and many others were convinced that levels of male

---

[55] Emsley, C., *Hard Men: the English and Violence since 1750*, (Hambledon), 2005, and ibid, Wood, J. Carter, *Violence and crime in nineteenth-century England: the shadow of our refinement*, provide an overview. See also, Stone, L., 'Interpersonal Violence in English Society 1300-1980', *Past and Present*, Vol. 101, (1983), pp. 22-33.

[56] On domestic violence, see, Hammerton, A. James, *Cruelty and companionship: conflict in nineteenth-century married life*, (Routledge), 1992, and D'Cruze, Shani, *Crimes of Outrage: Sex, Violence and Victorian Working Women*, (UCL Press), 1998. See also, Emmerichs, M. B. W., 'Trials of Women for Homicide in Nineteenth-Century England', *Women & Criminal Justice*, Vol. 5, (1), (1993), pp. 99-109.

violence were made worse by the consumption of alcohol; an analysis not exclusive to feminists as long-standing temperance societies show. Drink was often a cause of violence in the family, and outside. For example, in Dundee in the 1870s, the problem with drunkenness had become problematic, and one policeman would bring in between 60 and 70 drunken men and women on a Saturday night. In the late 1870s, the crime of 'shebeening', selling alcohol without a licence was committed by more women than men and in 1877, fines imposed on persons selling liquor without a licence raised almost £300 in revenue for the police. Some Victorian temperance reformers gave drink as the fundamental cause of all crime; the public house was the 'nursery of crime'. [57]

Others were less zealous and suggested only a connection between crimes of violence and drink. [58] There is some evidence to suggest that there were slight increases in figures for assault and drunkenness during years of prosperity: high wages and high employment led to a greater consumption of alcohol that, in turn, contributed to more violent crime. However, in the last quarter of the century the overall trend is markedly downwards. This may be explained, in part, by which contemporaries perceived as the civilisation or moralisation of the population. Perhaps also there was a decrease in anxiety about small-scale, drink-related violence. [59]

Why were offences against property feared?

The energies of law enforcement were focused on maintaining order and defending property. The late-eighteenth and early-nineteenth century saw major changes in Britain that had an impact on crime. [60]

---

[57] Burne, Peter, *The Teetotaler's Companion*, (Arthur Hall and Co.), 1847, p. 31-56.

[58] Rowbotham, Judith. "'Only when drunk': the stereotyping of violence in England, c. 1850-1900', in D'Cruze, Shani, (ed.), *Everyday Violence in Britain, 1850-1950, Gender and Class*, (Pearson Education Limited), 2000, pp. 155-169.

[59] Davies, A., 'Youth Gangs, Masculinity and Violence in Late Victorian Manchester and Salford', *Journal of Social History*, Vol. 32, (1998), pp. 349-369, and '"These viragoes are no less cruel than the lads": young women, gangs and violence in late Victorian Manchester and Salford', *British Journal of Criminology*, Vol. 39, (1999), pp. 72-89, and Pearson, G., *Hooligan: A History of Respectable Fears*, (Leicester University Press), 1983, consider one aspect of violence.

[60] Bailey, V., (ed.), *Policing and Punishment in Nineteenth century Britain*, (Croom Helm), 1981, contains several important essays and ibid, Philip, D., *Crime and Authority in Victorian England: The Black Country 1835-60*, and Jones, D., *Crime, Protest, Community and Police in Nineteenth Century*

Highway robbery died out as roads became less isolated with more traffic, more patrols and more turnpike gates. For example, the last series of prosecutions for highway robbery were heard at the Old Bailey were in 1830. In the next eighty years, only three more cases were tried; in 1832, 1877 and a final case in 1897. Robbing travellers on the railways was a new crime, especially before the introduction of corridor trains. [61]

Huge business venture, operating with little regulation, provided opportunities for crooked dealings and an extension of white-collar crime. [62] The working-classes were exploited as consumers by shop-keepers by the adulteration of food and other commodities. Many investors lost money in railway fraud scandals in the 1840s. In 1846, *The Railway Gazette* exposed several of these schemes: The West End and Southern Counties Railway spent all shareholders deposits before its Bill came up and was rejected in Parliament, equally the

---

Britain, (Routledge), 1982, and *Crime in Nineteenth Century Wales*, (University of Wales Press), 1992, are useful collections of thematic and regional essays.

[61] Ireland, R. W., '"An increasing mass of heathens in the bosom of a Christian land": the railway and crime in the nineteenth century', *Continuity and Change*, Vol. 12, (1997), pp. 55-78, focuses on Carmarthenshire in Wales between 1850 and 1880 and Quick, Michael, 'The Garrett Gang: luggage thefts in the 1840s', *Journal of the Railway & Canal Historical Society*, Vol. 187, (2004), pp. 437-445.

[62] Robb, George, *White-collar crime in modern England: financial fraud and business morality, 1845-1929*, (Cambridge University Press), 1992, and Taylor, James, *Boardroom Scandal: The Criminalization of Company Fraud in Nineteenth-Century Britain*, (Oxford University Press), 2013, provide detailed studies. Sindall, R. S., 'Middle-class crime in nineteenth century England', *Criminal Justice History*, Vol. 4, (1983), pp. 23-40, Barnes, Paul, 'A Victorian financial crisis: The scandalous implications of the case of Overend Gurney', in ibid, Rowbotham, Judith, and Stevenson, Kim, (eds.), *Criminal conversations: Victorian crimes, social panic, and moral outrage*, pp. 55-69. See also, Locker, John P., 'The Paradox of the 'Respectable Offender': Responding to the Problem of White-Collar Crime in Victorian and Edwardian England', in Johnston, Helen, (ed.), *Punishment and control in historical perspective*, (Palgrave), 2008, pp. 115-134, Wilson, Gary and Wilson, Sarah, '"Getting away with it" or "punishment enough"?: The problem of "respectable" crime from 1830', in Moore, James Robert, and Smith, John, (eds.), *Corruption in urban politics and society, Britain 1780-1950*, (Ashgate), 2007, pp. 57-78, Wilson, Sarah, 'Fraud and White-collar Crime: 1850 to the Present', in ibid, Kilday, Anne-Marie, and Nash, David, (eds.), *Histories of Crime in Britain 1600-2000*, pp. 141-159, and Colley, Robert, 'The Arabian Bird: A Study in Income Tax Evasion in Mid-Victorian Britain', *British Tax Review*, (2001), pp. 207-221.

Bristol and Liverpool line, the Northampton Bedford and Cambridge Line. If investors suspected fraud, it was up to them to sue the company in the bankruptcy court. George Hudson, 'the Railway King', was instrumental in developing railways in the 1830s and 1840s but was ruined by disclosure of fraud in the Eastern Railway and the discovery of his bribery of MPs. [63] Women made up a significant portion of investors during the nineteenth century, especially in such key areas of the economy as banking, railways and insurance. Yet, bourgeois notions of gentility required that women remain ignorant of money matters and refrain from active participation in business affairs, leaving women especially exposed to all manner of fraud. Financial literature, newspaper debates and popular fiction clearly demonstrate how women were victimised by white-collar crime. The phrase 'railway morals' became a term of derision after an article by Herbert Spencer, Victorian social Darwinist philosopher in the *Edinburgh Review* in 1854 while *Reynold's Newspaper* complained in 1856 that Britain was a 'paradise of knaves, provided they are rich ones'.

There were several banking crises during the 1820s and widespread fraud was uncovered: George Howarth, manager of the Rochdale Savings Bank into which many poor people put their savings, was discovered on his death in 1849 to have embezzled £72,000 through false accounting. Bank failures continued well into the nineteenth century and one of the largest in which false accounting was deployed, was the 1878 City of Glasgow Bank failure. The bank was one of the largest banks at the time with 133 branches and deposits of over £8m and collapsed with debts of over £8.5m. The directors had lent millions of pounds to friends and family without any collateral security and had then concealed the insolvency by fiddling the accounts so as to understate its loans by £3m. The directors were imprisoned for 18 months while thousands of small savers lost their money. In 1882, over a £1m was embezzled from Jardine Matheson and in 1890 poor investments in South America would have led to the failure of Baring Brothers Bank had not the government brokered a secret deal. Although the behaviour of corrupt businessmen and especially embezzling clerks led to social outrage and often long prison sentences, they were generally seen as 'rotten apples' rather than as members of the 'criminal classes'. From

---

[63] For contemporary comment, see, 'The Hudsonian Eclipse', *Tait's Edinburgh Magazine*, Vol. 16, (1849), pp. 319-324. Lambert, Richard S., *The Railway King 1800-1871, a study of George Hudson and the Business Morals of his Times*, (Allen and Unwin), 1964, and Arnold, A. J., and McCartney, S. M., *George Hudson: The Rise and Fall of the Railway King*, (Hambeldon), 2004.

the mid-nineteenth century through the early decades of the twentieth, the law put few obstacles in the paths of white collar criminals, trusting instead that the free market would regulate itself and that good business would drive out bad.

The sharp increase in crime figures after 1825 that continued until mid-century is well known, though not thoroughly explained. The increase in population was significant during these years but it was well below the increase measured in crime statistics. Moreover, the increase seems to have been as marked in rural counties like Bedfordshire as it was overall. What is noticeable about the peaks in crime, from 1825 to a peak in 1832, a decline followed by another upswing to a peak in 1842 and again in 1848 is that they coincided with years marked by economic depression and political unrest. The correlation suggests that victims might have been more ready to prosecute because of the general feeling of insecurity and offenders more likely to steal because of economic hardship. Political unrest weakened some of the usual factors that discouraged crime. The number of new magistrates increased from about 300 per year in 1820 to 400 by 1830. More active JPs meant more men available to hear complaints and issue warrants and the effective prosecution of crime increased.

Property crimes were frequently commented on in the Victorian press. Those who owned property and who, as a result, had the vote tended to live in areas where violence was less common. Britain's propertied classes felt themselves under attack from two directions. There was the potential for revolution to be export from the continent. There were revolutions in France in 1789, 1830 and 1848 and revolutions across other parts of Europe in 1830 and 1848. These created considerable fear that the same thing would happen in Britain. The late 1830s and early 1840s were years of acute anxiety fed by the economic depression as well as by Chartist and industrial agitation culminating in Newport rebellion in 1839, the Plug Plots in 1842 and the Kennington Common meeting in 1848. [64] Also, attacks were expected from the 'dangerous classes' in the growing slums of urban Britain. As towns grew, and the slum areas expanded the

---

[64] Royle, Edward, and Walvin, James, *English Radicals and Reformers 1760-1848*, (Harvester Press), 1982, Stevenson, John, *Popular Disturbances in England 1700-1870*, (Longman), 1979. Hunt, E. H., *British Labour History 1815-1914*, (Weidenfeld), 1981, and Wright, D. G., *Popular Radicalism: The Working-class Experience 1780-1880*, (Longman), 1988, contain useful material on radicalism. Thomis, Malcolm, and Holt, P., *Threats of Revolution in Britain 1789-1848*, (Macmillan), 1974, and Royle, Edward, *Revolutionary Britannia?*, (Manchester University Press), 2000, provide different perspectives on the threat of revolution.

middle-classes felt that they were losing control of these inner-city areas. Many people were convinced by the writings of Malthus and his pessimistic picture of the poor implying that it was their own improvidence and immorality that led to problems of over population, food shortage and, consequently, high poor rates.[65]

In the mid-nineteenth century, 60 per cent of larceny charges were for less than five shillings.[66] Larceny statistics in the second half of the century also show some link between the peaks of offences and years of high unemployment.[67] But, after the 1840s, the working-classes rarely had to contend with the coincidence of high food prices and economic depression that was so marked in the first half of the century. This was due, in part, to a rise in the export market for industrial goods that enabled firms to offset short-term contractions in the home market. At the same time stable, even declining food prices helped many section of the working-class to ride out short periods of unemployment. These elements help to explain the overall decline in theft and violence: put at its simplest, during this period the poor became less habituated to theft because they were less subjected to periods of severe unemployment coinciding with serious subsistence problems. In addition, the growth and professionalism of the new police force probably acted as a deterrent; the destruction of the rookeries for urban improvement removed some of the worst criminal areas; the Vagrancy Acts meant a stricter supervision of the casual poor.

The state and morality

Growth in population and in the corresponding preference for urban living mobilised an increasing degree of state intervention in the private lives of its citizens. Sanitation and housing, water supplies and the control of disease, all became subject to government intervention in some way during the century, alongside the cross-over from the

---

[65] Meier, William M., *Property Crime in London, 1850-Present*, (Palgrave Macmillan), 2011, pp. 13-40.
[66] Gatrell, V. A. C., 'The decline of theft and violence in Victorian and Edwardian England', Gatrell, V. A. C., et al, (eds.), *Crime and the law: a social history of crime in Western Europe since 1500*, (Europa Publications), 1980, pp. 238-370, and Godfrey, Barry S., and Locker, John P., 'The nineteenth-century decline of custom, and its impact on theories of "workplace theft" and "white collar crime"', *Northern History*, Vol. 38, (2001), pp. 261-273.
[67] Ferris, Graham, 'Larceny: Debating the "boundless region of dishonesty"', in ibid, Rowbotham, Judith, and Stevenson, Kim, (eds.), *Criminal conversations: Victorian crimes, social panic, and moral outrage*, pp. 70-90.

definitely public to the obviously private. Government's role was an increasingly prescriptive one laying down acceptable sexual behaviour and policing sexual relations through laws governing such areas as prostitution, homosexuality and contraception. In many respects, the state assumed the role previously played by the church. This can be seen in its sanctioning marriages and its pronouncements as to the grounds on which divorce was valid, in its defining the forms of licit and illicit sexual behaviour and in its treatment of prostitution.[68]

Prostitution and the Contagious Diseases Acts
In the urban context, increasing anxiety was expressed over an increase in prostitution and venereal disease. Military reports had reported a steady increase in venereal infections among the men since the 1820s. A series of government inquiries in the 1850s and 1860s testified to the seriousness with which the dual problems of venereal diseases and sexual immorality among the lower ranks was regarded in official circles. In 1862, 29 per cent of all army men admitted to hospital and 12.5 per cent of all naval hospital admissions were for sexually transmitted diseases.[69] From the 1840s, public anxiety had also been focused on prostitution, the 'great social evil', by studies from evangelical clerics and doctors and by rescue and reform societies campaigning for a police crackdown on the London streets.[70]

---

[68] The best starting point is Walkowitz, Judith, *Prostitution and Victorian Society: Women, Class and the State*, (Cambridge University Press), 1980, and MacHugh, Paul, *Prostitution and Victorian Social Reform*, (Croom Helm), 1980, deal specifically with the debate on the Contagious Diseases Acts. Bartley, Paula, *Prostitution: prevention and reform in England, 1860-1914*, (Routledge), 2000, and ibid, Mort, Frank, *Dangerous Sexualities: Medico-moral politics in England since 1830*, pp. 54-73 provide valuable background. Fisher, Trevor, *Prostitution and the Victorians*, (Alan Sutton), 1997 is a useful collection of sources.

[69] See, *Report of the Committee appointed to enquire into the Pathology and Treatment of the Venereal Disease with the view to Diminish its Injurious Effects on the men of the Army and Navy*, (Harrison and Sons), 1868, pp. xli-xlii, for statistical information for 1864. Hall, Lesley A., 'Venereal diseases and society in Britain, from the Contagious Diseases Acts to the National Health Service', in Davidson, Roger, and Hall, Lesley A., (eds.), *Sex, sin and suffering: venereal disease and European society since 1870*, (Routledge), 2001, pp. 120-136; Blanco, Richard L., 'The attempted control of venereal disease in the army of mid-Victorian England', *Journal of the Society for Army Historical Research*, Vol. 45, (1967), pp. 234-241.

[70] See, for example, *Social versus political reform: the sin of great cities: or, The great social evil a national sin: illustrated by a brief enquiry into its extent, causes, effects, and existing remedies*, (A. W. Bennett), 1859, and Spurgeon, Charles, *The Great Social Evil. A sermon*, [on *John*, viii, 10, 11], 1860,

Attempts to subject enlisted men to periodic genital examination met with considerable rank-and-file resistance and government turned instead to the regulation of the women with whom soldiers and sailors consorted leading to the passage of the Contagious Diseases Acts of 1864, 1866 and 1869.

The 1864 Contagious Diseases Act applied to a number of naval ports and army garrison towns in England and Wales. Under its provisions, both police personnel and medical practitioners, acting under the direct supervision of the War Office and the Admiralty, rather than the local constabulary were empowered to notify a justice of the peace if they suspected a woman of being a 'common prostitute'. The woman would then be apprehended and taken to a certified hospital for medical examination, where she could be detained for up to three months to effect a treatment if the examination proved positive. A woman's refusal to co-operate with what was effectively a suspension of habeas corpus could lead to a prison sentence of one month, doubling for any subsequent offence. There were also penalties for brothel keepers. Further legislation in 1866 and 1869 extended the geographical locations covered by the regulations, while the Admiralty and War Office were now mandated to provide hospital facilities for inspection and treatment. Provision was also made within hospitals for adequate moral and religious instruction of the women and for regular fortnightly inspections of former detainees, while the period of compulsory detention was extended to six months. [71]

Supporters of the legislation did not see the principles of state hygiene as contradicting the moral emphases of the public health movement. Far from the state sanctioning male vice by providing men of the forces with a clean supply of women, it claimed that the acts were essentially moral in aim and intention. In reality, the acts were concerned with the regulation of the sexual and moral habits of two particular groups within the urban poor: female prostitutes and the lower ranks of the armed forces. But the tactics used to discipline these two groups were markedly different. [72]

---

[71] Ogborn, Miles, 'Law and discipline in nineteenth century English state formation: the Contagious Diseases Acts of 1864, 1866 and 1869', *Journal of Historical Sociology*, Vol. 6, (1), (1993), pp. 28-55, Smith, F. B., 'The Contagious Diseases Acts reconsidered', *Social History of Medicine*, Vol. 3, (1990), pp. 197-215, and 'Ethics and disease in the later 19th century: the Contagious Diseases Acts', *Historical Studies: Australia & New Zealand*, Vol. 15, (1971), pp. 118-135.

[72] See, Parliamentary Papers, *Report from the Select Committee on Contagious Diseases Act (1866)*, (1868-1869), *Report of royal commission upon the administration and operation of the Contagious Diseases Acts plus*

The legislation understandably angered women, and many men, the more so because of the opportunities it afforded the police to harass women. The Acts made the assumption that prostitution was a permanent and necessary evil. They condoned male sexual access to fallen women and were specifically directed at women in order to protect the health of men. If the priority had been to fight venereal infections, then inspecting the prostitutes' clients would also have been required by the Acts. However, the assumption was that, while men would be offended at the intrusion, the women were already so degraded that further humiliations were of no consequence. These acts became a feminist cause because they permitted the police to detain and inspect any woman suspected of venereal infection, and, it was claimed, innocent women found themselves forced to undergo humiliating inspections. One obvious problem lay in the fact that the law did not distinguish between prostitutes and other women of the lower classes and another was that, contrary to common Victorian belief that any extramarital sexual experience inevitably doomed women to a life of prostitution and dismal, lonely death, many women only worked intermittently as prostitutes.

Social Science Congresses were an important forum for reformers who wished to bring a social problem to national attention and public scrutiny. [73] Some of those who wished to campaign for the repeal of the Contagious Diseases Acts chose the Congress which was to meet at Bristol in the early autumn, 1869 as the platform from which to launch their campaign. At first the Congress Committee were loath to have the subject debated at Bristol, but changed their mind just before the Congress met. Some leaders of the movement arranged a preliminary meeting at the Royal Hotel, Bristol on 30 September 1869 attended by some seventy persons that passed a resolution strongly condemning the Regulation system with six

---

Minutes of evidence, (1871), and *Report from the Select Committee on the Contagious Diseases Acts plus Further reports*, (1880-1881), for the changing nature of the debate on the legislation. Hill, Berkeley, 'Statistical results of the Contagious Diseases Acts', *Journal of the Statistical Society of London*, Vol. 33, (1870), pp. 463-485, and Stansfeld, James, 'On the validity of the annual government statistics of the operation of the Contagious Diseases Acts', *Journal of the Statistical Society*, Vol. 39, (1876), pp. 540-561, give contemporary views on the ways the Acts operated.

[73] For the Social Science Association, see Goldman, Lawrence, '*The Social Science Association, 1857*-1886: a Context for mid-Victorian Liberalism', *English Historical Review*, Vol. 101, *(1986),* pp. 95-134, and *Science, reform, and politics in Victorian Britain: the Social Science Association, 1857-1886*, (Cambridge University Press), 2002.

dissentients. On Monday, 4 October 1869, Dr C. Bell Taylor [74] of Nottingham read his paper advocating the repeal of the Contagious Diseases Acts, while Dr W. P. Swain, Surgeon, Royal Albert Hospital, Devonport and Mr Berkeley Hill of the Extension Association read papers in favour of the Acts and of their extension. The meeting resolved by an overwhelming majority that the National Association for the Promotion of Social Science should protest against the Acts and take steps to resist their extension and the following day, The National Association for the Repeal of the Contagious Diseases Acts was established. [75] Initially women were excluded from the Association though it was quick to change this policy. Despite this, women led by Josephine Butler broke away to form the Ladies' National Association for the Repeal of the Contagious Diseases Act.[76] The LNA was well organised and vocal. The women's protest was received with expressions of outrage and puzzlement by men within the established political culture. Many LNA women came from a background of similar, if less explicitly sexual, moral reform campaigns, anti-slavery and temperance in particular. The recognition that class was an important consideration won them support from working-class men fearing the effects of the acts on their own wives and children. [77]

Middle-class evangelists had worked for the poor since the early part of the century, attempting to stamp out their alleged immorality. Leading repealers took a far more direct and, on occasions, dangerous

---

[74] Taylor, Charles Bell, *Observations on the Contagious Diseases Act, (women, not animals): showing how the new law debases women, debauches men, destroys the liberty of the subject, and tends to increase disease : being a reply to Mr. W. Paul Swain's paper on the working of the act at Devonport*, (Frederick Banks), 1869.

[75] Hamilton, M., 'Opposition to the Contagious Diseases Acts, 1864-1886', *Albion*, Vol. 10, (1978), pp. 14-27.

[76] L'Esperance, Jean, 'The Work of the Ladies' National Association for the Repeal of the Contagious Diseases Acts', *Bulletin for the Society for the Study of Labour History* (Spring, 1973), pp.14-16. Butler, Josephine, *Personal Reminiscences of a Great Crusader*, (H. Marshall), 1896. Jordan, Jane, *Josephine Butler*, (John Murray), 2001, Petrie, Glen, *A Singular Iniquity: The Campaigns of Josephine Butler*, (Viking Press), 1971, and Bell, E. Moberly, *Josephine Butler: Flame of Fire*, (Constable), 1962. See also, Mathers, Helen, 'Evangelicalism and feminism: Josephine Butler, 1828-1906', in Morgan, Sue, (ed.), *Women, religion and feminism in Britain, 1750-1900*, (Palgrave Macmillan), 2002, pp. 123-137, and 'The evangelical spirituality of a Victorian feminist: Josephine Butler, 1828-1906', *Journal of Ecclesiastical History*, Vol. 52, (2001), pp. 282-312.

[77] Blackwell, Elizabeth, *Wrong and right methods of dealing with social evil: as shown by English parliamentary evidence*, (A. Brentano), 1883.

action seeking out registered prostitutes and giving them practical help and moral support in opposing the legislation. Feminists of the LNA supported the contemporary campaign for female doctors and challenged male doctors, politicians and army men with a number of telling points. They denied the naturalness of male lust and the double standard of morality for the sexes rejecting the commonly held view that prostitutes protected virtuous females against unreasonable sexual demands. Also, activists condemned MPs' prurient interest in the sordid matters raised by the repeal campaign and criticised doctors' insistence on internally examining arrested prostitutes. The support for the Contagious Diseases Acts by Elizabeth Garrett, who, like male doctors, put checking disease before defending liberty, was an embarrassment to the LNA that was not concerned with the control of venereal disease. [78] Feminists resented the way in which women were defined only in relation to men and motherhood. Men predictably objected to changing a state of affairs from which they benefited considerably.

The campaign against the Contagious Diseases Acts did not destroy the double standard of morality for the sexes any more than it materially improved the position of prostitutes. Politicians may have become disenchanted with the Contagious Diseases legislation and tired of the struggle in provoked, but they had not been persuaded that Parliament should abandon other attempts to regulate vice. Women were divided on the issue. Rescue work attracted both feminists and non-feminists members of the LNA, and women outside the Association. It reinforced those notions about feminine mission and moral superiority that had encouraged female community and justified women's involvement in reform earlier in the century. During the 1880s and 1890s, it led some of them, mobilised in a host of social purity groups like the National Vigilance Association to believe that legislation could be used to 'force people to be moral'.

---

[78] See Garrett, Elizabeth, *An enquiry into the character of the Contagious Diseases Acts of 1866-69*, (Harrison and Sons), 1870.

Was there a 'new' morality?
From the early-nineteenth century, until absorbed by the new social purity movements of the 1880s, the Society for the Suppression of Vice (founded in 1802) remained the Victorian's basic legal force against the obscene. [79] Its work demonstrated the often close relationship between private vigilance and public authorities. It was the persuasion of the Vice Society that led to the Obscene Publications Act 1857. [80] Through the 1870s and 1880s, the 'abolitionists' were a major social force and the stimulus for the emergence of vigorous social-purity organisations such as the National Vigilance Association. Why was there a major attempt at moral restructuring in the last decades of the nineteenth and first decade of the twentieth centuries? Various causes can be identified. From the 1870s, following what was regarded as a decline in standards in the 1850s and 1860s, a new confidence in the moralistic ethic can be detected. [81] In the early years of the century, moral reformers had been sustained by the threat of revolution. No such fears limited them in the 1880s and 1890s but there were a series of causes and scandals that maintained their momentum: the iniquities of the Contagious Diseases Acts to the scandalous leniency meted out to high class 'madams'; from the exploitation and abduction of young girls in the White Slave Trade to the divorce cases of Charles Dilke in 1886 [82] and the Irish leader Parnell in 1890 [83]; the scandal of the Cleveland Street homosexual brothel 1889-1890 said to involve the duke of Clarence, eldest son of the heir to the throne [84] and the Tranby Croft

---

[79] Roberts, M. J. D., *Making English morals: voluntary association and moral reform in England, 1787-1886*, (Cambridge University Press), 2004, 2008, provides a valuable overview. See also, Hall, Lesley A., 'Hauling Down the Double Standard: Feminism, Social Purity and Sexual Science in Late-nineteenth-Century Britain', *Gender & History*, Vol. 16, (2004), pp. 36-56.

[80] Hunt, Alan, *Governing morals: a social history of moral regulation*, (Cambridge University Press), 1999, pp. 57-76.

[81] Fisher, Trevor, *Scandal: The Sexual Politics of Late Victorian Britain*, (Alan Sutton), 1995, is a useful and readable examination of this issue.

[82] Nicholls, David, *The lost prime minister: a life of Sir Charles Dilke*, (Continuum), 1995, pp. 177-194, Horstman, Allen, *Victorian Divorce*, (Croom Helm), 1985, p. 140.

[83] Ibid, Horstman, Allen, *Victorian Divorce*, pp. 140-141.

[84] On this see Chester, Lewis, Leitch, David, and Simpson, Colin, *The Cleveland Street Affair*, (Weidenfeld), 1976. This book demonstrates clearly the ambiguous attitudes to homosexuality by the Establishment. When the affair seemed likely to become the most explosive scandal of the nineteenth century and the taint of homosexuality came close to the royal household, it was quickly and quietly buried.

gambling scandal of 1891 that did involve the Prince of Wales. [85] Above all in 1895, there was the conviction and imprisonment of Oscar Wilde, the Irish dramatist. Wilde was in fact prosecuted three times for his homosexual behaviour, a sentence of two years hard labour was passed after the third trial and Wilde was imprisoned in Reading Jail. It was here that he wrote *De Profundis* and *The Ballad of Reading Gaol*. On his release from prison Wilde was bankrupt, divorced, his children had been taken from him and many of his friends had deserted him. He left the country to live a life of exile in France. [86]

There was a constituency ready to be stirred by such scandals, especially in the lower middle-class and the respectable working-class whose values were being attacked by radicals and libertarians. [87] Respectability, with its stress on values such as self-help and self-reliance, the value of work and the need for social discipline and the centrality of the family, was threatened by public immorality. Here was a strong basis for social purity. Behind this, giving the campaigns a tremendous dynamism was an evangelical revival, bringing large sections of the feminist movement into alliance with Nonconformity, an alliance sealed in outrage against double standards. Many of the leaders of the campaigns in the 1880s were products of this Christian revival. W. T. Stead described himself as 'a child of the revival of 1859-60' that had swept across the Atlantic and won hundreds of thousands of converts. He became editor of the *Pall Mall Gazette* in 1883 and soon gave the public a mix of moral outrage and salacious titillation. Social purity was also able to mine very deep fears of a more secular kind. 1885, an immensely important year in sexual politics, was also the year of the expansion of the electorate in the Third Reform Act, there were fears of national decline following the defeat and death of General Gordon, anxieties about Ireland and all this in the context of a socialist revival and feminist agitation. Social purity became a metaphor for a stable society and in 1885 was able to tap an anxiety that found a symbolic focus in the 'twin evils' of enforced prostitution and the exploitation of young girls.

---

[85] Havers, Michel, Grayson, Edward, and Shankland, Peter, *The Royal Baccarat Scandal*, 1977, (Souvenir Press), 1988
[86] Foldy, Michael, *The Trials of Oscar Wilde: Deviance, Morality and Late-Victorian Society*, (Yale University Press), 1997.
[87] Ibid, Hunt, Alan, *Governing morals: a social history of moral regulation*, pp. 140-191, and Roberts, M. J. D., *Making English morals: voluntary association and moral reform in England, 1787-1886*, (Cambridge University Press), 2004, pp. 245-289.

Largely as a result of the efforts of feminists and other social reformers, legislation, in the form of the Criminal Law Amendment Bill, was introduced into Parliament in the early 1880s with the intent of protecting young women. This was to be done through the dual means of increasing the age of female consent from thirteen to sixteen and bringing brothels under greater legal controls. For several years the Bill languished in Parliament. At a crucial moment, support for it was energised by a sensational report, *'The Maiden Tribute of Modern Babylon'* serialised in the daily *Pall Mall Gazette* in 1885, documenting the complexity and reach of organised prostitution as an industry and its reliance on sophisticated techniques for the entrapment of young girls. [88] W. T. Stead's sensational expose generated a sense of outrage with which a wide range of public opinion found itself in sympathy. The result was the Criminal Law Amendment Act that attempted to suppress brothels, raised the age of consent for girls to sixteen and introduced new penalties against male homosexuals in private as well as in public. Further changes, in the Vagrancy Act 1898 and the Criminal Law Amendment Act 1912, underlined the new legislative involvement with prostitution and homosexuality. Reformers in 1885 had no doubt that their cause was right: a crusade against 'a dark and cruel wrong'. Yet they were directing their energies at many of the wrong targets, illustrating the nineteenth century preference for moral campaigns rather than structural social reforms.

How safe was Victorian Britain?

There seems to be interplay between criminal statistics and periodic fears of crime and disorder and it is probable that the collection and publication of national crime figures led to the perception of crime as a major national and impersonal problem. Statistics made crime national and the criminal a national figure. Crime could be shown to be offences perpetrated on a large scale against respectable people by a group that, by being measured statistically, could be defined collectively as criminals or as the 'criminal classes'. For instance, crime rates in rural Warwickshire were consistently lower than those in

---

[88] Four articles which appeared in the *Pall Mall Gazette*, Monday, 6 July 1885, Tuesday, 7 July 1885, Wednesday, 8 July 1885 and Friday, 10 July 1885; the articles, though unsigned, were acknowledged to be the work of W. T. Stead, its editor. Stead was convicted of kidnapping and abetting indecent assault for procuring Eliza Armstrong and served three months in prison. See, Schults, Raymond L., *Crusader in Babylon: W. T. Stead and the Pall Mall Gazette*, (University of Nebraska Press), 1972, and Eckley, Grace, *Maiden Tribute: A Life of W. T. Stead*, (Xlibris Corporation), 2007.

Birmingham. However, from the 1860s, rural crime was rising in relation to the population whilst urban crime was falling.

Action against vagrants remained high with a special Vagrancy Committee later set up among the justices to keep an eye on the problem. Each police district had to submit quarterly reports on the state of vagrancy in their area. The chart above shows that levels of arrest remained high, to the extent that lodging-house keepers in Warwickshire complained that police action was depriving them of their customers. In towns such as Birmingham in contrast, the local authorities were content to leave well enough alone. Higher arrest rates in rural areas reveal the greater concern and self-interest of the ruling local gentry in this question, for whom vagrants roaming the countryside brought a direct sense of threat to the security of their property.

For many contemporaries, Britain was not safe, a situation given credence in the literature of the period. In *Oliver Twist*, written at the beginning of Queen Victoria's reign, the streets were plagued with gangs of juvenile pickpockets, dangerous housebreakers like Bill Sykes, loose women like Nancy being battered to death in dingy back-street alleys and the East End a den of thieves. At the end of her reign, George Gissing in his *The Nether World*, published in 1889, still painted a lurid picture of the East End whose inhabitants were as 'vile' as their surroundings. Despite evident improvements, perceptions of crime in the East End was magnified rather than diminished in the nineteenth century, a situation reinforced by writings such as John Hollingshead's *Ragged London* in 1861, Andrew Mearns' *The Bitter Cry of Outcast London* in 1883, Margaret Harkness' *In Darkest London* in 1889, Walter Besant's *East London* a decade later and Jack London's *The People of the Abyss* in 1903.

The extent to which these perceptions corresponded with actual levels of crime is difficult to quantify as many crimes such as domestic violence and infanticide often went unreported and it was not until 1869 that the precursor of the Criminal Records Office was established in London. Drunkenness and theft were rampant especially in the larger cities where levels of arrest and conviction were low. Mugging and its associated violence were rife. The helpless were especially vulnerable. The well-dressed might be waylaid, dragged down an alley, and stripped of their finery, or pet dogs kidnapped for ransom or simply filched for their skins. Around mid-century, and again in 1862, 'garrotting' or half-strangling unwary pedestrians from behind while accomplices stripped them of their valuables, caused great waves of panic. There were big-time criminals as well as gangs of street hooligans. In the 1890s, the 'Blind Beggar Gang', a group of twenty pickpockets, plied their trade in Petticoat Lane. In a new version of highway robbery, for instance, bankers' consignments might be snatched in transit. There was also a surge in gun crime in the 1880s and hardened burglars increasingly went armed. Protection rackets were widespread especially in the poorer areas of the East End with groups such as the Bessarabians in the 1880s and the 'Strutton Ground Boys' from Westminster in the 1890s demanding money with menaces. In both cases, local vigilante groups often made up of shopkeepers and tradesmen were formed to counter the threat and the police had to intervene to break up fights between the gangs and vigilantes. For individuals or whatever class, it was risky to gather anywhere were there were crowds of people or where there were few.

Despite the often gratuitously graphic description of crime in newspapers and 'penny dreadfuls', for which there was a seemingly insatiable demand, society as a whole became safer over the course of the nineteenth century. The police became a more effective deterrent and were certainly more popular than they had been in the 1830s and 1840s. The use of telegraphy, photography, and in the 1890s fingerprinting, made life more difficult for the habitual criminal. In addition to improved policing, social conditions improved with the clearing of the 'rookeries' or slums in the major cities and towns that had long been centres of crime. The introduction of compulsory elementary school after 1870 seems, at least initially, to have reduced levels of juvenile crime as did the provision of recreational opportunities for young men. Both theft and violence appear to have experienced a decline in late Victorian and Edwardian Britain. Crime and criminals remained but by 1914 their activities appear to have become less brutal and violent than three decades earlier.

14 Punishment

Between 1830 and 1914, there were three major alterations in the ways convicted offenders were treated. There was a change from death or transportation as the major punishments for felonies to imprisonment in custom-built prisons.[1] There was also a shift, admittedly less marked, from the personnel of the courts making all key decisions about the offender to the experts in the new prison system making some of those decisions. Finally, once it was agreed that most offenders should be sent to prison, the crucial arguments centred on to what extent prisons were places of punishment or reformation.

The traditional view of changes in punishment accepts that the 'Bloody Code' was arbitrary and savage and that the reformers' stance was moral unassailable. Penal reform began with the abolition of capital statutes urged by Romilly and Mackintosh and largely carried out by Sir Robert Peel and Lord John Russell when Home Secretaries in the 1820s and 1830s. It gathered pace as the government took an increasing role in the organisation and supervision of prisons with the opening of Millbank in 1816 and Pentonville in 1842, with the creation of the Prison Inspectorate in 1835 and the centralisation of the whole system under the Home Office in 1877.

Revisionist historians recognise the savagery of the 'Bloody Code' but have been more subtle in assessing its arbitrariness and see the emergence of the new prison system as a further institutional solution to the need for social control and discipline like the workhouse established under the new Poor Law. In many respects, the arguments of traditionalists and revisionists are the mirror image of each other. In the traditional Whig view, the humanitarian and progressive nature of penal reform fits with the humanitarian and progressive requirements of the liberal democratic society that emerged in the early-nineteenth century. In the revisionist account, there is a fit between the new system of prison and punishment and

---

[1] The most vivid revisionist study on prisons is Ignatieff, Michael, *A Just Measure of Pain: the penitentiary in the Industrial Revolution 1750-1850*, (Macmillan), 1978. Sharpe, J. A., *Judicial Punishment in England*, (Faber), 1990, covers a broader span of time. Gatrell, V. A. C., *The Hanging Tree. Execution and the English People 1770-1868*, (Oxford University Press), 1994, is a major study of changing sensibilities and debunks many myths about execution. See also, McConville, Sean, *A history of English prison administration, 1750-1877*, (Routledge), 1981, and Brown, Alyson, *English society and the prison: time, culture and politics in the development of the modern prison, 1850-1920*, (Boydell), 2003.

the control requirements of the developing capitalist system.

How was the 'Bloody Code' revised?

The 'Bloody Code' in 1800 had about 200 or so capital offences. The most serious offences against persons and property tried at Assizes or at the Old Bailey were punishable by death. Quarter Sessions and all but two borough sessions had no such power. Execution was usually by hanging. Individuals could claim benefit of clergy, a medieval right extended to men and women who could demonstrate basic literacy, until the law was abolished in 1827. [2] Gaols held the accused before trial and some petty offenders were sentenced to short periods of imprisonment but their function did not extend to long-term incarceration. Transportation, after 1787 to Australia, was seen as a solution for many criminals.

There was growing unease about the operation of the legal code that led to demands for reform of the criminal law. Campaigners such as Sir Samuel Romilly protested that there was a 'lottery of justice'. [3] There was uncertainty about the punishment for different offences and that even when the death sentence was passed it was far from certain that it would be carried out and, as a result, there was no lesson for the public. Judges, he feared, had too many discretionary powers and responded to different offences in their own individual ways. [4] Romilly and reformers like him have been portrayed as far-sighted humanitarians beset on all sides by die-hard reaction. But how great

---

[2] In 1512, Henry VIII had made certain offences 'felonies without benefit of clergy' and by the end of the sixteenth century, the list of unclergyable offences included murder, rape, poisoning, petty treason, sacrilege, witchcraft, burglary, theft from churches and pickpocketing. In the eighteenth century, increasing crime rate prompted Parliament to exclude some minor property crimes from benefit of clergy. Eventually, housebreaking, shoplifting goods worth more than 5 shillings and the theft of sheep and cattle all became felonies without benefit of clergy and earned their perpetrators automatic death sentences.

[3] *Memoirs of the Life of Sir Samuel Romilly written by himself, with a selection from his Correspondence*, edited by his sons, 3 Vols. (John Murray), 1840, and *The Speeches of Sir Samuel Romilly in the House of Commons*, 2 Vols. (J. Ridgway and Sons), 1820 provide contemporary material. See also, Medd, Patrick, *Romilly: a life of Sir Samuel Romilly, lawyer and reformer*, (Collins), 1968, and Gregory, C. N., 'Sir Samuel Romilly and criminal law reform', *Harvard Law Review*, Vol. 15, (1902), pp. 446-467.

[4] Romilly, Samuel, *Observations on the Criminal Law of England: as it relates to Capital Punishments, and on the mode in which it is administered*, (T. Cadell and W. Davies), 1810, pp. 8-23,

were their achievements?

By the late-eighteenth century, some of the more savage physical punishments of the medieval and early-modern period were rarely used. People were still whipped and the public whipping of women did not end until 1817. Also in decline were those punishments like the stocks or the pillory largely because they no longer worked. Some of those pilloried lost an eye or were even killed; some wore armour to protect themselves. On the other hand, someone such as the bookseller John Williams who sold newspapers criticising the government in 1765 was cheered in the pillory and was given £200 raised in a collection. The use of capital punishment as a solution had been questioned long before Romilly began his campaign. [5] In 1783, the procession to Tyburn for execution was abolished and after this, hangings took place outside Newgate Prison. In this context, Romilly 's achievement is perhaps less pronounced. Romilly and other reformers were able to get things done because increasingly parliamentary opinion supported their views. For instance, the bill to abolish the death penalty for pickpockets went through Parliament in six weeks in 1808 without a division. [6]

The debate between the Whigs and the Tories over law reform in the early-nineteenth century centred on the law's broad application of capital punishment for both violent and property crimes. [7] Whig reformers argued for sentences tailored to the severity of offenses, so as to project the image of law that is applied fairly, impersonally and impartially. The opponents of criminal law reform had a more coherent case than contemporaries or subsequent historians have given them credit. Anti-reformers insisted that justice was not a lottery and that judicial discretion was sensible and conscientiously practised. Reformers could point to injustices but anti-reformers could point to many instances showing that the system operated with mercy and moderation. The strongest argument of traditionalists concerned whether there could ever be a significant measure of certainty on the

---

[5] Potter, Harry, *Hanging in Judgment: Religion and the Death Penalty in England from the Bloody Code to Abolition*, (SCM Press), 1993, Bentley, David R., *Capital punishment in Northern England, 1750-1900*, (BPR Publishers), 2008, and McLeod, Hugh, 'God and the Gallows: Christianity and Capital Punishment in the Nineteenth and Twentieth Centuries', *Studies in Church History*, Vol. 40, (2004), pp. 330-356.

[6] Handler, Philip, 'Forgery and the end of the 'bloody code' in early-nineteenth-century England', *Historical Journal*, Vol. 48, (2005), pp. 683-702.

[7] See, McGowan, R., 'Images of Justice and Reform of the Criminal Law in early-nineteenth-century England', *Buffalo Law Review*, Vol. 32, (1), (1983), pp. 89-125.

way that a punishment was meted out to fit a particular crime. The Criminal Law Commissioners appointed in 1833 ran into major problems when they tried to establish a rational system of sentencing. In their *Second Report* in 1836, they specified four overall classes of crime each with two alternative penalties; by 1839, there were fifteen overall classes of crime each with a far greater range of penalties and by 1843, the scale of penalties had reached forty-five. The attempts of the Commission to establish precise offences and to codify the criminal law eventually foundered but its eight reports published by 1849 contain the most thorough and principled examination of English criminal law ever made by an official body.

Traditionalists were defending an aristocratic and paternalistic image of justice that focused on the practice of the courts and the use of mercy. Reformers focused on existing severity and proposed an image of Benthamite impersonal justice in which the law was administered equally to all and was above the suspicion of being dependent on the discretion of the judiciary. The problems for the opponents of reform were that moderate and influential Tories like Sir Robert Peel were sympathetic to the reformers' image of justice. However, what has to be recognised is the logic of the traditionalists' case and what has to be rejected is the notion that the reformers had a far-sighted vision of nineteenth century progress that would culminate in the modern legal system.

Reform of the criminal law began in the first decade of the nineteenth century and was associated with individual MPs such as Romilly. [8] Between 1810 and 1818, the House of Commons passed four Bills abolishing the death penalty for stealing 5 shillings from a shop but all were rejected by the House of Lords. In 1818, a House of Commons committee was appointed to report on capital offences and as a result some obsolete laws were repealed. In the ten years between 1815 and 1824, an average of 89 people were hanged each year, 16 for murder. The death penalty began to lose its central role in the criminal justice system with Peel's rationalisation of the law as Home Secretary in the 1820s even though numbers of capital convictions continued to rise roughly in line with the rise in criminal statistics until the early 1830s. Between 1823 and 1830, the death penalty was abolished for over a hundred offences and in the following decade was removed from other offences: in 1832, from house-

---

[8] Hostettler, John, *The politics of criminal law reform in the nineteenth century*, (Rose), 1992, Ford, T. H., 'English criminal law reform from Peterloo to Peel', *Durham University Journal*, Vol. 76, (1984), pp. 205-216, and Follett, Richard R., *Evangelicalism, penal theory and the politics of criminal law reform in England, 1800-30*, (Palgrave), 2001.

breaking, horse-stealing, sheep-stealing and coining false money; and in 1837, from all offences except murder, attempted murder and treason. The number of offences continued to be reduced in the 1830s and early 1840s and after this it was rare for anyone to be executed for any offence other than murder. Between 1845 and 1854, on average nine people were hanged each year, all for murder. In 1861, the death penalty was finally abolished for attempted murder.

At the same time there were reforms of both the criminal and civil court system. In 1813, Manchester appointed stipendiary magistrates, an example followed by Liverpool in 1836, Birmingham in 1856 and Leeds three years later. Court procedures were simplified in the early 1830s and in 1836, prisoners accused of felonies were allowed to have counsel to represent them in court. The problem of imprisonment for debt was addressed in 1844 when it was abolished for amounts less than £20 and was finally abolished for all debts in 1861. This development was aided by the establishment of a system of county courts in 1846 to allow people to sue cheaply for small debts.

The hardening attitude towards prison discipline coincided with further legal limitations on capital punishment and the final shift of physical punishment away from the public eye. In 1861, Parliament abolished the death penalty for all crimes other than murder and high treason. In 1856, a Select Committee recommended the ending of public executions and a Royal Commission made a similar suggestion ten years later. Why end public executions? The deterrent effect of public execution was recognised but contemporaries argued that this would still remain if executions were held in private and was far outweighed by the public order problems posed by the large crowds executions generated. The mid-Victorians increasingly took the view that public executions were morally wrong. Even if people believed in the deterrent effect of hanging, they did not believe it was right for men and especially women and children to see a person hanging at the end of a rope. The last public execution took place outside Newgate on 26 May 1868. [9] The removal of the convict and of punishment from the public gaze robbed the felon of any moment of glory or martyrdom. It was also in keeping with notions of dignity and decorum so important to Victorian sensibilities.

With the decline in the use of the death penalty, prisons of different varieties had a more central role to place in the punishment

---

[9] Cooper, D. D., *The Lesson of the Scaffold*, (Allen Lane), 1974, examines the debate about public executions. See also, McGowen, Randall, 'Civilizing punishment: the end of the public execution in England', *Journal of British Studies*, Vol. 33, (1994), pp. 257-282.

of offenders, though until the middle of the century transportation also remained an option for dealing with those deemed serious offenders. The transportation of convicts to English colonies had its origins in the late-sixteenth century.[10] Parliament gave magistrates the power to exile rogues and vagabonds 'beyond the seas' in 1597 and James I authorised pardons for condemned felons on condition that they went to the New World. From 1654 onwards, some prisoners who received a reprieve from the death sentence were sent to work on the plantations in North America and the West Indies and in 1678, Parliament approved the idea of sending prisoners to serve their sentences in the American colonies of Virginia and Maryland and in the West Indies where they could be used in developing those lands. However, it was not until the Transportation Act 1718 that Britain systematically adopted foreign exile as a punishment for serious crime. Between 1719 and 1776, some 50,000 people were transported. Transportation to the American colonies effectively ended in 1775 with the American War of Independence.[11] Such was the desperation of the British government over what to do with convicted felons that in the mid-1780s it decided to establish a penal colony in Australia.[12]

From the foundation of New South Wales in January 1788 until 1867, transportation was an important, though increasingly contentious, feature of colonial life.[13] More than 187,000 convicts were sent to Australia, most after 1815. Opposition to transportation

---

[10] Innes, Joanna, 'The role of transportation in seventeenth and eighteenth century English penal practice', in Bridge, Carl, (ed.), *New Perspectives in Australian History,* (Sir Robert Menzies Centre for Australian Studies, Institute of Commonwealth Studies, University of London), 1990, pp. 1-24.

[11] Ekirch, A. Roger, *Bound for America: The Transportation of British Convicts to the Colonies, 1718-1775*, (Oxford University Press), 1987, and Morgan, Gwenda, and Rushton, Peter, *Eighteenth-Century Criminal Transportation: The Formation of the Criminal Atlantic,* (Palgrave Macmillan), 2004, provide a detailed account of the operation of the transportation system.

[12] Martin, Ged, (ed.), *The Founding of Australia: The Argument about Australia's Origins*, (Hale and Iremonger), 1978, provides a convenient collection of materials on why Australia was chosen.

[13] Rudé, G., *Protest & Punishment: The Story of the Social and Political Protesters transported to Australia 1788-1868*, (Oxford University Press), 1978, and *Criminal and Victim: Crime and Society in Early-nineteenth-Century England,* (Oxford University Press), 1985, Shaw, Alan, *Convicts and the Colonies: a study of penal transportation from Great Britain and Ireland to Australia and other parts of the British Empire*, (Faber), 1966, and Hughes, R., *The fatal shore: a history of the transportation of convicts to Australia, 1787-1868,* (Collins Harvill), 1987.

grew in Britain and Australia during the 1830s and in 1840, it was discontinued to New South Wales but continued to Tasmania until 1853 and Norfolk Island until 1856. In 1849, transportation started to Western Australia.[14] Long-term transportation was retained in the 1853 Penal Servitude Act but finally abolished the 1857 Penal Servitude Act. Technically, transportation was replaced by penal servitude, a term of imprisonment that usually included hard labour and was served in British gaols. Ranging from 3 years to life, it was for those who would have been transported for less than 14 years and could also be used as an alternative sentence for those liable to transportation of 14 years or more. In practice, convicts were transported to Western Australia as late as 1867. With hangings greatly reduced and transportation slowed and then ended, prison was now the main punishment for criminals in Britain.[15]

Prisons and Reformers

Although the modern prison is generally regarded as a nineteenth century development, the change from traditional prisons to penitentiaries took place in the previous century.[16] Three major advantages of imprisonment became clearer during the eighteenth century. Previously, there had been no real alternative to sentencing offenders to death or transportation or releasing them back into the community. Many criminals who committed small offences got off without any punishment because juries were unwilling to convict when

---

[14] Ibid, Shaw, Alan, *Convicts and the Colonies* and Robson, L. L., *The Convict Settlers of Australia*, (Melbourne University Press), 1976, and Nicholas, Stephen, (ed.), *Convict workers: reinterpreting Australia's past*, (Cambridge University Press), 1988, examine the process and the participants. Smith, Babette, *Australia's birthstain: the startling legacy of the convict era*, (Allen & Unwin), 2008, considers why Australians are still misled by myths about their convict heritage. See also Brown, Richard, *Three Rebellions: Canada 1837-1838, South Wales 1839 and Victoria, Australia 1854*, (Clio Publishing), 2010, *Three Rebellions: Famine, Fenians and Freedom 1840-1882*, (Clio Publishing), 2011, and *Resistance and Rebellion in the British Empire 1600-1980*, (Clio Publishing), 2012.

[15] Smith, D., 'The demise of transportation: mid-Victorian penal policy', *Criminal Justice History*, Vol. 3, (1982), pp. 21-45. See also, Willis, James J., 'Transportation versus Imprisonment in Eighteenth- and Nineteenth-Century Britain: Penal Power, Liberty, and the State', *Law & Society Review*, Vol. 39, (1), (2005), pp. 171-210.

[16] Bender, John, *Imagining the Penitentiary: Fiction and the Architecture of Mind in Eighteenth-Century England*, (University of Chicago Press), 1987, examines how the attitudes expressed in narrative literature and art between 1719 and 1779 helped bring about this change.

the only available punishment was death. Imprisonment could be used to make the rehabilitation of the offender part of the punishment. Some people saw Houses of Correction as the means for reforming convicted criminals through making them work. Finally, prisons removed criminals from society and prison sentences deterred others from committing offences. By the end of the eighteenth century, imprisonment had become the punishment most commonly used for convicted criminals. In Surrey and Sussex, for example, 60 per cent and 43 per cent of criminals respectively were sentenced to prison.

There were different types of prisons but, in the eighteenth century, building and maintaining them was largely a matter of local initiative. The state played no part in the development or supervision of prisons and there was no national penal policy.[17] Profit was made by charging prisoners for services and from payment by the county for maintenance of those prisoners who could not pay. This meant that prisoners could purchase their own room, good food and drink and their friends and family could visit time if they had the money. Most communities, even villages, had a small 'lock-up' to hold serious prisoners until they were sent to larger gaols or to keep drunks overnight.[18] Houses of Correction [19] were established after the passage of Poor Law legislation in 1601 initially to deal with vagrants, beggars and the undeserving poor.[20] In Lincolnshire, for example, there were Houses of Correction at Folkingham, Louth, Spalding and Spilsby. In 1706, an Act of Parliament allowed judges to send criminals who had successfully claimed benefit of clergy to a house of correction for up to two years. Finally there were county gaols.

Prisons in the eighteenth and early-nineteenth centuries were very unpleasant places. All kinds of prisoners were thrown in together: convicts, those awaiting trial, lunatics, debtors, women and children. They were unhealthy, damp, overcrowded and insanitary, with no running water or sewage system. Many old castles were still used as gaols. 'Gaol-fever', probably typhus, killed many of the

---

[17] Webb, S., and B., *English Prisons under Local Government*, (Longman), 1922, contains a wealth of detail.
[18] On this see, Innes, J., 'Prisons for the Poor: English Bridewells 1555-1800', in Snyder, F., and Hay, D., (eds.), *Labour, Law and Crime: An Historical Perspective*, (Tavistock Publications), 1987, pp. 42-101, esp. 77-101.
[19] The first ever House of Correction was at the palace of Bridewell in London and the name 'bridewell' was often used as an alternative to 'House of Correction'.
[20] Van der Slice, Austin, 'Elizabethan Houses of Correction', *Journal of Criminal Law and Criminology*, Vol. 27, (1), (1936), pp. 45-67.

inmates. There were serious outbreaks during the assizes at Taunton in 1730, the Old Bailey in 1750 when sixty men died including the Lord Mayor and two judges and at Shrewsbury in 1774.

Historians have studied the ways in which Newgate Gaol operated in the eighteenth century in detail. [21] Other gaols were similar. A room on the 'Master Side' cost £3.33p a week. The charity wards were grossly overcrowded, built for 150 prisoners but containing 275. The day began at 7 am when the bell clanged, prisoners' leg-irons were unlocked and they saw to their own washing and breakfast. They were largely left alone by the warders until 9 pm when they were locked up again. Inmates elected their own 'Steward' and 'Wardsmen' to run the place. Anything was allowed, if you tipped the gaoler. Some prisoners kept pets; ale and tobacco could be bought. The gaoler estimated that he made £400 a year brewing his own ale. There was a chapel but ministers complained of poor behaviour during the services. The last sermon preached to a prisoner who was going to be hanged was a special occasions. The gaolers would sell tickets, at £20 each, to the public to hear it.

How significant were prison reformers?

Individual reformers had criticised the system of criminal punishment based on capital punishment and transportation since the 1770s. They had two motives. Prisons were cruel and unfair. Many of the reformers were Evangelicals who pointed out that convicts were God's creatures too. People's lives were being wasted, languishing in gaols when they could change their ways and become decent citizens. Goals were inefficient. Over half of the prisoners were either debtors or had served their sentence but could not afford to pay the gaoler the release fee. At Newgate Prison in 1729, the release fee was 34 pence. Sir William Eden [22] published the influential *Principles of Penal Law* in 1771 and John Howard's *The State of the Prisons in England and Wales* was published in 1777. In spite of the enthusiastic reception given to the work of Howard, much influenced by the writings of Cesare Beccaria and the boost given to reformers, change remained

---

[21] Babington, Anthony, *The English Bastille: A history of Newgate Gaol and prison conditions in Britain, 1188-1902*, (Macdonald and Co.), 1971, Grovier, K., *The Gaol: The Story of Newgate, London's most notorious prison*, (John Murray), 2008, Rumberlow, Donald, *The Triple Tree: Newgate, Tyburn and Old Bailey*, (Harrap), 1982, and Kalman, Harold D., 'Newgate Prison', *Architectural History*, Vol. 12, (1969), pp. 50-112.

[22] Draper, Anthony J., 'William Eden and leniency in punishment', *History of Political Thought*, Vol. 22, (2001), pp. 106-130, and Bolton, G. C., 'William Eden and the convicts, 1771-1787', *Australian Journal of Politics & History*, Vol. 26, (1980), pp. 30-44.

slow and continued to depend on the zeal and initiative of private individuals rather than on any government direction.[23] Howard, Sir George Paul, Elizabeth Fry and Jeremy Bentham were the most influential.

John Howard (1726-1790) was an English philanthropist and reformer in the fields of penology and public health.[24] On his father's death in 1742, Howard inherited considerable wealth and travelled widely in Europe. He then became High Sheriff in Bedfordshire in 1773. As part of his duties, he inspected Bedford Gaol and was appalled by the insanitary conditions there. He was also shocked to learn that the jailers were not salaried officers but depended on fees from prisoners and found that some prisoners had been acquitted by the courts but were kept in prison because they had not paid their release fees. In 1774, Howard persuaded the House of Commons to pass two acts that stipulated first that discharged persons should be set at liberty in open court and that discharge fees should be abolished and secondly, that justices should be required to see to the health of prisoners. Years afterward, however, Howard complained that the acts had not been 'strictly obeyed.' Howard continued to travel widely, touring Scotland, Ireland, France and the Netherlands, Germany, and Switzerland, often-visiting local prisons. He was influential in legislation in 1779 that authorised the building of two penitentiary houses where, by means of solitary confinement, supervised labour and religious instruction, the reform of prisoners might be attempted. The Penitentiary Act was an ambitious piece of legislation, designed to impose a national scheme for the punishment of offenders that could serve as an acceptable substitute for the temporary suspension

---

[23] On Beccaria, see Bellamy, Richard, (ed.), *On Crimes and Punishments and Other Writings*, (Cambridge University Press), 1995. Bellamy's introduction provides a brief biographical study as well as examining the significance of Beccaria's writings.

[24] Brown, James Baldwin, *Memoirs of the public and private life of John Howard, the philanthropist*, (T. and G. Underwood), 1818, 2nd edition, 1823, and Field, John, *The life of John Howard: with comments on his character and philanthropic labours*, (Longman, Brown, Green, and Longmans), 1850, remain useful sources. See also, Howard, D. L., *John Howard: prison reformer*, (C. Johnson), 1958, Gibson, John, *John Howard and Elizabeth Fry*, (Methuen), 1971, Ireland, Richard W., 'Howard and the paparazzi: painting penal reform in the eighteenth century', *Art, Antiquity and Law*, Vol. 4, (1999), pp. 55-62, Porter, Roy, 'Howard's beginning: prisons, disease, hygiene', in Creese, Richard, Bynum, William F., and Bearn, J., (eds.), *The health of prisoners: historical essays*, (Rodopi), 1995, pp. 5-26, and Morgan, Rod, 'Divine philanthropy: John Howard reconsidered', *History*, Vol. 62, (1977), pp. 388-410.

of transportation occasioned by the American Revolutionary War. [25] This act, however, like those of 1774, was never effectively enforced. He spent the last years of his life studying means of preventing plague and limiting the spread of contagious diseases. Travelling in Russia in 1790 and visiting the principal military hospitals that lay en route, he reached Kherson in Ukraine. In attending a case of camp fever that was raging there, he contracted the disease and died.

The power of Howard's representation of prisons and prison life in *The State of the Prisons in England and Wales* published in 1777 has led to a one-dimensional view of Hanoverian prisons grounded in their filth, petty corruption and insecurity and as places of contagious moral degeneration. [26] It neglected the attempts by early-eighteenth century legislators and some magistrates to introduce a measure of penal reform. Legislation in 1700 and 1720 allowed magistrates to levy county rates to meet the cost of building new gaols and, before Howard's intervention there was a sporadic prison rebuilding programme. Howard's influence consisted less in the novelty of his ideas as in the powerfully made case for reform that contributed to an existing debate on prison conditions. Elizabeth Fry, for example, was critical of his failure to address the issue of rehabilitation. Success was ultimately the result of the work of others especially Dr John Coakley Lettsom and James Neild, both of them Quakers. [27] It also galvanised widespread if embryonic local reform initiatives like those in Gloucestershire. Howard commented favourably on local prison building in Hertfordshire where local magistrates used their power to raise county rates to build a new prison that was opened in 1779 and on the work of Lancashire magistrates in the 1770s that resulted in the reconstruction of Lancaster gaol. [28] The late-eighteenth century saw a vigorous local movement for reform led by local magistrates that resulted in improvements in both the

---

[25] Throness, Laurie, *A Protestant Purgatory: Theological Origins of the Penitentiary Act, 1779*, (Ashgate), 2008, and Devereaux, Simon, 'The making of the Penitentiary Act, 1775-1779', *Historical Journal, Vol.* 42, (2), (1999), pp. 405-433.

[26] England, R. W., 'Who Wrote John Howard's Text: *The State of the Prisons* as a Dissenting Enterprise', *British Journal of Criminology*, Vol. 33, (1993), pp. 203-215, suggests that Howard played little role in writing his book but that the three (or possibly more) men who gave Howard extensive editorial help were not acknowledged since they were active Dissenters against the Church of England.

[27] See Neild, F. G., 'James Neild (1744-1814) and prison reform', *Journal of the Society of Medicine*, Vol. 74, (1981), pp. 834-840.

[28] DeLacey, Margaret, *Prison Reform in Lancashire, 1700-1850: a study in local administration,* (Stanford University Press), 1986, pp. 70-152

management and fabric of local gaols funded by ratepayers. [29]

Sir George Onesiphorus Paul was made High Sheriff of Gloucester in 1780 and reacted to the local prisons with much the same disgust as John Howard. [30] Howard's report on Gloucester prison was damning. Paul realised that he could not alter this and that the only option was to build a new prison and the Gloucestershire Act 1785 gave him the power to do this. He worked with an architect, William Blackburn, to turn his ideas into reality. The new prison had to be secure with walls 5.4 metres high with spikes on top. The buildings were arranged so the gaolers could easily see what was going on. It had to be healthy. People believed that disease was caused by bad air, so the gaol was built to suck in fresh air through large gateways, with open portcullises. The large, heated cells were reached by open balconies. Howard had admired the 'lazarettos' – isolation wards for health checks at the entrances of many Mediterranean ports. Paul put such a ward at the entrance to the gaol. The gaol had a house of correction for minor offenders, a gaol for prisoners on remand awaiting trial, and a penitentiary for those who had committed serious offences, with male and female sections for each.

Paul paid attention to the rules, as well as the building. There was a paid Governor, a chaplain and a surgeon who visited the sick each day and inspected every prisoner each week. Prisoners were to be reformed through work, education and religion. If they could not read they were taught and given religious books. Staff had to keep detailed journals on what prisoners said and did. They had to wear a yellow and blue uniform and keep clean; they were not allowed pets or to play games. They were, however well fed and not kept in irons. They spent long periods on their own, thinking about their life of crime. This separation of prisoners from each other was later taken further but at Gloucester it was only for the first nine months of the sentence. Paul's prison and rules became a model for other prisons.

Women's prisons were probably worse than men's. There was the same chaotic mixing of those awaiting trial and those convicted. Women prisoners were just as dependent on the gaoler for everything. Women's prisons usually had male gaolers, who often

---

[29] This was not without opposition, see Brown, Susan E., 'Policing and Privilege: The Resistance to Penal Reform in Eighteenth-Century London', in Goldgar, Anne, and Frost, Robert I., (eds.), *Institutional Culture in Early Modern Society*, (Brill), 2004, pp. 103-132.

[30] Whiting, J. R. S., *Prison reform in Gloucestershire, 1776-1820: a study of the work of Sir George Onesiphorus Paul, Bart.*, (Phillimore), 1975, and Cooper, R. A., 'Ideas and Their Execution: English Prison Reform', *Eighteenth-Century Studies*, Vol. 10, (1), (1976), pp. 73-93

exploited the women. Women convicts were the outcasts of society. The ideal woman at the time was an angel, a homebuilder, wife and mother, gentle and virtuous. Women in prison had obviously broken this code and few people pitied them. However, there was no shortage of women prisoners. In general, fewer women than men committed crimes. However, for some offence, like drunkenness, numbers of men and women were roughly equal and they were not far behind for murder. Elizabeth Fry (1780-1845) was a Quaker philanthropist and one of the major promoters of prison reform in Europe, who also helped to improve the British hospital system and the treatment of the insane. [31] The daughter of a wealthy Quaker banker and merchant, she married Joseph Fry, a London merchant in 1800 and combined her work with the care of a large family. Unstinting in her attendance of the poor, she was acknowledged as a 'minister' by the Quakers or Society of Friends (1811) and later travelled in Scotland, northern England, Ireland, and much of Europe. Quakers believe that there is something of God in everyone and that has drawn many into working with prisoners.

Just before Christmas 1813, Elizabeth Fry visited the women's section of Newgate Prison and was shocked with what she saw. There were 300 women crammed into three rooms. Some were ill but could not afford treatment. Some were freezing but could not afford to pay for bedding. Some were fighting'. There were many children among them. She never forgot the sight of two women fighting over a dead baby's clothes. She returned the next day with baby clothes and clean straw bedding. After these had been handed out she began to pray and many of the convicts joined her. She did not return to the prison until 1816. The chaplain and the gaoler both warned against going in. This time she appealed to the women to do something for their children. Her lack of fear and her directness made a huge impression and they started a school for the prison children. Elizabeth Fry formed a group of mainly Quaker women to visit the prison daily and make changes in the way it was run. A matron was appointed to run the women's section, the women were supplied with materials to work

---

[31] Fry, Elizabeth Gurney, Fry, Katharine. and Cresswell, Rachel Elizabeth, *Memoir of the Life of Elizabeth Fry: With Extracts from Her Journal and Letters*, 2 Vols. (J. Hatchard and Son), 1848, Kent, J. H. S., *Elizabeth Fry*, (Batsford), 1962, Hatton, Jean, *Betsy: the dramatic biography of prison reformer Elizabeth Fry*, (Monarch), 2005, Skidmore, Gil, (ed.), *Elizabeth Fry: a Quaker life: selected letters and writings*, (Altamira Press), 2005, Isba, Anne, *Excellent Mrs Fry: The Unlikely Heroine*, (Continuum), 2010, and Summers, Anne, 'Elizabeth Fry and mid-nineteenth century reform', in ibid, Creese, Richard, Bynum, William F., and Bearn, J., (eds.), *The health of prisoners : historical essays*, pp. 83-101.

at sewing and knitting to be sold and Bible readings were held. In 1818, Elizabeth Fry gave evidence to a parliamentary Select Committee. This reported that her efforts had made the women's section in Newgate an orderly and sober place.

Her courage in working with women prisoners, her religious motives and her success made her famous. [32] She was often asked to address meetings and was summoned to meet Queen Victorian in 1840. The Gaols Act of 1823 took up some of her many ideas: gaolers had to be paid, prisoners were to be separated into categories and women had to have female gaolers and warders. However, the Act did not go as far as she wished in forcing prisons to try to reform their inmates. Her own reforms cost money and she knew that many prisons would not take them up unless they were forced to.

Even in her lifetime her suggestions were increasingly acted upon throughout most of Europe. Later in her life she travelled widely in Europe and, especially in France and Ireland, she was welcomed and listened to with respect but this was not the case in England. [33] Fry spoke out against the Separate System arguing that her reforms gave women a sense of dignity and perhaps an honest skill but did not break people's spirits. Edwin Chadwick was highly critical of this saying that the reforms of Howard and Fry encouraged people to get into prison:

...the prisons have been so reformed...as to attract vagrants and others who preferred their comfort to labour. [34]

Elizabeth Fry died in 1845 and upper-class women could no longer wander casually into prisons and meddle in how they were run. However, three ideas still present in British prisons owe their origins to her: separate women's prisons with a female staff; volunteer prison visitors; and, a belief that prison is a place from which people can emerge rehabilitated. [35]

---

[32] See Fry, Elizabeth, *Observations on Visiting, Superintendence And Government of Female Prisoners*, (J. and A. Arch), 1827.

[33] For example, Elizabeth Fry inspected the state of Irish gaols in 1826; see comments in Fry, Elizabeth, and Gurney, Joseph John, *Report addressed to the Marquess Wellesley, Lord Lieutenant of Ireland, respecting their late visit to that country*, (Cumming), 1827.

[34] Finer, S. E., *The Life and Times of Sir Edwin Chadwick*, (Methuen), 1952, p. 165, citing an unpublished manuscript for the Constabulary Commission Report of 1839.

[35] Downing, Kevin, and Forsythe, Bill, 'The Reform of Offenders in England, 1830-1995: A Circular Debate', *Criminal Justice History*, Vol. 18,

The late-eighteenth century gave rise to a prison that was never actually built, at least not exactly as its creator intended: Jeremy Bentham's Panopticon, designed by the British philosopher in 1791 to serve as a place of incarceration intended to control prisoners by making them feel that they were under constant surveillance. According to Michel Foucault, whose *Discipline and Punish: The Birth of the Prison* (1975) used the idea of the Panopticon as a model for less tangible forms of social control, the Panopticon was the basis of all discussions of prison reform during the first half of the nineteenth century.[36]

The French Wars between 1793 and 1815 involved government departments in the organisation and administration of large numbers of prisoners on British soil. Even though central government became increasingly involved in penal administration and reform, Benthamism and Quakerism were two of the main pressures for penal reform during the early decades of the nineteenth century. However, there were important differences between Bentham's and Fry's ideas and those of their supposed supporters.[37] Both Bentham and Fry supported the classification of prisoners, productive labour in prisons and the maintenance of healthy prison conditions. Their supporters, however, were more pragmatic concerned with solitary confinement and hard labour as the focus of their desire to deter crime. In many respects, this was a generational difference. Bentham and Fry were reformers, like Howard, concerned with the salvation of prisoners while by 1830, Benthamites and Quakers active in penal reform were largely concerned with reducing levels of crime and by 1835 they had

---

(2003), pp. 145-162, and Forsythe, W. J., *The Reform of Prisoners, 1830-1900*, (Routledge), 1987.

[36] For Bentham's vision see, Bentham, Jeremy, *Panopticon or the inspection house: Containing The Idea of a New Principle of Construction applicable to any Sort of Establishment, in which Persons of any Description are to be kept under Inspection: And In Particular To Penitentiary-Houses, Prisons, Houses Of Industry, Work-Houses, Poor...,* (T. Payne), 1791, and *Panopticon: Postscript: Containing Further Particulars And Alterations Relative To The Plan Of Construction Originally Proposed; Principally adapted to the Purpose of a Panopticon Penitentiary-House*, 2 Vols. (T. Payne), 1791. Semple, Janet, *Bentham's prison: a study of the Panopticon penitentiary*, (Oxford University Press), 1993, and Schofield, Philip, *Utility and democracy: the political thought of Jeremy Bentham*, (Oxford University Press), 2006, pp. 80-83, 109-111, 254-260, provide critique.

[37] Cooper, R. A., 'Jeremy Bentham, Elizabeth Fry and English Prison Reform', *Journal of the History of Ideas*, Vol. 42, (4), (1981), pp. 675-690.

largely rejected Bentham's and Fry's ideas for prison reform. [38]

Why did a national prison system evolve?

The involvement of the Home Office in the administration of prisons evolved gradually during the nineteenth century until, by 1878, the Home Secretary became responsible for the administration of all prisons. The outbreak of the American War of Independence in 1775 ended transportation to the American colonies and created a major logistical problem for central government. The solution was the use of old sailing ships or 'hulks' as a 'temporary expedient' while government considered what to do with convicted prisoners. In 1779, legislation introduced a new concept of hard labour for prisoners in the hulks commencing with dredging the River Thames and made provision for the building of two penitentiaries. There was considerable delay in building these institutions and because transportation to Australia became possible in 1787 relieving the pressure on the hulks, it was not until 1813 that construction of convict prisons commenced under the direct responsibility of the Home Office with the penitentiary on Millbank. [39]

Millbank was designed according to principles laid down by Jeremy Bentham and he secured a contract to build it but was unable to obtaining funding. In 1813, the Home Office took over the contract and built a modified version of the prison that was completed in 1821. Initially, Millbank contained male and female convicts but legislation in 1823 limited its use to men. In the prison's early years, sentences of five to ten years were offered as an alternative to transportation to those thought most likely to reform. Millbank was severely criticised by contemporaries especially for its dietary regime and the health of inmates. [40] Reduction in prisoners' diets in 1822 led to an outbreak of scurvy and cholera was a problem in the early 1850s. [41] In 1843,

---

[38] Moore, J. M., 'Penal reform: a history of failure', *Criminal Justice Matters*, Vol. 77, (1), (2009), pp. 12-13, has some interesting if brief comments on Howard and Fry.

[39] Hulks continued to be used until 1859 and during the French Wars contained 70,000 prisoners, many French prisoners of war. They were brought under the control of the Home Office in 1850.

[40] See, for example, the comments in *Report on the discipline and management of the convict prisons, and disposal of convicts, 1852,* (George R. Eyre and William Spottiswoode), 1853, pp. 58-97, ibid, Mayhew, Henry, and Binny, John, *The criminal prisons of London, and scenes of prison life*, pp. 232-273, and *Reports of the Directors of Convict Prisons...For the Year 1862*, (George R. Eyre and William Spottiswoode), 1863, pp. 43-94.

[41] 'Cholera in its Relations to Sanitary Measures', *British and Foreign Medico-Chirurgical Review,* Vol. 7, (1851), pp. 9-11.

Millbank ceased to have a penitentiary function and, until it closed fifty years later, became an ordinary prison and holding centre for men and women awaiting transportation or in the case of sick prisoners, removal to one of the 'hulks'. Every person sentenced to transportation was sent to Millbank first, where they were held for three months before it was decided where to send them. [42] Millbank was generally regarded as a failure as a penitentiary. [43]

Home Office involvement in the building of Millbank marked a shift in penal policy and resulted in a dual system of Home Office prisons and local prisons until the two were finally amalgamated in 1878. From Peel onwards, Home Secretaries adopted an interventionist approach to penal questions and developed some sort of policy on the punishment of criminal offenders. [44] A prison for juvenile offenders opened in 1839 at Parkhurst followed by Pentonville prison in 1842 that was intended as a model on which local authorities could base their own schemes. Between 1842 and 1877, 90 new prisons were built in Britain. The District Courts and Prisons Act of 1842 laid down further regulations for building and running gaols. Plans for building a new gaol, by agreement between two or more authorities, were to be submitted to the Home Secretary. If he approved them an Order in Council would be issued constituting the prison a common gaol. The Act of 1844 authorised the appointment of a Surveyor General of Prisons to advise justices on the building or rebuilding of gaols and introduced controls over the building of new prisons. This was particularly significant for the future: in the six years after the building of Pentonville, fifty-four new prisons largely modelled on the Pentonville design were built providing 11,000 separate cells. The Convict Prisons Act 1850 gave the Home Secretary authority to appoint the Directors of Convict Prisons that was formed to replace various boards of commissioners that had previously managed the different convict prisons, to be responsible

---

[42] Holford, G. P., *An account of the general penitentiary at Millbank ; containing a statement of the circumstances which led to its erection, a description of the building, etc., to which is added an appendix, on the form and construction of prisons*, (C. & J. Rivington), 1828, Griffith, Arthur, *Memorials of Millbank, and Chapters in Prison History*, 2 Vols. (H. S. King), 1875, Vol. 1, pp. 27-70, and Wilson, David, 'Millbank, The Panopticon and Their Victorian Audiences', *Howard Journal of Criminal Justice*, Vol. 41, (2002), pp. 364-381.

[43] Ibid, Griffith, Arthur, *Memorials of Millbank, and Chapters in Prison History*, Vol. 1, pp. 289-310, puts the case against the penitentiary.

[44] Forsythe, B., 'Centralisation and Local Autonomy: The Experience of British Prisons 1820-1877', *Journal of Historical Sociology*, Vol. 4, (1991), pp. 317-345.

for the Convict Prison Service.

Parallel to the development of new prisons were attempts, largely unsuccessful, to impose some standards and uniformity in the running of local prisons. After 1815, there was an increase of parliamentary interest and activity in prisons. Legislation in 1815 required returns to be made of all persons committed and of their crimes. In 1819, the *Report of the Select Committee on the State and Description of Gaols* and an *Account Respecting Gaols, Penitentiaries etc. as to the Number of Prisoners Confined and the Management of them* were published. In 1820, the Commons received *Returns from Gaols of Persons Committed* and a Select Committee was set up to inquire into the laws relating to prisons and its *Report* appeared in 1822. Following a Select Committee report, Sir Robert Peel introduced the Gaol Act in 1823 and the Prison Discipline Act the following year that laid down rules for local prisons. Earlier legislation had been mainly permissive, but the 1823 Act made central control firmer. It dealt with only 130 prisons; county gaols and those in London, Westminster and in 17 other towns. It was hoped that the authorities in charge of other gaols would either improve them voluntarily or join with county authorities to build new ones. As a result of the Act, between 30 and 40 small towns either closed their gaols or let them fall into disuse. The legislation was informed by the idea of the penitentiary and spelled out health and religious regulations, required the categorisation of prisoners and directed magistrates to inspect prisons three times a year and demanded that annual reports be sent from each gaol to the Home Office. The reports appeared from 1826 listing gaols by counties, and for each entry contain information about the number and employment of prisoners and state of the buildings. They were declared to be no longer necessary in 1858 but had ceased to appear a decade earlier. Many local gaols ignored at least some of these regulations and Peel, reluctant to antagonise local sensibilities about independence, made no attempt to impose sanctions or a national system of inspection.

In 1835, a series of reports was made by a House of Lords' Committee on the State of Gaols containing appendices setting out much detailed information including gaols controlled by municipal corporations. These reports informed the drafting of the Prisons Act 1835 'for effecting greater uniformity of practice in the government of the several prisons in England and Wales'. The Act empowered Lord John Russell, the Home Secretary to establish a Prison Inspectorate of five with only limited powers to inspect local prisons. [45] The

---

[45] Stockdale, E. 'Short History of Prison Inspection in England', *British Journal of Criminology*, Vol. 23, (3), (1983), pp. 209-223.

Inspectorate was required to make an annual report for each of the establishments visited for the Home Secretary to present to parliament. The reports were initially divided between four districts (Home, Northern and Eastern, Southern and Western and Scotland with Northumberland and Durham), but this was reduced in 1853 to three (Northern, Midland and Southern), and to the Northern and Southern in 1863.

Colonial opposition to transportation built up in the 1830s and 1840s and this paralleled the emerging dominance of slightly different concepts of prison discipline from Westminster, the separate and silent systems. [46] Reformers discovered the prison as a place to teach order and discipline to the offenders, who were perceived as a fundamental threat to the stability of society. The basic idea was to hold prisoners in solitude to shield them from the supposed contaminating influence of other convicts. Being left in completely silence with only the company of one's conscience and the Bible was to bring about the spiritual rehabilitation of the offender. Also, a strict diet of work and military discipline would help to turn them into law-abiding citizens. Prison building aimed at transforming the prison from a physically and morally filthy place of confinement into a clean and rationally functioning reform-machine. Before 1830, attempts to enforce 'solitude' by separating prisoners in gaols had been largely unsuccessful. However, from the 1830s, separate confinement became an effective national policy largely because of the combination of new forms of state power through discipline, government and law with the notion of geographical uniformity. The connections between state power and effective centralised uniformity help to explain why the 'separate system' rather than alternative regimes was widely supported by prison reformers in the 1830s and 1840s and why it continued to be the lynchpin of penal policy even after its reformative claims had been rejected. [47]

The initial, practical application of the silent and separate

---

[46] Molesworth, William, *Report from the Select Committee of the House of Commons on Transportation: together with a letter from the Archbishop of Dublin on the same subject, and notes*, (H. Hooper), 1838, Ritchie, John, 'Towards ending an unclean thing: The Molesworth committee and the abolition of transportation to New South Wales, 1837-40', *Australian Historical Studies*, Vol. 17, (1976), pp. 144-164, and Townsend, N., 'The Molesworth Enquiry: Does the report fit the evidence', *Journal of Australian Studies*, Vol. 1, (1977), pp. 33-51.

[47] Ogborn, Miles, 'Discipline, Government and Law: Separate Confinement in the Prisons of England and Wales, 1830-1877', *Institute of British Geographers*, New Series, Vol. 20, (3), (1995), pp. 295-311.

systems occurred in the United States in the 1820s. [48] The Auburn system, also known as the New York System, evolved during the 1820s at Auburn Prison. Convicts worked during the day in groups and were kept in solitary confinement at night, with enforced silence at all times. This 'silent' system promised to rehabilitate criminals by teaching them personal discipline and respect for work, property and others. The 'separate' system, by contrast, was based on the principle of keeping prisoners in solitary confinement. [49] The first prison built according to the separate system was the Eastern State Penitentiary in 1829 in Philadelphia, Pennsylvania and its design was later copied by more than 300 prisons worldwide. Its revolutionary system of incarceration, dubbed the 'Pennsylvania System' encouraged separation of inmates from one another as a form of rehabilitation.[50] This was the basic idea behind the separate system favoured in the 1839 Prisons Act. [51] A group of experts, notably William Crawford a leading figure in the Prison Discipline Society and Reverend Whitworth Russell formerly chaplain at Millbank, advocated the separate system. [52] Lord John Russell, somewhat hesitantly,

---

[48] Gray, Francis C., *Prison Discipline in America*, (Charles C. Little and James Brown), 1847, Adshead, Joseph, *Prisons and Prisoners*, (Longman, Brown, Green and Longman), 1845, and Dix, Dorothea Lynde, *Remarks on Prisons and Prison Discipline in the United States*, (Kite), 1845, provide an interesting comparison of the American and British systems.

[49] Forsythe, W. J., 'The beginnings of the separate system of imprisonment 1835-1840', *Social Policy & Administration*, Vol. 13, (2), (1979), pp. 105-110, and 'The Aims and Methods of the Separate System', *Social Policy & Administration*, Vol. 14, (1980), pp. 249-256. See also Field, John, *Prison discipline: and the advantages of the separate system of imprisonment, with a detailed account of the discipline now pursued in the new County Gaol, at Reading*, 2 Vols. (Longman, Brown, Green, and Longmans), 1848, and Jebb, Joshua, *Observations on the Separate System of Discipline submitted to the Congress assembled at Brussels, on the subjects of Prison Reform, on the 20 September 1847*, (W. Clowes and Sones), 1847.

[50] Teeters, N. K., and Shearer, J. D., *The Prison at Philadelphia: the separate system of penal discipline, 1829-1913*, (Temple University Press), 1957, and Sellin, T., 'The Origin of the 'Pennsylvania System of Prison Discipline'', *The Prison Journal*, Vol. 50, (1970), pp. 13-21. See also, Packard, F. A., *A Vindication of the Separate System of Prison Discipline from the Misrepresentations of the North American Review, July, 1839*, (J. Dobson), 1839.

[51] This was strongly expressed in *Third Report of the [Prison] Inspectors*, 4 Vols. (W. Clowes and Sons), 1838, Vol. 1, pp. 13-32, while the 'futility' of the silent system was discussed, pp. 33-34.

[52] William Crawford's influence was felt particularly in *Report of William Crawford on the Penitentiaries of the United States, addressed to His*

authorised the construction of a new national prison in London and Captain Joshua Jebb, subsequently appointed Surveyor-General of Prisons in 1846 and favourably disposed to the separate system, was entrusted with the design. [53] The result was the opening of Pentonville in 1842. [54]

The objective of such a prison or 'penitentiary' was that of penance by the prisoners through silent reflection in separate cells. At exercise time each prisoner held on to a knot on a rope; the knots were 4.5 metres apart so that prisoners were too far apart to talk. They wore a mask, the 'beak', when they were moved around the building so that anonymity was preserved. At the required church services each convict was confined to a separate box so that communication with fellow inmates was all but impossible. The plan was for the solitary confinement and anonymity of Pentonville to last for 18 months before a man was transported. It was believed that in the quiet, contemplative state of the solitary cell, convicts, assisted by their Bibles and the ministrations of the chaplain would come to a realisation and repentance of their wrong doing:

> It cannot be questioned, then, on grounds of reasoning, independent of experience, that the Separate system is better calculated to promote that great object of Prison Discipline — the reformation of the offender. [55]

The problem was that not every convict was quite so malleable; some assaulted warders, other developed serious psychological disorders or attempted suicide. Between 1842 and 1850, 55 prisoners in Pentonville went mad, 26 had nervous breakdowns and three

---

Majesty's Principal Secretary of State for the Home Department, (Ordered, by The House of Commons, to be printed, 11 August 1834), 1834, and *Extracts from the second report of [William Crawford and Whitworth Russell] the inspectors of prisons for the Home District*, (William Clowes and Sons), 1838.

[53] Stockdale, E., 'The Rise of Joshua Jebb, 1837-1850', *British Journal of Criminology*, Vol. 16, (1976), pp. 164-170. See also, Jebb, Joshua, *Report of the Surveyor-General of Prisons on the construction, ventilation and details of Pentonville Prison*, (W. Clowes and Sons), 1844, *Second Report of the Surveyor-General of Prisons*, (W. Clowes and Sons), 1847, and *Reports and Observations on the Discipline and Management of Convict Prisons*, (Eyre and Spottiswoode), 1863.

[54] Tomlinson, Heather, 'Design and reform: the 'separate system' in the nineteenth century English prison', in King, Anthony D., (ed.) *Buildings and Society: Essays on the Social Development of the Built Environment*, (Routledge), 1984, pp. 94-119.

[55] *The Christian Examiner*, Vol. 40, (1846), p. 131.

committed suicide. [56] By the end of the 1840s, even the annual reports of the prison's commissioners were compelled to admit that there were problems with the system. [57]

In the 'silent system' prisoners were still confined to their cells for most of the first nine months and were forbidden from communicating with other prisoners. Prisoners who committed an offence could be put on a diet of bread and water, or chained up or whipped. The main elements of the regime were 'hard labour, hard fare and a hard board'. Gone was any idea about useful or saleable work. Hard labour was intended to be hard and deliberately pointless. There were various kinds of hard labour. The use of the treadmill on which prisoners did ten minutes on and five minutes off for several hours. Oakum-picking involved separating out the fibres of old ships' ropes so they could be re-used. The crank was usually in the prisoner's cell. The warder could see how many revolutions the prisoner had made. Finally shot-drill was where heavy cannon balls were passed from one to another down a long line of prisoners. The food or 'hard fare' was deliberately monotonous. Hard beds replaced hammocks. [58]

The initial, optimistic logic of the separate system, together with pressure form the Home Office for national uniformity led some local authorities to establish the system in existing or purpose-built prisons. However, the operation of the silent system did not need large-scale improvement or reconstruction of prison buildings and also allowed prisoners to labour in association. Bedfordshire justices, for example, originally ruled out reform of Bedford gaol on the grounds of cost and when they did decide to rebuild they faced vociferous protests from ratepayers. Crawford and Whitworth Russell both died in 1847 removing the two most ardent advocates of the separate system. It had never been implemented across the country with the uniformity

---

[56] Thomson, J. Bruce, 'The Effects of the Present System of Prison Discipline on the Body and Mind', *Journal of Mental Science*, Vol. 12, (1866), pp. 340-348, argued that 'the separate system of prison discipline is trying upon the mind and demands the most careful attention on the part of medical officers, inasmuch as mental diseases are most prominent among criminals in prisons...'

[57] See for example, Burt, J. T., *Results of the system of separate confinement, as administered at the Pentonville prison*, (Longman, Brown, Green and Longmans), 1852.

[58] Ibid, Brown, Alyson, *English Society and the Prison: Time, Culture and Politics in the Development of the Modern Prison, 1850-1920*, (Boydell), pp. 13-31, considers prisoners' perceptions of doing 'time'. See also, Priestley, Philip, *Victorian Prison Lives: English prison biography, 1830-1914*, (Methuen), 1985.

and rigour that they had wished leading to a mixture of both systems. However, within ten years the debate on prisons had shifted significantly and the issue was not whether the system should be silent or separate but whether the whole penal system was sufficiently severe.[59]

Toward the mid-nineteenth century, some authors became interested in the actual conditions of prisons. [60] Although eighteenth-century authors such as Daniel Defoe and John Gay had featured the image of the infamous Newgate Prison in their writings, Charles Dickens's explorations of the criminal world took a somewhat darker tone. Novels including *Oliver Twist* (1838), *Little Dorrit* (1857) and *Great Expectations* (1861) featured extended scenes in prison. [61] Writings from prison also gained greater visibility as more individuals who were literate were incarcerated. Prison biography became a genre in itself, allowing inmates to express the horror of their condition to a wider public. [62] By the time Oscar Wilde began writing about his experiences in prison from 1895-1897, prison writing was much more realistic, gritty and sordid. Wilde's *De Profundis* (1905), written during his prison term at Reading Gaol, reveals the witty Wilde completely altered by the utter humiliation and physical suffering of his punishment for 'indecency'. [63] In other writings, he describes the prison as 'built with bricks of shame' where 'what is good in Man...wastes and withers there.' [64] The subject of prison reform also took to the stage in 1865 with Charles Reade's drama *It Is Never Too Late To Mend*. Its première at the Princess' Theatre on 4 October 1865 saw one of the most memorable disturbances in the nineteenth century theatre occurred when the drama critics, led by Frederick

---

[59] Henriques, U. R. Q., 'The rise and decline of the separate system of prison discipline', *Past & Present*, Vol. 54, (1972), pp. 61-93.

[60] Alber, Jan, and Lauterbach, Frank, (eds.), *Stone of Law, Bricks of Shame: Narrating imprisonment in the Victorian Age*, (University of Toronto Press), 2009.

[61] See, Paroissien, 'Victims or Vermin?: Contradictions in Dickens' Penal Philosophy', and Grass, Sean C., '*Great Expectations*, Self-Narration and the Power of the Prison', in ibid, Alber, Jan, and Lauterbach, Frank, (eds.), *Stone of Law, Bricks of Shame*, pp. 25-45, 171-190.

[62] This was especially evident in the literature of Irish nationalism; see, for example, Mitchel, John, *Jail Journal, or, Five years in British prisons*, (Office of *The Citizen*), 1854, and Clarke, Thomas James, *Glimpses of an Irish Felon's Prison Life*, (Maunsel & Roberts), 1922, pp. 1-41.

[63] Harris, Frank, *Oscar Wilde: His Life and Confessions*, 2 Vols. (The author), 1916, Vol. 2, pp. 223-250.

[64] Wilde, Oscar, *The Ballad of Reading Gaol*, (T. B. Mosher), 1907, initially published anonymously in 1897.

Guest Tomlins of the *Morning Advertiser* demanded that the play be halted because of its offensive subject matter and one particularly shocking scene of prison torture. As a result, it did not remain in the play after the first night. [65] Increasingly, writings about prisons began to assert the rights of the criminal as a person with human dignity. The Howard Association was formed in 1866 with the intention of independently monitoring the prison system and the handling of convicts. [66]

The creation of the Directors of Convict Prisons and a Prisons Inspectorate in 1850 represented the beginnings of the later centralised service. Also in 1850, a Select Committee on Prison Discipline was established under Sir George Grey and is important because it examined the relative merits of the 'separate' and 'silent' systems. There had been intense arguments about these systems for thirty years and Grey's Committee found that some local prisons were still very unsatisfactory and that in them neither separation nor reformation was possible. With the ending of transportation to Tasmania in 1852, a crisis slightly eased by the cooperation of Western Australia that agreed to taking convicts, it was clear that the prison system needed to develop resources to cope with all long-sentence prisoners in England. [67] The result was a shift in thinking away from reformation as a major aim of imprisonment towards a more draconian system.

Administrators believed that the mere denial of freedom was not punishment enough and thought up various ways of intensifying the pains of imprisonment. Their industriousness made the hand crank and the treadwheel common features in prisons of the second half of the nineteenth century. 1863 can be singled out as a key year for the increasing severity of the penal system, though largely through coincidence. In 1862, London underwent a panic over the increased incidence of garrotting. Joshua Jebb, who had been under attack for being too soft on dangerous men, died. The 'silent system' was particularly associated with the new Assistant Director of Prisons, Sir

---

[65] Reade, Charles, *It is Never Too Late To Mend or The Horrors of a Convict Prison*, (Review of Reviews Office), 1864. See, Barrett, Daniel, '*It Is Never Too Late To Mend* (1865), and Prison Conditions in Nineteenth-Century England', *Theatre Research International*, Vol. 18, (1993), pp. 4-15.

[66] In 1921, it merged with the Prison Reform League to become the Howard League for Penal Reform. See, Rose, Gordon, *The Struggle for Penal Reform: the Howard League and its Predecessors*, (Stevens), 1961.

[67] Kerr, Margaret, 'The British Parliament and transportation in the eighteen-fifties', *Australian Historical Studies*, Vol. 6, (1953), pp. 29-44.

Edmund Du Cane, a firm disciplinarian, appointed in 1863.[68] The result of growing concerns about the institutional breakdown of the penal system and a widespread, if overblown, panic about levels of crime was a Select Committee of the House of Lords chaired by Lord Carnarvon. It presented its *Report on Gaol Discipline* in July 1863 stressing the importance of punishment over reformation and many of its recommendations were incorporated in the Penal Servitude Act 1864.[69] Lord Chief Justice Cockburn told the Committee that the primary object of the treatment of prisoners should be:

...deterrence, through suffering, inflicted punishment for crime, and the fear of the repetition of it.

The Select Committee also pointed out the deficiencies in the local operation of prisons. The Prisons Act 1865 aimed to enforce a strict, uniform regime of punishment in all 193 local prisons depriving county justices and municipal corporations of their independent authority over local gaols. The intention was not to try to reform prisoners through work or religion but to impose strict standards of discipline through 'hard labour, hard fare and a hard board'. Thirteen English borough or liberty prisons were closed and either sold or, with the Home Secretary's permission, used as police stations or lock-ups. Many smaller prison authorities gave up their gaols because of the expense of complying with the new regulations, leaving only 113 prisons under local control. The legislation made it possible for the grant from central government to the local authority to be withdrawn if the provisions of the Act were not implemented. Even this had little effect upon the urgent need to improve conditions of the local prisons and produce economy and efficiency in their management. [70]

The organisation and control of Britain's penal institutions had by 1865 been subjected to increasing centralisation and rationalisation through the mechanisms of State inspection in the 1835 Prison Act, regulation in Prison Acts in 1823 and 1844 and finance through the 1865 Prison Act. In essence, the 1865 Prisons Act sounded the death knell of the mainly privatised, locally administered prison system in England and Wales and the Prisons Act of 1877 put the finishing

---

[68] Hasluck, Alexandra, *Royal Engineer: a life of Sir Edmund Du Cane*, (Angus and Robertson), 1973.

[69] See, Tomlinson, M. Heather, 'Penal Servitude 1846-1865: a system in evolution', in Bailey, V., (ed.), *Policing and Punishment in Nineteenth Century Britain*, (Croom Helm), 1981, pp. 126-149.

[70] Glen, William C., *The Prison Act, 1865: with the other statutes and parts of statutes in force relating to goals and prisons, and an extensive index to the whole*, (Shaw and Sons), 1865.

touches to the centralisation and unification of the prison system. The 1877 legislation transferred the powers and responsibilities from the local justices to the Home Secretary who also took over from local rate payers the cost of the system. The detailed administration of the system was delegated to the Prison Commission, a new body of up to five members, assisted by inspectors. Sir Edmund Du Cane, Chairman of the Prison Commission, faced a formidable task in organising an efficient and uniform system. Resources and needs required review, staffing had to be rationalised, and the regimes in the various prisons awaited inspection. When the 1877 Act came into operation on 1 April 1878, this work was sufficiently advanced to enable the Commissioners immediately to close 38 out of a total of 113 local prisons. Within ten years, a further 19 had been closed.

The regime that Du Cane imposed in the local prisons was based on the principle of separate confinement that was justified on the grounds that an offender was more likely to see the error of his ways if left to contemplate his crime alone. It also reflected the view that imprisonment was a punishment intended to deter the offender from further crime. For the first month the prisoner was required to sleep on a plank bed and to work alone in his cell. The work would be tedious, unpleasant and unconstructive; at this stage it would usually consist of picking oakum. Later, he might find himself working the crank or treadwheel. Food was monotonous and unpalatable. No letters or visits were allowed for the first three months, and thereafter were permitted only at three monthly intervals. A convict was sentenced to penal servitude, not to imprisonment spent the first nine months of his sentence in solitary confinement. The convict crop and the prison uniform, its colour depending on the prisoner's classification with its broad arrows were intentionally demeaning and unsightly and facilities for personal hygiene were minimal. Under the Penal Servitude Act 1857, a convict serving more than three years was allowed to earn remission amounting to a quarter of his sentence. Marks were awarded for good behaviour and the amount of remission depended on the number of marks earned.

By the late 1880s, belief in punishment and deterrence as the main objects of imprisonment and confidence in the separate system as a desirable and effective means of dealing with prisoners came increasingly under question especially from a rabid campaign in the *Daily Chronicle*. [71] The result was the departmental committee

---

[71] See, Forsythe, W. J., *Penal discipline, reformatory projects and the English Prison Commission, 1895-1939*, (Exeter University Press), 1990, and Harding Christopher, ''The Inevitable End of a Discredited System'? The Origins of the Gladstone Committee Report on Prisons, 1895',

chaired by Herbert Gladstone in 1894 and 1895 reflecting changes in attitudes towards prisoners.[72] 'We start', said the Committee, 'from the principle that prison treatment should have as its primary and concurrent objects, deterrence and reformation'.[73] The Committee recommended that unproductive labour, in particular the crank and treadwheel should be abolished and that the principle of labour in association, practised for many years in the convict service, should be extended to local prisons. They argued that under proper conditions association for industrial labour relieved isolation was healthier, eased the task of providing industrial work in prison and, if regarded as a privilege that could be withdrawn, would not endanger control.[74] The Committee also recommended that further efforts should be made to classify prisoners, that books should be made more widely available and that educational facilities should be extended. They urged that the rules about visits should be exercised with discretion not rigidly applied, especially in circumstances where they would be beneficial to the prisoner. For convicts, the initial period of solitary confinement should be reduced, since its original reformatory purpose had long since deteriorated into one of pure deterrence. A juvenile reformatory should be established to take offenders up to the age of 23 for a period of between one and three years with the emphasis on individual treatment and special arrangements for after-care. For the 'habitual criminal' preventative detention was introduced to enable courts to impose an additional sentence of 5-10 years as a deterrent. More generally, the Committee emphasised the urgent need for aid and after-care to be available to prisoners on release and for the voluntary bodies concerned to have opportunities to establish contact with prisoners before their discharge.

On the publication of the report, Sir Edmund Du Cane, chairman of the Prison Commissioners resigned his post, something welcomed in the press as 'the inevitable end of a discredited system'.[75]

Historical Journal, Vol. 31, (3), (1988), pp. 591-608, and Hannum, E. Brown, 'The Debate on Penal Goals: Carnarvon, Gladstone and the harnessing of Nineteenth Century 'Truth', 1865-1895', *New England Journal on Prison Law,* Vol. 7, (1981), pp. 97-103.

[72] 'Report from the departmental committee on prisons', *Parliamentary Papers*, Vol. lvi, 1895 or the Gladstone Committee.

[73] Ibid, Gladstone Committee, para 25.

[74] In 1900, as part of the Gladstone reforms, prisons were instructed to allow conversation between prisoners at exercise but the reactions of prison governors was almost entirely unfavourable. 'Conversation', the *Prison Commissioners' Annual Report* in 1900 stated, 'at exercise is not sought after; prisoners prefer to exercise in the usual way.'

[75] *Daily Chronicle*, 15 April 1895.

The report is frequently used to mark a shift in penal policy away from a rigidly deterrent approach and a condemnation of 'useless' labour to one grounded in a more 'reformative' system of imprisonment and this has given it the appearance of a prospectus for radical change. [76] However, its recommendations were implemented slowly and piecemeal. [77] There were significant weaknesses in the report arising largely from its failure to address the issue of prison administration as well as conditions for prisoners and its indecisiveness, a reflection of the weakness and amateurish nature of the committee from the outset.[78] That the publication of the report came less than two months before the resignation of Rosebery's Liberal government and the Liberal defeat in a general election in 1895 meant that its impact was further limited. The result was that some of its recommendations were watered down while others were simply ignored. The momentum for change in penal policy dissipated and it was not until 1898 that legislation was passed. [79]

Few of the Gladstone recommendations required legislation since powers had already been delegated to the Home Secretary to frame and revise prison rules and this may explain why the Prisons Act 1898 had such a lengthy development. In addition, there was little parliamentary pressure for a legislative review of penal policy and although draft bills were written in 1896 and 1897, they were not seen as a priority The Prison Act 1898 dealt mainly with changes in the nature of prison labour, by providing for association in labour if this was practicable, for the phasing out of the crank and treadwheel and for the use of oakum picking only as a last resort. It led to a dilution of the separate system, the abolition of hard labour and established the idea that prison labour should be productive, not least for the prisoners, who should be able to earn their livelihood on release. The Act also made provision for the courts to classify into one of three divisions those sentenced to imprisonment. This novel development reflected the contemporary view that it was more appropriate that the sentencing court rather than the executive should decide the

---

[76] See, for example, Loucks, Nancy and Haines, Kevin, 'Crises in British Prisons: A Critical Review Essay', *International Criminal Justice Review*, Vol. 3, (1993), pp. 77-93, that stated at pp. 77-78 'The Gladstone Committee (1895) laid the framework for the aims of the modern prison service in England and Wales.'
[77] For contemporary criticism see, Morrison, W. D., 'The Progress of Prison Reform', *Law Magazine and Review*, Vol. 32, (1902-1903), pp. 32-33.
[78] Ibid, McConville, Sean, *English Local Prisons, 1860-1900: Next only to Death*, pp. 615-696, discusses the Gladstone report and its aftermath.
[79] Ibid, McConville, Sean, *English Local Prisons, 1860-1900*, pp. 697-757, examines the tortuous passage of legislation.

conditions under which an offender should serve his sentence. In practice, courts seldom used any but the third classification, the most severe but the provision was not repealed until 1948. The legislation made important structural changes by amalgamating the Prison Commissioners and the Directors of Convict Prisons and in establishing the principle of lay involvement in monitoring prisons through Boards of Visitors.

The Victorian prison:

...was a man's world; made for men, by men. Women in prison were seen as somehow anomalous: not foreseen and not legislated for. They were provided with separate quarters and female staff for reasons of modesty and good order - but not otherwise dealt with all that differently. [80]

The most common offences committed by women were linked to prostitution and were, essentially, 'victimless' crimes such as soliciting, drunkenness, drunk and disorderly and vagrancy that tended to be dealt with by the courts either by fines or short periods of imprisonment. Until Holloway became a female-only prison in 1903, women were held in separate sections of mixed prisons. However, the unlawful activities of the predominantly middle-class Suffragettes posed a major problem for the prison authorities especially when they began going on hunger strikes. What distinguished the suffragette hunger strike campaign was the calculated use of the press, especially after the government began to force-feed suffragettes. In reporting stories of determined women prisoners, newspapers presented a challenge to more docile images of women.[81]

On 24 June 1909, an artist Marion Wallace Dunlop was arrested and imprisoned after painting an extract of the 1689 Bill of Rights on the wall of the House of Commons. Like other suffragette prisoners, she refused political status in prison and, on 5 July, began a hunger strike in protest. After ninety-one hours of fasting, she was released. Other suffragettes followed her example and were also released. From September 1909, Herbert Gladstone, Home Secretary (1905-1910), introduced forcible feeding. [82] Historians are divided over the

---

[80] Ibid, Priestley, Philip, *Victorian Prison Lives*, pp. 69-70.

[81] Purvis, June, 'The prison experiences of the Suffragettes', *Women's History Review*, Vol. 4, (1), (1995), pp. 103-133.

[82] This was maintained Reginald McKenna (Home Secretary, 23 October 1911-25 May 1915). Winston Churchill was Home Secretary during the truce in 1910-1911 and it is interesting to speculate what he would have done about force-feeding, as he was a supporter of women's suffrage. On the attitude of the Home Office from 1906 to 1914 see, Crawford, Elizabeth,

importance of force-feeding. Some justify it simply on the grounds that it saved the lives of hunger strikers. On the other hand, suffragette propaganda portrayed it as oral rape and many feminist historians have agreed with this perspective. Over a thousand women endured, what Jane Marcus called 'the public violation of their bodies' and a contemporary doctor said that 'using the term 'medical treatment' as a cloak, commits an act which would be assault if done by an ordinary doctor'. [83] There was also a class dimension. Influential women like Lady Constance Lytton [84] were released, while working-class women were treated brutally. [85] As the number of suffragette prisoners' rose and suffragette propaganda continued to make capital out of forcible feeding, the government changed its strategy. In April 1913, the Prisoners' Temporary Discharge on Ill-Health Act was passed. This allowed the temporary discharge of prisoners on hunger strike combined with their re-arrest later once they had recovered and was

---

'Police, Prisons and Prisoners: the view from the Home Office', *Women's History Review*, Vol. 14, (3 & 4), (2005), pp. 487-505.

[83] *British Medical Journal*, 5 October 1915, p. 908.

[84] Constance Lytton, the daughter of the Earl of Lytton who had once served as Viceroy of India, joined the Suffragettes in 1909 and was arrested on several occasions for militant actions. However, on each occasion, she was released without being force-fed. Believing that she was getting special treatment because of his upper class background, she decided to test her theory. In 1911, she dressed as a working-class woman and was arrested in a protest outside Liverpool's Walton Gaol under the name 'Jane Wharton'. She underwent a cursory medical inspection and was passed fit. She was forcibly fed and became so ill she suffered a stroke that partially paralysed her. After her release, her story generated a great deal of publicity for the movement. See, Mulvey-Roberts, Marie, 'Militancy, masochism or martyrdom? The public and private prisons of Constance Lytton' in Purvis, June, and Holton, Sandra Stanley, (eds.), *Votes for Women*, (Routledge), 2000, pp. 159-180.

[85] Geddes, J. F., 'Culpable Complicity: the medical profession and the forcible feeding of suffragettes, 1909-1914', *Women's History Review*, Vol. 17, (1), (2008), pp. 79-94. The forcible feeding of suffragettes in prisons in Edwardian Britain was an abuse that had serious physical and psychological consequences for those fed, and one in which the medical profession was complicit, by failing as a body to condemn the practice as both medically unnecessary and dangerous. Sir Victor Horsley, an eminent but controversial figure, led opposition to forcible feeding, but, with relatively few male colleagues backing him, it continued unchecked. Undeterred, Horsley worked tirelessly to make his profession aware of the realities of the practice and recognise that, as the militant campaign had escalated, the Home Office had used the doctors administering it to punish, rather than treat, the hunger strikers.

soon described as the 'Cat and Mouse Act'.

Although there were several attempts before 1914 to define and improve the nature of convict life and changes in the ways that young offenders were treated, much of the structures of imprisonment followed the foundations laid down by Carnarvon and Du Cane and remained largely undisturbed by reformers, administrators and politicians for much of the following century. [86]

What happened to young offenders?

Juvenile crime was a concern before the beginning of the nineteenth century but a number of historians have argued that the late-eighteenth and early-nineteenth century was pivotal in the changes that occurred in the treatment of juvenile criminals. Some historians maintain that this represented an 'invention' of juvenile crime but there was not so much an 'invention' as a 'reconceptualisation' of the juvenile offender during the nineteenth century. [87] Farmers whose apples had been taken may have complained to the children's parents. The local constable might give them a severe telling off or a clip on the ear. Only the most difficult and persistent child criminals found themselves in court and when they did, they were punished like adults. Children were put in prisons, transported and hanged. In 1880, there were 6,500 children under 16 in adult prisons, of whom 900 were under 12. [88]

From the late 1810s, commentators were increasingly concerned by juvenile crime and this led to a convergence in policy by public and voluntary sectors. The private initiatives set up to deal with juvenile crimes, such as the Marine Society in 1756, the Philanthropic Society

---

[86] Ibid, McConville, Sean, *English Local Prisons, 1860-1900*, p. 549.

[87] Shore, Heather, *Artful dodgers: youth and crime in early-nineteenth-century London*, (Royal Historical Society), 1999, Duckworth, Jeannie, *Fagin's Children: Criminal Children in Victorian England*, (Hambledon), 2002, Horn, Pamela, *Young Offenders: Juvenile Delinquency 1700-2000*, (Amberley Press), 2010, and Abbott, Jane, 'The press and the public visibility of nineteenth-century criminal children', in ibid, Rowbotham, Judith, and Stevenson, Kim, (eds.), *Criminal conversations: Victorian crimes, social panic, and moral outrage*, pp. 23-39

[88] See, King, Peter and Noel, Joan, 'The origins of "the problem of juvenile delinquency": the growth of juvenile prosecutions in London in the late eighteenth and early-nineteenth centuries', *Criminal Justice History*, Vol. 14, (1993), pp. 17-41, King, Peter, 'The Rise of Juvenile Delinquency in England, 1780-1840: Changing Patterns of Perception and Persecution', *Past & Present*, Vol. 160, (1998), pp. 116-166, and Stack, John A., 'Children, urbanization and the chances of imprisonment in mid Victorian England', *Criminal Justice History*, Vol. 13, (1992), pp. 113-139.

in 1788, the Refuge for the Destitute in 1804, were not exclusively for juveniles but strongly involved with the rescue and reform of the young and the activities of individuals such as Mary Carpenter, Sydney Turner and Matthew Davenport Hill coincided with parliamentary penal policy. This fusion in thinking led individuals involved in the voluntary sector being involved in the public machinery of juvenile justice and providing evidence to parliamentary committees and commissions.

The publication of the *Report of the Committee for Investigating the Alarming Increases of Juvenile Crime in the Metropolis* in 1816 was of especial importance. Although many of its arguments having already been presented in the pamphlets of the Philanthropic Society, the report seems to have sparked a parliamentary debate about such crime. The Committee that produced it contained a number of Quaker social reformers who were important in the broader history of criminal justice. Thomas Fowell Buxton, an evangelical Whig politician, campaigned for an end to capital punishment in all cases but those of murder. Peter Bedford, the Spitalfields philanthropist was well-known for his work among the deprived silk workers of that area. Samuel Hoare, Quaker banker was Chairman of the Society for the Improvement of Prison Discipline and brother-in-law of Elizabeth Fry and William Crawford, from 1835 one of the first Inspector Generals of Prisons. Quakers put criminals, and particularly women and child criminals, at the heart of political debate promoting a more child-centred approach to juvenile criminals and their role in developing social and domestic policy was pivotal.

The focus for juvenile crime lay in London and the parliamentary debate was coloured by its understanding and perceptions of metropolitan delinquency. Contemporary reports commented on the swarms of ragged children infesting the metropolis and investigations by social and penal reformers were heavily influenced by a hard-core of juvenile offenders. People's awareness of juvenile crime was raised by the publication of *Oliver Twist* in 1837. Dickens shocked people with his description of the Artful Dodger and Fagin's trained gang of metropolitan pickpockets. His story may have been fiction but it was successful in stimulating thinking about child crime and how to deal with it. Discussion of juvenile offenders occurred in other parts of the country but it was rarely as influential as the metropolitan perspective. The factory was increasingly viewed as a site of disorder and delinquency and the work of the Reverend John

Clay with prisoners in Preston in the late 1830s and 1840s was widely regarded. [89]

By the 1860s, two alternative views of the nature of juvenile offenders had evolved. The more influential, apparent in the work on delinquents by both Henry Mayhew and John Binny, saw the juvenile criminal as exclusively male. [90] The female role was peripheral and then largely as a source of sexual corruption. Like the Dodger, the delinquent often had the manner of a small adult, a boy-man, a combination of innocence and experience, of immaturity and mature masculinity that seems to have both disturbed and attracted reformers and investigators. However, there was also an understanding that children were not just miniature adults but developing people who were influenced by their environment. Reformers such as Mary Carpenter, developing the child-centred attitudes of the Friends, began to ask important questions. [91] How and when does a child know what is right and wrong? What should be done about the fact that criminals and deprived backgrounds produced more child criminals? [92] Children were likely to become criminals by sending them to an adult prison. [93] What alternatives should there be?

The result was the gradual development of the juvenile justice system. Though early modern policy makers and welfare practitioners had not been unaware of the specific needs of children, separate institutions for youngsters, both at the level of trial and punishment, were an innovation of the nineteenth century. In 1838, a positive, but short-lived, step was taken of separating juvenile offenders when the former military prison on the Isle of Wight at Parkhurst was opened with a reformatory regime for convicts under eighteen prior to their transportation. The Juvenile Offenders Act of 1847 allowed children under the age of fourteen to be tried summarily before two magistrates, thus making the process of trial for children quicker and

---

[89] Clay, John, 'Annual Report of the Rev. John Clay, Chaplain to the Preston House of Correction, Presented to the Visiting Justices at the October Sessions, 1838', *Journal of the Statistical Society of London*, Vol. 1, (1839), pp. 84-113. See also, DeLacy, Margaret, *Prison reform in Lancashire, 1700-1850: a study in local administration*, (Manchester University Press), 1986, pp. 205-224, for discussion of Clay and the separate system.

[90] Ibid, Mayhew, Henry, and Binny, John, *The criminal prisons of London, and scenes of prison life*, pp. 376-397.

[91] Carpenter, Mary, *Juvenile delinquents: their condition and treatment*, (W. & F. G. Cash), 1856, pp. 15-49. She also included a valuable discussion of girls, pp. 81-117.

[92] Ibid, pp. 119-160.

[93] Ibid, pp. 161-205.

removing it from the public glare of the higher courts and the age limit was raised to sixteen in 1850. Acts in 1855, 1879 and 1899 extended summary provision for the young with the result that by 1899 all offences committed by children and young people could be dealt with summarily by magistrates, with the exception of murder charges. In 1853, a Select Committee on Criminal and Destitute Children recommended a degree of state assistance for reformatory schools. The result, between 1854 and 1857, was a series of Reformatory and Industrial School Acts that replaced prison with specific juvenile institutions. The Youthful Offenders Act 1854 provided for persons less than sixteen years to be sent to such schools for from two to five years following two weeks in a prison (perhaps as a shock). These reform schools were very tough but the clear intention was to separate the child from his or her bad home environment. In 1857, legislation sanctioned the sending to industrial schools of children between the ages of seven and fourteen who had been convicted of vagrancy. The perceived decline in juvenile crime after 1860 was often attributed to the reformatories and industrial schools by reformers. [94]

By the late-nineteenth century the new juvenile justice system was firmly in place. Various acts since 1850 had extended summary powers, and there were increasing calls for a separate juvenile court in which to process young delinquents. The first children's court was set up in Birmingham in April 1905, strongly influenced by the model of the Illinois Juvenile Court that had been established in America in 1899. Transportation had ended by 1867, though emigration of delinquent children continued. A number of Reformatory and Industrial Schools developed from the acts of the 1850s, a process completed by the Education Act of 1876, which put into place industrial day schools and truant schools. In 1902, an experimental school to try to reform repeating offenders aged 15-21 was started at Borstal in Kent. It was run like a public school, with lots of sport and residential houses. The plan for more such schools, called Borstals, was extended in 1908 and for a time they were very successful.

By the 1860s, the state was prepared to intervene directly in the lives of children. The Factory Acts removed children from some workplaces and introduced protections in others; the Education Act

---

[94] It is unlikely that this was the only cause of decline and taking the country as a whole there was no common sentencing policy with regard to juveniles. The majority of convicted juveniles continued to be sent to ordinary gaols. See, Shore, Heather, 'Punishment, Reformation, or Welfare: Responses to 'The Problem' of Juvenile Crime in Victorian and Edwardian Britain', in Johnston, Helen, (ed.), *Punishment and control in historical perspective*, (Palgrave), 2008, pp. 158-176.

1870 made elementary schooling compulsory. The Children's Charter of 1889, driven through Parliament by the NSPCC criminalised cruelty to children and enabled the state to intervene in family life. The 1908 Children's Act was an important move in the separate treatment of children. It stopped children under 14 being sent to prisons and created special Juvenile Courts to hear cases. After 1908, a child under seven was not held liable for his actions. This was raised to eight in 1933 and ten in 1963. In 1932, reformatory schools were replaced by Approved Schools for offenders under 15. A total of 86 boys' schools and 35 girls' schools were set up. As Radzinowitz and Hood pointed out, by the eve of the First World War, 'there was a network of 208 schools: 43 reformatories, 132 industrial schools, 21 day industrial schools and 12 truant schools'. [95]

The juvenile offender was not an invention of the nineteenth century. However, it is clear that in this period a reconceptualisation of youth crime and various developments in social policy, as well as the activities of certain individuals, resulted in a new language of youthful delinquency. By the late-nineteenth century, through a combination of state legislation and institutional projects, voluntary initiatives, and cultural concepts culled from a particular response to, and understanding of, such crime, the juvenile offender had become a central figure, fully entrenched in the British justice system.

---

[95] Radzinowicz, Leon, and Hood, Roger, *The Emergence of Penal Policy in Victorian and Edwardian England*, (Oxford University Press), 1990, pp. 618-620.

15 Policing

The medieval system of policing was based on community action where individuals were expected to aid neighbours and protect their communities from crime.[1] This pledge system was based around tithings, groups of ten families entrusted with policing minor problems such as disturbances, fire, wild animals and other threats.[2] The leader was called a tithingman and he was expected to raise the hue and cry to assemble his followers when the community was threatened. Ten tithings were grouped into a hundred and the hundredman, who later became the parish constable, dealt with more serious breaches of the law. At county level, the shire reeve, a royal official whose role evolved into that of sheriff, was responsible for public order in his area and soon began to pursue and apprehend criminals as part of his duties.[3] In the thirteenth century, a watch system was developed to protect property in larger towns and cities. Watchmen patrolled at night and helped protect against robberies, disturbances and fire reporting to the area constable.

In 1326, Justices of the Peace (JPs) were first appointed to assist the sheriff in controlling the county. Their judicial role developed later in addition to their primary role as peacekeepers.[4] Constables were appointed by Quarter Sessions and became the operational assistant to the justices.[5] Appointed for between three and ten years,

---

[1] See Jewell, Helen M., *English Local Administration in the Middle Ages*, (David and Charles), 1972, for context.

[2] Morris, W. A., *The Frankpledge System*, (Longman, Green and Co.), 1910, pp. 27-53.

[3] Morris, W. A., *The Medieval English Sheriff to 1300*, (Manchester University Press), 1927, and Gorski, Richard, *The Fourteenth-century Sheriff: English local administration in the late Middle Ages*, (Boydell), 2003.

[4] Burn, Richard, *The Justice of the Peace and Parish Officer*, 3rd edition, (Printed by Henry Lintot for A. Miller), 1756, provides detailed coverage of roles and operation. See also, Osborne, B., *Justices of the Peace 1381-1848: A History of the Justices of the Peace for the Counties of England*, (Sedgill Press), 1960, Milton, Frank, *The English Magistracy*, (Oxford University Press), 1967, McConville, S., 'Frustrated Executives: A Lost Opportunity for the English Magistracy', *Victorian Studies*, Vol. 33, (4), (1990), pp. 581-602, and Philips, David, 'A 'Weak' State?: The English State, the Magistracy and the Reform of Policing in the 1830s', *English Historical Review*, Vol. 119, (2004), pp. 873-891.

[5] Simpson, H. B., 'The Office of Constable', *English Historical Review*, Vol. 10, (1895), pp. 625-641 is, despite its age, still worth reading. See also, Kent, Joan, 'The English Village Constable, 1580-1642: The Nature and Dilemmas of the Office', *Journal of British Studies*, Vol. 20, (2), (1981), pp.

the constable faced a heavy fine if he refused to serve. The person appointed constable could pay someone to do the job for him and this became widespread in the sixteenth century and meant that, in some places, almost permanent 'professionals' were at work. The constable had to report to JPs on the state of roads and on public houses. He relied on his petty constables, operating in town and village, for his information. The constables had to use their own initiative and make regular presentments or reports to the court. They had no uniform or weapon. In towns, but also in some villages, watchmen patrolled the streets at night. In London, there were also two provost-marshals whose job including arresting vagrants and maintaining order on the highways round the capital. [6]

Maintaining law and order depends on some form of policing. Despite the institutional changes and innovations in procedure which made government in the localities more uniform, more professional and more accountable, by the early-eighteenth century, this system of policing was increasingly unable to cope with the growing population and the rising tide of crime. The only national police force that existed was the force of revenue or customs officer that specialised in catching smugglers. The old constable system was cheap to run and the government continued with it. However, it could not cope with the size of the new industrial towns like Birmingham, Manchester and Sheffield. What existed was a medieval system of policing in a modern world. Watchmen were poorly paid. Patrick Colquhoun, a critic of the system, argued 'the old and infirm were thus employed to keep them out of the workhouse'.

The City of London employed 1,000 night watchmen so it was an important source of employment. [7] Some watchmen were in league with criminals. They were rarely efficient in dealing with criminals and usually gave up the chase when a criminal went into a neighbouring parish. Some large towns employed thief-takers such as Jonathan Wild. They pocketed reward money after the successful prosecution of criminals. Large-scale disturbances or riots were deal with either by the professional army or by the local militia or yeomanry. [8] They were used across England to keep order in the

---

26-49, Storch, Robert D., 'The Old English Constabulary', *History Today*, Vol. 49, (11), (1999), pp. 43-49.

[6] Boynton, Lindsay, 'The Tudor Provost-Marshal', *English Historical Review*, Vol. 77, (1962), pp. 437-455.

[7] Reynolds, E. A., *Before the Bobbies: The Night Watch and Police Reform in Metropolitan London, 1720-1830*, (Stanford University Press), 1998.

[8] Dodsworth, F. M., 'The Idea of Police in Eighteenth-Century England: Discipline, Reformation, Superintendence, c. 1780-1800', *Journal of the History of Ideas*, Vol. 69, (2008), pp. 583-604, and '"Civic" police and the

1790s and 1810s. Local militias were used for local problems but they were often inexperienced and drawn largely from the middle-classes. The Peterloo Massacre of August 1819 during which Yeomanry attacked an unarmed and peaceful crowd resulting in fatalities shows just how inexperienced they could be. [9]

The traditional view of the system of policing before 1829 was that it was inefficient and corrupt and that the 'real' history of policing for London and England begins with the setting up of the Metropolitan Police in 1829. This was certainly the view of contemporary critics such as Patrick Colquhoun but Quarter Session and other local records suggest that to view policing simply from Westminster slanted the issue of law enforcement in the eighteenth and early-nineteenth century unjustifiably in favour of reformers. [10] Although there was ineffective policing before 1829, the same inefficiency was also evident after 1829. Magistrates and local administration in the eighteenth century was not hopelessly ineffective and local leaders in parochial and county administration were prepared to adopt effective methods of policing and this proved pivotal to the implementation of national policies. [11] There was:

---

condition of liberty: the rationality of governance in eighteenth-century England', *Social History*, Vol. 29, (2004), pp. 199-216.

[9] Paley, Ruth, '"An imperfect, inadequate and wretched system"?: policing London before Peel', *Criminal Justice History*, Vol. 10, (1989), pp. 95-130. See also, ibid, Dodsworth, F. M., 'The Idea of Police in Eighteenth-Century England: Discipline, Reformation, Superintendence, c. 1780-1800'.

[10] For 'traditional' teleological accounts of policing history, see Reith, Charles, *A Short History of the British Police*, (Oxford University Press), 1948, Ascoli, David, *The Queen's Peace: the Origins and Development of the Metropolitan Police 1829-1979*, (Hamish Hamilton), 1979, and Critchley, T. A., *A History of Police in England and Wales*, (Constable), 1978.

[11] See, for example, Kent, Joan R., 'The centre and the localities: state formation and parish government in England, circa 1640–1740', *Historical Journal*, Vol. 38, (1995), pp. 363-404, considers state formation at the base of the governmental system and examines the extent of, and reasons for, support of national policies at the parochial level. See also, Innes, Joanna, *Inferior Politics: Social Problems and Social Policies in Eighteenth-Century Britain*, (Oxford University Press), 2010, and Davies, Stephen, 'The Private Provision of Police during the Eighteenth and Nineteenth Centuries', in Beito, David T., Gordon, Peter, and Tabarrok, Alexander, (eds.), *The Voluntary City: Choice, Community and Civil Society*, (University of Michigan Press), 2002, pp. 151-181.

...a significant degree of continuity between the old and the new—the 'bobbies' of Scotland Yard carried on what the 'Charlies' on the night watch had begun.[12]

The problem of policing was at its most severe in London.[13] The result was the development of professional policing at local level from the initial use of paid watchmen in key West End parishes in 1735 through to the creation of the Metropolitan Police in 1829. By 1823, twenty-three parochial night watch acts has been passed largely before 1790. Even if policing was neither uniform nor centralised over the entire metropolitan area, London was far more extensively policed in 1828 than was the case a century earlier. In 1730, the government decided to appoint a chief magistrate for London to hold court at Bow Street.[14] The first was Sir Thomas de Veil. He was followed by two half-brothers, Henry and John Fielding. Henry Fielding had little faith in petty constables or watchmen and he appointed six men to act as full-time 'runners' or thief-takers.[15] They were paid a guinea a week plus a share of the reward for each successful prosecution. Later the blind Sir John Fielding, who succeeded his brother, established the Bow Street Runners on a permanent basis and ran it from 1754 to until his death in 1780.[16] The Fieldings transformed the role of the Bow Street magistracy, and provided the model on which the other London Police Offices were based.[17]

---

[12] Ibid, Reynolds, E. A., *Before the Bobbies*, p. 5, see also, pp. 148-166.

[13] Beattie, J. M., *Policing and Punishment in London, 1660-1750: Urban Crime and the Limits of Terror*, (Oxford University Press), 2001.

[14] Beattie, J. M. 'Sir John Fielding and Public Justice: The Bow Street Magistrates' Court, 1754-1780', *Law and History Review*, Vol. 25, (1), (2007), pp. 61-100, and *The First English Detectives: The Bow Street Runners and the Policing of London, 1750-1840*, (Oxford University Press), 2012.

[15] On Henry Fielding see, Fielding, Henry, *An Enquiry into the Causes of the late Increase of Robbers*, (A. Miller), 1751, and Bertelsen, Lance, *Henry Fielding at Work: Magistrate, Businessman, Writer*, (Palgrave), 2000.

[16] It was said that Sir John could recognise 3,000 criminals by their voices and that they were unnerved by this talent. There is no modern study of Sir John Fielding but see, Leslie-Melville, R., *The Life and Work of Sir John Fielding*, (Lincoln Williams), 1905, for useful, if on occasions, anecdotal material.

[17] In 1805 some of the runners were issued with blue coats and trousers, black boots and hats, white gloves and scarlet waistcoats – hence the name 'Robin Redbreasts'. Each carried a pistol, cutlass and truncheon. See, Cox, David J., *A Certain Share of Low Cunning: A history of the Bow Street Runners, 1792-1839*, (Willan Publishing), 2010, and Beattie, J. M., 'Early

The Bow Street Police Office and its personnel have long been regarded by many historians as little more than a discrete and often inconsequential footnote to the history of policing, leading to a partial and incomplete understanding of their work. The term Bow Street 'Runner' has caused much subsequent confusion with its frequent misapplication by numerous historians and commentators to the other forces based at Bow Street. These forces included a Foot Patrole, established on a permanent basis in 1790 by Sir Sampson Wright during his tenure as chief magistrate (1780-1797), and operative throughout sixteen districts of central London during the hours of darkness. This force continued in various guises until the advent of the Metropolitan Police in 1829. A Horse Patrole was permanently established in 1805 by Sir Richard Ford (chief magistrate 1800-1806), and this force continued under the aegis of Bow Street Public Office until it was finally placed under jurisdiction of the Metropolitan police in 1836. The Horse Patrole was responsible for patrolling the various turnpike roads leading into the metropolis. Finally, in 1821 a Day Patrole was created; this force operated in the area of the metropolis between the jurisdiction of the Horse Patrole and the Foot Patrole. [18]

The Bow Street principal officers were regarded by the Fieldings as more than simply a metropolitan force and they were willing to send the officers throughout Great Britain in order to investigate and detect crimes. Cox argues that in several ways the utilisation of Principal Officers, who alone were originally known as the 'Bow Street Runners', in provincially instigated cases paved the way for important subsequent developments in policing, especially with regard to detective practices. The principal officers did operate, on an admittedly small scale, as a *de facto* national force. Fielding also began a system of publishing information about serious crimes committed in London with descriptions of wanted criminals and in 1772 called for the collection, collation and circulation of information on a national basis. Information was sent to Bow Street from local magistrates and constables and then disseminated throughout Britain

---

Detection: The Bow Street Runners', in Emsley. Clive, and Shpayer-Makov, Haia, (eds.), *Police Detectives in History, 1750–1950*, (Ashgate), 2006, pp. 15-32. See also, Hetherington, F. P., *Chronicles of Bow Street Police-Office: With an Account of the Magistrates, Runners, and Police*, (Chapman & Hall), 1888.

[18] Styles, John, 'Sir John Fielding and the Problems of Criminal Investigation in Eighteenth-Century England', *Transactions of the Royal Historical Society*, Vol. 33, (1983), pp. 127-149 Reynolds, Elaine A., 'Sir John Fielding, Sir Charles Whitworth, and the Westminster Night Watch Act, 1770-1775', *Criminal Justice History*, Vol. 16 (2002).

by means of the *Hue & Cry* and *Police Gazette*, the official publication of Bow Street, founded in 1786 and eventually metamorphosing into the *Police Gazette*. Bow Street showed that there was an alternative to both the parish constabulary system that was increasingly perceived as outmoded and inefficient and the creation of a large, centralised police force. The Thames River Police was set up in 1800 to police the river and its banks. [19]

Much recent research concerning the history of policing has shown that the previously accepted teleological and linear progression from an old inefficient parish and watch system to an efficient and effective 'modern police' was not as clear-cut as many police historians of the earlier twentieth century would have had us believe.

What was the significance of different models of policing?

The English were suspicious of any notion of a powerful police that they equated with the Catholic absolutism of France. [20] Louis XIV had established a Royal Police in 1667 under with explicit aim of strengthening royal authority in all fields of life. Public Prosecutors were the King's agents. By contrast, in England the landowning aristocracy had checked the growth of centralised royal power and the organisation of justice reflected the local power of the landowner as much as that of the monarch. This led to the development of decentralised model of policing in the eighteenth century where the administration of justice and the policing was under local control. For the people, law and crime were rooted in everyday life and community rather than in systems where police and judges represented more distant royal power.

England was unique in having the victim as the initiator of criminal prosecutions and this only began to decline well into the nineteenth century. It was the victim, not state officials, who initiated investigation and prosecution. In this traditional system of localised, highly personalised justice the main instrument was the court and the trial. Crime detection and policing methods were elementary and crude. Courts waited for matters to be brought before them. This was a system of personal power in which landowners put in a good

---

[19] See, Colquhoun, P., *Treatise on the Commerce and Police of the River Thames*, (J. Mawman), 1800, pp. 157-208, and Budworth, G., *The River Beat: The Story of London's River Police since 1798*, (Historical Publications), 1997.

[20] Lenman, Bruce, and Parker, Geoffrey, 'The State, The Community and Criminal Law in Early Modern Europe', in Gatrell, V. A. C., Lenman, Bruce, and Parker, Geoffrey, (eds.), *Crime and the Law: The Social History of Crime in Western Europe Since 1500,* (Europa), 1980, pp. 11-48.

word for their labourers, something that helped consolidate their personal standing and power in the community. This was not an abstract system of justice but one where justice was perceived in terms of personal relationships and where justice was tempered with mercy.

In the late-eighteenth century, however, this informal, personal system began to break down before the increasing incidence of urban unrest and property crime, especially in London. [21] For the urban middle-classes, rising crime was a symptom of the need for new forms of control of the lower orders. The notion of the 'rule of law', an impartial application of the law between different social groups gained ground and displaced the older rural notion of deferential justice. This reflected the changing nature of urban capitalist society in which the relationship between the offender and the victim became more impersonal as the face-to-face society irretrievably broke down. Crime was no longer seen as simply a wrong, a personal interaction between individuals or individuals and their superiors, it became a disruption, in which an offence against the criminal law was a disruption of the public peace and of the effective working of society. This led to a shift from the centrality of the court to an emphasis on police and crime detection to minimise disruption to the working of society.

Fears of a continental style, state-controlled national police force remained and greatly increased during the Napoleonic Wars, when reported excesses of the militaristic *gendarmerie* were prominently reported in British newspapers and journals. Although this traditional fear was anathema to the English gentry and their notion of liberty, the urban middle-classes had a very different view of the problem of security:

> The squirearchy might treasure the discretion which the old system allowed them, to choose among a variety of punishments ranging from an

---

[21] Philips, David, "A New Engine of Power and Authority': The Institutionalization of Law-Enforcement in England, 1780-1830', in ibid, Gatrell, V. A. C., Lenman, Bruce, and Parker, Geoffrey, (eds.), *Crime and the Law: The Social History of Crime in Western Europe Since 1500*, pp. 155-189; Hay, Douglas, and Snyder, Francis, (eds.), *Policing and Prosecution in Britain, 1750-1850*, (Clarendon Press), 1989; Emsley, Clive, *The English Police: A Political and Social History*, 2nd edition, (Longman), 1996, pp. 15-23; McMullan, J. L., 'The Arresting Eye: Discourse, Surveillance, and Disciplinary Administration in Early English Police Thinking', *Social and Legal Studies*, Vol. 7, (1998), pp. 97-128. Gattrell, V., 'Crime, authority and the policeman-state', in ibid, Thompson, F. M. L., (ed.), *The Cambridge Social History of Britain 1750-1950: Vol. 3 Social Agencies and Institutions*, pp. 243-310, provides a good overview.

informal reprimand to death; but the urban shopkeeper wanted something which would efficiently protect his commercial property.[22]

The ruling classes increasingly feared the anarchy of the city and a war of all against all, a fear that reached its peak in the 1790s when they viewed events in France. This fear reflected concerns with political disorder and lack of the correct habits of restraint and obedience and criminality that merged into one another in a general fear of disorder. This was later eloquently expressed in the Tory *Blackwood's Magazine* that warned:

> ...the restraints of character, relationship and vicinity are...lost in the crowd...Multitudes remove responsibility without weakening passion. [23]

Police reformers, such as John Fielding and Patrick Colquhoun and the commercial and propertied middle-classes increasingly advocated rigorous control and surveillance of the lower classes by a more systematically organised and coordinated police force. [24] Such proposals were vehemently opposed by the gentry and the emerging industrial working-classes that feared that the government would form a powerful, centralised police force to ride roughshod over their liberties. With the crucial support of Tory backbenchers, they resisted efforts to establish French-style police methods in England. The most important development was the Middlesex Justices Act of 1792 that appointed stipendiary or paid magistrates in charge of small police forces. But the predominantly local system of policing was still in place in the 1820s.

Sir Robert Peel was responsible for introducing two approaches of policing in Britain. When Secretary of State for Ireland between 1812 and 1818, he established the Peace Preservation Force in 1814 and later the Irish Constabulary Act of 1822 established police forces in county areas and created a more militarised and centralised form of policing. [25] This body was a paramilitary police force whose aim was less the detection and prevention of crime than the wider political

---

[22] Philips, D., "A New Engine of Power and Authority' The Institutionalisation of Law Enforcement in England 1750-1830', in ibid, Gatrell, V. A. C., Lenman, Bruce, and Parker, Geoffrey, (eds.), *Crime and the Law*, p. 126.

[23] 'Causes of the Increase in Crime', *Blackwood's Magazine*, Vol. 56 (July 1844), p. 8.

[24] See, for example, Colquhoun, P., *A Treatise on the Police of the Metropolis*, (H. Fry), 1796.

[25] Palmer, S. H., *Police and Protest in England and Ireland, 1780-1850*, (Cambridge University Press), 1988, pp. 193-276.

task of subduing the Catholic Irish peasantry. There was less resistance to stern measures against agrarian protest and violence in Ireland. Then Peel, as Home Secretary from 1822 to 1827 and 1828 to 1830, used arguments based on the efficiency of the Irish police and the threat to liberty from disorder and crime to achieve police reform in England. Peel pushed the Metropolitan Police Act through Parliament in 1829 creating a paid, uniformed, preventive police for London headed by commissioners without magisterial duties and under central direction. The example of uniformed, professional police subsequently spread throughout England over the following decades, but they remained under local control and the extent to which the new police differed at least initially from the existing watchmen and constables should not be exaggerated. [26] These developments provided two different models for policing: a centralised, military styled and armed force of Ireland kept away from the local community in barracks; and, a consciously non-military, unarmed, preventive English police supposedly working in partnership with and with the consent of the local community. [27] More often than not elements from both models were employed by colonial police forces and adapted to suit local circumstances. Where the security of the state was threatened, the Irish approach was deployed, while English methods were more pervasive and influenced day-to-day policing of all aspects of social life.

During the 1950s and 1960s, historians of English policing argued that the introduction of the 'new police' received widespread community support. The few individuals, who opposed its introduction, it was argued, were soon won over by the force's ability to prevent crime and maintain social order, so securing it 'the confidence and the lasting admiration of the British people'. [28] The

---

[26] Styles, John, 'The Emergence of the Police: Explaining Police Reform in Eighteenth- and Nineteenth-Century England', *British Journal of Criminology*, Vol. 27, (1987), pp. 15-22.

[27] Brogden, Michael, 'An Act to Colonise the Internal Lands of the Island: Empire and the Origins of the Professional Police', *International Journal of the Sociology of Law*, Vol. 15, (1987), pp. 179-208; Anderson, D. M., and Killingray, David, (eds.), *Policing and the Empire: Government, Authority, and Control, 1830-1940*, (Manchester University Press), 1991.

[28] Jones, David, 'The New Police, Crime and People in England and Wales, 1829-1888,' *Transactions of the Royal Historical Society*, Vol. 33, (1983), p. 153. For discussions of this debate see, ibid, Emsley, Clive, *Policing and its Context, 1750-1870*, pp. 4-7; Bailey, V., 'Introduction', in ibid, Bailey, V., (ed.), *Policing and Punishment in Nineteenth Century Britain*, pp. 12-14; Fyfe, N. R., 'The Police, Space and Society: The Geography of Policing', *Progress in Human Geography*, Vol. 15, (3), (1991), pp. 250-252;

smooth transition from a locally based 'inefficient' parish constable system to an efficient and professional body of law enforcers formed the basis of this 'consensus' view. During the 1970s, historians using conflict and social control theories challenged the consensus view of widespread public acceptance. Concentrating on working-class responses, they argued that the 'new police' were resisted as an instrument of repression developed by the propertied classes to destroy existing working-class culture and impose 'alien values and an increasingly alien law' on the urban poor'. [29] Conflict historians argued that a preventive police system was developed in response to changes in the social and economic structure of British society. Storch, its foremost proponent contended that, the formation 'of the new police was a symptom of both a profound social change and deep rupture in class relations'. [30] The working-classes, it was argued, questioned the legitimacy of the 'new police' and responded to their interference in a variety of ways ranging from subtle defiance to open and, on occasions, violent resistance.

More recently the level of support that the 'new police' received from the propertied classes has been questioned. Weinberger argues that opposition to the 'new police':

...was part of a 'rejectionist' front ranging from Tory gentry to working class radicals against an increasing number of government measures seeking to regulate and control more and more aspects of productive and social life'.[31]

Palmer also argues that conflict historians 'have tended to ignore or down play the resistance within the elite to the establishment of a powerful police' and have over-emphasised the threat from below. [32] While accepting that the introduction of the 'new police' involved a

---

ibid, Brogden, M., 'An Act to Colonise the Internal Lands of the Island: Empire and the Origins of the Professional Police', pp. 181-183.
[29] Ibid, Jones, David, 'The New Police, Crime and People in England and Wales, 1829-1888', p. 153.
[30] Storch, R., 'The Plague of the Blue Lotus: Police Reform and Popular Resistance in Northern England, 1840-57', *International Review of Social History*, Vol. 20, (1975), p. 62.
[31] Weinberger, B., 'The Police and the Public in Mid-nineteenth-century Warwickshire', in ibid, Bailey, V., (ed.), *Policing and Punishment in Nineteenth Century Britain*, p. 66.
[32] Ibid, Storch R., 'The Plague of the Blue Lotus: Police Reform and Popular Resistance in Northern England, 1840-57', p. 61; ibid, Palmer S. *Police and Protest in England and Ireland, 1780-1850*, p. 8.

clash of moral standards, he argues that it should not be exaggerated.[33] These more recent studies therefore suggest that opposition to the 'new police' was also, but not equally, a response of the English upper- and middle-classes.

The broad generalisations regarding public opposition or acceptance of the 'new police' have tended to obscure the subtleties in community responses. Opposition did exist, at times resulting from police enforcement of 'unpopular edicts' or attempts to 'prevent mass meetings,' although they were also used and supported by many people 'as a fact of life' in their preventive and social order capacities.[34] While these studies have concentrated predominantly on the public's negative responses to the introduction of the 'new police', Stephen Inwood has considered how the police, administratively and functionally, dealt with the public. Too great a reliance on social control theories, Inwood argues, has led to over-simplification of the complex inter-relationships between the 'new police' and the wider community. While the 'new police' sought 'to establish minimum standards of public order,' it was not in their own interests 'to provoke social conflict by aspiring to unattainable ideals'. [35] Inwood sees relations between the police and the public as based on a calculated pragmatism in which it was acknowledged that attempts to impose unpopular laws rigidly would ultimately meet with resistance resulting in 'damage to the rule of law'. [36] Police administrators and the constables were required to tread carefully between the demands and expectations of 'respectable' society and the practical need for good relations with the working-classes. [37] While there has been a re-examination of public responses to the 'new police' and police responses to the public, these studies maintain that the police were, amongst particular groups, for varying reasons and at certain times, unpopular. Weinberger argues that this unpopularity stemmed from public:

---

[33] Storch, R., 'Policeman as Domestic Missionary: Urban Discipline and Popular Culture in Northern England, 1850-1880', *Journal of Social History*, Vol. 9, (4), (1976), pp. 481-509.

[34] Ibid, Jones, David, 'The New Police, Crime and People in England and Wales, 1829-1888', p. 166; ibid, Emsley, Clive, *The English Police*, pp. 5-6.

[35] Inwood, S., 'Policing London's Morals: The Metropolitan Police and Popular Culture, 1829-1850', *London Journal*, Vol. 15, (2), (1990), p. 144.

[36] Ibid, p. 134.

[37] Ibid, p. 131

...suspicion of the police as an alien force outside the control of the community; resentment at police interference in attempting to regulate traditionally sanctioned behaviour; [and] objections to expense. [38]

Policing in the nineteenth century

Between 1812 and 1822, six House of Commons' Select Committees affirmed broad, if qualified, satisfaction with the civic jigsaw of parish-based watch systems. However, resistance to the notion of a police force lessened in the 1810s and early 1820s largely because of growing moral panic among the ruling class about working-class insurrection. In addition, while rising crime and disorder were still attributed by the urban middle-classes to the moral decay of the masses, there was an increasing willingness to critique the old criminal justice system as inefficient both in controlling crime control and providing public order and regulation.

Peel certainly argued in Parliament when introducing his Metropolitan Police Bill in 1828 that it would be more efficient than the existing uneven systems. However, he was not focussed simply on the safety of the streets or the protection of property and the main task of the new police was not crime detection. Peel's reforms directly addressed the more general fear of the 'dangerous classes' and he saw crime as part of a more fundamental issue of public order. What was needed was moral discipline within the working-classes and this was going to be achieved by 'crime prevention'. The police targeted alehouses and the streets where legislation such as the 1824 Vagrancy Act enabled constables to arrest individuals not for crime committed but for 'loitering with intent', putting the burden of proof on the defendant rather than the police. The police were concerned not simply with those who committed crimes but with the poor as a whole who were seen as a 'criminal class'.

In starting from this broader conception of policing as general social control of the poor rather than simply crime control or even control of public disturbances, Peel was echoing an older tradition that had always seen policing in a wider context than crime control. Seeing the police as an essentially military force to secure the country against rebellion, rather than simply control crime and as a means of gathering intelligence was well established in Continental Europe. So those who saw the introduction of the police in the context of European developments had a point since Peel's view of the police owed something to the Continental tradition. Peel recognised that establishing the Metropolitan Police as a military force similar to his

---

[38] Ibid, Weinberger, B., 'The Police and the Public in Mid-nineteenth-century Warwickshire', p. 65.

reforms in Ireland would not be acceptable in England. He counted on the fears by the ruling class about revolution and of the middle-classes on the immorality of the working-classes to enable legislation to be successfully passed that combined the policing tasks of crime prevention and maintaining public order with moral regulation and instilling disciplined work and moral habits.

How was the Metropolitan Police developed?

In 1828, a new Select Committee was appointed and, largely because it was composed of individuals sympathetic to his ideas, Peel secured a report broadly sympathetic to his aims. The Committee confirmed Peel's earlier assessment of the system as intrinsically defective by virtue of its fragmented, non-uniform, and uncoordinated nature, something which would always defeat the best initiatives and efforts of individual parish forces. The proposed solution was predicable: a system of centrally directed and regulated police for the metropolis. The establishment of Peel's Metropolitan Police in 1829 embodied a conception of policing at odds with the discretionary and parochial procedures of eighteenth century law enforcement. However, he argued that a uniform system for the entire metropolis would mean that provision was not as dependent on the wealth of a parish. Full-time, professional, hierarchically organised, they were intended to be the impersonal agents of central policy. [39] The 1829 Metropolitan Police Act applied only to London and the jurisdiction of the legislation was limited to the Metropolitan London area, excluding the City of London and provinces. [40] This was an astute political decision

---

[39] Most critical studies of policing stop around 1870-1880: Miller, W. R., *Cops and Bobbies: Police Authority in New York and London 1830-1870*, (Ohio State University Press), 1977, ibid, Emsley, Clive, *Policing and its Context 1750-1870*, Taylor, David, *The new police: crime, conflict, and control in 19th-century England,* (Manchester University Press), 1997, and Steedman, C., *Policing the Victorian Community: The Formation of English Provincial Police Forces 1856-1880*, (Routledge), 1984. Later themes can be teased out of ibid, Critchley, T. A., *A History of Police in England and Wales 900-1966*, Emsley, C., *The English Police*, (Longman), 2nd edition, 1996, Emsley, Clive, *The Great British Bobby: A history of British policing from the 18th century to the present*, (Quercus), 2009, and ibid, Ascoli, D., *The Queen's Peace: The Metropolitan Police 1829-1979.*

[40] Mason, Gary, *The official history of the Metropolitan Police: 175 years of policing London*, (Carlton), 2004, Shpayer-Makov, Haia, *The making of a policeman: a social history of a labour force in metropolitan London, 1829-1914*, (Ashgate), 2001, Petrow, Stefan, *Policing morals: the Metropolitan Police and the Home Office, 1870-1914*, (Oxford University Press), 1994, and Smith, P. T., *Policing Victorian London: political*

on Peel's part since the City was fiercely independent and had resisted other attempts to unify London's police provision. Even today, the City of London had its own independent force, the result of a compromise in 1839. All London's police were the responsibility of one authority, under the direction of the Home Secretary, with headquarters at Scotland Yard. 1,000 men were recruited to supplement the existing 400 police. Being a policeman became a full-time occupation with weekly pay of 16/- and a uniform. Recruits were carefully selected and trained by the Commissioners. Funds came from a new police rate levied on parishes by overseers of the poor and a receiver was appointed to take charge of financial matters. John Wray was appointed to the post and served until 1860.

Parliament authorised the formation of the Metropolitan Police in July 1829 but the first constables did not take to the streets until September 1830. 'Bobbies' or 'Peelers' were not immediately popular.[41] Some parishes, especially the wealthier ones, objected to losing control over the ways they were policed complaining, not without justification, that they were required to pay for the police but had no say in their management or operation. Most citizens viewed constables as an infringement on English social and political life and people often jeered the police. There were suspicions that Lieutenant-Colonel Rowan, a veteran of Wellington's army, sought to establish a military force. However, both Peel and the Commissioners made deliberate attempts to ensure that the police did not take on the appearance of the military. Blue was deliberately chosen as the colour for uniforms to differentiate it from the red worn by the British army. Until 1864, top hats were worn by officers to emphasise their civilian character and beat officers were armed only with a truncheon. The preventive tactics of the early Metropolitan police were successful and crime and disorder declined. Their pitched battles with the Chartists in Birmingham and London in 1839 and 1848 proved the ability of the police to deal with major disorders and street riots. By 1851, attitudes to the police, at least in parts of London appear to have mellowed:

---

policing, public order, and the London Metropolitan Police, (Greenwood Press), 1985.

[41] Campion, David A., '"Policing the Peelers": Parliament, the public and the Metropolitan Police, 1829-33', in Cragoe, Matthew, and Taylor, Antony, (eds.), *London politics, 1760-1914*, (Palgrave), 2005, pp. 38-56.

The police are beginning to take that in the affections of the people that the soldiers and sailors used to occupy. In these happier days of peace, the blue coats, the defenders of order, are becoming the national favourites. [42]

The Metropolitan Police Act established the principles that shaped modern English policing. The primary means of policing was conspicuous patrolling by uniformed police officers. Police were to be patient, impersonal, and professional. Command and control were to be maintained through a centralised, pseudo-military organisational structure. The first Commissioners, Lieutenant-Colonel Sir Charles Rowan (1829-1850) and Richard Mayne (1829-1868), a lawyer, insisted that the prevention of crime was the primary aim of the police force. [43] During the 1830s, the Metropolitan Police absorbed several existing forces: the Bow Street Horse Patrol in 1836 and the Marine Police and the Bow Street Runners two years later. Finally, the authority of the English constable derived from three official sources: the Crown, the law and the consent and co-operation of the citizenry.

It has been suggested that as London's crime-rate fell, that of nearby areas increased. The number of offences did seem to increase in areas of London where the police were not allowed to go. For example, Wandsworth became known as 'black' Wandsworth because of the number of criminals who lived there. As Chadwick pointed out in 1853:

...criminals migrate from town to town, and from the towns where they harbour, and where there are distinct houses maintained for their accommodation, they issue forth and commit depredations upon the surrounding rural districts; the metropolis being the chief centre from which they migrate. [44]

How and why did the police force become a national institution?

Suspicions that the Metropolitan Police was a covert military force persisted across the political and social spectrum and the question of rising policing costs irritated parish authorities. Widespread complaints of inferior services delivered for higher charges were eventually met in 1833 by central government agreeing to fund a quarter of policing costs. The continuing political sensitivity of the new

---

[42] 'The Police and the People', *Punch*, Vol. 21, (1851), p. 173.
[43] The term 'commissioner' was given legislative legitimacy in the Metropolitan Police Act 1839. Before that, Rowan and Mayne were only Justices of the Peace.
[44] Second Report from the Select Committee on the Police with the Minutes and Appendix, *Parliamentary Papers*, Vol. 36, 1853, Appendix 5, pp. 170-171.

police led to persistent parliamentary scrutiny. Of particular importance was a Select Committee in 1834, consisting of Peel and many of the 1828 Select Committee, which concluded after looking at statistical evidence that the Metropolitan Police was achieving its objectives and that its:

...influence in repressing crime, and the security it has given to person and property [makes it] one of the most valuable modern institutions. [45]

Parliament now turned its attention to policing beyond the metropolis. [46] The Metropolitan Police acted as the model for the rest of England and Wales but the expansion of police forces to boroughs and to rural areas was gradual. Just as within London, provincial policing raised sensitive issues of local social influence and political power and the structural problems were the same. As a result of extensive local autonomy, there was an enormous variety of structures and degrees of sophistication in rural and urban policing, united principally by their common use of part-time constables and watchmen. The limitations of these diverse systems was highlighted by the agitation against the new Poor Law and the emergence of Chartism and soon the issue was not whether a national reformed police system should be adopted but what form that system should take.

As the idea of the new police spread to the provinces, they were often given very wide functions, understandable in terms of very general notions of regulation and inspection. [47] The Acts of 1839 and 1842 enabled the extension of police role and functions in the counties. This included the use of the police in the collection of rates, road surveying, weights and measures inspection and dealing with vagrants under Poor Law legislation. Carolyn Steedman commented that by:

...the 1860s and early 1870s witnessed something like an inspection fever...[with suggestions that] policemen be appointed as inspectors of taxes, of unemployed children not covered by the Factory Acts, of midwives and truants under the educational reforms of the 1870s. Carried away by the vision of a thoroughly policed and inspected society, some, including county chief

---

[45] Report of Select Committee on Police of the Metropolis, *Parliamentary Papers*, Vol. 16, 1834, p. 21.
[46] Philips, David, and Storch, Robert D., *Policing Provincial England 1829-1856: The Politics of Reform*, (Leicester University Press), 1999.
[47] One of the most effective local studies of policy is Taylor, David, *Policing the Victorian Town: The Development of the Police in Middlesbrough, c.1840-1914*, (Palgrave), 2002.

constables, suggested that the homes of the poor should be inspected by the police for cleanliness and against overcrowding. [48]

Growth in urban manufacturing centres had rendered local government structures generally inadequate. The 1835 Municipal Corporations Act helped older boroughs to sort out their administrative structures and allowed new towns to become incorporated. Towns that were incorporated were obliged to set up a Watch Committee responsible for appointing sufficient paid constables to keep the peace and prevent crime but few of them seemed eager to implement the law. Although, this was mandatory under the legislation, there was a complete lack of any regulations for government policing under the Act, a reflection of an absence of sufficient political support for further erosion of corporate autonomy. As a result, by 1837, only 93 of 171 boroughs had organised a police force; three years later, 108 of 171 boroughs had organised a police force but by 1848, 22 boroughs still had no police force. Municipal forces were about half the size of London, proportionate to population and remained grossly inadequate until after 1856.

Rural policing was generally regarded as ineffective and parish constables, uneducated, ignorant of their duties, lazy and corrupt. Rural disturbances in the early 1830s underscored the limitations of rural policing. The Swing Riots in rural southern England, combined with those in urban areas centring on the Reform Bill crisis at the beginning of the 1830s, led the Whig government to prepare a bill setting up a national police system but declining disorder and more pressing legislative priorities killed off this initiative. [49] However, these events, along with rising rates of local vagrancy, coupled with falling levels of social deference, encouraged local reform initiatives. Two approaches were available: private subscription forces, usually established by the local landed interests and action under the Lighting and Watching Act 1833 that gave parish councils powers to levy a special rate to employ sufficient watchmen of day and night. These aimed gently to encourage greater levels of rural policing without challenging local autonomy but the extent to which permissive powers were adopted depended on levels of local anxiety about crime and disorder and a willingness to fund reform.

---

[48] Ibid, Steedman, C., *Policing the Victorian Community: The Formation of English Provincial Police Forces 1856-1880*, p. 54.
[49] Philips, D., and Storch, R. D., 'Whigs and Coppers: the Grey Ministry's National Police Scheme, 1832', *Historical Research*, Vol. 67, (1994), pp. 75-90.

Local reforms did not satisfy the concerns of central government and in May 1836 Lord John Russell announced that a Rural Police Bill was in preparation. Rather than attempt to get contentious legislation through Parliament, Russell agreed with Chadwick's call for a Royal Commission 'to enquire into the Best Means of Establishing an effective [rural police]'. The 1839 *Report* proposed establishing a force of 8,000 national police under the control of the Home Office and the Metropolitan Police Commissioners. However, the establishment of a professional force in localities would be elective not prescriptive with each county's Quarter Sessions making the decision. To encourage adoption, the cost was to be shared with the county rate providing three-quarters and central funds the remaining quarter. There was widespread hostility to the *Report* and this allowed Russell to introduce responsive legislation that rapidly passed through Parliament. [50]

The 1839 Rural Constabulary Act did not meet the *Report*'s demands for a national police force, with the Metropolitan Police as the controlling power. It permitted JPs to appoint Chief Constables for the direction of the police in their areas and allowed for one policeman per 1,000 of the population. Response was poor. By 1853, only 22 counties out of 52 had police forces. Yorkshire was the poorest served. One division of the East Riding had only 9 policemen. By about 1855, there were only 12,000 policemen in England and Wales. The provinces were slow to implement the 1839 Act for several reasons. Chadwick saw the new police as a means of regulating the unpopular new Poor Law. There was opposition to the idea of police, as a challenge to the liberties of localities. The expense was deemed to be too great; there was considerable local government inertia and a lack of co-operation between the boroughs and the counties. Finally, no provision was made until 1856 for government inspection, audit or regulation.

One important factor in the transformation of the provincial police force after 1835 was the growing importance of 'surveillance' leading to changes in the conception of public space. [51] For example, the Portsmouth Borough police was significantly improved in the

---

[50] Brundage, Anthony, 'Ministers, magistrates and reformers: the genesis of the Rural Constabulary Act of 1839', *Parliamentary History*, Vol. 5, (1986), pp. 55-64. See, Emsley, Clive, 'The Bedfordshire police 1840-1856: a case study in the working of the Rural Constabulary Act', *Midland History*, Vol. 7, (1982), pp. 73-92.

[51] Ogburn, Miles, 'Ordering the city: surveillance, public space and the reform of urban policing in England 1835-56', *Political Geography*, Vol. 12, (1993), pp. 505-521.

period before 1856 through a series of locally initiated reforms to control public space for which there was substantial local middle-class support. This reflected the growing powers of the state at all levels and especially the growing regulatory and administrative powers that they could deploy to deny open public spaces to the working-classes. Numerous sites within and on the edges of towns were eliminated by the pressures of urban growth but attempts to control or exclude working people from using these sites led to frequent and often violent resistance. Whether this was a consequence of the perceived 'civilising mission' of the police or the emergence of an aggressive middle-class civic culture or a combination of the two, the traditional freedoms of working-class culture were first controlled and then gradually curtailed.

The Municipal Corporation Act 1835 and the Rural Constabulary Act 1839, in theory, spread the new police into the provincial boroughs and enabled counties or parts of counties to establish police forces. Unlike the Metropolitan Police, the borough and county forces ostensibly remained under local watch committee control. The chief constables of the counties tended to have greater independence from their police committees than the head constables of boroughs where, in some places, the police continued to be regarded as municipal servants carrying out a variety of administrative functions until well into the twentieth century. If police committees wanted their constables to collect market tolls or act as municipal mace bearers, there was nothing to prevent them.

However, even in the nineteenth century the parochial principle was being rapidly eroded in the interests of systematisation, collaboration and greater neutrality. The creation of Her Majesty's Inspectorate of Constabulary in 1856 whose certificates of efficiency led to treasury grants, and the subsequent growth of police experts within the Home Office, who speak directly to the experts who served as chief or head constables by-passing civilian police committees, resulted in further uniformity and a degree of centralisation before the First World War. In some boroughs such as Liverpool, chief constables achieved a significant degree of autonomy from their watch committees as early as the 1850s and elsewhere they gained their *de facto* independence during the 1870s as central government increasingly dictated their duties. [52] Following the recommendations

---

[52] Hart, Jennifer, 'Reform of the borough Police, 1835-56', *English Historical Review*, Vol. 70, (1955), pp. 411-427, Philips, David, 'A "Weak" State? The English State, the Magistracy and the Reform of Policing in the 1830s', *English Historical Review*, Vol. 119, (2004), pp. 873-891, and

of the 1853 Select Committee on Police, the County and Borough Police Act 1856 made police forces mandatory in counties and boroughs, subjected them to central inspection and sanctioned Exchequer grants to forces certified as 'efficient'. [53] From the 1870s onwards, Home Office rules helped to regulate pay, discipline and criteria for employment. The Police Act 1890 allowed mutual-aid agreement between forces to facilitate the borrowing of constables in times of severe, usually industrial unrest. [54]

Scotland Yard came to play an important role in the centralising process. The Home Office's direct control of metropolitan policing from 1829 onwards was turned to powerful effect. Most new police policies and practices were first developed in London and in this way Scotland Yard set the pace for an increasing specialisation and centralisation of police functions that Peel could never have foreseen. All provincial police forces were gradually affected by it. This can be seen in three respects. A plainclothes spy system was viewed with deepest suspicion in Peel's day. [55] The Home Office, however, established a small detective force of two inspectors and six sergeants in 1842. The detective force expanded in the 1860s boosted by a scare about ticket-of-leave men and the activities of Irish Fenians who were responsible for outrages in Manchester and London in 1867.

In the 1870s, there was a major corruption scandal within the detective branch. [56] Madame de Goncourt, a rich Parisian became the victim of Harry Benson and William Kurr, two confidence tricksters who persuaded her to part with £30,000. Scotland Yard was

---

Philips, David, and Storch, Robert D., *Policing provincial England, 1829-1856: the politics of reform*, (Leicester University Press), 1999.

[53] Hart, Jennifer, 'The County and Borough Police Act, 1856', *Public Administration*, Vol. 34, (1956), pp. 405-417.

[54] Morgan, Jane, *Conflict and Order: The Police and Labour Disputes in England and Wales, 1900-1939*, (Oxford University Press, 1987); Weinberger, Barbara, *Keeping the Peace?: Policing Strikes in Britain, 1906-1926*, (Berg), 1991.

[55] One of the main reasons for this was the role played by spies and agents provocateur during the radical disturbances of the 1810s. See, Pike, Alan R., 'A brief history of the Criminal Investigation Department of the London Metropolitan Police', *Police Studies*, Vol. 1, (1978), pp. 22-30. See also, Petrow, S., 'The rise of the Detective in London 1869-1914', *Criminal Justice History*, Vol. 14, (1993), pp. 91-108.

[56] Shpayer-Makov, Haia, *The Ascent of the Detective: Police Sleuths in Victorian and Edwardian England*, (Oxford University Press), 2011, explores the development of the police detective, a previously neglected subject. Stewart R. F., *The Great Detective Case of 1877: A study in Victorian Police Corruption*, (George A. Vanderburgh), 2000.

called in and Superintendent Adolphus Williamson sent Chief Inspector Nathaniel Druscovich to bring Benson back from Amsterdam where he had been arrested. Druscovich seemed to find the job surprisingly difficult. A sergeant and two others were sent to catch Kurr but he moved just as they expected to arrest him. Eventually he was arrested in Edinburgh, stood trial and was convicted. This led to questions about why the arrests had proved so difficult and Benson and Kurr began to explain. Inspector John Meiklejohn had been in Kurr's pay since 1873 accepting large sums of money to tip him off when his crimes were about to lead to his arrest. Meiklejohn had offered Druscovich the opportunity to borrow money from Kurr to repay his brother's debts and as a result, Druscovich was also implicated as was Chief Inspector Palmer, who appears to have been duped into going along with his colleagues. The three were sentenced to two years in prison, and the scandal nearly wrecked Williamson's career.

Although his integrity was unquestioned, Williamson's supervision of subordinates seemed wanting, and following the Committee of Inquiry, the Home Office took the opportunity to overhaul the existing system and to establish the CID under Howard Vincent in 1878. By 1884, the Metropolitan Police district CID had expanded from 280 to 800 officers though this constituted only 2.4 per cent of the police in London. A higher percentage of detectives were found in the major provincial cities: Liverpool and Glasgow 3.5 per cent and Birmingham 4.5 per cent. The number of arrests by metropolitan detectives rose from 13,000 to 18,000 in five years and this success ensured the continuance of the CID. The legitimacy of secret detection was seldom challenged again.

In 1869, the Home Office and Scotland Yard instituted a criminal records system. Initially it was primitive and unwieldy but improved with an increasing use of photography and, after 1901, fingerprinting. The regular circulation of simple information sheets to provincial forces brought satisfying results. In 1883, the Special Irish Branch was established in response to Fenian bomb outrages. But by the late 1880s it had become involved in broader questions of national security. In these ways the state was learning to keep closer tabs on its unrespectable citizens and political dissidents. [57]

Peel's police had been concerned largely with enforcing the common law. His late Victorian successors were able to act under

---

[57] Porter, Bernard, *The origins of the vigilant state: the London Metropolitan Police Special Branch before the First World War*, (Weidenfeld and Nicolson), 1987. See also, Allason, R. *The Branch: A History of the Metropolitan Police Special Branch, 1883-1983*, (David & Charles), 1983.

statute or regulations as Parliament and the Home Office extended police control over a wide array of social groups, from habitual criminals to abused children, from pornographer to drunks. [58] The state assumed an increasing direction of the penal system, notably in the Prison Act 1877, and of the ancient judicial discretion in sentencing with the establishment of the Court of Criminal Appeal in 1907. The police themselves after 1850 very gradually became the main agents of prosecution while Whitehall's assumption of a central position in the process was symbolised by the creation of the office of Director of Public Prosecutions in 1879. The criminal department of the Home Office was set up in 1870 and by 1906 was dealing with a third of all Home Office business.

In respect of central control of the criminal justice system, as in other spheres of government activity, the forty years after 1870 saw important innovations. This was evident in the increase in both the number of police and the costs. In 1861, there was one policeman to every 937 people in England and Wales, by 1891, one for every 731 and by 1951, one for every 661. Costs rose from £1.5 million in 1861 to over £3.5 million in 1891 and £7.0 million in 1914. As a result, by 1914, what policemen, magistrates and even judges could do even in remote areas of the country was effectively being dictated from Westminster and Whitehall. However, the parochial principle still remained more than merely cosmetic.

Who became policemen?

By 1900, working as a police constable meant a steady job with low income but attractive benefits. Employment was independent of the business cycle and pay was not linked to individual performance. Such work was in demand and only one-in-five applicants were accepted. In the Metropolitan Police during the nineteenth century, only about 10 per cent of the force was born in London. This reflected the preference of senior officers for countrymen because they were regarded as healthier, tougher and more willing to take orders and they did not have the conflicting loyalties exhibited by some Londoners who policed their own neighbourhood. The first recruits to the Metropolitan Police were between the ages of 18 and 35 years but as policing became more attractive recruitment was limited to

---

[58] See, for example, Croll, Andy, 'Street disorder, surveillance and shame: Regulating behaviour in the public spaces of the late Victorian British town', *Social History*, Vol. 24, (3), (1999), pp. 250-268, Stevenson. S. J., 'The Habitual Criminal in 19th century England: some observations on the figures', *Urban History Yearbook*, 1986, pp. 44-53.

those between 20 and 27. Most were still labourers though the number of recruits from non-manual backgrounds increased, a process aided by the increasing status of the job and with the provision of pensions from 1890, its job security. [59]

The early constables were usually recruited from the agricultural labour force or from the army, were paid low wages and were often quick to leave the force. For instance, in Whitechapel, the 1851 Census shows that the majority of policemen came from outside London of whom 23 per cent came from Ireland. Almost half had previously been labourers who were offered the possibility or security and a regular income in the police and who were less likely than skilled men to leave. Men who left on their own will tended to be from more skilled occupations, with a background of better work before joining the force. In the early-twentieth century, economic pressures encouraged more of these men to join the force. Veterans tended to be men from unskilled or semi-skilled backgrounds, for whom the police service was an avenue to upward mobility. Although men from poorer backgrounds remained longest in the police, those from better-off backgrounds who did remain were most likely to rise through the system into the higher ranks. Others were dismissed for drunkenness. A parliamentary Select Committee in 1834 heard that 80 per cent of dismissals were for drunkenness.

Initial formal training was about three to five weeks by 1900 and about half that in 1850. Until the early-twentieth century, most training was military drill for purposes of crowd control, with only brief training dedicated to behaviour on the beat and this was largely remembering laws and instructions. What counted was the informal training learned on the beat and the habits picked up from established officers. Isolated by uniform, discipline and function from the working-class communities and upholding 'order' often in the face of chronic hostility and abuse within those communities, career policemen developed a distinct occupational culture with its own values and standards that strengthened bonds between fellow officers. The police generated their own, often discretionary, operational standards on the streets, passed on via 'apprenticeship' from officer to officer, that were often less respectable and at odds with those of the

---

[59] Martin, John, and Gail Wilson, Gail, *The Police, A Study in Manpower: Evolution of the Service in England and Wales, 1829-1965*, (Heinemann), 1969, and Shpayer-Makov, H., *The Making of a Policeman: A Social History of a Labour Force in Metropolitan London, 1829-1914*, (Ashgate), 2002.

rulebooks and the letter of the law. [60]

Some degree of tension between the command structure and the ordinary station-men was endemic in British policing. It stemmed from grievances about working conditions. In 1848, a number of constables petitioned their superiors that their pay was not sufficient to support a family. In 1872, when over 3,000 constables and sergeants turned up for a meeting to discuss demands for a pay rise. Senior officers at Scotland Yard were so concerned that a pay rise was quickly granted but later 109 men involved in the action were sacked. There were abortive Metropolitan Police strikes in 1879 and 1890. In 1890, there was an attempt to form the Metropolitan Police Union, but granting of pensions removed a major source of complaint. Since the police were used against industrial unrest the fact that officers were appropriating the language of trade unionism was viewed as a potential threat to discipline and in conflict with the demands of the job. A further attempt to unionise occurred in September 1913 with the resurrection of the Metropolitan Police Union that the following year changed its name to the National Union of Police & Prison Officers. A police order was issued in December 1913 threatening the dismissal of officers associated with the union.

In addition, there was the remoteness of commissioners and chief constables, often trained in the military or colonial services, from the lower-rank notions of 'good policing' that focused on detection rather than deterrence, action rather than service, physical engagement rather than administration. [61] There were sporadic campaigns against their corruption and malpractice. These surfaced during the trials of 1877 and of Inspector White in 1880 and during the public disquiet that resulted in the issuing of Judges' Rules on interrogation and arrest procedures in 1912. The 1906-1908 Royal Commission was initiated over the alleged wrongful arrest of Madame Eva D'Angely, a lady of dubious reputation but a lady nonetheless for 'riotous and indecent behaviour'. In this case, her husband protested her innocence, newspapers published her story and the Home Secretary was questioned in the House of Commons. [62]

---

[60] Taylor, David, 'The standard of living of career policemen in Victorian England: the evidence of a provincial borough force', *Criminal Justice History*, Vol. 12, (1991), pp. 108-131, and Lowe, W. J., 'The Lancashire Constabulary, 1845-1870: the social and occupational function of a Victorian police force', *Criminal Justice History*, Vol. 4, (1983), pp. 41-62.
[61] Wall, David, *The Chief Constables of England and Wales: a socio-legal history of a criminal justice elite*, (Ashgate), 1998, pp. 13-86.
[62] Clapson, Mark, and Emsley, Clive, 'Street, Beat, and Respectability: The Culture and Self-Image of the Late Victorian and Edwardian Urban Policeman', *Criminal Justice History*, Vol. 16, (2002), pp. 107-131.

A high number of complaints were brought against the Metropolitan Police in their early years. Between 1831 and 1840, the average number of complaints against the police was 411 per annum. The number of complaints was at its highest, at 511, in 1840. Of these, 273 were made against individual officers; the remainder concerned the small strength of the force and the frequency of robberies. The 1906-1908 Royal Commission upon the Duties of the Metropolitan Police found that only nineteen of the complaints it invited were worth examining and only a few proven satisfactorily. The impoverished public that did not matter but might have known better about police malpractice did not speak out; when it did, hostile questioning discredited it. What is clear from the evidence of the Royal Commission is the long-standing system of wheeling and dealing between police and underworld that had its own unwritten rules and at which command officers had no choice but to connive. Blind eyes were turned, favours exacted and reciprocated, informers employed, bribes exchanged and some brutality was standard practice. Relations between police and law-breakers were necessarily close and it would be surprising then as now, if they were not also contaminating. Witnesses before the 1878 confidential detective committee drew a thin veil over the implications of detectives 'using' a certain class of people among the criminal class from whom to get information by small payments or other means. Officials recurrently compromised in their efforts to police the streets.

Was there a 'policeman state'?

The strength and cost of the policing developed continuously throughout the nineteenth century. The extension of the function of the police to encompass broad areas of human activity and the growing surveillance of the working-classes in particular led to the pervasive presence of the 'bobby' across society and a growing belief that Britain had become a regulatory and policeman state. The police became a central element of state power and, for some historians, 'domestic missionaries' charged with bringing order and discipline to the disorderly and robust nature of working-class attitudes and culture. Different sections of the community were united in their initial opposition to the establishment of the Metropolitan Police. Some Whigs and aristocratic Tories saw the centralised police as an attack on the liberties of Englishmen. Radicals commonly regarded the police as a ruling-class instrument that could be used to combat calls by disenfranchised middle- and working-class groups for wider participation in the political system. Parish vestries and magistrates objected to the reduction of their power and influence and some ratepayers opposed the cost of the new force. Yet as the nineteenth century progressed, the work of the police was viewed more favourably by many sections of society.

The poor expected little sympathy from the police and had always been the targets of the law. [63] Several statutory weapons put poor people on the centre of law enforcement. The Vagrancy Act 1824, the Metropolitan Police Act 1839, police acts and bye-laws, the Habitual Criminals legislation of 1869-1871 combined to give police immense discretionary powers of arrest on suspicion of intent to commit a felony. The police had equal discretionary powers of defining obstruction, breach of the peace, and drunkenness. They could decide whether or not to arrest, whether to bring charges and what charges. Against these powers the poorer people had little defence. Early police orders told constables not to interfere with 'respectable' working people. Stop-and-search powers resulted in the arrest of vagrants, suspicious people and, with luck, some actual criminals. This resulted in vulnerable and accessible people being driven into courts. Magistrates convicted or committed them for trial on very little evidence often, little more than police testimony as to character.

In the nineteenth century, many more people had a direct experience of the disciplinary and coercive effects of policing and the law than is widely believed. When arrests or summonses in any one-year are considered as well as convictions, the results are even more startling. In 1861, 1 in 29 of men and 1 in 120 of women were either arrested or summonsed. By 1901, the figures respectively were 1 in 24 and 1 in 123. Summary prosecutions rose by 73 per cent between 1861 and 1901. The immediate threat that the police offered to the social life of the poor had greatly increased in those decades when the policeman state was making its major bureaucratic advances. [64] The Edwardian working-classes were in this sense more closely regulated and supervised than their parents and grandparents but there was

---

[63] Storch, R. D., 'The policeman as domestic missionary: urban discipline and popular culture in northern England, 1850-80', *Journal of Social History*, Vol. 9, (1976), pp. 481-509, and 'The plague of the blue locusts: police reform and popular resistance in northern England, 1840-57', *International Review of Social History*, Vol. 20, (1975), pp. 61-91, and Swift, R., 'Urban policing in early Victorian England, 1835-86: a reappraisal', *History*, Vol. 73, (1988), pp. 211-237.

[64] See, for example, Bramham, Peter, 'Policing and the police in an industrial town: Keighley 1856-1870', *Local Historian*, Vol. 36, (2006), pp. 175-184, and Sheldon, Nicola, 'Policing Truancy: Town versus Countryside: Oxfordshire 1871-1903', *History of Education Researcher*, Vol. 77, (2006), pp. 15-24.

inevitably resentment. In the second quarter of the nineteenth century, anti-police riots had expressed this frame of mind forcefully. These confrontations declined after 1850 but the significance of this can be misconstrued. It indicated less the growing acquiescence of an incorporated working-class than the isolation, marginalisation and defeat of its poorest and most turbulent sectors. The decline of their collective opposition to police reflected growing effectiveness of crowd control by the police and the obligation imposed on an increasingly marginalised residuum to come to terms with the permanence of the social order, even when they benefited little from it.

Many working-class communities were becoming more settled and the regularly employed working-class assimilated to bourgeois standards of order and indeed conceptions of criminality. Those in stable employment were distanced from the street economy of social crime and consciousness of the value of property acquired from wages and from savings led to attitudes to crime among the working-classes that were shared with the middle-classes. During the second half of the nineteenth century, the modern 'moral panic' about crime and violence becomes a feature of urban life, especially in London during the garrotting panic of 1862 and the Jack the Ripper murders of 1888. The street thieves were just as likely to rob workers of their pay packets as the middle-classes of their wallets and murderers preyed on the vulnerable of all classes. The earlier middle-class panic about the lower orders in general was displaced by a fear, shared across the social classes, of the marginal criminal stranger and the middle-class fear of the 'underclass'.

By 1914, the police had established their authority and presence in the working-class communities dealing with crime but also with the wider task of surveillance and disciplining of working-class daily life. Working-class life had become regularised and disciplined. The police were an agent of the Victorian middle-classes and their fear of working-class exuberance as examples of the behaviour of the 'dangerous classes' who needed to be habituated to an ordered and disciplined working life. They were part of mechanisms of social control and by 1914 this task was largely completed, at least for the better-off sections of the working classes.

16 Leisure

The late-eighteenth and first half of the nineteenth century saw two major changes in the cultural experience of English society.[1] There was erosion of the older popular culture as a result of the withdrawal of patronage by the governing elite, the gradual dismantling of the agrarian social and economic frameworks that gave it justification by widespread industrialisation and the attacks on its public expression by a combination of religious evangelicalism and a secular desire to promote work discipline. By contrast, a more commercial culture developed, entrepreneurial, market-led and largely urban and bourgeois. This involved modification of both the content and transmission of high culture and, in the nineteenth century, the promotion of popular cultural products like circuses, prize and cock-fights for profit. Cultural experiences, like economic and social ones, were adaptable.

Why attack cultural experience?

The attack on popular culture was part of the assault on the life-styles and recreations of the labouring population that had been gathering pace since the sixteenth century. It had two linked thrusts: a religious belief that popular culture was profane, irreligious and immoral and a secular concern that it was detrimental to economic efficiency and public order. The desire to turn people into sober, virtuous and godly citizens motivated by an interest in work and social discipline is generally held to have been resolved by the mid-Victorian turn to recreation and sport, 'justifying God to the people' through the 'soft-hearted benevolence' of cricket, cycling and football. Erdozain argues that the problem of pleasure was inflamed by the ecclesiastical remedy. Just as the early Victorians came to identify sin with 'vice',

---

[1] Easton, S., Howkins, A., Laing, S., Merrick L., and Walker, H., *Disorder and Discipline: Popular Culture from 1550 to the Present*, (Temple Smith), 1988, and Borsay, Peter, *A History of Leisure: The British Experience since 1500*, (Palgrave), 2006, are good general surveys. Malcolmson, R.,W., *Popular Recreation in English Society 1700-1850*, (Cambridge University Press), 1973, and Cunningham, H., *Leisure in the Industrial Revolution*, (Allen and Unwin), 1980, provide perspectives on the issue of custom and leisure. Bailey, P., *Leisure and Class in Victorian England: rational recreation and the contest for control 1830-1885,* (Routledge), 1978, takes the arguments forward into the late-nineteenth century. Holt, R., *Sport and the British: A Modern History*, (Oxford University Press), 1989, and Tranter, N., *Sport, Economy and Society in Britain, 1750-1914*, (Cambridge University Press), 1998, are the best introduction to this area of leisure.

their successors came to associate salvation with an increasingly social and physical sense of 'virtue'. The problem of overdrawn boundaries between church and world gave way to a new and subtle confusion of gospel and culture resulting in a sense of cultural crisis, a challenge to the hegemony that called for moral regeneration and stricter disciplining of the lives of the labouring population. Sport became the perfect vehicle for the humanistic, 'unmystical' morality that defines the secularity of the twentieth century. [2]

Attacks on popular culture after 1830 can be seen as a response to pressures on existing forms of social control, of demographic and urban growth and the consequent erosion of paternalism. Evangelicalism played a major role in this critique of popular culture and succeeded in obtaining some agreement across the governing elite to its central moral tenets through groups such as the Society for the Reformation of Manners and the Society for the Suppression of Vice.[3] Its views had their greatest success with the mercantile, commercial and professional groups, who looked with distaste at the irrational and sinful nature of much popular culture and were appalled by the gratuitous cruelty to animals this involved. Methodism had greater impact on the working population and on artisans and small shopkeepers through its incessant attacks on the worldliness and sensuality of popular culture. Distaste for present pleasures was also a characteristics of secular radicalism. For articulate radicals, popular culture was too closely linked to the paternalistic social order. It offended their emphasis on reason and their stress on moral and intellectual self-improvement; books, education and debating rather than bear baiting, races and circuses. Secular radicals, no less than evangelicals, sought to redeem the working population.

This ideological attack was combined with Thomas Carlyle's 'abdication on the part of the governors'. The aristocracy and gentry gradually withdrew from participation in popular culture and no longer championed it against reformers. Society was becoming less face-to-face, except on special occasions, with social groups confined to their own cultural worlds. The layout of country houses and gardens demonstrated a move towards domestic privacy. This was more than just symbolic and reflected a much broader 'cutting-off' of the lives of aristocracy and gentry from the lives of the labouring population. Rural sports, customary holidays and apprenticeship

---

[2] On this issue see, Erdozain, Dominic, *The Problem of Pleasure: Sport, Recreation and the Crisis of Victorian Religion*, (Boydell Press), 2010.
[3] See, Harrison, Brian, 'Religion and recreation in nineteenth-century England', *Past & Present*, Vol. 38, (1967), pp. 98-125.

rituals came to be seen not as socially desirable but as wasteful distractions from work and threats to social order.

What was popular culture?

In 1830, popular culture was public, robust and gregarious, largely masculine and involved spectacle and gambling with an undercurrent of disorder and physical violence. The distinction between high and popular culture, between opera and drama on the one hand and spectacle, circus and showmanship on the other had broken down: Shakespeare, melodrama and performing animals not merely co-existed but intermingled.

The eighteenth century pleasure fairs had played a major role in this process and many major actors started their careers in their theatrical booths. English theatre and opera was produced not only for the cultivated and informed but for mass audiences for whom melodrama, lavish stage sets and live animals were essential and whom managers and actors bored at their peril. Expanding audiences funded the extensive rebuilding of Covent Garden, Drury Lane and Sadler's Wells as well as theatres outside the West End and entrepreneurs gave melodrama a legitimate place on the stage as well as developing the modern pantomime. Provincial theatres followed the example of London. [4] By 1830, however, there had been some decline in theatre going among the provincial bourgeoisie, the result as much of the rougher audiences frightening them away as the impact of evangelicalism.

Developments in sport showed the same commercialism and capacity to survive in the face of the hostility of authority. [5] Shooting and hunting were the only sports to remain exclusively elitist. Until 1831, shooting was legally restricted to owners of land worth more than £100 and the Games Laws ensured that poaching was severely punished. [6] While shooting demonstrated a horizontal cleavage in rural society, foxhunting had a far greater community interest. Although dominated by the landed aristocracy and country gentlemen, it was open to urban gentry and professionals and the poorer sections of the community followed the spectacle on foot. Some hunts were the property of single great landowners but were

---

[4] Borsay, Peter, *The English Urban Renaissance: Culture and Society in the Provincial Town 1660-1770*, (Oxford University Press), 1991, pp. 117-149.
[5] Ibid, Borsay, Peter, *The English Urban Renaissance: Culture and Society in the Provincial Town 1660-1770*, pp. 173-196.
[6] Munsche, P. B., *Gentlemen and poachers: the English game laws 1671-1831*, (Cambridge University Press), 1981.

expensive to maintain and subscription hunts became more common: there were 69 packs of hounds in Britain in 1812, 91 by 1825. [7]

Horseracing was the sport of both the rich and poor. It could not maintain its exclusiveness though different prices charged for the stands, the paddocks and the ordinary enclosures were as much an expression of social hierarchy as different class of railway travel. Horseracing combined two obsessions: the love of horses and gambling. Professional bookmakers appeared around 1800; by 1815, the 'classic' races, the Derby, the Oaks, the One Thousand and Two Thousand Guineas, the St Leger and the Ascot Gold Cup, were all established and by 1837, there were 150 places in Britain where race meetings were held. [8] By 1850, off-course betting had been established, further broadening participation.[9] Pugilism or prize fighting began as a sport of the labouring population but attracted aristocratic patronage by 1800. Like horseracing it was increasingly commercialised and its champions such as Tom Spring, [10] Tom Crib and Dutch Sam were full-time professionals. Both flourished as industries with their own specialist newspapers yet they were also evocative of an older, perhaps imaginary, culture where sporting squires and labourers rubbed shoulders in a common appreciation of animals and physical prowess. Upper-class support for prize fighting waned after 1830 but it retained its popularity among the working population and its real decline did not occur until after 1860.[11] Other sports like cricket, rowing and pedestrianism had similar

---

[7] On this issue see Carr, Raymond, *English Fox Hunting: A History*, (Weidenfeld), 1976, and Itzkowitz, David C., *Peculiar privilege: a social history of English foxhunting, 1753-1885*, (Harvester Press), 1977.

[8] Church, Michael, *The Derby Stakes: the complete history 1780-2006*, (Raceform Ltd), 2006, Seth-Smith, Michael, and Mortimer, Roger, *Derby 200: the official story of the blue riband of the turf*, (Guinness Superlatives), 1979, Tolson, John, and Vamplew, Wray, 'Facilitation Not Revolution: Railways and British Flat Racing 1830-1914', *Sport in History*, Vol. 23, (2003), pp. 89-106, and Huggins, Mike *Flat racing and British society, 1790-1914: a social and economic history*, (Cass), 2000.

[9] See, Clapson, Mark, *A bit of a flutter: popular gambling in England, c.1820-1961*, (Manchester University Press), 1992.

[10] Hurley, Jon, *Tom Spring: bare-knuckle Champion of All England*, (Stadia), 2007.

[11] See, Anderson, Jack, 'The Legal Response to Prize Fighting in Nineteenth Century England and America', *Northern Ireland Legal Quarterly*, Vol. 57, (2006), pp. 265-287, and Sheard, K. G., '"Brutal and degrading": the medical profession and boxing, 1838-1984', *International Journal of the History of Sport*, Vol. 15, (3), (1998), pp. 74-102.

characteristics to horse-racing and prize fighting.[12] They became more organised and professional, more dependent on attracting spectators and accompanied by extensive gambling. Cricket originated as an activity of the labouring population in southern England and was then take up by the aristocratic elite.[13] Pedestrianism and rowing also began as popular sports before moving up the social scale late in the nineteenth century.[14]

Many traditional customs continued until well after 1850. There is evidence for the large unchanged New Year mumming festivals in northern England until the 1870s. Guy Fawkes' Night was still celebrated despite attempts by various authorities to suppress bonfires and the burning of effigies.[15] Changes to traditional customs were not easily enforced even in areas, like Lancashire, where factory discipline was most firmly established. The Lancashire Wakes Weeks, traditionally the most important event of the recreational year, were forced on millowners rather than freely given.[16] It was not simply employers who attacked wakes and fairs. Moral reformers, the magistracy, and later the police recognised that these acted as a focus for criminal activity, could potentially lead to violence and threatened public order. That they continued until the late-nineteenth century was due not to lack of opposition but to disagreement about what action to take.

By 1830, a clear distinction was apparent between the nature of much popular recreation and the dominant intellectual movements of the day, rational liberalism and evangelicalism with their argument for a self-conscious and moralistic cultivation of respectability. This produced much of the impetus for reform. From the formation of the Proclamation Society in 1787, the campaign for reform gathered momentum. By the 1830s, there were societies for preventing cruelty to animals, the Lord's Day Observance Society founded in 1831 and the British and Foreign Temperance Society. Parliamentary reform in 1832 gave such societies slightly more influence over Parliament

---

[12] Wigglesworth, Neil, *A social history of English rowing*, (Routledge), 1992, pp. 1-91, and Halladay, Eric, *Rowing in England: a social history: the amateur debate*, (Manchester University Press), 1990

[13] See Underdown, David, 'The History of Cricket', *History Compass*, Vol. 4, (1), (2006), pp. 43-53, and Birley, Derek, *A Social History of English Cricket*, (Aurum Press), 1999.

[14] Lile, Emma, 'Professional Pedestrianism in South Wales during the Nineteenth Century', *The Sports Historian*, Vol. 20, (2000), pp. 94-105.

[15] Sharpe, J. A., *Remember, remember the fifth of November: Guy Fawkes and the gunpowder plot*, (Profile), 2005, looks at remembrance.

[16] Poole, Robert, 'Lancashire wakes week', *History Today*, Vol. 34, (8), (1984), pp. 22-29.

and as the police force extended they gained the means to enforce legislation. Betting was an early and obvious target for reform but lotteries were not made illegal until 1823 and 1825 and further measures to discourage gambling had to wait until the 1840s and 1850s. [17] Reform was not achieved easily, quickly or completely. Neither was it the prerogative, nor was it dictated by the interests, of any one social group. It traversed class boundaries, dividing all groups, especially the working-classes, internally.[18]

Changing attitudes: some case studies

The emergence of 'respectability' as the defining characteristic of acceptable forms of behaviour was a major feature of the changed attitudes to traditional forms of social behaviour. This can be seen in the cases of cruelty to animals, temperance and the growing problem of drug addiction. These three examples of changing attitudes to popular culture illustrate the importance of pressure, either voluntary or through legislation, to control and modify aspects of people's lives. To those, from all sections of society, who argued for change the issue was one of improving the quality of economic and social life, enhancing respectable attitudes and removing potential tensions and disorder. To those affected, reform attacked what they maintained was their traditional right to enjoy themselves and to escape, if momentarily, from their social conditions.

Why and how did people react against cruelty to animals?

The staging of contests between animals was still one of the most common and popular forms of recreation in England in the early-nineteenth century. [19] Cock fighting was the normal feature at fairs and race meetings involving the mingling of all social groups, though only men, and accompanied by heavy betting and often local and

---

[17] Munting, R., 'Social opposition to gambling in Britain: an historical overview', *International Journal of the History of Sport*, Vol. 10, (1993), pp. 295-312, Raven, James, 'The abolition of the English state lotteries', *Historical Journal*, Vol. 34, (1991), 371-389, and Woodhall, Robert, 'The British state lotteries', *History Today*, Vol. 14, (7), (1964), pp. 497-504.

[18] Itzkowitz, David C., 'Victorian bookmakers and their customers', *Victorian Studies*, Vol. 32, (1988), pp. 7-30.

[19] Ritvo, H., *The Animal Estate: the English and other creatures in the Victorian Age*, (Penguin), 1990, and Harrison, B., 'Animals and the State in Nineteenth Century England', *English Historical Review*, Vol. 88 (1973), pp. 786-820, reprinted in his *Peaceable Kingdoms: Stability and Change in Modern Britain*, (Oxford University Press), 1982, on cruelty to animals.

regional rivalries. [20] Hunting and hawking were widespread. Small children were notorious for amusing themselves in torturing living creatures but they were merely reflecting the standards of the adult world. This was largely what Keith Thomas calls 'the cruelty of indifference' as animals were outside the terms of their moral reference. [21]

During the eighteenth century the feelings of animals became a matter of very great concern and led to agitation in the early-nineteenth century culminating in the formation in 1824 of the Society (later Royal Society) for the Prevention of Cruelty to Animals and the passage of legislation against cruelty to horses and cattle in 1822, to dogs in 1839 and 1854 and against animal baiting and cock-fighting in 1835 and 1849. There are various reasons why this changed occurred. There had long been a tradition that unnecessary cruelty to animals was wrong not because of any moral concern with animals but because of its brutalising effects on human character. [22] It did not go unnoticed that the poisoner William Palmer hanged in 1856 had conducted cruel experiments on animals as a boy.

In the early-nineteenth century there was a move away from this point of view towards one that regarded cruelty to animals as morally wrong whether it had human consequences or not. At a less philosophical level animal sports were associated with noise, gambling and disorder. Hunting proved to be a more difficult issue and there is something in the contemporary argument that in the long war against blood sports it was the most plebeian activities that were criminalised and those sports with gentry and upper-class support that survived.

Should people drink?

In the early-nineteenth century ale, wine and spirits were cheap and consumed in large quantities. [23] With the dangers of disease from untreated water it was natural for town-dwellers to rely increasingly on alcohol and on water that had been boiled with tea and coffee. As Chadwick's inspectors found out from London slum-dwellers in the 1840s people did not believe that local water would ever be safe to

---

[20] Jobey, George, 'Cock-fighting in Northumberland and Durham during the eighteenth and nineteenth centuries', *Archaeologia Aeliana*, 5th series, Vol. 20, (1992), pp. 1-25, is a good local study.
[21] Thomas, Keith, *Man and the natural world: changing attitudes in England 1500-1800*, (Allen Lane), 1983, p. 148.
[22] Li, C. H., 'A union of Christianity, humanity, and philanthropy: the Christian tradition and the prevention of cruelty to animals in nineteenth-century England', *Society & Animals*, Vol. 8, (2000), pp. 265-285.
[23] Burnett, John, *Liquid pleasures: a social history of drinks in modern Britain*, (Routledge), 1999, provides an excellent overview.

drink. The scarcity of drinking water even created the profession of water-carrier. There were alternatives to alcohol: milk, though this was considered a dangerous drink even when fresh; soda-water was not made commercially until 1790 and ginger-beer was not sold in London until 1822. Tea [24] had become a necessity for the working-classes by 1830 and per capita coffee consumption increased faster than tea between 1820 and 1850. [25] But alcohol was more than just a thirst-quencher; it was thought to impart physical stamina, extra energy and confidence. Agricultural labourers, for example, believed that it was impossible to get in the harvest without their 'harvest beer'. Alcohol was regarded as a painkiller: it assisted dentists and surgeons before the use of anaesthetics, quietened babies and gave protection against infection. It also relieved psychological strain, moderating the sense of social isolation and gloom and enhanced festivity.

Drinking places provided a focus for the community. [26] Before 1800, drinking was not rigidly segregated by rank. Squires, for instance, often drank with their social inferiors. However, by 1830 a measure of social segregation had developed and by 1860 no respectable urban Englishman entered an ordinary public house.[27] Private, as opposed to public, drinking was becoming the mark of respectability. Drinking was also a predominantly male preserve and encouraged men to enjoy better living standards than their wives. On paydays drinking houses were often besieged by wives anxious to get money to feed and clothe their children before it was drunk away. The drinks trade comprised a large complex of different interests. [28] Of particular importance was the powerful landed interest that helps to explain the regional variations in support for the temperance movement. The barley crop was important to farmers and without the distillers' demands for grain, land in Scotland and Ireland might not have been cultivated. Politically the drinks trade drew its prestige

---

[24] Fromer, Julie E., *A necessary luxury: tea in Victorian England*, (Ohio University Press), 2008, and the broader Griffiths, John, *Tea: the drink that changed the world*, (André Deutsch), 2007.

[25] Bramah, Edward, *Tea and coffee: a modern view of three hundred years of tradition,* (Hutchinson), 1972.

[26] Holt, Mack P., (ed.), *Alcohol: a social and cultural history*, (Berg), 2006, provides an overview.

[27] Jennings, Paul, *The local: a history of the English pub*, (Tempus), 2007, Haydon, Peter, *The English pub: a history,* (Hale), 1994, and Kneale, James, "'A problem of supervision': moral geographies of the nineteenth-century British public house', *Journal of Historical Geography*, Vol. 25, (1999), pp. 333-348.

[28] Gourvish, T. R., and Wilson, R. G., *The British brewing industry, 1830-1980*, (Cambridge University Press), 1994.

from the reliance government placed on drink taxes for national revenue. Attitudes to alcohol were deeply ingrained in British society. Abandoning drinking was, for the working-classes, more than simply not going to public houses. It isolated workers from much popular culture and from a whole complex of recreational activities.

The Reformation Societies that emerged in the eighteenth and early-nineteenth centuries were enthusiastic about temperance but their main platform was the suppression of vice. The temperance movement that emerged in the 1830s differed from them in its concentration on the single issue of spirits, its belief in total abstinence and repudiation until after 1850 of legislative support.[29] The anti-spirits movement that developed in the 1830s was not a planned movement, at least initially and arose independently in different places. It was one of several attempts to propagate a middle-class style of life and arose at a time when drunkenness was already becoming unfashionable. Sobriety received the support of influential groups. Medical opinion, since the 1790s, had increasingly attacked the physical and psychological effects of alcohol. Evangelicals saw excessive drinking as a sin. Radicals attacked alcohol for its effects on the standard of living of the working-classes and coffee trades wished to popularise their product. The movement would not have made such an impact in the 1830s without the techniques of agitation and mass persuasion used by evangelical humanitarians, especially the anti-slavery campaign. Though any clear link between industrialisation and temperance is difficult to establish, the earliest anti-spirits societies originated in textile manufacturing areas in Ulster and Glasgow and spread to England though the textile centres of Preston, Leeds and Bradford. Some employers welcomed the more reliable workforce that temperance encouraged. Money not spent on drink could be spent on home-produced goods and some industrialists welcomed the movement as a means of accelerating economic growth and educating people on where to spend their wages.

Throughout the 1830s and 1840s, a debate within the temperance movement raged between those whose attack was focused on spirits while advocating moderation elsewhere and those who believed in total abstinence. But while these approaches gained support among those sections of the working population for whom respectability was an objective, the appeal of temperance was of more limited appeal for the poor, for whom alcohol provided temporary

---

[29] Greenaway, J. R., *Drink and British politics since 1830: a study in policy-making*, (Palgrave Macmillan), 2003, and Nicholls, James, *The Politics of Alcohol: A History of the Drinks Question in England*, (Manchester University Press), 2009

escape.[30] Representing the ideals of self-control and self-denial, the temperance movement epitomised middle-class Victorian values. Its values were shaped by the Evangelical movement that was concerned with salvation and the Utilitarian movement that was concerned with efficiency and valued self-control and self-denial. Joseph Kidd, a late-Victorian journalist for the *Contemporary Review* wrote:

> To be able to rule self and transmit to children an organisation (society) accustomed to self-restraint and moderation in all things is one of the chief delights and aspirations to the moral nature of a true man.[31]

Who were the 'opium eaters'?

The importance and impact of drug-taking across social boundaries in the nineteenth century has only recently become a subject of serious historical study.[32] Opium or opiate compounds were used widely in the first half of the nineteenth century and, though the main features of addiction and withdrawal had been known since the 1750s, most doctors still thought of opium not as dangerous or threatening but central to effective medicine. Until the Pharmacy Act 1868, opium was on open sale and could be bought in any grocer's or druggist's shop. Regular 'opium eaters' were accepted in their communities and rarely the subject of medical attention. They were certainly not seen as 'sick', deviant or diseased as they were to be by 1900. Lack of access to medical care, suspicion of the medical profession and positive hostility to medical treatment ensured opium's position in popular culture as a major form of self-medication.[33] Society generally used opium for sleeplessness, headache or depression and these shaded subtly into non-medical or 'recreational' uses.

---

[30] Ibid, Harrison, B., *Drink and the Victorians: The Temperance Question in England 1815-1872*, and ibid, Lambert, W. R., *Drink and Sobriety in Victorian Wales*, provide the best analysis on the issue of temperance and take the story forward into the second half of the nineteenth century.

[31] Kidd, Joseph, 'Temperance and Its Boundaries,' *Contemporary Review*, Vol. 34, (1879), p. 353.

[32] See in particular Berridge, V., and Edwards, G., *Opium and the People: Opiate Use in Nineteenth Century England*, (Yale University Press), 1987, revised edition, (Free Association), 1999, and Foxcroft, Louise, *The making of addiction: the 'use and abuse' of opium in nineteenth-century Britain*, (Ashgate), 2007.

[33] Milligan, Barry, 'The opium den in Victorian London', in Gilman, Sander L., and Zhou, Xun, (eds.), *Smoke: a global history of smoking*, (Reaktion), 2004, pp. 118-125.

Opium consumption was particularly high in the Fens in the nineteenth century and, according to an analysis made in 1862, more opium was sold in Cambridgeshire, Lincolnshire and Manchester than in other parts of the country. The Fens were an unhealthy, marshy area where medical assistance, especially for the poor, was severely limited and where many of the working-classes were prone to ague, rheumatism and neuralgia. The habit was limited to the low-lying areas centring on the Isle of Ely and south Lincolnshire. [34] The largest consumers were the labourers who came from the outlying fens rather than village or town dwellers. There was a tradition of self-medication with opium used to treat both people and animals. The introduction of new methods of exploiting the land resulted in declining standards of child care and an increase in the doping of young babies with opiates: infant mortality in Wisbech was 206 per thousand in the 1850s, higher than urban centres like Sheffield. Doping young babies was essential as women could be away from home for long periods of time working on the itinerant 'gangs' that became a major source of employment after 1830. Opiates may have been used to dispose of unwanted children, though this was not peculiar to the Fens. Opium could be used as an escape from the perceived reduction of status for the agricultural labourer that resulted from enclosure and drainage. Certainly use for euphoric purposes was not uncommon in the Fens. Dr Rayleigh Vicars wrote in the 1890s:

...their colourless lives are temporarily brightened by the passing dreamland vision afforded them by the baneful poppy.[35]

It is very difficult to estimate the effect opiate use had in the Fens though there may be a connection between it and the high general death rate. In the 1850s, it stood at 22 per thousand in southern Lincolnshire, a figure as high as the industrial areas of Huddersfield and Keighley in Yorkshire. Reaction to opium eating in the Fens, with its population apparently able to control and moderate its consumption was markedly different from the concern expressed about the urban problem. The 'stimulant' use of drugs by the urban

---

[34] High opium consumption may have characterised areas like this: there is evidence, for instance, of similar practices among the poor in the Romney Marshes in Kent. See, Beveridge, Valerie, 'Opium in the Fens in Nineteenth-century England', *Journal of the History of Medicine and Allied Sciences*, Vol. 34, (1979), pp. 293-313.

[35] Vicars, G. Rayleigh, 'Laudanum drinking in Lincolnshire', *St George's Hospital Gazette*, Vol. 1, (1893), p. 24.

working-classes was perceived as a threat to public order in a way that did not apply in the Fens. This is indicative of the way in which views of opiate use were coloured by the social and class setting.

Behind this was a desire to remould popular culture into a more acceptable form and a critique of the basic pattern of child rearing by the working-classes. Using opium as a scapegoat led to criticism of its use being diverted away from the realities of the urban environment to the individual failings of working mothers. The uses of opium by adults and for children in the rest of society went unremarked or were viewed more tolerantly. The writings of Thomas De Quincey and Samuel Taylor Coleridge, both frequent users, attracted a great deal of attention after 1830 and by drawing attention to the habit may have led to a gradual change towards a harsher, more restrictive attitude. [36]

How did leisure develop after 1850?

There was a strong impression among some contemporaries that the attempt to abolish certain pastimes had done more harm than good because it had resulted in the working-classes being left with very few outlets for leisure, other than those of a debased kind. Drunkenness, violence and fornication, it was claimed, were on the increase. This alarm that moral standards were declining combined with the fear that the social stability of the country was being undermined. The MP Robert Slaney, argued that it was the duty of those governing the working-classes to provide suitable alternative recreations for those people who otherwise 'will fly to demagogues and dangerous causes.'[37] By the 1830s, there was a growing sense among reforming and Evangelical groups that, though the working-classes seemed to have an inbuilt disposition towards spending any free time they had in sexual excesses, gambling and drinking. The middle- and upper-classes were not entirely free from blame or responsibility for this situation.

There were several reasons for this feeling of guilt. Urbanisation and enclosures led to a loss of public open spaces and footpaths and hence restricted the scope of working-class leisure time activities. As a result, they were driven from comparatively healthy outdoor pastimes towards the numerous temptations offered by drinking houses. It was not until the opening of the Birkenhead and Manchester parks in the 1840s that serious consideration was given to

---

[36] See, Morrison, Robert, 'Opium-eaters and magazine wars: De Quincey and Coleridge in 1821', *Victorian Periodicals Review*, Vol. 30, (1997), pp. 27-40.

[37] See, Richards, Paul, 'R. A. Slaney, the industrial town, and early Victorian social policy', *Social History*, Vol. 4, (1979), pp. 85-101.

setting up places of amusement within the parks themselves for the playing of games and sports.[38] It was not until the 1850s and 1860s and in some places the 1870s, that municipal parks were established in most provincial towns and cities. Nearly all the places of cultural improvement from which the working-classes could benefit--art galleries, botanical gardens, libraries and museums--were denied to them, either because they could not afford the subscriptions or entrance fees or because they were, if not positively excluded, at least not welcomed. Both the Museums Act of 1845 and the Public Libraries Act of 1850 gave local authorities permission to build museums and libraries out of public funds.[39] By 1860, however, only 28 library authorities had been set up. The lower classes had been influenced and harmed by the lax manners and moral of their social superiors. It was the duty of the rich, Hannah More and others argued, to set a wholesome example through their own behaviour and this was not being done. Leisure was often associated with idleness, so while it was recognised that spare time could bring benefits its dangers were also acknowledged. In a society where the gospel of work was so deeply ingrained, it was perhaps inevitable that leisure time should be regarded with suspicion.

Leisure requires 'free' time. After 1800, there was probably an extension of working hours with factories imposing a twelve or thirteen hour day as opposed to the ten-hour day of pre-industrial

---

[38] See, for example, Elliott, Paul, 'The Derby Arboretum (1840): the first specially designed municipal public park in Britain', *Midland History*, Vol. 26, (2001), pp. 144-176, Taylor, A., "Commons-stealers, land-grabbers and jerry-builders': space, popular radicalism and the politics of public access in London, 1848-80', *International Review of Social History*, Vol. 40, (1995), pp. 383-407, and MacGill, Lynn, 'The emergence of public parks in Keighley, West Yorkshire, 1887-93: leisure, pleasure or reform?', *Garden History*, Vol. 35, (2007), pp. 146-159.

[39] On libraries, see, Hewitt, Martin, 'Extending the public library 1850–1930', in Black, Alistair, and Hoare, Peter, (eds.), *The Cambridge history of libraries in Britain and Ireland: Vol. 3: 1850-2000*, (Cambridge University Press), 2006, pp. 72-81, Peatling, Gary K., 'Public libraries and national identity in Britain, 1850-1919', *Library History*, Vol. 20, (2004), pp. 33-47, Johnman, W. A. P., and Kendall, H., 'A Commission Appointed to Inquire into the Condition and Workings of Free Libraries of Various Towns in England (1869)', *Library History*, Vol. 17, (2001), pp. 223-238, Fletcher, J., 'Public libraries, legislation and educational provision in nineteenth-century England', *Journal of Educational Administration & History*, Vol. 28, (1996), pp. 97-113, and Sturges, Paul, 'The public library and its readers 1850-1900', *Library History*, Vol. 12, (1996), pp. 183-200.

society. [40] Coalminers, whose hours in the eighteenth century were relatively short, six to eight hours a day, were by 1842 nearly all working a twelve hour day with only short breaks for refreshment. Agricultural workers too suffered an increase in hours in the 1830s. In mining, agriculture, domestic service and the 'dishonourable' sections of the artisan trades and in all domestic work, the eighteenth century norm had been breached and hours were longer. After 1850, the campaign for the nine-hour day started in the building trade, but success was limited until the economic boom of the early 1870s when most organised trades were able to breakthrough to a 54 hour week. Despite pressure in the 1890s, reduction in hours nationally was insignificant until 1919 and 1920 when seven million workers obtained reductions. Collective bargaining was unquestionably the chief means by which hours of work were reduced while legislation such in 1874 reducing the hours of factory textile workers to 56 and a half, in 1902 further reducing a week for factory workers by an hour and in 1909 restricting underground work in the coalmines to eight hours, had only a marginal effects on the overall national statistics. [41]

There had been a sharp decline in the number of holidays that were recognised and observed since the seventeenth century. They continued to be observed, with some regional variation, around Christmas or New Year, at Easter and Whitsuntide, at the local fair, feast or wake, and to some extent on such national days as the 5 November and Shrove Tuesday. There were as yet no holidays with pay. The Bank Holidays Acts of 1871 and 1875 were not the first legislative recognition of holidays but they were the first in which the state's intervention was widely recognised and applauded. [42] In the late-nineteenth and early-twentieth centuries employers increasing conceded holidays to their workforce. Brunner Mond, Lever Bros., the Gas Light and Coke Company, the London and North-Western Railway Company and the Royal Dockyards had done so by the 1890s. In 1897, the Amalgamated Society of Railway Servants negotiated one-week's paid holiday after five years' service. Other unionised workers, in coal and iron, for example, were putting forward similar claims before 1914.

---

[40] Hopkins, E., 'Working hours and the conditions during the Industrial Revolution: a re-appraisal', *Economic History Review*, 2nd series, Vol. 35, (1982), pp. 52-66.

[41] Johnson, Paul A., and Zaidi, Asghar, 'Work over the life course', in ibid, Crafts, Nicholas F. R., Gazeley, Ian, and Newell, Andrew, (eds.), *Work and pay in twentieth-century Britain*, pp. 98-116.

[42] See, Smart, Eynon, 'Bank holidays...and much else', *History Today*, Vol. 21, (12), (1971), pp. 870-876.

The hours of work for the working-classes are relatively easy to establish in comparison to those of the middle-classes. There are no national statistics and only the most scattered and perhaps unrepresentative data. Three trends may be distinguished. Within the professions and the civil service hours were relatively short and imprecise until the late-nineteenth century, perhaps six hours a day. In the private sector, clerks worked rather longer hours, generally 40 hours per week in five days. Among businessmen, the days of long hours occurred in the first half of the nineteenth century and by 1900 they too began to internalise the 9 to 5 norm. Finally, at the lower end of the middle-classes, amongst shop-workers, hours were notoriously long and remained so. After over fifty years of effort to curtail hours, a House of Lords Select Committee in 1901 could only confirm that many shops were working 80 or 90 hours a week. Pressure from the Shop-Assistants Twelve Hours' Labour League, founded in 1881, and from the Early Closing Association did result in some improvement but the shift towards a legislative solution was only very partially successful. The 1911 Act did, however, enact a half-day holiday. As far as annual holidays were concerned the middle-class workers undoubtedly had the advantage and in 1875 the Civil Service Inquiry Commission indicated that clerks working for insurance companies, solicitors, banks, railway companies and the civil service were at getting at least two week's holiday a year. They had achieved this some seventy-five years before the bulk of manual workers.

How did people spend their leisure time?

The choice of how to spend leisure time can be seen as distinctly personal. However, boundaries of class, of gender, of age and of geography were likely to be reproduced in leisure and may have reinforced those boundaries and not merely passively reflected them. The issue is not one of leisure but of different leisure cultures that were not hermetically sealed against each other but overlapped and influenced each other. Nor were any of these cultures ever static; they were constantly changing, both in themselves and in relation to other cultures.

The phrase 'the leisured or leisure classes' can be traced back to the 1840s and may well have existed earlier. In 1868, Anthony Trollope was confident that England possessed:

> ...the largest and wealthiest leisure class that any country, ancient or modern, ever boasted. [43]

---

[43] Trollope, A., (ed.), *British Sports and Pastimes*, (Virtue & Co.), 1868, p. 18.

At the end of the century Thorstein Veblen subjected them to trenchant analysis in his 1899 *The Theory of the Leisure Class*.[44] He argued:

> The fundamental reason for the development of a leisure class was that only in conspicuous leisure and in conspicuous consumption could the wealthy achieve the status they sought. [45]

The critical word is 'conspicuous'. Leisure for the leisure class demanded that it be seen both by fellow members of the class and by an envious or admiring excluded public. Display was fundamental to its social position and it is difficult to determine whether there was any separation of work and leisure within the class. At a national level, the leisure class could be most readily observed in the London Season and until the 1880s, this was a political as well as a social occasion. In the circumscribed political world, the numbers involved were relatively small, perhaps 500 families compared to the 4,000 families who participated in the more social London Season of the late-nineteenth century. Until then entry to London 'Society' was carefully guarded and its social functions were mostly private. Thereafter, it became easier to but one's way into 'Society'. [46] This reflected a change in the nature of the leisure class. It became less easy to identify a class whose members manifestly did not work. By contrast, public attention began to focus on the plutocracy whose male members worked, but so successfully that they could spend their fortunes in their leisure. The London Season formed one clearly demarcated phase in the annual life of the leisure class; the remainder of the year was centred on the country houses in a mixture of activities some of which were thoroughly exclusive while others entailed a carefully calculated patronage of more popular occasions. [47] Shooting was the

---

[44] Tilman, Rick, *Thorstein Veblen and His Critics, 1891-1963: Conservative, Liberal, and Radical Perspectives*, (Princeton University Press), 1992, is a good critique of Veblen's ideas.

[45] Cunningham, H., 'Leisure and culture', in ibid, Thompson, F. M. L., (ed.), *The Cambridge Social History of Britain, 1750-1950*, Vol. 2, p. 290.

[46] On this see Pullar, Philippa, *Gilded Butterflies: The Rise and Fall of the London Season*, (Hamish Hamilton), 1978, and Davidoff, L., *The Best Circles: Society, Etiquette and the Season*, (Taylor & Francis), 1973.

[47] Mandler, Peter, *The fall and rise of the stately home*, (Yale University Press), 1997, Sykes, Christopher Simon, *The big house: the story of a country house and its family*, (HarperCollins), 2004, Gardiner, Juliet, *The Edwardian country house*, (Channel 4 Books), 2002, and Wilson, Richard, and Mackley, Alan, *Creating paradise: the building of the English country house 1660-1880*, (Hambledon), 2000.

most exclusive of sports while foxhunting was, in ideology at least, open to peer and peasant. In the late-nineteenth century, as in London Society, the plutocracy began to supplant the aristocracy as its leaders.

From the mid-eighteenth century the London Season had its provincial counterparts. There existed in the larger provincial towns, perhaps particularly in southern England the 'urban gentry' who in a modest way provided the lower echelons of the leisure class. After 1830, such people living on income from capital tended to gravitate towards the spas and more select seaside resorts. They were disproportionately female and old. In contrast to the national leisure class, there was neither firm structure to their year nor any flamboyance in their leisure. They maintained their status by careful observance of formalities that helped to distinguish them from those who had to work for a living. In the late-nineteenth century a new category, the retired, began to fuse with this older, modest, provincial leisure class, to form a substantial proportion of the population of the southern and coastal towns in which they congregated.

By contrast, urban middle-class culture was distinctively provincial. Until 1800, it was a culture that was more obviously urban than middle-class, expressing many of the values of the urban gentry, who themselves, may be considered as part of the leisure class and its aristocratic way of life. It was inherently social rather than intellectual. Its existence can be documented from figures of theatre building: only ten purpose-built theatres were erected in the larger provincial towns between 1736 and 1760 but more than a hundred were built between the 1760s and the 1840s. [48] The music festivals in the provinces are another indicator. In London it was not until the 1830s that the patronage and market for classical music passed from the aristocracy to the upper middle-classes; the provinces can be said to have led the way. [49] The new culture was visible too in the classical style of its architecture and in the design of squares and boulevards that were emphatically the territory of the aristocracy. For this culture was unashamedly exclusive.

---

[48] See, Garlick, Görel, 'Theatre outside London', and Schoch, Richard W., 'Theatre and mid-Victorian society', in Donohue, Joseph, (ed.), *The Cambridge history of British theatre: Vol. 2, 1660 to 1895*, (Cambridge University Press), 2004, pp. 165-182, 331-351.

[49] Dale, Catherine, 'The Provincial Musical Festival in Nineteenth-century England: A Case Study of Bridlington', in Cowgill, Rachel, and Holman, Peter, (eds.), *Music in the British provinces, 1690-1914*, (Ashgate), 2007), pp. 325-348, and Sprittles, Joseph, 'Leeds musical festivals', *The Thoresby Miscellany*, Vol. 13, (1959-63), pp. 200-270, provide good case studies.

In the early-nineteenth century, the intellectual dimension of this urban culture became more pronounced. So also did its masculinity.[50] Like-minded men turned typically to the club or society as a forum within which they pursued their interests. If this culture is projected forward into the second quarter of the nineteenth century, its leaders can be seen turning away from a provincial pursuit of high culture towards a direct concern with the social and political problems of their own towns: they formed statistical societies and diffused useful knowledge. They became a culture anxious to influence the ways of life of the working-classes from their narrow but powerful middle-class bridgehead and were increasingly concerned with the supply of leisure to others than with the enjoyment of it themselves.

The emergence of this male, intellectual, socially concerned and distinctly middle-class urban culture marked part of the wider challenge to the lack of seriousness and the frivolity of the urban gentry. Leisure activities such as theatre-going or novel reading or cards or even cricket, now had to be scrutinised to see if they served any purpose that God, rather than Society, would approve. Many such activities ceased to be 'respectable'. The sociability that had been so highly prized in the eighteenth century ceased to be a virtue. The attraction of a life lived in public within a defined and exclusive society gave way to an emphasis on domesticity and away from frank enjoyment of leisure towards a more calculating performance of duty, towards a 'rational' view of recreation. This 'call to seriousness' began to be relaxed from the mid-nineteenth century. In the 1860s and 1870s the press and pulpit endlessly discussed the legitimacy of this or that activity and of leisure in general. The official view was that the purpose of leisure was justified not for its own sake but for its ulterior purpose of re-creating men for work. Under this umbrella, however, more and more activities became legitimate and were doubtless enjoyed for their own sake. It was in physical activity, however, that the change was greatest. Middle-class urban culture, especially the public schools, was able from 1850 to transform the nature and image of sport. Sport encouraged qualities of leadership; it took boys' minds off sex and was the best training for war. [51] As rules were drawn up

---

[50] Danahay, Martin A., *Gender at work in Victorian culture: literature, art and masculinity*, (Ashgate), 2005.
[51] Lowerson, John, *Sport and the English middle classes, 1870-1914*, (Manchester University Press), 1993, Huggins, Mike, 'Second-class citizens? English middle-class culture and sport, 1850-1910: a reconsideration', *International Journal of the History of Sport*, Vol. 17, (2000), pp. 1-35, and Lowerson, John, 'Sport and British Middle-Class Culture: Some Issues of Representation and Identity before 1940', *International Journal of the History of Sport*, Vol. 21, (2004), pp. 34-49.

and enforced, sport became increasingly an analogy for middle-class male life: a competitive struggle within agreed parameters. The middle-classes not only imposed a new ideology on sport; they were also the chief beneficiaries of the expansion of facilities. Up to 1914:

...the sporting revolution belonged, in the main, to the middle-classes in their leafy suburbs. [52]

Middle-class urban leisure culture was transformed. The eighteenth century urban pursuit of pleasure turned in the nineteenth century into an anxious scrutiny of the legitimacy of particular pursuits and to a corresponding emphasis on domesticity rather than sociability. Gradually there was a relaxation, but it occurred within the safe boundaries of school and suburb. Indeed the most obvious and continuing thrust of the culture was towards social exclusivity. Within the wide middle-class boundary, lines to demarcate status were carefully drawn and upper and lower middle-classes would never meet in leisure. What they had in common was an attitude to leisure and a view of its social function: in leisure people could meet others of similar social status in environments, whether public or private, that were in accordance with the canons of respectability of the day.

Artisan leisure culture was based on a particular type of work and its rise and decline paralleled that of the artisans. In the first half of the nineteenth century it flourished, but as artisans were absorbed into the structure of capitalist industry they began to lose the characteristic feature of their culture: independence. Independence in the workplace was paralleled in the leisure culture where it took the form of a rejection of any patronage from above. Artisans made their own goods and also made their own culture. If the workplace was one factor leading to independence, masculinity and age were others; this was a leisure culture of adult males. Women were admitted rarely and then only on sufferance and the young apprentices, who had once had a culture of their own, were now firmly subordinated. In Birmingham, artisans formed debating societies and clubs and attended the theatre. [53] The friendly societies and the trade union both had their strongest roots among the artisans, and they were instinctively radical in their politics. But it was not an expansive

---

[52] Meller, H. E., *Leisure and the Changing City 1870-1914*, (Routledge), 1976, p. 236.
[53] See Money, J., *Experience and Identity: Birmingham and the West Midlands 1760-1800*, (Manchester University Press), 1977, pp. 80-120, Tholfsen, T. R., 'The artisan and the culture of early Victorian Birmingham', *University of Birmingham Historical Journal*, Vol. 4, (1954), pp. 146-166.

culture and had no missionary zeal to spread its way of life more widely. By 1850, the heavy drinking artisan culture was restricted to certain trades and regions and a more respectable, even family-based, culture began to replace it. In perception the artisan was now becoming the 'labour aristocrat', a respectable, hard-working member of society who took his pleasures seriously. In Edinburgh, the clubs that artisans joined for horticulture, golf and bowling and their participation in the patriotic Volunteer Force, suggested a new conformity to the values and norms of middle-classes. These clubs, however, retained their own independence. Artisan culture may have become more respectable, but it was a respectability generated from within the class and for the class not one imposed from outside. [54]

Urban popular culture in the nineteenth and early-twentieth centuries developed three important dimensions. It was a mass culture that permeated across communities. There were activities that people paid to attend as spectators, audience or readers. This included theatres, circuses and fairs and later in the century, music halls, professional football, horseracing, the popular press, seaside excursions and cinemas. [55] This was a commercial leisure in which the size of crowds with consequent financial returns was important to pay the stars and professionals. People also generated leisure activities within their own communities. Some were commercial, others voluntary but activities were of and for the people. The pub played a pivotal role and was the location for much more than the consumption of alcohol. The activities included brass bands, mass choirs, flower shows and the allotments that provided the basis for them, fishing and pigeon fancying. Competitiveness was one of the hallmarks of this type of culture: pub against pub, club against club; stars and professionals were absent; there was little formal separation of performers and spectators; and, the participants were mainly adult males. Finally, women focused not on activities, but on space, in particular the space of the home and the street. Women's leisure was not seen as leisure but something that accompanied work. In its more social aspect, in the street, its most typical form was chatting, was not distinguished from other forms of talk and was a culture heavily based on a sense of neighbourhood.

After 1800, a print culture developed that complemented and eventually superseded the existing oral popular culture. Events were

---

[54] Beaven, Brad, *Leisure, Citizenship and Working-class Men in Britain, 1850-1945*, (Manchester University Press), 2005, pp. 16-124.
[55] See, Russell, Dave, 'Popular entertainment, 1776-1895', in ibid, Donohue, Joseph, (ed.), *The Cambridge history of British theatre: Vol. 2, 1660 to 1895*, pp. 369-387.

advertised and news was conveyed in print. The expanding newspaper press of the eighteenth century had reached a largely middle-class audience primarily because of cost, but during the first half of the nineteenth century, a new literate popular culture emerged grounded in the radical and often 'unstamped' press and in the growth of melodramatic 'penny dreadfuls'. [56] It is difficult to establish an accurate profile of the readership of this expanding quantity of print by age, gender and class. Men, until after 1870, had a higher rate of literacy than women and they may have had easier access to literature. They were probably the main readers of the popular Sunday newspapers that by 1850 were read by one adult in twenty; for Sunday was much more a day of leisure for men than women. [57] Sporting literature was a genre of popular literature, and with its emphasis on 'manly' sports, also reached a dominantly male audience. Similarly, participation in and spectating of commercialised sports was largely, though not exclusively, male. Horseracing was immensely popular despite attempts to control its spread by law.

After 1850, figures for attendance become more reliable and their general trend is upwards. Music hall was the first new form of entertainment to make its mark. [58] Charles Morton's opening of the Canterbury Hall in Lambeth in 1851 was to gain him immediate and

---

[56] On the press Read, D., *Press and People 1790-1850: Opinion in Three English Cities*, (Edward Arnold), 1961, is excellent on the impact of the middle-class press while Hollis, P., *The Pauper Press: A Study in Working-Class Radicalism of the 1830s*, (Oxford University Press), 1970, Wickwar, W. H., *The Struggle for the Freedom of the Press 1819-1832*, (Allen & Unwin), 1928, and Weiner, J., *The War of the Unstamped: the movement to repeal the British newspaper tax, 1830-1836*, (Cornell University Press), 1969, on the popular press.

[57] See, Kamper, D. S., 'Popular Sunday newspapers, respectability and working-class culture in late Victorian Britain', in Huggins, Mike, and Mangan, James Anthony, (eds.), *Disreputable pleasures: less virtuous Victorians at play*, (Cass), 2004, pp. 83-102, and 'Popular Sunday newspapers, class, and the struggle for respectability in late Victorian Britain', Hewitt, Martin, (ed.), *Unrespectable recreations*, (Leeds Centre for Victorian Studies), 2001, pp. 81-94.

[58] On music generally, see, Russell, Dave, *Popular Music in England 1840-1914: A Social History*, (Manchester University Press), 1987, 2nd edition, 1997. Bratton, J. S., (ed.), *Music hall: performance and style*, (Open University Press), 1986, Till, Nicholas, '"First-Class Evening Entertainments": Spectacle and Social Control in a Mid-Victorian Music Hall', *New Theatre Quarterly*, Vol. 20, (2004), pp. 3-18, Scott, Derek B., 'Music and social class in Victorian London', *Urban History*, Vol. 29, (2002), pp. 60-73, and Kift, Dagmar, *The Victorian music hall: culture, class and conflict*, (Cambridge University Press), 1996.

retrospective attention, but there were important precedents in the saloon theatres that had flourished since the 1830s and in the 'music halls' that already existed in the larger provincial towns. What is striking about the 1850s and 1860s was the multiplicity of forms in which people could experience what was eventually to become standardised as 'music hall'. The focus on songs has distracted attention from the range of entertainment on offer in the halls; dance, acrobatics, mime drama and clowning as well as the occasional associated facility a museum, art gallery or zoo, were part of the 'variety' of the halls from the beginning. The emergence of music halls that were architecturally similar to theatres came relatively late during the second great wave of music hall building in the late 1880s and 1890s when chains of ownership were becoming common. It was in the 1890s, too, that there was a partially successful attempt to win middle-class audiences. Cinema can be seen as superseding music hall as the most popular form of mass entertainment, but there was a long period of overlap. Music hall was indeed the commercial cinema's first home. From 1906, onwards, however, cinemas acquired their own homes, some 4,000 of them by 1914. [59] There are no accurate figures for admission before 1934 but an average of 7 or 8 million a week is plausible in the years immediately before 1914 or 400 million admissions a year.

The seaside holiday represented escape from the city urban popular culture was also transposed to the coast. The seaside holiday was not something initiated by the middle-classes and imitated by the working-classes. [60] Escape to the sea by workers preceded the coming of the railway. The major increase in demand, however, came only in the late-nineteenth century and it was only then that the seaside holiday became a recognisable part of urban popular culture though there were regional variations. The week at the seaside that many working-class Lancastrians had come to enjoy by the 1880s was unusual and elsewhere the norm was the day trip. Demand expanded

---

[59] Much of the research on early cinema is in the form of studies of particular localities or entrepreneurs but see, Hiley, Nicholas, '"Nothing more than a 'craze'": cinema building in Britain from 1909 to 1914', in Higson, Andrew, (ed.), *Young and innocent? The cinema in Britain, 1896-1930*, (University of Exeter Press), 2002, pp. 111-127, and McKernan, Luke, 'A fury for seeing: Cinema, audience and leisure in London in 1913', *Early Popular Visual Culture*, Vol. 6, (2008), pp. 271-280.

[60] Walton, John K., 'The demand for working-class seaside holidays in Victorian England', *Economic History Review*, 2nd series, Vol. 34, (1981), pp. 249-265, and 'The seaside and the holiday crowd', in Toulmin, Vanessa, Russell, Patrick, and Popple, Simon, (eds.), *The lost world of Mitchell and Kenyon: Edwardian Britain on film*, (BFI Publishing), 2004, pp.158-168.

with the number of visitors to Blackpool rising from 1 million in 1883 to two million ten years later and to 4 million in 1914. [61]

Spectating at professional sport was already common by 1850 but the next half century saw a shift in popularity. Rowing ceased to be a major spectator sport and amateur athletics never achieved the crowds of the professional pedestrianism that it replaced. Football, on the other hand, attracted numbers that rose from the late-nineteenth century to 1914 and beyond.[62] The average football cup tie attendance rose from 6,000 in 1888-1889 to 12,000 in 1895-1896 and to over 20,000 in the first round in 1903. In 1908-1909, in the English First Division 6 million people watched matches, with an average crowd size of 16,000. It was dominantly a male pastime and was regionally concentrated in the Lowlands of Scotland, northern and Midland England and to a lesser extent London.

The pub had close ties to this commercialised aspect of urban popular culture and was the main location of what was by far the largest single item of leisure expenditure, alcohol. It was itself a commercial undertaking, increasingly under the control of the major brewers. Despite this, the pub also managed to be the main organising centre for the self-generating culture. Publicans were often sponsors of activities that they viewed simply with an eye to profit. In addition, the pub offered a space for socialising and clubs of all kinds met in pubs. The community generated by the pub expressed itself in the annual outing. Above all, within the pub men could take part in a range of competitive activities: darts, draughts, bowls and card playing and gambling of all kinds. Participant competitiveness was a key feature of urban popular culture and its significance is underplayed in accounts that focus on music hall, cinema and spectating generally. As communications improved many of these competitions became regional and national. Brass bands, for example, were competitive from their beginnings on a significant scale in the 1840s. [63]

The urban popular culture focused on the home and the street offered different kinds of satisfaction to different sections of the

---

[61] Walton, John K., 'Resorts and Regions: Blackpool, Southport, Lancashire and Beyond', in Brown, Alyson, (ed.), *Historical perspectives on Social Identities*, (Cambridge Scholars), 2006, pp. 7-22.

[62] See, Taylor, Matthew, *The Association Game: a history of British football*, (Pearson Longman), 2008, and Gibbons, Philip, *Association Football in Victorian England: a history of the game from 1863 to 1900*, (Minerva), 2001.

[63] Herbert, Trevor, (ed.), *The British Brass Band: a musical and social history*, (Oxford University Press), 2000.

population. [64] The dominant masculinity of the world of participant competition had parallels among women. Most working-class women were confined to the home and the street and there is increasing evidence that they created their own separate culture there and was a key component of the 'traditional working-class culture' from 1870 to 1950. This female network of support was based on the separation of male and female world after marriage. Popular urban leisure was to a considerable degree fractured along lines of gender.

Who supplied leisure and why?

Leisure activities were made available in four main ways and as a result provided employment in leisure. The state, whether at local or national level, created a legal framework and acted as a direct supplier. In the first half of the nineteenth century, its main concern was to control supply through licensing, but later its role was more positive and it became a direct supplier of such facilities as parks, libraries and playing fields. One reason why the state intervened was prestige that came from supporting both the production of high culture in the present and the preservation of the high culture of the past. By the 1830s, state aid was necessary to maintain or at least subsidise museums throughout the country and from the 1860s governments drew back from subsidising high culture. Public funding required more justification than the royal patronage that dominated support for culture in the first half of the nineteenth century. The public could not be denied right of access. In 1810, admission to the British Museum was made free resulting in an increase in the number of visitors from 128,000 in 1824-1825 to 230,000 in 1835 and 826,000 by 1846. It is easy to exaggerate the amount of state supply. Central government provided a legal framework within which museums or libraries could be built and run out of the rates but it was as concerned to protect ratepayers as to encourage the provision of a facility. Until 1914, libraries were largely the result of philanthropy than from the rates and were within reach of only 60 per cent of the population. The same was true of museums and parks. Local authorities played an increasingly important role and shared the same motives as central government: a concern for prestige in relation to other local authorities and concerns about social order. [65] A more compelling

---

[64] Johnes, Martin, 'Pigeon Racing and Working-class Culture in Britain, *c.* 1870-1950', *Cultural and Social History*, Vol. 4, (2007), pp. 361-383, examines one aspect of urban community leisure.

[65] See, for example, Morrison, John, 'Victorian municipal patronage: the foundation and management of Glasgow Corporation Galleries 1854-1888', *Journal of the History of Collections*, Vol. 8, (1996), pp. 93-102.

motive was to stimulate prosperity. Seaside resorts led the way after 1875, investing in sea defences, promenades, piers, golf courses and concert halls in an attempt to improve their attractiveness to potential visitors.

A major element in the state's supply of leisure was its concern to regulate the use of space. The home, as a private space, was beyond its physical reach. Licensing the sale of alcohol was the state's major intervention and was intended to preserve public order and provide some means of monitoring the leisure of the poorer sections of society. [66] Public parks, museums and libraries were supported precisely because they were public, open to scrutiny and controlled by bye-laws. The space provided by theatre, music hall and cinema was potentially more dangerous, but the power or threat of licensing of both building and activity made them relatively acceptable. [67] The censorship of both plays and films ensured that public entertainment adhered to acceptable moral and political values. Fire regulations, for example those imposed on music halls in 1878, not only reduced the dangers of fire, but drove many of the smaller, less salubrious halls out of business. In the cinema, the industry formally established its own form of censorship in 1912 with the British Board of Film Censors. [68] In horse-racing, by contrast, the government banned off-course betting in the Street Betting Act of 1906. [69]

There was much self-made leisure, whether communal or associational or personal and family. In its communal or associational forms it was a major means of supply of leisure for the middle-class urban culture, typically in the form of subscription concerts and libraries and of clubs, for example, for chess. In Bradford in 1900, there were 30 choral societies, 20 brass bands, an amateur orchestra, six concertina bands and a team of hand-bell ringers. In Rochdale, and elsewhere, the churches and chapels were crucial suppliers of

---

[66] Mutch, Alistair, 'Shaping the Public House, 1850-1950: Business Strategies, State Regulation and Social History', *Cultural and Social History*, Vol. 1, (2004), pp. 179-200.

[67] See, Ley, A. J., *A history of building control in England and Wales, 1840-1990*, (RICS Books), 2000, and Gaskell, S. Martin., *Building control: national legislation and the introduction of local bye-laws in Victorian England,* (British Association for Local History), 1983. Harper, R. H., *Victorian building regulations: summary tables of the principal English building acts and model by-laws, 1840-1914,* (Mansell), 1985, shows the extent of regulation.

[68] Robertson, J. C., *The British Board of Film Censors: film censorship in Britain, 1896-1950*, (Croom Helm), 1985, pp. 1-18.

[69] Dixon, David, *From Prohibition to Regulation: Bookmaking, Anti-gambling, and the Law*, (Oxford University Press), 1991.

leisure up to 1914 with their young men's and ladies' classes, their debating societies and numerous other activities. [70] Much leisure within the family relied on commercial sources of supply, of games, pianos, books and a wide array of hobbies. In music and hobbies in particular, there was considerable activity in working-class homes: by 1910 there was one piano for every fifteen people, far more than the middle-classes could absorb. [71]

Voluntary bodies and philanthropists were key agents in the supply of leisure for others. They were less single-minded than the state, but as with the latter the supply of leisure fell into two groups, a negative controlling one and a positive supply one. The Vice Society (1802), the Royal Society for the Prevention of Cruelty to Animals (1824), the Lord's Day Observance Society (1831), numerous temperance and teetotal societies and the National Council for Public Morals (1911) were in the first group. The second group included philanthropists and employers who funded parks, libraries, brass bands and football clubs, the Mechanics' Institutes, the Pleasant Sunday Afternoon Association, the Girls' Friendly Society (1874) and the Boys' Brigade (1883). What united these two approaches was a concern to direct and mould other people's leisure by control of some sort over its supply.

The hope of weaning people away from bad habits by the provision of respectable alternatives initially became important during the 1830s. The solution was 'rational recreation', quiet and elevating pursuits, modelled on the best contemporary middle-class practice. As a result, not only would the bad habits themselves disappear or at least diminish, but in the process people, largely men of good will from different classes would meet fraternally and come to understand each other's point of view. The amount of leisure provided was enormous. Parks, libraries and similar institutions were frequently the outcome of philanthropy. In Glasgow where ratepayers on three occasions in the second half of the century refused to fund a public library, Stephen Mitchell, a tobacco magnate, left £70,000 for a library that opened in 1877. In Manchester, T. C. Horsfall raised the funds for an Art Museum opened in 1884. Bristol acquired a municipally owned museum, library and art gallery between 1895 and 1905, all through private funding. Much church and chapel activity was

---

[70] See, for example, Cusack, Janet, 'Bible classes and boats: church and chapel rowing clubs at Plymouth and Devonport in the early twentieth century', *Mariner's Mirror*, Vol. 87, (2001), pp. 63-75.

[71] McKibbin, R., 'Work and hobbies in Britain 1880-1950', in Winter, J. M., (ed.), *The working class in modern British history: essays in honour of Henry Pelling*, (Cambridge University Press), 1983, pp. 127-146.

organised from above for people deemed to be in need. Of these, the most important were the young. The real problem arose when they left Sunday Schools and it was partly to keep a hold on these children that William Smith established the Boys' Brigade in Glasgow in 1883. Thereafter uniformed youth movements, particularly for boys, attracted a high proportion of the youth population. [72] The Boys' Brigade had its denominational rivals and from 1908 faced serious competition from the Boy Scouts. By 1914, between a quarter and a third of the available youth population was enrolled in a youth movement. The provision of leisure probably served females less well than males, doubtless in part because the former were thought to pose less of a problem. The Girls' Friendly Society, formed in 1874, was predominantly rural and Anglican in outlook and many of its members were young domestic servants. Two further organisations came into being to meet their needs as they grew older: the Mothers' Union founded in 1885 expanded to 7,000 branches by 1911 and the Women's Institutes begun in 1915.

Finally, leisure was supplied on a commercial basis and played an increasingly significant role in the supply of leisure between 1830 and 1914. In 1830, it was provided largely for the middle-classes but had diffused into the working-classes by the 1870s. There was a shift in the nineteenth century from the patron-client relationship that characterised the employment of professionals in cricket and music in 1800 to an employment relationship more akin to that of the industrial world. This was in part because of the seasonal nature of much of such employment, but also because of the lack of control over entry to leisure jobs. The numbers employed were growing, certainly after 1870. Between 1871 and 1911, the population of England and Wales rose on average by 0.8 per cent per year and the number employed in the arts and entertainment by 4.7 per cent per year. The number of actors and actresses peaked in 1911 at over 19,000, having quadrupled in the previous thirty years. [73] In nearly every section of the leisure industries there were attempts to raise the status of entertainers. The outcome was the achievement of stardom for the select few while the rank and file had to be content with wages at roughly semi-skilled level. The best actors and actresses were already getting £150 per week in the 1830s. In 1890, at least ten jockeys were earning £5,000 per season and the better professional

---

[72] See, Springhall, John, *Youth, empire and society: British youth movements, 1883-1940*, (Croom Helm), 1977, for an excellent summary of developments with a detailed bibliography.
[73] Pécastaing-Boissière, Muriel, *Les actrices victoriennes: Entre marginalité et conformisme*, (L'Harmattan), 2003.

cricketers were earning £275 per year. Between 1906 and 1914, the wages of performing musicians doubled reaching £200 per year. The best professional footballers could not earn high wages: the Football Association set the maximum wages at £208 per year but only a minority got that amount. On the whole, however, complaints about wages and conditions of service within the entertainment and sports world were muted. The lure of acceptance as a profession, the hope of stardom for the individual and the sense that to be in entertainment was unlike any other job, for the most part curtailed any open conflict.

The importance of leisure in giving people a sense of national and social identity is matched by a greater significance placed on leisure in people's individual life-choices. Leisure preference is normally assumed to have been a feature of pre-industrial society and could not survive the greater emphasis on consumerism of an industrialised society. Between 1830 and 1914, as hours of leisure grew longer, leisure activities took on a more central role in people's lives. 'Rational recreationalists' wanted to 'control' what people, and especially the working-classes, did in their spare time and they were successful, to a degree, in mitigating the worst excesses of pre-industrial leisure with its potential violence and cruelty. Yet the persistence of large-scale spectating, especially of football and horse-racing showed the limits of that success. Alcohol and gambling remained key working-class leisure activities and, despite increased controls by the state, continued to play a major part in defining working-class consciousness throughout this period. Leisure was in 1914, as it had been in 1830, largely male-dominated and escapist.

17 Government

It is not, perhaps, unreasonable to conclude, that a pure and perfect democracy is a thing not attainable by man, constituted as he is of contending elements of vice and virtue, and ever mainly influenced by the predominant principle of self-interest. [1]

𝕴n what ways did Government influence the lives of citizens in late-eighteenth century England, their behaviour and conditions of life according to which principles and with what effects? [2] A central assumption was that the government's role was at most strictly limited and that it should not and could not determine the structure and working of society. Its role was to provide a firmly established and clearly understood framework within which society could very largely run itself. This view of the state came increasingly under pressure when faced by the problems created by political, social and economic change from the 1780s. Britain possessed highly effective central government institutions, but unlike other European countries did not develop a strong and professional bureaucracy with powerful interests of its own until after the 1850s. The critical issue was the relationship between the state and the individual: when should the state intervene to regulate people's lives and when should it not? The Victorian central state involved itself in the lives of its citizens in many ways and had a clear vision of its role, but its approach was often indirect and discreet. A range of buffer institutions, both official and voluntary, developed between the central state and the citizen. [3]

The belief in local responsibility for local needs was strong and local government not intrusively controlled by central government. Closely associated with it was the conviction that all members of the community possessed certain rights, enforceable at law. However

---

[1] Tytler, Lord Woodhouselee, Alexander Fraser, *Universal History: From the Creation of the World to the Beginning of the Eighteenth Century*, Vol. 1, (Petridge and Company), 1854, p. 216

[2] The extension of the role of the state is best approached through Corrigan, P., and Sayer, D., *The Great Arch: English State Formation as Cultural Revolution*, (Basil Blackwell), 1985. It can be read in conjunction with Poggi, G., *The Development of the Modern State: A Sociological Introduction*, (Hutchinson), 1978, Jordan, B., *The State: Authority and Autonomy*, (Basil Blackwell), 1985, and Dunleavy, P. and O'Leary, B., *Theories of the State: The Politics of Liberal Democracy*, (Macmillan), 1987.

[3] Harling, Philip, and Mandler, Peter, 'From 'fiscal-military' state to laissez-faire state, 1760-1850', *Journal of British Studies*, Vol. 32, (1993), pp. 44-70, examines the evolution of the state.

weakly, burgesses and landowners felt it was their responsibility to uphold these rights primarily through the agency of the magistracy. Those holding governing responsibility generally did not try to exclude the mass of the population from participation in the regulation of their own lives. Even non-ratepayers could influence decisions on such matters as policing and poor relief policy through the courts, through petitions to those in authority and attendance at parish meetings. A similar intervention of non-voters in parliamentary elections in which voting was not secret until 1872 allowed even the working-classes to express their views and exert some influence. It was only in the 1820s, that a strategy of constructing a firm regulatory state within which a free economy and free individuals could flourish took precedence in government circles. [4] However, some argue that local power did not rest on conceptions of community or on pluralist notions of local democracy and rights but a view of central-local relations as part of the modern state's extension of surveillance across its territory. Ogburn suggests that the shaping of the Police Bill 1856 was the result of a strategic engagement by national and local state agencies and that local social policy outcomes were the result of negotiation within structures of administrative rules and resources. [5] Society in 1830 was not 'democratic' in any meaningful sense, but nor was it in 1914.

The combination of strength and overall control by central government linked to decentralised institutions enshrining a strong sense of local community created a distinctive type of state. The intellectual context for a 'revolution in government' is important. [6] It encompassed a new way of looking at economics grounded in the 'free market' and a philosophical system for examining the 'utility' of

---

[4] Harling, Philip, 'The powers of the Victorian state', in Mandler, Peter, (ed.), *Liberty and authority in Victorian Britain*, (Oxford University Press), 2006, pp. 25-50, and 'The State', in ibid, Williams, Chris, (ed.), *A Companion to Nineteenth-Century Britain*, (Blackwell), 2004, pp. 110-124, provide an excellent, succinct overview. Jupp, Peter, *The governing of Britain, 1688-1848: the executive, Parliament and the people*, (Routledge), 2006, and Harling Philip, *The Modern British State: An Historical Introduction*, (Polity), 2001, are more detailed. See also, Roberts, David F., *The Social Conscience of the early Victorians*, (Stanford University Press), 2002, pp. 375-456.

[5] Ogborn, Miles, 'Local power and state regulation in nineteenth century Britain', *Transactions of the Institute of British Geographers*, Vol. 17, (2), (1992), pp. 215-226.

[6] On changing philosophies of government see Pearson, R., and Williams, G., *Political Thought and Public Policy in the Nineteenth Century: an introduction*, (Longman), 1984.

existing institutions and procedures. These were popularised during the 1840s and 1850s and combined in the middle-class notion of 'respectability'.

A 'revolution in government'?

The first half of the nineteenth century, and especially the 1830s, saw an expansion in the role of government. This 'revolution in government' has long been an area of historiographical controversy. [7] People sought to understand the dramatic economic changes that were occurring leading to the development of new ideas in economic and social affairs. [8]

A 'revolution' contextualised?

In 1776, Adam Smith in his *Wealth of Nations* called for the freeing of the economy from regulation either in the form of restrictive tariffs or of the anti-social monopolies that had been created. [9] He

---

[7] On the nineteenth century 'revolution in government', see, Cromwell, V., *Revolution or Evolution: British Government in the Nineteenth Century*, (Longman), 1977, and Taylor, A. J., *Laissez Faire and State Intervention in Nineteenth Century Britain*, (Macmillan), 1972, for the historiographical debate to the early 1970s.

[8] Jones, Kathleen, *The Making of Social Policy in Britain 1830-1990*, (Athlone Press), 1991, and Laybourn, Keith, *The Evolution of British Social Policy and the Welfare State*, (Keele University Press), 1995, are good surveys. See also, Fraser, D., *The Evolution of the British Welfare State*, fourth edition, (Macmillan Palgrave), 2009, Henriques, U., *Before the Welfare State*, (Longman), 1981, MacDonagh, O., *Early Victorian Government*, (Weidenfeld), 1977, Roberts, D., *Victorian Origins of the British Welfare State*, (Archon Books), 1968, Parris, H., *Constitutional Bureaucracy*, (Allen and Unwin), 1969, Sutherland, G., (ed.), *Studies in the Growth of Nineteenth Century Government*, (Routledge), 1972, and Chester, N., *The English Administrative System 1780-1870*, (Oxford University Press), 1981, McLeod, Roy, (ed.) *Government and Expertise: Specialists, administrators and professionals 1860-1919*, (Cambridge University Press), 1988, has an excellent introduction and contains many valuable papers on later developments. Checkland, S., *British Public Policy 1776-1939: an economic, social and political perspective*, (Cambridge University Press), 1984, is a valuable study. Lagan, Mary, and Schwarz, Bill, *Crisis in the British State 1880-1930*, (Hutchinson), 1986, contains some excellent essays from a radical perspective.

[9] Campbell, R. H., Skinner, Andrew S., and Todd, W. B., (eds.), *The Glasgow Edition of the Works and Correspondence of Adam Smith: Inquiry into the Nature and Causes of the Wealth of Nations*, 2 Vols. (Oxford University Press), 1976, is the best edition. On Smith, see Haakonssen,

wanted trade and economic forces to work in a free market that, he maintained in a wider context, allowed individuals to fulfil their full potential. Smith's conception of society as a collection of individuals for whom self-interest was the driving force marked a move from the reciprocally structured hierarchy based on land. He envisaged a positive role for the state in providing public services that individuals alone could maintain. Later writers such as Malthus and Ricardo built on Smith's work. Malthus focused on the pressure on resources occasioned by population growth while Ricardo demonstrated the central role of capital in a society. Ricardo has been seen as the high priest of the capitalist middle-classes contrasting their position with the image of the parasitic privileged landlord. [10] He strengthened the case for freeing the commercial classes from a protected market in which agriculture had a self-perpetuating dominance. [11]

Parallel to economic theories was the emergence of an alternative social philosophy associated with Jeremy Bentham who accepted the free market economy and recognised that the state might have to ensure that a real community of interest was catered for. [12] He and his followers wished to apply the test of utility to all institutions: were they economical, efficient and above all conducive to 'the greatest happiness to the greatest number'? His supporters, the Utilitarians envisaged collective state action geared to the needs of individuals. The issue for Bentham's disciples, especially James Mill and his son John Stuart Mill, was how far should laissez-faire go and what intervention by the state was acceptable. To the Mills, laissez-faire was an ideal and every intervention by the state was a step away from that ideal. In his *Principles of Political Economy,* published in 1848, J. S. Mill maintained that government intervention was only justifiable in exceptional cases where an overwhelming need existed

---

Knud, (ed.), *The Cambridge Companion to Adam Smith*, (Cambridge University Press), 2006.
[10] Ricardo, David, *On the principles of Political Economy and Taxation*, 3rd edition, (John Murray), 1821, is his most important work. See also, Henderson, John P., *The life and economics of David Ricardo*, (Kluwer Academic Publishers), 1997, and Hollander, S., *The Economics of David Ricardo*, (University of Toronto Press), 1979.
[11] See especially, Ricardo, David, *On Protection to Agriculture*, 4th edition, (John Murray), 1822.
[12] Schofield, Philip, *Utility and democracy: the political thought of Jeremy Bentham*, (Oxford University Press), 2006, is the best study of Bentham's political thinking. Halevy, E., *The Growth of Philosophical Radicalism*, (Faber), 1952, still contains much of value on Benthamism. See also, Lieberman, David, 'From Bentham to Benthamism', *Historical Journal*, Vol. 28, (1985), pp. 199-224.

for state action. [13]

Gradually the ideas of the political economists and Utilitarians were popularised, percolated to all levels of society and by the 1850s had been synthesised into that body of attitudes and values often known critically as 'Victorianism'.[14] Samuel Smiles and others crystallised this social philosophy into work, thrift, self-help and respectability. [15] This was not a static social philosophy but a means for individuals to climb the social ladder through industry and initiative. This was extended from the 1870s into a Darwinian social theory in which people found their place in society in proportion to their talents: the fittest reached the top, those inferior remained at the bottom. [16] In this context, a deterrent Poor Law had both logical and justifiable. This social ideology was certainly middle-class in both its origins and application but its impact lay across society. Service, respectability and, at least in public, a stricter religious observance and moral code permeated upwards into the ranks of the landed elite. There is some disagreement about the extent of middle-class hegemony. Perkin saw a triumph for the middle-class entrepreneurial ideas while Burns maintained that it is 'extravagant' to maintain that England was governed by and in the interests of the middle-classes. [17] But there is no doubt that there was a blending in politics and society of aristocratic and middle-class interests, of property and capital to form a new dominant ruling class

The self-help philosophy moved downwards as well as upwards. Given the unequal distribution of wealth it is surprising that a shared

---

[13] See Mill, John Stuart, *Principles of Political Economy with some of their applications to Social Philosophy*, 2 Vols. (C. C. Little & J. Brown), 1848, Vol. 2, pp. 567-591, and *On Liberty*, (Henry Holt & Co.), 1859, pp. 44-55. See also, Reeves, Richard, *John Stuart Mill: Victorian Firebrand*, (Atlantic Books), 2007.

[14] Smout, T. C., (ed.), *Victorian values*, (Oxford University Press), 1992, and Marsden, Gordon, *Victorian values: personalities and perspectives in nineteenth-century society*, 2nd edition, (Longman), 1998. See also, Day, Gary, *Varieties of Victorianism: the uses of a past*, (Macmillan), 1998.

[15] Jarvis, Adrian, *Samuel Smiles and the Construction of Victorian Values*, (Sutton), 1997, considers the issue of respectability from a revisionist perspective.

[16] Hawkins, Mike, *Social Darwinism in European and American Thought 1860-1945*, (Cambridge University Press), 1997, pp. 3-60, and Paul, Diane B., 'Darwin, social Darwinism and eugenics', in Hodge, Jonathan, and Radick, Gregory, (eds.), *The Cambridge Companion to Darwin*, (Cambridge University Press), 2003, pp. 214-239.

[17] Perkin, Harold, *The Origins of Modern English Society, 1780-1880*, (Routledge), 1972, pp. 271-339, Burn, W. L., *The Age of Equipoise: a study of the mid-Victorian generation*, (Allen & Unwin), 1964, p. 8.

social philosophy became dominant. There were alternative anti-capitalist theories, associated with Thomas Paine, [18] Thomas Spence[19] and Charles Hall [20] and in the 1820s, Robert Owen [21] and Thomas Hodgskin, [22] that challenged Smith's concept of individuals pursuing their own self-interests. [23] Hall, for instance, argued that inequalities in wealth and the production of luxuries led to the exploitation of the poor and their suffering and claimed that their exploitation was so severe that they 'retained only the product of one hour's work out of eight'. He was a strong advocate of progressive taxation to even out the inequalities of society. Many of these theories were evident in the Chartist movement, though whether the movement was anti-capitalist is debatable but after the mid-1840s some working people were affected by middle-class values as they became concerned to get a better deal from capitalism. 'New model' trade unionism, adult

---

[18] Keane, John, *Tom Paine: a political life*, (Bloomsbury), 1996, provides insight into Paine's life while Claeys, Gregory, *Thomas Paine: social and political thought*, (Allen and Unwin), 1989, considers the development of his thinking. Butler, Marilyn, (ed.), *Burke, Paine, Goodwin and the revolution controversy*, (Cambridge University Press), 1984, provides a thematic discussion of the debate in the 1790s while Hampsher-Monk, Iain, (ed.), *The impact of the French Revolution*, (Cambridge University Press), 2005, is an excellent selection of critical texts.

[19] Dickinson, H. T., (ed.), *The Political Works of Thomas Spence*, (Avero), 1982.

[20] Hall, Charles, *The Effects of Civilization on the People in European States, with Observations on the Principal Conclusion in Mr. Malthus's Essay on Population* (Printed by the author), 1805.

[21] On Robert Owen see, Thompson, Noel, (eds.), *Robert Owen and His Legacy*, (University of Wales Press), 2011, and Donnachie, Ian, *Robert Owen: social visionary*, (John Donald), 2005. On Owenism the most valuable study remains Harrison, J. F. C., *Robert Owen and the Owenites in Britain and America*, (Routledge), 1969. Claeys, G., *Machinery, money and the millennium: from moral economy to socialism 1815-1860*, (Princeton University Press), 1987, and *Citizens and saints: Politics and anti-politics in early British socialism*, (Cambridge University Press), 1989, are major studies of Owenism. Claeys, Gregory, (ed.), *Selected Works of Robert Owen*, 4 Vols. (Pickering & Chatto), 1993, contains the most important primary materials.

[22] Thompson, Noel W., *The People's Science: The popular political economy of exploitation and crisis 1816-34*, (Cambridge University Press), 1984, and *The Real Rights of Man: Political Economies for the Working-class, 1775-1850*, (Pluto Press), 1998. On Hodgskin see, Stack, David, *Nature and artifice: the life and thought of Thomas Hodgskin (1787-1869)*, (Boydell & Brewer), 1998.

[23] Krishnamurthy, Aruna, (ed.), *The Working-Class Intellectual in Eighteenth- and Nineteenth-Century Britain*, (Ashgate), 2009.

education, friendly societies and co-operatives among the working population suggests an increasingly shared value system.

Towards a regulatory state

In the simplified 'self-help' view of the ideal society, the state had a purely negative role. A. V. Dicey and Samuel Smiles could have agreed that the period from 1825 to 1870 was one dominated by Benthamism or individualism.[24] But their view of the limits of state activity is difficult to reconcile with the activities that in practice the state adopted. The age of laissez-faire and individualism apparently saw the emergence of the centralised administrative state. This seeming paradox can be resolved in a variety of ways.[25]

Laissez-faire may have been the ideal but the problems posed by urban and industrial society necessitated an extension of the activities of the state locally and nationally. This discrepancy was not between theory and practice in general terms but between theory and practice in different areas of policy. There was also inconsistency between the utilitarian approach to law and politics, in which intervention was justifiable to ensure a harmony of interests and the call for the free operation of the market in economic matters. The problem with this explanation is that the line between society and economic was far from clear. Poor Law, public health and factory reform involved economic as much as social questions. Even in economic matters, such railways and the nature of companies, the state introduced regulatory supervision. There was certainly a greater reluctance to interfere in economic matters, but the distinction is far from absolute.

Benthamite utilitarianism was an amalgam of laissez-faire and interventionist ideas and not exclusively individualist. Some argue that it was the archetype of British collectivism. Perkin maintained that entrepreneurial and professional ideals combined and that while the former roughly corresponds to the self-help ideology, the latter involved the professionalisation of government, the solution of problems by the application of reason and the creation of the administrative state.[26] The root of the tension between these two ideals lay in the conflict between Smith's natural harmony of interests in the market and the need in certain circumstances to create an artificial harmony through intervention. Laissez-faire or intervention could be

---

[24] Dicey, A.V., *Lectures on the relation between law & public opinion in England during the nineteenth century*, (Macmillan), 1905, pp. 126-210.
[25] Ibid, Fraser, D., *The Evolution of the British Welfare State*, pp. 106-115.
[26] Ibid, Perkin, Harold, *The Origins of Modern English Society, 1780-1880*, pp. 308-339.

equally Benthamite depending on the specific context.

These explanations are all concerned in some way with the implications and contradictions of Benthamite theory. In MacDonagh's analysis of growing state involvement in emigration and shipping in the first half of the nineteenth century Benthamism has no central role. What was meant by the term 'Benthamite'? [27] Did it apply to people who had read Bentham or his followers or who were influenced directly or indirectly by him or them? He suggests that the expanding role of government followed a five-stage model that rests on pressure of 'intolerable facts' and an expediential administrative momentum. [28] In the first stage some 'intolerable evil' is identified that, it was believed, could be legislated out of existence by a prohibitory Act. Shortcomings in this legislation were recognised in the second stage leading to new laws creating government inspectors for enforcement. The impetus created professionals with intimate knowledge of the problem that led to growing centralisation and superintendence by a central agency. This brought awareness that the problem could not be swept away and that slow regulation and re-regulation was needed. Finally, a bureaucratic machine pursued research to produce preventive regulation that passed almost unnoticed into law. Whether or not this model can be applied to other areas of social policy, it is important in explaining how government grew more regulatory and intrusive in character.

The final explanation takes MacDonagh's model a stage further and argues that the evolving administrative state had little to do with either individualism and collectivism but with conflict between two views of the role of government, a traditional and an incrementalist view and that these models conditioned the response of the state to intolerable evils. [29] The traditional model put great faith in the historic rights and customs enshrined in past constitutional practice, with a particular emphasis on local self-government and saw growing centralisation as an attack on the traditional freedom of English

---

[27] See, for example, Hume, L. J., 'Jeremy Bentham and the Nineteenth-Century Revolution in Government', *The Historical Journal*, Vol. 10, (3), (1967), pp. 361-375, and Conway, Stephen, 'Bentham and the nineteenth-century revolution in government', in Bellamy, Richard, (ed.), *Victorian Liberalism: Nineteenth-century political thought and practice*, (Routledge), 1990, pp. 71-90.

[28] MacDonagh, Oliver, *A Pattern of Government Growth 1800-60: The Passenger Acts and their Enforcement*, (McGibbon & Kee), 1961. See the debate with Parris, H., *Government and the Railways in Nineteenth Century Britain*, (Routledge), 1965.

[29] Lubenow, W. C., *The Politics of Government Growth: Early Victorian Attitudes to State Intervention 1833-48*, (David & Charles), 1971.

institutions. The incrementalist model reacted to problems hesitantly and pragmatically without preconceived policy. Lubenow examined Poor Law and public health reform, railways and the factory question and although his model applies well to public health, it is less certain for the other areas. His approach does, however, highlight the importance of the local perspective in the growth of the administrative state.

Despite these contradictory views, it is possible to highlight four aspects of the emerging administrative state. Its initial response to social and economic reform was largely ad hoc, practical, unplanned and pragmatic. It was the pressure of the real world to resolve real problems rather than abstract theories that produced administrative growth. In addition, the relationship between central and local government cannot be ignored. Centralisation was seen as leading to the end of real local government but also as an evil to be feared more than the problem it was attempting to overcome. The problem was not whether the state should act to deal with social problems such as public health, but what the agency of intervention should be. On issues where they had common interests, central and local government worked together. However, in other areas, there was also an alliance between voluntary and state action. Many contemporaries saw intervention as a means for individuals to evade their responsibilities or as a means through which the central state could impose its will on an unconvinced populace. Combining voluntary and state action was the only way many felt that progress could be made. Finally, there was the vital element of administrative momentum, whether it was or was not grounded in Benthamism. The bureaucracy grew and attracted extended powers because of the growing realisation of how much needed to be done to create a state in which meaningful liberty could flourish. Many contemporaries recognised that there was a case for intervention to create the conditions in which mutual self-help and competition could operate freely. Laissez-faire was the ideal, state intervention the pragmatic reality.

An effective and efficient machinery of government was created with the emergence of inspection as the means of ensuring bureaucratic control. The administrative revolution made widespread use of executive powers created before 1830. Regulation by the Privy Council through Orders-in-Council remained important, sometimes legitimated by statute. The new Board of Trade, replacing that abolished in 1782, developed from a Committee of the Privy Council on Trade and Plantations formed in 1784, reorganised by an Order-in-Council in 1786. But its officers and responsibilities were established by statute law with the creation of a vice-president in 1817 and a president in 1826. From 1839, education was 'organised' by a Committee of the Privy Council but its single officer and some of its responsibilities and financial regulation were established by statute. A similar process of statutory definition occurred in the Treasury and the Home Office. [30] The Foreign Office, by contrast, owed as most of its power to prerogative and privilege rather than to statute. By the late 1830s, it is possible to talk of a machinery of central government in ways that were not possible a century earlier.

The emergence of the statistical ideal, the collection of 'facts', was used to justify centralist policies and was essential to the transformation of the relationship between local and central government. [31] Walter Bagehot asserted the necessity for British government to investigate as well as act and that the 'great maxim of modern thought is not only the toleration of everything but the examination of everything'. [32] Commissions of inquiry increased rapidly after 1800, in part of result of the movement for economical reform, in part by the needs of war. Between 1832 and 1846, over a hundred Royal Commissions were established. Commissions and committees of inquiry operated with a set agenda, controlled membership, defined forms of inquiry, relationship between gathered evidence and the legitimation of certain 'facts' that formed the basis for reports and recommendations. [33] For example, law reformers with the goal of codification found royal commissions particularly well-suited to their objectives, initiating inquiries into criminal, property, and evidence laws, among others. This was paralleled by the emergence of state inspectors for factories from 1833, the Poor Law from 1834, prisons from 1835, schools from 1839 and for mines from 1850. Their annual reports generated further legitimate 'facts'. They were charged with inspecting and reporting on the implementation of Acts, the legitimate operation of local institutions and the 'efficiency'

---

[30] Pellew, Jill, *The Home Office 1848-1914, from clerks to bureaucrats*, (Associated University Presses), 1982, pp. 5-120.

[31] See Cullen, M. J., *The statistical movement in early Victorian Britain the foundations of empirical social research*, (Harvester), 1975, and more generally, Poovey, Mary, *A History of the Modern Fact: Problems of knowledge in the sciences of wealth and society*, (University of Chicago Press), 1998.

[32] Bagehot, Walter, *The English Constitution*, (Chapman and Hall), 1867, p. 210.

[33] Clokie, H. M., and Robinson, J. W., *Royal Commissions of Inquiry: the significance of investigations in British politics*, (Stanford University Press), 1937, pp. 54-79, Lauriat, Barbara, "The Examination of Everything': Royal Commissions in British Legal History', *Statute Law Review*, Vol. 31, (1), (2010), pp. 24-46,

of those in receipt of central funding. [34] State inspectors were the vanguard of central intervention in two important respects. They sought to secure national minimum provision in their different areas. The structure of administration adopted by the British state was heavily influenced by its capacity to secure a consensus within industry on the nature of the risks that existed and also on what legal redress might be offered to those who suffered from disease as a consequence of their employment. They also acted to establish and standardise a range of civic institutions that symbolised the extension of the state beyond the efforts of either individuals or local groupings. These civic institutions were either 'objects of terror' like workhouses or police stations or new public institutions including parks and gardens that celebrated local civic character and pride and characterised respectable and cultured citizenship.

The emergence of the modern state was largely the result of the demographic and economic changes that occurred in Britain in the late-eighteenth and early-nineteenth centuries. Why there was a the 'revolution in government' is far less clear. Contemporary perceptions of particular policies and the consequent extension of the role of the state varied. It was possible for the same policy to be regarded at the same time as benevolent, a solution to a practical problem, an effective bureaucratic expedient, a prop to the existing social and political order, an asset to the middle-classes and yet also a legitimate popular demand. Social reform in the eighteenth and nineteenth centuries, the emergence of the 'policing' and 'inspectorial' functions of the 'surveillance' state and the parallel centralising of bureaucratic control was rarely motivated by one thing. Policies were the result of the consideration of different, often conflicting, perspectives.

---

[34] See, for example, Bartrip, P. W. J., and Fenn, P. T., 'The Evolution of Regulatory Style in the Nineteenth Century British Factory Inspectorate', *Journal of Law and Society*, Vol. 10, (2), (1983), pp. 201-222, Bartrip, P. W. J., *The Home Office and the dangerous trades: regulating occupational disease in Victorian and Edwardian Britain*, (Rodopi), 2002, ibid, Pellew, Jill, *The Home Office 1848-1914, from clerks to bureaucrats*, pp. 121-182, Dunford, J. E., *Her Majesty's Inspectorate of Schools in England and Wales, 1860-1970*, (Museum of the History of Education, University of Leeds), 1980, and Edmonds, E. L., *The School Inspector*, (Routledge), 1962, 1998, pp. 114-136

The state in action 1830-1880

Although the Whigs had defended political and civil liberty against the arbitrary rule of the state, during the 1830s they were more interventionist than their predecessors. [35] Mandler summed up their position in the following way:

> They exhibited great impatience with endless debates over the abstract question of state intervention. They preferred a case-by-case judgement on the merits. [36]

The moral language of the old Tory society was increasingly reflected in the liberal ideals of self-determination, advancement, improvement and innovation. [37]

Within these broad principles the Whigs promoted constitutional reform in 1832. The Reform Act defined clearly distinguished between those who were and those who were not sanctioned to wield power and did so entirely in terms of property ownership, entrenching the power of landed wealth while acknowledging the new sources of power. [38] They also reconstructed essential institutions of government especially the serious delays in the higher courts by restructuring the House of Lords and Privy Council appeal systems and simplifying the rules of pleading at common law in 1832 and 1833. Social questions were investigated with unprecedented thoroughness providing a grounding for reform. Royal Commissions, with their ability to investigate problems as well as take oral evidence from witnesses, took over from Select Committees as the chief means of official investigation: 41 were

---

[35] See Parry, J., *The Rise and Fall of Liberal Government in Victorian Britain*, (Yale University Press), 1993, Southgate, Donald, *The Passing of the Whigs, 1832-1886*, (Macmillan), 1962, and Brent, R., *Liberal Anglican Politics: Whiggery, Religion and Reform 1830-1841*, (Oxford University Press), 1987. Finlayson, G., *England in the Eighteen Thirties*, (Edward Arnold), 1969, Llewellyn, A., *The Decade of Reform: The 1830s*, (David & Charles), 1972, Newbould, I., *Whiggery and Reform 1830-41: the politics of government*, (Macmillan), 1990, and Mandler, P., *Aristocratic Government in the Age of Reform*, (Oxford University Press), 1990, are useful for the Whig reforms.

[36] Mandler, P., 'Cain and Abel: Two Aristocrats and the Early Victorian Factory Acts', *Historical Journal*, Vol. 27, (1984), p. 96.

[37] Burns, Arthur, and Innes, Joanna, (eds.), *Rethinking the Age of Reform: Britain 1780-1850*, (Cambridge University Press), 2003, contains several revisionist essays on this period.

[38] Pearce, Robert, *The Great Reform Act*, (Cape), 2003, is an excellent narrative.

established between 1832 and 1841.

State intervention had to cope with existing vested interests. State entry into the field of working-class education was faced with opposition from Anglicans and Nonconformists over who should run schools and controversy about costs The Whigs' only success was the introduction of annual grant from 1833 that was administered by the religious societies without subordination to government control. The Factory Act 1833 encountered similar opposition and was modified following pressure from mill owners. The Factory Inspectorate was an attempt to create an enforcement mechanism independent of existing institutions but there were initially only four inspectors and the act was widely evaded.[39] More effective enforcement would have been resisted on the grounds of costs, opposition in principle to state intrusion in the operation of industry and the liberty of mill owners and parents. Yet, in the next twenty years, inspectors were appointed to regulate the poor law, prisons, mines, public health and schools. Education and factory reform were new areas of state action while reforming the Poor Laws in 1834 dealt with an already existing area of intervention. The central state sought to imposed a uniform national system led to opposition that was unsuccessful in preventing implementation but did lead to a local flexibility.

An important limitation on effective government intervention from the 1830s through to the 1860s was the absence of reformed local institutions capable of administering new national initiatives. The 1834 Act had taken such a step in relation to the poor law in establishing 'unions'. The Municipal Corporations Act 1835 was a further step in making councils accountable to their male ratepayers; women ratepayers were not given the municipal franchise until 1869.[40]

---

[39] Bartrip, Peter W. J., and Fenn, P. T., 'The Evolution of Regulatory Style in the Nineteenth Century Factory Inspectorate', *Journal of Law and Society*, Vol. 10, (1983), pp. 201-222, and 'The Administration of Safety: the Enforcement Policy of the Early Factory inspectorate, 1844-64', *Public Administration*, Vol. 58, (1980), pp. 87-102. See also, Crooks, Eddie, *The factory inspectors: a legacy of the industrial revolution*, (Tempus), 2005, and Martin, Bernice, 'Leonard Horner: a portrait of an inspector of factories', *International Review of Social History*, Vol. 14, (1969), pp. 412-443.

[40] Finlayson, Geoffrey, 'The Municipal Corporation Commission and Report, 1833-5', *Bulletin of the Institute of Historical Research*, Vol. 36, (1963), pp. 36-52, and 'The politics of municipal reform, 1835', *English Historical Review*, Vol. 81, (1966), pp. 673-692; Phillips, John A., and Wetherell, Charles, 'Probability and political behaviour: a case study of the Municipal Corporations Act of 1835', *History and Computing*, Vol. 5, (1993), pp. 135-153.

The role of the reformed corporations was not initially seen as primarily governmental or administrative although they had the right to appoint a watch committee responsible for the establishment and conduct of a police force. Their main function was representing local opinion on national and local issues in Parliament. Whig ambitions to satisfy conflicting constituencies aroused more opposition than support in the later 1830s. Popular expectations had been raised and then dashed by parliamentary reform, by education and factory reform and the widely disliked poor law. The outcome was both working-class Chartism and the election of Peel's Tory government in 1841.

Peel remained unconvinced of the importance of constitutional matters or of party and his administration from 1841 to 1846 notably neglected them. [41] Peelremained unresponsive to demands for constitutional reform from the Chartists extending the machinery of public order through the increasing creation of local police forces. He was prepared to divide his own party in 1846 over Corn Law repeal in pursuit of the higher goal of economic liberalism. He pursued further liberalisation of the economy. Tariffs were further reduced and income tax reintroduced in 1842 and the annual Budget began to take on a central political role. [42] Peel also moved towards the construction of a framework of government designed to enhance business efficiency by providing a more reliable banking system and moving towards an enforceable commercial law that safeguarded contracts and provided protection against fraud. [43] In 1843, district bankruptcy courts were established and in 1846, county courts were created. [44] Peel believed that it was important to minimise state intervention in personal lives while establishing economic policy designed to facilitate free economic activity. However, he recognised that intervention was a necessity to maintain social stability. He was hostile to the Ten Hours movement on economic grounds though he was prepared to introduce mining legislation where he saw that there

---

[41] For Peel's ministry see Crosby, T. L., *Sir Robert Peel's Administration 1841-1846*, (David & Charles), 1970.

[42] Daunton, M. J., *Trusting Leviathan; the Politics of Taxation in Britain, 1799-1914*, (Cambridge University Press), 2001, is excellent on Peel's fiscal policies.

[43] Molyneux, Catherine, 'Reform as process: the parliamentary fate of the Bank Charter Act of 1844', in Turner, Michael J., (ed.), *Reform and reformers in nineteenth century Britain*, (University of Sunderland Press), 2004, pp. 63-80.

[44] Batzel, V. M., 'Parliament, businessman and bankruptcy, 1825-1883: a study in middle-class alienation', *Canadian Journal of History*, Vol. 18 (1983), pp. 171-186.

was a moral case. [45] The 1844 Factory Act was a remodelled Whig measure and it was the Whigs in 1847 that introduced ten hours legislation. [46] The Tories resisted Chadwick's pressure for public health reform after 1843 and the first major national legislation in 1848 by the Whigs.

The minimal regulatory state was not widely experienced as intrusive or oppressive and government presented itself as working for the common good, with improved standards of living as its aim. Popular radicalism was not hostile to economic liberalism provided that it did not undermine living standards. However, by the late 1840s, there was a full revolt against the principle of centralisation. [47] Parliament's experiments in centralised administration had almost all ended in failure. The independent Poor Law Commission had given way, in 1847, to a more timid Poor Law Board under ministerial and parliamentary control. A strong Board of Health was shorn of much of its influence when, in 1854, Chadwick was forced to resigned. *The Times* responded to this event with a jubilant leader that announced:

> If there is such a thing as a political certainty among us, it is that nothing autocratic can exist in this country....Mr Chadwick and Dr Southwood Smith, have been deposed, and we prefer to take our chance of cholera and the rest than be bullied into health. [48]

Constitutional questions lost their importance in the 1850s and government growth slowed after the Whig government fell in 1852. Coalition with the Peelites brought an end to Whig intervention in pursuit of social progress. [49] The General Board of Health, established in 1848, was wound up in 1858 and public health was left

---

[45] See, Heesom, Alan, 'The Coal Mines Act of 1842, social reform, and social control', *Historical Journal*, Vol. 24, (1981), pp. 69-88, and 'The northern coal-owners and the opposition to the Coal Mines Act of 1842', *International Review of Social History*, Vol. 25, (1980), pp. 236-271.

[46] Stewart, R., 'The Ten Hours and Sugar Crises of 1844: Government and the House of Commons in the Age of Reform', *Historical Journal*, Vol. 12, (1969), pp. 35-57.

[47] See, Gutchen, Robert M., 'Local Improvements and Centralization in Nineteenth-Century England', *Historical Journal*, Vol. 4, (1961), pp. 85-96, and Bartrip, P. W. J., 'State Intervention in Mid-Nineteenth Century Britain: Fact or Fiction?', *Journal of British Studies*, Vol. 23, (1), (1983), pp. 63-83.

[48] *The Times*, 17 August 1854.

[49] Conacher, J. B., *The Peelites and the Party System, 1846-1852*, (David & Charles), 1972 and Jones, W. D., & Erikson, Arvel B., *The Peelites 1846-1857*, (Ohio State University Press), 1972, consider Peel and his supporters after repeal in 1846.

largely to localities that gradually and unevenly extended their powers.[50]

The Peelite ideal of government reached its zenith after 1853 in the hands largely of William Gladstone who believed that the direct links between government and economy should be minimal. As Chancellor of the Exchequer, he restored fiscal policy to its pre-1846 direction by progressively dismantling duties and tariffs and reconstructing income tax. [51] He made the annual Budget central to politics and encouraged the Treasury to assert fiscal control over the activities of the civil service. [52] This process was a gradual, if slow, success aided by the civil service reforms initiated in the 1850s with Treasury primacy was recognised in 1867 when its Permanent Secretary was granted seniority over heads of other departments. [53] Gladstone was also committed to continued institutional change. He was closely involved in the reform of Oxford University in the 1850s[54] and his support for Cardwell's army reforms in 1871 was partly rooted in his desire to create a professional service comparable with that of Prussia. [55] But his approach was cautious and in reforming Oxford,

---

[50] Perkins, Clarence, 'The General Board of Health, 1848-1854', in *Facts and factors in economic history: articles by former students of Edwin Francis Gay*, (Harvard University Press), 1932, pp. 240-260. See also, Smith, H. J., 'Local reports to the General Board of Health', *History*, Vol. 56, (1971), 46-49.

[51] Buxton, S. C., *Mr. Gladstone as Chancellor of the Exchequer: a study*, (J. Murray), 1901.

[52] Roseveare, Henry, *The Treasury, 1660-1870: the foundations of control*, (Allen & Unwin), 1973, and Wright, Maurice, 'Treasury control 1854-1914', in ibid, Sutherland, Gillian (ed.), *Studies in the growth of nineteenth-century government*, pp. 195-226.

[53] Wright, Maurice, *Treasury control of the Civil Service, 1854-74*, (Oxford University Press), 1969, Greenway, J. R., 'Parliamentary reform and civil service reform: a nineteenth-century debate reassessed', *Parliamentary History*, Vol. 4, (1985), pp. 157-169, Hughes, Edward, 'Sir Charles Trevelyan and Civil Service Reform, 1853-5', *English Historical Review*, Vol. 64, (1949), pp. 53-88, 206-234, and 'Postscript to the Civil Service reforms of 1855', *Public Administration*, Vol. 33, (1955), pp. 299-306 and Clark, G. Kitson, '"Statesmen in disguise": reflexions on the history of the neutrality of the Civil Service', *Historical Journal*, Vol. 2, (1959), pp. 19-39.

[54] Harvie, Christopher, 'Reform and expansion, 1854-1871', in ibid, Brock, M. G., and Curthoys, Mark C., (eds.), *The History of the University of Oxford, Vol. 6: Nineteenth-century Oxford, part I*, pp. 697-730.

[55] Strachan, Hew, *Wellington's Legacy: The Reform of the British Army 1830-1854*, (Manchester University Press), 1984, Tucker, A. V., 'Army and society in England, 1870-1900: a reassessment of the Cardwell reforms',

he rejected radical proposals to replace the collegiate system with a faculty structure. In 1853, he asked Sir Stafford Northcote and Sir Charles Trevelyan of the Treasury to investigate and report on the civil service to take forward the development of a more efficient system. [56] The Northcote-Trevelyan report of 1854 recommended recruiting an efficient, professional, apolitical service based on promotion by merit rather than seniority. The changes spread slowly through the service, especially in the more elite departments, jealous of their independence. The reforms were completed theoretically by Orders in Council under Gladstone's premiership in 1870 when all departments, save the Foreign Office, were to observe the new norms. The Treasury avoided open competition until 1878 and few officials were appointed by this route in the 1880s and 1890s. The coalition and Liberal governments of the 1850s and 1860s carried other institutional reforms forward. The Common Law Procedure Acts of 1854 and 1860 sought to further speed up proceedings; the Court of Chancery Acts, 1852 and 1858, to speed up the notorious slowness pilloried by Dickens. [57]

In the Gladstonian State, Parliament's role was to check the excesses of government rather than debating and sanctioning the actions of the executive. Gladstone kept expenditure firmly in ministerial hands and the Public Accounts Committee established in 1862 had powers only to check abuses of expenditure retrospectively. Gladstone's was a minimal state that was to be a strong, decisive and efficient firmly moulding the framework within which the moralised citizenry would enjoy their freedom. But he was no democrat and constitutional reform had as little appeal for him as for Peel. His conversion to reform in the 1860s was based in a pragmatic realisation that moderate artisans, if allowed to vote, would strengthen Liberalism. His 1866 proposals for electoral reform were designed with this in mind and he believed that the 1867 household franchise introduced by Disraeli went too far and he viewed the introduction of

---

Journal of British Studies, Vol. 2, (1963), pp. 110-141, and Bond, Brian, 'Edward Cardwell's army reforms, 1868-74', *Army Quarterly & Defence Journal*, Vol. 84, (1962), pp. 108-117.

[56] Hart, Jenifer, 'The genesis of the Northcote-Trevelyan Report', in ibid, Sutherland, Gillian, (ed.), *Studies in the growth of nineteenth-century government*, pp. 63-81.

[57] Lobban, Michael, 'Preparing for Fusion: Reforming the Nineteenth-Century Court of Chancery', *Law and History Review*, Vol. 22, (2004), pp. 389-428, 565-600, and comments by Getzler, Joshua, 'Chancery Reform and Law Reform', *Law and History Review*, Vol. 22, (2004), pp. 601-608, and Oldham, James, 'A Profusion of Chancery Reform', *Law and History Review*, Vol. 22, (2004), pp. 609-614.

the secret ballot in 1872 as a regrettable necessity. However, Gladstone recognised that market forces alone could not promote a just society and that some interference was acceptable and necessary, at least at the margins, on grounds of social justice. Factory legislation remained in place but was not significantly pushed forward. In the field of social welfare, government accepted overall responsibility for public health and poor laws, but in both cases left a high level of discretion to the localities. The minimal state was based on the capacity of a vast network of voluntary organisations, in co-operation with local government, to superintend moral, charitable, education and welfare services.

The defence of local autonomy against central state intervention remained influential and the powers and activities of local government expanded in the mid-Victorian period. [58] Local government affected people's lives more visibly than the central state. However, the direction of local government expansion varied considerably. For the large towns, there were local battles over incorporation under the 1835 Act and struggles for control of guardians, vestries, police, improvement and highways commissioners and over church rates. [59] By 1861, towns as large as Bury, Merthyr Tydfil and Birkenhead, with populations of 87,000, 84,000 and 42,000 respectively had no municipal corporation. Even reluctant corporations were not left entirely to their own devices by central government. Policing and public health were important for maintaining public order and social stability and from 1856 central government paid a quarter of the cost of local police forces on condition that the Home Office Inspectorate recognised them as efficient. [60] Until 1871, Tom Taylor chivvied along local sanitary improvements at the Local Government Act Office. [61] Where local initiatives occurred, they were less often a response to intolerable evils than to environmental crises such as outbreaks of infectious disease. In general, local authorities were more willing to

---

[58] Weinstein, B. J., "Local Self-Government Is True Socialism': Joshua Toulmin Smith, the State and Character Formation', *English Historical Review*, Vol. 123, (2008), pp. 1193-1228.

[59] Beckett, J. V., *City Status in the British Isles, 1830-2002*, (Ashgate), 2005, pp. 43-72, examines Manchester and its quest for city status between 1836 and 1888.

[60] Vine, Sir John Richard Somers, *English Municipal Institutions: their growth and development from 1835 to 1879*, (Waterlow), 1879, Weinbaum, Martin, *The Incorporation of Boroughs*, (Manchester University Press), 1937.

[61] Lambert, Royston, 'Central and local relations in mid-Victorian England: the Local Government Act Office, 1858-71', *Victorian Studies*, Vol. 6, (1962), pp. 121-150.

accept central government advice on technical problems than central involvement in policing.

Non-urban areas had no all-purpose elected authority. The Poor Law Boards accumulated a wide range of responsibilities and provided a kind of embryo-elected local government in the countryside. They administered the Vaccination Acts, [62] became registrars of births, marriages and deaths from 1837, were responsible for registering voters and administering elections and were involved in rural police and highways administration. Between 1844 and 1874, 'poor law' spending on these non-poor law purposes rose from 27 to 40 per cent of the total. Boards of Health were separately established with separate elections and with separate rating powers. From 1852, Burial Boards could be set up to provide cemeteries and from 1862, Highway Boards to maintain roads. After 1870, School Boards were established on a householder franchise that included women; and shortly after women gained the right to be elected to Boards of Guardians. [63] Often rural and urban local authorities had different and overlapping boundaries but local government activity remained uneven largely because of the reluctance of ratepayers to pay its growing costs. In 1868, national taxation raised £67,800,000 and local rates in England and Wales £19,800,000. Local spending amounted to over £30 million, the gap being made up by loans, government subsidies and the rent on properties owned by local authorities.

Concern about the complexity and cost of local government, for example, a suburban property assessed at £1,100 attracted 87 separate rate demands in a year was such that in 1869 Gladstone established a Royal Commission to look at the structure of local government in England and Wales. Its report, in 1871, made recommendations that were gradually implemented over the next fifty years. It established certain principles: it discredited the policy of establishing separate local authorities for each major task; it proposed the consolidation of local powers in the hands of single local authorities to be established throughout the country; but, it failed to find a solution to the rating problem. Gladstone imposed greater uniformity of practice on local authorities and in 1871 set up the Local Government Board with

---

[62] Brunton, Deborah, *The politics of vaccination: practice and policy in England, Wales, Ireland, and Scotland, 1800-1874*, (University of Rochester Press), 2008. See also, Lambert, R. S., 'A Victorian national health service: state vaccination, 1855-71', *Historical Journal*, Vol. 5, (1962), pp. 1-18.

[63] On the expanding role of women see Hollis, Patricia, *Ladies Elect: Women in English Local Government 1865-1914*, (Oxford University Press), 1987.

responsibilities for public health, the poor law and other local activities. [64] The new central department set about trying to achieve greater uniformity. George Goschen, the first President of the Board, initiated a policy of striving to co-ordinate publicly funded poor relief. The Public Health Act 1872 compelled local authorities to act, whereas the new poor law policy only advised local Boards.

Variability in local government provision continued because there were limits to the control central government could exert without rousing opposition. This points to the limitations of minimal state and by the 1870s, local and voluntary bodies were unable to bear the full weight of social responsibility placed on them. Gladstone and his contemporaries accepted, at least in principle that market forces alone would not necessarily create a good society and, as a result, left the door ajar for the disintegration of the minimal regulatory state. [65]

Towards a welfare state 1880-1914

Conservative governments held office for twenty-three years between 1874 and 1906. This did not mean that there was a fundamental change in attitudes to government. Disraeli and most of his colleagues shared Toryism's traditional stress on the role and responsibilities of established authority, devotion to public service and general welfare were of greatest significance. Like Gladstone, Disraeli recognised the need for the constant adaptation of institutions rather than their radical transformation as the structure of society changed. [66] The Conservative interpretation of the proper role of the state in respect of social intervention was more flexible than Gladstone's. They remained wedded to economic liberalism until 1914 and beyond despite the tariff reform challenge of Joseph Chamberlain after 1903. But Toryism had never been averse in principle to the use of power as a means to enhance social welfare. Disraeli's second government from 1874 to 1880 was prepared to take social intervention further

---

[64] Macleod, R. M., *Treasury control and Social Administration: A Study of Establishment Growth at the Local Government Board, 1871-1905*, (London School of Economics), 1968

[65] Stebbings, C., '"Officialdom": Law, bureaucracy, and ideology in late Victorian England', in Lewis, Andrew D. E., and Lobban, Michael, (eds.), *Law and history*, (Oxford University Press), 2004, pp. 317-342, Moore, James Robert, and Rodger, Richard, 'Municipal Knowledge and Policy Networks in British Local Government, 1832-1914', *Jahrbuch für europäische Verwaltungsgeschichte*, Vol. 15, (2003), pp. 29-58.

[66] On the ideas underlying political parties see Greenleaf, W. H., *The British Political Tradition: Volume 2: The Ideological Heritage*, (Methuen), 1983.

than Gladstone had done, not least in order to win votes. [67]

Disraeli came to office after his victory in the 1874 General Election with no concrete plans but his government produced an unusually large amount of reforming legislation. Much of it either continued existing trends or was of very limited effect and there was little sign that Disraeli wished to go further or was motivated by any Conservative philosophy of paternalism. Anti-interventionism was still the predominant attitude of the government and of the party. [68] Lord Salisbury, Disraeli's successor, shared the Victorian promise of clear leadership combined with strong if minimal central government linked to economic liberalism, decentralisation and limited social intervention. Major structural changes in Britain after 1880 increased pressure on government to adapt constitutional structures and to extend the social role of the state. The country's economic stability and global economic and political position was less assured and international rivalries were intensifying. The spread of mass communications and the existence of a more prosperous and better educated working population meant that steps were needed to maintain internal stability, to bind all who safely could be into the constitution and to secure a sense of national cohesion overriding sectional interests. In 1884, rural householders were given the vote on the same terms as voters in the boroughs. The following year, constituency boundaries were redrawn creating single-member constituencies establishing the principle of 'one man, one vote'. However, women and about 40 per cent of adult males were still

---

[67] Ghosh, P. R., 'Disraelian Conservatism: A Financial Approach', *The English Historical Review* Vol. 99, (1984), pp. 268-296, Smith, Paul, *Disraelian Conservatism and Social Reform*, (Routledge), 1967, and Shannon, R., *The Age of Disraeli, 1868-1881: The Rise of Tory Democracy*, (Longman), 1992.

[68] Thane, P., (ed.), *The Origins of British Social Policy*, (Croom Helm), 1978, provides a series of useful articles. Harris, J., *Unemployment and Politics 1886-1914*, (Oxford University Press), 1972, examines government responses of unemployment, while her *William Beveridge*, (Oxford University Press), 2nd edition, 1997, provides a definitive biography of a 'key player'. Semmel, B., *Imperialism and Social Reform: English Social-Imperial Thought, 1895-1914*, (Oxford University Press), 1960, gives a different slant. Mommsen, W., *The Emergence of the Welfare State in Britain and Germany 1850-1950*, (Croom Helm), 1981, provides a comparative analysis. Jones, Helen, *Health and Society in Twentieth-Century Britain*, (Longman), 1994, contains an excellent chapter on health before 1914 while Cherry, Steven, *Medical services and the hospitals in Britain 1860-1939*, (Cambridge University Press), 1996, considers how medical services were organised in the years before the welfare state.

excluded in 1914.

The absence of elected local government in the counties and the ancient system of non-elected landowner authority appeared more antiquated when rural householders acquired the parliamentary vote in 1884.[69] There was also the problem of London whose governance could no longer be left to the Corporation of the City of London and an assortment of vestries and ad hoc bodies. The Tories introduced elected county councils and a council for London in 1888 elected on a household franchise. [70] In 1894, urban and rural district councils were established and in 1899, the London boroughs became second tier authorities. The minimal property qualification for membership of these authorities was in 1895 opened to all householders increasing the numbers of women and workingmen eligible to stand. Women were playing an increasingly important role in extending the social functions of local authorities, especially on Poor Law and School Boards. They were debarred until 1907 from seats on county and municipal councils, though if they were independent ratepayers, as very large numbers of widows and single women were, they might vote for both.[71] The number of workingmen elected to local authorities was small because of their lack of time and loss of income but 86 were elected in 1907 and 196 in 1913. Involvement of women and workingmen in local politics contributed to the organisational growth of the political labour movement. This did not mean that their demands for state intervention were more advanced than radical Liberals or Tories. Suspicion of the central state and attachment to independence and voluntary effort was strong among working people. The more politically active tended to favour more state action in housing and unemployment provided that it remained, as far as possible, under local control.

These changes stimulated the uneven growth of local government activity but left the rating problem unresolved. [72] Local government spending rose from £27.3m in 1870 to £42.2m in 1890

---

[69] Chandler, J. A., *Explaining local government: local government in Britain since 1800*, (Manchester University Press), 2007 provides an overview.

[70] Dunbabin, J. P. D., 'The Politics of the Establishment of County Councils', *Historical Journal*, Vol. 6, (1963), pp. 226-252.

[71] Boussahba-Bravard, Myriam, '"To Serve and to Elect": The Women's Local Government Society, Britain 1888-1918', Body-Gendrot, Sophie, Carré, Jacques, and Garbaye, Romain, (eds.), *A city of one's own: blurring the boundaries between private and public*, (Ashgate), 2008, pp. 181-200.

[72] See, Travers, Tony, and Esposito, Lorena, *The decline and fall of local democracy: A history of local government finance*, (Policy Exchange), 2003, and Cannan, Edwin, *A History of Local Rates in England*, (P. S. King & Co.), 1912.

and reached £125.8m by 1910. By the mid-1880s, government recognised the need for central subsidies to local government that did not undermine their sense of autonomy. In 1888, separate central grants was abolished and local authorities were 'assigned' revenues totalling £4.8m and were free to choose where the revenues should be spend. This did not, however, solve the problem. Ratepayers continued into the 1900s to resist the cost of the decentralisation that they in principle defended. Further municipalisation was one solution. Many authorities began to run their own services estimating that they could run them more effectively and profitably than private enterprise. By 1910, UK local governmentwas £6,000m in debt. Increased capital expenditure, especially on housing, hospital building and transport and further municipalisation of services characterised the activities of the more energetic authorities in the 1890s. Rates rose by between 30 and 50 per cent in London between 1891 and 1906 and municipalisation was blamed. But this was not unopposed and it is unclear whether municipalisation provided better or cheaper services. Local government by 1914 was more active in social and economic intervention, somewhat more uniform in its activities and somewhat less independent of central government than fifty years earlier.

The principles underlying the consensus on the minimal state, liberal economy, decentralisation and political participation of citizens was questioned during the 1890s. Serious social problems remained and there were fears that unless action was taken by the central state the social stability, one of the main achievements of mid-Victorian Britain, could break down. There were ominous signs: riots in Trafalgar Square in 1887, more militant actions by a minority of trade unionists and the formation of an Independent Labour Party.[73] This represented a general 'crisis' of the state and of liberalism that began in the 1880s and became acute between 1910 and 1926. [74] The 'collectivist' forms of state organisation and regulation that developed were different from the laissez-faire response of the mid-Victorian state. The problem is that this view of 'crisis' overstates the discontinuity between the situation before and after the 1880s perpetuating the view that an age of individualism was followed by one of collectivism. However, the 1880s did see the beginnings of a serious challenge to prevailing social and political orthodoxies and

---

[73] Humberstone, T. L., *Battle of Trafalgar Square*, (Ridgill Trout), 1948.
[74] Ibid, Lagan, Mary and Schwarz, Bill, *Crisis in the British State 1880-1930*.

Liberalism found itself under most threat.[75]

There were growing concerns that a substantial minority of the population were not sharing the general rise in living standards and were falling behind because of age and infirmity and who could not enter the over-stocked labour market.[76] Joseph Chamberlain sought an alternative approach to government to ward off what he saw as the unavoidable rise of labour and of pressures for an unacceptable degree of state intervention. He first put forward his views for a national policy in his 'Unauthorised Programme' of the 1880s. He did not envisage increasing centralisation arguing that initiatives from central government should be administered by elected local authorities in association with voluntary organisations rather than directly through national agencies. He made minor steps towards their implementation during his brief tenure as President of the Local Government Board in the Liberal government of 1886, permitting local authorities to establish public works to provide employment rather than poor relief for the unemployed with minimal effects. Chamberlain developed his ideas further as a Liberal Unionist in the Conservative Party of the 1890s but their impact of party policy was small. The Conservatives of the 1880s and 1890s initiated Royal Commissions into a wide range of social problems but their legislative outcome was slight and taxpayer resistance to legislation favouring the working-classes remained highly influential within the Conservative party. When Chamberlain put forward his tariff reform programme of 1903, he divided the Conservative and Unionist Party and lost.[77]

The Conservatives acted more positively in the field of industrial relations to strengthen 'responsible' unionism.[78] Central government

---

[75] See, Bailkin, Jordanna, *The culture of property: the crisis of liberalism in modern Britain*, (Chicago University Press), 2004, Vincent, Andrew, 'Classical liberalism and its crisis of identity', *History of Political Thought*, Vol. 11, (1990), pp. 143-161.

[76] On the Liberal Party, see, Searle, G. R., *The Liberal Party: triumph and disintegration, 1886-1929*, 2nd edition, (Palgrave), 2001, Moore, James R., *The transformation of urban liberalism: party politics and urban governance in late-nineteenth century England*, (Ashgate), 2006, and Lynch, Patricia C., *The Liberal Party in rural England 1885-1910: radicalism and community*, (Oxford University Press), 2003.

[77] Cain, Peter J., 'Political economy and Edwardian England: the tariff-reform controversy', in O'Day, Alan (ed.), *The Edwardian age: conflict and stability 1900-1914*, (Macmillan) 1979, pp. 35-60, and Sykes, Alan, *Tariff Reform in British Politics 1903-1913*, (Oxford University Press), 1979.

[78] On the Conservative Party, see, Ramsden, John, *An appetite for power: a history of the Conservative Party since 1830*, (HarperCollins), 1998, Smith, Jeremy, *The taming of democracy: the Conservative Party 1880-1924*,

took on an entirely new role of conciliation and arbitration in labour disputes following the Conciliation Act 1896. The Labour Department of the Board of Trade formed to administer the act and more generally to examine working conditions, appointed officials with trade union experience in a conscious effort to promote notions of a community of interest between capital and labour. The Workmen's Compensation Act 1897 made employers liable for accidents at work but, until 1906, was confined to certain dangerous occupations. Parallel to this 'liberalisation' of relations with unions, there was a series of legal decisions, culminating in the Taff Vale case in 1901 that severely limited the legal rights unions believed that they had gained in the 1870s. [79] This led to increasing disillusionment among respectable trade unionists with the Conservative Party.

This framework was put to a further test by the Boer War. The early military setbacks, the cost, together with the revelations of the physical unfitness of volunteer recruits gave new urgency and new sources of support to fears of relative national decline. Calls came from across party boundaries for 'national efficiency'. [80] The main outcome was the introduction of school meals and medical inspections and treatment for school children after 1906, and some increased local and voluntary activity in the field of child and maternal welfare. The Conservatives responded by keeping further social intervention to a minimum but could not be totally unresponsive to demands for change that developed in the 1890s and revived after the war. The Education Act 1902 was their most decisive step, though it antagonised Nonconformists and also ratepayers by increasing further their commitments. The Unemployed Workmen Act 1905 was a minimal response to a problem of increasingly urgency. The equally urgent problem of reforming the poor law, increasingly a focus for labour and radical Liberal criticism, was met by the establishment of

---

(University of Wales Press), 1997, and Green, E. H. H., 'The Conservative Party, the state and social policy, 1880-1914', in Francis, Martin, and Zweiniger-Bargielowska, Ina, (eds.), *The Conservatives and British society, 1880-1990*, (University of Wales Press), 1996, pp. 226-239.

[79] See McCord, Norman, 'Taff Vale Revisited', *History*, Vol. 78, (1993), pp. 243-260, and Davidson, Roger, 'The Board of Trade and Industrial Relations 1896-1914', *Historical Journal*, Vol. 21, (3), (1978), pp. 571-591.

[80] Searle, G. R., '"National efficiency" and the "lessons" of the war', in Omissi, David Enrico, and Thompson, Andrew Stuart, (eds.), *The Impact of the South African War*, (Palgrave), 2002, pp. 194-211, and more generally *The quest for national efficiency: a study in British politics and political thought, 1899-1914*, (Oxford University Press), 1971.

a Royal Commission in 1905.[81]

The Liberals came to power in 1906 after a landslide electoral victory but offered few promises of social legislation.[82] Between 1906 and 1908, their pact with Labour resulted in the Trade Disputes Act 1906 but social legislation such as the introduction of school meals by a Labour backbencher or medical inspections because of civil service pressure was initiated outside the cabinet. Any further initiatives were constrained by the hostility of the Conservative-dominated Lords and by shortage of government revenue compounded by rising prices. Rates were unpopular and by-election gains made by Conservatives from mobilising around ratepayer discontent removed one means of financing social measures. Hence Liberal legislation was either very cheap or funded from new sources, such as the National Insurance contributions introduced in 1911.[83]

Graduated income tax, in place of the flat-rate previously employed, was a means of increasing revenue that was compatible with free trade. Asquith's 1907 budget distinguished between earned and unearned income reducing the rate on the former from 1s to 9d in the pound. He also introduced compulsory returns for all classes of taxable income. The yield was small but the move marked the way to Lloyd George's more dramatic budgets from 1909 and marked an important break with Gladstonian principles. The 'class politics' that Gladstonian tax policy had been designed to keep at bay now seemed inescapable. Asquith also took the first step towards innovative and popular social reform and was responsible for the Old Age Pensions Act 1908. Social reform for the next four years was primarily the work of Lloyd George and Winston Churchill. Labour exchanges, minimum wages and protection of working conditions in 'sweated'

---

[81] See, Woodroofe, Kathleen, 'The Royal Commission on the Poor Laws, 1905-9', *International Review of Social History*, Vol. 22, (1977), pp. 137-164.

[82] Powell, David, *The Edwardian crisis: Britain, 1901-1914*, (Macmillan), 1996.

[83] There are a range of works on the Liberal governments between 1906 and 1914 and useful biographies of Campbell-Bannerman, Asquith, Winston Churchill and especially Lloyd George. These all consider the Liberal social reforms. Hay, J. R., *The Origins of the Liberal Welfare Reforms*, (Macmillan), 1975, is a short synopsis of historians' interpretations though in need of revision; Brooks, David, *The age of upheaval: Edwardian politics 1899-1914*, (Manchester University Press), 1995, is a useful study. Gilbert, Bentley B., *The Evolution of National Insurance in Great Britain: The Origins of the Welfare State*, (Joseph), 1966, and his two published volumes of his biography of Lloyd George are standard. Crowther, Anne, *British Social Policy 1914-1939*, (Macmillan), 1988, has a useful opening chapter.

female labour and unemployment and health insurance followed. This social legislation left many problems unresolved. There was no attempt to reconstruct the poor law despite the recommendations of the Royal Commission in 1909. The measures were also economical, and not, or intended to be, significantly redistributive. The most striking characteristic of the social legislation was the effectiveness with which it was implemented due, in part, to the larger and more efficient bureaucratic resources of central and local government. In 1851, there were 39,000 civil servants, in 1881, 51,000, in 1901 116,400, and, by 1911, there were 172,000.

Between the 1870s and 1914, there was an important shift of opinion on the proper role of government at local and national levels. The minimal regulatory state was found increasingly unsuitable to deal with the growing plethora of social problems that threatened not only social stability but also the continued power of the Liberal Party. Changing attitudes were a combination of political expediency and social awareness. There was also a significant shift in the degree that people were prepared to tolerate intervention and recognition that individual rights had to be weighed against the more general rights of the community.

18 Churches under pressure

The Church of England system is ripe for dissolution. The service provided by it is of a bad sort: inefficient with respect to the ends or objects professed to be aimed at by it: efficient with respect to the divers effects which, being pernicious, are too flagrantly so to be professed to be aimed at. [1]

In the first half of the nineteenth century British society became increasingly polarised and an important part in that process was religious adherence:

> So, in the nineteenth century religion was itself a major source of conflict in west-European societies; it also reflected the other fundamental lines of division. The battles between the official churches and their opponents initially brought together coalitions of those from different social classes. [2]

British society was intensely religious in 1780 and, despite the pessimistic conclusions contemporaries read into the Religious Census of 1851, it remained so. The Bible dominated thought and culture to a considerable extent.[3] Even among those openly antagonistic to the Bible, Scripture was still important to their lives. Secularists and atheists often regarded Scripture as being important in terms of their own loss of faith. This did not mean that religious institutions were not under pressure. The state religions, Presbyterianism in Scotland and Anglicanism in England, Wales and Ireland, faced threats from within and without and sought to widen their popular appeal and reinforce their defences against hostile forces. [4] The eighteenth century had seen the beginnings of a populist evangelicalism that energised Anglicanism and existing Dissenting sects and, after 1800, led to their rebranding as Nonconformity. In Ireland, and to a lesser extent mainland Britain, Roman Catholicism formed the third religious community. These religions made absolute claims for themselves and attempted to demarcate clear boundaries

---

[1] Bentham, Jeremy, *Church of Englandism and the Catechism Examined*, (E. Wilson), 1818, pp. 198-199.
[2] McLeod, H., *Religion and the People of Western Europe 1789-1970*, (Oxford University Press), 1981, p. 22.
[3] Larsen, Timothy, *A People of One Book: the Bible and the Victorians*, (Oxford University Press), 2011, demonstrates the extent to which the Bible dominated Victorian thought and culture.
[4] Brown, Stewart, J., *The National Churches of England, Ireland and Scotland, 1801-1846*, (Oxford University Press), 2001.

between their own communities and the world beyond. [5] This was, as Hugh McLeod has rightly said, 'the age of self-built ideological ghettos' maintained a network of institutions, a body of collective memories, particular rites, hymns and legendary heroes over several generations.[6] As the authority of the state churches was challenged, these groups sought to impose the same degree of control within their own sphere of influence that the state churches had once exercised. [7] This competition was exported to Britain's colonies and replicated especially in the predominantly white-settler communities and was also evident in the burgeoning missionary activities of the different denominations. [8]

---

[5] Paz, Denis G., (ed.), *Nineteenth-Century English Religious Traditions: Retrospect and Prospect*, (Greenwood Publishing Group), 1995, contains essays summarising the different religious traditions and the tensions they faced. See also, Melnyk, Julie, *Victorian Religion: Faith and Life in Britain*, (Praeger), 2008.

[6] Ibid, McLeod, H., *Religion and the People of Western Europe 1789-1970*, p. 36.

[7] Yates, Nigel, *Eighteenth Century Britain: Religion and Politics 1714-1815*, (Longman), 2007, and Brown, Stewart, *Providence and Empire 1815-1914*, (Longman), 2008, provide a recent summary of developments. Gay, J. D., *The Geography of Religion in England*, (Duckworth), 1971, is valuable especially for its maps, Gilbert, A. D., *Religion and Society in Industrial England 1740-1914*, (Longman), 1976, and Ward, W. R., *Religion and Society 1790-1850*, (Batsford), 1972. Currie, R. R., Gilbert, A. D., and Horsley, L. S., *Churches and Churchgoers: Patterns of Church Growth in the British Isles since 1700*, (Oxford University Press), 1977, provides a statistical treatment of national religious trends but does little on trends for regions and localities. *Religion in Victorian Britain*, 4 Vols. (Manchester University Press), 1988: Parsons, Gerald, (ed.), Vol. 1, *Traditions*, Vol. 2, *Controversies* and Vol. 4, *Interpretations*, and Moore, J. R., (ed.), Vol. 3, *Sources*, is of immense value for detailed analysis. Brown, Stewart, and Tackett, Timothy, (eds.), *Cambridge History of Christianity: Volume 7, Enlightenment, Reawakening and Revolution 1660-1815*, (Cambridge University Press), 2006, and Gilley, Sheridan, and Stanley, Brian, (eds.), *Cambridge History of Christianity: Volume 8, World Christianities c.1815-c.1914*, (Cambridge University Press), 2005, give a global perspective. Morgan, Sue and de Vries, Jacqueline, (eds.), *Women, Gender and Religious Cultures in Britain, 1800-1940*, (Routledge), 2010, contains several relevant papers.

[8] Cox, Jeffrey, *The British Missionary Enterprise since 1700*, (Routledge), 2008, and Porter, Andrew N., *Religion versus empire?: British Protestant missionaries and overseas expansion, 1700-1914*, (Manchester University Press), 2004 provide good summaries. See also, Carey, Hilary M., *God's Empire: Religion and Colonisation in the British World, c.1801-1908*, (Cambridge University Press), 2011, and Carré, J., (ed.), *Le monde*

The Church of England 1800-1851

The Church of England found itself in an uncomfortable position in 1800 largely because it had been slow to recognise the significance of the changes taking place in the population structure of the country. [9] Fully integrated into the social environment with village and parish normally coterminous, its strength lay in southern England where the bulk of the population and wealth was located. [10] The situation in northern England was less favourable and there was a long-term failure to retain the loyalty and affections of the industrialising areas. Parishes were large, often poorly endowed and so attracted few clergy and many livings were held in plurality or by non-resident incumbents. [11] For example, in 1831 Leeds, with a population of over 70,000 people, had only three places of Anglican worship. [12] The elaborate legal procedure for creating new parishes further hindered its ability to cope with the rapidly changing situation. The church hierarchy had little comprehension of the nature of the city and of the 104 bishops between 1783 and 1852, only 17 had ever held an urban living. The diocesan system of the north was equally inflexible and unable to meet the new situation. Until 1836, Lancashire, large parts of Cumberland and Westmoreland and the north-west part of Yorkshire were all included in the unwieldy Diocese of Chester. [13]

---

britannique: Religion et cultures (1815-1931), second edition, (Sedes), 2009.

[9] On the Church of England see Norman, E. R., *Church and Society in England 1770-1970,* (Oxford University Press), 1976, and Knight, Frances, *The Nineteenth-Century Church and English Society,* (Cambridge University Press), 1999. On social attitudes, Soloway, R. A., *Prelates and People: Ecclesiastical Social Thought in England 1783-1852,* (Routledge), 1969, Clark, G. Kitson, *Churchmen and the Condition of England,* (Methuen), 1973.

[10] Gregory, Jeremy, and Chamberlain, Jeffrey Scott, (eds.), *The National Church in Local Perspective: the Church of England and the regions, 1660-1800,* (Boydell), 2003, especially, pp. 1-28, illustrates the range of responses to the problems facing religious communities.

[11] Gibson, William T., 'Nepotism, family, and merit: the Church of England in the eighteenth century', *Journal of Family History,* Vol. 18, (1993), pp. 179-190.

[12] Royle, Edward, 'The Church of England and Methodism in Yorkshire, c.1750-1850: from monopoly to free market', *Northern History,* Vol. 33, (1997), pp. 137-161.

[13] Early attempts at reform are considered in Burns, R. Arthur, 'A Hanoverian legacy?: diocesan reform in the Church of England, c.1800-1833', in Walsh, John, Haydon, Colin, and Taylor, Stephen, (eds.), *The*

There was no bishop based in Lancashire and the West Riding until the dioceses of Ripon and Manchester were established in 1836 and 1847 and Liverpool and Newcastle did not gain episcopal status until 1880 and 1882. [14]

It was not just in the large towns that the Anglican Church's position was parlous. Excessive emphasis has been placed on the alienation of urban society and this has tended to deflect attention away from the situation in the countryside. [15] The real tragedy for the Church was not the failure to meet the needs of people in the growing cities but rather its failure in the countryside where all its resources were concentrated. Among the lower clergy, the curates and the holders of small benefices, there remained a degree of poverty that continued to cause hardship, despite legislation that sought to regulate curates' stipends. Many church buildings were in disrepair and pluralism and absenteeism were rife. Where Dissent established support, competition from the Church was often limited. Enclosure had reduced the hold of the Church since improvements in farming led to the commutation of tithes for land and many believed that the increase in the clergy's land was at the expense of the small tenant farmer. [16] An even worse reaction against the Church of England resulted from the collection of the tithe in kind, generally regarded as the ideal way of alienating the parson from his flock. [17]

An unresponsive and less than efficient pastoral system was exacerbated by a widespread belief that the Church must defend its position. Like the unreformed Parliament, the unreformed Church had its own elaborate defence of the status quo. The French

---

Church of England, c.1689-c.1833: from toleration to Tractarianism, (Cambridge University Press), 1993, pp. 265-282.

[14] Jacob, W. M., *The Clerical Profession in the Long Eighteenth Century, 1680-1840*, (Oxford University Press), 2007, examines the concept of 'profession' during the later-Stuart and Georgian period, with special reference to the clergy of the Church of England.

[15] See, for example, Brown, Callum G., 'The mechanism of religious growth in urban society: British cities since the eighteenth century', in McLeod, Hugh, *European Religion in the Age of the Great Cities, 1830-1930*, (Routledge), 1994, pp. 237-260, a synoptic overview. See also, Burns, Arthur, *The Diocesan Revival in the Church of England c.1800-1870*, (Oxford University Press), 1999.

[16] Lee, Robert, *Rural society and the Anglican clergy, 1815-1914: encountering and managing the poor*, (Boydell), 2006, considers the church in Norfolk.

[17] On this issue see Evans, E. J., *The Contentious Tithe: The Tithe Problem and English Agriculture 1750-1830*, (Routledge), 1976, pp. 16-41 and 94-114.

Revolution had frightened the propertied classes and strengthened their belief that the society under their control must be defended as a divinely ordained hierarchy. [18] In this situation suggested reforms, including modest ones, could easily by identified with revolution and revolution with the destruction of Christianity. Even those who avoided the extremes of reaction felt it was their religious duty to preserve the constitution, the social order and the morality now under threat. In 1834, a fifth of the magistrates in England were Anglican clergymen, embodying an enormous investment in social stability.

To critics such as the journalist John Wade, whose polemic the *Black Book* appeared in 1820 and in a revised form as *The Extraordinary Black Book* in 1831, the abuses of the Church, its ineffective organisation and its conservative views were in need of reform. [19] This was not the view of the Church: its property rights had to be defended; it was not accountable to the public; it had, as an established institution, a prescriptive right to authority. By a series of instinctive, but ill-judged actions, the Church identified itself with extreme Toryism and alienated opinion further in the 1820s and early 1830s. [20] Abused by the radicals from outside Parliament, events in 1828 and 1829 showed how little the Church could expect from its political friends. With Daniel O'Connell's Catholic Association campaigning for emancipation in Ireland and the threat of widespread public disorder, Wellington's Tory government concluded that Emancipation was the only practical solution and legislation was passed in April 1829. The repeal of the Test and Corporation Acts and Catholic Emancipation ended the special relationship between the Church and Parliament establishing, in effect, free trade in religion. Dissenters and Catholics would now participate in legislation affecting the Church. [21] The attitude of the bishops during the

---

[18] See, Stafford, William, 'Religion and the doctrine of nationalism in England at the time of the French Revolution and Napoleonic wars', in Mews, Stuart, (ed.), *Religion and national identity: papers read at the nineteenth summer meeting and twentieth winter meeting of the Ecclesiastical History Society*, (Oxford University Press), 1982, pp. 381-395.

[19] Clayson, Jim, Frow, Edmund, and Frow, Ruth, 'John Wade and *The Black Book*', *Labour History Review*, Vol. 59, (2), (1994), pp. 55-57.

[20] Simon, W. G., 'The bishops and reform', *Historical Magazine of the Protestant Episcopal Church*, Vol. 32, (1963), pp. 361-370, considers the period between 1820 and 1850.

[21] O'Ferral, *Catholic Emancipation: Daniel O'Connell and the birth of Irish democracy 1820-30*, (Gill & Macmillan), 1985, and Reynolds, J. A., *The Catholic Emancipation Crisis in Ireland, 1823-9*, (Yale University Press), 1954, provide contrasting studies. Kerr, Donal, 'Catholic Emancipation Act

reform agitation of 1830-1832 further tarnished the reputation of the Church and reinforced its identification in the eyes of the public with reaction.

What was the nature of individual action?

The Church was unable to resist the pressures for reform since it was not united in maintaining its authoritarian and conservative position. Critical opinion from evangelicals and from the laity led to concentration on the reform and reinvigoration of the parish. The Church of England and the Church of Ireland had been joined by the Act of Union. It became increasingly necessary to reform the gross abuses and alter the political position of the Church of Ireland and this, by extension, raised the same question in relation to the Anglican Church. Since it had no governing body of its own, the Church depended on Parliament and party politicians for support in its reactionary attitudes. The Church might claim to be aloof from public opinion, but after 1832 politicians could not afford to be.

Initially, reform of the Church was left to individuals. The Church of England still commanded considerable support among lay people who remained willing to donate large sums of their money, time and skill, to maintaining and extending its fabric. Charles Simeon, the Vicar of Holy Trinity, Cambridge, sought to improve the quality of those entering the Church.[22] In the late-eighteenth century there was little professional training for clergymen and Simeon supplied the need in Cambridge with instruction to improve the quality and delivery of sermons. His example probably encouraged the establishment of the first specialist theological colleges at St. Bees in 1816 and Lampeter in 1828. Simeon maintained that good evangelical clergymen were necessary but he also believed in the need to ensure that there was continuity of 'gospel ministers' in livings if the work of the Church was to be maintained. The idea of a corporation or trust to secure advowsons had already been operated

---

of 1829', *Seanchas Dhroim Mór*, Vol. 1, (1980), pp. 57-75, looks at the legislation and Machin, G. I. T., *The Catholic Question In English Politics 1820-1830*, (Oxford University Press), 1964, views the question through the refracting mirror of English politics.

[22] Carus, William, (ed.), *Memoirs of the life of... Charles Simeon...with a selection from his writings and correspondence*, (Hatchard and Son), 1847, is an essential if partial source. Moule, H. C. G., *Charles Simeon*, (Methuen), 1892, and Hopkins, H. E., *Charles Simeon of Cambridge*, (Hodder & Stoughton), 1977, remain good studies of his life. Piper, John, *Roots of Endurance: Invincible Perseverance in the Lives of John Newton, Charles Simeon and William Wilberforce*, (Crossway Books), 2006, places Simeon in his evangelical context.

but in 1817, Simeon began his trust with the purchase of the patronage of Cheltenham. He was perhaps more aware than many of his contemporaries of the need to secure a foothold in the growing industrial towns. His most important successes came after the Municipal Corporations Act of 1835 that compelled corporations to give up their patronage. After he died in 1836, his successors secured two parishes in Liverpool and parishes in Bath, Derby, Macclesfield, Bridlington and Beverley. He was very conscious of the need to operate within the framework of the Church of England and disliked the insistence of evangelicals who believed that their commission to preach the gospels meant that they could override parochial boundaries. He insisted on church order and this probably deterred many Anglican Evangelicals leaving the Church of England.

Lay influence on the Church of England was felt from the systematic nationwide penetration of the Anglican evangelicals associated loosely with William Wilberforce. The British and Foreign Bible Society [23] and the Church Missionary Society, [24] founded in 1803 and 1811, independently of the success they enjoyed abroad, played a major part in extending evangelical influence in Britain. The Bible Society sought to disseminate copies of the Bible without note or comment; by 1825 it had issued over four million. Many non-evangclical clergymen disliked this. They emphasised the importance of the Book of Common Prayer as well as the Bible and were suspicious of the co-operation with Dissent that the Society encouraged. The Evangelical campaign sought to bring the working population within the orbit of the Established Church with the aim of keeping them in their place.

Evangelicalism was seen as an antidote to revolution from the 1790s. Hannah More (1745-1833) and her sister Martha played a considerable role in educating people for their place in society. [25] In

---

[23] Canton, William, *The History of the British and Foreign Bible Society*, 5 Vols. (Murray), 1904-1910, Howsam, Leslie, *Cheap bibles: nineteenth-century publishing and the British and Foreign Bible Society*, (Cambridge University Press), 1991, and Batalden, Stephen, Cann, Kathleen, and Dean, John, (eds.), *Sowing the word: the cultural impact of the British and Foreign Bible Society, 1804-2004*, (Sheffield Phoenix), 2004.

[24] Elbourne, Elizabeth, 'The foundation of the Church Missionary Society: the Anglican missionary impulse', in ibid, Walsh, John, Haydon, Colin, and Taylor, Stephen, (eds.), *The Church of England, c.1689-c.1833: from toleration to Tractarianism*, pp. 247-264, and Stock, Eugene, *The History of the Church Missionary Society: its Environment, its Men and its Work*, 4 Vols. (Church Missionary Society), 1899-1916.

[25] Stott, Anne, *Hannah More: The First Victorian*, (Oxford University Press), 2003, is an excellent biography; pp. 169-190, consider the *Cheap*

1795, she started the Cheap Repository Tracts in response to cheap radical literature. All 114 tracts had the same evangelical and conservative intention and an annual circulation of over two million copies. By 1830, the evangelicals had directed their attention at all sections of society. Wealth, social and political contacts and the crisis occasioned by the French Revolution helped them to spread their ideas among the aristocratic elite. The anti-slavery campaigns mobilised middle-class opinion and the Cheap Repository Tracts provided 'proper' reading for the working population.

Joshua Watson (1771-1855) was concerned to improve the ability of the Church to appeal to the growing urban population.[26] A successful wine merchant with wide commercial and financial interests, he retired from business in 1814 to devote himself to good works. He appealed to High Churchmen, in contrast to the Evangelicals, and the group that gathered at his house in Hackney became known as the Hackney Phalanx and publicised their activities through the *British Critic*. Watson was prominent in the formation of the National Society for Promoting the Education of the Poor in the Principles of the Established Church in 1811. Its purpose was to encourage parishes to start their own schools and within three years it had raised sufficient contributions to establish 360 schools in that there were 60,000 pupils and nearly a million twenty years later. It did not receive state support until government grants were introduced in 1833. Though the 1839 Whig educational proposals were mangled by Anglican opposition, a Committee of the Privy Council did take over the supervision of education and Watson's resignation in 1842 coincided with the assertion of the authority of the State in education.

The other charitable effort that Watson led was the building of new churches. There was little point in educating children into the Anglican faith if, when they grew up, they could not become regular churchgoers. This was a very difficult enterprise for private charity, even if money could be found. Until 1818, a new parish had to be created by Parliament and to build a new church in an existing parish required the consent of the patron and the incumbent, either of whom might feel their rights were being infringed. In 1818, Watson formed an Incorporated Church Building Society and in the same year, the Prime Minister, Lord Liverpool established an official

---

Repository Tracts. See also, Pedersen, Susan, 'Hannah More meets Simple Simon: tracts, chapbooks, and popular culture in late eighteenth-century England', *Journal of British Studies*, Vol. 25, (1986), pp. 84-113.

[26] Churton, Edward, *Memoir of Joshua Watson*, 2 Vols. (J. H. and J. Parker), 1861, and Webster, A. B., *Joshua Watson: the story of a layman, 1771-1855*, (SPCK), 1954.

commission with a grant of £1 million with a further £0.5 million added in 1824. [27] Parliamentary grants were virtually used up by 1828 and were not renewed, but such was the stimulus given to private subscribers that the commission did not finish its work until 1857. By then, it had built 612 new churches accommodating 600,000 people. This figure does not exhaust the total number of churches built as many were built or rebuilt by private means.

How far did institutional reform resolve the problems facing the Church?

By the early 1830s, despite the work of these individuals and groups, there was a feeling that the Church was faced with the choice between reform or 'complete destruction'. [28] This fear was sufficient to remove the obstacles to organisational change and pastoral renewal that had long prevented its adjustment to industrial and urban society. The ecclesiastical and political crises of 1828-1832 were closely connected. The repeal of the Test and Corporation Acts in 1828, though they had little impact on the lives of Anglicans and Nonconformists, gave legitimacy to the 'de facto' situation. Catholic Emancipation in 1829 ended the civil disabilities against Catholics even if it had little impact on anti-Catholic sentiments and arguably may have increased them. This dramatically symbolised the failure of the old monopolistic and exclusive conception of the Establishment and its replacement by a pluralistic conception of religion. The blind conservatism of the Church of England's leadership during the reform agitation, a conservatism motivated by a fear that the country was near revolution and that the church faced disestablishment, the 1832 Reform Act and the Whig electoral landslide meant that moderate reform could no longer be avoided. [29] The State increasingly took control of this 'metamorphosis' and the initiative for reform. The restructuring of the Establishment was something imposed by a Parliament that could not afford to wait for some consensus on reform to emerge from within the Church itself. [30]

---

[27] Port, M. H., *600 New Churches: the Church Building Commission, 1818-1856*, 1961, revised edition, (Spire Books), 2006.
[28] On the problem of church reform see, Virgin, P., *The Church in an Age of Negligence: ecclesiastical structure and the problems of church reform*, (Cambridge University Press), 1989.
[29] Burns, R. Arthur, 'The authority of the church', in Mandler, Peter, (ed.), *Liberty and authority in Victorian Britain*, (Oxford University Press), 2006, pp. 179-200.
[30] For the role of the state see Brose, O., *Church and Parliament: The Reshaping of the Church of England 1828-1860*, (Cambridge University Press), 1959, Thompson, K. A., *Bureaucracy and Church Reform: A Study*

In June 1832, an Ecclesiastical Revenues Commission was established, but for two and a half years it had achieved little concrete. It investigated the Church's financial structures but, as the debate about the Church intensified outside Parliament, proposals for reform were either defeated or allowed to lapse. The breakthrough came with the setting up of a new Commission to 'consider the State of the Established Church' in early 1835 during Peel's minority 'Hundred Days' administration. It consisted of senior churchmen and Anglican politicians, including Peel, whose task was to prepare bills ready to present to Parliament to tackle the abuses that had been shown to be widespread in the Church of England. For Peel, it was essential for there to be 'judicious reform' to give 'real stability to the Church in its spiritual character...I believe enlarged political interests will be best promoted by strengthening the hold of the Church of England upon the love and veneration of the community'. [31] Peel recognised that unless something was done quickly church reform might fall into the hands of politicians less sympathetic to the Anglican cause and possibly jeopardise the position of the Church as an Established body. By establishing a permanent body that involved the Church of England in initiating its own reform, Peel sought to encourage a greater sense of responsibility among Anglican leaders and hopefully shield the Church against further damaging attacks. [32]

The Ecclesiastical Commission survived the change in government in April 1835 and in 1836, the Whig Prime Minister Lord Melbourne established it on a permanent basis as the Ecclesiastical Commission and, under the chairmanship of Charles James Blomfield, bishop of London, it quickly became the main instrument of organisational improvement in the Church. [33] It never became a government department answerable to Parliament through a minister and retained a degree of independence thought necessary if reform was to triumph over the opposition of vested interests in the

---

of the Church of England 1800-1965, (Oxford University Press), 1970, and Machin, G. I. T., *Politics and the Churches in Great Britain 1832 to 1868*, (Oxford University Press), 1977.

[31] Parker, C. S., (ed.), *Sir Robert Peel: from his private papers*, 3 Vols. (John Murray), 1899, Vol. 2, p. 266.

[32] Dibdin, L. T., and Downing, S. E., *The Ecclesiastical Commission: a sketch of its history and work*, (Macmillan), 1919. See also, Manning, H. E., *The Principle of the Ecclesiastical Commission examined*, (J. G. & F. Rivington), 1838.

[33] Blomfield, Alfred, (ed.), *A memoir of Charles James Blomfield, Bishop of London (1828-56), with selections from his correspondence*, 2 Vols. (John Murray), 1863, and Johnson, Malcolm, *Bustling intermeddler? The life and work of Charles James Blomfield*, (Gracewing), 2001.

House of Lords and in the Church at large. But, since the Church possessed no effective assembly or courts of its own, the initiative at the most vital points in the development of this body had to come from government. Major reforms of the Church's structure occurred in the second half of the 1830s and during Peel's ministry (1841-1846). The boundaries of existing dioceses were modified and new dioceses created in 1836; severe restrictions were placed on pluralism in 1838 and in 1840, excess revenues were distributed from cathedrals to those with greater needs. The Whigs also introduced the Registration Act in 1836 placing the registration of births, marriages and deaths in the hands of civil officials and not the Church and in 1838 the Dissenters' Marriage Act ended the obligation of Nonconformists to marry in Anglican churches. [34] A Populous Parishes Act was passed in 1843 empowering the Ecclesiastical Commission to create new parishes and providing the necessary stipends out of Church funds but it was clear to Peel that the cost of building new churches would have to be covered by the more efficient use of the Church's existing resources and charitable contributions. [35] An impressive fund-raising campaign resulted in £25 million being spent on building and restoration work between 1840 and 1876. Improving the quality of the clergy proved a gradual process and the ideal of a fully-resident clergy remained difficult to put into practice and pluralism and non-residence remained relatively common until the 1870s. It should not be assumed that this necessarily resulted in poor standards of clerical attention to their parochial duties. Many of the rural clergy lived only a short distance from their parishes and were as efficient as they would have been had they been technically resident.

Of crucial importance in attempting to re-establish the popular position of the Church was resolving its financial grievances caused by the unpopularity of church rates and tithes. Though compulsory church rates were not abolished until 1868, legal judgements made it clear that they could only be collected where authorised by the churchwardens and a majority of the vestry. As Nonconformists were eligible to vote for both, in some towns such as Birmingham the rate

---

[34] Cullen, M. J., 'The making of the Civil Registration Act of 1836', *Journal of Ecclesiastical History*, Vol. 25, (1974), pp. 39-60, and Ambler, R. W., 'Civil registration and baptism: popular perceptions of the 1836 act for registering births, deaths and marriages', *Local Population Studies*, Vol. 39, (1987), pp. 24-31.

[35] Welch, P. J., 'Blomfield and Peel: a study in cooperation between Church and State, 1841-6', *Journal of Ecclesiastical History*, Vol. 12, (1961), 71-84.

lapsed. This was preferable to Nonconformists than the scheme that the House of Commons seriously considered for repairing all parish churches from public funds. [36] The Tithe Commutation Act 1836 ended tithes in kind replacing them with money payments based on the average prices of corn, oats and barley over the previous seven years.

The approach of the Commission was both radical and realistic. The decision to use excessive endowments to help poorer parishes resulted in 5,300 parishes being assisted in this way between 1840 and 1855. By 1850, the numbers of non-resident clergy had fallen significantly strengthening the work of the Anglican ministry. The increase in the pastoral efficiency of the clergy was accompanied by a decline in their status relative to other professions. The number of clergymen in the magistracy fell. The Church was saved in the 1830s and 1840s by giving up some of its social and secular administrative functions and by a further surrendering of its autonomy to the State. The religious dimension of the priestly office had become paramount. However, these initiatives did little to stem the numerical slide of the Church of England in urban and increasingly rural areas.

How was the Church reformed from within?

In the vanguard of the Church's reaction to change since the 1790s, the High Church 'party' may well have inhibited reformist tendencies before 1830. They distrusted their more evangelical colleagues, whose pastoral concerns seemed to threaten the unreformed Establishment and were horrified by the structural and administrative reforms of Blomfield and Peel. The problem of the Church of Ireland led to the emergence of the Tractarian or Oxford movement. [37] The

---

[36] Brent, Richard, 'The Whigs and Protestant dissent in the decade of reform: the case of church rates, 1833-1841', *English Historical Review*, Vol. 102, (1987), pp. 887-910.

[37] Nockles, Peter B., *The Oxford Movement in Context: Anglican High Churchmanship, 1760-1857*, (Cambridge University Press), 1997, Yates, N., *The Oxford Movement and Anglican Ritualism*, (The Historical Association), 1983, and Faber, G., *Oxford Apostles*, (Faber), 1933, and Church, R.W., *The Oxford Movement: Twelve Years 1833-1845*, (Macmillan), 1891, a classic, loyalist account in a modern edition edited by G. F. A. Best in 1970. Skinner, Simon A., *Tractarians and the 'condition of England': the social and political thought of the Oxford movement*, (Oxford University Press), 2004, is an invaluable modern study but see also, Carter, Grayson, *Anglican Evangelicals: Protestant secessions from the via media, c.1800-1850*, (Oxford University Press), 2001, pp. 249-311. Brown, Stewart J., and Nockles, Peter B., *The Oxford Movement: Europe and the*

1833 Church Temporalities Act reformed the Church of Ireland, reducing its archbishops from four to two and its bishops by ten and creating a body of ecclesiastical commissioners to control a substantial part of the Church's revenue. These reforms did not spell disaster for Irish Anglicanism and it remained the religion of a socially advantaged but numerically weak minority. [38] However, in the 1830s, many Anglicans were outraged and it was the imminent passage of the Irish Temporalities Bill that prompted John Keble to preach his sermon on 'National Apostasy' on Sunday 14 July 1833. It marked the formal beginnings of the Oxford movement.

The Hadleigh conference in late July led to agreement over the principles of the new movement: to proclaim the doctrine of the apostolic succession; the belief that it was sinful to give the laity a say in church affairs; to make the Church more popular; and, to protest against attempts to disestablish the Anglican Church. [39] The Oxford movement was a reaction against prevailing religious attitudes. It was part of the general and widespread revival of the 'corporate' against the 'individual' evangelical spirit of the day. It was a reaction against the Church as a department of state: as Keble said 'let us give up a national Church and have a real one'. [40] It was essentially a spiritual movement, concerned with the invisible world and was not only anti-liberal but also paradoxically intensely political. Newman opposed liberalism and erastianism as both struck at the spiritual dimension, the former by enslaving its spiritual guardian, the latter by destroying its dogmatic foundations. The Tractarians diagnosed an age blighted

---

Wider World, 1830-1930, (Cambridge University Press), 2012, paints a broader perspective. Chadwick, O., *Newman*, (Oxford University Press), 1983, is a brief biography focussing on his ideas and his *The Spirit of the Oxford Movement*, (Cambridge University Press), 1990, contains a collection of important essays. Ker, I., *John Henry Newman*, (Oxford University Press), 1990, is the definitive biography.

[38] Kriegel, Abraham D., 'The Irish Policy of Lord Grey's Government', *English Historical Review*, Vol. 86, (1971), pp. 22-45, Condon, Mary D., 'The Irish Church and the Reform Ministries', *Journal of British Studies*, Vol. 3, (1964), pp. 140-162, and Davis, R. W., 'The Whigs and religious issues, 1830-35', in Davis, R. W., and Helmstadter, R. J., (eds.), *Religion and Irreligion in Victorian Society: Essays in honour of R. K. Webb*, (Routledge), 1992, pp. 29-50.

[39] Nockles, Peter B., 'The Oxford Movement as Religious Revival and Resurgence', *Studies in Church History*, Vol. 44, (2008), pp. 214-224.

[40] On attitudes to the state, see Nockles, P. B., 'Pusey and the Question of Church and States', in Butler, P., (ed.), *Pusey Rediscovered*, (SPCK), 1982, pp. 255-297, Rowlands, J. H. L., *Church, State and Society: The Attitudes of John Keble, R. H. Froude and J. H. Newman, 1827-45*, (Churchman Publishing), 1989.

by worldliness and that contemporary Protestantism was incapable of rescuing it from spiritual decay.

The principal objective of the Oxford movement was the defence of the Church of England as a divinely-founded institution, of the doctrine of the Apostolic Succession and of the *Book of Common Prayer* as a 'rule of faith'. The movement postulated the branch theory, which states that Anglicanism along with Orthodoxy and Roman Catholicism form three 'branches' of the one 'Catholic Church'. Many in the movement argued for the inclusion of traditional aspects of liturgy from medieval religious practice, as they believed the church had become too 'plain'. The method of the Tractarians was to concentrate on a single article of the Christian creed: 'I believe in one Catholic and Apostolic Church', by which they meant the maintenance of apostolic order in the Church through the episcopacy. They used *Tracts for the Times* to disseminate their views, the first published in September 1833. By the end of 1833, 20 tracts had been published; 50 by the end of 1834 and 66 by July 1835. Tracts were nothing new: John Wesley had used tracts and the Evangelicals had their Religious Tract Society. What was novel about the *Tracts* of the Oxford movement was that they were written and circulated by dons and addressed not to the poor but to educated minds.

For many the Oxford movement raised the threat of Popery. [41] The papist and bigoted perceptions of the movement was partially confirmed by the Hampden case of 1835-1836 when leading Tractarians unsuccessfully opposed the appointment of Renn Dickson Hampden as Regius Professor of Divinity in 1836.[42] Hampden symbolised both the liberal and erastian face of the Church of England. His liberal views had already attracted the attention of the leaders of the Oxford movement after his return to Oxford in 1829. In his *Observations on Religious Dissent* published in August 1834, he defended the right of non-Anglicans to attend Oxford and this led to a response from Newman in the *Elucidations*

---

[41] See, Freeman, Peter, 'The response of Welsh Nonconformity to the Oxford movement', *Welsh History Review*, Vol. 20, (2001), pp. 435-465, and 'The effect of the Oxford Movement on some election campaigns in Wales in the mid-nineteenth century', *National Library of Wales Journal*, Vol. 31, (2000), pp. 369-380.

[42] Jebb, Richard, *A report of the case of the Right Rev. R. D. Hampden, D.D., Lord Bishop elect of Hereford: in Hereford Cathedral, the ecclesiastical courts, and the Queen's Bench*, (William Benning and Co.), 1849, Cratchley, W. J., 'The trials of R. D. Hampden', *Theology*, Vol. 35, (1937), pp. 211-226, and Thomas, Stephen, *Newman and Heresy: The Anglican Years*, (Cambridge University Press), 1991, pp. 71-79.

and an acrimonious debate persisted between the two scholars for two years. Newman's attack had two strands: he opposed the appointment of a clergyman with what he saw as suspect rationalist views especially one who threatened the Anglican hegemony at Oxford, something Newman saw as a threat to Christianity itself and also opposed his appointment by the patronage of a Whig prime minister. His nomination by Lord John Russell to the vacant see of Hereford in December 1847 was again the signal for organised opposition and his consecration in March 1848 took place despite a remonstrance by many of the bishops.

By the end of 1837, Newman in effect led a 'party' within the establishment and this gave anti-Catholic groups further evidence of the increasing Catholicity of the Tractarians. [43] In 1841, Newman published Tract 90, *Remarks on Certain Passages in the Thirty-Nine Articles* concluding that the doctrines of the Roman Catholic Church, as defined by the Council of Trent, were compatible with the Thirty-Nine Articles of the sixteenth century Church of England. Newman's conversion to Roman Catholicism in 1845, followed by that of Henry Edward Manning in 1851, had a profound effect upon the movement, strengthening the argument of opponents that the movement sought to 'Romanise' the Church but also pointing to its limitations. Originating within Oxford University, its approach was academic, clerical and conservative. [44] Its appeal was restricted to the educated classes, not so much from deliberate intention as from the interests and sympathies of its protagonists. It was not until after 1845 that the Anglo-Catholic revival reached out to the poor and got a footing in the slums. [45] Partly because bishops refused to give livings to Tractarian priests, many of them ended up working in the slums.

---

[43] On Newman's journey to Catholicism, see, Cameron, J. M., 'John Henry Newman and the Tractarian movement', in Smart, N., et al., (eds.), *Nineteenth Century Religious Thought in the West*, (Cambridge University Press), 1985, pp. 69-111, Ramsey, A. M., 'John Henry Newman and the Oxford Movement', *Anglican and Episcopal History*, Vol. 59, (1990), pp. 330-344, Blehl, Vincent Ferrer, *Pilgrim journey: John Henry Newman, 1801-1845*, (Burns & Oates), 2001, and Short, Edward, *Newman and his Contemporaries*, (Continuum), 2011.

[44] Nockles, Peter B., '"Lost causes and...impossible loyalties": the Oxford Movement and the university', in ibid, Brock, M. G., and Curthoys, Mark C., (eds.), *The History of the University of Oxford, Vol. 6: Nineteenth-century Oxford, part I*, pp. 195-267.

[45] Simpson, W. J. S., *The history of the Anglo-Catholic revival from 1845*, (Allen & Unwin), 1932, and Reed, J. S., '"Ritualism rampant in East London": Anglo-Catholicism and the urban poor', *Victorian Studies*, Vol. 31, (1988), pp. 375-403.

From their new ministries they developed a critique of British social policy, both local and national. It was predominantly clerical and, though it did acquire some support from eminent laymen, the *Tracts* were addressed to clergymen. [46] The movement had to be clerical because if the clergy did not accept its message it is certain no one else would. Its success in interesting the country's clergy in theological questions and church principles was one of its major achievements. Finally, it was inevitable that the standpoint of the movement was backward-looking. The problem for Newman started with the Reformation: 'a limb badly set, it must be broken again in order to be righted'. [47] This retrospection could, and was, seen as conservatism if not reaction by many.

Newman left the Anglican Church for Rome because he concluded that secular interference had tarnished the Church of England's apostolic character. The Gorham case in the late 1840s seemed to reinforce the claims being made by the movement. There were two distinct strands in the controversy. There was considerable anxiety in the Established Church over the breadth of views that members might hold and still remain members of the Church; how far was the Church of England a 'broad' church? The case also raised questions about the relationship between Church and State and particularly the extent to which the State could legitimately wield influence over doctrine and ritual that the Church maintained were its exclusive domain. To what extent could the Church maintain its independence from the political arm of the State? [48]

Despite concerns that some of his views were at odds with Anglican doctrine, George Gorham had been ordained in 1811, held curacies in several parishes and had been made vicar of St. Just in the Exeter diocese in 1846. The following year, Gorham was recommended for Brampford Speke. Upon examining him, Bishop

---

[46] Hutchison, W. G., (ed.), *The Oxford Movement, Being a selection from Tracts for the Times*, (The Scott Library), 1906, and Fulweiler, H. W., 'Tractarians and Philistines: the *Tracts for the Times* versus Victorian middle-class values', *Historical Magazine of the Protestant Episcopal Church*, Vol. 31, (1962), pp. 36-53.

[47] Froude, Richard H., *Remains of the late Reverend Richard Hurrell Froude*, 2 Vols. (J. G. & F. Rivington), 1838, Vol. 1, p. 433.

[48] Jordan, Andrew, 'George Cornelius Gorham, Clerk v Henry Phillpotts, Bishop of Exeter: A Case of Anglican Anxieties', *Ecclesiastical Law Journal*, Vol. 5, (1998), pp. 104-111. See also, Search, John, [Thomas Binney], *The Great Gorham Case: A History in Five Books including Expositions of the Rival Baptismal Theories by a Looker-On*, (Partridge and Oakey), 1850, and Nias, J. C. S., *Gorham and the Bishop of Exeter*, (SPCK), 1951.

Henry Phillpotts, who had the previous year instituted him at St. Just, took exception to Gorham's attacks on Tractarianism and particularly his evangelical view that baptismal regeneration was conditional on a conscious experience to confirm the sacrament's validity. Phillpotts decided that Gorham was unsuitable for the post. Gorham appealed to the ecclesiastical Court of Arches to compel the bishop to institute him but the court confirmed the bishop's decision and awarded costs against Gorham. This reassured Tractarian fears that Anglican apostolicity was being corrupted by secular authority. But, Gorham then appealed to the Privy Council, which caused great controversy about whether a secular court should decide on the doctrine of the Church of England. Ecclesiastical lawyer Edward Badeley, a member of the Oxford movement, appeared before the Council to argue the Bishop's cause but eventually on 9 March 1850, the Council in a split decision reversed the previous decisions granting Gorham his institution. Bishop Phillpotts repudiated the judgment and threatened to excommunicate the Archbishop of Canterbury and anyone who dared to institute Gorham. Fourteen prominent Anglicans, including Badeley and Henry Edward Manning called upon the Church of England to repudiate the views that the Privy Council had expressed on baptism. Since there was no response from the Church, apart from Phillpotts' protest, they left the Church of England and joined the Roman Catholic Church. Most Tractarians remained within the Church giving rise to the Anglo-Catholic party that stressed the role of ritual in fostering a sense of the Church as a distinctive, religious community.

The impact of the Oxford movement on the Anglican Church was essentially ecclesiastical. [49] It led to the establishment of Anglican religious orders, both of men and women. It incorporated ideas and practices related to the practice of liturgy and ceremony in a move to bring more powerful emotional symbolism and energy to the church. Its effects were widespread and the Eucharist gradually became more central to worship, vestments became common and numerous Catholic practices were re-introduced into worship. This led to controversies within churches that ended up in court, as in the dispute about ritualism. The Tractarians also played an important role in the provision of theological training for the clergy. Chichester (1839),

---

[49] Knight, Frances, 'The influence of the Oxford Movement in the parishes, c.1833-1860: a reassessment', in Vaïss, Paul, (ed.), *From Oxford to the people: reconsidering Newman & the Oxford Movement*, (Gracewing), 1996, pp. 127-140. Ibid, Chadwick, O., *The Spirit of the Oxford Movement*, pp. 289-306, and Yates, Nigel, *The Oxford Movement and parish life: St Saviour's, Leeds, 1839-1929*, (St Anthony's Hall Publications), 1975.

Wells (1840), Cuddesdon (1854) and Salisbury (1860) were all founded on definite high church principles. [50] Before 1830, the role of clergymen within society can best be described as 'social' rather than 'spiritual'. The Oxford movement provided clergy with a new concept of their social role that was not quasi-political but profoundly spiritual. This new concept of priestly vocation goes a long way to explain clerical support for Tractarianism. Evangelical assertions that the laity was becoming priest-ridden were not without foundation. [51]

Evangelicalism within Anglicanism

The Evangelical Revival in the eighteenth century was partly a consequence of the increasing frustration felt by individuals like the Wesleys with the intense conservatism of Anglican high churchmen.[52] Not all of those who supported Wesleyan Methodism left the Church of England in the 1790s. From 1750, another group of Evangelical clergy and laity also began to attack the conservatism of the established church from within. They took a considerable initiative in missionary work and campaigns for social and 'moral' reform and by the 1820s were beginning to establish a foothold in the parishes of some larger towns. [53] By 1830, three Evangelicals had been made bishops. Despite their emphasis on spiritual conversion and the absolute supremacy of Scripture over the traditions of the Church, they were not anti-sacramental encouraging frequent communion services. Theirs was a simple and unmysterious form of worship. People are all in a state of natural depravity, weighed down by sin and life is an arena of moral and spiritual trial in which people are tempted, tested and ultimately sorted into saints and sinners. There is a spiritual contract between each soul and God in which intermediaries like the clergy are of relatively little importance. Redemption comes through the faith of the individual in Christ's Atonement on the Cross. This was an evangelical 'scheme of salvation'. Within the Anglican middle-

---

[50] See, Chapman, Mark D., (ed.), *Ambassadors of Christ: commemorating 150 years of theological education in Cuddesdon, 1854-2004*, (Ashgate), 2004.

[51] Toon, P., *Evangelical Theology, 1833-1856: A Response to Tractarianism*, (Marshall, Morgan & Scott), 1979, considers this issue.

[52] Noll, Mark A., *The Rise of Evangelicalism: The Age of Edwards, Whitefield and the Wesleys*, (IVP), 2004, and Walsh, John, '"Methodism" and the origins of English-speaking evangelicalism', in Noll, Mark A., Bebbington, D. W., and Rawlyk, George A., (eds.), *Evangelicalism: Comparative studies of popular Protestantism in North America, the British Isles and beyond, 1700-1990*, (Oxford University Press), 1994, pp. 19-37.

[53] Scotland, Nigel, *Evangelical Anglicans in a revolutionary age 1789-1901*, (Paternoster), 2004.

classes, evangelicalism spread rapidly from the mid-1820s because of economic alarms, Catholic Emancipation, constitutional crises, cholera and other signs of impending divine intervention. [54]

By the 1820s, Anglicans were speaking about Anglican Evangelicals as 'the Evangelicals' as if they were the only ones. [55] This division between Anglican and non-Anglican evangelicals had not existed during the first phase of evangelicalism before the 1780s when people moved freely across the formal boundaries between denominations. The division developed as a result of Wesleyan Methodists separating from the Established Church in the 1790s and because Anglican Evangelicals were the ones who mattered socially and politically. If an ability to excite 'the affections' enabled evangelicalism to transcend the inertia of eighteenth century religion, a corresponding suspicion of 'worldly' pleasures slowly brought it down to earth. Originally the movement was premised on religious freedom, but as instinctive suspicion developed into the increasing hostility in the early-nineteenth century, it became coercive and alienating. It was in the wounded conscience of evangelicalism that the crisis of Victorian religion began. This was evident in the second phase of evangelicalism that began with the conversion of William Wilberforce and Hannah More in the 1780s. [56] These individuals brought a social distinction and respectability and conservatism that it had previously not enjoyed. Under their banner of the 'Evangelical Party', in itself an ambiguous term given the diversity of Anglican Evangelicalism, this group became the most dynamic and ambitious element in the Established Church.

Evangelical Anglican clergy worked within the Establishment claiming, much to the annoyance of bishops during the early-

---

[54] Smith, Mark A., and Taylor, Stephen, (eds.), *Evangelicalism in the Church of England c.1790-c.1880: a miscellany*, (Boydell), 2004. See also, Balleine, George R., *A History of the Evangelical Party in the Church of England*, (Longmans, Green and Co.), 1908, and Hylson-Smith, Kenneth, *Evangelicals in the Church of England, 1734-1984*, (Continuum), 1989, pp. 109-224.

[55] Hilton, R. Boyd, *The Age of Atonement: The Influence of Evangelicalism on Social and Economic Thought 1785-1865*, (Oxford University Press), 1988, is essential. See also, Best, G., 'Evangelicalism and the Victorians', in Symondson, A., (ed.), *The Victorian Crisis of Faith*, (SPCK), 1970, pp. 37-56, and Smyth, C., 'The evangelical movement in perspective', *Cambridge Historical Journal*, Vol. 7, (1941-3), pp. 160-174. Bebbington, D. W., *Evangelicalism in Modern Britain*, (Unwin Hyman), 1987, pp. 75-150, covers the whole of the period.

[56] Wolffe, John, *The Expansion of Evangelicalism: The Age of Wilberforce, More, Chalmers and Finney*, (IVP), 2007.

nineteenth century that they represented the central Anglican tradition established during the mid-sixteenth century. The Islington Clerical Conference, which first convened in 1827, provided an annual forum for Anglican evangelicals laying an important role in keeping them together by acting as a check on bitter disagreements and failings out. By the 1830s, Evangelicals were in control of most of the national and local religious societies, though the latter were more interdenominational than their national headquarters. They published the bulk of the popular Christian literature: the Bible in all languages; classics of the Evangelical point of view such as *The Pilgrim's Progress*; soul-arousing works of every kind, and, periodicals such as *The Christian Observer* and *The Eclectic Review*. It was developing, through the work of Charles Simeon, parochial organisation designed to maintain an intense religious life and to channel the charitable impulse to promote social and religious discipline. By the 1830s, its national leadership was consolidated among peers, MPs, bishops and the leading figures of the ecclesiastical and business world. [57]

This diffusion of Anglican Evangelicalism was not achieved without some loss of vigour. This process has been called one of 'accommodation' making Evangelicalism palatable and manageable for the cultivated classes, an attractive and exemplary model for a combination of piety and social position. It is difficult to estimate the extent to which this was a conscious aim of Wilberforce and his supporters or a reflection of the level of its success. But there is little doubting its influence throughout British society touching those who were not evangelically-minded and who may not have liked its theology: for example, Sunday observance, the enforcement of the blasphemy laws, especially in the 1820s, and the encouragement of Sunday and day schools. The moral revolution was accomplished and overt sexuality for the middle-classes was driven into a private underworld or into lower-class life. Victorian respectability predated the accession of the Queen in 1837. [58]

The existence of the Establishment meant that relations between Anglican and non-Anglican evangelicals became increasingly difficulty

---

[57] Holladay, J. D., 'English Evangelicalism, 1820-1850: diversity and unity in "Vital Religion"', *Historical Magazine of the Protestant Episcopal Church*, Vol. 51, (1982), pp. 147-157. See also, Wolffe, J., *The Protestant Crusade in Great Britain, 1829-1860*, (Oxford University Press), 1991.
[58] On the moral revolution, see Jaeger, M., *Before Victoria: Changing Standards and Behaviour 1787-1837*, (Chatto and Windus), 1956, and Wilson, Ben, *Decency & Disorder: The Age of Cant 1789-1837*, (Faber), 2007.

after 1820. During the 1820s and 1830s, Nonconformists moved from a reluctant acceptance of Establishment to an attitude of general dislike of it. By the 1840s, disestablishment became a major issue with Nonconformists wishing to reduce the Church of England to an equality of status with their own denominations, competing freely in an open 'religious' market. [59] This view of the Establishment was known as 'voluntarism' and was an attitude increasingly sympathised with by Methodists of every kind, by many Presbyterians in England as well as Scotland and by Irish Roman Catholics. Although some Evangelicals such as Lord Shaftesbury never hesitated to co-operate with Nonconformists and few left the Church, most Anglican Evangelicals persisted in seeing the Establishment as an advantageous and necessary condition.

While the existence of an Establishment was a cause of division within evangelicalism, the principle of 'No Popery' was a ground of unity. This has been seen as one of the causes of the lowering of the tone of evangelicalism and a resurgence of anti-Catholic feelings in the 1840s and 1850s. Some change in the relationship between public men and public opinion may partially explain what happened to Evangelicalism after 1830. Post-reform politics saw the emergence of a more politically conscious public with worries, real or imaginary, about which that public wanted something done. [60] By 1836, Wilberforce, Hannah More and Charles Simeon had died and their successors, Shaftesbury and Fowell Buxton were not personally inferior but Evangelicalism seems to have moved into a lower gear. [61] Best argues:

> It is almost as if its greatest contribution had by then been made and as if it was felt to lack the breadth and tone of distinction that could satisfy many of its natural leaders in the post-revolutionary age. [62]

---

[59] Macintosh, W. H., *Disestablishment and Liberation: The movement for the separation of the Anglican Church from state control*, (Epworth Press), 1972.

[60] For the significance of the evangelical mission, see Lewis, D. M., *Lighten their Darkness: the Evangelical Mission to Working-class London, 1828-1860*, (Greenwood Press), 1986.

[61] Follett, Richard R., 'After Emancipation: Thomas Fowell Buxton and Evangelical Politics in the 1830's', *Parliamentary History*, Vol. 27, (2008), pp. 119-129.

[62] Best, G., 'Evangelicalism and the Victorians' in ibid, Symondson, A., (ed.), *The Victorian Crisis of Faith*, p. 48, and Bradley, C., *The Call to Seriousness: The Evangelical Impact on the Victorians*, (Jonathan Cape), 1976.

Evangelicalism, as a religion of duty placed service above doctrine and appealed to women in particular. Wilberforce argued in *A Practical View* that women were more favourably disposed to religion and good works than men.[63] The activities and restrictions of nineteenth century family life and female education tended to focus the affections and raise philanthropy to the level of obedience to God.[64] Though some women found Christianity restrictive, most female reformers saw it as an emancipatory influence heightening women's self-esteem and giving them a sense of place and direction. Christianity confirmed that women had a rightful and important place in the charitable world; a place that particularly to men was a subordinate one. [65] Female Evangelical piety did not threaten the social order. Clare Lucas Balfour wrote in 1849:

> ...the history of every religious and benevolent society in the civilised world shows the female sex pre-eminent in numbers, zeal and usefulness, thus attesting the interest women take in Christian labours for the welfare of society. [66]

Historians acknowledge the importance of evangelicalism in shaping the mentality of the first half of the nineteenth century but recognise the problem in defining that role precisely. Evangelicalism's middle-class piety fostered concepts of public probity and national honour based on the ideals of economy, professionalism and 'respectability'. [67] Though many prominent Evangelicals were paternalists and bitterly opposed to the prevailing 'laissez-faire' ethos of the period, many contemporaries thought of evangelicalism as synonymous with philanthropy. Boyd Hilton argues that Evangelicals helped to create and buttress capitalist philosophy then under attack.

---

[63] Wilberforce, William, *A Practical View of the Prevailing Religious System of Professed Christians: in the Higher and Middle Classes in this Country: contrasted with Real Christianity*, 19th edition, (Crocker and Brewster), 1829, pp. 286-289.

[64] Ibid, Wilberforce, William, *A Practical View*, pp. 229, 270-271.

[65] Elliott, D. W., *The Angel out of the House: Philanthropy and Gender in Nineteenth-century* England, (University of Virginia Press), 2002, pp. 111-134. See also, Bowpitt, Graham, 'Evangelical Christianity, Secular Humanism and the Genesis of British Social Work', *British Journal of Social Work*, Vol. 28, (5), (1998), pp. 675-693.

[66] Balfour, C. L., *Women and the Temperance Reformation*, (Houlston and Stoneman), 1849, p. 6.

[67] Tolley, C., *Domestic Biography: The Legacy of Evangelicalism in four Nineteenth-century Families*, (Oxford University Press), 1997, looks at the Macaulays, Stephens, Thorntons and Wilberforces.

They wanted society to operate as closely to 'nature' as possible by repealing interventionist laws leaving people to work out their own salvation and spiritual life in the course of their ordinary lives. In that evangelical ethos, suffering seemed to be part of God's plan and governments took a harsh attitude to social underdogs in order not to interfere with such dispensations of providence. 'Self-help' was both an economic and spiritual means of achieving salvation.

While unreformed the Anglican Church claimed the allegiance of the whole society. It was thoroughly integrated within the mainstream culture and social structure and monopolistic in its attitude to religious rivals. As long as political sanctions against religious deviance were firmly upheld, widespread support for alternative religious perspectives could be held in check but from 1689 onwards British society moved gradually towards a pluralist, religious voluntarism. By the 1830s, Britain had become an increasingly pluralistic society containing not one but a plurality of cultural systems. The reforms of the 1830s and 1840s represented a decisive turning point for Anglicanism. Though still the Established Church in England, Wales and Ireland, it had accommodated itself to the reality of permanent competition with other 'churches' within its boundaries. The State might intervene to support the Establishment but there was no chance that it would restore the Church to its constitutionally prescribed role as a monopoly religion. Like the landed elite, the Church, though it fought a skilled rearguard action for the rest of the century, was increasingly prepared to compromise to preserve its remaining privileges. The change was one of metamorphosis, not restoration, a recognition of the shift in the character of the Church to being one denomination among several.

Nonconformity 1800-1850

The metamorphosis within the Established Church was bound to have significant effects on the Dissenting churches after 1830. [68] But Anglicanism was not the only form of organised religion undergoing fundamental changes in the first half of the nineteenth century. There

---

[68] Watts, Michael R., *The Dissenters, Volume 1: From the Reformation to the French Revolution*, (Oxford University Press), 1978, and *The Dissenters, Volume 2: The expansion of Evangelical Nonconformity 1791-1859*, (Oxford University Press), 1995, are the most valuable surveys. See also, Sellers, I., *Nineteenth Century Nonconformity*, (Edward Arnold), 1977, for a general survey and Thompson, D. M., *Nonconformity in the Nineteenth Century*, (Routledge), 1972, and Briggs, J. H. Y., and Sellers, I., *Victorian Nonconformity*, (Edward Arnold), 1973, for documentary studies.

was a shift within Methodist, Congregational and Baptist communities away from the sect-type religious culture of the eighteenth century towards a new and patently denominational orientation to the wider society. Methodism in particular ceased to be a movement and became an organisation. The term 'Dissent' gradually evolved into 'Nonconformity' and 'dissenters' to 'Nonconformists.' [69] The movement towards denominationalism had its origins in the late-eighteenth century and was organisational and 'clerical'. Denominational organisation was the result of the need and desire to pursue new goals. It arose out of the evangelical revival in the eighteenth century and was not a reaction to it. The new goal was evangelism in the form of missionary activities both abroad and at home and was possible because of the theological shift away from the Calvinist doctrine of the elect that would have rendered such activity pointless. In this situation, the church could and should be open to all.

The growth of denominations

The formation of the Northamptonshire Association in 1764 among Particular (Calvinistic) Baptists marked a turning point. In 1797, the Baptist Home Mission Society was formed in London. Area or County Associations of Churches were formed among the Independents, but generally later than among Baptist, in Warwickshire in 1793, Wiltshire and East Somerset in 1797, Hampshire in 1797, Lancashire in 1806 and Hertfordshire in 1810. In due course, a Congregational Home Missionary Society was formed in 1819 working mainly in those areas where County Associations were weak or non-existent. Village preaching depended on support from elsewhere and united action by a number of churches was an obvious way of achieving this. Itinerancy challenged isolationism but during the second and third decades of the nineteenth century, the freedom enjoyed by the early itinerants succumbed to the institutionalisation of the organisations. [70]

Evangelism came to be seen as a denominational rather than local responsibility. Despite this development, the 1820s saw the first signs of formalism that later sapped the dynamism and recruiting power of English Nonconformity. It was possible for the central organisations of the different churches to exercise control and

---

[69] Thompson, D. M., *Denominationalism and Dissent 1795-1835: a question of identity*, (Friends of Dr William's Library), 1985.
[70] On itinerancy, Lovegrove, D. W., *Established Church, Sectarian People: Itinerancy and the Transformation of Dissent 1780-1830*, (Cambridge University Press), 1988, especially pp. 142-165, is valuable.

discipline. Denominationalism also had expression in an increasingly 'clerical' approach. Jabez Bunting and his Wesleyan colleagues gradually strengthened the distinction between travelling and local preachers, not only by developing the doctrine of the 'pastoral office' but also by enforcing the commitment to permanent itinerancy and corporate discipline among the travelling preachers. [71]

Excessive spontaneity was seen as a threat to the integrity of Wesleyanism and a theological basis for the differentiation of roles and functions between ministers and laymen was elaborated. This redirection of the Methodist movement under ministerial control imposed immense internal strains resulting in a prolonged period of conflict and schism, beginning with the New Connection breakaway in 1797 and ending with the major disruptions and realignments between 1849 and 1857. 'Primitive Methodists', 'Bible Christians', Tent Methodists' and 'Wesleyan Reformers' all contained sectarian overtones in their names and were significant in capturing an element of protest against the institutionalisation and consolidation that underpinned the crumbling of the Methodist version of evangelical Nonconformity. Other Nonconformists lacked both the will and the machinery to sharpen the clerical-lay distinction in this way.

The movement from sects to denominationalism, from a 'unity of experience' to a 'unity of organisation', can be seen as a response to the need for some form of social control. In this view, denominationalism has been seen as the failure by Nonconformity to respond to popular religion and of the anxiety and potential dangers to the country if it got out of control. This view seems to draw too stark a distinction between lay or undenominational and clerical or denominational. The move to denominationalism was caused by the need to maintain the constituencies of the different Nonconformist groups within an increasingly open religious 'free-market'. Between 1780 and 1815, Nonconformity was preoccupied with rural society where it tested the Established Church's power. Congregationalist County associations and regional Baptist bodies devoted their energies to the hinterlands rather than the larger centres of population. Even national bodies pursued similar aims. By 1823, the Baptist Western Association numbered 78 member churches, an increase of 44 since 1780. With the spread of urban awareness came recognition of the problems involved in establishing effective contact with urban populations. Neither the individualism of the pioneering preachers or the rudimentary organisation of

---

[71] Brown, K. D., *A Social History of the Nonconformist Ministry in England and Wales, 1800-1930*, (Oxford University Press), 1988, pp. 19-79.

the regional societies could cope with the scale of the problem. The result was a move to national networks under the control of denominational bodies that were alone capable of providing planning and giving the organisations direction. Denominationalism was a consequence of the need to mobilise resources effectively to deal with the urban problem.

The impetus for structural definition stemmed from the need for more efficiency and a growing sense of denominational identity accompanied the return to peace after 1815. There was an increasing demand for religious places with the attendant financial problems of their provision and maintenance. By the 1830s, this material interest had combined with rising ministerial status as an expression of contemporary concerns for 'respectability' and this hastened the change from individual spontaneity to a more formal assumption of responsibility for further expansion. By 1840, the shape of the movement had visibly altered with the old emphasis on free-ranging, outdoor evangelism supplanted by indoor, more controlled, gatherings. [72]

Older Nonconformist sects

Presbyterianism had slowly moved away from the doctrine of the Trinity and by 1830, a majority of its members were Unitarian in creed. [73] Unitarianism had developed from the 'rational theology' of the eighteenth century but its association with free thought, radical politics and its defence of people such as Richard Carlile made orthodox Dissent suspicious. Increasingly the doctrinal differences between Unitarians and Trinitarians mattered. [74] In 1816, the minister of the Wolverhampton Unitarian chapel was discovered to be a Trinitarian and his congregation dismissed him. In the ensuing legal case the vice-chancellor held that the chapel was built when it was illegal to be a Unitarian and that the law could therefore have upheld no endowment to support Unitarian worship. The Wolverhampton case put in jeopardy the chapel and endowment of every Unitarian congregation founded before 1813, when Unitarian opinion ceased to

---

[72] Johnson, Dale A., *The changing shape of English Nonconformity, 1825-1925*, (Oxford University Press), 1999.

[73] Bolan, C. G., et al, *The English Presbyterians*, (Beacon Press), 1968, remains important.

[74] Unitarianism is a non-trinitarian Christian theology which holds that God is only one person, in contrast to the doctrine of the Trinity (God as three in one, 'Father, Son and Holy Ghost'). Richey, R. E., 'Did the English Presbyterians become Unitarian?', *Church History*, Vol. 42, (1973), pp. 58-72, Schulman, Frank, *'Blasphemous and wicked': the Unitarian struggle for equality 1813-1844*, (Manchester College, University of Oxford), 1997.

be illegal. A similar decision in favour of Trinitarians occurred over the fund left by Lady Hewley in 1704 to provide endowments in the six northern English counties. The vice-chancellor's court confirmed that only Trinitarians were eligible for endowments from the fund in 1833 and this judgement was maintained respectively by the Lord Chancellor and the House of Lords in 1836 and 1842. These cases divided English dissenters and in March 1836, a majority of Unitarian congregations in London separated themselves from the Protestant dissenting deputies, splitting the alliance of 'Old' Dissent.

The legal uncertainty for Unitarians created by the Lady Hewley case was exacerbated by a suit over the richly endowed Eustace Street chapel in Dublin in 1843-1844 when Irish Trinitarians sought to acquire the chapels and endowments of Irish Unitarians. The result, that followed the 1836 precedent, meant that every Unitarian chapel might now become the subject of litigation. Peel attempted to resolve the problem by introducing a Dissenters Chapels Bill. This said that where there was no trust deed determining doctrine or usage that the usage of twenty-five years should be taken as conclusive evidence of the right of any congregation to possess a chapel and its endowments and that any suits pending should have the benefit of the act. Peel was surprised by the depth of opposition from Nonconformists and from the evangelical clergy of the Church of England. Its passage was important as a further extension of the 1813 Toleration Act to others besides orthodox Trinitarians. [75]

Surviving Trinitarian congregations looked to Scotland for support but the Church of Scotland was reluctant and in 1839, the General Assembly acknowledged that the Presbyterian Church of England was independent. The Unitarians were not an expanding religious grouping but the Trinitarians, their numbers swelled by Scottish immigration into England, were. In 1836, the congregations of Lancashire and the north-west agreed to form a synod of two presbyteries and adopted the Westminster confession of faith. The synod expanded during the late 1830s and 1840s: London and Newcastle were brought in 1839; Berwick in 1840; Northumberland in 1842 and Birmingham in 1848. The changing attitude of the synod was reflected in the change of name: in 1839, it was the 'Presbyterian Church of England in connection with the Church of Scotland' and in 1849 the 'Presbyterian Church in England'. Not until 1876 did it

---

[75] Bebbington, D. W., 'Unitarian Members of Parliament in the Nineteenth Century', *Transactions of the Unitarian Historical Society*, Vol. 24, (3), pp. 153-175, examines the elite within the Church who were generally successful businessmen, Liberal in politics and progressive in social attitudes.

become the Presbyterian Church of England. The 1851 *Religious Census* showed that the distribution of Presbyterianism was almost entirely a reflection of Scottish immigration into England. Half of total attendances were recorded in the three northern counties of Northumberland, Durham and Cumberland. Lancashire and London each accounted for about 20 per cent each and the remaining 10 per cent included isolated congregations in Staffordshire, Cheshire, Warwickshire and Worcestershire, Westmoreland and Yorkshire. [76]

Between 1830 and 1860, the Congregationalists turned from a loose federation into something like a modern denomination. [77] This was a major achievement since a denomination meant some form of central authority and Independents had always held that each chapel was sovereign. The force that moved Independents in this direction was the recognition that their rights over marriage or burial or church rates were better protected by county associations than by small sovereign units and the need for central support for colleges and to make stipends adequate for ministers. An attempted union in 1811 failed but in 1831 a Congregation Union was tentatively established. During the 1830s, the Union survived uneasily. County associations joined slowly: Oxford and West Berkshire in 1841, Cornwall in 1846 and Hampshire in 1848 were among the latest to join, but they sent no money. The union was saved by the skill of Algernon Wells, secretary from 1837 until his death in 1850. [78] He put the Union on a sound financial and organisational footing with profits from its publications. After 1845, the Union ran into problems caused by the conflict within Wesleyan Methodism that brought its central government into question. Many Independents sided with Bunting's opponents and the death of Algernon Wells in 1850 removed an important force for moderation within the Union.

---

[76] For Presbyterianism in Ireland see, Holmes, A. R., *The shaping of Ulster Presbyterian belief and practice, 1770-1840*, (Oxford University Press), 2006.

[77] Jones, R., *Congregationalism in England 1662-1962*, (Independent Press), 1962, and Pope, Robert, (ed.), *Congregationalism in Wales*, (University of Wales Press), 2004, are important studies. Rimmington, Gerald T., 'Congregationalism in Rural Leicestershire and Rutland, 1863-1914', *Midland History*, Vol. 31, (1), 2006, pp. 94-104, is a good case study. Thorne, Susan, *Congregational Missions and the Making of an Imperial Culture in Nineteenth-century England*, (Stanford University Press), 1999, considers the impact of foreign missionary societies.

[78] Wells, Algernon, *The Principles and Position of the Congregational Churches: A Discourse delivered at the recognition of the Rev. J. Gill*, (John Snow), 1849.

Although the Union diminished the variety of uses in chapels, the pressure had always been towards free worship and the breadth of Independent doctrine. Congregational churches were faithful to Calvinism but could not observe the advances of Methodism without adopting some of its devices and missionary enthusiasm. They gained from Sunday schools and village preaching but there was a thinning in the upper and educated ranks of society. Political disputes between church and dissent in the 1830s and 1840s [79] raised fears that Independents were natural allies of Irish and radicals and this meant that by 1850, Congregational churches had a more broadly lower middle-class composition than they had in 1800, though they housed more worshippers. [80]

The 1851 *Religious Census* revealed the same geographical pattern that existed in 1700. Congregationalism was most important in a line of counties stretching eastward from Cornwall and Devon to Essex and Suffolk. Whatever hold Dissent had in the largest urban complexes was due largely to the Wesleyan Methodists. The exception was London where Congregationalists had a more dominant role but even here the picture was patchy. There were few congregations in Kensington, Chelsea and Bayswater where Anglicanism was dominant. The East End also proved poor soil. There were few Congregational chapels apart from a number of missions supported by wealthy suburban congregations. In the middle-class suburbs, especially south of the Thames, the field was left clear for Baptists and Methodists. It was in the prosperous and expanding suburbs like Hampstead, Brixton, Highbury and Clapham that Congregationalism had its real base.

The Baptists were Independent congregations that practised the baptism of believers and there was little to distinguish them from Congregationalists. [81] But this outward harmony concealed considerable diversity. Congregational chapels contained few

---

[79] See, for example, Salter, F. R., 'Congregationalism and the 'Hungry Forties'', *Transactions of the Congregational Historical Society*, Vol. 17, (1955), pp. 107-116, in relation to the Anti-Corn Law League.

[80] Brown, K. D., 'The Congregational ministry in the first half of the 19th century: a preliminary survey', *Journal of the United Reformed Church History Society*, Vol. 3, (1983), pp. 2-15.

[81] Underwood, A. C., *A History of the English Baptists*, (Kingsgate Press), 1947, Briggs, John H. Y., *The English Baptists of the 19th century*, (Baptist Historical Society), 1994, and George, Timothy, *Baptists: A Brief History*, (B. & H. Publishing), 2009. Ellis, Christopher, 'Baptists in Britain', in Wainwright, Geoffrey, Westerfield Tucker, and Karen B., (eds.), *The Oxford History of Christian Worship*, (Oxford University Press), 2006, pp. 560-573, provides a succinct overview.

labourers, while many Baptist chapels were composed of people from the lower levels of society. Baptist congregations had less educated pastors, more illiterate members, held their Calvinism more firmly, were doctrinally more conservative and sought to retain their independence more vehemently. Congregationalists were moderate Calvinists but Baptists were divided into three groups: General or Arminian Baptists; Particular Baptists who were moderate Calvinists and Strict and Particular Baptists who were Calvinist but not moderate. [82] Most of the General Baptist congregations went back to the seventeenth century and had faded into Unitarian belief but since 1770 a small group, the General Baptists of the New Connection, preserved the orthodox Arminian faith. [83]

The nineteenth century saw a coming together among Baptists and as early as 1813 a Baptist Union was created to provide a common meeting ground for Particular and General Baptists. [84] To create a 'union' proved more difficult than among Congregationalists even though the same needs for union existed; a missionary society in need of money and direction, training of ministers, stipends for pastors and chapels in debt. The General Baptists were only lukewarm in their support for the 1813 union and, though it was reorganised in 1832, support for it grew more slowly than that for the contemporary Congregational Union.[85] The 1851 *Religious Census* showed that about 366,000 Baptists attended services. Particular Baptists had 1,491 chapels in England and 456 in Wales. New Connection of General Baptists had 179 chapels in England and three in Wales. Old General Baptists had 93 chapels. The Baptists' main strength lay in the block of counties stretching from the East Midlands to the coast of East Anglia. Except in Dorset and Methodist Cornwall, Baptists increased in all the southern counties of England after 1800. By contrast, there were few Baptists in the northern counties apart from the West Riding.

The major expansion of the Society of Friends (the Quakers) took place in the eighteenth century and they were numerically strongest in the north (Lancashire, Yorkshire and Westmoreland), in

---

[82] Breed, G. R., *Particular Baptists in Victorian England and their strict communion organizations*, (Baptist Historical Society), 2003, and Dix, Kenneth, *Strict and particular: English strict and particular Baptists in the nineteenth century*, (Baptist Historical Society), 2001.

[83] Oliver, Robert W., *History of the English Calvinistic Baptists 1771-1892: from John Gill to C. H. Spurgeon*, (Banner of Truth Trust), 2006.

[84] Briggs, John H. Y., *The English Baptists of the 19th century*, (Baptist Historical Society), 1994.

[85] Ward, W. R., 'The Baptists and the Transformation of the Church, 1780-1830', *Baptist Quarterly*, Vol. 25, (1973), pp. 167-184.

the south-west and in London, Bristol and Norwich.[86] Most Quakers came from the rural and urban 'petite bourgeoisie' with few from the upper-classes or the lower orders. But this trend was reversed in the first half of the nineteenth century. Contemporaries identified three major causes of this. The evangelical revival had the effect of dividing Quakers into those who adopted an evangelical approach to their belief and those for whom discussion of the Bible (its reading aloud at meetings did not occur until 1860) was unthinkable.[87] The dispute came to a head in 1835-1837 and led to about 300 Friends of Lancashire and Kendal leaving the Society. For a time they maintained a separate denomination as Evangelical Friends but soon found little to divide them from other denominations and some joined the Church of England and others the Plymouth Brethren. Quaker religious education was extremely poor. It was seen as secondary to simply waiting upon the word and was consequently undeveloped. Quaker Sunday schools were not begun until the 1840s. Marriage discipline was strict and when it was broken, the individual was bound to be expelled. John Bright's brother and two sisters were expelled for marrying outside the Society. Perhaps a third of the Friends who married between 1809 and 1859 had, according to one contemporary, been expelled for marrying outside the Society. The conservatism of the Quakers led to decline and this was not arrested until the 1860s when marriage discipline became less draconian, religious education was improved and there was recognition of the positive value of evangelism.

During the nineteenth century, a number of religious movements grew up in the United States and that were brought to Britain. Before 1850, only the Church of Jesus Christ of Latter Day Saints or the Mormons was of any significance.[88] Founded in the 1820s, the Mormons claimed to be the only true and valid church and first appeared in Britain in 1837 when seven Mormon missionaries landed at Liverpool. A second mission in 1840, led by its leader Brigham Young, proved equally successful. Based on Liverpool, Mormon missions were sent round the country and it is small wonder that many of the early converts were the poor for whom the 1840s was

---

[86] Walvin, James, *The Quakers: money and morals*, (John Murray), 1997, is a good overview while Isichei, Elizabeth Allo, *Victorian Quakers*, (Oxford University Press), 1970, is more focussed.

[87] Bright, Simon, "Friends have no cause to be ashamed of being by others thought non-evangelical': unity and diversity of belief among early-nineteenth-century British Quakers', *Studies in Church History*, Vol. 32, (1996), pp. 337-350.

[88] See, Jensen, Richard L., and Thorp, Malcolm R., (eds.), *Mormons in early Victorian Britain,* (University of Utah Press), 1989.

a period of intense hardship. Furthermore the Mormons organised a very efficient emigration system out of Liverpool. [89] Between 1841 and 1843, nearly 3,000 emigrants left Liverpool and, despite the suspension of all emigration in 1846 and 1847, by 1850 the number of emigrants had risen to nearly 17,000.

In the 1851 *Religious Census* 16,628 Mormons attended the evening service of Sunday. [90] The 1850s saw Mormonism is decline throughout Britain. In part this was the result of improved conditions for the working population. More important was the announcement by Brigham Young in 1852 that polygamy was God's will. Outside the Mormon mission house in Soham (Cambridgeshire) 1,200 people watched as village youths enacted a Mormon wedding, to which seven brides rode on donkeys. Polygamy exposed Mormonism to charges of immorality and vice and was fatal to evangelism in Britain and the number of Mormons fell back slowly to 2,000 by the 1860s.

How did Methodism develop under Jabez Bunting?

Between 1800 and 1830, Wesleyan Methodism faced threats from outside and from within as it sought to find 'respectability' and acceptance throughout British society. [91] Three problems dominated discussions: the problem of Methodist loyalty; how and

---

[89] Shepperson, W. S., 'The place of the Mormons in the religious emigration of Britain, 1840-60', *Utah Historical Quarterly*, Vol. 20, (1952), pp. 207-218, Taylor, P. A. M., 'Why did British Mormons emigrate?', *Utah Historical Quarterly*, Vol. 22, (1954), 249-270, and Taylor, P. A. M., *Expectations Westward: the Mormons and the Emigration of their British converts in the 19th century*, (Cornell University Press), 1966.

[90] Benson, E. C., and Doxey, C., 'The ecclesiastical census of 1851 and the Church of Jesus Christ of Latter-day Saints', *Local Historian*, Vol. 34, (2), (2004), pp. 66-79.

[91] Methodism between 1820 and 1914 can be approached in the following general works: Davies, R. E., George, A. S., and. Rupp, E. G., (eds.), *A History of the Methodist Church in Great Britain*, Vol. 2, (Epworth Press), 1978, Vol. 3, (Epworth Press), 1980, and the documentary Vol. 4, (Epworth Press), 1987, Hempton, David, *Methodism: empire of the spirit*, (Yale University Press), 2005, Semmel, B., *The Methodist Revolution*, (Heinemann), 1974, and Hempton, D., *Methodism and Politics in British Society 1750-1850*, (Hutchinson), 1984. More specific older studies include Edwards, M., *After Wesley: a study of the social and political influence of Methodism in the middle period, 1791-1849*, (Epworth Press), 1948, Taylor, E. R., *Methodism and Politics 1791-1851*, (Cambridge University Press), 1935, and Wearmouth, R. F., *Methodism and the Working-class Movements of England 1800-1850*, (Epworth Press), 1937. Currie, R., *Methodism Divided: A Study in the Sociology of Ecumenicalism*, (Faber), 1968, gives full weight to the secessions.

where should Methodism grow; and finally, how should Methodism respond to popular radicalism. Methodism seemed particularly revolutionary since enthusiasm and evangelism tapped strong emotions and was believed to have genuinely dangerous potential. Methodists were therefore suspected of radical tendencies, even when their leaders were at great pain to demonstrate their support for the Tory establishment. Within Methodism the struggle was between 'conservative' and broadly 'liberal' wings both convinced they were being faithful to Wesley's principles and intentions.

On Wesley's death in 1791, 'Church Methodism' was still an option and those who advocated it could use Wesley's refusal to separate himself from the Church of England as a conclusive argument. [92] Though theoretically an option, it was soon replaced by the determination to build a church more strongly organised than the Church of England. The Methodist Conference of preachers was to be the 'living' Wesley, entitled to govern autocratically as he had governed but delegating its power to local superintendent ministers appointed by it. With this hierarchical conception of church government went a 'no politics' rule that in practice meant no radical politics. A 'liberal' wing opposed this view of government arguing that they were faithful to Wesley's own impatience with rules, loyal to his appeal to the poor over the heads of the existing dominant aristocratic elite. Ministers were regarded as servants rather than masters and laymen had to be included at every level of government from national to local level. The minister's function was to evangelise and bring new recruits into the Christian family where all were equal. Implied in this alternative view of Methodism was a revolutionary vision of Britain not, as the conservatives maintained, acceptance of the existing social structure.[93]

Between the 1790s and 1820s, the aristocracy suffered from a growing paranoia and political radicalism and widespread economic distress caused government to be apprehensive. [94] This was

---

[92] Lloyd, Gareth, '"Croakers and Busybodies": The Extent and Influence of Church Methodism in the Late 18th and Early 19th Centuries', *Methodist History*, Vol. 42, (1), (2003), pp. 20-32.

[93] Bowmer, J. C., *Pastor and people: a study of church and ministry in Wesleyan Methodism from the death of John Wesley (1791) to the death of Jabez Bunting (1858)*, (Epworth Press), 1975.

[94] Vickers, J. A., *Thomas Coke: An Apostle of Methodism*, (Epworth Press), 1969, and *Thomas Coke and world Methodism*, (World Methodist Historical Society), 1976, are good studies of a neglected figure who led the movement between Wesley and Bunting. See also, Smith, W. T., 'Thomas Coke's doctorate', *Proceedings of the Wesley Historical Society*, Vol. 41, (1978), pp. 169-173, and Lloyd, Gareth, 'The papers of Dr Thomas Coke: a

also the period when Methodism, that was about 100,000 strong in 1791, reached its point of organisational take-off. Methodists claimed, though probably with some exaggeration, that there were 200,000 members by 1802, 270,000 by 1806 and 367,000 by 1812. A more moderate, and more reliable, claim saw 167,000 members in England alone in 1815 with 631 preachers and 1,355 chapels, with over half a million members and hearers combined. Figures apart, there is evidence of the Connection moving boldly into the more settled towns and villages of rural England posing a direct challenge to the Established Church.

For many, Methodism seemed a great threat to stability and Anglican clergy were especially disconcerted by what they saw as its 'levelling principles'. Popular religious feeling was, to those who governed, synonymous with fanaticism and fanaticism was an enemy to stability. The response from the Connection was twofold. Methodists continued, following Wesley, to insist that their religious beliefs made loyalty to the established order a spiritual imperative. Methodist sermons, conference resolutions and tracts continually emphasised loyalty, for conscience sake, to the government and the Crown. The preachers of the Connection also argued that Methodism reduced the discontent of the lower orders and that its influence was consciously exerted to bring about 'peace and good order'. By 1830, these arguments, which corresponded with Wilberforce's views on the practical, political effects of 'vital Christianity', were becoming more widely accepted outside Methodism but it was a slow process.

The second problem that Methodism faced was how it could increase its membership and what direction that growth should take. There was a fine line between acceptable mass evangelism and revivalist excesses that had on occasions worried Wesley and increasingly concerned Wesleyan preachers in the early decades of the nineteenth century. Though some expressed theological doubts about revivalism, more important was the political pressure from government and the Church of England about growing Methodist extremism. The problem was exacerbated by two things. American Methodism that was trying to introduce frontier-style revivalism into eastern cities was introduced into England by Lorenzo Dow. Also Methodist revivalist offshoots in Britain began to organise themselves into some kind of connectional system. Arriving in England in late 1805, Dow soon made contact with revivalist Methodists in Lancashire, Cheshire and the Potteries. Under his influence Hugh

---

catalogue', *Bulletin of the John Rylands University Library of Manchester*, Vol. 76, (2), (1994), pp. 205-320.

Bourne and William Clowes adapted the 'camp-meeting' technique of the American frontier. Camp meetings were condemned by the Methodist Conference and many chapels were closed to Dow and his followers but they won considerable support. The result, in 1811, was the formation of the Primitive Methodists that seceded from the parent body. It spread quickly through the Midlands and between 1819 and 1824 its membership quadrupled from 7,842 to 33,507. A roughly similar movement, the Bible Christians flourished in Devon and Cornwall with revival meetings that lasted several days and nights and its application to join the Wesleyan Connection was refused. [95] Foremost among those who opposed revivalism was Jabez Bunting which he saw as divisive. In their opposition to revivalism Bunting and others failed to distinguish between the temporary outbreaks of zealous revivalism in some northern towns and the massive rural support for the brand of Methodism offered by Bourne and Clowes. Revivalism was not a monolithic entity but had degrees of acceptability and unacceptability but, as in 1797, the Wesleyan leadership decided that the best method of control was expulsion.

Bunting dominated Wesleyan Methodism until his death in 1858. In 1811, Bunting, then only 34 years old, was stationed at Leeds as an itinerant preacher serving under the superintendence of George Morley; stationed nearby was Richard Watson. Although Watson and briefly been a Wesleyan itinerant, he had joined the New Connection in 1804. They formed a close friendship and Bunting urged Watson to seek readmission to the Wesleyans and, because of Bunting's support this occurred in 1812. [96] Bunting, Watson and Morley planned the organisation of the Leeds Missionary Society as a model for the Connection. The appeal of this initiative to the rank-and-file was recognised at the 1814 Conference and led to the introduction of a new rule in relation to the Legal Hundred, the 100 senior ministers who could veto the decisions of the Conference.

---

[95] See, Kendall, H. B., *The Origins and History of the Primitive Methodist Church*, 2 Vols. (Robert Bryant), 1919, Milburn, G. E., *Primitive Methodism*, (Epworth Press), 2002, and Wilkinson, J. T., *Henry Bourne 1772-1852*, (Epworth Press), 1952, examine the major secession, Shaw, T., *The Bible Christians*, (Epworth Press), 1975, a less important one. See also, Walford, John, *Memoirs of the life and labours of the late venerable Hugh Bourne: Founder of the English Camp Meetings, and the Originator, and for Twenty-two Years Editor of the Primitive Methodist Magazines*, 2 Vols. (T. King), 1855-1856, reprinted Antliff, W., (ed.), 2 Vols. (Berith Publications), 1999, and Brittain, J. N., 'Hugh Bourne and the Magic Methodists', *Methodist History*, Vol. 46, (2008), pp. 132-140.

[96] See, Bunting, Jabez, *Memorials of the late rev. Richard Watson, including the funeral sermon and brief biographical notices*, (John Mason), 1833.

Previously ministers were admitted by a system of strict seniority but from 1814, though three out of four vacancies were filled by seniority, the fourth would be a nominee of all the preachers of the Conference. Bunting was the first minister to benefit from the new system and the extent of his success may be seen in his immediate election as Secretary of the Conference.

The final problem that Methodism faced was popular radicalism. [97] The Conference and the Committee of Privileges were vocal in their support for the existing social order, but the number of circulars they issued testifies to their ineffectiveness among rank-and-file members. In 1812, preachers, including Bunting fought a campaign against Luddites, refusing to conduct Luddite funerals and closing chapels to Luddite orators. The ineffectiveness of institutional solutions came home to Bunting when six Luddites, whose fathers were Methodists, were hanged at York in 1813. [98] Throughout the Midlands and the north Methodism faced competition from, and was influenced by, the new generation of political clubs. Also in 1812 Wesleyans in the hosiery districts of the East Midlands became involved in the anti-war petitioning of the Friends of Peace. [99] The changing fortunes of war in late 1812 and 1813 spared the Conference from further embarrassment. Between 1815 and 1820, Methodism was attacked on two fronts. The radical press claimed it was too reactionary, while the government accused it of hiding radicals. Wesleyan leaders transferred responsibilities to local preachers and the result was a fall in membership as individuals were expelled for radical actions. Growth in the northern manufacturing districts came to a halt and even went into temporary decline in 1819 and 1820. In Rochdale, for instance, there was a 15 per cent fall in members between 1818 and 1820. Events between 1800 and 1830 had led to a closer definition of Methodism in both a denominational and social sense. Government pressure, revivalism and radicalism and administrative and financial difficulties led to changes in its structure and organisation. Wesleyan conservatism was now well

---

[97] Dolan, John, *The Independent Methodists: A History*, (James Clarke Company), 2005. The early Independent Methodist societies broke away from Wesleyan Methodism over involvement in radical politics and the refusal to allow writing to be taught in Wesleyan Sunday Schools. Other societies came into being through the attraction of a 'free' ministry, particularly in communities where poverty was prevalent; this attracted some dissident Primitive Methodists.

[98] Hargreaves, John A., 'Methodism and Luddism in Yorkshire, 1812-1813', *Northern History*, Vol. 26, (1990), pp. 160-185.

[99] Cookson, J. E., *The Friends of Peace: Anti-war Liberalism in England 1793-1815*, (Cambridge University Press), 1982, pp. 190-191, 245-249.

rooted among those with influence in the movement; Methodism was becoming respectable.[100]

Bunting was sincere in his support for the Methodist mission at home and abroad, but he was also convinced that he was vital to that mission's success.[101] Though the formal basis of his power was not large, his control over the direction that Methodism took after 1820 was both absolute and clerical and he was often called the 'Pope of Methodism'.[102] He was secretary of the Methodist Conference after 1814 and of the nationwide missionary society. He was President of the Conference in 1820, 1828, 1836 and 1844. He was a member of every important committee, speaker at every Conference, edited the *Wesleyan Methodist Magazine*, and had a decisive influence on the 'stationing' of ministers. He managed Conference because most people supported his policies, because he mastered every subject, because he was more moderate in proposals than in manner and because he was a realist. He persuaded the Wesleyans to open a 'theological institution' with himself as active president in 1834. Bunting established both a spiritual ideal and a disciplinary system, pitilessly punishing any who dared to criticise him.

Bunting redefined the government of the Connection. The Conference, consisting of the Legal Hundred and other preachers, had been reformed in 1814. But the Connection remained under Bunting's control and senior churchmen and Conference saw strong government as the only way of directing Methodist expansion. The burden and responsibility over the local Methodist societies and

---

[100] Engemann, T. S., 'Religion and political reform: Wesleyan Methodism in nineteenth-century Britain', *Journal of Church & State*, Vol. 24, (1982), pp. 321-336, provides a good summary.

[101] Hempton, David, *The Religion of the People: Methodism and Popular Religion c. 1750-1900*, (Routledge), 1996, pp. 91-108, considers Bunting's formative years to 1820.

[102] Ward, W. R., (ed.), *The Early Correspondence of Jabez Bunting*, (Royal Historical Society), 1972, and Ward, W. R., (ed.), *Early Victorian Methodism: The Correspondence of Jabez Bunting 1830-1858*, (Oxford University Press), 1976. See also, Hayes, A. J., and Gowland, D. A., (eds.), *Scottish Methodism in the early Victorian period: the Scottish Correspondence of the Rev. Jabez Bunting 1800-57*, (Edinburgh University Press), 1981, and Bunting, T. P., and Rowe, G. S., *The life of Jabez Bunting, D.D.*, 2 Vols. (Harper & Brothers), 1859, 1887. For contrary views on Bunting see, Kent, J. H. S., *Jabez Bunting: The Last Wesleyan*, (Epworth Press), 1955, and *The Age of Disunity*, (Epworth Press), 1966, and ibid, Currie, R., *Methodism Divided*, is more hostile. Ibid, Bowmer, J. C., *Pastor and People*, recognises Bunting's arrogance but regards him as essentially a defender of 'classical' Wesleyan church order.

chapels was carried by local laymen though Conference chose district committees to act during the year. To overrule decisions by local officers who controlled the money invited collision between Conference and its congregations and between clerics and laymen. Bunting's control over the Stationing Committee enabled him to press the authority of itinerant ministers and diminish that of congregations. In 1818, preachers were authorised to call themselves 'the Reverend' and in 1836, Conference approved the laying on of hands in all ordinations of ministers. High Methodists preferred clerical costume but opposition from anti-ritualists in the northern congregations led to the Conference banning them in 1842.

As Conference met for only a few days a year and most of the preachers who attended lacked experience of business, real power lay with a permanent executive dominated by Bunting. When Bunting was absent from sessions of the Conference, such was his dominance that it was found that it could not conduct sensible business. The problem with this control was that it allowed little room for opposition or independence. Conference tended to agree with what the executive proposed. The consequence of this was a growing conflict between central government and local initiative. For those who did not wish to be expelled from Methodism it seemed safer to let Bunting dominate and define Wesleyanism. In any local dispute, Bunting upheld the right of ministers to instruct and to discipline their members. In 1827, for example, he insisted that the Brunswick Chapel in Leeds should have an organ, though most of the Methodists there considered it a symbol of clericalism, if not Popery, and in protest formed their own denomination, the Protestant Methodists.[103] In 1835, Samuel Warren of Manchester was expelled by Conference and the decision was upheld by the Lord Chancellor. Warren and his supporters wanted local societies to have more independence, Methodist money controlled by laymen, no legislation without the consent of a majority of the local societies and the theological institution to be abandoned. These two groups joined forming the Wesley Methodist Association. Teetotalism posed a further threat to Methodist unity in the late 1830s and early 1840s. In England it was usually led by Methodists and old Dissenters and in Cornwall resulted in members deserting ministers who would not sign the pledge and give the sacraments with unfermented wine.[104]

---

[103] Hughes, J. T., 'The story of the Leeds 'non-cons': formation of the Wesleyan Protestant Methodists', *Proceedings of the Wesley Historical Society*, Vol. 39, (1973), pp. 73-76.

[104] Lander, John K., 'The early days of teetotalism in Cornwall', *Journal of the Royal Institution of Cornwall*, ns, Vol. II, (2002), pp. 85-100, and Rule,

Conference banned this wine in 1841 but a prudent Cornish superintendent prevented schism by turning a blind eye to some usage of the banned wine. In 1842, however, about 600 members separated from Conference and became the Teetotal Wesleyan Methodists. [105]

By the 1840s, worship within Methodism were as diverse as those in the Established Church. Some chapels were solemn and liturgical and used the Book of Common Prayer; in others worship was revivalist. Irrespective, women did not become eminent as local preachers in Wesleyan Methodism, though they did among Primitive Methodists and Bible Christians.[106] Bunting, though he stood for order, recognised the rightfulness of revivals. It was the extent of revivalism that, by the 1840s, he questioned. He disapproved of ranting and was careful to disassociate himself from the emotionalism of Primitive Methodists. The most serious opposition came in the 1840s with both the *Wesleyan Times* and anonymous pamphlets or *Fly Sheets* attacking Bunting's personality and policies. Although he never acknowledged authorship, James Everett, a disgruntled preacher and satirist, was accused and in 1849 expelled along with two contributors to the *Wesleyan Times*. The dispute was venomous and reflected widespread discontent with Bunting's regime. The result was the formation of the Wesleyan Reformers and up to a third of Wesleyans left the Conference. Some seceders formed Wesleyan Congregationalist chapels, some supported the Primitive Methodists and in 1857 Everett was successful in joining with those who had walked out with Warren in forming the United Methodist Free Church, Liberal in politics and lay in emphasis. Everett became the first president of almost 40,000 members. [107]

The Wesleyan splits left the seceders more radical and those who remained more conservative. But they also aroused feelings of

---

John, 'Explaining revivalism: the case of Cornish Methodism', *Southern History*, Vol. 20-21 (1998-1999), pp. 168-188.
[105] Small, William, *Methodism versus Teetotalism: The Despotism of modern Wesleyan Methodism*, (Ingram and Cooke), 1841, is a witty attack on Bunting over the issue.
[106] Lloyd, Jennifer M., *Women and the Shaping of British Methodism: Persistent Preachers, 1807-1907*, (Manchester University Press), 2010, considers the experience of Bible Christian and Primitive Methodist female evangelicals especially before 1850.
[107] Beckerlegge, Oliver A., *The United Methodist Free Churches: a study in freedom*, (Wesley Historical Society Lecture), 1957, and Gowland, D. A., *Methodist Secessions: The origins of Free Methodism in three Lancashire towns, Manchester, Rochdale, Liverpool*, (Manchester University Press), 1979.

bitterness and cynicism. Wearmouth called it a 'spiritual earthquake that shook the very foundations'. [108] They may also have diverted Methodism among working people from evangelism. Even at the nadir of the reaction in 1855, there were still some 260,000 adult Wesleyans who accepted Bunting's control of their national life and the local rule of ministers acceptable to him. His policies of establishing Wesleyan Methodism as a religious grouping between Dissent and the Established Church had been bought at the cost of theological repression and expulsion but many people found an acceptable spiritual home in the Methodism he had refashioned.

Methodism accounted for nearly a quarter of the total attendance in the 1851 *Religious Census*. It was most dominant in the belt of arable farming stretching from the south Midlands into Lincolnshire and Yorkshire, and in Cornwall and the Isle of Wight. Its influence was least felt in three regions: south-east of a line from Bournemouth to Great Yarmouth; in the three northern counties of Northumberland, Westmoreland and Cumberland; and, in the counties bordering the Bristol Channel extending north across the Welsh Marches. Sussex, Surrey, Hampshire and large parts of Wiltshire and Berkshire were devoid of Wesleyan Methodism in 1851 and no sustained effort was made to introduce it till 1865. Why this area was a 'Methodist Desert' was partly a result of Wesley's policy of concentrating on urban areas where the Church of England was failing in its functions and in areas that would readily accept his message. The situation in the south-east was less responsive since the Anglican parochial system had not broken down as it had in the north. By contrast, Methodism was highly successful in the Isle of Wight and Cornwall after 1800 when it stepped in to fill the vacuum left by the Church of England. By 1851, Methodist influence was at its peak and all branches of the original Connection were represented. Wesley also paid frequent visits to Devon but it was not until after 1850 that Methodism took off but never to the same extent as Cornwall. The strong position of Dissent in Devon before 1740 helps to explain this compared to the existence of fewer Dissenting chapels in Cornwall.

Methodism was never a monolithic denomination. During Wesley's lifetime the only division within Methodism was between those who subscribed to a Calvinist theology led by George Whitefield and the Arminian Wesleyans. The nineteenth century saw its progressive decline as individual churches either rejoined mainstream Methodism or became Congregational churches. In England the only

---

[108] Wearmouth, R. F., *Methodism and the struggle of the working classes, 1850-1900*, (Epworth Press), 1964, p. 91.

focus of Calvinistic Methodists was in a belt from Cambridgeshire and Huntingdonshire, south through London into Kent. The Methodist New Connection, formed into a separate denomination in 1797, was virtually identical to the parent body, except for the power it gave to the laity.[109] It drew its membership almost exclusively from north of the Severn-Wash line and in 1851 there were only nine churches south of that line: five in London, three in Cornwall and one in Norfolk. The New Connection was essentially a phenomenon of the Midlands and the north and its greatest strength lay in Cheshire, Nottinghamshire, Worcestershire, Staffordshire and the West Riding and into the north-east.

Primitive Methodism originated in Staffordshire and spread quickly between 1810 and 1850. From its original home it expanded along the line of the River Trent, having significant success in the East Riding spreading northwards into Durham and south through Lincolnshire into Norfolk. On reaching the Bible Christian strongholds in south-east and south-west England Primitive Methodism lost its impetus. By 1851, it was firmly established making up over a fifth of all Methodists, and the second largest Methodist group. Primitive Methodism was largely rural in character and, with the exception of Durham and the Potteries, its main strength was in the predominantly agricultural counties of England. Primitive Methodism was used, to a certain extent, by nineteenth century agricultural labourers as a means through that they could fight for social and economic recognition and their chapels provided the rural worker with a symbol of independence and defiance of the established social order. It was not until after 1850 that its appeal to the urban worker increased.

The Bible Christians were a product of the West Country and, unlike the other branches of Methodism they were not a breakaway body.[110] Although they adopted features similar to Methodism when they applied for membership of the Wesleyan Connection it was rejected because of the independent character of its charismatic leader William O'Bryan. The Bible Christians opened their first chapel at Shebbear in north Devon in 1815 and four years later held their first Conference. In the early 1820s, the leaders of the movement sent a mission to Kent and London and also accepted an invitation to take their cause to Somerset. By 1851, there were small groups of Bible Christians all along the south coast from Cornwall to Kent. However,

---

[109] Larsen, Timothy, 'Methodist New Connexionism: lay emancipation as a denominational *raison d'etre*', in Lovegrove, Deryck W., (ed.), *The Rise of the Laity in Evangelical Protestantism*, (Routledge), 2002, pp. 153-164.
[110] Ibid, Shaw, T., *The Bible Christians*.

over large parts of England there was little success. The appeal of Bible Christianity, like Primitive Methodism, was to rural society and provided a religious position from which to attack the economic system symbolised by the Church of England and Anglican landowners. The Bible Christians found industrial towns difficult to evangelise. Both Primitive Methodism and Bible Christianity arose in response to the need to fill the religious vacuum left by the Church of England among rural workers. The spread of Primitive Methodism was halted when it reached the Bible Christian strongholds and the converse was true. The similarities between them made it unlikely that both groups could flourish in the same locality though this did occur in Hampshire and Cornwall. [111]

The Protestant Methodists, formed in 1827, united with the followers of Samuel Warren to make the Wesley Methodist Association in the 1830s. It was, with the exception of Cornwall, weak everywhere south of the Severn-Wash line. The main concentrations were in Cheshire, Lancashire, Cumberland and Westmoreland, with eastern extensions into Durham and Yorkshire and then south in Nottinghamshire and Leicestershire. It made little headway in the strongly revivalist counties of the east: Norfolk, Lincolnshire, the North and East Ridings of Yorkshire. The Wesleyan Methodist Reformers, formed when James Everett was expelled in 1849, was barely organised by 1851. They complemented the Association in geographical distribution and in 1857 joined with the Association to form the United Free Methodist Church with an initial membership of around 40,000.

The 1851 *Religious Census* shows a resurgent Nonconformity and a defensive Anglicanism but though most contemporaries accepted this, it is deceptively simple. By the 1840s, Nonconformity was beginning to enter a phase of limited growth that eventually led to decline. The economic, demographic and cultural conditions of the previous one hundred years had been highly receptive to Nonconformist recruitment. But three separate conditions began to alter this situation. Effective Anglican competition gradually emerged with the resurgence of the Church of England after 1832. Society was changing in ways hostile to Nonconformity. The decline of traditional support among urban artisans and tenant farmers and agricultural labourers meant that Victorian Nonconformity depended heavily for support on those social groups, like the middle-classes, least insulated from the influence of the religious Establishment. Finally,

---

[111] See, Few, Janet, 'Uproar and Disorder?: The Impact of Bible Christians on Communities of Nineteenth Century North Devon', *Family and Community History*, Vol. 12, (1), (2009), pp 37-50.

Nonconformist religious culture was evolving institutional and denominational priorities that slowed down the rate of growth and by 1851 Nonconformity was just passed the zenith of its power.

Roman Catholicism 1800-1850

The period between 1780 and 1850 has been characterised by John Bossy as representing the 'birth of a denomination' for Catholicism.[112] As with Protestant Dissent, Catholicism went through a period of growth in membership, conflict between lay and clerical influences and organisational change. Bossy has called into question two ideas about nineteenth century English Catholicism. He maintains that the notion propagated by Newman, Wiseman and others in mid-century of a 'Second Spring', a miraculous rebirth of Catholicism dating from about 1840 is a piece of tendentious ecclesiastical propaganda. He also argues that, though commonly accepted by historians, the view that modern English Catholicism was:

> ...a cutting from the Catholicism of Ireland transplanted by emigration into an alien land that had long ceased to have anything worth mentioning to offer in the way of an indigenous Catholic tradition.[113]

This view is in need of substantial modification if only because it neglects the evidence for a vibrant, if not always successful, tradition of English Catholicism that went back to the sixteenth century.

In 1770, there were about 80,000 Catholics in England. By 1850, this had multiplied tenfold to about three quarters of a million, a radical transformation. Geographical distribution was also transformed, though less radically. Catholicism developed in areas where it had been barren since the Reformation: in the industrial areas of the West Riding and south-east Lancashire, in the east Midlands, in south Wales and, to a certain extent, in London. Its focus in its areas of traditional strength, the rest of Lancashire, the north-east and west Midlands moved from the countryside to towns and manufacturing districts. These changes brought about social

---

[112] On Catholicism in the nineteenth century see Norman, E. R., *Roman Catholicism in England*, (Oxford University Press), 1985, and Bossy, J., *The English Catholic Community*, (Darton, Longman and Todd), 1975. Norman, E. R., *The English Catholic Church in the Nineteenth Century*, (Oxford University Press), 1984, and his *Anti-Catholicism in Victorian England*, (Allen and Unwin), 1968, are more detailed. Paz, D. G., *Popular Anti-Catholicism in Mid-Victorian England*, (Stanford University Press), 1992, and Arnstein, W. L., *Protestant versus Catholic in mid-Victorian England*, (University of Missouri Press), 1982, on anti-popery.

[113] Ibid, Bossy, J., *The English Catholic Community*, p. 297.

change and congregations of labourers, artisans, tradesmen and the poor topped up with some business and professional families replaced congregations of gentry, farmers, agricultural labourers and rural craftsmen. [114]

This represented a transformation of the English Catholic community and would have occurred had no Irish immigrants arrived. By 1770, English Catholicism was already expanding because of growing population and the efforts of Catholic clergy and its social structure was already in the process of change. Irish immigration reinforced trends already evident. [115] By 1851, in urban Lancashire there was a ratio of three Irish-descended to one English-descended Catholic. Irish immigrants and English Catholics were initially divided to a certain extent by language, by economic status though this should not be over-exaggerated since both groups contained people of a wide range of incomes and occupations, with different social and political attitudes and different attitudes to the clergy and by mutual dislike. They were unified by intermarriage, by common schooling and by the process of assimilation. In some areas such as Cardiff and south Wales, in Cumberland and the West Riding purely Irish communities, with Irish priests and nationalistic self-consciousness did not have any real contact with English Catholicism until after 1851. They were, however, the exception and the norm especially in larger cities was a mixed and stratified community. [116] This numerical change upset the balance of power within the Catholic community. In 1770, it was still dominated by its secular aristocracy but by 1850 it was dominated by its clergy. It was a paradox of the movement for Catholic Emancipation that, although lay Catholics who conducted the campaign went to great lengths to emphasise their detachment from papal jurisdiction, it was the clergy who really gained in authority. Appeals to Rome to decide on the acceptability of new oaths, the need for organisation and the emergence of a Catholic middle-class divorced from the old landed families tended to give the clergy an enhanced role and prepared the way for the centralisation of the Church in the mid-nineteenth century.

---

[114] Jordan, Sally, 'Paternalism and Roman Catholicism: the English Catholic Elite in the Long Eighteenth Century', *Studies in Church History*, Vol. 42, (2006), pp. 272-281.

[115] Gilley, Sheridan, 'Roman Catholicism and the Irish in England', in ibid, MacRaild, Donald M., (ed.), *The Great Famine and beyond: Irish migrants in Britain in the nineteenth and twentieth centuries*, pp. 147-167.

[116] Mullett, Michael A., *Catholics in Britain and Ireland, 1558-1829*, (Macmillan), 1998, provides a valuable overview.

In 1820, the English Catholic clergy was only 400 strong. There had been little increase in the number of priests since 1770, a consequence of the disintegration of the continental training establishments. Three secular-clergy seminaries at Ware, Ushaw and Oscott were functioning by 1810 but they were unable to provide more that a trickle of new priests. The years after 1830 saw a new mood of self-confidence among Catholic seculars as they sought a return to ordinary government of the Church by canon law and territorial episcopate and some degree of independence from the rule of Rome. The first half of the century was marked by continued antipathy between the secular clergy and the regulars, priests of one of the Catholic religious orders. In 1838, Rome issued two decrees that gave new privileges to the regular clergy operating in England and allowed them to open chapels without the permission of bishops. In 1840, the seculars petitioned Rome requesting that in future no regulars should be appointed as Vicars Apostolic. [117] There was a widespread belief among seculars that regular clergy were anti-episcopal. The dispute between them was not resolved until 1881 when the regulars had to conduct their missions on the same basis of others and their chapels and schools were placed under episcopal control.

The movement towards the 'restoration of a hierarchy' in England can be seen, in part, as a secular attempt to gain full control over the English Church. In 1837, the Vicars Apostolic approached Pope Gregory XVI but, though he was willing to increase the number of Vicariates to increase efficiency, he was unwilling to re-establish a hierarchy for fear of Crown interference in appointments. In 1840, the Eastern, Central, Welsh and Lancastrian Districts were established: the number of Vicariates was doubled. Full restoration was still sought by English bishops because of the need to bring Roman discipline and influence to bear on the centralising of missions and because of the need for additional armour against the regulars. In 1847, Pius IX was persuaded of the case but it was not until 1850 that the hierarchy was restored.[118] The following year, the government passed the Ecclesiastical Titles Act that reinforced the

---

[117] On Vicars Apostolic between 1550 and 1850, see, Hemphill, Basil, 'The vicars apostolic of England', *Clergy Review*, ns, Vol. 31, (1949), pp. 35-41, 99-106, 165-173, 247-254, 394-400; Vol. 32, (1949), pp. 38-45, 180-187, 249-256, 323-330.

[118] Ralls, W., 'The Papal Aggression of 1850: A Study in Victorian Anti-Catholicism', *Church History*, Vol. 32, (1974), pp. 242-256, and Paz, D. G., 'Popular Anti-Catholicism in England, 1850-1851', *Albion*, Vol. 11, (1979), pp. 331-359

existing prohibition of Catholics assuming territorial titles held by the clergy of the Church of England. For 'Old' Catholics and the remnants of the Catholic gentry the restored hierarchy marked the final eclipse of their power over the Church. It was the symbol of Roman hegemony.

Why was the state of working-class religion a problem in the mid-century?

In his report on the 1851 *Religious Census*, Horace Mann noted:

> ...a sadly formidable proportion of the English people are habitual neglecters of the public ordinances of religion. [119]

Mann's report emphasised that a large section of the population was absent from church and that the absentees were drawn mainly from the working-classes that had become 'thoroughly estranged from our religious institutions'. He analysed the causes of this estrangement and suggested six reasons: social inequalities within the churches, for example class arranged and rented pews; the depth of class divisions within society that meant that working-class people would not wish to worship with members of other classes; the apparent lack of interest on the part of the churches in the material well-being of the poor; suspicion of the clergy; the effects of poverty: many working-class people lacked time or space for reflection and were too preoccupied with immediate problems to give much thought to religion; and, the lack of 'aggressive' missionary activity. [120]

There is significant disagreement among historians about the role and importance of religion in the lives of the working population. One reason for this confusion lies in the difficulty of interpreting the census but some firm observations were made. [121] Vast numbers of

---

[119] Mann, Horace, *Census of Great Britain, 1851: Religious Worship in England and Wales*, (G. Routledge), 1854, p. 93. *Census of Great Britain, 1851: Religious worship in England and Wales, abridged from the official report made by H. Mann.* 1854, *Census of Great Britain, 1851: religious worship, England and Wales: reports and tables* [1690] H.C., (1852-3), Vol. LXXXIX, 1, [1852-3] and *Census of Great Britain, 1851: Religious worship and education: Scotland: reports and tables* [1764] H.C., (1854), Vol. LIX, 301, [1854]. The census material for particular localities, for example, Kent and Bedfordshire, has been published by local history record societies.

[120] Williams, Sarah, 'The language of belief: an alternative agenda for the study of Victorian working-class religion', *Journal of Victorian Culture*, Vol. 1, (1996), pp. 303-317.

[121] Thompson, David M., 'The 1851 Religious Census: Problems and Possibilities', *Victorian Studies*, Vol. 11, (1), (1967), pp. 87-97, Pickering,

people did not attend formal religious services, especially the working population in the large industrial and manufacturing cities and towns that were apparently largely beyond the influence of church or chapel. The Church of England could no longer claim to be the 'national' church. It remained strongest in the counties round London and in eastern England, but in some northern and western areas and in Wales chapel-goers were in the majority. [122]

The 1851 *Religious Census* is widely regarded as evidence for widespread religious apathy but it simply provides a snapshot of attendance on one day in one year. However, the work of Wickham on Sheffield and Inglis with their negative treatment of religion among the labouring population with their stress on 'indifference' and 'apathy' remains influential. [123] What, constituted 'high' as opposed to 'low' attendance? How far can people's religious beliefs be learned from whether they attended on a particular day or not? How is it possible to resolve the problem of religious apathy highlighted by many contemporary observers, who equated religious belief with regular church attendance with working-class autobiographies suggesting that their authors were strongly interested in religion? [124]

The impact of religion on the working population in the first half of the nineteenth century was multi-faceted. The working-classes had their own different, but equally valid approach to religion that was strongly practical and concerned especially with mutual aid and with maintaining standards of 'decent' behaviour. Any interpretation has to deal with the contradictory notions of secularising trends and

---

W. S. F., 'The 1851 religious census: a useless experiment', *British Journal of Sociology*, Vol. 18, (1967), pp. 382-407. See also, the detailed analysis of the 1851 Religious Census in Snell, Keith D. M., and Ell, Paul S., *Rival Jerusalems: the geography of Victorian religion*, (Cambridge University Press), 2000, and Crockett, Alasdair, 'Rural-Urban Churchgoing in Victorian England', *Rural History*, Vol. 16, (1), (2005), pp. 53-82.

[122] On the issue of working-class 'indifference' and antagonism towards the churches see McLeod, H., *Religion and the Working-class in Nineteenth Century Britain*, (Macmillan), 1984, for a brief bibliographical study and Gill, Robin, *The 'empty' church revisited*, (Ashgate), 2003, pp. 69-134. On the position of the Church of England see Coleman, B. I., *The Church of England in the Mid-Nineteenth Century: A Social Geography*, (The Historical Association), 1980, and 'Religion in the Victorian City', *History Today*, Vol. 31, (8), (1980), pp. 25-31.

[123] Wickham, E. R., *Church and People in an Industrial City*, (Lutterworth), 1957, and Inglis, K. S., *Churches and the Working-classes in Victorian England*, (Routledge), 1963, remain important studies.

[124] Wolffe, John, 'Elite and Popular Religion in the Religious Census of 30 March 1851', *Studies in Church History*, Vol. 42, (2006), pp. 360-371.

the continuing strength of working-class religiosity. Austin Freeman wrote of the spiritual effects of industrialisation:

...it has destroyed social unity and replaced it by social disintegration and class antagonism... [125]

The weakening of the Established churches was evident in the century before the 1851 *Religious Census*. The prevailing style of religion tended to be rational and moralistic and commitment required was fairly low. Indifference and scepticism was widespread and 'enthusiasm' was viewed with suspicion. Religion failed to satisfy the emotional needs of large sections of society who either conformed because it was expected of them or who left the parish church to form their own religious groups sometimes with a separate place of worship. From the 1730s throughout Britain, there was a steady stream of defections from the church questioning both its latitudinarianism and erastianism and its rationalist and unemotional nature. Evangelicalism and the emergence of groups within the church and outside it, Methodism for instance, raised the level of religious awareness and emotional commitment.

Parallel to this revolution in sentiment was a failure on the part of the establishment to provide sufficient new churches, especially in urban centres. This was believed by contemporaries to have encouraged the spread of Nonconformity and non-churchgoing. The 1790s saw a polarisation of religious attitudes with the addition of a political dimension. The Established churches were seen as vital agencies for the defence of a paternalistic, hierarchical society, a conservatism that discredited them in the eyes of those who favoured radical reform. Both Nonconformists and millenarians reflected the hopes of those who believed that events in France heralded a new era of equality and social justice. [126] Millenarians like Richard Brothers, a naval officer living in London who was imprisoned as a lunatic after 1795 and Joanna Southcott who from 1801 until her death in 1814 enjoyed a widespread following. [127] They maintained

---

[125] Freeman, R. Austin, *Social Decay and Regeneration*, (Constable), 1921, p. 284.

[126] On 'infidelism', Royle, E., *Victorian Infidels: the origins of the British secularist movement, 1791-1866*, (Manchester University Press), 1974, and his documentary collection *Radical Politics 1790-1900: Religion and Unbelief*, (Longman), 1971. Budd, S., *Varieties of Unbelief*, (Heinemann), 1977, takes the 1850s as its starting point.

[127] Matthews, Ronald, *English Messiahs. Studies of six English religious pretenders, 1656-1927*, (Methuen), 1936, pp. 127-195, considers Brothers and Southcott but see also, Brown, Frances, *Joanna Southcott: the woman*

that the violent events of the 1790s and 1800s had their place in God's plan for the salvation of mankind and that the millennial kingdom was coming soon. Millenarianism was a very old tradition but the 1790s saw the emergence of a new phenomenon, organised irreligion.[128] Many clergy saw non-churchgoing as evidence for 'infidelism' but this neglects the extent to which there were simply insufficient places in churches. [129]

So did the involvement of the working population in religion increase or decline after 1830? The splits within Methodism, the church building of various denominations and the growing assurance of the Established Church calls into question the view often expressed that religious adherence was in decline. Most denominations did not have reliable lists of members until 1851. Gilbert suggests that the great expansion of Nonconformity ground to a halt in the 1840s but that there were also 'crisis points' when individuals turned to religion because of the widespread belief that many human problems could not be solved by natural means. After 1850, he argues both church and chapel appealed to the middle-classes. [130] Wickham, by contrast, defined the second half of the nineteenth century as a 'religious boom' in Sheffield with the building of new churches and chapels. [131] He too stressed the middle-class character of most congregations but he implied an increase in working-class congregations. Gilbert's analysis overstates the degree to which the third quarter of the nineteenth century was one of decline but there is no doubt that important changes were taking place in the religion of the working population.

If the statistical argument is inconclusive how far does 'identity' with established denominations provide a solution? Membership of

---

clothed with the sun, (Lutterworth), 2002, Hopkins, J. K., *A woman to deliver her people: Joanna Southcott and English millenarianism in the era of revolution*, (University of Texas Press), 1982, and Lockley, Philip J., *Visionary Religion and Radicalism in early industrial England: from Southcott to socialism*, (Oxford University Press), 2013.

[128] Harrison, J. F. C., *The Second Coming: Popular Millenarianism, 1780-1850*, (Routledge), 1979, is standard. For an important local study see, Bell, Karl, ''The Humbugg of the World at an End': the apocalyptic imagination of the uses of collective fantasy in Norfolk in 1844', *Social History*, Vol. 31, (4), (2006), pp. 454-468.

[129] Turner, F. M., 'The religious and the secular in Victorian Britain', in Turner, F. M., *Contesting cultural authority: essays in Victorian intellectual life*, (Cambridge University Press), 1993, pp. 3-37.

[130] Ibid, Gilbert, A. D., *Religion and Society in Industrial England 1740-1914*, pp. 125-175.

[131] Ibid, Wickham, E. R., *Church and People in an Industrial City*, pp. 107-134.

the Established churches symbolised membership of civil society. The parish church, where the most people were baptised, married and buried, was the symbol of community. In Scotland, disputes over lay patronage and over ritual in England were a reflection of the feeling that the parish church belonged to the people. Orthodoxy meant citizenship and deliberately to cut oneself off from the parish church was viewed with intense suspicion and meant limiting oneself to the status of a second-class citizen. Orthodoxy was a public affirmation of belief in the existing social system even if beliefs were private. The emergence of religious pluralism and the movement away from legislative limitations on Nonconforming groups had a deeply divisive effect. In the nineteenth century sectarian identity influenced most areas of life and even those less interested in religion found themselves in situations where an identity was forced upon them. Sectarian conflict took two major forms in Britain. It was the result of the decline of established social systems and the transition to more open and pluralistic society. It was also the product of the mixing of different populations following social movement from rural to urban environments. By 1850, most British cities had distinct Irish Catholic neighbourhoods and anti-Catholicism reinforced the inner cohesion of these communities and the Catholic identity of their members.

Political radicalism often grew out of religious heterodoxy. Unitarians with their congregational autonomy and non-Trinitarian doctrines developed a number of working-class chapels. The most important aspect of the political implications of religious heterodoxy was the role of secularism from the 1790s onwards. [132] The freethinking tradition established in the 1790s largely raised the issue of the freedom of the press to publish anti-Christian or radical literature and newspapers. Pitt's actions against the radical press in 1798 and 1799 as well as the more general conservative backlash forced freethinking underground but it re-emerged as a vibrant force after 1815. The leading figure in its revival was Richard Carlile and between 1817 and 1825 he campaigned against Liverpool's administration and moral reformers. [133] By the early 1830s, Carlile's influence on the 'infidel' tradition was declining and the anti-Christian component of Owenism came to the fore. Owen's opposition to

---

[132] Brown, Callum G., *The death of Christian Britain: understanding secularisation, 1800-2000*, (Routledge), 2000, pp. 16-34.
[133] Wiener, Joel H, *Radicalism and freethought in nineteenth-century Britain: the life of Richard Carlile*, (Greenwood Press), 1983. See also, Marsh, Josh, *Word Crimes: blasphemy, culture, and literature in nineteenth-century England*, (University of Chicago Press), 1998, pp. 18-77.

Christianity was grounded in the argument that it seemed to produce division rather than harmony in society. Denominations were 'competitive' rather than 'co-operative' and for Owen this prevented the creation of his 'new moral world'. The growth of secularism from the late 1830s was the result of a split within Owenism precipitated by Charles Southwell who attacked Owen as a wrong-headed dreamer and in 1841 began the *Oracle of Reason* in which he proclaimed the rational truths of atheism. Southwell's arrest and prosecution led to Malthus Ryall and George Jacob Holyoake setting up the Anti-Prosecution Union. [134] Peel and Russell could use the courts to punish freethinkers but this could not silence them. In London, intense activity led to the development of the London Atheistical Society to agitate for a change in the law for 'infidels' and a Free Thinkers Tract Society was formed to disseminated radical literature. By 1850, there had been a significant weakening of infidel organisations, as much a result of internal disagreement as external pressures, and this led Holyoake to set up a new movement that in 1852 he called 'Secularism'. The appeal of freethinking was never very wide and in the first half of the nineteenth century the choice for the working population was between 'orthodox' churches and none at all.

How religious was the working-class after 1850? How widespread was irreligion among working people? In 1936, R. C. K. Ensor wrote:

No-one will ever understand Victorian England who does not appreciate that among highly civilised...countries it was one of the most religious the world has ever known. [135]

This orthodoxy prevailed until around 1960. Historians debated as to whether this religiosity was a good or bad thing; they discussed when and why it went into decline; but no-one doubted that it was a reality.[136] The challenge to the consensus came from E. R. Wickham and K. S. Inglis. Wickham was concerned with the lack of involvement in the church by the working-classes and led him to trace

---

[134] McLaren, Angus, 'George Jacob Holyoake and the Secular Society: British popular freethought, 1851-8', *Canadian Journal of History*, Vol. 7, (1972), pp. 235-251. See also, ibid, Marsh, Josh, *Word Crimes: Blasphemy, Culture, and Literature in Nineteenth-Century England*, pp. 78-126.
[135] Ensor, R. C. K., *England 1870-1914*, (Oxford University Press), 1936, p. 137.
[136] For analysis of the literature see McLeod, H., *Religion and the Working-class in Nineteenth century Britain*, (Macmillan), 1984, and *Religion and Irreligion in Victorian England*, (Headstart History), 1993.

the roots of this apparent indifference back to the nineteenth century. Inglis' interest was in Christian evangelistic and social reform movements of the later-nineteenth century ranging from the Salvation Army to the Settlements, to various forms of Christian Socialism. He concluded that there was a common thread running through all these movements: they were a response to a general working-class alienation from churches. Both Wickham and Inglis did not deny that the Victorian period witnessed a 'religious boom' but insisted that it was overwhelmingly middle-class and passed the working-classes by. They challenged existing assumptions about the nature of Victorian religion because of their use of two largely neglected sources: the censuses of church attendance conducted nationally by government and locally by newspapers at various points, notably in the 1880s. Especially important was Inglis' analysis of the national *Religious Census* of 1851 that, he argued, demonstrated that none of the churches made a significant impact on the urban working-classes.[137]

A series of local studies and thematic articles in the 1960s and 1970s reached broadly similar conclusions: the great majority of Victorian working people were indifferent, if not hostile, to organised religion, and the many attempts to convert the working-classes were a massive failure. By the 1970s, developments in social history and 'history from below' led historians to ask whether the definition of religion was too narrow. Was too much emphasis being placed on church-going as a measure of working-class religiosity? There was a growing interest in popular religion, a term used to describe a wide range of beliefs that were religious but diverged from the official orthodoxy of church and chapel.[138] There was also an attempt to relate religious changes more closely to their economic and social context. Gilbert suggested that industrialisation aided secularisation in the long run but in the short term it helped trigger a temporary religious revival that petered out by the 1840s.[139] Yeo's study of Reading suggested that it was not industrialisation or urbanisation that undermined organised religion, but the specific form of capitalism that was emerging in the early-twentieth century.[140]

---

[137] Inglis, K. S., 'Patterns of religious worship in 1851', *Journal of Ecclesiastical History*, Vol. 11, (1960), pp. 74-86.
[138] This definition of popular religion comes from Obelkevich, James, *Religion in Rural Society: South Lindsey 1825-1875*, (Oxford University Press), 1976.
[139] Ibid, Gilbert, A. D., *Religion and Society in Industrial England 1740-1914*, pp. 152-167.
[140] Yeo, S., *Religion and Voluntary Organisations in Crisis*, (Croom Helm), 1976, pp. 117-184.

The Wickham-Inglis thesis was further challenged during the 1980s. Most influential was Jeffrey Cox in his study of the south London borough of Lambeth. [141] He accepted that working-class attendance at church and chapel was low but in many other respects he challenged existing assumptions. He recognised the wide-ranging social role of the Victorian churches that entered people's lives at many points and could exercise a pervasive influence even in communities were church attendance was low. He suggested that the decline of English churches was not the inevitable consequence of industrialisation and urbanisation but a result of the specific ways in which people chose to respond to these developments. Finally, Callum Brown rejected Wickham and Inglis on just about every points. Big towns were not significantly less church-going than small towns. Working-class participation in church life was more significant than has generally been assumed; the nineteenth century was a period of religious growth not decline. In the late-nineteenth century, when the church lost the middle-classes that it had successfully won as the cities grew in the nineteenth century, it was associated with suburbanisation not urbanisation. [142]

There are four rival chronologies of Victorian working-class religion. Inglis suggests that working-class religious involvement was consistently low. Wickham argues that there was some increase in working-class involvement between about 1850 and 1870 during a period of relative prosperity but accepts that the level was generally low. Gilbert sees religious involvement reaching a peak in the 1830s and 1840s and declining as living standards improved. Finally, Callum Brown suggests the peak came much later, perhaps as late as the 1890s taking a relatively positive view of the achievements of the Christian evangelicals and social reformers. Archbishop Cosmo Lang claimed that the period from about 1880 to 1914 marked the 'golden age of parochial work in the cities of England'. [143] Different views of when working-class religion declined are linked to rival views about why it declined. These different views support the conclusion that there is a strong case for interpreting Victorian working-class life in secular terms.

---

[141] Cox, J., *English Churches in a Secular Society: Lambeth 1870-1930*, (Oxford University Press), 1982. See also, Williams, S. C., *Religious Belief and Popular Culture in Southwark, c.1880-1939*, (Oxford University Press), 1999.

[142] Brown, Callum, G., 'Did Urbanisation Secularise Britain?', *Urban History Yearbook*, (1988), pp. 1-14.

[143] Cit, Bowen, Desmond, *The Idea of the Victorian Church: A Study of the Church of England, 1833-1881*, (McGill University Press), 1968, p. 421.

However, the use of new forms of evidence and re-evaluation of material that had previously been regarded as relatively unimportant has called this into question. There is a growing body of statistics on the occupational composition of Nonconformist chapels. Comparison of attendance lists with census schedules suggest that most Nonconformist chapels had a substantial working-class element among their members. Gilbert's analysis of Nonconformist baptismal and burial records between 1800 and 1837 shows that artisans formed the largest occupational group and that, with smaller numbers of labourers and miners, made up about three-quarters of Methodists, Baptists and Congregationalists. He concludes that the dramatic expansion of Nonconformity between 1780 and 1840 was mainly due to recruitment among the working-classes and that chapels only became more middle-class after 1850. More recent studies maintain that the pattern described by Gilbert lasted much longer and that it was after 1900 than Methodism became largely middle-class. The most thorough study has been undertaken by Rosemary Chadwick into Bradford chapels in the 1880s.[144] She found that they tended to include large numbers of working-class women and of working-class men in skilled occupations but that there was an under-representation by men in semi-skilled and unskilled occupations.

More wide-ranging but more difficult to interpret is the evidence of oral history. Elizabeth Roberts concluded from her oral history of the working-classes in Barrow and Lancaster between 1880 and 1930:

> The most striking and obvious act about religion during the first part of this period is the significant part it played in all but one family's life. [145]

The use of oral evidence has undermined existing orthodoxy in several ways. It suggests that the proportion of working-class people who went to church or chapel with some degree of frequency is rather higher than anyone might have guessed. Thompson and Vigne found that about 40 per cent of the interviewees from working-class families in industrial regions of England claimed their mother attended church or chapel with some degree of frequency. [146] In London, the north Midlands, the Potteries and the north-east the figure for fathers was

---

[144] See, Chadwick, Rosemary, *Church and people in Bradford and district 1880-1914*, D.Phil thesis, University of Oxford, 1986.

[145] Robert, Elizabeth, *Working-class Barrow and Lancaster 1890-1930*, (University of Lancaster: Centre for North-West Regional Studies), 1976, p. 62.

[146] See, Thompson, Paul, *The Edwardians: the remaking of British society*, (Weidenfeld and Nicolson), 1975, (Routledge), 1992, and *The voice of the past: oral history*, (Oxford University Press), 1978.

around 20 per cent, but it was higher in Lancashire (32 per cent) and Yorkshire (40 per cent). The average for both sexes is thus around 30 per cent, a figure somewhat higher than censuses taken on a single Sunday might suggest. The probable explanation is that because of illness, tiredness or child-care problems, working-class church-goers were less likely than their middle-class counterparts to attend every week and that the 1851 Census under-represent the extent of working-class attendance. Oral evidence illustrates Cox's argument that the churches had a pervasive social influence even in communities where church-going was low.

Churches and chapels were social centres for wide sections of the population, providing in one way or another for both sexes and all age groups. The most striking example of the inescapable presence of the church and chapel was the fact that the overwhelming majority of working-class children went to Sunday school. There have been many different views among historians as to the causes and consequences of this. Thompson stressed the indoctrination and 'religious terrorism practised by Sunday Schools and saw them as an effective means of training a new generation of docile factory hands.[147] Lacquer agreed that Sunday Schools were effective but he presented a much more sympathetic view of their objectives and methods and stressed their popularity both with working-class parents and many of their children.[148] Roberts saw Sunday Schools as popular, though principally because of the treats they provided. Humphries thought children resented going to Sunday school and did their best to disrupt classes.[149] Cox argued that, while enjoyably chaotic from the children's point of view, the schools were ineffective as a means of inculcating religion or anything else.

These divergent interpretations arise from the very varied character of an institution that was sponsored by many very different religious denominations in social environments of many different kinds that evoked many different kinds of individual responses. One generalisation can, however be made: the almost universal exposure of Victorian working-class children to Sunday schools meant that the great majority of the population grew up with a basic acquaintance

---

[147] Ibid, Thompson, E. P., *The Making of the English Working-class*, pp. 412-416.
[148] Lacquer, T. W., *Religion and Respectability: Sunday Schools and Working-class Culture 1780-1850*, (Yale University Press), 1976, chapters 6-7.
[149] Humphries, Stephen, *Hooligans or Rebels? An Oral History of Working-Class Childhood and Youth 1889-1939*, (Basil Blackwell), 1981, pp. 130-134.

with the Bible, Christian hymns and Christian doctrine. For many people this acquaintance remained basic and the resulting sense of Christian identity was largely passive. Most important of all, the oral evidence highlights aspects of religious belief and practice otherwise hidden from public view. Contemporary observers were too ready to assume that those who seldom or never went to church were 'secular' or 'indifferent' in their religious outlook. There were indeed people who could be described in such terms but there were also a good many people whose religious views were far more complex.

Is it possible to reconcile such a diversity of interpretations? It has to be recognised that all types of sources contain their inherent weakness and biases. For instance, the large body of commentary on working-class life by middle-class observers is limited in value both by the fact that the comments are those of outsiders and by the fact that these observers were often looking for evidence to support their own religious and social biases. Historians have been far too willing to take Engels' view on working-class religion at face value. The divergence between historians' interpretations of nineteenth century working-class religion is also partly explicable by the diversity of the Victorian working-classes. There were important religious differences between regions, between ethnic groups, between occupational groups and between men and women.

19 Religion in decline?

The Victorian age was self-consciously religious. [1] Britain's greatness, Victorians believed that its prosperity, political liberties and Empire was rooted in Christian and Protestant faith. Yet if religion flourished, it did not bring harmony and the transition to pluralism brought conflict and controversy with Protestants ranged against each other and against Catholics, evangelical against high churchman and Christian against unbeliever. Nor were the conflicts limited to the religious sphere. Both politics and social life were riven by the clashes of churches and creeds. The churches' biggest problem, however, was not their disputes with each other but changes in the wider society especially the continued spread of industry and large towns and deepening class divisions. The churches responded with characteristic energy and determination, making religion more relevant to British society in 1850 than it had been a century earlier. But despite their best efforts they largely failed to win the allegiance of the urban working-classes and by 1900 they were losing their hold on the respectable middle-classes as well. [2]

How far was the Church of England in decline after 1850?

The most important, if least expected development in this period was the resurgence of the Church of England. After the crises of the 1820s and 1830s, it belatedly reformed itself, fought back against the Nonconformists and regained some of the initiative it had lost. In towns, new churches were built even though the country parish remained the Anglican ideal and by 1900, the number of clergy had doubled. The clergy played the central role in the Anglican revival. [3] They began to receive professional training that brought a more energetic and combative approach to their work. In urban parishes, they served not only as priests and pastors but as social organisers as well setting up social and recreational activities, mobilising the laity

---

[1] For the development of religion in the Victorian period see Chadwick, Owen, *The Victorian Church*, 2 Vols. (SCM Press), 1970, 1972, for the standard reading with ibid, Gilbert, A. D., *Religion and Society in Industrial England*, for a different interpretation. For the period after 1900, see, Robbins, Keith, *England, Ireland, Scotland, Wales: The Christian Church 1900-2000*, (Oxford University Press), 2008, pp. 1-96.

[2] Field, Clive D., ''The Faith Society?': Quantifying Religious Belonging in Edwardian Britain, 1901-1914', *Journal of Religious History*, Vol. 37, (1), (2013), pp. 39-63.

[3] Haig, Alan, *The Victorian clergy*, (Routledge), 1984, considers the professionalising of the clergy.

while keeping control in their own hands and conducting services with smooth professionalism. With the Church now showing some 'aggression' of its own and using some of the weapons of Dissent against Dissent, it steadily improved its share of the religious market. A slow-moving establishment recast itself as a church militant. The 1830s also saw a new departure in its life. As evangelicalism had revived its Protestant and Puritan traditions, the Oxford movement now reinvigorated its Catholic traditions, rescuing them from Protestant contempt and restoring them to the life of the church. Spiritual renewal brought discord in the 1840s when Newman and some of his followers went over to Rome and in the 1850s when the younger Tractarian clergy began to introduce incense, vestments and other 'Catholic' ritual practices into their services.

From the 1840s, Anglicanism was torn by conflict between its rival 'parties'. The broad churchmen, liberal in theology and politics were caught in the middle. The Anglo-Catholics, as they later came to call themselves, formed a virtual sect within the church, complete with heroes if not heroines, martyrs, seminaries, organisations and periodicals. Outraged Protestants reacted with sermons, lawsuits, legislation and even mob violence in a long and futile campaign to halt the 'ritualist' plague. [4] Disraeli, denouncing the 'mass in masquerade', passed the Public Worship Regulation Act 1874 under which five ritualist clergymen were convicted and sent to jail. [5] Though their best known efforts were in slum parishes, where they hoped to win over the poor with their colourful ritual and self-sacrificing pastoral work, it was eventually the middle-classes, especially in London and the south-east, who provided the bulk of their support. The Anglo-Catholics nevertheless brought change to Anglicanism as a whole. [6] Their insistence that communion was the central act of worship and the badge of active church membership, gradually came to be accepted by nearly all sections of the Church. The doubling of the

---

[4] Yates, Nigel, *Anglican ritualism in Victorian Britain, 1830-1910*, (Oxford University Press), 1999, Whisenant, James, *A fragile unity: anti-ritualism and the division of Anglican evangelicalism in the nineteenth century*, (Paternoster Press), 2003, and Whisenant, James, 'Anti-ritualism and the moderation of evangelical opinion in England in the mid-1870s', *Anglican and Episcopal History*, Vol. 70, (2001), pp. 451-477.

[5] Bentley, James, *Ritualism and politics in Victorian Britain: the attempt to legislate for belief*, (Oxford University Press), 1978, and Palmer, Bernard, *Reverend rebels: five Victorian clerics and their fight against authority*, (Darton, Longman & Todd), 1993.

[6] Reed, J. S., *Glorious battle: the cultural politics of Victorian Anglo-Catholicism*, (Vanderbilt University Press), 1996.

numbers of communicants in the decades before 1914, even as attendance declined, was a reflection of their influence.

If the Anglican Church was to be successful during the second half of the nineteenth and early-twentieth century then it had to be successful in the cities where population was increasingly concentrated. The traditional view of the growth of the Victorian cities focussed on the increasing breakdown of community, individual isolation, poor housing, social deprivation and an ever growing class divide. In this context, organised religion struggled to survive and this led to the belief that the 'industrial revolution divided men from God' but Chadwick suggests that this view may be misplaced and that the city dwellers were never committed churchgoers. [7] Eighteenth century visitations, for instance, show that as few as 1-2 per cent of parishioners took communion, this perhaps being a better indication of true religiosity than attendance.

Urbanisation actually aided the growth of the church in certain sections of society, especially the new and rapidly growing middle-classes. Cox suggests:

> Even its greatest success is sometimes regarded as a failure...the Church of England succeeding in capturing or maintaining the allegiance of the new urban as well as the old rural elites. [8]

Nonetheless the church of the 1850s became increasingly aware, through the writings of Dickens, Kingsley and the work of the Poor Law Commission, that the working-classes were largely alienated from the established church. In the 1880s, Charles Booth estimated that the upper- or middle-classes, who represented 12 per cent of the population, made up the majority of the church, especially the Church of England. The churches were not inactive in their response to urbanisation. The dramatic need for more buildings to accommodate the burgeoning population was recognised by Joshua Watson and his Incorporated Church Building Society in 1818 and by Horace Mann after his *Religious Census* in 1851. There was an unprecedented mobilisation of resources through the charitable activities of the churches in areas of social deprivation. Despite this, the churches continued to decline in significance for many in the working-classes suggesting that decline was less to do with change itself but with the ways in which the Church responded to that change.

---

[7] Chadwick, Owen, *The Secularisation of the European Mind in the Nineteenth Century*, (Cambridge University Press), 1975, p. 95.
[8] Ibid, Cox, Jeffrey, *The English churches in a Secular Society: Lambeth, 1870-1930*, p. 5.

Just how effective the Church of England was in urban centres depends on what determined success. Church attendance statistics were used as the major source of information about the state of nineteenth century Christianity and a successful church was therefore one that was full. The problem is that the impact of beliefs on any one section of society did not necessarily correspond with institutional statistics whose accuracy is difficult to corroborate. In addition, it depends on which indices of religiosity are used. For instance the number of Anglican marriages declined from 90.7 per cent of all marriages in 1844 to 64.25 per cent in 1904, yet baptisms increased from 62.35 per cent in 1885 to 65.8 per cent in 1902. As a result, different historians have judged the church of the nineteenth century in different lights. Some have deemed the decline in attendance a failure of the church to reach the urban masses while others see the church holding its own, if not growing. What is clear is that the response to the Anglican Church varied by gender and region as well as by class. Attendance by women was higher across all classes and, for both working- and middle-classes women played a central role in maintaining their families' religious values. Regional variations were also important but where the church had historically been strong, it remained so. London, the focus of much contemporary concern, was exceptionally secularised. In the 1880s, 15-20 per cent of London's working-classes attended a church compared with 40 per cent of middle-classes while in Bristol this was probably 40 per cent and 66 per cent respectively.

Why were the working-classes alienated from the Church of England? There was a cultural gap between the church and the working classes. The rural dean of Kennington quoted by Charles Booth said in the 1890s: 'Working men don't go to church for the same reason that I don't go to the races'.[9] Certainly clergy in the East End of London were regarded as missionaries. McLeod commented:

> The Church of England in Bethnal Green was a missionary church, its ministers isolated by the suspicion of the natives and by the differences in language and custom that made the life of the local population repugnant to them.[10]

Respectability was part of that cultural gap. The need to wear one's best clothes to church was a bar to the poor but it was also an attraction. Working women who went to church were 'respectable'.

---

[9] Ibid, p. 105.
[10] McLeod, Hugh, *Class and Religion in the Late Victorian City*, (Croom Helm), 1974, p. 104.

There were also few positions of responsibility available to the working-classes in the church. The Anglican clergy were almost entirely upper middle-class and three-quarters 75 per cent had degrees in 1870. Lay leadership was limited as well; in Lewisham, for instance, although the church was 50 per cent working-class, they were never represented as churchwardens. This lack of involvement was also evident in the charitable activities of the church. The problem was that the church did much for the people but little with them.

The Church of England embarked on a massive programme of church building and over 600 new churches were built between 1818 and 1884. The number of clergy increased significantly from 14,613 in 1841 to 24,232 in 1891. Building churches was one thing but filling them quite another. There were deeper structural problems that the church failed to recognise and so it began to blame the infidelity of the working classes rather than their own conservatism. The evangelical emphasis on industry, sobriety and thrift appealed to the upwardly mobile middle-classes but had little resonance among working people while its social conservatism simply alienated them. Relief offered by frequently condescending district visitors was frequently resented by the poor who in turn resented the poor's ingratitude. Yet despite the immense amount of activity and effort the Victorian church poured into philanthropy, second in cost and manpower only to church building, it did little to encourage the working-classes to attend church.

Traditionally the urban contribution of the Church of England has been regarded as one of failure. The church failed to reach the working-classes and, despite initial success with the middle class, a subsequent failure to hold them in the face of rising secularism. Yet, in 1901, the Census showed attendance by 47,000 men and 61,000 women in the East End and in London as a whole one in five attended church. The church was an inescapable and intrusive part of the urban landscape. Individual clergy made heroic efforts to identify and communicate with the local community. The High churchman Osborne Jay of Jago took up boxing in Shoreditch, Weldon Champneys of Whitechapel gave weekday lectures in a school where he felt it was less off-putting for the working man than the church and he supported the coalwhippers fight for justice over employment. The Sunday school movement was on a huge scale and maintained a notion that the Church of England was 'our church'. At Christ Church, Gypsy Hill, the one poor street in the parish provided 10 per cent of all baptisms. The Anglican Church did have internal structural obstacles to reaching the entire urban populations and inevitably failed to attain this target. Yet its attempts to do so were not insignificant.

Why was Nonconformity successful after 1850?

The Victorian period was one of the high points in Nonconformist history. The different groups matched their Anglican rivals in numbers and in the mid-1880s their combined membership, excluding adherents, was about 1.4 million, much the same as the number of Anglican Easter communicants, while their huge Sunday school enrolments easily surpassed those of the Anglicans. They were largely successful in their campaign to remove their disabilities but it did not become clear until near the end of the period that with political gains there was a loss of evangelical fervour.[11]

In the 1830s and 1840s, however, Nonconformity was still expanding rapidly. Carefully planned yet intensely emotional revival meetings produced thousands of conversions and enabled it to keep pace with the increase in population. After 1850, however, as British society stabilised, religious revivals gradually ceased (the Welsh revival of 1904-1905[12] was the last) and growth rates slackened. Recruitment was also affected by competition from the Church of England and by the further spread of factory industry that left fewer of the independent artisans who had flocked to the chapels in the past. As the supply of adult converts dwindled, Nonconformists were forced to recruit from within, concentrating on children of existing members; the Sunday school replaced the revival meeting. In the 1880s, Nonconformity began to decline relative to the total population and in the decade before 1914 there was a fall in absolute numbers.

Nonconformity's social composition changed little. The core of membership still came from the lower middle and upper working-classes. Not even Primitive Methodism, the most plebeian of the larger churches, made much headway with factory workers. Each of the main denominations could boast its rich businessmen such figures as W. H. Lever (Congregationalist), Thomas Cook (Baptist), George Cadbury (Quaker), Jesse Boot (Wesleyan Methodist) and Samuel Courtauld (Unitarian) and solid middle-class prosperity was well represented among the leading lights in the chapels. It was often said that such people eventually went over to the social superior Church of England that 'the carriage only stops for one generation at the

---

[11] Johnson, Dale A., *The changing shape of English Nonconformity, 1825-1925*, (Oxford University Press), 1999, pp. 77-163.

[12] On this see, Morgan, John Vyrnwy, *The Welsh religious revival, 1904-5: a retrospect and a criticism*, (Chapman & Hall), 1909, Harvey, John, 'Spiritual emblems: the visions of the 1904-1905 Welsh revival', *Llafur*, Vol. 6, (1993), pp. 75-93, and Gitre, Edward J., 'The 1904-05 Welsh Revival: Modernization, Technologies, and Techniques of the Self', *Church History*, Vol. 73, (2004), pp. 792-827.

chapel door'.[13] Nevertheless, a significant minority of the provincial urban elite were Nonconformists, and though socially untypical of chapel-goers as a whole, they did much to give Nonconformity its characteristic form: its energy, its confidence and also its resentment towards the Establishment.

Being a Nonconformist always involved more than accepting certain religious beliefs or attending a particular chapel. They were Nonconformists by choice and principle and prided themselves on their independence and refusal to defer to authority. At the very least it meant a determination to uphold their faith regardless of legal disabilities or social snobbery. In most denominations they chose their own ministers, paid their stipends and managed chapel affairs with a minimum of interference from outside.[14] Nonconformity also brought with it a social network and public identity. Nonconformists did business with each other, married into each other's families and come to be known as Nonconformists in the local community. From their preachers and denominational press, they gained a distinctive perspective on the wider world and its problems. More than a religious commitment, Nonconformity involved a way of life and an outlook on life.[15]

At the centre of that outlook was the principle of religious freedom. Nonconformists condemned Anglicanism as a 'state church' and argued that there should be 'free trade' in religion as there was in the economy. A free and fair competition in religion, they believed, was one they would expect to win, one that would confirm that they and not the Anglicans were the true national church. The 'nonconformist conscience' gave them a belief in their role as the arbiters of the nation's morals and they brought it to bear on all

---

[13] Cit, Obelkevich, J., *Religion and Rural Society*, (Oxford University Press), 1993, p. 333. However, in the *Parliamentary Debates*, (Reuter's Telegram Co.), 1907, p. 127, it was 'Many of her bishops and archbishops had been not only men of high birth and....that the carriage never stopped for three generations at the chapel door'.

[14] Tensions, however, remained with the Church of England especially over burials; see, Stevens, C., 'The Burial Question: Controversy and Conflict, c.1860-1890', *Welsh Historical Review*, Vol. 21, (2002), pp. 328-356.

[15] Bebbington, D. W., 'Nonconformity and electoral sociology, 1867-1918', *Historical Journal*, Vol. 27, (1984), pp. 633-656, Valentine, Simon Ross, 'The role of Nonconformity in late Victorian politics', *Modern History Review*, Vol. 9, (2), (1997), pp. 6-9, Hancock, W. C. R., 'No compromise: Nonconformity and politics 1893-1914', *Baptist Quarterly*, Vol. 36, (2), (1995), pp. 56-69, and Smith, Leonard, *Religion and the rise of labour: Nonconformity and politics in Lancashire and the West Riding, 1880-1914*, (Ryburn), 1994.

manner of public and private issues, especially on the drink problem. Temperance became, after 1850, not only their favourite moral reform but part of their identity and part of their claim to moral superiority.[16]

As Nonconformity prospered, it became more settled and dignified. New chapels were larger and more expensive, built increasingly after the 1850s in the Gothic style. Cushioned pews replaced the older wooden ones reflecting a taste for comfort and luxury that marked Nonconformity's 'mahogany age'. Ministers received academic training and became 'reverends'. From the 1890s, 'connections' or 'unions' were replaced by the collective name of Free Churches. In the process much of their former vigour and control over discipline was lost. Services became shorter and auxiliary activities like literary societies and cricket clubs multiplied. The punitive God of old gave way for the kind father who understood and made allowances. Inward experience of sin and conversion faded; everyone had their own spark of the divine spirit. Yet Nonconformity helped many thousands of ordinary people lead lives of dignity and self-respect, giving them opportunities for self-improvement and responsibility in the life of their chapels.

A Catholic revival?

Neither the Anglican Church nor its Protestant rivals changed as profoundly as Roman Catholicism. Its devotional life was transformed by the ultramontanism of the continent. From Ireland came the immigrants who increased the Catholic population from 750,000 in 1851 to over 2 million by 1914; the great majority of Catholics were now urban, Irish and working-class. From Anglicanism, finally, came a small but significant stream of converts, of whom Newman and Manning were the best known, bringing new blood into the clergy and the promise of further gains amongst the educated classes. As English Catholicism entered its 'second spring' some hoped for nothing less than the 'reconversion' of England to Rome.

The arrival of the Irish posed enormous problems for English Catholics. The Catholicism that had served them well enough in rural Ireland did not hold up for long in London or Liverpool and a high proportion of immigrants lost all contact with the church. Priests carried out what amounted to a 'devotional revolution' to prevent

---

[16] Bebbington, D. W., *The nonconformist conscience: chapel and politics, 1870-1914*, (G. Allen & Unwin), 1982, and Larsen, Timothy, 'A nonconformist conscience? Free churchmen in Parliament in nineteenth-century England', *Parliamentary History*, Vol. 24, (2005), pp. 107-119.

further seepage abandoning the cool, restrained piety of the eighteenth century and adopting an unashamedly emotion, almost missionary, approach. Their preaching matched the fervour of Protestant revivalists; their new churches, with the candles, incense, plaster statues and other props of ultramontane piety, emulated those of Rome or Naples.

Victorian Catholicism was dominated by the clergy. The role of the old Catholic gentry was minimal, nor was there any challenge to the priests from the small, Catholic middle-class. In the poor, inner city parishes, the priests were dedicated, dominant, often paternalist figures, laying down the law to their parishioners as well as bringing them faith and the sacraments. 'Improvement' was not ignored, but this was a church of the unskilled, where unlike most Protestant churches, it was no disgrace to be and remain poor. [17] Whatever the church's dreams of reconverting England, its immediate strategies were realistic and defensive. Mixed marriages were condemned; great sacrifices were made to build a Catholic school system. The aim was to shield Catholics from all Protestant and secular influence, to keep them in self-enclosed communities where the church was the focus of social as well as religious identity. The presence of a large Catholic population was an important factor in the Catholic revival in major urban centres especially in London. [18] Cardinals Wiseman and Manning, archbishops of Westminster, restructured the expanding Catholic Church in Britain. Impoverished Irish immigrants contributed to the building of local Catholic churches. Catholicism was an important medium of both Celtic and proletarian culture. [19]

What most Protestants knew of Catholicism was the bold triumphalist ultramontanism of its public stance and its effects on

---

[17] The Salvation Army, founded by General Booth in the late 1870s, specifically targeted both its evangelical mission and its social work on the very poor. In part, this was a response to the success of Catholic evangelism.
[18] On the Irish and Roman Catholicism in London, see the following papers by Gilley, Sheridan, 'Papists, protestants and the Irish in London, 1835-70', in Cuming, G. J., and Baker, Derek, (eds.), in *Studies in Church History, Volume 8: Popular belief and practice*, (Cambridge University Press), 1972, pp. 259-266, 'Heretic London, holy poverty and the Irish poor, 1830-1870', *Downside Review*, Vol. 89, (1971), pp. 64-89, 'Protestant London, no Popery and the Irish poor, 1830-60', *Recusant History*, Vol. 10, (1970), pp. 210-230, Vol. 11, (1971), pp. 21-46, and 'The Roman Catholic mission to the Irish in London', *Recusant History*, Vol. 10, (1969), pp. 123-145.
[19] Quinn, Dermot A., *Patronage and piety: the politics of English Roman Catholicism, 1850-1900*, (Macmillan), 1993.

them was to deepen alarm into panic. [20] This was triggered by the appearance of Catholic fellow travellers in the Church of England. When bishops were restored to the Catholic Church in 1850, Cardinal Wiseman provoked near-hysterical charges of 'papal aggression'; in Stockport in 1852 anti-Catholic and anti-Irish feelings erupted into violence. [21] Many Protestants regarded the pope as antichrist, the mass as 'idolatry', the Irish Famine as just punishment for the rejection of Protestant truth. They surrounded Catholicism with a kind of religious pornography, dwelling especially on the horrors of the confessional, where priests insinuated 'impure' thoughts into the minds of innocent girls and turned wives against their husbands. Good Protestant families felt shame and disgrace when one of their members 'perverted' to Rome. Anti-Catholic prejudice flowered in this period and was widespread in every social class. The religious conflicts of the Victorian period were fought out not only in pulpits and pamphlets but also in the political arena. The churches during much of the period did more to mobilise political feeling than the political parties themselves. The antagonism between Protestants and Catholics intensified in a period that saw heavy Irish immigration, the nationalist struggle in Ireland and the adoption of aggressive tactics both by the Catholic Church and by its Protestant opponents. [22] It had its effect at national level on such issues as the Maynooth grant in 1845, the Fenian 'panic' following the Clerkenwell bombing in late 1867 and Irish Home Rule; locally, in areas with large Irish Catholic populations, it led to party divisions along religious lines.

A 'crisis of faith'?

The crisis of faith has dominated discussions of religion and the Victorians. One problem with the 'crisis of faith' narrative is that it excluded much of the religious life of the period and has, too often, become the main story. Many Victorians may have experienced doubt about religion but many more did not. The 'crisis of faith' was a by-product of Victorian religiosity and in particular the influence of

---

[20] On this subject ibid, Paz, D. G., *Popular Anti-Catholicism in Mid-Victorian England*.
[21] Ralls, W., 'The Papal Aggression of 1850: A Study in Victorian Anti-Catholicism', *Church History*, Vol. 32, (1974), pp. 242-256, and Paz, D. G., 'Popular Anti-Catholicism in England, 1850-1851', *Albion*, Vol. 11, (1979), pp. 331-359. On the Vatican Decrees in 1870 see, Von Arx, J. P., 'Interpreting the Council: Archbishop Manning and the Vatican decrees controversy', *Recusant History*, Vol. 26, (2002), pp. 229-242.
[22] See, Ruotsila, Markku, 'The Catholic Apostolic Church in British Politics', *Journal of Ecclesiastical History*, Vol. 56, (2005), pp. 75-91.

evangelicalism. Victorians wrote and discussed this crisis but many did so because they prized faith and feared and cared about its loss. In that respect, the widespread debate over faith was less a measure of the extent of the crisis as a measure of the extent of their concern.[23]

Stories are frequently told of prominent Victorians such as George Eliot losing their faith. This crisis is often presented as demonstrating the intellectual weakness of Christianity as it was assailed by new lines of thought such as Darwinism and biblical criticism. The second half of the nineteenth century was certainly marked by bitter and prolonged controversies primarily precipitated by the intellectual polemics of the Tractarians, the publication of Charles Darwin's *Origin of Species* in 1859, [24] the provocative theological symposium *Essays and Reviews* in 1860 [25] and its milder successor *Lex Mundi* in 1889 and the promulgation of the Vatican Decrees in 1870. [26] Poets and novelists portrayed the trauma of the loss of faith by individuals and editors of newspapers and journals provided a forum for the religious elite that grappled very publicly with questions of doubt and disbelief. [27] However, these articulate individuals were not a cross-section of their society. They were the talented, well-educated and the kind of people whose beliefs and values were recorded either by themselves or others. It is not easy to generalise from what they wrote and what was written about them to the attitudes of society as a whole. Was their 'crisis of faith' part of a new phenomenon of ideological secularisation that set the Victorian

---

[23] Helmstadter, Richard J., (ed.), *Victorian Faith in Crisis: Essays on Continuity and Change in Nineteenth-century Religious Belief*, (Stanford University Press), 1990.

[24] See, for example, Lyon, John, 'Immediate reactions to Darwin: the English Catholic press' first reviews of the *Origin of the Species*', *Church History*, Vol. 41, (1972), pp. 78-93.

[25] Altholz, J. F., *Anatomy of a controversy: the debate over 'Essays and reviews', 1860-1864*, (Scolar), 1994.

[26] Fitzsimons, R., 'The Church of England and the First Vatican Council', *Journal of Religious History*, Vol. 27, (2003), pp. 29-46, Von Arx, J.P., 'Interpreting the Council: Archbishop Manning and the Vatican decrees controversy', *Recusant History*, Vol. 26, (2002), pp. 229-242, and Altholz, J. F., and Powell, J., 'Gladstone, Lord Ripon, and the Vatican decrees, 1874', *Albion*, Vol. 22, (1990), 449-459.

[27] Larsen, Timothy, *Crisis of doubt: honest faith in nineteenth-century England*, (Oxford University Press), 2006, serves as a corrective to the 'crisis of faith' narrative. It focuses on freethinking and Secularist leaders who came to faith. As sceptics, they had imbibed all the latest ideas that seemed to undermine faith; nevertheless, they went on to experience a crisis of doubt and then to defend in their writings and lectures the intellectual cogency of Christianity.

age apart from earlier periods of English religious history? If it was, can the decline in religious observance after 1850 be attributed, at least in part, to the gradual erosion of religious practice by this tide of doubt and disbelief?

Was faith simply a matter of class?

Religious practice, to most churchmen, was synonymous with Sunday attendance. But when attendance was measured, as in the 1851 Religious Census, results were disconcerting. Church-going was influenced by a wide variety of social and geographical circumstances. Attendance was higher in Scotland than England and highest of all in Wales. Within England it was higher in the countryside than in the towns, though this should not be exaggerated. [28] There were considerable variations between regions, but the strongest influence was that of class.[29]

Religion never simply reflected class divisions: none of the larger churches was the preserve of any single group or class; all cut across class lines. However, class had a bearing not only on attendance at church but at what church people worshipped in and more importantly, on the content and character of their religiosity and on the place religion had in their lives. Among the gentry and aristocracy, there was a sense that the Anglican Church deserved support precisely because it was part of a social order in which they had a privileged position. They attended partly to set an example to their social inferiors and gave large amounts of money to build and restore churches, working with the clergy to promote Anglican interests and their own. The rural labouring piety of the 1850s crumbled in the 1870s and 1880s, not because of 'irreligion', but because of the enforced migration and collapse of archaic community structures brought about by the agricultural depression. Falling land values also eroded the status and social prestige of the Anglican clergy who were from the 1880s sliding inexorably downwards from the lesser ranks of the landed gentry into the urban middle-classes. [30]

---

[28] Crockett, Alasdair, 'Rural-Urban Churchgoing in Victorian England', *Rural History*, Vol. 16, (2005), pp. 53-82, Green, Simon J. D., 'Secularization by default?: urbanisation, suburbanisation and the strains of voluntary religious organisation in Victorian and Edwardian England', *Hispania Sacra*, Vol. 42, (1990), pp. 423-433, and Pugh, D. P., 'The strength of English religion in the nineties: some evidence from the north west', *Journal of Religious History*, Vol. 12, (1983), pp. 250-265.
[29] Williams, Sarah C., 'Victorian Religion: A Matter of Class or Culture?', *Nineteenth Century Studies*, Vol. 17, (2003), pp. 13-17.
[30] Smith, J. T., *Victorian class conflict?: schoolteaching and the parson, priest and minister, 1837-1902*, (Sussex Academic Press), 2009.

It was among the middle-classes that the Victorian religious boom had the biggest impact. Religion was the opiate not of the masses but of the bourgeoisie and their heavy involvement in church life was one of the distinctive features of the British religious scene. [31] It was in the middle-classes that religion was most strongly sustained by social pressure: regular church attendance and keeping the Sabbath were felt to be essential for a family's respectability. Yet deep and genuine religious commitment was evident in this and other classes in Victorian society and should not be underestimated. Middle-class religiosity, despite variations in church-going, reveals some common themes. Religion was treated as a family matter. Husband, wife and children formed a religious unit not only at church but at home, in family prayers and grace before meals. [32] Middle-class people also tended to regard their church as a social centre, where they could meet others of similar outlook and join in the various recreational and philanthropic activities and where young people could meet suitable partners of the opposite sex. By the 1870s, the integrative function of Nonconformity was waning, as economic tensions rose, and as issues like Empire, feminism and Irish Home Rule split Nonconformists into rival political allegiances. Moreover, the lower middle-class, the backbone of Nonconformity, was changing in character and there was a world of difference between the religious outlook of superior artisans and small shopkeepers of the 1850s and the office-workers of 1900. For the former, religion was often an expression of solidarity with the local community. For the latter it was often an expression of separateness and difference and increasingly likely to take the form, if not of Anglicanism, then of suburban Nonconformity than had been common forty years before.

As for the urban working-classes, the common view was that they rarely attended church and were therefore 'spiritually destitute'. The obsession of churchmen and the middle-classes with Sunday attendance meant that they overlooked the fact that the working-classes came into contact with the churches on a great many occasions and had religious notions of their own, however unorthodox. The churches were alien, middle-class institutions where people like themselves, lacking good clothes and unable to afford pew rents, felt

---

[31] Twells, Alison, *The civilising mission and the English middle class, 1792-1850: the "heathen" at home and overseas*, (Palgrave), 2009.
[32] See, for example, Tiller, Kate, Thomas, Terry, and Collins, Brenda, 'Family, community and religion', in Golby, John, (ed.), *Communities and families*, (Cambridge University Press), 1994, pp. 155-193, and Pawley, Margaret, *Faith and family: the life and circle of Ambrose Phillipps de Lisle*, (Canterbury), 1993.

out of place. Church-goers tended to be regarded as snobs and hypocrites and a member of the working-class going to church was liable to be condemned for putting on airs and setting himself above his neighbours. Social pressure did as much to deter church-going in the working-classes as it did to encourage it in the middle and upper-classes. Although neither regular attenders nor total strangers to the churches most considered themselves Christian. [33] Contemporary surveys often underestimated the piety of the poor and that outside London as many as a fifth of the Edwardian working-classes may have attended churches on a more or less regular basis. Most married in church; many mothers up to 1914 insisted on being 'churched' after giving birth; and most had their babies christened.

Most working-class children went to Sunday school. Children looked forward to the summer treat as one of the high points of the year; the Sunday school anniversary, particularly in Nonconformity, was a major festival. Many children received religious instruction in church day schools. The elaborate pomp of working-class funerals, popular resistance to the spread of cremation and the universal fear of the pauper's grave, suggest no lack of interest in the resurrection of the body and prospect of everlasting life. [34] The working-classes also looked to the churches and to Anglican parsons in particular for charity. [35] Most urban churches set up extensive welfare schemes, doling out food, blankets, money and Bibles, even if such charity was only a degree less shameful than going to the workhouse. Working people dealt with the churches on their own terms, taking what they wanted and ignoring the rest.

---

[33] Entwistle, Dorothy, '"Hope, colour, and comradeship": loyalty and opportunism in early twentieth-century church attendance among the working class in north-west England', *Journal of Religious History*, Vol. 25, (2001), pp. 20-38.

[34] See, for example, Stevens, Catrin, '"The funeral made the attraction": the social and economic functions of funerals in nineteenth-century Wales', in Gramich, Katie and Hiscock, Andrew, (eds.), *Dangerous diversity: the changing faces of Wales: essays in honour of Tudor Bevan*, (University of Wales Press), 1998, pp. 83-104.

[35] This can be explored in Shapely, Peter, 'Saving and salvation: charity and the Anglican church in Victorian Manchester', in Ford, Chris, Powell, Michael, and Wyke, Terry J., (eds.), *The Church in Cottonopolis: essays to mark the 150th anniversary of the Diocese of Manchester*, (Lancashire & Cheshire Antiquarian Society), 1997, pp. 72-84.

Why was religion so important in Victorian politics?

The religious conflicts of the Victorian period were fought out not only in pulpits and pamphlets but also in the political arena. [36] The churches during much of the period did more to mobilise political feeling than the political parties themselves. The antagonism between Protestants and Catholics intensified in a period that saw heavy Irish immigration, the nationalist struggle in Ireland and the adoption of aggressive evangelising tactics both by the Catholic Church and by its Protestant opponents. [37] It had its effect at national level on such issues as the Maynooth grant in 1845 and Irish Home Rule; locally, in areas with large Irish Catholic populations, it led to party divisions along religious lines. No less hard-fought were the battles over the established churches. The Church of Ireland was a leading issue in the election of 1868 before being disestablished the following year by Gladstone and in Wales, disestablishment was the chief aim of the Liberal Nonconformist majority and a central political issue from the 1860s to 1914. [38] But it was England that saw the conflict between church and chapel in its classic form.

On one side were the Nonconformists, allied with Whigs and Liberals, seeking to remove their disabilities; on the other were the Anglicans, allied with the Conservatives defending the privileges of the establishment. They clashed at national and especially at local levels where Nonconformists entered municipal politics in large numbers after 1835. The struggle to turn the confessional state into a secular state was a long one. The Whig governments of the 1830s did little to whittle down Anglican privileges. It introduced civil registration, allowed Nonconformists to perform their own marriages, but compulsory church rates remained in force despite bitter local struggles. In the 1850s, the church courts lost their jurisdiction over

---

[36] Ibid, Machin, G. I. T., *Politics and the Churches in Great Britain, 1832 to 1868*, and *Politics and the churches in Great Britain 1869-1921*, (Oxford University Press), 1987.

[37] See, Ruotsila, Markku, 'The Catholic Apostolic Church in British Politics', *Journal of Ecclesiastical History*, Vol. 56, (2005), pp. 75-91.

[38] See, Machin, Ian, 'Disestablishment and democracy, c.1840-1930', Biagini, Eugenio F., (ed.), *Citizenship and community: liberals, radicals and collective identities in the British Isles, 1865-1931*, (Cambridge University Press), 1996, pp. 120-147, Bell, P. M. H., *Disestablishment in Ireland and Wales*, (SPCK), 1969, and O'Leary, Paul, 'Religion, nationality and politics: disestablishment in Ireland and Wales, 1868-1914', in Guy, John R., and Neely, W. G., (eds.), *Contrasts and comparisons: studies in Irish and Welsh Church history*, (Welsh Religious Historical Society), 1999, pp. 89-113.

divorce and wills was abolished. The main breakthrough came with Gladstone's first government: it abolished church rates in 1869 and opened Oxford and Cambridge up to Nonconformists the following year. The last disability was removed by the Burials Act 1880 that allowed Nonconformist ministers to perform their own funeral services in parish churchyards. [39] But the establishment itself remained a matter for dispute as did a variety of other issues above all the closely related and bitterly contested issue of education. Any attempt to channel public money into denominational schools or to give the Church of England a privileged position in state schools provoked intense opposition from Nonconformity. That England was late in creating a system of public education was mainly due to rivalry and mistrust between the churches. The Education Act 1902, that favoured the Anglicans, spurred a large Nonconformist vote for the Liberals in the 1906 general election. By this time, however, religious issues were being replaced by class ones, the 'social gospel' attracted little interest and support grew for the notion that the churches should stay out of politics altogether.

Was there a civil religious culture after 1830?

Some aspects of Victorian religious culture cut across denominational lines and tended to escape denominational control altogether. Virtually all clergymen, Catholic as well as Protestant, regarded the threat of eternal punishment as essential to Christian faith and morals in 1850. However, by the 1870s, this increasingly seemed inconsistent with God's love and was quietly pushed into the background. The churches had to adapt to a moral consensus they could no longer control. There was also general agreement, among Protestants at least, about public worship. Yet the sermon lost its pre-eminent position shrinking from an hour in length in 1830 to twenty-five minutes or less by 1914 [40] and was replaced by church music that took a more central role in worship. [41] Hymns, long established in Nonconformity, quickly caught on in Anglican churches and *Hymns Ancient and*

---

[39] Stevens, Catrin, 'The "burial question": controversy and conflict, c.1860-1890', *Welsh History Review*, Vol. 21, (2002), pp. 328-356, and Wiggins, Deborah, 'The Burial Act of 1880, the Liberation Society and George Osborne Morgan', *Parliamentary History*, Vol. 15, (1996), pp. 173-189.
[40] Francis, Keith A., and Gibson, William, (eds.), *The Oxford Handbook of the British Sermon, 1689-1901*, (Oxford University Press), 2012, pp. 3-45.
[41] See Ellison, Robert H., *The Victorian pulpit: spoken and written sermons in nineteenth-century Britain*, (Susquehanna University Press), 1998, on the importance of the sermon and preaching in Victorian religion

Modern first appeared in 1861 rekindling the spirit of worship even when the objects of worship were becoming problematic. [42]

Sabbatarianism was a major force in this period. [43] The Lord's Day Observance Society, founded by Anglican evangelicals in 1831, acted as the main pressure group. [44] Most of its attempts to impose its views by legislation failed but in 1856 it scored a major success in ensuring Sunday closing for the British Museum and National Gallery. The churches were less successful in keeping control of holidays and the holiday calendar. Christmas, in its modern form largely a Victorian invention, had less to do with Christianity than with the middle-class cult of the family. The harvest festival, though introduced by high church Anglicans in the 1840s, was essentially pagan in spirit. National days of prayer and thanksgiving fell into disuse while Bank Holidays, created in 1871 by-passed Christianity altogether.

Churches became social as well as religious institutions. Sunday schools alone were a major industry. [45] Membership of the Band of

---

[42] Phillips, C. S., 'The beginnings of 'Hymns Ancient and Modern'', *Theology*, Vol. 38, (1939), pp. 276-284, and Watson, J. R., 'Ancient or Modern, *Ancient and Modern*: The Victorian Hymn and the Nineteenth Century', *Yearbook of English Studies*, Vol. 36, (2), (2006), pp. 1-16. Dibble, Jeremy, 'Musical trends and the Western Church: A collision of the 'ancient' and 'modern'', in ibid, Gilley, Sheridan, and Stanley, Brian, (eds.), *World Christianities, c. 1815-1914*, pp. 121-135, and Routley, Erik, *A short history of English church music*, (Mowbrays), 1977, provide the context. See also, Yamke, S. S., *Make a joyful noise unto the Lord: Hymns as a reflection of Victorian social attitudes*, (Ohio University Press), 1978.

[43] Wigley, J., *The rise and fall of the Victorian Sunday*, (Manchester University Press), 1980, Murray, Douglas M., 'The Sabbath question in Victorian Scotland in context', in Swanson, Robert Norman, (ed.), *The use and abuse of time in Christian history*, (Boydell), 2002, pp. 319-330, Robertson, C. J. A., 'Early Scottish railways and the observance of the sabbath', *Scottish Historical Review*, Vol. 57, (1978), pp. 143-167, Brooke, David, 'The opposition to Sunday rail services in north eastern England, 1834-1914', *Journal of Transport History*, Vol. 6, (1963), pp. 95-109, and Harrison, B. H., 'The Sunday trading riots of 1855', *Historical Journal*, Vol. 8, (1965), pp. 219-245.

[44] Vervaecke, Philippe, 'Les loisirs dominicaux contestés: La Lord's Day Observance Society et le respect du 'Sabbat', 1831-2006', *Revue française de civilisation britannique*, Vol. 14, (2007), pp. 135-145.

[45] Cliff, P. B., *The rise and development of the Sunday School Movement in England 1780-1980*, (National Christian Educational Council), 1986, and Rosman, Doreen M., 'Sunday schools and social change in the twentieth century', in Orchard, Stephen, and Briggs, John H. Y., (eds.), *The Sunday*

Hope, Boy's Brigade, Men's Societies, the Girls' Friendly Society and the Young Men's and Young Women's Christian Associations ran into millions. Other church activities included literary and debating societies; recreation, including cricket and football teams from which professional clubs like Aston Villa and Everton later emerged; and philanthropy. These activities, however, carried with them a danger of diverting the church from its primary religious role, particularly as they became vulnerable to the expansion of commercial leisure and to the growing provision of welfare by the state. In the 1870s, the first signs appeared that the long period of growth was coming to an end. Though membership was still increasing, it failed to keep pace with the growth in population and church-going actually began to decline. Such hallmarks of Victorian religiosity as strict Sunday observance and family prayers were being abandoned and the churches condemned but were unable to curb the middle-class practice of birth control. Criticism of Christian doctrine was openly published and agnosticism and 'secular religions' won support. Behind the statistics of falling attendance lay a deeper disaffection with the churches and their message.

The decline of the appeal of churches has had many explanations, no one of them sufficient by itself. The most general argument is simply that modern industrial society made secularisation inevitable. But this says little about the specific causes and processes of decline. The effect of scientific discoveries is difficult to estimate. At the level of ideas it was less the scientific than the moral critique of Christianity that did the most damage. There could be morality, people now believed, without the fear of hell and without religion altogether. A more persuasive argument is that the social pressures that had encouraged middle-class church-going earlier in the century were weakening. In an economy of large firms and professional qualifications attending church to demonstrate one's moral credentials no longer seemed so necessary. Yet the decline of the churches did not necessarily mean a decline of religion in a broader sense. Those who drifted away from orthodox belief were sometimes attracted to successor faiths like nationalism that themselves had a religious quality and dimension. Queen Victoria's jubilees in 1887 and 1897, the increasingly elaborate coronations and the cult of Empire were the rituals of an 'invented' civil religion. [46] For the first time, religious impulses found expression on a large scale outside the

---

school movement: studies in the growth and decline of Sunday schools, (Paternoster), 2007, pp. 149-160.

[46] See Kuhn, William M., 'Queen Victoria's Jubilees and the Invention of Tradition', *Victorian Poetry*, Vol. 25, (1987), pp. 107-114.

churches and outside Christianity, though probably not enough to make up for the decline in the churches themselves.

Was there a Victorian 'crisis of faith'?

The intellectual ferment of the second half of the nineteenth century differed from that of earlier periods in important aspects of tone and substance and in the ways that it implicated the ordinary church-going population as well as the religious intelligentsia. It was the percolation downwards of theological uncertainty into the ranks of ordinary believers that marked the Victorian period off from the doubt and disbelief of Hanoverian society. Radical and potentially subversive ideas were popularised across society and this added a new dimension to the relationship between the Churches and the wider intellectual world. Victorian laymen, judged by popular religious newspapers, periodicals and sermons, were capable of considerable theological subtlety, but even those who were less subtle could be caught up in the crises of Darwinism and biblical criticism. [47] The popularisation of controversy and the involvement of the general public in religious debates was what contemporaries often found noteworthy.

What was novel was the emergence of popular theological speculation within the Churches. Popular infidelity was not new, but in the past its hostility to the Christian tradition had militated against its chances of subverting the faith of the church-going population. City Mission workers found in the late-nineteenth century that there was a strong undercurrent of plebeian secularism, Paineite in the bold invective and blunt ribaldry through which it was expressed. This augmented the more urbane secularism of people such as Charles Bradlaugh, George Jacob Holyoake and Annie Besant. [48] But the Victorian 'crisis of faith' was not precipitated by such counter-religious propaganda. It was not secularists but devout Christians who were its most effective proponents. The controversial *Essays and Reviews* of 1860 was the work of six Anglican clergymen and a devout layman.

There were profound misgivings in all the Churches that the traditional tenets of belief and faith were being questioned in an attempt to come to terms with wider intellectual tendencies. The

---

[47] Knight, P., *The Age of Science*, (Basil Blackwell), 1986, places the Darwinian dispute in its nineteenth century context while the monumental biography Desmond, Adrian and Moore, James, *Darwin*, (Michael Joseph), 1991, is a major study of this enigmatic figure.
[48] On Holyoake and Annie Besant, see Grugel, Lee E., *George Jacob Holyoake: a study in the evolution of a Victorian radical*, (Porcupine Press), 1976, and Taylor, Ann, *Annie Besant: a biography*, (Oxford University Press), 1992.

periodical *The Sword and the Trowel* brought tensions to a head among Baptists in 1887, publishing a series of articles accusing radicals in the denomination of virtual apostasy. Similar crises occurred in Wesleyanism in the early 1880s when Rev. W. H. Dallinger was prevented from delivering the Fernley lecture advancing the synthesis of Methodist theology and evolutionary theory. [49] Similar problems arose amongst Congregationalists as the result of the airing of advanced theological opinions during a meeting during the autumn session of the Congregational Union held in Leicester in October 1877. [50] Despite the tensions that the popularisation of these issues generated and the fascination they held for denominational editors, preachers and pamphleteers, controversy was less significant within the Churches than the absence of permanent division. The 'crisis of faith' was contained and produced very little actual loss of faith. While there were notable cases of apostasy, doubt generally led not to disbelief but to theological revision or accommodation of one kind or another.

The decline of religious adherence in modern English society was not caused by the loss of existing members. Membership retention has not been a major problem. From the 1830s, a growing number of English religious organisations had collected and collated data on aspects of recruitment and loss. A similar picture emerges in each case. Religious organisations had a high turnover in membership with losses by expulsion, lapsing and leakage but these were offset by extremely rapid recruitment. But as their growth rates declined, so did membership turnover. In Wesleyanism, for example, annual losses of total membership were 14.1 per cent of the total membership in 1880-1881 but only 6.8 per cent in 1932. However, in 1881 it had attracted enough new members to offset the loss but by 1932 losses greatly exceeded new member. Recruitment rather than loss was the crucial variable in declining support.

What were the links between the Victorian 'crisis of faith' and the growing inability of the Churches to draw new members from the broader society? The intellectual tensions occasioned by theological revisionism and Darwinian Theory did not produce significant levels

---

[49] Haas, J. W., 'The Reverend Dr William Henry Dallinger, F.R.S. (1839-1909)', *Notes & Records of the Royal Society*, Vol. 54, (2000), pp. 53-65.

[50] Ledger-Lomas, Michael, '"Glimpses of the Great Conflict": English Congregationalists and the European Crisis of Faith, circa 1840-1875', *Journal of British Studies*, Vol. 46, (2007), pp. 826-860, Thompson, D. M., 'R. W. Dale and the "civic gospel"', in Sell, Alan P. F., (ed.), *Protestant nonconformists and the west Midlands of England: papers presented at the first conference of the Association of Denominational Historical Societies and Cognate Libraries*, (Keele University Press), 1996, pp. 99-118.

of defection among existing adherents largely because of the strong social and cultural pressures that existing among Victorian Christians to reach some sort of ideological compromise. The heat was generally taken out of the crises by an almost irresistible imperative towards accommodation with the wider intellectual world. In a society that was no longer dominated by a pervasive religious belief, there was a distinctively modern religious-cultural preoccupation with making the Christian faith relevant. The quest for relevance is a characteristic of neither churches in which relevance is assured by social domination, nor of sects that accepted cultural marginality but is a preoccupation of denominational type religion. It is essential for the survival of denominations that depend on the voluntary allegiance of members who adhere in general to the prevalent ideas and intellectual fashions of their age. Victorian Christianity's attempts to come to terms with biological and geological science, social science, archaeology, comparative religion, historical scholarship and philosophical theology can be seen in this light. The alternative to ideological accommodation was the increasing marginality and cultural isolation of organised religion within English society.

Denominations do not have the control over their members of either churches or sects. Membership does not exclude other commitments and denominational life is only one of a variety of associational activities. The denomination must compete for members with other recreational, social, cultural and vocational activities. The transition to denomination means that the organisation could no longer demand levels of participation from its members previously regarded as normal. In fact, the membership's beliefs and values were increasingly moulded by 'worldly' associations as by 'religious' ones. There was a decline in commitment, especially evident among Nonconformists. The Church of England had long accommodated people willing to worship in church but unwilling to tolerate too intense or too disciplined a religious life. The pervasive nature of Nonconformity to its adherents, especially falling attendance at weekday prayer, preaching and class meetings, was beginning to decline by the early 1850s. By 1900, many church leaders felt that they were fighting a losing battle to rival 'the social party, the secular concert or the tennis club'. [51] The choices facing them were bleak.

---

[51] Cit, ibid, Gilbert, A. D., *Religion and Society in Industrial England*, p. 181. See also, Hennell, Michael, 'Evangelicalism and worldliness, 1770-1870', in Cuming, G. J., and Baker, D., (eds.), *Popular belief and practice; papers read at the ninth summer meeting and the tenth winter meeting of the Ecclesiastical History Society*, (Cambridge University Press), 1972, 229-236.

On one side religion was growing increasingly worldly where recreational activities went alongside and often were more important than spiritual ones. The alternative was alienation both from the wider culture and from the great majority of Victorians and Edwardians who were prepared for accommodation with the changing spirit of the times. It was the worldliness of accommodation rather than the alienation of reaction that was the norm.

The Victorian 'crisis of faith' was a matter of the Churches coming to terms ideologically with the secularising tendencies within the wider culture. But this was only partially successful. What was a 'crisis of faith' for believers was for outsiders a 'crisis of plausibility' and the failure of the Churches to deal effectively with this that hindered their ability to maintain an adequate rate of recruitment from the broader society. Far more important for the future of English religion than the specific challenges of Darwinism or biblical criticism, or the internal adjustments that these challenges demanded of the Churches, was the gradual divergence, increasingly evident after 1860, between religious and secular modes of interpreting reality. Previously there had been something like a consensus between believers and unbelievers about the plausibility of the religious worldview. Religious definitions of reality had been credible even to those who had rejected or ignored them. This was not the case in the cultural milieu of modern industrial England. Well before 1900, commentators insisted that the most serious threat to English religion was not the incompatibility between science and religion but the growing tendency for people without much knowledge of theology or interest in it becoming alienated from the modes of thought and definitions of reality that made religiosity explicable and relevant.

Two powerful forces were operating in society to produce this fundamental secularisation of the values and beliefs of the population outside the Churches. There was a popularisation of the 'scientific spirit'. [52] Increasingly after 1850 science dominated popular definitions of reality. The scientific ethos as a popular philosophy tended to stultify all forms of metaphysical thinking, despite the fact that many of the scientists putting forward these views were themselves

---

[52] Fyfe, Aileen, 'Science and Religion in Popular Publishing in 19th Century Britain', in Meusburger, Peter, Welker, Michael, and Wunder, Edgar, (eds.), *Clashes of Knowledge: Orthodoxies and Heterodoxies in Science and Religion*, (Springer Science), 2008, pp. 121-132, and Ruse, Michael, 'The relationship between science and religion in Britain, 1830-1870', *Church History*, Vol. 44, (1975), pp. 505-522.

Christians. [53] Also, popular materialism emerged as a major social force. There is a significant link between the economic changes that occurred after 1750 and the growing secularisation of society. Poverty, scarcity and disease had been the common lot of all but the fortunate few in pre-industrial societies. But in nineteenth century England, the material wealth of a whole society began steadily to improve. The self-sustaining economic growth of a maturing industrial society and economy had already undermined attitudes and values that had taken shape amidst the poverty and economic insecurity of generations before the Industrial Revolution.

The crisis of plausibility produced by the emergence of industrial society in England made its presence felt early in the Victorian period. Increasingly the Churches were becoming estranged from modern English society, though this was not brought home fully until the experience of the First World War. Victorian fears about the alienation of the working-classes from organised religion, though grounded in the definition of religiosity as attendance, were not groundless. It was also becoming apparent that for the middle and upper-classes, religion was an increasingly irrelevant activity and cultural influence. The denominational compromises of the Victorian churches in their search for relevance undermined their evangelical verve just as the crisis of plausibility undermined their influence on wider society. In seeking to understand why religious adherence declined after 1850, science and theology provide only part of the answer.

---

[53] See, Lucas, J. R., 'Wilberforce and Huxley: a legendary encounter', *Historical Journal*, Vol. 22, (1979), pp. 313-330, Gilley, Sheridan, 'The Huxley-Wilberforce debate: a reconsideration', in Robbins, Keith, (ed.), *Religion and humanism: papers read at the eighteenth summer meeting and the nineteenth winter meeting of the Ecclesiastical History Society*, (Oxford University Press), 1981, pp. 325-340, and James, Frank A. J. L., 'An 'Open Clash between Science and the Church'?: Wilberforce, Huxley and Hooker on Darwin at the British Association, Oxford, 1860', in Knight, David M., and Eddy, Matthew, (eds.), *Science and beliefs: from natural philosophy to natural science, 1700-1900*, (Ashgate), 2005, pp. 171-194.

20 Class

All societies are, to some degree, stratified or divided into different social groups. These groups may be in competition with each other for social control or wealth. They may be functional, defined by their contribution to society as a whole. They may share common 'values', have a common 'national identity' or they may form part of a pluralistic society in which different 'values' coexist with varying degrees of consensus or conflict. They have different names like 'castes' or 'ranks' or 'classes'. British society in the nineteenth and early-twentieth century has been called a 'class society' but there are some differences between historians about its precise meaning or whether it is meaningful at all.[1] Were there two classes or three or five or any classes at all? Were there any common values? They do, however, agree that society in 1914 was different from the society that existed in the 1780s. It is important to have some understanding of the 'wholeness' of society, whether nationally or within a given locality because it was the overall structure of society that people were reacting against or attempting to preserve. Individuals and the diversities of their experiences must be understood, given meaning and significance, not in isolation but within their web of social relationships.

How far was society paternalist?

The underlying basis of the elitism of the aristocracy in the 1830s was one of mutual and reciprocal obligation within a hierarchical framework. Harold Perkin maintained:

> The old society, then was a finely graded hierarchy of great subtlety and discrimination, in which men were acutely aware of their exact relation to those immediately above and below them, but only vaguely conscious except at the very top of their connections with those on their own level....There was one horizontal cleavage of great import, that between the 'gentleman' and the 'common people', but it could scarcely be defined in economic terms.[2]

This view of society was paternalist and hierarchical. What mattered was not what was later parodied as 'forelock tugging' but

---

[1] On methodology see Burke, P., *History and Social Theory*, (Polity), 1992, Abrams, P., *Historical Sociology*, (Open Books), 1982, and two books by Lloyd, C., *Explanation in Social History*, (Basil Blackwell), 1986, and *The Structures of History*, (Basil Blackwell), 1993.
[2] Perkin, H., *The Origins of Modern English Society 1780-1880*, (Routledge), 1969, p. 24.

sympathetic and active involvement by the elites in the lives of the rest of society. There was an expectation of reciprocity, a common outlook and identification of interests and, if necessary, sheer coercion to maintain the civil stability of a hierarchical social structure. A Christian faith and moral code was a common possession of all of society and rank, station, duty and decorum were central social values. A paternalist saw society in the following ways. It should be authoritarian, though tempered by adhesion to the common law and ancient 'liberties'. It should be hierarchical and should be 'organic' with people knowing their appointed place within a defined 'social order'. Finally, it should be 'pluralistic' consisting of different hierarchical 'interests' making up the organic whole. [3]

Within this structure, paternalists had certain duties and held certain assumptions. There was the duty to rule, a direct result of wealth and power and an obligation to help the poor, not passively but with active assistance. Paternalists also believed in the duty of 'guidance', a firm moral superintendence. Paternalism governed relationships at all levels of society and continued to play an important role even in innovative areas of the economy. [4] Apprenticeship, for instance, was more than induction into craft particular skills; it was an immersion in the social experience or common wisdom of the community. Practices, norms and attitudes were, as a result, reproduced through successive generations within an accepted framework of traditional customs and rights grounded in the vaguely defined notion of 'the moral economy'. [5]

Patronage was central to the paternalist ethic and it retained its importance throughout the nineteenth century. [6] It was a key feature of an unequal face-to-face society, crossing social barriers and bringing together potentially hostile groups. Patronage involved a 'lopsided' relationship between individuals, a patron and a client of unequal status, wealth and influence. It could be called a 'package deal' of

---

[3] Roberts, David, *Paternalism in Early Victorian England*, (Croom Helm), 1979, pp. 2-10.
[4] Revill, George, '"Railway Derby": occupational community, paternalism and corporate culture, 1850-90', *Urban History*, Vol. 28, (2001), pp. 378-404, and 'Liberalism and paternalism: politics and corporate culture in "Railway Derby", 1865-75'. *Social History*, Vol. 24, (1999), pp. 196-214, provide a valuable case study.
[5] Thompson, E. P., 'The Moral Economy of the Crowd in the Eighteenth Century', *Past and Present*, Vol. 50, (1971), pp. 76-136, reprinted in his *Customs in Common*, (Merlin Press), 1991, pp. 185-259, with 'The Moral Economy Reviewed', pp. 259-351.
[6] Bourne, J. M., *Patronage and Society in Nineteenth-Century England*, (Edward Arnold), 1986, remains an essential study.

reciprocal advantage to the individuals involved. It is true that by the 1830s much of the 'politically useful' forms of patronage such as jobs for electors and rewards for political supporters had already decayed but to assume that there was a general decline in patronage is to fundamentally misconceive the issue. [7] Patronage remained central to the Church of England with successive prime ministers exercising considerable influence over episcopal appointments [8] and in the Arts.[9] The nineteenth century is often seen as an age in which professionalism replaced patronage in British political and social life but this is too stark a distinction. Careers were opened up to the talents as the upwardly-mobile middle-classes gained entry into the old preserves of the aristocracy and gentry. Fewer and fewer places were 'reserved' just because they were within the gift and bequest of those with wealth and property. Elections and examinations, especially after 1850, made steady inroads into elitism and merit was substituted for manipulation and management. But patronage remained an important feature of British society and gained important footholds in Britain's growing empire.

Many of the political, social and economic changes of the first half of the nineteenth century, however, greatly increased the amount of patronage that was available. There was a dramatic growth in the number of 'administratively necessary' offices. [10] The prison, factory, health and schools Inspectorate were all staffed, at least initially, through patronage. This was paralleled in local government where

---

[7] Harling, Philip, *The waning of 'Old Corruption': the politics of economical reform in Britain, 1779-1846*, (Oxford University Press), 1996.

[8] See, for example, Gibson, William T., '"A Great Excitement": Gladstone and church patronage, 1860-1894', *Anglican and Episcopal History*, Vol. 68, (1999), pp. 372-396, Disraeli's church patronage, 1868-1880', *Anglican and Episcopal History*, Vol. 62, (1992), pp. 197-210, and 'The Tories and church patronage: 1812-1830', *Journal of Ecclesiastical History*, Vol. 41, (1990), pp. 266-274.

[9] See, Morrison, John, 'Victorian municipal patronage: the foundation and management of Glasgow Corporation Galleries 1854-1888', *Journal of the History of Collections*, Vol. 8, (1996), pp. 93-102, and Wolff, Janet and Arscott, Caroline, '"Cultivated Capital": patronage and art in nineteenth-century Manchester and Leeds', in Marsden, Gordon, (ed.), *Victorian values: personalities and perspectives in nineteenth-century society*, (Longman), 1998, pp. 29-41.

[10] This is evident in Clifton, G. C., *Professionalism, patronage and public service in Victorian London: the staff of the Metropolitan Board of Works, 1856-1889*, (Athlone Press), 1992, and Porter, Dale H., and Clifton, G. C., 'Patronage, professional values and Victorian public works: engineering and contracting the Thames embankment', *Victorian Studies*, Vol. 31, (1988), pp. 319-349.

'efficient' patronage was used by rival elites within communities as an extension of party politics. Finally, offices may have been filled by personal nomination but individuals had to possess some basic competence. This notion of 'merit' received wider application after the Northcote-Trevelyan report of 1854, though patronage comfortably withstood much of the onslaught of merit until the 1870s.[11] Only the urban middle-classes of the north were indifferent to patronage though it was still evident in, for example, the promotion of science.[12] The bulk of the middle-classes were located in the genteel world of the professions and of propertyless independent incomes, far less entrepreneurial and competitive than their industrial equivalents. As long as a common area of shared values existed patronage continued to have broad application and utility.

How and why did the nature of society change?

For a variety of reasons this paternalist view of society began to break down from the early-nineteenth century. An 'abdication on the part of the governors' had been recognised as early as the 1820s though it was Carlyle who popularised it in the 1840s.[13] This process had the following features. The changing focus of the economy away from land and towards manufacturing and service industries led to a gradual decline in the economic power of the paternalist landed elite and the fabric of state paternalism was gradually dismantled. Paternalism was grounded in reciprocal obligations, like 'just wages' and 'fair prices', many of which were given a statutory basis in Tudor and Stuart legislation. From the 1770s, this legislation was either allowed to lapse or deliberately repealed. The principles of 'the free market' could not accommodate the protectionism inherent in paternalism. The critical issue is whether the notion of the caring landlord existed in reality and how far there was an actual 'abdication' or whether it was simply thought that there was an 'abdication' by those fighting to retain older values in the face of social and economic change. While there is no doubt that society changed, to view change solely in terms of a

---

[11] This was particularly evident in the Indian Civil Service: Compton, J. M., 'Open Competition and the Indian Civil Service, 1854-1876', *English Historical Review*, Vol. 83, (1968), pp. 265-284, and Moore, R. J., 'The abolition of patronage in the Indian Civil Service and the closure of Haileybury College', *Historical Journal*, Vol. 7, (1964), pp. 246-257.

[12] Cardwell, D. S. L., 'The patronage of science in nineteenth-century Manchester', in Turner, Gerard L'Estrange, (ed.), *The patronage of science in the nineteenth century*, (Noordhoff International Publishing), 1976, pp. 95-113.

[13] Ibid, Perkin, H., *The Origins of Modern English Society 1780-1880*, pp. 183-196, discusses this issue.

shift from paternalistic solidarity to unbridled individualism is too stark. Nineteenth century society contained elements of both but despite this there remained a widespread belief that there had been a shift from a paternalist to a capitalist society.

Agriculture may have declined relative to other sectors of the economy but the aristocratic tone of British society was still set by the great houses and the large landowners. As J. F. C. Harrison says:

> Landed England did not survive unchanged. Had there not been flexibility in coming to terms with the economic realities of the industry state, and a willingness to retreat gradually and quietly from untenable positions of political privilege, landed society might not have outlived the end of the century. In fact it displayed remarkable powers of tenacity and adaptation: it sought to engulf and change some of the new elements in society, though in the process it was itself changed. [14]

Urbanisation occurred broadly outside the paternal net. There is evidence that many people moved to towns because they perceived them as 'free' from the social constraints of rural society. In addition, as towns and cities burgeoned in size after 1850 they ceased to be face-to-face societies and became places of anonymity. Changing religious observance broke the 'bond of dependency' between squire, parson and labourer. The aristocracy and gentry gradually 'cut' their lives off from those of their labouring workers. The layout of country houses and gardens that evolved from the mid-seventeenth century demonstrated a move towards domestic privacy.[15] Client relationships became less important as labour became more mobile and centred in urban communities.

The economic and political power of the landed elite came from their ownership and control of land while for industrial entrepreneurs it came from their ownership and control of manufacturing. For both these elites the nineteenth century saw important changes. The emergence of managers as a segment of the economic elite reflected

---

[14] Harrison, J. F. C., *The Early Victorians 1832-1851*, (Panther), 1973, p. 123.

[15] See, for example, Pollock, Linda A., 'Living on the stage of the world: the concept of privacy among the elite of early modern England', in Wilson, Adrian, (ed.), *Rethinking social history: English society, 1570-1920 and its interpretation*, (Manchester University Press), 1993, pp. 78-96, Meldrum, Tim, 'Domestic service, privacy and the 18th century metropolitan household', *Urban History*, Vol. 26, (1999), pp. 27-39, and Taylor, William M., 'Visualising comfort: aspect, prospect, and controlling privacy in *The Gentleman's House* (1864)', in Taylor, William M., (ed.), *The geography of law: landscape, identity and regulation*, (Hart Publishing), 2006, pp. 65-83.

changing rates and channels of social mobility.[16] Education became a more important medium as a channel of recruitment into managerial occupations and consequently the chances of those from working- or especially middle-class backgrounds of moving into the economic elite improved. The emergence of a managerial sector introduced an important source of potential conflict within the economic elite as a whole. The moral solidarity of the old property-owning elite was undermined. The separation of ownership and control in industry resulted in the emergence of two different roles as individuals moved apart in their outlook on and attitudes towards society in general and towards enterprise in particular. The 'individualistic', profit-seeking entrepreneur is contrasted with the managerial executive, whose values stressed efficiency and productivity rather than profits. Such a difference in ideals and values reinforced divergence in styles of life and social contacts. This in turn produced a certain conflict of interests, sometimes leading to open struggles, since the pursuit of maximum returns on capital was not always compatible with safeguarding the productivity and security of the enterprise.[17] Finally, the separation of ownership and control was held to introduce important shifts in the structure of economic power. Within the large joint-stock companies that emerged in the 1850s and 1860s, effective power increasingly devolved into the hands of managers and the sanctions held by the 'owners' of the enterprise were merely nominal.[18]

This separation of ownership and control is not the only factor that led to the disintegration of the old ruling class. There was a general rise in rates of mobility, particularly intergenerational mobility, into elite positions in many institutional spheres during the last thirty years of the nineteenth century. There was some redistribution of wealth and income after 1850 as levels of 'real' wages rose that

---

[16] Pollard, Sidney, 'The genesis of the managerial profession: the experience of the Industrial Revolution in Great Britain', *Studies in Romanticism*, Vol. 4, (1965), pp. 57-80.

[17] This was evident in agriculture after 1870: Hunt, E. H., and Pam, S. J., 'Managerial failure in late Victorian Britain?: land use and English agriculture', *Economic History Review*, second series, Vol. 54, (2001), pp. 240-266, and 'Responding to agricultural depression, 1873-96: managerial success, entrepreneurial failure?', *Agricultural History Review*, Vol. 50, (2002), pp. 225-252.

[18] Alborn, Timothy L., *Conceiving companies: joint-stock politics in Victorian England*, (Routledge), 1998, Taylor, James, *Creating capitalism: joint-stock enterprise in British politics and culture, 1800-1870*, (Boydell), 2006, and Johnson, Paul, *Making the Market: Victorian Origins of Corporate Capitalism*, (Cambridge University Press), 2010.

benefitted some in the working-classes. Parliamentary reform in 1832, 1867 and 1884-1885 initially gave the middle-classes and latterly some in the working-classes a stake in the existing political structure. This needs to be seen in relation to the rights of organisation in the industrial and political sphere for the mass of the population. The growth of trade unions, especially after 1851, the expansion in the range of political pressure groups and the emergence of the Labour Party in the early years of the twentieth century constituted both potential limitations on the power of elite groups as well as perhaps changing the structure of those elite groups themselves.

Perkin characterised the late-eighteenth and early-nineteenth century as a 'one-class society'.[19] Only the aristocratic elite could, he maintained, be seen as a 'class'. This view of a unitary capitalist ruling class certainly did not exist by 1830. Marx viewed the British ruling class as an 'antiquated compromise' in which, while the aristocracy 'ruled officially', the bourgeoisie ruled 'over all the various spheres of civil society in reality'.[20] The aristocracy, that Marx thought had 'signed its own death warrant' as a result of the Crimean War (1853-1856), proved to be much more resilient in maintaining a strong presence in the Cabinet, Parliament and the Civil Service. The proprietary fortunes and power of the large landowners remained virtually intact until the end of the century and the relatively amicable inter-penetration of aristocratic landowners and wealthy industrialists remains one of the striking features of British society in the latter half of the century.

What did contemporaries understand by the idea of 'class'?

An alternative to the vertical relationships of a paternalistic hierarchical society lay in the horizontal solidarities of 'class'.[21] Richard Dennis, in his study of nineteenth century industrial cities, sums up the problem of class in the following way:

> Evidently the road to class analysis crosses a minefield with a sniper behind every bush.... it may not be possible to please all the people all of the

---

[19] Ibid, Perkin, H., *The Origins of Modern English Society 1780-1880*, pp. 36-38.
[20] Marx, Karl, 'The Crisis in England and the British Constitution', in Marx, K., and Engels, F., *On Britain*, (Moscow State Publishing House), 1953, pp. 410-411.
[21] The literature on 'class' is immense but theoretical perspectives can be found in Calvert, P., *The Concept of Class*, (Hutchinson), 1983, Giddens, A., *The Class Structure of Advanced Societies*, (Hutchinson), 1973, and especially Neale, R. S., (ed.), *History and Class: essential readings in theory and interpretation*, (Basil Blackwell), 1984.

time... [22]

How many classes were there? What do historians understand by 'class consciousness' and how, if at all, did it differ from 'class perception'? When did a working-class come into existence? Despite all the literature on the subject, the years since the publication of E. P. Thompson's elegant *The Making of the English Working-Class* in 1963, have done little to clarify the situation. Answers to the central questions of 'when?', 'how?' and 'why?' have been surprisingly inconclusive. [23]

'Two nations'?

Many contemporaries interpreted early Victorian society in terms of two classes. Disraeli popularised the idea of 'two nations', the rich and the poor. [24] Elizabeth Gaskell wrote of Manchester that she had

---

[22] Dennis, R., *English Industrial Cities in the Nineteenth Century: A Social Geography*, (Cambridge University Press), 1984, pp. 187-188.

[23] Neale, R. S., *Class in British History 1680-1850*, (Basil Blackwell), 1983, and *Class and Ideology in the Nineteenth Century*, (Routledge), 1972, the useful bibliographical essay by Morris, R. J., *Class and Class Consciousness in the Industrial Revolution*, (Macmillan), 1980, and his 'The industrial revolution: Class and Common Interest', *History Today*, Vol. 33, (5), (1983), pp. 31-35, are good starting points for the period before 1850. See also, Briggs, A., 'The language of 'class' in early-nineteenth century England', in Briggs, A., and Saville, J., (eds.), *Essays in labour history in memory of G. D. H. Cole*, revised edition, (Macmillan), 1967, pp. 43-73, and Jones, G. Steadman, *Languages of Class*, (Cambridge University Press), 1983. Joyce, Patrick, *Visions of the People: Industrial England and the question of class 1840-1914*, (Cambridge University Press), 1991, takes the question of language further and questions the veracity of a view of society grounded simply in 'class'. Other studies include Prothero, I., *Artisans and Politics in Early Nineteenth-Century London*, (Dawson), 1979, Smith, D., *Conflict and Compromise: Class Formation in English Society 1830-1914*, (Routledge), 1982, and Calhoun, C., *The Question of Class Struggle*, (Basil Blackwell), 1982. Reid, Alastair J., *Social Classes and Social Relations in Britain 1850-1914*, (Macmillan), 1992, is the best and briefest starting-point for this period. Benson, J., *The Working-class in Britain 1850-1939*, (Longman), 1989, is a sound general survey. McKibbin, R., *The Ideologies of Class: Social Relations in Britain 1880-1950*, (Oxford University Press), 1990, is an excellent collection of articles. Perkin, H., *The Rise of Professional Society: England since 1880*, (Routledge), 1989, extends his earlier work in a masterful study. Meacham, Stanish, *A Life Apart: The English Working-class 1890-1914*, (Thames & Hudson), 1977, and Bourne, Joanna, *Working-class Cultures in Britain 1890-1960*, (Routledge), 1994, are excellent.

[24] See Disraeli, Benjamin, *Sybil or The two nations*, (B. Tauchnitz), 1845.

'never lived in a place before where there were two sets of people always running each other down.' [25] Tory Radicals were not alone in using the two-class model. Engels referred to the working-class in the singular and offered a model dominated by two classes, the bourgeoisie and the proletariat, in which other classes existed but were becoming increasingly less important. [26] Marxist historians, E. P. Thompson and John Foster, have also used this model.

For Thompson, class experience was largely the result of the productive relations into which people entered. The essence of class lay not in income or work but in class-consciousness, the product of contemporary perceptions of capital and labour, exploiter and exploited. But Thompson enlarged the horizons of working-class history to include not simply trade unions, real wages and popular political traditions but the broader cultural experience of working people. His was a cultural and experiential view of class as much as an economic one. Class, Thompson stated, 'is defined by men as they live their own history, and, in the end, this is its only definition.' [27] Class was the outcome of the inherited or shared, active and conscious experiences of working people. His was not an economically determinist view of class but one in which workers' voice and wills and feelings led them towards collective identity, struggle and action. For Thompson, no consciousness, no class. *The Making* has been extensively debated in the half century since it was published especially by those who advantaged radical language over Thompson's collective action.[28]

John Foster, in his study of Oldham, South Shields and Northampton, found that 12,000 workers sold their labour to 70 capitalist families. [29] There was a middle-class of tradesmen,

---

[25] Gaskell, Elizabeth, *North and South*, (B. Tauchnitz), 1855, p. 48.
[26] McLellan, D., *Engels*, (Fontana), 1977, Carver, T., *Engels*, (Oxford University Press), 1981, and Hunt, Tristram, *The Frock-coated Communist: The Revolutionary Life of Friedrich Engels*, (Allen Lane), 2009, provide valuable critiques.
[27] Ibid, Thompson, E. P., *The Making of the English Working Class*, p. 11.
[28] Palmer, Bryan, *The Making of E. P. Thompson: Marxism, Humanism and History*, (University of Toronto Press), 1981, Kaye, H. J., *The British Marxist Historians*, (Polity), 1984, pp. 167-220, and Kaye, H. J., and McClelland, D., (eds.), *E. P. Thompson: Critical Perspectives*, (Polity), 1990. See also, Palmer, Bryan D., et al, 'E. P. Thompson's The Making of the English Working Class at Fifty', *Labour/Le Travail*, Vol. 71, (2013), pp. 149-192, and Fieldhouse, Roger, and Taylor, Richard, (eds.), *E. P. Thompson and English radicalism*, (Manchester University Press), 2013.
[29] Foster. J., *Class Struggle and the Industrial Revolution: early industrial capitalism in three English towns*, (Weidenfeld), 1974.

shopkeepers and small masters but despite deep divisions in their social and political behaviour they aligned with the working-class on most political issues. [30] The working-class, Foster argues, went through three stages of developing consciousness. Initially it was 'labour conscious' when consumer prices ceased to be a major concern for workers and the focus shifted to the levels of their own wages. [31] Then 'class conscious' where attempts to resolve industrial and economic problems, initially by a vanguard of skilled workers, became politicised. This can be seen in the 1830s and 1840s in working-class support for the Chartist movement. [32] Political reform was seen as a necessary prerequisite for the resolution of economic problems: only a Parliament elected on the Charter would be prepared to legislate in favour of working-class concerns. Foster argues that the movement was a victim of its own success and that the bourgeoisie was alerted to the threat from the potentially revolutionary masses and adopted a policy of economic liberalisation by conceding some proletarian demands specifically mentioning the Ten Hour Act 1847 and the offer of household suffrage in 1849. This, he maintained, represented a major tactical victory and led to a 'liberalised consciousness' by which the bourgeoisie, aided by growing economic prosperity after 1850, was able to attach important sections of the working population to its consensus ideology grounded in individualism and 'respectability'. [33] Skilled workers who had previously formed the revolutionary vanguard became reformist in attitude, accepting the economic situation as it was and working to get the best deal out of it they possibly could though individual and collective bargaining.

It is possible to criticise the two-class model in a variety of ways. It assumes a model for change based on conflict or 'class war' between two competing classes for economic dominance. It accepts other social groups, but subsumes them within the two-class perspective. It recognises that although there may have been a significant degree of ideological homogeneity in the vibrant and volatile social magma of the industrial factory towns, this was less evident in rural areas and the

---

[30] Foster's view of the petit bourgeoisie and his attempts to explain it away have been criticised by historians such as R. S. Neale who interpose a 'middling' class between the middle and working-classes in his 'five-class model': Neale, R. S., 'Class and class-consciousness in early-nineteenth century England: three classes or five?', *Victorian Studies*, Vol. 12, (1968-9), pp. 5-32.
[31] Ibid, Foster. J., *Class Struggle and the Industrial Revolution: early industrial capitalism in three English towns*, pp. 47-72.
[32] Ibid, pp. 73-125.
[33] Ibid, pp. 203-249.

older urban areas where class consciousness was less well formed and where older patterns of social interaction retained their importance. Diversity of experience within the working population led to diversity of responses.

'Three classes'?

Others saw society differently. The majority of contemporary and modern analysts have adhered to the three-class model. David Ricardo, the economist, identified three economic classes based on rent, capital and wages broadly 'upper', 'middle' and 'working' classes. The journalist Henry Mayhew went further dividing society in the late 1840s into 'those who will work, those who cannot work, those who will not work and those who need not work'. [34] Contemporary attitudes have been complicated by lack of agreement among historians on when a 'class system' came into being and how far the older values survived into the Victorian period. Perkin argued that, as the result of industrialisation, urbanisation and the midwifery of religion, a class society emerged between 1789 and 1833 or, more precisely between 1815 and 1820. Class was characterised:

...by class feeling, that is, by the existence of vertical antagonism between a small number of horizontal groups, each based on a common source of income. [35]

The paternal view of society was not, however, destroyed by these class antagonisms and the potential conflict of emergent class society was contained by modification of existing institutions. For Perkin, compromise was a central reason for the persistence of older social values and structures and that only an 'immature' class society was characterised by violence. Each class developed its own 'ideal' and, by 1850, he believed, three can be clearly seen: the entrepreneurial ideal of the middle-classes, a working-class ideal and an aristocratic ideal based respectively on profits, wages and rent. The 'struggle between ideals' was:

...not so much that the ruling class imposes its ideal upon the rest, but that the class that manages to impose its ideal upon the rest becomes the ruling class. [36]

---

[34] Mayhew, Henry, *London Labour and the London Poor: A Cyclopaedia of the Condition and Earnings of Those That Will Work, Those That Cannot Work, and Those That Will Not Work*, 4 Vols. (Griffin, Bohn and Co.), 1861.
[35] Ibid, Perkin, H., *The Origins of Modern English Society 1780-1880*, p. 37.
[36] Ibid, pp. 218-270, for discussion on the 'struggle between ideals'.

The mature class society that emerged by the 1850s was, despite the differences that existed between classes, not marked by overt conflict but by tacit agreement and coexistence under the successful entrepreneurial ideal. The same destination as John Foster but by a different route.

Between 1880 and 1914, class society reached its zenith.[37] The rich, both large landowners and capitalists, consolidated into a new plutocracy that had already begun to emerge in the 1850s. The middle-classes, ever more graduated in income and status, came to express those finer distinctions in prosperity and social position physically, both in outward appearance, in dress, furnishings and housing and in their geographical segregation from one another and the rest of society in carefully differentiated suburbs. So too did the working-classes, in part involuntarily because they could only afford what their social betters left for them, but also, within that constraint, because those working-class families who could chose to differentiate themselves equally, by Sunday if not every day dress and by better and better furnished houses in marginally superior areas. Only the very poor, the 'residuum' as Charles Booth called them, had no choice at all and were consigned to the slums. They were the most segregated class of all because all the rest shunned them and their homes.

For Perkin, class society in Britain in 1880 already contained the seeds of its own decay. The three classes each had their own powerful ideals of what society should be and how it should be organised to recognise and reward their own unique contribution to the welfare of the community. Each class in a segregated society believed that its contribution was most vital and should be rewarded accordingly.[38] The landowners, capitalists and middle-classes saw themselves as providing the resources and organising ability that drove the economic system to provide the goods necessary for the survival and civilised life for the whole community. Those in the working-classes who thought about it saw themselves as providing the labour, the sole source of value, without which the resources and management would be in vain. The increasing class conflict of the late-Victorian and Edwardian period was the struggle for income, status and power arising from this clash of incompatible ideals. It was into this tripartite struggle that 'the professional class' came contributing both to the struggle and to the means of resolving it.[39]

Between the constitutional crisis between 1909 and 1911 and the

---

[37] Perkin, H., *The Rise of Professional Society: England since 1880*, (Routledge), 1990, pp. 27-63.
[38] Ibid, pp. 62-114.
[39] Ibid, pp. 171-217.

General Strike in 1926, class society in Britain underwent a profound crisis largely between the classes of capital and labour, in which the government became reluctantly involved, by no means wholly on the side of capital. Fear of social revolution was raised before 1914 by the co-existence of threats of from the Suffragettes and from Irish Nationalists and Ulstermen over the future status of Ireland and from the more aggressive trade unionists. It was further complicated by the outbreak of war in 1914 and its consequences especially revolution in Russia, Germany, Austria-Hungary and Turkey. The war ruthlessly laid bare the shortcomings and deficiencies of society, the economy and the political system. [40]

A class society?

If it is legitimate to speak of a class only when a group is united in every conceivable way then the concept is rendered meaningless. Classes are not and never were monolithic blocks of identical individuals. Class helped working people describe themselves in relation to society they experienced as well as to society as a whole. It provided identity for workers no longer bound by paternalist values as well as consciousness of that class identity. It evolved in response to growing population, greater social mobility, urban growth and new patterns of work based in the factory or workshop. But when the working-classes came into existence remains unclear. For some workers, the popular radicalism and conservatism of the 1790s marked its beginnings while for others it was the radicalism between 1815 and 1821 that gave class substance. What people did, where they lived and the significant divisions within the working-classes between skilled, semi-skilled and unskilled, working men and women and rural and industrial workers were perhaps more important in defining how workers viewed class than an overarching sense of 'classness'. It was the diversity of their lived experience as much as their unity of purpose that marked the working-classes by 1850.

Despite all the literature on the subject, the half-century since the publication of Edward Thompson's *The Making of the English Working Class* has done little to clarify the situation. Answers to the central questions of 'when?', 'how?' and 'why?' have been surprisingly inconclusive. The critical question is whether working people in the nineteenth and early-twentieth centuries consciously acted as members of a class as well as in other roles. Historians have interpreted class in different ways. At one extreme are those who argue that class and class action were abnormal and that individual interest was always more powerful than class loyalty. On the other,

---

[40] Ibid, pp. 218-285.

some historians see social developments in which class conflict played an integral and inevitable role. The postmodernist debates of the late 1980s and early 1990s demolished, at least temporarily, any notion of grand narratives as a means of explaining agency and change reducing it to part of the 'linguistic turn'. Marxist writers and labour historians maintain the hegemonic status of class while others have suggested that work and religion united people in large numbers but that class as a unifying force bringing large numbers of people together never really existed.[41] Nevertheless, the importance of class and political development within the realm of social movement history remained largely untouched by its semantic niggling and methodological extremes of the deconstructionist arguments.[42] The debate did, however, result in a gradual shift away from class as the only significant explanation of working-class action and towards a recognition that the working-classes shared diverse identities—gender, age, religion, race and ethnicity and location—that also played their part in defining who the working-classes were.

The industrial revolution was not simply a transition from an agricultural and domestic economy to one eventually dominated by factory regimes but rather a restructuring of economy and society. Where people lived and the spaces they inhabited played a critical part in how they defined their own senses of class. The community— whether rural or urban—included family and kin, houses and streets, churches and chapels and pubs, places of work, cultural opportunities and political organisations that acted and reacted upon individuals and groups developing, defining and redefining their identities. Communities were not necessarily defined in territorial terms but often by the experience of social interaction among those of similar attitudes, beliefs and interests. They were an amalgam of competing and contradictory and consensual and conflicting networks of people, places and spaces that made up localities, regions and nations.

---

[41] See, for instance, Joyce, Patrick, *Work, Society and Politics*, (Harvester Press), 1980, and Joyce, Patrick, (ed.), *The Historical Meaning of Work*, (Cambridge University Press), 1987.

[42] Croll, Andy, 'The impact of postmodernism on modern British social history', Berger, Stefan, (ed.), *Labour and Social History: Historiographical Reviews and Agendas, Mitteilungsblatt des Instituts für Soziale Bewegungen*, Vol. 27, (2002), pp. 137-152.

21 The working-classes

It is difficult to overestimate the importance of work in working-class life between 1780 and 1914. Work helped determine two fundamental features of working-class existence: the ways in which workers spent most of their waking hours and the amounts of money they had at their disposal.[1] It also determined most other aspects of working-class life: the standards of living they enjoyed, standards of health, the type of housing they lived in, the nature of family and neighbourhood life and the ways in which leisure time was spent and the social, political and other values that were held.[2]

Changing nature of work

The swing away from domestic forms of production can be roughly explained by three developments: the growth of population, the extension of enclosure with its consequent reduction in demand for rural labour and the advent of mechanised production boosting productivity and fostering the growth of new towns and cities. The result was a change in the structure of the labour market.[3]

---

[1] The literature on the labouring population is immense. Ibid, Hunt, E. H., *British Labour History 1815-1914*, Rule, J., *The Labouring Classes in Early Industrial England 1750-1850*, (Longman), 1986, Benson, J., *The Working-class in Britain 1850-1939*, (Longman), 1989, Hopkins, E., *A Social History of the English Working-classes 1815-1945*, (Edward Arnold), 1977, Belchem, J., *Industrialisation and the Working-class*, (Scolar), 1990, Savage, M., and Miles, A., *The remaking of the British working class, 1840-1940*, (Routledge), 1994, and Brown, K. D., *The English Labour Movement 1700-1951*, (Gill and Macmillan), 1982, are good starting points.

[2] Ibid, Benson, John, *The Working-class in Britain 1850-1939*, pp. 9-38, is the best introduction to this issue. Joyce, Patrick, (ed.), *The Historical Meanings of Work*, (Cambridge University Press), 1987, is an excellent collection containing a seminal introduction by the editor. Joyce, Patrick, 'Work', in Thompson, F. M. L., (ed.), *The Cambridge Social History of Britain 1750-1950: Vol. 2 People and their Environment*, (Cambridge University Press), 1990, pp. 131-194, is a short overview.

[3] Hopkins, E., 'Working hours and conditions during the industrial revolution: a reappraisal', *Economic History Review*, 2nd series, Vol. 35, (1982), pp. 52-66, and Reid, D. A., 'The decline of Saint Monday 1776-1876', *Past and Present*, Vol. 71, (1976), pp. 76-101, and 'Weddings, weekdays, work and leisure in urban England 1791-1911: the decline of Saint Monday revisited', *Past and Present*, Vol. 153, (1996), pp. 135-163, and Schwarz, L., 'Custom, wages and workload in England during industrialization', *Past and Present*, Vol. 197, (2007), pp. 143-175, cover important topics. Voth, H. J., *Time and work in England 1750-1830*, (Oxford University Press), 2000, asks whether working hours in England

The enclosure of common lands from the 1770s had a profound impact on the livelihood of rural workers and their families. It led to a contraction of resources available for many workers and a greater reliance on earnings. The spread of enclosure especially in southern England thrust rural labourers on to the labour market in a search for work that was made the more acute by falling arable farm prices and wages between 1815 and 1835. [4] The result of the growth in labour supply and agricultural depression was the collapse of farm service in the south and east of the country. It had been customary for farm workers to be hired for a year, to enter service in another household and to live with another family, receiving food, clothes, board and a small annual wage in return for work, only living out when they wished to marry.

The development of factory-based textile production had a profound effect on outwork, the other source of earned income for rural workers. Different parts of the country were associated with different products with lace-making round Nottingham, stocking-knitting in Leicester, spinning and weaving of cotton and wool in Lancashire and Yorkshire. The appearance of the mills damaged the status and security of some very skilled branches of outwork. People in many rural households were thrown into poverty as such work contracted and became available only at miserably low rates of pay. The fate of the handloom weavers, stocking-frame knitters and silk weavers in the 1830s and 1840s, all reflected the impact of technological change on the distribution of work.[5] Textiles were not the only industry to experience such structural changes. In both town and country, mechanisation had a marked impact on a wide variety of employment and the position of some skilled workers was undermined while the demand for new skills grew.

---

increased as a result of the Industrial Revolution while Steedman, Carolyn, *An Everyday Life of the English Working Class: Work, Self and Sociability in the Early Nineteenth Century*, (Cambridge University Press), 2013, suggests that historians have overstated the importance of work to the working man's understanding of himself as a creature of time, place and society.

[4] Richardson, T. L., 'Agricultural labourers' wages and the cost of living in Essex, 1790-1840: a contribution to the standard of living debate', in Holderness, B. A., and Turner, M. E., (eds.), *Land, labour and agriculture, 1700-1920: essays for Gordon Mingay*, (Hambledon), 1991, pp. 69-90.

[5] See Bythell, Duncan, *The Handloom Weavers*, (Cambridge University Press), 1969, and *The Sweated Trades: Outworks in Nineteenth-Century Britain*, (Batsford), 1978, for a detailed discussion of this issue.

Apprenticeship and dilution

Urban workers had always been more reliant on cash wages than had their rural counterparts. Pre-industrial towns were generally commercial and market centres rather than places of manufacture and employment was more specialised than elsewhere. The service sector was important with lawyers, accountants, bankers and merchants. Small units of production of skilled artisans provided local services and goods rather than commodities for export or the mass market operating largely on a domestic basis. They were frequently under the control of the craft guilds that controlled recruitment and training and the quality of products and established the vocabulary of the rights of 'legal' or 'society' men who worked in 'legal' shops that permeated craft unions into the nineteenth century. The position of the skilled urban artisan increasingly under threat from semi-skilled and less well-trained workers after 1800. [6]

The Elizabethan Statute of Artificers (or Apprentices) 1563 provided a legal framework of craft regulations but had fallen into abeyance long before its apprenticeship clauses were finally repealed in 1811. [7] Under the old system of apprenticeship, the pupil was formally indentured normally at age ten (or seven for the navy) and joined a master's house traditionally for seven years before being recognised as a journeyman qualified to practice the trade. It was also usual for journeymen to 'live in', entitled to bed, board and wages in return to work, only moving out on marriage. Often journeymen 'tramped' the country in search of work in part to extend their experience and knowledge of their trade but also to escape increasingly uncertain employment prospects in their immediate locality. [8] To become a master the journeyman had to produce his 'masterpiece', demonstrating his mastery of the skills of the specific trade as well as the capital necessary to establish his own workshop.

---

[6] Sheeran, George, 'Conflicting images: portrayals of the factory and the country in the nineteenth century', in *Rural and urban encounters in the nineteenth and twentieth centuries: regional perspectives,* (Conference of Regional and Local Historians), 2004, pp. 23-40.

[7] Lane, Joan, *Apprenticeship in England, 1600-1914*, (UCL Press), 1996, and Wallis, Patrick, 'Apprenticeship and Training in Pre-modern England', *Journal of Economic History*, Vol. 68, (2008), pp. 832-861, provide background.

[8] See Hobsbawm, E. J., 'The tramping artisan' in his *Labouring Men*, (Weidenfeld and Nicolson), 1964, pp. 34-63, and ibid, Thompson, E. P., *The Making of the English Working-class*, and 'Time, Work-Discipline and Industrial Capitalism', *Past & Present*, Vol. 38, (1967), pp. 56-97, reprinted in *Customs in Common*, (Merlin Press), 1991, pp. 352-403.

From the early-nineteenth century, fewer apprentices were completing their indentures and journeymen's wages were falling, both signs that employers were no longer bothered about hiring only men who had served their time. This led to a dilution in the labour force and a blurring of the boundaries between 'society' and 'non-society' men, a situation made worse by the mechanisation of production that required fewer skills than handwork. [9]

The nature of training for skilled work changed; apprenticeships were shortened and concentrated on specific skills rather than on an extensive understanding of all aspects of production. Lads worked alongside journeymen rather than being attached to a master's household with various adverse results. The new system bore heavily on apprentices' families, who frequently still paid for indentures while the apprentice lived at home and could expect little or no wages for his efforts until his time was served. The old stipulated ratios between journeymen and boys were increasingly ignored and apprentices became a cheap alternative for adult labour further depressing the adult labour market. Such developments were resented by the journeymen expected to train recruits, souring relations and often making training uncooperative. Many boys were dismissed as soon as they were old enough to command an adult rate, a practice more common during economic downturns.[10] This abuse of apprenticeship provoked sporadic industrial disputes as skilled workers tried to

---

[9] Humphries, Jane, 'English Apprenticeship: A Neglected Factor in the First Industrial Revolution', in David, Paul A., and Thomas, Mark, (eds.), *The economic future in historical perspective*, (Oxford University Press), 2001, pp. 73-102. Rose, Mary B., 'Social policy and business; parish apprenticeship and the early factory system, 1750-1834', *Business History*, Vol. 31, (1989), pp. 5-32, Lane, J., 'Apprenticeship in Warwickshire cotton mills, 1790-1830', *Textile History*, Vol. 10, (1979), pp. 161-174, and a valuable comparative study Elbaum, Bernard, 'Why apprenticeship persisted in Britain but not in the United States', *Journal of Economic History*, Vol. 49, (1989), pp. 337-349.

[10] Honeyman, Katrina, *Child workers in England, 1780-1820: parish apprentices and the making of the early industrial labour force*, (Ashgate), 2007, Steinberg, Marc W., 'Unfree Labor, Apprenticeship and the Rise of the Victorian Hull Fishing Industry: An Example of the Importance of Law and the Local State in British Economic Change', *International Review of Social History*, Vol. 51, (2006), pp. 243-276, and Reinarz, Jonathan, 'Learning By Brewing: Apprenticeship and the English Brewing Industry in the Late Victorian and Early Edwardian Period', in Munck, Bert De, Kaplan, Steven L., and Soly, Hugo, (eds.), *Learning on the shop floor: historical perspectives on apprenticeship*, (Berghahn Books), 2007, pp. 111-130, and 'Fit for management: apprenticeship and the English brewing industry, 1870-1914', *Business History*, Vol. 43, (2001), pp. 33-53.

protect their position and to prevent their trade from being flooded by excess labour. The independence of their 'aristocratic' status was upheld through the rhetoric of custom and the invention of 'tradition' to sanction and legitimise current practice. This excluded employers and market calculations from the opaque world of custom, tradition, craft mystery and skill, a separate culture upheld by secrecy, theatrical ceremony and, when necessary, ritualised violence. Through these means skilled workers defended their position at the 'frontier of control'.

Reduced to wage-earning proletarians without rights to the materials and product of their labour, skilled workers fought hard to retain some control over the 'labour process' and to defend their workplace autonomy against the new labour disciplines favoured by political economists and employers. [11] Even in new forms of work organisations, they often succeeded in safeguarding their status despite 'deskilling' technology and increased division of labour. But in defending or reconstructing skilled status, their actions were divisive: not just a line drawn against employers but against unfair or unskilled competition in the labour market. [12] Skill as property became skill as patriarchy that left women defenceless against the increasingly marginalised nature of their labour. At the same time, new mechanised processes facilitated cheaper forms of bulk production. As a result, the market became saturated with semi-skilled workers, who knew something of the trade but did not possess the full range of skills expected of the qualified man. Henry Mayhew, chronicling London's labour market in the 1840s, contrasted the position of the 'honourable' tradesman with the 'slop' workers whose wages and products undercut old recognised prices and reduced job security long assumed to belong to the man with an established craft. [13]

---

[11] That this was often unsuccessful is explored in Green, David R., *From artisans to paupers: economic change and poverty in London, 1790-1870*, (Scolar & Ashgate), 1995. See also, Levene, Alysa, '"Honesty, sobriety and diligence": master-apprentice relations in eighteenth- and nineteenth-century England', *Social History*, Vol. 33, (2008), pp. 183-200.

[12] This was especially evident in attacks, widespread in the late eighteenth and early-nineteenth centuries, on new technology where it posed a threat to employment but was especially focused on the use of unskilled labour. See, for example, Brodie, Marc, 'Artisans and dossers: the 1886 West End riots and the East End casual poor', *London Journal*, Vol. 24, (1999), pp. 34-50.

[13] Mayhew, Henry, *London Labour and the London Poor*, 4 Vols. (Griffin, Bohn, and Company), 1861-1862, and Thompson, E. P., and Yeo, E., (eds.), *The Unknown Mayhew: Selections from the Morning Chronicle 1849-50*, (Penguin), 1971, provide evidence for the 1850s and should be used in conjunction with Mayhew, Henry, *The Morning Chronicle Survey of Labour*

The most obvious impact of industrialisation was found in the more intense and strictly disciplined nature of work in those industries transformed by the new technology: textiles, coal-mining, metal-processing and engineering. Early mills were manned by pauper labour, mostly children because the regularity of work was alien to the adult population used to a greater degree of autonomy in conducting their working lives. [14] The higher wages available in factories provided insufficient compensation for this loss of 'freedom'. Impoverished handloom weavers would send their daughters to work on the power looms but resisted the prospect themselves. Hours in the early factories were probably no longer than those in the domestic trades but what made it far less acceptable was the mind-numbing tedium of the work involved, the loss of public feast days and holidays and, for middle-class commentators, the physical consequences of long hours and the appalling conditions in the factory towns.

Changes in labour market conditions during the nineteenth century made it difficult to make clear distinctions between the employed, the unemployed, the underemployed, the self-employed and the economically inactive. Subcontracting was rife, notably in the clothing trade where middlemen 'sweated' domestic women to earn a profit. The 'slop' end of the fashion and furnishing trades competed frantically for such orders as were available at almost any price. Casualism became more visible towards 1900 as cities spread in size. Short-term engagements and casual employment were particularly associated with the docks and the construction industries. The casual labour of the old East End was trapped within an economy of declining trades. Conditions of employment deteriorated. By the early 1870s, London's shipbuilding had slumped beyond the point of recovery and by the 1880s most heavy engineering, iron founding and metal work had gone the same way. [15] Competition from provincial furniture, clothing and footwear factories could only be met by

---

and the Poor, 1849-50, 6 Vols. (Caliban), 1980. Humpherys, Anne, *Travels into the Poor Man's Country: The Work of Henry Mayhew*, (University of Georgia Press), 1977, is a valuable study.

[14] Honeyman, Katrina, 'The Poor Law, the Parish Apprentice, and the Textile Industries in the North of England, 1780-1830', *Northern History*, Vol. 44, (2007), pp. 115-140.

[15] Rankin, Stuart, (ed.), *Shipbuilding on the Thames and Thames-Built Ships: a symposium for researchers and authors held on Saturday 2 September 2000: supported by London Borough of Southwark, Department of Education & Leisure and the Greenwich Maritime Institute to mark the 130th anniversary year of the launch of "Lothair", last large vessel built in Rotherhithe, 1870,* (Rotherhithe & Bermondsey Local History Group), 2000.

reducing labour costs and this led to the increasing importance of metropolitan sweated trades.

Variations in standards of living, wages and working conditions were at least as great in towns as in the countryside. Average urban wages were certainly higher but so were rent and food so that urban dwellers were not necessarily better off than their rural counterparts. Women's wages were invariably well below those of men and families dependent on a sole female wage earner were among the poorest of the urban population. Jobs guaranteeing a regular weekly wage, with little cyclical unemployment, were rare, highly prized and jealously guarded. Cyclical unemployment was the norm for most workers and was a major factor in the urban labour market and in turn had a significant impact on standards of living, quality of housing and the residential areas to which people could aspire.

Categorising urban workers

The urban population was organised in hierarchical terms, largely in terms of levels of skill. At the base of the hierarchy were the genuinely casual workers who formed a residual labour force that often migrated to a town when no other work was available. Such work as hawking and street trading, scavenging, street entertainment, prostitution and some casual labouring and domestic work fell into this category. Below these were begging and poor relief. Casual trades were largely concentrated in large cities, especially London, and the number fluctuated considerably. Very low and irregular incomes condemned families dependent on casual work to rooms in slums, but in London they would emerge from the rookeries of St. Giles to sell their goods in the cities or in middle-class residential districts. Large numbers of street traders in prosperous middle-class areas caused antagonism and sometimes fear. The police were often called to control street trading activities helping to reinforce middle-class stereotypes of a dirty and dangerous sub-class that should be confined to the slums.

Above the casual street traders were unskilled mainly casual occupations in which workers were hired for a few hours at a time and could be laid off for long periods without notice. These included labourers in the building trades, in sugar houses and other factories, carters, shipyard workers and especially dockers. All towns had such workers but they were especially important in port cities such as London, Liverpool, Bristol and London and in industries like coal mining or clothing that had a partly seasonal market. Precise numbers involved in casual work are impossible to determine. In Liverpool over 22 per cent of the employed population in 1871 were general, dock or warehouse labourers, many casual. When in work Liverpool dockers earned high weekly wages, ranging from 27s for quay porters to 42s for a stevedore but few maintained such earnings for any length of time and in a bad week many earned only a few shillings. Conditions changed little between 1830 and 1914. These workers were frequently in debt and regularly pawned clothes. In good times they would eat meat or fish but normally their diet consisted largely of bread, margarine and tea. Illness or industrial injury (common in dangerous dockland working conditions) would have led to financial disaster. Casual workers needed to live close to their workplace since employment was often allocated on a first-come, first-served basis. Liverpool dockers mostly lived close to the docks and this limited their housing choice to old, insanitary but affordable accommodation.

Factories provided more regular employment after 1830 as did public services as railway companies and many commercial organisations. Skilled manual labour was relatively privileged: a Lancashire skilled cotton spinner earned 27-30s per week in 1835 and a skilled iron foundry worker up to 40s. [16] In coal mining, skilled underground workers earned good wages and in key jobs such as shot-firing, putting, hewing and shaft sinking usually had regular employment although this often meant moving from colliery to colliery and between coalfields. Textile towns like Manchester, Bradford and Leeds and metal and engineering centres such as Sheffield and the Black Country tended to suffer less from poverty from irregular earnings than cities like Glasgow, Cardiff, Liverpool or London. Skilled engineering trades were amongst the earliest to unionise, along with artisans and craftsmen, particularly in London and northern industrial towns. [17] They protected their interests jealously and, despite some dilution in their position, they commanded higher wages and regular employment. This conferred many advantages: renting a decent terrace house in the suburbs avoiding the squalor of Victorian slums but with a long walk to work or, later in the century, the use of the 'workmen's trains'.

After 1850, the numbers working in white-collar occupations increased and a lower middle-class emerged among the petit-bourgeoisie of small shopkeepers and white-collar salaried occupations of clerks, commercial travellers and schoolteachers. White-collar employment increased from 2.5 per cent of the employed population in 1851 to 5.5 per cent by 1891. Such

---

[16] Boot, H. M., 'How skilled were Lancashire cotton factory workers in 1833?', *Economic History Review*, 2nd series, Vol. 48, (1995), pp. 283-303.
[17] On the emergence of trade unions, see Rule, John, (ed.), *British Trade Unions 1750-1850: The Formative Years*, (Longman), 1988, and Reid, Alistair, J., *United We Stand: A History of Britain's Trade Unions*, (Allen Lane), 2004.

employment was found in all towns but especially in commercial and financial centres such as Glasgow, Manchester, Liverpool and Bristol. White-collar workers were a diverse group: insurance and bank clerks commanded the highest incomes of over £3 per week and the greatest prestige; in contrast railway clerks often earned little more than skilled manual workers but had greater security of employment. White-collar employees certainly perceived themselves, and were perceived by others, to be in a secure and privileged position. They could afford not only a decent terraced house, but by 1880 could commute over longer distances by public transport, especially after the suburban railway and tram networks were established. Despite long hours of work for clerks and shopkeepers, their occupations were less hazardous than most factory employment and, with more regular incomes and healthier housing, they were more likely to enjoy better health and living standards than most industrial workers.

Women were employed in all categories of work and in textile districts female factory employment was very significant.[18] Single women often entered domestic service but married women who needed to supplement a low male wage or widows supporting several children, were severely limited in choice. Away from the textile districts, most found work as domestic cleaners, laundry workers, in sewing, dressmaking, boot and shoemaking and other trades carried on either in the home of small workshops. The notions of 'a woman's job' and 'a woman's rate' were regarded by employers, trade unions and often by women workers themselves as a 'natural' phenomenon throughout this period. The consequence of this was low pay and a sexual division of labour leading to sexual segregation. Patterns of segregation were by no means fixed throughout the country. Brick-making was a woman's trade in the Black Country where men worked in ironworks and coal-pits. In Lancashire where women worked in cotton and where openings for men were scarce, it was dominated by men. It was, however, rare not to see a clear dividing line between women and men's jobs within occupations and between women and men's processes. Not only was there vertical segregation at work with men's and women's processes clearly distinguished but there was a trend to horizontal segregation increasing after 1851 with women working in lower grade occupations, at a lower wage.[19]

---

[18] Humphries, Jane, "The most free from objection...': The sexual division of labour and women's work in nineteenth-century England', *Journal of Economic History*, Vol. 47, (1987), pp. 929-949.

[19] Bradley, Harriet, *Men's Work, Women's Work*, (Polity), 1989, is a useful survey and critique of sexual divisions of labour. It contains valuable case studies of a variety of occupations.

Women's work commanded a woman's rate, even when they were involved in the same processes as men. In manufacturing occupations, with the exception of textiles, women generally earned about half the average weekly earnings of men. New methods of wage payment introduced in the late-nineteenth and early-twentieth centuries reinforced the idea of a woman's rate. Women were more often paid by piece rate than men and found their rates lowered or they earned 'too much'. Wages were always low with piece rates producing incomes ranging from 5s to 15s a week. Non-manual workers generally earned a higher percentage of the average male earnings: women shop assistants earned about 65 per cent as much as men in 1900 and women teachers 75 per cent their male colleagues. In all-female occupations, women did worst of all. Nineteenth century nurses were often paid little more than domestic servants.[20] Indeed their pay was actually reduced to encourage middle-class applicants who did not need the money. Middle-class parents were roundly condemned by feminists for allowing their daughters to work for pocket money because they considered it to be more respectable and genteel. Theirs was voluntary rather than real work.

The proportion of women in industry declined from the 1890s, except in unskilled and some semi-skilled work but their role in higher professional, shop and clerical work increased. The introduction of the telephone and typewriter from the 1870s saw the army of male clerks replaced by female office workers. The revolution in retailing provided additional employment for women and by 1911 one-third of all shop assistants were female. The number of women in commerce and many industries increased between 1891 and 1911, but the proportion of women in paid employment hardly changed and remained around 35 per cent. But the characteristics of female employment changed substantially. Before 1914, domestic service was still the overwhelming source of employment for women and girls, though the clothing and textile trades employed more women than men. Women, however, were also beginning to infiltrate the lower grade clerical and service occupations. In 1901, 13 per cent of clerks were women, but by 1911 this had risen to 21 per cent, though the higher clerical grades remained almost exclusively male. Nevertheless the employment status of women remained inferior to that of men: in 1911, 52.1 per

---

[20] Sweet, Helen M., 'Establishing Connections, Restoring Relationships: Exploring the Historiography of Nursing in Britain', *Gender & History*, Vol. 19, (2007), pp. 565-580.

cent of women occupied semi-skilled or unskilled jobs compared to 40.6 per cent of men.

The industrial revolution was not a simple transition from an agricultural and domestic economy to one dominated by factory regimes but rather as a restructuring of economy and society. For individual workers this meant the abandoning of old skills as well as the development of new ones, while increasing regional specialisation of industry created differing impacts from one locality to another. Although contemporaries placed considerable emphasis on the development of large-scale factory production, domestic production and small workshops dominated manufacture until the mid-nineteenth century. A major restructuring of the British economy after 1890 brought significant changes in the working conditions and operation of the labour market. Women played an increasingly important role in the workforce, new technology and machinery created different jobs demanding new and often less individually crafted skills. Older workers, particularly in heavy industries, often found it difficult to adjust to new work practices. The years between 1890 and 1914 were a transitional period that retained many of the characteristics of the nineteenth century economy whilst signs of the new work patterns of the inter-war years began to develop.

Did standards of living rise or fall between 1780 and 1850?

Discussion of living standards is bedevilled by a range of methodological problems.[21] What is the meaning of living standards? Is it a qualitative or quantitative concept? What evidence can be used? Statistics, one of the main fuels in the debate, obscure much of the diversity and harshness of working-class experience. Should historians be using 'actual' wages or 'real' wages as the basis for their arguments?[22] These issues have given rise to a debate, especially

---

[21] Rubinstein, W. D., *Wealth and Inequality in Britain*, (Faber), 1986, provides a sound introduction. Taylor, A. J., (ed.), *The Standard of Living in the Industrial Revolution*, (Methuen), 1975, contains articles by the major protagonists in the debates before the 1970s. Floud, R., Wachter, K., and Gregory, A., *Height, health and history: Nutritional status in the United Kingdom 1750-1980*, (Cambridge University Press), 1990, a major contribution to the debate. Crafts, N. F. R., 'Some dimensions of the 'quality of life' during the British industrial revolution', *Economic History Review*, Vol. 50, (1997), pp. 617-639, is valuable. Humphries, Jane, 'Standard of Living, Quality of Life', in Williams, Chris, (ed.), *A Companion to Nineteenth-Century Britain*, (Blackwell Publishers), 2004, pp. 287-304, summarises the debate.

[22] Crafts, N. F. R., and Mills, Terence C., 'Trends in real wages in Britain, 1750-1913', *Explorations in Economic History*, Vol. 31, (1994), pp. 176-

over the decades between 1780 and 1850, on not simply whether living standards fell or rose, but over the whole revolutionary experience. [23]

There was a decline in real wages starting in the 1750s that persisted through the price peak of 1812-1813 and the distress of the post-war years. In London this downward trend was not reversed until the 1820s, though it was not until the 1840s that the levels of the 1740s were regained and exceeded. The national index compiled by Lindert and Williamson also situates the upturn in the 1820s but their figures are far more optimistic suggesting that real wages nearly doubled between 1820 and 1850. [24] By 1830, therefore the worst excesses of the pessimist scenario seem to have been at an end and real wages for the bulk of the working population seem to have been rising, though whether Lindert and Williamson's optimistic assessment is entirely valid is questionable. So what did people earn? In the 1760s most high-wage counties were in the south east. By 1850, they were in the Midlands and north: in Lancashire wages were more than a third higher than in Buckinghamshire, a differential that continued until the end of the century. This North-South divide [25] and wage payments must be assessed in the context of family income and the higher cost of living for the working-classes, a hardship aggravated by the family poverty cycle and the devastating impact of recurrent short-term crises. [26]

Standard of living statistics conceal important structural changes

---

194, and Feinstein, C. H., 'Pessimism perpetuated: real wages and the standard of living in Britain during and after the Industrial Revolution', *Journal of Economic History*, Vol. 58, (1998), pp. 625-658, and 'What really happened to real wages?: trends in wages, prices, and productivity in the United Kingdom, 1880-1913', *Economic History Review*, second series, Vol. 43, (1990), pp. 329-355.

[23] Weaver, Stewart, 'The Bleak Age: J. H. Clapham, the Hammonds and the standard of living in Victorian Britain', in Taylor, Miles, and Wolff, Michael, (eds.), *The Victorians since 1901: histories, representations and revisions*, (Manchester University Press), 2004, pp. 29-43.

[24] Crafts, N. F. R., 'English workers' real wages during the industrial revolution: some remaining problems'; with reply by Peter Lindert and Jeffrey Williamson, *Journal of Economic History*, Vol. 45, (1985), pp. 139-153.

[25] On this issue, see Baker, Alan R. H., and Billinge, Mark, (eds.), *Geographies of England: the North-South divide, material and imagined*, (Cambridge University Press), 2004.

[26] Harison, Casey, 'The standard of living of English and French workers, 1750-1850', in Rider, Christine, and Thompson, Michael, (eds.), *The industrial revolution in comparative perspective*, (Krieger), 2000, pp. 165-178, provides a useful comparative study.

in the composition of working-class family income before 1850.[27] The assumption on which the figures were based, especially the dominance of money-wages and of the male breadwinner, lack validity until 1850 by which time workers had been deprived of traditional perks and rights and the working-class family had been forced to redefine gender roles and functions.[28] The imposition of monetary form of wage payment marked a fundamental change in employers' attitudes to property and labour. Age was probably the most important factor in determining output and earnings. In the 1830s, the youngest and fittest of the handloom weavers could earn 25 per cent more wages in the same time as a weaker person could earn on the same machine. Throughout the trades, the elderly or rather the prematurely old were often forced to give up the better-paid tasks as they were affected by various forms of occupational disorder. For instance, the Sheffield fork-grinding industry killed off no less than a quarter of its workforce every five years.[29] Differences in output and earnings were kept to a minimum where group solidarity and trade societies were strong, but this did not apply to the so-called 'dishonourable' trades or in the over-stocked outwork industries. Here, in the absence of day rates, opportunistic middlemen and commercially minded masters were able to exploit cheap, unskilled labour through the piece-rate system. Even in 'honourable' trades, few workers were fortunate enough to enjoy full-time work throughout the year.

The focus on the adult male 'breadwinner' has diverted attention away from the notion of the family income. Earnings in this period were assessed in family, not individual, terms with the family often functioning as a unit of production. By 1830, however, the prospects for women and hence family earnings deteriorated considerably. The first victims of technological or structural unemployment were women who encountered the new prejudice and sexual division of labour and the harsh economic costs of the new

---

[27] Voth, Hans-Joachim', Living standards and the urban environment', in ibid, Floud, Roderick, and Johnson, Paul A., (eds.), *The Cambridge economic history of modern Britain, Volume 1: industrialisation, 1700-1860*, pp. 268-294.

[28] Horrell, Sara, and Humphries, Jane, 'The origins and expansion of the male breadwinner family: the case of nineteenth-century Britain', *International Review of Social History, Supplement*, Vol. 5, (1997), pp. 25-64, summarises the debates.

[29] Williams, Naomi, 'The reporting and classification of causes of death in mid-nineteenth-century England: the example of Sheffield', *Historical Methods*, Vol. 29, (1996), pp. 58-71.

male breadwinner ideal.[30] Sexual segregation was rigorously enforced in the textile mills where women were denied access to the best-paid skilled jobs. Skill was a male preserve in the modern factory, protected by trade union organisation and internal subcontracting that gave mule spinners a supervisory role for which women were deemed ineligible. Textile mills apart,[31] mechanisation and the factory system brought few new opportunities for women: female employment was derisory in iron and steel, railways, chemicals and the expanding heavy industries. Sexual segregation was by no means restricted to the factory districts and occurred wherever men were confronted with changes in the location or process of work. In rural England, for example, female participation was limited to haymaking and weeding the corn by 1830.[32]

The family income suffered as a result but most men on their own economic grounds welcomed the new sexual specialisation. They were increasingly vulnerable to seasonal unemployment with the expansion of production that was less labour intensive and they were determined to restrict cheap female competition.[33] Yet in many cases the wife's contribution to the family income remained indispensable but the force of the new convention against working women confined their employment to the lowest paid 'dishonourable' and sweated

---

[30] Horrell, Sara, and Humphries, Jane, 'Women's labour force participation and the transition to the male-breadwinner family, 1790-1865', *Economic History Review*, Vol. 48 (1995), pp. 89-117, and '"The exploitation of little children": child labour and the family economy in the industrial revolution', *Explorations in Economic History*, Vol. 32, (1995), pp. 485-516.

[31] There were severe limitations on women's roles in textiles; see, Valverde, Mariana, '"Giving the female a domestic turn": the social, legal and moral regulation of women's work in British cotton mills, 1820-1850', *Journal of Social History*, Vol. 21, (1987-8), pp. 619-634.

[32] Verdon, Nicola, *Rural women workers in nineteenth-century England: gender, work and wages*, (Boydell), 2002, provides an overview while Ulyatt, Donna J., *Rural women and work: Lincolnshire c.1800-1875*, (Anderson Blake Books), 2005, and MacKay, John, 'Married women and work in nineteenth-century Lancashire: the evidence of the 1851 and 1861 census reports', in Goose, Nigel, (ed.), *Women's work in industrial England: regional and local perspectives*, (Local Population Studies), 2007, pp. 164-181, provide valuable case studies. See also, Sharpe, Pamela, 'The female labour market in English agriculture during the Industrial Revolution: expansion or contraction?', in ibid, Goose, Nigel, (ed.), *Women's work in industrial England: regional and local perspectives*, pp. 51-75.

[33] Clark, Gregory, 'Farm wages and living standards in the industrial revolution: England, 1670-1869', *Economic History Review*, Vol. 54, (2001), pp. 477-505, provides a valuable longitudinal study.

trades.[34] Their cheap labour was exploited to reinforce still further male hostility towards 'unfair' competition. Relations between the sexes in the London tailoring trades were at crisis point in the early 1830s when the Owenite socialists championed the rights of working women and called on the London tailors union to adopt a policy of 'equalisation' in order to unite all the workforce. The resulting strike was, however, a disastrous failure and led to further marginalisation of female workers in the trades.[35]

The expenditure for working-class families was significantly higher than for the middle and upper-classes.[36] Food was by far the most important item, accounting for up to three-quarters of the wage packet. Working people bought poor quality food in small quantities for immediate consumption and rarely received value for money. Food was often obtained from the Saturday night markets where dealers were able to off-load their otherwise unsaleable produce: Engels commented that 'the workers get what is too bad for the property-holding class.'[37] They were often dependent on credit and had to pay the higher prices of the obliging small shopkeepers. Provisions were dearer still where workers were victims of the truck system and the poor quality, adulterated foods of the 'Tommy shops'.[38] Despite stringent legislation from 1831, the truck system remained common practice into the 1850s in south Staffordshire and in much of rural East Anglia where gangmasters supplied subcontract

---

[34] Blackburn, Sheila, *A fair day's wage for a fair day's work?: sweated labour and the origins of minimum wage legislation in Britain*, (Ashgate), 2007, '"Between the devil of cheap labour competition and the deep sea of family poverty?": sweated labour in time and place, 1840-1914', *Labour History Review*, Vol. 71, (2006), pp. 99-121, and '"Princesses and sweated-wage slaves go well together": images of British sweated workers, 1843-1914', *International Labor and Working-Class History*, Vol. 61, (2002), pp. 24-44.

[35] Schmiechen, J. A., *Sweated industries and sweated labour: the London clothing trades: 1860-1914*, (Taylor & Francis), 1984.

[36] Horrell, S., and Humphries, J., 'Old questions, new data, and alternative perspectives: families' living standards in the industrial revolution', *Journal of Economic History*, Vol. 52, (1992), pp. 849-880.

[37] Ibid, Engels, Frederick, *The condition of the working class in England*, p. 104.

[38] On the operation of the truck system see, Hilton, G. W., 'The British truck system in the 19th century', *Journal of Political Economy*, Vol. 65, (1957), pp. 237-256, and *The truck system, including a history of the British Truck Acts, 1465-1960*, (W. Heffer), 1960.

labour at the cheapest daily rates. [39]

As with food, so with housing: those at the bottom end of the market received scant value for money.[40] Accommodation accounted for anything up to a quarter or even a third of a labourer's wages compared to about a sixth of the income of the middle-classes. The nuclear family, the sacred cow of English social history, was too expensive for many families who lived with kin or in lodgings for the first few years of marriage. Foster found that the proportion of families living with relatives ranged from a third in Northampton to over two-thirds in South Shields while in Preston in 1851, lodgers were present in 23 per cent of all households.[41] Many urban workers were also subject to the 'house trucking' system where housing was dependent on their employers, an extension of the 'tied' cottage system of rural England.

For working-class teenagers, clothes and accessories were the first call on income after they had paid their contribution to the family income. Many poor families, however, relied on cast-off, second-hand or stolen goods.[42] Clothes could be easily pawned or fenced and there are many recorded cases of petty theft: in Manchester there was an average of 210 reports a year of stolen clothing from hedges or lines. Extra income was often spent on clothes since they were easily pawnable as well as providing immediate enjoyment.[43]

Skills, work and management, 1850-1914

Craft-like control persisted in amended form in the mid-Victorian factory, a privilege enjoyed by a new 'aristocracy of labour'. Foster argues that these workers derived their status from a change in employer strategy. Skilled workers were incorporated in a new authority structure designed to strengthen discipline and increase productivity. The introduction of the 'piece master' system in the engineering factories brought the skilled engineer into active

---

[39] Verdon, Nicola, 'The employment of women and children in agriculture: a reassessment of agricultural gangs in nineteenth-century Norfolk', *Agricultural History Review*, Vol. 49, (2001), pp. 41-55.

[40] Williams, Samantha, 'Poor relief, labourers' households and living standards in rural England c.1770-1834: a Bedfordshire case study', *Economic History Review*, Vol. 58, (2005), pp. 485-519.

[41] Ibid, Foster. J., *Class Struggle and the Industrial Revolution: early industrial capitalism in three English towns*, pp. 125-131.

[42] Richmond, Vivienne, *Clothing the Poor in Nineteenth-Century England*, (Cambridge University Press), 2013, pp. 52-92.

[43] Tebbutt, Melanie, *Making Ends Meet: Pawnbroking and Working-Class Credit*, (Leicester University Press), 1983, and Hudson, K, *Pawnbroking: an aspect of British social history*, 1982.

involvement in the work of management as group leader and technical supervisor. In cotton factories, spinners retained skilled status as a crucial group after the introduction of the self-acting mule. These male workers intensified the labour of juvenile and female time-paid assistants, an effective adaptation of traditional gender and family roles to the factory environment. [44]

There is some disagreement over the extent to which this position was secure. Stedman Jones insists that real control had already passed to employers with the restructuring of industry on 'modern' lines.[45] Skilled workers became defensive seeking to preserve their status and differentials through the benevolence of their employers. In the absence of technical expertise, employers were often forced to concede considerable autonomy to skilled workers, though they generally derived some benefit from the arrangement. Allowing spinners to appoint their own piercers relieved employers of direct responsibility for labour recruitment and discipline. Apprenticeship operated in a similar way, providing employers with a skilled workforce trained at worker expense. This pragmatic compromise between skilled workers and employers was usually informally negotiated locally. Capital made production possible, but the actual details of production, workers insisted was their responsibility.

Where no independence was allowed, workers were often reluctant to enter employment whatever wages it offered. Domestic service, a comparatively well-paid occupation largely unaffected by cyclical unemployment, was shunned by working-class girls in factory districts and urban areas. Lancashire marriage registers show that servants tended to marry husbands from a lower social-economic status than their peers, an indication of the social stigma attached to service in an area where alternative female employment was readily available. [46] The middle-classes of the factory districts relied on rural migrants for domestic servants and some obtained cheap live-in

---

[44] Ibid, Foster. J., *Class Struggle and the Industrial Revolution: early industrial capitalism in three English towns*, pp. 224-238.

[45] Jones, Gareth Stedman, *Outcast London: a study in the relationship between classes in Victorian society*, (Oxford University Press), 1971, pp. 19-51. See his critique of Foster 'Class Struggle and the Industrial Revolution', in his *Languages of Class*, (Cambridge University Press), 1983, pp. 25-74.

[46] Anderson, Michael, 'What can the mid-Victorian censuses tell us about variations in married women's employment?', *Local Population Studies*, Vol. 62, (1999), pp. 9-30.

servants from the local workhouse. [47]

Factory employment offered women some independence but they seldom held the most well-paid and responsible jobs especially supervisory tasks that carried skilled status and workplace authority. These male preserves were jealously protected by 'closed' trade unionism. Women were denied access to the well-paid spinning sector not because they were physically incapable of operating self-acting mules but they often lacked the necessary technical skills and experience. [48] They had been excluded from the spinning factories in the 1810s and 1820s when the use of 'doubled' mules put a premium on male physical strength. Without recent practical experience, women became the victims of discontinuity in the transmission of craft skills and knowledge from one generation to another. The cult of domesticity that sought to limit female paid employment to the brief period before marriage further hindered the acquisition of workplace skills. In some parts of Lancashire, married women went out to work in substantial numbers, but not in its spinning belt where the well-paid spinners and engineers feared a loss of status should their wives return to paid employment.

Unable to restrict labour supply, male and female weavers united in trade unionism, a development resisted by paternal employers. The Preston lock-out of 1853-1854 brought conflict between employers and workers in an attempt to reverse the 10 per cent wage cuts of 1847. [49] The cotton workers were starved back to work after twenty-eight weeks, a decisive defeat that marked a turning-point in strategy as union leaders cultivated an image of moderation and respectability to secure recognition from reluctant employers. Blackburn employers granted union recognition and negotiating rights

---

[47] Horn, Pamela, *The rise and fall of the Victorian servant*, revised edition, (Sutton Publishing), 2004, Higgs, Edward, 'The tabulation of occupations in the nineteenth-century census with special reference to domestic servants', in ibid, Goose, Nigel, (ed.), *Women's work in industrial England: regional and local perspectives*, pp. 250-259, Drake, Michael, 'Aspects of domestic service in Great Britain and Ireland, 1841-1911', *Family & Community History*, Vol. 2, (1999), pp. 119-128, and Jamieson, Lynn, 'Rural and urban women in domestic service', in Gordon, Eleanor, and Breitenbach, Esther, (eds.), *The world is ill-divided: women's work in Scotland in the nineteenth and early twentieth centuries*, (John Donald), 1990, pp. 136-157.

[48] Freifeld, Mary, 'Technological change and the "self-acting" mule: a study of skill and the sexual division of labour', *Social History*, Vol. 11, (1986), pp. 319-343.

[49] See, Dutton, H. I., and King, J. E., '*Ten Per Cent and no surrender*': the Preston strike, 1853-1854, (Cambridge University Press), 1981.

on the strict understanding that union officials would 'police' the agreement. [50] Though recognition was elsewhere delayed until the 1880s, the Blackburn weavers pointed the way forward towards modern collective bargaining. In already unionised industries, similar conciliation and arbitration schemes enjoyed considerable success in the late 1860s and early 1870s. They were first introduced in the Nottingham hosiery industry and were of mutual benefit to unions and employers, an institutional expression of the mid-Victorian compromise in labour relations. [51] New sliding wage-scales were welcomed in the coal and iron trades where wage disputes had broken many unions: conciliation boards now automatically adjusted wages to product price. [52] Some of the other schemes clearly favoured employers. In the building trade, for instance, employers took advantage of mutual negotiation to reassert and redefine managerial powers thereby curtailing the autonomous regulation of the trade. [53]

Culture and community in the factory became the concern of 'scientific management', an approach significantly more sophisticated than the paternalism of the 1850s and 1860s. The working environment improved as employers implemented new factory legislation and extended the range of welfare programmes, but other initiatives were less benevolent. Pioneer forms of Taylorism provided new managerial techniques to raise labour productivity and curb the power of organised labour and were pursued with some vigour as international competition increased and prices fell. [54] The design and

---

[50] Beattie, Derek, *Blackburn: the development of a Lancashire cotton town*, (Ryburn), 1992, provides the context but see also, Daumas, Jean-Claude, et al, 'Trade unionism in textiles towns and areas', in Robert, Jean-Louis, Prost, Antoine, and Wrigley, Chris, (eds.), *The emergence of European trade unionism*, (Ashgate), 2004, pp. 56-57, 64-65 and 70-73.

[51] Church, R. A., 'Technological change and the Hosiery Board of Conciliation and Arbitration, 1860-84', *Yorkshire Bulletin of Economic & Social Research*, Vol. 15, (1963), pp. 52-60.

[52] Loftus, Donna, 'Industrial conciliation, class co-operation and the urban landscape in mid-Victorian England', in Morris, R. J., and Trainor, R. H., (eds.), *Urban governance: Britain and beyond since 1750*, (Ashgate), 2000, pp. 182-197, and Porter, J. H., 'Wage bargaining under conciliation agreements, 1860-1914', *Economic History Review*, second series, Vol. 23, (1970), pp. 460-475.

[53] Price, Richard, *Masters, Unions, and Men: Work control in building and the rise of labour, 1830-1914*, (Cambridge University Press), 1980, pp. 94-197, looks at the development of industrial relations from the late 1860s.

[54] 'Taylorism' originated in the United States and represented the logical development of the division of labour. The different aspects of manufacture were identified and then applied to an assembly line structure. See, Taylor, Frederick Winslow, *The principles of scientific management*, (Harper &

planning of production processes became a managerial prerogative, a task undertaken by new production engineers, while shop-floor operatives were kept under constant surveillance by foremen. This challenged the skilled workers' belief that they had autonomy in the sphere of production. Supervision was often accompanied by new methods of payment and incentive schemes such as bonus systems. Employers wished to take advantage of the technological developments of the 'second industrial revolution': semi-automatic machines, standardised and interchangeable parts and the increasing use of semi-skilled labour on tasks previously the preserve of a skilled elite. [55] These innovations threatened to undermine skilled status and craft organisations but, in the English context at least, they proved highly resilient.

The consequences of attempts to reorganise production varied from industry to industry. Craft organisation remained stronger where employers were hindered by market forces, inelasticity of demand for the product or its perishable nature. Hand compositors in the newspaper industry gained control of the linotype machines for their own exclusive 'craft' use, a privilege extracted from employers in the competitive market for a perishable product. [56] Some employers decided against reorganisation when faced by threats of craft resistance, a sensible, if short-term, solution for family-owned firms making satisfactory profits. Also the product market for British-made capital goods was often highly individualised, a significant obstacle to the introduction of standardised mass-production techniques. Ships, machines and railway engines were constructed to fulfil the individual needs of customers. It was not until the bicycle boom of the mid-1890s that a broad-based demand for a product with standardised parts emerged and at this point engineering employers began to introduce American-style machine tools and lathes.

Mechanisation was implemented in the midst of workplace conflict, as employers combined in a national organisation, the Engineering Employers Federation [57] to reverse the gains secured by

---

Brothers), 1911, and Hounshell, David A., *From the American System to Mass Production, 1800-1932: The Development of Manufacturing Technology in the United States*, (JHU Press), 1985.

[55] See, Zeitlin, Jonathan, 'The meaning of managerial prerogative: industrial relations and the organisation of work in British engineering, 1880-1939', in Harvey, Charles E., and Turner, John, (eds.), *Labour and business in modern Britain*, 1989, pp. 32-47.

[56] See, Duffy, Patrick, *The skilled compositor, 1850-1914: an aristocrat among working men*, (Ashgate), 2000.

[57] Zeitlin, Jonathan, 'The internal politics of employer organization: the Engineering Employers' Federation, 1896-1939', in Tolliday, Steven, and

the Amalgamated Society of Engineers during the craft militancy of the 1889-1892 boom. [58] In the lock-out of 1897, the EEF insisted on their absolute right to manage but their victory did not mean the crushing of the union or a thorough transformation of the division of labour. The aim of employers was to boost output and reduce labour costs without major capital spending rather than the new rationalising Taylorist mode. Throughout the 1890s, there were similar disputes in other major industries as employers reasserted their authority in pursuit of lower costs and more efficient use of labour. [59] Between 1892 and 1897, 13.2 million days were lost through disputes compared to 2.3 million between 1899 and 1907 when new systems of national collective bargaining, similar to those in engineering, took effect. [60] Conflict was particularly intense in the coalfields. [61] The collective bargaining arrangements of the 1890s, the outcome of national strikes and lock-outs, recognised and confirmed the role and functions of craft trade unions, while also making clear the power and prerogatives of employer authority.

The compromise workplace relationships of the 1850s and 1860s were reconstructed in different forms. Skilled workers had to resolve whether they could or should retain their exclusive status. Some workers were prepared to shed some of their exclusivism to strengthen their position against modernising employers. The aristocratic boilermakers set the example, preventing a major reorganisation of steel ship production by a flexible union policy that kept the boundaries of membership under constant review. When

---

Zeitlin, Jonathan, (eds.), *The Power to Manage?: Employers and Industrial Relations in Comparative Historical Perspective*, (Routledge), 1991, pp. 46-70, especially 47-55.

[58] Burgess, K., 'New Unionism for old? The Amalgamated Society of Engineers in Britain', in Mommsen, W. J., and Husung, H.-G., (eds.), *The development of trade unionism in Great Britain and Germany, 1880-1914*, (German Historical Institute), 1985, pp. 166-184.

[59] This is evident in Smith, D. N., 'Managerial strategies, working conditions and the origins of unionism: the case of the tramway and omnibus industry, 1870-91', *Journal of Transport History*, third series, Vol. 8, (1987), pp. 30-51, and Lester, V. Markham, 'The employers' liability/workmen's compensation debate of the 1890s revisited', *Historical Journal*, Vol. 44, (2001), pp. 471-495.

[60] Cronin, James E., 'Strikes 1870-1914', in Wrigley, Chris, (ed.), *A history of British industrial relations, Vol. 1: 1875-1914*, (Harvester), 1982, pp. 74-98.

[61] Church, Roy A., and Outram, Quentin, *Strikes and Solidarity: Coalfield Conflict in Britain, 1889-1966*, (Cambridge University Press), 2002, pp. 38-58, 95-112.

the need arose, semi-skilled workers were granted membership, an important step towards the establishment of a closed shop. Attitudes to unskilled workers depended on circumstances: some were admitted, others were not. This redefinition of their boundaries of exclusion to admit previously prohibited groups of workers proved highly effective in allowing skilled workers to retain their aristocratic status in the new conditions of late-Victorian England. It helps to explain why the Alliance Cabinet-Makers' Association succeeded while the older Friendly Society of Operative Cabinet-Makers withered away into narrow craft restrictionism. [62] Old-fashioned prejudice was probably most difficult to abandon where gender was concerned. Craft organisation in the Potteries remained narrow and sectional, powerless to prevent displacement as cheap female labour was put to work on new machines. [63]

The persistence of exclusive status reflecting the interplay between 'genuine skill' (a necessary exercise of dexterity, judgment and knowledge) and 'socially constructed skill' (the status upheld by organisational control). [64] Managerial control was exerted over the technical expertise previously located on the shop-floor. A distinction emerged between planning and execution, the implementation of which depended on supervisory workers, trained technicians who owed their position to knowledge acquired at night school. Shop-floor skills were increasingly limited and specialised despite the continued existence of apprenticeship that passed on knowledge of the trade. Formal, indentured arrangements in the older crafts steadily declined but apprenticeship expanded in several growing industries such as building and printing where there was considerable agreement between employers and workers over training methods. [65] With the greater specialisation of work and skill, apprentice labour was quickly turned to profit by employers, a source of cheap labour that, as earlier in the century, undermined the position of adult men in the labour

---

[62] Betjemann, Peter, 'Craft and the Limits of Skill: Handicrafts Revivalism and the Problem of Technique', *Journal of Design History*, Vol. 21, (2008), 183-193.

[63] Anderson, G., 'Some aspects of the labour market in Britain 1870-1914', in ibid, Wrigley, Chris, (ed.), *A history of British industrial relations, Vol. 1: 1875-1914*, pp. 1-19.

[64] Griffiths, Trevor, *The Lancashire working classes: c.1880-1930*, (Oxford University Press), 2001, is an excellent case-study.

[65] Powell, Christopher G., *The British building industry since 1800: an economic history*, second edition, (Spon), 1996, pp. 74-98. Skingsley, T. A., 'Technical training and education in the English printing industry: a study of late 19th century attitudes', *Journal of the Printing Historical Society*, Vol. 13, (1978-9), pp. 1-25; Vol. 14, (1979-80), pp. 1-58.

market.[66]

Despite the persistence of skill differentials, the working-classes became more homogeneous in late-Victorian England. The proportion of the occupied population engaged in farming fell from 15 per cent in 1871 to 7.5 per cent in 1901 as rural migrants entered the most rapidly expanding sections of the domestic economy, transport and mining marking a major shift from worse to better paid jobs and from less to more regular employment. Small units continued to proliferate in some sectors of the economy but the factory was finally established as the predominant form of organisation even in the sweated and shoemaking trades leaving some poor outworkers stranded in old centres of small-scale workshop production.[67]

Diversity and standards of living, 1850-1914

Improved standards of living during the mid-Victorian period owed more to greater stability in employment than a marked increase in wages.[68] The economy was characterised by high, relatively stable prices and high levels of consumption. This was, however, punctuated by inflation between 1853 and 1855 and 1870 and 1873. Food prices rose less than most other prices resulting in marked increases in the consumption of tea, sugar and other 'luxuries'. In dietary terms, however, there was no significant advance in the standard of living until the falling prices of the 1880s.[69] Brewing apart, food remained a largely unrevolutionised industry in production and retailing until 1900. Real wages kept pace with food price rises, but rent proved increasingly expensive with particularly sharp increases in the mid-1860s. For some workers substantial and lasting advances in

---

[66] See, for example, Wilcox, Martin, 'Opportunity or Exploitation? Apprenticeship in the British Trawl Fisheries, 1850-1936', *Genealogists' Magazine*, Vol. 28, (2004), pp. 135-149.

[67] See, Gazeley, Ian, 'Manual work and pay, 1900-70', in ibid, Crafts, Nicholas F. R., Gazeley, Ian, and Newell, Andrew, (eds.), *Work and pay in twentieth-century Britain*, pp. 55-79.

[68] Church, Roy, *The Great Victorian Boom, 1850-1873*, (Macmillan), 1975, summarises research position in the mid-1970s.

[69] See, Clayton, Paul, and Rowbotham, Judith, 'An unsuitable and degraded diet? Part one: public health lessons from the mid-Victorian working class diet', *Journal of the Royal Society of Medicine*, Vol. 101, (6), (2008), pp. 282-289, 'An unsuitable and degraded diet? Part two: realities of the mid-Victorian diet', *Journal of the Royal Society of Medicine*, Vol. 101, (7), (2008), pp. 350-357, and 'An unsuitable and degraded diet? Part three: Victorian consumption patterns and their health benefits', *Journal of the Royal Society of Medicine*, Vol. 101, (9), (2008), pp. 454-462.

real wages did not occur until the late 1860s. The real wages of Black Country miners actually fell by a third during the mid-1850s and did not recover fully until 1869, after which there was a major advance carrying real wages some 30-40 per cent above the 1850 level. Money earnings in cotton displayed a similar chronology with the relatively modest advances in the 1850s followed by some spectacular advances after 1865: between 1860 and 1874, weavers' wages rose by 20 per cent and spinners by between 30 and 50 per cent. [70]

In this period, skilled workers earned twice those who were unskilled and they were less vulnerable to unemployment. For skilled trade unionists in the metal, engineering and shipbuilding industries, there were only two occasions, in 1858 and 1868, when the unemployment rates reached double figures. For agricultural labourers, the mid-Victorian boom brought no real improvement in standards of living and ironically, when improvement occurred in the 1870s and 1880s, it was against the backdrop of falling farming profitability. [71] George Bartley's study of *The Seven Ages of a Village Pauper* suggested that three out of four inhabitants of the typical village required public relief at some stage in their lives. [72] In some industrial areas there was a similar lack of material advance. In the Black Country, only the skilled building trades enjoyed an increase in real wages despite peak production in local coal and iron industries. On Merseyside, wage rates for skilled and unskilled workers remained stable until eroded by high food prices in the early 1870s. Women workers in sweated trades and casual employment probably gained least during the mid-Victorian period, though there is some evidence for an improvement in day rates for charring and washing in the 1870s.

Despite the greater stability of employment and the belated improvement in earnings, few working-class families rose above economic insecurity and bouts of periodic poverty. At critical moments in the family cycle even the differential enjoyed by skilled workers proved inadequate to prevent considerable hardship. This was particularly severe at times of general distress when a downturn in the trade cycle or a harsh winter led to short-time working and unemployment. The can be seen particularly in the Lancashire

---

[70] Hunt, E. H., *Regional wage variations in Britain, 1850-1914*, (Oxford University Press), 1973.
[71] See, for example, Williams, L. J., and Jones, D., 'The wages of agricultural labourers in the nineteenth century: the evidence from Glamorgan', *Bulletin of the Board of Celtic Studies*, Vol. 29, (1982), pp. 749-761, and Horn, Pamela, 'Northamptonshire agricultural labourers in the 1870s', *Northamptonshire Past and Present*, Vol. 4, (1971), pp. 371-377.
[72] Bartley, George, *The Seven Ages of a Village Pauper*, (Chapman and Hall), 1874, pp. 2-5.

Cotton Famine of 1861-1865, a protracted period of distress and unemployment.[73] During the winter of 1862-1863, 49 per cent of all operatives in the 28 poor law unions of the cotton district were unemployed with a further 35 per cent on short-time. The depth and persistence of such mass unemployment was unprecedented: at Ashton the worst hit town where there was little industrial diversification, 60 per cent of the operatives remained unemployed as late as November 1864, while at Salford the unemployment rate stood at 24 per cent.[74]

Unemployment on this scale had a disastrous impact on standards of living and posed considerable problems for the relief agencies, both Poor Law and philanthropic once workers had exhausted their savings. The Poor Law and the charities were unsuited to the needs of unemployed factory workers.[75] They had already come under scrutiny following events in London during the harsh winter of 1860-1861 when the temperature remained below freezing for a month causing severe privation for the casual work force. Across the East End, the Poor Law system simply broke down as the number of paupers increased from about 96,000 to over 135,000. To meet the emergency charitable funds had to be distributed without investigation, an exercise condemned in the investigative journalism of John Hollingshead as indiscriminate 'stray charity'.[76] The Poor Law Board, already under investigation by the parliamentary Select Committee, was determined to prevent similar problems by insisting on the strict compliance with the Outdoor Relief

---

[73] Arnold, R. A., Sir, *The History of the Cotton Famine: From the Fall of Sumter to the passing of the Public Works Act*, (Saunders, Otley and Co.), 1864, Henderson, W. O., *The Lancashire Cotton Famine, 1861-1865*, (Manchester University Press), 1934, and Farnie, Douglas A., 'The cotton famine in Great Britain', in Ratcliffe, B. M., (ed.), *Great Britain and her World 1750-1914: Essays in honour of W. O. Henderson*, (Manchester University Press), 1975, pp. 153-178.

[74] For the impact of the famine see, Holcroft, Fred, *The Lancashire Cotton Famine around Leigh*, (Leigh Local History Society), 2003, Peters, Lorraine, 'Paisley and the cotton famine of 1862-1863', *Scottish Economic & Social History*, Vol. 21, (2001), pp. 121-139, Henderson, W. O., 'The cotton famine in Scotland and the relief of distress, 1862-64', *Scottish Historical Review*, Vol. 30, (1951), pp. 154-164, and Hall, Rosalind, 'A poor cotton weyver: poverty and the cotton famine in Clitheroe', *Social History*, Vol. 28, (2003), pp. 227-250. See below, pp. 288-289.

[75] Tanner, Andrea, 'The casual poor and the City of London Poor Law Union, 1837-1869', *Historical Journal*, Vol. 42, (1999), pp. 183-206.

[76] Hollingshead, John, *Ragged London in 1861*, (Smith, Elder & Co.), 1861, p. 244.

Regulation Order. However, local Guardians refused to force the respectable unemployed to perform demeaning work tasks in the company of idle and dissolute paupers. They paid out small weekly allowances of between 1s and 2s per head on the assumption that this meagre non-pauperising sum would be augmented from other sources, short-time earnings, income from other members of the family or charitable aid.

After 1865, Lancashire operatives began to benefit from the mid-Victorian boom but others were less fortunate. Workers in the East End were hit hard by the crisis of 1866-1868, the result of an unfortunate conjunction of circumstances. The shipbuilding industry was dependent on government favour and foreign orders but this collapsed after the banking failures of 1866, a financial panic that brought an end to the boom in railway and building construction. The winter of 1866-1867 was extremely harsh and was accompanied by high food prices and the return of cholera. This added to the hardship and caused a breakdown of the seasonal economic equilibrium. The overall effect was to augment the casual labour problem.

Working-class real wages rose dramatically from the mid-1870s to the mid-1890s, while unemployment remained close to the levels of the mid-Victorian boom. [77] The decisive factor in improved living standards was not money wages, even though they continued upwards, but the dramatic fall in food prices that accounted for much of the working-class budget. Prices tumbled by over 40 per cent, drawing real wages up in the most substantial and sustained increase of the nineteenth century. Allowing for unemployment, the real wages of the average urban worker stood some 60 per cent higher in 1900 than in 1860. [78]

There was considerable diversity in living standards. The advance in living standards was not evenly spread. All types of workers had to endure economic fluctuations of one kind or another, not least in the troughs in the economy in 1878-1879, 1884-1887 and 1892-1893, but their severity diverged markedly. Shipbuilding felt the full impact of the world trade depression. There was an oversupply

---

[77] Saul, S. B., *The Myth of the Great Depression 1873-1896*, (Macmillan), second edition, 1988, summarises research.

[78] Ibid, Feinstein, C. H., 'What really happened to real wages?: trends in wages, prices, and productivity in the United Kingdom, 1880-1913', and 'New estimates of average earnings in the United Kingdom, 1880-1913', *Economic History Review*, Vol. 43, (1990), pp. 595-632, and Gourvish, T. R., 'The standard of living 1890-1914', in O'Day, Alan (ed.), *The Edwardian age: conflict and stability 1900-1914*, (Macmillan), 1979, pp. 13-34.

of ships in the early 1870s and stockpiling was not an option during the depression. Over 20 per cent boilermakers and shipbuilders earned 40s or more in the early-twentieth century, the income available for consumption was substantially less than these wages suggest. At times of full employment, skilled workers paid off debts incurred during the last spell of unemployment and saved for the next interruption in earnings. Workers in the building trades were subject to a different rhythm, longer than the five to seven year trade and investment cycle experienced in capital goods industries. Swings in the building industry lasted twenty years or more: from a peak in 1876, earnings and work levels were reduced until the mid-1890s, the start of the next boom that reached a double peak in 1898 and 1903. During booms, full employed builders' labourers were economically independent and were able to live above the poverty line without supplementary income. Within the long cycles, building activity remained at the mercy of the weather, with a seasonal trough from November to February pushing those without savings back into poverty.

Winter remained a slack season in many other trades, bringing hardship to the casually employed in the docks, on the streets and in the sweatshops. This was particularly evident when trade was depressed and, in 1879 and 1886, led the unemployed to riot. Charles Booth's survey found that it was the irregularity of work rather than low rates of pay that accounted for working-class impoverishment. [79] Employment in the clothing trades was still seasonal and sweated. Female workers in the cheap 'slop' end of the market in the London tailoring trade worked no more than two and a half days a week at a daily rate of 2s 6d to 4s for machinists and 1s 6d to 3s 6d for button-holers. Wages were higher in the West End bespoke trade. Up to 30s per week was paid during brisk periods especially during the 'season' but milliners and dressmakers and tailoresses were frequently driven into prostitution during the slack season returning to the shops with the advent of the new season's trade. Morals, contemporaries observed, fluctuated with trade. [80]

---

[79] For Booth's residuum, see, Welshman, John, *Underclass: A History of the Excluded, 1880-2000*, (Continuum International Publishing Group), 2006, pp. 1-44.
[80] The phrase originated in Sherwell, Arthur, *Life in West London*, (Methuen), 1897, p. 146.

Working-class women in the economy

Between 1780 and 1914 there were significant and radical changes in many areas of British economic and social life. [81] The critical question is whether there were parallel changes in the world of women's work. In the first half of the nineteenth century, the main employment open to women in Britain were in agriculture, domestic service, dressmaking and textile manufacture. After 1860, however, young women began to enter previously all-male areas like medicine, pharmacy, librarianship, the civil service, clerical work and hairdressing, or areas previously restricted to older women like nursing, retail work and primary school teaching. There was a sexual division of labour and, for the most part, women did 'women's work' defined in terms of low wages. For example, in the Glasgow tailoring industry in the 1890s, men were paid 3/6d and women 9d for making the same garment.

Women had a reproductive rather than a productive role and as reproductive work was unpaid, society regarded it as having no economic value. This perception was translated into the labour market and a gender hierarchy of labour developed whereby women's work was given a lower social and economic value than that of men. The sexual division of labour split the unity of the working-classes by gender and often the enmity between the two groups was seen in trade union activity. [82] Women were also regarded as a cheap reserve pool of labour that could be brought in and out of the workforce to suit the requirements of capital and/or the state. Finally, the Industrial Revolution brought about a decisive separation between home and work. In pre-industrial society women were engaged in production at home. The way femininity was defined in the first half of the nineteenth century blinded most employers in the new industries to the suitability of young female labour. Industrialisation shifted large areas of production into factories or workshops and many women became factory workers or 'sweated labour'. [83] Cheap labour is a fundamental element of the capitalist mode of production and female labour was and is cheap labour.

---

[81] I have explored this issue in greater detail in my *Sex, Work and Politics: Women in Britain, 1830-1918*, (Authoring History), 2012, pp. 75-122.

[82] See, Pedersen, J. S., 'Victorian liberal feminism and the 'idea' of work', in Cowman, Krista, and Jackson, Louise A., (eds.), *Women and work culture: Britain c. 1850- 1950*, (Ashgate), 2005, pp. 27-47.

[83] Hewitt, Margaret, *Wives and Mothers in Victorian Industry*, (Greenwood Press), 1958, is useful for information. Ibid, Bythell, D., *The Sweated Trades: Outwork in Nineteenth Century Britain*, is the standard work while Pennington, Shelley, and Westover, Belinda, *A Hidden Workforce:*

Many aspects of women's work were controversial. Women, single, married or widowed had always worked. [84] However, by the mid-nineteenth century, working wives and mothers were often regarded especially by middle-class commentators as unnatural, immoral and inadequate homemakers and parents. These criticisms arose from contemporary assumptions about women's work and about the inherent nature of women themselves. The problem is that these assumptions were not always clearly expressed, were ambivalent and contradictory and not universally shared. It is clear that the upper and middle-class critics of working-class women did not object to work as such. Most objections arose from the location of work and when women were seen working away from their own, or someone else's home what contemporaries regarded as their proper sphere.

Many women saw paid work, not as an alternative to housework, but as a way of enabling them better to fulfil their duty as wives, mothers and homemakers. In general, however, working-class women did not regard full-time paid work as something they would undertake all their adult lives. Married women who, for financial reasons, were compelled to work rarely continued to work when the financial crisis had ended. It was poverty that drove many working-class women into wage-earning work and it was widespread poverty that to some extent helps to explain men's defensive attitude against women's work. E. H. Hunt wrote of the period 1850-1914:

> Men believed that a limited amount of work was available and suspected that allowing women to share work would cause some families to be without pay as a consequence of other families taking more than their fair share. [85]

Homeworkers in England 1850-1985, (Macmillan), 1989, examines a specific area.

[84] Useful studies of working women writing and speaking for themselves include: Burnett, John, (ed.), *Useful Toil: Autobiographies of Work People from the 1820s to the 1920s*, (Routledge), 1994, Chew, Doris Nield, *Ada Nield Chew: The Life and Writings of a Working Woman,* (Virago), 1982, Black, Clementina, *Married Women's Work Being the Report of an Enquiry undertaken by the Women's Industrial Council*, (G. Bell and Sons, Ltd.), 1915, especially for rural work and charwomen and Reeves, Maud Pember, *Round About a Pound a Week*, (G. Bell and Sons, Ltd.), 1913, (Virago), 1979, a survey of families living on an income of 18-26 shillings a week in Lambeth, south London carried out by the Fabian Society's Women's Group.

[85] Hunt, E. H., *British Labour History 1815-1914*, (Weidenfeld), 1981, p. 24.

This confusion between private and public spheres can be seen in a variety of ways such as women taking in lodgers or selling food from their back kitchens or acting as a domestic servant. For instance, in Dunstable in the 1841 Census, there were 332 lodgers out of a total population of 2,582 people. All were female and most were concerned with the seasonal straw plaiting or hatting industry providing important income for householders. For working-class women, there could be no clear distinction between the public and private spheres, whatever they would have ideally liked.

Women's work

The notions of 'a woman's job' and 'a woman's rate' were regarded by employers, trade unions and by women workers themselves as a 'natural' phenomenon throughout this period. Its consequence was low pay and a sexual division of labour leading to segregation. Patterns of sexual segregation were by no means fixed throughout the country. Brick-making was a woman's trade in the Black Country where men worked in ironworks and coalpits. In Lancashire where women worked in cotton and where openings for men were scarce, it was a male preserve. It was, however, rare not to see a clear dividing line between women and men's jobs within occupations and between women and men's processes with women working in lower grade occupations for lower wages.[86]

Women's work commanded a woman's rate, even when they were involved in the same processes as men. In manufacturing occupations, women generally earned about half the average weekly wages of men. Only in textiles did women earn significantly above 50 per cent of male earnings. New methods of wage payment introduced in the late-nineteenth and early-twentieth centuries reinforced the idea of a woman's rate. Women were more often paid by piece rate than men. They also found their rates lowered or they earned 'too much'. Non-manual workers generally earned a higher percentage of the average male earnings: women shop assistants earned about 65 per cent and women teachers 75 per cent their male colleagues. In all-female occupations, women often did worst of all. Nurses were often paid little more than domestic servants.[87] Indeed their pay was actually lowered to encourage middle-class applicants who did not

---

[86] Bradley, Harriet, *Men's Work, Women's Work*, (Polity), 1989, is a useful survey and critique of the available research material on the sexual division of labour and contains valuable case studies of a variety of occupations.

[87] Sweet, Helen M., 'Establishing Connections, Restoring Relationships: Exploring the Historiography of Nursing in Britain', *Gender & History*, Vol. 19, (2007), pp. 565-580.

need the money. Middle-class parents were roundly condemned by feminists for allowing their daughters to work for pocket money because they considered it to be more respectable and genteel. Theirs was voluntary work rather than real work.

Both employers and male trade unionists denied women access to the means of acquiring real skills by their exclusion from training and apprenticeship programmes. This pattern of male dominance and control at the workplace must be related to the power dynamics within the family. It has been suggested that male dominance over the pre-industrial family work unit and the practice of sexually segregating tasks was carried over into the factory when the workplace separated from the home. The boundary between men's and women's work was defended in the face of technological change, which threatened to blur the distinction between sexual boundaries, by means of union exclusiveness and the control skilled men managed to exert over apprenticeship and via their power to subcontract work. The conclusions reached as to what was suitable work for women differed from area to area and between social classes but male workers, employers, government and women workers themselves largely shared it.

There are difficulties defining the 'working-classes' but generally the term is used to cover women who worked with their hands, who were paid wages, not salaries, and who did not employ other people; also, and most importantly, the wives and daughters of men who fitted this description. Women worked full-time or part-time either outside the home in a workshop or factory or on the land or worked in their own homes or in other people's. However, a very large numbers of women worked full-time in the home for no wages at all. A contrast was made between 'real' work and work in the home which, since it has never been paid, was somehow assumed not to be 'real' work at all and consequently had become devalued in the eyes of many men and women. Working wives and mothers were often regarded as unnatural, unfeminine, immoral and inadequate homemakers and parents. Unmarried women were also criticised. They were attacked by male workers who feared the loss of work but who wrote petitions full of apparent concern for women and their children. Men also believed that a limited amount of work was available and suspected that allowing women to share work would cause some families to be without pay as a result of other families taking more than their fair share.

Was Pinchbeck right?

To what extent were changes in the nature of work, especially the development of the factory system, significant in allowing women into the labour market as independent wage earners? [88] Favourably reviewed when published in 1930, it was not until the 1980s that Pinckbeck's *Women Workers in the Industrial Revolution* received greater attention when it earned the valid if unenviable reputation as a 'classic text'. Rendall claims that 'Pinchbeck's work is still of great importance, and remains a 'major survey of the impact of industrialisation on women workers in Britain.'[89] Many works on women's history begin with a reference to Pinchbeck. Bythell, for instance, contrasts Pinchbeck's optimistic view of women's opportunities to Eric Richards' more pessimistic view. [90]

Pinchbeck argued that economic changes between 1750 and 1850 transformed women's employment opportunities and made women better off. Initially women suffered from declining employment opportunities but after 1800, there was an increase in the availability of employment outside the home, improving women's status and conditions and acting as a vital element in the development of the notion of the 'family wage'. Pinchbeck saw the opportunity to specialise in housework as a privilege and the withdrawal of some married women from the labour force as an improvement. Noting that many women lost their economic independence, she considered the gains to be sufficient to make up for this loss. Noting the withdrawal of farmers' wives from productive employment, she claimed:

> In the change she sacrificed her former economic independence according to the extent to which she ceased to manage her household and

---

[88] The classic works are Pinchbeck, Ivy, *Women Workers in the Industrial Revolution*, (Routledge), 1930, reprinted (Virago), 1985, and ibid, Drake, B., *Women in Trade Unions,*. For working women, see Sharpe, Pamela, *Adapting to Capitalism: Working Women in the English Economy, 1700-1850*, (Palgrave), 2000, Roberts, E., *Women's Work 1840-1940*, (Macmillan), 1987, Richards, E., 'Women in the British Economy since 1700', *History*, Vol. 59, (1974), pp. 337-357, and Rose, S., *Limited Livelihoods: Class and Gender in Nineteenth Century England*, (Routledge), 1992. Burnette, Joyce, *Gender, Work and Wages in Industrial Revolution Britain*, (Cambridge University Press), 2008, is an important revisionist study that considers gender and wages in relation to market forces. John, A. V., (ed.), *Unequal Opportunities: Women's Employment in England 1800-1950*, (Basil Blackwell), 1986, is a useful collection of papers.
[89] Rendall, Jane, *Women in an Industrializing Society: England 1750-1880*, (Blackwell), 1991, p. 7.
[90] Bythell, Duncan, 'Women in the Work Force', in O'Brien, Patrick, and Quinault, Roland, (eds.), *The Industrial Revolution and British Society*, (Cambridge University Press), 1993, pp. 31-54.

contributed to the wealth of her family, but for her, the new conditions meant an advance in the social scale and did not entail any material hardship. [91]

For Pinchbeck, the move toward a 'family wage' allowed men to support their families, allowed wives to withdraw from the labour force and this was a clear advance.

Women who remained in the labour force were better off in 1850. Pinchbeck noted that, while contemporaries thought factory conditions were bad, conditions were actually better than those in alternative employments in domestic industry. Women entering factories did not leave behind ideal circumstances, but domestic industries with low pay and poor working conditions. Pinchbeck concluded:

...the Industrial Revolution has on the whole proved beneficial to women. It has resulted in greater leisure for women in the home and has relieved them from the drudgery and monotony that characterised much of the hand labour previously performed in connection with industrial work under the domestic system. For the woman workers outside the home it has resulted in better conditions, a greater variety of openings and an improved status. [92]

Pinchbeck relied on non-quantitative sources to describe patterns and trends in women's work and later historians using statistical analysis generally agree with her descriptions. Horrell and Humphries argue that there was a downward trend in female labour force participation throughout the first half of the nineteenth century leading them to conclude that 'Sixty-five years on we find that our evidence largely supports Pinchbeck's views.' [93] Other historians support Pinchbeck's claims. Snell concludes that farmers hired fewer workers as annual servants in the early-nineteenth century, supporting Pinchbeck's assertion that 'the custom of employing annual servants who lived in the farm declined in favour of day labourers who were responsible for their own board and lodging'. [94] He also confirmed Pinchbeck's observation that women were apprenticed to a wide variety of trades. [95] Investigating the employment of day-labourers,

---

[91] Ibid, Pinchbeck, Ivy, *Women Workers in the Industrial Revolution*, p. 42.
[92] Ibid, Pinchbeck, Ivy, *Women Workers in the Industrial Revolution*, p. 4.
[93] Horrell, Sara, and Humphries, Jane, 'Women's Labour Force Participation and the Transition to the Male-breadwinner Family, 1790-1865', *Economic History Review*, Vol. 48 (1995), pp. 89-117, at p. 113.
[94] Ibid, Pinchbeck, Ivy, *Women Workers in the Industrial Revolution*, p. 37.
[95] Ibid, Snell, K., *Annals of the Labouring Poor: Social Change and Agrarian England 1660-1900*, 270-319.

Burnette found that the patterns of agricultural female employment at a farm near Sheffield coincided with what Pinchbeck described: declining female employment between 1815 and 1834 followed by increasing female employment.[96]

Pinchbeck has not been without her critics. She concluded that the Industrial Revolution made women better off, something Rendall argues was 'unduly optimistic' and other historians saw this period as one during which women lost rather than gained.[97] The notion that the Industrial Revolution increased the participation of women in general outside the home is difficult to sustain. Davidoff and Hall noted that 'the loss of opportunities to earn increased the dominance of marriage as the only survival route for middle-class women.'[98] Levels of female activity varied according to area and occupation. In the north-eastern coalfields, women ceased to work underground in the eighteenth century and none had worked below ground in Staffordshire, Shropshire, Leicestershire and Derbyshire for some time before it was banned in the Mines Act of 1842.[99] The wives and daughters of migrant Scottish farmers astonished farmers in East Anglia in the 1880s by doing work that had been done exclusively by men there for almost a century. But few women had sufficient income to make themselves independent of either their parents or husbands. Contemporaries may have been impressed by the 'freedom' of the lasses of the mill towns who secured a reputation for flashy dressing and an undeserved one for sexual promiscuity but they were atypical. In 1851, domestic service accounted for 37.3 per cent of female occupations aged 15 or over, textiles 18.5 per cent, dressmaking 18 per cent and farming 7.7 per cent. Most of these occurred in the home where constraints on emancipation were very real and where women's wages were at a level that was assumed to be supplementary.[100]

---

[96] Burnette, Joyce, 'Laborers at the Oakes: Changes in the Demand for Female Day-Labourers at a Farm near Sheffield during the Agricultural Revolution', *Journal of Economic History*, Vol. 59, (1999), pp. 41-67.
[97] Ibid, Rendall, Jane, *Women in an Industrializing Society: England 1750-1880*, p. 7.
[98] Davidoff, Leonore and Hall, Catherine, *Family fortunes: men and women of the English middle class 1780-1850*, (Hutchinson), 1987, p. 273.
[99] John, A. V., *By the Sweat of their Brow: Woman Workers at Victorian Coalmines*, (Croom Helm), 1980, pp. 19-35.
[100] Mark-Lawson, Jane, and Witz, Anne, 'From 'family labour' to 'family wages'? The case of women's labour in nineteenth-century coalmining', *Social History*, Vol. 13, (1988), pp. 151-174, and Horrell, Sara, and Humphries, Jane, 'The Origins and Expansion of the Male Breadwinner Family: The Case of Nineteenth-Century Britain', in Janssens, Angélique,

Male exclusiveness largely explains why changes in social attitudes to women's employment had remained largely unaltered by 1850. Traditionally, manufacturing skill had been largely associated with men and this had created a sense of male solidarity that extended beyond the workplace into community and home. Men's struggles to maintain their skilled place in the workforce against machinery and against the encroachment of unskilled women was an important part of their efforts to maintain their social status within the community and their families. This patriarchal ideology was used to justify keeping women away from the new technology, as in a petition from the Staffordshire potters in 1845:

> To maidens, mothers and wives we say machinery is your deadliest enemy...It will destroy your natural claims to home and domestic duties....[101]

It also limited men's incomes, as cotton spinner pleaded in 1824:

> The women, in nine cases out of ten, have only themselves to support, while the men generally have families...The women can afford their labour for less than men.... Keep them at home to look after their families. [102]

These contemporary criticisms of working women were based on an ideological consideration of a proper women's sphere, not on an investigation of actual working conditions. With the exception of skilled artisans, whose status generally ensured an income sufficient to support a wife and family, most women in the working-classes worked not merely to 'top up' the family budget but to ensure basic levels of family subsistence.

Identifying participation

The 1851 Census suggests that just over a quarter of the female population--some 2.8 million out of 10.6 million--were at work and that women made up 30.2 per cent of the country's labour force. [103] These figures, however, suggest that female participation in the labour force was low but these figures are misleading. [104] More

---

(ed.), *The Rise and Decline of the Male Breadwinner Family?* (Cambridge University Press), 1998, pp. 25-64.
[101] Cit, ibid, Drake, Barbara, *Women in Trade Unions*, p. 6.
[102] *Manchester Guardian*, 20 November 1824.
[103] Mitchell, B. R., *Abstract of British Historical Statistics*, (Cambridge University Press), 1962, p. 60.
[104] Enumerators did not always clearly distinguish between the terms 'housekeeper' and 'housewife': see, Higgs, Edward, 'Domestic Service and

women were actually employed than are listed in the census, possibly by as much as a third. Domestic service, the textile trade and the clothing trades accounted for 80 per cent of all women in recorded occupations in 1851. By contrast, the number of women in agriculture halved between 1851 and 1881 and there was a new and expanding category of professional occupations and subordinate offices. Most other occupations employed few women, though at a regional level there were still significant numbers in the metal trades, in food and drink manufacture and also in printing and stationery work.

The proportion of the female labour force remained remarkably constant between the 1870s and the 1910s. Between 1871 and 1914, women were concentrated in certain 'women's jobs'.[105] In 1881, four main occupations accounted for 76 per cent of employed working-class women and this changed only slightly before 1914. When these figures are broken down by region and occupation, it is apparent that participation rates varied considerably over the country. The proportion was over a third in Lancashire, Nottingham, Leicestershire, Bedfordshire and Buckinghamshire but fell to less than one-fifth in Northumberland, Durham, Lincolnshire, Cambridgeshire, Monmouth and Kent. Such disparities were not simply reflections of a particular age-structure because women's participation in work varied greatly even for the 15-24 age-group whose members were mostly unmarried and therefore notionally available for work.

Agriculture accounted for 12 per cent of women workers in the 1840s, but had already ceased to be a major employer of women by 1881.[106] The decline in the number of women involved after 1861 reflects growing mechanisation but the census figures neglect the seasonal nature of much of the work. In nineteenth-century England, women worked on farms at many different tasks and frequently did laborious, repetitive work in the fields. In the 1860s, this labour was defined as unfeminine by the middle-class and women who did it were frequently described as unsexed and immoral. Working-class

---

Household Production', in John, Angela V., (ed.), *Unequal Opportunities: Women's Employment in England 1800-1950*, (Basil Blackwell), 1986, pp. 125-150, and John, Angela V., 'Women, Occupations and Work in the Nineteenth Century Censuses', *History Workshop*, Vol. 23, (1987), pp. 59-80.

[105] Bailey, Timothy J., and Roy E., 'Women's work in census and survey, 1911-1931', *Economic History Review*, second series, Vol. 54, (2001), pp. 87-107

[106] Verdon, Nicola, *Rural women workers in nineteenth-century England: gender, work and wages*, (Boydell), 2002, is essential.

radicals took up and adopted this imagery in order to demand a male breadwinning wage when they fought their employers. However, the women also directly challenged their employers' authority and were frequently at odds with the development of that new male working-class respectability which stressed women's role as wives and mothers. Sayer looks at the resistances of the field women and the response to their action by the radical, mainstream and feminist press of the second half of the nineteenth century and highlights the complex relationship between class and gender. [107] Increasing numbers of young rural women went into domestic service, where they were better paid, £12-£15 per year rather than £10 as a fieldworker and were also given board and lodgings.

Domestic service was the most common occupation for working-class girls and women throughout this period. [108] Between 1851 and 1871, there was an increase in the numbers employed rising from 9.8 to 12.8 per cent of the total female population in England and Wales. After 1871, there was a slight decline down to 11.1 per cent by 1911. It has been frequently stated that domestic servants were usually country girls who has few alternative forms of work and certainly many country girls did follow this route. The vast majority of domestic servants had in common a heavy workload but they did not all share the same social status. All servants were affected by the social status of their employers and within a household there were considerable differences in power of influence of, for example, the housekeeper or the kitchen maid and there were also male and female status hierarchies involved. [109] By 1900, there were increasing complaints about the shortage of servants from members of the middle- and upper-classes. It was not simply a matter of wages since these increased steadily during the second half of the nineteenth century. The wages still appeared to be low: average annual wages for 1907 were £19 10s for general servants and £26 8s for parlour maids. Despite this, an increasing number of women regarded the wages as insufficient compensation for what were regarded as long hours, the hard physical effort and lack of independence. There was

---

[107] Sayer, Karen 'Field-faring women: the resistance of women who worked in the fields of nineteenth-century England', *Women's History Review*, Vol. 2, (2), (1993), pp. 185-198.

[108] McBride, Theresa, *The Domestic Revolution: The Modernization of Household Service in England and France 1820-1920*, (Croom Helm), 1976, is a valuable comparative work. Horn, Pamela, *The Rise and Fall of the Victorian Servant*, (Gill & Macmillan), 1975, is an important work on the subject.

[109] Higgs, E., 'Domestic Servants and Households in Victorian England', *Social History*, Vol. 8, (1983), pp. 203-210.

also an increase in alternative employment. While town girls preferred to have different employment to domestic service, for country girls it represented an easily available and acceptable occupation.

Textile workers increased in number throughout the period especially in the cotton industry in England. This expansion was accompanied by the steady decline of the Scottish cotton industry as it became more concentrated in Lancashire. In the Lancashire industry women had more equality with men than on most other industries. The only major process from which they were excluded was mule-spinning. Women were also excluded from being tacklers or overlookers, the person in charge of a group of weavers. Women weavers were paid well compared with most other women workers. Oral evidence suggests that they could and did earn more than unskilled men in other areas of employment and a good woman weaver could earn as much as her male counterpart. However, in most mills this was not the case and the aggregated figures show that women weavers earned less than men.

The tendency for women working in urban trades was to see their condition decline after 1830 and the sweated trades expanded. The drive towards increasing mass production in urban trades forced male skilled craftsmen to defend their position as their livelihood was threatened. The outcome for most women workers in these trades could only be exclusion from skilled work and employment in subdivided or unskilled work at lower, often very low, wages. In the printing industry, women were effectively excluded by 1880. By contrast women bookbinders preserved their skill and status, though also their low wages relative to skilled men, until changes in the 1880s. By the 1850s, except in large cities like Manchester and Leeds, homework had disappeared from the North of England. In the Midlands and the South, however, the pattern was very different. For instance, in Birmingham many women made nails and chains in sheds attached to their homes; Northampton women made boots and shoes. One of the largest concentrations of homeworkers was in London where women worked in the various garment trades, a situation aided by the marketing of the sewing machine after 1851.

In trying to assess the number of working women during this period, we run up against a number of confusing problems. The change of work-base from the home to the factory or workshop led to changing, though never fully clarified definitions of the meaning of 'work', 'employment' and 'occupation'. In effect, 'work' became shorthand for waged work. Yet formal employment was a minority theme in the social history of working-class women in this period. When the Census of 1881 excluded unpaid household work as a category of gainful employment, there was a dramatic drop in the female work rate figure from around 98 per cent (and almost the same as the work rate for men) to 42 per cent. In reality, however, working-class women worked in large numbers and often for a considerable proportion of their lives in both paid and unpaid position. This, despite the howls of middle-class protest raised periodically in parliament and in the press against their involvement in the world of work with their consequent neglect of husband, family and home.

Unemployment

It is difficult to superimpose twenty-first century notions of unemployment on the late-eighteenth and nineteenth century labour market. There are no statistics, national or otherwise. Patterns of work were very diverse, varying between different industries and trades but also within the same industry in different parts of the country. [110] The enormous variation in the nature of waged work is not the only difficulty. Industrialisation separated work from home and this reduced the wage-earning capacity of married women who were increasingly tied down by household duties. The age limits of the working population were determined simply by physical capacity. Statutory attempts to impose restrictions on the use of child labour in the 1830s and 1840s initially proved unsuccessful. Both employers and parents colluded in their evasion, the former because child labour was cheap and more easily disciplined; the latter because children's earnings were vital in the constant battle against poverty. [111] Larger families tended to be poorer families and family size grew during the first half of the century.

Victorian England did not recognise a common age of retirement from working life that was determined by the requirements

---

[110] On this issue see, Whiteside, Noel, *Bad Times: Unemployment in British Social and Political History*, (Faber), 1991, and Burnett, John, *Idle hands: experience of unemployment, 1790-1990*, (Routledge), 1994.

[111] For the debate on the effectiveness of enforcement see, Peacock, A. E., 'The successful prosecution of the Factory Acts, 1833-55', *Economic History Review*, second series, Vol. 37, (1984), pp. 197-210, Nardinelli, C., 'The successful prosecution of the Factory Acts: a suggested explanation', *Economic History Review*, second series, Vol. 38, (1985), pp. 428-430, and Bartrip, Peter W. J., 'Success or failure? The prosecution of the early Factory Acts', *Economic History Review*, second series, Vol. 38, (1985), pp. 423-427.

of the job and the physical capacity of the worker. [112] Work was overwhelmingly manual and premium was placed on physical strength and stamina that faded with age, especially when accompanied by a poor diet consequent on low earnings and as a result, the age at which workers 'retired' varied considerably. In the 1840s, Engels observed how working conditions in mines bred chronic illness and that miners needed a high level of physical fitness and were forced to stop work at 35-45 rarely living beyond 50. [113] At the same time, Mayhew documented the case of a 70 year old London needlewoman who was refused help by the relieving officer because she was considered fit to earn her own living. [114] In all branches of the labour market, advancing years spelt reduced earnings and irregular work and, if death did not intervene, eventual reliance on children, charity or the poor law. [115]

No respectable worker or his family would turn to the Poor Law in time of distress except when absolutely essential to survival. [116] By 1850, the name 'pauper' carried a social stigma second only to that of the convicted criminal. This explains the huge expansion of clubs, societies and associations that collected contributions from working people in order to help them cope in the event of a crisis. [117] Insurance

---

[112] See, for instance, Goose, Nigel, 'Farm service, seasonal unemployment and casual labour in mid-nineteenth-century England', *Agricultural History Review*, Vol. 54, (2006), pp. 274-303, focuses of Hertfordshire.

[113] Ibid, Engels, Frederick, *The condition of the working class in England*, pp. 247-262.

[114] Mayhew, Henry, *London Labour and the London Poor: The Condition and Earnings of Those that will work, cannot work, and will not work*, (George Woodfall and Son), 1851, Vol. 1, p. 404. Millinery and dressmaking constituted the higher end of female employment with the needle; they were 'respectable' occupations for young women from middle-class or lower middle-class families. The number of women involved in dressmaking alone in the early 1840s was estimated to be 15,000: House of Commons, *Reports from Commissioners: Children's Employment, Trade and Manufactures*, Sessional Papers, Vol. XIV, (1843), p. 555.

[115] Strange, Julie-Marie, 'Only a pauper whom nobody owns: reassessing the pauper grave c. 1880-1914', *Past & Present*, Vol. 178, (2003), pp. 148-175.

[116] Boot, H. M., 'Unemployment and Poor Law relief in Manchester, 1845-1850', *Social History*, Vol. 15, (1990), pp. 217-228, provides a valuable local study.

[117] Fisk, Audrey, *Mutual self-help in southern England, 1850-1912*, (Foresters Heritage Trust), 2006, and ibid, Cordery, Simon, *British friendly societies, 1750-1914*, Gorsky, Martin, 'Friendly society health insurance in nineteenth-century England', in Gorsky, Martin, and Sheard, Sally, (eds.), *Financing medicine: the British experience since 1750*, (Routledge), 2006,

against unemployment was less common and was largely confined to skilled men in printing, construction, engineering, metal-working, shipbuilding and some of the older crafts in leather-working, bookbinding and furniture-making. It operated through trade unions and was principally designed to prevent union men being forced to work below the recognised rate when desperate for want of work. In other sectors of the economy, notably mining and textiles, unions negotiated work-sharing schemes as an alternative form of protection against the threat of recession. In this way, the negotiation of working practices was designed to protect jobs as well as maintain wages. [118]

By 1906, unions that did provide help for those out of work covered about a million workers, but did not distinguish very clearly between those idle due to strikes and those unemployed because of a depression in trade. For the vast majority of the workforce there was no automatic support to fall back on when recession struck and, in trying to maintain their self-esteem, resorted to various things. Credit played a major role within working-class families and loans were obtained from money-menders or relatives and neighbours on the understanding that debts would be repaid when times were not so hard. [119] The local pawnshop was a familiar resort of many who pledged items on Monday and redeemed them on Friday when (and if) the wages arrived. The unemployment of the husband frequently pushed the wife into taking in more washing, more cleaning, child-minding and sewing and, in the last resort, into prostitution in order to supplement dwindling family resources. Working-class households survived on a precarious structure of credit that tended to collapse when employment was scarce, debts mounted, the rent was unpaid and creditors at the door. By various strategies, the families of unskilled labourers 'got by' most of the time, but without any security outside the informal help of family or friends. The only other option for the unemployed was migration from depressed to prosperous

---

pp. 147-164, and Alborn, Timothy L., 'Senses of belonging: the politics of working-class insurance in Britain, 1880-1914', *Journal of Modern History*, Vol. 73, (2001), pp. 561-602.

[118] Hatton, Timothy J., 'Unemployment and the labour market, 1870-1939', in ibid, Floud, Roderick, and Johnson, Paul A., (eds.), *The Cambridge economic history of modern Britain, Vol. 2: economic maturity, 1860-1939*, pp. 344-373, and Boyer, George R., and Hatton, Timothy J., 'New estimates of British unemployment, 1870-1913', *Journal of Economic History*, Vol. 62, (2002), pp. 643-675.

[119] Finn, Margot C., *The character of credit: personal debt in English culture, 1740-1914*, (Cambridge University Press), 2003, pp. 278-315, and O'Connell, Sean, *Credit and Community: Working-Class Debt in the UK since 1880*, (Oxford University Press), 2009.

areas within Britain or emigration to colonies such as Canada, New Zealand and South Africa where labour was still scarce. Emigration, whether assisted [120] or not, was an option for the young and skilled since colonies were not prepared to be used as a dumping ground for Britain's surplus labour and colonial governments had as little desire for British paupers as for British convicts. [121]

By the late-nineteenth century, urban expansion concentrated unemployment and underemployment in unprecedented fashion and made social distress more visible. With the migration of the middle-classes and the skilled working-class to the suburbs, those unable to find regular employment were left behind, forming the backbone of an 'inner city' problem. The new visibility of disorganisation in the labour market, at a time of German and American economic expansion, the extension of the vote to most working men in 1884, the growth of trade and labour organisation and the inability of traditional institutions to cope with the situation combined to promote the unemployment question as a key issue in national politics for the first time. [122] It took over twenty years to convert emergency intervention into permanent government policy. [123]

An 'aristocracy of labour'?

In 1870 George Potter, a prominent unionist and radical journalist wrote:

---

[120] Howells, Gary, '"On account of their disreputable characters": parish-assisted emigration from rural England, 1834-1860', *History*, Vol. 88, (2003), pp. 587-605, considers Bedfordshire, Norfolk and Northamptonshire. See also, Haines, R., 'Nineteenth century government-assisted immigrants from the United Kingdom to Australia: schemes, regulations and arrivals 1831-1900, and some vital statistics 1834-1860', *Flinders Occasional Papers in Economic History*, Vol. 3, (1995), pp. 1-171.
[121] See, for example, Richards, Eric, 'How Did Poor People Emigrate from the British Isles to Australia in the Nineteenth Century?' *Journal of British Studies*, Vol. 32, (1993), pp. 250-279, and Gray, Peter, '"Shovelling out your paupers": the British state and Irish famine migration 1846-50', *Patterns of Prejudice*, Vol. 33, (4), (1999), pp. 47-66.
[122] On this issue, see, Harris, José, *Unemployment and Politics: A study in English social policy, 1886-1914*, (Oxford University Press), 1972, Davidson, Roger, *Whitehall and the Labour Problem in late-Victorian and Edwardian Britain: A study in official statistics and social control*, (Routledge), 1985, and Walters, William, *Unemployment and Government: Genealogies of the Social*, (Cambridge University Press), 2000, pp. 12-53.
[123] Gazeley, Ian, and Newell, Andrew, 'Unemployment', in ibid, Crafts, Nicholas F. R., Gazeley, Ian, and Newell, Andrew, (eds.), *Work and pay in twentieth-century Britain*, pp. 225-263.

The working man belonging to the upper-class of his order is a member of the aristocracy of the working-classes. He is a man of some culture, is well read in politics and social history....His self-respect is also well developed. [124]

His view of the 'aristocracy of the working-classes', distinguished from other workers by their way of life, values and attitudes and seen as a moderating influence on the politics of popular protest, is scattered widely through contemporary accounts of the working-class in the third quarter of the nineteenth century. In 1869, for instance:

Labour should be elevated into an aristocracy, and if all mechanics and...An aristocracy of labour would produce merit, virtue, and intelligence...[125]

While, two decades later:

All have reached a certain level of professional skill; they are not chance comers, they form an aristocracy. Like all aristocracies, they have a desire, unintelligent it may be, for exclusiveness and like all aristocracies they form an elite. [126]

How valid are attempts to identify a distinct upper stratum within the working-classes? How far did these divisions affect the militancy and class consciousness of the labour movement in this period? [127]

---

[124] *The Reformer*, 5 November 1870.
[125] Unsworth, William, *Self-culture and Self-reliance, Under God the Means of Self-elevation*, (Elliot Stock), 1869, p. 55.
[126] De Rousiers, Paul, and Herbertson, Fanny Dorothea, *The Labour Question in Britain*, (Macmillan & Co.), 1896, p. 55.
[127] Gray, Robert, *The Aristocracy of Labour in Nineteenth-century Britain c.1850-1914*, (Macmillan), 1981, is an excellent summary of early research on the subject but needs to be read in conjunction with the relevant sections of ibid, Reid, Alastair J., *Social Classes and Social Relations in Britain 1850-1914*, and Lummis, Trevor, *The Labour Aristocracy, 1851-1914*, (Scolar), 1994. See also, Shepherd, M. A., 'The origins and incidence of the term "labour aristocracy"', *Bulletin of the Society for the Study of Labour History*, Vol. 37, (1978), pp. 51-67, Moorhouse, H. F., 'The Marxist theory of the labour aristocracy', *Social History*, Vol. 3, (1978), pp. 61-82, and 'The significance of the labour aristocracy', *Social History*, Vol. 6, (1981), pp. 229-233, and Reid, Alastair J., 'Politics and economics in the formation of the British working class: a response to H. F. Moorhouse', *Social History*, Vol. 3, (1978), pp. 347-361, and McLennan, Gregor, 'The labour aristocracy and 'incorporation': notes on some terms in the social history of the working class', *Social History*, Vol. 6, (1981), pp. 71-81.

Hobsbawm provided the starting-point for the modern debate when he said that there was:

> ...a distinctive upper strata of the working-class, better paid, better treated and generally regarded as more 'respectable' and politically moderate than the mass of the proletariat. [128]

Nineteenth century industry was diverse in terms of mechanisation, scale of operation and subdivision of processes. 'Traditional' unmechanised production, largely unaffected by the processes of industrial change, continued to manufacture individual items for clients. Equally features of the 'craft' division of labour were reproduced in large-scale mechanised production. Economic differences within the working-classes have to be placed in the context of the social and technical organisation of work. [129] The heavy dependence of key sectors of nineteenth century industry on skilled labour can be seen very clearly but does this provide a case for an aristocracy of labour? [130]

Engineering is often regarded as central to the formation of a labour aristocracy.[131] The expansion of the industry was associated with the expansion of skilled employment, much of it highly paid. Skilled engineering workers had been under pressure in the 1840s culminating in the lock-out of 1852. Thereafter, however, the pace of technical change slackened, at least until the 1890s, and there was a spread of techniques from their narrow base in Lancashire and the West Riding. The industry was heavily dependent on the skilled labour of turners and fitters. Management's authority was limited by craft custom and foremen retained their trade affiliations, often

---

[128] See, Hobsbawm, E. J., 'The Labour Aristocracy in Nineteenth-century Britain', in ibid, *Labouring Men: Studies in the History of Labour*, p. 272. See also, Hobsbawm, E. J., 'Artisan or labour aristocrat?', *Economic History Review*, second series, Vol. 37, (1984), pp. 355-372.

[129] Harrison, Royden, and Zeitlin, Jonathan, (eds.), *Divisions of labour: Skilled workers and technological change in nineteenth century England*, (Harvester), 1977, and More, Charles, *Skill and the English working class, 1870-1914*, (Taylor & Francis), 1980, provide the context.

[130] Matsumura, Takao, *The labour aristocracy revisited: the Victorian flint glass makers, 1850-80*, (Manchester University Press), 1983.

[131] Musson, A. E., 'The Engineering Industry' in Church, Roy, (ed.), *The Dynamics of Victorian Business: Problems and Perspectives to the 1870s*, (Routledge), 1980, pp. 87-106, and Saul, S. B., 'The Mechanical Engineering Industries in Britain, 1860-1914', in Supple, Barry, (ed.), *Essays in British Business History*, (Oxford University Press), 1977, pp. 31-48.

belonging to the same craft unions and were only gradually transformed into a distinct supervisory stratum. There were attempts by some employers to respond to new competitive challenges from the 1870s and introduce further technical change but these developments were more marked in some regions than others and the entrenched position of apprentice-trained craftsmen remained intact in many engineering centres. [132]

Building is often cited as a classic case of a 'traditional' sector growing to provide the infrastructure of an industrial-urban society. [133] But, as with other sectors of Victorian industry, a focus on the absence of large-scale mechanisation can obscure important changes in the organisation of work and a resulting growth of specialisation and occupational subdivision. By 1900, wood-working and stone-cutting machines, new materials like concrete and steel and the acute depression were undermining craft controls. The piecemeal application of machines was typical of the changes occurring in labour-intensive crafts in the second half of the century, with effects on the pace of work, the versatility and initiative of skilled labour and the possibility of 'dilution'. The position of building craftsmen depended on their ability to maintain trade boundaries in the face of these pressures. [134]

A number of skilled trades such as building had a close relationship to an expanding urban market with the most skilled employment in the luxury or bespoke end of that market. There may not have been widespread mechanisation but this did not mean that there were no changes in methods of production. In Edinburgh, a major centre of publishing, divisions emerged between the minority of compositors paid on time-rates and a larger group of less regularly employed men paid on piece-rates. [135] In clothing and shoemaking, the use of casuals was more marked, with a substantial sector of sweated labour working at home with no customary or trade union control of wages or conditions. Other urban crafts were more

---

[132] Zeitlin, Jonathan, 'Engineers and compositors: a comparison', in ibid, Harrison, Royden, and Zeitlin, Jonathan, (eds.), *Division of labour: Skilled workers and technological change in nineteenth-century Britain*, pp. 185-250.

[133] Cooney, E. W., 'The Building Industry', in ibid, Church, Roy, (ed.), *The Dynamics of Victorian Business: Problems and Perspectives to the 1870s*, pp. 142-160.

[134] See Crossick, Geoffrey, .The labour aristocracy and its values: a study of mid-Victorian Kentish London', *Victorian Studies*, Vol. 19, (1976), pp. 301-328.

[135] Gray, R. Q., *The Labour Aristocracy in Victorian Edinburgh*, (Oxford University Press), 1976.

successful in retaining some control over the restructuring of the labour process, adapting to and partly shaping changes in the division of labour. Workers in such trades were often employed in very small units with limited application of machines or steam-power. Their security rested on their ability to control changes in the division of labour. [136]

Who were the 'Labour Aristocrats'? Were improvements in conditions restricted to a small upper stratum of 10 per cent of the working-classes? This may, or may not, be a critical issue but it does require some attempt to identify who this group were and what distinguished them from the remainder of the working-class. Hobsbawm mentioned a number of criteria by which to distinguish members of the labour aristocracy:

> First, the level and regularity of a worker's earnings; second, his prospects of social security; third, his conditions of work including the way he was treated by foremen and masters; fourth, his relations with the social strata above and below him; fifth, his general conditions of living; lastly, his prospects of future advancement and those of his children. [137]

His focus is on the persistence of craft methods in many sectors of British industry, the potential bargaining power this afforded to key groups of workers and the significance of 'artisan' cultures and modes of activity in the formation of the working-class.

The debate has, however, centred on issues of work organisation and especially the continuities and discontinuities of industrial development in the early- and mid-nineteenth centuries. While Hobsbawm concentrated on textile workers, the labour aristocracy for writers such as Foster are piece-workers in engineering, spinners in cotton and checkweightmen in mining. [138] All these, he suggests, represent new forms of industrial authority emerging in the 1850s and acted very much as the agents of capital in supervising, 'pacesetting' and disciplining the rest of the workforce. Stedman Jones argues that the transition to a more stable industrial capitalism with an expanding sector of mechanised production involved the adaptation of all parts

---

[136] See, McClelland, Keith, 'Masculinity and the "representative artisan" in Britain, 1850-1880', in Roper, Michael, and Tosh, John, (eds.), *Manful assertions: masculinities in Britain since 1800*, (Routledge), 1991, pp. 74-91.
[137] Ibid, Hobsbawm, E. J., *Labouring Men*, p. 273.
[138] Musson, A. E., 'Class struggle and the labour aristocracy, 1830-60', *Social History*, Vol. 3, (1976), pp. 335-356, and the response Foster, John, 'Some comments on "Class struggle and the labour aristocracy, 1830-60"', *Social History*, Vol. 3, (1976), pp. 357-366.

of the labour force to effective employer control of production.[139] The traditional autonomy of craftsmen was destroyed, but divisions of skills were then re-created and maintained by groups with the necessary bargaining-power. The impact of capitalist development, especially in the nineteenth century, did not simply to destroy skills, but created new forms of skilled labour within which craft methods and traditions could assert themselves. There were attempts to rationalise production by employers but these were hampered by lack of managerial technique and experience as well as by the strength of skilled labour. This gave 'control' to the skilled workers and there were few groups of skilled workers whose position did not involve control of some specialised technique indispensable to their employers and this provided the basis for their bargaining power.

The debate on the labour aristocracy allows four issues to be addressed. Was the labour aristocracy simply a perpetuation of the earlier artisan traditions or was it a consequence of the formation of new skilled groupings within the working-class? This is a question of continuity or discontinuity. The earliest uses of the term 'aristocracy of labour' referred to hierarchies within certain crafts, like coach-making, in the 1830s and 1840s and the labour aristocracy described in the third quarter of the century may represent the expansion of these groups under the favourable conditions of the mid-Victorian boom. What impact did the changing nature of work have on the labour aristocracy? There is no doubt of the cultural importance of traditions drawn from artisan cultures of the 1830s and earlier or of the economic importance of apprenticed skills drawn from these older trades. However, there were newer trades, especially associated with engineering, shipbuilding and the rapid expansion of capital goods that altered the occupational make-up of the working-classes. How willing was the labour aristocracy to adapt to changing economic conditions? The tenacity of craft methods in the older trades did not indicate an absence of adaptation to change. Some trades managed to stabilise their position and exert some control over the processes of mechanisation. Those that failed to do this succumbed to technological unemployment or the casualisation of employment. Finally, the notion of a labour aristocracy is not simply an economic concept. Working-class behaviour and experience was not confined to the workplace and the basis for a cohesive upper stratum within the working-classes can also be sought within local communities. Labour

---

[139] Jones, Gareth Stedman, 'Working-class culture and working-class politics in London, 1870-1900: notes on the remaking of a working class', *Journal of Social History*, Vol. 7, (1974), pp. 460-508, and ibid, *Languages of class: studies in English working class history, 1832-1982*, pp. 179-238.

aristocracy was not simply about 'control' in the workplace but about culture and community, values and life-styles and above all status. The formation of a labour aristocracy or 'artisan elite' drew together men from a range of trades within communities that set them apart from the less advantaged sections of the working-classes.

Conclusions

Class identity was remarkably strong in nineteenth century England, reinforced through networks of collective and associational culture. There are, however, some problems in whether to use the singular or plural form. Some argue that it is misleading and unnecessary to adopt the plural form simply to acknowledge strata of workers differentiated by income, occupations, region or some other variable. This view neglects the gulf that existed between skilled, semi-skilled and unskilled workers between whom there were considerable cultural as well as economic differences.

Workers may well have identified themselves in terms of their common class but there were other concepts than played a significant, perhaps even more important, role. 'Skill' and 'status' were crucial concepts for male workers and the retention of skilled status was an ideal to which all workers aspired. 'Work' was defined narrowly and took little account of unpaid housework. 'Community' increasingly replaced kin as the crucial welfare network for the urban working-classes between 1830 and 1914. Settled and stable, especially after the 1850s, most envisaged a future spent within the narrow confines of the town or city in which they had been brought up, secure in the protection of the customs and mores of a particular district. Communities were not necessarily defined in territorial terms but often by the experience of social interaction among those of similar attitudes, beliefs and interests. The community combined pubs, churches, chapels, co-ops and various special interest groups that were locality-based and served the needs of relatively independent urban villages, delineating districts within which the working-classes moved and married. Men who travelled out of the neighbourhood to work hurried back to their 'local' for a drink, now patronised in preference to the trade pub close to the workplace. Community meant a convivial communality of interests.

There were wide differences within the working-classes but whether either within the workplace or the community there was a clearly identifiable group of working-class 'aristocrats' is still unclear. The working-class or working-classes was marked by its divisions and sub-divisions on the basis of levels of skill, wages, gender, levels of control and so on. This highlights the unsatisfactory nature of any simple division between aristocrats and plebeians, between skilled and unskilled labour or between men and women. Most workers found themselves on complex wage ladders with many steps along which they generally expected to move, in both directions, at different stages of their working lives. [140]

---

[140] Breuilly, John, 'The labour aristocracy in Britain and Germany: a comparison', in Breuilly, John, (ed.), *Labour and Liberalism in 19th-century Europe: essays in comparative history*, (Manchester University Press), 1992, pp. 26-75, provides a valuable perspective.

22 The middle-classes

Who were the 'middle-classes'? [1] George Kitson Clark rightly counselled caution when he pointed out:

> Of course, the general expression 'middle-class' remains useful, as a name for a large section of society.... [but] it is necessary to remember that a belief in the importance and significance of the middle-class in the nineteenth century derives from contemporary opinion.... They do not always say clearly whom they have in mind, and since the possible variants are so great a modern writer should follow them with great caution.... [2]

The middle-classes can be distinguished from the aristocracy and gentry not so much by their income as by the necessity of earning a living, and at the bottom from the working-classes not by their higher income but by their property, however small, represented by stock in trade, tools or by their educational investment in skills or expertise. Yet, the divide that was emerging was not the Marxist division between aristocracy and bourgeoisie but:

> ...a cultural one, between the patrician landowner, banker, lawyer, clergyman or merchant on the one hand and the plebeian tradesman and manufacturer on the other. [3]

---

[1] James, Lawrence, *The middle class: a history*, (Little, Brown), 2006, is a detailed study. Wahrman, Dror, *Imagining the Middle Class. The Political Representation of Class in Britain c.1780-1840*, (Cambridge University Press), 1995, analyses the emergence of middle-class consciousness. Nossiter, T. J., *Influence, Opinion and Political Idioms in Reformed England: Case Studies from the North-East 1832-1874*, (Harvester), 1975 and Crossick, G., and Hauge, H. G., *Shopkeepers and Master Artisans in Nineteenth-Century Europe*, (Methuen), 1984 contain some useful comments on the 'shopocracy'. Ibid, Bourne, J. M., *Patronage and Society in Nineteenth Century England*, is excellent for the changing notion of 'patronage' and its effects on the middle-classes. Crossick, G., (ed.), *The Lower Middle Class in Britain 1870-1914*, (Croom Helm), 1977, is the most useful collection of papers and Anderson, G., *Victorian Clerks*, (Manchester University Press), 1976, deals with one occupational group. See also, Searle, G. R., *Entrepreneurial Politics in Mid-Victorian Britain*, (Oxford University Press), 1993, and *Morality and the Market in Victorian England*, (Oxford University Press), 1998.

[2] Clark, G. Kitson, *The Making of Victorian England*, (Methuen), 1965, p. 96.

[3] Clark, J. C. D., *English Society 1688-1832*, (Cambridge University Press), 1985, p. 71; see also his *The Language of Liberty 1660-1832*, (Cambridge University Press), 1993.

There may have been considerable room for agreement between capital and labour in attacking the political monopoly of the aristocracy, an agreement that was frequently reinforced by shared local, political and religious loyalty. The alliance between capital and labour was, however, often fraught by fears of bourgeois dominance and by suspicion of 'betrayal'. [4] Paradoxically it was often the aristocracy that provided legislative support for the working-classes against opposition from manufacturers and industrialists.

The middle-classes of the mid-nineteenth century were an extremely heterogeneous body embracing at one end bankers and large industrialists with incomes from investment and profits of over £1,000 per year and at the other end small shopkeepers and clerks with annual earnings of under £50. The middle-classes can be divided into two broad groupings. The upper middle-class was divided into two fairly distinct groups: the financiers and merchants of London and the manufacturers of the North and Midlands. The former were generally wealthier, of higher social status and closer to the landed elites than the industrialists. [5] London bankers and City merchants were among the wealthiest people in the country. Most of the largest fortunes, such as those of the Rothschilds, Morrisons, Barings or Sassoons, came from commerce or finance and not from manufacturing and industry. [6] The latter were dominated by the provincial elites, those men and families controlling the growing industrial complex. Factory owners were usually wealthy but not immensely wealthy.[7] By 1880, and perhaps earlier, Britain was as much the 'Clearing House of the World' as the 'Workshop of the World'.

A lower middle-class emerged in the first half of the century and consisted of three main groups: smaller manufacturers, shopkeepers,

---

[4] This can best be seen in the agitation between 1830 and 1832 that led to the Reform Act. Those sections of the working-class that had supported reform got little or nothing. This led to a powerful sense of betrayal that fed into the demands of the Chartists for universal suffrage.

[5] See, Nenadic, S., 'Businessmen, the urban middle classes, and the "dominance" of manufacturers in 19th century Britain', *Economic History Review,* Vol. 44, (1991), pp. 66-85.

[6] On banking and the middle-class, see, Cassis, Y., 'Bankers and English society in the late 19th century' *Economic History Review,* Vol. 38, (1985), pp. 210-229, and *City bankers, 1890-1914,* (Cambridge University Press), 1994, 2009. See also, Camplin, Jamie, *The rise of the plutocrats: wealth and power in Edwardian England,* (Constable), 1978.

[7] Crouzet, François, *The First Industrialists: The Problem of Origins,* (Cambridge University Press), 1985, 2008, pp. 99-115, Howe, A., *The Cotton Masters 1830-1860,* (Oxford University Press), 1984, pp. 50-89.

dealers, milliners, tailors, local brewers; the rapidly expanding ubiquitous 'clerk' in both business and government; and finally, the growing professionals, schoolteachers, railway officials, an emergent managerial class, accountants, pharmacists and engineers. [8] Middle-class 'occupations' grew from 6.5 per cent of the working population in 1851 to 7.8 per cent by 1871. Structural changes towards a larger service sector in the late-Victorian economy resulted in a growth in the number of clerical and administrative employees. [9]

Aware of their 'caste', they maintained an important distinction between themselves as salaried or fee-earning employees and wage-earning manual workers. Dorothy Marshall argues:

> Some of these employments were lucrative, some poorly paid, but the men who engaged in them were united in the conviction that they were socially superior to the manual worker, however skilled. The struggling clerk, who earned less than the expert fine cotton spinner, underlined his superiority by his dress, his speech and his manners. These, and not his income, were what distinguished him from the working-class. [10]

Little had changed when E. M. Forster wrote prosaically of Leonard Bast a clerk:

> The boy, Leonard Bast, stood at the extreme verge of gentility. He was not in the abyss, but he could see it and at times people whom he knew had dropped in and counted no more. He knew that he was poor and would admit it: he would have died sooner than confess any inferiority to the rich.... [11]

While sharing the aspirations and values of the class above them, the lower middle-class was under constant pressure to differentiate itself from the working-classes whose ways of life they rejected but into whose clutches they could easily fall. There was an unresolved tension

---

[8] Crossick, G., 'The Emergence of the Lower Middle Class in Britain: a discussion', in ibid, Crossick, G., (ed.), *The lower middle class in Britain, 1870-1914,* pp. 11-60; Savage, Michael, 'Career mobility and class formation: British banking workers and the lower middle classes', in ibid, Miles, Andrew, and Vincent, David, (eds.), *Building European society: occupational change and social mobility in Europe, 1840-1940,* (Manchester University Press), pp. 196-216.

[9] Anderson, G. I., 'The Social Economy of Late-Victorian Clerks', in ibid, Crossick, G., (ed.), *The lower middle class in Britain, 1870-1914,* pp. 113-133.

[10] Marshall, D., *Industrial England 1776-1851*, (Routledge), 1973, p. 96.

[11] Forster, E. M., *Howards End*, 1910, (Forgotten Books), 1958, p. 42.

between the need to maintain the symbols of status and the constraints of economic reality. [12]

There was an obsession with religious certainty, moral zeal and purity and respectability but above all keeping up appearances at all costs throughout the middle-classes and this led the children and grandchildren of the late-Victorians to accuse them of hypocrisy. [13] But this was not the only or perhaps the most abiding character trait of the middle-classes:

> A person of the middle class appreciates the value of the position he occupies; and he will not marry, if marriage will so impoverish him as to render it necessary to resign his social position. [14]

Their search was for security, comfort and peace of mind and above all for that social acceptance and approval denoted by respectability.[15] These were, as J. F. C. Harrison says:

> ....not perhaps very noble strivings, especially when pursued in a competitive and individualist spirit. Materialism in an undisguised form seldom appears very attractive.... (Yet) in retrospect the years 1890-1914 have come to seem like a golden age of the middle-classes.... It was a basically conservative civilisation, alternately complacent and fearful.... Yet it should not be forgotten that criticism of the middle-class was largely endogenous. The brilliant collection of writers, intellectuals, socialists and feminists who exposed and attacked bourgeois civilisation in the 1880s and 1890s were for the most part themselves raised within it. [16]

Being respectable meant maintaining a reputable facade and encouraged all the hypocrisies highlighted by contemporary social commentators and novelists. There is now a more subtle appreciation

---

[12] Hammerton, A. James, 'The English weakness? Gender, satire and "moral manliness" in the lower middle class, 1870-1920', in Kidd, Alan J., and Nicholls, David, (eds.), *Gender, civic culture, and consumerism: middle-class identity in Britain, 1800-1940*, (Manchester University Press), 1999, pp. 164-182, and 'Pooterism or partnership?: marriage and masculine identity in the lower middle class, 1870-1920', *Journal of British Studies*, Vol. 38, (1999), pp. 291-321.

[13] Bailey, Peter, 'White collars, gray lives?: the lower middle class revisited', *Journal of British Studies*, Vol. 38, (1999), pp. 273-290.

[14] Fawcett, Henry, *The Economic Position of the British labourer*, (Macmillan & Co.), 1865, p. 44.

[15] The briefest discussion of respectability can be found in Best, G., *Mid-Victorian Britain 1851-1875*, (Fontana), 1979, pp. 279-286.

[16] Harrison, J. F. C., *Late Victorian Britain 1875-1901*, (Fontana), 1991, pp. 65-66.

of middle-class values and the extent of 'hypocrisy' now depends on examining particular values rather than the middle-class ideology as a whole.

The emergence of the middle-classes in the first half of the nineteenth century and the growing importance of its entrepreneurial values has often been used in ways that imply it was the dominant group after 1850. [17] In fact, what characterised the middle-classes was its aspiration for economic, political and cultural power rather than the achievement of that aspiration. The relative power of the aristocracy and the emergent bourgeoisie illustrates this. Rubinstein[18] used the value of individual property at death as recorded in probate calendars and assessments of incomes in different districts made by the Inland Revenue for the purposes of taxation to analyse the relative wealth of different groups of property owners. [19] Each of these sources is subject to some technical qualifications for, even before the imposition of heavy death duties on inherited wealth, the rich had reasons to dispose of some of their property before death. Tax assessment of the living promises a solution to this problem but the measurement of income by area of residence is likely to undervalue the importance of capital holdings in other districts. Despite this, it is clear that the wealth of landowners was predominant for longer than

---

[17] There is less literature on the middle-classes in the nineteenth and early-twentieth century than for the labouring population. Ibid, James, Lawrence, *The Middle-class: A History*, is an exhaustive study. Bradley, I., *The English Middle-classes are Alive and Kicking*, (Collins), 1982, takes a longer perspective but contains a few pages of assistance. Read, D., *The English Provinces c.1760-1960: a study in influence*, (Edward Arnold), 1964, is a tentative attempt to explore provincial society where the middle-classes were at their strongest. See also, Trainor, Richard H., 'The middle class', in ibid, Daunton, Martin J., (ed.), *The Cambridge urban history of Britain, Vol. 3: 1840-1950*, pp. 673-713.

[18] Rubinstein, W. D., *Men of Property: The Very Wealth in Britain since the Industrial Revolution*, (Croom Helm), 1981, *Elites and the Wealthy in Modern British History*, (Methuen), 1987, and ibid, *Wealth and Inequality in Britain*, provide valuable analyses of wealth-holding, point to the relatively low standing of manufacturers and argue that few businessmen brought landed estates and that the aristocracy was a closed elite. See also, Rubinstein, William D., 'Wealth making in the late-nineteenth and early twentieth centuries: a response', *Business History*, Vol. 42, (2000), pp. 141-154, and Nicholas, Tom, 'Wealth making in the nineteenth and early twentieth century: the Rubinstein hypothesis revisited', *Business History*, Vol. 42, (2000), pp. 155-168.

[19] Ibid, Rubinstein, W. D., *Men of Property: The Very Wealth in Britain since the Industrial Revolution*, pp. 9-26, considers the methodological problems in studying the wealthy.

has been assumed. Among the increasingly important non-landed wealth-holder, industrial employers came third behind bankers and merchants with only 30-40 per cent of non-landed fortunes at their peak in 1850. [20]

Until the 1880s, over half of the very wealthiest still had the bulk of their property in land. [21] Even when income from rents began to fall from the 1870s, large landowners were able to increase their incomes from coal and mineral royalties and from urban rents, while landowners of all sizes were able to supplement their incomes by diversifying into commercial and financial activities in the City of London, then experiencing rapid growth because of its emergence as the major service centre for the world economy. As a result, there was a marked concentration of non-landed wealth in London, particularly the City and this was to be found at the level of the middle-classes as well as the very rich. [22] Within the industrial regions much the same pattern is repeated: centres of commerce like Liverpool contained the highest general levels of wealth and even in a city like Manchester only one out of six recorded millionaires was a cotton manufacturer, the others were bankers and merchants. [23]

The growth of manufacturing employment and the wealth of employers in the northern industries was important but their fortunes were only impressive a small town level. [24] Their patronage of the Arts

---

[20] Nicholas, Tom, 'Wealth making in nineteenth- and early twentieth-century Britain: industry v. commerce and finance', *Business History*, Vol. 41, (1999), pp. 16-36.

[21] Berghoff, Hartmut, 'British businessmen as wealth-holders, 1870-1914: a closer look', *Business History*, Vol. 33, (1991), pp. 222-240.

[22] Green, David R., 'To do the right thing: gender, wealth, inheritance and the London middle class', in Laurence, Anne, Maltby, Josephine, and Rutterford, Janette, (eds.), *Women and their money, 1700-1950: essays on women and finance*, (Routledge), 2009, pp. 133-150, Rubinstein, W. D., 'The role of London in Britain's wealth structure, 1809-99: further evidence', in Stobart, Jon, and Owens, Alastair, (eds.), *Urban fortunes: property and inheritance in the town, 1700-1900*, (Ashgate), 2000, pp. 131-152.

[23] Ibid, Stobart, Jon, and Owens, Alastair, (eds.), *Urban fortunes: property and inheritance in the town, 1700-1900*, highlights the importance of property and inheritance in shaping social, cultural, economic and political structures and interactions within and between towns and cities.

[24] Morris, R. J., 'The middle class and the property cycle during the industrial revolution', in Smout, Christopher, (ed.), *The search for wealth and stability: essays in economic and social history presented to M. W. Flinn*, (Macmillan), 1979, pp. 91-113, *Class, sect and party: the making of the British middle class, Leeds, 1820-1850*, (Manchester University Press),

drew positive comments, as, for example, in 1857:

> The taste of the middle classes, then, for modern pictures is a wholesome fact – good for painters, good for art, good for honesty and truth, which is the cause of all true art. [25]

This was partly the result of the limited extent of the ambitions of prosperous family-based firms, as well as of the greater uncertainty and lower rate of return from productive activity in comparison with landownership and finance and it was closely connected with manufacturers' general avoidance of heavy fixed investment in plant and equipment. Even in their own regions, manufacturers were still overshadowed by the landowning classes.

The Reform Act 1832 is traditionally regarded as the beginnings of middle-class political power.[26] The new franchise increased the representation of the urban middle-class but it was also designed to reduce the power of newly wealthy owners of corrupt boroughs and to restore and give fresh legitimacy to the traditional influence of the landed interest. As late as the 1860s, almost two-thirds of the country's MPs came from landed backgrounds, over one-third, hereditary aristocrats and around half of the cabinets of both parties were still aristocratic.[27] It was not until after the Reform Act 1867 that major changes in the nature of the political elite emerged. The Act extended the franchise to certain sections of the urban working-classes and this led to a shift from local patterns of influence to professionally organised political machines. This was enhanced by further extensions of the franchise in 1884 but also by the Secret Ballot Act 1872 and the restriction of candidates' spending on elections by the Corrupt Practices Act 1883. After 1885, there was a further dilution in aristocratic power through awards of peerages in recognition of

---

1990, and *Men, women and property in England 1780-1870,* (Cambridge University Press), 2005, consider Leeds as an example.

[25] *A handbook to the gallery of British paintings in the Art treasures exhibition, a repr. of notices orig. publ. in 'The Manchester guardian': Being a Reprint of Critical Notices Originally Published in The Manchester Guardian,* (Manchester art treasures exhib), 1857, p. 14.

[26] Garrard, John Adrian, 'The middle classes and nineteenth century national and local politics', in Garrard, John Adrian, Jary, David, Goldsmith, Michael, and Oldfield, Adrian, (eds.), *The middle class in politics,* (Saxon House), 1978, pp. 35-66, and Briggs, Asa, 'Middle-class consciousness in English politics, 1780-1846', *Past & Present,* Vol. 9, (1956), pp. 65-74, provide a brief overview.

[27] Ibid, Searle, G. R., *Entrepreneurial Politics in Mid-Victorian Britain,* is the clearest statement of the position of the middle-classes in politics.

wealth and political service and the introduction of elections for local government in the counties in 1888 and 1894.

There was a major restructuring of the British Establishment from the 1870s but the extent to which the middle-classes as a whole benefitted from this was limited. It did not give provincial manufacturers an enhanced position at national level. [28] Membership of the ruling elite was extended to include larger numbers of bankers and merchants but contained few manufacturers. The great country houses remained important and the network of power and influence remained firmly based in the south of the country and the aristocracy was still the leading group within the ruling classes. The industrial middle-classes was able to exert pressure on the nation's political elite to get the kind of government it wanted. However, restructuring the Establishment was owed less to industrialists than occupationally-based pressure groups among both the professional middle-classes and the working-classes that had won major reforms in the 1860s and 1870s and made further advances in the 1890s and 1900s.

Lancashire factory owners became a substantial group in the House of Commons after 1832 but their effectiveness was limited by internal political divisions and by their failure to create external alliances with other parliamentary groupings. [29] In the longer term, factory owners became less active in politics and more conservative in their social behaviour and their attachment to the Tory Party echoed the traditional allegiance of the Lancashire aristocracy. The debate over the Corn Laws and their repeal in 1846 was apparently an assertion of industrial against the landed interest. Repeal was beneficial to manufacturers who had a direct interest in reducing food prices and tariffs on their products but it was by no means disadvantageous to the aristocracy much of whose land was devoted to pastoral farming and whose rents from arable land were largely maintained during the long mid-century boom. It was tenant farmers, caught between the need to pay their rents and fear of falling grain prices, who stood to suffer most from repeal and were its most vocal opponents. Repeal was a result of aristocratic concession to popular opinion during a short-term crisis rather than an expression of the

---

[28] The economic strength of this group, measured in terms of their share of the national wealth, began to decline from the 1870s under pressure from foreign competition.

[29] Kadish, A.', Free trade and high wages: the economics of the Anti-Corn Law League', and Lloyd-Jones, Roger, 'Merchant city: the Manchester business community, the trade cycle, and commercial policy, c.1820-1846', in Marrison, Andrew (ed.), *Freedom and trade, Vol. 1: Free trade and its reception, 1815-1960*, (Routledge), 1998, pp. 14-27, 86-104.

long-term growth of middle-class political power. [30] The middle-class 'victory' of 1846 was atypical of their success in this period and did not mark the beginnings of middle-class control of the political system.

So if the position of manufacturers within the British ruling elite was limited, what power did they have within their own industrial regions? Given their wealth, they exercised considerable local power but, there were limitations on their political power. Aristocratic influences persisted in many industrial towns until at least the 1870s offsetting the economic and political impact of the factory elite. There was also competition from non-landed groups, especially mercantile, retailing and professional middle-classes, who were more active in local urban politics than manufacturers. In Bolton and Salford, for instance, in the 1840s over half the councillors were manufacturers but this had fallen to under 40 per cent by the 1870s. The political dominance of manufacturers was confined to the smaller industrial towns but even there it was not unlimited. The growing powers of local government led to the creation of regulatory and democratic local procedures.

The middle-classes had a relatively low status in terms of wealth-holding and political power, but how far did they mould society in their own image and indirectly influence the behaviour of the more prominent actors? Perkin contrasted the 'entrepreneurial ideal' of the emergent middle-classes with the 'aristocratic' ideal but it is difficult to define 'bourgeois' as opposed to 'aristocratic' values. It is perhaps better to focus on whether the specific interests of manufacturers were represented in the attitudes and values of the ruling classes. [31] Literary culture suggests that manufacturers, far from reshaping dominant

---

[30] McCord, N., *The Anti-Corn Law League 1838-1846*, (Allen and Unwin), 1958, and Pickering, Paul A., and Tyrrell, Alex, *The People's Bread: A History of the Anti-Corn Law League*, (Leicester University Press), 2000, provide different perspectives but Prentice, Archibald, *History of the Anti-Corn Law League*, 2 Vols. (W. & F. G. Cash), 1853, new edition with an introduction by W. H. Chaloner, (Cass), 1968, is still a valuable source. The political strategies of the League can be approached through Hamer, D. A., *The Politics of Electoral Pressure*, (Harvester), 1977, pp. 58-90, .

[31] Gunn, Simon, *The public culture of the Victorian middle class: ritual and authority in the English industrial city, 1840-1914*, (Manchester University Press), 2000, and Kidd, Alan J., and Nicholls, David, (eds.), *Gender, civic culture, and consumerism: middle-class identity in Britain, 1800-1940*, (Manchester University Press), 1999, Green, S., 'In search of bourgeois civilisation: institutions & ideals in 19th century', *Northern History*, Vol. 28, (1992), pp. 228-245, and Morgan, S., "'A sort of land debatable': Female influence, civic virtue and middle-class identity, c.1830-c.1860', *Women's History Review*, Vol. 13, (2004), pp. 183-210.

attitudes, were consistently rejected unless they conformed to existing social values.

Economic success beyond the exploitation of land was viewed with some suspicion and the belief that money was without the reciprocal obligations and duties of landowning retained its influence. Until the 1760s, attitudes were ambiguous, but subsequently the trend was towards literary condemnation of new wealth that reached its peak in the rejection of provincial manufacturers between the 1840s and the 1930s. The only route to acceptance and 'respectability' was to adopt the values of civilised culture and public service associated with the 'gentleman', and later the professional man and to abandon the money-making and sectional interest associated with new wealth. [32] These elite values had an effect on the industrial middle-classes many of whom lived in town houses or holidayed at coastal resorts located on large landed estates. Most sought acceptance by the Establishment and the wealthier sent their sons to public schools and bought their own landed estates. Those who were active in political life did so in the Conservative and Liberal parties led by the aristocracy. [33] There was, however, a significant space for the cultural influence of non-landed groups within the industrial regions. Merchants, retailers and professionals were more active than manufacturers and there were important political and religious differences within local middle-classes with Nonconformists beyond Wesleyan Methodists largely supporting a liberal or radical stance while Anglicans were more conservative in their politics.

Entrepreneurs

During the economic revolutions after 1780, entrepreneurs were viewed as the main instruments of change because of their enterprise, organisational innovation skill and their ability to exploit commercial opportunities. [34] Many industrial pioneers operated in a uniquely favourable economic environment; an expanding domestic market buttressed, especially in cotton, by a flourishing overseas demand. This allowed entrepreneurs such as Robert Owen, Benjamin Gott[35]

---

[32] See one dimension in Jeremy, David J., (ed.), *Religion, business, and wealth in modern Britain*, (Routledge), 1998.

[33] MacLeod, Dianne Sachko, *Art and the Victorian middle class: money and the making of cultural identity*, (Cambridge University Press), 1996.

[34] See this issue from a literary perspective, McKinstry, Sam, 'The positive depiction of entrepreneurs and entrepreneurship in the novels of Sir Walter Scott', *Journal of Scottish Historical Studies*, Vol. 26, (2006), pp. 83-99.

[35] See, Heaton, Herbert, 'Benjamin Gott and the industrial revolution in Yorkshire', *Economic History Review*, Vol. 3, (1931-2), pp. 45-66.

and his partners, George Newton and Thomas Chambers to exploit profit potentials. In favourable economic conditions, substantial profits could be achieved without effective use of power supplies or optimal factory layouts. However, successful entrepreneurs such as Arkwright, Strutt and Peel were perhaps not typical of contemporary businessmen. More representative were individuals such as the Wilsons of Wilsontown Ironworks [36] or the Needhams of Litton [37] whose businesses suffered from serious entrepreneurial shortcomings coupled with gross mismanagement. Such was the strength of the home and overseas markets, the former benefiting from railways and gradually rising living standards that entrepreneurs had no great inducement to alter the basic economic structure that had evolved before 1830.

Without change in the scale of operations, the relatively slow enlargement of the labour forces of individual enterprises and the close coincidence of firm and plant, meant that the nature of entrepreneurship and the structure of the firm changed little in the middle decades of the century. However, some firms that traced their origins to the Industrial Revolution were already declining in relative importance and some were disappearing altogether. Marshall's of Leeds declined from the 1840s, though it lingered on for another forty years by which time many of its leading competitors in flax spinning had already gone: Benyons in 1861, John Morfitt and John Wilkinson a few years later. The Ashworth cotton enterprises, built up between 1818 and 1834 by Henry and Edward Ashworth, began their relative decline in the 1840s. In iron, Joshua Walker & Co. did not long survive the end of the French Wars, its steel trade being formally wound up in 1829 and its iron trade finally wasted away in the 1830s. Other ironmasters fared little better: John Darwin, one of Sheffield's leading industrialists, had gone bankrupt by 1828. The Coalbrookdale Company lacking managerial guidance after Abraham and Alfred Darby retired in 1849 and Francis Darby died in 1850, faltered and was sustained only continuing demand for its products.[38]

---

[36] Donnachie, Ian L., and Butt, John, 'The Wilsons of Wilsontown ironworks, 1779-1813: a study in entrepreneurial failure', *Explorations in Entrepreneurial History*, second series, Vol. 4, (1967), pp. 150-168.

[37] MacKenzie, M. H., 'Cressbrook and Litton mills, 1779-1835', *Derbyshire Archaeological Journal*, Vol. 88, (1969 for 1968), pp. 1-25, Chapman, Stanley D., 'Cressbrook and Litton mills: an alternative view', *Derbyshire Archaeological Journal*, Vol. 89, (1970 for 1969), pp. 86-90, and MacKenzie, M. H., 'Cressbrook and Litton Mills: a reply', *Derbyshire Archaeological Journal*, Vol. 90, (1972 for 1970), pp. 56-59.

[38] Thomas, Emyr, *Coalbrookdale and the Darby family: the story of the world's first industrial dynasty*, (Sessions), 1999.

How competent were entrepreneurs in late-Victorian and Edwardian Britain? [39] The view of entrepreneurs in the late-nineteenth century as having declining initiative and flagging drive rests on the dynamism of their predecessors of the classical industrial revolution. [40] From the 1870s, growth in industrial production declined, there was a relative deterioration in Britain's international economic status and a sluggish rise in productivity that have, to some degree, been blamed on declining entrepreneurial spirit. [41] Landes, for instance, supported this position suggesting that British enterprise reflected a:

...combination of complacency. Her merchants, who had once seized the markets of the world, took them for granted; the consular reports are full of the incompetence of British exporters, their refusal to suit their goods to the taste and pockets of the client, their unwillingness to try new products in new areas, their insistence that everyone in the world ought to read in English and count in pounds, shillings and pence. Similarly, the British manufacturer was notorious for his indifference to style, his conservatism in the face of new techniques, his reluctance to abandon the individuality of tradition for the conformity implicit in mass production. [42]

British entrepreneurial failure suggests an adverse comparison with performance elsewhere, usually in Germany and America. However, McCloskey [43] found that the British iron and steel masters exploited technology before 1914 as well as their competitors but was

---

[39] Payne, Peter, 'Entrepreneurship and British economic decline', in Collins, Bruce, and Robbins, Keith, (eds.), *British culture and economic decline*, (St. Martin's Press), 1990, pp. 25-58.

[40] Payne, P. L., *British Entrepreneurship in the Nineteenth Century*, (Macmillan), second edition, 1988, is a brief bibliographical study. Dintenfass, Michael, *The Decline of Industrial Britain 1870-1980*, (Routledge), 1992, and Dormois, Jean-Pierre, and Dintenfass, Michael, (eds.), *The British industrial decline*, (Routledge), 1999, provide a challenging account of Britain's long-term decline since the 1870s.

[41] Westall, O. M., 'The competitive environment of British business 1850-1914', in Kirby, M. W., and Rose Mary B., (eds.), *Business enterprise in modern Britain: from the eighteenth to the twentieth century*, (Routledge), 1994, pp. 207-235, and Kirby, M. W., *The Decline of British Economic Power Since 1870*, (Taylor & Francis), 1981, pp. 1-24, provides a valuable context.

[42] Landes, D., *The Unbound Prometheus*, (Cambridge University Press), 1969, p. 564.

[43] McCloskey, D. N., *Economic maturity and entrepreneurial decline: British iron and steel, 1870-1913*, (Harvard University Press), 1973, pp. 1-21, 56-72, 125-130.

less convinced by the potential of the British coal industry. [44] Similar studies of the cotton industry found that failure to introduce newer technology and reliance on mule-spinning did not lead to a decline in productivity. [45] On the basis of these and other studies, McCloskey argued that there was 'little left of the dismal picture of British failure painted by historians'. [46] Nevertheless doubts remain. British entrepreneurs failed to confront organisational weakness or enter more vigorously new manufacturing industries. However, they did move into the service sector, whose relatively rapid rate of growth and high productivity between 1870 and 1914 was superior to the old staples and provided resilience in Britain's aggregate economic growth. Entrepreneurial hesitation were always present, even during the Industrial Revolution and this became more apparent after 1870.[47]

There is a deep-seated conviction that British culture was the root cause of Britain's industrial decline. Central is the belief that the British people, especially the middle-classes, have long been averse to industry. Those businessmen who could forsake industry and trade for a life of gentility have eagerly done so. This 'gentrification' of the English middle-classes caused a dulling of industrial energies and led to a decline in Britain's economic prowess. [48] Politicians and civil servants whose actions shaped policies within which private enterprise operated were drawn from the gentry or educated in the ideals of

---

[44] McCloskey, D. N., *Enterprise and Trade in Victorian Britain*, (Allen & Unwin), 1981, pp. 74-93.

[45] Chapman, S. D., 'The Textile Industries', in Roderick, G. W., and Stephens, M. D., (eds.), *Where did we go wrong? Industrial performance, education and the economy in Victorian Britain*, (Taylor & Francis), 1981, pp.125-138.

[46] Ibid, McCloskey, D. N., *Enterprise and Trade in Victorian Britain*, p. 106.

[47] See, for example, Brown, K. D., 'Entrepreneurial Failure and Retailing: a case-study', *Journal of Industrial History*, Vol. 5, (2002), pp. 71-88, Toms, Steven, 'Windows of opportunity in the textile industry: the business strategies of Lancashire entrepreneurs, 1880-1914', *Business History*, Vol. 40, (1998), pp. 1-25.

[48] The classic modern exposition of this view can be found in Wiener, Martin, *English Culture and the Decline of the Industrial Spirit 1850-1980*, (Cambridge University Press), 1981. See also, Trainor, Richard, 'The gentrification of Victorian and Edwardian industrialists', in Stone, Lawrence, Beier, A. L., Cannadine, David, and Rosenheim, James M., (eds.), *The First modern society: essays in English history in honour of Lawrence Stone*, (Cambridge University Press), 1989, pp. 167-197, and Thomson, F. M. L., *Gentrification and the Enterprise Culture: Britain 1780-1980*, (Oxford University Press), 2003, pp. 19-142, and Robbins, Keith, *Politicians, diplomacy, and war in modern British history*, (Hambledon), 1994, pp. 67-84, on British culture versus British industry.

service at a public school or one of the ancient universities. The financiers and traders of London to whom they looked for economic expertise were also imbued with the same anti-industrial spirit. In reality, however, the middle-classes were far less hostile to manufacturing. The upper middle-classes sent a significant number of their sons into business and their flow into manufacturing and commerce was not limited to genteel pursuits like merchant banking. Sons of landowners and professionals accounted for a quarter of British steel manufacturers active between 1865 and 1914 and both groups were substantially over-represented in this heavy industry in comparison with their incidence in the population as a whole.

The decline of industrial Britain after 1870 was a matter of the decisions about tools and techniques, education and training and advertising and sales that the men who remained in the offices and on the shop-floors made. There is little direct evidence linking the choices entrepreneurs and managers made about production and marketing with the anti-industrial values to which they supposedly succumbed. If there was a 'gentry cast' to their minds, that strongly influenced business decision-making, there are few traces of it in the records of British enterprises.

The professions

The development of a substantial and powerful professional group within the middle-classes gathered considerable pace in the later Victorian period. [49] Britain had an increasing, and increasingly prosperous, population. It grew by a third in the last three decades of the century, a higher growth rate than for 1841-1871 though here the rate was influenced by the Irish famine and its aftermath. Increasingly population was concentrated in urban settings. In 1841, 48 per cent of the population of England and Wales lived in settlements of 2,500 people or more; by 1871, this had risen to 65 per cent and by 1901, 78 per cent. There was also diversification of the industrial structure with an increased emphasis on the service sectors whose share of the national income rose from 44 per cent in 1841 to 54 per cent by 1901.

It was in the urban centres that the middle-classes mushroomed. Those with incomes over £150 per year increased by about 170 per

---

[49] Corfield, P., *Power and the professions in Britain, 1700-1850*, (Routledge), 1995, provides context. Reader, W. J., *Professional Men: The Rise of the Professional Classes in Nineteenth-Century England*, (Basic Books), 1966, is still the best short introduction to the subject but needs to be read in relation to Gourvish, T. R., 'The Rise of the Professions' in Gourvish, T. R., and O'Day, Alan, (eds.), *Later Victorian Britain 1867-1900*, (Macmillan), 1988, pp. 13-36.

cent: from 307,000 in 1860-1861 to 833,000 in 1894-1895. A 'service class' emerged from the traditional professional occupations in religion, law, medicine and education and other occupations connected with the demands of the industrialising society such accounting, surveying, civil and mechanical engineering . [50] For Perkin, the professions constituted the 'forgotten middle-class', temporarily ignored in the early stages of the industrial revolution as the aristocratic, entrepreneurial and working-class ideals vied for supremacy. [51] This neglected group nevertheless benefited from the expanded opportunities provided by industrialisation and by the expansion of education. [52]

In 1851, certain occupations had acquired social status through their control of a particular area of knowledge and expertise combined with a license to use this knowledge and expertise. The activities of a 'profession' were controlled and regulated by the profession itself through monopolistic restrictive practices. The 'professional class' embraced not only those in the 'learned professions' plus 'literature, art and science' but also those engaged in government and defence. This classification excluded accountants, architects and surveyors who were included on the list of industrial occupations. However, it was the notion of service to the community that was held to justify a privileged position of trust:

> This great class includes those persons who are rendering direct service to mankind and satisfying their intellectual, moral and devotional wants. [53]

The late-nineteenth century saw considerable competition for professional status as emerging occupations tried to join their more established colleagues. The numbers in this group rose from about 345,000 in 1861 to 515,000 in 1881 and 735,000 in 1901, an increase of 113 per cent across the period. The professional elements in society increased from about 2.5 per cent in 1861 to 4.0 per cent in 1901 as a percentage of the occupied population.

Between 1861 and 1901, the growth in the established professions was slight. Numbers in religion, law and medicine rose by 30-60 per cent, compared to an overall increase in population of

---

[50] The civil service and armed forces may also be seen as part of this group but, equally, they may be seen as part of 'government'.
[51] Ibid, Perkin, Harold, *The Rise of Professional Society*, p. xxii.
[52] See, Schwarz, Leonard D., 'Professions, elites, and universities in England, 1870-1970', *Historical Journal*, Vol. 47, (2004), pp. 941-962.
[53] 'Remarks on the Industrial Statistics of 1861', *Return on Poor Rates and Pauperism*, July 1864.

61 per cent and an increase of 170 per cent in those with incomes over £150. However, some occupations exhibited much higher growth rates. Dentistry established itself as a recognised activity after the Medical Act 1858 [54] and the Dentists Act 1878. [55] Writing and journalism and music and entertainment expanded reflecting the growth of leisure activities and their commercial exploitation in the late-nineteenth century. Teaching was stimulated by the expansion of both public and state schools and the 'industrial professions' of architecture, engineering and surveying also expanded. After 1881, the growth of most professional occupations was more modest but two occupations experienced considerable growth. Most of the increase in the numbers of physicians and surgeons were concentrated after 1881 while acting continued to exhibit above-average growth, its 174 per cent increase between 1881 and 1901 receiving special attention in the 1901 Census Report. Employment opportunities for women remained limited in the major professions especially in the more prestigious posts but dominated three occupations, teaching, midwifery and nursing, where status was usually low: of the 230,000 teachers listed in 1901, 172,000 or three-quarters were women.

Between 1860 and 1900, new, protective organisations were established in the predominantly male professionalising occupations and there was a considerable increase in educational and training activities but this built on critical earlier decisions. For instance, the British Medical Association was founded in 1856. [56] After 1860, earlier advances were strengthened and local and provincial bodies combined to form national associations. Royal Charters were conferred on existing institutions and other elements of enhanced status were evident in statutory recognition, regulation and privilege. In the law, separation of barristers from the subordinate branch of solicitors and attorneys remained. Barristers took steps to defend restrictive practices through a Bar Committee of 1883, reorganised in 1894 as the Bar Council. Solicitors, who had obtained a monopoly of conveyancing in 1804, obtained more work with the creation of

---

[54] Roberts, M. J. D., 'The Politics of Professionalization: MPs, Medical Men, and the 1858 Medical Act', *Medical History*, Vol. 53, (2009), pp. 37-56. See also, Lawrence, Christopher, *Medicine in the Making of Modern Britain 1700-1920*, (Routledge), 1994,.

[55] Campbell, J. M., 'A brief survey of British dentistry: Charles Allen - Dentists' Act, 1878', *British Dental Journal*, Vol. 52, (1950), pp. 175-181.

[56] Little, E. M., *History of the British Medical Association 1832-1932*, (BMA), 1932, republished, 1984, Pyke-Lees, Walter, *Centenary of the General Medical Council, 1858-1958: the history and present work of the Council*, (General Medical Council), 1958, and Oswald, Arthur, *The Royal College of Surgeons of England*, (Country Life), 1962.

country courts in 1846. [57] Their association, the 'Incorporated Law Society' was entrusted with registration in 1843, given a new charter in 1845, the right to conduct its own examinations in 1877 and established its own Law School in London in 1903. The number of members of the Law Society increased fourfold to reach 77,000 by 1901 and the number of practising solicitors rose by 60 per cent over the same period to 16,300. [58] The creation of the 'industrial professions' was, by contrast, emphatically a creation of the nineteenth century. Railways acted as a major stimulus encouraging change in engineering, accounting, surveying and architecture as well as in specialist branches of the law. Two organisations were established before 1860: the Institution of Civil Engineers in 1818 and a similar body for Mechanical Engineers in 1847. [59] Between 1860 and 1900, a dozen further bodies were established, six in 1860-1873 and six more in 1889-1897. Membership of engineering institutions rose from about 1,700 in 1860 to 23,000 in 1900.

The development of professional activities sought to raise their status, increase financial rewards and provide occupational security by means of differentiation, regulation and an emphasis on the gentlemanly virtues of education and middle-class morality. The transformation of the older professions and the emergence of newer branches were part of the general process of socio-political change. Professional activities, whether stimulated by internal factors such as new knowledge, or by external changes like industrial growth, urbanisation and the railways, were a major element in the process by which middle-class elites established and protected their position in an industrial society. This involved a separation from the working-classes and a power-sharing and partial empathy with the old aristocratic order. The rise of the professions pointed both backward

---

[57] Christian, E. B. V., *A short history of solicitors*, (Reeves & Turner), 1896, and Garrard, J. A., and Parrott, Vivienne, 'Craft, professional and middle-class identity: solicitors and gas engineers, c.1850-1914', in Kidd, Alan J., and Nicholls, David, (eds.), *The making of the British middle class? Studies of regional and cultural diversity since the eighteenth century*, (Sutton), 1996, pp. 148-168.

[58] Sugarman, David, *A brief history of the Law Society*, (Law Society), 1995.

[59] Pullin, John, *Progress through mechanical engineering: the first 150 years of the Institution of Mechanical Engineers*, (Quiller), 1997. See also, Reader, W. J., *History of the Institution of Electrical Engineers, 1871-1971*, based on research by Rachel Lawrence, Sheila Nemet, and Geoffrey Tweedale, (Peregrinus on behalf of the Institution of Electrical Engineers), 1987, and Buchanan, R. A., 'Institutional proliferation in the British engineering profession, 1847-1914', *Economic History Review*, second series, Vol. 38, (1985), pp. 42-60.

and forward: backward since the professions failed to shake off the trappings of aristocratic values; forward in encouraging a greater degree of government intervention in the economy, the hallmark of the modern twentieth century state.

Middle-class women: the ideal explored

The emergence of the middle-classes has been treated as 'male' and accounts of middle-class consciousness structured round public events in which women have generally been seen as playing little part.[60] The place of women in conventional historiography lay at the heart of middle-class notions of family and home. Their role was essentially domestic, dependent and private while the male role was one of having dependants and public. Was 'the separation of spheres' and the division between the public and private a given or was it constructed as an integral part of middle-class culture and self-identity? Catherine Hall maintains:

> But one of the ways in which the middle-class was held together, despite many divisive factors, was their ideas about masculinity and femininity. Men came to share a sense of what constituted masculinity and women a sense of what constituted femininity....masculinity meant having dependants, femininity meant being dependent...the idea of a universal womanhood is weak in comparison with the idea of certain types of sexual differentiation being a necessary part of class identity.[61]

There was no middle-class equivalent to the working-class idea of the 'family wages' that established a notion of economic dependence. The middle-classes took on the aristocratic notion of patrilineal rights to property even though they broke with them at many other points. The Birmingham *Trade Directories* demonstrate clearly the growing dependence of women after 1780 and their increasingly marginal economic role. By the 1840s, however, women were seen as lacking the knowledge and expertise to enter into business: jobs were being redefined as managerial and skilled and therefore masculine. Women could manage the home and the family but not the workshop or the factory.

---

[60] On the emergence of the middle-classes Davidoff, L., and Hall, C., *Family Fortunes: Men and Women of the English middle-class 1780-1850*, (Hutchinson), 1987, second edition, (Routledge), 2002, is a major contribution to women's history.

[61] Hall, C., 'Gender Divisions and Class Formation in the Birmingham Middle-class 1780-1850', in Samuel, R., (ed.), *People's History and Socialist Theory*, (Routledge), 1981, p. 165

How were middle-class women represented? The concept of 'respectability' was a complex combination of moral, religious, economic and cultural systems that helped defined the individual's proper relationship with their worlds. The notion of respectability was defined for women in terms of dependency, delicacy and fragility. Independence was unnatural; it signified boldness and sexual deviancy. Female dependency was secured through economic, legal, medical and cultural discourses. Dependency should not be seen in terms of a repressive exercise of power but as a natural and gratifying part of respectable femininity. Male veneration upheld the delicacy and purity of women and, far from oppressing them elevated them to a superior position. Baptist Noel, an evangelical writer stated:

> Women deserve all tenderness; and, made of a more delicate organisation, and of less strength, they need respect and courtesy, protection in danger, the supply of their wants, and above all affection to repay affection.[62]

The characteristics of ideal femininity were a part of a woman's normal biological development. The supposed fragility of middle-class femininity was contrasted with the image of working-class women as inherently healthy, hardy and robust. This myth served the interests of the medical profession and of many middle-class men. The definition of female respectability was part of the wider formation of the domestic ideology and the development of home and family values, the notion of the 'Angel in the House'.[63]

A cult of domesticity developed with the separation of the home and the workplace during the late-eighteenth and early-nineteenth century and a reconstruction of gender identities.[64] Women were defined 'naturally' as domestic beings, suited to the duties of the home and children. Men were associated with a public sphere, the world of work and politics. The home, for the middle-classes, was emptied of its association with work and was seen in terms of privacy. The home became a haven from the speculation, competition and conflicts of

---

[62] Noel, Baptist, *The Fallen and their Associates*, (James Nisbet and Co.), 1860, pp. 7-8.
[63] Patmore, Coventry, *The Angel in the House: The Betrothal*, (J. W. Parker & Son), 1854.
[64] Hall, Catherine, 'The Early Formation of Victorian Domestic Ideology', in ibid, Hall, Catherine, *White, Male and Middle-class,* (Basil Blackwell), 1994, pp. 75-93, provides a valuable discussion of the development of this central concept between the 1790s and 1840s. It provides a fundamental context for later developments.

business and public life. It was 'domesticated'. It was, however, much more than:

> The Home is the crystal of society -- the very nucleus of national character; and from that source, be it pure or tainted, issue the habits, principles and maxims, which govern public as well as private life. The nation comes from the nursery; public opinion itself is for the most part the outgrowth of the home. [65]

Regulation, control and peace in the home ensured national security and prosperity. The breakdown of domestic order was seen in terms of a total social disintegration. The ideologies of the home and separate spheres were fundamental elements in the formation of an ideal for the middle-class 'Perfect Lady'. This presupposed a plentiful supply of money, provided by working husbands, to create the cosy sanctuary, the home. However, the vast majority of women were in the working-classes for whom the ideal corresponded little to the reality of their lives. The economic realities of life for the great majority of the middle-classes meant that they had insufficient income to employ a legion of cooks, maids, nannies and governesses. The lot of many, perhaps most, middle-class women was often one of hard work and making ends meet, whilst helped in the house often by a single young maid-of-all work.

Most middle-class women could not afford the idleness or other trappings of this stereotype. In reality, there are doubts whether many women indulged in the hypersensitivity with which the Perfect Lady is usually accredited. Ill health among lower middle-class women was far more likely to arise from overwork and from non-stop childbearing than from inertia. Yet, this sickly facet of the Perfect Woman stereotype is important. [66] The view of women as consumptive weaklings could not have been projected without the active support of the medical profession that attempted to exert social control over their lives by producing medical arguments in favour of the 'traditional female role'. Their views on the health of women actually differed enormously according to class. Middle-class women were regarded as inherently sick if they tried to step outside their prescribed role; working women, on the other hand, were themselves health hazards, who harboured the germs of cholera, typhoid and venereal disease and who bore numerous sickly working-class babies. Economic and

---

[65] Smiles, Samuel, *Self-Help*, (John Murray), 1859, p. 274
[66] See in particular Duffin, Lorna, 'The conspicuous consumptive: woman as invalid', in Delamont, Sara, and Duffin, Lorna, (eds.), *The Nineteenth Century Woman*, (Croom Helm), 1978, pp. 26-56.

social conditions made it impossible for working-class women to attain the ideal of the Perfect Lady and there was rarely a separation between work and home. Yet many in the working-classes admired the ideal.

Middle-class writers who were popular among the working-classes wrote about the moral purity of the reputable working-class and the deserving poor. Dickens, Mrs Gaskell and George Eliot portrayed the sanctity of the working-class home in the face of the moral carelessness of upper-class men who thought they could freely dally with women beneath them. In most respects the Perfect Lady represented only a very small minority but there is no doubt of the influence of the ideal. The idea of the wife at home to look after the house and family became increasingly desirable and even if she could not afford servants or idleness, she could be respectable, chaste and virtuous.

This message was widely projected from the pulpit, in religious tracts, in poems, in magazines, in painting and in manuals on the behaviour of women. The Perfect Lady had to acknowledge and inwardly assimilate the fact that she was inferior to men. Mrs Sarah Stickney Ellis, author and mid-century commentator, put the message succinctly:

> As women, then, the first thing of importance is to be content to be inferior to men -- inferior in mental power, in the same proportion that you are in bodily strength. [67]

The young girl would be educated in her role of service to the male and in childhood she could practise this submissive and servile role upon her demanding brothers. As for the Victorian woman who really could not dupe herself into believing that she was inferior to man, there was the persuasive and pervasive doctrine of the 'separate spheres'. John Ruskin, in a series of lectures given to women in Manchester in 1864 and later published under the precious and obscure title *Sesames and Lilies*, shied away from the reality that man ruled and women were his subjects. He could not countenance:

> ...the idea that woman is only the shadow and attendant image of her lord owing him thoughtless servile obedience. [68]

She was, according to Ruskin, man's complement and helpmate. Man was the doer of deeds and the great function of women was to

---

[67] Ellis, Sarah Stickney, *The Daughters of England: Their Position in Society, Character and Responsibilities*, (Appleton), 1843, p. 6.
[68] Ruskin John, *Sesames and Lilies*, (John Wiley & Sons), 1867, p. 77.

praise. So much for 'separate but equal', an insidious doctrine designed to subvert women from seeking change.

The proper sphere of the Perfect Lady was the home and it was she who converted mere bricks and mortar into that bastion of Victorian cosiness. The outside world was a wicked place, full of terrors and it was small wonder that Victorian businessman sought refuge close to his own warm hearth. Within the home the male willingly submitted to the devoted ministrations of his dear wife--the angel in the house. She was totally untainted by the grimy realities of industrial capitalism. If the outside world was dark, discordant and evil, the angel in the home brought light and harmony to the secure domestic world. Victorian magazines, many with the word 'Home' in the title, glorified the domestic role and reinforced the dominant female image. Paintings on show at the Royal Academy did the same. George Elgar Hick's painting *Woman's Mission: Companion of Manhood*, exhibited in 1863, projected this ideology very effectively. In it the loving wife comforts her grief stricken husband, in whose hand is held a black-bordered letter. The painter demonstrates not only this specific act of comfort, but the wife's general concern for her husband is shown in the neat room, clean table-cloth, shining cutlery and crockery and in the vase of flowers on the mantel.

The Perfect Lady stereotype was gradually rejected by women who felt themselves suffocated by its cloying image. Middle-class women launched the attack on the inactivity and economic dependence that was expected of them. They demanded control over property, economic independence and admission to education and to the professions, wider employment opportunities and the franchise. There were several economic and social reasons why feminism emerged and why it often focused on the Sex Question. Some argue that feminism was the result of the break-up of the old productive family unit that left single women redundant. Others pursue the sex ratio theory, showing that a 'surplus' female population existed by the 1840s and that these surplus, unsupported spinsters broke down the barriers to entry into the professions. The emergence of a distinct middle-class effectively closed many of what would previously have been middle-class female occupations. It was this group of middle-class women, dissatisfied with their assigned place that sought to redefine women's social position. They provided the overwhelming majority of 'New Women'. It was these bourgeois women whom John Stuart Mill had in mind when he pleaded for equality of the sexes in *The Subjection of Women* in 1869 and it was they who took up the challenge.

The 'New Women' were in part the product of changed socio-economic conditions and in part the result of the efforts of individual women who suffered social ostracism for their beliefs. The suffrage movement, educational reform, the campaign against the Contagious Diseases Acts and the fight to distribute birth control information all contributed to the decline of hypocrisy and rigidity. Women increasingly demanded and gained constructive and useful roles in society. Job opportunities were opening to every class and the typewriter and telephone had a profound impact of work for women. Social attitudes were beginning to change: in the 1880s and 1890s, W. S. Gilbert was far softer in his satire of middle aged spinsters than his predecessors in the music halls and in popular literature independent women became heroines for the first time. But this was a slow process.

The New Woman was lampooned and shown in a variety of 'unladylike' postures such as playing golf and riding bicycles. The pages of *Punch*, a journal renowned for its anti-feminism, peddled the popular caricature of the 'New Woman'. Her aspirations to education were derided in its pages throughout the 1890s. The entry of women to the professions was similarly a great joke. On the women's campaign for the vote, *Punch* was equally biting: Suffragettes were uniformly old, ugly, butch and bespectacled. In Thomas Hardy's novel *Jude the Obscure* (1896) there can be no happiness for Sue Bridehead: she recoiled from marriage to a good man, Jude; her children die horribly and she finally breaks down. George Gissing's portrayal of spinsters in *The Odd Women* (1892) showed the unhappiness to which their course had led them. The images that are most frequently presented of the New Woman were cruel, mocking and hostile. However, others took a more understanding attitude towards 'new women'. [69]

It is difficult to know how satisfied women were with their lot. A woman who was discontented would seek an individual rather than a group solution to her predicament. Clearly the limited choice of employment, especially before the 1890s, and low pay for all classes of women meant that marriage was the most attractive option. But the fluidity of society meant that women could not remain within a static role of domesticity. Even the most contented could not help but be affected by the intense debate on the position of women that swirled about them. By the 1860s, middle-class women were taking on an

---

[69] Ledger, Sally, 'The New Woman and feminist fictions', in Marshall, Gail, (ed.), *The Cambridge Companion to the Fin de siècle*, (Cambridge University Press), 2007, pp. 153-168, Bickle, Sharon, '"Kick(ing) Against the Pricks": Michael Field's *Brutus Ultor* as Manifesto for the "New Woman"', *Nineteenth Century Theatre and Film*, Vol. 33, (2006), pp. 12-29.

increasingly large number of tasks that required public agitation while a few hoped to broaden the definition of women's 'proper sphere'. Yet respectability remained the goal of outsiders, from actresses to shopkeepers and its possession the prize of even the most militant feminist. In 1914, women were still largely excluded from circles of power, authority and prestige; marriage was still held out as the goal of every young woman. It was the First World War and its immediate aftermath that, for a time, provided women with a significant degree of emancipation but by the mid-1920s feminism was again in retreat.

Middle-class women and employment

The distinction between public and private was never absolute. Among business owners listed in commercial directories between 1780 and 1860, about 10 per cent were female. Women were active businesswomen in towns, many of whom had served an apprenticeship and had earned the 'freedom' of the trade from the appropriate guild. Women were apprenticed to a wide variety of trades, including butchery, bookbinding, brush making, carpentry and rope-making and as silver-smiths. Single women, married women and widows are included in these numbers. Sometimes widows carried on the businesses of their deceased husbands, not simply as figureheads but because they had been active in management of the business while their husband was alive and wished to continue. [70] Most firms were small family partnerships and there is evidence of the important role played by wives and daughters, especially behind the scenes, in retailing, book keeping, correspondence and dealing with clients.

By the 1830s, although many middle-class women had successfully entered trades, they faced growing obstacles. The number of females apprenticed declined but this may not have been an important barrier to employment. Women generally received less education than men though the extent to which this restricted their access to trade is questionable given the limited practical use of education. Women found it more difficult than men to raise the necessary capital because English law did not consider a married woman to have any legal existence; she could not sue or be sued. A

---

[70] Tradesmen considered themselves lucky to find a wife who was good at business. In his autobiography James Hopkinson, a cabinetmaker, said of his wife, 'I found I had got a good and suitable companion one with whom I could take sweet council and whose love and affections was only equall'd by her ability as a business woman': Goodman, J. B., (ed.), *Victorian Cabinet Maker: The Memoirs of James Hopkinson, 1819-1894*, (Routledge), 1968, p. 96.

married woman was a *feme covert* and technically could not make any legally binding contracts and this may have discouraged others from loaning money to or making other contracts with married women. However, this law was not as limiting in practice as it would seem to be in theory because a married woman engaged in trade on her own account was treated by the courts as a *feme sole* and was responsible for her own debts. [71]

Finding suitable employment

By the 1850s, there was a rapid growth in the ranks of middle-class women for whom marriage was to prove unattainable and the increasing failure of middle-class families to maintain large retinues of unproductive and unmarried daughters. The number of single women between the ages of 15 and 45 rose by 72 per cent, from 2.76 million to 3.29 million in the twenty years between 1851 and 1871. This situation was exacerbated by the rising age of marriage that also left more single women waiting for, and often not achieving, marriage. In 1851, a question about marital status on the British census sparked concern about the decline of the family as the moral and reproductive basis of British society triggering the debate about the 'surplus woman' problem. The census viewed single women who were not reproducing as one among many unproductive groups within the nation. [72] For such women who would be regarded as 'ladies', the spectre of a double failure loomed large: the inability to attract a husband and not fulfil their proper role in life as wives and mothers marked them out in the circles of Victorian gentility, while their upbringing and education did not prepare them for the world of work. [73]

The feminist campaigns of the late-1850s and 1860s were concerned with the problem of finding suitable employment for single women. Theodosia, Lord Monson hired and furnished at her

---

[71] In 1764, James Cox and his wife Jane were operating separate businesses, and both went bankrupt within the space of two months. Jane's creditors sued James' creditors for the recovery of five fans, goods from her shop that had been taken for James' debts. The court ruled that, since Jane was trading as a *feme sole*, her husband did not own the goods in her shop, and thus James' creditors had no right to seize them. See, Blackstone, William, *Reports of Cases determined in the several Courts of Westminster-Hall, from 1746 to 1779*, London, 1781, pp. 570-575.

[72] See Levitan, Kathrin, 'Redundancy, the 'Surplus Woman' Problem, and the British Census, 1851-1861', *Women's History Review*, Vol. 17, (3), (2008), pp. 359-376.

[73] I have explored this issue in greater detail in my *Sex, Work and Politics: Women in Britain, 1830-1918*, (Authoring History), 2012, pp. 122-148.

town expense new offices for the *English Woman's Journal* at 19 Langham Place, an extensive property in which she also created a committee room, reading room and coffee shop that was open from 11 am to 10pm. [74] In 1860, it was advertised as 'The Ladies Institute' and it soon became the meeting place for a group of liberal, politically-minded women who became known as the Langham Place group or circle and included Helen Blackburn, novelist Matilda Hays, Emily Faithfull, champion of women's education Emily Davies, Jessie Boucherett and Lady Manson. It offered a central metropolitan conduit from which a variety of radical and feminist experiments flowed and was the earliest feminist group to be involved in the area of women's employment.

Central to the activities of the Langham Place group was its role in developing journals in which feminist issues were discussed.[75] The *English Women's Review* was established two years before the Langham Place Group and marked the beginning of a prolific decade of feminist periodicals. In 1857, it changed its name to the *English Women's Review* and after four issues, Bessie Rayner Parkes and writer Matilda Hays, who had been trying to found a feminist publication for ten years took over as editors. They moved it from Edinburgh to London and one of the essays it published was a hard-hitting article by Barbara Leigh Smith Bodichon entitled 'Women and Work'. The cost of purchasing the magazine proved too high and in March 1858 Bessie Rayner Parkes and Barbara Leigh Smith Bodichon founded the *English Woman's Journal* in its place. Published monthly, it ran for six years with an impressive circulation: from 1860, it was printing 1,000 copies a month to sell and 250 to store to cover demand for back copies. It ceased publication in August 1864 and Parkes then founded the short-lived *Alexandra Magazine and Woman's Social and Industrial Advocate* that was refounded as the *Alexandra Magazine and Englishwoman's Journal* in 1864-1865. Jessie Boucherett took over the magazine in 1866 and it was renamed the *Englishwoman's Review*. [76]

---

[74] Alexander, Sally, 'Why feminism? The women of Langham Place' in Alexander, S., (ed.), *Becoming a woman*, (Virago), 1994, pp. 135-148, and Lacey, C. A., (ed.), *Barbara Leigh Smith Bodichon and the Langham Place Group*, (Routledge), 1987.

[75] Herstein, Sheila, 'The Langham Place circle and feminist periodicals of the 1860s', *Victorian Periodicals Review*, Vol. 26, (1993), pp. 24-27, and relevant articles in *Dictionary of Nineteenth-Century Journalism in Great Britain and Ireland*, (Academia Press and The British Library), 2009.

[76] Jordan, Ellen, and Bridger, Anne, '"An Unexpected Recruit to Feminism': Jessie Boucherett's 'Feminist Life' and the importance of being wealthy', *Women's History Review*, Vol. 15, (2006), pp. 385-412, examines how she

The major theme of the *English Women's Review* was employment and the associated need to improve the education of women of all classes. The reading room set up at Langham Place became the first of the women's employment societies.[77] Founded in 1859 by Jessie Boucherett, Barbara Bodichon and Adelaide Proctor, the Society for Promoting the Employment of Women (SPEW) had two stated aims: to train women and to find employment for them. It established a register of women seeking employment and also established classes in arithmetic and bookkeeping, skills of increasing social value.[78] SPEW proved highly effective in maintaining a high profile for its activities in the press and by lobbying influential MPs as well as using its considerable social networks to persuade influential figures to employ women. It was successful in having women accepted into the clerical branches of the Civil Service, made it possible for many girls to be apprenticed in a wide variety of occupations previously only available for men such as china-painting, gilding, hairdressing, photography, telegraphy and watch-making.[79] Although SPEW did succeed in placing women in jobs, initially the number was small. However, the organisation brought a fresh and set of attitudes into prominence based not on the threat of poverty but on the dignity and fulfilment that waged-work could offer.[80]

Another important aspect of later feminist involvement in employment campaigns was the continued establishment of feminist periodicals devoted principally either to this issue or at least offering coverage of new trades for women, as well as carrying job applications. Emily Faithfull, for example, published a weekly, eight page journal *Women and Work* from 1874 to 1876 as 'a complete and reliable organ for women seeking employment and employers seeking workers.'[81] As there were limited ways in which women could find available work, these feminist ventures played an important role. They were cheap with *Women and Work* selling for

---

used her wealth to fund the initial women's suffrage campaign and to direct the strategies of the activist groups to which she belonged.

[77] Bridger, Anne, and Jordan, Ellen, *Timely Assistance: The Work of the Society for Promoting the Training of Women, 1859-2009*, (Society for Promoting the Training of Women), 2009.

[78] *The Times*, 8 June 1860.

[79] SPEW was renamed the Society for Promoting the Training of Women (SPTW) in 1926 and is still in existence.

[80] On this issue, see, Jordan, Ellen, *The women's movement and women's employment in nineteenth century Britain*, (Routledge), 1999, pp. 3-21.

[81] *Women and Work*, 6 June 1874.

ld encouraging and informative and introduced women to a whole range of related feminist issues. [82]

The tightrope of respectability was only one of a host of problems by feminist campaigners. Parkes, as editor of the *English Women's Review*, and SPEW sought to broaden the range of occupations that women of different classes might take up beyond the saturated markets for governesses and needlewomen. Increasingly, however, Parkes condemned the work of married women outside the home, though Boucherett and Faithfull argued that 'every woman should be free to support herself by the use of whatever faculties God has given her', without obstruction by prejudice or legislation. [83] Middle- and working-class women shared the problem of limited fields of opportunity. The 'governess problem' encapsulated the difficulties imposed since because there was a dearth of employment available for middle-class women, governesses rapidly became an overstocked and hugely exploited field of labour and there was a real risk that they would become destitute and slide into prostitution. [84] The campaign around the employment of middle-class women centred on the opportunities and choices open to single women, and implicit in this was her choice of whether or not to marry. [85] There was also a potential conflict with orthodox political economy, which argued that women's work depressed the wages of men when they were in free competition. Some, like Boucherett were prepared to face the consequences of a free market in labour. Parkes and others adopted a more cautious position suggesting ways in which

---

[82] This was, for example, also evident in the publication of guides for women searching for work such as Grogan, Mercy, *How women may earn a living*, (Cassell & Co.), 1883, and Davidson, J. E., *What our daughters can do for themselves: a handbook of women's employments*, (Smith, Elder, & Co.), 1894.

[83] Faithfull, E., 'Open council', *English Woman's Journal*, Vol. 10, (1862), pp. 70-71, at p. 70.

[84] On the issue of governesses see Hughes, Kathryn, *The Victorian Governess*, (Hambledon), 1993, Renton, Alice, *Tyrant or victim? A history of the British governess,* 1991, Raftery, Deirdre, 'The nineteenth-century governess: image and reality', in Whelan, Bernadette, (ed.), *Women and paid work in Ireland, 1500-1930* (Four Courts), 2000, pp. 57-68, and Horn, Pamela, 'The Victorian governess', *History of Education*, Vol. 18, (1989), pp. 333-344.

[85] Faithfull, Emily, *Choice of a Business for Girls*, (Victoria Press), 1864, and Faithfull, Emily, 'On some of the Drawbacks connected to the present Employment of Women: paper read before the National Association for the promotion of social science, in London, June 11th, 1862', *Transactions of the National Association for the Promotion of Social Science*, (John W. Parker), 1863, pp. 809-810.

association and co-operation among women might moderate the harshness of the free market.

Professionalising women's work

The most potent way in which activist women could extend the cause of women's employment was by moving into new areas of opportunity. [86] Many prominent feminists did this by taking up employment in government jobs as factory and sanitary inspectors, in the new female professions of nursing and teaching or by fighting for entry to hitherto closed professions such as medicine and the Law though the breakthrough into the professions should not be exaggerated. The problems became more acute for women entering nursing or teaching, precisely because they were the areas that rapidly became associated with and almost defined, women's professionalism. The care of the sick and of children was, of course, an acceptable area of activities for women. Nursing was an exclusively female profession in the latter half of the century, unlike teaching, where the tendency was for women employees to be concentrated in the lower ranks of the profession and paid less than their male counterparts.

The 'white-blouse' revolution

The 1851 Census listed only fourteen women as commercial clerks in England and Wales but by 1921, 46 per cent of Britain's clerks were women. This represented a massive shift in the gender composition. In the mid-nineteenth century, clerks were men generally employed in the counting-houses of merchants and manufacturers as well as in the growing bureaucracies of central and local government. Although in some instances their income of perhaps £50 a year in the 1850s was often less than skilled workers, most clerks saw themselves as socially superior, had higher levels of literacy and educational achievement. Before the 1880s, male clerks pursued their careers largely untroubled by serious competition in the labour market increasing from 2.5 per cent of all occupied males in 1851 to over 7 per cent in 1911. However, women began to be recruited in increasing numbers especially in the two decades before the First World War but though they made major inroads into the commercial office, they were largely absent in the male reserves of banking, railways and the law. This was the 'white-blouse

---

[86] On this issue, see Witz, A., 'Patriarchy and professions: the gendered politics of occupational closure', *Sociology*, Vol. 24, (1990), pp. 675-690.

revolution'.[87] Why this occurred was the result of changes in the organisation of the office, technological developments and better education for girls. Changes in business organisations especially the growth of joint-stock companies and amalgamation of companies created larger and more complex structures from the smaller counting-houses. The increased volume of office work saw an increase in the size of the office workforce. Employing more male clerks was an option but this would have led to a rising wages bill at the same time that Boards of Directors were trying to curtail costs. Employing women as office workers was cheaper but even so in 1911, male clerks outnumbered female workers by four to one.

Telegraphy and the telephone speeded up communications but it was the typewriter that from the 1880s revolutionised the production of documents in offices. The first Remington model was sold in Britain in 1878; 304 Remington Model IIs were sold in 1880, 27,000 in 1887 and 65,000 in 1890. Although typewriting is gender-free, few male clerks learned typing skills especially when it became clear that typists were unlikely to be promoted. However, once shorthand was linked with typewriting, it was quickly feminised and explains why girls, initially largely from the better educated middle-classes, became the backbone of office work. By the 1890s, working-class boys and girls, as well as those from less secure middle-class backgrounds were taking evening continuation classes in commercial subjects provided by local School Boards and by voluntary organisations increasing the number of suitably qualified young women who could become clerks. The economic benefits of office work motivated large numbers of young women to invest in classes in shorthand and typewriting. In 1910, female clerks earned on average a £1 a week in commerce and more in insurance compared to the 12 and 18 shillings a week paid to female cotton workers. In other female white-collar occupations, nurses earned between £24 and £40 a year and only in school teaching did women earn substantially more than clerks. A small percentage of female clerks earned higher wages than almost all women and most men with the elite private secretaries in top London offices by 1911 earning between £150 and £220 a year.

Office work fulfilled the middle-class requirement of genteel and economically secure employment and apart from nursing and teaching and the higher reaches of shop work was the only occupation that allowed women to be 'ladylike' in and outside work. It is also clear that female clerks generally left the labour market when they

---

[87] Anderson, Gregory, (ed.), *The White-Blouse Revolution: Female Office Workers since 1870*, (Manchester University Press), 1988, especially pp. 1-66.

married. The process of feminisation of office work was slow and women only made up slightly more than a fifth of clerks in 1911 largely because they were not hired to replace men.

Nursing

In the early-nineteenth century, nursing in hospitals was almost exclusively working-class in character, a century later it was a profession composed largely of middle-class women. [88] The professionalisation of nursing drew on established social norms of female behaviour and nurses were increasingly seen as paragons of female virtue: dedication to duty, reliability and efficiency. These existed in the context of total obedience to male doctors, their asexual character reinforced by nurses living in segregated lodgings and a dedication to a vocation that was almost religious in intensity. Although it provided important opportunities for middle- and working-class employment, the professionalisation of nursing provided little liberation from male-domination. In fact, Florence Nightingale was anxious not to rouse male opposition in the medical profession by equating nursing with feminism. [89]

The Nightingale nurse did not emerge as the standard model for nursing until the 1890s. It took time for new concepts on nurse training and discipline to gain support in hospitals. Contemporaries and later historians have considered Florence Nightingale, with her training school established at St. Thomas' Hospital in 1860 as the founder of modern nursing. The Nightingale school has not been judged a great success by historians, but its achievement was to associate her name in the public mind with a particularly disciplined form of nurse training. [90] Nightingale nursing built on these two earlier reforms: doctor-driven reform that came to be called the 'ward system' and the reforms of the Anglican Sisters, known as the 'central

---

[88] Hawkins, Sue, *Nursing and Women's Labour in the Nineteenth Century*, (Routledge), 2010, places nursing in the context of women's wider role in British society.
[89] Abel-Smith, Brian, *A History of the Nursing Profession*, (Heinemann), 1960, and Maggs, C. J., *The Origins of General Nursing*, (Croom Helm), 1983, provide valuable studies of the development of nursing in the nineteenth century.
[90] Baly, Monica, 'The Nightingale nurses: the myth and the reality', in Maggs, C., (ed.), *Nursing History, the state of the art* (Croom Helm), 1987, pp. 33-59, and her more extensive *Florence Nightingale and the nursing legacy*, (Croom Helm), 1986. See also, McDonald, Lynn, 'Florence Nightingale a Hundred Years on: why she was and what she was not', *Women's History Review*, Vol. 19, (2010), pp. 721-740.

system' of nursing. [91]

Historians of nursing have ascribed the nineteenth century reforms to two main causes: hospital doctors whose medical knowledge was developing found the old independent nurse practitioners a threat and the spread of middle-class values by philanthropists. By contrast, Helmstadter and Godden argue that the real cause of nursing reform was the development of the new scientific medicine that emphasised supportive therapies and became heavily dependent on skilled nursing for successful implementation of these treatments. The old hospital nurses could not meet the requirements of the new medicine. It was difficult to recruit educated women or 'ladies' and there were intricate interactions between the requirements of clinical nursing under hospital medicine's new regime and the contemporary ideal of a lady.

The importance of Florence Nightingale, forever fixed in the public imagination as the 'Lady with the Lamp' in the Crimea, lies in her contribution in establishing a set of rules and expectations of what a nurse should be. Her view of nursing was based on moral rather than scientific principles. Candidates for her training schemes had to demonstrate that they had the stamina and character to fulfil her highest moral requirements. Cleanliness was next to godliness so nurses had to have the highest standards of hygiene but apart from that, the major objective was complete dedication to patient care. Even nurses' uniforms were modelled on those of nursing sisters in religious orders. Nursing was less a profession than a calling.

Before 1861, there were fewer than a thousand women acting as hospital nurses but by 1901, this had risen to 12,500 nurses in general hospitals. The reasons for this are clear. The nursing profession was based on a hierarchical system based on the domestic sphere of women's accepted world and middle-class women were attracted to a role without any loss of social status and this was reflected in their pay and conditions. Matrons were given low salaries because it was assumed that they were from affluent families and had a private income. Nursing also attracted working-class girls because, though it resembled domestic service, it was not limited by the confines of a household and had a degree of freedom and independence. They too were poorly paid but this was balanced by living in and by professional status especially after the establishment of formal training and certification for nurses after 1881. Without

---

[91] Helmstadter, Carol, and Godden, Judith, *Nursing before Nightingale, 1815-1899*, (Ashgate), 2011. See also, Helmstadter, Carol, 'Building a New Nursing Service: Respectability and Efficiency in Victorian England', *Albion*, Vol. 35, (4), (2004), pp. 590-621.

working-class nurses the problem of recruiting sufficient nurses would have proved impossible but this was not without difficulties. Most working-class nurses had little education and most training courses did little to address this issue. There were also important openings in nursing beyond hospitals with the emergence of district nurses from the 1860s and especially after 1880. [92]

The fight for female doctors

Florence Nightingale transformed the image and practice of nursing in the 1860s but it was still assumed that doctors would be male. It is ironic that the campaign fought by women to become doctors, one of the great epics of the women's movement, is less known than the professionalising of nursing. [93] Women would feel more comfortable and confident if, at times of illness, they could be attended by women doctors. Although Florence Nightingale was a Victorian icon and popularly endured in poem and story book, Sophia Jex-Blake who pioneered female doctors is a less familiar figure. Yet, both women had a number of features in common. They had social status and financial security, refused to be intimidated, were able publicists and had the devoted admiration of individuals of both sexes. But while images of the Lady with the Lamp were widespread and popular, no female doctor achieved the same level of instant recognition.

Elizabeth Blackwell, a Nonconformist who had trained in America, was able to practise in England after the 1858 Act recognised foreign degrees though the following year this was rescinded and spoke of the loneliness of being the only woman doctor. [94] It was a decade later when the first female medical students, led by Sophia Jex-Blake entered the University of Edinburgh but the University refused to award them degrees. Jex-Blake and the other female students took the University to court but lost their case in

---

[92] Howse, Carrie, "The Ultimate Destination of All Nursing': The Development of District Nursing in England, 1880-1925', *Nursing History Review*, Vol. 15, (2007), pp. 65-94.
[93] Blake, Catriona, *The Charge of the Parasols: Women's Entry to the Medical Profession in Britain,* (Women's Press), 1990, examines how women fought for and obtained entry into the medical profession.
[94] See, Baker, Rachel, *The First Woman Doctor: The Story of Elizabeth Bakewell, M. D.*, (George C. Harrap and Co. Ltd.), 1946, and Chambers, P., *A Doctor Alone: A Biography of Elizabeth Blackwell: The First Woman Doctor*, (Bodley Head), 1956.

1873. [95] Several then went abroad to qualify. [96] In 1864, the University of Zurich had admitted female students and universities in Paris, Berne and Geneva followed suit in 1867. Jex-Blake went to Switzerland to study medicine at the University of Berne. Elizabeth Garrett Anderson managed to have her name entered on the medical register in 1865 by gaining the diploma of the Apothecaries Society and obtained a degree from the University of Paris in 1870. [97] Elizabeth Garrett and Sophia Jex-Blake were able to establish the London School of Medicine for Women in 1874 and gradually there were enough courses and lecturers for women to gain a good medical education.

In 1876, British examining bodies were permitted to include women if they wished and by slow stages, first licences and then university degrees were open to medical women. The following year the Royal Free Hospital admitted female students for clinical training and the University of London adopted a new charter in 1878 that allowed women to graduate from their courses. Individual institutions were slowly forced to permit women to hold their degrees, though some, like Oxford and Cambridge, resisted until 1920 and 1948 respectively. One by one, often with great personal difficulty and dedication, a handful of women were able to qualify through this indirect route. By 1880, there were five of them, such a modest achievement after so much effort. The numbers were small but rising. In the 1881 Census there were 25 women doctors in England and Wales or 0.17 per cent of all doctors. By 1891, 101 women doctors were in practice in the British Isles and the following year, the British Medical Association was finally forced to admit women doctors. In the 1911 Census, there were 495 women practitioners or 1.98 per cent of all doctors. [98]

The problem faced by women doctors, unlike nurses, was that they could not be accommodated into existing female stereotypes.

---

[95] Roberts, Shirley, *Sophia Jex-Blake: A woman pioneer in nineteenth century medical reform*, (Routledge), 1993, pp. 78-137, considers this issue.
[96] On Jex-Blake's women, their education and careers, see Crowther, M. Anne, and Dupree, Marguerite W., *Medical Lives in the Age of Surgical Revolution*, (Cambridge University Press), 2007, pp. 152-175.
[97] Anderson, Louisa, *Elizabeth Garrett Anderson, 1836-1917; by her daughter*, (Faber & Faber), 1939, and Manton, Joan, and Manton, Grenville, *Elizabeth Garrett Anderson*, (Methuen), 1965.
[98] Little, E. M., *History of the British Medical Association 1832-1932*, (BMA), 1932, republished, 1984, Pyke-Lees, Walter, *Centenary of the General Medical Council, 1858-1958: the history and present work of the Council*, (General Medical Council), 1958, and Oswald, Arthur, *The Royal College of Surgeons of England*, (Country Life), 1962.

They demonstrated that, contrary to existing medical wisdom, they had the necessary intellectual abilities to qualify even if as contemporaries believed it would develop their brains at the expense of their reproductive organs. In fact, medicine was one of the few professions in which women could combine motherhood and a career. Jex-Blake remained single but Elizabeth Garrett Anderson combined marriage and motherhood with her private practice and later with running the London School of Medicine for Women. Married women could also combine their profession with domesticity in general practice. The first female doctors married men who were either practitioners themselves or had substantial middle-class incomes: in either case, they were well supported with domestic help for child-care. All practised in towns, with the surgery usually attached to their residence and did not undertake the arduous rounds of the country practitioner.

Controlling entry

In professional and white-blouse work, employers tended to play a more direct role in maintaining sexual segregation and women, particularly those in the professions, experienced rather more direct discrimination by employers in respect to recruitment and promotion than manual workers. In the higher professions, employers were also the men who controlled entry to the profession. Until 1914, very few teaching hospitals admitted women wishing to train as doctors despite the opening of the Medical Register to women several decades earlier. If the medical profession at least proved malleable in this period, the law remained unassailable before 1914. As the number of qualified women increased, and it became usual for middle-class girls to work on leaving school, the lines of sexual segregation were vigorously defended. Ideas about the proper role of married women lay behind the introduction of the marriage bar, particularly after 1918. They assumed that married women could be treated as a reserve army of labour because of their primary responsibility to home, family and husband. [99]

Women were first employed as clerks in the Post Office and the Playfair Commission 1874-1875 maintained that, because this

---

[99] Ibid, Holcombe, Lee, *Victorian Ladies at Work: Middle-class working women in England and Wales 1850-1914*, and Vicinus, Martha, *Independent Women: Work and community for single women 1850-1920*, (Virago), 1985, provide a much needed focus on the problems facing middle-class women who either did not wish to enter into marriage or for whom work was necessary within marriage.

had been successful, women's employment could be extended to other departments if they 'could be placed in separate rooms, under proper female supervision'. This view was reiterated by the Ridley Commission in 1890. Initially women were recruited by nomination to the clerical level or they joined the service by open competition to posts in the lower grades and rose to the clerical level by promotion. Although the MacDonnell Royal Commission recommended that women should be eligible for administrative situations, it was not until 1925 that the first woman was recruited to the administrative class in the Civil Service. [100]

Many male teachers were incensed by the growth in the number of women teachers. [101] Between 1875 and 1914, the number of women elementary teachers increased by 862 per cent compared to a 292 per cent increase in men. This led to the proportion of female teachers rising from 54 per cent in 1875 to 75 per cent by 1914. Unlike doctors and top civil servants, male teachers were not in a position to control recruitment that was in the hands of school boards and then local authorities after 1902. The nineteenth century pupil-teacher system had encouraged the entry of working-class girls into teaching. [102] Like nurses, they learned on the job. Pupil teaching did not enjoy high status and it was not unusual for such girls to be considered in the same bracket as shop assistants or clerks. Many female teachers remained uncertificated: in 1913 the ratio for women was 1 in 9 compared to 1 in 3 for men. After 1907, the bursary system of teacher training replaced the pupil-teacher scheme. Boys or girls intending to become teachers had to stay on longer at school and become student teachers at seventeen. As a result, more middle-class women entered the profession and its status rose.[103]

---

[100] Martindale, Hilda, *Women Servants of the State, 1870-1938: A History of Women in the Civil Service,* (George Allen & Unwin), 1938, pp. 15-86, considers women's involvement to 1918.

[101] Oram, Alison, *Women Teachers and Feminist Politics, 1900-39,* (Manchester University Press), 1996, and Phipps, Emily, *History of the National Union of Women Teachers,* (National Union of Women Teachers), 1928

[102] See, *Report of the departmental committee on the pupil teacher system,* 2 Vols. (HMSO), 1898.

[103] See, Trouvé-Finding, Susan, 'Unionized Women Teachers and Women's Suffrage', Boussahba-Bravard, Myriam, (ed.), *Suffrage outside suffragism: women's vote in Britain, 1880-1914,* (Palgrave), 2007, pp. 205-230, Oram, Alison, ''Men must be educated and women must do it': the National Federation (later Union) of Women Teachers and contemporary feminism 1910-30', *Gender & Education,* Vol. 19, (6), (2007), pp. 663-667, and Kean, Hilda, *Deeds not words: the lives of suffragette teachers,* 1990.

In 1911, of the 117,057 female commercial clerks, 114,429 were single and 95 per cent under thirty-five. Most of these girls only expected to work until they married and employment practices in both private and public sectors were based on this expectation. Discrimination was not solely the prerogative of employers and male-dominated trade unions and in some occupations, single women in the public sector insisted on excluding married women. For instance, in 1921, female civil servants passed a resolution asking for the banning of married women from their jobs and the resulting ban was enforced until 1946. There were other setbacks. During World War One, hospitals had accepted female medical students but in the 1920s, women were again rejected on the grounds of modesty. The National Association of Schoolmasters campaigned against the employment of female teachers. In 1924, the London County Council make its policy explicit when it changed the phrase 'shall resign on marriage' to 'the contract shall end on marriage'. In the private sector, the same exclusionary policy tended to be informal but nonetheless universal.

Reforming women's lives

The symbolic importance of the vote has meant that women's broader political culture and history has been obscured. The possession of the vote qualified women finally to enter the purely masculine and public world of national politics from which they had so long been excluded. Women's interest in securing access to political rights was not limited to the campaign for parliamentary suffrage. Feminists agitated on a range of issues that affected public policy from education through official attitudes to prostitution. [104] Nineteenth century Britain was a society in which class boundaries were increasingly complex and gender was one of the influences determining women's loyalties and interests. [105] There were other loyalties, most obviously to class and community.   Nineteenth and early-twentieth century women

---

[104] Women's participation in public life is explored in ibid, Hollis, Patricia, *Ladies Elect: Women in English Local Government 1865-1914*, and in the collection of documents Hollis, Patricia, (ed.), *Women in Public: The Women's Movement 1850-1900*, (Allen & Unwin), 1979, and in Jalland, Pat, *Women, Marriage and Politics 1860-1914*, (Oxford University Press), 1986. Rendall, Jane, (ed.), *Equal or Different: Women's Politics 1800-1914*, (Basil Blackwell), 1987, contains a variety of papers on the politicisation of women in the nineteenth and early-twentieth centuries.
[105] On this issue see Pedersen, Joyce S., 'The historiography of the women's movement in Victorian and Edwardian England: varieties of contemporary liberal feminist interpretation', *The European Legacy*, Vol. 1, (1996), pp. 1052-1057.

employed the language of their own experience, of motherhood, of domestic labour, of religious commitment, whether their links were primarily with other women or when they were operating in male-dominated social institutions or political movements. While challenging injustice, many drew their considerable strength from what they regarded with pride as their most fulfilling tasks, as wives and mothers. [106]

Before 1850 women, especially if married, had few legal rights. Under the Common Law, married women had no legal identity apart from that of their husbands. Their position was defined by the doctrine of coverture under which a woman lost all rights to economic independence and property during marriage. William Blackstone, the eighteenth century jurist laid down the legal relationship:

> By marriage, the husband and wife are one person in law; that is, the very being or legal existence of the women is suspended during the marriage, or at least is incorporated and consolidated into that of the husband: under whose wing, protection and cover, she performs everything. [107]

Under the law, men gained considerable control over their wives. A husband assumed legal possession or control of all property that belonged to his wife on marriage and of any property that might come to her during marriage. The law distinguished between real property, mainly freehold land that the husband could not dispose of without his wife's permission though he could control it and its income and personal property that passed into his absolute possession and which he could use in any way he chose. The husband's rights also extended to any children of the marriage; they were his children and where a marriage was dissolved custody was automatically ceded to the man. Married women could neither sue nor be sued, nor enter into contracts and her debts and legal wrangles were her husband's responsibility. He could even set aside her will on her death. Husbands had the right to decide where and how to live. They were legally entitled to beat their wives and could, and sometimes did, lock them up.

Women were not allowed any responsibility or competence within marriage and were tied to a moral standard to which their partners were not expected to adhere. Before 1857, responsibility for

---

[106] I have explored ways in which women's 'public' lives were reformed in my *Sex, Work and Politics: Women in Britain, 1830-1918*, (Authoring History), 2012, pp. 149-225.

[107] Blackstone, William, *Commentaries on the Laws of England in Four Books*, 1765-1769, Vol. 1, chapter 15

divorce lay in the hands of the church. [108] Since ecclesiastical law recognised very few grounds for divorce, the only other recourse was the obscure and costly one of a private petition to parliament. Consequently it remained a rare and restricted option with only about 200 such petitions ever being granted. In cases heard in parliament before the marriage reforms of the 1850s, few women came forward as petitioners. Where they did present cases involving adultery by their husbands, their bid for divorce was rejected, while adultery on the part of the wife was always sufficient grounds for a husband's petition.

Feminists campaigning centred on inequalities and problems relating to the institution of marriage and on efforts to wipe out the double standard of morality based on gender that licensed male freedom but suppressed women, a double standard enshrined in matrimonial legislation. [109] The centrality of marriage in most women's lives made it an obvious feminist concern. In 1854, Barbara Leigh Smith published a tract on women's legal disabilities entitled *A Brief Summary, in plain language, of the most important laws of England concerning Women, together with a few observations thereon.* It began the campaign that was to become one of the more prominent and indeed successful of all feminist agitation. [110] In 1856, a petition bearing 3,000 signatures demanding a change in the law affecting married women's property was presented to both Houses of Parliament. The Divorce and Matrimonial Causes Act was hurriedly passed in 1857 to head off the more alarming prospect of a proposed married women's property bill. Legislation affecting divorce arose largely from the government initiated Royal Commission on Divorce

---

[108] Stone, Lawrence, *Road to divorce: England, 1530-1987*, (Oxford University Press), 1990.

[109] Gibson, Colin, *Dissolving Wedlock*, (Routledge), 1994, provides valuable insight into this area of women's experience looking at divorce over a long period. Horstman, Allen, *Victorian Divorce*, (St Martin's Press), 1985, and Stone, Lawrence, *Road to Divorce: England 1530-1987*, (Oxford University Press), 1990, are more specific. Holcombe, Lee, *Wives and Property: Reform of the Married Women's Property Law in nineteenth-century England*, (Toronto University Press), 1983, and Shanley, Mary Lyndon, *Feminism, Marriage and the Law in Victorian England 1850-1895*, (Princeton University Press), 1989, provide an entree into how the law was changed. Doggett, Maeve, *Marriage, Wife-Beating and the Law in Victorian England*, (University of South Carolina), 1993, looks at a neglected subject.

[110] Burton, Hester, *Barbara Bodichon 1827-1891*, (John Murray), 1949, and Herstein, Sheila, *Mid-Victorian Feminist: Barbara Leigh-Smith Bodichon*, (Yale University Press), 1985.

set up in 1850 whilst the less successful attempts to change the law on married women's property arose directly from feminist lobbying. [111]

The 1857 Act was unsatisfactory in three respects. It had been used as an alternative to more controversial legislation and set back the cause of married women's property by more than a decade. Its provision for deserted wives was inadequate and it enshrined a double standard in the grounds in established for securing a divorce. Women's access to divorce was limited to cases where the husband's adultery was compounded by further sexual misdemeanours (bigamy, cruelty, desertion or incest) while for the man his wife's adultery was sufficient cause. There were some 150 divorces per year in the 1860s following the 1857 Act, a surprisingly high proportion of them perhaps as many as half among the working- and lower middle-classes. For 1890 to 1900, this had risen to 582 annually. The major deficiencies in the 1857 Act only surfaced again when organisations like the Women's Emancipation Union made divorce reform a plank of their policies in the early 1890s. [112] The Clitheroe case of 1891 was also instrumental in re-opening the wider question of women's status within marriage. Mr and Mrs Jackson had lived apart throughout their brief marriage and when Jackson returned from New Zealand, his wife refused to live with him. He abducted her and held her captive in his sister's house in Blackburn while a legal suit was set in train. The judges initially upheld Jackson's claim but this was overturned by the Court of Appeal that set Mrs Jackson free. A husband could no longer physically compel his wife to live with him. [113]

---

[111] Shanley, M. L., "One must ride behind': married women's rights and the divorce act of 1857'. *Victorian Studies*, Vol. 25, (1982), pp. 355-376; Anderson, Olive, 'Hansard's hazards: an illustration from recent interpretations of married women's property law and the 1857 Divorce Act', *English Historical Review*, Vol. 112, (1997), pp. 1202-1215; Shanley, Mary Lyndon, *Feminism, Marriage, and the Law in Victorian England*, (Princeton University Press), 1993, pp. 22-48.

[112] See, for example, *Women's Emancipation Union: women and the law courts: paper read at the Birmingham Conference, 25th October, 1892*, 1892, and *The Women's Emancipation Union: its origin and its work*, (Guardian Printing Works), 1892

[113] Elmy, E. C. Wolstenholme, *The decision in the Clitheroe case and its consequences: a series of five letters by Mrs Wolstenholme Elmy*, (Guardian Print), 1891, ibid, Shanley, Mary Lyndon, *Feminism, Marriage, and the Law in Victorian England*, pp. 156-188, and Frost, Ginger, 'A shock to marriage? The Clitheroe Case and the Victorians', Robb, George, and Erber, Nancy, (eds.), *Disorder in the court: trials and sexual conflict at the turn of the century*, (Macmillan), 1999, pp. 100-118.

In the previous thirty years, the marriage debate had centred on the property issue.[114] The first married women's property committee was set up in 1855 but it failed in its legislative attempts in 1856-1857. It was an issue that raised interest across class barriers, more particularly in relation to a husband's rights over his wife's earnings. The property campaign combined parliamentary manoeuvre with bills and amendments through the late 1860s and 1870s and hard propaganda and lobbying. When the first and inadequate instalment of the Married Women's Property Act was passed in 1870, the campaigners were not mollified and maintained their attacks.[115] Women could now keep up to £200 of the money they earned. Bills and amendments came before parliament in 1873, 1874, 1877, 1878, 1880 and 1881 before finally becoming law in August 1882. The 1882 Act was widely regarded as a victory equalising the rights and responsibilities of women irrespective of marital status.[116] Legislation two years later finally allowed women to keep all their personal property that they brought to the marriage or acquired during it but it was not until 1893 that the rights of married women to property were

---

[114] Ibid, Holcombe, Lee, *Wives and property: reform of the married women's property law in nineteenth-century England*, is a detailed study.

[115] The 1870 Act allowed all wives to retain any property or earnings acquired after marriage rather than, as before, losing them to their husbands. For contemporary details of the legislation see, *The Married Women's Property Act, 1870: its relations to the doctrine of separate use, with notes*, (Stevens and Haynes), 1873. See, ibid, Shanley, Mary Lyndon, *Feminism, Marriage, and the Law in Victorian England*, pp. 49-78, Combs, Mary Beth, 'The Price of Independence: How the 1870 Married Women's Property Act Altered the Investment Risks Faced by Lower Middle Class British Women', *Journal of Economics*, Vol. 30, (2), (2004), pp. 1-26,'Cui Bono? The 1870 British Married Women's Property Act, Bargaining Power, and the Distribution of Resources within Marriage', *Feminist Economics*, Vol. 12, (2006), pp. 51-83, and 'A Measure of Legal Independence'': The 1870 Married Women's Property Act and the Portfolio Allocations of British Wives', *Journal of Economic History*, Vol. 65, (4), (2005), pp. 1028-1057, and Morris, R. J., 'Men, women and property: the reform of the Married Women's Property Act, 1870', in Thompson, F. M. L., (ed.), *Landowners, capitalists and entrepreneurs: essays for Sir John Habakkuk* (Oxford University Press), 1994, pp. 171-191.

[116] The 1882 Act allowed women to retain any property possessed at the time of their marriage, thus extending to all women with property a right which the better-off had previously been able to acquire through establishing a trust in equity. See, Thicknesse, Ralph, *The Married Women's Property Act, 1882*, (W. Maxwell & Son), 1884, and ibid, Shanley, Mary Lyndon, *Feminism, Marriage, and the Law in Victorian England*, pp. 103-130.

assimilated to those of unmarried women. A woman was no longer a 'chattel' but an independent and separate person. Even after 1884, relatively few women had sufficient income or property on which to live conformably alone or with children after divorce. [117]

Of growing concern in the 1870s was anxieties over violence within marriage.[118] Legal opinion did little to prohibit male violence. It was Frances Power Cobbe's denunciation of wife-abuse, an act she saw as resulting in large part from the degrading pressure of poverty that re-opened the marriage debate in the late 1870s.[119] She argued that the new divorce courts remained an option beyond the reach of poor women, whom she felt to be more at risk. The passage of the Matrimonial Causes Act in 1878 established a class distinction: wealthier women could still obtain full divorces under the 1857 Act, while working women were offered the cheaper but more restricted alternative of a separation order granted through a magistrate's court that prohibited the option of re-marriage. Women could now secure a separation on the grounds of cruelty and claim custody of their

---

[117] Redman, Joseph H., *A concise view of the law of husband and wife as modified by the Married women's property acts: with an appendix of statutes*, (Reeves & Turner), 1883 and Brown, A., and Griffith, J. R., *The married women's property acts, 1870, 1874, 1882, 1884: with copious and explanatory notes and an appendix of acts relating to married women*, (Stevens and Haynes), 1891.

[118] On domestic violence, see, Hammerton, A. James, *Cruelty and companionship: conflict in nineteenth-century married life*, (Routledge), 1992, and 'Victorian marriage and the law of matrimonial cruelty', *Victorian Studies*, Vol. 33, (1990), pp. 269-292; D'Cruze, Shani, *Crimes of outrage: sex, violence and Victorian working women*, (UCL Press), 1998, Savage, Gail, "A State of Personal Danger': Domestic Violence in England, 1903-1922', in Watson, K. D., (ed.), *Assaulting the past: violence and civilization in historical context*, (Cambridge Scholars), 2007, pp. 269-285, Edwards, Susan, "Kicked, beaten, jumped on until they are crushed', all under man's wing and protection: The Victorian dilemma with domestic violence', in Rowbotham, Judith and Stevenson, Kim, (eds.), *Criminal conversations: Victorian crimes, social panic, and moral outrage*, (Ohio State University Press), 2005, pp. 247-266, and Tomes, Nancy, 'A 'torrent of abuse': crimes of violence between working-class men and women in London, 1840-75', *Journal of Social History*, Vol. 11, (1978), pp. 328-345.

[119] *Life of Frances Power Cobbe: By herself*, (S. Sonnenschein & Co.), 1904, pp. 556-634, considers 'the claims of brutes' and gives a clear statement of her views. See also, Mitchell, Sally, *Frances Power Cobbe: Victorian feminist, journalist, reformer*, (University of Virginia Press), 2004, pp. 267-304, Williamson, Lori, *Power and protest: Frances Power Cobbe and Victorian society*, (Rivers Oram), 2005, and Hamilton, Susan, *Frances Power Cobbe and Victorian feminism*, (Palgrave Macmillan), 2006.

children. Magistrates even authorised protection orders to wives whose husbands have been convicted of aggravated assault. Cobbe saw the 1878 Act as a means of empowering women. Yet her suggestions were more far-reaching than those actually implemented in the legislation. She argued that the right of separation should be amplified by automatic maternal custody of children and by maintenance orders for a wife and children against the offending husband. From 1883, about 8,000 separation orders per year were being granted. The subsequent history of these changes shows that the option of separation was utilised largely by women while divorce remained primarily a vehicle used by men. The social stigma attaching even to an 'innocent' divorced woman in respectable circles, though not to a separated wife in the working-class, figures suggest may have remained a considerable deterrent to ending a marriage.

The growing challenge to the conventions of marriage among the middle-classes appears to have coincided with a peak of enthusiasm for formal marriage and associated religious ritual among the working-classes. Older irregular customs of co-habitation and separation were disappearing except in remote rural areas and illegitimacy rates were exceptionally low. The argument that working-class women promoted formal marriage as a source of security does not take account of the enthusiasm of working-class men for stable partnerships. Both men and women were dependent for a reasonable standard of living upon a stable relationship. Gradually, it seems, divorce court judges were moving towards a conception of marriage as a contract between husband and wife embodying reciprocal rights and obligations, rather than as a relationship of patriarchal dominance and dependence. Nevertheless, divorce was still not an easy path for a woman to take and in the circumstances it is surprising that so many had the courage and determination to end their marriages.

Conclusions

Whether in the economy, society, politics or culture, the nineteenth century is often portrayed as one of growing middle-class hegemony in which the entrepreneurial ideal became the dominant social ideology. The problem is that the middle-classes were remarkably diverse ranging from financiers and businessmen who were wealthier than many landowners to clerks whose income differed little from skilled workers. The notion of respectability that distinguished it from the excesses of the aristocracy and the working-classes is no longer regarded as the exclusive characteristic of the middle-classes as it dispersed across society. Defining masculinity and femininity in terms of separate spheres played an important part in marking off the middle-classes from other social groups and different sections of the bourgeoisie could agree on the subordinate position of women if nothing else creating a homogeneous ideology between the disparate groups within the middle-classes. However, the lived experience of many in the middle-classes created a gulf between the ideal, the rhetoric and the reality. The view that all groups of property owners, landed and non-landed were increasingly integrated into a new ruling class after 1850 is questionable. Given the diverse economic functions, different geographical locations and access to wealth and power, it is difficult to establish a viable case for middle-class political hegemony. It is true that the middle-classes were given the vote in 1832, municipal government was reformed in 1835, they managed to get the Corn Laws repealed in 1846 and their ideological stance, characterised by 'respectability', was of growing significance. But this occurred within a framework of aristocratic economic and political power. The 'power' of the middle-classes, however it is construed, did increase and they became more influential in determining policy directions and agendas. However, this does not mean that they acquired political power in any meaningful sense. In 1914, political power, especially at national level remained, to a considerable degree, where it had been in 1832 with the aristocratic elite.

23 The upper-classes

Between 1780 and 1914, manufacturing industry grew steadily in importance to become dominant within the economy and this was reflected in the structure of class relations. The relationship between agriculture and industry changed tilting the economic balance of power in favour of the manufacturing class while Britain's central position of in the international flow of commodities and capital ensured the continuing importance of the financiers and merchants of the City of London.[1] The landed interest was forced to come to terms with its changed circumstances. The nineteenth century saw the development of a closer relationship between property owners whether in agriculture or industry. The distinction between the two had never been complete, even in the eighteenth century successful industrialists bought themselves landed estates and landowners exploited the mineral reserves beneath their land. Although by 1900, the landed, manufacturing and commercial classes had moved closer together in economic, cultural and political terms, they had not yet coalesced into a unified propertied class.[2]

Changes in the banking system in the second half of the century stimulated a closer relationship between the two groups. In 1780, three different types of bank together formed the British banking system.[3] At the heart of the London financial system were the private banks such as Hoares, Childs, Coutts and Martins that had often developed out of older goldsmith businesses.[4] The private banks of

---

[1] On this issue see Chapman, S. D., *Merchant Enterprise in Britain*, (Cambridge University Press), 1992.

[2] See, for example, Rothery, Mark, 'The shooting party: the associational cultures of rural and urban elites in the late-nineteenth and early twentieth centuries', in Hoyle, Richard W., (ed.), *Our hunting fathers: field sports in England after 1850*, (Carnegie), 2007, pp. 96-118.

[3] On the development of banking in the nineteenth century see Collins, Michael, *Banks and Industrial Finance in Britain 1800-1939*, (Macmillan), 1995, and Quinn, Stephen, 'Money, finance and capital markets', in ibid, Floud, Roderick, and Johnson, Paul A., (eds.), *The Cambridge economic history of modern Britain, Volume 1: industrialisation, 1700-1860*, pp. 147-174 and Cottrell, P. L., 'Domestic finance, 1860-1914', in ibid, Floud, Roderick, and Johnson, Paul A., (eds.), *The Cambridge economic history of modern Britain, Volume 2: industrialisation, Economic Maturity, 1860-1939*, pp. 253-279.

[4] Hutchings, Victoria, *Messrs Hoare bankers: a history of the Hoare banking dynasty*, (Constable), 2005, and Temin, Peter, and Voth, Hans-Joachim, 'Credit rationing and crowding out during the industrial revolution: evidence from Hoare's Bank, 1702-1862', *Explorations in*

the West End had many landed clients and were often heavily involved in the long-term mortgage business of the landed class. By contrast, the private banks of the City itself were more concerned with the provision of short-term credit for merchant firms and, to a much lesser extent, manufacturing business. The Bank of England and, perhaps less importantly, the Scottish chartered banks were embroiled in the management of government finances but also carried out some private banking transactions for the merchant houses that comprised its major shareholders. The Bank was by no means a central bank regulating the rest of the banking system; its main role was to facilitate the formation of the financial syndicates that purchased government stock. The third type of bank was the country bank, private banks located outside London. [5] These often arose as adjuncts of mercantile concerns and had strong banking links with both local landowners and industrialists. Though their businesses were highly localised, the country banks were tied into the national system of capital mobilisation through their use of London agents and correspondent offices, generally one of the London private bankers.

Major changes in the financial system began with the repeal of the 'Bubble Act' in 1825 and the two Companies Acts of 1856 and 1862. [6] These changes made limited liability and transferable shares more easily available to businesses and did much to stimulate the establishment of joint-stock banks in London and the provinces. The country banks were often involved in the formation of joint-stock banks, a number of these being in London. Agency arrangements

---

Economic History, Vol. 42, (2005), pp. 325-348, and ibid, Temin, Peter, and Voth, Hans-Joachim, *Prometheus Shackled: Goldsmith Banks and England's financial revolution after 1700*, pp. 39-72.

[5] Dawes, M. and Ward-Perkins, C. N., *Country banks of England and Wales: private provincial banks and bankers, 1688-1953*, (Chartered Institute of Bankers), 2000, Brunt, Liam, 'Rediscovering Risk: Country Banks as Venture Capital Firms in the First Industrial Revolution', *Journal of Economic History*, Vol. 66, (2006), pp. 74-102, Caunce, Stephen, 'Banks, communities and manufacturing in West Yorkshire textiles, c.1800–1830', in Wilson, John Francis, and Popp, Andrew, (eds.), *Industrial clusters and regional business networks in England, 1750-1970*, (Ashgate), 2003, pp. 112-129, Cottrell, P. L., 'Britannia's sovereign: Banks in the finance of British shipbuilding and shipping, c. 1830-1894', in Akveld, L. M., Loomeijer, Frits R., and Hahn-Pedersen, Morten, (eds.), *Financing the maritime sector: proceedings from the fifth North Sea history conference*, (Fiskeri- og Sofartsmuseet), 2002, pp. 191-254.

[6] Alborn, Timothy L., *Conceiving Companies: Joint-stock Politics in Victorian England*, (Routledge), 1998, pp. 87-143, examines the development of joint-stock and deposit banking from 1826.

between London and country banks were, in many cases, formalised in mergers to form large joint-stock banks. The tightening up of the banking system, especially in the 1844 Bank Act, enabled it to become more closely involved in capital mobilisation. [7] Agricultural wealth filtered through the country banks to London from where the money went to finance the industries of the north and midlands and to finance landowners' mortgages. [8]

By the 1860s and 1870s, the City of London had become the centre of a global monetary system, with a particularly important group of 'merchant banks' specialising in financing foreign trade and funding foreign government loans. [9] Such prominent merchant bankers as Rothschild and Baring, together with others such as Goshen and Hambros, were generally based around the businesses of émigré merchants and bankers and often continued with their merchant businesses alongside their banking activities.[10] The merchants and merchant bankers of the City formed a tightly integrated group with numerous overlapping business activities: they joined together to syndicate loans and to run the major dock, canal and insurance companies and dominated the board of the Bank of England. This City group was united through bonds of business, kinship and friendship and its cohesion was increased by the frequency and informality in the exchanges, coffee-houses and other meeting-places in the square mile itself. [11]

---

[7] Horsefield, J. K., 'The Origins of the Bank Charter Act, 1844', *Economica*, Vol. 11, (1944), pp. 180-189. See also, Torrens, Robert, *The Principles and Practical Operation of Sir Robert Peel's Act of 1844*, (Longmans), 1857.

[8] Ackrill, Margaret and Hannah, Leslie, *Barclays: the business of banking, 1690-1996*, (Cambridge University Press), 2001.

[9] Kynaston, David, (ed.), *The Bank of England: money, power and influence 1694-1994*, (Oxford University Press), 1995, and Cottrell, P. L., 'The Bank of England in transition, 1836-1860', in Bosbach, Franz, and Pohl, Hans, (eds.), *Das Kreditwesen in der Neuzei, Banking System in Modern History*, (K.G. Saur), 1997.

[10] See, for example, Burk, Kathleen, *Morgan Grenfell, 1838-1988: the biography of a merchant bank*, (Oxford University Press), 1989.

[11] Collins, Michael, 'English banks and business cycles, 1848-1880', in Cottrell, P. L., and Moggridge, D. E., (eds.), *Money and power: essays in honour of L. S. Pressnell*, (Macmillan), 1988, pp. 1-40, Capie, F. H., and Collins, Michael, 'Banks, industry and finance, 1880-1914', *Business History*, Vol. 41, (1999), pp. 37-62, and 'Industrial lending by English commercial banks, 1860s-1914: why did banks refuse loans?', *Business History*, Vol. 38, (1996), pp. 26-44, Cottrell, P. L., 'The domestic commercial banks and the City of London, 1870-1939', in Cassis, Youssef, (ed.), *Finance and financiers in European history, 1880-1960*, (Cambridge University Press), 1992, pp. 39-62.

A propertied elite

In the eighteenth century, the distinction between landlords and capitalist farm tenants had been sharpened by the continuing process of agricultural improvement.[12] By 1850, the enclosure movement was all but completed and a third rural class of agricultural wage labourers had been created. The three classes of landlord, tenant farmer and labourer characterised Victorian rural society and formed the basis of contemporary images of the rural world. [13]

Landlords were dominant in terms of wealth, power and prestige while tenant farmers were under increasing economic pressure and their social status had fallen below manufacturers and merchants. [14] In 1850, rentier landowners held about 75 per cent of the land in England and a considerably higher proportion in Scotland and Wales. Running a great landed estate was a matter of efficient economic management. [15] The estate was treated as a unit of capital and was administered through procedures similar to those used in the larger mines and ironworks. In landed estates, there was a partial separation of ownership from control. General supervision of the affairs of the estate remained with the landowner while day-to-day administration was delegated to agents and stewards who collected rents, kept accounts and supervised the tenants. Large estates employed both a resident land agent with delegated authority but often also a chief agent with a subordinate staff to handle specialised tasks such as timber, minerals and so on. [16] Where land was let out to tenants, strategic

---

[12] Thompson, F. L. M., *English Landed Society in the Nineteenth Century*, (Routledge), 1963, remains an important work. Stone, L., and Stone, J. C. Fautier, *An Open Elite? England 1540-1880*, (Oxford University Press), 1984, Mingay, G. E., *The Gentry*, (Longman), 1976, and Beckett, J. C., *The Aristocracy in England 1660-1914*, (Basil Blackwell), 1986, second edition, 1989, cover broader periods. These should now be supplemented by Carradine, D., *The Decline and Fall of the British Aristocracy*, (Yale University Press), 1990, and *Aspects of Aristocracy: Grandeur and Decline in Modern Britain*, (Yale University Press), 1994. General views, with sociological emphasis, can be found in Powis, J., *Aristocracy*, (Basil Blackwell), 1984, and Scott, J., *The Upper-classes*, (Macmillan), 1980.

[13] Lindert, Peter H., 'Who owned Victorian England?: the debate over landed wealth and inequality', *Agricultural History*, Vol. 61, (1987), pp. 25-51.

[14] See, Moore, D. C., 'The Landed Aristocracy', in ibid, Mingay, G. E., (ed.), *The Victorian countryside*, Vol. 2, pp. 367-382.

[15] Spring, David, *The English landed estate in the 19th century: its administration*, (John Hopkins Press), 1963, remains important.

[16] See, for example, Richards, E., 'The Land Agent', in ibid, Mingay, G. E., (ed.), *The Victorian countryside*, Vol. 2, pp. 439-456, Webster, Sarah A.,

control was shared between the landowner and the tenant. The landowner and his agents exercised supervision over tenants and made decisions over the renewal of tenancies as well as contributing to the capital requirements of the farms. The relationship between landowner and tenant was cemented in their financial arrangements with tenants receiving the profits from their farming activity and using it to pay his rent to the landowner. [17]

Family strategy was an important mechanism in economic life helping to maintain the traditional family life-style and the family estate. During the nineteenth century, farming offered a relatively poor return compared to the investment opportunities available in industry. Many landowners diversified into investments in minerals, in urban property, in railways and docks and in overseas mining concerns to supplement their largely static agricultural earnings. [18] The Duke of Sutherland, the Marquess of Bute and the Earl of Dudley were prominent as mineral developers. [19] Many landowners began to develop those parts of their estates that were well-sited for urban growth. [20] Until 1850, apart from London, these were relatively small and localised, but the pace of development soon increased. In London the major landowners included the Duke of Portland, the Duke of Westminster in Pimlico, Belgravia and Mayfair and the Duke of Bedford in Bloomsbury and Covent Garden. [21] In smaller cities and towns, prominent landowners included the Duke of Norfolk and Earl Fitzwilliam in Sheffield, the Marquess of Salisbury and the Earls of Derby and Sefton in Liverpool, the Marquess of Bute in Cardiff

---

'Estate Improvement and the Professionalisation of Land Agents on the Egremont Estates in Sussex and Yorkshire, 1770-1835', *Rural History*, Vol. 18, (2007), pp. 47-70, and Colyer, Richard J., 'The land agent in nineteenth-century Wales', *Welsh History Review*, Vol. 8, (1977), pp. 401-425.

[17] See, Moore, D. C., 'The gentry', in ibid, Mingay, G. E., (ed.), *The Victorian countryside*, Vol. 2, pp. 383-398, and Rothery, Mark, 'The wealth of the English landed gentry, 1870-1935', *Agricultural History Review*, Vol. 55, (2007), pp. 251-268.

[18] See, for example, Ward, J. T., 'West Riding Landowners and Mining in the Nineteenth Century', *Bulletin of Economic Research*, Vol. 15, (1), (1963), pp. 61-74.

[19] Davies, John, *Cardiff and the Marquesses of Bute*, (University of Wales Press), 1981, Richards, Eric, *The Leviathan of Wealth: the Sutherland fortune in the Industrial Revolution*, (Routledge & Kegan Paul), 1973.

[20] A good introduction to this subject is Cannadine, David, *Lords and Landlords: the Aristocracy and the Towns 1774-1967*, (Leicester University Press), 1980, and Cannadine, David, (ed.), *Patricians, power and politics in nineteenth-century towns*, (Leicester University Press), 1982.

[21] See, for example, Sheppard, F. H. W., 'The Grosvenor estate, 1677-1977', *History Today*, Vol. 27, (1977), pp. 726-733.

and the Calthorpes in Birmingham. As fashion shifted from the spa towns to seaside resorts in the 1880s and 1890s, landowners such as the Duke of Devonshire profited from the growth of centres such as Eastbourne, Brighton, Hastings and Scarborough. In 1886, 69 of the 261 provincial towns were largely owned by great landowners and a further 34 were owned by smaller landowners.

Rugby's headmaster Thomas Arnold saw railways as heralding the downfall of the aristocracy and initially many landowners saw them as an interference with their territorial rights and strenuously opposed their construction. However, railways offered opportunities not only through investment but through the sale of land to railway companies and through compensation:

> 'There is nobody so violent against railroads as George...he organised the whole of our division against the Marham line!' 'I rather counter on his', said Lord de Mowbray, 'to assist me in resisting this joint branch here; but I was surprised to learn he had consented.' 'Not until the compensation was settled', innocently remarked Lady Marney; 'George never opposes them after that. He gave up his opposition to the Marham line when they agreed to his terms'. [22]

The 1850 edition of Bradshaw's *General Railway Directory* listed only 24 peers and 25 sons of peers as railway directors and during the last twenty-five years of the century the number of directors in the House of Lords did not rise above fifty-one at any one time. Where landowners did invest heavily in railways, this tended not to be in main-line companies but in the secondary lines that connected their mineral interests to the main arteries of the railway network. In this way, landowners saw railway investment as a way of improving the income from the agricultural and mineral resources of their own estates. [23] As his rents fell in the depression, the Earl of Leicester invested about £170,000 in railways between 1870 and 1891, about half of his non-landed investment.

Landowners complemented their estate business with interests in industrial and commercial ventures, a diversification eased by their close business links with City financiers. Railways were giant enterprises whose capital requirements outweighed those of all other businesses together. London bankers, especially Glyn Mills, acted as active promoters for railway companies and brought together the masses of 'anonymous' investors, many from the professions and

---

[22] Ibid, Disraeli, Benjamin, *Sybil: or The two nations*, p. 106.
[23] Ward, J. T., 'West Riding Landowners and the Railways', *Journal of Transport History*, Vol. 4, (1960), pp. 242-251.

'widows and orphans', who provided much of the railway capital. [24] By the 1850s, over 200 railway companies, both domestic and foreign, banked with Glyn, Mills, and Co. The railway boom in the 1840s resulted in the 15 largest companies controlling 75 per cent of railway revenue and by the boom of the 1860s the top four companies had 44 per cent of revenue. [25] As a result, from the 1860s, many landowners began to take portfolio investments in the big main-line companies, a move away from their previous commitment only to local lines. The railway booms brought together some of the interests of the financial community and the landowners.

The development of railways also had an indirect impact on industrial funding. Limited liability had rarely been thought necessary by industrial entrepreneurs but, as the capital requirements of some industries increased, trusts and partnerships gave way to the joint-stock company. [26] This enabled manufacturers to draw on a wider pool of capital and to provide for the various members of their families by issuing shares to them. [27] For instance, the Pease family held several firms in the North of England including Joseph Pease & Partners, coal-owners, J. W. Pease & Co. that dealt in iron and limestone and the banking business was carried by J & J. W. Pease. Extensive woollen mills were run under the name of Henry Pease & Co. The headquarters of all these firms was in Northgate, Darlington. By the mid-1860s, about a thousand new joint-stock companies were being registered annually, though the majority were still run as partnerships. The spread of railway shareholding encouraged the growth of the London and provincial stock exchanges and made it easier for expanding industrial enterprises to raise capital and for landowners to

---

[24] Gore-Browne, Eric, *The history of the house of Glyn, Mills and Co.*, (Privately Printed), 1933

[25] Irving, R. J., 'The capitalisation of Britain's railways, 1830-1914', *Journal of Transport History*, third series, Vol. 5, (1984), pp. 1-24.

[26] See, Bryer, R. A., 'The Mercantile Laws Commission of 1854 and the political economy of limited liability', *Economic History Review*, second series, Vol. 50 (1997), pp. 37-56, and Loftus, Donna, 'Limited Liability, Market Democracy, and the Social Organization of Production in Mid-Nineteenth-Century Britain', in Henry, Nancy, and Schmitt, Cannon, (eds.), *Victorian investments: new perspectives on finance and culture*, (Indiana University Press), 2009, pp. 79-97.

[27] Rose, Mary B., 'The family firm in British business 1780-1914', in Kirby, M. W., and Rose, Mary B., (eds.), *Business enterprise in modern Britain: from the eighteenth to the twentieth century*, (Routledge), 1994, pp. 61-87, and Nenadic, Stana, 'The Small Family Firm in Victorian Britain', in Jones, Geoffrey, and Rose, Mary B., (eds.), *Family Capitalism*, (Routledge), 1993, pp. 86-114, provide the context.

invest.

The move towards joint stock capital was linked to an increase in the levels of economic concentration.[28] In the 1880s, the hundred largest industrial firms accounted for less than 10 per cent of the total market. However, a spate of company amalgamation led to greater concentration in the 1890s as merger activity outpaced the growth of the market. Companies were floated on the Stock Exchange and might then grow by taking over their competitors or rival firms might combine to float a common holding company. Families whose firms were floated or merged at this time often retained ordinary, voting shares for themselves and allowed debentures and non-voting shares to be sold to the wider public. As a result, family control could be maintained through relatively small capital investment. The flotation of firms allowed capital to be raised from outside the family circle while the joint-stock firm allowed family wealth to be diversified and made more secure. Large amalgamation of family firms occurred in a rapid burst between 1898 and 1900, but the rate of flotation and merger remained high until 1914.

As a result, some family firms continued to prosper. In 1848, for instance, Thomas Barlow founded Barlow & Co. in Manchester, manufacturing and trading in textiles in Britain. From the mid-1850s, the firm started importing cotton from America and began exporting textiles to India and the Far East. In 1864, he founded Thomas Barlow & Bro. and during the 1870s and 1880s established his own trade agencies in Calcutta, Shanghai and Singapore to export goods from Britain, to import tea and coffee, and to acquire his own plantations in these regions. During the last two decades of the nineteenth century, Thomas's eldest son John Emmott Barlow steered the family firm away from textiles to develop its interests in agency work, in the export of iron and steel, and in tea and coffee, which led to the acquisition of a bonded tea warehouse in London. In 1891, the Barlows took over the ailing textile importers Scott & Co. in Singapore and began to extend their business to coffee estates. When the crop failed in the late 1890s, business was diversified to planting rubber trees. In 1906, a number of estates combined to form the Highlands and Lowlands Para Rubber Co., with Barlow & Co. as its agents in Singapore and Kuala Lumpur, while Thomas Barlow & Bro. acted as Secretaries in England. Diversification was one route to family success. But, in the case of W. D. & H. O. Wills in the tobacco industry, family control was maintained through a combination of technical innovation and organisational change in the 1890s. This

---

[28] Johnson, Paul, *Making the Market: Victorian Origins of Corporate Capitalism*, (Cambridge University Press), 2010.

strengthened the firm and did not lead to a haemorrhage of capital and ability from the organisation into landownership and politics. [29]

Because of family loyalties and priorities, those larger companies that succeeded in adopting a more centralised structure were generally either those in which one constituent firm was considerably larger than the others or those in which a particular family managed to subordinate its fellows in the struggle for control. The families who lost out in the struggle for control in the amalgamated firms were faced with the choice of either retiring into land or politics or moving into new business ventures. Families that wished to leave business often decided to sell out to a company promoter prior to the Stock Exchange flotation. These families sometimes retained a stake in the firm but were not involved in active control. [30] Promoters were often keen to recruit peers to the board of companies that they had floated, feeling that a 'lord on the board' would help the sale of shares. [31] The number of the aristocracy on the board of the Great Western Railway rose from eight of the forty-nine directors in 1856-1875 to thirteen out of thirty-six between 1896 and 1915. From the 1870s, landowners joined the boards of joint-stock companies and by 1896, a quarter of all peers had directorship. Many of these men would have been invited on to a board to provide kudos but many landowners found that their directorships provided a significant supplement to their income. Companies may even have benefited from the 'managerial' expertise of the landowners since the managerial problems of large firms and the need for delegated administration were similar to those faced on their estates.

The declining return of agriculture as a proportion of the returns of the economy as a whole was aggravated by the agricultural depression of 1873-1896. [32] Smaller landowners were hit more severely than the larger landowners who had been able to diversify into non-agricultural activities. This exacerbated growing awareness and criticism of the accumulation of wealth in land, commerce and

---

[29] Alford, B. W .E., *W. D. & H. O. Wills and the Development of the UK Tobacco Industry, 1786-1965*, (Taylor & Francis), 2006, pp. 304-306.
[30] Casson, Mark, 'The economics of the family firm', *Scandinavian Economic History Review*, Vol. 47, (1999), pp. 10-23.
[31] See, Jeremy, David, J., 'Anatomy of the British Business Elite, 1860-1980', *Business History*, Vol. 26, (1), (1984), pp. 3-23, Channon, G, 'The recruitment of directors to the board of the Great Western Railway', www.manchesteruniversitypress.co.uk/uploads/docs/200001.pdf
[32] See, Channing, Francis Allston, *The Truth about Agricultural Depression: an economic study of the evidence of the Royal Commission*, (Longman, Green and Co.), 1897, pp. 29-52, on evidence for successful farming.

industry. [33] The result of this controversy and criticism was the establishment of an official investigation to scotch the claim that most land was owned by 30,000 people. This backfired and the investigation discovered that the land was owned by a much smaller number of people. The results of the survey for 1873 were published in the *Returns of Owners of Land* (the 'New Domesday Book') and, although there is some confusion in the various summaries of the *Returns*, certain conclusions about the ownership of land are clear. [34] 80 per cent of land was owned by 7,000 people, of whom 4,200 in England and Wales and 800 in Scotland held 1,000 acres or more. Among these people, 363 held 10,000 acres or more and 44 had 100,000 acres or more. Most of the largest estates were in Scotland: there were a total of 35 estates larger than 100,000 acres, of which the 25 Scottish estates accounted for a quarter of the Scottish land. In total, large landowners held about 24 per cent of the land, smaller rentiers held about 55 per cent and owner-occupiers held a further 10 per cent with the Church of England and the Crown holding a similar amount. Finally, this national picture was repeated at local level: in East Anglia, for example, 350 people owned 55 per cent of the agricultural land in Norfolk, Suffolk and Cambridgeshire.

In terms of income, 2,500 people had an annual rental income of £3,000 or more in 1873 of whom 866 had an income of £10,000 or more and 76 £50,000 or more. Sixteen people received a rental income in excess of £100,000, the largest incomes going to the Dukes of Norfolk and Buccleuch and the Marquess of Bute. There was not a perfect correlation between income and acreage. Only 7 people had both 100,000 acres and £100,000 annual income: the Dukes of Buccleuch, Devonshire, Northumberland, Portland and Sutherland, the Marquess of Bute and the Earl Fitzwilliam. The survey did not extend to the rental income derived from urban rents and the wealth of men such as the Duke of Westminster was underestimated. [35] To identify Britain's richest landowners more closely it is necessary to include the Dukes of Norfolk and Westminster, who had large incomes from relatively small estates and six men with massive estates

---

[33] Burrows, A. J., *The agricultural depression and how to meet it; hints to landowners and tenant farmers: By Alfred J. Burrows ...Reprinted, with considerable additions, from 'The Journal of Forestry and Estate Management'*, (William Rider & Son), 1882, was one, of several, self-help books.
[34] See Bateman, John, *The Great Landowners of Great Britain and Ireland*, (Harrison and Sons), 1879, fourth edition, (Harrison and Sons), 1883.
[35] Ibid, Rubinstein, W. D., *Men of Property: The Very Wealth in Britain since the Industrial Revolution*, pp. 193-226, provides analysis based on the *Returns of Owners of Land*; see especially Table 7.1, pp. 194-195.

with less than £100,000 rental: the Duke of Richmond, the Earls of Breadalbane, Fife and Seafield, Alexander Matheson and Sir James Matheson. These fifteen people were the core of the British landed class and the continuing overlap between the rich and the peerage is obvious. Of the 363 people with both £10,000 income and 10,000 acres, together holding almost a quarter of Britain's land, 246 were members of the peerage; and a further 350 peers had smaller estates.

Landed wealth-holders 1809-1899			
	1809-1858	1858-1879	1880-1899
Millionaires	75	33	32
Half-millionaires	150	50	n/a
Total	225	83	--

It is clear that the number of landed millionaires fell between the first and second half of the century in relation to wealthy merchants and industrialists. [36] Perkin estimated that there were, in 1850, 2,000 businessmen with profits of £3,000 or more; 338 of these people received £10,000 or more and 26 £50,000 or more. [37] In 1867, the wealthiest 0.5 per cent of the population received 26.3 per cent of the total income. By 1880, the number of businessmen with Schedule D profits of £3,000 or more had risen to 5,000 of whom 987 received £10,000 or more and 77 £50,000 or more.

Top British wealth-holders outside land 1809-1914				
	1809-58	1858-79	1880-99	1900-14
Millionaires	9	30	59	75
Half-millionaires	47	102	158	181
Total	56	132	217	256

By 1880, the commercial and manufacturing classes had overtaken the landed classes in economic terms. The financial sector consistently accounted for between 20 and 40 per cent of all non-landed millionaires. Both of the main industries of the industrial revolution were well-represented among millionaires. Textiles accounted for about 10 per cent, a slight increase from earlier in the century while metals accounted for the same percentage in both of the earlier periods and then fell away. In the later periods, the food, drink and tobacco industries together accounted for about a fifth of all non-landed millionaires, and from 1858 the distributive trades accounted

---

[36] Spring, David, and Spring, Eileen, 'Debt and the English aristocracy', *Canadian Journal of History*, Vol. 31, (1996), pp. 377-394.
[37] Ibid, Perkin, H., *The Origins of Modern English Society 1780-1880*, pp. 414-420.

for one-tenth. The wealthy men of land, commerce and manufacturing drew closer together during the Victorian period, though landowners still tended to denigrate merchants and manufacturers as 'middle-class' and concerned with 'trade'. [38] This status exclusion was eased by the existence of a vast number of clerks, shopkeepers and tradesmen who were oriented towards the commercial and manufacturing classes and appeared to form a continuous social class with them. In fact, the economic gulf between them was immense.

Deference and decline

The involvement of landowners on boards of manufacturing and commercial companies was complemented by the continuing movement of industrial and commercial wealth into land and an increase in intermarriage between the classes. By 1830, London bankers and merchants such as Lloyd, Baring, Drummond and the Rothschilds, brewers such as Barclay, Hanbury and Whitbread had bought into land, as had wealthy lawyers. Entry into land through purchase or through marriage continued after 1830 at very much the same rate as in the previous century. Later in the century industrialists such as Tennant, Armstrong, Coats and Wills also bought into land. This can be explained by the continued status land brought since alternative and more profitable investment outlets were available. How typical these industrial magnates were is questionable since entry into the landed elite remained remarkably restricted. Most sons of manufacturers inherited the family firm not a country mansion. [39]

The cultural blending of the privileged social classes was marked by a reassertion of the status of the 'gentleman' with its associated life-style. [40] Tocqueville had noted this process in the 1850s:

...if we follow the mutation of time and place of the English word 'gentleman...we find its connotation being steadily widened in England as the classes draw nearer to each other and intermingle. In each successive century we find it being applied to men a little lower in the social scale... [41]

---

[38] See, Spring, Eileen, 'Business men and landowners re-engaged', *Historical Research*, Vol. 72, (1999), pp. 77-91.
[39] Speck, W. A., *A Concise History of Britain, 1707-1975*, (Cambridge University Press), (1993), pp. 59-60.
[40] In this see, Mason, P., *The English gentleman*, (André Deutsch), 1982, and Raven, S. A. N., *The English gentleman: an essay in attitudes*, (A. Blond), 1961.
[41] Tocqueville, Alexis de, *The Old Regime and the French Revolution*, (Harper & Brothers), 1856, p. 108, (Doubleday), 1955, pp. 82-83.

What characterised a 'gentleman' was instinctively known and defined though their very indefinability. [42] This inherently vague notion had long marked a fundamental status divide in society and, as the number of manufacturers and merchants increased so it took increasing significance in social control. The small size of the peerage meant that even the admission of their most wealthy manufacturers into the peerage could only operate as a mechanism of social control if the peerage continued to be associated with the more informal and flexible concept of the gentleman. Acceptance as a gentleman by those who were already recognised as gentlemen defined a person as someone who mattered socially and politically. That status could be given or withdrawn without justification by influential social circles made it a subtle and effective mechanism of social control.

The life-style of the gentleman had to be accommodated to the practices of the manufacturing and commercial classes. The round of visiting the great country houses, the meetings of the Quarter Sessions, and rural pursuits such as fox-hunting and racing were already integrated into the London-based 'Season' of activities in which all members of 'Society' participated. After 1830, this became more formalised and acquired a new authority over those who regarded themselves as gentlemen. Davidoff is correct when she states:

> Society can be seen as a system of quasi-kinship relationships that was used to 'place' mobile individuals during the period of structural differentiation fostered by industrialisation and urbanisation. [43]

In this period 'Society' was rapidly growing in size and directories listing the families of gentlemen found a growing market. In 1833, John Burke published the first edition of his genealogical directory of county families: initially called *Burke's Commoners*, it was subsequently given the more acceptable title of *Burke's Landed Gentry*. The 1833 volume listed 400 county families, the qualification for inclusion being possession of at least 2,000 acres of land. The 1906 volume had grown to 5,000 families, of whom 1,000 were of industrial background. *Burke's General Armory* was published in various editions from 1842 and listed all those families claiming the right to bear heraldic arms. Most of the 60,000 families included in

---

[42] For the evasiveness of the Victorians in defining 'gentleman' see, Osborne, Hugh, 'Hooked on Classics: Discourses of Allusion in the Mid-Victorian Novel', in Ellis, Roger, and Oakley-Brown, Liz, (eds.), *Translation and nation: towards a cultural politics of Englishness*, (Multilingula Matters), 2001, especially pp. 144-149.

[43] Davidoff, L., *The Best Circles*, (Croom Helm), 1973, p. 15.

the definitive 1844 edition owned little or no land. Such were the changes that were occurring to Society.

Presentation at court was regarded as central to the life of a gentleman and his family. By 1850, it was the essential entré into Society and the needs of the newcomers were met by the publication of manuals of instruction and by Certificates of Presentation.[44] The London Season, together with such events as yachting at Cowes and grouse-shooting on the Scottish moors, were central features of the life-style of the gentleman. It was, however, the Victorian public school that forged a cultural unity between the landed classes and the newcomers. The educational changes initiated by Thomas Arnold at Rugby were intended to produce 'Christian Gentlemen', a blend of the traditional notion of the gentleman with the humanitarianism of evangelical Christianity. The public school reforms of the 1860s led to the formation of the 'Headmasters' Conference' as the central forum through which the major schools could exert control and influence over the lesser schools. The rise of new men aspiring to social leadership, the expansion of the number of suitable posts in government service and the increasing use of competitive examinations for recruitment, all reinforced the benefits of a public school education. By the 1870s, the route to top positions via public school and Oxbridge had been established.

The code of gentlemanly behaviour passed on through the public schools defining what was 'done' and what was 'not done'. The gentleman had definite duties and obligations towards other members of society who had a corresponding obligation to defer to his 'natural' superiority. This marked a restoration of the 'bonds of dependency' that had existed in the eighteenth century but within an industrial and urban context. Deferential behaviour was expected of subordinates as a sign of the legitimacy of the prevailing patterns of inequality. The public school ethos was, in part, a response to the reforms of recruitment and promotion in the civil service, the law and the army but it ran counter to the rationality, efficiency and functionality of trade and industry. In some respects, the ethos pronounced by public schools represented a balance between the rationalised organisation of economic change and traditional power, a compromise between landed and entrepreneurial ideals.

The dominance of the values of the gentleman and the associated cult of amateurism has been important in the arguments

---

[44] Ellenberger, N. W., 'The transformation of London "society" at the end of Victoria's reign: evidence from the court presentation records', *Albion*, Vol. 22, (1990), pp. 633-653.

about entrepreneurial decline after 1870.[45] A. J. P. Taylor explained Britain's decline:

> The simplest answer, which remains true to the present day, was the public schools. They taught the classics when they should have been teaching sciences. [46]

The view that 'gentlemanly' culture was privileged over science and technology and that middle-class entrepreneurship was diluted by mirroring the values and lifestyle of landed society is central to this interpretation of decline. The constant flow of successful businessmen from the ungentlemanly field of trade and industry to the more acceptable fields of politics and the land is held to have resulted in a haemorrhage of talent. In fact, the attendance by the children of businessmen at public schools did not produce a drift from business life and many manufacturers saw the creation of a successful family business as the first step in a longer-term strategy of establishing a landed family. Once they had accumulated sufficient wealth, successful businessmen would become 'gentlemen', with country seats, perhaps even a knighthood or peerage, seats in Parliament for themselves or their Oxbridge educated sons. They ceased to be 'players' in the entrepreneurial field and became 'gentlemen'. The major problem with this view is that the aristocracy had emerged from the world of business and had never rejected the idea of making money through capital investment and commerce was a good thing. Some of the commercial elite certainly were 'gentrified' during the second half of the nineteenth century but they were primarily London financiers and bankers whose entrepreneurial performance remained confident well into the twentieth century. The cultural attack on entrepreneurial attitudes in late-Victorian Britain is far from convincing especially when Britain's attitude to entrepreneurialism and business life was far less hostile than in the rest of Europe and there is little evidence that, despite the importance they attached to the classics, public schools were opposed to the teaching of science. [47]

Victorian society was characterised by a move towards unity among the privileged social classes, but there was never complete

---

[45] Rubinstein, W. D., *Capitalism, culture and decline in Britain 1750-1990*, (Routledge), 1993, pp. 102-139, examines education, the 'gentleman' and British entrepreneurship. See also, ibid, Thomson, F. M. L., *Gentrification and the Enterprise Culture: Britain 1780-1980*, pp. 122-142.
[46] Taylor, A. J. P., *Essays in English History*, (Pelican), 1976, p. 37.
[47] Ibid, Rubinstein, W. D., *Capitalism, culture and decline in Britain 1750-1990*, p. 49.

integration. Landowners and the City may have come closer together but manufacturers and provincial merchants remained apart. By the 1870s, autonomous and assertive industrial dynasties were entrenched in areas such as Glasgow, Manchester, Liverpool, Birmingham, Cardiff and Newcastle. It was at this provincial level that manufacturers and merchants came closer together. The distinction between three privileged classes that had been self-evident in the 1830s was far less clear by 1914. Although each class was based round a particular kind of property, they entered into ever more extensive business and personal relationships with each other. Each class also included people who were not active participants in the control and use of property, but who drew their income from this and had family links with the core of their class. Such people were to be found in politics, the professions and the intelligentsia and these occupations constituted major areas of overlap between the fringes of the three privileged classes.

Creating the establishment

It was in politics that the new patterns of class alignment were their clearest. Between 1800 and 1850, the national political rulers were drawn exclusively from the landed classes and the City faction of the commercial class, with the manufacturers and provincial merchants pursuing their interests in the towns and cities. [48] From mid-century, this patrician approach to national politics was gradually diluted by the changing balance of power between the privileged classes and led to changes in the composition of the political leadership. [49]

The policy of the ruling Tory elite that dominated politics between the 1780s and 1830 was grounded in a negative protection of the established social order: no parliamentary reform and no concessions to working-class or middle-class radicalism. However, the changing balance of power between the landed and manufacturing classes led government to bolster agriculture. In 1813-1814, the state finally abandoned Elizabethan wage and apprenticeship regulations freeing up the labour market but in 1815, it introduced the Corn Laws

---

[48] Boyd Hilton, R., *A Mad, Bad, and Dangerous People? England 1783-1846*, (Oxford University Press), 2006, and Derry J. W., *Politics in the Age of Fox, Pitt and Liverpool: Continuity and Transformation*, (Macmillan), 1990, provides an overview.

[49] Hoppen, K. Theodore, *The mid-Victorian generation, 1846-1886*, (Oxford University Press), 1998, and Searle, G. R., *A new England?: peace and war 1886-1918*, (Oxford University Press), 2004.

to support arable farmers. [50] More economic controls were dismantled in the 1820s but the pace of economic change was not as rapid as many manufacturers demanded. [51] It was not until the Whigs came to power in late 1830 that this changed.

The Whig government faced with tensions between maintaining the political hegemony of the landed class and satisfying the demands of their commercial and manufacturing supporters, speeded the move towards a laissez-faire if regulatory state and succeeded in passing a conservative measure of parliamentary reform in 1832. But the major area of political activity for the middle-classes was at the local level. Local politics was seen as more important than national politics and the Municipal Corporations Act 1835 more important than 1832. The major line of division was not, however, between town and country but within towns.[52] A county group of established merchants and manufacturers, generally Anglican and Tory, were oriented towards the local gentry. They competed with a metropolitan group of newer manufacturers, often Nonconformists and oriented towards the Whigs, for control of the council and the magistracy and to determine the choice of MPs. [53] In Oldham, there was a separation between the cotton manufacturers who looked towards the merchant dynasties of Manchester and the older capitalists, especially colliery-owners who looked towards the local landowners. [54]

---

[50] Fay, C. R., *The Corn Law and Social England*, (Cambridge University Press), 1932, remains the most valuable discussion of the nature of the Corn Laws while Barnes, Donald Grove, *A History of The English Corn Laws from 1660-1846*, (George Routledge & Sons, Ltd.), 1930, takes a broader approach. See also, Kadish, Alan, (ed.), *The Corn Laws: the formation of popular economics in Britain,* 6 Vols. (William Pickering), 1996.
[51] Boyd Hilton, R., *Corn, Cash, Commerce: the economic policies of the Tory governments 1815-1830*, (Oxford University Press), 1977.
[52] Roberts, Matthew, *Political movements in urban England, 1832-1914*, (Palgrave), 2009, and Miskell, Louise, 'Urban Power, Industrialisation and Political Reform: Swansea Elites in the Town and Region, 1780-1850', in Roth, Ralf, and Beachy, Robert, (eds.), *Who ran the cities?: city elites and urban power structures in Europe and North America, 1750-1940*, (Ashgate), 2007, pp, 21-36.
[53] See, for example, Garrard, John Adrian, 'The middle classes and nineteenth century national and local politics', in ibid, Garrard, John Adrian, Jary, David, Goldsmith, Michael, and Oldfield, Adrian, (eds.), *The middle class in politics*, pp. 35-66, Taylor, Peter, 'A divided middle class: Bolton, 1790-1850', *Manchester Region History Review*, Vol. 6, (1992), pp. 3-15, and ibid, Morris, R. J., *Class, sect and party: the making of the British middle class: Leeds, 1820-1850*.
[54] Price, Sarah, 'Governing the community: the rise of popular radicalism in Oldham, Lancashire, 1790-1837', *Family & Community History*, Vol. 4,

The landed class that saw itself as the natural rulers of society and regarded itself as having the right to exercise such power and to speak on behalf of those who were not entitled to participate in the exercise of political power themselves. This oligarchic representation ran from the level of national government, through county politics, to the level of the parish. The aristocratic elite were dominant at national level leaving the gentry to control local politics. This hegemony was challenged from the 1840s by the emergence of 'electoral' politics. MPs were elected by those whom wished to have their interests represented in the 'public sphere', where public opinion could be formed and decisions reached. This led to the development of central organisations for the Conservative and Whig parties that handled electoral registration, selection of candidates and liaised between local and national leadership. In addition, pressure group politics, whether by 'societies', 'leagues' or 'unions' became central in metropolitan and provincial politics and the political interests of business were expressed in the Chambers of Commerce that were formed in the larger cities and spread more widely in the 1840s and 1850s. [55] At the heart of the elitist system of representation was the notion of deference but this could not easily be transferred to an expanding urban context and so could not be relied on to provide an effective guarantee for the continuing political rule of the landed class. Elitist politics therefore came under increasing strain as urban influences grew. Between 1840 and 1870, there was a period of confrontation between elitist and electoral politics. [56] However, the outcome was not simply the replacement of elitist by electoral politics but a compromise between the landed class and the manufacturing classes and the structure of political representation reflected the nature of this compromise.

The system of deference was apparent in the social backgrounds

---

(2001), pp. 125-137, Winstanley, Michael J., 'Oldham radicalism and the origins of popular Liberalism, 1830-1852', *Historical Journal*, Vol. 36, (1993), pp. 619-643, and Gadian, D. S., 'Class consciousness in Oldham and other north-west industrial towns', *Historical Journal*, Vol. 21, (1978), pp. 161-172.

[55] Taylor, Miles, 'Interests, parties and the state: the urban electorate in England, c.1820-72', and Lawrence, Jon, 'The dynamics of urban politics, 1867-1914' in Lawrence, Jon, and Taylor, Miles, (eds.), *Party, state and society: electoral behaviour in Britain since 1820*, (Scolar), 1997, pp. 50-78, 79-105. See also, Mitchell, Jeremy C., *The organization of opinion: open voting in England, 1832-68*, (Palgrave), 2008, and Machin, Ian, *The rise of democracy in Britain, 1830-1918*, (Macmillan), 2001.

[56] Hoppen, K. Theodore, 'The franchise and electoral politics in England and Ireland 1832-1885', *History*, Vol. 70, (1985), pp. 202-217.

of the political rulers of the period. Reform in 1832 opened up the system a little, but elitist patterns of representation remained largely unaltered. Of the 13 Cabinets formed between 1830 and 1868, peers and commoners were each dominant in six and the two Houses balanced in one. [57] Those Cabinets in which the Lords had a majority tended to be relatively short-lived Conservative administrations and this could suggest that the Commons was the more important institution. To some extent this is true, but those who entered the Commons were not substantially different from those in the Lords. In the Parliament of 1833, there were 217 MPs who were sons of peers or who were themselves baronets. [58] By 1880, the number had only fallen slightly to 170. Of the 103 men holding Cabinet office between 1830 and 1868, 68 were major landowners, 21 merchant bankers and 14 were from the legal and medical professions.

Not only were there close links between the Commons and Lords but the landowners who were active in Parliament were drawn heavily from those who had diversified into other economic activities. Between 1841 and 1847, the total of 815 MPs in seats at some time included 234 non-peerage landowners. [59] The 166 heads of landowning families in parliament included 26 who had active business interests and many more who held directorships in railways, insurance and joint-stock banks. Most of those with active business interests were private or merchant bankers, only 6 were manufacturers. This elitist pattern of representation was not confined to central government or Parliament and pervaded local government and played a central role in the military. The pattern of recruitment to the officer corps meant that the structure of authority in the army mirrored the wider society and created a pool of suitable recruits for

---

[57] Laski, Harold, 'The personnel of the English cabinet, 1801-1924', *American Political Science Review*, Vol. 22, (1928), pp. 12-31.

[58] See Woolley, S. F., 'The personnel of the parliament of 1833', *English Historical Review*, Vol. 54, (1938), pp. 240-262.

[59] Aydelotte, W. O., 'A statistical analysis of the Parliament of 1841: some problems of method', *Bulletin of the Institute of Historical Research*, Vol. 27, (1954), pp. 141-155, and 'The business interests of the gentry in the parliament of 1841-7', in ibid, Clark, G. Kitson, *The making of Victorian England*, pp. 290-305, McLean, Iain, 'Interests and ideology in the United Kingdom Parliament of 1841-7: an analysis of roll call voting', in Lovenduski, Joni, & Stanyer, Jeffrey, (eds.), *Contemporary political studies 1995*, 3 Vols. (Political Studies Association of the United Kingdom), 1995, Vol. 1, pp. 1-20, and Schonhardt-Bailey, Cheryl, 'Ideology, Party and Interests in the British Parliament of 1841-47', *British Journal of Political Science*, Vol. 33, (2003), pp. 581-605.

political careers. [60] Military participation was an important part of the experience of a large proportion of the landed class and was proportionately more important in the higher ranks of the peerage.

Conservatives and Whigs competed for the support of the privileged classes. [61] The Conservatives depended on landowners and farmers, together with the support of the colonial and shipping interest and those attached to the Established Church. The Whigs, or Liberals as they became in the late 1850s, were also drawn from the landed class, but attempted to express the interests of the manufacturing and commercial classes. [62] During the 1840s, the Conservatives began to broaden the base of their support in the commercial and manufacturing classes but the repeal of the Corn Laws led to this Peelite group splitting-off from the rest of the party.

Patronage had always played a major role in enabling governments to manage their support. However, by the 1830s, the decline of the 'influence of the Crown' and especially its capacity to use sinecure positions to garner support for its government made the management of Parliament and especially the House of Commons more problematic. This combined with an absence of effective party discipline often made it difficult for governments to control their supporters, though there is ample evidence to show that most MPs either supported one party or the other or voted accordingly. [63] The resurgence of a Conservative Party during the 1850s and the final emergence of a Liberal Party by 1860 reflected a redefinition of 'party' as an effective electoral machine for achieving political power. This was reflected in the recognition by both parties that electoral politics now central to the political system and led to the creation of national Registration Associations by both parties to replace the more informal

---

[60] Clayton, Anthony, *The British officer: leading the army from 1660 to the present*, (Pearson Longman), 2006, pp. 92-160.

[61] On the emergence of political parties see Evans, E. J., *Political Parties in Britain 1783-1867*, (Methuen), 1985, O'Gorman, F., *The Emergence of the British Two-Party System 1760-1832*, (Edward Arnold), 1982, and Hill, B.W., *British Parliamentary Parties 1742-1832*, (Allen and Unwin), 1985. See, for the later period, Jenkins, T. A., *Parliament, party and politics in Victorian Britain*, (Manchester University Press), 1996, and Hawkins, Angus, *British party politics, 1852-1886*, (Macmillan), 1998.

[62] Jenkins, T. A., *The liberal ascendancy, 1830-1886*, (Macmillan), 1994.

[63] See, Jenkins, T. S., 'The whips in the early-Victorian House of Commons', *Parliamentary History*, Vol. 19, (2000), pp. 259-286, and Sainty, John Christopher, and Cox, Gary W., 'The identification of government whips in the House of Commons, 1830-1905', *Parliamentary History*, Vol. 16, (1997), 339-358.

services provided by the political clubs.[64] The emergence of a national party system, in which party discipline played an increasingly important role, strengthened government control over parliament and restored a degree of political stability that had been lacking in the 1850s. With the increase in the franchise in 1867 and 1884, what became central for both parties was getting their supporters out to vote and, although the two political parties remained largely undemocratic in nature, this represented the beginnings of genuinely 'popular' politics. The creation of a National Liberal Federation in Birmingham in 1877 by a caucus of local activists was important in furthering the process by which parties, as vote-getting machines, became the dominant feature of political representation. [65] The gradual build-up of electoral organisations, the introduction of the secret ballot in 1872, the influence of the press on public opinion and the advent of major political campaigns broke the old elitist system of representation and the period from the second and third Reform Acts saw alternating party governments under Disraeli and Gladstone. [66]

The emergence of electoral politics saw political representation gradually reflect the changing balance of power among the privileged classes. [67] The old elitist pattern was modified not destroyed and the landed class remaining an important social and political force. The result, in the last third of the century, was the emergence of the 'establishment' as the newly prominent manufacturers and their party machines were admitted to the sphere of informality and personal connections that characterised the landed classes. In return for accepting the hegemony of the values and life-style of the landed class, the most prominent manufacturers were admitted as full members of the status group of 'gentlemen'. The public schools, the professions

---

[64] Jaggard, Edwin, 'Managers and Agents: Conservative Party Organisation in the 1850s', *Parliamentary History*, Vol. 27, (2008), pp. 7-18, and Rix, Kathryn, 'Hidden workers of the party: The professional Liberal agents, 1885-1910', *Journal of Liberal History*, Vol. 52, (2006), pp. 4-13.

[65] Watson, R. S., *The National Liberal Federation: from its commencement to the general election of 1906*, (T. Fisher Unwin), 1907, Herrick, Francis H., 'The Origins of the National Liberal Federation', *Journal of Modern History*, Vol. 17, (2), (1945), pp. 116-129, and ibid, Hanham, H. J. *Elections and Party Management: Politics in the time of Disraeli and Gladstone*.

[66] Rix, Kathryn, '"The Elimination of Corrupt Practices in British Elections"? Reassessing the Impact of the 1883 Corrupt Practices Act', *English Historical Review*, Vol. 123, (2008), pp. 65-97.

[67] Lawrence, Jon, *Speaking for the people: party, language, and popular politics in England, 1867-1914*, (Cambridge University Press), 1998, and *Electing Our Masters: The Hustings in British Politics from Hogarth to Blair*, (Oxford University Press), 2009.

and the Church became essential supports for the establishment that now dominated British public life.

Between the 1880s and 1914, there was a fundamental restructuring of party politics as the Conservatives became the true party of the establishment.[68] As the Liberals became more identified with intervention and reform, the Conservative party was a safe haven for those who feared the idea of the increasing political power of the working-classes.[69] In 1886, the old Whigs and the Liberal Unionists split from the official Liberals over Ireland and made an electoral pact with the Conservatives and in 1912 entered into full merger. The Conservatives became the Imperial party, the party of Queen and Empire, 'social justice' and 'social reform'. The traditional landed and agrarian groups gravitated towards the Conservatives as did the commercial and financial interests and eventually the manufacturers. The establishment party drew support, not only from the privileged classes, but also from the middle stratum of clerks, shopkeepers and from sections of the working-classes whom Disraeli referred to as the 'angels in the marble'.

The establishment dominated all aspects of the state. In the period after 1868, there was a greater representation of new wealth in parliament. In 1885, 16 per cent of MPs were landowners, 12 per cent from the military but 32 per cent were from the law and other professions and 38 per cent from industry and commerce. Between 1868 and 1886, 27 out of the 49 men holding Cabinet office were landowners, but between 1886 and 1914 the proportion fell to 49 out of 101. The fall in the representation of landowners was not simply a fall in the number of landowning MPs but also a fall in the average size of their estates. There was also a declining number of hereditary titles represented in parliament but the number of knights remained constant until 1918 when the numbers increased. Businessmen were increasingly given knighthoods and baronetcies rather than full

---

[68] Shannon, Richard, *History of the Conservative Party, Vol. 3: The age of Salisbury, 1881-1902, unionism and empire*, (Longman), 1996, Ramsden, John, *History of the Conservative Party, Vol. 4: The age of Balfour and Baldwin, 1902-1940*, (Longman), 1978, Green, E. H. H., *The Crisis of Conservatism: The Politics, Economics and Ideology of the British Conservative Party, 1880-1914*, (Routledge), 1996, and ibid, Smith, Jeremy, *The taming of democracy: the Conservative Party, 1880-1924*.

[69] See, for instance, Roberts, Matthew, '"Villa toryism" and popular conservatism in Leeds, 1885-1902', *Historical Journal*, Vol. 49, (2006), pp. 217-246, and Lynch, Patricia C., *The Liberal Party in rural England 1885-1910: radicalism and community*, (Oxford University Press), 2003.

peerages. [70] It was Queen Victoria who regarded the baronetcy as appropriate for the middle-classes who might find difficulty in coping with the expense and responsibility of a peerage. In 1895, there were 31 millionaire MPs and by 1906 only 22 that links to the decreasing importance of land as a source of millionaires. [71]

The establishment still monopolised the most important national and local political positions as well as recruitment to the army and to the important professions of the church and law. But even here there is evidence of change. By 1900, there were 60 bishops, 26 with seats in the Lords of whom only 30 per cent were recruited from the landed classes. Half the bishops had wives who came from the landed classes and 90 per cent of bishops were educated at Oxford or Cambridge. [72] Similarly, three quarters of all judges between 1876 and 1920 came from the landed or business classes. [73] At the heart of the establishment was the peerage. No longer allocated through political patronage, peerage gradually came to be seen as indicators of achievement in politics and public service. Thus, the accommodation between the landowners and the manufacturing and commercial classes was reflected in the awarding of peerage and other titles to non-landowners.

Of the 463 people awarded peerages between 1837 and 1911, 125 were neither magnates nor gentry. These men made up 10 per cent of the new peerage at the beginning and 43 per cent at the end. The annual rate of peerage creation increased rapidly from the 1860s with new entrants drawn from the politically active elements of the new commercial and manufacturing classes. Only after 1885, when the brewers Allsopp, Guinness and Bass and the railway contractor Brassey entered the Lords, did businessmen enter the peerage in any numbers. Between 1880 and 1914, 200 new peers were created: a quarter from the land, a third from industry and a third from professions such as the army and the law. Between 1875 and 1904, 162 peerage and 300 baronetcies were created. 2,659 knighthoods were granted in the same period and new orders of knighthoods were created for diplomatic and Indian services, the Royal Victorian Order for special public services and the grade of knight bachelor was

---

[70] Smith, E. A., *The House of Lords in British politics and society, 1815-1911*, (Longman), 1992.
[71] Rush, Michael, *The role of the Member of Parliament since 1868: from gentlemen to players*, (Oxford University Press), 2001.
[72] Beeson, Trevor, *The bishops*, (SCM Press), 2002, provides a valuable collective biography since 1800.
[73] See, Duman, Daniel, 'A social and occupational analysis of the English judiciary, 1770-1790 and 1855-1875', *American Journal of Legal History*, Vol. 17, (1973), pp. 353-364.

expanded. The mixture of 'old' and 'new' in the establishment is evident in that between 1880 and 1914, more than a half of all knights had fathers who were peers, baronets, knights or landowners.

The 'establishment' was a tightly knit group of intermarried families that formed the political rulers of Britain and that monopolised recruitment to all the major social positions. The new party organisations were a part of this establishment, with the party headquarters and parliamentary leadership being drawn into the pattern of exclusivity of the London gentleman's club where the ethos and values of the public schools were carried into adult life. In economic terms, however, the privileged classes remained relatively distinct and a unified propertied class had not been created by 1914.

24 The end of the nineteenth century

If forced to find a metaphor for writing about Victorian and Edwardian social history I should prefer something like Penelope's web—a garment endlessly woven by day and unpicked again by night.[1]

Neither the death of Queen Victoria in 1901 or of her successor Edward VII nine years later marked an end to the issues and values that had been debated since the late-eighteenth century. The 'long' nineteenth century extended until the outbreak of war in August 1914. That there was considerable change during this period is undoubted but, when faced with a confusing diversity of beliefs and styles of life, few of the long-held views about the Hanoverians, Victorians and Edwardians survive close scrutiny.

At the beginning of the nineteenth century, the bulk of Britain's population still lived in the countryside and most industry was located within an essentially rural society. Industrial growth drew in the surplus population from other regions into towns and cities. By the middle of the century, half the population lived in the countryside, but by the end it was only a third. Britain had become an industrialised and urbanised society and the rural world became increasingly that of a declining minority. The decades between the 1860s and the First World War transformed Britain swiftly and profoundly. British society became urbanised and suburbanised, secularised, democratised; general assumptions about social relationships and politically legitimate behaviour shifted from the basis of vertical hierarchical community groupings to stratified classes: in a word, it became 'modern'.[2]

The total occupied workforce grew from approximately 5 million to 13 million between 1830 and 1914 and the female work force from nearly 2 million to about 5½ million. Expanding industries accommodated a substantial proportion of this new workforce: 3 per cent of the extra male jobs were in metal manufactures or in mining and quarrying. The creation of new jobs from the growth of a new industry was supplemented by the demand for people to service these industries and their workers, from builders and craftsmen, to shop-workers and sellers of food and drink. Furthermore, the geographical

---

[1] Harris, Jose, *Private Lives, Public Spirit: A Social History of Britain, 1870-1914*, (Oxford University Press), 1992, (Penguin), 1993, p. 251.
[2] Shannon, Richard, *The Crisis of Imperialism, 1865-1915*, (Paladin), 1974, p. 11.

concentration of industries generating new jobs attracted growing numbers of people to these areas. Glamorgan and Durham were important centres for coal and iron and steel and both counties experienced substantial growth in population. Each of these counties gained an extra million inhabitants between 1831 and 1911, with Glamorgan increasing its population by 6½ times and Durham 4½ times.

The textile industry employed a substantial part of the population of adults and young persons over 10 with 3.3 per cent of this group engaged in the cotton industry and 2.2 per cent male and 1.4 per cent female in the woollen industry. However, national statistics do not reflect the localised impact of the textile industries. In 1838, 60 per cent of all cotton workers in Britain lived in Lancashire and this grew to 76 per cent by 1900. The local economy depended massively on the cotton industry, directly in terms of employment in cotton workers and indirectly for those who provided other goods and services. Despite technological changes supporting mass production, the British textile industry of this period still maintained many traditional and local characteristics and these were reflected in regional specialisation. In 1865, the coal mines employed nearly a third of a million people before a rapid expansion took place in the industry in the 1870s reaching a peak of 1.1 million workers in 1914. The number of large-scale mines increased during the nineteenth century dug either in new coal seams or in existing small or shallow family mines. The new deep mines needed a new workforce, many of whom were housed in rows of new terraced cottages that became typical of coal-mining villages. D. H. Lawrence, who grew up in the Nottinghamshire coalfield at the end of the nineteenth century, described the development of the landscape at the start of his novel, *Sons and Lovers*. At this time, despite the building of these new mines, the mines and villages were still surrounded by the countryside, like 'black studs on the countryside, linked by a loop of fine chain, the railway'. [3]

These dramatic economic and industrial changes caused equally dramatic population changes in terms of growth and especially in population distribution. Wealth creation associated with industrial growth allowed the maintenance of a larger population while the concentration of new industries in certain areas saw widespread population movements. Massive social change rarely occurs uneventfully and the growth and shifts in population were accompanied by a wide range of problems as demands for housing,

---

[3] Lawrence, D. H., *Sons and Lovers*, 2 Vols. (B. Tauchnitz), 1929, Vol. 1, p. 4.

sewerage, water, food, labour and leisure all expanded. Britain was becoming a predominantly urbanised and industrial society with all the problems, as well as benefits that this entailed. Rather than this being a source of pride or optimism, contemporary largely middle-class observers feared that the city was becoming a place of 'dreadful delight'. Manchester was 'Coke Town', London the 'modern Babylon'. At a physical level, urbanisation compounded existing social problems of sanitation, disease, and housing and gave rise to new ones that contemporaries linked to crime, prostitution and poverty. Cities were seen as sites of moral corruption and violence inhabited by criminals, drug addicts, prostitutes, homosexuals and immigrants. But some Victorians saw cities as places of excitement and many took advantage of the growing leisure opportunities on offer. Others went 'slumming', exploring working-class districts, slums and rookeries either in pursuit of excitement or to offer charity.

By 1914, Britain had become a society in which individuals' class determined their life expectancies. Class structure was so important that it was mirrored in the structure of ocean liners. The wealthier passengers were separated from the poorer for practically the whole journey. The very wealthy passengers paid the most for their tickets and stayed in first-class accommodation. The slightly less wealthy middle-classes and upper-working class paid less and stayed in second-class accommodation. The poor third class passengers paid the least amount for their tickets and stayed in third-class or what used to be called 'Steerage'. On the *Titanic*, Decks A-D were reserved for the first-class passengers while second-class passengers were on Decks D-G. Third-class passengers were on Deck G situated near the ship's engines. Each class of passenger had their own entrance to the ship and could sit on their designated decks to relax. This was put in place to stop the different classes from mixing. The only time that people from all social classes came together was during the church service held in the first-class quarters on Sunday. In terms of accommodation, food and facilities available on the liner, there was a clear class division. In third-class, there were only two baths to share between the 710 passengers while the first-class suites had their own bathing facilities. When the *Titanic* sank in April 1912, a far higher proportion of third-class passengers perished than in first- and second-class.[4]

The ship became a refracting prism, a metaphor for the problems and tensions facing society. Everyone found ammunition in the *Titanic* and put their own spin on it: suffragists and their

---

[4] Biel, Steven, *Down with the Old Canoe: A Cultural History of the Titanic Disaster*, (W. W. Norton & Co.), 1996.

opponents; radicals, reformers, and capitalists; critics of technology and modern life; racists and xenophobes and champions of racial and ethnic equality; editorial writers, preachers and poets. Fundamentalists saw the iceberg as divine punishment for worldly pride and self-indulgence. Protestant sermons used the Titanic to condemn the budding consumer society and working-class ballads made the ship emblematic of the foolishness and greed of the rich. Yet early accounts of the disaster focused largely, and with little evidence on the heroism of well-to-do passengers like John Jacob Astor, who put 'women and children first' in the lifeboats and anti-suffragist agitators used this as evidence that women were too weak to be allowed the vote. This myth of first-class heroism was used to trumpet a good deal of racist cant about heroic Anglo-Saxon manhood, at the expense of foreigners, blacks, and lower-class *Titanic* passengers, who were often depicted in early accounts as cowards though others chose to celebrate the noble workers who went down with the ship.

The economic and social changes of the late-Victorian and Edwardian years contributed to crisis but it is unclear what the crisis represented. Christianity had been shaken by Darwinism and problems in the economy, the revelation of enduring poverty and the alteration of the social structure called many Victorian ideas into doubt. To many men and women, especially younger people Victorian ideas and values no longer seemed satisfying. Consequently, the years between 1870 and 1914 were filled with exploration and speculation as people searched for new ordering principles. Fundamental assumptions about the economic and social systems came under attack and new ones emerged. Britain's experience in the First World War was its first taste of 'total war' when around six million British people had direct experience of trench warfare while most of the remaining population became involved in the war effort in some way. This meant change and upheaval in some way. There is, however, a debate about the nature and extent of the change produced by the war. This centres on whether the war is seen as the cause of fundamental change or whether, alternatively, it can be seen as a catalyst that accelerated existing political, social and economic trends. [5]

---

[5] There are several valuable books on the ways in which the war affected Britain. Bourne, John, *Britain and the Great War 1914-18*, (Edward Arnold), 1989, and Constantine, Stephen, Kirby Maurice W., and Rose, Mary B., (eds.), *The First World War in British History*, (Edward Arnold), 1995, provide an excellent introduction. Marwick, Arthur, *The Deluge:*

The emotional trauma suffered by many men who were conscripted to serve in the Armed Forces. There was widespread bereavement because of the death of family and friends. [6] There were changes in diet and habits resulting from food rationing. People lived in a society in which government propaganda and government controls were more extensive than in pre-war society. Many upper and middle-class women gained new experience from taking up paid employment for the first time. [7] The social, cultural and emotional impact of the war was such that it has led some historians to argue that the period after 1918 witnessed a fundamental realignment of moral and social attitudes while others emphasise continuity between pre- and post-war experiences. [8]

British Society and the First World War, 2nd edition, (Macmillan), 1991, was the first study to really examine the impact of 'total war'.
[6] Seldon, Anthony, and Walsh, David, *Public Schools and the Great War*, (Pen & Sword Military), 2013, examines its impact on public schools. Of those public schoolboys who fought in the war, a fifth were killed.
[7] Molinari, Véronique, 'Le droit de vote accordé aux femmes britanniques à l'issue de la Première Guerre mondiale: une récompense pour les services rendus?', *La revue LISA*, vol. 6, (4), (2008), pp. 71-87.
[8] Reynolds, David, *The Long Shadow: The Great War and the Twentieth Century*, (Simon & Schuster), 2013, considers the long-term tranformative effects of the war.

Further Reading

This is a brief and general guide; more detailed references can be found in the footnotes. Many of the references to primary sources are available on Google Books or Internet Archive either to be read or downloaded.

For detailed bibliographical references see, Brown, L. M., and Christie, I. R., *Bibliography of British History 1789-1851*, (Oxford University Press), 1977, and Hanham, H. J., *Bibliography of British History 1851-1914*, (Oxford University Press), 1976. Cannon, John, *A Dictionary of British History*, 2nd ed., (Oxford University Press), 2009, and Cook, Chris, *The Routledge Companion to Britain in the Nineteenth Century, 1815-1914*, (Routledge), 2005, provide important references. Langton, J., and Morris, R. J., *Atlas of Industrialising Britain 1780-1914*, (Methuen), 1986, and Pope, R., (ed.), *Atlas of British Social and Economic History since c.1700*, (Routledge), 1989, provide a valuable spatial dimension.

For primary sources see, Aspinall, A., and Smith, E. A., (eds.), *English Historical Documents, Volume XI, 1783-1832*, (Eyre and Spottiswoode), 1959, Young, G. M., and Handcock, W. D., (eds.), *English Historical Documents, Volume XII, (1), 1832-1874*, (Eyre and Spottiswoode), 1956, Handcock, W. D., (ed.), *English Historical Documents, Volume XII, (2), 1874-1914*, (Eyre and Spottiswoode), 1977, and Hanham, H. J., *The Nineteenth Century Constitution 1815-1914: documents and commentary*, (Cambridge University Press), 1969.

Brown, Callum G., and Fraser, W. Hamish, *Britain since 1707*, (Longman), 2010, provides an excellent synopsis of developments. Hilton, Boyd, *A Mad, Bad & Dangerous People? England 1783-1846*, (Oxford University Press), 2005, Hoppen, K. Theodore, *The Mid-Victorian Generation 1846-1886*, (Oxford University Press), 1998, and Searle, G. R., *A New England?: Peace and War, 1886-1918*, (Oxford University Press), 2005, are more detailed. Daunton, M. J., *Progress and Poverty: An Economic and Social History of Britain 1700-1850*, (Oxford University Press), 1995, and *Wealth and welfare: an economic and social history of Britain, 1851-1951*, (Oxford University Press), 2007, are the most up-to-date studies. Thompson, F. M. L., (ed.), *The Cambridge Social History of Britain 1750-1950*, 3 Vols. (Cambridge University Press), 1990, adopts a thematic approach to social developments.

Index

Agricultural Children Act 1873, 370
Agriculture. *See* Farming
Aristocracy, 29, 43, 106, 173, 197, 455, 478, 479, 493, 564, 575, 600, 612, 614, 616, 618, 641, 667, 668, 669, 670, 671, 672, 673, 674, 675, 676, 679, 682, 684, 717, 724, 727, 729, 733
Arnold, Thomas, 343, 344, 724, 732
Australia, 126, 129, 137, 317, 318, 406, 416, 420, 430, 438, 667
Bank Holidays, 78, 200, 490, 605
Bank Holidays Act, 490
Bankers, 140, 203, 414, 628, 676, 680, 682, 719, 720, 721, 724, 730, 733, 737
Banks, 191, 305, 306, 308, 402, 455, 491, 719, 720, 721, 737
Barnardo, Thomas, 126, 296, 297, 301, 303
Beale Dorothea, 355
Bedfordshire, iii, 28, 38, 113, 122, 131, 208, 209, 265, 275, 324, 379, 383, 398, 403, 424, 436, 467, 577, 641, 661, 667
Bentham, Jeremy, 272, 424, 429, 430, 508, 512, 532
Benthamism, 156, 272, 273, 350, 429, 508, 511, 512, 513
Besant, Annie, 97, 98, 100, 101, 174, 175, 176, 607
Besant, Walter, 188, 413, 504
Birkbeck George, 350
Birmingham, 7, 17, 26, 28, 43, 59, 77, 78, 79, 101, 113, 114, 124, 140, 172, 182, 186, 187, 191, 192, 197, 202, 207, 209, 212, 213, 226, 228, 247, 254, 256, 291, 298, 308, 349, 364, 365, 377, 378, 413, 419, 448, 451, 463, 470, 495, 542, 558, 663, 692, 714, 724, 734, 739
Black Country, 9, 18, 59, 226, 384, 394, 395, 400, 633, 634, 649, 655
Black immigrants, 127
Blackpool, 200, 201, 499
Bloody Code, 415, 416
Booth, Charles, 187, 189, 259, 260, 261, 263, 292, 310, 398, 590, 591, 623, 652
Bow Street, 453, 454, 464
Bradford, 103, 182, 196, 201, 203, 205, 228, 237, 279, 291, 364, 485, 501, 585, 633
Bradlaugh, Charles, 100, 101, 607
Brighton, 49, 68, 73, 198, 201, 228, 724
Bristol, 6, 24, 94, 114, 175, 198, 217, 227, 231, 236, 250, 306, 341, 349, 377, 402, 407, 502, 562, 571, 591, 632, 634
British and Foreign School Society, 320, 327
Budd, William, 235, 236, 250, 579
Bunting, Jabez, 556, 559, 563, 564, 566, 567, 568, 569, 570, 571
Buss, Frances Mary, 355
Butler, Josephine, 259, 343, 408, 544
Caird, James, 34, 222
Cambridge, 341, 345, 346, 347, 348, 349, 356, 357, 367, 376, 377, 378, 456
Canada, 126, 129, 137, 139, 667
Capital, 13, 14, 15, 16, 20, 22, 23, 24, 31, 36, 42, 48, 54, 55, 56, 57, 61, 62, 63, 66, 70, 89, 125, 152, 154, 184, 185, 192, 202, 203, 209, 254, 255, 267, 320, 321, 327, 360, 417, 423, 444, 446, 451, 493, 508, 509, 527, 529, 617, 620, 622, 624,

748

628, 645, 646, 652, 653, 671, 672, 676, 679, 698, 719, 720, 721, 722, 723, 724, 725, 726, 727, 733
Cardiff, 140, 182, 208, 233, 377, 575, 633, 723, 734
Carlyle, Thomas, 82, 132, 133, 478, 615
Carpenter, Mary, 299, 389, 446, 447
Chadwick, Edwin, 154, 214, 215, 227, 233, 234, 239, 241, 242, 243, 244, 245, 246, 247, 248, 249, 250, 252, 253, 254, 262, 266, 267, 269, 270, 271, 272, 273, 282, 287, 331, 388, 428, 464, 467, 483, 519, 544, 548, 590
Chamberlain, Joseph, 187, 188, 197, 212, 215, 254, 255, 291, 365, 524, 528, 534
Charity Organisation Society (COS), 213, 291, 292, 295, 301, 302, 303, 304, 310
Chartism, 154, 156, 157, 278, 285, 323, 324, 325, 390, 403, 463, 510, 518, 621, 676
Child labour, 37, 142, 144, 145, 147, 148, 149, 150, 151, 152, 370, 639, 664
Children, 29, 37, 81, 87, 88, 89, 91, 92, 93, 94, 95, 100, 103, 104, 105, 107, 108, 112, 113, 114, 116, 125, 126, 135, 142, 143, 144, 145, 146, 147, 149, 150, 151, 153, 154, 155, 158, 159, 160, 161, 162, 163, 164, 165, 166, 167, 169, 172, 209, 220, 221, 232, 249, 254, 257, 260, 261, 262, 263, 279, 285, 288, 296, 298, 299, 301, 304, 305, 307, 312, 313, 314, 317, 318, 320, 321, 322, 323, 326, 327, 328, 329, 330, 331, 332, 333, 336, 339, 340, 341, 343, 354, 359, 360, 361, 362, 364, 365, 366, 368, 369, 370, 373, 374, 375, 378, 379, 380, 381, 409, 411, 427, 445, 446, 447, 448, 449, 465, 471, 484, 486, 487, 488, 503, 529, 539, 586, 594, 601, 602, 631, 634, 639, 641, 656, 664, 665, 671, 678, 693, 697, 703, 712, 716, 717, 746
Class, 612-25
 a changing society, 615-18
 class society, 624-25
 class-consciousness, 312, 620, 621
 nature of, 618-24
Coal Mines Inspection Act 1850, 158, 167
Cobbe, Frances Power, 399, 716, 717
Cobbett, William, 151, 274, 277
Colquhoun, Patrick, 144, 388, 451, 452, 455, 457
Communications
 bicycle, 49, 50, 51, 645
 canals, 16, 18, 22, 23, 25, 26, 27, 28, 29, 52, 53, 60, 61, 65, 68, 80, 90, 132, 138, 317, 721
 economic impact of railways, 60-63
 horse-drawn transport, 35, 37, 46, 47, 51, 480, 483
 motor transport, 45, 46, 50, 51
 railways, 3, 4, 5, 16, 18, 20, 21, 23, 25, 26, 27, 28, 29, 35, 45, 46, 47, 50, 52, 53, 54, 55, 56, 57, 58, 59, 60, 61, 62, 63, 64, 65, 66, 67, 68, 69, 70, 71, 72, 73, 74, 75, 76, 77, 78, 79, 80, 123, 124, 138, 179, 198, 200, 202, 205, 343, 401, 402, 511, 513, 605,639, 685, 691, 703, 723, 724, 725, 737
 roads, 9, 18, 23, 25, 26, 45, 47, 48, 49, 50, 51, 52, 53, 72, 73, 78, 138, 183, 205, 207, 401, 451, 454, 523
 social impact of railways, 63-80
 turnpikes, 26, 47, 48, 317, 382, 401, 454

749

Contagious Diseases Act, 406, 407, 408
Corn Laws, 36, 41, 162, 164, 682, 718, 734, 735, 738
Cotton textiles, 2, 3, 11, 12, 13, 14, 16, 18, 23, 24, 27, 41, 44, 108, 142, 143, 144, 145, 146, 148, 149, 152, 155, 165, 174, 178, 192, 226, 261, 289, 290, 331, 627, 629, 633, 634, 639, 642, 643, 644, 649, 650, 655, 660, 663, 671, 677, 680, 684, 685, 687, 704, 726, 735, 744
County and Borough Police Act 1856, 469
Coventry, 18, 49, 51, 208, 227, 261
Crawford, William, 434, 435, 436, 446
Crewe, 205, 207
Crime, 382-414
  criminal courts, 384-87
  levels of crime, 394-96
  nature of criminal classes, 387-94
  offences against people, 396-400
  offences against property, 404
  theft, 281, 382, 387, 394, 404, 413, 414, 416, 641
Darwin, Charles, 509, 599, 607, 611, 685
Darwinism, 393, 509, 599, 607, 610, 746
Davies, Emily, 356, 357
Deference, 466, 736
Dickens, Charles, 69, 147, 284, 295, 310, 321, 322, 327, 390, 396, 437, 446, 521, 590, 695
Disease, 83, 116, 134, 135, 137, 196, 226, 230, 231, 232, 233, 234, 236, 239, 242, 243, 249, 258, 262, 298, 302, 404, 405, 406, 408, 409, 424, 425, 426, 483, 515, 522, 611, 694, 745
  cholera, 83, 87, 88, 133, 225, 226, 230, 231, 232, 233, 234, 235, 236, 239, 242, 245, 246, 248, 249, 252, 309, 430, 519, 550, 651, 694
  nature of urban disease, 229-39
  smallpox, 221, 231, 232, 236, 249, 251, 290
  tuberculosis, 88, 233, 237, 247, 304
  typhus, 133, 230, 231, 232, 233, 236, 237, 245, 247, 422
Disraeli, Benjamin, v, 8, 163, 167, 287, 365, 368, 521, 524, 525, 589, 614, 619, 724, 739, 740
Divorce, 405, 410, 604, 713, 714, 716, 717
Divorce and Matrimonial Causes Act 1857, 713
Domestic service, 102, 103, 104, 114, 117, 138, 172, 174, 177, 354, 490, 503, 634, 635, 642, 643, 653, 655, 659, 662, 663, 706
Domesticity, 110, 494, 495, 643, 693, 697, 709
Doncaster, 207, 218
Du Cane, Sir Edmund, 439, 440, 441, 445
Dunstable, 28, 122, 208, 655
East Anglia, 17, 104, 140, 223, 275, 561, 640, 659, 728
Ecclesiastical Commission, 541
Ecclesiastical Titles Act 1851, 576
Edinburgh, 26, 37, 77, 83, 92, 156, 209, 242, 295, 309, 315, 331, 356, 368, 387, 402, 470, 496, 568, 670, 700, 707
Education, 323-81, 389, 392, 514, 517, 518, 522, 529
  Clarendon Commission, 342, 343, 344
  Cockerton judgment 1899, 372
  elementary education, 314, 328, 329, 331, 332, 333, 358, 364, 366, 367, 369, 370
  factory schools, 314, 321, 330, 333

girls' education, 353-58, 378-81
grammar schools, 317, 340, 341, 342, 344, 348, 354, 356, 371, 372, 374, 375, 381
mechanics' institutes, 350
Minutes of 1846, 331, 335
monitorial system, 320, 321, 327, 328, 334,
Newcastle Commission, 333, 335, 336, 339, 363
public schools, 340, 341, 342, 343, 344, 346, 374, 375, 376, 381
reformatory schools, 362, 389
Revised Code, 335, 337, 338, 364, 368, 339, 352
Sunday schools, 314, 319, 326, 329, 389
Taunton Commission, 341, 356
technical education, 350-53
universities, 345-50, 357, 376-78
Education Act 1870, 359-67
Education Act 1876, 369
Education Act 1880, 369
Education Act 1902, 367, 370, 375, 529
Eight Hours Act 1908, 179
Electricity, 204, 206, 217
Eliot, George, 599, 695
Elites, 4, 255, 343, 344, 346, 590, 613, 615, 616, 676, 679, 689, 691, 719, 735
Endowed Schools Act 1869, 342
Engels, Friedrich, 108, 115, 133, 147, 191, 192, 220, 390, 587, 618, 620, 640, 665
Engineering, 7, 17, 28, 41, 43, 44, 58, 59, 65, 79, 190, 207, 216, 244, 349, 614, 631, 633, 641, 645, 646, 649, 666, 669, 670, 671, 672, 689, 690, 691
Enlightenment, the, 5, 30, 31, 111, 533
Entrepreneurs, 18, 31, 150, 200, 211, 240, 344, 388, 479, 498,
616, 684, 685, 686, 687, 688, 715, 725
Factories and Workshops Act 1901, 172
Factory, 18, 142, 143, 149, 150, 151, 153, 154, 156, 160, 166, 168, 169, 179, 205, 208, 222, 241, 277, 625, 627, 631, 634, 636
Factory Act 1819, 149
Factory Act 1833, 154, 148-55, 330, 333, 517
Factory Act 1844, 159-60, 330, 519
Factory Act 1847, 161-63
Factory Act 1850, 163
Factory Act 1874, 167
Factory Act 1878, 167, 171
Factory Acts Extension Act 1864, 165
Factory Acts Extension Act 1867, 166
Factory Movement, 148, 149, 152, 156, 162
Faithfull, Emily, 700, 701, 702
Family, 1, 28, 34, 37, 38, 43, 53, 64, 67, 76, 77, 94, 96, 97, 98, 99, 100, 101, 102, 103, 104, 105, 106, 107, 108, 109, 114, 116, 118, 119, 120, 126, 144, 150, 165, 180, 186, 202, 203, 205, 211, 220, 224, 238, 262, 297, 298, 299, 313, 315, 333, 359, 360, 362, 381, 399, 400, 402, 411, 422, 427, 449, 473, 492, 496, 501, 502, 534, 553, 564, 585, 601, 605, 606, 625, 626, 627, 637, 638, 639, 640, 641, 642, 645, 649, 651, 656, 657, 658, 659, 660, 664, 665, 666, 681, 685, 692, 693, 695, 696, 698, 699, 709, 723, 725, 726, 727, 730, 732, 733, 734, 744, 747
Famine, Irish Potato, 129, 131, 136, 137, 138, 139, 140, 575, 598, 650
Farming, 11, 23, 27, 33, 34, 35, 36, 37, 38, 39, 40, 60, 84, 93,

INDEX

94, 95, 146, 223, 261, 535, 571, 648, 649, 659, 682, 723, 727
  agricultural depression, 33, 35, 377, 600, 617, 627, 727, 728
  dairy farming, 33, 35, 36, 39, 40, 218
  High Farming, 37, 39, 40, 41
  market gardening, 38
  rural society, 219-24
Farr, William, 83, 87, 236, 250
Fee Grant Act 1891, 369
Femininity, 119, 653, 692, 693, 717
Fielden, John, 148, 156, 162, 287
Fielding, Henry, 453
Fielding, Sir John, 453, 454, 457
Finance, 22, 24, 25, 27, 183, 186, 209, 255, 353, 439, 526, 676, 680, 681, 719, 720, 721, 725
Financiers, 31, 140, 676, 688, 717, 719, 721, 724, 733
First World War, 7, 449, 468, 470, 611, 698, 703, 743, 746
Food, 17, 21, 30, 37, 41, 44, 81, 82, 85, 87, 88, 189, 224, 233, 237, 238, 241, 252, 258, 260, 261, 275, 282, 285, 306, 307, 382, 387, 401, 404, 422, 436, 602, 627, 632, 640, 641, 648, 649, 651, 655, 661, 682, 729, 743, 745, 747
  adulteration of, 237, 238, 401
Football, 74, 477, 496, 499, 502, 504, 606
Forster, W. E., 113, 364, 365, 366, 367, 368, 677
Foster, John, 37, 64, 620, 621, 623, 641, 642, 671
Franchise, 4, 7, 227, 319, 517, 521, 523, 526, 681, 696, 736, 739
Free Place Regulations 1907, 374
Friendly societies, 6, 200, 262, 305, 306, 307, 308, 495, 511, 665
Fry, Elizabeth, 297, 424, 425, 427, 428, 429, 430, 446

Garrett, Elizabeth, 409, 708, 709
Gas, 204, 206, 214, 217, 252
Gaskell, Elizabeth, 8, 71, 113, 619, 620, 695
Gaskell, Peter, 115, 116
Gentleman, 347, 612, 684, 730, 731, 732, 733, 742
Gentry, 275, 287, 294, 324, 325, 334, 344, 346, 378, 396, 413, 456, 457, 459, 478, 479, 483, 493, 494, 575, 577, 597, 600, 614, 616, 675, 687, 688, 723, 735, 736, 737, 741
Germany, 7, 19, 25, 42, 66, 76, 128, 182, 205, 254, 353, 357, 424, 525, 624, 646, 674, 686
Gissing, George, 71, 188, 189, 413, 697
Gladstone, William, 56, 62, 64, 167, 252, 302, 363, 365, 520, 521, 522, 523, 524, 525, 599, 603, 604, 614, 739
Glasgow, 6, 7, 73, 74, 79, 87, 124, 134, 138, 139, 140, 156, 171, 194, 200, 207, 212, 228, 232, 254, 256, 350, 402, 470, 485, 500, 502, 614, 633, 634, 653, 734
Government, 505-31
  a reforming state, 516-31
  ideas of government, 507-11
  regulatory state, 511-15
Graham, Sir James, 88, 129, 159, 160, 161, 230, 286, 287, 315, 330, 333
Great Depression 1878-1896, 7, 39, 42, 44, 651
Great Exhibition 1851, 29, 37, 73, 351, 352
Hill, Octavia, 213, 297, 301, 355
Holyoake, George Jacob, 582, 607
Home Office, 48, 91, 129, 155, 158, 164, 168, 251, 252, 291, 415, 430, 431, 432, 436, 443, 444, 462, 467, 468, 469, 470, 471, 514, 515, 522

Hospitals, 86, 95, 194, 253, 290, 307, 377, 406, 425, 525, 705, 706, 707, 709, 711
Housing, 9, 21, 70, 80, 86, 88, 124, 133, 152, 181, 186, 187, 196, 203, 205, 206, 208-19, 221, 222, 228, 233, 239, 240, 243, 250, 254, 255, 256, 296, 297, 299, 305, 308, 355, 393, 404, 526, 527, 590, 623, 626, 632, 641, 684, 744, 745
Housing of the Working-class Act 1890, 211
Howard, Ebenezer, 40, 206
Howard, John, 423, 424, 425, 426, 428
Industrial Revolution, iii, 2, 10, 11, 12, 13, 16, 19, 20, 22, 23, 25, 29, 41, 108, 111, 130, 135, 144, 147, 148, 152, 182, 249, 323, 415, 477, 490, 611, 617, 619, 620, 621, 627, 629, 636, 637, 639, 641, 642, 653, 657, 658, 659, 679, 685, 687, 720, 723, 728
Industrialists, 27, 154, 192, 240, 348, 485, 618, 676, 682, 685, 687, 719, 720, 729, 730
Inequality, 256, 261, 722, 732
Infanticide, 88, 89, 90, 91, 92, 94, 95, 397, 413
Investment, 14, 20, 22, 23, 27, 36, 37, 38, 39, 47, 48, 55, 56, 66, 67, 151, 199, 201, 214, 217, 308, 317, 320, 353, 536, 652, 675, 676, 681, 723, 724, 726, 730, 733
Ireland, 38, 84, 85, 95, 104, 120, 124, 125, 129, 130, 131, 132, 133, 134, 135, 136, 138, 140, 192, 222, 228, 230, 232, 251, 298, 316, 397, 401, 411, 420, 424, 427, 428, 457, 459, 462, 472, 480, 484, 489, 523, 532, 536, 537, 543, 554, 559, 574, 575, 588, 596, 598, 603, 624, 643, 700, 702, 728, 736, 740
Iron industry, 10, 11, 12, 14, 15, 16, 17, 18, 19, 23, 24, 25, 27, 28, 38, 41, 42, 43, 52, 54, 57, 58, 59, 65, 68, 69, 73, 79, 102, 123, 126, 132, 136, 140, 190, 276, 490, 631, 633, 639, 644, 649, 685, 686, 725, 726, 744
Jebb, Joshua, 434, 435, 438, 545
Jewish immigrants, 128
Jex-Blake, Sophia, 707, 708, 709
Juvenile Offenders Act, 385
Labour market, v, 145, 174, 180, 193, 260, 267, 270, 273, 528, 626, 627, 629, 630, 631, 632, 636, 639, 647, 648, 653, 657, 664, 665, 666, 667, 703, 704, 734
Lancashire, 9, 14, 17, 20, 35, 38, 40, 44, 103, 108, 137, 145, 148, 149, 156, 158, 159, 162, 167, 174, 192, 198, 201, 207, 211, 226, 247, 261, 277, 278, 289, 306, 317, 333, 350, 351, 425, 447, 473, 481, 499, 534, 555, 558, 561, 565, 570, 573, 574, 575, 586, 595, 627, 633, 634, 637, 639, 642, 643, 644, 647, 649, 650, 651, 655, 661, 663, 669, 682, 687, 735, 744
Landed class, the, 279, 296, 720, 729, 732, 734, 735, 736, 738, 739, 741
Landed interest, 34, 41, 280, 484, 681, 682, 719
Landowners, 18, 38, 72, 182, 195, 200, 203, 209, 214, 221, 222, 227, 280, 240, 286, 296, 455, 479, 506, 526, 573, 616, 618, 623, 675, 679, 680, 688, 717, 719, 720, 721, 722, 723, 724, 725, 727, 728, 730, 735, 737, 738, 740, 741, 742
Langham Place Group, 700
Leeds, 14, 100, 103, 150, 153, 182, 184, 191, 192, 193, 201, 203, 207, 224, 227, 228, 234, 247, 254, 278, 291, 334, 340, 349, 350, 364, 377, 419, 485, 493, 497, 534, 548, 566, 569, 614, 633, 663, 680, 685, 735, 740

753

Leisure and recreation, iv, vi, 49, 60, 73, 76, 80, 178, 196, 197, 198, 220, 370, 477, 488, 489, 491, 492, 493, 494, 495, 496, 497, 498, 499, 500, 501, 502, 503, 504, 606, 626, 658, 690, 745
  attack on, 477–79
  attitude to animals, 482–83
  leisure after 1850, 488–504
  nature of popular culture, 482
Lingen, Ralph, 336
Literacy, 313–23, 350, 353, 354, 365, 370, 416
Liverpool, 6, 7, 24, 28, 45, 52, 54, 70, 77, 78, 79, 113, 114, 123, 124, 130, 134, 138, 139, 140, 184, 191, 192, 198, 201, 206, 207, 209, 210, 211, 212, 214, 216, 217, 227, 228, 232, 233, 244, 247, 259, 278, 291, 349, 364, 377, 402, 419, 444, 468, 470, 535, 538, 562, 570, 581, 596, 632, 633, 634, 680, 723, 734
Local government, 363, 513, 522, 523, 524, 526, 527, 528, 531
Local Government Act 1875, 229
Local Government Act 1888, 49, 229
Local Government Act 1894, 49, 229
Local Government Board, 48, 87, 229, 238, 252, 282, 291, 332, 523, 524, 528
Local Government Boundaries Act 1887, 229
Loch, C. S., 300, 303
London, 6, 7, 9, 17, 18, 24, 25, 26, 28, 35, 46, 48, 49, 51, 52, 56, 59, 60, 66, 68, 72, 73, 74, 75, 77, 78, 79, 80, 83, 88, 90, 91, 93, 96, 102, 103, 112, 114, 121, 122, 123, 124, 126, 127, 128, 130, 131, 132, 133, 134, 138, 140, 160, 175, 176, 177, 182, 183, 184, 185, 186, 187, 188, 189, 190, 183–91, 191, 192, 193, 195, 196, 201, 202, 204, 205, 207, 209, 210, 211, 212–14, 224, 225, 227, 228, 229, 230, 231, 232, 233, 234, 235, 236, 242, 245, 246, 247, 248, 250, 251, 254, 255, 259, 274, 277, 281, 282, 287, 290, 291, 297, 299, 300, 301, 302, 303, 309, 310, 321, 327, 328, 349, 350, 351, 355, 357, 361, 366, 368, 369, 372, 375, 376, 377, 378, 380, 386, 390, 391, 394, 395, 396, 397, 398, 404, 405, 407, 413, 420, 422, 423, 426, 427, 430, 432, 435, 438, 445, 446, 447, 451, 452, 453, 454, 455, 456, 458, 460, 462, 463, 464, 465, 466, 469, 470, 471, 472, 476, 479, 483, 486, 489, 490, 492, 493, 497, 498, 499, 526, 527, 541, 546, 552, 555, 558, 560, 562, 572, 574, 578, 579, 582, 584, 585, 589, 591, 592, 596, 597, 602, 614, 619, 622, 630, 631, 632, 633, 637, 640, 642, 650, 652, 654, 663, 665, 670, 672, 676, 680, 688, 691, 699, 700, 702, 704, 708, 709, 716, 719, 720, 721, 723, 724, 725, 726, 730, 732, 733, 742, 745
Lowe, Robert, 319, 337, 365
MacDonagh, Oliver, 159, 507, 512
Malthus, Thomas, 81, 82, 83, 265, 266, 310, 404, 508, 510
Manchester, 22, 28, 45, 52, 53, 54, 70, 74, 77, 78, 79, 92, 113, 115, 123, 124, 133, 134, 135, 136, 138, 144, 145, 184, 191, 192, 203, 207, 214, 215, 216, 224, 226, 228, 231, 241, 242, 247, 254, 290, 291, 307, 329, 331, 341, 348, 349, 350, 351, 357, 364, 365, 379, 400, 419, 447, 451, 469, 480, 487, 488, 497, 502, 533, 535, 569, 570, 579, 602, 614, 615, 616, 619,

620, 633, 634, 641, 660, 663, 665, 669, 674, 677, 678, 680, 681, 682, 695, 704, 710, 726, 734, 735, 745
Mann, Horace, 328, 577, 590
Manual workers, 180, 491, 634, 635, 655, 677, 709
Manufacturers, 30, 36, 53, 115, 150, 151, 152, 153, 154, 155, 161, 333, 351, 676, 679, 681, 682, 683, 684, 688, 703, 722, 725, 730, 731, 733, 734, 735, 737, 739, 740
Marriage, 82, 85, 96, 98, 102, 103, 104, 108, 110, 113, 114, 116, 117, 120, 121, 184, 265, 316, 354, 500, 559, 562, 628, 641, 642, 643, 659, 678, 697, 698, 699, 709, 711, 712, 713, 714, 715, 716, 717, 730
Married women's property, 355, 713, 714, 715
Married Women's Property Act 1870, 715
Marx, Karl, 108, 618
Masculinity, 118, 447, 494, 495, 500, 692, 717
Matchgirls' strike 1888, 175-77
Mayhew, Henry, 133, 134, 391, 392, 430, 447, 622, 630, 631, 665
Mearns, Andrew, 186, 187, 258, 413
Medical profession, 87, 99, 100, 225, 247, 250, 251, 444, 480, 486, 693, 694, 705, 707, 709
Merchants, 29, 31, 202, 209, 224, 628, 676, 680, 682, 686, 703, 719, 721, 722, 729, 730, 731, 734, 735
Metal industries, 10, 17, 42, 43, 44, 52, 146, 165, 189, 190, 316, 631, 633, 649, 661, 666, 743
Metropolitan Police Act 1839, 475
Middle-classes, 323, 326, 351, 378, 381, 390, 508, 509, 515, 675-718

clerks, 101, 315, 345, 402, 491, 514, 515, 633, 634, 635, 676, 703, 704, 705, 709, 710, 711, 717, 730, 740
entrepreneurs, 684-88
lower middle-class, 202, 341, 345, 411, 560, 601, 633, 665, 676, 677, 694
professions, the, 688-92
shopocracy, 255, 675
status of women, 692-98
upper middle-class, 297, 592, 676
women and work, 698-711
women's rights, 711-17
Middlesbrough, 79, 103, 123, 124, 208, 465
Midlands, 36, 38, 44, 60, 121, 137, 172, 193, 197, 205, 207, 233, 495, 561, 566, 567, 571, 572, 574, 585, 608, 637, 663, 676
Migration, 5, 8, 18, 22, 82, 84, 85, 102, 117, 120, 121, 122, 123, 124, 126, 129, 130, 131, 134, 137, 138, 139, 140, 182, 184, 185, 221, 222, 224, 292, 600, 632, 666, 667
 depopulation, 38, 121, 122, 208
 emigration, 84, 85, 96, 102, 117, 120, 125, 130, 136, 137, 138, 292, 448, 512, 563, 574, 667
 immigration, iv, 85, 128, 130, 133, 137, 138, 185, 232, 558, 559, 575, 598, 603
 Irish migration, 129-41
Mill, John Stuart, 169, 272, 508, 509, 696
Millbank prison, 234, 415, 430, 431, 434
Mines and Collieries Act 1842, 158
Mining, 10, 15, 16, 17, 42, 44, 65, 79, 85, 102, 124, 136, 158, 166, 167, 168, 179, 276, 291, 325, 348, 361, 490, 518, 631,

632, 633, 648, 666, 671, 723, 743, 744
'Moral economy', 151, 223, 510, 613
Moral reform, 410-12
Morant, Sir Robert, 371, 372, 374
More, Hannah, 489, 538, 539, 550, 552
Municipal Corporations Act 1835, 228, 240, 468, 517, 735
National Education League, 365, 367
National Education Union, 366
National Society, 318, 320, 321, 322, 327
New Zealand, 303, 406, 667, 714
Newgate prison, 392, 417, 419, 423, 427, 428, 437
Newman, John Henry, 347, 544, 545, 546, 547, 548, 574, 589, 596
Newspapers, 72, 91, 141, 183, 196, 315, 390, 402, 497, 645
Nightingale, Florence, 296, 297, 705, 706, 707
North-East England, 8, 9, 52, 136, 175, 247, 319, 361, 675
Nursing, 81, 88, 653, 690, 703, 704, 705, 706, 707
Oastler, Richard, 107, 148, 149, 150, 151, 152, 155, 156, 157, 160, 163, 284
Old age, 262, 263, 294
Old age pensions, 530
Opium, use of, 486-88
Owen, Robert, 149, 156, 205, 308, 312, 325, 510, 581, 582, 684
Oxford, 341, 345, 346, 347, 348, 349, 356, 357, 376, 377, 378, 520
Oxford Movement, 543, 544, 545, 548, 549, 543-49, 589
Paternalism, 18, 152, 154, 164, 169, 182, 205, 278, 295, 478, 525, 597, 612, 613, 615, 616, 624, 644

Patronage, 198, 201, 206, 270, 273, 280, 281, 295, 336, 367, 477, 480, 492, 493, 495, 500, 538, 546, 581, 597, 613, 614, 615, 675, 680, 738, 741
Paul, Sir George, 426
Peel, Sir Robert, 152, 157, 158, 159, 160, 161, 286, 330, 385, 418, 432, 452, 457, 458, 461, 462, 463, 465, 482, 518, 519, 541, 542, 543, 558, 582, 721
Peerage, the, 681, 729, 731, 733, 737, 738, 741
Penitentiary Act 1779, 424, 425
Pentonville prison, 415, 431, 435, 436
Perkin, Harold, 45, 509, 511, 612, 615, 618, 619, 622, 623, 683, 689, 729
Philanthropy, 178, 186, 254, 294-304, 310, 424, 483, 500, 502, 553, 592, 606
Police Act 1890, 469
Policing, 450-76
    Metropolitan Police, 183, 452, 453, 454, 458, 460, 461, 462, 463, 464, 465, 467, 468, 469, 470, 471, 473, 474
    models of policing, 455-60
    national policing, 464-71
    policing before 1829, 450-55
    policeman state, 474, 475
    social composition, 471-74
Political parties
    Conservative, 128, 152, 166, 167, 203, 212, 215, 292, 319, 330, 363, 492, 524, 525, 528, 529, 530, 684, 736, 737, 738, 739, 740
    Labour, 6, 7, 527, 618
    Liberal, 53, 186, 203, 212, 252, 293, 330, 342, 347, 363, 365, 366, 369, 442, 492, 505, 516, 521, 528, 529, 530, 531, 558, 570, 603, 684, 738, 739, 740
    Tory, 148, 149, 150, 151, 154, 215, 265, 274, 275, 277, 278, 330, 363, 417, 418,

INDEX

457, 459, 474, 516, 518, 519, 525, 526, 536, 564, 614, 620, 682, 734, 735
Whig, 151, 154, 155, 266, 275, 276, 287, 330, 417, 466, 474, 516, 517, 519, 542, 543, 544, 603, 735, 738, 740
Poor Law, 147, 184, 186, 241, 244, 257, 258, 260, 262, 263, 264, 265, 266, 267, 268, 269, 270, 272, 273, 274, 277, 278, 279, 280, 281, 282, 283, 284, 285, 290, 291, 292, 294, 304, 331, 332, 339, 374, 517, 518, 523, 524, 529, 530, 531, 650, 665
  after 1847, 288-93
  Andover scandal, 286, 287
  Gilbert's Act 1782, 264
  how cruel?, 283-85
  opposition, 274-78
  organisation after 1834, 278-83
  Poor Law Amendment Act 1834, 272, 267-74
  Poor Law Amendment Act 1847, 272
  Poor Law Guardians, 186, 251, 271, 276, 280, 281, 282, 283, 286, 287, 289, 290, 291, 292, 293, 302, 331, 523, 651
  Poor Law Unions, 9, 186, 276, 278, 291
  reasons for reform, 263-67
  Speenhamland, 223, 265
  workhouse, 88, 90, 91, 238, 257, 265, 267, 269, 273, 274, 275, 276, 277, 279, 282, 283, 284, 285, 286, 287, 288, 289, 291, 319, 321, 331, 332, 360, 415, 451, 602, 643
Population, iv, v, 4, 6, 8, 17, 18, 20, 21, 22, 26, 27, 29, 40, 46, 66, 78, 79, 81-109, 137, 138, 139, 140, 183, 184, 185, 189, 193, 197, 199, 201, 204, 207, 208, 209, 211, 212, 216, 218, 219, 221, 225, 227, 228, 238, 250, 257, 258, 259, 280, 306, 310, 315, 317, 318, 319, 323, 324, 350, 353, 354, 368, 374, 375, 390, 397, 403, 404, 413, 451, 466, 467, 477, 478, 480, 481, 485, 498, 503, 506, 508, 511, 525, 528, 534, 539, 556, 563, 577, 578, 580, 586, 590, 594, 597, 606, 607, 610, 618, 621, 624, 631, 632, 633, 637, 648, 655, 660, 662, 664, 677, 688, 689, 696, 729, 743, 744, 746
  birth control, 85, 97, 98, 99, 100, 101, 102, 120-24, 126, 128, 129, 130, 133, 136, 606, 697
  fertility, 82, 83, 85, 96, 97, 98, 99, 101, 102, 104, 105, 107, 116
  illegitimacy, 90, 92, 93, 94, 104, 113, 114, 115, 117, 284, 717
  life expectancy, 85, 86, 87, 233,
  mortality, 82, 83, 85, 86, 87, 88, 102, 104, 137, 185, 229, 232, 235, 238, 487,
Post Office, 74, 308, 709
Poverty, 4, 18, 82, 101, 126, 128, 137, 144, 222, 224, 228, 233, 237, 254, 257, 258, 259, 260, 261, 262, 263, 269, 271, 272, 273, 274, 277, 289, 292, 294, 293, 300, 301, 303, 310, 567, 577, 597, 611, 627, 630, 633, 637, 640, 649, 650, 652, 654, 664, 701, 716, 745, 746
Privacy, 97, 120, 203, 204, 214, 221, 478, 616, 693
Prostitution, 89, 104, 119, 385, 393, 405, 407, 405-9, 411, 412, 443, 632, 652, 666, 702, 711, 745
Public Health, 212, 241, 240, 245, 250, 251, 252, 253, 262
  reasons for slow pace of reform, 240-41

757

Public Health Act 1848, 241, 244-49
Public Health Act 1872, 229, 252
Public Health Act 1875, 253
Public Health Act 1890, 238
Public Libraries Act 1850, 316, 489
Punishment, 415-49
  juvenile punishment, 445-49
  prison reformers, 423-30
  prisons, 392, 421-45, 514, 517
  separate and silent, 433-38
Reform Act 1832, 4, 681
Reform Act 1867, 4, 319, 365
Reform Act 1884, 4
Religion
  and working-classes, 577-87
  Anglican. *See* Church of England
  Anglicanism. *See* Church of England
  Baptists, 254, 555, 556, 560, 561, 594, 595
  Church of England, 5, 126, 149, 152, 159, 160, 318, 323, 331, 346, 348, 349, 355, 367, 373, 425, 532, 534, 535, 537, 538, 540, 541, 543, 545, 546, 547, 548, 549, 550, 552, 534-54, 558, 559, 562, 564, 565, 571, 573, 577, 578, 584, 588, 590, 591, 592, 594, 595, 598, 599, 604, 609, 614, 728
  Congregationalist, 254, 363, 556, 570, 594
  crisis of faith?, 598-611
  Evangelicalism, 298, 408, 418, 477, 478, 479, 481, 532, 538, 549, 550, 551, 552, 553, 579, 589, 599, 609
  Methodism, 326, 550, 552, 555, 556, 560, 561, 563, 564, 565, 566, 567, 568, 569, 570, 571, 572, 573, 585, 594, 608, 684

Nonconformist, 5, 76, 160, 254, 323, 556, 557, 573, 574, 585, 594, 595, 603, 604, 707
Nonconformity, 31, 154, 318, 373, 411, 532, 545, 554, 555, 556, 557, 573, 574, 579, 580, 585, 594, 595, 596, 601, 602, 604, 609
Primitive Methodism, 556, 566, 567, 570, 572, 573, 594
Quakers, 67, 205, 206, 254, 297, 427, 446, 562, 594
religiosity, 579, 582, 583, 590, 591, 598, 600, 601, 606, 610, 611
Roman Catholic, 5, 134, 139, 318, 323, 329, 347, 373, 455, 458, 532, 536, 537, 540, 545, 546, 548, 550, 552, 574, 575, 576, 577, 581, 589, 596, 597, 598, 599, 603, 604
secularisation, 73, 101, 581, 583, 599, 606, 610, 611
Religious Census 1851, 532, 559, 560, 561, 563, 571, 573, 577, 578, 579, 590, 600
Religious societies, 320, 327, 329, 517
Rent, 186, 210, 211, 212, 213, 238, 632
Respectability, 114, 117, 118, 119, 267, 318, 345, 358, 398, 399, 481, 482, 484, 485, 495, 496, 497, 507, 509, 550, 551, 553, 557, 563, 601, 621, 643, 662, 678, 684, 693, 698, 702, 717, 718
Ricardo, David, 508, 622
Romilly, Sir Samuel, 383, 415, 416, 417, 418
Rowntree, Seebohm, 214, 224, 259, 260, 262, 263, 310
Royal Commission, 154, 158, 167, 168, 172, 179, 184, 186, 213, 228, 252, 266, 292, 304
Rural Constabulary Act 1839, 467, 468

Rural Constabulary Act 1839, 468
Ruskin, John, 68, 695
Russell, Lord John, 415, 432, 434, 467, 546
Sabbatarianism, 605
Sadler, Michael, 150, 153, 277
Sanitary Act 1866, 241, 252
Sanitation, 182, 210, 227, 228, 229, 239, 241, 250, 253
Scotland, 4, 7, 20, 38, 44, 66, 74, 77, 83, 84, 92, 95, 102, 104, 121, 124, 125, 131, 132, 134, 135, 137, 138, 139, 140, 144, 152, 156, 174, 207, 211, 220, 222, 228, 230, 231, 242, 247, 251, 289, 294, 322, 357, 368, 372, 379, 387, 397, 424, 427, 433, 453, 463, 469, 473, 484, 499, 523, 532, 549, 552, 558, 577, 581, 588, 600, 605, 643, 650, 722, 728
Scotland Yard, 469, 470
Self-help, iv, 1, 6, 296, 300, 303, 305, 307, 309, 310, 328, 411, 509, 511, 513, 665, 728
Sexuality, 95, 97, 99, 109, 111, 112, 113, 114, 116, 118, 119, 120, 226, 551
Shaftesbury, Lord, Anthony Ashley Cooper, 107, 116, 147, 148, 151, 153, 155, 157, 158, 159, 160, 161, 162, 163, 164, 165, 212, 213, 245, 296, 297, 299, 324, 325, 552
Sheffield, 43, 70, 101, 114, 192, 217, 228, 246, 254, 349, 351, 377, 395, 451, 487, 538, 578, 580, 633, 638, 659, 685, 723
Shipbuilding, 17, 43, 44, 190, 631, 649, 651, 666, 672, 720
Shopkeepers, 66, 101, 103, 193, 247, 280, 396, 414, 478, 601, 621, 633, 634, 640, 676, 698, 730, 740
Shops Act 1912, 174
Shuttleworth, James Kay, 115, 116, 133, 160, 233, 242, 320, 324, 325, 331, 332, 334, 335, 336, 337, 338, 339, 389
Simeon, Charles, 537, 538, 551, 552
Simon, Sir John, 250, 251, 252, 253
Skills, 31, 43, 44, 125, 143, 152, 174, 313, 315, 316, 319, 326, 355, 360, 361, 379, 380, 613, 627, 628, 629, 630, 636, 643, 647, 656, 672, 675, 701, 704
Smiles, Samuel, 201, 309, 509, 511, 694
Smith, Adam, 16, 507, 508
Snow, John, 83, 226, 250, 251
Social control, 312, 319, 325, 363, 415
Society for Promoting the Employment of Women (SPEW), 701, 702
Society for the Diffusion of Useful Knowledge, 322
Southend, 198, 200
Southey, Robert, 19, 151
Sport, 199, 448, 477, 479, 480, 494, 495, 499
Standards of living, 3, 83, 137, 238, 379, 519, 626, 632, 636-41, 648, 649, 650, 648-52
Status, 30, 31, 57, 105, 108, 121, 123, 148, 163, 181, 190, 202, 226, 227, 271, 283, 288, 306, 312, 342, 343, 345, 354, 360, 443, 472, 487, 492, 493, 495, 503, 522, 535, 543, 552, 557, 575, 581, 600, 613, 623, 624, 625, 627, 630, 635, 636, 641, 642, 643, 645, 646, 647, 657, 658, 660, 662, 663, 673, 676, 678, 683, 686, 689, 690, 691, 699, 706, 707, 710, 714, 715, 722, 730, 731, 739
Stead, William T., 97, 98, 176, 187, 411, 412
Steam power, 2, 3, 11, 14, 15, 16, 19, 29, 37, 41, 50, 55, 63, 66, 143, 198, 316, 364, 671
Storch, Robert, 315, 451, 459, 460, 465, 466, 469, 475

Sunderland, 27, 44, 231, 247, 518
Sweated Industries Act 1909, 173
Sweated trades, 43, 171, 172, 188, 190, 632, 640, 649, 663
Swindon, 28, 65, 79, 205, 207
Swing Riots 1830, 466
Teachers, 140, 314, 320, 321, 326, 327, 330, 331, 332, 334, 335, 336, 337, 338, 380, 635, 655, 690, 710, 711
Teaching, 297, 318, 320, 321, 326, 327, 334, 335, 337, 338, 339, 340, 345, 346, 352, 357, 367, 377, 379, 434, 653, 690, 703, 704, 709, 710, 733
Temperance, 351, 400, 483-86
Ten Hour movement. *See* Factory movement
Tenants, 38, 39, 40, 70, 127, 211, 535, 573, 682, 722, 723, 728
Textiles, 7, 10, 11, 13, 14, 16, 23, 24, 25, 41, 42, 44, 54, 164, 631, 635, 639, 644, 655, 659, 666, 720, 726
Thomas Hardy, 73, 147, 697
Thompson, E. P., 144, 388, 586, 613, 619, 620, 624, 628, 630
Tithe Commutation Act 1836, 543
Trade union, 6, 108, 164, 167, 173, 174, 177, 178, 305, 306, 495, 529, 618, 620, 633, 634, 639, 646, 653, 655, 666, 670, 711
Transportation, 392, 433, 447
Unemployment, 18, 128, 139, 143, 153, 257, 261, 264, 269, 273, 289, 290, 291, 292, 293, 294, 306, 310, 331, 404, 525, 526, 531, 632, 638, 639, 642, 649, 650, 651, 652, 664, 665, 666, 667, 672
United States, 24, 128, 129, 137, 139, 309, 313, 351, 434, 562, 629, 644
Upper-classes, 719-42

Urban society, 137, 181, 225, 535, 540, 670
Urbanisation, 181-219
  governing towns, 226-29
  leisure resorts, 197-201
  market towns, 29, 124, 228
  regional centres, 191-97
  suburbanisation, 51, 74, 80, 87, 106, 122, 123, 124, 186, 202, 203, 201-5, 523, 560, 601
  town planning, 205-7
Utilitarianism, 511
Vaccination Act 1853, 249
Vagrancy, 388, 404, 448
Vagrancy Act 1824, 412, 461, 475
Vestry, 9, 49, 185, 240, 542
Wages. *See* Standards of Living
Wales, 5, 8, 9, 17, 18, 20, 21, 25, 26, 29, 33, 35, 38, 39, 44, 48, 49, 54, 61, 71, 72, 74, 75, 77, 78, 81, 83, 84, 85, 88, 95, 96, 104, 114, 121, 122, 123, 124, 125, 132, 134, 137, 140, 144, 191, 198, 199, 200, 207, 211, 216, 217, 220, 221, 223, 228, 230, 232, 233, 241, 251, 256, 263, 267, 275, 276, 278, 327, 328, 329, 334, 335, 340, 352, 361, 365, 367, 370, 371, 377, 383, 384, 385, 388, 389, 395, 397, 401, 406, 411, 423, 425, 432, 433, 439, 442, 452, 458, 459, 460, 462, 465, 467, 469, 471, 472, 473, 481, 486, 501, 503, 510, 515, 523, 529, 532, 545, 554, 556, 559, 561, 574, 575, 577, 578, 588, 600, 602, 603, 662, 688, 703, 708, 709, 720, 722, 723, 728
Water, 12, 13, 14, 15, 27, 34, 52, 86, 87, 88, 144, 164, 185, 193, 195, 197, 210, 211, 214, 215, 216, 217, 230, 231, 232, 234, 235, 237, 238, 240, 241, 243, 244, 246, 248, 250, 251, 252, 254, 255, 404, 422, 436, 483, 484, 745

Watson, Joshua, 324, 348, 397, 539, 590, 605, 716, 739
Whitechapel, 184, 189, 210, 233, 302, 472, 592
Wilberforce, William, 537, 538, 550, 551, 552, 553, 565
Women, 143, 158, 160, 163, 166, 184, 296, 631, 634, 635, 653-64, 688-717
and trade unionism, 174-78
Women's Co-operative Guild, 97
Wordsworth, William, 68, 69, 151
Working conditions, 147, 158, 164, 165, 174, 175, 176, 473, 529, 530, 632, 633, 636, 646, 658, 660, 665
Working-classes, 626-74
agricultural labourers, 487
apprenticeship, 107, 145, 147, 478, 628, 629, 647, 656, 698, 734
aristocracy of labour, 43, 641, 667, 668, 669, 672, 667-73
artisan, 10, 17, 18, 43, 108, 188, 189, 258, 341, 342, 490, 495, 496, 671, 672, 673
casual workers, 43, 80, 128, 180, 184, 188, 190, 261, 264, 404, 630, 631, 632, 649, 650, 651, 665
factory workers, 44, 144, 145, 151, 222, 305, 490, 594, 633, 650, 653
nature of work, 626-36
unskilled labour, 43, 57, 86, 124, 133, 135, 139, 144, 175, 176, 179, 184, 306, 472, 585, 597, 624, 630, 632, 635, 636, 638, 647, 649, 660, 663, 666, 673, 674
working women, 653-64
Workmen's Compensation Act 1906, 180
York, 69, 83, 149, 184, 208, 230, 259, 260, 262, 263, 297, 434, 462, 567
Yorkshire, 8, 9, 14, 17, 101, 103, 137, 148, 149, 150, 152, 154, 155, 156, 174, 199, 208, 222, 277, 278, 279, 282, 290, 306, 308, 317, 338, 350, 351, 467, 487, 489, 534, 559, 561, 567, 571, 573, 586, 627, 644, 684, 720, 723
Youthful Offenders Act 1854, 448

About the Author

Richard Brown was, until he retired, Head of History and Citizenship at Manshead School in Dunstable, and has published thirty print and Kindle books and 50 articles and papers on nineteenth century history. He is a Fellow of both the Royal Historical Society and the Historical Association.

Other recent books by Richard Brown

'A Peaceable Kingdom': Essays on Nineteenth Century Canada, (Authoring History), 2013.

Settler Australia, 1780-1880, Volume 1: Settlement, Protest and Control, Volume 2: Eureka and Democracy, (Authoring History), 2013. Also available in a Kindle version.

Resistance and Rebellion in the British Empire, 1600-1980, (*Rebellion Trilogy*, Clio Publishing), 2013. Also available in a Kindle version.

Rebellion in Canada, 1837-1885, Volume 1: Autocracy, Rebellion and Liberty, Volume 2: The Irish, the Fenians and the Métis, (Authoring History), 2012. Also available in a Kindle version.

Sex, Work and Politics: Women in Britain, 1830-1918, (Authoring History), 2012. Also available in a Kindle version.

Famine, Fenians and Freedom 1840-1882, (*Rebellion Trilogy*, Clio Publishing), 2011. Also available in a Kindle version.

Three Rebellions. Canada 1837-1838, South Wales 1839 and Victoria, Australia 1854, (*Rebellion Trilogy*, Clio Publishing), 2010. Also available in a Kindle version.

Printed in Great Britain
by Amazon.co.uk, Ltd.,
Marston Gate.